Citation Classics from the Journal of Business Ethics

Advances in Business Ethics Research

A Journal of Business Ethics Book Series

For further volumes:
http://www.springer.com/series/8805

Alex C. Michalos • Deborah C. Poff
Editors

Citation Classics from the Journal of Business Ethics

Celebrating the First Thirty Years of Publication

Springer

Editors
Alex C. Michalos
Professor Emeritus, Political Science
University of Northern British Columbia
(home) Brandon, MB, Canada

Deborah C. Poff
President and Vice Chancellor
Brandon University
Brandon, MB, Canada

ISBN 978-94-007-4125-6 ISBN 978-94-007-4126-3 (eBook)
DOI 10.1007/978-94-007-4126-3
Springer Dordrecht Heidelberg New York London

Library of Congress Control Number: 2012942912

Printed on acid-free paper

Springer is part of Springer Science+Business Media (www.springer.com)

Contents

Chapter 1
Introduction*

Alex C. Michalos and Deborah C. Poff (eds.)

This citation classics monograph in the ABER series marks over 30 years of publishing academic articles in the *Journal of Business Ethics*. As you read the introduction to this book, you will note that we address the strengths and limitations of using various citation indexes and indicators as tools for assessing the scholarly quality and impact of articles in any particular field.

Before we begin that discussion, however, we would like to discuss other indicators of importance for the articles that appear in this collection besides that of citations. In order to do so, let us take you back to our then nascent journal, which first appeared in print in 1982. It was one of the first academic peer-reviewed journals dedicated to the interdisciplinary field of business ethics and over 30 years later remains the only rank A business ethics journal in the *Financial Times 45*. In fact, we believe that its early establishment as an academic venue for the publication of research in the interdisciplinary field of business ethics is an historically significant event or marker that played a critical role in establishing this new field. Further, it continues to play a pivotal role in the evolution of the field and its cognate interdisciplinary research areas. Our view in this is shared by a number of our past and current editors of the *Journal* as well as scholars whose articles appear in this book.

If we use Kuhn's (1970) discussion of a paradigm in scientific theory (leaving aside the criticisms of Kuhn's famous tract on scientific revolutions), he described a number of notable and recognizable features of an area of intellectual inquiry and

---

*The first third of this essay is excerpted with some revisions from Michalos (2005). We are grateful to Chis Hurst for his bibliographic help.

A.C. Michalos (✉)
Professor Emeritus, Political Science, University of Northern British Columbia,
(home) 463 13th Street, Brandon, R7A 4P9, MB, Canada
e-mail: michalos@brandonu.ca

D.C. Poff (eds.)
President and Vice Chancellor, Brandon University, 18th Street,
R7A 6A9, Brandon, MB, Canada

A.C. Michalos and D.C. Poff (eds.), *Citation Classics from the Journal of Business Ethics*, Advances in Business Ethics Research 2,
DOI 10.1007/978-94-007-4126-3_1,

discovery that are germane here. The manner in which a paradigm transforms a group of scholars into a field or profession, according to Kuhn, includes the enhancement of scholarly careers and reputation through the publication of journal articles and the initiation of those specialized journals where articles are "addressed only to professional colleagues, the men whose knowledge of a shared paradigm can be assumed…" (Kuhn 1970, p. 20). Further, Kuhn noted that the establishment of learned societies, the establishment of curriculum and fields of study as legitimate disciplines within universities and colleges are additional indicators of the acceptance and adoption of a paradigm. As well, monographs on theory and methodology that are innovative and contribute new knowledge to the field count as indicators of the establishment of the paradigm. Finally, the production of textbooks, which are seen as less prestigious because of their didactic role in teaching the norms and established questions in the field are later indicators of the normal and accepted premises of the field.

As you read the articles in this contribution to the ABER book series, it is important to note that in the articles and in the reflections of authors and editors, we have powerful confirmation of the importance of these authors and editors who did precisely what Kuhn itemizes in his list of recognizable contributions and key indicators of the establishment of a new paradigm for a field of inquiry. These scholars contributed to the knowledge creation in the field through their research and publications. They contributed to the reputation of the journal, not only through publication but through service as referees and editors. They established and served on the executives of new learned societies and they contributed to the establishment of other learned journals with different and complementary missions and foci. Finally, many wrote, edited or co-edited the texts that became the standard material for the academic courses and programs of study which they frequently designed, introduced in their university curricula and in which they taught. To all of these contributors, for all of their diverse contributions, we express our sincere thanks. Together we have built the foundation of a field of research whose importance can only increase with time.

Citation Classics

Eugene Garfield was the founder of the Institute for Scientific Information (ISI), the *Science Citation Index*, *Social Sciences Citation Index* and several other important works. According to Garfield (1985), "By definition, a *Citation Classic* is a paper or book that has been highly cited in its field" (p. 404). Because different fields are characterized by different institutional arrangements (e.g., numbers and kinds of communication media, practitioners, standardized practices and rules of procedure), different numerical thresholds are used to identify classics in each field. In an earlier paper, Garfield (1976) wrote that

> …less than 25% of all papers will be cited ten times in all eternity! …any paper cited ten times in one year is *ipso facto* significant. Occasionally there is an anomaly. But a paper cited ten times in each of two successive years is well on its way to citation stardom. Whether the author is on the way to immortality depends on how well he or she does in other papers (p. 419).

An average paper in the *Science Citation Index* is cited about 1.7 times per year (Garfield 1972). For the years 1955–1987, Garfield (1989) claimed that for the whole *Index* database,

> …more than 56 percent of the source items are uncited – not even self-cited. (Many of these source items are abstracts, letters, and editorials, of limited interest; nevertheless, a huge number of papers go uncited.) (p. 7).

In 1973 Garfield distinguished three kinds of "uncitedness", namely, "the uncitedness of the mediocre, the unintelligible, the irrelevant", then that "of the meritorious but undiscovered or forgotten", and finally that

> of the *distinction* that comes to those whose work has become so well known (and presumably been previously so heavily cited) that one finds it at first tedious, then unnecessary, and finally actually gauche to cite such men at all (p. 413).

Hamilton (1990) reported that ISI data revealed that about 55% of the "papers published between 1981 and 1985 in journals indexed by the institute received no citations at all in the 5 years after they were published" (p. 1331). In response, Pendlebury (1991) wrote that the precise figures were "47.4% uncited for the sciences, 74.7% for the social sciences, and 98.0% for the arts and humanities". However, more importantly, he explained that

> "These statistics represent every type of article that appears in journals indexed by the Institute for Scientific Information (ISI) in its *Science Citation Index*, *Social Sciences Citation Index*, and *Arts & Humanities Citation Index*. The journals' ISI indexes contain not only articles, reviews, and notes, but also meeting abstracts, editorials, obituaries, letters like this one, and other *marginalia*, which one might expect to be largely un-cited. In 1984, the year of the data quoted by Hamilton, about 27% of the items indexed in the *Science Citation Index* were such *marginalia*. The comparable figures for the social sciences and arts and humanities were 48% and 69%, respectively.
>
> If one analyzes the data more narrowly and examines the extent of uncited articles alone (this information was not yet available when Hamilton wrote his articles), the figures shrink, some more than others: 22.4% of 1984 science articles remained uncited by the end of 1988, as did 48.0% of social sciences articles and 93.1% of articles in arts and humanities journals" (pp. 1410–1411).

Table 1.1 illustrates a few thresholds for citation classics from different fields, ranging from papers with 50 or more citations covering the fields of geography and marine biology to 500 or more citations covering all fields listed in the *Science Citation Index*. Plomp (1990) used a threshold of 25 citations to identify "highly cited papers", which is a more modest label than 'citation classic' and perhaps not quite the same idea. As others had before him (e.g., Garfield 1972), Plomp noticed, for example, that because in 1982 the 40 core biochemistry journals produced 13,500 articles while the 25 core astrosciences journals produced 4,500 articles, there were many more opportunities for citations in the former field than in the latter. In fact, "the most cited biochemistry papers obtained ten times as many citations as the most cited astrosciences papers", although there were only three times as many biochemistry papers than astrosciences papers.

In the *Encyclopedia of Library and Information Science*, the entry for 'citer motivations' says

> Citations are examples of unobtrusive or nonreactive social science measures. Unobtrusive measures are physical evidences of activity that exist independently of their source: the private act of authorship produces citations that are public objects available for scrutiny and analysis. As with many of these unobtrusive measures, it is difficult to ascertain in any given application what social or psychological construct the citation counts are measuring (Brooks 1988, p. 48).

Merton (1977), a highly productive and respected sociologist of science, believed that the status of any scientist's research output

> ...resides only in the recognition accorded his work by peers in the social system of science through reference to his work...Since recognition of the worth of one's work by qualified peers is, in science, the basic form of reward (all other rewards deriving from it) and since it can only be widely accorded within the social system of science when the attributed work is widely known, this provides institutional incentive for the open publication, without direct financial reward, of scientific work (pp. 47–48, as quoted by Lawani and Bayer 1983).

Lawani and Bayer (1983) claimed that

> Despite the ambiguities of citation practices, the difficulties of ascertaining why a paper is or is not cited, and the potential malpractices in citing, considerable evidence has been accumulated to suggest that citations do indeed provide an objective measure of what is variously termed "productivity," "significance," "quality," "utility," "influence," "effectiveness," or "impact" of scientists and their scholarly products (pp. 60–61).

The evidence takes many forms. For example, Narin (1976) reviewed 24 studies published between 1957 and 1975 that generally confirmed the hypothesis that citation counts are positively correlated with peer rankings of the quality of scientific articles, eminence of scientists, graduate schools, graduate departments, editor evaluations, Nobel prizes and other awards, authors' incomes, access to resources, initial appointments and mobility. Brooks (1985) reported that Virgo (1977)

> ...found citation analysis to be a consistent and accurate predictor of important scientific papers, better on the average than the individual scientist's judgment which 'is a reasonable conclusion if one considers that citations actually reflect a consensus of a large group of readers as compared to the evaluation of a single individual' [Virgo 1977, p. 423].

Lawani and Bayer (1983) undertook a very thorough study comparing peer assessments of cancer research papers with the papers' citation rates and concluded that "Highly rated papers are more highly cited than average papers".

Notwithstanding such supporting evidence for the usefulness of citation counts in the evaluation of published research, Garfield has often published cautionary remarks about the use of such counts. For example, he wrote that

> Counts of this sort are strictly quantitative and objective. But even admitting this limitation, an author's or a paper's frequency of citation has been found to correlate well with professional standing. It is certainly not the *only* measure, nor one that can be used, for any purpose, in isolation. We do not claim for it the absolute reliability that critics of citation analysis have wrongly imputed to us when they have attacked it. The fact does remain, however, that it provides a useful objective criterion previously unavailable (Garfield 1981, p. 135, reprinted in Garfield 1983).

Among the problems with using citation counts in the ISI databases to evaluate publications, Garfield (1983) mentioned the following.

> …there are undoubtedly highly useful journals that are not cited frequently [e.g., Scientific American]. Scientists read many such journals for the same reason people read newspapers and other non-scientific periodicals – to keep up with what is going on generally…Another consideration is that citation frequency is sometimes – indeed to some extent must be – a function of variables other than scientific merit. Some such variables may be an author's reputation, the controversiality of subject matter, a journal's circulation and its cost, reprint dissemination, its coverage by current-awareness and indexing and abstracting services, society memberships, the availability and extent of libraries' journal collections, national research priorities (p. 137); see also Garfield (1977, 1988).

While some features of published citation counts have been improved, in a series of papers MacRoberts and MacRoberts (1986, 1987, 1989a, b) challenged the use of citation counts on a variety of grounds. From their papers and others we constructed the following list of criticisms. (1) Many individuals and works that have had an influence on the development of published papers are not cited in those papers (they estimated that "about 15% of the influence on a paper is contained in its references"); (2) sometimes important influences are mentioned in the text of published papers but not in their bibliographies; (3) the motivation for self-citations is suspect (Self-citations are generally estimated to be about 10–30% of all citations; Bonzi and Snyder (1991) surveyed 51 self-citing authors and found "very few differences in motivation" between self- and other-citations.); (4) when review papers are cited, it is unclear exactly who is being "rewarded"; (5) general references within a text also have unclear referents, e.g., "Mendelian genetics"; (6) ISI indexes contain many errors, e.g., when authors' names are spelled in different ways, or written sometimes with and sometimes without middle initials, separate entries may made for the same document; when page and/or volume numbers are changed, separate entries may be made; when page numbers alone or page numbers and volume numbers are inverted, new entries may be made; (7) ISI indexes cover only about 10% of scientific literature; (8) "English language journals and western science are clearly over-represented, whereas small countries, non-western countries, and journals published in non-Roman scripts are under-represented."; (9) different disciplines are more or less well represented (e.g., 6% of biology journals are included, compared to 14% of clinical medicine journals); (10) politics seems to have influenced inclusions and exclusions (e.g., *Review of Radical Political Economy* is excluded, but *Public Interest* is included); (11) later proponents of views may be cited as the views' inventers; (12) proponents of views may be cited as opponents, and vice-versa; (13) people often cite material that "they have not seen or that they have seen but have not read"; (14) people make ceremonial and perfunctory citations (Moravcsik and Murugesan (1975) estimated about 40% of the references in a sample of high energy physics papers were perfunctory); (15) private communications are often influential but do not provide a published title to cite; (16) authors are notorious for repeating themselves in different papers, each of which may be cited as an additional contribution to research; (17) people sometimes select only one of several similar papers that influenced them; (18) they also redundantly cite several similar papers because they are similar, although they may have read and/or been influenced by one (Moravcsik and Murugesan (1975) estimated about one-third of the references in their sample were redundant); (19) they may cite a well-known or fail to cite a relatively unknown author because these practices are perceived to impress their readers; (20) about 70% of citations appear to be "multi-motivated"; (21) different disciplines have different typical rates of citation, which are typically neglected by citation analysts (e.g., engineering and mathematics papers average 5–6 references per publication, psychology and biology average 8–10, earth and space science, physics, chemistry and clinical medicine average 12–15 and biomedical research papers average 18–20); (22) citation rates vary with countries of origin; (23) rates vary with the "size of the pool of available citers"; (24) methods and review papers "receive disproportionately more citations than theoretical or empirical papers"; (25) citation counts cannot allocate credit for papers with several authors; (26) researchers from some countries tend to be aware of and cite papers coming from their countries (e.g., Americans tend to cite papers by Americans); (27) citation counts do not distinguish positive or negative reasons for the citations; (28) authors tend to search the literature for and cite those papers that agree with their views; (29) citation rates vary with the physical accessibility of cited material; (30) changes in editors and editorial boards have produced changes in citation patterns (Sievert and Haughawout 1989); (31) recent papers are cited more than older ones because there are relatively more of the former (Oppenheim and Renn, 1978); (32) rapidly developing fields like molecular biology and biochemistry are "more dependent on fresh data" and therefore generate relatively more citations (Vinkler 1987).

Given the evidence just reviewed for and against the use of citation counts as measures of quality, reasonable people may come to different conclusions about their usefulness. In our view, such counts must be used with caution, recognizing that a wide variety of plausible assessment criteria are available and that use of a more robust array of such criteria may lead to different conclusions. Citation counts are used here with this caveat.

Table 1.1 shows that we have some flexibility in specifying a threshold figure for citation classics.

Classics in the *Journal of Business Ethics*

Our data were extracted from the total Web of Science database which, according to Thomson Reuters (2011), "contains 760 million+cited references…[drawn from] 12,032 high impact journals". On the basis of data taken from the Web of Science (and available to anyone), we found that in the 30 year period from 1982 to 2011 (June) there were a total of 4,747 titles published in the *Journal of Business Ethics*. Since the journal seldom published book reviews, editorials or letters, most of those titles represented articles. One thousand and eighty-four articles (22.8%) were not cited at all, which is fewer half of the 55–57% general average for the whole *Index* database, lower than the 74.7% for all social sciences material and the 48%

Table 1.1 Citation classics, diverse definitions and fields

Required cites, ≥	No. of classics	Maximum cites	Fields/Journals	Source
500	3	1255	All Sci.Cit.Index	Johnston (2003)
100	36	1255	All Sci.Cit.Index	Johnston (2003)
50	150	Na	Geography Js	Bodman (2003)
158[a]	100	705	J Am. Med. A	Garfield (1987)
100[b]	50		Anaesthesia & Pain Js	Terajima and Åneman (2003)
75	28	405	Chesap. Bio. Lab	Waring (2000)
50	21	868	Marine Bio. Js	Fuseler-McDowell (1988)
25[c]	na	Na	Medicine	Plomp (1990)

Source: Michalos 2005, p. 29
[a]Top 100 most cited articles selected, minimum citation frequency was 158
[b]Top 50 most cited articles selected, minimum citation frequency was 100
[c]Highly cited articles

for social science articles alone. The 3,663 (77.2%) cited articles generated 33,750 citations, with a classic hyperbolic distribution curve in which relatively few articles attract many citations and relatively many articles attract few citations. The mean number of citations per published article was 7.1, with a mode of 0, a median of 3, and a standard deviation of 12.1. There were 100 articles with 43 or more citations each (i.e., the mean of 7+3 standard deviations), and those 100 (2.1%) articles attracted 6,518/33,750 = 19.3%. of all citations. Fifty-one (1.0%) articles with 55 or more citations (i.e., 7+4 standard deviations) attracted 4,150/33,750 = 12.3% of all citations. Thirty-three (0.7%) articles with 67 or more citations (i.e., 7+5 standard deviations) attracted 3,077/33,750 = 9.1% of all citations.

Since articles with citation rates of 43 or more are 3 standard deviations above the mean, those articles form a fairly distinguished lot. Those with rates of 4 (55 citations), 5 (67 citations) or more standard deviations above the mean form an even more impressive group. If an article has more citations than 99% of all articles published in the journal, that is an outstanding achievement. Accordingly, we designated articles with citation rates at least 4 standard deviations above the mean as *citation classics*.

Comparing our threshold with those in Table 1.1, our bar has been set at over twice the height of Plomp's medical journals, and bit higher than Bodman's geography journals and Fuseler-McDowell's marine biology journals. The other five thresholds are higher than ours and some considerably higher. Our threshold of 55 citations produces more classics than five of the seven given in Table 1.1 and our paper with the greatest number of citations (210) is lower than that of the five studies providing maximum numbers. If our threshold was set at 5 standard deviations above the mean (67), our number of classics would have been higher than three of the seven entries in Table 1.1.

Table 1.2 contains a breakdown of the 100 most distinguished articles according to their age and citation counts. One would expect that the longer an article is available for citation, the better its chances of being cited and turning up in a list of citation classics. However, examination of the publication dates of the 100

Table 1.2 Age of article and citation rates

Group	1982–1991 (%)	1992–2001 (%)	2002–2011 (%)
Top 100	39.0	44.0	17.0
51 classics	41.2	49.0	9.8
18 4-sd classics	33.3	61.1	5.6
33 5-sd classics	45.5	42.4	12.1

articles examined to produce Table 1.2 reveals that this expectation is at best only partially confirmed. Table 1.2 gives a complete picture.

For the top 100, 51 classics and 18 4-standard deviation classics, the expectation is disconfirmed. In these three cases, the relative frequency of publications runs from those in the period 1992–2001 to 1982–1991 to 2001–2011. Among the 100 articles, 39% were published in the period from 1982 to1991 period, 44% in 1992–2001, and 17% in 2002–2011. Among the 51 citation classics, the gap between the 1992–2001 and 1982–1991 figures is larger than the gap for the same periods for the group of 100 articles, i.e., 7.8 vs. 5 percentage points. For the 18 articles whose rates are exactly 4 standard deviations above the mean, the gap is still larger, i.e., 27.8 vs. 7.8 percentage points. When we reach the 33 articles with rates of 5 or more standard deviations above the mean, the expected progression appears, i.e., 45.5% in the earliest period, 42.4% in the middle period and 12.1% in the last. Generally, age is probably an advantage, but not a sufficient condition for achieving the status of a classic.

Table 1.3 lists the 51 citation classics for the 1982–2011 (June) period. Ninety-four authors produced the 51 citation classics, for an average of 1.84 authors per article. For the 18 articles with rates between 55 and 66, there were 29 authors averaging 1.61 authors per article. For the elite 33 articles, there were 65 authors averaging 1.97 authors per article. Apparently, then, on average there is some advantage in having more authors per paper.

We identified the 51 classics' country origins by the country of the lead author. It hardly mattered because the lead authors of 86% (44) of the articles lived in the USA. Besides these, there were two articles coming from the Netherlands and Spain, and one each from the UK, Hong Kong and Israel.

Sixty-seven percent (34) of the classics involved some sort of quantitative analysis, e.g., surveys of consumers, business students and managers, as well as meta-analyses, development of new standardized measures and some modeling. There is no logically tidy way to distinguish theoretical from philosophical analyses. So, the best we can do is report that the remaining 33% were largely theoretical and/or philosophical.

We tried a variety of ways of sorting articles by topics and/or types, but there are too many articles that might plausibly be characterized in several different ways. Very roughly, about 51.0% of the classics involve some sort of analyses of moral virtue and behaviour, 17.6% are literature reviews, 15.7% are concerned with modeling ethical decision making, 9.8% concern some feature of codes of ethics and 5.9% are about corporate social and financial performance.

Table 1.3 *Journal of Business Ethics* Citation classics 1982–2011 (June)

Citations	Title	Author(s)	Vol.	Year
210	Ethical decision-making: a review of the empirical literature	Robert C Ford Woodrow D Richardson	13	1994
147	Toward the development of a multidimensional scale for improving evaluations of business ethics	R Eric Reidenbach Donald P Robin	9	1990
124	Corporate social responsibility theories: mapping the territory	Elisabet Garriga Domenec N Mele	53	2004
123	A behavioral model of ethical and unethical decision-making	Michael Bommer Clarence Gratto Jerry Gravander Mark Tuttle	6	1987
118	The effects of culture on ethical decision-making: an application of Hofstedes typology	Scott J Vitell Saviour L Nwachukwu James H Barnes	12	1993
111	Moral reasoning and business ethics: implications for research, education and management	Linda Klebe Trevino	11	1992
110	Organizational dissidence: the case of whistle-blowing	Janet P Near Marcia P Miceli	4	1985
106	The social desirability response bias in ethics research	Donna M Randall Maria F Fernandes	10	1991
106	Methodology in business ethics research: a review and critical assessment	Donna M Randall Annetta M Gibson	9	1990
105	A review of the empirical decision-making literature: 1996–2003	Michael J O'Fallon Kenneth D Butterfield	59	2005
100	Judging the morality of business practices: the influence of personal moral philosophies	Donelson R Forsyth	11	1992
98	A review of empirical studies assessing ethical decision-making in business	Terry W Loe Linda Ferrell Phylis Mansfield	25	2000
98	A study of the effect of age and gender upon student business ethics	Durwood Ruegger Earnest W King	11	1992
97	Some initial steps toward improving the measurement of ethical evaluations of marketing activities	R Eric Reidenbach Donald P Robin	7	1988
95	Differences in ethical perceptions between male and female managers: myth or reality	Jeaneen M Kidwell Robert E Stevens Art L Bethke	6	1987
88	Business ethics: a literature review with a focus on marketing ethics	John Tsalikis David J Fritzsche	8	1989
86	An integrative model for understanding and managing ethical behavior in business organizations	W Edward Stead Dan L Worrell Jean Garner Stead	9	1990
82	Concerns of college students regarding business ethics	Richard F Beltramini Robert A Peterson George Kozmetsky	3	1984

(continued)

Table 1.3 (continued)

Citations	Title	Author(s)	Vol.	Year
79	Gender differences in proclivity for unethical behavior	Michael Betz Lenahan O'Connell Jon M Shepard	8	1989
77	Predicting unethical behavior: a comparison of the theory of reasoned action and the theory of planned behavior	Man Kit Chang	17	1998
77	Consumer ethics: an investigation of the ethical beliefs of elderly consumers	Scott J Vitell James R Lumpkin Mohammed YA Rawwas	10	1991
73	The role of moral intensity in moral judgments: an empirical investigation	Sara A Morris Robert A McDonald	14	1995
73	Will the ethics of business change: a survey of future executives	Thomas M Jones Frederick H Gautschi	7	1988
73	Situational ethics: an empirical study of differentiators of student attitudes	Charles W McNichols Thomas W Zimmerer	4	1985
72	The relationship between corporate social performance and organizational size, financial performance and environmental performance	Peter A Stanwick Sarah A Stanwick	17	1998
71	Business codes of multinational firms: what do they say?	Muel Kaptein	50	2004
70	Consumer ethics: an empirical investigation of factors influencing ethical judgments of the final consumer	Scott J Vitell James Muncy	11	1992
70	The morality of software piracy: a cross-cultural analysis	William R Swinyard Heikki Rinne Au Keng Kau	9	1990
69	The association between corporate social responsibility and financial performance: the paradox of social cost	Moses L Pava Joshua Krausz	15	1996
68	Corporate ethics practices in the mid-1990s: an empirical study of the *Fortune 1000*	Gary R Weaver Linda Klebe Trevino Philip L Cochran	18	1999
67	Concepts and definitions of CSR and corporate sustainability: between agency and communion	Marcel van Marrewijk	44	2003
67	An experimental examination of the effects of individual and situational factors on unethical behavioral intentions in the workplace	Gwen E Jones Michael J Kavanagh	15	1996
67	Pinto fires and personal ethics: a script analysis of missed opportunities	Dennis A Gioia	11	1992
66	Toward an understanding of ethical climate: it's relationship to ethical behavior and supervisory influence	James C Wimbush Jon M Shepard	13	1994
65	The influence of stated organizational concern upon ethical decision-making	Eugene R Laczniak Edward J Inderrieden	6	1987

(continued)

Table 1.3 (continued)

Citations	Title	Author(s)	Vol.	Year
64	The nature of the relationship between corporate codes of ethics and behavior	Mark Schwartz	32	2001
63	Professional codes: why, how and with what impact	Mark S Frankel	8	1989
63	Ethical beliefs and behavior among managers: a cross-cultural perspective	Dove Izraeli	7	1988
61	Business ethics: conflicts, practices and belief of industrial executives	Scott J Vitell Troy A Festervand	29	2001
60	Codes of ethics as signals for ethical behavior	Janet S Adams Armen Tashchian Ted H Shore	26	2000
60	The impact of national culture on software piracy	Bryan W Husted	6	1987
59	Religiosity, ethical ideology and intentions to report a peer's wrongdoing	Tim Barnett Ken Bass Gene Brown	15	1996
59	Demographic and related differences in ethical views among small businesses	Paul J Serwinek	11	1992
58	An analysis of corporate ethical code studies: where do we go from here	Betsy Stevens	50	2004
58	Managers' personal values as drivers of corporate social responsibility	Christine A Hemingway Patrick W Maclagan	13	1994
57	Ethical values of individuals at different levels in the organizational hierarchy of a single firm	James R Harris	17	1998
57	Business students and ethics: a meta-analysis	Susan C Borkowski Yusuf J Ugras	9	1990
56	The challenge of ethical behavior in organizations	Ronald R Sims	11	1992
56	Personal characteristics in college students' evaluations of business ethics and corporate social responsibility	Peter Arlow	11	1992
56	Business ethics judgments: a cross-cultural comparison	Thomas W Whipple Dominic F Swords	10	1991
55	Corporate codes of ethics and sales force behavior: a case study	William A Weeks Jacques Nantel	11	1992

Comparisons with Business Ethics Quarterly, 2001–2011

Since people often make comparisons between the *Journal of Business Ethics* and *Business Ethics Quarterly*, we thought it would be useful to do some quantitative analysis. Because JOBE existed 10 years before BEQ, it would not have been reasonable or fair to compare the two journals for the life of each one. The best we could do is roughly compare outputs from the years 2001–2011.

For that period of time, JOBE published 2,753 articles, compared to 430 for BEQ, i.e., a bit over six articles were published in the former for every one published in the latter. The total numbers of citations for JOBE and BEQ were 12,697 and 1,895, respectively, again representing a bit over a six to one advantage. The mean citation rates and standard deviations for the two journals are remarkably similar. For JOBE the mean was 4.6 and the standard deviation was 8.0. For BEQ the comparable figures were 4.4 and 8.4. The maximum number of citations for a JOBE article was 124, compared to 90 for BEQ. Thirty-two percent of JOBE articles were not cited at all, compared to 38% of BEQ articles. So articles published in JOBE had a somewhat greater chance of being cited.

When we compared the top 20 articles in JOBE for the longer and shorter periods, we were surprised to find that only two appeared in both sets. In the 1982–2011 period, the Garriga and Mele (2004) article was in third place and the O'Fallon and Butterfield (2005) article was tenth. In the 2001–2011 period, the Garriga and Mele article placed first and O'Fallon and Butterfield came second. The differences in the two lists provide additional evidence of the insufficiency of article age as an explanation for citation status. The fact that the two articles appearing in both lists are literature review articles provides additional support to one of the most frequently noticed findings from citation research.

Comparing the JOBE and BEQ lists of the 20 most frequently cited articles by articles' lead authors, there is only one name appearing in both lists. The author is Geoff Moore. His JOBE article appeared in 2004 ("The fair trade movement: parameters, issues and future research") and his BEQ article appeared in 2005 ("Humanizing business: a modern virtue ethics and the virtuous corporation"). The JOBE article is a descriptive review of the fair trade movement and the BEQ article is a philosophical analysis. The fact that there is only one name in both lists supports the generally accepted view that the two journals serve somewhat overlapping but different research communities.

The articles by Garriga and Mele (2004) and Moore (2004) appeared in a Special Issue of JOBE based on the 16th Annual Conference of the European Business Ethics Network, edited by Laszlo Zsolnai and Laszlo Feteke. Apparently, then, very high quality articles may appear in Special Issues as well as in regular issues.

Because we believe in the soundness of most of the 25 arguments offered by Seglen (1997) showing that Journal Impact Factors are invalid measures of journal quality, we have not presented any such figures here. The comparisons explained earlier of the differences in the top ranked articles in JOBE for longer and shorter periods reveals an important time-related dimension for the use of citation rates for any purpose. Articles with impressive citation rates in the short run may have less or more impressive rates in the long run, and there is no rule book to help researchers decide exactly what length time-runs are most appropriate. Since one publishes to be read, if all other things are equal, the longer one's material is read, the better. Some philosopher said, with exaggeration no doubt, that one should write for all eternity, meaning not take an eternity to write but to be read for eternity. From this point of view, which we accept, it would be preferable to be well-cited over 30 years versus 20 or 2.

One of the most interesting things we found by examining the top 20 articles in JOBE and BEQ for the 2001–2011 period was the very long lag time for citation of articles in both journals. For JOBE, among the top 20 articles, there was one article from 2006, and for BEQ there was one article from 2007, i.e., the article with the nearest publication date to 2011 in the top 20 for JOBE came out 5 years earlier and for BEQ 4 years earlier. If these lag times are anywhere representative of most of the articles published in these two journals, then it would clearly be a serious mistake to suppose that a Journal Impact Factor carries any useful information at all. A Journal's Impact Factor is calculated by dividing of the number of times articles are cited in any year by the number of articles, reviews, proceedings or notes published in the 2 previous years, e.g., the Impact Factor for JOBE or BEQ for 2011 would be the result of dividing the number of citations to articles in those journals that year by the number of publications in those journals for 2009 and 2010. If it usually takes at least 4 or 5 years before the top articles in these journals are cited, the 2-year basis used for Journal Impact Factors makes such measures irrelevant. Seglen (1997, p. 506) remarked that "far from being a quality indicator, citation impact is primarily a measure of scientific utility, rather than of scientific quality". We would add the qualification "*short term* scientific utility".

Appendix: Articles with Citation Rates Greater than 3 and Less than 4 Standard Deviations Above the Mean, 1982–2011 (June)

Citations	Title	Author(s)	Vol.	Year
54	Supply chain specific? Understanding the patchy success of ethical sourcing initiatives	Sarah Roberts	44	2003
54	Evolution and implementation: a study of values, business ethics and corporate social responsibility	Brenda E Joyner Dinah Payne	41	2002
54	Measuring the impact of teaching ethics to future managers – a review, assessment and recommendations	James Weber	9	1990
53	Enron ethics (or: culture matters more than codes)	Ronald R Sims Johannes Brinkmann	45	2003
53	A cross-cultural comparison of the ethics of business students	Steven Lysonski William Gaidis	10	1991
53	Ethical attitudes of students and business professionals – a study of moral reasoning	John A Wood Justin G Longenecker Joseph A McKinney Carlos W Moore	7	1988

(continued)

Appendix (continued)

Citations	Title	Author(s)	Vol.	Year
52	An empirical investigation of the relationship between change in corporate social performance and financial performance: a stakeholder theory perspective	Bernadette M Ruf Krishnamurty Muralidhar Robert M Brown Jay J Janney Karen Paul	32	2001
52	The institutionalization of organizational ethics	Ronald R Sims	10	1991
52	Toward a profile of student software piraters	Ronald R Sims Hsing K Cheng Hildy Teegen	15	1996
52	Ethical decision-making in the medical profession – an application of the theory of planned behavior	Donna M Randall Annetta M Gibson	10	1991
51	The perceived role of ethics and social responsibility: a scale development	Anusorn Singhapakdi Scott J Vitell Kumar C Rallapalli Kenneth L Kraft	15	1996
51	Situational determinants of software piracy: an equity theory perspective	Richard S Glass Wallace A Wood	15	1996
51	A comparative analysis of ethical beliefs – a 4 country study	Mee-Kau Nyaw Ignace Ng	13	1994
50	Consumers' perceptions of corporate social responsibilities: a cross-cultural comparison	Isabelle Maignan	30	2001
50	Empiricism in business ethics – suggested research directions	Diana C Robertson	12	1993
50	Ethical behavior of marketing managers	David J Fritzsche Helmut Becker	2	1983
49	Corporate legitimacy as deliberation: a communicative framework	Guido Palazzo Aandreas G Scherer	66	2006
49	Ethical codes of conduct and organizational context: a study of the relationship between codes of conduct, employee behavior and organizational values	Mark J Somers	30	2001
49	Issue-contingent effects on ethical decision making: a cross-cultural comparison	Mark A Davis Nancy Brown Johnson Douglas G Ohmer	17	1998
49	Softlifting – a model of motivating factors	Penny M Simpson Debasish Banerjee Claude L Simpson	13	1994
48	The Fair Trade movement: parameters, issues and future research	Geoff Moore	53	2004
48	Environmental marketing: a source of reputational, competitive and financial advantage	Morgan P Miles Jeffrey G Covin	23	2000
48	Toward an understanding of cross-cultural ethics – a tentative model	William A Wines Nancy K Napier	11	1992

(continued)

Appendix (continued)

Citations	Title	Author(s)	Vol.	Year
48	Ethical behavior among marketing researchers – an assessment of selected demographic characteristics	SW Kelley OC Ferrell SJ Skinner	9	1990
48	An empirical study of moral reasoning among managers	Robbin Derry	8	1989
48	Implementing business ethics	Patrick E Murphy	7	1988
48	Business ethics – a cross-cultural comparison of managers	Helmut Becker David J Fritzsche	6	1987
48	The status of business ethics – past and future	Richard T DeGeorge	6	1987
47	The maturing of socially responsible investment: a review of the developing link with corporate social responsibility	Russell Sparkes Chirstopher J Cowton	52	2004
47	Behind the mask: revealing the true face of corporate citizenship	Dirk Matten Andrew Crane Wendy Chapple	45	2003
47	Consumer ethics research: review, synthesis and suggestions for the future	Scott J Vitell	43	2003
47	The role of consumers' trust in online-shopping	Sonja Grabner-Kraeuter	39	2002
47	Professional ethics – business students perceptions	James R Davis Ralph E Welton	10	1991
47	The moral authority of transnational corporate codes	William C Frederick	10	1991
47	Ethical beliefs differences of males and females	John Tsalikis M Ortiz-buonafina	9	1990
47	Correlates of salespeoples' ethical conflict – an exploratory investigation	Alan J Dubinsky Thomas N Ingram	3	1984
46	What will consumers pay for social product features?	Pat Auger Paul Burke Timothy M Devinney Jordan J Louviere	42	2003
46	Should trees have managerial standing – toward stakeholder status of nonhuman nature	Mark Starik	14	1995
46	Software piracy – is it related to level of moral judgment	Jeanne M Logsdon Judith Kenner Thompson Richard A Reid	13	1994
46	Oppositionists and group norms – the reciprocal influence of whistle-blowers and coworkers	David B Greenberger Marcia P Micheli Debra J Cohen	6	1987
45	Social accountability and corporate greenwashing	William S Laufer	43	2003
45	Learning from the literature on collegiate cheating: a review of empirical research	Deborah F Crown M Shane Spiller	17	1998

(continued)

Appendix (continued)

Citations	Title	Author(s)	Vol.	Year
44	Corporate social responsibility in the twenty-first century: a view from the world's most successful firms	Jamie Snider Ronald P Hill Diane Martin	48	2003
44	Corporate communication and impression management – new perspectives why companies engage in corporate social reporting	Reggy Hooghiemstra	27	2000
44	Observer judgments about moral agents' ethical decisions: the role of scope of justice and moral intensity	MS Singer Alan E Singer	16	1997
44	The influence of ethical fit on employee satisfaction, commitment and turnover	Randi L Sims KGalen Kroeck	13	1994
44	Approaches to organizational culture and ethics	Amanda Sinclair	12	1993
43	Codes of ethics	George CS Benson	8	1989
43	Differences in research ethics judgments between male and female marketing professionals	Ishmael P Akaah	8	1989

References

Bodman, A.R. 2003, Citation classics in geography journals (Abstract), Association of American Geographers. http://convention.allacademic.com/aag2003/view_paper_info.html?pub_id=2274. Accessed 19 Dec 2003.

Bonzi, S., and H.W. Snyder. 1991. Motivations for citation: A comparison of self-citation and citation to others. *Scientometrics* 21(2): 245–254.

Brooks, T.A. 1985. Private acts and public objects: An investigation of citer motivations. *Journal of the American Society for Information Science* 36(4): 223–229.

Brooks, T.A. 1988. Citer motivations. In *Encyclopedia of library and information science*, ed. A. Kent, 48–59. New York: Marcel Dekker.

Fuseler-McDowell, E. 1988. Documenting the literature of marine biology. In *Marine science information throughout the world*, ed. C.P. Winn, R.W. Burkhart, and J.C. Burkhart. Charleston: International Association of Aquatic and Marine Science Libraries and Information Centers.

Garfield, E. 1972. Citation analysis as a tool in journal evaluation. *Science* 178: 471–479.

Garfield, E. 1973. Uncitedness III – The importance of *not* being cited. *Current Contents* 24(February 21): 413–414.

Garfield, E. 1976. Is the ratio between number of citations and publications cited a true constant? *Current Contents* 6(February 9): 419–421.

Garfield, E. 1977. Restating the fundamental assumptions of citation analysis. *Current Contents* 39(September 26): 232–239.

Garfield, E. 1981. Why the *Journal Citation Reports*? In *Science citation index: Journal citation reports*, ed. E. Garfield. Philadelphia: Institute for Scientific Information.

Garfield, E. 1983. How to use *Journal Citation Reports*, including a special salute to the *Johns Hopkins Medical Journal. Current Contents* 17(April 25): 131–138.

Garfield, E. 1985. Uses and misuses of citation frequency. *Current Contents* 43(October 28): 403–409.

Garfield, E. 1987. 100 citation classics from the *Journal of the American Medical Association. Journal of the American Medical Association* 257(1): 52–59.

Garfield, E. 1988. The impact of citation counts – A UK perspective. *Current Contents* 37(September 13): 296–298.
Garfield, E. 1989. Citation behavior – An aid or a hindrance to information retrieval? *Current Contents* 18(May 1): 3–8.
Garriga, E., and D. Mele. 2004. Corporate social responsibility theories: Mapping the territory. *Journal of Business Ethics* 53: 51–71.
Hamilton, D.P. 1990. Publishing by – And for? – The numbers. *Science* 250: 1331–1332.
Johnston, G.A.R. 2003. Citations in science citation index. http://www.usyd.edu.au/pharmacology/aalab/Citations.html. Accessed 19 Dec 2003.
Kuhn, T. 1970. *The structure of scientific revolutions*. Chicago: University of Chicago Press.
Lawani, S.M., and A.E. Bayer. 1983. Validity of citation criteria for assessing the influence of scientific publications: New evidence with peer assessment. *Journal of the American Society for Information Science* 34(1): 59–66.
MacRoberts, M.H., and B.R. MacRoberts. 1986. Quantitative measures of communication in science: A study of the formal level. *Social Studies of Science* 16: 151–172.
MacRoberts, M.H., and B.R. MacRoberts. 1987. Testing the Ortega hypothesis: Facts and artifacts. *Scientometrics* 12(5–6): 293–295.
MacRoberts, M.H., and B.R. MacRoberts. 1989a. Problems of citation analysis: A critical review. *Journal of the American Society for Information Science* 40(5): 342–349.
MacRoberts, M.H., and B.R. MacRoberts. 1989b. Citation analysis and the science policy arena. *Trends in Biochemical Sciences* 14(1): 8–10.
Merton, R.K. 1977. The sociology of science: An episodic memoir. In *The sociology of science in Europe*, ed. R.K. Merton and J. Gaston, 3–141. Carbondale: Southern Illinois University Press.
Michalos, A.C. (ed.). 2005. *Citation classics from social indicators research*. Dordrecht: Springer.
Moore, G. 2004. The fair trade movement: parameters, issues and future research. *Journal of Business Ethics* 52: 73–86.
Moore, G. 2005. Humanizing business: A modern virtue ethics and the virtuous corporation. *Business Ethics Quarterly* 15: 237–255.
Moravcsik, M.J., and P. Murugesan. 1975. Some results on the function and quality of citations. *Social Studies of Science* 5: 86–92.
Narin, F. 1976. *Evaluative Bibliometrics: The use of publication and citation analysis in the evaluation of scientific activity*. Washington, DC: Computer Horizons.
O'Fallon, M.J., and K.D. Butterfield. 2005. A review of the empirical ethical decision-making literature: 1996–2003. *Journal of Business Ethics* 59: 375–413.
Oppenheim, C., and S.P. Renn. 1978. Highly cited old papers and the reasons why they continue to be cited. *Journal of the American Society for Information Science* 29: 225–231.
Pendlebury, D.A. 1991. Science, citation and funding. *Science* 251: 1410–1411.
Plomp, R. 1990. The significance of the number of highly cited papers as an indicator of scientific prolificacy. *Scientometrics* 19(3–4): 185–197.
Seglen, P.O. 1997. Why the impact factor of journals should not be used for evaluating research. *British Medical Journal* 314: 497–506.
Sievert, M.E., and M. Haughawout. 1989. An editor's influence on citation patterns: A case study of *Elementary School Journal*. *Journal of the American Society for Information Science* 40(5): 334–341.
Terajima, K., and A. Åneman. 2003. Citation classics in anaesthesia and pain journals: A literature review in the era of the internet. *Acta Anaesthesiologica Scandinavica* 47(6): 655–663.
Thomson Reuters. 2011. Real facts: Real numbers: Real knowledge, http://wokinfo.com/realfacts/qualityandquantity/.
Vinkler, P. 1987. A quasi-quantitative citation model. *Scientometrics* 12(1–2): 47–72.
Virgo, J.A. 1977. A statistical procedure of evaluating the importance of scientific papers. *The Library Quarterly* 47(4): 415–430.
Waring, E. 2000. Citation classics Chesapeake Biological Laboratory, 1925–2000, UM Center for Environmental Science Libraries, Summer. http://www.cbl.umces.edu/Library/history.php3. Accessed 19 Dec 2003.

Chapter 2
Ethical Decision Making: A Review of the Empirical Literature

Robert C. Ford and Woodrow D. Richardson

Ethical decision making is a topic of great interest in the literature of business ethics. A number of authors have proposed a variety of theoretical models in the effort to explain and predict the process by which a manager makes an ethical decision. These range from the situational-individual interaction model of Trevino (1986) to the contingency framework of Ferrell and Gresham (1985) to the moral intensity model of Jones (1991). While any of these models might serve as a basis for undertaking empirical study of the ethical decision process, there is surprisingly limited effort directed toward theory testing (Randall and Gibson 1990). Indeed, most of the writing on this topic has been nonempirical (Trevino 1986). The paucity of empirical research grounded on theory has substantially impeded the development of the field.

The purpose of this article is to examine the available empirical literature on ethical decision making. By reviewing the extent to which empirical work supports or refutes the ethical decision making models, it will be possible to better understand the extent to which these models are predictive and descriptive of an individual's ethical decision behavior. Further, it will be possible to identify the factors that have been found associated with such behavior and those factors that are not. It is not our purpose to propose another model of ethical decision making behavior but rather to rely on those already developed to identify those factors which merit further study. Thus, the contribution of this paper is to organize the available empirical information in order to see what we know and need to know about the factors which are hypothesized as determinants of ethical decision behavior.

R.C. Ford (✉)
Department of Management, College of Business Administration,
University of Central Florida, Orlando FL 32816-1400, USA
e-mail: rford@bus.ucf.edu

W.D. Richardson
Harry F. Byrd, Jr. School of Business, Shenandoah University, Winchester VA 22601, USA

A.C. Michalos and D.C. Poff (eds.), *Citation Classics from the Journal of Business Ethics*, Advances in Business Ethics Research 2,
DOI 10.1007/978-94-007-4126-3_2,

In general, the ethical decision making models divide the postulated influences on an individual's decision behavior into two broad categories (for a review of those theoretical models which have been proposed see Ford and Hansen 1991; Jones 1991; Randall and Gibson 1990). The first category includes variables associated with the individual decision maker. The second category consists of variables which form and define the situation in which the individual makes decisions.

This paper uses these two broad categories as an organizational scheme to review empirical studies that have been published on the ethical decision process. While it could be argued that the second category should actually be divided into situation specific versus general environmental variables (cf. Bommer et al. 1987), the transitory influences of such variables across decision dilemmas makes such a categorization problematic. Although using only two broad categories may sacrifice specificity for the sake of parsimony, we feel that this approach is preferable to creating "another" model of the process. This general approach should allow researchers to better assess the existing body of empirical work and its applicability to their own theoretical efforts.

Individual Factors

Individual factors have received by far the most research attention in the empirical literature. This category includes all those factors that are uniquely associated with the individual decision maker. Thus, these factors include those variables that are a result of birth (e.g. nationality, sex, age, etc.) as well as those that are a result of the human development and socialization process (e.g. personality, attitudes, values, education, religion, employment, etc.). These factors, then, represent the sum total of the life experiences and circumstances of birth that a particular individual brings to the decision making process.

Table 2.1 depicts the variety of factors which have been investigated. The table is divided into categories representing an individual's personal attributes, education and employment background, and personality.

Personal Attributes

The first four factors reported on Table 2.1 deal with variables associated with an individual's personal attributes. These factors include attributes determined by the circumstances of an individual's birth (religion and nationality) as well as those that are set by birth (age and sex).

Religion

The four studies reported here investigated religious value orientation (Hegarty and Sims 1978, 1979) strength of religious belief (McNichols and Zimmerer 1985),

Table 2.1 Empirical evidence relating the effect of individual factors on ethical behavior

Variable Study (Year)	Sample	Method	Finding
Personal attributes			
Religion			
Hegarty and Sims (1978, 1979)	Grad stud.	Lab experiment	Not significant
Kidwell et al. (1987)	Managers	Ques. Newstrom and Ruch (1975)	No relationship between denomination or church attendance and perceptions of what is ethical
McNichols and Zimmerer (1985)	UG stud.	Scenarios	Strong religious beliefs assoc. with negative attitude toward the acceptability of behaviors
Nationality			
Abratt et al. (1992)	Managers	Questionnaire	No difference in the responses of managers from S. Africa and Australia
Becker and Fritzche (1987)	French, German and U.S. Mgrs.	Questionnaire	French mgrs. believed more strongly in the efficacy of codes of conduct
Hegarty and Sims (1978, 1979)	Grad stud.	Lab experiment	Non-U.S. citizen were more unethical
Whipple and Swords (1992)	U.S. and U.K. bus. stud.	Questionnaire	Not significant
White and Rhodeback (1992)	U.S. and Taiwanese	Vignettes	U.S. managers tended to provide higher ethicality ratings
Sex			
Beltramini et al. (1984)	UG students	Questionnaire	Females more concerned with ethical issues
Browning and Zabriskie (1983)	Members of Pur. Assoc.	Questionnaire	Not significant
Callan (1992)	State emp.	Questionnaire	Not significant
Chonko and Hunt (1985)	Managers	Questionnaire	Males saw fewer ethical problems than females
Dubinsky and Levy (1985)	Salespeople	Questionnaire	Not significant
Ferrell and Skinner (1988)	Marketing researchers	Questionnaire	Females exhibited higher levels of ethical behavior
Hegarty and Sims (1978, 1979)	Grad stud.	Lab experiment	Not significant

(continued)

Table 2.1 (continued)

Variable Study (Year)	Sample	Method	Finding
Jones and Gautschi (1988)	MBA stud.	Open-ended questions	Females less likely to be company loyal in an ethically questionable environment
Kidwell et al. (1987)	Managers	Ques. Newstrom and Ruch (1975)	Males and females differed on only 1 of 17 items Males more likely to conceal their errors
McNichols and Zimmerer (1985)	Students	Scenarios	Not significant
Ruegger and King (1992)	Students	Questionnaire	Females more ethical than males
Serwinek (1992)	Insurance employees	Questionnaire	No difference on three of four ethical indices
Whipple and Swords (1992)	Students	Questionnaire	Females more critical of ethical issues than male counterparts
Age			
Browning and Zabriskie (1983)	Members of Put. Assoc.	Questionnaire	Younger mgrs. had a more ethical viewpoint than older mgrs.
Callan (1992)	State emp.	Questionnaire	Not significant
Izraeli (1988)	Managers	Questionnaire	Not significant
Jones and Gautschi (1988)	MBA students	Open-ended questions	Weak significance on 2 of 14 items
Kidwell et al. (1987)	Managers	Questionnaire	Not significant
Ruegger and King (1992)	Students	Questionnaire	Older students were more ethical
Serwinek (1992)	Insurance employees	Questionnaire	Older workers had stricter interpretations of ethical standards
Stevens (1984)	Students and executives	Questionnaire Clark (1966)	Not significant
Education and employment background			
Type of education			
Beltramini et al. (1984)	Students	Questionnaire	Business majors more concerned with ethical issues than other majors
Chonko and Hunt (1985)	Managers	Questionnaire	Technical majors more ethical than nontechnical majors
Dubinsky and Ingram (1984)	Salespeople	Questionnaire	Not significant

Goodman and Crawford (1974)	Students	Scenarios	Not significant
Hawkins and Cocanoughec (1972)	Students	Scenarios	Bus. majors more tolerant of questionable practices
Laczniak and Inderrieden (1987)	MBA stud.	In-basket	Technical vs. Nontechnical educ. had no effect
McNichols and Zimmerer (1985)	Students	Scenarios	Not significant
Stevens et al. (1989)	Stud., Mgrs. Attorneys	Ques. Newstrom and Ruch (1975)	Few differences in the views of managers, bus. stud., attorneys, and law students
Years of education			
Browning and Zabriskie (1983)	Members of Put. Assoc.	Questionnaire	Managers with Higher Educ. viewed gifts as unethical
Dubinsky and Ingram (1984)	Salespeople	Questionnaire	Not significant
Jones and Gautschi (1988)	MBA students	Open-ended questions	Graduate degree respondents were less likely than Undergraduate to exhibit loyalty response
Kidwell et al. (1987)	Managers	Questionnaire	Not significant
Lane et al. (1988)	G/UG stud.	Questionnaire	Statistical differences on only 4 of 12 items
Serwinek (1992)	Insurance employees	Questionnaire	Not significant
Employment			
Arlow and Ulrich (1980)	Students and executives	Questionnaire Clark (1966)	Executives more ethical than students
Dubinsky and Gwin (1981)	Sales and Purch. Mgrs.	Scenarios	Purchasing mgrs. see more questionable business practices than do Sales mgrs.
Goodman and Crawford (1974)	MBAs and Mgrs.	Scenarios	Not significant
Stevens (1984)	Students/executives	Questionnaire Clark (1966)	Executives more ethical than students
Stevens et al. (1989)	Stud., Mgrs. Attorneys	Ques. Newstrom and Ruch (1975)	Not significant
Years of employment			
Callan (1992)	State employees	Questionnaire	Length of service not related to ethical values
Dubinsky and Ingram (1984)	Managers	Questionnaire	Not significant
Kidwell et al. (1987)	Managers	Questionnaire	Those with more years employed tended to exhibit more ethical responses

(continued)

Table 2.1 (continued)

Variable Study (Year)	Sample	Method	Finding
Serwinek	Ins. emp.	Questionnaire	Not significant
Personality/Beliefs/Values			
Machiavellian			
Hegarty and Sims (1978, 1979)	Grad stud.	Lab experiment	High Machiavellian assoc. with unethical beh.
Singhapakdi and Vitell (1990)	Marketing managers	Questionnaire	High Mach. mgrs. perceived ethical problems as less serious and were less likely to take action
Neuroticism, extroversion and value orientation			
Hegarty and Sims (1978, 1979)	Grad stud.	Lab experiment	Neuroticism, extrov. and political orien - n.s.; econ. orien assoc. with unethical behavior
Locus of control			
Hegarty and Sims (1978, 1979)	Grad stud.	Lab experiment	Not significant
Zahra (1989)	Managers	Questionnaire	External LOC mgrs. perceived organizational politics as ethical
Role conflict and ambiguity			
Dubinsky and Ingram (1984)	Salespeople	Questionnaire	Not significant
Acceptance of authority			
Ferrell and Skinner (1988)	Marketing researchers	Questionnaire	Not significant

denomination, and a behavior, frequency of church attendance (Kidwell et al. 1987). Of these factors, only strength of religious belief was significantly and positively related to strength of ethical standards (McNichols and Zimmerer 1985).

Nationality

The second personal attribute is nationality. Again, the results are mixed. As in the studies of religion, the studies and their results are not directly comparable. Abratt et al. (1992) found no difference in the responses of managers from South Africa and Australia while the Hegarty and Sims (1978, 1979) and White and Rhodeback (1992) studies showed a significant correlation between unethical behavior and non-U.S. citizenship. The Becker and Fritzsche (1987) study investigated the degree to which French, German, and U.S. managers differed in believing that codes of conduct were effective in influencing managerial behavior with the French having the greatest faith in these ethical devices.

Sex

Sex is reported in more empirical studies than any other single variable. Fourteen are listed on Table 2.1. Of these, seven reveal that females are likely to act more ethically than males; at least in some situations (Beltramini et al. 1984; Chonko and Hunt 1985; Ferrell and Skinner 1988; Jones and Gautschi 1988; Kidwell et al. 1987; Ruegger and King 1992; Whipple and Swords 1992). While seven other studies found that sex had no impact on ethical beliefs (Browning and Zabriskie 1983; Callan 1992; Dubinsky and Levy 1985; Hegarty and Sims 1978, 1979; McNichols and Zimmerer 1985; Serwinek 1992).

Age

The last personal attribute found measured in the empirical literature is age. Here, there are eight studies (Browning and Zabriskie 1983; Callan 1992; Izraeli 1988; Jones and Gautschi 1988; Kidwell et al. 1987; Ruegger and King 1992; Serwinek 1992; Stevens 1984) to report. Only three found a significant relationship between older and younger respondents and their ethical beliefs. Browning and Zabriskie (1983) reported that younger purchasing managers had a more ethical viewpoint than older managers. However, Serwinek (1992) found that older workers had stricter interpretations of ethical standards, and Ruegger and King (1992) found older students to be more ethical than younger students.

Overall, the mixed results for some personal attributes that have been tested and the lack of a significant correlation in many studies between such factors and ethical beliefs, suggests:

Summary

Personal attributes are related to an individual's ethical beliefs and decision making behavior in some studies but not in others.

Education and Employment Background

The next four individual factors reported in Table 2.1 are those relating to educational background and employment experience. These factors include type of education, years of education, type of employment, and years of employment. Here, studies report some significant relationships but, unfortunately, they tend to contradict one another.

Type of Education

Hawkins and Cocanoughec (1972) compared business students with other majors and report that business students are more tolerant of unethical behavior than non-business students. On the other hand, Beltramini and his associates (1984) report that business majors are more concerned about ethical issues than others. Since the two studies were asking different questions and used different methods, these results are not necessarily inconsistent (e.g. business majors may be more concerned than others even though they are more tolerant). In a different approach to the education issue, Chonko and Hunt (1985) found managers with technical backgrounds to be more ethical than managers with non-technical backgrounds, while Laczniak and Inderrieden (1987) found no difference in ethical beliefs for MBA students with technical versus those with non-technical educational backgrounds. Likewise, Stevens and his associates (1989) found few differences between the ethical beliefs of managers and business students or attorneys and law students. Two other studies (Goodman and Crawford 1974; McNichols and Zimmerer 1985) reported in Table 2.1 found no significant differences in type of education.

Years of Education

The number of years of education also exhibited mixed results. Browning and Zabriskie (1983) found that purchasing managers with more education viewed gifts and favors to be more unethical than less educated purchasing managers. This was partially supported by Jones and Gautschi (1988) and Lane et al. (1988). In three other studies (Dubinsky and Ingram 1984; Kidwell et al. 1987; Serwinek 1992) however, no significant relationship was found.

Employment and Years of Employment

For the next two groupings reported on Table 2.1, employment versus student status and years of employment, the results are again mixed. Two studies comparing students and managers found that managers were more ethical than students (Arlow and Ulrich 1980; Stevens 1984). In a similar study using Newstrom and Ruch's (1975) questionnaire, Stevens et al. (1989) found few differences in ethical beliefs between managers, business students, attorneys, and law students, although the professionals' ethical beliefs were generally higher than their student counterparts.

In addition to these studies, Dubinsky and Gwin (1981) report a comparison between managers from two different functional areas. This comparison between purchasing managers and salespeople shows a significantly different ethical perspective between the two and reveals the need to consider such comparisons in future work. Brenner and Molander (1977) report responses from a variety of functional areas but do not report any statistical analysis of the importance, if any, these functional identifications may have on ethical behavior. Also, a study by Bowman (1976) sought to compare results of a survey of public administrators with the data from an earlier, nearly identical, study by Carroll (1975) of business administrators. Although there are no statistical tests of differences reported (for this reason these studies are not included in Table 2.1), a number of comparisons are reported where the percentage agreement with an ethical issue is clearly different between the two groups of respondents. Finally, a study by Kidwell and her associates (1987) found a relationship between years of employment and. ethical beliefs.

Here, the scarcity of empirical work makes it difficult to conclude anything other than further study is warranted on both age and employment related factors. Intriguingly, such data may be already available from the reported studies since these items are frequently included in the data collection methods used in the majority of the studies reported above. Authors of these studies might easily reanalyse their data to discover any significant differences due to any of these factors. However, it is very likely that age and years of employment would be highly intercorrelated as would managerial position, education, and age (Posner and Schmidt 1987). This makes isolating the primary effects (if any) of such factors very difficult and leads to:

Summary

In some instances, type and years of education and type and years of employment are related to an individual's ethical beliefs and decision making behavior. However, in other situations, ethical beliefs and decision making are independent of education and employment.

Personality, Beliefs and Values

The last group of individual factors reported in the empirical literature on ethical behavior focuses on the personality factors, values and beliefs of the decision maker. Here, only a half dozen studies have appeared. By far the most extensive work in this area is reported in two articles by Hegarty and Sims (1978, 1979). In their lab experiments, they included measures of a variety of personality factors including the Allport-Vernon-Lindzey Scale of Values, the Rotter External-Internal Locus of Control Scales, Eysenck Neuroricism-Extroversion Scales, and the Machiavellianism Scale.

Machiavellianism

In their investigation of the covariates of ethical decision behavior Hegarty and Sims (1978, 1979) found that Machiavellianism explained significant variance in ethical behavior in both studies. A later study by Singhapakdi and Vitell (1990) supports this by finding that Machiavellian managers perceive ethical problems as less serious than others and were less likely to take action to correct the problem.

Values

The Allport-Vernon-Lindzey measure of economic value orientation was significant in the Hegarty and Sims (1978, 1979) studies, while the political value orientation was significant in the 1978 study but not the 1979 study. The Eysenck measures of neuroticism and extroversion showed no significant relationship to ethical behavior (Hegarty and Sims 1978, 1979).

Locus of Control

In the measure of Internal versus External Locus of control, the results were again mixed with significant results in 1978, but no significance was found in the 1979 study (Hegarty and Sims). In a more recent study, Zahra (1989) supports the significance of the earlier results by finding that external locus of control managers viewed organization politics as ethical behavior.

Other Variables

Beyond these few studies, there is little else to report on personality related variables. Dubinsky and Ingram (1984) found no relationship with role conflict – role ambiguity measures in their study and Ferrell and Skinner (1988) found no significant relationship with an acceptance of authority measure they used.

It seems intuitively obvious that certain personality traits should be related to ethical decision behavior. There are many well accepted measures that offer fruitful opportunities for future empirical investigation. Indeed, even replication of the studies noted above could contribute greatly to a better understanding of the relationship between various dimensions of the individual's personality and that person's ethical decision making behavior. In light of the limited evidence, we offer the following:

Summary

Some personality traits of the decision maker are related to his/her ethical beliefs and behavior. Interestingly, the trait which would have the strongest predicted theoretical relationship (i.e. Machiavellianism) to ethical beliefs and decision making has been verified in the empirical work.

Situational Factors

The second category of factors included in most theoretical models are associated with the situation. While several theoretical models make the distinction between situation specific, overall organizational, and general environmental variables, these have been combined together in this review as noted earlier. This category includes a variety of situational forces that are conceptually distinct from the individual factors listed in Table 2.1. These forces, then represent the situational pressures which come to bear on the individual to encourage or discourage ethical decision making. Thus, in our review, this category would include the individual's referent groups, the ethical values and practices of the supervisor, organizational culture, industry norms, and overall social values.

Referent Groups

The studies investigating referent group factors include studies of both peer groups, top management influences on ethical decision behavior, and the use of rewards and sanctions.

Peer Group Influence

The peer group studies listed on Table 2.2 are essentially those of Mary Zey-Ferrell. She reports (Zey-Ferrell et al. 1979) that respondent's perceptions of the beliefs of his or her peers is the best predictor of the respondent's ethical behavior. In a later study with Ferrell (Zey-Ferrell and Ferrell 1982), they found that this predictive

Table 2.2 Empirical evidence relating factors not specific to the individual and ethical decision making

Variable Study (Year)	Sample	Method	Finding
Referent Groups			
Peer group influence			
Dubinsky and Loken (1989)	Salespeople	Questionnaire (Ajzen and Fishbein Model)	Intenders more likely to feel pressure from referents especially top mgmt. and supervisors
Izraeli (1988)	Israeli managers	Ques. Newstrom and Ruch (1975)	What peers do was the best predictor of ethical behavior
Pratt and McLaughlin (1989)	Students	Questionnaire	Students more sensitive to their professors' beliefs as ethical benchmark than peer beliefs
Zey-Ferrell and Ferrell (1982)	Advertising managers	Ques. Newstrom and Ruch (1975)	Interorganizational referent groups less likely to influence behavior
Zey-Ferrell *et al.* (1979)	Marketing managers	Questionnaire	Perceptions of peers' behavior influenced unethical beh. more than respondents own beliefs
Top management influence			
Akaah and Riordan (1989)	Marketers	Scenarios – (Crawford 1970)	Absence of top mgmt. actions against unethical behavior resulted in stronger approval of questionable practices
Murphy et al. (1992)	Managers	Questionnaire	Actions of Top Mgrs. had minimal influence on organizational ethical behavior
Zey-Ferrell and Ferrell (1982)	Managers	Ques. Newstrom and ruch (1975)	Mixed Results
Zey-Ferrell et al. (1979)	Managers	Questionnaire	Not significant
Rewards & sanctions			
Fritzsche and Becker (1983)	Marketers	Vignettes	Severe consequences leads to actions that are perceived to be supported by top management
Hegarty and Sims (1978)	Grad stud.	Lab experiment	Rewarding unethical behavior increases unethical behavior
Hunt et al. (1984)	Market researchers	Questionnaire	Top Mgmt. actions reduce ethical problems
Laczniak and Inderrieden (1987)	MBA stud.	In-basket	Mixed discipline leads to ethical behavior

Codes of conduct			
Akaah and Riordan (1989)	Marketers	Scenarios – (Crawford 1970)	Not significant
Chonko and Hunt (1985)	Managers	Questionnaire	Codes affect mgrs. perception of the extent of ethical problems
Ferrell and Skinner (1988)	Marketing researchers	Questionnaire	Enforced Codes assoc. w/higher levels of ethical behavior for data subcontractors and research firms, but not corp. researchers
Hegarty and Sims (1979)	Grad stud.	Lab experiment	Codes of conduct were positively related to ethical behavior
Hunt et al. (1984)	Marketing researchers	Questionnaire	Not significant
Laczniak and Inderrieden (1987)	Students	In-basket	Codes + sanctions leads to more ethical behav. weak support
Murphy et al. (1992)	Managers	Questionnaire	
Singhapakdi and Vitell (1990)	Marketing managers	Questionnaire	Ethical policy determines extent to which sales executives see ethical problems
Weeks and Nantel (1992)	Salespeople	Questionnaire	Well communicated code of ethics related to ethical sales force behavior
Type of ethical conflict			
Fritzsche and Becker (1983)	Marketing managers	Scenarios	Rejected hypothesis that managerial behavior was invariant across types of ethical problems
Weber (1990)	Managers	Interview	Dilemma type affected moral reasoning of mgrs.
Organizational factors			
Organization effects			
Akaah (1992)	Marketers	Questionnaire	Strong identity w/the org. assoc. w/higher ethical behavior. Org. Warmth assoc. w/unethical behavior
Akaah and Riordan (1989)	Marketers	Scenarios – (Crawford 1970)	Results suggest that healthier ethical env. leads to strong ethical stands
Delaney and Sockell (1992)	Columbia U. alumni	Questionnaire	Ethics training has a positive effect on ethical behavior

(continued)

Table 2.2 (continued)

Variable Study (Year)	Sample	Method	Finding
Ferrell and Skinner (1988)	Marketing researchers	Questionnaire	More formalization assoc. w/ethical decisions Centralization related to higher perceived ethical behavior in research firms
Victor and Cullen (1987)	MBA students and managers	Questionnaire	Sig. differences in the ethical climate of four sample populations
Organization size			
Browning and Zabriskie (1983)	Members of Pur. Assoc.	Questionnaire	Larger firm respondents more accepting of gifts and favors from ex-suppliers
Murphy et al. (1992)	Managers	Moral Dilemmas	Moral judgement varied by size
Weber (1990)	Managers	Interview	Relationship between org. size and level of moral reasoning
Organizational level			
Akaah and Riordan (1989)	Marketers	Scenarios – (Crawford 1970)	Not significant
Chonko and Hunt (1985)	Managers	Questionnaire	Higher level mgrs. less likely to see ethical problems
Delaney and Sockell (1992)	Columbia U. alumni	Questionnaire	Lower level mgrs. perceived greater need to be unethical to get ahead than upper level mgrs.
Izraeli (1988)	Israeli managers	Ques. Newstrom and Ruch (1975)	Not significant
Mitchell et al. (1992)	Bank employees	Interview	Knowledge of ethical problems and perceived seriousness of ethical problems was influenced by level in the hierarchy
Posner and Schmidt (1987)	Managers	Questionnaire	Lower level mgrs. were more pessimistic concerning the ethical character of their org.
Industry factors			
Industry type			
Akaah and Riordan (1989)	Marketers	Scenarios – (Crawford 1970)	Not significant

Dornoff and Tankersley (1975–1976)	Retailers	Scenarios	Significant perceptual differences among retailers toward the actions taken in purchase conflict situations
Laczniak and Inderrieden (1987)	MBA stud.	In Basket	No diff. in respondents working public vs. private orgs.
Business competitiveness			
Dubinsky and Ingram (1984)	Salespeople	Questionnaire	No relationship between increased competitiveness and unethical behavior
Hegarty and Sims (1978)	Grad stud.	Lab experiment	Increased comp. resulted in unethical behavior

relationship did not hold for managers whose contacts with their peers were less intense or less frequent. These findings would, then, lead to the belief that the influence of the person's peers was related to both the intensity and frequency of contact with that person's peers. Izraeli's (1988) findings lend further support for the importance of the person's peer group in determining that person's ethical decision behavior.

Interestingly, there are a number of studies (Brenner and Molander 1977; Baumhart 1961; Ferrell and Weaver 1978; Hunt et al. 1984; Izraeli 1988; Jones and Gautschi 1988; Kidwell et al. 1987; Krugman and Ferrell 1981; Newstrom and Ruch 1975; Stevens et al. 1989; Vitell and Festervand 1987) that all report that respondents saw themselves as more ethical than their peers, supervisors, or other people they knew. The weight of the evidence that the peer group has a significant influence on ethical behavior coupled with the evidence that individual managers see themselves as more ethical than peers or colleagues leads to:

Summary

The direct influence of the person's peers increases as the intensity and frequency of contact with that person's peers increases. People see themselves as more ethical than their peers, co-workers, and supervisors in their ethical beliefs and decision making behavior.

Top Management Influence

Another type of referent group influence is that exerted by top management on the decision maker. The actions of top management can influence a decision maker in several ways. First, top management actions can serve as a model or referent for desired behavior. Second, what top management rewards and punishes can also influence behavior. Several of the many studies investigating the influence of top management follow the Brenner and Molander (1977) and Baumhart (1961) approach. These two studies surveyed *Harvard Business Review* readers who were asked to indicate what they believed most influenced their own ethical behavior. By a wide percentage margin, the responding managers ranked the behavior of superiors as the most important in both the 1961 and 1977 studies. Much less frequently mentioned influences (in descending order) included the existence of a formal company policy, the industry's ethical climate, and the behaviors of one's equals (peers) in the company. These rankings were supported in later studies by Posner and Schmidt (1984) and by Vitell and Festervand (1987). Posner and Schmidt (1984) reported, for example, that the managers surveyed believed that their ethical behavior was directly dependent upon their supervisor's ethical behavior. While the evidence derived from these descriptive studies would indicate that top management does play a very important role in influencing an individual's ethical decision making, other studies using more rigorous methods provide only mixed support for this conclusion.

Akaah and Riordan (1989) found that the absence of top management actions against unethical behavior resulted in stronger approval of questionable practices in the organization. However, Murphy and his colleagues (Murphy et al. 1992) report that leadership has minimal influence on ethical behavior. Two additional studies reported either no significance (Zey-Ferrell et al. 1979) or mixed results (Zey-Ferrell and Ferrell 1982), respectively regarding the influence of top management on ethical behavior.

Rewards and Sanctions

While the influence of top management is frequently seen through its manipulation of the reward and sanctions available through its organizational position as discussed above, some research has been done which specifically investigates the influence of rewards and sanctions on ethical decision making behavior. All the studies noted in the rewards and sanctions section of Table 2.2 found a relationship between rewards and the ethical behavior of the individual decision maker (Fritzsche and Becker 1983; Hegarty and Sims 1978; Hunt et al. 1984; Laczniak and Inderrieden 1987). If top management can be considered a special case of group influence then the findings concerning top management influence amplifies the findings on the importance of peer influence. It is clear that top management does have an impact on an individual's ethical decision making over and above an employee's peers both through how it acts and through its granting or withholding organizational rewards and sanctions.

Summary

An individual's ethical beliefs and decision making behavior will increasingly become congruent with top management's beliefs as defined through their words and actions as rewards provided for compliance congruency are increased.

Codes of Conduct

Codes of conduct have been examined in a large number of studies (9 are listed on Table 2.2) in the empirical literature. Here, for the most part, the existence of a code of conduct or corporate policy statement on ethical behavior has been found to be consistently and significantly related to ethical behavior. If top management is thought of as a special case of peer and group influences, then the existence or non-existence of a code of conduct can be thought of as a special case of top management support for ethical behavior. Obviously, if top management takes the trouble to develop a code, they are trying to influence ethical behavior in a positive way. Laczniak and Inderrieden (1987) reported that sanctions coupled with codes of conduct resulted in more ethical behavior for students participating in an in-basket exercise. Their results support earlier studies by Hegarty and Sims

(1979) and coincide with more recent work by Singhapakdi and Vitell (1990) and Weeks and Nantel (1992).

It may be that corporate codes are surrogate indications of top management's commitment to ethical behavior. However, the efficacy of codes in an organization will be determined by top management's willingness to enforce such codes. This leads to:

Summary

The existence of corporate codes of conduct will positively increase an individual's ethical beliefs and decision behavior. The existence of corporate codes and top management's use of rewards and sanctions for code adherence and violations will increase ethical beliefs and decision making more than the existence of codes.

Type of Ethical Decision

Fritzsche and Becker (1983) found that managerial decision behavior would vary across types of ethical problems. Their findings were based on a series of scenarios developed to see if different types of dilemmas would lead to variations in a manager's ethical decision making. In a similar study, Weber (1990) found that the type of dilemma also affected the manager's moral reasoning.

A number of studies (Izraeli 1988; Kidwell et al. 1987; Stevens et al. 1989; Zey-Ferrell and Ferrell 1982) utilizing the Newstrom and Ruch (1975) questionnaire supported the notion that some activities (e.g. falsifying reports, passing blame for errors versus giving gifts, not reporting others' violations) are viewed as more unethical than other activities.

Organizational Factors

The next three factors of Table 2.2 are related to organization characteristics. These studies examine various organization effects (e.g., climate, structure, etc.), the size of the organization, and employee's level in the organization.

Organization Effects

Five studies examine different organization effects relating to ethical decisions. Delaney and Sockell (1992) noted that company ethics training programs had a positive effect on ethical behavior based on their survey of Columbia Business School alumni. Akaah and Riordan (1989) concluded that healthier ethical environments, as defined by the extent of ethical problems within an organization, would improve the chances that marketing professionals would make ethical decisions. Victor and

Cullen (1987) tested for and found the presence of distinct, different ethical climates by examining military, academic, and corporate organizational members. Akaah (1992) studied social inclusion as an ethics correlate by using Litwin and Stringer's (1968) operationalization of organizational climate. Two variables, organizational warmth and organizational identity, were used in the study. Akaah (1992) found marketing professionals with higher organizational identity to have higher ethical behavior while professionals in warm organizations were less ethical.

The number of empirical studies investigating the influence of structural factors is very limited. In a major study of market researchers in three different types of organizations (data subcontractors, marketing research firms, and corporate research departments), Ferrell and Skinner (1988) found a number of organizational factors that were related to ethical behavior. The authors examined formalization, centralization, and controls using scales adapted from John (1984). They also examined acceptance of authority using a scale developed by Withey (1965). Ferrell and Skinner (1988) report that higher levels of formalization are related to greater perceived ethical behavior in all three types of firms. Centralization is related to higher perceived ethical behavior in research firms only. The measures on acceptance of authority and control were not found to be related to ethical behavior.

While there is some evidence of a relationship between the ethical climate and ethical decision making behavior, there is a need for further research to better understand the relationships found here. This is especially true in light of the increasing body of literature on organizational culture. Further, the significant relationships found in the Ferrell and Skinner work (1988) indicate a fertile opportunity for investigation which could build on a large body of knowledge in the organizational structure and design literature.

Summary

The more ethical the climate and culture of an organization is, the more ethical an individual's ethical beliefs and decision behavior will be. The strength of this influence may be moderated by the structure and design of some organizations.

Organization Size

Three studies examined organization size and found that firm size impacted ethical perception and moral judgement. Browning and Zabriskie (1983) found that respondents from larger firms were more accepting of gifts and favors from ex-suppliers. The Murphy et al. (1992) study showed that smaller companies tended to avoid unethical behavior in marketing issues while larger firms tended to avoid unethical issues in operational areas. Although no statistical analysis was performed, Vitell and Festervand (1987) found that respondents from smaller firms believed unethical practices were more common in their industries. They (Vitell and Festervand 1987) concluded that smaller firms might be under greater pressure to engage in unethical behavior in order to remain competitive with larger firms.

Weber (1990) in analyzing responses to moral dilemmas found that there was a small but consistent relationship between organization size and stage of moral reasoning. Weber suggested that members of large bureaucratic organizations are more likely to perceive themselves as cogs in a machine, and may use a lower level of moral reasoning in their decision making. Further, employees of smaller companies may face fewer rules and feel a greater sense of importance to the firm resulting in a higher level of moral reasoning. In spite of the contradictory arguments made concerning the relationship between organization size and ethical decision behavior, the limited empirical evidence suggests the following:

Summary

As the size of an organization increases, individual ethical beliefs and decision making behavior decreases.

Organization Level

The studies investigating organization level have yielded mixed results. On one hand, Chonko and Hunt (1985) found that higher level managers were less likely to perceive ethical problems, and studies by Posner and Schmidt (1987) and Delaney and Sockell (1992) looking at the issue from the other end of the organization tended to support this by finding lower level managers were more pessimistic concerning the ethical character of the organization. On the other hand, Mitchell et al. (1992) found that higher level bank employees were more aware of ethical problems than lower level employees. Two other studies (Akaah and Riordan 1989 and Izraeli 1988) found no relationship between organization level and ethical behavior. These findings lead to:

Summary

As an employee's level in the organization increases, that employee's ethical beliefs and decision making behavior decreases.

Industry Factors

The last two factors discussed in Table 2.2 investigate factors associated with industry type and the level of overall business competitiveness.

Industry Type

Each of the three studies listed under industry type found no difference in responses by industry. It seems possible that the variable has not been properly tested for its effect. In the case of Akaah and Riordan (1989), for example, the authors acknowledge that their broad classification scheme may have dissipated the variable's effect. Dornoff and Tankersley (1975–1976) study had only three different types of retailers, while Laczniak and Inderrieden (1987) were able to only divide respondents into public versus private organizations. At issue here is the attitude of the industry itself. While this may be a product of industry survival needs, it is likely to also reflect a long history of accepted industry practices and customs. The crudeness of the operationalization of this factor in the available studies may have led to obfuscation of significant industry differences. However, it appears to be an important issue worthy of further investigation.

Summary

Industry ethical standards are not related to an individual's ethical beliefs and decision making behavior.

Business Competitiveness

The final factor considered is closely related to industry type and has been labeled business competitiveness. The rationale underlying the study of this factor is that increased market place competition is likely to bring greater pressure to sacrifice ethical ideals for the sake of survival. The two studies cited here provide mixed results. In their lab experiment, Hegarty and Sims (1978) found that competitiveness tends to decrease ethical decision behavior, while Dubinsky and Ingram (1984) found no such relationship. It seems reasonable to believe that the influence of such a situation where the survival of the organization and hence the security of the decision maker's job may rest on acting unethically, the pressure to act unethically would be strong.

Summary

The level of overall business competitiveness may influence an individual's ethical beliefs and decision making behavior.

Discussion

There is a great deal of work to be done in better understanding the influence of the many factors discussed here on the ethical approach used by the decision maker. Indeed, there are even some obvious factors for which no studies are apparently available. Such demographic factors as marital status, children, and career type are not mentioned in any studies reported here. Other obvious factors, including level of education, age, number of years employed, and income level are seldom reported and poorly understood. Since many studies rely on questionnaires to gather data, it seems that these factors would be relatively easy to capture in future studies allowing a considerable expansion in the body of knowledge about how these demographic variables influence ethical decision behavior. While such factors may ultimately hold little explanatory power, further research on these factors is warranted to test the existing models.

The study of personality factors while more complex than demographic variables is again an area with enormous potential for ethical decision research. Many instruments already exist to measure a variety of individual traits. Many of these measures lend themselves to paper and pencil tests that could be easily incorporated into the questionnaire formats frequently used in ethics research. Indeed, studies of the ethical decision-making process using the available standard measures could readily be implemented with student samples without severely threatening generalizability and offer the advantage of laboratory research designs (Randall and Gibson 1990). Even more surprising is the omission of the many attitudinal factors frequently noted in the behavior literature. No study found in this review, for example, investigated the relationship between such obvious factors as job or organizational commitment and ethical decision making behavior.

The factors not specific to an individual have received even less empirical attention than individual factors. If we are to learn more pertaining to ethical decision processes, the context in which ethical decisions are made must be examined. Many of these variables might be obtained from archival data. Presence of ethical codes, professional codes, and the specifics of reward systems might be obtained from annual reports, company publications, and case studies. Given the level of interest in decision making in general and ethical decision making in particular, it is surprising how few organizational variables have in fact been studied. Such factors as the general economic climate, level of industry competitiveness, existence of professional codes of conduct, or other aspects of the task and organizational structure have not been studied and offer fertile opportunities for future research.

One additional note concerns the general lack of common terminology. Most studies on ethical decision making offer no clear definition of "ethical" behavior or conduct (Randall and Gibson 1990). While defining ethics may be like "nailing jello to a wall" (Lewis 1985), meaningful progress in this field will continue to be impeded by the lack of clear constructs upon which cumulative efforts can be built. These comments are also related to our opening remarks concerning model development. The study of ethics does not currently need additional models of ethical behavior just as it does not need additional definitions of key constructs. What is needed is further testing of plausible existing models (Ferrell and Gresham 1985; Jones 1991; Trevino 1986) and usage of clearly stated terminology (Bowman 1976; Brenner and Molander 1977; Browning and Zabriskie 1983; Jones 1991).

Finally, a comment concerning the focus of the studies on ethical issues. Based on the review of the literature it appears safe to say that people perceive themselves to be more ethical than their peers. Future studies focusing on respondents' beliefs as compared to their perception of peer beliefs do not seem warranted without examining interaction effects with other factors. Future research comparing the beliefs of students and practitioners fall into the same category. However, studies examining the decision processes of students might be quite informative. Well-designed lab experiments might be useful in exploring factors impacting ethical decision processes.

Conclusion

This review of the empirical literature offers a number of opportunities for researchers to consider in their future efforts. In this review we have indicated areas that could easily be incorporated into the typical questionnaire study design. Further, there are a number of issues that have been investigated but the results are inconclusive or contradictory. Regardless of the difficulty of defining what ethical behavior is, there have been a number of studies which have attempted to operationalize this factor and then test its relationship to a variety of dependent variables noted in this review. In a sense, this review is discouraging in that the number of empirical studies is distressingly small. In another sense, this review is exciting in that it identifies a large number of opportunities for fruitful research in an area in which we still know so little and need to know so much.

References

Abratt, R., D. Nel, and N.S. Higgs. 1992. An examination of the ethical beliefs of managers using selected scenarios in a cross-cultural environment. *Journal of Business Ethics* 11: 29–35.

Akaah, I.P. 1992. Social inclusion as a marketing ethics correlate. *Journal of Business Ethics* 11: 599–608.

Akaah, I.P., and E.A. Riordan. 1989. Judgements of marketing professionals about ethical issues in marketing research: A replication and extension. *Journal of Marketing Research* 26(1): 112–120.

Arlow, P., and T.A. Ulrich. 1980. Business ethics, social responsibility and business students: An empirical comparison of Clark's study. *Akron Business and Economic Review* 11(3): 17–23.

Baumhart, R. 1961. Problems in review: How ethical are businessmen? *Harvard Business Review* 39(July-August): 6–9.

Becker, H., and D.J. Fritzche. 1987. Business ethics: A cross-cultural comparison of managers' attitudes. *Journal of Business Ethics* 6: 289–295.

Beltramini, R.F., R.A. Peterson, and G. Kozmetsky. 1984. Concerns of college students regarding business ethics. *Journal of Business Ethics* 3: 195–200.

Bommer, M., C. Gratto, J. Gravander, and M. Tuttle. 1987. A behavioral model of ethical and unethical decision making. *Journal of Business Ethics* 6: 265–280.

Bowman, J. 1976. Managerial ethics in business and government. *Business Horizons* 19: 48–54.

Brenner, S.N., and E.A. Molander. 1977. Is the ethics of business changing? *Harvard Business Review* 55(January-February): 57–71.

Browning, J., and N.B. Zabriskie. 1983. How ethical are industrial buyers? *Industrial Marketing Management* 12: 219–224.
Callan, V.J. 1992. Predicting ethical values and training needs in ethics. *Journal of Business Ethics* 11: 761–769.
Carroll, A.B. 1975. Managerial ethics: A post Watergate view. *Business Horizons* 18(April): 75–80.
Chonko, L.B., and S.D. Hunt. 1985. Ethics and marketing management: An empirical examination. *Journal of Business Research* 13(August): 339–359.
Clark, J. 1966. *Religion and moral standards of American businessmen*. Cincinnati: South-Western Publishing.
Crawford, M.C. 1970. Attitudes of marketing executives toward ethics in marketing research. *Journal of Marketing* 34: 46–52.
Delaney, J.T., and D. Sockell. 1992. Do company ethics training programs make a difference? An empirical analysis. *Journal of Business Ethics* 11: 719–727.
Dornoff, R.J., and C.B. Tankersley. 1975–1976. Do retailers practice social responsibility? *Journal of Retailing* 51(4): 33–42.
Dubinsky, A.J., and J.M. Gwin. 1981. Business ethics: Buyers and sellers. *Journal of Purchasing and Materials Management* 17(Winter): 97–103.
Dubinsky, A.J., and T.N. Ingram. 1984. Correlates of salespeople's ethical conflict. An exploratory investigation. *Journal of Business Ethics* 3: 343–353.
Dubinsky, A.J., and M. Levy. 1985. Ethics in retailing: Perceptions of retail salespeople. *Journal of the Academy of Marketing Science* 13(1): 1–16.
Dubinsky, A.J., and B. Loken. 1989. Analyzing ethical decision making in marketing. *Journal of Business Research*. 19(2): 83–107
Ferrell, O.C., and L.G. Gresham. 1985. A contingency framework for understanding ethical decision making in marketing. *Journal of Marketing* 49(Summer): 87–96.
Ferrell, O.C., and S.J. Skinner. 1988. Ethical behavior and bureaucratic structure in marketing research organizations. *Journal of Marketing Research* 25(February): 103–109.
Ferrell, O.C., and K.M. Weaver. 1978. Ethical beliefs of marketing managers. *Journal of Marketing* 42(July): 69–73.
Ford, R.C., and R. S. Hansen. 1991. Intent and opportunity as predictors of a comprehensive ethical decision-making model. Paper presented at Association of Business Ethics, Miami.
Fritzsche, D.J., and H. Becker. 1983. Ethical behavior of marketing managers. *Journal of Business Ethics* 1: 291–299.
Goodman, C.S., and C.M. Crawford. 1974. Young executives: A source of new ethics? *The Personnel Journal* 53(March): 180–187.
Hawkins, D.I., and A.B. Cocanoughec. 1972. Student evaluations of the ethics of marketing practices: The role of marketing education. *Journal of Marketing* 36(April): 61–64.
Hegarty, W.H., and H.P. Sims Jr. 1978. Some determinants of unethical decision behavior. An experiment. *Journal of Applied Psychology* 63(4): 451–457.
Hegarty, W.H., and H.P. Sims Jr. 1979. Organizational philosophy, policies and objectives related to unethical decision behavior. A laboratory experiment. *Journal of Applied Psychology* 64(3): 331–338.
Hunt, S.D., L.B. Chonko, and J.B. Wilcox. 1984. Ethical problems of marketing researchers. *Journal of Marketing Research* 21(August): 304–324.
Izraeli, D. 1988. Ethical beliefs and behavior among managers: A cross-cultural perspective. *Journal of Business Ethics* 7: 263–271.
John, G. 1984. An empirical investigation of some antecedents of opportunism in a marketing channel. *Journal of Marketing Research* 21(August): 278–289.
Jones, T.M. 1991. Ethical decision making by individuals in organizations: An issue-contingent model. *Academy of Management Review* 16(2): 366–395.
Jones, T.M., and F.H. Gautschi III. 1988. Will the ethics of business change? A survey of future executives. *Journal of Business Ethics* 7: 231–248.

Kidwell, J.M., R.E. Stevens, and A.L. Bethke. 1987. Differences in the ethical perceptions between male and female managers: Myth or reality. *Journal of Business Ethics* 6: 489–493.

Krugman, D.M., and O.C. Ferrell. 1981. The organizational ethics of advertising corporate and agency views. *Journal of Advertising* 10(1): 21–30.

Laczniak, G., and E.J. Inderrieden. 1987. The influence of stated organizational concern upon ethical decision making. *Journal of Business Ethics* 6: 297–307.

Lane, M.S., D. Schaupp, and B. Parsons. 1988. Pygmalion effect. An issue for business education and ethics. *Journal of Business Ethics* 7: 223–229.

Lewis, P.V. 1985. Defining business ethics: Like nailing Jello to a wall. *Journal of Business Ethics* 4: 377–383.

Litwin, G., and R. Springer. 1968. *Motivation and organization climate*. Boston: Harvard University Press.

McNichols, C.W., and T.W. Zimmerer. 1985. Situational ethics: An empirical study of differentiators of student attitudes. *Journal of Business Ethics* 4: 175–180.

Mitchell, W.J., P.V. Lewis, and N.L. Reinsch Jr. 1992. Bank ethics: An exploratory study of ethical behaviors and perceptions in small, local banks. *Journal of Business Ethics* 11: 197–205.

Murphy, P.R., J.E. Smith, and J.M. Daley. 1992. Executive attitudes, organizational size and ethical issues: Perspectives on a service industry. *Journal of Business Ethics* 11: 11–19.

Newstrom, J.W., and W.A. Ruch. 1975. The ethics of management and the management of ethics. *MSU Business Topics* 23(Winter): 29–37.

Posner, B.Z., and W.H. Schmidt. 1984. Values and the American manager. An update. *California Management Review* 26(3): 202–216.

Posner, B.Z., and W.H. Schmidt. 1987. Ethics in American companies: A managerial perspective. *Journal of Business Ethics* 6: 383–391.

Pratt, C.B., and G.W. McLaughlin. 1989. An analysis of predictions of college students' ethical intentions. *Research in Higher Education* 30(2): 195–219.

Randall, D.M., and A.M. Gibson. 1990. Methodology in business ethics research: A review and critical assessment. *Journal of Business Ethics* 9: 457–471.

Ruegger, D., and E.W. King. 1992. A study of the effect of age and gender upon student business ethics. *Journal of Business Ethics* 11: 179–186.

Serwinek, P.J. 1992. Demographic & related differences in ethical views among small businesses. *Journal of Business Ethics* 11: 555–566.

Singhapakdi, A., and S.J. Vitell. 1990. Marketing ethics: Factors influencing perceptions of ethical problems and alternatives. *Journal of Macromarketing* 10(Spring): 4–18.

Stevens, G.E. 1984. Business ethics and social responsibility. The response of present and future managers. *Akron Business and Economic Review* 15(Fall): 6–11.

Stevens, G. E., W. D. Richardson, and A. E. Abramowitz. 1989. Perceptual differences of ethical decision situations business vs. law: A difference of opinion? *Southern Management Association Proceedings*, 199–201.

Trevino, L.K. 1986. Ethical decision making in organizations: A person-situation interactionist model. *Academy of Management Review* 11(3): 601–617.

Victor, B., and J.B. Cullen. 1987. A theory and measure of ethical climate in organizations. In *Research in corporate social performance and policy*, ed. W.C. Frederick and L.E. Preston, 51–71. Greenwich: JAI Press.

Vitell, S.J., and T.A. Festervand. 1987. Business ethics: Conflict, practices and beliefs of industrial executives. *Journal of Business Ethics* 6: 111–122.

Weber, J. 1990. Managers' moral reasoning: Assessing their responses in three moral dilemmas. *Human Relations* 43(7): 687–702.

Weeks, W.A., and J. Nantel. 1992. Corporate codes of ethics and sales force behavior. A case study. *Journal of Business Ethics* 11: 753–760.

Whipple, T.W., and D.F. Swords. 1992. Business ethics judgments: A cross-cultural comparison. *Journal of Business Ethics* 11: 671–678.

White, L.P., and M.J. Rhodeback. 1992. Ethical dilemmas in organization development a cross-cultural analysis. *Journal of Business Ethics* 11: 663–670.

Withey, S. 1965. The US and USSR: A report of the public's perspective on the United States-Russian relations in late 1961. In *Components of defense policy*, ed. D. Bobrow, 164–174. Chicago: Rand McNally.

Zahra, S.A. 1989. Executive values and the ethics of company politics: Some preliminary findings. *Journal of Business Ethics* 8: 15–29.

Zey-Ferrell, M.K., and O.C. Ferrell. 1982. Role-set configuration and opportunity as predictors of unethical behavior in organizations. *Human Relations* 35(7): 587–604.

Zey-Ferrell, M.K., M. Weaver, and O.C. Ferrell. 1979. Predicting unethical behavior among marketing practitioners. *Human Relations* 32(7): 557–569.

Chapter 3
Toward the Development of a Multidimensional Scale for Improving Evaluations of Business Ethics

R. Eric Reidenbach and Donald P. Robin

As both the subject and consequence of unethical business behavior grow in importance, so too does our need to study its antecedents, dynamics, and impacts. Several models of ethical decision-making already exist (Trevino 1986; Hunt and Vitell 1986; Ferrell and Gresham 1985) and wait to be informed and tested. Crucial to this process of testing and informing the models, which in turn leads to a better understanding of the ethical decision-making process, is a valid and reliable measuring device.

Current measurement practices are inadequate for studying this complex process. For example, a common measuring approach is to ask individuals to respond to a situation or an action having ethical consequence on a single item scale, typically, but not exclusively, anchored by "very ethical" and "very unethical" (e.g., Hawkins and Cocanougher 1972; Krugman and Ferrell 1981; George 1985; Browning and Zabriskie 1983). Variations on this type of measuring approach exist and the use of a single item measure is more pervasive than the four studies identified as examples.

The benefits of a multidimensional measure of ethics in business begin this presentation. It is followed by a brief review of the major moral philosophies that are used in the development of a multidimensional scale. The scale development procedure is described and is followed by an application of the scale. Finally, the authors identify several additional areas in which the use of the scales may prove beneficial for increasing understanding of ethical decision-making, both by researchers and practitioners.

R.E. Reidenbach • D.P. Robin (✉)
Center for Business Development and Research,
University of Southern Mississippi, Hattiesburg, MS 39406, USA
e-mail:Robind@wfu.edu

A.C. Michalos and D.C. Poff (eds.), *Citation Classics from the Journal of Business Ethics*, Advances in Business Ethics Research 2,
DOI 10.1007/978-94-007-4126-3_3, © Springer Science+Business Media B.V. 2013

Value of a Multidimensional Scale

To develop a valid measure of individual ethical judgment it is important to begin with as complete an understanding of the content of the construct as possible (e.g., see Nunnally 1969). Then the breadth and complexity of the construct dictates the breadth and complexity of the measure used to capture it. A very specific and narrow construct only needs a specific and narrow measure, but a broad and complex measure needs more.

A reasonable beginning assumption is that individuals use more than one rationale in making ethical judgments, and that the importance of those rationales is a function of the problem situation faced by the individual. The result is a fairly broad and moderately complex construct. Each rationale used represents a necessary dimension in any measure that expects to capture a true sense of that ethical judgment. Thus, a multidimensional and multi-item measure seems to be needed to adequately represent this latent construct.

This approach for measuring the ethical judgment construct also allows the researcher to go beyond a simplistic understanding of "what" the respondent believes and begins the process of understanding "why" he/she believes it. It thus fosters a scientific understanding of the process. The importance of this aspect of the measure is illustrated in a later example developed in this article.

The Use of Contemporary Normative Philosophies

Following the preliminary work of Reidenbach and Robin (1988), five ethical philosophies were selected as the basis for developing the multidimensional scale. In the "Appendix" to this article each philosophy is described in moderate depth. Further, examples are provided of how the language and ideas of these philosophies have been applied in the everyday lives of individuals. The idea of the popularization of these world views is not new. The ethical behavior models of Ferrell and Gresham (1985), and Hunt and Vitell (1986) both state that such popularization exists. Further, these five philosophies encompass most of the "great" ideas for social survival, not just from the area of moral philosophy, but also from religion. Ideas of fairness, justice, contract, duty, consequence, greatest good and many others that come from the five philosophies can also be found in the Bible, the Koran, the writings of Buddha, and in other religions. Thus, the use of these philosophies provides a substantial beginning point for the development of a multidimensional scale to measure ethical judgments.

Each philosophy enjoys a well-recognized and heavily debated tradition. However, while each philosophy has its own unique conceptual core, there does exist a certain conceptual overlap among them. These major contemporary normative moral philosophies include theories of justice (Rawls 1971; Nozick 1974; Kristol 1978), relativism (Hoffman and Moore 1984, pp. 3–5; Stace 1937; Brandt 1959), utilitarianism, for which several variations exist (Smart 1973; Sartorios 1975; Singer 1976), egoism (Beauchamp and Bowie 1983; Donaldson and Werhane 1983, pp. 21–23), and deontology (Ross 1930; Kant trans. 1964).

Normative Philosophies as a Base for Measure Development

Two factors, common to all of the moral philosophies, are important to the development of measurement items. While the normative philosophies were described as "theories" in the preceding section, an important distinction between the normative and scientific use of the term theory must be made. Normative theories are prescriptive and usually not empirical, while the scientific use of the term is descriptive and at least suggestive of how the theory might be empirically tested.

Normative philosophies are idealizations much like the Ten Commandments and accordingly make much stronger statements about what ought to be rather than what actually is. This presents a problem for measure development, an activity designed to provide measures of what people believe is. When WHAT IS does not conform to WHAT OUGHT TO BE, are the measures invalid? The answer is not necessarily; no more invalid than the results of comparing measures of actual corporate behavior, for example, to codes of ethics developed by the corporation.

A second issue of using normative moral philosophies as a basis for scale development concerns the extent to which individuals are aware or knowledgeable of the different philosophies. It has been suggested that individuals, in varying degrees and extents, seem to rely, either knowingly or unknowingly, on the different strains of moral philosophy, typically teleology and deontology, for making assessments of the ethical content of a particular action (Ferrell and Gresham 1985; Hunt and Vitell 1986). The extent of this knowledge is not known. Certainly the language of some of the different philosophies, taught through fairy tales, fables, and early life experiences with family, friends, church, and other social institutions, is represented in our ethical evaluative process. The question remains, however, as to which philosophies have had the most impact on Western culture, and which have been incorporated into the ethical evaluative process of individuals.

Initial Scale Development Procedures

The development of the multidimensional scale followed the procedures outlined by Nunnally (1969), Churchill (1979), and Campbell and Fiske (1959). From a content analysis of the contemporary normative moral philosophies discussed in a previous section and in the appendix, initial items were developed (see Beauchamp and Bowie 1983; DeGeorge 1986; Donaldson and Werhane 1983; Hoffman and Moore 1984). For example, the egoist strain of moral philosophy relies heavily on the ideas

Table 3.1 A priori normative philosophy scales[a]

Justice scales:
Just/unjust
Fair/unfair
Does result/does not result in an equal distribution of good and bad
Relativist scales:
Culturally acceptable/unacceptable
Individually acceptable/unacceptable
Acceptable/unacceptable to people I most admire
Traditionally acceptable/unacceptable
Acceptable/unacceptable to my family
Egoism scales:
Self promoting/not self promoting
Selfish/not selfish
Self sacrificing/not self sacrificing
Prudent/not prudent
Under no moral obligation/morally obligated to act otherwise
Personally satisfying/not personally satisfying
In the best interests of the company/not in the best interests of the company
Utilitarian scales:
Efficient/inefficient
Ok/not ok if actions can be justified by their consequences
Compromises/does not compromise an important rule by which I live
On balance, tends to be good/bad
Produces the greatest/least utility
Maximizes/minimizes benefits while minimizes/maximizes harm
Leads to the greatest/least good for the greatest number
Results in a positive/negative cost-benefit ratio
Maximizes/minimizes pleasure
Deontology scales:
Violates/does not violate an unwritten contract
Violates/does not violate my ideas of fairness
Duty bound/not duty bound to act this way
Morally right/not morally right
Obligated/not obligated to act this way
Violates/does not violate an unspoken promise

[a]The actual form of the scale was as follows:
Just_:_:_:_:_:_:_ Unjust
The instructions that followed each scenario and preceded each listing of the 33 scale items were as follows: "Please give your beliefs to the action described in the scenario by placing a check (√) between each of the opposites that follow. Thank you"

of prudence, self promotion, acting in the best interest of the individual, selfishness, and personal satisfaction. Identifying the key concepts of each moral philosophy in this manner produced the original pool of 33 items shown in Table 3.1 along with the particular moral philosophy from which they were extracted.

As indicated earlier, each moral philosophy has a conceptual core, but certain aspects of each philosophy may embrace similar terminologies. To the extent possible, overlapping terms have been eliminated leaving those ideas and concepts which are central to a particular philosophy. The 33 items were submitted to a panel of three individuals knowledgeable of the five different moral philosophies. Table 3.1 represents a consensus of the individual judges. As a consensus it is recognized that Table 3.1 does not reflect a rigid and clearly nonexclusive partitioning of moral philosophical concepts. Such a discrete partitioning is unlikely because the terminologies of the different philosophies are not themselves discrete.

A pretest of the measure involving a sample of 218 business students was conducted. The pretest utilized the three scenarios shown in Fig. 3.1 (adapted from Dornoff and Tankersley 1975) as stimuli for the evaluation process, and the results of that effort are reported in an earlier *Journal of Business Ethics* article (Reidenbach and Robin 1988).

These three scenarios were selected because of the variety of ethical problems they presented and because of the variability of individual reactions to them. The principal purpose of this pretest was to resolve any item ambiguity or misunderstanding and to rectify any problems with the selected scenarios. Only four scale items were eliminated at this stage.

At this point the scale items were subjected to a second and third stage distillation process. Stage two involved a sample of 108 retail managers and owners divided randomly into two equal groups. One group evaluated the scenarios using the 29 items on a 5 point Likert-type scale while the other group evaluated the scenarios using a 7 point bipolar format. Factor patterns indicated that scale type did not influence the results and the 29 items were reduced to 14 items. The a priori criteria used in purging the items included: (l) consistency of the loadings across all scale/scenario data sets; (2) size of the loadings for each structure set; (3) low inter-item correlations with other dimension items; and (4) respondent's ability to apply the individual item. With respect to criteria 1 through 3, objective decision rules were developed for item deletion. Respondent debriefings and questionnaire comments also guided item classification and deletion decisions.

Three factors emerged from this stage and were subjected to a fourth distillation stage. In this iteration, 105 small business operators in a different but contiguous state evaluated the scenarios using the 14 scale items. Using the same analysis and item reduction criteria, the 14 items were reduced to 8 items, which formed the three factor structures shown in Table 3.2, and used in the current study.

Testing the Measures

Again proceeding along the guidelines established by Nunnally (1969), Churchill (1979), and Campbell and Fiske (1959), a final study testing the items was undertaken. Questionnaires were sent to 218 managers in a different type of business association

Fig. 3.1 Scenarios used in the study

Auto Scenario:

A person bought a new car from a franchised automobile dealership in the local area. Eight months after the car was purchased, he began having problems with the transmission. He took the car back to the dealer, and some minor adjustments were made. During the next few months he continually had a similar problem with the transmission slipping. Each time the dealer made only minor adjustments on the car. Again, during the thirteenth month after the car had been bought the man returned to the dealer because the transmission still was not functioning properly. At this time, the transmission was completely overhauled.

Action: Since the warranty was for only one year (12 months from the date of purchase), the dealer charged the full price for parts and labor.

Sales Scenario:

A young man, recently hired as a salesman for a local retail store, has been working very hard to favorably impress his boss with his selling ability. At times, this young man, anxious for an order, has been a little over-eager. To get the order, he exaggerates the value of the item or withholds relevant information concerning the product he is trying to sell. No fraud or deceit is intended by his actions, he is simply over-eager.

Action: His boss, the owner of the retail store, is aware of the salesman's actions but he has done nothing to stop such practice.

Retail Scenario:

A retail grocery chain operates several stores throughout the local area including one in the city's ghetto area. Independent studies have shown that prices do tend to be higher and there is less of a selection of products in this particular store than in the other locations.

Action: On the day welfare checks are received in the area of the city the retailer increases prices on all of his merchandise.

who had agreed to participate in the study. This was done to reduce any bias that might be associated with occupation. One hundred fifty-two questionnaires were returned for a 69.7% response rate. Respondents were also asked to indicate the probability of their undertaking the same action described in each scenario on a seven point scale anchored with "highly probable" and "highly improbable." In addition, respondents were asked to evaluate the ethics of the action on a seven point scale anchored with "ethical/unethical."

Table 3.2 Factor structures for the three scenarios

	Factor one			Factor two			Factor three		
Variables	*R*[a]	*S*	*A*	*R*	*S*	*A*	*R*	*S*	*A*
Fair/unfair	0.05	0.05	0.05	0.18	0.28	0.12	0.10	0.15	0.16
Just/unjust	0.05	0.05	0.05	0.24	0.34	0.18	0.12	0.14	0.17
Morally right/not morally right	0.05	0.05	0.05	0.18	0.22	0.12	0.15	0.17	0.01
Acceptable/unacceptable to my family	0.05	0.05	0.05	0.15	0.24	0.26	0.08	0.25	0.13
Traditionally acceptable/unacceptable	0.21	0.29	0.07	0.05	0.05	0.05	0.05	0.09	0.03
Culturally acceptable/unacceptable	0.24	0.38	0.14	0.05	0.05	0.05	0.10	0.14	0.03
Violates/does not violate an unspoken promise	0.08	0.12	0.09	0.06	0.09	0.06	0.05	0.05	0.05
Violates/does not violate an unwritten contract	0.16	0.24	0.16	0.08	0.10	0.07	0.05	0.05	0.05

Percent of variance explained by three factor solution:
[a]*R* = Retail scenario = 80.9%, *S* = Sales scenario = 82.8%, *A* = Auto scenario = 74.0%

The scale items were submitted to a principal components factors analytic procedure utilizing a varimax rotation. A natural three factor solution, identical to the one produced in the last distillation stage and shown in Table 3.2, was generated.

The three dimensions that emerged in the evaluations of the three scenarios were then subjected to a variant of the multitrait-multimethod analysis (Campbell and Fiske 1959). The method used in this case is more appropriately referred to as a multitrait-multicontext analysis with the three scenarios representing the different contexts. This approach has precedence in the research literature (Heeler and Ray 1972, p. 365) and has been employed previously by Robertson and Meyers (1969). The purpose of both the multitrait-multimethod and multitrait-multicontext approaches is to establish convergent and discriminant validity.

The purpose of convergent validity is to confirm that the constructs or traits are independent of the approaches used to measure them. The concern is that the results are not an artifact of the measuring instrument. This concern was addressed in stage two of this analysis when a split sample produced identical results using different measurement scales. At least for the two measures tested, the constructs do not seem to be an artifact of the scaling procedure.

The multitrait-multicontext approach used in this study tests what is perhaps a more interesting and important concern. In this analysis the convergent validity question is concerned about whether the constructs or traits are dependent on the different scenarios used. The use of scenarios as "contexts" allows the researchers to introduce what is potentially greater variability than is usually used as different "measures" of the traditional approach. Thus, if the traits selected are appropriate for evaluating only one ethical situation, their usefulness is severely limited; and no convergent validity will occur in the matrix. However, if the multitrait-multicontext analysis produces a convergence of constructs, the research has exhibited the first indication that the constructs are independent of the situation to which they are applied. The benefits from developing universal constructs are apparent, and no further justification seems necessary.

Discriminant validity measures the extent to which the traits or constructs are unique, and are reflections of the same dimension. The use of either "contexts" or "measures" makes little difference to the tests of discriminant validity because the focus is on the traits or constructs. However, the application of discriminant validity tests is somewhat different in this research. Instead of totally unique traits or constructs, the intent of this research is to search for unique "dimensions" of the same construct – ethical judgment. For this reason, absolute uniqueness (discriminant validity) is not as important as in the traditional analysis. The resultant multitrait-multicontext matrix is shown in Table 3.3.

Measure Reliability

The summated item scores evidence a high degree of reliability with coefficient alphas ranging between 0.71 and 0.92 with an average reliability of 0.8 and appear along the diagonal of the matrix in Table 3.3. These reliabilities compare favorably

Table 3.3 Multitrait-multicontext matrix

		RD_1	RD_2	RD_3	SD_1	SD_2	SD_3	AD_1	AD_2	AD_3
Retail scenario	RD_1	0.92								
		(0.0001)								
	RD_2	0.46	0.80							
		(0.0001)	(0.0001)							
	RD_3	0.28	0.19	0.71						
		(0.001)	(0.01)	(0.0001)						
Sales scenario	SD_1	0.27	0.12	0.07	0.92					
		(0.001)	(NS)	(NS)	(0.0001)					
	SD_2	0.12	0.41	0.05	0.64	0.86				
		(NS)	(0.0001)	(NS)	(0.0001)	(0.0001)				
	SD_3	0.17	0.13	0.47	0.42	0.29	0.74			
		(0.02)	(NS)	(0.0001)	(0.0001)	(0.0001)	(0.0001)			
Auto scenario	AD_1	0.41	0.17	0.11	0.42	0.23	0.23	0.83		
		(0.0001)	(0.02)	(NS)	(0.0001)	(0.002)	(0.0003)	(0.0001)		
	AD_2	0.17	0.49	0.11	0.11	0.37	0.17	0.28	0.72	
		(0.02)	(0.0001)	(NS)	(NS)	(0.0001)	(0.02)	(0.0001)	(0.0001)	
	AD_3	0.12	0.12	0.41	0.12	0.02	0.45	0.24	0.04	0.72
		(NS)	(NS)	(0.0001)	(NS)	(NS)	(0.0001)	(0.002)	(NS)	(0.0001)

RD retail scenario dimensions, *SD* sales scenario dimensions, *AD* auto scenario dimensions

with other tests of reliability reported in the various business literature and are certainly well above the 0.5 or 0.6 standard of acceptability established by Nunnally (1969, p. 226) for early stages of scale development.

Measure Validity

Churchill (1979) identifies four idealized criteria in the Campbell and Fiske (1959) methodology for demonstrating validity within a multitrait-multi-method analysis which are equally applicable to the multitrait-multicontext derivation of that procedure.

> (1) Evidence of the convergent validity of a measure is provided in the validity diagonal by the extent to which the correlations are significantly different from zero and sufficiently large to encourage further examination of validity (p. 71).

The coefficients in the validity diagonal are all significantly different from zero. They range in size from 0.27 to 0.49 with an average correlation of 0.41. Accordingly, there exists sufficient empirical evidence to suggest the presence of convergent validity.

> (2) Entries in the validity diagonal should be higher than the correlations that occupy the same row and column in the heteromethod (heterocontext) block (p. 71).

Inspection of Table 3.3 indicates that this condition is satisfied.

> (3) The validity coefficients should be higher than the correlations in the heterotrait-monomethod (monocon text) triangles which suggests that the correlation within a trait measured by different methods (contexts) must be higher than the correlations between traits which have method (context) in common (p. 71).

The entries in Table 3.3 satisfy this condition with two exceptions. The correlation between dimension 1 and 2 in the retail scenario and the sales scenario is greater than the corresponding correlation in the validity diagonal. We believe that in part this is due to the high internal consistency of the items but also in part to the conceptual linkage between the two dimensions. Dimension 1 is comprised of two justice concepts (fair, just), one broad-based morality item (morally right), and one relativistic item (acceptable to my family). Dimension 2 is a relativistic dimension comprised of two items, culturally acceptable and traditionally acceptable. Our notions of justice, fairness, morality and what is acceptable to our families are defined in a broader sense by what is both culturally and traditionally acceptable. In essence, dimension 1 depends in part on the parameters defined in dimension 2. Since the Campbell and Fiske methodology produces idealized criteria for discriminant validity, it is felt that this exception does not negate the conceptual arguments for validation.

> (4) The patterns of correlations should be the same in all of the heterotrait triangles (p. 71).

A visual inspection of Table 3.3 indicates that this condition is generally met. Correlations tend to be larger between dimensions 1 and 2, lower between dimensions 1 and 3, and lowest between dimensions 2 and 3. In most cases, the correlations between dimensions 2 and 3 are nonsignificant or very weak.

In sum, there exists strong but not complete discriminant validity. The fact that dimension 1 and dimension 2 are correlated suggests, in this case, a tempering relationship wherein dimension 2 helps define the meaning of dimension 1.

Dimension Identification

The three factors (Table 3.2) explain 74% of the item variance in the auto scenario, 81% of the variance in the retail scenario, and 83% of the variance in the sales scenario.

Dimension One – A Broad-based Moral Equity Dimension

Dimension one is the most complex of the three ethical dimensions. We would suggest that this dimension, comprised of the four items:

1. Fair/unfair
2. Just/unjust
3. Acceptable/unacceptable to my family
4. Morally/not morally right

Describes a broad-based, moral equity dimension. Our use of the term moral reflects the meaning ascribed to it by Tom Beauchamp (1982, p. 5).

> In its broadest and most familiar meaning morality is concerned with many forms of belief about right and wrong human conduct. These normative beliefs are expressed through such general terms as 'good,' 'bad,' Virtuous,' 'praiseworthy,' 'right,' 'ought,' 'blameworthy.'

This broad dimension is dominated by two items clearly associated with notions of the moral philosophy of justice: fair and just. In addition, it contains what has been classified as a deontological item (morally right/not morally right) and a relativistic concept (acceptable/not acceptable to my family). There is some question as to how clearly deontological the notion of "morally right/not morally right" actually is in its everyday usage. Its classification as a deontological item comes from a more theoretical interpretation made by the judges and may not reflect its more popular meaning. Consequently, it may represent a broader based notion of good and bad and may depict a more ecumenical concept of ethics than is suggested by its deontological classification. The same argument might be made for the item "acceptable to my family" which the judges classified as relativistic in a philosophical sense. Evidently, the respondents ascribed a different sense to the item, incorporating it within the more fundamental notion of moral equity along with ideas of fairness and justice.

Embedded in this dimension appears to be a basic, almost fundamental decision rule for evaluating the moral content of business situations. Decisions are evaluated essentially in terms of their inherent fairness, justice, goodness and rightness. Moreover, this dimension incorporates the idea of family acceptance. By extension, we would suggest that this dimension relies heavily on lessons from our early training that we receive in the home regarding fairness, right and wrong as communicated through childhood lessons of sharing, religious training, morals from fairy tales, and fables.

Dimension Two – A Relativistic Dimension

Dimension two is comprised of the two items:

1. Traditionally acceptable/unacceptable.
2. Culturally acceptable/unacceptable.

This, according to the judges' consensus categorization of concepts, suggests a relativistic dimension. This dimension seems to be more concerned with the guidelines, requirements, and parameters inherent in the social/cultural system than with individual considerations. These items suggest that the social and cultural systems are important in helping us define our ethical beliefs. These beliefs are relativistic in the sense that beliefs are subject to the dictates of society. It would seem, however, that the social system parameters implied in this dimension go beyond a purely legal structure of society to include a traditional, historical, and culturally learned understanding of "how the game is played." By extension, it is suggested that this is a dimension that one acquires later in the development stages as the individual experiences adequate and sufficient social intercourse to develop greater understanding of cultural and traditional norms. Depending on the universality of this dimension, it may account for differing ethical evaluations of business activities across cultures and subcultures. Trevino (1986) acknowledges the impact of culture on the ethical behavior of managers. Her propositions are limited to organizational rather than societal impacts but nonetheless define the relationship between culture and ethical behavior.

The relationship between one's societal environment and the ethical evaluative process is made more manifest in the Hunt and Vitell Model (1986) which posits an indirect relationship between cultural influences and evaluative norms. The findings in this instance suggest that beliefs about what is culturally and traditionally acceptable play a more direct role in the evaluative process. Ferrell and Gresham (1985) treat the social and cultural environment as exogenous in their model. The presence of this dimension within the evaluative structure of individuals would suggest at least a partial respecification of their model concerning the role that society and culture play in the ethical evaluative process. That is, society and culture both play a determinant role and an evaluative role.

Examination of the multitrait-multicontext matrix in Table 3.3 indicates that in two of the three scenarios (retail and sales), dimensions 1 and 2 were highly correlated. This, in part, may be explained by the high inter-item correlations among the individual variables and the relatively high coefficient alphas. This is to be expected when the construct being studied (ethical judgment) is comprised of a number of overlapping theoretical dimensions which are inherent in the different moral philosophies.

Conceptually, another plausible explanation exists for the relationship between dimensions 1 and 2. Essentially, our notions of justice, fairness, morality, and what is acceptable to our families are, in large part, tradition and culture based. Notions of moral equity are tempered by an experiential and social process bounded by our traditions and culture. Tradition and culture shape our beliefs, values, and attitudes in all aspects of life and certainly influence our notions of what are right and wrong.

Dimension Three – A Contractualism Dimension

Dimension three, comprised of the items:

1. Violates/does not violate an unspoken promise
2. Violates/does not violate an unwritten contract

is, according to Table 3.1, a purely deontological dimension wherein notions of implied obligation, contracts, duties, and rules are present. This dimension resembles most closely the ideas inherent in contractualism, most specifically the idea of a "social contract" that exists between business and society. Most, if not all, business exchanges incorporate either implicit or explicit promises or contracts. Business exchanges involve a *quid pro quo* wherein one party is obligated to provide a product, service, employment, or perform some action in return for something of value. Individuals appear to take this idea of exchange one step further to include an ethics of exchange. This broadened view of exchange includes obligations which may go beyond a purely economic nature and include notions of fair play, truth telling, duty, and rights. Violation of these implicit ideas would result in the condemnation of the exchange process or at least part of the process as unethical.

Two aspects of the three dimensions are noteworthy. First, noticeably absent from the three dimensions are ideas which are most closely associated with utilitarianism and egoism. All references to cost/benefit types of ethical calculus were purged during second and third stage item distillation procedures on the basis of minimal contribution to the explanatory power of the multidimensional measures. Moreover, in debriefing analyses it was obvious that respondents had a difficult time in understanding and applying the concepts inherent in utilitarian thinking.

Second, the items that comprise the relativism dimension appear to be both sources of and standards for ethical evaluation. That is, culture and tradition shape or define our value systems and appear also to play an evaluative role in the ethical decision-making process. An analogous situation might involve a father teaching a son right from wrong. As the son matures and confronts an action which contains an ethical dilemma, the son might ask himself, "I wonder what my father would think of me if I chose this action." In this case the father is both the source of, and a standard for, the evaluative process. This also appears to apply to the item "acceptable to my family" which loads on dimension one.

Using the Dimensions

Two tests of the measure's explanatory and predictive power using the data collected in stage four demonstrate the utility of the multidimensional scale. First, factor scores for each dimension were regressed against a univariate evaluation of the perceived ethics of the action depicted in each scenario. This procedure follows that employed in the testing of multiattribute attitude models (e.g., Wilson et al. 1975; Harrell and Bennett 1974). Factor scores were used instead of the sum- mated item scores because of the inherent multi- collinearity present among the dimensions of the same construct and its resultant obscuring effects when attempting to establish the respective roles of each.

Second, the scores indicating the intention of individuals to act in the same manner depicted in each scenario action were also regressed against the factor scores for each dimension. The results of these two multiple regressions are shown in Table 3.4. The three dimensions comprising the overall ethics construct explain 79, 55, and 83% of the variance in the univariate measure of ethics with an average R^2 of 0.72. Thus, the three dimensions capture, on average, 72% of the variance in the univariate evaluative variable, further suggesting strong evidence of construct validity. Moreover, the beta weights shed some additional light on the role that each dimension plays in the evaluative process.

Dimension 1, the broad-based moral equity dimension, has the greatest relative impact in the evaluative process. Dimensions 2 and 3, the relativistic and contractualism dimensions respectively, play lesser roles. This relationship supports the idea mentioned earlier that these two dimensions temper or support the principal evaluative role of Dimension 1. In other words, the broad-based moral equity

Table 3.4 Dimension relationships with univariate ethics measure and intention scores

	Ethics				Intention			
	R^2	B_1	B_2	B_3	R^2	B_1	B_2	B_3
Sales	0.79	0.82	0.26	0.23	0.29	0.46	0.25	0.16
	(0.0001)	(0.0001)	(0.0001)	(0.0001)	(0.0001)	(0.0001)	(0.0005)	(0.03)
Auto	0.55	0.68	0.21	0.18	0.39	0.57	0.21	0.14
	(0.0001)	(0.0001)	(0.0004)	(0.003)	(0.0001)	(0.0001)	(0.003)	(0.05)
Retail	0.83	0.87	0.18	0.17	0.34	0.57	0.11	0.11
	(0.0001)	(0.0001)	(0.0001)	(0.0001)	(0.0001)	(0.0001)	(NS)	(NS)

dimension is the principal evaluative dimension aided by notions of relativism and contractualism. The second and third dimensions seem to become more or less important depending on the nature of the ethical problem. However, the dominance of the first dimension is intuitively understandable in making an ethical/unethical evaluation since it seems to represent a less specific and broader based moral judgment criterion. Moreover, its impact is congruent with the propositions concerning the role of justness and fairness posited by Kohlberg (1976, Chapter 2).

Dimension Roles in Predicting Behavior Intentions

Table 3.4 also offers evidence of predictive validity of the three dimensions in "explaining" an individual's intention to behave in the same manner as depicted in the action statements of the scenarios. R^2s ranged between 0.29 (sales scenario) and 0.39 (auto scenario) with an average R^2 of 0.34. On average then, the measures explain 34% of the variance in the managers' intention to behave in the same manner as the scenario action described.

While Trevino does not incorporate behavioral intention in her model, the Hunt and Vitell model posits that individual intentions are a function of ethical judgments. The Ferrell and Gresham model, on the other hand, suggests that other cognitive factors such as knowledge, values, and attitudes and significant others, as well as opportunities, impact the individual's intention to behave. Empirically, the measures explain only a portion of an individual's intention suggesting that other variables or other ethical evaluative criteria do come into play in predicting intention. Looking at the relative contributions of the three dimensions indicates that Dimension One, the broad-based moral equity dimension, as would be expected, makes the largest relative contribution in all three scenarios and again seems to be tempered by the second and third dimensions.

For example, in the scenario judged most unethical, the retail scenario, behavioral intention was due almost exclusively to dimension one. Neither the idea of social contract nor cultural acceptance seemed important in deciding if managers would behave in the same manner. However, these beliefs did play a role in helping to understand behavioral intention in the other two scenarios. In the least unethical scenario (sales) the relativistic dimension exerted its greatest impact in explaining behavioral intention. In this scenario the employee was simply overeager, and the manager was unwilling to correct the behavior. A greater degree of social acceptance for the behavior of the employee is easy to justify in this scenario and so is the role of that acceptance in understanding intention. Similarly, the idea of a social contract seems to mediate behavioral intention in both the sales and auto scenario. In both of these scenarios the managers seemed to believe that an implied (unspoken/unwritten) promise or contract existed and that its existence influenced their behavioral intention. In the auto scenario an actual contract did exist in the form of a warranty which was never fulfilled. In the sales scenario the implication is that there does exist a social contract between business and its customers not to cheat them.

Table 3.5 Difference in explanatory power of multidimensional scale items over univariate measure

Scenario		Intention
Sales (least unethical)	Univariate	0.28
	Multidimensional	0.29
	Difference	+0.01
Auto	Univariate	0.22
	Multidimensional	0.39
	Difference	+0.17
Retail (most unethical)	Univariate	0.17
	Multidimensional	0.34
	Difference	+0.17

One final indication of the utility of the multidimensional measures is evidenced by the increased power in explaining behavioral intentions they afford over the univariate measure of ethics. Behavioral intention R^2s for the univariate measure are compared with those of the multidimensional measures in Table 3.5.

In two of the three cases, the multidimensional measures explained a substantially greater amount of variance in the intention scores. In only one case, the sales scenario, which was judged least unethical by the respondents, was there essentially equal explanatory power. In the scenario judged most unethical (retail) the scales doubled the explanatory power of the univariate measure. Within the limited context of these three scenarios, this finding suggests that the predictive power of the multidimensional measure is directly related to the perception of the ethical consequences.

Conclusions and Recommendations for Future Research

This study has presented a multidimensional scale evidencing substantial reliability and validity for evaluating the perceptions of the ethical content of business activities. The items and dimensions that make up this scale are shown in Table 3.6. The procedure used to develop the items suggests that they represent a set of ethical evaluative criteria with general application.

The three positive dimensions do not correspond strictly to the normative moral philosophies and tend to disagree with several of the hypothesized relationships in recently developed models of ethical decision-making. This finding is not surprising since the models are based on normative moral philosophies which represent idealized prescriptive sets of norms rather than positive descriptive sets of evaluative criteria.

The potential applications of this scale to the study of business ethics are manifold, but future users must proceed with the caution due any new measuring instrument. Psychometric measures more realistically evolve rather than burst forth full blown and complete. While these scales have been through four developmental stages, the validation and development process is never ending.

Table 3.6 The proposed multidimensional ethics scale

Construct 1 – The broad-based moral equity construct		
Just	-------	Unjust
Fair	-------	Unfair
Morally right	-------	Not morally right
Acceptable to my family	-------	Not acceptable to my family
Construct 2 – The relativist construct		
Culturally acceptable	-------	Culturally unacceptable
Traditionally unacceptable	-------	Traditionally unacceptable
Construct 3 – The social contract construct		
Violates an Unspoken promise	-------	Does not violate an Unspoken promise
Violates an Unwritten contract	-------	Does not violate an Unwritten contract

The findings do present the opportunity to inform the various ethics models, principally with regard to the combinatorial process involved in making ethical evaluations. While an identifiable but limited deontological dimension was found, the results do not support the contention that individuals rely upon a set of teleological principles (utilitarian or egoist) in making ethical evaluations. Instead, individuals tend to rely on a broad sense of moral equity dominated by concerns for fairness and justice, tempered by relativistic and social contract dimensions.

Another interesting application of the scales is to examine their potential relationship between an individual's ethical evaluative criteria and their stage of moral development. Studies specifically examining the linkages between moral development and resulting sets of evaluative criteria might enhance the predictability of Kohlberg's work. The dominance of the ideas of fairness and justice in dimension 1 is congruent with the notion of Kohlberg that these two concepts are involved in all ethical decision-making regardless of stage of moral development. This finding provides some support for the Trevino model. The use of the three different scenarios to provide varying contexts for testing the scales and the consistent performance of the dimensions with respect to the differing contexts suggests that the measures are situation independent. It seems plausible that the dimensions could maintain their validity across a wide variety of business ethics applications, but this requires continual testing. If the measures are independent of context, then the diversity of potential applications expands gready.

For example, managerial applications of multiple context scales might provide an aid in conducting ethical audits, a tool in addressing specific ethical problems, a means of sampling customer, employee, community, and industry reactions to determine if corporate values are maintained by employees and an aid in designing ethical training for business personnel. The scales would seem to be useful when incorporated within the "parallel planning systems" approach proposed by Robin and Reidenbach (1987). Information is needed to develop their "ethical profile", to "identify impacted publics", to determine "actionable ethical core values", to "enculturate-integrate core values into the corporate culture", and to "monitor and control... for ethical effectiveness" (pp. 52–56).

Further, the multidimensional nature of the scales can provide information as to why a particular business activity is judged unethical. Global measures cannot provide this information. Specifically, the use of the scales can give a manager insight as to whether the activity contemplated or undertaken is perceived as fair, just, or whether it violates certain cultural or traditional values. This latter information would be particularly beneficial in multinational business settings as would that concerning the ideas of contracts and duties in dimension three, which might vary significantly from country to country.

Appendix

Five Ethical Theories

Each of the following ethical theories seems to provide important ideas and language for modern societies. It is that characteristic that made them the beginning point for this research.

Justice Theory

Much of the most influential and fundamental concepts of justice theory comes from the writings of Aristotle. He developed the "principle of formal justice" which states simply that equals ought to be treated equally, and unequals ought to be treated unequally. It provides a minimum rule of justice, but it does not explain how to determine equality or how to proportion when people or performances are unequal. To establish the latter, philosophers often refer to six principles of distributive justice, usually recognizing that others could be added to the list. These six principles are: (1) to each person an equal share; (2) to each person according to individual need; (3) to each person according to that person's rights; (4) to each person according to individual effort, (5) to each person according to societal contribution; (6) to each person according to merit (Beauchamp and Bowie 1983, pp. 41–42).

It is not necessary that a society adopt one principle of distributive justice and exclude the others. Societies often use different principles in different situations. For example, in the United States transfer payments to the poor and unemployed are based on some measure of need, while promotions and salary increases are usually based on merit. In still another application, it is society's intention to provide an equal opportunity for public education to all.

Finally, there is the concept of procedural justice. As the name implies, its purpose is to develop rules or procedures that result in fair or just outcomes. There are three forms of procedural justice – "pure," "perfect," and "imperfect." if the rules, as in a game, guarantee just outcomes in every occurrence, they produce "pure" procedural justice. "Perfect" procedural justice provides a fair result in every case. In "imperfect" procedural justice the rules represent the best attempt to produce fair results but sometimes the outcomes are unjust.

The moral development literature of Kohlberg relies heavily on concepts of justice. It permeates all six of their stages and the last three stages are tied to specific concepts of justice (Rest 1979, pp. 35–36). Their stage four, law and order, can be paired with the idea of "formal justice." Their stage five fits nicely with the concepts of "procedural justice" described above, and they match stage six with what is called "substantive justice." Thus, this literature relies heavily on concepts of justice.

Relativism

The basic concept of relativism is that all normative beliefs are a function of a culture or individual, and therefore, no universal ethical rules exist that apply to everyone. The argument continues that since ethical rules are relative to a specific culture, the values and behavior of people in one culture need not govern the conduct of people in another culture. Varied and apparently contradictory values between many cultures have been reported by anthropologists, and this evidence is offered as a justification of relativism. The concept of cultural relativism has been extended to ideas of individual relativism in which the value differences of individuals are recognized. In this form, fundamental and ultimate disagreements between individuals, or an individual and his/her society, are cited as the reason for believing in the concept.

Arguments against relativism seem to be preferred over the preceding arguments by most ethicists. One argument against relativism is simply that, as a philosophy, it does not achieve the main task of ethics. That main task is described by J.S. Mill and Aristotle as the development and maintenance of conditions that allow people to pursue a stable and happy life. A somewhat different view comes from Kant who believed that the objective of ethics is to create a "good will" toward others. Relativism, according to its critics, is not likely to achieve these objectives.

Other arguments against relativism suggest that there is no real basic difference between moral beliefs, in spite of the findings of the anthropologists. This argument is based on the common needs and fears of humans, and suggests that if researchers dug deep enough in trying to understand why different beliefs are held, they would reach a point where the basic rationales were the same. Still another argument against relativism is that, even if a belief or behavior is accepted in a society, that doesn't mean it is right. Additional arguments exist but these are sufficient to explain why philosophers have not fully adopted the relativistic arguments. Even so, many of these philosophers also recognize that unresolved disagreements in moral beliefs may be inevitable (Brandt 1959, pp. 100–103, 285–288).

Many managers cite as a defense against alleged unethical behavior in international settings, the cultural differences in methods for doing business. "La mordida" or "baksheesh" – bribery or kickbacks – are two culturally acceptable behaviors in some countries. Specifically, this justification was used by Boeing in defense of its actions in Japan.

Deontology

Deontology suggests that individuals have a duty, the root word for the term, to satisfy the legitimate claims or needs of others as determined by applying logic to an ethical rule. These duties to others are many and diverse. Under this philosophy it is our duty to pay our debts, care for our children, and tell the truth because it is the "right" thing to do. The most prominent ethical rule comes from Immanuel Kant and it's called the "Categorical Imperative" (Immanuel Kant, *Foundations of the Metaphysics of Morals*, Beck, trans., 1959, pp. 9–28). The most popular formulation says, "I ought never to act except in such a way that I can also will that my maxim should become a universal law." With this rule and the use of logic any action can be evaluated to determine if it is ethical or unethical. These duties on the part of one individual toward another create rights for the other. Thus, the duty of parents creates rights for children, and the duty of debtors creates rights for the lender. A popular understanding of these ideas comes to the general public through the church, the Bill of Rights, the boy and girl scout pledges, and even the military (duty, honor, country).

Deontology may be the most preferred ethical philosophy today, but it also has its critics. The most important complaint against deontology is that, whatever rule might be constructed, exceptions can almost always be found to be necessary. Applying the categorical imperative and logic, most people would agree that lying is unethical. However, it is easy to imagine situations in which lying seems to be the most ethical thing to do. W. D. Ross (1930) gave one solution to this problem by suggesting that the rules created are *prima facie* and that we should recognize exceptions. In effect, this approach shifts the burden of proof to the individual that would break the rule.

An interesting adaptation of Kantian Deontology was developed by John Rawls. His approach has become labeled "contractarianism" or "contractualism" because of the manner in which he uses the idea of a social contract. Bayles and Henley (1983) describe the connection as follows:

> The contemporary American philosopher John Rawls, for instance, has developed an account of justice that has roots in Locke, Rousseau, and Kant. The guiding idea behind this account is the social contract in a form similar to that underlying the fifth formulation of Kant's categorical imperative: 'Every rational being must act as if he, by his maxims, were at all times a legislative member in the universal realm of ends.' In this formula Kant uses the conception of the social contract found in Jean-Jacques Rousseau (1712–1778), although he interprets it in his own distinctive way. (pp. 59–60)

Teleology – Egoism

Teleological, or consequentialist theories include all of those theories that measure morality based on the consequences of actions. The two most commonly discussed teleological theories in modern philosophy can be illustrated by asking if evaluation of the consequences should focus solely on the individual or if the evaluation should encompass all of society. If the answer is that the evaluator should consider only the consequences to the individual, then the ethical theory is called egoism. If the answer is to consider all of society, then the theory is called utilitarianism.

One presentation of egoism suggests that an act is ethical when it promotes the individual's long-term interests. There are many variations of the theory which focus on short-term hedonism, or in the case of psychological egoism, which contends that everyone is psychologically programed to behave only in their own self interest. However, the presentation of egoism using long-term interests is taken most seriously by modern philosophers. In this formulation, it is possible for an individual to help others, help formulate and follow the rules of society, and even give gifts if that person feels that those actions are in his or her own best interests. It should also be noted that the theory states that people *should* behave as egoists and not that they *do* behave that way.

The philosophy of ethical egoism is usually attacked on the basis that it ignores what most people would agree are blatant wrongs. It also has no way of solving conflicts of egoistic interests, and therefore like relativism, does not satisfy the goals of ethical philosophy. Egoism has been important in business because of the well-known work of Adam Smith who believed that through an "invisible hand" businesses operating in their own self interest would produce the greatest economic good for society. The concern for society is utilitarian, and Smith's work provides a link between the two teleological theories.

Teleology–Utilitarianism

Utilitarianism is the teleological theory which states that individuals should act so as to produce the greatest possible ratio of good to evil for all of society. It forces the actors to consider all of the outcomes of their action or inaction and to weigh one against another to determine that which is best for society. Since one action is compared to another, utilitarianism promotes efficiency. That is, a less efficient action is likely to produce less utility than a more efficient action, and is therefore less ethical. As suggested in the preceding section, much of the justification for capitalism is based in utilitarianism. In addition, the general public learns about the ideas of utilitarianism through the concept of the democratic process which focuses on majority rule.

The two most important complaints against utilitarianism are that it is impossible to project and measure the consequences of many important actions, and that important harms to individuals or small groups can be averaged with small gains to a large number and appear to be acceptable. The first complaint is less troublesome because individuals are constantly making important decisions with less than perfect information. The second complaint has caused an important problem for the theory, and even though it still has a large following among philosophers, the theory has lost some stature because of its failure to deal with the complaint.

References

Bayles, Michael D., and Kenneth Henley. 1983. *Right conduct: Theory and applications*. New York: Random House.

Beauchamp, Tom. 1982. *Philosophical ethics*. New York: McGraw Hill.

Beauchamp, Tom L., and Norman E. Bowie. 1983. *Ethical theory and business*, 2nd ed. Englewood Cliffs: Prentice-Hall.

Brandt, Richard. 1959. *Ethical theory*. Englewood Cliffs: Prentice-Hall.

Browning, John, and Noel B. Zabriskie. 1983. How ethical are industrial buyers? *Journal of Marketing* 42(July): 69–73.

Campbell, Donald T., and Donald W. Fiske. 1959. Convergent and discriminant validation by the multitrait-multimethod matrix. *Psychological Bulletin* 56(March): 81–105.

Churchill, Gilbert A. 1979. A paradigm for developing better measures of marketing constructs. *Journal of Marketing Research* XVI(February): 64–73.

DeGeorge, Richard R. 1986. *Business ethics*, 2nd ed. New York: MacMillan.

Donaldson, Thomas, and Patricia H. Werhane. 1983. *Ethical issues in business*, 2nd ed. Englewood Cliffs: Prentice-Hall.

Dornoff, Ronald J., and Clint B. Tankersley. 1975. Perceptual differences in market transactions: A source of consumer frustration. *Journal of Consumer Affairs* 9(Summer): 97–103.

Ferrell, O.C., and Larry G. Gresham. 1985. A contingency framework for understanding ethical decision-making in marketing. *Journal of Marketing* 49(Summer): 87–96.

George, Richard J. 1985. The ethical perceptions of present and future corporate executives'In *Proceedings of the Southwest Marketing Association Conference* (March), 143–146.

Harrell, Gilbert D., and Peter D. Bennett. 1974. An evaluation of the expectancy value model of attitude measurement for physician prescribing behavior. *Journal of Marketing Research* XI(August): 269–278.

Hawkins, Del I., and Benton Cocanougher. 1972. Student evaluations of the ethics of marketing practices: The role of marketing education. *Journal of Marketing* 36(April): 54–61.

Heeler, Roger M., and Michael L. Ray. 1972. Measure validation in marketing. *Journal of Marketing Research* 9(November): 456–464.

Hoffman, W.Michael, and Jennifer Mills Moore. 1984. *Business ethics: Readings and cases in corporate morality*. New York: McGraw-Hill.

Hunt, S.D., and S. Vitell. 1986. A general theory of marketing ethics. *Journal of Macromarketing* 6(Spring): 5–16.

Kant, Immanuel. 1964. *Foundations of the metaphysics of morals*. Trans. H. J. Paton. New York: Harper and Row Publishers.

Kohlberg, Lawrence. 1976. Moral stages and moralization: The cognitive development approach. In *Moral development and behavior: Theory research and social issues*, ed. Lickona Thomas. New York: Holt, Rinehart, and Winston.

Kristol, Irving. 1978. A capitalist conception of justice. In *Ethics, free enterprise and public policy: Original essays on moral issues in business*, ed. Richard T. DeGeorge and Joseph A. Pichler. Oxford: Oxford University Press.

Krugman, Dean M., and O.C. Ferrell. 1981. The organizational ethics of advertising: Corporate and agency views. *Journal of Advertising* 10(1): 21–30. 48.

Nozick, R. 1974. *Anarchy, state and Utopia*. New York: Basic Books.

Nunnally, J.C. 1969. *Psychometric methods*. New York: McGraw-Hill.

Rawls, John. 1971. *A theory of justice*. Cambridge, MA: The Belknap Press of Harvard University Press.

Reidenbach, Reidenbach E., and Donald P. Robin. 1988. Some initial steps toward improving the measurement of ethical evaluations of marketing activities. *Journal of Business Ethics* 7: 871–879.

Rest, J.R. 1979. *In judging moral issues*. Minneapolis: University of Minnesota Press.

Robertson, Thomas S., and James H. Meyers. 1969. Personality correlation of opinion leadership and innovation buying behavior. *Journal of Marketing Research* VI(May): 164–168.
Robin, Donald P., and R.Eric Reidenbach. 1987. Social responsibility, ethics, and marketing strategy: Closing the gap between concept and application. *Journal of Marketing* 51(January): 44–58.
Ross, W. 1930. *The right and good.* Oxford: Clarendon.
Sartorios, R.E. 1975. *Individual conduct and social norms: A utilitarian account of social union and rule of law.* Belmont: Dickenson Publishing.
Singer, Peter. 1976. Freedom and utility in the distribution of health care. In *Ethics and health policy*, ed. R. Veatch and R. Bronson. Cambridge, MA: Boelinger Publishing.
Smart, J.J.C. 1973. Distribution, justice and utilitarianism. In *Justice and economic distribution*, ed. Arthur John and William H. Shaw. Englewood Cliffs: Prentice-Hall.
Stace, W.T. 1937. *The concept of morals.* New York: MacMillan.
Trevino, Linda Klebe. 1986. Ethical decision making in organizations: A person-situation interactionist model. *Academy of Management Review* 11: 601–617.
Wilson, David T., H.Lee Mathews, and James W. Harvey. 1975. An empirical test of the Fishbein behavioral intention model. *Journal of Consumer Research* 1(March): 39–48.

Chapter 4
Corporate Social Responsibility Theories: Mapping the Territory

Elisabet Garriga and Domènec Melé

Introduction

Since the second half of the twentieth century a long debate on corporate social responsibility (CSR) has been taking place. In 1953, Bowen (1953) wrote the seminal book *Social Responsibilities of the Businessman.* Since then there has been a shift in terminology from the social responsibility of business to CSR. Additionally, this field has grown significantly and today contains a great proliferation of theories, approaches and terminologies. Society and business, social issues management, public policy and business, stakeholder management, corporate accountability are just some of the terms used to describe the phenomena related to corporate responsibility in society. Recently, renewed interest for corporate social responsibilities and new alternative concepts have been proposed, including corporate citizenship and corporate sustainability. Some scholars have compared these new concepts with the classic notion of CSR (see Van Marrewijk (2003) for corporate sustainability; and Matten et al. (2003) and Wood and Lodgson (2002) for corporate citizenship).

Furthermore, some theories combine different approaches and use the same terminology with different meanings. This problem is an old one. It was 30 years ago that Votaw wrote: "corporate social responsibility means something, but not always the same thing to everybody. To some it conveys the idea of legal responsibility or liability; to others, it means socially responsible behavior in the ethical sense; to still others, the meaning transmitted is that of 'responsible for' in a causal mode; many simply equate it with a charitable contribution; some take it to mean socially conscious; many

E. Garriga (✉)
Business Policy Department, FADA Business School, Arago, 204, 08011 Barcelona, Spain
e-mail: egarriga@eada.edu

D. Melé
Department of Business Ethics, IESE Business School, University of Navarra,
AVD Pearson, 21, 08034 Barcelona, Spain
e-mail: mele@iese.edu

A.C. Michalos and D.C. Poff (eds.), *Citation Classics from the Journal of Business Ethics*, Advances in Business Ethics Research 2,
DOI 10.1007/978-94-007-4126-3_4, © Springer Science+Business Media B.V. 2013

of those who embrace it most fervently see it as a mere synonym for legitimacy in the context of belonging or being proper or valid; a few see a sort of fiduciary duty imposing higher standards of behavior on businessmen than on citizens at large" (Votaw 1972, p. 25). Nowadays the panorama is not much better. Carroll, one of the most prestigious scholars in this discipline, characterized the situation as "an eclectic field with loose boundaries, multiple memberships, and differing training/perspectives; broadly rather than focused, multidisciplinary; wide breadth; brings in a wider range of literature; and interdisciplinary" (Carroll 1994, p. 14). Actually, as Carroll added (1994, p. 6), the map of the overall field is quite poor.

However, some attempts have been made to address this deficiency. Frederick (1987, 1998) outlined a classification based on a conceptual transition from the ethical-philosophical concept of CSR (what he calls CSRl), to the action-oriented managerial concept of social responsiveness (CSR2). He then included a normative element based on ethics and values (CSR3) and finally he introduced the cosmos as the basic normative reference for social issues in management and considered the role of science and religion in these issues (CSR4). In a more systematic way, Heald (1988) and Carroll (1999) have offered a historical sequence of the main developments in how the responsibilities of business in society have been understood.

Other classifications have been suggested based on matters related to CSR, such as Issues Management (Wartick and Rude 1986; Wood 1991a) or the concept of Corporate Citizenship (Altman 1998). An alternative approach is presented by Brummer (1991) who proposes a classification in four groups of theories based on six criteria (motive, relation to profits, group affected by decisions, type of act, type of effect, expressed or ideal interest). These classifications, in spite of their valuable contribution, are quite limited in scope and, what is more, the nature of the relationship between business and society is rarely situated at the center of their discussion. This vision could be questioned as CSR seems to be a consequence of how this relationship is understood (Jones 1983; McMahon 1986; Preston 1975; Wood 1991b).

In order to contribute to a clarification of the field of business and society, our aim here is to map the territory in which most relevant CSR theories and related approaches are situated. We will do so by considering each theory from the perspective of how the interaction phenomena between business and society are focused.

As the starting point for a proper classification, we assume as hypothesis that the most relevant CSR theories and related approaches are focused on one of the following aspects of social reality: economics, politics, social integration and ethics. The inspiration for this hypothesis is rooted in four aspects that, according to Parsons (1961), can be observed in any social system: adaptation to the environment (related to resources and economics), goal attainment (related to politics), social integration and pattern maintenance or latency (related to culture and values).[1] This hypothesis permits us to classify these theories in four groups:

1. A first group in which it is assumed that the corporation is an instrument for wealth creation and that this is its sole social responsibility. Only the economic aspect of the interactions between business and society is considered. So any supposed social activity is accepted if, and only if, it is consistent with wealth

creation. This group of theories could be call instrumental theories because they understand CSR as a mere means to the end of profits.

2. A second group in which the social power of corporation is emphasized, specifically in its relationship with society and its responsibility in the political arena associated with this power. This leads the corporation to accept social duties and rights or participate in certain social cooperation. We will call this group political theories.
3. A third group includes theories which consider that business ought to integrate social demands. They usually argue that business depends on society for its continuity and growth and even for the existence of business itself. We can term this group integrative theories.
4. A fourth group of theories understands that the relationship between business and society is embedded with ethical values. This leads to a vision of CSR from an ethical perspective and as a consequence, firms ought to accept social responsibilities as an ethical obligation above any other consideration. We can term this group ethical theories.

Throughout this paper we will present the most relevant theories on CSR and related matters, trying to prove that they are all focused on one of the fore mentioned aspects. We will not explain each theory in detail, only what is necessary to verify our hypothesis and, if necessary, some complementary information to clarify what each is about. At the same time, we will attempt to situate these theories and approaches within a general map describing the current panorama regarding the role of business in society.

Instrumental Theories

In this group of theories CSR is seen only as a strategic tool to achieve economic objectives and, ultimately, wealth creation. Representative of this approach is the well-known Friedman view that "the only one responsibility of business towards society is the maximization of profits to the shareholders within the legal framework and the ethical custom of the country" (1970).[2]

Instrumental theories have a long tradition and have enjoyed a wide acceptance in business so far. As Windsor (2001) has pointed out recently, "a leitmotiv of wealth creation progressively dominates the managerial conception of responsibility" (Windsor 2001, p. 226).

Concern for profits does not exclude taking into account the interests of all who have a stake in the firm (stakeholders). It has been argued that in certain conditions the satisfaction of these interests can contribute to maximizing the shareholder value (Mitchell et al. 1997; Ogden and Watson 1999). An adequate level of investment in philanthropy and social activities is also acceptable for the sake of profits (McWilliams and Siegel 2001). We will return to these points afterwards.

In practice, a number of studies have been carried out to determine the correlation between CSR and corporate financial performance. Of these, an increasing number show a positive correlation between the social responsibility and financial performance of corporations in most cases (Frooman 1997; Griffin and Mahon 1997; Key and Popkin 1998; Roman et al. 1999; Waddock and Graves 1997) However, these findings have to be read with caution since such correlation is difficult to measure (Griffin 2000; Rowley and Berman 2000).

Three main groups of instrumental theories can be identified, depending on the economic objective proposed. In the first group the objective is the maximization of shareholder value, measured by the share price. Frequently, this leads to a short-term profits orientation. The second group of theories focuses on the strategic goal of achieving competitive advantages, which would produce long-term profits. In both cases, CSR is only a question of enlightened self-interest (Keim 1978) since CSRs are a mere instrument for profits. The third is related to cause-related marketing and is very close to the second. Let us examine briefly the philosophy and some variants of these groups.

Maximizing the Shareholder Value

A well-known approach is that which takes the straightforward contribution to maximizing the shareholder value as the supreme criterion to evaluate specific corporate social activity. Any investment in social demands that would produce an increase of the shareholder value should be made, acting without deception and fraud. In contrast, if the social demands only impose a cost on the company they should be rejected. Friedman (1970) is clear, giving an example about investment in the local community: "It will be in the long run interest of a corporation that is a major employer in a small community to devote resources to providing amenities to that community or to improving its government. That makes it easier to attract desirable employees, it may reduce the wage bill or lessen losses from pilferage and sabotage or have other worthwhile effects." So, the socio-economic objectives are completely separate from the economic objectives.

Currently, this approach usually takes the share-holder value maximization as the supreme reference for corporate decision-making. The Agency Theory (Jensen and Meckling 1976; Ross 1973) is the most popular way to articulate this reference. However, today it is quite readily accepted that shareholder value maximization is not incompatible with satisfying certain interests of people with a stake in the firm (stakeholders). In this respect, Jensen (2000) has proposed what he calls 'enlightened value maximization'. This concept specifies long-term value maximization or value-seeking as the firm's objective. At the same time, this objective is employed as the criterion for making the requisite tradeoffs among its stakeholders.

Strategies for Achieving Competitive Advantages

A second group of theories are focused on how to allocate resources in order to achieve long-term social objectives and create a competitive advantage (Husted and

Allen 2000). In this group three approaches can be included: (a) social investments in competitive context, (b) natural resource-based view of the firm and its dynamic capabilities and (c) strategies for the bottom of the economic pyramid.

(a) Social Investments in a Competitive Context

Porter and Kramer (2002) have recently applied the well-known Porter model on competitive advantage (Porter 1980) to consider investment in areas of what they call competitive context.[3] The authors argue that investing in philanthropic activities may be the only way to improve the context of competitive advantage of a firm and usually creates greater social value than individual donors or government can. The reason presented – the opposite of Freidman's position – is that the firm has the knowledge and resources for a better understanding of how to solve some problems related to its mission. As Burke and Logsdon (1996) pointed out, when philanthropic activities are closer to the company's mission, they create greater wealth than others kinds of donations. That is what happens, e.g., when a telecommunications company is teaching computer network administration to students of the local community.

Porter and Kramer conclude, "philanthropic investments by members of cluster, either individually or collectively, can have a powerful effect on the cluster competitiveness and the performance of all its constituents companies" (2002, pp. 60–61).

(b) Natural Resource-Based View of the Firm and Dynamic Capabilities

The resource-based view of the firm (Barney 1991; Wernelfelt 1984) maintains that the ability of a firm to perform better than its competitors depends on the unique interplay of human, organizational, and physical resources over time. Traditionally, resources that are most likely to lead to competitive advantage are those that meet four criteria: they should be valuable, rare, and inimitable, and the organization must be organized to deploy these resources effectively.

The "dynamic capabilities" approach presents the dynamic aspect of the resources; it is focused on the drivers behind the creation, evolution and recombination of the resources into new sources of competitive advantage (Teece et al. 1997). So dynamic capabilities are organizational and strategic routines, by which managers acquire resources, modify them, integrate them, and recombine them to generate new value-creating strategies. Based on this perspective, some authors have identified social and ethical resources and capabilities which can be a source of competitive advantage, such as the process of moral decision-making (Petrick and Quinn 2001), the process of perception, deliberation and responsiveness or capacity of adaptation (Litz 1996) and the development of proper relationships with the primary stakeholders: employees, customers, suppliers, and communities (Harrison and St. John 1996; Hillman and Keim 2001).

A more complete model of the 'Resource-Based View of the Firm' has been presented by Hart (1995). It includes aspects of dynamic capabilities and a link with the external environment. Hart argues that the most important drivers for new resource and capabilities development will be constraints and challenges posed by the natural biophysical environment. Hart has developed his conceptual framework with three main interconnected strategic capabilities: pollution prevention, product stewardship and sustainable development. He considers as critical resources continuous improvement, stakeholder integration and shared vision.

(c) Strategies for the Bottom of the Economic Pyramid

Traditionally most business strategies are focused on targeting products at upper and middle-class people, but most of the world's population is poor or lower-middle class. At the bottom of the economic pyramid there may be some 4,000 million people. On reflection, certain strategies can serve the poor and simultaneously make profits. Prahalad (2002), analyzing the India experience, has suggested some mind-set changes for converting the poor into active consumers. The first of these is seeing the poor as an opportunity to innovate rather than as a problem.

A specific means for attending to the bottom of the economic pyramid is disruptive innovation. Disruptive innovations (Christensen and Overdorf 2000; Christensen et al. 2001) are products or services that do not have the same capabilities and conditions as those being used by customers in the mainstream markets; as a result they can be introduced only for new or less demanding applications among non-traditional customers, with a low-cost production and adapted to the necessities of the population. For example a telecommunications company inventing a small cellular telephone system with lower costs but also with less service adapted to the base of the economic pyramid.

Disruptive innovations can improve the social and economic conditions at the "base of the pyramid" and at the same time they create a competitive advantage for the firms in telecommunications, consumer electronics and energy production and many other industries, especially in developing countries (Hart and Christensen 2002; Prahalad and Hammond 2002).

Cause-Related Marketing

Cause-related marketing has been defined as "the process of formulating and implementing marketing activities that are characterized by an offer from the firm to contribute a specified amount to a designated cause when customers engage in a revenue-providing exchanges that satisfy organizational and individual objectives" (Varadarajan and Menon 1988, p. 60). Its goal then is to enhance company revenues and sales or customer relationship by building the brand through the acquisition of, and association with the ethical dimension or social responsibility dimension (Murray and Montanan 1986; Varadarajan and Menon 1988). In a way, it seeks product differentiation by creating socially responsible attributes that affect company reputation (Smith and Higgins 2000). As McWilliams and Siegel (2001, p. 120) have pointed out: "support of cause related marketing creates a reputation that a firm is reliable and honest. Consumers typically assume that the products of a reliable and honest firm will be of high quality". For example, a pesticide-free or non-animal-tested ingredient can be perceived by some buyers as preferable to other attributes of competitors' products.

Other activities, which typically exploit cause-related marketing, are classical musical concerts, art exhibitions, golf tournaments or literacy campaigns. All of these are a form of enlightened self-interest and a win-win situation as both the company and the charitable cause receive benefits: "the brand manager uses consumer concern for business responsibility as a means for securing competitive advantage. At the same time a charitable cause receives substantial financial benefits" (Smith and Higgins 2000, p. 309).

Political Theories

A group of CSR theories and approaches focus on interactions and connections between business and society and on the power and position of business and its inherent responsibility. They include both political considerations and political analysis in the CSR debate. Although there are a variety of approaches, two major theories can be distinguished: Corporate Constitutionalism and Corporate Citizenship.

Corporate Constitutionalism

Davis (1960) was one of the first to explore the role of power that business has in society and the social impact of this power.[4] In doing so, he introduces business power as a new element in the debate of CSR. He held that business is a social institution and it must use power responsibly. Additionally, Davis noted that the causes that generate the social power of the firm are not solely internal of the firm but also external. Their locus is unstable and constantly shifting, from the economic to the social forum and from there to the political forum and vice versa.

Davis attacked the assumption of the classical economic theory of perfect competition that precludes the involvement of the firm in society besides the creation of wealth. The firm has power to influence the equilibrium of the market and therefore the price is not a Pareto optimum reflecting the free will of participants with perfect knowledge of the market.

Davis formulated two principles that express how social power has to be managed: "the social power equation" and "the iron law of responsibility". The social power equation principle states that "social responsibilities of businessmen arise from the amount of social power that they have" (Davis 1967, p. 48). The iron law of responsibility refers to the negative consequences of the absence of use of power.

In his own words: "Whoever does not use his social power responsibly will lose it. In the long run those who do not use power in a manner which society considers responsible will tend to lose it because other groups eventually will step in to assume those responsibilities" (1960, p. 63). So if a firm does not use its social power, it will lose its position in society because other groups will occupy it, especially when society demands responsibility from business (Davis 1960).

According to Davis, the equation of social power-responsibility has to be understood through the functional role of business and managers. In this respect, Davis rejects the idea of total responsibility of business as he rejected the radical free-market ideology of no responsibility of business. The limits of functional power come from the pressures of different constituency groups. This "restricts organizational power in the same way that a governmental constitution does." The constituency groups do not destroy power. Rather they define conditions for its responsible use. They channel organizational power in a supportive way and to protect other interests against unreasonable organizational power (Davis 1967, p. 68). As a consequence, his theory is called "Corporate Constitutionalism".

Integrative Social Contract Theory

Donaldson (1982) considered the business and society relationship from the social contract tradition, mainly from the philosophical thought of Locke. He assumed that a sort of implicit social contract between business and society exists. This social contract implies some indirect obligations of business towards society. This approach would overcome some limitations of deontological and teleological theories applied to business.

Afterwards, Donaldson and Dunfee (1994, 1999) extended this approach and proposed an "Integrative Social Contract Theory" (ISCT) in order to take into account the socio-cultural context and also to integrate empirical and normative aspects of management. Social responsibilities come from consent. These scholars assumed two levels of consent. Firstly a theoretical macrosocial contract appealing to all rational contractors, and secondly, a real microsocial contract by members of numerous localized communities. According to these authors, this theory offers a process in which the contracts among industries, departments and economic systems can be legitimate. In this process the participants will agree upon the ground rules defining the foundation of economics that will be acceptable to them.

The macrosocial contract provides rules for any social contracting. These rules are called the "hyper-norms"; they ought to take precedence over other contracts. These hyper-norms are so fundamental and basic that they "are discernible in a convergence of religious, political and philosophical thought" (Donaldson and Dunfee 2000, p. 441). The microsocial contracts show explicit or implicit agreements that are binding within an identified community, whatever this may be: industry, companies, Or economic systems. These microsocial contracts, which generate 'authentic norms', are based on the attitudes and behaviors of the members of the norm-generating community and, in order to be legitimate, have to accord with the hyper-norms.

Corporate Citizenship

Although the idea of the firm as citizen is not new (Davis 1973) a renewed interest in this concept among practitioners has appeared recently due to certain factors that have had an impact on the business and society relationship. Among these factors, especially worthy of note are the crisis of the Welfare State and the globalization phenomenon. These, together with the deregulation process and decreasing costs with technological improvements, have meant that some large multinational companies have greater economical and social power than some governments. The corporate citizenship framework looks to give an account of this new reality, as we will try to explain here.

In the 1980s the term "corporate citizenship" was introduced into the business and society relationship mainly through practitioners (Altman and Vidaver-Cohen 2000). Since the late 1990s and early twenty-first century this term has become more and more popular in business and increasing academic work has been carried out (Andriof and McIntosh 2001; Matten and Crane 2005).

Although the academic reflection on the concept of "corporate citizenship", and on a similar one called 'the business citizen', is quite recent (Matten et al. 2003; Wood and Logsdon 2002; among others), this notion has always connoted a sense of belonging to a community. Perhaps for this reason it has been so popular among managers and business people, because it is increasingly clear that business needs to take into account the community where it is operating.

The term "corporate citizenship" cannot have the same meaning for everybody. Matten et al. (2003) have distinguished three views of "corporate citizenship": (1) a limited view, (2) a view equivalent to CSR and (3) an extended view of corporate citizenship, which is held by them. In the limited view "corporate citizenship" is used in a sense quite close to corporate philanthropy, social investment or certain responsibilities assumed towards the local community. The equivalent to CSR view is quite common. Carroll (1999) believes that "Corporate citizenship" seems a new conceptualization of the role of business in society and depending on which way it is defined, this notion largely overlaps with other theories on the responsibility of business in society. Finally, in the extended view of corporate citizenship (Matten et al. 2003; Matten and Crane 2005), corporations enter the arena of citizenship at the point of government failure in the protection of citizenship. This view arises from the fact that some corporations have gradually come to replace the most powerful institution in the traditional concept of citizenship, namely government.

The term "citizenship", taken from political science, is at the core of the "corporate citizenship" notion. For Wood and Logsdon "business citizenship cannot be deemed equivalent to individual citizenship-instead it derives from and is secondary to individual citizenship" (2002, p. 86). Whether or not this view is accepted, theories and approaches on "corporate citizenship" are focused on rights, responsibilities and possible partnerships of business in society.

Some theories on corporate citizenship are based on a social contract theory (Dion 2001) as developed by Donaldson and Dunfee (1994, 1999), although other approaches are also possible (Wood and Logsdon 2002).

In spite of some noteworthy differences in corporate citizenship theories, most authors generally converge on some points, such as a strong sense of business responsibility towards the local community, partnerships, which are the specific ways of formalizing the willingness to improve the local community,[5] and for consideration for the environment.

The concern for local community has extended progressively to a global concern in great part due to the very intense protests against globalization, mainly since the end of the 1990s. This sense of global corporate citizenship led to the joint statement "Global Corporate Citizenship – the Leadership Challenge for CEOs and Boards", signed by 34 of the world largest multinational corporations during the World Economic Forum in New York in January 2002. Subsequently, business with local responsibility and, at the same time, being a global actor that places emphasis on business responsibilities in a global context, have been considered as a key issue by some scholars (Tichy et al. 1997; Wood and Lodgson 2002).

Integrative Theories

This group of theories looks at how business integrates social demands, arguing that business depends on society for its existence, continuity and growth. Social demands are generally considered to be the way in which society interacts with business and gives it a certain legitimacy and prestige. As a consequence, corporate management should take into account social demands, and integrate them in such a way that the business operates in accordance with social values.

So, the content of business responsibility is limited to the space and time of each situation depending on the values of society at that moment, and comes through the company's functional roles (Preston and Post 1975). In other words, there is no specific action that management is responsible for performing throughout time and in each industry. Basically, the theories of this group are focused on the detection and scanning of, and response to, the social demands that achieve social legitimacy, greater social acceptance and prestige.

Issues Management

Social responsiveness, or responsiveness in the face of social issues, and processes to manage them within the organization (Sethi 1975) was an approach which arose in the 1970s. In this approach it is crucial to consider the gap between what the organization's relevant publics expect its performance to be and the organization's actual performance. These gaps are usually located in the zone that Ackerman (1973, p. 92) calls the "zone of discretion" (neither regulated nor illegal nor sanctioned) where the company receives some unclear signals from the environment. The firm should perceive the gap and choose a response in order to close it (Ackerman and Bauer 1976).

Ackerman (1973), among other scholars, analyzed the relevant factors regarding the internal structures of organizations and integration mechanisms to manage social issues within the organization. The way a social objective is spread and integrated across the organization, he termed "process of institutionalization". According to Jones (1980, p. 65), "corporate behavior should not in most cases be judged by the decisions actually reached but by the process by which they are reached". Consequently, he emphasized the idea of process rather than principles as the appropriate approach to CSR issues.

Jones draws an analogy with the political process assessing that the appropriate process of CSR should be a fair process where all interests have had the opportunity to be heard. So Jones has shifted the criterion to the inputs in the decision-making process rather than outcomes, and has focused more on the process of implementation of CSR activities than on the process of conceptualization.

The concept of "social responsiveness" was soon widened with the concept "Issues Management". The latter includes the former but emphasizes the process for making a corporate response to social issues. Issues management has been defined by Wartick and Rude (1986, p. 124) as "the processes by which the corporation can identify, evaluate and respond to those social and political issues which may impact significantly upon it". They add that issues management attempts to minimize "surprises" which accompany social and political change by serving as an early warning system for potential environmental threats and opportunities. Further, it prompts more systematic and effective responses to particular issues by serving as a coordinating and integrating force within the corporation. Issues management research has been influenced by the strategy field, since it has been seen as a special group of strategic issues (Greening and Gray 1994), or apart of international studies (Brewer 1992). That led to the study of topics related with issues (identification, evaluation and categorization), formalization of stages of social issues and management issue response. Other factors, which have been considered, include the corporate responses to media exposure, interest group pressures and business crises, as well as organization size, top management commitment and other organizational factors.

The Principle of Public Responsibility

Some authors have tried to give an appropriate content and substance to help and guide the firm's responsibility by limiting the scope of the corporate responsibility. Preston and Post (1975, 1981) criticized a responsiveness approach and the purely process approach (Jones 1980) as insufficient. Instead, they proposed "the principle of public responsibility". They choose the term "public" rather than "social", to stress the importance of the public process, rather than personal-morality views or narrow interest groups defining the scope of responsibilities.

According to Preston and Post an appropriate guideline for a legitimate managerial behavior is found within the framework of relevant public policy. They added that "public policy includes not only the literal text of law and regulation but also the broad pattern of social direction reflected in public opinion, emerging issues, formal legal requirements and enforcement or implementation practices" (Preston and Post 1981, p. 57). This is the essence of the principle of public responsibility.

Preston and Post analyzed the scope of managerial responsibility in terms of the "primary" and "secondary" involvement of the firm in its social environment. Primary involvement includes the essential economic task of the firm, such as locating and establishing its facilities, procuring suppliers, engaging employees, carrying out its production functions and marketing products. It also includes legal requirements. Secondary involvements come as consequence of the primary. They are, e.g., career and earning opportunities for some individuals, which come from the primary activity of selection and advancement of employees.

At the same time, these authors are in favor of business intervention in the public policy process especially with respect to areas in which specific public policy is not yet clearly established or it is in transition: "It is legitimate – and may be essential –that affected firms participate openly in the policy formation" (Preston and Post 1981, p. 61).

In practice, discovering the content of the principle of public responsibility is a complex and difficult task and requires substantial management attention. As Preston and Post recognized, "the content of public policy is not necessarily obvious or easy to discover, nor is it invariable over time" (1981, p. 57). According to this view, if business adhered to the standards of performance in law and the existing public policy process, then it would be judged acceptably responsive in terms of social expectations.

The development of this approach was parallel to the study of the scope regarding business-government relationship (Vogel 1986). These studies focused on government regulations – their formulation and implementation – as well as corporate strategies to influence these regulations, including campaign contributions, lobbying, coalition building, grass-roots organization, corporate public affairs and the role of public interest and other advocacy groups.

Stakeholder Management

Instead of focusing on generic responsiveness, specific issues or on the public responsibility principle, the approach called "stakeholder management" is oriented towards "stakeholders" or people who affect or are affected by corporate policies and practices. Although the practice of stakeholder management is long-established, its academic development started only at the end of 1970s (see, e.g., Sturdivant 1979). In a seminal paper, Emshoff and Freeman (1978) presented two basic principles, which underpin stakeholder management. The first is that the central goal is to achieve maximum overall cooperation between the entire system of stakeholder groups and the objectives of the corporation. The second states that the most efficient strategies for managing stakeholder relations involve efforts, which simultaneously deal with issues affecting multiple stakeholders.

Stakeholder management tries to integrate groups with a stake in the firm into managerial decision-making. A great deal of empirical research has been done, guided by a sense of pragmatism. It includes topics such as how to determine the best practice incorporate stakeholder relations (Bendheim et al. 1998), stakeholder salience to managers (Agle and Mitchell 1999; Mitchell et al. 1997), the impact of stakeholder management on financial performance (Berman et al. 1999), the influence of stakeholder network structural relations (Rowley 1997) and how managers can successfully balance the competing demands of various stakeholder groups (Ogden and Watson 1999).

In recent times, corporations have been pressured by non-governmental organizations (NGOs), activists, communities, governments, media and other institutional forces. These groups demand what they consider to be responsible corporate practices. Now some corporations are seeking corporate responses to social demands by establishing dialogue with a wide spectrum of stakeholders.

Stakeholder dialogue helps to address the question of responsiveness to the generally unclear signals received from the environment. In addition, this dialogue "not only enhances a company's sensitivity to its environment but also increases the environments understanding of the dilemmas facing the organization" (Kaptein and Van Tulder 2003, p. 208).

Corporate Social Performance

A set of theories attempts to integrate some of the previous theories. The corporate social performance (CSP) includes a search for social legitimacy, with processes for giving appropriate responses.

Carroll (1979), generally considered to have introduced this model, suggested a model of "corporate performance" with three elements: a basic definition of social responsibility, a listing of issues in which social responsibility exists and a specification of the philosophy of response to social issues. Carroll considered that a definition of social responsibility, which fully addresses the entire range of obligations business has to society, must embody the economic, legal, ethical, and discretionary categories of business performance. He later incorporated his four-part categorization into a "Pyramid of Corporate Social Responsibilities" (Carroll 1991). Recently, Schwartz and Carroll (2003) have proposed an alternative approach based on three core domains (economic, legal and ethical responsibilities) and a Venn model framework. The Venn framework yields seven CSR categories resulting from the overlap of the three core domains.

Wartick and Cochran (1985) extended the Carroll approach suggesting that corporate social involvement rests on the principles of social responsibility, the process of social responsiveness and the policy of issues management. A new development came with Wood (1991b) who presented a model of corporate social performance composed of principles of CSR, processes of corporate social responsiveness and outcomes of corporate behavior. The principles of CSR are understood to be analytical forms to be filled with value content that is operationalized. They include: principles of CSR, expressed on institutional, organizational and individual levels, processes of corporate social responsiveness, such as environmental assessment, stakeholder management and issues management, and outcomes of corporate behavior including social impacts, social programs and social policies.

Ethical Theories

There is a fourth group of theories or approaches focus on the ethical requirements that cement the relationship between business and society. They are based on principles that express the right thing to do or the necessity to achieve a good society. As main approaches we can distinguish the following.

Normative Stakeholder Theory

Stakeholder management has been included within the integrative theories group because some authors consider that this form of management is a way to integrate social demands. However, stakeholder management has become an ethically based theory mainly since 1984 when Freeman wrote *Strategic Management: A Stakeholder Approach.* In this book, he took as starting point that "managers bear a fiduciary relationship to stakeholders" (Freeman 1984, p. xx), instead of having exclusively fiduciary duties towards stockholders, as was held by the conventional view of the firm. He understood as stakeholders those groups who have a stake in or claim on the firm (suppliers, customers, employees, stockholders, and the local community). In a more precise way, Donaldson and Preston (1995, p. 67) held that the stakeholder theory has a normative core based on two major ideas (1) stakeholders are persons or groups with legitimate interests in procedural and/or substantive aspects of corporate activity (stakeholders are identified by their interests in the corporation, whether or not the corporation has any corresponding functional interest in *them*) and (2) the interests of all stakeholders are of *intrinsic value* (that is, each group of stakeholders merits consideration for its own sake and not merely because of its ability to further the interests of some other group, such as the shareowners).

Following this theory, a socially responsible firm requires simultaneous attention to the legitimate interests of all appropriate stakeholders and has to balance such a multiplicity of interests and not only the interests of the firm's stockholders. Supporters of normative stakeholder theory have attempted to justify it through arguments taken from Kantian capitalism (Bowie 1991; Evan and Freeman 1988), modem theories of property and distributive justice (Donaldson and Preston 1995), and also Libertarian theories with its notions of freedom, rights and consent (Freeman and Phillips 2002).

A generic formulation of stakeholder theory is not sufficient. In order to point out how corporations have to be governed and how managers ought to act, *a normative core* of ethical principles is required (Freeman 1994). To this end, different scholars have proposed differing normative ethical theories. Freeman and Evan (1990) introduced Rawlsian principles. Bowie (1998) proposed a combination of Kantian and Rawlsian grounds. Freeman (1994) proposed the doctrine of fair contracts and Phillips (1997, 2003) suggested introducing the fairness principle based on six of Rawls' characteristics of the principle of fair play: mutual benefit, justice, cooperation, sacrifice, free-rider possibility and voluntary acceptance of the benefits of cooperative schemes. Lately, Freeman and Phillips (2002) have presented six principles for the guidance of stakeholder theory by combining Libertarian concepts and the Fairness principle. Some scholars (Burton and Dunn 1996; Wicks et al. 1994) proposed instead using a "feminist ethics" approach. Donaldson and Dunfee (1999) hold their 'Integrative Social Contract Theory'. Argandoña (1998) suggested the common good notion and Wijnberg (2000) an Aristotelian approach. From a practical perspective, the normative core of which is risk management, The Clarkson Center for Business Ethics (1999) has published a set of *Principles of Stakeholder Management.*

Stakeholder normative theory has suffered critical distortions and friendly misinterpretations, which Freeman and co-workers are trying to clarify (Phillips et al. 2003). In practice, this theory has been applied to a variety of business fields, including stakeholder management for the business and society relationship, in a number of textbooks Some of these have been republished several times (Carroll and Buchholtz 2002; Post et al. 2002; Weiss 2003; among others).

In short, stakeholder approach grounded in ethical theories presents a different perspective on CSR, in which ethics is central.

Universal Rights

Human rights have been taken as a basis for CSR, especially in the global market place (Cassel 2001). In recent years, some human-rights-based approaches for corporate responsibility have been proposed. One of them is the UN Global Compact, which includes nine principles in the areas of human rights, labor and the environment. It was first presented by the United Nations Secretary- General Kofi Annan in an address to The World Economic Forum in 1999. In 2000 the Global Compact's operational phase was launched at UN Headquarters in New York. Many companies have since adopted it. Another, previously presented and updated in 1999, is The Global Sullivan Principles, which has the objective of supporting economic, social and political justice by companies where they do business. The certification SA8000 (www.cepaa.org) for accreditation of social responsibility is also based on human and labor rights. Despite using different approaches, all are based on the Universal Declaration of Human Rights adopted by the United Nations general assembly in 1948 and on other international declarations of human rights, labor rights and environmental protection.

Although for many people universal rights are a question of mere consensus, they have a theoretical grounding, and some moral philosophy theories give them support (Donnelly 1985). It is worth mentioning the Natural Law tradition (Simon 1992), which defends the existence of natural human rights (Maritain 1971).

Sustainable Development

Another values-based concept, which has become popular, is "sustainable development". Although this approach was developed at macro level rather than corporate level, it demands a relevant corporate contribution. The term came into widespread use in 1987, when the World Commission on Environment and Development (United Nations) published a report known as "Brutland Report". This report stated that "sustainable development" seeks to meet the needs of the present without compromising the ability to meet the future generation to meet their own needs" (World Commission on Environment and Development 1987, p. 8). Although this report originally only included the environmental factor, the concept of "sustainable development" has since expanded to include the consideration of the social dimension as being inseparable from development. In the words of the World Business Council for Sustainable Development (2000, p. 2), sustainable development "requires the integration of social, environmental, and economic considerations to make balanced judgments for the long term".

Numerous definitions have been proposed for sustainable development (see a review in Gladwin and Kennelly 1995, p. 877). In spite of which, a content analysis of the main definitions suggests that sustainable development is "a process of achieving human development in an inclusive, connected, equiparable, prudent and secure manner" (Gladwin and Kennelly 1995, p. 876).

The problem comes when the corporation has to develop the processes and implement strategies to meet the corporate challenge of corporate sustainable development. As Wheeler et al. (2003, p. 17)have stated, sustainability is "an ideal toward which society and business can continually strive, the way we strive is by creating value, creating outcomes that are consistent with the ideal of sustainability along social environmental and economic dimensions".[6]

However, some suggestions have been proposed to achieve corporate ecological sustainability (Shrivastava 1995; Stead and Stead 2000; among others). A pragmatic proposal is to extend the traditional "bottom line" accounting, which shows overall net profitability, to a "triple bottom line" that would include economic, social and environmental aspects of corporation. Van Marrewijk and Werre (2003) maintain that corporate sustainability is a custom-made process and each organization should choose its own specific ambition and approach regarding corporate sustainability. This should meet the organization's aims and intentions, and be aligned with the organization strategy, as an appropriate response to the circumstances in which the organization operates.

The Common Good Approach

This third group of approaches, less consolidated than the stakeholder approach but with potential, holds the common good of society as the referential value for CSR (Mahon and McGowan 1991; Velasquez 1992). The common good is a classical concept rooted in Aristotelian tradition (Smith 1999), in Medieval Scholastics (Kempshall 1999), developed philosophically (Maritain 1966) and assumed into Catholic social thought (Carey 2001) as a key reference for business ethics (Alford and Naugthon 2002; Melé 2002; Pope John Paul II, 1991, #43). This approach maintains that business, as with any other social group or individual in society, has to contribute to the common good, because it is a part of society. In this respect, it has been argued that business is a mediating institution (Fort 1996, 1999). Business should be neither harmful to nor a parasite on society, but purely a positive contributor to the well-being of the society.

Business contributes to the common good in different ways, such as creating wealth, providing goods and services in an efficient and fair way, at the same time respecting the dignity and the inalienable and fundamental rights of the individual. Furthermore, it contributes to social well-being and a harmonic way of living together in just, peaceful and friendly conditions, both in the present and in the future (Melé 2002).

To some extent, this approach has a lot in common with both the stakeholder approach (Argandoña 1998) and sustainable development, but the philosophical base is different. Although there are several ways of understanding the notion of common good (Sulmasy 2001), the interpretation based on the knowledge of human nature and its fulfillment seems to us particularly convincing. It permits the circumnavigation of cultural relativism, which is frequently embedded in some definitions of sustainable development.

The common good notion is also very close to the Japanese concept of Kyosei (Goodpaster 1999; Kaku 1997; Yamaji 1997), understood as "living and working together for the common good", which, together with the principle of human dignity, is one of the founding principles of the popular "The Caux Roundtable Principles for Business"(www.cauxroundtable.org).

Discussion

The preceding description, summed up on Table 4.1, leads to the conclusion that the hypothesis considered in the introduction about the four basic focus employed by CSR theories and related approaches is adequate. Consequently, most of the current theories related to CSR could be broadly classified as instrumental, political, integrative and ethical theories.

Donati (1991), a contemporary sociologist, has reviewed many aspects of the work of Parsons. He suggests that adaptation, goal attainment, integration and latency presented by Parsons (1961) as rigid functions, have to be understood as four interconnected dimensions present in every social phenomenon. This suggests that the concept of business and society relationship must include these four aspects

Table 4.1 Corporate social responsibilities theories and related approaches

Types of theory	Approaches	Short description	Some key references
Instrumental theories (focusing on achieving economic objectives through social activities)	Maximization of shareholder value	Long-term value maximization	Friedman (1970) and Jensen (2000)
	Strategies for competitive advantages	Social investments in a competitive context	Porter and Kramer (2002)
		Strategies based on the natural resource view of the firm and the dynamic capabilities of the firm	Hart (1995) and Litz (1996)
		Strategies for the bottom of the economic pyramid	Prahalad and Hammond (2002), Hart and Christensen (2002) and Prahalad (2002)
	Cause-related marketing	Altruistic activities socially recognized used as an instrument of marketing	Varadarajan and Menon (1988) and Murray and Montanan (1986)
Political theories (focusing on a responsible use of business power in the political arena)	Corporate constitutionalism	Social responsibilities of businesses arise from the amount of social power that they have	Davis (1960, 1967)
	Integrative social contract theory	Assumes that a social contract between business and society exists	Donaldson and Dunfee (1994, 1999)
	Corporate (or business) citizenship	The firm is understood as being like a citizen with certain involvement in the community	Wood and Lodgson (2002), Andriof and Mcintosh (2001), and Matten and Crane (2005)
Integrative theories (focusing on the integration of social demands)	Issues management	Corporate processes of response to those social and political issues which may imp act significantly upon it	Sethi (1975), Ackerman (1973), Jones (1980), Vogel (1986), and Wartick and Mahon (1994)
	Public responsibility	Law and the existing public policy process are taken as a reference for social performance	Preston and Post (1975, 1981)
	Stakeholder management	Balances the interests of the stakeholders of the firm	Mitchell et al. (1997), Agle and Mitchell (1999), and Rowley (1997)
	Corporate social performance	Searches for social legitimacy and processes to give appropriate responses to social issues	Carroll (1979), Wartick and Cochran (1985), Wood (1991b), and Swanson (1995)

Ethical theories (focusing on the right thing to achieve a good society)	Stakeholder normative theory	Considers fiduciary duties towards stakeholders of the firm. Its application requires reference to some moral theory (Kantian, Utilitarianism, theories of justice, etc.)	Freeman (1984, 1994), Evan and Freeman (1988), Donaldson and Preston (1995), Freeman and Phillips (2002), and Phillips et al. (2003)
	Universal rights	Frameworks based on human rights, labor rights and respect for the environment	The Global Sullivan Principles (1999) and UN Global Compact (1999)
	Sustainable development	Aimed at achieving human development considering present and future generations	World Commission on Environment and Development (Brutland Report) (1987) and Gladwin and Kennelly (1995)
	The common good	Oriented towards the common good of society	Alford and Naugthon (2002), Melé (2002) and Kaku (1997)

or dimensions and some connection among them must exist. This must be reflected in every theory. In some authors, such as Friedman, it is relatively easy to discover these dimensions and connections, in other theories it is not so easy.

In fact, although the main concern in the Friedman view (Friedman 1970; Friedman and Friedman 1962) is for wealth creation, as we have pointed out above, this concern is rooted in certain cultural values regarding the free market, private property and the fact that wealth creation is good for society. This shows us that certain values are present, even though they are frequently questioned. At the same time, he accepts the rules of the free market, laws and ethical customs in each place. Friedman and, above all, Jensen (2000) also accept the integration of some social demands into the company if it is profitable in the long-term. Regarding politics, underpinning the Friedman view there is a functional conception of the social with clear political consequences. Society is understood as a mechanism with monofunctional groups, each with a concrete purpose. Thus, the exclusive purpose of business organizations is the creation of wealth. It is held that business operating in a free market is the best way to allocate scarce resources because society can achieve an optimum situation in the sense of Pareto (Pareto Optimum). This means that the satisfaction of all people involved in the situation is the greatest possible or, at least, the situation satisfies most of them without being detrimental for others. However, in the presence of externalities, when decision-makers do not take into account secondary effects of their actions that burden or benefit others, the market is inefficient and the equilibrium is not a Pareto optimum. When externalities appear, another system of society, the political system, should act. The political system must confront these externalities through taxes, regulation and minimum package of rights. So, business contributes to the welfare of society through the market mechanism and in compliance with the law. Of course, outside business, the manager can spend any quantity of personal money on social activities according to his or her personal preferences. However, the social objectives and demands come under business consideration only through the law applied by the political system.

A contrasting theory, in which the four dimensions mentioned and their connections are not so easy to discover, is "the principle of public responsibility" of Preston and Post (1975). However, these dimensions are implicit. In fact, this theory presupposes a certain conception of society and values. The political dimension is clear, since public policy is assumed as basic criterion. Regarding wealth creation, undoubtedly the application of this theory would have consequences for profit generation. Actually, these scholars recognize that what they call secondary relationships (related to secondary involvements) "as essential to effective management over the long term" (Preston and Post 1981, p. 57).

It is not our aim to review all theories described, but what has been said regarding the four dimensions in the approaches of Friedman and Preston and Post, could probably be extended to other theories. If our intuition is correct, a proper concept of the business and society relationship should include these four aspects or dimensions, and some mode of integration of them. Although most theories studied do not make it explicit, one can appreciate a tendency to overcome this deficit.

In fact, in the last few years, some theories have been proposed in which two or even more of these dimensions and their interconnection have been considered. That is the case, e.g., of Wood's Corporate Social Performance model (1991b). This model basically focuses on integrating social demands, however, it also considers institutional legitimacy, accepting that "society grants legitimacy and power to business" (Davis 1973, p. 314). In this manner, Wood introduces both political and integrative dimensions while economic and ethical dimensions are implicit. Regarding the latter, the stated principles of corporate responsibility assumed are based on social control rather than on prescriptive responsibility coming from ethics. This is precisely the criticism Swanson (1995) made of Wood's model. As an alternative, Swanson (1995, 1999) proposed a derived model in which she tried to include the ethical dimension explicitly, through a theory of values. Following Frederick (1992) she accepted that business organizations have responsibilities related to economizing and ecologizing. Furthermore executive decision-making should forego power-seeking in favor of directing the firm to economize and ecologize.

More recently, Wood and Lodgson (2002), dealing with the corporate or business citizen model, have introduced the ethical dimension in their model. They focus on the political dimension but also incorporate universal rights into their vision of corporate behavior.

Theories on CSR, which take long-term profits as the main goal normally, use an empirical methodology and are descriptive, although explicitly they also present a conditional prescription. Their generic statement might take the form: "if you want to maximize profits you must assume CSR in the way proposed by this theory". In contrast, ethical theories are prescriptive and use a normative methodology. Integrating empirical and normative aspects of CSR, or economic and ethics, is great challenge. Some authors (Brandy 1990; Etzioni 1988; Quinn and Jones 1995; Swanson 1999; Treviño and Weaver 1994 among others) have considered this problem, but it is far from being resolved. This lack of integration has been denounced as the cause of the lack of a paradigm for the business and society field (Swanson 1999).

Finally, the current situation presents many competing ethical theories. This very often produces confusion and skepticism. The problem is especially serious in the case of ethical theories, and even within each group of theories. Considering, for instance, the stakeholder normative theory. As we have explained above, this can be developed using a great number of different ethical theories. Although each of these theories states universal principles, in practice, the global effect is one of unabashed relativism: "If you are Utilitarian, you'll do this, if you are Kantian you'll do that" (Solomon 1992, p. 318).

Conclusion

We can conclude that most of current CSR theories are focused on four main aspects: (1) meeting objectives that produce long-term profits, (2) using business power in a responsible way, (3) integrating social demands and (4) contributing to a good society by doing what is ethically correct. This permits us to classify the most relevant theories on CSR and related concepts into four groups, which we have called instrumental, political, integrative and value theories. Most of the theories considered do not make explicit the implications of each specific approach for the aspects considered in others groups of theories.

Further research could analyze these four dimensions and their connection in the most relevant theories and consider their contributions and limitations. What seems more challenging, however, is to develop a new theory, which would overcome these limitations. This would require an accurate knowledge of reality and a sound ethical foundation.

Notes

1. Parsons considers the existence of four interconnected problems in any action system: (1) the problem mobilizing of resources from the environment and then distributing them throughout the system, which requires adaptation to environment; (2) the problem of establishing priorities among system goals and mobilizing system resources for the attainment of the goals; (3) the problem of coordinating and maintaining viable relationships among system units and (4) the problem of assuring that the actors in the social system display the appropriate values. This entails motivation and other characteristics (pattern maintenance) and dealing with the internal tensions and strain of the actors in the social system (tension management). That means preserving the basic structure of the system and adjusting to changing conditions within the framework that the basic structure provides. According to Parsons these problems necessitate four requisites or imperatives for the maintenance of a social system: adaptation (A), goal attainment (G), integration (I) and pattern maintenance or latency (L).
2. Some years before, T. Leavitt, a Harvard Business School professor, expressed this approach in an even more radical way: “Corporate welfare makes good sense if it makes good economic sense – and not infrequently it does. But if something does not make economic sense, sentiment or idealism ought not to let it in the door” (Leavitt 1958, p. 42).
3. According to Porter and Kramer (2002), a competitive context consists of four interrelated elements of the local business environment that shape potential productivity. The first element is the factor condition, which involves employee education, natural resources, high quality technological institutions and physical infrastructure. The second element is related to demand conditions; that is to say, how the firm can influence the quality and the size of local market by, for example, developing educated and demanding customers. The third, the context for strategy and rivalry involves how the firm can invest in incentives and norms that rule competition as for example all the efforts for reducing corruption, preventing the formation of cartels and opening markets. The last is the firm’s investment in related and supporting industries, for example, strengthening the relationship with suppliers of services, components and machinery.

4. According to Davis, "markets leave business theoretically without any social power and hence, no social responsibility (balanced zero equation). This zero equation of no power and no responsibility is a proper theoretical model for pure competition, but it is theory only and it's inconsistent with the power realities of modern organizations. They posses such a great initiative, economic assets, and power in their actions do have social effects" (Davis 1967, p. 49).
5. In fact, different models have been constructed in order to explain how and why partnerships are built and how to determine, measure, evaluate partnerships (Andrioff 2001; Zadek 2001).
6. That is not the only problem. According to Gladwin and Kennelly (1995, p. 876), the concept of sustainable development is "fuzzy, elusive, contestable and/or ideologically controversial" and with multiple objectives and ingredients, complex interdependencies and considerable moral thickness. But, in spite of everything, the concept is becoming more and more popular and has introduced an important element to the CSR debate.

References

Ackerman, R.W. 1973. How companies respond to social demands. *Harvard University Review* 51(4): 88–98.

Ackerman, R., and R. Bauer. 1976. *Corporate social responsiveness*. Virginia: Reston.

Agle, B.R., and R.K. Mitchell. 1999. Who matters to CEOs? An investigation of stakeholder attributes and salience, corporate performance and CEO values. *Academy of Management journal* 42(5): 507–526.

Alford, H., and M. Naugthon. 2002. Beyond the shareholder model of the firm: Working toward the common good of a business. In *Rethinking the purpose of business. Interdisciplinary essays from the catholic social tradition*, ed. S.A. Cortright and M. Naugthon, 27–47. Notre Dame: Notre Dame University Press.

Altman, B.W. 1998. Corporate community relations in the 1990s: A study in transformation. *Business and Society* 37(2): 221–228.

Altman, B.W., and D. Vidaver-Cohen. 2000. Corporate citizenship in the new millennium: Foundation for an architecture of excellence. *Business and Society Review* 105(1): 145–169.

Andriof, J., and M. McIntosh (eds.). 2001. *Perspectives on corporate citizenship*. Sheffield: Greenleaf.

Andrioff, J. 2001. Patterns of stakeholder partnership building. In *Perspectives on corporate citizenship*, ed. J. Andriof and M. McIntosh, 200–213. Sheffield: Greenleaf.

Argandoña, A. 1998. The stakeholder theory and the common good. *Journal of Business Ethics* 17: 1093–1102.

Barney, J. 1991. Firm resource and sustained competitive advantage. *Journal of Management* 17: 99–120.

Bendheim, C.L., S.A. Waddock, and S.B. Graves. 1998. Determining best practice in corporate-stakeholder relations using data envelopment analysis. *Business and Society* 37(3): 306–339.

Berman, S.L., A.C. Wicks, S. Kotha, and T.M. Jones. 1999. Does stakeholder orientation matter? The relationship between stakeholder management models and the firm financial performance. *Academy of Management journal* 42(5): 488–509.

Bowen, H.R. 1953. *Social responsibilities of the businessman*. New York: Harper & Row.

Bowie, N. 1991. New directions in corporate social responsibility. *Business Horizons* 34(4): 56–66.

Bowie, N. 1998. A Kantian theory of capitalism. Special issue, Ruffin series, *Business Ethics Quarterly*, no. 1: 37–60.
Brandy, F.N. 1990. *Ethical managing: Rules and results*. London: Macmillan.
Brewer, T.L. 1992. An issue area approach to the analysis of MNE-government relations. *Journal of International Business Studies* 23: 295–309.
Brummer, J. 1991. *Corporate responsibility and legitimacy*. New York: Greenwood Press.
Burke, L., and J.M. Logsdon. 1996. How corporate social responsibility pays off. *Long Range Planning* 29(4): 495–503.
Burton, B.K., and C.P. Dunn. 1996. Feminist ethics as moral grounding for stakeholder theory. *Business Ethics Quarterly* 6(2): 133–147.
Carey, J.B. 2001. The common good in catholic social thought. *St. John's Law Review* 75(2): 311–313.
Carroll, A.B. 1979. A three-dimensional conceptual model of corporate performance. *Academy of Management Review* 4(4): 497–505.
Carroll, A.B. 1991. The pyramid of corporate social responsibility: Towards the moral management of organizational stakeholders, *Business Horizons*, July/August, 39–48.
Carroll, A.B. 1994. Social issues in management research. *Business and Society* 33(1): 5–25.
Carroll, A.B. 1999. Corporate social responsibility. Evolution of definitional construct. *Business and Society* 38(3): 268–295.
Carroll, A.B., and A.K. Buchholtz. 2002. *Business and society with infotrac: Ethics and stakeholder management*, vol. 5. Cincinnati: South-Western.
Cassel, D. 2001. Human rights business responsibilities in the global marketplace. *Business Ethics Quarterly* 11(2): 261–274.
Christensen, C.M., and M. Overdorf. 2000. Meeting the challenge of disruptive change. *Harvard Business Review* 78(2): 66–75.
Christensen, C., T. Craig, and S. Hart. 2001. The great disruption. *Foreign Affairs* 80(2): 80–96.
Davis, K. 1960. Can business afford to ignore corporate social responsibilities? *California Management Review* 2: 70–76.
Davis, K. 1967. Understanding the social responsibility puzzle. *Business Horizons* 10(4): 45–51.
Davis, K. 1973. The case for and against business assumption of social responsibilities. *Academy of Management journal* 16: 312–322.
Dion, M. 2001. Corporate citizenship and ethics of care: Corporate values, codes of ethics and global governance. In *Perspectives on corporate citizenship*, ed. J. Andriof and M. McIntosh, 118–138. Sheffield: Greenleaf.
Donaldson, T. 1982. *Corporations and morality*. Englewood Cliff: Prentice-Hall.
Donaldson, T., and T.W. Dunfee. 1994. Towards a unified conception of business ethics: Integrative social contracts theory. *Academy of Management Review* 19: 252–284.
Donaldson, T., and T.W. Dunfee. 1999. *Ties that bind: A social contracts approach to business ethics*. Boston: Harvard Business School Press.
Donaldson, T., and T.W. Dunfee. 2000. Precis for ties that bind. *Business and Society* 105(Winter): 436–444.
Donaldson, T., and L.E. Preston. 1995. The stakeholder theory of the corporation: Concepts, evidence, and implications. *Academy of Management Review* 20(1): 65–91.
Donati, P. 1991. *Teoria relazionale della societa*. Milano: Franco Agnelli.
Donnelly, J. 1985. *The concept of human rights*. London: Croom Helm.
Emshoff, J.R., and R.E. Freeman. 1978. Stakeholder management. Working Paper from the Wharton Applied Research Center Quly. Quoted by Sturdivant (1979).
Etzioni, A. 1988. *The moral dimension. Towards a new economics*. New York: The Free Press.
Evan, W.M., and R.E. Freeman. 1988. A stakeholder theory of the modern corporation: Kantian capitalism. In *Ethical theory and business*, ed. T. Beauchamp and N. Bowie, 75–93. Prentice Hall: Englewood Cliffs.
Fort, T.L. 1996. Business as mediating institutions. *Business Ethics Quarterly* 6(2): 149–164.
Fort, T.L. 1999. The first man and the company man: The common good, transcendence, and mediating institutions. *American Business Law Journal* 36(3): 391–435.

Frederick, W.C. 1987. Theories of corporate social performance. In *Business and society: Dimensions of conflict and cooperation*, ed. S.P. Sethi and C.M. Flabe, 142–161. New York: Lexington Books.
Frederick, W.C. 1992. Anchoring values in nature: Towards a theory of business values. *Business Ethics Quarterly* 2(3): 283–304.
Frederick, W.C. 1998. Moving to CSR4. *Business and Society* 37(1): 40–60.
Freeman, R.E. 1984. *Strategic management: A stakeholder approach*. Boston: Pitman.
Freeman, R.E. 1994. The politics of stakeholder theory: Some future directions. *Business Ethics Quarterly* 4(4): 409–429.
Freeman, R.E., and W.M. Evan. 1990. Corporate governance: A stakeholder interpretation. *Journal of Behavioral Economics* 19(4): 337–359.
Freeman, R.E., and R.A. Phillips. 2002. Stakeholder theory: A libertarian defence. *Business Ethics Quarterly* 12(3): 331–349.
Friedman, M. 1970. The social responsibility of business is to increase its profits. *New York Times Magazine*, September 13th, 32–33, 122, 126.
Friedman, M., and R. Friedman. 1962. *Capitalism and freedom*. Chicago: University of Chicago Press.
Frooman, J. 1997. Socially irresponsible and illegal behavior and shareholder. *Business and Society* 36(3): 221–250.
Gladwin, T.N., and J.J. Kennelly. 1995. Shifting paradigms for sustainable development: Implications for management theory and research. *Academy of Management Review* 20(4): 874–904.
Goodpaster, K.E. 1999. Bridging East and West in management ethics: Kyosei and the moral point of view. In *International business ethics. Challenges and approaches*, ed. G. Enderle, 151–159. Notre Dame: University of Notre Dame Press.
Greening, D.W., and B. Gray. 1994. Testing a model of organizational response to social and political issues. *Academy of Management journal* 37: 467–498.
Griffin, J.J. 2000. Corporate social performance: Research directions for the 21st century. *Business and Society* 39(4): 479–493.
Griffin, J.J., and J.F. Mahon. 1997. The corporate social performance and corporate financial performance debate: Twenty-five years of incomparable research. *Business and Society* 36(1): 5–31.
Harrison, J.S., and C.H. St. John. 1996. Managing and partnering with external stakeholders. *Academy of Management Executive* 10(2): 46–61.
Hart, S.L. 1995. A natural-resource-based view of the firm. *Academy of Management Review* 20(4): 986–1012.
Hart, S.L., and C.M. Christensen. 2002. The great leap. Driving innovation from the base of the pyramid. *MIT Sloan Management Review* 44(1): 51–57.
Heald, M. 1988. *The social responsibilities of business: Company and community, 1900–1960*. New Brunswick: Transaction Books.
Hillman, A.J., and G.D. Keim. 2001. Shareholder value, stakeholder management, and social issues: What's the bottom line. *Strategic Management Journal* 22(2): 125–140.
Husted, B.W., and D.B. Allen. 2000. Is it ethical to use ethics as strategy? *Journal of Business Ethics* 27(1–2): 21–32.
Jensen, M.C. 2000. Value maximization, stakeholder theory, and the corporate objective function. In *Breaking the code of change*, ed. M. Beer and N. Nohria, 37–58. Boston: Harvard Business School Press. Repr., (2002) as Value maximization, stakeholder theory, and the corporate objective function. *Business Ethics Quarterly* 12(2): 235–256.
Jensen, M.C., and W. Meckling. 1976. Theory of the firm: Managerial behavior, agency cost, and capital structure. *Journal of Financial Economics* 3(October): 305–360.
Jones, T.M. 1980. Corporate social responsibility revisited, redefined. *California Management Review* 22(2): 59–67.
Jones, T.M. 1983. An integrating framework for research in business and society: A step toward the elusive paradigm? *Academy of Management Review* 8(4): 559–565.
Kaku, R. 1997. The path of Kyosei. *Harvard Business Review* 75(4): 55–62.

Kaptein, M., and R. Van Tulder. 2003. Toward effective stakeholder dialogue. *Business and Society Review* 108(Surmmer): 203–225.
Keim, G.D. 1978. Corporate social responsibility: An assessment of the enlightened self-interest model. *Academy of Management Review* 3(1): 32–40.
Kempshall, M.S. 1999. *The common good in late medieval political thought*. Oxford: Oxford University Press.
Key, S., and S.J. Popkin. 1998. Integrating ethics into the strategic management process: Doing well by doing good. *Management Decision* 36(5–6): 331–339.
Leavitt, T. 1958. The dangers of social responsibility. *Harvard Business Review* 36(September–October): 41–50.
Litz, R.A. 1996. A resourced-based-view of the socially responsible firm: Stakeholder interdependence, ethical awareness, and issue responsiveness as strategic assets. *Journal of Business Ethics* 15: 1355–1363.
Mahon, J.F., and R.A. McGowan. 1991. Searching for the common good: A process-oriented approach. *Business Horizons* 34(4): 79–87.
Maritain, J. 1966. *The person and the common good*. Notre Dame: Notre Dame University Press.
Maritain, J. 1971. [c 1943], *The rights of man and natural law*. New York: Gordian Press.
Matten, D., and A. Crane. 2005. Corporate citizenship: Towards an extended theoretical conceptualization. *Academy of Management Review* 30(1): 166–179.
Matten, D., A. Crane, and W. Chapple. 2003. Behind the mask: Revealing the true face of corporate citizenship. *Journal of Business Ethics* 45(1–2): 109–120.
McMahon, T.F. 1986. Models of the relationship of the firm to society. *Journal of Business Ethics* 5: 181–191.
McWilliams, A., and D. Siegel. 2001. Corporate social responsibility: A theory of the firm perspective. *Academy of Management Review* 26(1): 117–127.
Melé, D. 2002. *Not only stakeholder interests. The firm oriented toward the common good*. Notre Dame: University of Notre Dame Press.
Mitchell, R.K., B.R. Agle, and D.J. Wood. 1997. Toward a theory of stakeholder identification and salience: Defining the principle of who and what really counts. *Academy of Management Review* 22(4): 853–886.
Murray, K.B., and J.R. Montanan. 1986. Strategic management of the socially responsible firm: Integrating management and marketing theory. *Academy of Management Review* 11(4): 815–828.
Ogden, S., and R. Watson. 1999. Corporate performance and stakeholder management: Balancing shareholder and customer interests in the U.K. privatized water industry. *Academy of Management Journal* 42(5): 526–538.
Parsons, T. 1961. An outline of the social system. In *Theories of society*, ed. T. Parsons, E.A. Shils, K.D. Naegle, and J.R. Pitts. New York: Free Press.
Petrick, J., and J. Quinn. 2001. The challenge of leadership accountability for integrity capacity as a strategic asset. *Journal of Business Ethics* 34: 331–343.
Phillips, R.A. 1997. Stakeholder theory and a principle of fairness. *Business Ethics Quarterly* 7(1): 51–66.
Phillips, R.A. 2003. Stakeholder legitimacy. *Business Ethics Quarterly* 13(1): 25–41.
Phillips, R.A., E. Freeman, and A.C. Wicks. 2003. What stakeholder theory is not. *Business Ethics Quarterly* 13(1): 479–502.
Pope John Paul II. 1991. *Encyclical 'Centesimus Annus'*. London: Catholic Truth Society, and www.vatican.va
Porter, M.E. 1980. *Competitive strategy: Techniques for analyzing industries and competitors*. New York: Free Press.
Porter, M.E., and M.R. Kramer. 2002. The competitive advantage of corporate philanthropy. *Harvard Business Review* 80(12): 56–69.
Post, J.E., L.E. Preston, S. Sauter-Sachs, and S. Sachs. 2002. *Redefining the corporation: Stakeholder management and organizational wealth*. Stanford: Stanford University Press.
Prahalad, C.K. 2002. Strategies for the bottom of the economic pyramid: India as a source of innovation. *Reflections: The SOL Journal* 3(4): 6–18.

Prahalad, C.K., and A. Hammond. 2002. Serving the world's poor, profitably. *Harvard Business Review* 80(9): 48–58.
Preston, L.E. 1975. Corporation and society: The search for a paradigm. *Journal of Economic Literature* 13(2): 434–454.
Preston, L.E., and J.E. Post. 1975. Private management and public policy. In *The principle of public responsibility*. Englewood Cliffs: Prentice Hall.
Preston, L.E., and J.E. Post. 1981. Private management and public policy. *California Management Review* 23(3): 56–63.
Quinn, D.P., and T.M. Jones. 1995. An agent morality view of business policy. *Academy of Management Review* 20(1): 22–42.
Roman, R., S. Hayibor, and B.R. Agle. 1999. The relationship between social performance and financial performance. *Business and Society* 38(1): 109–125.
Ross, S. 1973. The economy theory of the agency: The principal's problem. *American Economic Review* 63: 134–139.
Rowley, T.J. 1997. Moving beyond dyadic ties: A network theory of stakeholder influences. *Academy of Management Review* 22(4): 887–911.
Rowley, T., and S. Berman. 2000. New brand of corporate social performance. *Business and Society* 39(4): 397–412.
Schwartz, M.S., and A.B. Carroll. 2003. Corporate social responsibility: A three-domain approach. *Business Ethics Quarterly* 13(4): 503–530.
Sethi, S.P. 1975. Dimensions of corporate social performance: An analytical framework. *California Management Review* 17(3): 58–65.
Shrivastava, P. 1995. The role of corporations in achieving ecological sustainability. *Academy of Management Review* 20: 936–960.
Simon, Y.R. 1992 (1965). In *The tradition of natural law. A philosopher's reflections*, ed. V. Kuic. New York: Fordham University Press
Smith, T.W. 1999. Aristotle on the conditions for and limits of the common good. *American Political Science Review* 93(3): 625–637.
Smith, W., and M. Higgins. 2000. Cause-related marketing: Ethics and the ecstatic. *Business and Society* 39(3): 304–322.
Solomon, R.C. 1992. Corporate roles, personal virtues: An Aristotelian approach to business ethics. *Business Ethics Quarterly* 2(3): 317–340.
Stead, J.G., and E. Stead. 2000. Eco-enterprise strategy: Standing for sustainability. *Journal of Business Ethics* 24(4): 313–330.
Sturdivant, F.D. 1979. Executives and activist: Test of stakeholder management. *California Management Review* 22(Fall): 53–59.
Sulmasy, D.P. 2001. Four basic notions of the common good. *St. John's Law Review* 75(2): 303–311.
Swanson, D.L. 1995. Addressing a theoretical problem by reorienting the corporate social performance model. *Academy of Management Review* 20(1): 43–64.
Swanson, D.L. 1999. Toward an integrative theory of business and society: A research strategy for corporate social performance. *Academy of Management Review* 24(3): 506–521.
Teece, D.J., G. Pisano, and A. Shuen. 1997. Dynamic capabilities and strategic management. *Strategic Management Journal* 18(7): 509–533.
The Clarkson Center for Business Ethics. 1999. *Principles of stakeholder management.* Toronto: Joseph L. Rotman School of Management. Reprinted (2002) on, *Business Ethics Quarterly* 12(4), 257–264.
The Global Sullivan Principles. 1999. http://globalsullivanprinciples.org, September 2003.
Tichy, N.M., A.R. McGill, and L. St. Clair. 1997. *Corporate global citizenship*. San Francisco: The New Lexington Press.
Treviño, L.K., and G.R. Weaver. 1994. Normative and empirical business ethics. *Business Ethics Quarterly* 4(2): 129–143.
United Nations. 1999. Global compact. www.unglobalcompact.org

Van Marrewijk, M. 2003. Concept and definitions of CSR and corporate sustainability: Between agency and communion. *Journal of Business Ethics* 44: 95–105.
Van Marrewijk, M., and M. Werre. 2003. Multiple levels of corporate sustainability. *Journal of Business Ethics* 44(2/3): 107–120.
Varadarajan, P.R., and A. Menon. 1988. Cause-related marketing: A coalignment of marketing strategy and corporate philanthropy. *Journal of Marketing* 52(3): 58–58.
Velasquez, M. 1992. International business, morality and the common good. *Business Ethics Quarterly* 2(1): 27–40.
Vogel, D. 1986. The study of social issues in management: A critical appraisal. *California Management Review* 28(2): 142–152.
Votaw, D. 1972. Genius became rare: A comment on the doctrine of social responsibility Pt 1. *California Management Review* 15(2): 25–31.
Waddock, S.A., and S.B. Graves. 1997. The corporate social performance-financial performance link. *Strategic Management Journal* 18(4): 303–320.
Wartick, S., and P.L. Cochran. 1985. The evolution of corporate social performance model. *Academy of Management Review* 10(4): 758–769.
Wartick, S.L., and J.F. Mahon. 1994. Towards a substantive definition of the corporate issue construct: A review and synthesis of literature. *Business and Society* 33(3): 293–311.
Wartick, S.L., and R.E. Rude. 1986. Issues management: Corporate fad or corporate function? *California Management Review* 29(1): 124–132.
Weiss, J.W. 2003. *Business ethics: A stakeholder and issues management approach*, 3rd ed. Ohio: Thomson - South-Western.
Wernelfelt, B. 1984. A resource based view of the firm. *Strategic Management Review* 5: 171–180.
Wheeler, D., B. Colbert, and R.E. Freeman. 2003. Focusing on value: Reconciling corporate social responsibility, sustainability and a stakeholder approach in a network world. *Journal of General Management* 28(3): 1–29.
Wicks, A.C., D.R. Gilbert Jr., and R.E. Freeman. 1994. A feminist reinterpretation of the stakeholder concept. *Business Ethics Quarterly* 4(4): 475–497.
Wijnberg, N.M. 2000. Normative stakeholder theory and Aristotle: The link between ethics and politics. *Journal of Business Ethics* 25: 329–342.
Windsor, D. 2001. The future of corporate social responsibility. *International Journal of Organizational Analysis* 9(3): 225–256.
Wood, D.J. 1991a. Social issues in management: Theory and research in corporate social performance. *Journal of Management* 17(2): 383–406.
Wood, D.J. 1991b. Corporate social performance revisited. *Academy of Management Review* 16(4): 691–718.
Wood, D.J. and J.M. Lodgson. 2002. Business citizenship: From individuals to organizations. Ruffin series, no. 3, *Business Ethics Quarterly*, 59–94.
World Business Council for Sustainable Development. 2000. *Corporate social responsibility: Making good business sense*. Geneve: World Business Council for Sustainable Development.
World Commission on Environment and Development. 1987. *Our common future*. Oxford: Oxford University Press.
Yamaji, K. 1997. A global perspective of ethics in business. *Business Ethics Quarterly* 7(3): 55–71.
Zadek, S. 2001. Partnership alchemy: Engagement, innovation, and governance. In *Perspectives on corporate citizenship*, ed. J. Andriof and M. McIntosh, 200–212. Sheffield: Greenleaf.

Chapter 5
A Behavioral Model of Ethical and Unethical Decision Making

Michael Bommer, Clarence Gratto, Jerry Gravander, and Mark Tuttle

Introduction

Well-conceived schematic models are useful devices in understanding behavior, especially in situations where the individual is subjected to multiple forces. The decision-making dynamics of an individual faced with choices involving ethical issues are complex. However, current models of ethical and unethical behavior within organizations are generally not very helpful in understanding and explaining that behavior.

The absence of well-developed models of ethical and unethical behavior in organizations reflects a dearth of research on the factors affecting this behavior and on the ways in which these factors enter into the underlying decision process. Not only is there little relevant research, but what there is does not lend itself to model building. For example, business and professional ethics, a rapidly developing sub-discipline which concerns itself primarily with the social and professional aspects of ethical and unethical behavior in business and professional contexts, has seen little research directed toward uncovering the factors leading to ethical (and unethical) behavior in various situations. Instead, there is a considerable body of descriptive material of two main types: first, accounts of particular cases of actual decisions to act ethically or unethically (study of unethical actions predominates) and, second, surveys of managers about their attitudes toward certain ethical

M. Bommer • M. Tuttle
Department of Management, Clarkson University, Potsdam, NY 13676, USA
e-mail: michalos@brandonu.ca

C. Gratto
School of Business, Clarkson University, Potsdam, NY 13676, USA

J. Gravander (✉)
School of Liberal Arts, Clarkson University, Potsdam, NY 13676, USA
e-mail: jgravand@clarkson.edu

A.C. Michalos and D.C. Poff (eds.), *Citation Classics from the Journal of Business Ethics*, Advances in Business Ethics Research 2,
DOI 10.1007/978-94-007-4126-3_5, © Springer Science+Business Media B.V. 2013

dilemmas, their perceptions about the circumstances within which these dilemmas currently must be resolved, and their beliefs about changes in these circumstances which would make resolution of the dilemmas easier. However, case studies do not always indicate why particular decisions were made, let alone indicate general causes behind ethical and unethical behavior. For example, Anderson et al. (1980) concluded in their study of the Bay Area Rapid Transit (BART) case that one could not be sure about what happened, much less that one could know who acted correctly and who incorrectly and why. Moreover, survey studies, like the one conducted by Flores (1982) about safety-related decisions in design and product development, typically stop with an account of what people say they would do in certain situations rather than determine directly which actual unethical and ethical behaviors would occur in those situations. Since this descriptive information does not identify the various environmental and individual factors which influence decisions to act ethically or unethically, it cannot indicate the relative importance of these factors in determining the outcomes of decisions.

The purpose of this paper is to propose and describe a conceptual model of ethical and unethical behavior in organizations. Although this model must be viewed as a first attempt to identify and relate the various factors which influence managers' decisions to act ethically or unethically, we believe that it will increase the understanding of such behavior as related to the many factors which affect the manager's decision–making process. We further believe that this conceptual model of the decision process underlying ethical and unethical actions would be of considerable use to those who are seeking to develop and implement programs which would facilitate ethical behavior on the part of decision makers, as well as to those who desire to turn their research from the descriptive study of ethical and unethical behavior to an investigation of the underlying structure of such behavior and the process leading to it.

A schematic diagram of the model appears as Fig. 5.1. This model groups under several categories a wide range of factors which the literature lists as possible influences on managers' decisions when they are confronted by ethical dilemmas. These categories include a decision–maker's social environment, government and legal environment, professional environment, work environment, personal environment, and individual attributes. The model links these influences with ethical and unethical behavior via the mediating structure of the individual's decision-making process. The decision process in the model functions as a central processing unit with its own internal characteristics, such as the individual's cognitive style, type of information acquisition and processing, and perceived levels of loss and reward, that influence the decision. The model also distinguishes between the degree of influence which the decision maker perceives the various factors to have and the influence they actually have.

Given that the literature is scanty, it is at best suggestive about the influences on managers' ethical (and unethical) behavior, and it most definitely does not afford an exhaustive identification of the relevant factors nor of patterns of possible interaction among these. The categorization adopted for the model should thus be taken as tentative. Moreover, as each of the major categories of the model, along with the decision process function, are described and discussed in turn, the reader should remember both the paucity of relevant research and its inaptness for model building.

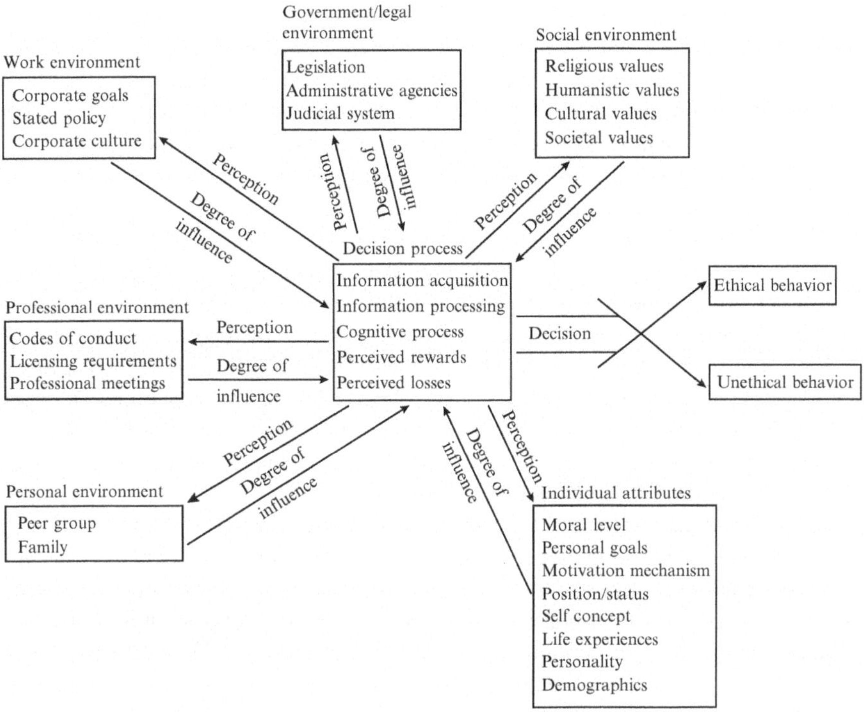

Fig. 5.1 A behavioral model of ethical/unethical decision making

Concepts and Definitions

This paper is not prescriptive with respect to ethical and unethical behavior, that is, it does not attempt to establish which behaviors are objectively morally correct and incorrect in given situations. However, it does more than merely describe decision makers' beliefs and attitudes about their actions. It is an epidemiological investigation which aims to identify the factors which influence decision makers to behave in certain situations, either ethically or unethically. Some of these factors enter into the decision makers' moral reasoning about the situations, whereas others do not. The paper will attempt to identify which factors play a role in decision makers' moral reasoning about the ethical situations in which they are involved, and it will suggest the nature of the role these factors play.

Clearly the key concepts involved in the paper are "ethical" and "unethical," and a central conceptual issue is how "ethical behavior" is identified and in what sense it is "ethical." There is a longstanding tradition in ethics which holds that "ethical behavior" is behavior which is shown to be objectively morally correct via appeal to a theory of morally correct (or permissible, obligatory, desirable, etc.) action, and that it is "ethical" precisely because it is the behavior which is required by the theory.

However, many ethicists maintain that the question of which ethical theory is correct is itself answered by appeal to certain ethical behaviors, that is, that some behaviors in certain situations are so clearly morally correct that they provide a moral intuition with which any theory must correspond if it is to be considered correct (see, for example, Bowie 1982). This paper understands "ethical behaviors" to be those behaviors the correctness of which constitutes the moral intuition in business and the professions.

The remaining question is which behaviors the paper understands to be these litmus-test behaviors in the business and professional contexts. They are those which have been identified by experienced managers and professionals as clear and exemplary instances of "ethical behavior." Such instances are recorded and identified in, for example, the cases published by the Board of Ethical Review of the National Society of Professional Engineers, the awards given for exemplary ethics in engineering by the Institute for Electrical and Electronics Engineers, and the citations for ethics in business given by the Values in Business Management Program at the C. W. Post Center of Long Island University.

A final issue is what exactly is meant by saying environmental and individual factors influence a decision maker's selection of ethical and unethical behavior. This paper does not presuppose strict behaviorism. First, one of its objectives is to elucidate the patterns of moral reasoning used by decision makers and the way in which various factors enter into their decisions to choose ethical and unethical behavior. Second, although the model postulates that a variety of environmental and individual factors influence decisions, it does not assume that these factors are sufficient conditions for the selection of particular behaviors. On the contrary, the model assumes the factors are – individually and in various combinations – necessary conditions in the sense that were the factors impinging on any given individual to change, that individual's ethical and unethical behavior would be different. The environmental and individual factors establish a context within which decision makers must choose to act, and from this point of view the primary purpose of the paper should be interpreted as the identification of factors which are such that changing them would facilitate decision makers in choosing ethical over unethical behaviors in given situations.

Social Environment

The social environment of a manager is the set of humanistic, religious, cultural, and societal values generally shared by the members of his or her society, and in particular those values of that society's sub-groupings to which the manager belongs. Two aspects of the influence of the social environment on managers' decisions will be discussed in this section. First, although it is a truism that values affect behavior, evidence seems to indicate that with respect to ethical and unethical behavior on the job, many managers will not adhere to general social values unless these are also incorporated within their professional or work environment. Second, some ethicists have recently argued that some general social values are not necessarily appropriate guides to behavior in certain managerial and business situations. Brady (1985) has recently proposed a model to aid in the understanding of how a society's values and business interplay. Brady argues that often the type of ethical dilemma influences how strongly society's values effect the decision. In some situations (for example, equal employment) often a formalist view is taken where the decision maker does use society's value system in the decision-making process, while in other situations (for example, nuclear power or genetic engineering) individuals tend to be more pragmatic and concrete or do not use society's value systems as a guide.

Case upon case report on managers who make on-the-job decisions that violate general social values. Many critics take this as evidence that business and ethics do not mix, that is, that managers deliberately choose to abandon general social values in the conduct of their managerial duties. However, a manager's failure to follow his or her general social values while on the job is probably more complex than this. Managers do not appear to make on-the-job decisions that they believe are unethical within the job-related context in which the decisions are made, as can be concluded from the analysis of numerous cases of ethical and unethical behavior in the business context (see, for example, Fairweather 1980; Cohan and Whitcover 1980; Vandivier 1980). In these cases, managers who have been accused of unethical on-the-job behavior will say such things as, "I am not that type of person. I am an elder in my church, active in community affairs, a good family man, a Boy Scout leader, and so on. I just thought this was the way you were supposed to act in this business." Such statements imply that managers are ethical segregationists, that is, that they segregate on-the-job ethical behavior from off-the-job ethical behavior and apply different sets of values to each. This implies, in turn, that managerial decisions will correspond more closely to the humanistic, religious, cultural, and societal values of society-at-large only when these values are made part of the job environment. This would occur either by incorporating these general social values into the codes of conduct which are part of managers' professional environment, including them in the corporate culture and policy of their work environment, or both.

Before general social values could be incorporated into managers' professional and work environment, the question of which social values are appropriate to the job context must be answered. The traditional answer from ethicists has been, "All of them." For example, some writers on professional ethics have argued that separate codes of conduct for the professions are unnecessary; all that is needed is the simple statement that generally held social values apply to professional decisions (Pavlovic 1980; Oldenquist and Slowter 1979). Recently this traditional wisdom has been challenged. For example, with respect to the value of truth-telling, some critics have argued that although truth-telling is a value that should have broad application in business, there are certain business and managerial situations to which it should not be applied (Carr 1983; Gravander 1982). They argue that there may be a species of business behavior which is properly labeled "business bluffing," which although it is not the truth, should not be condemned through an application of a truth-telling value. They base their case on an analogy to poker bluffing, which is not the truth, but also is never condemned as a lie. This entire area of inquiry, however, needs more development before one could decide, first, how much of an exemption from general social values these critics want to give business and, second, whether their position is valid.

Government and Legal Environment

Laws are values and mores of society that have the force of its formal authority. "Legal" and "ethical" are not necessarily synonymous. Nevertheless, the legal dimension is an important determinant in many ethical decisions. Some individuals are not dissuaded from a course of action by its illegality or the threat of punishment, but they are the exception. Most individuals feel compelled to refrain from an action which is specifically prohibited by law. This effect of legal considerations on managers' ethical decisions is due not just to the legal consequences which follow from breaking the law, but also to the strong social stigma associated with the label "illegal," as well as the desire to comply with the moral force behind the law.

In order to be effective, laws need to be actively enforced. However, because of their complexities, business-related crimes by managers are often not rigorously prosecuted. It is frequently difficult for investigating officers, prosecutors, judges, and jurists to understand the intricacies of the offense. Further, since the harm is often of an economic nature rather than physical, and because the crime's victim may be an insurance company or other corporation that does not elicit sympathy, the cases may be given low priority by prosecutors (McGowan 1983). Thus, the actual enforcement policy may result in low risk of detection, token enforcement and prosecution, and relatively light sentences with only short if any imprisonment in a minimum security institution (Geis and Stotland 1980). In contrast to their relative legal insignificances, crimes by managers hold out the possibility of very large personal or corporate financial rewards. Thus, managers, who refrain from business-related crime may be more motivated by the moral force behind the law and the social stigma of breaking it than by the legal consequences.

Crimes by managers cannot be attributed to ignorance of the law. It is true that from the perspective of the individual decision maker within a large organization, most of the law's institutions are remote. Consequently, the individual's perception of what the law requires has likely been obtained informally. For example, notions of what "the law" is come from conversations with other non-professionals, and many of the subtleties and reasons for the law are lost. Further, the individual's information is often dated. However, ignorance of what is required appears to be a factor in only a very few "white collar" crimes (Meier and Geis 1982), and this finding can probably be extended to the full range of illegal actions open to managers.

Of greater influence on a manager contemplating committing a crime is the probability of detection. This influence stems from two distinct factors. First, expectations about the probability of an event's detection are more important in determining risk taking than is the magnitude of the expected consequence (Dickson 1978).

Thus, though the punishment for the crime might be small, the certainty of detection is a powerful deterrent. This may be due to the social stigma which is associated with detection, since even when managers escape severe punishment for their business-related crimes, they often become pariahs among their former friends and associates. Second, while the research indicates that there is deterrent effect from rigorous prosecution of crime (Geis and Stotland 1980), the converse undoubtedly is true, also. Lack of vigorous prosecution of certain violations indicates to the decision-maker that the particular conduct is being condoned. That is, low probability of detection due to lackadaisical enforcement robs the law of its moral force.

Of interest in connection with this latter point is the relative effect of governmental agencies. Because of their broad powers, they can change the probability of detection for certain crimes. For example, the FBI's enforcement priorities were shifted by the Reagan administration to reflect less concern with "white collar" crimes such as embezzlement and fraud. There was concern at the time in the justice Department that wrongdoers would tailor their crimes so as to fall short of the amounts that would attract investigation by federal agents and, thus, that "white collar" crime would increase (Taylor 1984).

Professional Environment

The professional environment of a manager is the institutionalized professional context within which a manager practices. This is quite different than the vague and informal identification of a person as "professional," by which is meant the person is competent and responsible. While persons who see themselves as professional in this sense may strive to bring high ethical standards to their decisions, such efforts are best understood as attempts by individuals to adhere to their personal values. Fields of activity are properly designated professions only if they are characterized by (a) professional associations, (b) established licensing procedures, or (c) both.

To say that a licensing procedure is established is to say that at least some aspects of the profession are closed to individuals who are not licensed via a formal licensing process. In a field with an established licensing procedure, individuals cannot identify themselves as members of that profession unless they hold a license. Though the possibility of loss of one's license is a powerful deterrent to unethical behavior, management is not a licensed profession.

Professional associations play an important role in both regulating the professions and controlling entry to them. For example, the American Bar Association and the major engineering professional associations accredit law and engineering degree programs, and it is impossible (in the case of law) or very difficult (in the case of engineering) to practice in these areas without graduating from an accredited program. Not all fields have professional associations which are this dominant, but even in those which do not the relationship between the individual and the professional organization is such that the individual has the self-image and social status of professional by virtue of membership in the association. Professional associations typically have formal and published standards of professional conduct (Flores 1980; Layton 1981), and recent court rulings have been based on the principle that the public perceives membership in a professional association as a guarantor of members' adherence to these standards (May 1983).

Professional associations typically demand ethical behavior via formal codes of ethics. Some critics argue that these codes should be taken as merely suggestive of what various professions take to be morally important, since attempts to follow these codes forces professionals into unacceptable moral quandries (Leugenbiehl 1983). For example, engineering codes require that engineers be loyal to their clients and employers and also blow the whistle on them, and since it seems impossible to do both simultaneously, engineers are forced to choose between different violations of the code (Gravander 1981). Moreover, it is not always clear what course of action complies with the codes in specific situations. A recent survey of chemical engineers revealed considerable differences of opinion about what was ethically correct when they were asked to apply their professional code of ethics to a set of case studies (Kohn and Hughson 1980).

In spite of these difficulties with codes of ethics, professionals exhibit considerable interest in complying with the ethical standards established by their codes. For example, the National Society of Professional Engineers regularly publishes hypothetical cases in which its Board of Ethical Review applies the NSPE Code to the type of ethical problem encountered in engineering, and there has recently been considerable activity within the engineering community directed toward formulating a clear, "unified" code by which all engineers can easily regulate their professional conduct (Oldenquist and Slowter 1979). Moreover, professional associations, especially in engineering, have increasingly taken to enforcing their codes via expulsion of violators (Martin and Schinzinger 1983; Unger 1982), and this sanction, even though it really involves only loss of status, has been perceived as so extremely undesirable by some members that presumably it has some general effectiveness in forcing compliance (see, for example, Fairweather 1980). In addition to sanctions to force compliance with the codes, professional associations in engineering have begun developing support mechanisms for members who have followed the codes and in so doing have clashed with their employer's or client's wishes. Many advocates argue that such support mechanisms will be the decisive factor in tipping the balance toward ethical behavior (Unger 1982; Broome 1983).

Managers have a professional environment insofar as they are members of a profession. Several of the professional associations which are open to managers have formal codes of ethics and discuss ethics at meetings and in journals of their professional societies. Although it does not have developed enforcement procedures in the way that professional associations in other fields have, the American Assembly of Collegiate Schools of Business will only accredit programs that have significant course work dealing with "ethical considerations and social and political influences as they affect" business organizations (AACSB 1983). Moreover, some managers are members of a second profession by virtue of being lawyers, accountants, engineers, and so on. When enforcing codes of ethics, these professions have not distinguished between managerial behavior on the one hand and legal, accountancy, and engineering behavior on the other. Therefore, for managers, especially those who are also members of another profession, the factors discussed in this section will be important determinants in their ethical behavior. Moreover, it is likely that this causal effect is not dependent on the individual's awareness of the extent to which he or she is affected by the professional environment, since the standards of the profession are internalized over time and followed implicitly without an explicit awareness of the sanctions which are a force behind compliance.

Work Environment

Several factors in the work environment strongly influence managers' decisions on whether to act ethically or unethically. These are corporate goals, stated policy, and corporate culture. Unfortunately for the individual managers, these three factors can each support conflicting decisions in a given situation. For example, short-term corporate goals and the corporate culture may point in one direction, and long-term goals and stated policies point in another. Which direction managers turn often depends on which factor is more dominant in their work environment.

Short-term goals for profit and similar measures of performance are often emphasized in companies. When an acceptable rate of return on investment or similar monetary measure is the dominant goal, being ethical will be an important sub-goal only insofar as it does not detract from the primary goal. Yet an emphasis on short-term profitability which leads to unethical actions can have substantial long-term negative effects, to the point of threatening the corporation's very existence. Good examples of this can be found in the insufficient standards concerning the handling of asbestos by Johns-Manville and the operation of the Three Mile Island nuclear power plant (Wheelen and Hunger 1984).

Many business entities have formal policies that prohibit unethical conduct and prescribe punishment for it. Statements of these are typically found in operating and policy manuals and in supervisor's workplace statements, and they are disseminated in training programs and posters in the workplace. What real effect do these have? Would those people who profess that they are affected by these statements have acted ethically anyway? Do the stated policies simply reinforce or restate values that the individuals have already internalized?

There is considerable evidence to support the notion that a company's stated policies do in fact foster and increase the frequency of ethical behavior. For example, in a simulated decision-making exercise, a letter from the fictitious company's president supporting ethical behavior and warning of dismissal for unethical behavior resulted in increased ethical behavior (Hegarty and Sims 1979). Similarly, a significant determinant as to whether purchasing officers accepted gratuities was the existence of a written company policy (Staff 1979).

Several factors affect the efficacy of stated policies in leading managers to make ethical decisions (Mautz et al. 1979). First, the more decentralized the decision-making function, and consequently the less direct the supervision of managers, the greater the likelihood of inadvertent non-compliance. Some companies, for example those with outside sales forces, are inherently decentralized and run a greater risk of non-compliance with stated company policy. Second, the stated policies can be unclear, with the consequence that there are conflicting or incompatible messages. For example, the policies might set levels of performance and goals that are unattainable without the individual resorting to behavior that is prohibited by the policy. Third, organic changes in a company such as mergers, rapid growth, and the addition of foreign operations can lead to situations which the formulators of the policy did not have in mind. In such cases, the policies can no longer effectively guide action.

While stated policies on ethical behavior are generally voluntary, some are required by law. For example, the Securities and Exchange Commission Rule 17j-1 under the Investment Company Act of 1940 requires that registered companies and other certain closely associated entities must have written codes of ethics in which the companies articulate prohibited practices and implement detection and enforcement procedures (Gillis 1981).

Corporations have their own 'cultures', just as societies do. The culture is reflected in the "... attitudes and values, management styles and problem-solving behavior of its people" (Schwartz and Davis 1981). Corporate norms are the products of this culture. It is often contended that in a capitalist system humanistic, compassionate, and egalitarian values tend to be left behind as the business enterprise pursues its profit motive. Within this context the fact that business enterprises generally act only in their self-interest is not surprising. "As one comes across occasional corporate good works, it should not be forgotten that corporations are not eleemosynary (charitable) institutions and cannot be expected to act in ways contrary to their dominant ethos, which is profit" (Hodges 1963).

The conduct of the Board of Directors, CEO and other senior management can signal subordinate managers as to which behaviors are acceptable. An individual's supervisor has significant power over his or her behavior. There is a great deal of research showing that authority figures can influence others to behave unethically. An individual's supervisor often has the capacity for rewarding and punishing and, therefore, is an authority figure for the individual in the work environment. Social psychologists (Freedman et al. 1981) have found that one way to maximize compliance to a set of norms is to put an individual in a well-controlled situation and make noncompliance difficult. The well known Milgram studies (1963, 1965) are examples of how authority figures can exert extreme pressure to comply to orders even when compliance is unethical.

Policies that have been suggested as encouraging ethical behavior include the presence of effective procedures for monitoring compliance to company policy and ascertaining what is actually occurring in those areas where policies have been established. These procedures need to be sufficient for determining or detecting when improper acts have taken place, as well as for identifying the transgressor. Since existence of easy opportunities to act unethically facilitates the occurrence of unethical acts, systems and controls need to be implemented that will both decrease the ease and eliminate the opportunities. Screening prospective employees for trust and responsibility and instituting appropriate limits on access to information and tangible items are also important (Mautz et al. 1979).

There are other organizational characteristics associated with a reduced frequency of unethical activity. The presence of systems to facilitate communication, both vertically and horizontally in the managerial hierarchy, is one. To be effective, such communication needs to be timely, clear, and accurate, as well as open and frank. Such channels of communication apparently help prevent senior management from becoming distant or insulated from wrongdoers at lower levels in the organization. Managers are thus more likely to know who is doing what and by which means. Under such circumstances it is more difficult for managers to ignore unethical behavior within their organizations (DeGeorge 1978).

Personal Environment

The variables in this segment of the model – the family and peer groups – relate to the individual's personal life outside of the organization. Although the research in this area is very limited, it raises a number of conceptual issues.

Research on the relation between an individual's family and occupational situations has focused almost exclusively on the influence of occupation on the family (Mortimer 1980; Donald and Bradshaw 1981). For example, Donald and Bradshaw (1981) found that work and occupational stress tends to produce family problems whereas there is little or no research on how the family affects on-the-job ethical and unethical behavior. McLean (1978) has taken a different approach to the relationship between the family and ethical and unethical behavior. His theory of reference groups stresses that ethicists have failed to account for the pressure which multiple roles exert on members of modern society when they undertake ethical analyses. He notes that one of the multiple roles not often taken into account is that of family member.

Peer group pressure seems to be a significant variable in predicting deviant behavior (Grasmick and Green 1980; Burkett and Jensen 1975) among adolescent youth. There seems to be a strong relationship between peer group attitude and behavior and the propensity of illegal activity by youthful offenders. Other research indicates that peer group pressure may cause the group to make faulty and often immoral decisions (Janis 1972; Allison 1971; Halberstam 1972).

The individual's home environment also seems to guide moral development. Kagan (1984) has argued for a non-environmental approach. He advances a genetic explanation for the development of moral values, but at the present he seems to be in the minority. The opposing view, supported by a large body of literature within developmental psychology, postulates the theory that the individual's family and peers have a large influence on moral development (Bandura 1971, 1977). The child goes through a complex socialization process which is an important determinant of moral thinking. The family and peer groups are both important in this process (Cohen 1976; Clausen 1968). Although the literature in the area emphasizes the child's moral actions, the individual's family and peer environment surely also has a continuing influence into adulthood. However, the lack of relevant research on many of the topics limits the conclusions that can be drawn.

Individual Attributes

The individual component of the model comprises moral level, personal goals, motivation mechanisms, position/status, self concept, life experiences, personality, and demographic variables. The research connecting individual attributes with ethical and unethical behavior is fairly limited and tends to concentrate on moral level, demographics, motivation mechanisms, and self concept.

Kohlberg's influence is found throughout most of the research on the individual and moral development. Kohlberg (1969, 1971) defines six stages of moral development, which he groups into three general categories, two stages per category. The first general category is the preconventional (or pre-moral). Individuals in this category do not base judgement of right and wrong on society's standards, but on their own physical needs. Fear of punishment is the main reason rules are followed by people in this category. Kohlberg's second category is the conventional level. Children usually reach this category around the age of ten, and it is also the most prevalent moral category for adults. The basic criteria for right and wrong in this category are the norms and regulations of society. Kohlberg's final category is the postconventional. An individual in this category does not reject the legitimacy of rules in society, but at times finds society's prescriptions wanting. The postconventional individual has the capacity for reflection, logical reasoning, responsibility, and an inner source of morality and justice.

Kohlberg has developed an instrument for assessing an individual's level of moral reasoning. Many of the studies relating to the individual attributes in this segment of the model use a Kohlberg-type instrument to determine moral level and then study moral level as a dependent variable influenced by the other individual attributes as independent variables. Kohlberg-type instruments use a series of ethical dilemmas as an ambiguous stimulus for subjects who are then asked to describe how they would behave in the situation. The level of moral reasoning is determined from the rationale used in explaining the hypothetical actions.

Maqsud (1980) for example, studies the effect of the personality characteristic of locus of control on moral level. Locus of control refers to the degree one relies on oneself (internal) vs. others (external) for reinforcement (Rotter 1966). Maqsud found a significant concentration of internal locus of control individuals in the postconventional (higher order) level of moral reasoning. Others (Adams-Weber 1969; Johnson and Gormly 1972) have reported similar findings. Other studies have used a variety of personality measures and related them to level of moral reasoning. Authoritarianism, neuroticism, and level of anxiety have all been related to differing indices of moral reasoning (Elliott 1976).

Demographic variables, for example, sex, age, and education, have been used to predict moral reasoning in a number of studies. A number of authors (Lyons 1982; Braverman et al. 1972) have studied the effect of sex differences on moral level. They found that females tend not to progress to post-conventional morality as often as males because of differential societal pressures on females, even though at younger ages females tend to be more advanced in terms of moral reasoning (Freeman and Giefink 1979). Age and education level also are related to moral reasoning. Older individuals tend to score lower on moral reasoning scales, while the more educated tend to score higher (Dortzbach 1975; Rest 1976; Crowder 1976; Coder 1975).

Ward and Wilson (1980) have studied the effect of motivational orientation (safety vs. esteem). They found that esteem-motivated individuals do not submit to group pressure, that is, they display a consistent moral posture across situations. Safety-motivated subjects tend to acquiesce to group pressure and exhibit inconsistent moral action. When acting as individuals, there was no difference between the moral actions of the safety and esteem subjects.

There have been many studies in criminology that attempt to identify characteristics that distinguish criminals from non-criminals (Lykken 1957; Frost and Frost 1962; Peterson et al. 1961). For example, Mednick and co-workers (1977) found that criminals exhibited the following characteristics: low intelligence, poorer impulse control, emotional immaturity, lack of ability to learn by experience, poorer work habits, and lower nervous activity. However, crime in corporations does not fit the profile of crime at large. So-called "white collar" crime is committed by people of high social status and, usually, high income level. Many of the other variables which identify criminals at large do not generalize to the corporate criminal, for example, low intelligence or personality disorganization. Different characteristics seems to identify the corporate criminal. For example, Aubert (1952) found that individuals at the corporate level who behave unethically have in general a negative attitude toward legal regulations, although they admit that certain types of law are necessary. Moreover, many who have been convicted of "white collar" crime do not perceive that they have behaved inappropriately (Geis 1973).

Individual attributes do seem to relate to the level of moral reasoning. However, the research reported in this section does have a number of problems. First, the level of moral reasoning is the dependent variable in ethics research, not ethical behavior. This clearly assumes that it is obvious that the post-conventional individual is going to act ethically. But does the capability for ethical reasoning guarantee ethical action or behavior? The real dependent variable should be ethical behavior, not level of moral reasoning. Second, the research is not realistic. Most of the research is done in academia, with little relevance toward ethics in the real world (especially the business world). Designs need to be developed that realisticaly simulate real world environments, and research needs to be done in more applied settings. Third, the research tends to focus on the isolated individual. However, there is some evidence (Nichols and Day 1982) that individuals interacting in a group produce group decisions at a higher level of moral reasoning than the average of the individual members when acting alone. Since many business decisions relating to ethics are made in the corporate context, this effect needs further study.

Decision Process

In recent years a variety of different models have emerged which outline the major steps or functions involved in a rational decision-making process. Rationality here is defined as the best selection of means to achieve an objective consistent with the value system of the decision maker (Steiner et al. 1982). Most of the models encompass the following steps in one form or another: setting managerial objectives; searching for alternatives; evaluating alternatives; choosing an alternative; implementing the decision; and monitoring and controlling the results. Associated with each of these steps is the gathering and processing of information within a value construct and the cognitive limitations of the decision maker.

Ethical issues may arise in any step of the decision-making process. For example, in setting managerial objectives, it is necessary to consider ethical concerns relating to the choice of pursuing various directions. In comparing various alternatives, ethical considerations often arise as part of the valuation process. In the implementation step the potential consequences to resources (human and physical) which will be affected by the decision must be considered from an ethical perspective (Boulding 1966).

In making these types of decisions involving ethical considerations a manager draws upon his/her basic personal values and those acquired values derived from his/her role in the environments previously discussed. In making these decisions value conflicts are inevitable, and the particular resolution of these conflicts depends on the relative degree of influence of the various environments on the decision maker. For example, at any point the values of the decision maker may conflict with the values of the organization. A study of 238 managers revealed that they "experience pressure, real or perceived, to compromise their personal moral standards to satisfy organizational expectations" (Carroll 1975). A study by England (1967) revealed that managers place a great deal of importance on organizational goals and have a strong group orientation. A further study by Senger (1971) found that managers tend to evaluate their subordinates with respect to their degree of acceptance of organizational values. These findings would tend to support a hypothesis that in event of a conflict of values, organizational and group values may assume greater emphasis in comparison to personal values. However, in resolving this conflict between the personal values of the manager and the goals of the organization, Monsen et al. (1966) argue that the manager most frequently resolves this conflict by emphasizing his/her own personal goals. This seems to imply that in the event of a conflict, managers pursue a path that they perceive will enhance their own self interests especially with respect to career advancement.

In making various decisions at each step in the decision-making process the manager acquires and processes a myriad of information. Some of this information is problem specific whereas other information relates to the previously discussed environmental factors. This information ranges from hard data, such as laws and stated corporate policies, to soft data, such as an individual's self concept and peer group with a range of information in between these states. The manager must then

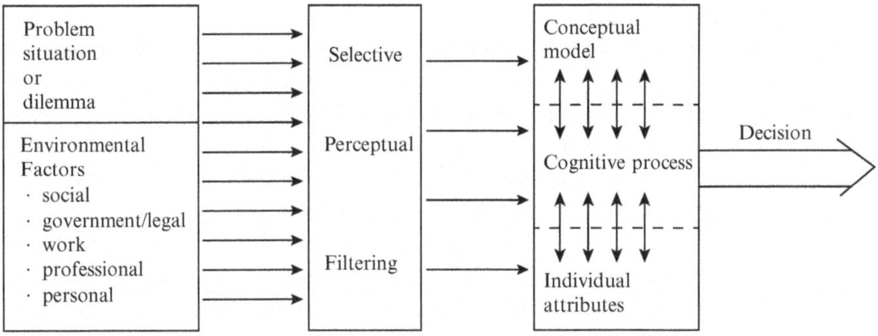

Fig. 5.2 The decision process

synthesize and analyze this information to determine a rational decision to the problem situation. A simplified model of the more important elements in this process are depicted as Fig. 5.2. The two information inputs – the parameters of the problem situation and the environmental factors impinging on the decision maker – are filtered by the manager in a selective perception process. The manager then builds a conceptual model, which goes through an iterative process affected by the individual attributes and mediated by the individual's unique cognitive process. Since environmental factors and individual attributes have been discussed in previous sections of this article, this section will focus on the remaining aspects of the decision process.

Hogarth (1980) notes that people have limited information-processing capacity. The consequence of this limitation affects the manager's (1) perception of information, (2) style of information processing, and (3) memory as follows:

1. Perception of information is selective. The decision maker, influenced by a number of different forces, may or may not select the information which is most relevant to the problem situation.
2. Since people cannot simultaneously integrate a great deal of information, processing is mainly done in a sequential manner. The sequence in which information is processed may bias a person's judgement and limit the evaluation of interrelated elements.
3. Finally, people have limited memory capacity. This limits the access to information which might be relevant to the problem.

Given this limited information-processing capacity, managers tend to select information and process it in a sequential manner. What we select depends on the information stimulus and on our internal representation of the problem situation.

As a way of dealing with the complexity of the situation, managers appear to form a conceptual model of the problem. Simon (1976) notes that decision makers cannot comprehend all alternatives, probabilities, consequences, values, and the evaluation of these and so construct an internal representation or model of the situation.

The model may be simplistic or complex, depending on the cognitive capabilities and capacity of the manager. New information modifies our internal representation model which, in turn, directs our activities to further sample information from the environment, which further modifies our internal representation, which directs exploration, etc., in a cyclical fashion. Only that information that fits is incorporated into the model. Features that fit well into the model are more readily selected and more likely to be incorporated than those that do not fit easily. In any case, the model is never a complete representation of the real world problem situation, which limits the manager's ability to make a truly rational decision (bounded rationality). Consequently, judgments or choices made reflect not only the structure of the problem situation but also the capabilities and limitations of the decision maker.

In the past few years a number of conceptual and empirical articles have appeared in the literature regarding the effect of a manager's cognitive style of problem solving and decision making (see, for example, Benbasat and Taylor 1978; Blaylock and Rees 1984; Henderson and Nutt 1979; Kilman and Mitroff 1976; and Taggart and Robey 1981). Simon (1960, p. 72) defines cognitive style as "the characteristic, self consistent mode of functioning which individuals show in their perception and intellectual activities." There are many dimensions of cognitive style (Goldstein and Blackman 1978) just as there are many dimensions of an individual's personality. The difference between the personality and cognitive style of an individual is "a distinction between what an individual thinks (personality) and the way the individual thinks (cognitive style)" (Pratt 1980, p. 502). Although there is general acknowledgement that the construct of cognitive style is multidimensional, the number and identity of such dimensions and the relationship between these dimensions are not clear (Zmud 1979).

In recent years there has been a surge of interest about the impact of cognitive style on managerial problem solving and decision making. Some of the most cited cognitive measures which would seem to affect ethical and unethical decision making include: Myers-Briggs Type Indicator (Myers 1962); Witkin's Embedded Figures Test (Witkin et al. 1971); Cognitive Complexity (Bieri et al. 1966) and Tolerance of Ambiguity (Budner 1962). The Myers-Briggs Indicator, which is based on Carl Jung's theory of type, purports to assess differences in behavior as to how an individual uses perception and judgement. Witkin's Embedded Figures test assesses whether one is more field dependent (relies more on external referents for behavior) or field independent (relies more on internal referents for behavior). Cognitive complexity is a measure of one's ability to evaluate multiple dimensions or aspects of a problem situation. Budner's Scale for Tolerance-Intolerance of Ambiguity assesses one's degree of tolerance for dealing with ambiguous, uncertain situations. Such factors as personality traits, psychological needs, self concept, demographic factors, value systems, as well as one's memory of experiences shape the selection process and internal representation of the problem situation. Actions become consistent with the internal cognitive process of an individual which is shaped by these many forces rather than by the reality of the problem situation.

In deciding whether or not to pursue a given course of action, the rational decision maker is further influenced by both the perceived consequences and the perceived risks involved. Many times an individual's perception of a consequence or risk differs significantly from the actual consequence or risk as a result of a minimization or exaggeration process. Few individuals have the luxury of perfect information when making a decision or even knowing the degree of information to which they are knowledgeable. The decision is further influenced by the subjective weights applied to the consequences according to the individual's unique value system or utility function.

Finally, in making a final choice or decision for the problem situation, the manager may or may not resort to using a decision tool or aid. In recent years a number of decision tools and aids have been developed ranging in complexity from highly structured computer-based models to simple rules of thumb. These aids provide the opportunity of extending the limited information processing and cognitive capabilities of the managers.

The ultimate decision of choice (ethical or unethical) to a problem situation is dependent on a number of factors affecting the decision process. These factors include the available information (hard and soft), the individual attributes and cognitive capabilities of the managers, the perceived consequences and risks of a decision, the value or utility assigned to these consequences, as well as the degree of reliance on structured models by the manager.

Conclusions

The model developed in this article must be recognized as a first attempt to identify and relate the environmental factors and influences in decision making, where an individual is faced with a choice that has ethical implications. We expect this model to evolve as further research expands the body of knowledge relating to this field.

While substantial research has been done concerning ethical issues, clearly much more needs to be done. Most urgently needed is a series of empirical studies of specific decision-making situations involving ethical issues. The behaviors of individuals and their interaction with their environments should be systematically observed so as to determine which factors lead to a particular decision. Components of the model could be manipulated in order to ascertain the importance of each component. Undoubtedly such a complex undertaking would require substantial time and resources. The results of such a series of experiments would allow further refinement and understanding of the model and its components.

While this representation and description is preliminary, it can still provide valuable assistance in the understanding, development and evaluation of intervention and awareness programs in industry. Likewise it can be useful in academic settings, in courses that deal with ethical issues in business and industry, by providing a multidimensional framework to assist in the comprehension of the variety and magnitude of the factors that need to be considered.

References

Adams-Weber, J.R. 1969. Generalized expectancies concerning locus of control reinforcements and the perception of moral sanctions. *The British Journal of Social and Clinical Psychology* 8: 340–343.

Allison, G.T. 1971. *Essence of decision: Explaining the Cuban missile crisis.* Boston: Little, Brown & Company.

American Assembly of Collegiate Schools of Business Accreditiation. 1983. Council Procedures and Standards. 1983. AACSB, St. Louis, MO.

Anderson, R., R. Petrucci, D. Schendel, and L.E. Trachman. 1980. *Divided loyalties: Whisle blowing at BART.* West LaFayette: Purdue University Press.

Aubert, U. 1952. White-collar crime and social structure. *The American Journal of Sociology* 58: 263–271.

Bandura, A. 1971. Analysis of modeling process. In *Psychological modeling*, ed. A. Bandura. Chicago: Atherton, Aldine.

Bandura, A. 1977. *Social learning theory.* Englewood Cliffs: Prentice-Hall.

Benbasat, I., and R.N. Taylor. 1978. The impact of cognitive styles on information systems design. *Management Information Systems Quarterly* 2: 43–54.

Bieri, J., A.L. Atkins, S. Briar, R.L. Leaman, H. Miller, and T. Tripodi. 1966. *Clinical and social judgement.* New York: Wiley.

Blaylock, B.K., and L.P. Rees. 1984. Cognitive style and the usefulness of information. *Decision Sciences* 15: 74–91.

Boulding, K. 1966. The ethics of rational decision. *Management Science* 12: 161–169.

Bowie, N. 1982. *Business ethics.* Englewood Cliffs: Prentice-Hall.

Brady, F.N. 1985. A Janus-Head model of ethical theory: Looking two ways at business/society issues. *Academy of Management Review* 10(3): 568–576.

Braverman, I., S. Vogel, D. Braverman, F. Clarkson, and P. Rosenkrantz. 1972. Sex-role stereotypes: A current appraisal. *Journal of Social Issues* 28: 58–78.

Broome, T.H. 1983. New developments in engineering ethics: The AAES plan. In *Beyond whistle-blowing*, ed. V. Weil, 228–242. Chicago: Illinois Institute of Technology.

Budner, S. 1962. Intolerance of ambiguity as a personality variable. *Journal of Personality* 30: 29–50.

Burkett, S.R., and E. Jensen. 1975. Conventional ties, peer influence, and the fear of apprehension: A study of adolescent marijuana use. *The Sociological Quarterly* 16: 523–553.

Carr, A.Z. 1983. Is business bluffing ethical? In *Moral issues in business*, ed. B. Vincent, 17–24. Belmont: Wadsworth.

Carroll, A.B. 1975. Managerial ethics: A post-Watergate view. *Business Horizons* 18: 75–80.

Clausen, J.A. 1968. Perspectives on childhood socialization. In *Socialization and society*, ed. J. Clausen. Boston: Little, Brown & Company.

Coder, R. 1975. Moral judgement in adults. Unpublished doctoral dissertation, University of Minnesota.

Cohan, R.M., and J. Whitcover. 1980. A heartbeat away. In *Ethical problems in engineering: Cases*, pp, vol. 2, 2nd ed, ed. R. Baum, 52–57. Troy: Rensselaer Polytechnic Institute.

Cohen, S.E. 1976. *Social and personality development in childhood.* New York: Macmillan.

Crowder, J.W. 1976. The defining issues test and correlates of moral judgment. Unpublished master's thesis, University of Maryland.

DeGeorge, R.T. 1978. *Ethics, free enterprise and public policy.* New York: Oxford Press.

Dickson, J.W. 1978. Perceptions of risk as related to choice in a two-dimensional risk situation. *Psychological Reports* 44: 1059–1062.

Donald, J., and P. Bradshaw. 1981. Occupational and life stress and the family. *Small Group Behavior* 12: 329–375.

Dortzbach, J.R. 1975. Moral judgment and perceived locus of control: A cross-sectional developmental study of adults, aged 25–74. Unpublished doctoral dissertation, University of Oregon.

Elliott, A. 1976. Fakers: A study of managers: Responses on a personality test. *Personnel Review* 5: 33–37.
England, G.W. 1967. Personal value systems of American managers. *Academy of Management Journal* 10: 53–68.
Fairweather, V. 1980. $80,000 in payoffs. In *Ethical problems in engineering: Cases*, pp, vol. 2, 2nd ed, ed. R.J. Baum, 50–51. Troy: Rensselaer Polytechnic Institute.
Flores, A. 1980. The problem of professionalism: A code of ethics'. In *Ethical problems in engineering: Readings*, vol. 1, 2nd ed, ed. A. Flores, 1–6. Troy: Rensselaer Polytechnic Institute.
Flores, A. (ed.). 1982. *Designing for safety: Engineering ethics in organizational contents*. Troy: Center for the Study of the Human Dimensions of Science and Technology, Renssalaer Polytechnic Institute.
Freedman, J.L., D.O. Sears, and J.M. Carlsmith. 1981. *Social psychology*. Englewood Cliffs: Prentice Hall.
Freeman, S.J.M., and J.W. Giefink. 1979. Moral judgment as a function of age, sex, and stimulus. *Journal of Psychology* 102: 43–47.
Frost, B.P., and R.K. Frost. 1962. The pattern of WISC scores in a group of juvenile sociopaths. *Journal of Clinical Psychology* 18: 354–355.
Geis, G. 1973. Deterring corporate crime. In *Deterring corporate crime*, ed. R. Nader and M.J. Green, 182–197. New York: Grossman.
Geis, G., and E. Stotland. 1980. *White-collar crime theory and research*. Beverly Hills: Sage.
Gillis, J.G. 1981. Securities law and regulation. *Financial Analysts Journal* 37: 14.
Goldstein, K.M., and S. Blackman. 1978. *Cognitive style: Five approaches and relevant research*. New York: Wiley-Interscience.
Grasmick, H., and E. Green. 1980. Legal punishment, social disapproval, and internalization as inhibitors of illegal behavior. *The Journal of Criminal Law and Criminology* 71: 325–335.
Gravander, J.W. 1981. The origin and implications of engineers' obligations to the public welfare. In *PSA 1980*, vol. 2, ed. P.D. Asquith and R.N. Giere, 443–455. East Lansing: The Philosophy of Science Association.
Gravander, J.W. 1982. When in Rome, do as who? *The Liberal Studies Educator* 4: 23–28.
Halberstam, D. 1972. *The best and the brightest*. New York: Random House.
Hegarty, W.H., and H. Sims. 1979. Organizational philosophy, policies, and objectives related to unethical decision behavior: A laboratory experiment. *Journal of Applied Psychology* 64: 331–338.
Henderson, J.C., and P.C. Nutt. 1979. The influence of decision style on decision making behavior. *Management Science* 26: 371–386.
Hodges, L. 1963. *The business conscience*. Englewood Cliffs: Prentice-Hall.
Hogarth, R. 1980. *Judgement and choice: The psychology of decision*. New York: Wiley.
Janis, I. 1972. *Victims of groupthink*. Boston: Houghton Mifflin.
Johnson, C.K., and J. Gormly. 1972. Academic cheating: The contribution of sex, personality, and situational variables. *Developmental Psychology* 6: 320–325.
Kagan, J. 1984. *The nature of the child*. New York: Basic.
Kilman, R.H., and I.I. Mitroff. 1976. Qualitative versus quantitative analysis for management science: Different forms for different psychological types'. *Management Science* 22: 19–32.
Kohlberg, L. 1969. Stage and sequence: The cognitive-developmental approach to socialization. In *Handbook of socialization theory and research*, ed. D. Goslin, 347–480. Chicago: Rand McNally.
Kohlberg, L. 1971. From is to ought (How to commit the naturalistic fallacy and get away with it in the study of moral development). In *Cognitive development and epistemology*, ed. T. Mischel, 151–235. New York: Academic.
Kohn, P.M., and R.V. Hughson. 1980. Perplexing problems in engineering ethics. *Chemical Engineering* 75: 132–147.
Layton, E.T. 1981. *The revolt of the engineers*. Cleveland: Case Western Reserve University.
Leugenbiehl, H.C. 1983. Moral education and the codes of ethics. In *Beyond whistleblowing: Defining engineers' responsibilities*, ed. V. Weil, 284–299. Chicago: Illinois Institute of Technology.

Lykken, D.T. 1957. A study of anxiety in the sociopathic personality. *Journal of Abnormal and Social Psychology* 55: 6–10.
Lyons, N. 1982. Conceptions of self and morality and modes of moral choice. Unpublished doctoral dissertation, Harvard University.
Maqsud, M. 1980. Locus of control and stages of moral reasoning. *Psychological Reports* 46: 1243–1248.
Martin, M., and R. Schinzinger. 1983. *Ethics in engineering*. New York: McGraw-Hill.
Mautz, R., R. Reilly, and M. Maher. 1979. Personnel failure: The weak link in internal control. *Financial Executive* 47: 22–25.
May, L. 1983. Professional action and professional liability. In *Beyond whistleblowing: Defining engineers' responsibilities*, ed. V. Weil, 211–227. Chicago: Illinois Institute of Technology.
McGowan, W. 1983. The great white-collar crime coverup. *Business and Society Review* Spring 1983: 25–31.
McLean, S.D. 1978. Ethics, reference group theory, and the root metaphor analysis. *Andover Newton Quarterly* 14: 211–221.
Mednick, S.A., L. Kirkegaard-Sorensen, B. Hutchings, J. Knop, R. Rosenburg, and F. Schulsinger. 1977. The interplay of socioenvironmental and individual factors in the etiology of criminal behavior. In *Biosocial bases of criminal behavior*, ed. S. Mednick and K.O. Christiansen. New York: Gardner Press.
Meier, R.F., and G. Geis. 1982. The psychology of the white-collar offender. In *On white-collar crime*, ed. G. Geis. Lexington: Lexington.
Milgram, S. 1963. Behavioral study of obedience. *Journal of Abnormal and Social Psychology* 67: 317–378.
Milgram, S. 1965. Some conditions of obedience and disobedience to authority. *Human Relations* 18: 57–76.
Monsen, R.J., B.O. Saxberg, and R.A. Sutermeister. 1966. The modern manager: What makes him run? *Business Horizons* 9: 23–24.
Mortimer, J.T. 1980. Occupational-family linkages as perceived by men in the early stages of professional and managerial careers. *Research in the Interweave of Social Roles* 1: 99–117.
Myers, I.B. 1962. *Manual for the Myers-Briggs type indicator*. Princeton: Educational Testing Service.
Nichols, M.L., and V.E. Day. 1982. A comparison of moral reasoning of groups and individuals on the "defining issues test". *Academy of Management Journal* 25: 201–208.
Oldenquist, A.G., and E.E. Slowter. 1979. Proposed: A single code of ethics for all engineers. *Professional Engineer* 49: 8–11.
Pavlovic, K.R. 1980. Autonomy and obligation: Is there an engineering ethics? In *Ethical problems in engineering: Readings*, vol. 1, 2nd ed, ed. A. Flores, 89–93. Troy: Rensselaer Polytechnic Institute.
Peterson, D.R., H.C. Quay, and T.L. Tiffany. 1961. Personality factors related to juvenile delinquency. *Child Development* 32: 355–372.
Pratt, J. 1980. The effects of personality on a subject's information process: A comment. *The Accounting Review* 55: 501–506.
Rest, J.R. 1976. *Moral judgment related to sample characteristics* (Final report to NIMH), Minneapolis: University of Minnesota.
Rotter, J.B. 1966. Generalized expectancies for internal versus external control of reinforcement. *Psychological Monographs 80* (Whole no. 609).
Schwartz, H., and S.M. Davis. 1981. Matching corporate culture and business strategy. *Organizational Dynamics* 10: 36.
Senger, J. 1971. Managers' perceptions of subordinates' competence as a function of personal value orientations. *Academy of Management Journal* 14: 415–423.
Simon, H. 1960. *The new science of management*. New York: Harper and Row.
Simon, H. 1976. *Administrative behavior: A study of decision making processes in administrative organization*. New York: Free Press.

Staff. 1979. Gifts to buyers. *Purchasing*, April 11, 19.

Steiner, G., J. Miner, and E. Gray. 1982. *Management policy and strategy*. New York: MacMillan.

Taggart, W., and D. Robey. 1981. Mind and managers: On the dual nature of human information processing and management. *Academy of Management Review* 6: 187–195.

Taylor, R.E. 1984. White collar crime getting less attention. *The Wall Street Journal* 203(23): 27.

Unger, S.H. 1982. *Controlling technology: Ethics and the responsible engineer*. New York: Holt, Rinehart and Winston.

Vandivier, K. 1980. Engineers, ethics, and economics. In *Ethical problems in engineering: Cases*, vol. 2, 2nd ed, ed. R. Baum, 136–138. Troy: Rensselaer Polytechnic Institute.

Ward, L., and J.P. Wilson. 1980. Motivation and moral development as determinants of behavioral acquiescence and moral action. *Journal of Social Psychology* 112: 271–286.

Wheelen, L., and J.D. Hunger. 1984. *Strategy management*. Reading: Addison-Wesley.

Witkin, H.A., P.K. Oltman, R.K. Ruskin, and S.A. Karp. 1971. *The embedded figures test*. Palo Alto: Consulting Psychologist Press.

Zmud, R.W. 1979. Individual differences in MIS success: A review of the empirical literature. *Management Science* 25: 966–979.

Chapter 6
The Effects of Culture on Ethical Decision-Making: An Application of Hofstede's Typology

Scott J. Vitell, Saviour L. Nwachukwu, and James H. Barnes[†]

Over the last decade, the topic of social responsibility and ethics in business has been of significant interest to scholars. However, few studies have been cross-cultural in content, even though existing theoretical models recognize the importance of this factor (e.g., Ferrell and Gresham 1985; Hunt and Vitell 1986, 1992). Bartels (1967) was one of the first to note the importance of the role of culture in ethics decision-making identifying cultural factors such as values and customs, religion, law, respect for individuality, national identity and loyalty (or patriotism), and rights of property as influencing ethics. In their general theory of marketing ethics, Hunt and Vitell (1986, 1992) incorporated cultural norms as one of the constructs that affect one's perceptions in ethical situations. The influence of cultural and group norms/values on individual behavior was also noted by Ferrell and Gresham (1985) in their contingency framework for understanding ethical decision making within a business context. However, neither these theoretical conceptualizations of ethical decision-making nor subsequent empirical investigations tell us *how* culture influences ethics and ethical decision-making.

In the present paper, the authors provide a conceptual framework as to *how* culture influences one's perceptions and ethical decision-making in business. In order to accomplish this task, the authors have adopted the cultural typology proposed by Hofstede (1979, 1980, 1983, 1984) regarding the differences between countries based on certain cultural dimensions. With respect to business ethics, the authors have adopted the revised model proposed by Hunt and Vitell (1992). Our overall objective is to develop research propositions that involve the relationship

S.J. Vitell (✉)
Department of Marketing, School of Business Administration,
University of Mississippi, University, MS 38677, USA
e-mail: svitell@bus.olemiss.edu

S.L. Nwachukwu
Department of Marketing and Management, Southern University,
New Orleans, Louisiana 70126, USA

J.H. Barnes (†Deceased)

A.C. Michalos and D.C. Poff (eds.), *Citation Classics from the Journal of Business Ethics*, Advances in Business Ethics Research 2,
DOI 10.1007/978-94-007-4126-3_6,

between the cultural component and other elements of decision-making in situations involving ethical issues.

The Cultural Typology

Hofstede argues that societies differ along four major cultural dimensions: power distance, individualism, masculinity, and uncertainty avoidance. This cultural typology is based on the findings of several studies (i.e., Hofstede 1979, 1980, 1983, 1984). According to Hofstede (1984), power distance is the extent to which the less powerful individuals in a society accept inequality in power and consider it as normal. Although inequality exists within every culture, the degree to which it is accepted varies from culture to culture. Hofstede defines individualist cultures as being those societies where individuals are primarily concerned with their own interests and the interests of their immediate family. Collectivist cultures, in contrast, assume that individuals belong to one or more "in-groups" (e.g., extended family, clan, or other organization) from which they cannot detach themselves. The "in-group" protects the interest of its members, and in turn expects their permanent loyalty.

Masculinity, according to Hofstede, is the extent to which individuals in a society expect men (as opposed to women) to be assertive, ambitious, competitive, to strive for material success, and to respect whatever is big, strong and fast. Masculine cultures expect women to serve and to care for the non-material quality of life, for children, and for the weak. Feminine cultures, on the other hand, define relatively overlapping social roles for both sexes with neither men nor women needing to be overly ambitious or competitive. Masculine cultures value material success and assertiveness while feminine cultures value qualities such as interpersonal relationships and concern for the weak.

Uncertainty avoidance is defined as the extent to which individuals within a culture are made nervous by situations that are unstructured, unclear, or unpredictable, and the extent to which these individuals attempt to avoid such situations by adopting strict codes of behavior and a belief in absolute truth. Cultures with strong uncertainty avoidance are active, aggressive, emotional, security-seeking, and intolerant. On the other hand, cultures with weak uncertainty avoidance are contemplative, less aggressive, unemotional, accepting of personal risk, and relatively tolerant.

All four of these cultural dimensions relate to ethics in the sense that they may influence the individual's perception of ethical situations, norms for behavior, and ethical judgments, among other factors. The implication is that as societies differ with regards to these cultural dimensions so will the various components of their ethical decision-making differ. The specific manner in which these cultural dimensions may influence ethical decision-making is discussed later, however.

A Framework for Marketing Ethics Decision-Making

In the field of moral philosophy, ethical theories have generally been classified into two major types, deontological and teleological (e.g., Beauchamp and Bowie 1979;

Murphy and Laczniak 1981). The major difference between these two theories is that, whereas deontological theories focus on the specific actions or behaviors of an individual, teleological theories focus on the consequences of those actions or behaviors (Hunt and Vitell 1986). In other words, deontological theories are concerned with the inherent righteousness of a behavior or action, whereas teleological theories are concerned with the amount of good or bad embodied in the consequences of the behavior or action.

In their general theory of marketing ethics, Hunt and Vitell proposed that "cultural norms affect perceived ethical situations, perceived alternatives, perceived consequences, deontological norms, probabilities of consequences, desirability of consequences, and importance of stakeholders" (1986, p. 10). However, they did not specify *how* cultural norms affect ethical decision-making. The revised Hunt-Vitell (1992) general theory of ethics does not specify *how* cultural norms influence ethical decision-making either. Nor have empirical tests of the theory examined the influence of cultural norms on ethical decision-making (e.g., Vitell and Hunt 1990; Mayo and Marks 1990; Singhapakdi and Vitell 1990, 1991).

The primary task of this paper is the conceptualization of the impact of culture on the deontological and teleological evaluation of business practitioners. For example, with respect to one's deontological evaluation, how important are factors such as organizational norms, industry norms, professional norms and personal experiences? Likewise, with respect to one's teleological evaluation, how important are the various stakeholder groups such as the individual, his/her family, the organization, or other social units to which the individual is a member? Several propositions are formulated by applying Hofstede's cultural typology to the proposals of the revised general theory of marketing ethics (Hunt and Vitell 1986, 1992). While Hunt and Vitell are specifically concerned with marketing ethics, their model is easily generalized to apply to all business situations. Figure 6.1 depicts their revised theory of ethics.

Propositions

Individualism/Collectivism Dimension

Based on Hofstede's conceptualization of the individualism/collectivism construct, it is suggested that business practitioners from countries that are low on individualism would tend to be more susceptible to group and intraorganizational influence than their counterparts from countries that are high on this construct. Since individuals in these "collectivism" societies cannot easily distance themselves from the various groups to which they belong (including industry, professional and business groups) they will most likely be influenced by the norms of these groups. According to Hofstede, these groups protect the interests of their members, but in turn expect permanent loyalty (i.e., adherence to group norms). However, persons from more "individualist" societies, who are more concerned with their own self-interest, will tend to be influenced less by group norms.

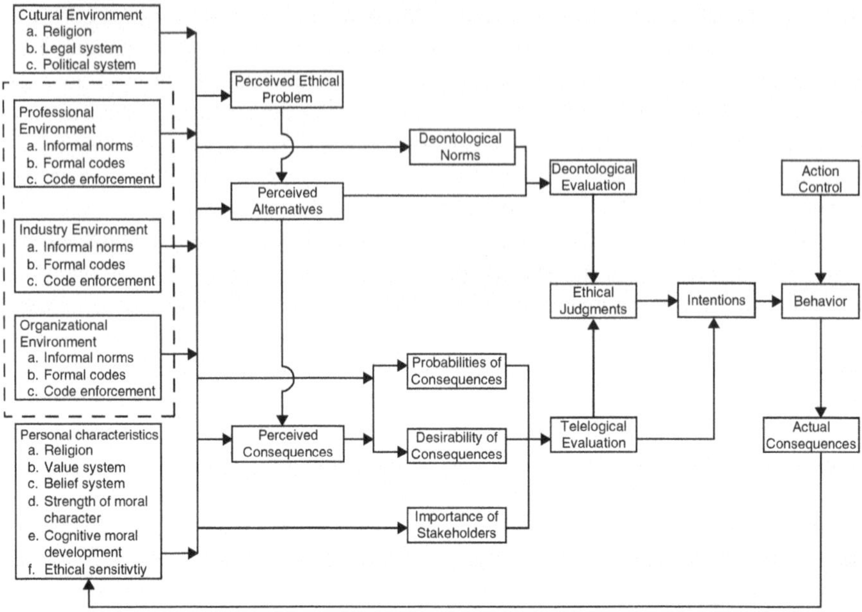

Fig. 6.1 Hunt-Vitell theory of ethics (Source: Hunt and Vitell 1992 revised from Hunt and Vitell 1986). The portion of the model outside the *dashed lines* constitutes the general theory. The portion inside the *dashed lines* individuates the general model for professional and managerial contexts

According to Hofstede's examination of various cultures and regions, Japan is characterized as low on individualism and high on collectivism, whereas the United States is high on individualism and low on collectivism. In support of this characterization of the United States, Robin and Reidenbach (1987) noted that the myriad of codes of ethics developed by organizations in the United States do not seem to have an effect on behavior. Additionally, Chonko and Hunt (1985) reported that codes of ethics are often developed and then put away; they are often not even introduced into the corporate culture. Consequently, their mere existence, without enforcement, is insufficient to affect ethical behavior. Based on the above rationale, and supporting empirical results, the following propositions were developed:

Proposition 1: *Business practitioners in countries that are high on individualism (i.e., the U.S. or Canada) will be less likely to take into consideration informal professional, industry and organizational norms when forming their own deontological norms than business practitioners in countries that are high on collectivism (i.e., Japan).*

Proposition 2: *Business practitioners in countries that are high on individualism (i.e., the U.S. or Canada) will be less likely to take into consideration formal professional, industry and organizational codes of ethics when forming their own deontological norms than business practitioners in countries that are high on collectivism (i.e., Japan).*

In a study conducted in the U.S. by Hegarty and Sims (1979), the personal desire for wealth was found to be positively related to unethical behavior. However, organizational profit goals, by themselves, did not have any significant influence on ethical behavior. Thus, U.S. marketers, appear more willing to behave unethically for personal gain than for corporate gain. On the other hand, in his work with respect to corporate culture, Ouchi (1981) noted that the typical Japanese organizational structure (the type Z organization) elicits significant organizational commitment from employees. Based on this and the preceeding arguments, the following propositions were formulated:

Proposition 3: *Business practitioners in countries that are high on individualism (i.e., the U.S. or Canada) will be likely to consider themselves as a more important stakeholder*[1] *than owners/stockholders and other employees.*

Proposition 4: *Business practitioners in countries that are high on collectivism (i.e., Japan) will be likely to consider the owners/stockholders and other employees as more important stakeholders than themselves.*

Power Distance Dimension

This dimension suggests that business practitioners in countries with a large power distance are more likely to accept the inequality in power and authority that exists in most organizations, and, thus, they are more likely to accord individuals in prominent positions undue reverence compared to business practitioners in countries with a small power distance. The concept of power distance has been incorporated in studies of business ethics in different forms. Ferrell et al. (1983) used differential association theory to describe ethical/unethical behavior. This theory assumes that behavior is learned through the process of interacting with persons who are a part of intimate personal groups (Sutherland and Cressey 1970) such as one's peers rather than one's superiors. While this would be true in any society, it would be most likely in one with a small power distance where less reverence is given to the opinions of one's superiors.

Ferrell and Gresham (1985) used both differential association theory as well as role-set theory to describe similar behavior patterns. A role-set refers to the relationship which focal persons have by virtue of their status in an organization. It is defined as the mixture of characteristics of significant others who form the role set, and may include their position and authority within the organization, as well as their perceived beliefs and behaviors (Ferrell and Gresham 1985).

These studies of the impact of differential association and the role-set constructs on behavior have reported that differential associations with peers (that is, the referent others closest to the focal person) were the strongest predictor of ethical/unethical behavior (Zey-Ferrell et al. 1979; Zey-Ferrell and Ferrell 1982). These findings can be interpreted to mean that, in countries such as the United States or Canada with a small or medium power distance, individuals look more to both their peers and informal norms than to their superiors and formal norms, for guidance on appropriate behavior. This does not mean that superiors do not influence ethical behavior; instead it simply means that in countries with a small distance their influence may be lessened.

However, in countries with a large power distance, superiors are expected to act autocratically without consulting subordinates. This would tend to indicate that a greater importance is given to both the cues of superiors and more formal norms in countries with a large power distance. Thus, the following propositions are presented:

Proposition 5: *Business practitioners in countries with a small power distance (i.e., the U.S. or Canada) are more likely than business practitioners in countries with a large power distance (i.e., France) to take their ethical cues from fellow employees.*

Proposition 6: *Business practitioners in countries with a large power distance (i.e., France) are more likely than business practitioners in countries with a small power distance (i.e., the U.S. or Canada) to take their ethical cues from superiors.*

Proposition 7: *Business practitioners in countries with a small power distance (i.e., the U.S. or Canada) are likely to consider informal professional, industry and organizational norms as more important than formal codes of ethics when forming their own deontological norms.*

Proposition 8: *Business practitioners in countries with a large power distance (i.e., France) are likely to consider formal professional, industry and organizational codes of ethics as more important than informal norms when forming their own deontological norms.*

Uncertainty Avoidance Dimension

Based on Hofstede's conceptualization of this dimension, it is suggested that business practitioners from societies that are strong on uncertainty avoidance are more likely to be intolerant of any deviations from group/organizational norms than their counterparts from countries that have weak uncertainty avoidance. As an example, the United States and Canada are characterized by Hofstede as having weak uncertainty avoidance, whereas Japan is characterized as strong on this dimension. This characterization suggests that business practitioners in Japan are more likely to be intolerant of any deviations from group/organizational norms than their North American counterparts. Since deviants are not expected to be tolerated, membership in most organizational groups in Japan is expected to be composed of mostly non-deviants in comparison to the United States or Canada.

This reasoning concurs with Ouchi's (1981) theory regarding organizational cultures in Japanese and American firms. Ouchi states that type Z organizations (i.e., Japanese firms) have a high degree of consistency in their internal cultures.

These firms involve intimate associations of people who are tied together through a variety of bonds. In contrast to a hierarchical organization (i.e., American firms) where there is a great deal of mistrust, the individual in the type Z organization naturally seeks to do that which is in the common good.

In a study of U.S. research firms, data subcontractors, and corporate research departments, Ferrell and Skinner (1988) reported that in the absence of formalized standards and codes of conduct, the acceptability of various activities and procedures (ethical or unethical) was ambiguous. Thus, business and marketing research practitioners in the U.S. may sometimes accept unethical behavior, especially where there is no formal standard or rule to guide that behavior. According to the theories of both Hofstede and Ouchi, this would be much less likely within a Japanese firm. Thus, the following propositions have been formulated:

Proposition 9: *Business practitioners in countries that are high in uncertainty avoidance (i.e., Japan) will be more likely to consider formal professional, industry and organizational codes of ethics when forming their own deontological norms than business practitioners in countries that are low in uncertainty avoidance (i.e., the U.S. or Canada).*

Proposition 10: *Business practitioners in countries that are high in uncertainty avoidance (i.e., Japan) will be less likely to perceive ethical problems*[2] *than business practitioners in countries that are low in uncertainty avoidance (i.e., the U.S. or Canada).*

Related to the concept of uncertainty avoidance is the belief that one can predict the actions of members of a social unit, such as a family or social group, of which one is a member. Societies that are strong in uncertainty avoidance and, therefore, intolerant of deviants, can be expected to have a high degree of accuracy in predicting the actions of individuals who share the membership of any social unit. Therefore, it is expected that for individuals to continue to be members of a social group, the consequences of their actions must be perceived by the membership to be desirable to the majority of the group members. For example, it is not uncommon for a Japanese CEO to relinquish his position if he perceives that his actions have had undesirable consequences for the firm. However, in the United States, this is seldom the case. Irrespective of the consequences of their actions for the firm, the typical U.S. CEO is likely to resign only when compelled to do so. Thus, we have developed the following propositions:

Proposition 11: *Business practitioners in countries with high uncertainty avoidance (i.e., Japan) will be more likely to perceive the negative consequences of their "questionable" actions than business practitioners in countries with low uncertainty avoidance (i.e., the U.S. or Canada).*

Proposition 12: *Business practitioners in countries with high uncertainty avoidance (i.e., Japan) will be likely to consider the owners/stockholders and other employees as more important stakeholders than themselves.*

Proposition 13: *Business practitioners in countries with low uncertainty avoidance (i.e., the U.S. or Canada) will be likely to consider themselves as more important stakeholders than the owners/stockholders and other employees.*

Masculinity/Femininity Dimension

The masculinity/femininity dimension suggests that there are some cultural environments that are more conducive to unethical conduct than others. Societies that are characterized as masculine encourage individuals, especially males, to be ambitious, competitive and to strive for material success. These factors may contribute significantly to one's engagement in unethical behavior.

Sweden, for example, is classified by Hofstede as a feminine culture, whereas the United States and Japan are classified as masculine cultures. This characterization implies that, compared to the United States and Japan, Sweden defines more overlapping social roles for both men and women, and neither gender needs to be overly ambitious or competitive. In fact, some practices, such as high pressure selling, that are seen as just good business in a "masculine" culture may be considered as unethical by many in a more "feminine" culture. Thus, decision-makers in some cultures (i.e., masculine) may not even perceive certain ethical problems because they are *not* defined by their culture as involving ethics. Given this characterization, the following propositions were formulated relative to the masculinity/femininity dimension:

Proposition 14: *Business practitioners (both males and females) in countries high in "masculinity" (i.e., the U.S. or Japan) will be less likely to perceive ethical problems than business practitioners (both males and females) in countries characterized as high in "femininity" (i.e., Sweden).*

Proposition 15: *Business practitioners (both males and females) in countries high in "masculinity" (i.e., the U.S. or Japan) will be less likely to be influenced by professional, industry and organizational codes of ethics than business practitioners (both males and females) in countries characterized as high in "femininity" (i.e., Sweden).*

Testing the Propositions

One of our objectives in developing this synthesis of business ethics and culture was to derive testable propositions. However, before these propositions can be tested, they must first be transformed into research hypotheses by adding specificity to them and by developing a taxonomy of moderator variables involving the other factors than can affect ethical decision-making in the workplace such as the industry environment, the organizational environment, the professional environment and personal characteristics.

Because of the nature of the propositions, the authors believe that survey procedures would be more appropriate than experimentation for testing them. Surveys used in empirical studies involving marketing ethics (e.g., Reidenbach et al. 1991; Mayo and Marks 1990; Singhapakdi and Vitell 1991) have been shown to be an efficient and practical method of examining various propositions. Irrespective of the survey instrument used, it is hoped that appropriate measures will be taken in translating the instrument into foreign languages, while at the same time retaining the original meanings of the items in the instruments (Dant and Barnes 1989).

Ideally, business practitioners from several countries would need to be included in any study so that the individual effects of the four different dimensions could be accurately measured. While we understand the difficulty in doing this, and the fact that several studies may actually be needed, we, nevertheless, consider it to be a worthwhile research endeavor.

Conclusions

Most studies on ethical issues in business, while focusing on moral philosophies, merely provide descriptive statistics about ethical beliefs and significant covariations of selected variables. In the context of theory building, there are a number of models that have been offered; however, few empirical tests of these models have been attempted and none have adequately examined the cultural dimension.

The objective of this paper has been to integrate the conceptual propositions of theory in business ethics with a typology of cultural dimensions. However, while the cultural dimensions were developed after extensive research involving several different countries and cultures, only parts, of the selected models of business ethics have been tested and supported.

While recognizing that there are many factors (e.g., cultural environment, industry environment, organizational environment, personal characteristics and professional environment) that can influence ethical decision-making, since the primary objective of this paper was to show how the different cultural dimensions impact on the ethical decision-making process across different societies, the propositions offered concern only the influence of culture. The propositions derived are sufficiently explicit so as to be used to generate empirically testable research hypotheses, and we offer them for that purpose.

These propositions, if tested, could help individual firms that are operating in multinational markets to identify some of the inherent differences in the behavior of their employees across different cultures. It might also help in identifying those management actions that will most likely result in "ethical" behavior on the part of employees, management actions that may differ from culture to culture. For example, management may wish to emphasize formal codes of ethics in some countries and more informal ones in other countries.

Notes

1. A specific individual or group of individuals perceived by the decision-maker to be affected by his/her decisions.
2. A problem or dilemma, facing the decision-maker, that is perceived by the decision-maker as involving an ethical issue.

References

Bartels, R. 1967. A model for ethics in marketing. *Journal of Marketing* 31: 20–26.

Beauchamp, T.L., and N.E. Bowie. 1979. *Ethical theory and business*. Englewood Cliffs: Prentice-Hall.

Chonko, L.B., and S.D. Hunt. 1985. Ethics and marketing management: An empirical examination. *Journal of Business Research* 13: 339–359.

Dant, R., and J.H. Barnes. 1989. Methodological concerns in cross-cultural research: Implications for economic development. In *Marketing and development: Toward broader dimensions, research in marketing supplement*, vol. 4, ed. E. Kumcu and A.F. Firat, 149–171. Greenwich: JAI Press.

Ferrell, O.C., and L.G. Gresham. 1985. A contingency framework for understanding ethical decision making in marketing. *Journal of Marketing* 49: 87–96.

Ferrell, O.C., and S.J. Skinner. 1988. Ethical behavior and bureaucratic structure in marketing research organizations. *Journal of Marketing Research* 25: 103–109.

Ferrell, O.C., M. Zey-Ferrell, and D. Krugman. 1983. A comparison of predictors of ethical and unethical behavior among corporate and agency advertising managers. *Journal of Macromarketing* 3: 19–27.

Hegarty, W.H., and H.P. Sims. 1979. Organizational philosophy, policies, and objectives related to unethical decision behavior: An laboratory experiment. *Journal of Applied Psychology* 64(3): 331–338.

Hofstede, G. 1979. Value systems in forty countries: Interpretation, validation, and consequences for theory. In *Cross-cultural contributions to psychology*, ed. L.H. Eckensberger, W.J. Lonner, and Y.H. Poortinga, 398–407. Lisse: Swets & Zeitlinger.

Hofstede, G. 1980. *Culture's consequences: International differences in work-related values*. Beverly Hills: Sage.

Hofstede, G. 1983. Dimensions of national culture in fifty countries and three regions. In *Expiscations in cross-cultural psychology*, ed. J.B. Deregowski, S. Dziurawiec, and R.C. Annios, 335–355. Lisse: Swets & Zeitlinger.

Hofstede, G. 1984. The cultural relativity of the quality of life concept. *Academy of Management Review* 9(3): 389–398.

Hunt, S.D., and S. Vitell. 1986. A general theory of marketing ethics. *Journal of Macromarketing* 8: 5–16.

Hunt, S.D., and S. Vitell. 1992. The general theory of marketing ethics: A retrospective and revision. In *Ethics in marketing*, ed. J. Quelch and C. Smith. Chicago: Richard D. Irwin.

Mayo, M.A., and L.J. Marks. 1990. An expirical investigation of a general theory of marketing ethics. *Journal of the Academy of Marketing Science* 18(2): 163–171.

Murphy, P., and G.R. Laczniak. 1981. Marketing ethics: A review with implications for managers, educators and researchers, *Review of Marketing*, 251–266.

Ouchi, W.G. 1981. *Theory* Z. Reading: Addison-Wesley.

Reidenbach, R.E., D.P. Robin, and L. Dawson. 1991. An application and extension of a multi-dimensional ethics scale to selected marketing practices and marketing groups. *Journal of the Academy of Marketing Science* 19(2): 83–92.

Robin, D.P., and R.E. Reidenbach. 1987. Social responsibility, ethics, and marketing strategy: Closing the gap between concept and application. *Journal of Marketing* 51: 44–58.

Singhapakdi, A., and S.J. Vitell. 1990. Marketing ethics: Factors influencing perceptions of ethical problems and alternatives. *Journal of Macromarketing* 10: 4–18.

Singhapakdi, A., and S.J. Vitell. 1991. Research note: Selected factors influencing marketers' deontological norms. *Journal of the Academy of Marketing Science* 9(1): 37–42.

Sutherland, E., and D.R. Cressey. 1970. *Principles of criminology*, 8th ed. Chicago: Lippincott.

Vitell, S.J., and S.D. Hunt. 1990. The general theory of marketing ethics: A partial test of the model. *Research in Marketing* 10: 237–265.

Zey-Ferrell, M., and O.C. Ferrell. 1982. Role-set configuration and opportunity as predictors of unethical behavior in organizations. *Human Relations* 35(7): 587–604.
Zey-Ferrell, M., K.M. Weaver, and O.C. Ferrell. 1979. Predicting unethical behavior among marketing practitioners. *Human Relations* 32: 557–569.

Chapter 7
Moral Reasoning and Business Ethics: Implications for Research, Education, and Management

Linda Klebe Treviño

During the last decade, a number of business ethics researchers have turned to moral psychology for theory, constructs, and measures that could be applied to social scientific research in the business ethics domain. The search for moral character, a stable personality trait that would predict immoral behavior began with the classic classroom cheating studies of Hartshorne and May (1928). However, because these studies seemed to demonstrate that immoral behavior was situation specific, the subject of moral character was neglected by psychologists for some time.

Beginning in 1958, Kohlberg revived interest in moral psychology. His theory of cognitive moral development (Kohlberg 1969) emphasized the cognitive basis of moral judgment and its relationship to moral action. A number of business ethics researchers have been guided by Kohlberg's (1969) cognitive moral development (CMD) theory. Although not without its critics (see Kohlberg et al. (1983) for a synopsis of and reply to criticisms), Kohlberg's CMD theory has become the most popular and tested theory of moral reasoning, and it remains among the most cited work in contemporary behavioral science (Endler et al. 1978). This paper will review CMDresearch, focusing in particular on related business ethics research. It will draw implications from this research for future business ethics research, for business ethics education, and for the management of ethical decision-making behavior in organizations.

L.K. Treviño (✉)
Smeal College of Business Administration, Pennsylvania State University,
University Park, PA 16802, USA
e-mail: LTreviño@psu.edu

A.C. Michalos and D.C. Poff (eds.), *Citation Classics from the Journal of Business Ethics*, Advances in Business Ethics Research 2,
DOI 10.1007/978-94-007-4126-3_7,

Moral Reasoning – Cognitive Moral Development

Rest (1986, p. 3) posed the question, "when a person is behaving morally, what must we suppose has happened psychologically to produce that behavior?" He proposed that, in such a situation, a person would perform at least four basic psychological processes: (1) interpret the situation in terms of the actions possible, and the effects of these actions on the self and others; (2) judge which course of action is morally right; (3) give priority to what is morally right over other considerations; (4) demonstrate the strength and skills to follow through on the intention to behave morally.

CMD theory focuses primarily on the cognitive processes involved in number two, judging what is morally right. The research has been concerned with discovering people's moral judgment strategies by presenting them with hypothetical moral dilemmas, and then asking them to judge what is right and wrong and to explain their justifications. Their explanations and justifications are then used to characterize how they reason about moral dilemmas. Theory and research have also linked moral judgment to moral action (Blasi 1980). How people think is related to what they do.

The groundwork for CMD theory was laid by Jean Piaget (1932) in his seminal study of moral development in children. Piaget challenged social influence views of morality (Durkheim 1925). He viewed morality as cognitive and developmental. Moral rules developed through the child's active role in constructing moral judgments as well as through interactions with the social environment. Piaget identified two separate moralities that characterize children from ages 6 through 12. The first type of morality, characteristic of young children, can be described as a morality of constraint or heteronomy (subject to another's law) where right is defined as obedience to authority. This morality is gradually replaced by a morality of cooperation or autonomy where children begin to comprehend rules separate from adult authority figures. Through peer interaction and cognitive development, the child eventually begins to see morality as a necessity of the social system, and rules are viewed as mutually beneficial. The child becomes more autonomous and less dependent on externally imposed rules.

Kohlberg (1969) built on Piaget's work with his longitudinal research on children and young adults. Kohlberg followed 58 American boys ranging from 10 to 16 years of age, interviewing them every 3 years over a 12 year period. His research, based upon the boys' open-ended responses to hypothetical moral dilemmas, delineated a structure of moral reasoning and its gradual transformation from middle childhood to adulthood. According to the theory, changes in moral reasoning result from cognitive disequilibrium that occurs when an individual perceives a contradiction between his or her moral reasoning level and the next higher one (Turiel 1969).

Over 20 years of research has provided considerable support for Kohlberg's model. In general, this research supports the major components of the model, that is: (1) moral judgment has a cognitive base; (2) stages represent qualitative differences in modes of thinking – hierarchical, integrated systems of thought, each representing a structured whole; (3) individuals develop through an invariant sequence of stages; (4) individuals prefer problem solution at the highest stage available to them (Kohlberg 1969).

Kohlberg's CMD framework provides three broad levels of CMD, each composed of two stages. Within each level, the second stage is a more advanced and organized form of the level's general perspective Individuals move forward through an invariant sequence of stages, each representing a qualitatively different mode of thought. The stages are considered to be structured wholes in the sense that an individual's moral reasoning is expected to form a coherent system that can best be described by one stage or by a combination of at most two adjacent stages. The stages are also hierarchical integrations, meaning that people comprehend reasoning at all stages below their own, but not more than one stage above their own. The basic structural element in the development of moral maturity is social perspective – or the view one has of his or her relationship to society and its moral rules and expectations. Although six stages are identified, few people reach the highest stages (Colby et al. 1983).

At level one (labeled the preconventional level), a person views rules as imposed and external to himself or herself. Moral decisions are explained and justified in terms of one's own hedonistic interests, and particularly in terms of rewards and punishments, and the exchange of favors. Stage one individuals are guided by obedience for its own sake. Punishment avoidance is the key consideration. At stage two, a marketplace orientation develops. Fairness is interpreted in terms of a "you scratch my back, I'll scratch yours" reciprocity.

At level two (the conventional level) the individual has internalized the shared moral norms of society or some segment like a family or peer group. What is right is explained in terms of living up to roles and what is expected by relevant others, fulfilling duties and obligations, and following rules and laws. Kohlberg's research placed most American adults at this conventional level. More, specifically, at stage three, good behavior is thought to be what pleases or helps others and what is approved by them. Motives and intentions also become important at this stage. The stage three individual is interested in interpersonal trust and social approval. At stage four, the individual's perspective broadens to consider the society of which s/he is a part. Fulfilling agreed upon duties becomes important. At this stage, moral judgments consider the rules and laws of social, legal, or religious systems that are designed to promote the common good.

The level three (postconventional) individual has gone beyond identification with others' expectations, rules, and laws. S/he sees beyond law for law and order's sake. More specifically, stage five individuals are aware of the relativism of personal values. The emphasis is still on laws and rules because they represent the social contract, but stage five thinking considers the possibility of changing the law for socially useful purposes. At stage six, the individual is guided by self-chosen ethical principles of justice and the rights of human beings. These principles may be consistent with society's expectations but they are not selected for that reason. Some values and rights must be upheld regardless of what others think. When laws and one's own principles conflict, one acts in accord with the principles. According to

Kohlberg, less than 20% of American adults reach principled level thinking. In his reformulation of moral stages, Kohlberg (Colby et al. 1983, p. 60) stated that stage six is not supported by the longitudinal data. "Stage 6 has disappeared as a commonly identifiable form of moral reasoning." The theoretical definition of stage six, derived from the writings of a very small sample of society's moral leaders, represents a terminal stage that very few individuals are expected to reach.

In a somewhat controversial stance, Kohlberg (1981) claimed that higher stage judgments are objectively "better" and therefore more desirable than lower stage judgments according to both cognitive and moral criteria. In terms of cognitive criteria, he argued that stage five judgments are more cognitively complex (more differentiated) and more cognitively inclusive (include lower stage judgments). In terms of moral criteria, he argued that stage five judgments "come closer to the formal criteria distinguishing moral from nonmoral judgments. These criteria have been elaborated by a tradition of 'formalist' moral philosophy running from Kant to contemporaries such as Hare, Frankena, Brandt, Rawis, and Raphael" (Kohlberg 1981, p. 191). Thus, Kohlberg found philosophers' justifications of moral reasoning to be consistent with his explanations of developmental movement to a principled thinking stage.

Measurement of Cognitive Moral Development

The ability to conduct solid social scientific research relies upon the availability of valid and reliable measurement instruments. During the 1970s CMD researchers developed a number of instruments to measure CMD, perhaps motivated by Kurtines and Grief's (1974) critical review of Kohlberg's original measurement methods. Kohlberg and colleagues (Colby et al. 1983) published their longitudinal study of moral judgment along with an in depth treatment of the measurement issue. Gibbs and colleagues (Gibbs and Widaman 1982; Gibbs et al. 1984; Basinger and Gibbs 1987) continue the development of measures that are easier to administer and score. At the same time, Rest (1979) developed a different approach to measuring CMD, the Defining Issues Test.

Standard Issue Scoring

Kohlberg's method of assessing subjects' CMD is termed standard issue scoring (Colby et al. 1983). Standard issue scoring evolved over a number of years from earlier approaches. It specifies stage criteria and defines the moral concepts that are used within each stage. The interview and its scoring are designed to "elicit a subject's: (1) construction of his/her own moral reasoning, (2) moral frame of reference or assumptions about right and wrong, and (3) the way these beliefs and assumptions are used to make and justify moral decisions" (Colby and Kohlberg 1987, p. 61). Standard hypothetical dilemmas are used to elicit subjects' reasoning. Kohlberg and colleagues (Colby et al. 1983) presented substantial evidence supporting the reliability and validity of the standard issue scoring method.

The most famous dilemma, known as the Heinz dilemma, takes place in Europe. It asks subjects to react to a situation where Heinz is the husband of a woman dying from a special kind of cancer. A very expensive drug might save her. However, Heinz has only half of the $4,000 he needs. The druggist will not sell it cheaper or let Heinz pay later. Heinz considers breaking into the drugstore to steal the drug for his wife. Through systematic analysis of responses to a series of 9–12 standardized probe questions, the standard issue scoring method elicits the cognitive organization or patterning of subjects' responses.

To score CMD, subjects' responses to these standard hypothetical moral dilemmas and standardized probe questions are first classified into two standard issue categories. For example, in the Heinz dilemma, responses are classified as upholding the life issue if they argue in favor of stealing the drug, and as upholding the law issue if they argue against stealing the drug. Responses are then further analyzed in terms of the content of the justification of the choice and the value content appealed to in the justification. Finally, formal stage structures are identified. The focus is on a subject's competence. Probe questions are designed to elicit the upper limits of the subjects' thinking (Colby and Kohlberg 1987; Kohlberg et al. 1983).

Although the validity and reliability of Kohlberg's standard issue scoring system has been criticized (Cortese 1984), the most serious limitation to its use in research may be the significant amount of time required to conduct lengthy interviews with each research subject, and the substantial training needed to prepare researchers to conduct interviews and score responses. These limitations have led to the development of measures that can be group administered and more objectively scored.

Sociomoral Reflection Measure

Gibbs and Widaman (1982) developed a non-interview, open-ended written measure called the sociomoral reflection measure (SRM). This measure retains the qualitative nature of interview responses, but answers are written in response to a printed open-ended questionnaire rather than being verbalized in an interview setting. Like the interview, the SRM is a production task. Subjects make decisions in response to hypothetical moral dilemmas, and then justify these decisions. Researchers can train themselves to administer and score the instrument and it can be administered in groups. The developers report psychometric properties comparable to those of the moral judgment interview and the standard issue scoring method. A correlation of 0.85 with the standard interview method was reported in an age-heterogeneous sample.

One benefit of these open-ended measures, oral or written, is that social desirability of responses is not considered to be a problem. According to CMD theory, subjects who are asked to spontaneously generate responses to hypothetical questions are cognitively incapable of generating responses at a higher level than their highest stage of moral development.

Sociomoral Reflection Objective Measure

The sociomoral reflection objective measure (SROM) reflects a further contribution to the assessment of moral reasoning. Based upon the SRM, Gibbs and colleagues (Gibbs et al. 1984) developed an objective, multiple-choice measure of reflective sociomoral reasoning. The measure is a group-administered recognition task that assesses the developmental status of justifications for moral decisions. It presents dilemmas adapted from Kohlberg's Moral Judgment Interview and a series of stage-significant response options representative of stage one through five. The measure can be completed in about 45 min. The developers reported acceptable reliability and validity of the measure for adults and most adolescents. In addition, there was no significant correlation with the Marlow-Crowne measure of social desirability. Finally, the SROM was found to have substantial concurrent validity with the SRM and Kohlberg's moral judgment interview, although scores on the recognition task were generally slightly higher than spontaneously produced responses.

Because this measure provided little advantage over the SRM in terms of administration time, Basinger and Gibbs (1987) conducted a study to determine whether a shortened version of the objective measure would achieve acceptable reliability and validity. The shortened form presents two moral dilemmas and a series of response options representative of stages one through four. Subjects indicate whether these options are "close" or "not close" to their own reasoning, and which option is closest to their own thinking. The short form takes 20 min less to administer and it is quicker to score. The shortened form evidenced acceptable validity and reliability for eleventh graders, but not for sixth graders or juvenile delinquents and there was no evidence that higher moral judgment scores reflected social desirability bias. Because it excludes stage five items, the SROM may be inappropriate for research with adults.

Defining Issues Test

The Defining Issues Test (DIT) (Rest 1979) is the most widely used assessment technique for studying moral judgment (Gibbs and Widaman 1982). Like the more recent work of Gibbs and colleagues (Gibbs et al. 1984; Basinger and Gibbs 1987), the DIT is a recognition task rather than a production task. It does not require the subject to produce responses to open-ended questions. Rather, it presents the subject with six hypothetical moral dilemmas and for each, a list of considerations for determining what is right. Subjects rank the four most important considerations, and these are used to create the P score. The measure shows how a subject construes a moral dilemma by indicating those issues the subject perceives as most important for decision making. A high P score indicates that the subjects give more importance to principled considerations. Because of the very different measurement approaches, scores on the DIT are not expected to be equivalent to scores on Kohlberg's open-ended test. Thus, it is considered to be inappropriate, based on the DIT, to make statements about what specific Kohlberg stage (i.e., one through six) a subject is in (Gibbs and Widaman 1982). However, based upon the P score, subjects can be characterized as more or less principled. In addition, Rest provides suggested cut-off scores that can be used to divide samples into groups. For example, subjects can be divided into principled and non-principled categories. The DIT measure has been used in over 500 studies and has been found to have favorable psychometric properties (Davison and Robbins 1978). In addition, Rest incorporated a check for socially desirable responses and appropriate test-taking set. For example, he recommended computation of the M score. The M score indicates to what extent the subject is choosing items that are lofty sounding but meaningless. Protocols with M scores of 8 or higher are eliminated from further analyses (Rest 1979).

A number of the measures, described above, have been used or adapted for business ethics research designed to understand managers' moral reasoning and moral behavior. This research is reviewed below.

Research on Cognitive Moral Development and Business Ethics

Adult Moral Reasoning

CMD research provides overwhelming evidence that moral reasoning scores increase with age. This research has been replicated many times and with many samples in the U.S. and abroad. In addition, the age trend has been demonstrated with Kohlberg's interview measurement techniques as well as with the more objective DIT measure (Rest 1983). However, more is known about CMD in children than in adults. Research has found that some subjects at lower stages of moral judgment (stages one to three) continued to develop toward stage four from ages 16–24. Other research has suggested that higher-stage subjects (stages four to six) became more consistently high stage (Kohlberg and Kramer 1969). Kohlberg argued that stages five and six (when it exists) are adult stages, typically not reached until the late twenties or beyond (Kohlberg and Turiel 1973).

Continuing adult development has been linked to higher education. The longitudinal research found significant positive correlations between adult CMD and educational level ranging from 0.54 to 0.69. In fact, years of formal education has been one of the most consistent correlates of CMD, although it is not clear what accounts for this relationship (Rest and Thoma 1985; Rest and Deemer 1986). Rest and Deemer (1986, p. 57) argued that education is a proxy variable for other kinds of life experience. They suggested that moral judgment accompanies "a growing awareness of the social world and one's place in it."

In recent theorizing about adult moral reasoning, Kohlberg and colleagues (Kohlberg et al. 1983) have distinguished between the notions of hard and soft stages. Four criteria are used to identify hard stages. Hard stages represent qualitatively different modes of thinking. They follow an invariant sequence, are structured wholes, and are hierarchically integrated. Unlike hard stages, soft stages do not depend on the unconscious emergence of new cognitive functions. Rather, they depend on more conscious "formal reflection" and the adult's focus on the self as a whole system of meaning in relation to an ethical philosophy and a more complete world view. Kohlberg and his colleagues concluded that soft stages may be more useful than hard stages for characterizing the hierarchical levels of positive development in adulthood. "The strict Piagetian stage construction may need to be abandoned in the study of adult development but the idea of soft stages of development in adulthood should not be" (Kohlberg et al. 1983, p. 40). Additional research will be required to more fully understand adult moral development.

Manager's Moral Reasoning

A number of researchers have proposed that Kohlberg's CMD stages can be used to characterize managers' moral reasoning in business ethics situations (Derry 1989; Manning 1981; Stratton et al. 1981; Treviño 1986; Weber 1990). For example, Manning (1981) hypothesized that CMD theory could be applied to explain and predict a manager's reasoning in a performance appraisal situation where a salespersons' productivity had decreased due to emotional problems. He proposed that a stage one manager would reason through the situation in terms of potential consequences for him/her (the manager) if discipline wasn't imposed. Alternatively, a stage four manager would be expected to take into account broader issues such as the salesperson's past loyalty.

Stratton et al. (1981) empirically tested a similar proposition. They used Kohlberg's six CMD stages to classify management students' responses in an ethical dilemma involving padding an expense account. They found that subjects who recommended padding the expense account were more likely to use a rationale categorized in the first three moral reasoning stages. Students who recommended not padding the account were much more likely to use higher level arguments.

Recent theory and research suggest that moral reasoning may vary depending upon the context. Higgins et al. (1984) argued that individuals' moral judgments operate within a range of moral development stages. Because situational cues are salient in real situations, moral judgments in these situations can be expected to be lower than they are in hypothetical dilemma situations that are less personally involving. Treviño (1986) applied this argument to managers in business settings. She proposed that managers' moral reasoning level would be lower in actual work-related decision situations compared to the hypothetical non-work related dilemmas typical of Kohlberg's research. Weber's (1990) research supported this hypothesis in an interview study with 37 managers. Each manager was confronted with three ethical conflicts, one taking place outside of the business context and two within a corporate context. Based upon Kohlberg's standard issue scoring (Colby et al. 1983), Weber (1990) developed two hypothetical business dilemmas so that managers' moral reasoning in business dilemma situations could be compared to their reasoning in response to Kohlberg's Heinz dilemma. He also developed a reliable abbreviated adaptation of Kohlberg's standard issue scoring method. Weber (1990) found that conventional level (stages three and four) reasoning predominated in the business context dilemmas. Consistent with the hypothesis, the reasoning level in the two business-related conflicts was significantly lower than the reasoning level for the non-business dilemma.

The finding that managers use lower level moral reasoning to resolve business context dilemmas is consistent with an understanding of human behavior based upon cultural anthropology. Cultural anthropology has found that individuals play highly differentiated roles that allow them to accept different values, norms and behaviors in different life domains (e.g., work and home). This context-specificity allows human beings to cognitively organize their experience while limiting cognitive dissonance and felt contradiction (Barrett 1984; Treviño 1990). Given Weber's (1990) findings, this context-specificity notion may have important implications for our understanding of moral reasoning in organizations. Future research should delve further to understand these differences between managers' moral reasoning in business versus other settings. For example, managers may feel pressured to rely upon justifications that are consistent with the reward structure of the business organization rather than the highest stage available to them. Obedience to authority, conformity to the group, and maintenance of the status quo may be more salient considerations in the business organization setting, constraining and limiting the expression of managers' moral reasoning capacity.

In a study of managers that investigated the relationship between age, education, and CMD, Elm et al. (1990) found that older managers and those with longer tenure with the firm had lower moral reasoning scores, as measured by the DIT. This finding was not due to differences in educational level. The study found no significant relationship between education and moral reasoning level. Given the previous evidence for a strong relationship between age and CMD, and educational level and CMD, these findings must be considered cautiously. However, it is possible that in situations that constrain an individual's freedom to select and consider various moral points of view, moral reasoning may be retarded rather than facilitated. For example, if the business organizational context focuses the individual's attention on quantitative analysis of numbers rather than more qualitative moral issue considerations, or on obedience and conformity rather than broader issues of rights and justice, moral growth may not be supported.

Moral Reasoning and Gender

With more women in the work force, it becomes important to address the question of CMD and gender. Do men and women differ in terms of moral reasoning? And, if so, what implication, if any, does this difference hold for the business setting?

Carol Gilligan (1977) has become widely recognized for her criticism of Kohlberg's justice perspective on moral reasoning as it applies to women. Kohlberg developed his justice-based theory using an all-male longitudinal sample, but argued that the theory was applicable to both genders. Gilligan's interviews with women about their experiences of moral conflict in an abortion decision situation led her to claim that Kohlberg's justice perspective on moral reasoning was gender-biased and inadequate for capturing women's moral reasoning. She argued that Kohlberg's justice perspective places the self as moral agent against a background of social relationships. Judgments about the conflicting claims of self and others are made against a standard of equality. Alternatively, in Gilligan's proposed "care" perspective that she argued is more likely to be used by women, relationships become the focus. For example, the public abortion debate centers on a justice perspective. Claims of the fetus and the pregnant woman are either balanced or placed in opposition in terms of rights and respect for individuals. However, when framed as a problem of care, the focus shifts to questions of the connection between the women and the fetus and whether it is caring or careless to end the connection (Gilligan and Attanucci 1988).

Gilligan and Attanucci (1988) summarized two studies in which they conducted interviews to determine whether men and women differ in terms of the moral concerns they raise when discussing actual moral conflicts in their lives. Interview data was scored in terms of the most frequent mode of moral reasoning, care only or justice only. One study of 11 women and 10 men matched for high levels of education and professional occupations supported the idea that men are more likely to raise justice concerns and women are more likely to raise care concerns. However, a second study of medical students did not support the hypothesized relationship between gender and moral orientation. The moral reasoning of medical students, both men and women, seemed to be strongly influenced by the powerful cultural norms of medical practice.

Reporting on DIT-related research, Rest (1986) reported that sex differences on the DIT are trivial, and that when they exist, females score higher. Sex differences explain less than one-half of 1% of the variance in DIT scores. Thus, he argued that Gilligan's view regarding gender differences is not at all supported by DIT-based research (Rest et al. 1986).

Derry (1987, 1989) conducted a study of business managers based upon Gilligan's work. She hypothesized that male and female business managers would differ in moral reasoning – that females would voice a morality of care more frequently and men would more frequently voice a morality of justice. She interviewed first level managers ranging in age from 32 to 62. Her findings did not support the gender difference hypothesis. She found no significant differences in the moral reasoning of men and women managers. In fact, all but one of the managers who described a moral conflict at work used primarily rights reasoning.

Derry concluded that the gender differences that have been found in other research may be context specific and do not carry over into careers and organizational cultures where men and women are trained to think in certain ways. Women business managers are simply using the reasoning processes that are consistent with their organizational roles and responsibilities and that they believe will be rewarded in the business context. Like Weber's (1990) work, this research suggests that the norms and roles of the business context may have a powerful influence on managers' moral reasoning. And, consistent with the findings for medical students (Gilligan and Attanucci 1988), these norms and roles appear to similarly influence men and women.

Moral Reasoning and Culture

CMD theory argues that moral judgment development is universal. Human beings follow a similar developmental course in terms of how they judge right and wrong in moral dilemma situations. The underlying conceptions and categories are proposed to be common across all human cultures. Snarey (1985) conducted a literature review pertaining to the cross cultural research. He reviewed 44 studies conducted in 26 cultural areas. Forty-four percent of the samples represented non-European populations that have been influenced by the West (e.g., India, Japan). Thirty-three percent included tribal or village folk populations. Many of the samples included adults. Based upon the evidence provided in these studies, Snarey concluded that the cross-cultural research supports the invariant sequence proposition. The full range of stages was represented in the data. Stages one to four were universally in evidence. Stage skipping and stage regressions were rarely found. Although stage five was rare, it was evident in approximately two-thirds of the populations that included subjects aged 18–60 and older. Nearly all samples from urban cultures or middle-class populations exhibited some principled reasoning.

Rest et al. (1986) examined research findings from 20 DIT-based studies conducted in 15 cultures. In their review, they found that the similarities between cultures were much more striking than the differences, suggesting additional support for the universality claim, as well as support for the portability of the DIT for cross-cultural research.

Cross-cultural research in business ethics could benefit from the application of Kohlberg's CMD model. This research would provide a common theory base for comparing managerial cognitions in ethical dilemma situations. Stage definitions could be used as a common basis for categorizing and explaining how managers from different cultures think about ethical dilemmas in their work. The emphasis, as always with Kohlberg's model, would be on managers' thought processes, their rationales, justifications, and explanations for why a particular action is right or wrong. For this research to be conducted effectively, work will be required to adapt CMD measures to the languages and cultures to be studied (Treviño 1988).

CMD theory would also support the development of hypotheses and empirical research to investigate the influence of culture on the moral reasoning of managers. For example, Kohlberg (1969) argued that development derives in part from participation in decision making and role-taking opportunities. Therefore, cultures oriented toward group decision making, active involvement of the individual, and mutual responsibility, may contribute to moral judgment development (Treviño 1988).

Managers' Moral Reasoning and Behavior

Although moral cognition is an important and interesting field of study in itself, the question of a possible link between cognition and behavior has been the focus of much CMD research. The proverb, "As a man thinketh, so is he" suggests that thoughts and behaviors are related. However, others have argued that thoughts and words have little relationship to deeds. Mischel and Mischel (1976, p. 107) argued that "history is replete with atrocities that were justified by involving the highest principles ... in the name of justice, of the common welfare, of universal ethics, and of God, millions of people have been killed and whole cultures destroyed." Despite this skepticism, Kohlberg (1969) argued that cognition and action should be related due to the individual's drive to achieve consistency between thought and behavior. Thus, he proposed that higher stages of CMD should be related to more ethical behavior.

The empirical research on the relationship between moral judgment and behavior supports a moderate relationship between the two. For example, CMD has been found to be significantly related to cheating behavior (Grimm et al. 1968; Malinowski 1979; Malinowski and Smith 1985), resistance to pressure from an authority figure (Kohlberg 1969), helping behavior (Kohlberg and Candee 1984), and whistleblowing (Brabeck 1984). In a critical review of the moral cognition/moral action empirical literature, Blasi (1980) concluded that: (1) considerable support exists for a moderate statistical relationship between moral reasoning and moral action; (2) moral reasoning is important, but does not fully explain delinquent behavior; (3) weaker support exists for the relationship between CMD and stage honesty or altruism; (4) less support exists for the hypothesis that principled individuals are more likely to resist social conformity pressures in moral dilemma situations.

More recently, Thoma (1985) reviewed about 30 studies based upon the DIT measure. The behaviors studied varied broadly from naturally occurring phenomena such as delinquency to laboratory simulations of behavior such as cheating. Similar to Blasi's (1980) finding, the link between moral judgment and behavior was pervasive, but moderate, with correlations of about 0.30. In a particularly interesting finding, moral judgment, as measured by the DIT, was significantly related to the quality of medical interns' overall job performance (Candee 1985). Although it is arguable that moral judgment is more important to the physician's work than to other work roles, this research raises questions about the potential relationship between moral judgment and managerial performance or perhaps moral judgment and effective leadership. Words like integrity and values are frequently used to characterize effective business leaders. Empirical research will be required to investigate the potential relationship between CMD and leadership or management effectiveness.

Several research studies have demonstrated a significant relationship between moral reasoning level and behavior in business situations. For example, Vecchio (1981) hypothesized and found that CMD level moderated inequity resolution. In overpayment conditions, individuals higher in CMD were more likely to maximize work performance quality and minimize quantity. In addition, in two in-basket decision-making studies, Treviño and colleagues (Treviño et al. 1985; Treviño and Youngblood 1990) found that moral reasoning level, as measured by the DIT, was significantly related to ethical decision behavior. More principled subjects made significantly more ethical decisions. Similarly, Ponemon (1990) demonstrated that auditor underreporting was systematically related to the level of moral reasoning. Underreporting refers to the underreporting of chargeable time where auditors report fewer hours than they actually utilized to complete a task. In an experimental laboratory study of 88 auditors from a national public accounting firm, those with lower DIT scores underreported most severely.

Given support for the moderate relationship between moral judgment and moral action, researchers have begun to consider additional variables that are proposed to mediate this relationship. Higgins et al. (1983) presented evidence regarding the importance of judgments of responsibility as potential mediators between judgments of what is right and moral action in a particular situation. Judgments of responsibility may serve as important mediators between moral judgment and action in actual job situations. Responsibility judgments may be influenced by role expectations. For example, within a work organization, professionals and individuals at higher hierarchical levels may be held to stricter moral standards (Hamilton and Sanders 1981). Thus, a physician is likely to feel personally responsible for the consequences of a medical decision. However, for lower level workers, responsibility may be more easily diffused to peers or superiors, making correspondence between moral thought and moral action less likely. The social psychological literature has documented this diffusion of responsibility phenomenon in bystander intervention studies. With diffusion of responsibility, if an individual is one of many observing an emergency, he feels his own responsibility for taking action lessened and he is less likely to help the victim (Darley and Latane 1968; Latane and Darley 1986). Similarly, this phenomenon may occur in organizational settings where someone else (generally a superior) is supposed to be responsible. Thus, organizations wishing to promote moral behavior that is consistent with moral reasoning may need to find managerial structures and systems that encourage individual managers to take personal responsibility for their decisions and actions (Treviño 1986, 1990; Turiel and Smetana 1984).

Influencing Moral Reasoning

Given the research support for a relationship between moral cognition and moral action, it is appropriate to ask whether moral reasoning can be influenced. The next sections will focus on research suggesting that moral judgments can be affected by the work itself, by training interventions, and by group decision-making and leadership.

The Work Itself

Moral reasoning is thought to be a distinct cognitive domain that can be influenced through interaction with one's environment. Thus, it is reasonable to suggest that an adult's work may influence the development of moral reasoning. Kohlberg and colleagues found that some adults continued to advance in moral reasoning after leaving formal schooling (Colby et al. 1983). They proposed that two characteristics of the work itself may play a role in the continuing development of moral reasoning: role taking opportunities and responsibility for the resolution of moral dilemmas. Role taking means taking account of the perspective of others. Thus, according to the theory, individuals whose work affords them the opportunity to hear and consider others' viewpoints, will be more likely to advance in moral reasoning as a result of their work. Similarly, individuals whose work requires them to be responsible for resolving moral conflicts (e.g., physicians) would be more likely to advance. Little research has been conducted to test these propositions. However, a study by Armstrong (1987) is suggestive. Armstrong compared the moral reasoning scores (as measured by the DIT) of practicing accountants with an average of 1 year of graduate education with the moral reasoning scores of college students, graduate students, and adults in general as reported in Rest's data. CPA respondents' scores were significantly lower than both college student scores and graduate student scores, suggesting that accountants' moral reasoning scores were more like those of adults in general. She concluded that accountants' college education may not have fostered moral growth. However, it is also possible that the work of accountants is in some way related to a loss or regression in moral growth. Longitudinal research will be required to test this possibility. Management researchers may wish to ask the question, does the work of business managers generally contribute to development in moral reasoning or not?

Training and Education

Many managers assume that any individual of good character should be able to function effectively, making the moral decisions required of a manager in today's complex business environment. However, Rest (1988, p. 24) argued that "to assume that any 20 year old of good general character can function ethically in professional situations is no more warranted than assuming that any logical 20 year old can function as a lawyer without special education." The basic disposition of good general character requires additional special education in the profession's unique problems and the approaches to solving them.

Thus, one potential practical approach to influencing moral reasoning is through CMD-based education and training interventions. The moral education literature suggests that moral education programs based upon moral development theory have succeeded in producing substantial gains in moral reasoning especially with participants in their twenties and thirties. These training programs are aimed at helping participants to think through moral controversy by raising hypothetical ethical dilemmas. The purpose of the training is to promote movement through moral reasoning stages by exposing participants to reasoning one stage higher than the one the participant generally uses. Theoretically, the discussion will promote internal cognitive conflict, leading the participant to question his or her own reasoning, and consider the next higher stage reasoning. This begins a restructuring of cognitive patterns and positive change (Rest 1988). These strategies have been tested and supported with children as well as adults in dental, medical, and business education settings (Boyd 1981–1982; Candee 1985; Goldman and Arbuthnot 1979; Penn and Collier 1985; Power et al. 1989). Many of these studies have demonstrated increases in moral judgment in a relatively concentrated period of time (Power et al. 1989). A meta-analytic review of over 50 DIT-based studies (Rest and Thoma 1986) included 12 studies with adult students. This review suggested that the most effective educational programs are those that involve dilemma discussions and those that last from 4–12 weeks. In addition, adult groups advanced more than younger groups. Future research is needed to investigate whether these advances that result from educational interventions bring about concomitant changes in behavior. Additional research will also be needed to determine whether educational interventions can influence other aspects of moral decision making such as the identification of a situation as a moral dilemma, a skill that has been overlooked in most moral education programs (Candee 1985).

Kohlberg and colleagues (Power et al. 1989) have recently addressed what they perceive to be some limitations of these moral education programs. First, most traditional moral education programs direct attention to hypothetical dilemmas rather than to real world problems. Second, although moral education programs have been shown to increase moral judgment scores, behavior is not likely to change until stage five, principled thinking (Blatt and Kohlberg 1975). At lower stages, the influence of the social context is extremely important. An underlying theoretical tenet of CMD theory argues that moral judgment development occurs through the interaction of the individual with his or her environment. Thus, Kohlberg proposed that moral development and behavior could be positively influenced via participation in “just communities,” schools that treat their students justly and encourage them to take an active role in making their community more just. These schools are governed democratically, holding weekly community meetings to discuss issues of moral concern. At these meetings, students are exposed to various points of view. Students also participate in the development of a social contract that defines the rights and responsibilities of community members. Finally, students and teachers have the same basic rights of freedom of expression, respect from others, and freedom from physical or verbal harm. The underlying assumption is that the institutional climate created in these just communities will provide the conditions that are necessary for moral growth. Studies comparing several just community high schools with comparison schools found the just community schools to be higher on a measure of moral culture. In addition, students from several of these schools scored higher on measures of individual CMD (Power et al. 1989).

Based upon this research, Higgins and Gordon (1985) have begun to develop a theory of the climate of work organizations. Their study of worker-owned companies suggests that informal educational processes in work organizations can be made more explicit and formal. In addition, they argue that educational experiences in the workplace should promote individual moral development. They have developed a method that allows workplace norms to be assessed in terms of CMD theory and suggest that it may be applicable to the many recent attempts at democratization of the workplace in the U.S.

This research has potential implications for business ethics education as well as for management. First, a typical discussion about how business ethics education should be conducted often resolves around the question of whether business ethics should be taught via a separate course or by integrating business ethics content across the curriculum, or perhaps whether cases or some other pedagogical approach should be used. The research reviewed above suggests that CMD based education has the potential to significantly influence moral reasoning and could be used in both higher education and corporate training contexts. In addition, Kohlberg's just community concept suggests that business school educators should be directing their attention to how the moral development of their students is affected through the "hidden curriculum," the norms and values that regulate social relationships in the school or educational program. Can business educators envision the development of just communities in business education programs? The creation of a just community requires faculty and administrators to willingly change their behavior, letting go of their positions of unquestioned authority and opening themselves to the challenges of a truly democratic community.

Group Decision Making and Group Leadership

The foregoing discussion and most of the research has emphasized moral reasoning at the individual level of analysis. However, in organizations, complex decision making is often accomplished in group settings. Recent research has addressed the influence of group processes and leadership on moral reasoning. For example, building on the work of Nichols and Day (1982), Dukerich et al. (1990) explored the impact of group discussion and group leadership on moral reasoning. In two studies, they found that, in general, individuals benefited from a consensus-oriented group discussion of DIT dilemmas. Individual moral reasoning scores on a DIT post-test were significantly higher than individual scores on the pre-test. However, additional analyses suggested that subjects who were initially lowest on moral reasoning advanced significantly while those who were highest actually had lower post-test scores. More research will be needed to determine if these changes in individual moral reasoning resulting from group discussion are transitory or permanent. Perhaps most interesting were the findings regarding the role of the group leader. When less principled individuals played the leadership role, group performance decreased. Groups with leaders higher in moral reasoning either improved or stayed the same. These research results suggest that managers interested in supporting ethical behavior in the organization may wish to encourage group decision making. However, it may also be important to influence group leadership. In the research, more principled individuals were not any more likely to emerge as leaders than were individuals lower in moral reasoning. Thus, organizations may wish to provide leadership training for these individuals and/or assign them to leadership positions in decision-making groups.

Conclusion

The study of ethical behavior has been guided by a number of paradigms and approaches, most prominent among them a normative approach rooted in philosophy and a descriptive/predictive approach rooted in the social sciences (Fleming 1987; Kahn 1990). This special issue has chosen to focus on the social scientific approaches. Kohlberg's work is somewhat unique in the sense that his theory represents something of an integration of these normative and descriptive/predictive approaches (Kohlberg 1981). Kohlberg's highest stages are thought to be more desirable in that they are consistent with moral philosophers' moral reasoning justifications (Kohlberg 1981). The normative and descriptive/predictive approaches can be expected to continue to exist side by side, each making its distinctive contribution to the study of business ethics.

This paper has focused on CMD theory and research, suggesting important implications for future theorizing and research in the area of business ethics. More CMD-based research will be required to understand how managers reason about ethical dilemmas in the work setting and how these reasoning processes influence their behavior in actual managerial situations. In particular, research is needed to understand whether and how the work itself and the work setting influence continuing adult moral development. The evidence thus far suggests that managerial work in business settings may not support moral reasoning at one's CMD capacity. Powerful organizational norms, reward systems, and structures may serve to constrain or even retard moral reasoning. This evidence may point future research in the direction of socialization theories of morality. These theories emphasize the external social system as the primary source of morality rather than the individual as in Kohlberg's work (Gibbs and Schnell 1985).

Clearly, CMD theory and research represent only one research stream within the descriptive/predictive approaches to studying business ethics. In order to more fully understand ethical behavior in an organizational context, it will likely be necessary to investigate additional influences on ethical behavior beyond CMD. For example, Rest (1986) proposed that the psychology of morality is comprised of four component processes of which moral judgment is only one. Future research should investigate other important processes such as the ability to recognize moral concerns in actual business decision-making situations and the ability to follow through on one's intentions (Rest 1986). Treviño (1986) proposed an interactionist model of ethical decision-making behavior in organizations. Treviño's model places CMD within the more complex context of other potentially important personality variables (e.g., locus of control, self-monitoring, ego strength) and situational influences (e.g., reward systems). Others have proposed ethical decision-making models that take into account values and the important role of significant others (Ferrell and Gresham 1985). Payne and Giacolone (1990) proposed the application of a number of social psychological approaches to understanding how ethical dilemmas are perceived. Research has just begun to test these more complex models (Treviño and Youngblood 1990). Further development and testing of these broader approaches will contribute to our understanding of moral judgment and behavior in organizations and will have implications for ethics education and the effective management of ethical behavior in business organizations.

References

Armstrong, M.B. 1987. Moral development and accounting education. *Journal of Accounting Education* 5: 27–43.

Barrett, R.A. 1984. *Culture and conduct: An excursion in anthropology*. Belmont: Wasworth.

Basinger, K.S., and J.C. Gibbs. 1987. Validation of the sociomoral reflection objective measure – short form. *Psychological Reports* 61: 139–146.

Blasi, A. 1980. Bridging moral cognition and moral action: A critical review of the literature. *Psychological Bulletin* 88: 1–45.

Blatt, M., and L. Kohlberg. 1975. The effects of classroom moral discussion upon children's moral development. *Journal of Moral Education* 4(2): 129–161.

Boyd, D.P. 1981–1982. Improving ethical awareness through the business and society curriculum. Business and Society *20–1* and *20–1*:27–31.

Brabeck, M. 1984. Ethical characteristics of whistle blowers. *Journal of Research in Personality* 18: 41–53.

Candee, D. 1985. Classical ethics and live patient simulations in the moral education of health care professionals. In *Moral education: Theory and application*, ed. M.W. Berkowitz and F. Oser, 297–320. Hillsdale: Erlbaum.

Colby, A., and L. Kohlberg. 1987. *The measurement of moral judgment: Theoretical foundations and research validations, and standard issue scoring manual*, vol. 1 and 2. Cambridge, MS: Cambridge University Press.

Colby, A., L. Kohlberg, J. Gibbs, and M. Lieberman. 1983. A longitudinal study of moral development. Monographs of the Society for Research in Child Development *48*(1, 2, Series # 200): 1–107.

Cortese, A. 1984. The internal consistency of moral reasoning: A multitrait-multimethod assessment. *The Journal of Psychology* 121(4): 373–386.

Darley, J.M., and B. Latane. 1968. Bystander intervention in emergencies: Diffusion of responsibility. *Journal of Personality and Social Psychology* 8: 377–383.

Davison, M.L., and S. Robbins. 1978. The reliability and validity of objective indices of moral development. *Applied Psychological Measurement* 2: 389–401.

Derry, R. 1987. Moral reasoning in work-related conflicts. In *Research in corporate social performance and policy*, vol. 9. Greenwich: JAI Press.

Derry, R. 1989. An empirical study of moral reasoning among managers. *Journal of Business Ethics* 8: 855–862.

Dukerich, J.M., M.L. Nichols, D.R. Elm, and D.A. Vollrath. 1990. Moral reasoning in groups: Leaders make a difference. *Human Relations* 43(5): 473–493.

Durkheim, E. 1925. *Moral education*. Paris: Libraire Felix Alcan (paperback reprint).

Elm, D., and M.L. Nichols. 1990. Influences on the moral reasoning of managers. Discussion paper # 139. Strategic Management Research Center, University of Minnesota.

Endler, N.S., J.P. Rushton, and H.L. Roediger. 1978. Productivity and scholarly impact. *American Psychologist* 33: 1064–1082.

Ferrell, O.C., and L.G. Gresham. 1985. A contingency framework for understanding ethical decision making in marketing. *Journal of Marketing* 49: 87–96.

Fleming, J.E. 1987. A survey and critique of business ethics research, 1986. *Research in Corporate Social Performance and Policy* 9: 1–23.

Gibbs, J.C., and S.V. Schnell. 1985. Moral development "versus" socialization. *American Psychologist* 40: 1071–1080.

Gibbs, J.C., and K.F. Widaman. 1982. *Social intelligence: Measuring the development of sociomoral reflection*. Englewood Cliffs: Prentice-Hall.

Gibbs, J., K.D. Arnold, R.L. Morgan, E.S. Schwartz, M.P. Gavaghan, and M.B. Tappan. 1984. Construction and validation of a multiple-choice measure of moral reasoning. *Child Development* 55: 527–536.

Gilligan, C. 1977. In a different voice: Women's conceptions of the self and morality. *Harvard Educational Review* 49: 431–446.

Gilligan, C., and J. Attanucci. 1988. Two moral orientations: Gender differences and similarities. *Merrill-Palmer Quarterly* 34(3): 223–237.

Goldman, S.A., and J. Arbuthnot. 1979. Teaching medical ethics: The cognitive developmental approach. *Journal of Medical Ethics* 5: 171–181.

Grimm, P.F., L. Kohlberg, and S.H. White. 1968. Some relationships between conscience and attentional processes. *Journal of Personality and Social Psychology* 8: 239–252.

Hamilton, V.L., and J. Sanders. 1981. The effect of roles and deeds on responsibility judgments: The normative structure of wrongdoing. *Social Psychological Quarterly* 44: 237–254.

Hartshorne, H., and M.S. May. 1928. *Studies in the nature of character*, Studies in S4-Control, vol. 1. New York: Macmillan.

Higgins, A., and F. Gordon. 1985. Work climate and socio-moral development in two worker-owned companies. In *Moral education: Theory and application*, ed. M.W. Berkowitz and F. Oser, 241–268. Hillsdale: Erlbaum.

Higgins, A., C. Power, and L. Kohlberg. 1984. The relationship of moral atmosphere to judgments of responsibility. In *Morality, moral behavior, and moral development*, ed. W.M. Kurtines and J.L. Gewirtz, 74–106. New York: Wiley.

Kahn, W.A. 1990. Toward an agenda for business ethics research. *Academy of Management Review* 15: 311–328.

Kohlberg, L. 1969. Stage and sequence: The cognitive-developmental approach to socialization. In *Handbook of socialization theory and research*, ed. D.A. Goslin. Chicago: Rand McNally.

Kohlberg, L. 1981. *Essays on moral development*, The Philosophy of Moral Development, vol. 1. San Francisco: Harper & Row.

Kohlberg, L., and D. Candee. 1984. The relationship of moral judgment to moral action. In *Morality, moral behavior and moral development*, ed. W.M. Kurtines and J.L. Gewirtz, 52–73. New York: Wiley.

Kohlberg, L., and R. Kramer. 1969. Continuities and discontinuities in childhood and adult moral development. *Human Development* 12: 93–120.

Kohlberg, L., and E. Turiel. 1973. *Moralization, the cognitive development approach*. New York: Holt, Rinehart, & Winston.

Kohlberg, L., C. Levine, and A. Hewer. 1983. *Moral stages: A current formulation and a response to critics*. Basel: Karger.

Kurtines, W., and E. Grief. 1974. The development of moral thought: Review and evaluation of Kohlberg's approach. *Psychological Bulletin* 81: 453–470.

Latane, B., and J. Darley. 1986. Group inhibition of bystander intervention in emergencies. *Journal of Personality and Social Psychology* 10: 215–221.

Malinowski, C. 1979. Cheating as a function of moral judgment and selected personality and situation variables. *Dissertation Abstracts International* 39: 5143B–5144B. University Microfilms No. 7908462.

Malinowski, C.I., and C.P. Smith. 1985. Moral reasoning and moral conduct: An investigation prompted by Kohlberg's theory. *Journal of Personality and Social Psychology* 49: 1016–1027.

Manning, F.V. 1981. *Managerial dilemmas and executive growth*. Reston: Reston.

Mischel, W., and H.N. Mischel. 1976. A cognitive social learning approach to morality and self-regulation. In *Moral development and behavior*, ed. T. Lickona, 84–107. New York: Holt, Rinehart & Winston.

Nichols, M.L., and V.E. Day. 1982. A comparison of moral reasoning of groups and individuals on the "defining issues test". *Academy of Management Journal* 25: 201–208.

Payne, S.L., and R.A. Giacolone. 1990. Social psychological approaches to the perception of ethical dilemmas. *Human Relations* 43: 649–665.

Penn, W.Y., and B.D. Collier. 1985. Current research in moral development as a decision support system. *Journal of Business Ethics* 4: 131–136.

Piaget, J. 1932. *The moral judgment of the child*. London: Kegan Paul.

Ponemon, L.A. 1990. Auditor underreporting and moral reasoning: An experimental lab study. Unpublished manuscript (SUNY-Albany).

Power, F.C., A. Higgins, and L. Kohlberg. 1989. *Lawrence Kohlberg's approach to moral education*. New York: Columbia University Press.

Rest, J. 1979. *Development in judging moral issues*. Minneapolis: University of Minnesota Press.

Rest, J. 1983. Morality. In *Manual of child psychology*, ed. P. Mussen, 556–629. New York: Wiley.

Rest, J. 1986. *Moral development: Advances in research and theory*. New York: Praeger.

Rest, J. 1988. Can ethics be taught in professional schools? The psychological research. *Easier Said than Done* (Winter).

Rest, J., and D. Deemer. 1986. Life experiences and developmental pathways. In *Moral development: Advances in research and theory*, ed. R. Rest, 28–58. New York: Praeger.

Rest, R., and S.J. Thoma. 1986. Educational programs and interventions. In *Moral development: Advances in research and theory*, ed. R. Rest. New York: Praeger.

Rest, R., S.J. Thoma, Y.L. Moon, and I. Getz. 1986. Moral judgment, behavior, decision making, and attitudes. In *Moral development: Advances in research and theory*. New York: Praeger.

Snarey, J.R. 1985. Cross-cultural universality of social-moral development: A critical review of Kohlbergian research. *Psychological Bulletin* 97: 202–232.

Stratton, W.E., W.R. Flynn, and G.A. Johnson. 1981. Moral development and decision making. A study of student ethics. *Journal of Enterprise Management* 3: 35–41.

Thoma, S.J. 1985. On improving the relationship between moral reasoning and external criteria: The utilizer/nonutilizer dimension. Unpublished doctoral dissertation, University of Minnesota, Minneapolis, Minnesota.

Treviño, L.K. 1986. Ethical decision making in organizations: A person-situation interactionist model. *Academy of Management Review* 11(3): 601–617.

Treviño, L.K. 1988. Reasoning about business ethics: A cross-cultural research perspective. *Proceedings of the Pan-Pacific Conference V; A Business Economic, and Technological Exchange*, Singapore.

Treviño, L.K. 1990. A cultural perspective on changing and developing organizational ethics. In *Research in organizational change and development*, vol. 4, ed. R.W. Woodman and W. Passmore, 194–230. Greenwich: JAI Press.

Treviño, L.K., and S.A. Youngblood. 1990. Bad apples in bad barrels: A causal analysis of ethical decision-making behavior. *Journal of Applied Psychology* 75(4): 378–385.

Treviño, L.K., C.D. Sutton, and R.W. Woodman. 1985. Effects of reinforcement contingencies and cognitive moral development on ethical decision making behavior: An experiment. Paper presented at the annual meeting of the academy of management, San Diego.

Turiel, E. 1969. Developmental processes in the child's moral thinking. In *Trends and issues in developmental psychology*, ed. P. Mussen, J. Langer, and M. Covington. New York: Holt, Rinehart, & Winston.

Turiel, E., and J.G. Smetana. 1984. Social knowledge and action: The coordination of domains. In *Morality, moral behavior, and moral development*, ed. W.M. Kurtines and J.L. Gewirtz, 261–280. New York: Wiley.

Vecchio, R.P. 1981. An individual difference interpretation of the conflicting predictions generated by equity theory and expectancy theory. *Journal of Applied Psychology* 66(4): 470–481.

Weber, J. 1990. Managers' moral reasoning: Assessing their responses to three moral dilemmas. *Human Relations* 43(7): 687–702.

Chapter 8
Organizational Dissidence: The Case of Whistle-Blowing*

Janet P. Near and Marcia P. Miceli

Consider an example of an increasingly common phenomenon: a disgruntled employee reports to the press that top management refuses to correct flaws in the construction or operation of its nuclear power facility. What is the appropriate response? The allegation could be ascribed to a 'sour grapes' attitude and discounted; the case might be ignored on the grounds that the flaws were minor 'technicalities', representing unimportant infractions that happen too frequently to be considered; or the complaint might be investigated and vigorously prosecuted, legally and/or organizationally.

Such cases recently have been dramatized in motion pictures, but they were based on incidents that actually occurred in America. All three responses were supported by different subgroups of the American public, reflecting a more general phenomenon: the unavailability of clear legal and organizational methods for responding to whistle-blowers.

Until recently the problem has been viewed exclusively from legal and policy perspectives. The courts have shown some inconsistency in their rulings on the rights of employees and employers in whistle-blowing cases (Ewing 1983; Malin 1983). Legislators have also considered the problem, with the result that a few states have passed in legislation to protect whistle-blowers (Malin 1983).

* The authors wish to thank H. Randolph Bobbitt and Jeffrey Ford for their comments on an earlier draft of this manuscript.

J.P. Near (✉)
Kelley School of Business, Indiana University, Bloomington, IN, USA
e-mail: near@indiana.edu

M.P. Miceli
McDonough School of Business, Georgetown University, Washington, D.C., USA

A.C. Michalos and D.C. Poff (eds.), *Citation Classics from the Journal of Business Ethics*, Advances in Business Ethics Research 2,
DOI 10.1007/978-94-007-4126-3_8, © Springer Science+Business Media B.V. 2013

The popular press has described famous cases, arguing both implicitly and explicitly for the development of public policy for defending responsible whistle-blowers (e.g., Ewing 1977; Nader et al. 1972; Peters and Branch 1972; Westin 1981).

Yet, the organizational implications have rarely been considered. There is a basic dilemma for any organization. The whistle-blower may provide valuable information helpful in improving organizational effectiveness; Clinard (1983) cites data showing that the prevalence of illegal activity in organizations is associated with declining organizational performance. At the same time, condoning the challenge of the organization's authority structure (specifically, the manager's right to make decisions) may push the organization into chaos and anarchy. Heller (1983) has documented the decline in authority of organizations and their leaders and its effects: reduced loyalty, commitment, and task performance. Thus, while some writers have encouraged organizations to consider the benefits of whistle-blowing (e.g., Ewing 1983), others have explored the threatening implications of whistle-blowing for organizations' authority structures and operations (e.g., Weinstein 1979).

If whistle-blowing is indeed on the rise, sparked by the consumer and civil rights movements and other factors (Ewing 1983; Westin 1981), then organization analysts require a theoretical framework for investigating the phenomenon (Farrell and Petersen 1982). The framework needs to be sufficiently specific as to allow predictions about whistle-blowing. The first step in developing such a framework is to recognize that whistle-blowing represents a process, rather than an event. We assume a process view, first defining the elements of the process and then suggesting a set of propositions for predicting the direction that the process will take, in a given organization. Our goal is to begin to develop a theoretical framework that will support systematic empirical exploration of an issue that is of increasing concern to organizations and managers alike. We know of no such framework of whistle-blowing *per se*. However, theories that have guided research in other areas within organizational behavior and organization theory are useful here. Since whistle-blowing involves the use of power in organizations and the actors' motivation to make whistle-blowing attempts, theories of power and dependency, and of motivation, are appropriate. Further, although there is little empirical research devoted exclusively to the whistle-blowing process, research on related topics, such as upward communication, is relevant in some cases. Therefore, we attempt to integrate this work into a preliminary model of the whistle-blowing process.

Defining Whistle-Blowing

If whistle-blowing is to be viewed as a process, then it is clear that it involves at least four elements: the whistle-blower, the whistle-blowing act or complaint, the party to whom the complaint is made, and the organization against which the complaint is lodged. Earlier definitions of whistle-blowing were consistent with regard to the characteristics of some but not all elements.

The Whistle-Blower

At least four defining characteristics of whistle-blowers may be observed. First, most authors, either implicitly or explicitly, have agreed that the whistle-blower must at some time be a member of the organization to which wrongdoing is ascribed (e.g., Farrell and Petersen 1982; Janis and Mann 1977; USMSPB 1981). However, the whistle-blower may leave the organization before blowing the whistle (Elliston 1982a). Second, the whistle-blower is an individual who lacks the authority to change the organization's activities; that is, the whistle-blower lacks a legitimate base of power for making the change and must rely on other informal bases of power (Elliston 1982a; Weinstein 1979). Third, it has been argued that the whistle-blower sometimes remains anonymous, as did Deep Throat of Watergate fame and as it currently encouraged through the establishment of 'hotlines' to the Inspectors General within many Federal agencies and departments. Anonymity may affect the nature of the whistle-blowing act and the credibility with which it is received; the ethical and practical implications of anonymous whistle-blowing are considered elsewhere (Elliston 1982a).

Fourth, although it has not been noted elsewhere, some whistle-blowers may occupy roles where such activity is prescribed. For example, internal auditors, omsbudsmen, and others in 'overseer' roles may be officially required to blow the whistle if they observe certain kinds of organizational wrongdoing, although unofficial pressure may be placed on them to remain silent. A recent case involved a Defense Department auditor who charged that he was involuntarily transferred after he reported price-fixing by a federal contractor for aircraft parts (Columbus Dispatch 1983). In this case, the whistle-blowing was officially role-prescribed. Other organization members occupy roles lacking such specific prescription, although they may feel accountable in a general sense for the activities of their organization. Thus, whistle-blowers are current or former organization members or persons whose actions are under the control of the organization, who lack authority to prevent or stop the organization's wrongdoing, whether or not they choose to remain anonymous in blowing the whistle and whether or not they occupy organizational roles which officially prescribe whistle-blowing activity when wrongdoing is observed.

The Whistle-Blowing Act

Blowing the whistle on an organization is an act of dissidence somewhat analogous to civil disobedience (Elliston 1982b). In Hirschman's (1970) terms, it represents expression of 'voice' by the dissident, as opposed to other methods by which dissidence might be expressed (e.g., exit from the organization). The whistle-blowing act has been variously construed as the giving of information concerning organizational activities that 'harm third parties' (Elliston 1982a) or "jeopardize the public interest" (Farrell and Petersen 1982). The activity itself may involve "misconduct, neglect or irresponsibility" (Farrell and Petersen 1982); "corrupt, socially harmful or illegal activity" (Janis and Mann 1977) or "wasteful activities" (USMSPB 1981). Obviously, the illegitimacy of organization activities is in the eye of the beholder, namely the whistle-blower. "Legitimacy", in the Weberian sense, refers to those activities which organizations have authority to commit. The basis of this authority is the acceptance by organization members and society that such organizational actions are appropriate (Weber 1947). If some segment of the organization members considers the activity illegitimate, then whistle-blowing may occur.

For example, some firms once required employees to buy their products, but this is no longer considered a legitimate organizational activity because employees refuse to accept the rule. Thus, although Weinstein (1979) describes whistle-blowing as an attempt to change the organization, this wide-ranging definition seems too general. When organization members attempt to change the organization's actions which are legitimate, this is not whistle-blowing. The concept of legitimacy (again in the Weberian sense) therefore seems critical, if organization members report 'wrongdoing' which they believe to be illegitimate acts outside the organization's purview to authority, then this is truly whistle-blowing. If the organization members simply provide suggestions to improve organization actions they dislike, this may represent some other form of dissidence.

We do not view whistle-blowing as an act of employee deviance. Whistle-blowing activities are not "unauthorized acts by employees which are intended to be detrimental to the formal organization", such as theft, embezzlement, restriction of output, etc. (Hollinger and Clark 1982). Consequently, the deviance literature (e.g., Hollinger and Clark 1982; Johnson and Douglas 1978) may be useful in determining why organizational wrongdoing – which may trigger whistle-blowing – occurs, but that is not the focus of this paper. Although whistle-blowing itself may be viewed as deviant in some organizations, this perception is not consistent or generalizable; for this reason, it is best not to consider whistle-blowing as deviant behavior, unless information to the contrary is provided in a specific case.

The Complaint Receiver

There is substantial disagreement concerning one of the elements of the whistle-blowing process, namely the nature of the person or agency who received the complaint. Most case studies (e.g., Nader et al. 1972; Perrucci et al. 1980; Weinstein 1979) focused on whistle-blowers who made their complaints public, by informing some person or agency external to the organization. It has been argued that this represents the only true case of whistle-blowing, because complaints that are voiced internally within the organization do not represent the same process (Farrell and Petersen 1982; Janis and Mann 1977). Yet, other authors (Elliston 1982a; Hirschman 1970; Nader et al. 1972; USMSPB 1981; Weinstein 1979; Westin 1981) have suggested that the complaint may be lodged internally, externally or some combination of the two; the process is largely the same so long as a complaint is made to someone other than or in addition to the immediate supervisor. That is, making the complaint through other than prescribed channels (i.e., the chain of command) represents going public, insofar as all groups outside the immediate work group are viewed as the public.

Conceptually, the act represents a challenge to the organization's authority structure and therefore threatens its basic mode of operation; it is this characteristic which makes the spectre of whistle-blowing anathema to organizations (Ewing 1983; Weinstein 1979) since the authority structure represents the basis for operation of any organization (Weber 1947). Empirically, however, there is a question here: as Kolarska and Aldrich (1980) point out, both the process and outcome of the use of "direct voice" (i.e., appealing within the organization) may be different from those involved in "indirect voice" (i.e., going outside the organization). Further, without empirical substantiation, we cannot be certain that reporting within the chain of command is entirely different from other reporting. One's reporting of suspicious organizational activity to anyone may be sufficiently threatening: it demonstrates that someone is aware of wrongdoing and intends to stop it. Possible differences and similarities can be discovered only if all types of whistle-blowers are investigated in future studies, since they have not been studied in the past.

The Organization

Any organization may be the target of a whistle-blowing attempt: large or small, public or private, young or old. The type of organization may affect its response to the attempt; preliminary indications are that public agencies respond somewhat differently than do private firms (Near et al. 1981). Perhaps more importantly, the nature of the organization's response may increase or decrease its own effectiveness. Ewing (1983) argues that those organizations that encourage valid whistle-blowing will gain additional information that may be used to improve their operations.

We, therefore, define whistle-blowing to be the disclosure by organization members (former or current) of illegal, immoral or illegitimate practices under the control of their employers, to persons or organizations that may be able to effect action. We next consider the steps involved in this process.

Steps in the Whistle-Blowing Process

The whistle-blowing event really represents a process comprised of four decisions made by the whistle-blower and the organization against which the complaint is lodged (Fig. 8.1). First, the observer must decide whether the activity observed is actually wrongful; that is, illegal, immoral or illegitimate. Observers are more likely to consider the activity wrongful if it conflicts with their own values or those stated by the organization and if the evidence concerning the activity is unambiguous.

Variables potentially affecting whistle-blowing and its outcomes			
Observer's Decision 1: Is the observed activity illegal, immoral or illegitimate?	Observer's Decision 2 (if the first question is answered affirmatively): Should the activity be reported?	Organization's Decision 1 (if the second question is answered affirmatively: Should the questioned activity be halted?	Organization's Decision 2 (if the second question is answered affirmatively): Should the whistle-blower be punished?
Variable potentially leading to affirmative decisions			
– Individual values opposing activity – Unambiguous evidence – Knowledge of conflict with organizational norms, values standards	– Serious impact of observed activity – Adequate knowledge of complaint channels – Observer's personal characteristics (e.g., youth, internal locus of control, high self-esteem, high initiative) – Availability of employment alternatives and/or emotional support – No alternative action available – Belief that whistle-blowing would be efficacious – Belief that whistle-blowing would result in few personal costs	– Alternatives to questioned activity – High perceived likelihood of substantial costs associated with inaction	– Low dependence upon the whistle-blower – Frivolous charge – No alternatives to questioned activity

Fig. 8.1 Variables potentially affecting whistle-blowing and its outcomes

Even under these circumstances, many observers do not blow the whistle. The decision to report the activity (Step 2) depends upon several factors. Whistle-blowers are likely to act only if the wrongdoing is perceived to be serious and if they know where to report it; further, they must believe that reporting it will be efficacious and that no alternative action would obtain the objective (i.e., discontinuation of wrongful action). Finally, whistle-blowers' personal situations must influence their decisions: whether they have alternative sources of financial and emotional support, what the costs will be to them personally, and whether their individual characteristics are such that they would be likely to take such a step.

Once the decision has been made to blow the whistle the organization must respond in some way. Conceivably it could do nothing; such inaction is likely to be perceived as very costly, however, and often it is costly in actuality. Given this problem the organization is confronted with the decision as to whether it should continue the allegedly wrongful action. It should be noted that there may be some dispute as to the legitimacy of the activity. What may appear illegitimate to some group of organization members, including the whistle-blower, may seem perfectly correct to the dominant coalition, because one of the two parties operates with a different set of decision rules or possesses additional information. Regardless of whether the whistle-blowing case in considered valid, the organization must take some action.

In the final step, the organization may decide to ignore the whistle-blower or to take steps to silence him. This may be quite legitimate, if the organization's dominant coalition believes the charge to be frivolous or invalid. It may reflect the inability of the organization to accomplish its objective through some other method, that is, no alternative action will accomplish the necessary ends. Finally, the organization may have relatively greater power over the whistle-blower (i.e., low dependence) so that the least costly strategy is to discredit her charge.

It should be noted that this whole cycle may be repeated in various forms. For example, some whistle-blowers make their complaint first within the organization (e.g., to an omsbudsman) and, if no suitable action is taken then begin the process again by going public. Other whistle-blowers may go through the cycle and, having felt that the organization's retaliation against them was illegal, they begin the process again, but now blowing the whistle on a different misdeed, that is, their alleged victimization. Although variations in the process are likely, we argue that every whistle-blowing incident must follow this sequence of steps, in this order. Since the steps obviously require the passage of time, this also is an important variable; if the legal system becomes involved, the time period during which these steps are played out may be lengthy indeed.

We now consider in greater detail the factors influencing these steps.

Factors Influencing the Whistle-Blowing Process and Its Outcomes

Several factors may influence whistle-blowing and its outcomes. These include motivation for action, the circumstances and individual characteristics affecting the power relations between the social actors.

The Motivation to Act

The observer of wrongdoing may be concerned with the potential efficacy of her actions, and with the level of expected retaliation. Efficacy has been called the perceived ability to influence (Gamson 1971). Farrell and Petersen (1982, p. 409) stated that "those who perceive their efficacy within the organization to be low will, in the long run, engage in little political behavior". Nader et al. (1972) proposed that observers who expect that they will suffer retaliation from management should be less likely to act than observers who do not. To understand the nature of these predictions, it is useful to draw upon motivation theory.

According to expectancy theorists (e.g., Vroom 1964), an individual's force to blow the whistle is a function of the perceived likelihood (expectancy) that outcomes such as managerial attention to the complaint, recognition of the whistle-blower's identify, public attention to the wrongdoing, etc., would follow action. Further, the evaluation of the outcomes is a function of the extent to which each is instrumental in achieving outcomes having desirable or undesirable consequences (valences) for the individual. These outcomes could include the desired changes in managerial practices, as well as experienced retaliation, support (or lack of it) from family, friends, co-workers, or other observers. If an individual expected that his blowing the whistle would be likely to result in a cessation of wrongdoing – which he highly desired – and that he would likely not experience retaliation – which he wished to avoid – he would be more likely to blow the whistle than if the outcomes were reversed as to probability of occurrence.

In a reinforcement theory framework (e.g., Skinner 1953), the wrongdoing serves as a discriminative stimulus for action when similar wrongdoing (stimuli) have been consistently followed by successful opposition in the past and have been consistently followed by positive managerial reaction. If wrongdoing is tolerated or encouraged, and if previous whistle-blowing attempts have been met with retaliation, the wrongdoing setting serves only to signal 'don't act'.

These simple examples are based on assumptions that (1) efficacy and retaliation are the major outcomes pertinent to whistle-blowing decisions, and (2) that there are no conflicts in environmental cues. The results of a survey conducted by the United States Merit Systems Protection Board (1981) indicate that the first assumption is probably realistic, at least for federal employees. About 80% of the respondents (a sample representing 65% of the 12,000 randomly selected employees of 15 departments and agencies) noted that efficacy was one of the two most important motivating factors, and about 40% of the respondents chose protection from retaliation as another.

However, the second assumption is probably less realistic. How do observers of wrongdoing make decisions when the cues for action signal efficacy coupled with retaliation – or, a lack of probable efficacy but no retaliation? Near and Jensen (1983) and Near et al. (1983) found that perceived efficacy and willingness to file a future complaint were closely related to perceived change in managerial attitudes, but not to retaliation. Potential efficacy therefore, seems to be more important. It may be that efficacy serves as a necessary condition for action; if the situational conditions suggest that whistle-blowing will not be effective, potential retaliation becomes irrelevant. If the observer believes a complaint will be successful in changing the wrongdoing, however, then the observer considers the likelihood and nature of expected retaliation. From the expectancy and reinforcement models of motivation, we see that these beliefs are a function of the organizational environment (including the power relationships among actors and actions) and the individuals's reinforcement histories or personality characteristics. Thus, those situational circumstances that suggest that whistle-blowing will be efficacious should generally evoke more whistle-blowing than circumstances that suggest otherwise. Such circumstances pertain to whether the objectionable viewed as act is clearly wrongful, whether the observer knows about efficious complaint channels, and the degree of seriousness in the alleged wrongdoing.

Circumstances Surroundings the Questionable Activity

An antecedent to whistle-blowing occurs either when (1) an act committed by at least one member – or outsider whose actions are under the control of the employer – is viewed by another member as wrongful; or, (2) outcomes perceived to be wrongful by one member result from inaction by another member or connected outsider. Without these antecedents, there is no discriminative stimulus for whistle-blowing. For the observer to be efficacious, he will need to assure that at least some powerful others will perceive an act as wrongful; if he blows the whistle on an act that no other would question, no change will be forthcoming. The whistle-blower – by definition – does not have the power to correct the perceived wrong himself. Therefore, the degree of clarity or ambiguity in the stimuli surrounding the triggering situation (hereinafter referred to as 'wrongdoing') may determine how an observer behaves in response to it. Observers may be reluctant to notify authorities if they have not directly observed the organization's wrongdoing, or if they are not sure that the action was wrong, according to personal, reference group, or societal standards.

Further, individuals who lack knowledge concerning appropriate channels of complaint may not act (Kolarska and Aldrich 1980). An awareness of complaint channels would increase the force to act, because the channel has been established as a vehicle for change. The publicized existence of a potential complaint recipient within the organization cues the observer that correction of wrongdoing may be desired by organizational leaders; hence, whistle-blowing would be efficacious. It may also convince the observer that she personally would not be personally punished. Knowledge of extra-organizational channels would stimulate whistle-blowing by signalling that society desired and would support legitimate whistle-blowing. However, to the extent that the observer distrusts the capacity of the complaint receiver to effect a change, the perceived efficacy will be reduced, as will the force to act. The degree of trust is a function of environmental events known to the observer, such as the experiences of other whistle-blowers, the backlog of complaints, the stated views of top management, and other events.

If whistle-blowing through the chain of command is viewed as communication of problem matters, Gaines' (1980) findings are relevant. She found that ambitious subordinates who trust their superiors exhibit more upward communication on problem matters than do other employees. Given that greater trust and confidence results when subordinates perceive the leader to be successful in upward interactions (Jones et al. 1975), we expect that greater trust would be associated with higher perceptions of efficacy and more use of internal channels of whistle-blowing.

The perceived seriousness of the wrongdoing observed may have an impact on whether it is reported within or outside the organization. In both cases, the degree of seriousness of the wrongdoing increases perceived efficacy, and hence the force to act, because serious acts are more likely to be perceived both by the observer and others as worthy of attention and potential change. Evidence of this linkage has been provided by Clinard (1983), whose interviews with executives revealed that they were more supportive of whistle-blowing when the acts were viewed as seriously wrong. Glausser (1982, p. 19) noted that "relevant and important messages, as perceived by the subordinate, tend to be communicated up the hierarchy more frequently than irrelevant and unimportant messages". An observer of wrongdoing considering 'going outside' may also perceive that public support may be withheld if the complaint is not serious and important. Thus, we expect few external complaints to involve minor or poorly substantiated incidents. Therefore,

Proposition 1: *Whistle-blowing is more likely to occur where: (a) observers of wrongdoing can verify that questionable activity has occurred; (b) it is viewed as clearly wrong by the observer; (c) there exist known complaint channels; and (d) it is seen as serious and/or recurring, than when none of these conditions is met.*

Proposition 2: *Observers will be more likely to blow the whistle when such action is expected to result in the desired change in managerial behavior (i.e., is efficacious), than when it is not.*

Proposition 3: *Observers will be more likely to blow the whistle when they believe that the wrongdoing they witness is of sufficient importance that they are prepared to endure retaliation.*

Proposition 4: *Organizations can modify the observer's stated beliefs and other behavior by encouraging or discouraging whistle-blowing in policies and actions; that is, observers of wrongdoing will be more likely to blow the whistle when the organization climate is conducive of dissidence.*

Individual Characteristics

Characteristics that individuals may bring to the organization affect the whistle-blower's decision to blow the whistle. One factor that would seem to be critically relevant to the individual's determining (1) that an act is wrong, and (2) that he should take action to correct it, is the individual's level of moral development (e.g., Kohlberg 1969). Dozier and Miceli (1984) have described evidence that suggests that individuals with higher levels of moral reasoning would see different activities as wrong than would other observers, and that they would be more likely to blow the whistle.

Personality factors, such as self-esteem, may play an important role (Farrell and Petersen 1982; Janis and Mann 1977). Observers who have low self-esteem may be apathetic about most organizational activities or may withdraw from situations; they would be less likely to blow the whistle than would persons with adequate self-esteem (Kolarska and Aldrich 1980). They may not perceive that they would be believed or that they could motivate others to bring about change. Thus, their perceptions of efficacy would be lower given the same environmental conditions. The individual who has an internal locus of control (LOC) may also blow the whistle when his or her external LOC counterpart would not. There are several reasons for this prediction. According to Rotter (1966), internal LOC individuals believe themselves to be largely in control of their outcomes, while the external LOC individuals believe that fate, luck, or chance determines much of what happens to them. Internal LOC's may see whistle-blowing as a step they must take to control an activity they cannot sanction, while external LOC's may see the questionable activity as controlled by powerful others, whom they cannot stop. Thus, internals' expectancies that they would be efficacious would be more pronounced than would externals. They may also downplay the likelihood of managerial retaliation, since they are less likely to attribute their fate to powerful others. Spector's (1982) recent review of studies of LOC's in organizational contexts revealed that externals may also be more compliant to authority, which suggests further that they would not blow the whistle. In a review of the literature on upward communication in organizations, Glausser (1982) proposed that internal LOC's would engage in more upward communication than would enternals. Thus, internal LOC's should be more likely to blow the whistle within the organization, i.e., to use 'direct voice', than would external LOC's.

Males may be more likely than females to blow the whistle; the reported case histories have been dominated by males. This may be a function of personality characteristics of the populations; males may, for a number of reasons, have higher self-esteem, a more internal locus of control, and/or more initiative than do females. Males may also have more opportunities to observe wrongdoing, because as a group they are more widely distributed across different job categories than are females, who tend still to be occupationally segregated. Finally, there is evidence (e.g., Costanzo and Shaw 1966) that females tend to conform more to a majority opinion than do males. If whistle-blowing is viewed as behavior deviating from majority opinion, then females should be less likely to blow the whistle than should males.

Proposition 5a: *Whistle-blowing is more likely to occur when observers of wrongdoing are male and have high self-esteem, an internal locus of control, and a high level of moral reasoning, than when they do not.*

Proposition 5b: *Internal LOC's will be more likely than external LOC's to attempt whistle-blowing through channels within the organization.*

Power Relations

Greater understanding of the whistle-blowing process requires an understanding of other variables affecting both (1) the motivation of an observer to blow the whistle and (2) the responses of powerful others to the complaint. A power-dependency framework provides a basis for understanding these variables.

Since whistle-blowing is a political action an organization member may take against an organization (Farrell and Petersen 1982), it should be described in the context of the power relations it entails. Power, according to Emerson (1962), may be defined as the inverse of dependency. Therefore, individuals or units are said to have power within their organizations when the organization depends on them (Hickson et al. 1971).

The whistle-blowing process always involves two sets of social actors: the organization members who blow(s) the whistle and the organization. Predictions as to how the process of whistle-blowing will play out must be based on the degree of dependency of each social actor on the other. The behavior of each social actor involved will vary as a function of dependence on the other (i.e., the whistle-blower on the organization and the organization on the whistle-blower) and the dependence on the situation (i.e., ability to change behavior or resist change in behavior). The whistle-blower's power in the situation depends on her relationship to the organization and the nature of change being suggested.

If a serious, clear case of wrongdoing were observed, the observer's actions would likely be affected by two factors, according to Emerson's (1962) theory of power (see also Pfeffer and Salancik 1978): the criticality of her dependence on the organization and the availability of alternative sources of support. Compliance to the organizations's objectives is thus not merely a function of moral development (e.g., Kohlberg 1969) or need to comply with authority (e.g., Milgram 1955) but rather a response to dependence on some other social actor.

Since the psychological and financial rewards employers provide are critical to nearly every employee (that is, they need these rewards to survive), we agree with Farrell and Petersen (1982) in that we expect whistle-blowing to occur with greater frequency when employment alternatives are perceived to be available and acceptable than when they are not. The whistle-blowers's perception of the employment opportunities is critical, since some may underestimate these opportunities and others may overestimate them.

Younger employees may be more likely than older employees to blow the whistle. Older employees tend to have a high personal investment of resources (such as time) in their organization and they may suspect they risk losing their "investments" and their future outcomes (Farrell and Petersen 1982). Senior employees' low turnover rate (Porter and Steers 1973) may attest to this.

However, younger employers with "lofty executive ambitions" (e.g., who wish to advance their careers in the organization) may be less likely to blow the whistle (Hacker 1975, p. 7). Glausser (1982, p. 8), citing Athanassiades (1973, 1974; see also Maier et al. 1963; O'Reilly 1978; Read 1962; Roberts and O'Reilly 1974), argued that employees who had "high mobility aspirations engage in more communication with their superiors, and are more precise and accurate about important task matters", than are other employees. However, he also reported (p. 9) that research conducted in non-organizational settings suggested that subordinates would "tend to withhold and/or distort information which is bad news for the superior". Since the superior may punish the subordinate who reports the bad news of perceived wrongdoing, by thwarting the subordinates' career progress, this second finding would appear to be particularly relevant for the 'fast track' junior employee. Such an employee is very powerless relative to the junior employee who does not have such aspirations and is willing to exit the organization.

Although some researchers have posited that observers who feel a great sense of loyalty or commitment to the organization may decide against whistle-blowing (Kolarska and Aldrich 1980), Farrell (1983) has found conflicting results on this point.

In some cases the employee may view whistle-blowing as disloyal because it involves criticism; in other cases the employee may believe that the dominant coalition does not know about the wrongdoing so that informing them may reflect greater loyalty than not informing them. Westin's (1981) earlier in-depth examination of case studies supported this point, as noted by Baker (1983). The great majority of corporate whistle-blowers considered themselves to be very loyal employees who tried to use 'direct voice' (internal whistle-blowing), were rebuffed and punished for this, and then used 'indirect voice' (external whistle-blowing). They believed initially that they were behaving in a loyal manner, helping their employers by calling top management's attention to practices that could eventually get the firm in trouble.

This research calls into question the nature and causes of loyalty. Loyalty itself is not a 'personality characteristic'; it is more properly viewed as a function of the interactions between employee and employer. Other employees may feel indebted to (and hence, relatively powerless in relation to) their employer. As suggested by equity theory (e.g., Adams 1963) indebtedness can arise from the employer's bestowing of rewards on employees to a greater extent than either they believed they deserved, or they believed another employer would provide, leading to a perception of few employment alternatives. Thus, while an observer may, at the time of the initial complaint, feel a great deal of loyalty, she may change her views of the employers and the situation after experiencing the outcomes of direct voice. Thus, we expect that early in the process whistle-blowers – especially those whistle-blowers using 'direct voice' exclusively – should express a great deal of loyalty. Later in the process, if the whistle-blowing attempt has been unsuccessful in terms of its halting the wrongdoing or retaliation, we expect lowered self-reports of loyalty.

Observers with social and/or financial support from family or friends are also more likely to blow the whistle (Janis and Mann 1977; Weinstein 1979); in fact, one study of whistle-blowers found that virtually all had received emotional support from family or friends (Near et al. 1980). Provision of alternative sources of support from spouses or other family members thus decreases the dependency of the whistle-blower on the organization.

Observers who are members of professional groups whose norms support whistle-blowing may feel sufficient support to take action (Janis and Mann 1977; Perrucci et al. 1980). We also expect that a high unemployment rate in the observer's relevant labor market (determined by industry, geographical location, or occupation) will chill whistle-blowing, because it is an indicator that fewer employment alternatives are available. Since the unemployment rate for professional employees is generally lower than the rate for non-professionals, they may also have more alternative sources of financial support.

Proposition 6: *Whistle-blowers are likely to be less dependent on their employers, relative to other employees: This should be reflected in their lower age, aspiration, and experience levels; their expressions of loyalty to persons or institutions other than their employer, such as professional groups; their higher levels of support from family or friends; and the rates of employment in their relevant labor markets.*

Dependence on the Whistle-Blowing Channel

Observers of wrongdoing will blow the whistle if they are dependent on this form of political action, i.e., if they believe that the organization's behavior must be changed and alternative methods are not perceived to be available. When individuals believe they are directly harmed by a policy or practice (e.g., as in the case of unfair employment discrimination or unsafe working conditions), they may be more likely to act than those who would act 'in the public good' or in support of their professional norms (e.g., engineers who wish to prevent the production of unsafe goods: Perrucci et al. 1980). We predict that they will choose external whistle-blowing rather than internal whistle-blowing when internal complaints have failed, when they fear the results of internal complaints, when they believe that internal complaints will not be as effective in changing the situation, or when they do not know the procedure for making internal complaints (Kolarska and Aldrich 1980). Their dependence upon external, public channels may result from their observation that the organization rarely changes without scrutiny; and/or that public backing will likely provide them with greater influence in changing their organization's behavior (Farrell and Petersen 1982), with protection from retaliation (Elliston 1982a), or with financial support or cost-sharing (e.g., EEOC may act as one's attorney; individuals hearing of the case may send money or letters of support).

Proposition 7: *Whistle-blowing is more likely to occur when observers of wrongdoing are highly dependent on the method of whistle-blowing as a form of political action; that is, when they feel that alternative actions are not possible.*

The Organization's Dependence

An organization may respond to the whistle-blowing attempt in several ways (Parmerlee et al. 1982). It may acknowledge and correct the wrongdoing, and reward the whistle-blower for providing useful information. It may attempt to coopt the whistle-blower, to buy compliance. It may isolate the whistle-blower from others, to prevent the flow of information to the individual and the communication of observed wrongdoing to others. The organization may challenge the credibility of the whistle-blower, thus decreasing the amount of public attention received. Finally, the organization may retaliate in a punitive way, as an example to other would-be whistle-blowers (Kolarska and Aldrich 1980).

The organization that is dependent on a whistle-blower, because she is critical to operations or not easily replaced, has less freedom to retaliate against the whistle-blower than against a whistle-blower who is less critical. The powerful whistle-blower may exit from the organization, taking with him knowledge and experience valued by the organization. Further, a powerful organization member may have higher credibility. The organization may be more likely to acknowledge and correct wrongdoing alleged by a credible observer, perhaps because its leaders may fear the observer's credibility will evoke public support for the complaint. One previous investigation of this relationship (Parmerlee et al. 1982) used crude measures of organizational dependency and yielded mixed results.

The perception that organizations are dependent may also affect the observer's decision to blow the whistle. In a laboratory study in which subjects assumed the role of inequitably treated employees, Martin et al. (1983) found that subjects who were told that their position was critical to the organization were more likely to attempt to fight the inequity than were subjects given other information. This effect occurred regardless of the magnitude of the perceived wrongdoing. However, criticality covaried with other 'mobilization resources', and the effect occurred with respect only to 'less legitimate' means of fighting, e.g., work slowdowns. The uses of 'indirect voice' and other types of 'direct voice' were not tested. Thus, the degree of organizational dependence may play a role both in the individual's decision to act and the organization's decisions to respond, but more precise testing is needed.

Structural characteristics of the organization may also be related to the degree of organizational dependence on the whistle-blower. The role of structural characteristics in upward communication, although infrequently investigated (Jabin 1982), is discussed by Glausser (1982). Several appear to be related to the size of the organization. Large organizations are presumably less dependent upon any one individual than are smaller organizations, because it may be easier for large organizations to reassign the responsibilities of an employee who has exited. The upward communication literature (see Glausser for a review) provides evidence that distance between parties to a communication and the number of sequential 'links' it must travel, inhibit communication flow. Further, it may be more difficult for large organizations than for small organizations to communicate the existence of established channels for reporting wrongdoing. Finally, whistle-blowers may feel greater loyalty to smaller organizations and therefore choose to blow the whistle internally, since this action may be less damaging to the organization. Thus, we would expect that fewer 'direct voice' or internal whistle-blowing attempts would be made in a large organization than in other organizations. Further, large organizations, as a result of their lesser dependence on the whistle-blower, will be more likely to retaliate against whistle-blowers than will small organizations.

Proposition 8a: *Organizations are more likely to engage in reprisal against the whistle-blower when they are not highly dependent upon the whistle-blower, because the whistle-blower is powerful or the organization is small.*

Proposition 8b: *Large organizations that are less dependent upon the whistle-blower will experience fewer internal whistle-blowing attempts than will organizations that are highly dependent on the whistle-blower.*

The Organization's Dependence Upon the Questioned Activity

The organization's response to the whistle-blower is likely influenced by the criticality of the questioned method of operation (i.e., whether it is necessary for survival) and the availability of alternative methods of operation. For example, a multinational corporation may find that it is expected to bribe local officials of a foreign country, in order to be allowed to operate sales offices in that country. If it is impossible to find other legal methods to substitute for the bribery (for example, offering jobs to the children of these officials), it will resist changing its questionable behavior. It has been found that organizations are more likely to engage in illegal behavior when they require the resources so obtained because their environments are not munificent in providing the resources (Staw and Szwajkowski 1975). Further, the criticality of the wrongdoing may determine the degree of threat to the organization; the higher the degree of threat, the more likely the organization is to punish or silence the whistle-blower (Weinstein 1979).

The costs imposed by an informed public may alter the criticality of the questioned activity, however. For example, if an organization learns via an internal whistle-blower that one of its products may cause injury to individuals, it may halt production to avoid the risks of consumers' litigation that might follow external whistle-blowing. Thus, the formerly critical activity becomes more costly potentially than alternatives.

The organization's dependence on the questioned activity is likely to enter into the observer's decision to blow the whistle, although its influence may not be as easy to trace as in the case of the organizational response to whistle-blowing. Where the observer believes that the organization is dependent upon the wrongdoing, and thus, unlikely to alter its behavior, the observer may be less likely to blow the whistle. Therefore, the effects of these factors may be difficult to disentangle. Nevertheless:

Propositions 9: *Organizations are more likely to refuse to halt wrongdoing and to engage in reprisal against the whistle-blower when they are highly dependent upon their wrongful behavior.*

Toward a Research Agenda

Research regarding whistle-blowing has been hampered by two problems: lack of a theoretical framework for interpreting the phenomenon and lack of appropriate methods for observing the phenomenon. Because whistle-blowing is a function of the individual's characteristics and reinforcement history, the environment within the organization, the external environment(s) in which the organization and the individual operate, and interactions among them, predicting its occurrence and effects is complex. The propositions given above represent an attempt to predict this process; methodological problems in potential tests of these propositions are considered below.

The Need for Multiple Methods

To date, empirical studies of whistle-blowing have relied almost exclusively on case studies, which may limit the generalizability of findings so obtained. Results from two survey studies have proved inconsistent with those obtained in case studies. Nader et al. (1972) argued that the threat of retaliation would prevent would-be whistle-blowers from taking action. Yet Near and Jensen (1983) and Near et al. (1983) found, using survey results, that whistle-blowers' beliefs that they would take the same action again were uncorrelated with their experience of retaliation. The use of case studies in this particular field may be even more risky than usual since there is no possibility of finding a 'typical' whistle-blower. Each case is unique, when it comes to whistle-blowing.

While case study results are limited in generalizability, survey results also suffer from three serious limitations with regard to the respondents: (1) they rely on recall to reconstruct events that may have occurred some time earlier; (2) they provide the only measures of their own behavior and of its antecedents; and (3) they speculate as to why they behaved as they did. The potential for error inherent in this method is obvious.

To eliminate these problems, laboratory studies of whistle-blowing might be used. The major difficulty here is in designing a study wherein subjects react to a wrongdoing action in the same way that they would if exposed to such an action in 'real' organizations.

Field experimentation is virtually impossible as many organizations would resist investigation in such sensitive areas. Company records are unlikely to yield data concerning organizational climate or consequences of action or inaction. Archival data cannot identify would-be whistle-blowers and why they decide not to act. Any investigation focusing on one or a few organizations is suspect regarding generalizability, especially when the organization has volunteered to participate (see Campbell and Stanley 1966).

The problem is not easily resolved. Studies utilizing multiple methods to explore the validity of results obtained are needed. Secondly, researchers must recognize that field studies should include a wide variety of different types of whistle-blowers. Some initial studies of homogeneous samples of whistle-blowers have been completed; these provide a standard against which heterogeneous samples may be compared. At this time no statistics concerning the whistle-blowing process are available (e.g., the incidence or success rate). Thus, we lack even the most rudimentary information about the effect of whistle-blowers on organizations.

Obviously, multiple approaches are required for studying whistle-blowing. A second possibility is to follow the steps recommended by McKelvey and Aldrich (1983) for organizational research. Following their argument, a taxonomy of whistle-blowers should be developed and an effort made to study whistle-blowers falling into the various categories (i.e., in separate and independent studies). While whistle-blowers do undoubtedly differ from one another, the discovery of any systematic similarities among categories of whistle-blowers would depend on comparisons within such categories. Unfortunately, since the focus in this research must be the interactions between two social actors (or so we have argued), probably a separate taxonomy should be developed to classify the organizations involved as well. Research then should focus on the various cells of the matrix created by combination of the two taxonomies, one for the whistle-blower and one for the organization.

First steps in this direction are seen in the research efforts focusing on a type of whistle-blowers – complainants in sex discrimination cases (e.g., Parmerlee et al. 1982) – and in studies of whistle-blowers in public agencies, a type of organization (e.g., Miceli and Near 1984). However, the typologies implicit in such classifications have not been developed in any systemic (i.e., taxonomic) way, nor have any studies to date focused on the interaction between type of whistle-blower and type of organization. Research along these lines would better support the development of theory concerning similarities across types of whistle-blowing cases that also recognizes the unique nature of each whistle-blowing incident.

Conclusion

Whistle-blowing in organizations is an issue which has only recently received public attention and systematic study. There are various reasons for earlier inattention: lack of public concern with whistle-blowing perhaps linked to low relative incidence of whistle-blowing; the focus of organization theory on explaining stability in organizations, and compliance to authority, rather than change and noncompliance (e.g., Benson 1977; Pfeffer 1981); and the difficulty involved in studying a problem which lacks either a well-developed theoretical framework to support it or an obviously appropriate research method to facilitate its exploration. Availability of data concerning such sensitive issues has also been a problem (Ewing 1980). By proposing an empirically testable model, we hope to stimulate more concern with the whistle-blowing process, its causes and its effects for the social actors involved.

References

Adam, J.S. 1963. Toward an understanding of inequity. *Journal of Abnormal and Social Psychology* 67: 422–424.

Athanassiades, J.C. 1973. The distortion of upward communication in hierarchical organizations. *Academy of Management Journal* 16: 207–236.

Athanassiades, J.C. 1974. An investigation of some communication patterns of female subordinates in hierarchical organizations. *Human Relations* 27: 195–209.

Baker, M. 1983. Employer response to professional complaints and alarms: Can corporate scientists and engineers speak out? Presented at the Annual Institute for Chemists, Atlantic City, NJ, May 1983.

Benson, J.K. 1977. Organizations: A dialectical view. *Administrative Science Quarterly* 22: 1–21.

Campbell, D.T., and J. Stanley. 1966. *Experimental and quasi-experimental designs for research*. Chicago: Rand McNally.

Clinard, M.B. 1983. *Corporate ethics and crime: The role of middle management*. Beverly Hills: Sage.

Columbus Dispatch. 1983. 'Pratt & Whitney prices spur federal inquiry', Originally in the Chicago Tribune, reported in the *Columbus Dispatch*, Mar 27, A7.

Costanzo, P.R., and M.E. Shaw. 1966. Conformity as a function of age level. *Child Development* 37: 967–975.

Dozier, J.B., and M.P. Miceli. 1984. Whistle-blowing as prosocial behavior: A review of potential predictors. Working Paper 84–88. College of Administrative Science, Ohio State University, Columbus.

Elliston, F.A. 1982a. Anonymity and whistle-blowing. *Journal of Business Ethics* 1: 167–177.

Elliston, F.A. 1982b. Civil disobedience and whistle-blowing: A comparative appraisal of two forms of dissent. *Journal of Business Ethics* 1: 23–28.

Emerson, R.E. 1962. Tower-dependence relations. *American Sociological Review* 27: 31–41.

Ewing, D.W. 1977. *Freedom inside the organization*. New York: Dutton.

Ewing, D.W. 1980. A proposed bill of rights. In *Current issues in personnel management*, ed. K.M. Rowland, M. London, G.R. Ferris, and J.L. Sherman, 94–99. Boston: Allyn and Bacon.

Ewing, D.W. 1983. *Do it my way – or you're fired!* New York: Wiley.

Farrell, D. 1983. Exit, voice, loyalty, and neglect as response to job dissatisfaction: A multi-dimensional scaling study'. *Academy of Management Journal* 26: 596–607.

Farrell, D., and J.C. Petersen. 1982. Patterns of political behavior in organizations. *Academy of Management Review* 7: 403–412.

Gaines, J. 1980. Upward communication in industry: An experiment. *Human Relations* 33: 929–942.

Gamson, W.H. 1971. Political trust and its remifications. In *Social psychology and political behavior*, ed. G. Abcarian and J. Soule, 40–55. Columbus: Merrill.

Glausser, M.J. 1982. Factors which facilitate or impede upward communication in organizations. Presented at the 42nd annual meeting of the Academy of Management, New York, August, 1982.

Hacker, A. 1975. Loyalty – and the whistleblower. *Across the Board* 67: 4–8.

Heller, F. 1983. Changing autocracy patterns: A cultural perspective. Presented at the 43rd annual meeting of the Academy of Management, Dallas, August, 1983.

Hickson, D.J., C.R. Hinings, R.W. Lee, R.W. Schneck, and J.M. Pennings. 1971. A strategic contingencies' theory of inter organizational power. *Administrative Science Quarterly* 16: 216–229.

Hirschman, A.O. 1970. *Exit, voice, and loyalty: Responses to decline in firms, organizations, and states*. Cambridge, MA: Harvard University Press.

Hollinger, R.C., and J.P. Clark. 1982. Formal and informal social controls of employee deviance. *The Sociological Quarterly* 3: 333–343.

Jabin, F.M. 1982. Formal structure characteristics of organizations and superior/subordinate communication. *Human Communication Research* 8: 338–347.

Janis, I.L., and L. Mann. 1977. *Decision making*. New York: Free Press.

Johnson, J.M., and J.D. Douglas. 1978. *Crime at the top: Deviance in business and the professions*. Philadelphia: Lippincott.

Jones, A.P., L.R. James, and J.R. Bruni. 1975. Perceived leadership behavior and confidence in the leader as moderated by job involvement. *Journal of Applied Psychology* 60: 146–149.

Kohlberg, L. 1969. *Stages in the development of moral thought and action*. New York: Holt, Rinehart and Winston.

Kolarska, L., and J. Aldrich. 1980. Exit, voice, and silence: Consumers' and managers' responses to organizational decline. *Organization Studies* 1: 41–58.

Maier, N.E.F., R.L. Hoffman, and W.H. Read. 1963. Superior-subordinate communication: The relative effectiveness of managers who held their subordinates' positions. *Personnel Psychology* 16: 1–11.

Malin, M.H. 1983. Protecting the whistle-blower from retaliatory discharge. *University of Michigan Journal of Law Reform* 16: 277–318.

Martin, J., P. Brickman, and A. Murray. 1983. Psychological and sociological barriers to collective action in organizations. Presented at the 43rd annual meeting of the Academy of Management, Dallas, August, 1983.

McKelvey, B., and H. Aldrich. 1983. Populations, natural selection and applied organizational science. *Administrative Science Quarterly* 28: 101–128.

Miceli, M.P., and J.P. Near. 1984. The relationships among beliefs, organizational position and whistle-blowing status: A discriminant analysis. *Academy of Management Journal* 27: 687–705.
Milgram, S. 1955. Some conditions of obedience and disobedience to authority. *Human Relations* 18: 57–75.
Nader, R., P.J. Petkas, and K. Blackwell (eds.). 1972. *Whistle-blowing: The report on the conference on professional responsibility*. New York: Grossman.
Near, J.P., and T.C. Jensen. 1983. The whistle-blowing process: Retaliation and perceived expectiveness. *Work and Occupations* 10: 3–28.
Near, J.P., M.A. Parmerlee, R.W. White, and T.C. Jensen. 1980. Effectiveness of sex discrimination complaints. Proceedings: Association for Women in Psychology. Los Angeles: CA.
Near, J.P., M.A. Parmerlee, R.W. White, and T.C. Jensen. 1981. Blowing the whistle on sex discrimination. A comparison of public and private organizations. Presented at the 41st annual meeting of the Academy of Management.
Near, J.P., M.P. Miceli, and T.C. Jensen. 1983. Variables associated with the whistle-blowing process. Working Paper 83–11, The Ohio State University, March, 1983.
O'Reilly, C.A. 1978. The intentional distortion of information in organizational communication: A laboratory and field investigation. *Human Relations* 31: 173–193.
Parmerlee, M.A., J.P. Near, and T.C. Jensen. 1982. Correlates of whistle-blowers' perceptions of organizational retaliation. *Administrative Science Quarterly* 27: 17–34.
Perrucci, R., R.M. Anderson, D.E. Schendel, and L.E. Trachtman. 1980. Whistle-blowing: Professionals' resistance to organizational authority. *Social Problems* 28: 149–164.
Peters, C., and T. Branch. 1972. Blowing the whistle: Dissent in the public interest, *Washington Monthly*, New York.
Pfeffer, J. 1981. *Power in organizations*. Marshfield: Pittman.
Pfeffer, J., and G.R. Salancik. 1978. *The external control of organizations*. New York: Harper and Row.
Porter, L.W., and R.M. Steers. 1973. Organizational, work, and personal factors in employee turnover and absenteeism. *Psychological Bulletin* 80: 151–176.
Read, W.H. 1962. Upward communication in industrial hierarchies. *Human Relations* 15: 3–15.
Roberts, K.H., and C.A. O'Reilly. 1974. Failures in upward communication: Three possible culprits. *Academy of Management Journal* 17: 205–215.
Rotter, J.B. 1966. Generalized expectancies for interval vs. external control of reinforcement. *Psychological Monographs* 80: 1–28.
Skinner, B.F. 1953. *Science and human behavior*. New York: Macmillan.
Spector, P.E. 1982. Behavior in organizations as a function of employee's locus of control. *Psychological Bulletin* 91: 482–497.
Staw, B.M., and E. Szwajkowski. 1975. The scarcity-munificence component of organizational environments and the commission of illegal acts. *Administrative Science Quarterly* 20: 345–354.
United States Merit Systems Protection Board (USMSPB). 1981. *Whistle-blowing and the federal employee*. Washington, D.C: U.S. Government Printing Office.
Vroom, V.H. 1964. *Work and motivation*. New York: Wiley.
Weber, M. 1947. *The theory of social and economic organization*. New York: Free Press.
Weinstein, D. 1979. *Bureaucratic opposition*. New York: Pergamon Press.
Westin, A.F. (ed.). 1981. *Whistleblowing*. New York: McGraw-Hill.

Chapter 9
The Social Desirability Response Bias in Ethics Research

Donna M. Randall and Maria F. Fernandes

Since the early 1950s researchers in the organizational sciences (e.g., Edwards 1953) have expressed concern that self-report questionnaires may contain response sets biasing observed relationships between variables. One artifact, in particular, which may impair the results of survey research and policy capturing (Arnold and Feldman 1981; Bishop et al. 1986; Mazen 1990) is a social desirability response set. Social desirability (SD) is broadly understood as the tendency of individuals to deny socially undesirable traits and behaviors and to admit to socially desirable ones (Zerbe and Paulhus 1987).

Researchers in business ethics, a rapidly developing subdiscipline within the field of management, need to be particularly sensitive to the potential effects of a social desirability response bias. Observation and measurement of business ethics is difficult (Trevino 1986). While self-report questionnaires are very commonly used as an observation technique in business ethics research, empirical studies have noted a high degree of sensitivity on the part of managers to questions about ethics (e.g., Victor and Cullen 1988). Respondents are frequently asked to express their agreement or disagreement with a statement such as, "Ethical practices are good business in the long-run" (Brown and King 1982, p. 15) or express their opinion about a behavior such as "Rejection of qualified job applicant because he is Jewish" (Goodman and Crawford 1974, p. 182). The socially desirable answer in such statements is quite apparent.

Due to the sensitive nature of ethics research, the presence of a social desirability response bias may pose an even greater threat to the validity of findings in ethics research than in more traditional organizational behavior research topics. However, little effort has been directed toward determining the impact of a response bias in ethics research.

D.M. Randall (✉)
Office of the President, Albion College, Albion, MI 49224-1831, USA
e-mail: drandall@albion.edu

M.F. Fernandes
7445 W. Devonwood Drive, 83703 Boise, ID, USA
e-mail: ffernadeseidahopower.com

A.C. Michalos and D.C. Poff (eds.), *Citation Classics from the Journal of Business Ethics*, Advances in Business Ethics Research 2,
DOI 10.1007/978-94-007-4126-3_9, © Springer Science+Business Media B.V. 2013

A recent review of business ethics research (Randall and Gibson 1990) revealed that self-report data were relied upon in almost 90% of empirical journal articles. However, only one of 96 empirical research articles since 1960 has attempted to assess the impact of a social desirability response bias. This paper seeks to examine the relationship between conceptually distinct measures of social desirability responding and self-reported ethical conduct.

Social Desirability

Individuals may have some attributes that are negatively valued by general societal norms (e.g., abuse of alcohol, abuse of drugs, drunken driving) and other attributes that are positively valued (e.g., voting in elections, church attendance) (Groves 1989). In an effort to conform to societal norms, individuals may present themselves in a favorable light, regardless of their "true" feelings or "actual" behavior. Specifically, individuals may under-report those activities perceived to be socially or culturally undesirable and may over-report those activities deemed to be socially or culturally desirable (Ganster et al. 1983).

From the early 1930s, researchers have expressed interest in the effects of a social desirability response set (e.g., Bernreuter 1933; Humm and Humm 1944). Results from these early tests raised the suspicion that test-takers who scored high on these tests were "faking in order to look good." Ganster et al. (1983) viewed this tendency as problematic because it may mask the relationship between two or more variables (a suppressor effect), provide a false correlation between independent and dependent variables (a spurious effect), or moderate the relationship between those variables (a moderator effect).

Dimensions of Social Desirability

Organizational science literature today generally depicts the social desirability construct as composed of two independent dimensions. When viewed as a personality characteristic, social desirability is frequently termed "need for social approval," and when viewed as an item characteristic, it is labelled "trait desirability" (Gove and Geerken 1977; Phillips and Clancy 1972).

SD as a Personality Characteristic

When viewed as a personality characteristic, a social desirability response is frequently operationalized using the Marlowe-Crowne (M-C) Scale (Crowne and Marlowe 1960). The scale consists of items drawn from a set of behaviors which are "culturally sanctioned and approved, but which are improbable of occurrence," such as "Before voting, I thoroughly investigate the qualifications of all candidates"

(Crowne and Marlowe 1960, p. 23). Compared with low scorers, high scorers on the M-C scale respond more to social reinforcement, restrain aggressive feelings, and are more amenable to social influence. Their performance on tasks is strongly influenced by how others evaluate them. They prefer to engage in low-risk behaviors and avoid evaluations by others (Crowne 1979).

When the M-C scale was published in 1960, it was intended as a general measure of social desirability in self-reports and assumed to reflect a need for social approval. However, questions have been raised about the validity of the M-C scale as a measure of need for approval. For instance, a series of studies were conducted investigating the relationship between frequency and amount of cheating behavior and M-C scores (Jacobson et al. 1970; Millham 1974). As predicted, those who cheated scored higher on the M-C scale than non-cheaters when detection was perceived to be unlikely (Millham 1974). In addition, those who scored high on the M-C scale cheated only enough to avoid disapproval, but did not cheat when approval could be won. These findings supported Crandall's (1966) conclusion that the M-C scale appears to be more appropriate for measuring the impulse to avoid disapproval rather than the need to seek social approval.

More recently, Paulhus (1984) contended that the scale contains, and fails to differentiate between, two distinct factors: self-deception and impression management. Self-deception refers to an unconscious tendency to see oneself in a positive light and is manifested in self-descriptions that are socially desirable, biased, and believed to be true by the respondent (Zerbe and Paulhus 1987). In self-reporting behavior, the respondent is assumed to be motivated to protect self-beliefs, including self-esteem (Paulhus 1986). Conversely, impression management refers to a conscious presentation of a false front, manifested by deliberately falsifying test responses to create a positive impression (Zerbe and Paulhus 1987). The respondent's behavior is assumed to be instrumental (Paulhus 1986).

Due to perceived limitations of the M-C scale, Paulhus (1984, 1988) developed the Balanced Inventory of Desirable Responding (BIDR) scale which contains two distinct subscales for self-deception and impression management. The BIDR is a descendant of the Self- and Other-Deception Questionnaires developed by Sackeim and Gur (1978). While the original self-deception items were developed under the assumption that individuals with a propensity for self-deception tend to deny having psychologically threatening thoughts or feelings, the most recent version of the scale (Paulhus 1988) emphasizes exaggerated claims of positive cognitive attributes.

The impression management items were selected under the assumption that some respondents consciously tend to over-report performance of desirable behaviors and under-report undesirable behaviors. Because the claims involve overt behaviors (e.g., I have never dropped litter on the street), any distortion can be presumed to be a conscious lie (Paulhus 1989). It is assumed that self-deception is minimized because the questions are concerned with the behavior of the respondent rather than the respondent's thoughts.

The preceding discussion reveals that social desirability as a personality trait has been reconceptualized in two highly distinct ways – a propensity for self-deception and a propensity for impression management – and that each conceptualization is independently related to self-reported conduct. Applying these findings to the ethics literature, the following hypotheses can be set forth:

H_1: The greater the propensity for self-deception, the greater the extent to which individuals will self-report ethical behaviors.

H_2: The greater the propensity for impression management, the greater the extent to which individuals will self-report ethical behaviors.

SD as an Item Characteristic

The second approach to a social desirability response bias, perceived desirability of the item, considers various behaviors or traits to be more or less socially desirable and thus discusses social desirability in relation to particular items. Strong support exists for the conclusion that social desirability effects are heavily influenced by characteristics of the item (Groves 1989).

In an early study, Edwards (1953) provided empirical support for the relationship between the judged desirability of a response in a self-report study and the likelihood of an individual giving that response. Edwards' findings were replicated in a series of investigations focusing on the influence of perceived item desirability on responses to various personality measures (e.g., Cowen and Tongas 1959; Rosen 1956; Wiggins and Rumrill 1959). Several years later, Phillips and Clancy (1972) again demonstrated that respondents consistently reported themselves as possessing characteristics they saw as desirable.

As a consequence, one can hypothesize:

H_3: The greater the perceived desirability of behavior, the greater the extent to which individuals will self-report ethical behavior.

Phillips and Clancy (1972) also examined the joint influence of need for approval and item characteristic measures on self-reported attributes. Contrary to what might be expected, the two possible response determinants (need for approval and item desirability) were found to be generally unrelated to each other but independently related to individuals' responses to various sociological measures. Further, they determined that item desirability exerted a greater influence than need for approval on individuals' responses. While Phillips and Clancy's measurement of trait desirability has recently been criticized for its complexity by Gove and Geerken (1977), the latter researchers did support the finding that item desirability and need for approval are largely independent and their effects additive.

It appears that while the personality of some individuals may predispose them toward a general pattern of socially desirable responding, their answers will be more strongly influenced by the situational influences – their perception of the desirability of engaging in specific behaviors. Thus,

H_4: Perceived desirability of behavior will exercise a stronger influence on self-reported ethical behavior than will propensity for self-deception or impression management.

Questioning the Existence of a Social Desirability Response Set

Several researchers (e.g., Groves 1989; Nunnally 1978; Paulhus 1988) have raised the possibility that any association between personality characteristics, item desirability, and self-reported behavior may accurately reflect the true state of affairs. That is, different levels of self-deception, impression management, or item desirability may be associated with actual differences in ethical conduct. This conduct is, in turn, accurately reported within surveys.

To test this alternative explanation, it would be desirable to observe actual behavior. As this is difficult to do, Phillips and Clancy (1972) developed an overclaiming scale to give researchers confidence that respondents actually do not perform claimed behaviors. Their scale seeks to measure the tendency to assert that one has accomplished some task when, in fact, this is not true. Phillips and Clancy asked respondents about their use of several new products, books, television programs, and movies (all of which were nonexistent), and the desirability of being the kind of person who uses these items. They found that those respondents who viewed the use of the items as highly desirable were more than twice as likely to give inaccurate responses (to overclaim) than those viewing the characteristics as highly undesirable. Phillips and Clancy concluded that the desirability of performing the behaviors influenced reporting of the behaviors and argued that the alternative explanation, that individuals' self-reported responses are accurate, cannot be fully supported.

However, Bradburn and his colleagues (1979) disagreed with Phillips and Clancy's conclusion. They determined that those individuals scoring high on need for approval actually behaved differently on a number of measures and that there are "pervasive real-world differences in the way persons with high and low MC scores behave and relate to other people" (p. 105). As DeMaio (1984) noted, findings from Phillips and Clancy's study and Bradburn et al.'s study can be reconciled as the former study is based on an item desirability measure of social desirability, while the latter is based on a personality characteristic measure of social desirability.

As a consequence, one can hypothesize:

H_5: Overclaiming will be more closely associated with the perceived desirability of ethical behavior than with propensity for self-deception or impression management.

Finally, two exploratory analyses will be conducted. On occasion, researchers have attempted to assess the influence of a social desirability response bias in ethics questionnaires (e.g., Stevens 1984) by incorporating the M-C scale into the study. As discussed above, despite the current popularity of the M-C scale, its validity has been called into question and other, more valid, scales (e.g., the BIDR) have been developed to identify the existence of a social desirability response bias. This study proposes to examine the relationship between scores on the M-C scale to measures of self-deception, impression management, item desirability, and self-reported ethical conduct.

Second, despite heavy reliance on self-report methodology, minimal effort in ethics research has been directed toward an assessment of the impact of a social desirability response bias on ethics scales commonly included in self-report questionnaires. This study also proposes to explore the impact of a SD response bias on one of the most popular ethics scale, the Ruch and Newstrom scale (1975).

Methods

A survey instrument was designed which included the following measures: the Marlowe-Crowne scale, the BIDR (with self-deception and impression management subscales), perceived item desirability of unethical behavior, an overclaiming scale, self-report unethical conduct, and Ruch and Newstrom's (1975) ethics scale. Prior to administering the survey, a pretest of the instrument was conducted using 43 junior and senior level students at a large state university. Items identified as either confusing, through a debriefing of pretest subjects, or lacking variability, through analysis of pretest results, were modified.

The revised questionnaire was then administered to students enrolled in an introductory management class. The students were asked to fill out a brief questionnaire in exchange for extra credit. Numerous precautions were taken by the researchers to promote disclosure of unethical conduct: assuring anonymity, asking that no name or identification mark be put on the survey, requesting participants to write their identification number only on a separate cover sheet (to receive extra credit), providing clearly visible and separate public drop boxes for the cover sheet and survey, administering the survey in a public auditorium, and asking for no identifying information in the survey other than level in school and gender. The questionnaire was completed by 348 students (50% female and roughly equal numbers of juniors and seniors).

The survey instrument contained the following seven scales (discussed in the order in which they appeared in the questionnaire):

Overclaiming

The procedure to detect overclaimers set forth by Phillips and Clancy (1972) was modified to allow for the use of an overclaiming scale with more items and items of greater relevance to students. On a scale of 1 to 5 (1 = not at all familiar, 3 = somewhat familiar, and 5 = very familiar), respondents were asked to rate their degree of familiarity with items in several categories: newly released movies, products, music albums, television programs, and designer label clothing. Each category contained five items, two of which were non-existent.

All affirmative responses to behaviors which could not possibly have occurred were tabulated to arrive at an overclaiming score. Possible values on the overclaiming scale ranged from 10 to 50. A score of 10 indicated the respondent was not at all familiar with any of the 10 fake items. A score of 50 indicated the respondent reported being very familiar with each of the 10 fake items. The internal consistency coefficient (alpha) for the scale was 0.70. Appendix A presents the 10 items composing the scale.

Respondents are often unwilling to admit their ignorance in areas they believe themselves to be experts (Bradley 1981). In a study of fictitious public affairs issues, Bishop et al. (1986) hypothesized that people can be pressured into giving an opinion on a fictitious issue when the topic seemed familiar to them. However, they found the more a person knew about a subject, the less likely he or she was to make such a mistake. In fact, the more respondents knew about a subject, the more easily they could recognize what was familiar and what was not. Therefore, the less knowledgeable a subject is about a topic, the more easily the person can be confused and pressured to give an opinion about it. As a consequence, the overclaiming scale was rescored after controlling for respondents' alleged expertise in each of the five areas. This was done by dividing the familiarity rating of non-existent items by the total familiarity ratings within each topic area. The respondent's total score is the sum across the five topics. As the results were highly correlated with the original scoring method, all subsequent analyses of the overclaiming scale used the original scoring method.

Marlowe-Crowne Scale

The Marlowe-Crowne Scale (Crowne and Marlowe 1960) was incorporated into the study for exploratory purposes. Respondents were asked to express their agreement by responding true or false to 33 items (15 of which were negatively coded). This instrument included such items as, "I am always courteous, even to people who are disagreeable," and "I never hesitate to go out of my way to help someone in trouble."

In past research, the average internal consistency coefficients of the Marlowe-Crowne Scale have ranged from 0.73 to 0.88 (Crowne and Marlowe 1964; Fisher 1967; Paulhus 1984; Tanaka-Matsumi and Kameoka 1986). A test-retest correlation of 0.88 over 1 month was reported by Crowne and Marlowe (1964), and 0.84 over a 1-week interval was reported by Fisher (1967). In the present study, the internal consistency coefficient (alpha) was 0.74.

Self-Report Behaviors

Students were asked to report whether they had engaged in a series of 10 unethical behaviors by responding true or false to each of the behaviors. The 10 behaviors had been previously identified in a study of students by Stem and Steinhorst (1984) and included such behaviors as, "exchanging answers with another student during an exam," "plagiarizing on a term paper," "receiving help on a take-home exam," and "turning in the same paper for two classes." The internal consistency coefficient (alpha) for the scale was 0.65.

Self-Deception and Impression Management

The Balanced Inventory of Desirable Responding (BIDR) contains two 20-item subscales measuring self-deception (an honest positivistic bias) and impression management (purposeful self-presentation) (Paulhus 1989). Respondents were asked to rate how each of 40 statements applied to themselves on a seven-point scale (1 = not true at all, 4 = neither true or false, and 7 = very true). Ten items in each subscale were reverse coded. As set forth by Paulhus (1989), all 40 items on the BIDR were summed to yield an overall measure of socially desirable responding. In addition, separate subscale scores were computed by summing the 20 items composing the self-deception subscale and the 20 items composing the impression management subscale.

Past research has shown that the average internal consistency coefficient for the full BIDR is 0.83, 0.68–0.80 for the self-deception subscale, and 0.75–0.86 for the impression management subscale (see Paulhus 1988). Average test-retest correlations of 0.69 and 0.65 over a 5 week period were reported by Paulhus (1988) for the self-deception and impression management scales, respectively. The complete BIDR demonstrates concurrent validity in correlating 0.71 with the M-C scale (Paulhus 1988) and 0.80 with Jacobson et al.'s (1970) Multidimensional Social Desirability Inventory. In the present study, the internal consistency coefficient for the full BIDR was 0.79, 0.60 for the self-deception subscale, and 0.79 for the impression management subscale.

Item Desirability

Following a procedure set forth by Dohrenwend (1966) and Phillips and Clancy (1972), item desirability was assessed by having respondents rate each self-reported unethical behavior on a nine-point scale of desirability (1 = very undesirable, 5 = neither undesirable or desirable, and 9 = very desirable). The less desirable respondents believed a behavior to be, the lower the assigned number. The internal consistency coefficient of the scale (alpha) in the present study was 0.83.

Ruch and Newstrom Scale

One of the most frequently used scales in the ethics literature to measure perceptions of unethical conduct was developed by Ruch and Newstrom (1975) (e.g., Ferrell and Weaver 1978; Izraeli 1988; Kidwell et al. 1987; Krugman and

Ferrell 1981; Newstrom and Ruch 1975, 1976). In completing the scale, students were asked to report how unethical they perceived a series of 17 business practices to be using a five-point scale (1 very unethical, 2=basically unethical, 3=ethically neutral, 4=basically ethical, and 5=very ethical). Examples of scale items include: "Using company services for personal use," and "padding an expense account up to 10%" (Ruch and Newstrom 1975, p. 18). High values indicate that respondents consider the questionable practices to be highly ethical. The 17 items were summed to yield a scale score. The internal consistency coefficient (*alpha*) for the scale in the present study was 0.83.

As the intent of the research was to examine the impact of socially desirable responding on self-reported ethical conduct, the hypotheses were tested using a series of zero order correlations or multiple regressions.

Results

Hypotheses

The first hypothesis examined the relationship between propensity for self-deception and self-report ethical conduct. It was expected that the greater the propensity for self-deception, the greater the extent to which individuals will report ethical behavior. As reflected in the correlation matrix in Table 9.1, the correlation between scores on the self-deception subscale and self-reported ethical conduct was 0.10 ($p<0.05$). The first hypothesis was supported.

Table 9.1 Pearson correlations between social desirability measures, overclaiming, and self-reported ethical conduct[a]

Variables	1	2	3	4	5	6	7	8
1. Self-reported ethical behavior	–							
2. Desirability of ethical behavior	0.68***	–						
3. M-C scale	0.24***	0.26***	–					
4. BIDR	0.42***	0.39***	0.64***	–				
5. Self-deception subscale	0.10*	0.11*	0.45***	0.76***	–			
6. Impression management subscale	0.53***	0.49***	0.59***	0.88***	0.36***	–		
7. Overclaiming scale	–0.07	–0.09	0.18***	0.13**	0.14**	0.11*	–	
8. Ruch and Newstrom's scale[b]	–0.16***	–0.29***	–0.17***	–0.19***	–0.05	–0.24***	0.14**	–

* $p<0.05$; ** $p<0.01$; *** $p<0.001$

[a] $N=319–341$

[b] High values = acceptance of unethical behavior

Table 9.2 Magnitude of influence of item desirability and personality characteristic measures on self-report behavior

Variable	*B*	*SEB*	*Beta*	*T*	*SigT*
Impression management subscale	0.0372	0.0063	0.2895	5.91	0.00
Self-deception subscale	–0.0127	0.0077	–0.0706	–1.65	0.10
Desirability of ethical behavior	0.0828	–0.0072	0.5322	11.58	0.00
(Constant)	7.5121	0.7716		9.74	0.00

Multiple *R* 0.71
R Square 0.50
Adjusted *R* Square 0.50
Standard Error 1.48

The second hypothesis examined the relationship between propensity for impression management and self-report ethical conduct. It was expected that the greater the propensity for impression management, the greater the extent to which individuals will report ethical behavior. The correlation between scores on the impression management subscale and self-reported ethical conduct was 0.53 ($p<0.001$). The second hypothesis was supported.

The third hypothesis set forth that the more desirable individuals assess ethical behavior, the greater they will self-report the behavior. The results in Table 9.1 indicated that the correlation between perceived desirability of ethical behavior and self- reported ethical conduct was 0.68 ($p<0.001$). The third hypothesis was supported.

The fourth hypothesis set forth that trait desirability will exercise a stronger influence on self-reported behavior than propensity for self-deception or propensity for impression management. To examine this hypothesis, self-reported ethical behavior was regressed on perceived item desirability, the impression management subscale, and the self-deception subscale. Table 9.2 reveals that the three independent variables explained 50% of the variation in self-reported unethical conduct. Perceived item desirability explained the largest share of that variance with the impression management subscale making a small, additional contribution. Further, addition of variables into the regression equation did not appreciably change the beta weights for those variables, reducing concern about the moderate level of association between independent variables. In sum, the fourth hypothesis was strongly supported.

The fifth hypothesis proposed overclaiming would be more strongly associated with perceived desirability of ethical behavior than with propensity for self-deception or impression management. The mean score on the overclaiming scale was 13.5. Of the 348 individuals responding, 103 (30%) did not overclaim on any of the 10 nonexistent items. As reflected in Table 9.1, overclaiming was significantly correlated with the self-deception subscale ($r=0.14$, $p<0.01$) and with the impression management subscale ($r=0.11$, $p<0.05$), but was not significantly correlated with the perceived desirability of engaging in ethical conduct ($r=-0.09$). Hence, Hypothesis 5 was rejected.

Exploratory Analyses

Marlowe-Crowne Scale

The Marlowe-Crowne scale was significantly correlated with self-reported ethical behavior ($r=0.24$), the perceived desirability of ethical behavior ($r=0.26$), the self-deception subscale ($r=0.45$), the impression management subscale ($r=0.59$), the overclaiming scale ($r=0.18$), and Ruch and Newstrom's scale ($r=-0.17$). All correlations were significant at the 0.001 level. However, entering the M-C scale into the regression equation in Table 9.2 reveals that the scale failed to make a significant contribution to the prediction of self-reported ethical conduct over that of the three variables previously entered into the equation.

Ruch and Newstrom's Scale

Ruch and Newstrom's scale was significantly correlated with self-reported ethical behavior ($r=-0.16$, $p<0.001$), the perceived desirability of ethical behavior ($r=-0.29$, $p<0.001$), the Marlowe-Crowne scale ($r=-0.17$, $p<0.001$), the impression management subscale ($r=-0.24$, $p<0.001$), and the overclaiming scale ($r=0.14$, $p<0.01$). However, it was not significantly correlated with the self-deception subscale ($r=-0.05$).

Discussion

As set forth in the first and second hypotheses, propensity for self-deception and impression management were significantly correlated with self-reported ethical behavior. As anticipated, the strength of the correlation varied measurably with the operationalization of the SD personality characteristic, confirming the importance of separating the two dimensions of the BIDR conceptually and analytically. The self-deception subscale was only weakly correlated with self-reported ethical behavior, while the impression management subscale of the BIDR reflected a stronger correlation. Thus, it appears that self-reported ethical conduct is more closely associated with a conscious over-reporting of desirable behaviors and under-reporting of undesirable behaviors, than it is associated with an unconscious tendency as measured by the self-deception subscale.

It was interesting to note that the self-report behavior scale had a relatively low internal consistency estimate ($alpha=0.65$). Subsequent item analysis revealed that the deletion of any item from the scale failed to increase the scale's consistency estimate. Hence, it appears that respondents differentiate between various unethical activities. Such a conclusion is consistent with the finding by Bradburn and colleagues

(1979) that social desirability effects are heavily influenced by characteristics of the item. As Grover (1990) has suggested, researchers may need to examine ethical conduct at the molecular level, i.e., study a single element of unethical behavior, as opposed to examining conduct at the molar level, i.e., viewing unethical behaviors as interchangeable.

As predicted in the third and fourth hypotheses, perceived desirability of ethical behavior and self-reported ethical conduct were positively and strongly correlated, with item desirability exerting a significantly stronger influence on self-reported ethical behavior than propensity for self-deception or impression management. In the present study, the addition of an impression management subscale to the regression equation minimally contributed to explained variation in self-reported behavior, and the addition of a self-deception subscale added very little to a regression equation containing an item desirability measure.

As discussed earlier, one could argue that self- reported ethical conduct accurately reflects the behavior of individuals with certain personality characteristics and with certain perceptions of item desirability. However, findings from the present study indicate that those who report what we know to be false familiarity with a series of items have higher levels of self-deception and impression management. Yet, unexpectedly, overclaiming was not significantly related to perceived desirability of ethical behavior, leading to the rejection of Hypothesis 5. It may be the case that the tendency to overclaim is more closely associated with a personality trait than with item desirability.

The magnitudes of the self-deception-overclaiming correlation and the impression management-overclaiming correlation are not large. Overclaiming clearly does not account for all variance in self-reported ethical behavior. A psychological patterning (ethical individuals provide socially desirable responses which agree with their behavior) appears to explain a majority of our findings, yet it does not explain all. At least a portion of the variance in self-reported ethical conduct appears to be due to a social desirability response bias.

In terms of exploratory analyses, the commonly used M-C scale revealed a weak correlation with self-reported ethical behavior. It appears that self-reported ethical conduct is more closely associated with impression management and perceived desirability of behavior than with a tendency to avoid disapproval as measured by the M-C scale. After taking into consideration other SD measures, the M-C scale adds little to explained variation in self- report ethical conduct.

Finally, exploratory analyses revealed that responses to Ruch and Newstrom's ethics scale were significantly correlated with all measures of social desirability except the self-deception subscale. Those individuals who identified a series of questionable business practices as highly unethical had significantly higher levels of impression management and perceived item desirability. Such a pattern of findings may indicate that responses to Ruch and Newstrom's scale, and possibly other ethics scales, may be influenced more by a conscious tendency to over-report desirable behaviors and a desire to project a particular image than by an unconscious tendency measured by the self-deception subscale.

Implications

The examination of the effects of a social desirability response bias on self-reported ethical conduct has a number of research and practical implications. First, as past social science research has convincingly demonstrated that people tend to report behavior in light of what they feel others will expect is appropriate (e.g., Cicourel 1964; Friedman 1967; Riecken 1962; Rosenthal 1966), it is imperative that researchers dealing with such a value-laden topic as ethical conduct be sensitized to the possibility of a strong social desirability bias. Managers are often reluctant to have their ethics observed or measured, and few employees may agree to provide information to researchers that might be incriminating to them or to their friends.

Previous research has convincingly demonstrated that observed levels of socially desirable responding vary with the level of anonymity. The more anonymity seems assured, the less socially desirability responding is detected (Bradburn et al. 1979; Nederhof 1985; Paulhus 1984; Wiseman 1972). In an experiment contrasting anonymous and public conditions, Paulhus (1984) determined that impression management scales were more sensitive to situational changes in anonymity than self-deception scales.

However, it is likely that steps that ethics researchers commonly take to minimize a social desirability response bias (e.g., asking that names not be placed on the survey instrument itself or assuring respondents that their names will never be associated with their findings) will not completely reduce the influence of a social desirability response bias. Although generalizations may be speculative, our research demonstrated that a social desirability bias persists even if a survey is administered in a non-threatening situation. Despite the numerous precautions we took to assure a totally anonymous survey administration, a significant social desirability response bias, largely due to impression management, was still observed. (However, one might argue that, as reflected by scores on the overclaiming scale, 30% of the respondents did not give any evidence of a social desirability bias.)

It is possible that had we not followed these precautionary measures, stronger relationships between the measures of social desirability (particularly, the impression management subscale) and individuals' responses would have been observed. As business ethics researchers do not commonly build in as many precautions as we did, we might argue that our findings reflect a floor for the influence of a social desirability response bias. Hence, the results presented here raise serious questions about the validity of self-report ethics research.

If a social desirability response bias persists after anonymous testing conditions, it may be possible to eliminate the influence of a social desirability response bias through the use of alternative methodologies such as randomized response methods, forced-choice items, proxy subjects, or computer administration (for a discussion of these techniques see Aupperle 1984; Lautenschlager and Flaherty 1990; Martin and Nagao 1989; Nederhof 1985; Paulhus 1984). However, if the use of these techniques is not possible or advisable, business ethics researchers could control for or partial out socially desirable response effects from hypothesized relationships (unless the influence of a social desirability response bias is of theoretic interest, see Zerbe and Paulhus 1987). To aid in this effort, Ganster et al. (1983) have detailed a procedure for identifying how the social desirability response set influences the relationship between independent and dependent variables. The results of the present study provide a useful complement to Ganster et al.'s research in that the latter did not explore how the SD response bias should be measured, only the type of influence a SD response bias (as measured by the Marlowe-Crowne scale) has on the relationship between independent and dependent variables.

From the present study one might conclude that further use of the M-C scale is not advisable. Zerbe and Paulhus (1987) also contended that studies using the M-C scale may underestimate the actual relationship between social desirability responding and organizational behavior constructs. Hence, business ethics studies which have incorporated the M-C scale in an effort to detect a social desirability bias and failed to find such an effect (e.g., Stevens 1984) may have utilized a weak measure. Findings from the present study indicate that if researchers desire to investigate social desirability as a personality characteristic, use of the impression management subscale of the BIDR is preferable. Furthermore, since item desirability consistently exerted a stronger influence than any personality characteristic measure in our study, an assessment of perceived item desirability of the dependent variable appears to be preferable in future research.

Inclusion of an overclaiming scale into a questionnaire may provide a less cumbersome method of detecting a social desirability response bias than an item desirability assessment when the number of items to be rated is large. An overclaiming scale constitutes a direct and unambiguous measure of an individual's attempt to deceive on a questionnaire (as the items are known to be non-existent). However, in the present study the scale failed to explain any additional variation over that of item desirability and impression management when entered into a multiple regression equation. Further, as overclaiming was only correlated with SD personality characteristics, overclaiming may not tap a social desirability response bias due to perceived item desirability.

The lack of a strong correlation between overclaiming and the various measures of social desirability incorporated into the present study may be attributable to either questionable construct validity of the other SD scales (for the overclaiming scale does ultimately represent a direct measure of deception) or to unreliability of the overclaiming scale itself (as the coefficient alpha is moderately low at 0.70). Before further empirical work with the overclaiming scale is conducted, it is desirable that theoretical linkages between various SD personality characteristic measures, item desirability, and overclaiming be specified. On the one hand, it may be that overclaiming mediates the linkage between personality characteristics and self-reported behavior and the linkage between item desirability and self-reported behavior. On the other hand, overclaiming may have a direct and unique impact as an independent variable on unethical behavior. More research needs to explore why individuals claim knowledge when they lack it and whether overclaiming is an unconscious or conscious tendency.

As noted earlier, studies on overclaiming report discrepant findings. Whereas Phillips and Clancy (1972) determined a clear linkage between overclaiming and item desirability and Bradburn and colleagues (1979) found no linkage between overclaiming and the M-C scale, we found a significant linkage between overclaiming and all SD personality characteristic measures, but no significant linkage between overclaiming and item desirability. Findings from the present study would indicate that overclaiming is more closely associated with a personality characteristic than with item desirability. Thus, overclaiming may only mediate the personality characteristic-self-reported behavior relationship.

Whenever a student sample is used, a caveat regarding the issue of generalizability is necessary. Due to the nature of the present sample, extrapolation of these results to employees in different organizations and to research on other sensitive topics should be undertaken with some caution. Nevertheless, the study was designed to provide a high degree of realism in regard to survey design and administration. Future research is needed to develop a nomological net for the overclaiming construct, to validate the scale developed within this study, and to replicate findings from our study with different samples and with a different set of unethical behaviors. The results reported here highlight the need for and can facilitate further investigation into the influence of social desirability in business ethics research.

Appendix A: Overclaiming Scale

How familiar are you with each of the following newly released movies?

1. Turned to Gold
2. Katherine's Mistake

How familiar are you with each of the following products?

1. Microsoft Statistical Assistant
2. New Life Spices

How familiar are you with each of the following albums?

1. Cosmic Being
2. Offender After Dark

How familiar are you with each of the following TV programs?

1. The Adventures of Johnnie
2. Chicago Heat

How familiar are you with each of the following designer labels?

1. Ocean City
2. Jones L. A.

All answers provided with a five point Likert scale (1 = not at all familiar, 3 = somewhat familiar, and 5 = very familiar).

References

Arnold, J.H., and D.G. Feldman. 1981. Social desirability response bias in self-report choice situations. *Academy of Management Journal* 24: 377–385.

Aupperle, K.E. 1984. An empirical measure of corporate social orientation. *Research in Corporate Social Performance and Policy* 6: 627–654.

Bernreuter, R.G. 1933. Validity of the personality inventory. *Personality Journal* 11: 383–386.

Bishop, G.F., A.J. Tuchfarber, and R.W. Oldendick. 1986. Opinions on fictitious issues: The pressure to answer survey questions. *Public Opinion Quarterly* 50: 240–250.

Bradburn, N.M., S. Sudman, and Associates. 1979. *Improving interview method and questionnaire design: Response effects to threatening questions in survey research*. San Francisco: Jossey-Bass.

Bradley, J.V. 1981. Overconfidence in ignorant experts. *Bulletin of the Psychonomic Society* 17(2): 82–84.

Brown, D.J., and K.B. King. 1982. Small business ethics: Influences and perceptions. *Journal of Small Business Management* 20: 11–18.

Cicourel, A.V. 1964. *Method and measurement in sociology*. New York: Free Press.

Cowen, E., and P. Tongas. 1959. The social desirability of trait descriptive terms. *Journal of Consulting Psychology* 3: 361–365.

Crandall, V. 1966. Personality characteristics and social achievement behaviors associated with children's social desirability response tendencies. *Journal of Personality and Social Psychology* 4: 447–486.

Crowne, D.P. 1979. *The experimental study of personality*. Hillsdale: Erlbaum.

Crowne, D.P., and D. Marlowe. 1960. A new scale of social desirability independent of psychopathology. *Journal of Consulting Psychology* 24: 349–354.

Crowne, D.P., and D. Marlowe. 1964. *The approval motive*. New York: Wiley.

Demaio, T.J. 1984. Social desirability and survey measurement: A review. In *Surveying subjective phenomena*, vol. 2, ed. C.F. Turner and E. Martin, 257–282. New York: Russell Sage.

Dohrenwend, B.P. 1966. Social status and psychiatric disorder: An issue of substance and an issue of method. *American Sociological Review* 23: 361–365.

Edwards, A. 1953. The relationship between the judged desirability of a trait and the probability that the trait will be endorsed. *Journal of Applied Psychology* 37: 90–93.

Ferrell, O.C., and K.M. Weaver. 1978. Ethical beliefs of marketing managers. *Journal of Marketing* 42(3): 69–73.

Fisher, G. 1967. Normative and reliability data for the standard and the cross-validated Marlowe-Crowne social desirability scale. *Psychological Reports* 20: 174.

Friedman, N. 1967. *The social nature of psychological research*. New York: Basic.

Ganster, D.C., H.W. Hennessy, and F. Luthans. 1983. Social desirability response effects: Three alternative models. *Academy of Management Journal* 26(2): 321–331.

Goodman, C.S., and M. Crawford. 1974. Young executives: A source of new ethics? *The Personnel Journal* 53: 180–187.

Gove, W.R., and M.P. Geerken. 1977. Response bias in surveys of mental health: An empirical examination. *The American Journal of Sociology* 82: 1289–1317.

Grover, S. L. 1990. The influence of professional role conflict and moral maturity on professionals' reporting accuracy. Paper presented at the 1990 Academy of Management meetings, San Francisco, CA, August 12–15.

Groves, R.M. 1989. *Survey errors and survey costs*. New York: Wiley.

Humm, D.G., and K.A. Humm. 1944. Validity of the Humm-Wadsworth temperament scale: With consideration of the effects of subjects' response-bias. *Journal of Psychology* 18: 55–64.

Izraeli, D. 1988. Ethical beliefs and behavior among managers: A cross-cultural perspective. *Journal of Business Ethics* 7: 263–271.

Jacobson, L.I., S.E. Berger, and J. Millham. 1970. Individual differences in cheating during a temptation period when confronting failure. *Journal of Personality and Social Psychology* 15: 48–56.

Kidwell, J.M., R.E. Stevens, and A.L. Bethke. 1987. Differences in ethical perceptions between male and female managers: Myth or reality? *Journal of Business Ethics* 6: 489–493.

Krugman, D.M., and O.C. Ferrell. 1981. The organizational ethics of advertising. *Journal of Advertising* 10(1): 21–30.

Lautenschlager, G.J., and V.L. Flaherty. 1990. Computer administration of questions: More desirable or more social desirability? *Journal of Applied Psychology* 75(3): 310–314.

Martin, C.L., and D.H. Nagao. 1989. Some effects of computerized interviewing on job applicant responses. *Journal of Applied Psychology* 74(1): 72–80.

Mazen, A.M. 1990. The moderating role of social desirability, age, and experience in human judgment: Just how indirect is policy capturing? *Organizational Behavior and Human Decision Processes* 45: 19–40.

Millham, J. 1974. Two components of need of approval score and their relationship to cheating following success and failure. *Journal of Research in Personality* 8: 378–392.

Nederhof, A.J. 1985. Methods of coping with social desirability bias: A review. *European Journal of Social Psychology* 15: 263–280.

Newstrom, J.W., and W.A. Ruch. 1975. The ethics of management and the management of ethics. *MSU Business Topics* 23(Winter): 29–37.

Newstrom, J.W., and W.A. Ruch. 1976. Managerial values underlying intra-organizational ethics. *Atlanta Economic Review* 26 (May–June): 12–18.

Nunnally, J.C. 1978. *Psychometric theory*, 2nd ed. New York: McGraw-Hill.

Paulhus, D.L. 1984. Two-component models of socially desirable responding. *Journal of Personality and Social Psychology* 46: 598–609.

Paulhus, D.L. 1986. Self-deception and impression management in test responses. In *Personality assessment via questionnaire: Current issues in theory and measurement*, ed. A. Angleitner and J.S. Wiggins. Berlin: Springer.

Paulhus, D.L. 1988. Development of the balanced inventory of desirable responding. Unpublished manuscript, University of British Columbia.

Paulhus, D.L. 1989. Measurement and control of response bias. In *Measures of social-psychological attitudes*, ed. J.P. Robinson, P.R. Shaver, and L. Wrightsman. New York: Academic.

Phillips, D.L., and K.J. Clancy. 1972. Some effects of 'social desirability' in survey studies. *The American Journal of Sociology* 77(5): 921–940.

Randall, D.M., and A.M. Gibson. 1990. Methodology in business ethics research: A review and critical assessment. *Journal of Business Ethics* 9(6): 457–472.

Riecken, H.W. 1962. A program for research on experiments in social psychology. In *Values and groups*, ed. N.F. Washburn. New York: Pergamon.

Rosen, E. 1956. Self-appraisal, personal desirability, and perceived social desirability of personality traits. *Journal of Social Psychology* 52: 151–158.

Rosenthal, R. 1966. *Experimental effects in behavioral research*. New York: Appleton.

Ruch, W.A., and J.W. Newstrom. 1975. How unethical are we?, *Supervisory Management*, pp. 16–21.

Sackeim, H.A., and R. Gur. 1978. Self-deception, self- confrontation and consciousness. In *Consciousness and self-regulation: Advances in research*, vol. 2, ed. G.E. Schwartz and D. Shapiro, 139–197. New York: Plenum.

Stem Jr., D.E., and R.K. Steinhorst. 1984. Telephone interview and mail questionnaire applications of the randomized response model. *Journal of the American Statistical Association* 79(387): 555–564.

Stevens, G.E. 1984. Business ethics and social responsibility: The responses of present and future managers. *Akron Business and Economic Review* 15(3): 6–11.

Tanaka-Matsumi, J., and V.A. Kameoka. 1986. Reliabilities and concurrent validities of popular self-report measures of depression, anxiety, and social desirability. *Journal of Consulting and Clinical Psychology* 54: 328–333.

Trevino, L.K. 1986. Ethical decision making in organizations: A person-situation interactionist model. *Academy of Management Review* 11(3): 601–611.

Victor, B., and J.B. Cullen. 1988. The organizational bases of ethical work climates. *Administrative Science Quarterly* 33: 101–125.

Wiggins, J., and C. Rumrill. 1959. Social desirability in the MMPI and Welsh's factor scales A and R. *Journal of Consulting Psychology* 23: 100–106.
Wiseman, F. 1972. Methodological bias in public opinion surveys. *Public Opinion Quarterly* 36: 105–108.
Zerbe, W.J., and D.L. Paulhus. 1987. Socially desirable responding in organizational behavior: A reconception. *Academy of Management Journal* 12(2): 250–264.

Chapter 10
Methodology in Business Ethics Research: A Review and Critical Assessment

Donna M. Randall and Annetta M. Gibson

At present, little is known about the quality of empirical research on the ethical beliefs and conduct of organization members. The purpose of this paper is to provide a critical review of the methodology in business ethics articles and to suggest methodological refinements. Using published empirical articles in academic journals as a data base, methodological decisions made by business ethics researchers in each of the eight major stages of the research process depicted in Fig. 10.1 are summarized. When weaknesses are noted, suggestions for a more defensible methodology are offered.

Methodology

An attempt was made to locate all published studies that empirically investigated ethical beliefs and behavior in organizations. Three computerized data bases were searched: *Management Contents*, the *Social Sciences Citation Index* (SSCI), and the *Business Periodicals Index* (BPI). *Management Contents* indexes 500 U.S. and international journals on a variety of business-related topics from 1974 to present. Using titles and descriptors, the following key words were searched: ethical conduct, ethical decision(s), and ethical situation(s). The SSCI contains over one million citations from articles in key social science journals and selected journals in related fields from 1972 to present. Using titles and descriptors, the following key words were searched: ethical conduct, ethical decision(s), ethical situation(s),

D.M. Randall (✉)
Office of the President, Albion College, Albion, MI 49224-1831, USA
e-mail: drandall@albion.edu

A.M. Gibson
School of Business, Andrews University, Berrien Springs, MI 49104, USA
e-mail: gibson@andrews.edu

A.C. Michalos and D.C. Poff (eds.), *Citation Classics from the Journal of Business Ethics*, Advances in Business Ethics Research 2,
DOI 10.1007/978-94-007-4126-3_10,

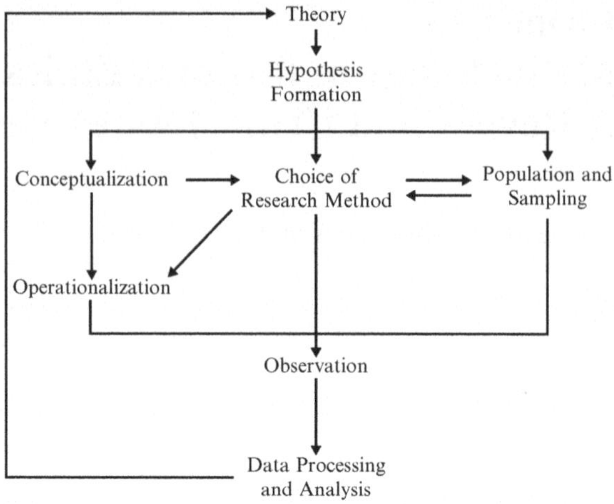

Fig. 10.1 An overview of stages in the research process (Adapted from Babbie 1986)

business ethics, managerial ethics, ethical beliefs, ethical conflict, ethical judgment, ethical attitudes, ethical perceptions, ethical standards, unethical behavior, unethical decision(s), immoral behavior, managerial morality, organizational ethics, and business philosophies. The BPI was accessed on CD/Rom using a Wilsondisc PC-Rom information retrieval system through the key word, "business ethics." The data base indexes 304 periodicals on virtually every subject area related to business from 1982 to the present.

In addition to the three computer searches, *The Readers Guide to Periodical Literature* from 1960 to present and the *Business Periodicals Index* from 1958 to the present were searched manually using "business ethics" as a key word. *The Readers Guide to Periodical Literature* is a cumulative subject index to approximately 175 periodicals published in the U.S. Finally, bibliographies in all relevant articles were reviewed to identify additional citations not obtained through the computer or manual searches.

Each article was screened using clearly defined, prespecified criteria. Each article was reviewed to determine if: (1) the article contained an empirical research study, and (2) the study dealt with ethical beliefs (defined by Bowman (1976), as judgments about what is right and wrong and whether or not these judgments are good or bad) or ethical behavior (defined by Runes (1964), as "just" or "right" standards of behavior between parties in a situation) of organizational employees (employees, peers, or managers). As the focus of the study was on ethical beliefs and behavior, related articles on social responsibility, corporate codes of conduct, and whistle-blowing were excluded from the study.

Of the over 700 citations obtained, 94 articles met these two criteria and were included in the study.[1,2] Each of the 94 articles was analyzed in depth. A code sheet was developed which consisted of a series of questions regarding key components of the research process depicted in Fig. 10.1. Such questions included: Was a theory presented? Were hypotheses specified? Were key constructs clearly defined?

Were the instruments used to measure the key constructs reliable and valid? Were the instruments pretested? What research design was selected? How was the sample selected? Did the researchers seek to generalize to a larger population? What observation techniques were used? What statistical techniques were used to analyze the data?

Further, using *Cabell's Directory of Publishing Opportunities in Business and Economics* (1988 edition), data were gathered on the acceptance rate of each journal publishing business ethics research (reflected in Table 10.1). When a range of acceptance rates was provided, the mean of that range was used to calculate the acceptance rate. Due to a skewed distribution, the median acceptance rate was used to classify acceptance rates of the journals as high (26% or above) or low (25% or lower). As analysis revealed that including studies from journals with nonavailable acceptance rates (18 studies) into the high acceptance rate category did not significantly change the findings, all subsequent analyses were run excluding the unrated studies.

The code sheet was pretested for comprehensiveness and clarity. Ten articles were coded independently by the first and second authors. After agreement was reached on coding discrepancies and refinements, all 94 articles were coded onto a revised code sheet by the second author. Using a random numbers table, the first author selected 15% (14 articles) and independently coded the articles. The interrater reliability between the two authors on the subsample of articles was 97.1%.

Overview of Articles

Empirical research on ethical beliefs and behavior in business organizations spans three decades beginning with a well-known study of attitudes of executives toward business ethics (Baumhart 1961). As Fig. 10.2 illustrates, academic interest in business ethics remained fairly constant until the mid 1970s. The 1980s reflected great interest in business ethics with over 60% (66) of the articles published during this period. Interest has been particularly strong in recent years, as reflected by the peak of published articles in 1987 and 1988.

Over the past three decades, a surprising variety of journals have published research on business ethics. As reflected in Table 10.1, the most popular publication outlet is the *Journal of Business Ethics,* publishing over one third (32) of the empirical articles on ethical beliefs and behavior of organizational members. With the exception of the *Journal of Marketing*, each of the remaining journals referenced in Table 10.1 published a maximum of three relevant articles.

Methodological Critique

While one might anticipate that empirical articles published in academic journals would provide fairly detailed methodological description, the review of articles revealed that this was not the case. There was a surprizing amount of missing detail.

Table 10.1 Journals publishing articles on ethical beliefs and behavior in business

Name of journal	# of articles	(%)	Acceptance rate[a]
1. *Journal of Business Ethics*	32	34.0	21–30%
2. *Journal of Marketing*	5	5.3	10% or less
3. *Akron Business and Economic Review*	3	3.2	11–20%
4. *Business Horizons*	3	3.2	20–25%
5. *Harvard Business Review*	3	3.2	5% or less
6. *Journal of Applied Psychology*	3	3.2	6–10%
7. *Journal of Business Research*	3	3.2	6–10%
8. *Psychological Reports*	3	3.2	na
9. *Journal of Retailing*	2	2.1	21–30%
10. *Management Review*	2	2.1	6–10%
11. *Business and Society Review*	2	2.1	10%
12. *Journal of Small Business Management*	2	2.1	21–30%
13. *Human Relations*	2	2.1	na
14. *Journal of Academy of Marketing Science*	2	2.1	11–20%
15. *Journal of Purchasing and Materials Management*	2	2.1	21–30%
16. *MSU Business Topics*	2	2.1	na
17. *Personnel Journal*	2	2.1	6–10%
18. *California Management Review*	1	1.1	6–10%
19. *Public Personnel Management Journal*	1	1.1	11–20%
20. *Academy of Management Journal*	1	1.1	6–10%
21. *Atlantic Economic Review*	1	1.1	na
22. *Conference Board Record*	1	1.1	15–18%
23. *Industrial Marketing Management*	1	1.1	11–20%
24. *Journal of Advertising*	1	1.1	6–10%
25. *Organizational Dynamics*	1	1.1	6–10%
26. *Personnel Administration*	1	1.1	na
27. *Purchasing*	1	1.1	na
28. *Review of Business and Economic Research*	1	1.1	11–20%
29. *Supervisory Management*	1	1.1	na
30. *Journal of Purchasing*	1	1.1	na
31. *Supervision*	1	1.1	50% or more
32. *Business and Society Review*	1	1.1	10%
33. *Direct Marketing*	1	1.1	na
34. *Canadian Business*	1	1.1	na
35. *European Journal of Marketing*	1	1.1	na
36. *Southern Business Review*	1	1.1	na
37. *Management Decision*	1	1.1	na
38. *Marketing Education*	1	1.1	na
Total	94	100.0	

[a]As reported in Cabell's *Directory of Publishing Opportunities in Business and Economics*, 1988 ed
na not available

Full methodological description appeared in less than one half (45) of the 94 articles. While several studies neglected to report only one or two methodological details, other studies (e.g., Allen 1980; Bezilla et al. 1976) reported only two methodological

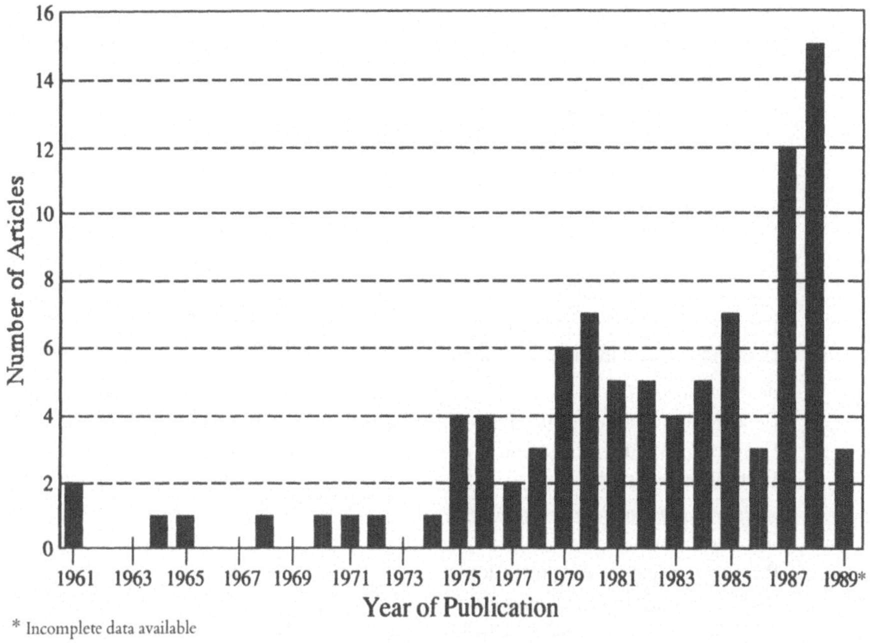

Fig. 10.2 Business ethics articles by year

details – who was sampled and the number of participants in the study – without any other methodological description.

A complete disclosure of methods in any empirical study is essential for an accurate appraisal of the research findings. Without full disclosure of research methods, it will be difficult to evaluate the significance of the research findings and dangerous to draw any practical implications from the study.

From the methodological description which was provided, the following conclusions about empirical research on ethical beliefs and conduct can be drawn:

Theoretic Framework

Theory is a necessary component of the research process. Positivists advocate a deductive approach to theory development in which a theoretic framework is the appropriate starting place for empirical research. Once a theoretic base has been established, business ethics researchers can make predictions about what beliefs and behavior would likely occur under given conditions, logically develop a research program to examine those predictions, interpret findings in light of the specified theory, and revise the theory, if necessary. The business ethics articles reviewed were characterized by a distinct absence of theory. As reflected in Table 10.2,

Table 10.2 Summary of methodological decisions

Theoretic framework	#	%
No theory development	60	64
Unclear if theory present	2	2
Weak theory development	8	9
Strong theory development	24	26
Hypothesis offered		
No	71	75
Yes	23	25
Conceptualization		
Definition offered to readers of article	21	22
Definition offered to study participants	7	7
Operationalization		
Concern for reliability of instrument mentioned	18	19
Concern for validity of instrument mentioned	18	19
Instrument pretested	19	20
Population and sampling decisions		
Study population		
Practicing managers and professionals	63	67
Students (graduate and undergraduate)	24	26
Combination of managers and students	7	7
Sample design		
Design not specified	13	14
Other	11	12
Convenience sampling	39	42
Random sampling	31	33
Response rate		
Not reported	10	11
Below 10%	0	0
10–19%	2	2
20–29%	10	11
30–39%	8	9
40–49%	10	11
50–59%	4	4
60–69%	4	4
Above 70%	4	4
Not applicable	42	45
Research design		
Survey research	76	81
Lab experiment/simulation	6	6
In-person interviews	4	4
In-person interviews and survey	3	3
Not reported	5	5
Analytic techniques		
Univariate techniques	33	35
Bivariate techniques	43	46
Multivariate techniques	18	19

64% (60) of the studies did not cite any previously established theoretic framework nor seek to develop one.

In an effort to move beyond descriptive research, it is desirable that researchers specify a theoretic framework. Researchers need not develop their own theoretic framework; a large number of theoretic models currently await empirical testing (e.g., Bommer et al. 1987; Trevino 1986). Empirical studies by Hegarty and Sims (1978) and Zey-Ferrell and Ferrell (1982) provide excellent examples of how previously existing theoretic frameworks can be used to guide empirical research on business ethics.

Hypotheses

Once a theoretic framework has been established, researchers typically develop and specify hypotheses or propositions predicting a particular relationship between two or more variables. Just as few empirical articles on ethical beliefs and behavior presented a theoretic framework, few presented testable hypotheses (Table 10.2).

As business ethic researchers move beyond exploratory research, it will be necessary to develop specific research hypotheses. Hegarty and Sims (1978, 1979) aptly illustrated how testable hypotheses can be derived from a theoretic framework.

Conceptualization

The conceptualization phase of the research process involves defining the meaning of theoretic constructs. This stage is particularly troublesome in ethics research as there is little consensus regarding what constitutes "ethical" beliefs or "ethical" behavior in an organizational setting (Baumhart 1961; Ferrell and Gresham 1985; Vitell and Festervand 1987). Not only are ethical standards constantly changing over time, but they vary from one situation or organization to another (Barnett and Karson 1987; Ferrell and Gresham 1985). As an illustration of the conceptual confusion characterizing business ethics research, Lewis (1985) identified 308 different definitions of the term "business ethics" in 254 articles, books, and textbooks.

Rather than offering a wide variety of definitions of ethical beliefs and behavior, the majority of business ethics articles reviewed offered no definition of ethical beliefs or conduct to study participants or readers of the article (Table 10.2). For instance, Allen (1980) asked survey respondents to indicate which organizations and institutions were likely to encourage poor ethics on the part of their members, without defining "poor ethics" or asking respondents what "poor ethics" meant to them. Such an approach allows readers and study participants to create and respond to their own definitions of ethical beliefs and conduct.

To build a cumulative data base of business ethics research, key constructs in business ethics research need to be clearly defined. Without a commonly shared understanding of what is meant by ethical beliefs and conduct, these terms will be ultimately defined by study participants and their definition will remain unknown to researchers and readers of business ethic articles. Examples of clearly stated definitions of ethical beliefs and conduct can be found in Bowman (1976), Brown and King (1982), Brenner and Molander (1977), and Browning and Zabriskie (1983).

Operationalization

Operationalization decisions involve finding reliable and valid measures for theoretical constructs. The articles reviewed reflected surprisingly little concern for either the validity or reliability of the research instruments (Table 10.2). It appears that most business ethics researchers assumed that their instruments were reliable and had face validity. Unfortunately, as little consensus exists about the definition of ethical beliefs and conduct, one researcher's judgment of validity of an instrument may not be the same as another's. In addition, if ethical beliefs and conduct are multidimensional constructs, face validity will not assure that an instrument taps all relevant dimensions.

Some researchers did demonstrate a concern for the reliability and validity of the research instruments. For instance, Chonko and Hunt (1985) sought to enhance the reliability of their instruments by using interrater reliability checks, while Dubinsky and Ingram (1984) reported the Cronbach's Coefficient alpha for all scales used in their research. Similarly, in seeking to enhance the content validity of their instrument, Fritzsche and Becker (1984) developed a number of vignettes in each of five representative categories of ethical problems.

Pretesting can help increase the reliability and validity of measures (as well as encourage scrutiny of question wording, question order, redundant questions, missing/inappropriate questions, confusing response categories, and poor scale items (Bailey 1982)). Yet, no pretest was conducted in 78% (73) of the business ethics articles. While some of these articles (23) had adopted measures from other studies, 50 of the articles utilized newly developed measures without any reported pretest.

When pretests were conducted they were appropriately conducted in the target population. For example, Fritzsche and Becker (1984) pretested vignettes on a sample of marketing managers (the relevant population) by drawing a random sample from a local chapter of the American Marketing Association. Similarly, Dubinsky and Gwin (1981) pretested descriptions of ethical situations with the assistance of purchasing and field sales personnel across several industries (the relevant population).

In sum, business ethics researchers need to develop reliable and valid instruments, to conduct pretests of those instruments, and to continue to conduct pretests in the target population. The reliability of the instruments can be fairly easily assessed using measures of interrater reliability, internal consistency, or test-retest reliability. Whereas the validity of instruments is typically more difficult to ascertain, possible options might include the use of a validation procedure set forth by Churchill (1979), a multitrait-multimethod matrix (Campbell and Fiske 1959), or a nomological net (Cronbach and Meehl 1955).

Population and Sampling Decisions

Population and sampling decisions concern identification of the group about which conclusions are to be drawn and the group that will be observed for that purpose. Population and sampling decisions generally involve four issues: who is sampled, what type of sample is drawn, what an acceptable response rate is, and what size of sample is needed.

Study Population

The bulk of articles on ethical beliefs and conduct used practicing managers and professionals as a sample (see Table 10.2). It was particularly interesting to note the heavy reliance upon samples of marketing managers. Over one-quarter (25) of the 94 articles explored ethical practices in marketing-related professions (sales, purchasing, and advertising). This was undoubtedly due to the belief that marketing managers encounter more situations that result in decisions with ethical impact than do executives in other functional areas of the firm (Chonko and Hunt 1985; Dubinsky and Gwin 1981; Dubinsky and Levy 1985; Levy and Dubinsky 1983; Trawick and Darden 1980).

It was also surprising to note that relatively few business ethics articles used student samples. Whereas the use of student samples has been heavily criticized in organizational research due to problems of generalizability (see Rosenthal and Rosnow 1975), student samples are appropriate if they comprise the population of interest or if the population of interest is similar to the student sample on theoretically relevant variables and the study is part of a research program investigating generalizability to the population of interest (Gordon et al. 1987). Furthermore, while studies examining attitudes have found sizeable discrepancies between students and other subjects, studies focusing on decision-making have found considerable similarities in the decisions and assumed behavior of student and nonstudent samples (Ashton and Kramer 1980; Remus 1986).

On those occasions when students were used as subjects in business ethics research, the purpose of the study was not to generalize to managers, but to determine attitudes held specifically by business students toward ethical dilemmas (e.g., Beltramini et al. 1984; Jones and Gautschi 1988), the influence of individual difference variables on ethical decision-making (e.g., McNichols and Zimmer 1985; Tsalikis and Nwachukwsu 1988), the impact and effectiveness of business ethics courses (e.g., Hawkins and Cocanougher 1972; Martin 1981), and the willingness of students to engage in unethical practices (e.g., Rosenberg 1987; Worrell et al. 1985).

Hence, the use of managerial samples for understanding the ethical beliefs of managers appears to be highly appropriate. In those instances where researchers are interested in exploring the ethical decision-making process, student samples can be substituted without a major threat to generalizability.

Sampling Design

Once a study population was selected, business ethics researchers relied primarily upon random or convenience sampling to select individuals for inclusion in the study (Table 10.2). Historically, random samples have been preferred over convenience samples as they offer the best assurance against sampling bias (e.g., Lazernitz 1968). Convenience or "captive audience" samples offer no assurance of representativeness and do not permit generalization to a larger population. (However, when expert opinion surveys are conducted (e.g., Schutte 1965), a convenience sampling design is highly appropriate.)

In business ethics research, generalizations from convenience samples to a larger population were frequently made. For instance, Rizzo and Patka (1981) generalized from a convenience sample of middle managers in public agencies in south Florida to all public managers; Trawick and Darden (1980) generalized from a convenience sample of marketing practitioners and educators (with an unspecified selection strategy) to all practitioners and educators; and, Dubinsky and Ingram (1984) similarly generalized from a convenience sample of salespersons (with an unspecified selection strategy) to all sales personnel.

Ideally, business ethics researchers should seek to decrease their reliance on convenience samples and increase the use of random samples. Random samples can be drawn using such techniques as membership lists of professional associations or a directory of manufacturers. As random sampling may not always be feasible due to time and resource constraints, at minimum, generalizations from convenience samples to the larger population need to be curtailed.

It was interesting to note that managerial and student samples are associated with distinct sampling designs. A majority of the 63 studies involving managers or professionals as the study population were conducted using a random sampling technique, through mail surveys, and had a mean sample size of 411. On the other hand, a majority of 24 studies involving students as the study population selected respondents through convenience sampling, utilized questionnaires administered in a research setting, and had a mean sample size of 560.

Sample Size

A large sample size can help minimize sampling error. Many researchers view 100 subjects as a minimum sample size (Bailey 1982). If one compares sample sizes in business ethics research against this standard, ethics research clearly surpasses the minimum. The mean number of subjects in the studies reviewed was 434, with a range from 4 to 2,856 subjects. As the mean was skewed by four particularly large samples, the median of 196 presents a better estimate of typical sample size.

However, adequacy of sample size is not simply a function of the number of subjects, but rather depends on such factors as how the respondents were selected (random or convenience), the distribution of the population parameter (the variable of interest), the purpose of the research project (exploratory or applied), and the intended data analytic procedures (to ensure adequate cell sizes for statistical analysis). Despite the importance of such factors, they were infrequently taken into consideration in the determination of appropriate sample size. It appears, as is true of most social science research (Simon and Burstein 1985), that the sample size was fixed by the amount of money available or the sample size that similar pieces of research used in the past (e.g., Krugman and Ferrell 1981; Posner and Schmidt 1987). For example, although Hogarth (1978) determined that under certain conditions groups with 8–12 experts have predictive ability close to the optimum, in the two surveys of expert opinion (Schutte 1965), a limited number of experts—seven and four, respectively—were approached.

It would be desirable for business ethics researchers to consider more carefully the issue of sample size. Attention to the purpose of the research, sampling design, and likely data analytic techniques can aid in this effort. A pretest can help determine how the population parameter is distributed in the population. Such techniques as a Monte Carlo experiment or step-wise sample-size determination (Simon and Burstein 1985) may also aid in determining appropriate sample size.

Response Rate

A low response rate in any type of research is troubling as the data may not be representative of the population surveyed. For most studies, Babbie (1986) advised that a response rate of at least 50% is adequate for analysis and reporting, a response rate of 60% is good, and 70% or more is very good. However, in research on sensitive topics, a response rate of even 70% may be a severe problem, as nonrespondents are more likely to be similar in important characteristics, thus introducing substantial nonrandom error. Moreover, factors such as cost of reducing the nonresponse bias need to be taken into consideration.

The typical response rate to surveys in the business ethics articles was low (Table 10.2). The mean response rate was 43%, ranging from 10% in a *Business and Society Review* survey (1975) to 96% in a study by McNichols and Zimmer (1985), with a median of 40%. A large number of factors may contribute to the low response rate. Bailey (1982) contended that response rates to social science research are declining due to saturation. However, the articles reviewed revealed an insignificant relationship between time and response rate to ethics research ($r = -0.08$, $p > 0.31$, $n = 42$).

The cause of the low response rate to surveys in business ethics research probably lies more in the nature of the research topic. Business ethics is a particularly delicate topic to research. Managers may not want to have their "ethics" observed or measured directly (Trevino 1986), and few employees may be willing to divulge information to researchers that might be incriminating to them or to their friends. Thus, people willing to participate in an experiment or survey about ethics might have very different attitudes than people more reticent to respond.

Due to the importance of acquiring an adequate response rate, business ethics researchers may want to consider three suggestions. First, they may want to use "stronger" techniques to encourage a higher response rate. These techniques might include personal interviewing (which typically has a higher response rate than survey research), targeting and intensively surveying a subpopulation (for a more personalized appeal), persuading respondents of the importance of the research topic and their candid answers (in the cover letter as well as on the questionaire), or free gifts provided with the survey (such as financial incentives or donations to charities) (see Dillman 1978, for a more complete discussion of these and other techniques to enhance the response rate).

Second, researchers could seek to determine if nonrespondents differ in any significant way from respondents. For example, Armstrong and Overton (1977) discussed the feasibility of using subjective estimates and extrapolation methods to estimate nonresponse bias. Of the business ethics studies reporting a response rate less than 60%, only one study (Chonko and Hunt 1985) compared demographics of respondents and nonrespondents to assess the possibility of a response bias. A number of other studies (e.g., Browning and Zabriskie 1983; Carroll 1975; Fritzsche and Becker 1984; Vitell and Festervand 1987) cited extensive demographic detail on the respondents, but failed to state how those data compared with characteristics of nonrespondents.

Finally, when a low response rate is obtained and comparable data on respondents are not available, researchers may want to warn readers not to generalize beyond the sample. For instance due to an unexpectedly low (40%) response rate, Lincoln et al. (1982) cautioned readers not to generalize to firms beyond those in the sample. However, even if a caveat is incorporated into the article, one might question the utility of the study and its contribution to the literature.

Selection of Research Design

As reflected in Table 10.2, survey research was clearly the most common research design used by business ethics researchers (81% of the studies). Other designs, utilized much less frequently, included lab experiments and simulations (6%), in-person interviews (4%), and a combination of in-person interviews and surveys (3%).

Survey Research

Survey research used either a direct question format or scenarios. When a direct question format was used, researchers typically asked respondents how they felt about a particular issue or if they would engage in a particular practice. Respondents were presented with an average of 19 questions one sentence in length. When scenarios were used, respondents were typically presented with a hypothetical situation and asked to indicate how they would behave in that situation. Most often respondents were presented with 12 scenarios (with as few as 1 scenario and as many as 37), with each scenario averaging five sentences in length.

The key problem with both the direct question and scenario formats is vagueness and generality. The problem situation is described so briefly to the respondent that it is difficult for him or her to evaluate and for the researcher to attain any reasonable degree of within-subject reliability. Ethical choice is commonly believed to be situationally specific; the "best" action is not based on pre-existing values, but upon specifics of the action choice (Barnett and Karson 1987). Contextual variables, such as the influence and actions of peers and managers, available rewards and punishments, and the probability of detection, may be essential pieces of information for realistic decision-making.

Two examples from the literature illustrate the problem of ambiguous and vague questions and scenarios. Using a previously developed instrument, Norris and Gifford (1988) asked respondents to express their agreement or disagreement with the action taken in the following situation: "A customer calls the retailer to report that her refrigerator purchased 2 weeks ago is not cooling properly and that all the food has spoiled. Action: The customer should be reimbursed for the value of the spoiled food." Hawkins and Cocanougher (1972) asked students how ethical or unethical the following situation was: "A large manufacturer of technical equipment requires that all its salesmen dress 'conservatively' in dark suits with white shirts." When provided with such one-sentence descriptions and no other contextual information, the only defensible answer to the question, "What would you do?" is probably, "It depends." (Frederiksen et al. 1972).

Scenarios and questions clearly need to be developed with a greater concern for realism. Fredrickson (1986) suggested a detailed methodology for developing scenarios in strategy research which can also be very appropriate in business ethics research. Structured interviews are conducted to identify issues facing the industry and possible actions on the part of respondents. A scenario is developed using industry-specific terminology, usually with enough detail for five, single-spaced pages. A pilot test is then conducted to ensure that the scenario and accompanying questions are understandable and an accurate portrayal of the situation. The procedure provides all respondents with a standardized stimulus, sets forth a reasonably realistic, detailed situation, and the situation is written in such a way that it generates the respondent's interest and therefore "involvement" (Fredrickson 1986).

In addition to the problem of vague scenarios and questions, a secondary problem accompanying survey research methodology relates to the heavy use of close-ended questions. Respondents are frequently asked to describe what they would do in a given situation by responding to close-ended questions. The respondent does not have to devise a solution—he or she merely has to evaluate those presented to him or her (Frederiksen et al. 1972). Problems do not typically present themselves in multiple-choice form. Sometimes it is necessary to invent a solution rather than to choose one of several presented (Frederiksen et al. 1972). Furthermore, close-ended questions are most appropriate when researchers have a well-defined issue and know precisely what dimension of thought they want the respondent to use in providing an answer (Dillman 1978). As business ethics research is in an embryonic stage (Laczniak and Inderrieden 1987), feasible behavioral choices remain loosely defined.

Despite the recognized difficulty of evaluating essay answers and the possible biasing effect of verbal facility (Frederiksen et al. 1972), a free-response format to questions and scenarios may be superior to the close-ended format typically used in business ethics research. However, the review of empirical research revealed that a free-response format was used in only five articles (Fritzsche and Becker 1984; Laczniak and Inderrieden 1987; Mayer 1988; Posner and Schmidt 1987).

In brief, the questions and scenarios used in survey research are typically too vague and lack realism, while the close-ended questions force responses into pre-defined categories. Fredrickson's article (1986) provides a detailed description of how more valid questions and scenarios can be developed, and the use of more open-ended questions can help overcome difficulties posed by the use of close-ended questions.

Laboratory Designs

Unlike survey research, laboratory research permits the examination of causal relationships and the control of exogenous variables. Within the context of a lab experiment, in-basket exercises (e.g., Laczniak and Inderrieden 1987) and computer simulations (e.g., Hegarty and Sims 1978) can be used.

Despite the advantages of lab research, at present little is done from an experimental design point of view (Laczniak and Inderrieden 1987) (also see Table 10.2). While only 6 of the 94 articles utilized a laboratory design, these articles demonstrate the potential value of laboratory research. For instance, using a computer simulation, Hegarty and Sims (1978) measured the effects of potential rewards and punishments on students paying kickbacks in simulated business situations. The experimental design consisted of a 3×3 factorial analysis of variance with selected personality and demographic variables as co-variates. Subjects entered decisions into an on-line time-shared computer program, allowing experimental control over key variables and an assessment of causal relationships.

In-person Interviews

In-person interviews can be very useful in exploratory stages of a research project for developing an understanding of a phenomenon. However, only 7 of the 94 articles used in-person interviews as a research design. Four of these articles relied solely upon in-person interviews for data collection (Bird and Waters 1987; Mayer 1988; Waters and Bird 1987; Waters et al. 1986), while the three other studies used a combination of in-person interviews and survey research (Avlonitis 1983; Rudelius and Buchholz 1979; Schutte 1965).

For in-person interviews to be useful, a complete description of findings is needed. All four studies relying exclusively on in-person interviews contained an extensive discussion of the findings from open-ended interviews. Of the studies using a combination of in-person interviews and surveys, Schutte (1965) and Avlonitis (1983) also provided a fair amount of methodological detail and discussion of findings from the personal interviews. However, the remaining study (Rudelius and Buchholz 1979) offered little detail about who and how many individuals were interviewed and the results of those personal interviews. In brief, in-person interviews can serve a valuable role in exploratory research on ethical beliefs and conduct if findings are sufficiently detailed.

In business ethics research, self-report data are almost invariably used as an observation technique as few alternative techniques exist. In fact, the review of empirical research revealed that self-report data were relied upon in almost 90% of the research articles (all research designs involving surveys or interviews).

Unfortunately, major differences often occur between what people say they would do and what they actually do. The use of self-report data raises problems in that respondents may organize their responses in light of what they feel "others" will expect is appropriate for someone like them in a particular kind of situation. Somewhat apprehensive about the confidentiality of their responses and the relationship of researchers to managers, respondents may be sensitive when answering questions about their ethical beliefs and conduct.

The tendency of respondents to deny socially undesirable traits, to claim socially desirable ones, and to say things which place the speaker in a favorable light has been termed a "social desirability" bias (Nederhof 1985). A social desirability bias may cause individuals to overreport actions that are perceived to be socially desirable ("ethical" conduct) and to underreport behavior ("unethical" conduct) perceived to be socially undesirable. It is also possible that respondents may overstate the difference between their ethical beliefs and actions and the beliefs and actions of others.

A number of empirical research articles have employed questions that are highly susceptible to a social desirability bias. For instance, Brown and King (1982) asked respondents to indicate agreement or disagreement with the following statement, "Ethical practices are good business in the long run." When asking respondents what they would do in a particular situation, Krugman and Ferrell (1981) gave respondents such options as, "Manipulating a situation to make a subordinate look bad," or "Divulging confidential information." The wording of such statements would clearly seem to encourage a social desirability bias.

It is admittedly difficult to counter social desirability biases. Phillips and Clancy (1970) contended that the usual precautions for eliminating the possible effects of the bias (e.g., assuring anonymity and stressing that there are no right or wrong answers) will typically not eliminate the influence of respondents' desire to place themselves in a favorable light. However, steps can and should be taken to reduce this bias. For example, the Crowne-Marlowe Social Desirability (SD) Scale

(Crowne and Marlowe 1964), used by Stevens (1984), can help detect a social desirability bias. In addition, Nederhof (1985) has provided a comprehensive review of techniques to reduce or prevent social desirability bias.

Analytic Techniques

Data processing and analysis refer to the transformation of data into a form suitable for analysis and drawing conclusions regarding the specified theory or hypotheses. One data analytic technique is not necessarily superior to another; the appropriateness of the technique depends primarily upon the theory, research hypotheses, and available data. In descriptive studies and especially exploratory ones, univariate statistics (means, modes, percentages, or standard deviations) may be in order. If the interrelation of two or more variables is the object of interest, a bivariate or a multivariate presentation of data may be more appropriate.

The business ethics articles reflected a heavy reliance on univariate and bivariate statistics (Table 10.2). Thirty-five percent (33) of the articles reported only univariate statistics (with 27 articles reporting only percentages, three articles reporting only means, and two articles reporting only rank orders). Forty-six percent (43) of the articles used some form of bivariate statistics (primarily t-tests), and 19% (18) of the articles used some form of multivariate analysis (e.g., analysis of covariance, multiple regression, or loglinear logit analysis.)

Without complete methodological detail and an understanding of the purpose of the research project, it is difficult to specify which form of statistical analysis should have been used. However, one might anticipate that as research on business ethics progresses, the reliance on multivariate statistics will increase. Indeed, a strong empirical relationship between the passage of time and use of multivariate statistics ($r=0.39$, $p<0.001$, $n=94$) can be detected.

Recommendations and Conclusions

After conducting structured personal interviews with more than 50 scholars in the area of ethics, Fleming (1987) concluded that researchers are somewhat dissatisfied with the present methodologies and are searching for new ones. From the review of empirical research, it appears that the dissatisfaction is justified; the methodology in business ethics research is clearly in need of improvement. However, in addition to searching for new methodologies, business ethics researchers may simply need to apply more conscientiously and to report more fully methodologies currently in use.

As summarized in Table 10.3, the critical review of methodological decisions has identified key weaknesses, strengths, and areas in need of improvement in business ethics research. Unfortunately, Table 10.3 reveals that decisions made early in the research process (specification of theory, development of hypotheses, conceptualization decisions, and operationalization decisions) are most susceptible

Table 10.3 Relative strengths and weaknesses of research decisions

Research stage	Relative strength	Possible improvements
Theory development	Weak	Specification of theory
Hypotheses	Weak	Specification of hypotheses
Conceptualization	Weak	Offer definition of ethical conduct to reader and study participants
Operationalization		
Reliability	Weak	Use more reliable instruments
Validity	Weak	Use more valid instruments
Pretesting	Weak	Use more pretests
Population and sampling decisions		
Study population	Strong	Managerial samples for beliefs; student samples acceptable for decision-making
Sample design	Moderate	Less reliance on convenience samples
Sample size	Moderate	Consider population parameters, design, purpose and analysis
Response rate	Weak	Use techniques to enhance response rate
Selection of the research design		
Survey research	Weak	Need more specific and realistic questions and scenarios
Laboratory research	Strong	Continue to use lab and simulations
In-person interviews	Moderate	Need fuller findings and description
Observation	Weak	Reduce social desirability bias
Data analysis and processing	Moderate	Less reliance on univariate statistics

to criticism, establishing a shaky foundation for decisions made in subsequent steps of the research process. Thus, methodological improvement in these initial steps in the research process should have the highest priority at this time.

To encourage more methodological rigor in empirical research, editors of journals publishing empirical business ethics research may consider adopting a structured referee rating form asking reviewers to assess the methodological rigor of the study. Such a form would not supplant traditional substantive reviews; it would be provided as supplemental to the open-ended responses typically solicited from reviewers.

Editors of journals might also invite a methodologist in addition to substantive reviewers to comment on papers submitted for review, ask that one of the substantive reviewers specifically review the paper for methodological adequacy, or solicit commentaries to be published along with the paper. Such modifications in the review process should encourage greater attention to and consideration of methodological issues on the part of potential authors, reviewers, and editors.

While all empirical articles need to demonstrate a concern for more methodologically rigorous articles, *The Journal of Business Ethics* may want to take a lead in this effort as it is regarded as the "flagship" journal in ethics research. Yet, a comparison of the 32 articles published in *Journal of Business Ethics* against the remaining 62 articles across all the methodological dimensions discussed above revealed no substantive methodological differences, with one exception. The *Journal of Business Ethics* tended to publish fewer studies using mail survey research than non-*Journal of Business Ethics* articles (i.e., 28% of *Journal of Business Ethics* articles used a mail survey approach vs. 56% of non-*Journal of Business Ethics* articles).

It was also interesting to note that the more "rigorous" journals, in terms of lower acceptance rates, did not generally publish more methodologically rigorous articles. No substantive methodological differences were detected between studies published in high and low acceptance journals, with again the one exception of research design. Journals with low acceptance rates (i.e., more rigorous journals) tended to publish more mail surveys than journals with high acceptance rates (i.e., less rigorous journals). Specifically, 68% of the articles in journals with low acceptance rates used a mail survey approach vs. 30% of the articles published in journals with high acceptance rates).

In sum, while it would be desirable to make all of the refinements suggested above, it is important to recognize that research in any area involves tradeoffs between the desirable and the practical (Bailey 1982). Due to difficulties presented by such a sensitive research topic as business ethics, researchers may never be able to approach the study of business ethics with an "ideal" scientific research process. However, with complete reporting of methodological decisions and the consideration of as many refinements in the review process as possible, a solid methodological foundation can be established and that foundation can make a substantial contribution to understanding and improving the ethical climate of organizations.

Notes

1. Because the search was not exhaustive, no argument is made that all empirical research articles on ethical beliefs and behavior have been included. For instance, research on business ethics appearing in books, book chapters, and conference papers have not been analyzed. The data gathering procedure also suffers from whatever limitations may be said to accompany the publication decisions of the journals incorporated within the data bases.
2. Limited empirical investigation of ethical beliefs and behavior has taken place (Trevino 1986). Most articles approach ethics from a nonempirical perspective, e.g., developing theoretic models of ethical decision-making (e.g., Trevino 1986; Bommer et al. 1987), specifying taxonomies of moral rules (e.g., Forsyth 1980), or providing practical guidance to managers (e.g., Laczniak 1983).

Acknowledgement The authors wish to thank J. Scott Armstrong for his comments on an earlier version of the manuscript.

References

Allen, R.F. 1980. IK in the office. *Organizational Dynamics* 8: 26–41.

Armstrong, J.S., and T.S. Overton. 1977. Estimating nonresponse bias in mail surveys. *Journal of Marketing Research* 14: 396–402.

Ashton, R.H., and S.S. Kramer. 1980. Students as surrogates in behavioral accounting research: Some evidence. *Journal of Accounting Research* 18: 1–15.

Avlonitis, G.J. 1983. Ethics and product elimination. *Management Decisions* 2: 37–45.

Babbie, E. 1986. *The practice of social research*, 4th ed. Belmont: Wadsworth.

Bailey, K.D. 1982. *Methods of social research*, 2nd ed. New York: Free Press.

Barnett, J.H., and M.J. Karson. 1987. Personal values and business decisions – An exploratory investigation. *Journal of Business Ethics* 6(5): 371–382.

Baumhart, R.C. 1961. How ethical are businessmen? *Harvard Business Review* 39(4): 6–8.

Beltramini, R.F., R.A. Peterson, and G. Kozmetsky. 1984. Concerns of college students regarding business ethics. *Journal of Business Ethics* 3(3): 195–200.

Bezilla, R., J.B. Haynes, and C. Elliott. 1976. Ethics in marketing research. *Business Horizons* 19: 83–86.

Bird, F., and J.A. Waters. 1987. The nature of managerial moral standards. *Journal of Business Ethics* 6: 1–13.

Bommer, M., C. Gratta, J. Gravendu, and M. Tuttle. 1987. A behavioral model of ethical and unethical decision-making. *Journal of Business Ethics* 6: 265–280.

Bowman, J.S. 1976. Managerial ethics in business and government. *Business Horizons* 19: 48–54.

Brenner, S.N., and A. Molander. 1977. Is the ethics of business changing? *Harvard Business Review* 55: 57–71.

Brown, D.J., and J.B. King. 1982. Small business ethics: Influences and perceptions [survey]. *Journal of Small Business Management* 20: 11–18.

Browning, J., and N.B. Zabriskie. 1983. How ethical are industry buyers? *Industrial Marketing Management* 12: 219–224.

Campbell, D.T., and D.W. Fiske. 1959. Convergent and discriminant validation by the multi-trait multi-method matrix. *Psychological Bulletin* 56(2): 81–105.

Carroll, A.B. 1975. Managerial ethics: A post-Watergate view. *Business Horizons* 18: 75–80.

Chonko, L.B., and S.D. Hunt. 1985. Ethics and marketing management: An empirical examination. *Journal of Business Research* 13: 339–359.

Churchill, G.A. 1979. A paradigm for developing better measures of marketing constructs. *Journal of Marketing Research* 16: 64–73.

Cronbach, L.J., and P.E. Meehl. 1955. Construct validity in psychological tests. *Psychological Bulletin* 52(4): 281–302.

Crowne, D.P., and D. Marlowe. 1964. *The approval motive*. New York: Wiley.

Dillman, D. 1978. *Mail and telephone surveys: The total design method*. New York: Wiley.

Dubinsky, A.J., and J.M. Gwin. 1981. Business ethics: Buyers and sellers. *Journal of Purchasing and Materials Management* 17: 9–16.

Dubinsky, A.J., and T.N. Ingram. 1984. Correlates of salespeople's ethical conflict: An exploratory investigation. *Journal of Business Ethics* 3: 343–353.

Dubinsky, A.J., and M. Levy. 1985. Ethics in retailing: Perceptions of retail salespeople. *Journal of the Academy of Marketing Science* 13(1): 1–16.

Ferrell, O.C., and L.G. Gresham. 1985. A contingency framework for understanding ethical decision making in marketing. *Journal of Marketing* 49(Summer): 87–96.

Fleming, J.E. 1987. Authorities in business ethics. *Journal of Business Ethics* 6(3): 213–217.

Forsyth, D.R. 1980. A taxonomy of ethical ideologies. *Journal of Personality and Social Psychology* 39(1): 175–184.

Frederiksen, N., O. Jensen, and A. Beaton. 1972. *Prediction of organizational behavior*. New York: Pergamon.

Fredrickson, J.W. 1986. An exploratory approach to measuring perceptions of strategic decision process constructs. *Strategic Management Journal* 7: 473–483.

Fritzsche, D.J., and H. Becker. 1984. Linking management behavior in ethical philosophy – An investigation. *Academy of Management Journal* 27: 166–175.

Gordon, M.E., L.A. Slade, and N. Schmitt. 1987. Student Guinea pigs: Porcine predictors and particularistic phenomena. *Academy of Management Review* 12: 160–163.

Hawkins, D.I., and A.B. Cocanougher. 1972. Student evaluations of the ethics of marketing practices: The role of marketing education. *Journal of Marketing* 36(2): 61–64.

Hegarty, W.H., and H.P. Sims Jr. 1978. Some determinants of unethical decision behavior. *Journal of Applied Psychology* 63(4): 451–457.

Hegarty, W.H., and H.P. Sims. 1979. Organizational philosophy, policies and objective related to unethical decision behavior: A laboratory experiment. *Journal of Applied Psychology* 64: 331–338.

Hogarth, R.M. 1978. A note on aggregating opinions. *Organizational Behavior and Human Performance* 21: 40–46.

Jones, T.M., and F.H. Gautschi. 1988. Will the ethics of business change? A survey of future executives. *Journal of Business Ethics* 7(4): 231–248.

Krugman, D.M., and O.C. Ferrell. 1981. The organizational ethics of advertising: Corporate and agency views. *Journal of Advertising* 10: 21–30.

Laczniak, G. 1983. Business ethics: A manager's primer. *Business* 3(1): 23–29.

Laczniak, G., and E.J. Inderrieden. 1987. The influence of stated organizational concerns upon ethical decision-making. *Journal of Business Ethics* 6(4): 297–307.

Lazernitz, B. 1968. Sampling theory and procedures. In *Methodology in social research*, ed. H.A. Blalock and A.B. Blalock, 278–328. New York: McGraw-Hill.

Levy, M., and A.J. Dubinsky. 1983. Identifying and addressing retail salespeople's ethical problems: A method of application. *Journal of Retailing* 59: 46–66.

Lewis, P.V. 1985. Defining 'Business Ethics': Like nailing jello to a wall. *Journal of Business Ethics* 4: 377–383.

Lincoln, D.J., M.M. Pressley, and T. Little. 1982. Ethical beliefs and personal values of top level executives. *Journal of Business Research* 10: 475–487.

Martin, T.R. 1981. Do courses in ethics improve the ethical judgment of students? *Business Society* 20: 18–26.

Mayer, J. 1988. Themes of social responsibility: A survey of three professional schools. *Journal of Business Ethics* 7(4): 313–320.

McNichols, L.W., and T.W. Zimmer. 1985. Situational ethics: An empirical study of differentiators of student attitudes. *Journal of Business Ethics* 4: 175–180.

Nederhof, A.J. 1985. Methods of coping with social desirability bias: A review. *European Journal of Social Psychology* 15: 263–280.

Norris, D., and J.B. Gifford. 1988. Retail store managers' and students' perceptions of ethical retail practices: A comparative and longitudinal analysis (1976–1986). *Journal of Business Ethics* 7(7): 515–524.

Phillips, D.L., and K.J. Clancy. 1970. Some effects of "Social Desirability" in survey studies. *The American Journal of Sociology* 77(5): 921–940.

Posner, B.Z., and W.H. Schmidt. 1987. Ethics in American companies: A managerial perspective. *Journal of Business Ethics* 6: 383–391.

Remus, W. 1986. Graduate students as surrogates for managers in experiments on business decision making. *Journal of Business Research* 14: 19–25.

Rizzo, A., and T.J. Patka. 1981. Organizational imperative and supervisory control: Their effects on managerial ethics. *Public Personnel Management* 10: 103–109.

Rosenberg, R. 1987. Managerial morality and behavior: The questionable payments issue. *Journal of Business Ethics* 6(1): 23–36.

Rosenthal, R., and R.L. Rosnow. 1975. *The volunteer subject*. New York: Wiley.

Rudelius, W., and R. Buchholz. 1979. What industrial purchasers see as key ethical dilemmas. *Journal of Purchasing and Materials Management* 15: 2–10.

Runes, D.D. (ed.). 1964. *Dictionary of philosophy*. Peterson: Littlefield, Adams & Company.

Schutte, T.F. 1965. Executives' perceptions of business ethics. *Journal of Purchasing* May: 38–52.

Simon, J.L., and P. Burstein. 1985. *Basic research methods in social science*, 3rd ed. New York: Random House.

Stevens, G.E. 1984. Business ethics and social responsibility: The responses of present and future managers. *Akron Business and Economic Review* 15(3): 6–11.

Trawick, F., and W.R. Darden. 1980. Marketer's perception of ethical standards in the marketing profession: Educators and practitioners. *The Review of Business and Economic Research* 16: 1–17.

Trevino, L.K. 1986. Ethical decision making in organizations: A person-situation interactionist model. *Academy of Management Review* 11(3): 601–617.

Tsalikis, J., and O. Nwachukwu. 1988. Cross-cultural business ethical beliefs between blacks and whites. *Journal of Business Ethics* 7(10): 745–755.

Vitell, S.J., and T.A. Festervand. 1987. Business ethics: Conflicts, practices and beliefs of industrial executives. *Journal of Business Ethics* 6: 111–122.

Waters, J.A., and F. Bird. 1987. The moral dimension of organizational culture. *Journal of Business Ethics* 6: 15–22.

Waters, J.A., F. Bird, and P.D. Chant. 1986. Everyday moral issues experienced by managers. *Journal of Business Ethics* 5: 373–384.

Worrell, D.L., W.E. Stead, J.G. Stead, and J.B. Spalding. 1985. Unethical decisions: The impact of reinforcement contingencies and managerial philosophies. *Psychological Report* 57(2): 355–365.

Zey-Ferrell, M., and O.C. Ferrell. 1982. Role-set configuration and opportunity as predictors of unethical behavior in organizations. *Human Relations* 35(7): 587–604.

Chapter 11
A Review of the Empirical Ethical Decision-Making Literature: 1996–2003

Michael J. O'Fallon and Kenneth D. Butterfield

The field of business ethics is commonly divided into two realms – normative ethics, which resides largely in the realm of moral philosophy and theology and guides individuals as to how they should behave, and descriptive (or empirical) ethics, which resides largely in the realm of management and business and is concerned with explaining and predicting individuals' actual behavior (e.g., Donaldson and Dunfee 1994; Treviño and Weaver 1994; Weaver and Trevino 1994). Although both realms of inquiry are important, this review focuses on empirical findings within the descriptive ethical decision-making literature.

During the mid 1980s and early 1990s, the field of descriptive ethics was advanced by a number of theoretical models (e.g., Jones 1991; Rest 1986; Trevino 1986). These models generally built on Rest's (1986) original framework, which views moral decision-making as involving four basic components, or steps – identifying the moral nature of an issue, making a moral judgment, establishing moral intent, and engaging in moral action. Researchers have since proposed and tested a wide variety of constructs that influence this four-step process, generally supporting the usefulness of Rest's framework. These include individual factors such as gender and cognitive moral development (e.g., Bass et al. 1999; Cohen et al. 2001), organizational factors such as codes of ethics and ethical climate/culture (e.g., Trevino et al. 1998), and moral intensity factors such as magnitude of consequences and social consensus (e.g., Jones 1991; Singhapakdi et al. 1999).

M.J. O'Fallon (✉)
School of Hospitality, Sport and Recreation Management, James Madison University, 800 South Main St., MSC 2305, Harrisonburg, VA 22807, USA
e-mail: ofallomj@jmu.edu

K.D. Butterfield
Department of Management, Information Systems and Entrepreneurship, Washington State University, Pullman, WA 99164-4736, USA

A.C. Michalos and D.C. Poff (eds.), *Citation Classics from the Journal of Business Ethics*, Advances in Business Ethics Research 2,
DOI 10.1007/978-94-007-4126-3_11,

The field of descriptive ethics has benefited from these theoretical and empirical contributions and has made important strides in describing how individuals actually think and act when faced with ethical situations. In 1994, Ford and Richardson published a comprehensive review of empirical literature prior to that year, and Loe et al. (2000) published a comprehensive review of empirical research prior to 1996. The present review has two primary objectives. One is to extend these previous reviews by summarizing and reviewing the empirical ethical decision-making literature from 1996 to 2003. It is informational, especially to empiricists, to have a summary of the ethical decision-making literature that takes up where the previous reviews left off. Our second objective is to compare the literature from 1996 to 2003 with conclusions drawn by Ford and Richardson and Loe et al. in order to surface trends and shed light on directions for future research. In addition, this review provides the reader with a sense of which independent and dependent variables have received the greatest amount of attention, which ones have been largely overlooked, and which variables have provided the most consistent findings in the ethical decision-making literature.

In order to achieve our objectives, studies were selected for inclusion if they met the following criteria. First, the studies were published during the period 1996–2003. 1996 was selected as the first year of inclusion as this was the last year in which studies were included in Loe et al.'s review (2000). Second, the studies were published in one of the journals included in the two previous reviews such as Academy of Management Journal, Administrative Science Quarterly, Business Ethics Quarterly, Human Relations, Journal of Academy of Marketing Science, Journal of Business Ethics, Journal of Business Research, Journal of Marketing, or Journal of Personal Selling & Sales Management. However, given the fact that ethics has become increasingly appealing across many domains, ethics researchers are finding other prominent outlets to submit their studies. Therefore, studies were also included in this review if they were published in one of the following journals: Accounting, Auditing, & Accountability Journal, Business & Society, European Journal of Marketing, International Journal of Management, Journal of American Academy of Business, Journal of Applied Social Psychology, Journal of Management Studies, Journal of Managerial Issues, Journal of Marketing, Journal of Organizational Behavior, Managerial Auditing Journal, or Organizational Behavior and Human Decision Processes. The studies were found by searching for the key word "ethical decision-making" in the ABI/Inform and PsycINFO search engines. Furthermore, an additional examination through the more well-known ethics journals such as journal of Business Ethics and Business Ethics Quarterly was conducted to determine if any studies were excluded from the original search process. Third, this review only included studies where the dependent variable(s) represented one or more of Rest's (1986) four steps of ethical decision-making. The four steps included: moral awareness – being able to interpret the situation as being moral; moral judgment – deciding which course of action is morally right; moral intent – prioritizing moral values over other values; and, moral behavior – executing and implementing the moral intention. Finally, studies were only included in this review if they examined decision making and behavior within an actual or simulated business environment. Therefore, studies examining topics such as academic dishonesty and consumer behavior were not included.

Empirical Research on Ethical Decision-Making

For the reader's convenience, a summary of empirical findings by category and dependent variable is provided in Table 11.1. Tables 11.2, 11.3, 11.4, and 11.5 list the studies by dependent variable – awareness (Table 11.2), judgment (Table 11.3), intent (Table 11.4), and behavior (Table 11.5). Within these tables, the studies are further sorted by independent variable (beginning with individual variables, followed by moral intensity, and ending with organizational factors), which are categorized alphabetically. In order to facilitate comparison with previous reviews, the following discussion is organized by independent variable – individual factors, organizational factors, and moral intensity factors. For purposes of presentation, we discuss these factors in order from the most comprehensively studied to the least studied and focus mainly on the variables that have received the greatest amount of research attention.

Table 11.1 Empirical studies examining direct effects by dependent variable

	Number of empirical studies by DV				
Construct	Awareness	Judgment	Intent	Behavior	Totals[a]
Individual factors					
Age	2	11	1	7	21
Awareness		2	3	2	7
Biases		2			2
CMD/Ethical judgment		4	11	8	23
Conflict	1	1			2
Ed., Emp., Job Sat. and Work exp.	4	24	5	8	41
Gender	3	33	4	9	49
Intent				1	1
Locus of control		5	6		11
Machiavellianism		5	4	1	10
Nationality	2	18	3	2	25
Need for cognition		2			2
Organizational commitment		1	2	1	4
Other individual effects	1	5	3	1	10
Philosophy/value orientation	3	22	12	5	42
Professional affiliation	1				1
Religion	1	6	2	1	10
Significant others		2	3	4	9
Moral Intensity	6	14	8	4	32
Organizational factors					
Business competitiveness	1	1		2	4
Codes of ethics	1	5	2	12	20
Ethical climate/culture	1	5	4	6	16

(continued)

Table 11.1 (continued)

Construct	Number of empirical studies by DV				
	Awareness	Judgment	Intent	Behavior	Totals[a]
External environment		1		2	3
Industry type		7	1	1	9
Opportunity			1	1	2
Organizational climate/culture		1		1	2
Organizational size		3	2	2	7
Other organizational effects		1	2	2	5
Rewards and sanctions		2	4	1	7
Significant others		1			1
Subjective norms			3		3
Training	1	1		1	3
Totals[a]	28	185	86	85	

[a] Totals do not indicate the total number of articles. It represents the total number of findings by each independent variable on the dependent variables. The total number of studies included is 174

Table 11.2 Empirical research examining direct effects on the dependent variable: awareness

Authors:Journal	Year	Findings
Individual factors: age		
Singhapakdi et al.:*JBE*	1996a	Significant predictor of perceived ethical problems in one of four scenarios
Karcher:*JBE*	1996	The relationship between ethical sensitivity and age is significantly positive
Individual factors: conflict		
Yetmar and Eastman:*JBE*	2000	Role conflict is negatively associated with ethical sensitivity
Individual factors: education, employment, job satisfaction and work experience		
Karcher:*JBE*	1996	No significant findings with respect to employment position or level of education
Sparks and Hunt:*JOM*	1998	Practitioners are more ethically sensitive than students
Yetmar and Eastman:*JBE*	2000	Job satisfaction is positively associated with ethical sensitivity
Cohen et al.:*JBE*	2001	No major differences between entry-level students and graduating students, as well as between students and professional accountants
Individual factors: gender		
Singhapakdi et al.:*JBE*	1996a	Significant predictor of perceived ethical problems in one of four scenarios

(continued)

Table 11.2 (continued)

Authors:Journal	Year	Findings
Ameen et al.:*JBE*	1996	Female subjects were more sensitive to and less tolerant of unethical activities than their male counterparts
Fleischman and Valentine:*JBE*	2003	No significant findings
Individual factors: nationality		
Singhapakdi et al.:*JBE*	2001a, b	There were significant differences between Australian and American marketers in two of four scenarios
Cherry et al.:*JBE*	2003	U.S. respondents had greater perception of an ethical issue than Taiwanese respondents
Individual factors: other individual effects		
Sparks and Hunt:*JOM*	1998	Perspective taking is correlated significantly with ethical sensitivity, while emotional contagion produced no significant results
Individual factors: philosophy/value orientation		
Singhapakdi et al.:*JBE*	1996a	Individuals with a high standard of professional values tend to recognize the ethical issues or problems more so than their counterparts
Sparks and Hunt:*JOM*	1998	Relativism is negatively related to ethical sensitivity
Yetmar and Eastman:*JBE*	2000	Relativism is negatively associated with ethical sensitivity
Individual factors: professional affiliation		
Yetmar and Eastman:*JBE*	2000	Professional commitment is positively associated with ethical sensitivity
Individual factors: religion		
Singhapakdi et al.:*JBE*	2000a, b	In three of four scenarios, there was a positive relationship between religion and perception of an ethical problem
Moral intensity		
Singhapakdi et al.:*JBR*	1996b	Moral intensity is a significant predictor of ethical perceptions
Singhapakdi et al.:*JAMS*	1999	Increases in perceived moral intensity increases the perception of an ethical problem
Butterfield et al.:*HR*	2000	Individuals are more likely to recognize the moral nature of the issue when it has negative consequences and when the individuals perceive social consensus
May and Pauli:*B&S*	2002	Probable magnitude of harm has a significant influence on moral recognition, but social consensus did not

(continued)

Table 11.2 (continued)

Authors:Journal	Year	Findings
Barnett and Valentine:*JBR*	2004	Magnitude of consequences was positively associated with ethical recognition in both scenarios, social consensus was significant in one scenario, and there were no significant findings for proximity and temporal immediacy
Valentine and Fleischman:*JBE*	2003	Marginally supported at $p<0.10$
Organizational factors: business competitiveness		
Butterfield et al.:*HR*	2000	When individuals perceive highly competitive practices, they become more aware of the moral issues
Organizational factors: codes of ethics		
Weaver and Trevino:*BEQ*	1999	Value and compliance ethics program orientations were both significant and positive predictors of ethical awareness
Organizational factors: ethical climate/culture		
VanSandt:*B&S*	2003	Benevolence and principle ethical criteria were associated with higher levels of moral awareness, while egoistic ethical criterion was associated with lower levels of moral awareness
Organizational factors: training		
Sparks and Hunt:*JOM*	1998	More training is negatively related to ethical sensitivity

Table 11.3 Empirical research examining direct effects on the dependent variable: judgment

Authors: Journal	Year	Findings
Individual *factors*: age		
Wimalasiri et al.:*JBE*	1996	There were significant differences in moral reasoning among different age groups
Deshpande:*JBE*	1997	In 5 of 17 situations with $p < 0.10$, older managers perceived the situation as being more unethical than younger managers
Eynon et al.:*JBE*	1997	Moral reasoning decreases with age
Larkin:*JBE*	2000	No significant findings
Latif:*JBE*	2000	Older individuals scored significantly lower on moral reasoning than younger individuals at $p = 0.10$
Roozen et al.:*JBE*	2001	Age has a negative effect on ethical attitude
Shafer et al.:*AAAJ*	2001	No significant findings
Singhapakdi et al.:*EJM*	2001a, b	No significant findings
Peterson et al.:*JBE*	2001	Responses to ethical issues were lower for younger respondents

(continued)

Table 11.3 (continued)

Authors: Journal	Year	Findings
Kracher et al.:*JBE*	2002	Age was negatively associated with moral development
Razzaque and Hwee:*JBE*	2002	Mixed findings. Younger purchasers tended to perceive three of six scenarios as more unethical than older purchasers
Individual factors: awareness		
Singhapakdi et al.:*JBE*	1996a	Individuals who perceive the situation as having an ethical problem will form a more ethical judgment
Valentine and Fleischman:*JBE*	2003	Recognition of the ethical issue was unrelated to ethical judgment
Individual factors: biases		
Sligo and Stirton:*JBE*	1998	Hindsight bias effects perceptions of ethical decision making
Chung and Monroe:*JBE*	2003	SD bias is higher when an action is judged to be more unethical
Individual factors: education, employment, job satisfaction and work experience		
Kaynama et al.:*JBE*	1996	The ethical perception of undergraduate students are stronger than those of MBA students
Malinowski and Berger:*JBE*	1996	No significant findings between majors
Verbeke et al.:*JBE*	1996	No relationship between career orientation and ethical decision making
Wimalasiri et al.:*JBE*	1996	There were significant differences in moral reasoning among different levels of education
Wimalasiri et al.:*JBE*	1996	There is no difference between a practicing managers and a students level of moral reasoning
Cole and Smith:*JBE*	1996	Students were more accepting of questionable ethical statements (7 of 10 statements) than business people
Deshpande:*JBE*	1997	Significance at $p<0.10$ was found in 1 of 17 situations
Green and Weber:*JBE*	1997	There was no difference in moral reasoning scores for accounting and other business major scores before taking an auditing course. However, after taking the auditing course, accounting majors scored higher than other business majors
Smith and Oakley:*JBE*	1997	Graduate students had higher responses to rule based scenarios than did undergraduates
Tse and Au:*JBE*	1997	Senior students were less ethical than junior students at $p<0.10$
Tse and Au:*JBE*	1997	No difference between business and non-business students
Reiss and Mitra:*JBE*	1998	There were no differences between business and non-business students

(continued)

Table 11.3 (continued)

Authors: Journal	Year	Findings
Reiss and Mitra:*JBE*	1998	Individuals that have work experience considered extra-organizational behaviors of an uncertain mature as more acceptable than individuals with no work experience
Weeks et al.:*JBE*	1999	There is a difference in ethical judgment across career stages. In general, individuals in the latter years of their career display higher ethical judgment
Larkin:*JBE*	2000	Overall, the ability to identify unethical behavior is related to experience
Latif:*JBE*	2000	First year pharmacy students scored higher on moral reasoning than pharmacists
Roozen et al.:*JBE*	2001	No significant findings with respect to work experience
Cohen et al.:*JBE*	2001	No difference between entry-level students and graduating students, as well as between students and professional accountants
Shafer et a1.:*AAAJ*	2001	Job position or education has no influence on judgment
Kaplan:*JBE*	2001	Overall, individuals assigned to the role of manager did not form more unfavorable ethically related judgments than individuals assigned to the role of shareholder
Latif:*JBE*	2001	As pharmacists gain tenure, their moral reasoning scores decline
Kracher et al.:*JBE*	2002	Education was positively associated with moral development scores
Razzaque and Hwee:*JBE*	2002	Education was a significant and positive influence on judgment in four of six scenarios
Wu:*JBE*	2003	In one of five scenarios, there was a significant difference in ethical recognition after receiving a Business ethics education
Individual factors: gender		
Okleshen and Hoyt:*JBE*	1996	Females were less tolerant of unethical situations than males
Wimalasiri et al.:*JBE*	1996	No significant findings
McDonald and Pak:*JBE*	1996	Significant gender differences existed in three of eight cognitive frameworks
Mason and Mudrack:*JBE*	1996	Women scored higher on an ethics scale than men
Rayburn and Rayburn:*JBE*	1996	No significant findings
McCuddy and Peery:*JBE*	1996	No significant findings
Schoderbek and Deshpande:*JBE*	1996	No significant findings
Malinowski and Berger:*JBE*	1996	In seven of nine scenarios, there was a difference between males and females
Cole and Smith:*JBE*	1996	No significant findings

(continued)

Table 11.3 (continued)

Authors: Journal	Year	Findings
Eastman et al.:*JBE*	1996	Men and women employ different ethical models to situations
Schminke and Ambrose:*JBE*	1997	Females scored significantly higher than males in 8 of 10 statements
Dawson:*JBE*	1997	There was a significant difference between males and females in 8 of 20 scenarios
Deshpande:*JBE*	1997	Significance at $p<0.10$ was found in 1 of 17 situations
Smith and Oakley:*JBE*	1997	No difference between gender regarding ethics related to legal or company policy issues, however, females had higher expectations for ethical behaviors in social and interpersonal concerns than males
Schminke:*JBE*	1997	No significant findings
Keyton and Rhodes:*JBE*	1997	Females identified more sexual harassment cues than males
Tse and Au:*JBE*	1997	Female students were more ethical than males students
Eynon et al.:*JBE*	1997	Females have higher moral reasoning scores than males
Reiss and Mitra:*JBE*	1998	Males tend to regard extra-organizational behaviors of uncertain ethical nature as more acceptable than females
Prasad et al.:*JBE*	1998	In 10 of 51 statements regarding perceptions of a just society, there were differences between female and male responses
Weeks et al.:*JBE*	1999	There is a difference between males and females in ethical judgment. Females reported to have higher ethical judgment in 7 of 19 scenarios, while males reported as having higher ethical judgment in 2 of 19 scenarios
Larkin:*JBE*	2000	four of six scenarios produced no significant findings. The other two scenarios indicated that females were more likely to identify the correct behavior than males
Deshpande et al.:*JBE*	2000	Moderate support. Females were more likely to perceive the activity as unethical in 7 of 17 activities at $p<0.10$
Roozen et al.:*JBE*	2001	No significant findings
Shafer et al.:*AAAJ*	2001	No significant findings
Singhapakdi et al.:*EJM*	2001a, b	In five of seven dimensions, there were gender differences
Ergeneli and Arikan:*JBE*	2002	Female and males perceptions of ethical behavior were different in 4 of 14 scenarios
Kracher et al.:*JBE*	2002	Males and Females reported similar levels of moral development
Razzaque and Hwee:*JBE*	2002	No significant findings

(continued)

Table 11.3 (continued)

Authors: Journal	Year	Findings
Baker and Hunt:*JMI*	2003	Moral orientation differed between all female and all male groups
Christie et al.:*JBE*	2003	There were significant gender differences in questionable business practice scenarios
Abdolmohammadi et al.:*JBE*	2003	No significant findings
Fleischman and Valentine:*JBE*	2003	Women judged the ethically questionable case more harshly than men
Individual factors: locus of control		
McCuddy and Peery:*JBE*	1996	Locus of control is negatively associated with ethical standards. Externals tended to regard uncertain ethical behaviors as more acceptable than internals
Reiss and Mitra:*JBE*	1998	No significant findings
Bass et al.:*BEQ*	1999	Internal individuals express more severe ethical judgments of an unethical behavior than externals
Cherry and Fraedrich:*JPSSM*	2000	No significant findings
Razzaque and Hwee:*JBE*	2002	Machiavellianism was negatively associated with ethical decision making
Individual factors: Machiavellianism		
Verbeke et al.:*JBE*	1996	Machiavellians are less ethically-oriented than non-Machiavellians
Rayburn and Rayburn:*JBE*	1996	Machiavellians are less ethically-oriented than non-Machiavellians
Bass et al.:*BEQ*	1999	High Machiavellian individuals judged the questionable selling practice as more acceptable in one of two scenarios
Razzaque and Hwee:*JBE*	2002	Machiavellianism is negatively related to judgment, but only significant in one of six scenarios
Schepers:*JBE*	2003	No significant findings
Individual factors: nationality		
Okleshen and Hoyt:*JBE*	1996	US students less tolerant of unethical situations than New Zealand students
Wimalasiri et al.:*JBE*	1996	There were no significant differences in moral reasoning among Chinese and non-Chinese individuals
McDonald and Pak:*JBE*	1996	There were differences in cognitive frameworks across cultures
Armstrong:*JBE*	1996	There is a difference in ethical judgments across three cultures; with Singapore students scoring lowest and Malaysia students scoring highest
McCuddy and Peery:*JBE*	1996	Race is associated with differences in ethical standards
Allmon et al.:*JBE*	1997	There was a significant difference in judgment across cultures in 11 of 16 situations

(continued)

Table 11.3 (continued)

Authors: Journal	Year	Findings
Clarke and Aram:*JBE*	1997	Spanish and U.S. respondents showed consistent differences in some situations evaluating aspects of entrepreneurial-ethical trade-offs
Jackson and Artola:*JBE*	1997	There were no differences between cultures in three of four situations
Davis et al.:*JBE*	1998	Culture effects decisions in ethical decision making
Goodwin and Goodwin:*JBE*	1999	In two of three scenarios, there were differences in ethical judgment between Malaysia and New Zealand students
Jackson:*HR*	2001	Ethical attitudes differ among national groups
Singhapakdi et al.:*JBE*	2001a, b	In two of four scenarios, Australian and American marketers differed in perception of ethical problems
Tsui and Windsor:*JBE*	2001	Moral reasoning between Chinese and Australian participants differed at $p=0.09$
Rittenburg and Valentine:*JBE*	2002	No significant findings
Volkema and Fleury:*JBE*	2002	Brazilian and U.S. respondents did not differ in perception of questionable negotiation behaviors
Kracher et al.:*JBE*	2002	Moral development scores between Indian and U.S. participants were not significantly different
Cherry et al.:*JBE*	2003	U.S. respondents had a more unfavorable ethical judgment of the unethical behavior than their Taiwanese counterparts
Christie et al.:*JBE*	2003	Attitude towards unethical decision-making differs across cultures
Individual factors: need for cognition		
Boyle et al.:*JBE*	1998	High need for cognition individuals are more prone to contextual biases then low need for cognition individuals
Singer et al.:*JBE*	1998	High need for cognition individuals utilize more issue-relevant information in decision making
Individual factors: organizational commitment		
Roozen et al.:*JBE*	2001	No significant findings
Individual factors: other individual effects		
Rayburn and Rayburn:*JBE*	1996	Individuals of high intelligence are less-ethically oriented than individuals of low intelligence
Rayburn and Rayburn:*JBE*	1996	Individuals of Type B personality are less ethically-oriented than individuals of Type A personality
Weber: *HR*	1996	As the nature of the harm decreases from physical to psychological, the stage of moral reasoning declines
Udas et al.:*JBE*	1996	Professional organization has no bearing on the perceptions of ethical issues

(continued)

Table 11.3 (continued)

Authors: Journal	Year	Findings
Abratt and Penman:*JBE*	2002	Questionable sales practices against customers and employers were judged as less ethical than similar practices against competitors
Individual factors: philosophy/value orientation		
Barnett et al.:*JBE*	1996	Idealism is positively associated and relativism was negatively associated with judgments that peer reporting is ethical
Butz and Lewis:*JBE*	1996	No significant findings with respect to leadership orientation
Keyton and Rhodes:*JBE*	1997	Situationists scored the lowest in identifying sexual harassment cues
Harrington:*JBE*	1997	Rule orientation significantly influences judgment
DeConinck and Lewis:*JBE*	1997	Although both were significant, deontology influenced sales managers' ethical judgments more than teleological
Bass et al.:*JPSSM*	1998	Idealism was the key dimension that explained differences in ethical judgments
Davis et al.:*JBE*	1998	Individuals who were idealistic contributed significantly to judgments of moral concern in two of four scenarios and judgments of immorality in two of four scenarios
Rallapalli et al.:*JBR*	1998	Ethical judgments are significantly affected by deontological norms and teleological evaluations
Rallapalli and Vitell:*JBR*	1998	Teleological evaluations significantly influenced ethical judgment
Barnett et al.:*JBE*	1998	Absolutists judgments were more harsh in the scenarios, where subjectivists judged the actions most leniently,
Fisher and Sweeney:*JBE*	1998	No significant findings with respect to political orientation
Bass et al.:*BEQ*	1999	Idealism was negatively associated with judgments
Boyle:*JBE*	2000	High relativists judged the ethically-questionable behavior as more ethical than low relativists and low and high idealists did not differ in their judgment of the ethically-questionable behavior
Cruz et al.:*JBE*	2000	Moral equity significantly influenced ethical judgments
Ashkanasy et al.:*JBE*	2000	Personal values, leniency and triviality, are significant predictors of ethical tolerance
Kujala:*JBE*	2001	Teleological thinking in general, and especially utilitarianism, plays an important role in Finnish managers' decision-making
Roozen et al.:*JBE*	2001	Instrumental values have a greater impact on ethical judgment than terminal values

(continued)

Table 11.3 (continued)

Authors: Journal	Year	Findings
Douglas et al.:*JBE*	2001	Ethical orientation did not significantly influence ethical judgments
Elias:*JBE*	2002	High idealists judged the earnings management actions as more unethical and high relativists judged them as more ethical
Kim:*JBE*	2003	Individuals with high idealism or less relativism tend to make stricter ethical judgments
Schepers:*JBE*	2003	Moral equity was a significant predictor of ethical judgment
Sivadas et al.:*JPSSM*	2003	Relativistic managers reported more positive ethical evaluations of controversial sales practices. No significant relationship with regard to idealistic managers
Individual factors: religion		
Wimalasiri et al.:*JBE*	1996	A significant relationship between higher stages of moral reasoning and higher degree of religious commitment existed
Clark and Dawson:*JBE*	1996	Intrinsically religious individuals judged the scenarios as less unethical than did non-religious individuals
Tse and Au:*JBE*	1997	The influence of religion on judgment was significant
Wagner and Sanders:*JBE*	2001	Individuals with high religious beliefs are less likely to evaluate an unethical act as being fair
Razzaque and Hwee:*JBE*	2002	Religiosity is positively and significantly correlated with four of six scenarios in one dimension (moralistic) but no correlations existed in the contractualism dimension
Giacalone and Jurkiewicz:*JBE*	2003	Spirituality negatively influences an individuals perception of a questionable business practice
Individual factors: significant others		
Tse and Au:*JBE*	1997	No significant findings with respect to father's or mother's occupation
Razzaque and Hwee:*JBE*	2002	No significant findings with respect to peer influence
Moral intensity		
Singer:*JBE*	1996	The overall ethicality of a manager can be predicted by social consensus, magnitude of consequences and likelihood of action
Weber:*HR*	1996	As the level of magnitude of consequences decreases, the stage of moral reasoning declines
Singer and Singer:*JBE*	1997	Social consensus and magnitude of consequences were significant predictors of judgments of overall ethicality in both the beneficial and harmful consequences conditions

(continued)

Table 11.3 (continued)

Authors: Journal	Year	Findings
Harrington:*JBE*	1997	Social consensus significantly influences judgment
Davis et al.:*JBE*	1998	Social consensus but not magnitude of consequences influences judgments of moral concern
Singer et al.:*JBE*	1998	Magnitude of consequence, social consensus and temporal immediacy were significant predictors of overall ethicality
Singhapakdi et al.:*JAMS*	1999	Idealistic individuals have higher perceptions of moral intensity, while relativistic individuals have lower perceptions of moral intensity
Barnett:*JASP*	2001	Issues having higher levels of perceived magnitude of consequences and lower perceived levels of social consensus were judged less ethical
Shafer et al.:*AAAJ*	2001	Probability of effect and magnitude of consequences significantly influenced judgments
McDevitt and Hise:*JBE*	2002	Materiality influences perception of act being ethical/unethical
Barnett and Valentine:*JBR*	2004	Magnitude of consequences was positively associated with ethical judgment in both scenarios, social consensus was significant in one scenario, and there were no significant findings for proximity and temporal immediacy
Carlson et al.:*JMI*	2002	Proximity of effect, but not the probability of effect nor the concentration of effect predicted moral judgment
Shaw:*JBE*	2003	Consensus and Magnitude of effect influences moral attitude
Valentine and Fleischman:*JBE*	2003	Strongly supported
Organizational factors: business competitiveness		
Verbeke et al.:*JBE*	1996	Competition didn't affect ethical decision making
Organizational factors: codes of ethics		
Udas et al.:*JBE*	1996	Codes of ethics has no bearing on perception of ethical issues
Nwachukwu and Vitell:*JBE*	1997	No significance between the existence of or nonexistence of a code of ethics on judgment
Stohs and Brannick:*JBE*	1999	In regards to issues dealing with the firm, a code of ethics influences a managers' perception of wrongness
Douglas et al.:*JBE*	2001	Codes of conduct did not significantly affect ethical judgments

(continued)

Table 11.3 (continued)

Authors: Journal	Year	Findings
Adams et al.:*JBE*	2001	Individuals employed in organizations with a code of ethics rated other members as more ethical than individuals in organizations that do not have a code of ethics
Organizational factors: ethical climate/culture		
Verbeke et al.:*JBE*	1996	Ethical climate positively affected ethical decision making
Upchurch:*JBE*	1998	Benevolence is the most predominant ethical climate in decision making
Singhapakdi et al.:*EJM*	2001a, b	Ethical climate strongly influences perceived importance of ethics
Douglas et al.:*JBE*	2001	Ethical culture did not directly influence ethical judgments. The external environment had a positive influence on attitudes toward questionable business practices
Weber and Seger:*JBE*	2002	Instrumental work ethical climate was the predominate climate in the ethical decision making process
Organizational factors: external environment		
Christie et al.:*JBE*	2003	The external environment had a positive influence on attitudes toward questionable business practices
Organizational factors: industry type		
Eynon et al.:*JBE*	1997	CPA's in small-firms scored significantly lower in moral reasoning than CPA's in Big 6 firms
Teal and Carroll:*JBE*	1999	Entrepreneurs may exhibit slightly higher moral reasoning skills than middle-managers
Latif:*JBE*	2000	Pharmacists scored lower on moral reasoning than other health professionals
Roozen et al.:*JBE*	2001	Employees in public sector and education reported a higher score on the most ethical profile than employees in private sector
Shafer et al.:*AAAJ*	2001	No significant findings
Ergeneli and Arikan:*JBE*	2002	There was a significant difference in the perceptions of salespeople working in the medical equipment and clothing sectors in 4 of 14 scenarios
Waller:*JBE*	2002	In three of five statements regarding ethics in political advertising, there was a significant difference in attitudes between advertising executives and federal politicians
Organizational factors: organizational climate/culture		
Razzaque and Hwee:*JBE*	2002	Org. culture is positive and significant in three of six scenarios
Organizational factors: organizational size		
Roozen et al.:*JBE*	2001	No significant findings

(continued)

Table 11.3 (continued)

Authors: Journal	Year	Findings
Shafer et al.:*AAAJ*	2001	No significant findings
Razzaque and Hwee:*JBE*	2002	No significant findings
Organizational factors: other organizational effects		
Verbeke et al.:*JBE*	1996	Internal communication positively affected ethical decision making
Organizational factors: rewards and sanctions		
Tenbrunsel and Messick:*ASQ*	1999	Weak sanctioning systems resulted in a focus on the business aspects in contrast to a focus on the ethical aspects when no sanctions were present
Cherry and Fraedrich:*JBR*	2002	Individuals who perceive higher levels of risk responded with more severe negative ethical judgments
Organizational factors: significant others		
Schoderbek and Deshpande:*JBE*	1996	Impression management positively influenced perceived unethical conduct
Organizational factors: training		
Eynon et al.:*JBE*	1997	Those who completed an ethics course reported significantly higher P- scores

Table 11.4 Empirical research examining direct effects on the dependent variable: intent

Authors: Journal	Year	Findings
Individual factors: age		
Shafer et al.: *AAAJ*	2001	No significant findings
Individual factors: awareness		
Singhapakdi et al.: *JAMS*	1999	Perceived ethical problem has a negative influence on intentions to act unethically
Singhapakdi: *JBR*	1999	The perception of an ethical problem positively influences ethical intentions
Singhapakdi et al.: *JBE*	2000a, b	Managers who perceived an ethical problem indicated that they were less likely to agree with the unethical intentions
Individual factors: cognitive moral development/ethical judgments		
Barnett et al.: *JBE*	1996	Ethical judgments were associated positively with behavioral intentions to report a peer's unethical behavior
Robin et al.: *JBR*	1996b	Perceive importance of an ethical issue positively relates to behavioral intentions
DeConinck and Lewis: *JBE*	1997	Ethical judgment was the biggest predictor of rewarding or punishing ethical/unethical behavior
Rallapalli et al.:*JBR*	1998	Ethical judgment significantly affected intentions

(continued)

Table 11.4 (continued)

Authors: Journal	Year	Findings
Bass et al.: *BEQ*	1999	Individuals were more likely to state intentions to perform an action if they judged it as ethical
Barnett: *JASP*	2001	Ethical judgments predicted behavioral intentions
Wagner and Sanders: *JBE*	2001	Those individuals who judge an unethical action as unethical indicated an intention not to behave unethically
Shafer et al.: *AAAJ*	2001	There was a positive relationship between judgments and intentions
Uddin and Gillett: *JBE*	2002	Low moral reasoners did not express higher intentions of fraudulent reporting
Shapeero et al.: *MAJ*	2003	No significant findings
Sivadas et al.: *JPSSM*	2003	The more just and fair an act was judged, the more likely the individual was hired
Individual factors: education, employment, job satisfaction and work experience		
Jones and Kavanagh: *JBE*	1996	Quality of work experiences positively influences behavioral intentions
Cohen et al.: *JBE*	2001	Accountants are more ethical than students
Shafer et al.: *AAAJ*	2001	Job position or education has no influence on intentions
Paolillo and Vitell: *JBE*	2002	No significant findings with respect to job satisfaction
Shapeero et al.: *MAJ*	2003	Senior and staff-level accountants are less likely to intend to ene in unethical behavior than supervisors and managers
Individual factors: gender		
Jones and Kavanagh: *JBE*	1996	No significant findings
Singhapakdi: *JBR*	1999	Women are more likely to disagree with the unethical actions
Cohen et al.: *JBE*	2001	Women are less willing to act unethically
Shafer et al.: *AAAJ*	2001	No significant findings
Individual factors: locus of control		
Jones and Kavanagh: *JBE*	1996	In one of two experiments, externals were more likely to report unethical intentions
Bass et al.: *BEQ*	1999	No significant findings
Cherry and Fraedrich: *JPSSM*	2000	Internal individuals indicate less intention to behave unethically than externals
Key: *JMI*	2002	Internals demonstrated greater perceed discretion, while externals demonstrated less perceived discretion
Shapeero et al.: *MAJ*	2003	Internals are less likely to intend to engage in unethical behavior
Granitz: *JBE*	2003	Internals are no more likely to participate/switch than Externals

(continued)

Table 11.4 (continued)

Authors: Journal	Year	Findings
Individual factors: Machiavellianism		
Jones and Kavanagh: *JBE*	1996	Individuals scoring high in Mach report higher unethical intentions
Bass et al.: *BEQ*	1999	High Machiavellian individuals reported greater intentions to perform the questionable actions
Schepers: *JBE*	2003	No significant findings
Granitz: *JBE*	2003	High Mach were more likely to participate/switch than low Mach's
Individual factors: nationality		
Singhapakdi et al.: *JBE*	2001a, b	In two of four scenarios, Australian and American marketers differed in intent to engage in unethical behavior
Volkema and Fleury: *JBE*	2002	In three of five situations, U.S. respondents were more likely to indicate a higher likelihood of engaging in questionable negotiating behaviors than Brazilian respondents
Cherry et al.: *JBE*	2003	U.S. respondents demonstrated less intention to perform the unethical behavior than Taiwanese respondents
Individual factors: organizational commitment		
Paolillo and Vitell: *JBE*	2002	No significant findings
Granitz: *JBE*	2003	Organizational commitment demonstrated no relationship to sharing
Individual factors: other individual effects		
Flannery and May: *AMJ*	2000	Intentions to engage in unethical behavior is positively influenced by their attitude to engage in that behavior
Flannery and May: *AMJ*	2000	No significant findings with respect to self-efficacy or moral obligation
Beams et al.: *JBE*	2003	Individuals who were more cynical about others unethical behavior were more likely to engage in the unethical behavior
Individual factors: philosophy/value orientation		
Morris et al.: *JBE*	1996	Personal values are inversely related to behavioral intentions
DeConinck and Lewis: *JBE*	1997	Deontology and Teleological were significant predictors of intention
Bass et al.: *JPSSM*	1998	No significant findings
Rallapalli et al.: *JBR*	1998	Intentions are affected by teleological evaluations
Bass et al.: *BEQ*	1999	No significant findings

(continued)

Table 11.4 (continued)

Authors: Journal	Year	Findings
Singhapakdi et al.: *JBE*	2000a, b	Idealism is a significant and positive predictor of Thai manager's ethical intentions in three of four scenarios, while relativism negatively and significantly influences intentions
Cruz et al.: *JBE*	2000	Intentions to behave ethically are based primarily on moral equity and contractualism
Eastman et al.: *JBE*	2001	No significant findings
Uddin and Gillett: *JBE*	2002	High self monitors did not express higher intentions of fraudulent reporting
Beams et al.: *JBE*	2003	Individuals who believed they would feel guilty were less likely to engage in the unethical behavior
Shapeero et al.: *MAJ*	2003	Deontological individuals are less likely to intend to engage in unethical behavior than teleological individuals
Sivadas et al.: *JPSSM*	2003	Relativistic managers were more likely to hire a salesperson who has performed an ethically questionable act. No significant relationship with respect to idealistic managers
Individual factors: religion		
Singhapakdi et al.:*JBE*	2000a, b	In two of four scenarios, religious Thai managers were likely to report more ethical intentions than their counterparts
Singhapakdi et al.: *JBE*	2000a, b	In three of four scenarios where $p<0.10$, there was a significant positive relationship between religion and ethical intentions
Individual factors: significant others		
Jones and Kavanagh: *JBE*	1996	In one of two experiments, peer influence and manager influence positively and significantly influenced behavioral intentions
Andersson and Bateman: *JOB*	1997	Individuals who were high in cynicism were more likely to indicate that they would perform unethical acts requested by management
Beams et al.: *JBE*	2003	Peer influence positively influenced the intent to behave unethically
Moral intensity		
Singhapakdi et al.: *JBR*	1996a, b	Moral intensity is a significant predictor of ethical intentions

(continued)

Table 11.4 (continued)

Authors: Journal	Year	Findings
Harrington: *JBE*	1997	Social consensus significantly influences intentions
Barnett: *JASP*	2001	Magnitude of consequences, social consensus, and proximity were predictors of behavioral intentions in at least one of two situations
Shafer et al.: *AAAJ*	2001	Probability of effect and magnitude of consequences significantly influenced intentions
Paolillo and Vitell: *JBE*	2002	Moral intensity is positively related to ethical decision-making intentions
May and Pauli: *B&S*	2002	Magnitude of consequence, social consensus and concentration of effect were positively related to moral intentions
Barnett and Valentine: *JBR*	2004	Magnitude of consequences was negatively associated with behavioral intentions in one of two scenarios, while social consensus, proximity and temporal immediacy had no significant influence
Granitz: *JBE*	2003	Individuals who perceived the issues to have low personal moral intensity were more likely to participate/switch
Organizational factors: codes of ethics		
Paolillo and Vitell: *JBE*	2002	Neither the existence or enforcement of codes of ethics influence ethical decision-making intentions
Granitz: *JBE*	2003	Individuals who shared in their perception of an applicable code, shared in ethical reasoning and moral intent
Organizational factors: ethical climate/culture		
DeConinck and Lewis: *JBE*	1997	No significant findings
Barnett and Vaicys: *JBE*	2000	Ethical climate did not directly affect intentions to behave ethically
Flannery and May: *AMJ*	2000	The instrumental climate deterred ethical intentions
Key: *JMI*	2002	Individuals who rated their organization as more ethical demonstrated greater perceived discretion, while those who rated their organization as less ethical had less perceived discretion
Organizational factors: industry type		
Shafer et al.: *AAAJ*	2001	No significant findings
Organizational factors: opportunity		
Powpaka: *JBE*	2002	A manager's intention to give a bribe is negatively influenced by his/her perceived choice

(continued)

Table 11.4 (continued)

Authors: Journal	Year	Findings
Organizational factors: organizational size		
Shafer et al.: *AAAJ*	2001	No significant findings
Paolillo and Vitell: *JBE*	2002	No significant findings
Organizational factors: other organizational effects		
Singhapakdi et al.: *JBE*	2000a, b	In three of four scenarios, Thai managers in organizations with higher levels of ethical values tend to have more ethical intentions than managers in organizations with lower levels of ethical values
Schepers: *JBE*	2003	No significant findings with regards to a focus on profit
Organizational factors: rewards and Sanctions		
Glass and Wood: *JBE*	1996	An individuals intention to engage in an unethical act is positively related to perceived favorable social outcomes
Cherry and Fraedrich: *JBR*	2002	Individuals who perceive higher levels of risk express less intent to engage in the unethical behavior
Beams et al.: *JBE*	2003	No significant findings with respect to likelihood of getting caught or the severity of the punishment. Individuals who expected higher gains were more likely to engage in unethical behavior
Shapeero et al.: *MAJ*	2003	Greater likelihood of reward results in intention to engage in unethical behavior
Organizational factors: subjective norms		
Gibson and Frakes: *JBE*	1997	Attitude toward the behavior and subjective norms explained a significant portion of unethical intentions
Flannery and May: *AMJ*	2000	Intentions to engage in unethical behavior is positively influenced by the subjective norms
Powpaka: *JBE*	2002	Intention to engage in unethical behavior s positively influenced by subjective norms

Table 11.5 Empirical research examining direct effects on the dependent variable: behavior

Authors: Journal	Year	Findings
Individual factors: age		
Hunt and Jennings:*JBE*	1997	Younger age teams tended to make the most unethical decisions
Glover et al.:*JBE*	1997	Age was not a predictor of ethical decision-making
Lund:*JBE*	2000	Older individuals acted more ethically in three of four scenarios
Honeycutt et al.:*JBE*	2001	Significant in one of five scenarios

(continued)

Table 11.5 (continued)

Authors: Journal	Year	Findings
Ross and Robertson:*JBE*	2003	No significant findings
Kim and Chun:*IJM*	2003	Younger generation individuals gave less ethical responses
Sankaran and Bui:*JAAB*	2003	The older an individual becomes, the less ethical he/she becomes
Individual factors: awareness		
Fleischman and Valentine:*JBE*	2003	The recognition of an ethical issue in an equitable relief case was negatively related to the decision to grant equitable relief
Valentine and Fleischman:*JBE*	2003	No significant findings
Individual factors: cognitive moral development/ethical judgment		
Green and Weber:*JBE*	1997	Higher levels of moral reasoning lead to more ethical behavior
Marnburg:*JBE*	2001	Individuals high in moral reasoning produced significantly more instability and inconsistency between policy-decisions and action-decisions
Ryan:*JBE*	2001	Moral reasoning was positively related to the helping and sportsmanship OCB behaviors, but not the civic virtue OCB behavior
Honeycutt et al.:*JBE*	2001	Ethical judgment was positively related to ethical behavior
Greenberg:*OBHDP*	2002	Individuals classified as conventional rather than preconventional stole significantly less money
Abdolmohammadi and Sultan:*JBE*	2002	Individuals with a lower P-score were more likely to engage in unethical behavior
Fleischman and Valentine:*JBE*	2003	No significant findings with regards to ethical judgments
Valentine and Fleischman:*JBE*	2003	Ethical judgment was significantly positively related to the decision to grant relief
Individual factors: education, employment, job satisfaction and work experience		
Malinowski and Berger:*JBE*	1996	No significant findings between majors
Glover et al.:*JBE*	1997	Mixed results
Lund:*JBE*	2000	Level of education did not significantly influence respondents' ethical/unethical behavior in three of four scenarios
Chavez et al.:*JBE*	2001	CEO tenure is negatively related to ethical decision making
Honeycutt et al.:*JBE*	2001	Salespeople whose compensation is commission based are more likely to engage in unethical behavior than those salespeople whose compensation is salary based. No significant findings with respect to education
Kim and Chun:*IJM*	2003	Mixed findings
Sankaran and Bui:*JAAB*	2003	Non-business majors tend to be more ethical
Tang and Chiu:*JBE*	2003	High income, pay dissatisfaction, and the number of job changes were not related to unethical behavior

(continued)

Table 11.5 (continued)

Authors: Journal	Year	Findings
Individual factors: gender		
Malinowski and Berger:*JBE*	1996	In seven of nine scenarios, there was a difference between males and females
Ameen et al.:*JBE*	1996	At $p<0.10$, men were more likely to have committed unethical behavior than women
Glover et al.:*JBE*	1997	Women make more ethical decisions than men
Libby and Agnello:*JBE*	2000	In five of six scenarios, there was a significant difference in responses between males and females
Radtke:*JBE*	2000	In 5 of 16 scenarios, there were significant differences in responses between males and females
Lund:*JBE*	2000	In three of four scenarios, men and women were not significantly different in their ethical/unethical behavior
Ross and Robertson:*JBE*	2003	Females are more likely to behave ethically
Chung and Trivedi:*JBE*	2003	Women have higher tax ethics than men
Sankaran and Bui:*JAAB*	2003	Women are more ethical than men
Individual factors: intent		
Wagner and Sanders:*JBE*	2001	Individuals who intend to not engage in an unethical act were unlikely to indicate having behaved unethically
Individual factors: Machiavellianism		
Ross and Robertson:*JBE*	2003	No significant findings
Individual factors: nationality		
Kennedy and Lawton:*JBE*	1996	Ukraine individuals were far more willing to engage in unethical business practices than American individuals
Whitcomb et al.:*JBE*	1998	Significant findings between Chinese and U.S. subjects in three of five dilemmas
Individual factors: organizational commitment		
Tang and Chiu:*JBE*	2003	Organizational commitment is not related to unethical behavior
Individual factors: other individual effects		
Sankaran and Bui:*JAAB*	2003	Individuals who are highly competitive tend to have lower levels of ethics, while there were no significant findings regarding personality type (A or B)
Individual factors: philosophy/value orientation		
Glover et al.:*JBE*	1997	A strong achievement orientation did not result in lower levels of ethical decision making, while a concern for honesty and fairness were not associated with higher levels of ethical decision making

(continued)

Table 11.5 (continued)

Authors: Journal	Year	Findings
Hoffman et al.:*JBE*	1998	The drop in mean scores suggest that when a person's economic well being is an issue, the tendency to act ethically diminishes
Nonis and Swift:*JEB*	2001	In three of four scenarios, differences in personal values did not enhance the propensity to make unethical business decisions
Tang and Chiu:*JBE*	2003	An individuals love of money was significantly related to unethical behavior
Fryxell and Lo:*JBE*	2003	Environmental values positively influenced behavior
Individual factors: religion		
Kennedy and Lawton:*JBE*	1996	Those who are more religious are somewhat less willing to engage in unethical behavior
Individual factors: significant others		
Glover et al.:*JBE*	1997	A high concern for others was not associated with ethical decision making
Sims and Keon:*JBE*	1999	The employee's perception of supervisor expectations was significantly related to ethical decision making
Jackson:*JMS*	2000	Top managements attitude influences a lower level managers behavior in ethical decision making
Robertson and Rymon:*BEQ*	2001	No significant findings with respect to commitment to relationship
Moral intensity		
Marshall and Dewe:*JBE*	1997	Moral intensity was not seen as an influencing factor in elicited responses of individuals
Greenberg:*OBHDP*	2002	Individuals stole more money when it was said to come from the organization, rather than an individual
Fleischman and Valentine:*JBE*	2003	Moral intensity in an equitable relief case was negatively related to the decision to grant equitable relief
Valentine and Fleischman:*JBE*	2003	Moral intensity was negatively associated with the decision to deny relief
Organizational factors: business competitiveness		
Hunt and Jennings:*JBE*	1997	High performing teams do not tend to make the most ethical decisions
Robertson and Rymon:*BEQ*	2001	Buyers who face a high pressure to perform are more likely to behave deceptively
Organizational factors: codes of ethics		
McCabe et al.:*BEQ*	1996	The existence of a code of ethics was significantly associated with lower levels of unethical behavior
Cleek and Leonard:*JBE*	1998	Codes of ethics does not influence ethical decision making behavior

(continued)

Table 11.5 (continued)

Authors: Journal	Year	Findings
Sims and Keon:*JBE*	1999	Mixed results. Informal/unwritten policies were significant in one of five scenarios as influencing ethical decision making while formal/written policies were significant in three of five scenarios
Hume et al.:*JBE*	1999	CPA's were not more likely to follow professional codes than unlicensed accountants
Weaver and Treviño:*BEQ*	1999	The perception that the company's ethics program is value and compliance based resulted in lower observed unethical conduct
Adams et al.:*JBE*	2001	Individuals in companies that have a code of ethics/ felt less pressure to behave unethically than those in an organization with no codes of ethics
Somers:*JBE*	2001	Unethical behavior is less prevalent in organizations that has a code of ethics versus. organizations that do not
Treviño and Weaver:*BEQ*	2001	Observed unethical conduct was higher when employees perceived less ethics program follow-through
Schwartz:*JBE*	2001	Codes have the potential to influence behavior
Greenberg:*OBHDP*	2002	Individuals who worked at an office with a corporate ethics program stole significantly less than individuals who do not work at an office with an ethics program
Peterson:*JBE*	2002	Codes of ethics were associated with less observed unethical behavior
McKendall et al.:*JBE*	2002	Did not lessen legal violations
Organizational factors: ethical climate/culture		
Bartels et al.:*JBE*	1998	Strong ethical climates are associated with less serious ethical problems
Treviño et al.:*BEQ*	1998	In code organizations, ethical culture was strongly associated with observed unethical behavior, where as in non-code organizations, ethical climate was strongly associated
Fritzsche:*JBE*	2000	Laws and codes was the dominant climate in high tech firms and lead to ethical behavior
Vardi:*JBE*	2001	Laws and rules was the most important climate type influencing OMB
Peterson:*JBE*	2002	Egoism climate correlated positively, while the benevolent and principled climates correlated negatively to unethical behavior
Weber et al.:*B and S*	2003	Organizations with a morally preferred ethical climate did not have known employee theft

(continued)

Table 11.5 (continued)

Authors: Journal	Year	Findings
Organizational factors: external environment		
Hunt and Jennings:*JBE*	1997	When facing a favorable environmental change, teams will not tend to make the most ethical decisions
Fryxell and Lo:*JBE*	2003	Mixed results. Environmental knowledge predicted behavior in two of three conditions
Organizational factors: industry type		
Oz:*JBE*	2001	IS professionals are more likely to engage in unethical behavior than other professionals in two of five statements
Organizational factors: opportunity		
Shafer:*JBE*	2002	Financial executives will be more likely to commit fraud when the financial risk is low and the dollar amounts are quantitatively immaterial
Organizational factors: organizational culture/climate		
Vardi:*JBE*	2001	The more positively the organizational climate is viewed, the less the reported misbehavior
Organizational factors: organizational size		
Bartels et al.:*JBE*	1998	Larger organizations tend to have more serious ethical problems
Chavez et al.: *JBE*	2001	Firm size is positively related to ethical decision making
Organizational factors: other organizational effects		
Trevino and Weaver:*BEQ*	2001	Observed unethical conduct was higher when employees perceived less general fairness
McKendall et al.:*JBE*	2002	Communication did not lessen legal violations
Organizational factors: rewards and sanctions		
Tenbrunsel:*AMJ*	1998	Individuals in a high incentive condition were more likely to engage in unethical behavior
Organizational factors: training		
McKendall et al.:*JBE*	2002	Did not lessen legal violations

Individual Factors

Gender. As shown in Table 11.1, 49 findings pertained to gender, with the greatest number of studies examining judgment as the dependent variable (33 studies), followed by behavior (9 studies), intent (4 studies) and awareness (3 studies). The results remain somewhat mixed. The majority of the recent literature reported few or no significant gender differences (23 studies) (e.g., Fleischman and Valentine 2003) or found women to behave more ethically than men, at least in certain situations (16 studies) (e.g., Cohen et al. 2001).

Comparison to past reviews – Ford and Richardson (1994) – Seven studies reported no significant findings, while another seven revealed that females are likely to act more ethically than males. Loe et al. (2000) – Nine studies reported no significant findings, while 12 reported that females are more ethical than males under certain circumstances.

Conclusion – The literature examining gender continues to produce fairly consistent findings. There are often no differences found between males and females, but when differences are found, females are more ethical than males.

Philosophy/value orientation. There were a total of 42 findings for philosophy/value orientation. These studies range from examining the differences between idealism and relativism (e.g., Singhapakdi et al. 1999) to deontological versus teleological perspectives (e.g., Cohen et al. 2001) to other value orientations, such as achievement and economic values. The research examining idealism and relativism has produced consistent results. That is, idealism and deontology are positively related to the ethical decision-making process, whereas relativism and teleology are negatively related.

Comparison to past reviews – Ford and Richardson (1994) – Reported only one finding regarding value orientation. Political orientation produced no significant findings, while economic orientation was associated with unethical behavior. Loe et al. (2000)–Rule deontologists rank higher on an ethical behavior scale than any other philosophy types and deontology and teleology have significant influences on the decision making process. There were no reported findings regarding idealism and relativism.

Conclusion – More than two decades of research reveal fairly consistent findings. Idealism and deontology are generally positively related to ethical decision-making, while relativism, teleology, and other factors, such as economic orientation are generally negatively related to ethical decision-making.

Education, employment, job satisfaction, and work experience. Forty-one findings were reported with respect to education (type and number of years of education), employment, job satisfaction, and work experience. Of these, six studies examined differences between student majors on the ethical decision-making process; five of which found no significant findings (e.g., Green and Weber 1997). However, Sankaran and Bui (2003) found that non-business majors were more ethical than business majors. In another 11 studies, years of education, employment or work experience did not significantly influence or marginally influenced ethical decision-making (e.g., Wu 2003). Other studies reported positive influences, such as individuals in the latter years of their career displayed higher ethical judgment (Weeks et al. 1999), while others reported negative influences. For example, CEO tenure was found to be negatively related to the ethical decision-making process (Chavez et al. 2001).

Comparison to past reviews – Ford and Richardson (1994) – Of the 23 studies included in their review, 8 examined type of education. Five of these studies reported little or no significant findings, while the remaining three studies produced mixed results. Of the remaining 15 studies with respect to years of education or employment, 8 discovered no significant findings. Four of the remaining studies produced results that favor more education, experience or employment.

Loe et al. (2000) – After eliminating the studies that were used in Ford and Richardson's review (total of 16), there were only two new studies that examined this variable. One study was in support of the notion that employment does influence ethical decision making, while the other found no relationship.

Conclusion – The research generally indicates that more education, employment or work experience is positively related to ethical decision-making (12 of 18 studies). However, type of education has little or no effect on the ethical decision-making process (10 of 14 studies). In addition, it is interesting to note that seven studies compared practitioners to students; three of which found students to be less ethical than practitioners. This has important implications for research, as many researchers study ethical decision making using student samples.

Nationality. In the 25 findings examining nationality, 5 studies found few or no differences across cultures. However, most studies and results are not directly comparable as, for the most part, each study examined different nations. Among the studies comparing the U.S. to other nations, the results have been mixed. Some suggest that U.S. respondents make better ethical decisions (e.g., Cherry et al. 2003), whereas other studies suggest that U.S. respondents may not make better ethical decisions (e.g., Volkema and Fleury 2002).

Comparison to past reviews – Ford and Richardson (1994) – In their review consisting of five studies, the results were mixed. Two of the five showed no significant findings. Of the three remaining studies, two indicated that U.S. respondents were more ethical than non-U.S. respondents. Loe et al. (2000) – After eliminating the five studies that overlapped with Ford and Richardson's review, six new studies were included in their review, all of which found significant differences. However, only one study compared the U.S. to another nation and found that U.S. managers consider ethical issues to be more important than U.K. managers.

Conclusion – Nationality appears to influence ethical decision-making. However, to what extent is still unclear. This is in part due to the fact that researchers have studied many different nations and it is difficult to make comparisons across studies.

Age. Twenty-one findings were reported regarding the effect of age on the decision-making process. Of these, eight found few or no significant age differences (e.g., Ross and Robertson 2003), whereas five studies reported a negative relationship to ethical decision-making (e.g., Sankaran and Bui 2003), and six reported a positive relationship (e.g., Kim and Chun 2003).

Comparison to past reviews – Ford and Richardson (1994) – Of the eight studies reviewed, only three reported significant findings. Two of these studies revealed that older participants were more ethical than younger participants. Loe et al. (2000) – Of the eight studies not included in Ford and Richardson's review, one study reported no significant findings. Five of the remaining studies indicated that older respondents tend to be more ethical in decision making than younger respondents.

Conclusion – Although previous reviews suggested that age appears to be positively correlated with ethical decision-making, this review calls this conclusion into question. The research on age has produced mixed and inconsistent results. Of the 37 findings included in this and past reviews, 14 produced no significant age differences,

10 studies found a positive relationship, while 6 studies found a negative relationship. These mixed results may suggest a more complex relationship between age and ethical decision making than is captured by these studies.

Cognitive moral development (CMD)/ethical judgment. In the 23 findings included in this review, all but 4 reported significant findings. Fifteen studies found a positive relationship between CMD and ethical judgment (e.g., Green and Weber 1997), or ethical judgment positively influenced the decision making process (e.g., Bass et al. 1999). In contrast, Au and Wong (2000) found a negative relationship between cognitive moral development and ethical judgment. The remaining three studies produced mixed results, or determined the strength of influence that ethical judgment or CMD plays in the decision making process (e.g., DeConinck and Lewis 1997).

Comparison to past reviews – Ford and Richardson (1994) – No studies reported. Loe et al. (2000) – Six studies examined this variable. One concluded that CMD influences ethical decision making, while other studies reported variables that either positively or negatively influenced CMD. They concluded that CMD is a difficult variable to study and report. This is partly due to the limited amount of research examining this variable.

Conclusion – Although there have been a few notable exceptions, the research generally suggests a positive relationship between CMD or ethical judgment and ethical decision-making.

Locus of control. Seven of the eleven findings included in this review suggest that internal locus of control tends to be positively associated with the ethical decision-making process, while external locus of control appears to be negatively associated (e.g., Shapeero et al. 2003). The other four remaining findings reported no significant differences.

Comparison to past reviews – Ford and Richardson (1994) – In two of three studies, there were no significant findings. In the third study, external managers perceived organizational politics as ethical. Loe et al. (2000) – In two additional studies, the findings were mixed, where one reported no significant results and the other reporting locus of control influences ethical decision-making directly and indirectly through outcome expectancies.

Conclusion – The findings are somewhat mixed. Several studies report no significant differences. Those that have found differences consistently report that internal locus of control is positively related to decision-making and external locus of control is negatively related.

Machiavellianism. The personality trait, Machiavellianism, produced fairly consistent results. In seven of ten findings, Machiavellianism was negatively related to the ethical decision-making process (e.g., Bass et al. 1999). The other three findings reported no significant results.

Comparison to past reviews – Ford and Richardson (1994) – In both reported studies, Machiavellianism was negatively associated with the ethical decision-making process. Loe et al. (2000) – In two supplementary studies, both findings indicated that Machiavellianism affects ethical-decision making.

Conclusion – The results consistently suggest that Machiavellianism is negatively related to the ethical decision-making process. In other words, high machs tend to be less ethical in their decision making than low machs.

Religion. In eight of the ten recent findings, religion, in some form or another, had a positive relationship to ethical decision-making (e.g., Singhapakdi et al. 2000a, b). On the other hand, Giacalone and Jurkiewicz (2003) found that spirituality negatively influences an individual's perception of a questionable business practice.

Comparison to past reviews – Ford and Richardson (1994) – In three of four studies, there were no significant findings. Only strength of religious belief was strongly related to ethical standards. Loe et al. (2000) – Did not include any new studies other than those already reported in Ford and Richardson.

Conclusion – Out of the 14 total findings, 9 reported a positive relationship with ethical decision-making. The results generally suggest that religion has a positive relationship with ethical decision-making.

Miscellaneous categories. The remaining areas of study (e.g., awareness, biases, conflict, intent, need for cognition, organizational commitment, other personality factors, professional affiliation, significant others) have received only a scant amount of research attention. As a result, these may represent areas for future research.

Summary. Individual factors have been widely examined in the ethical decision-making literature. The studies included in this review reported 270 findings with respect to individual level factors, compared to the roughly 120 findings reported in the Loe et al. article (2000). The most consistent findings appear in the studies that test for the direct effects of gender, ethical philosophies (i.e., idealism and relativism), cognitive moral development, locus of control, Machiavellianism, and religion. On the other hand, mixed findings were commonly found with regard to education level, work experience, nationality, and age

Organizational Factors

The five predominant organizational variables examined in the ethical decision-making literature are codes of ethics, ethical climate/culture, industry type, organizational size, and rewards and sanctions.

Codes of ethics. Of the 20 findings in this category, only 2 revealed no significant findings. Of the remaining 18 findings, 6 reported mixed results or suggested that the existence of a code of ethics did not influence ethical decision-making (e.g., Sims and Keon 1999), whereas 11 of the other 12 findings reported a positive effect on ethical decision-making (e.g., McDevitt and Hise 2002).

Comparison to past reviews – Ford and Richardson (1994) – Their review concluded that codes of ethics (conduct) are consistently and significantly related to ethical decision-making, with six of nine studies supporting this notion. Loe et al. (2000) – Of the ten studies that examined the influence of codes of ethics, seven studies supported the notion that codes of ethics are positively associated with ethical decision-making.

Conclusion – Although there have been few notable exceptions, the majority of studies support the idea that the existence of a code of ethics is positively related to ethical decision-making.

Ethical climate/culture. Sixteen findings reported the influence of ethical climate or ethical culture in the ethical decision-making process. Twelve of these reported that at least one or more dimensions of ethical culture or climate positively influenced ethical decision-making (e.g., Trevino et al. 1998). The remaining four studies found no influence in the decision making process (e.g., DeConinck and Lewis 1997) or reported the most dominant climate dimension in an organization (e.g., Upchurch 1998).

Comparison to past reviews – Ford and Richardson (1994) – No reported studies. Loe et al. (2000) – Only reported four studies that directly examined ethical climate. Of these studies, one identified different types of climate that exist in an organization, another stated that ethical climate is unrelated to moral reasoning, the third study concluded that ethical climate is negatively related to perceived ethical conflict, and one study was included in this review.

Conclusion – There is increasing support for the notion that ethical climates and cultures exist within organizations. The research generally supports the notion that ethical climates and cultures have a positive influence on ethical decision making.

Industry type. There were nine reported findings in this category. Only one study produced no significant findings (Shafer et al. 2001). The other eight findings are not directly comparable as different industries were chosen for each study.

Comparison to past reviews – Ford and Richardson (1994) – Three studies were reported, two of which resulted in no significant findings. The remaining study found significant differences among retailers toward actions taken in certain situations. Loe et al. (2000) – No additional studies reported.

Conclusion – Due to the fact that different industries were examined in various studies, no overall conclusions regarding the effect of industry can be drawn. However, of the 12 findings included in these reviews, 8 produced significant differences between industries.

Organizational size. Of the seven findings with regard to organizational size, five revealed no significant findings (e.g., Paolillo and Vitell 2002). The other two suggested mixed results – Bartels and colleagues (1998) found that larger organizations tend to have more serious ethical problems, whereas Chavez et al. (2001) found that firm size is positively related to the ethical decision making process.

Comparison to past reviews – Ford and Richardson (1994) – In the three studies reported, all indicated that size had a negative influence on ethical decision-making. One study found that larger firm respondents were more likely to accept gifts and favors from ex-suppliers, while the other two indicated that there was a difference between organizational size and moral reasoning and judgment. Loe et al. (2000) – No reported findings.

Conclusion – The research in this area generally suggests that organizational size has a detrimental effect on ethical decision making. However, given the mixed results, future research appears warranted.

Rewards and sanctions. The seven findings in this category were consistent, with only one study finding no significant results (Beams et al. 2003). In general, unethical behavior is more prevalent in organizations that reward unethical behavior and less prevalent in organizations that punish unethical behavior.

Comparison to past reviews – Ford and Richardson (1994) – The reported findings are consistent with current research. Rewards for unethical behavior induce such behavior, while sanctions prohibit unethical behavior. Loe et al. (2000) – For the most part, their review concurs with the literature presented in this review as well as Ford and Richardson's review. However, most of the studies reported in the review did not show a direct influence on behavior

Conclusion – The impact of rewards and sanctions is clear – rewarding unethical behavior tends to increase the frequency of such behavior, while effective sanctioning systems tend to decrease such behavior.

Miscellaneous. The remaining organizational variables were found in only a small number of studies. These include business competitiveness, external environment, opportunity, organizational climate/culture, other organizational effects, significant others, subjective norms, and training. Some of these variables are relatively new to the ethics literature (i.e., subjective norms and changes occurring in the external environment) and provide opportunities for future research.

Summary. Researchers in the past seven years have given less attention to organizational factors than to individual factors. Since 1996, there are a reported 82 findings with respect to organizational factors, compared to the 64 findings in Loe et al.'s review (2000). The most consistent findings were found in the studies testing for the effects of ethical climate/culture, codes of ethics, and rewards and sanctions. Mixed results were more common in studies examining industry type and organizational size.

Moral Intensity

In Loe et al.'s (2000) review, moral intensity was examined in only two studies. Since then, moral intensity has received quite a bit of research attention. In total, 32 findings were included in this review and have reported fairly consistent results. With the exception of Marshall and Dewe (1997), each study that examined moral intensity, or some component of moral intensity, found a relationship with at least one facet of ethical decision-making (e.g., May and Pauli 2002). Two of Jones' (1991) six issue-related factors produced the most consistent results. Social consensus and magnitude of consequences positively influenced ethical decision-making in 12 and 14 studies, respectively. Concentration of effect, temporal immediacy and proximity were examined in four studies, whereas probability of effect was examined in five studies.

With the exception of concentration of effect (which had a positive influence in each of the 3 studies), the findings for these other factors have been mixed.

Comparison to past reviews – Ford and Richardson (1994) – No reported studies. Loe et al. (2000) – Two studies, both of which support the notion that moral intensity influences the ethical decision-making process.

Conclusion – Although moral intensity is a relatively new construct in the business ethics literature, there seems to be strong support for its influence on the ethical decision-making process. Magnitude of consequences and social consensus represent the most consistent findings. As discussed below, additional research regarding the remaining four factors appears warranted.

Trends and Future Directions

In this section, we compare the past 7 years of empirical research with previous reviews in order to draw conclusions regarding trends in the ethical decision-making literature and to surface directions for future research. Overall, we observe that the field of descriptive ethics, particularly in the area of ethical decision-making, is a rapidly growing area of inquiry. Since 1996, a total of 174 empirical articles have been published in prominent business ethics journals. This can be compared to the roughly 110 articles over 30 years in the Loe et al. (2000) review. We consider this to be an indication that descriptive ethics is becoming an increasingly important topic in organizational and behavioral science.

The body of empirical research published over the past seven years has improved our understanding of the ethical decision-making process. However, upon critical examination of the literature, there are numerous areas that require further exploration or modification. The following discussion is not intended to be exhaustive. Rather, our intent is to surface trends and offer recommendations regarding issues that are common to empirical research articles (i.e., theoretical/conceptual and methodological issues) in order to guide future empirical ethical decision-making research.

Theoretical and Conceptual Issues

In Randall and Gibson's (1990) critique of methodology in business ethics research, they identified only 32 studies (roughly 35% of all studies included) that offered any type of theory development, and 71 studies (75%) lacked hypotheses. Although it is difficult to offer an exact count, we concur with Randall and Gibson that many studies over the past 7-year period lacked strong theoretical grounding and formal hypotheses. In place of theory, many researchers have opted to discuss construct development (i.e. culture, codes of ethics, locus of control, gender issues, etc.). Those studies that are grounded in theory often draw from social psychology, including Kohlberg's theory of cognitive moral development (1981) (e.g., Wimalasiri et al. 1996), Ajzen's theory of planned behavior (1985, 1989) (e.g., Flannery and

May 2000), equity theory (e.g., Glass and Wood 1996), and script theory (Boyle 2000). Other commonly used theories include Hunt and Vitell's (1986) general theory of marketing ethics (e.g., Rallapalli et al. 1996), theories of corporate illegality (e.g., McKendall et al. 2002), and theories of ethical climate/culture (e.g., Victor and Cullen 1988; Trevino et al. 1998).

If the field of descriptive ethics is to move forward to strengthen our understanding of the ethical decision-making process, it is imperative that future studies focus more attention on theory development. This includes developing and/or moving beyond Rest's framework, conceiving and testing additional individual, situational, and issue-related influences, and considering potential moderators of the ethical decision-making process.

Rest's Framework

Given the prominence of Rest's framework in the descriptive ethics literature, we encourage critical evaluation of this framework. Do these four steps truly capture the essence of the individual ethical decision-making process? Are there additional steps that precede, follow, or intervene between the other steps? Insight into these questions may be found in the variety of decision-making models found in the psychology and management literatures. Many models contain elements that might be useful in expanding or modifying Rest's basic framework. An example can be found in the notion of sensemaking, which refers to the idea that individuals are continuously bombarded by ambiguous environmental and organizational information that must be somehow noticed, interpreted, and acted upon (e.g., Milliken 1990; Weick 1979). As such, sensemaking involves the reciprocal interaction of scanning (i.e., information seeking), interpretation, and action (Gioia and Chittipeddi 1991). Although interpretation, which refers to the process by which the ambiguous information is structured so that it may provide meaning, significance, and a basis for action (Milliken 1990), and action are explicitly included in Rest's framework, the notion of scanning is not explicitly included. Scanning refers to the notion that people are not necessarily passive receivers of information. People are constantly searching for key environmental changes and events that may affect them (Daft and Weick 1984; Milliken 1990). Because moral situations often involve highly ambiguous environmental events, and because individuals are not always passive in receiving information about ethical issues, scanning appears to have clear application to the ethical decision making process. We encourage future research that explores such possibilities, along with other factors suggested by alternative models of human decision making.

Assuming that research continues within Rest's paradigm, additional work is needed to develop and test the three main direct relationships within the model and to otherwise examine the model's validity. To date, no empirical study has examined Rest's model in its entirety. Only a few studies have examined even one or two of the links, with most of the attention focusing on the relationship between moral judgment and moral intent (e.g., Barnett et al. 1996). We specifically encourage increased attention to the relationship between moral intent and moral behavior. Since 1996, only one study has investigated this relationship, finding that individuals who intended not to engage in the unethical act were unlikely to indicate behaving unethically (Wagner and Sanders 2001). Although the theory of planned behavior (Ajzen 1985, 1989) predicts a link between intent and action and has been supported in some domains (e.g., Beck and Ajzen 1991), recent ethics research has demonstrated that what an individual intends to do may not be what an individual actually does (Weber and Gillespie 1998). Weber and Gillespie further state, "although social psychologists (including Ajzen, Fishbein, and others) predict a linkage, their findings admittedly present weak to moderate correlation" (Weber and Gillespie 1998, pp. 462). Thus, additional exploration of this relationship appears warranted.

Compared to previous reviews, each of the four components of Rest's (1986) model has received an increasing amount of research attention. In our review, we counted 28 research findings for moral awareness, 185 for judgment, 86 for moral intent, and 85 for behavior. Although researchers have focused mainly on the last three steps, we would like to call for increased attention on the first step – moral awareness. The fact that moral awareness has received the least attention is not surprising, given that it is the first step in Rest's model and thus may be viewed primarily as an independent variable. Rest offered insight into the complexities of this step, stating that it involves the "interpretation of the particular situation in terms of what actions (are) possible, who (including oneself) would be affected by each course of action, and how the interested parties would regard such effects on their welfare" (1986, pp. 3). Future research might use these criteria as a basis for asking important questions about what precedes moral awareness – in other words, what factors influence an individual's realization "that she/he could do something that would affect the interests, welfare, or expectations of other people" (Rest 1986, pp. 5)?

Various individual, situational, and issue-related influences provide additional opportunities for future research on the moral awareness construct. For example, research might examine whether corporate ethics initiatives (e.g., training programs, values-oriented codes of conduct) can be designed to enhance employees' ability to recognize ethical issues. Future research could also examine the impact of ethical culture on moral awareness. Trevino (1990) defined ethical culture as a multidimensional construct consisting of various formal and informal systems of behavioral control. Formal systems are comprised of factors such as leadership, policies, authority structures and reward systems, while informal systems are comprised of norms, heroes, rituals, myths and language. Trevino argued that, to the extent that these systems encourage ethical conduct, individuals are likely to behave ethically. Similarly, if these systems are properly established in an organization, individuals may increase their ability to recognize ethical issues.

Influences on the Ethical Decision-Making Process

Within the descriptive ethics literature, there are a number of individual, situational, and issue-related variables that are garnering increased attention and may reflect new research trends. To date, the ethical decision-making literature has overwhelmingly examined individual factors in relation to contextual influences. Approximately 70% (270 out of the 384) of the variables examined in this review support this notion. For instance, a variable that has produced a great deal of recent attention is philosophy/value orientation – in particular, idealism versus relativism. In seven studies included in this review, idealistic individuals tended to be more ethical than relativistic individuals (e.g., Elias 2002; Singhapakdi et al. 2000a, b). Given this success, future research might examine additional philosophies or values, such as those suggested by moral philosophy or contemporary business practices (e.g., caring or sensitivity).

Of the various organizational-level influences, two that are gaining in interest are ethical climate and ethical culture. We were interested to find that there were no empirical studies of ethical climate or culture on ethical decision making reported in Ford and Richardson's (1994) review and only four reported in Loe et al.'s (2000) review. This was surprising, given that Victor and Cullen's (1988) initial development of the ethical climate construct and Trevino's initial theoretical treatment of the ethical culture construct occurred in the mid-to-late 1980s. Despite this late start, research connecting these constructs to the individual ethical decision-making process appears to be gaining momentum. Given the success of studies that have focused on contextual and organizational influences, this appears to represent an important but relatively untapped area of study. One suggestion for future research would be to examine the interaction between formal and informal aspects of ethical culture. Important questions might include: How can informal aspects undermine or enhance the power of formal aspects in curbing unethical behavior? How might a misalignment between formal and informal aspects affect unethical behavior? What elements of each are most effective in curbing unethical behavior?

Loe et al. (2000) called for additional empirical research on moral intensity. Since 1996, moral intensity has received increasing attention (a total of 32 findings). Since Jones' initial development of the construct (1991), empirical evidence has generally suggested that moral intensity, especially magnitude of consequences and social consensus, influences the ethical decision-making process. However, additional work needs to be conducted on the other four factors and on the validity of the model itself.

Moderators

Although many descriptive ethics models have been developed from an interactionist perspective (e.g., Trevino 1986), we were surprised that only 20 studies included in this review examined moderators (refer to Table 11.6) to the ethical decision-making process.

Examining interaction effects would broaden our understanding of the ethical decision-making process, and we encourage researchers to question the boundary conditions of the four-step model. Under what circumstances does moral awareness

Table 11.6 Empirical research examining interaction effects on each of the four dependent variables

Authors: Journal	Year	Findings
Dependent variable: awareness		
VanSandt:*B&S*	2003	Gender, age and ethics training were not significant moderating factors between ethical climate and moral awareness. Level of education was a significant moderator between ethical climate and moral awareness
Dependent variable: judgment		
Dawson:*JBE*	1997	Females reported higher scores than males at all experience levels
Harrington:*JBE*	1997	As social consensus weakens, the judgments of those who are more rule oriented decrease in ethicality quicker than those who are less rule-oriented
Tse and Au:*JBE*	1997	No interaction between major and gender, level of education, father's or mother's occupation, or religion
Rallapalli et al.:*JBR*	1998	Teleological evaluations have a greater influence on the ethical judgments in organizations with a less sensitive ethical environment
Mason and Mudrack:*JBE*	1996	There is a positive gender and employment status interaction effect on judgment
Boyle:*JBE*	2000	Male, low idealists rated the agent's actions considerably higher than female low idealists
Douglas et al.:*JBE*	2001	Codes of conduct affect ethical judgment in situations of high moral intensity
Douglas et al.:*JBE*	2001	Ethical culture is indirectly related to ethical judgments in high moral intensity situations, as it effects idealism, which affects ethical judgment
Douglas et al.:*JBE*	2001	Ethical orientation and judgment were only related in high moral intensity situations
Peterson et al.:*JBE*	2001	Younger respondents who were female demonstrated a higher level of ethics, while older males held a higher level of ethics
Roozen et al.:*JBE*	2001	Employees with a high organizational commitment and working in a company with an organizational goal of profit maximization behave less ethical than employees who are low in organizational commitment and work for the same company
Schepers:*JBE*	2003	Machiavellianism does not influence the relationship between profit and judgment
Sivadas et al.:*JPSSM*	2003	Absolutists and exceptionists judged the ethically controversial practices more critically
Dependent variable: intent		
Rallapalli et al.: *JBR*	1998	Individuals in a less sensitive organizational ethical environment tend to use teleological evaluations in stating intentions

(continued)

Table 11.6 (continued)

Authors: Journal	Year	Findings
Rallapalli et al.:*JBR*	1998	The influence of ethical judgments and teleological evaluations on intentions is positively moderated by a code of ethics
Barnett and Vaicys:*JBE*	2000	The interaction between ethical judgment and ethical climate on intentions was supported by social responsibility and rules/codes climates, but not egoism and team/friendship climates
Key:*JMI*	2002	The interaction between LOC and ethical culture did not predict perceived discretion
Sivadas et al.:*JPSSM*	2003	Absolutists were the least likely to intend to hire an individual who engages in ethically controversial practices
Dependent variable: behavior		
Deshpande:*JBE*	1996	Individuals who believed that their organization had a caring climate reported a significantly positive link between success and ethical behavior, while those in an instrumental climate perceived a significantly negative link between success and ethical behavior
Trevino and Weaver:*BEQ*	2001	As the ethics program changes from low to high follow-through, a smaller change in unethical behavior occurs in conditions of high perceived general fairness than conditions of low perceived general fairness
Greenberg:*OBHDP*	2002	Participants at the conventional level stole significantly less when an ethics program was in place than when no ethics program was in place
Chung and Trivedi: *JBE*	2003	Women in the friendly persuasion condition reported to be more ethical than men in the same condition
Ross and Robertson:*JBE*	2003	Men and younger persons were more likely to engage in unethical behavior
Fryxell and Lo:*JBE*	2003	The interaction between behavior, environmental knowledge and environmental values was only significant in one of three conditions

lead to moral judgment, moral judgment lead to moral intent, and moral intent lead to moral behavior?

An example of a promising individual-level moderating variable is locus of control, which refers to the degree to which individuals attribute causes of events to either internal or external sources (Rotter 1966). External individuals believe that outcomes and events in life are determined primarily by external forces (e.g., luck, fate, social context, other people), whereas internals view events and outcomes as being largely under their own control. In the descriptive ethics literature, internal locus of control has been associated with higher levels of cognitive moral development (e.g., Murk and Addleman 1992), higher levels of moral responsibility (e.g., Johnson et al. 1968), altruism/helping behavior, and resistance to expectations, requests, and other social pressures, especially those that violate their beliefs and principles (e.g., Lefcourt 1982). In fact, internals may react negatively to social influence, exhibiting a shift in attitudes in the opposite direction of the influence attempt (Biondo and MacDonald 1971). Researchers have argued that such findings are due largely to internals' views regarding causality and responsibility. When faced with a moral situation, internals are more likely to view that they are in control of the situation and to assume personal responsibility for outcomes. Thus, for example, we would expect that the positive relationship between moral intent and moral action would be stronger for an internal than for an external.

A promising contextual moderating variable is peer influence. Studies have generally found a positive direct effect for peer influence on the ethical decision-making process (e.g., Beams et al. 2003; Jones and Kavanagh 1996). Conceptually, it can also be argued that peer influence would have a moderating effect. Theoretical support for this contention is offered by previous models of ethical decision making (e.g., Trevino 1986). This assertion is also supported by social learning theory, which contends that individuals learn by observing and modeling the behavior of others (e.g., Bandura 1977), and by differential association theory, which argues that unethical behavior is passed from the reference group to the individual depending on the ratio of contacts the individual has with ethical behavior patterns compared to contacts with unethical behavior patterns (e.g., Sutherland and Cressey 1970). Thus, we might expect that the relationships between moral awareness, judgment, intent, and behavior will differ depending on peer influence. For example, one might argue that moral judgment is more likely to lead to moral intent if the individual's peer group provides normative support for ethical behavior.

Another emerging construct that may modesate aspects of the ethical decision-making process is moral imagination. Moral imagination has been defined as "articulating and examining alternatives, weighing them and their probable .implications, considering their effects on one's other plans and interests, and considering their possible effects on the interests and feelings of others" (Jacobs 1991, pp. 25). Moberg and Seabright (2000) postulated direct relationships between moral imagination and all four components' of Rest's model. However, one might also consider moderating effects. For example, once individuals establish moral awareness, they may be more likely to make a moral judgment if they are able to successfully imagine alternative actions and their implications for affected parties. Similarly, the relationship between judgment and intent may be strengthened if the individual is able to successfully identify and consider the other party's feelings and interests.

Methodological Issues

In addition to theoretical and conceptual issues, there are many methodology-focused insights that can be drawn from comparing the past 7 years of empirical literature to the conclusions drawn by Ford and Richardson, Loe et al. and various methodology-focused reviews (e.g., Randall and Gibson 1990; Weber 1992). These issues include the use of student samples, the use of scenario methodologies, the use of multivariate statistics, measuring ethical/unethical behavior, and the use of meta-analysis.

Student Samples

Since 1996, roughly 40% of empirical studies used a student sample or a combination of students and other individuals (70 of 174 studies). This is generally consistent with past reviews (e.g., Randall and Gibson 1990; Weber 1992). The appropriateness of using student samples has been widely debated among business ethics researchers. Some have argued that the use of student samples inhibits the generalizability of the results, whereas others have argued that student samples are appropriate for business ethics research if they "comprise the population of interest or if the population of interest is similar to the student sample on theoretically relevant variables" (Randall and Gibson 1990, pp. 463). We concur with Weber (1992), who stated that researchers should use appropriate samples and avoid using student samples simply because of their availability.

Scenario Methodology

Scenarios remain the most widely used method of assessing constructs in business ethics research. Of the 174 studies included in this review, 95 (55%) used scenarios or a variation of scenarios in their methodological approach. The justification for this is usually a statement such as "scenarios are widely used in business ethics research" or "several researchers have used the scenario approach successfully". Alexander and Becker (1978:103) stated that the use of scenarios "helps to standardize the social stimulus across respondents and at the same time makes the decision-making situation more real". The use of scenarios is also advantageous in that it allows researchers to manipulate the variables of interest while controlling for environmental factors. However, as noted by Marshall and Dewe (1997), when a scenario is used, two assumptions are implied: the situation described in the scenario actually presents an ethical dilemma for the respondent, and the context surrounding the situation is the same across all respondents. This clearly is not always the case. In addition, scenarios are often accompanied by closed-ended items, which may not tap an individual's actual response in a given situation. It has also been argued that too few scenarios may impact the researcher's ability to manipulate the variables of interest, which in turn could result in response biases. Too many scenarios, on the other hand, could result in overload and fatigue for the respondent (see Weber 1992). Only a few studies used a technique other than a scenario or questionnaire (e.g., simulations and lab experiments) over this time period. Research should carefully consider the purpose of their study and only use scenarios when appropriate.

Multivariate Statistics

The Ford and Richardson and Loe et al. reviews showed that most studies prior to 1996 used univarisate or bivariate statistical analyses, with little attention to multivariate techniques. The studies included in this review suggest that the use of multivariate statistical techniques is on the rise. Forty-two (24%) of the studies used univariate and bivariate statistics, while the remaining 76% used some form of multivariate statistics. Of these, 63 (36%) used ANOVA or a variation of ANOVA, 54 (31%) used regression or a form of regression, while the remaining studies used path analysis, LISREL or SEM (9%). However, it should be noted that one statistical technique is not necessarily superior to another technique. As noted by Randall and Gibson (1990:467), "the appropriateness of the technique depends primarily upon the theory, research hypotheses, and available data" (1990, pp. 467).

Measuring Ethical/Unethical Behavior

Due to issues such as social desirability bias, the relative infrequency in which unethical behavior occurs, and individuals' tendency to conceal information, measuring ethical–unethical behavior has been regarded as a difficult task (e.g., Treviño 1992). The articles in this review suggest that ethics researchers are seeking and devising creative ways to measure ethical-unethical behavior.

As mentioned previously, the dominant method used to collect data is scenarios/vignettes – roughly 55% of studies in this review used this approach. Many studies asked participants to put themselves in the position of a character portrayed in a hypothetical scenario. Participants generally were then asked what they would do in this particular situation. Although this method has advantages, a potential drawback is that it is unclear whether one is actually measuring behavior, or some other construct, such as intent. Given Rest's definitions of intent (deciding which action a person will attempt to pursue) and action (actually executing and implementing our intentions), the claim that one is tapping actual behavior is questionable.

In order to avoid this quandary, some researchers have begun to measure behavior in less conventional ways. Other approaches have included: (1) asking respondents to think of an ethical dilemma that they have encountered in their work environment (Marshall and Dewe 1997); (2) asking the respondents to answer the questions from other peoples' perspectives (Kim and Chun 2003); (3) asking the subjects to rate their own behavior in the workplace over the past year (McCabe et al. 1996); (4) classifying an organization as ethical/unethical based on recent internal audits (Weber et al. 2003); and, (5) asking respondents to rate the extent to which they have observed others engaging in unethical behavior (e.g., Trevino et al. 1998; Vardi 2001; Weaver and Trevino 1999). These approaches also have disadvantages, but they demonstrate creativity in measuring unethical behavior and offer future researchers additional options as they attempt to tap this difficult construct.

Another way to overcome these limitations is to use alternative methods such as lab studies, field experiments, in-basket exercises, and simulation Techniques (e.g., Randall and Gibson 1990; Treviño 1992). These methods not only allow researchers to tap actual behavior, their use also speaks to the oft-stated concern about the over-utilization of scenarios (e.g., Weber 1992). In this review, only about 4% (7 of 174 studies) used one of these techniques. Although experimental techniques have not gone without criticism (i.e., generalizability and realism), Trevino (1992) provides evidence in support of the strength of many of these techniques, arguing that if ethics researchers are able to identify variables that affect the ethical decision-making process in a controlled environment, it will enhance our ability to examine these variables in organizational contexts.

Meta Analysis

Although literature reviews are useful in summarizing and critiquing an overall body of literature, meta-analysis is better able to gather all quantitative data and derive statistically valid conclusions in a specific area of inquiry (Brierley and Cowton 2000). Although Robertson (1993) recommended that meta-analysis should be conducted more widely in the business ethics literature, we are aware of only three such analyses. Brierley and Cowton (2000) conducted a meta-analysis on organizational-professional conflict in accounting. Borkowski and Ugras (1998) published a meta-analysis examining the effects of age, gender, and undergraduate major on ethical attitudes and behavior among business students. Franke et al. (1997) analyzed gender differences in perceptions of ethical decision-making. Consistent with our conclusion regarding gender differences, both the Borkowski and Ugras and Franke et al. analysis indicated that women tend to be more ethical than men. We strongly encourage further use of meta-analytic procedures to advance our understanding of the ethical decision-making process.

Conclusion

This review offers two primary contributions. First, we summarized research articles published from 1996 to 2003, offering information regarding the findings, summary information on the number of published articles by the independent and dependent variables, and conclusions regarding the state of the research on each dependent variable. By doing so, we were able to identify and acknowledge which variables have received the most attention, as well as the variables that have been largely overlooked. Second, we compared this review with past reviews and surfaced a variety of trends and directions for future research. Overall, researchers have produced more empirical articles in the area of ethical decision making over the past 7 years than in the previous four decades combined. This has allowed us to view the current state of the field of ethical decision-making, enabling us to provide insight into the field's strengths and weaknesses. Strengths include increasing knowledge of individual, situational, and issue-related factors that influence ethical decision-making and the increasing use of multivariate statistics. Major weaknesses include a lack of theoretical grounding, problems in the operationalization and measurement of ethical/unethical behavior, and a lack of consideration of interaction effects.

This is an important time for the field of business ethics. The perceived prevalence of illegal and unethical corporate behavior is fueling skepticism and uncertainty about the role of ethics in modern business practice. We are encouraged to see increased attention to ethical decision making, as demonstrated by this review and by recent attention from prominent management journals (e.g., the upcoming special issue on organizational corruption in the Academy of Management Review). It is our hope that this review will stimulate additional research in this important area.

References

Abdolmohammadi, M., and J. Sultan. 2002. Ethical reasoning and the use of insider information in stock trading. *Journal of Business Ethics* 37(2): 165–173.

Abdolmohammadi, M.J., W.J. Read, and D.P. Scarbrough. 2003. Does selection-socialization help to explain accountants' weak ethical reasoning? *Journal of Business Ethics* 42(1): 71–81.

Abratt, R., and N. Penman. 2002. Understanding factors affecting salespeople's perceptions of ethical behavior in South Africa. *Journal of Business Ethics* 35(4): 269–280.

Adams, J.S., A. Taschian, and T.H. Shore. 2001. Codes of ethics as signals for ethical behavior. *Journal of Business Ethics* 29(3): 199–211.

Ajzen, I. 1985. From intentions to action: A theory of planned behavior. In *Action control: From cognition to behavior*, ed. J. Kuhl and J. Beckmenn, 11–39. New York: Springer.

Ajzen, I. 1989. Attitude structure and behavior. In *Attitude structure and function*, ed. S.J. Breckler and A.G. Greenwald, 241–274. Hillsdale/New York: Lawrence Erlbaum/Springer.

Alexander, C.S., and H.J. Becker. 1978. The use of vignettes in survey research. *Public Opinion Quarterly* 42: 93–104.

Allmon, D.E., H.C.K. Chen, T.K. Pritchett, and P. Forrest. 1997. A multicultural examination of business ethics perceptions. *Journal of Business Ethics* 16(2): 183–188.

Ameen, E.C., D.M. Guffey, and J.J. McMillan. 1996. Gender differences in determining the ethical sensitivity of future accounting professionals. *Journal of Business Ethics* 15(5): 591–597.

Andersson, L.M., and T.S. Bateman. 1997. Cynicism in the workplace: Some causes and effects. *Journal of Organizational Behavior* 18: 449–469.

Armstrong, R.W. 1996. The relationship between culture and perception of ethical problems in international marketing. *Journal of Business Ethics* 15(11): 1199–1208.

Ashkanasy, N.M., S. Falkus, and V.J. Callan. 2000. Predictors of ethical code use and ethical tolerance in the public sector. *Journal of Business Ethics* 25(3): 237–253.

Au, A.K.M., and D.S.N. Wong. 2000. The impact of guanxi on the ethical decision-making process of auditors – An exploratory study on Chinese CPA's in Hong Kong. *Journal of Business Ethics* 28(1): 87–93.

Baker, T.L., and T.G. Hunt. 2003. An exploratory investigation into the effects of team composition on moral orientation. *Journal of Managerial Issues* 15(1): 106–119.

Bandura, A. 1977. *Social learning theory*. Englewood Cliffs: Holt, Rinehart, and Winston.

Barnett, T. 2001. Dimensions of moral intensity and ethical decision making: An empirical study. *Journal of Applied Social Psychology* 31(5): 1038–1057.

Barnett, T., and C. Vaicys. 2000. The moderating effect of individuals' perceptions of ethical work climate on ethical judgments and behavioral intentions. *Journal of Business Ethics* 27(4): 351–362.

Barnett, T., and S. Valentine. 2004. Issue contingent and marketers' recognition of ethical issues, ethical judgments and behavioral intentions. *Journal of Business Research* 57: 338–346.

Barnett, T., K. Bass, and G. Brown. 1996. Religiosity, ethical ideology, and intentions to report a peer's wrong doing. *Journal of Business Ethics* 15(11): 1161–1174.

Barnett, T., K. Bass, G. Brown, and F.J. Hebert. 1998. Ethical ideology and the ethical judgments of marketing professionals. *Journal of Business Ethics* 17(7): 715–723.

Bartels, L.K., E. Harrick, K. Martell, and D. Strickland. 1998. The relationship between ethical climate and ethical problems within human resource management. *Journal of Business Ethics* 17(7): 799–804.

Bass, K., T. Barnett, and G. Brown. 1998. The moral philosophy of sales managers and its influence on ethical decision making. *The Journal of Personal Selling and Sales Management* 18(2): 1–17.

Bass, K., T. Barnett, and G. Brown. 1999. Individual difference variables, ethical judgments, and ethical behavioral intentions. *Business Ethics Quarterly* 9(2): 183–205.

Bateman, C.R., J.P. Fraedrich, and R. Iyer. 2003. The integration and testing of the Janus-Headed Model within marketing. *Journal of Business Research* 56: 587–596.

Beams, J.D., R.M. Brown, and L.N. Killough. 2003. An experiment testing the determinants of non-compliance with insider trading laws. *Journal of Business Ethics* 45(4): 309–323.

Beck, L., and I. Ajzen. 1991. Predicting dishonest actions using the theory of planned behavior. *Journal of Research in Personality* 25: 285–301.

Biondo, J., and A.P. MacDonald Jr. 1971. Internal-external locus of control and response to influence attempts. *Journal of Personality* 39: 407–419.

Borkowski, S.C., and T.J. Ugras. 1998. Business students and ethics: A meta-analysis. *Journal of Business Ethics* 17(11): 1117–1127.

Boyle, B.A. 2000. The impact of customer characteristics and moral philosophies on ethical judgments of salespeople. *Journal of Business Ethics* 23(3): 249–267.

Boyle, B.A., R.F. Dahlstrom, and J.J. Kellaris. 1998. Points of reference and individual differences as sources of bias in ethical judgments. *Journal of Business Ethics* 17(5): 517–525.

Brierley, J.A., and C.J. Cowton. 2000. Putting meta-analysis to work: Accountants' organizational professional conflict. *Journal of Business Ethics* 4(2): 343–353.

Butterfield, K.D., L.K. Trevino, and G.R. Weaver. 2000. Moral awareness in business organizations: Influences of issue-related and social context factors. *Human Relations* 53(7): 981–1018.

Butz, C.E., and P.V. Lewis. 1996. Correlation of gender-related values of independence and relationship and leadership orientation. *Journal of Business Ethics* 15(11): 1141–1149.

Carlson, D.S., K.M. Kacmar, and L.L. Wadsworth. 2002. The impact of moral intensity dimensions on ethical decision making: Assessing the relevance of orientation. *Journal of Managerial Issues* 14(1): 15–30.

Chavez, G.A., R.A. Wiggins III, and M. Yolas. 2001. The impact of membership in the ethics officer association. *Journal of Business Ethics* 34(1): 39–56.

Cherry, J., and J. Fraedrich. 2000. An empirical investigation of locus of control and the structure of moral reasoning: Examining the ethical decision-making processes of sales managers. *The Journal of Personal Selling and Sales Management* 20(3): 173–188.

Cherry, J., and J. Fraedrich. 2002. Perceived risk, moral philosophy and marketing ethics: Mediating influences on sales managers' ethical decision-making. *Journal of Business Research* 55: 951–962.

Cherry, J., M. Lee, and C.S. Chien. 2003. A cross-cultural application of a theoretical model of business ethics: Bridging the Gap between theory and data. *Journal of Business Ethics* 44(4): 359–376.

Christie, P.M.J., I.G. Kwon, P.A. Stoeberl, and R. Baumhart. 2003. A cross-cultural comparison of ethical attitudes of business managers: India, Korea and the United States. *Journal of Business Ethics* 46(3): 263–287.

Chung, J., and G.S. Monroe. 2003. Exploring social desirability bias. *Journal of Business Ethics* 44(4): 291–302.

Chung, J., and V.U. Trivedi. 2003. The effect of friendly persuasion and gender on tax compliance behavior. *Journal of Business Ethics* 47(2): 133–145.

Clark, J.W., and L.E. Dawson. 1996. Personal religiousness and ethical judgments: An empirical analysis. *Journal of Business Ethics* 15(3): 359–372.

Clarke, R., and J. Aram. 1997. Universal values, behavioral ethics and entrepreneurship. *Journal of Business Ethics* 16(5): 561–572.

Cleek, M.A., and S.L. Leonard. 1998. Can corporate codes of ethics influence behavior? *Journal of Business Ethics* 17(6): 619–630.

Cohen, J.R., L.W. Pant, and D.J. Sharp. 2001. An examination of differences in ethical-decision making between Canadian business students and accounting professionals. *Journal of Business Ethics* 30(4): 319–336.

Cole, B.C., and D.L. Smith. 1996. Perceptions of business ethics: Students vs. business people. *Journal of Business Ethics* 15(8): 889–896.

Cruz, C.A., W.E. Shafer, and J.R. Strawser. 2000. A multidimensional analysis of tax practitioners' ethical judgments. *Journal of Business Ethics* 24(3): 223–244.

Daft, R.L., and K.E. Weick. 1984. Toward a model of organizations as interpretation systems. *Academy of Management Review* 9: 284–295.

Davis, M.A., N.B. Johnson, and D.G. Ohmer. 1998. Issue-contingent effects on ethical decision making: A cross-cultural comparison. *Journal of Business Ethics* 17(4): 373–389.

Dawson, L.M. 1997. Ethical differences between men and women in the sales profession. *Journal of Business Ethics* 16(11): 1143–1152.

DeConinck, J.B., and W.F. Lewis. 1997. The influence of deontological and teleological considerations and ethical climate on sales managers' intentions to reward or punish sales force behavior. *Journal of Business Ethics* 16(5): 497–506.

Deshpande, S.P. 1996. Ethical climate and the link between success and ethical behavior: An empirical investigation of a non-profit organization. *Journal of Business Ethics* 15(3): 315–320.

Deshpande, S.P. 1997. Managers' perception of proper ethical conduct: The effect of sex, age, and level of education. *Journal of Business Ethics* 16(1): 79–85.

Deshpande, S.P., J. Joseph, and V.V. Maximov. 2000. Perceptions of proper ethical conduct of male and female Russian managers. *Journal of Business Ethics* 24(2): 179–183.

Donaldson, T., and T.W. Dunfee. 1994. Toward a unified conception of business ethics: Integrative social contracts theory. *Academy of Management Review* 19(2): 252–284.

Douglas, P.C., R.A. Davidson, and B.N. Schwartz. 2001. The effect of organizational culture and ethical orientation on accountants' ethical judgments. *Journal of Business Ethics* 34(2): 101–121.

Eastman, K.L., J.K. Eastman, and A.D. Eastman. 1996. The ethics of insurance professionals: Comparison of personal versus professional ethics. *Journal of Business Ethics* 15(9): 951–962.

Eastman, J.K., K.L. Eastman, and M.A. Tolson. 2001. The relationship between ethical ideology and ethical behavior intentions: An exploratory look at physicians' responses to managed care dilemmas. *Journal of Business Ethics* 31(3): 209–224.

Elias, R.Z. 2002. Determinants of earnings management ethics among accountants. *Journal of Business Ethics* 40(1): 33–45.

Ergeneli, A., and S. Arikan. 2002. Gender differences in ethical perceptions of salespeople: An empirical examination in Turkey. *Journal of Business Ethics* 40(3): 247–260.

Eynon, G., N.Y. Hill, and K.T. Stevens. 1997. Factors that influence the moral reasoning abilities of accountants: Implications for universities and the profession. *Journal of Business Ethics* 16(12/13): 1297–1309.

Fisher, D.G., and J.T. Sweeney. 1998. The relationship between political attitudes and moral judgment: Examining the validity of the defining issues test. *Journal of Business Ethics* 17(8): 905–916.

Flannery, B.L., and D.R. May. 2000. Environmental ethical decision making in the U.S. metal-finishing industry. *Academy of Management Journal* 43(4): 642–662.

Fleischman, G., and S. Valentine. 2003. Professionals' tax liability and ethical evaluations in an equitable relief innocent spouse case. *Journal of Business Ethics* 42(1): 27–44.

Ford, R.C., and W.D. Richardson. 1994. Ethical decision making: A review of the empirical literature. *Journal of Business Ethics* 13: 205–221.

Franke, G.R., D.F. Crown, and D.F. Spake. 1997. Gender differences in ethical perceptions of business practices: A social role theory perspective. *Journal of Applied Psychology* 82(6): 920–934.

Fritzshe, D.J. 2000. Ethical climates and the ethical dimension of decision making. *Journal of Business Ethics* 24(2): 125–140.

Fryxell, G.E., and C.W.H. Lo. 2003. The influence of environmental knowledge and values on managerial behaviours on behalf of the environment: An empirical examination on managers in China. *Journal of Business Ethics* 46(1): 45–69.

Giacalone, R.A., and C.L. Jurkiewicz. 2003. Right from wrong: The influence of spirituality on perceptions of unethical business activities. *Journal of Business Ethics* 46(1): 85–97.

Gibson, A.M., and A.H. Frakes. 1997. Truth or consequences: A study of critical issues and decision making in accounting. *Journal of Business Ethics* 16(2): 161–171.

Gioia, D.A., and K. Chittipeddi. 1991. Sensemaking and sense giving in strategic change initiation. *Strategic Management Journal* 12: 433–448.

Glass, R.S., and W.A. Wood. 1996. Situational determinants of software piracy: An equity theory perspective. *Journal of Business Ethics* 15(11): 1189–1198.

Glover, S.H., M.A. Bumpus, J.E. Logan, and J.R. Ciesla. 1997. Re-examining the influence of individual values on ethical decision making. *Journal of Business Ethics* 16(12/13): 1319–1329.

Goodwin, J., and D. Goodwin. 1999. Ethical judgments across cultures: A comparison between business students from Malaysia and New Zealand. *Journal of Business Ethics* 18(3): 267–281.

Granitz, N.A. 2003. Individual, social and organizational sources of sharing and variation in the ethical reasoning of managers. *Journal of Business Ethics* 42(2): 101–124.

Green, S., and J. Weber. 1997. Influencing ethical development: Exposing students to the AICPA code of conduct. *Journal of Business Ethics* 16(8): 777–790.

Greenberg, J. 2002. Who stole the money and when? Individual and situational determinants of employee theft. *Organizational Behavior and Human Decision Processes* 89: 985–1003.

Harrington, S.J. 1997. A test of a person-issue contingent model of ethical decision making in organizations. *Journal of Business Ethics* 16(4): 363–375.

Hoffman, J.J., G. Couch, and B.T. Lamont. 1998. The effect of firm profit versus personal economic well being on the level of ethical responses given by managers. *Journal of Business Ethics* 17(3): 239–244.

Honeycutt Jr., E.D., M. Glassman, M.T. Zugelder, and K. Karande. 2001. Determinants of ethical behavior: A study of auto sales people. *Journal of Business Ethics* 32(1): 69–79.

Hume, E.C., E.R. Larkins, and G. Iyer. 1999. On compliance with ethical standards in tax return preparation. *Journal of Business Ethics* 18(2): 229–238.

Hunt, T.G., and D.F. Jennings. 1997. Ethics and performance: A simulation analysis of team decision making. *Journal of Business Ethics* 16(2): 195–203.

Hunt, S.D., and S.J. Vitell. 1986. A general theory of marketing ethics. *Journal of Macro Marketing* 48: 30–42.

Jackson, T. 2000. Management ethics and corporate policy: A cross-cultural comparison. *Journal of Management Studies* 37(3): 349–369.

Jackson, T. 2001. Cultural values and management ethics: A 10-nation study. *Human Relations* 54(10): 1267–1302.

Jackson, T., and M.C. Artola. 1997. Ethical beliefs and management behavior: A cross-cultural comparison. *Journal of Business Ethics* 16(11): 1163–1173.

Jacobs, J. 1991. Moral imagination, objectively, and practical wisdom. *International Philosophical Quarterly* 31: 23–37.

Johnson, R.C., J.M. Ackerman, H. Frank, and A.J. Fionda. 1968. Resistance to temptation and guilt following yielding and psychotherapy. *Journal of Consulting and Clinical Psychology* 32: 169–175.

Jones, T.M. 1991. Ethical decision making by individuals in organizations: An issue-contingent model. *Academy of Management Review* 16(2): 366–395.

Jones, G.E., and M.J. Kavanagh. 1996. An experimental examination of the effects of individual and situational factors on unethical behavioral intentions in the workplace. *Journal of Business Ethics* 15(5): 511–523.

Kaplan, S.E. 2001. Ethically related judgments by observers of earnings management. *Journal of Business Ethics* 32(4): 285–298.
Karcher, J.N. 1996. Auditors' ability to discern the presence of ethical problems. *Journal of Business Ethics* 15(10): 1033–1050.
Kaynama, S.A., A. King, and L.W. Smith. 1996. The impact of a shift in organizational role on ethical perceptions: A comparative study. *Journal of Business Ethics* 15(5): 581–590.
Kennedy, E.J., and L. Lawton. 1996. The effects of social and moral integration on ethical standards: A comparison of American and Ukrainian business students. *Journal of Business Ethics* 15(8): 901–911.
Key, S. 2002. Perceived managerial discretion: An analysis of individual ethical intentions. *Journal of Managerial Issues* 14(2): 218–233.
Keyton, J., and S.C. Rhodes. 1997. Sexual harassment: A matter of individual ethics, legal definitions, or organizational policy? *Journal of Business Ethics* 16(2): 129–146.
Kim, Y. 2003. Ethical standards and ideology among Korean public relations practitioners. *Journal of Business Ethics* 42(3): 209–223.
Kim, S.Y., and S.Y. Chun. 2003. A study of marketing ethics in Korea: What do Koreans care about? *International Journal of Management* 20(3): 377–383.
Kohlberg, L. 1981. Essays in moral development. Vol. 1 The philosophy of moral development. New York: Harper and Row.
Kracher, B., A. Chatterjee, and A.R. Lundquist. 2002. Factors related to the cognitive moral development of business students and business professionals in India and the United States: Nationality, education, sex and gender. *Journal of Business Ethics* 35(4): 255–268.
Kujala, J. 2001. A multidimensional approach to Finnish managers' moral decision-making. *Journal of Business Ethics* 34(3/4): 231–254.
Larkin, J.M. 2000. The ability of internal auditors to identify ethical dilemmas. *Journal of Business Ethics* 23(4): 401–409.
Latif, D.A. 2000. Ethical cognition and selection-socialization in retail pharmacy. *Journal of Business Ethics* 25(4): 343–357.
Latif, D.A. 2001. The relationship between pharmacists' tenure in the community setting and moral reasoning. *Journal of Business Ethics* 31(2): 131–141.
Lefcourt, H.M. 1982. *Locus of control: Current trends in theory and research*, 2nd ed. Hillsdale: L. Erlbaum, London: Psychology Press.
Libby, B., and V. Agnello. 2000. Ethical decision making and the law. *Journal of Business Ethics* 26(3): 223–232.
Loe, T.W., L. Ferrell, and P. Mansfield. 2000. A review of empirical studies assessing ethical decision making in business. *Journal of Business Ethics* 25: 185–204.
Lund, D.B. 2000. An empirical examination of marketing professionals' ethical behavior in differing situations. *Journal of Business Ethics* 24(4): 331–342.
Malinowski, C., and K.A. Berger. 1996. Undergraduate student attitudes about hypothetical marketing dilemmas. *Journal of Business Ethics* 15(5): 525–535.
Marnburg, E. 2001. The questionable use of moral development theory in studies of business ethics: Discussion and empirical findings. *Journal of Business Ethics* 32(4): 275–283.
Marshall, B., and P. Dewe. 1997. An investigation of the components of moral intensity. *Journal of Business Ethics* 16(5): 521–530.
Mason, E.S., and P.E. Mudrack. 1996. Gender and ethical orientation: A test of gender and occupational socialization theories. *Journal of Business Ethics* 15(6): 599–604.
May, D.R., and K.P. Pauli. 2002. The role of moral intensity in ethical decision making. *Business & Society* 41(1): 84–117.
McCabe, D.L., L.K. Trevino, and K.D. Butterfield. 1996. The influence of collegiate and corporate codes of conduct on ethics-related behavior in the workplace. *Business Ethics Quarterly* 6(4): 461–476.
McCuddy, M.K., and B.L. Peery. 1996. Selected individual differences and collegians' ethical beliefs. *Journal of Business Ethics* 15(3): 261–272.

McDevitt, R., and J.V. Hise. 2002. Influences in ethical dilemmas of increasing intensity. *Journal of Business Ethics* 40(3): 261–274.

McDonald, G., and P.C. Pak. 1996. It's all fair in love, war, and business: Cognitive philosophies in ethical decision making. *Journal of Business Ethics* 15(9): 973–996.

McKendall, M., B. DeMarr, and C. Jones-Rikkers. 2002. Ethical compliance programs and corporate illegality: Testing the assumptions of the corporate sentencing guidelines. *Journal of Business Ethics* 37(4): 367–383.

Milliken, F.J. 1990. Perceiving and interpreting environmental change: An examination of college administrators' interpretation of changing demographics. *Academy of Management Journal* 33: 42–63.

Moberg, D.J., and M.A. Seabright. 2000. The development of moral imagination. *Business Ethics Quarterly* 10(4): 845–884.

Morris, M.H., A.S. Marks, J.A. Allen, and N.A. Peery Jr. 1996. Modeling ethical attitudes and behaviors under conditions of environmental turbulence: The case of South Africa. *Journal of Business Ethics* 15(10): 1119–1130.

Murk, D.A., and J.A. Addleman. 1992. Relations among moral reasoning, locus of control, and demographic variables among college students. *Psychological Reports* 70: 467–476.

Nonis, S., and C.O. Swift. 2001. Personal value profiles and ethical business decisions. *The Journal of Education for Business* 76(5): 251–256.

Nwachukwu, S.L.S., and S.J. Vitell. 1997. The influence of corporate culture on managerial ethical judgments. *Journal of Business Ethics* 16(8): 757–776.

Okleshen, M., and R. Hoyt. 1996. A cross cultural comparison of ethical perspectives and decision approaches of business students: United States of America versus New Zealand. *Journal of Business Ethics* 15(5): 537–549.

Oz, E. 2001. Organizational commitment and ethical behavior: An empirical study of information system professionals. *Journal of Business Ethics* 34(2): 137–142.

Paolillo, J.G.P., and S.J. Vitell. 2002. An empirical investigation of the influence of selected personal, organizational and moral intensity factors on ethical decision making. *Journal of Business Ethics* 35(1): 65–74.

Peterson, D.K. 2002. The relationship between unethical behavior and the dimensions of the ethical climate questionnaire. *Journal of Business Ethics* 41(4): 313–326.

Peterson, D., A. Rhoads, and B.C. Vaught. 2001. Ethical beliefs of business professionals: A study of gender, age and external factors. *Journal of Business Ethics* 31(3): 225–232.

Powpaka, S. 2002. Factors affecting managers' decision to bribe: An empirical investigation. *Journal of Business Ethics* 40(3): 227–246.

Prasad, J.N., N. Marlow, and R.E. Hattwick. 1998. Gender-based differences in perception of a just society. *Journal of Business Ethics* 17(3): 219–228.

Radtke, R.R. 2000. The effects of gender and setting on accountants' ethically sensitive decisions. *Journal of Business Ethics* 24(4): 299–312.

Rallapalli, K.C., S.J. Vitell, and J.H. Barnes. 1998. The influence of norms on ethical judgments and intentions: An empirical study of marketing professionals. *Journal of Business Research* 43: 157–168.

Randall, D.M., and A.M. Gibson. 1990. Methodology in business ethics research: A review and critical assessment. *Journal of Business Ethics* 9(6): 457–471.

Rayburn, J.M., and L.G. Rayburn. 1996. Relationship between Machiavellianism and type a personality and ethical-orientation. *Journal of Business Ethics* 15(11): 1209–1219.

Razzaque, M.A., and T.P. Hwee. 2002. Ethics and purchasing dilemma: A Singaporean view. *Journal of Business Ethics* 35(4): 307–326.

Reiss, M.C., and K. Mitra. 1998. The effects of individual difference factors on the acceptability of ethical and unethical workplace behaviors. *Journal of Business Ethics* 17(14): 1581–1593.

Rest, J.R. 1986. *Moral development: Advances in research and theory*. New York: Praeger.

Rittenburg, T.L., and S.R. Valentine. 2002. Spanish and American executives' ethical judgments and intentions. *Journal of Business Ethics* 38(4): 291–306.

Robertson, D.C. 1993. Empiricism in business ethics: Suggested research directions. *Journal of Business Ethics* 12(8): 585–599.
Robertson, D.C., and T. Rymon. 2001. Purchasing agents' deceptive behavior: A randomized response technique study. *Business Ethics Quarterly* 11(3): 455–479.
Robin, D.P., R.E. Reidenbach, and P.J. Forrest. 1996b. The perceived importance of an ethical issue as an influence on the ethical decision-making of Ad managers. *Journal of Business Research* 35: 17–28.
Roozen, I., P.D. Pelsmacker, and F. Bostyn. 2001. The ethical dimensions of decision processes of employees'. *Journal of Business Ethics* 33(2): 87–99.
Ross, W.T., and D.C. Robertson. 2003. A typology of situational factors: Impact on salesperson decision-making about ethical issues. *Journal of Business Ethics* 46(3): 213–234.
Rotter, J.B. 1966. Generalized expectancies for internal versus external control of reinforcement. *Psychological Monographs: General and Applied* 80: 1–28.
Ryan, J.J. 2001. Moral reasoning as a determinant of organizational citizenship behaviors: A study in the public accounting profession. *Journal of Business Ethics* 33(3): 233–244.
Sankaran, S., and T. Bui. 2003. Ethical attitudes among accounting majors: An empirical study. *Journal of American Academy of Business, Cambridge* 3(1/2): 71–77.
Schepers, D.H. 2003. Machiavellianism, profit, and the dimensions of ethical judgment: A study of impact. *Journal of Business Ethics* 42(4): 339–352.
Schminke, M. 1997. Gender differences in ethical frameworks and evaluation of others' choices in ethical dilemmas. *Journal of Business Ethics* 16(1): 55–65.
Schminke, M., and M.L. Ambrose. 1997. Asymmetric perceptions of ethical frameworks of men and women in business and nonbusiness settings. *Journal of Business Ethics* 16(7): 719–729.
Schoderbek, P.P., and S.P. Deshpande. 1996. Impression management, overclaiming, and perceived unethical conduct: The role of male and female managers. *Journal of Business Ethics* 15(4): 409–414.
Schwartz, M. 2001. The nature of the relationship between corporate codes of ethics and behavior. *Journal of Business Ethics* 32(3): 247–262.
Shafer, W.E. 2002. Effects of materiality, risk, and ethical perceptions on fraudulent reporting by financial executives. *Journal of Business Ethics* 38(3): 243–262.
Shafer, W.E., R.E. Morris, and A.A. Ketchand. 2001. Effects of personal values on auditors' ethical decisions. *Accounting Auditing & Accountability Journal* 14(3): 254–277.
Shapeero, M., H.C. Koh, and L.N. Killough. 2003. Underreporting and premature sign-off in public accounting. *Managerial Auditing Journal* 18(6/7): 478–489.
Shaw, T.R. 2003. The moral intensity of privacy: An empirical study of Webmasters' attitudes. *Journal of Business Ethics* 46(4): 301–318.
Sims, R.I., and T.L. Keon. 1999. Determinants of ethical decision making: The relationship of the perceived organizational environment. *Journal of Business Ethics* 19(4): 393–401.
Singer, M.S. 1996. The role of moral intensity and fairness perception in judgments of ethicality: A comparison of managerial professionals and the general public. *Journal of Business Ethics* 15(4): 469–474.
Singer, M.S., and A.E. Singer. 1997. Observer judgments about moral agents' ethical decisions: The role of scope of justice and moral intensity. *Journal of Business Ethics* 16(5): 473–484.
Singer, M., S. Mitchell, and J. Turner. 1998. Consideration of moral intensity in ethicality judgments: Its relationship with whistle-blowing and need-for-cognition. *Journal of Business Ethics* 17(5): 527–541.
Singhapakdi, A. 1999. Perceived importance of ethics and ethical decisions in marketing. *Journal of Business Research* 45: 89–99.
Singhapakdi, A., C.P. Rao, and S.J. Vitell. 1996a. Ethical decision making: An investigation of services marketing professionals. *Journal of Business Ethics* 15(6): 635–644.
Singhapakdi, A., S.J. Vitell, and K.L. Kraft. 1996b. Moral intensity and ethical decision-making of marketing professionals. *Journal of Business Research* 36: 245–255.

Singhapakdi, A., S.J. Vitell, and G.R. Franke. 1999. Antecedents, consequences, and mediating effects of perceived moral intensity and personal moral philosophies. *Journal of the Academy of Marketing Science* 27(1): 19–35.

Singhapakdi, A., J.K. Marta, K.C. Rallapalli, and C.P. Rao. 2000a. Toward an understanding of religiousness and marketing ethics: An empirical study. *Journal of Business Ethics* 27(4): 305–319.

Singhapakdi, A., S. Salyachivin, B. Virakul, and V. Veerayangkur. 2000b. Some important factors underlying ethical decision making of managers in Thailand. *Journal of Business Ethics* 27(3): 271–284.

Singhapakdi, A., K. Karande, C.P. Rao, and S.J. Vitell. 2001a. How important are ethics and social responsibility? A multinational study of marketing professionals. *European Journal of Marketing* 35(1/2): 133–152.

Singhapakdi, A., J.K.M. Marta, C.P. Rao, and M. Cicic. 2001b. Is cross-cultural similarity and indicator of similar marketing ethics? *Journal of Business Ethics* 32(1): 55–68.

Sivadas, E., S.B. Kleiser, J. Kellaris, and R. Dahlstrom. 2003. Moral philosophy, ethical evaluations, and sales manager hiring intentions. *Journal of Personal Selling & Sales Management* 23(1): 7–21.

Sligo, F., and N. Stirton. 1998. Does hindsight bias change perceptions of business ethics? *Journal of Business Ethics* 17(2): 111–124.

Smith, P.L., and E.F. Oakley III. 1997. Gender-related differences in ethical and social values of business students: Implications for management. *Journal of Business Ethics* 16(1): 37–45.

Somers, M.J. 2001. Ethical codes of conduct and organizational context: A study of the relationship between codes of conduct, employee behavior and organizational values. *Journal of Business Ethics* 30(2): 185–195.

Sparks, J.R., and S.D. Hunt. 1998. Marketing researcher ethical sensitivity: Conceptualization, measurement, and exploratory investigation. *Journal of Marketing* 62(2): 92–109.

Stohs, J.H., and T. Brannick. 1999. Codes of conduct: Predictors of Irish managers' ethical reasoning. *Journal of Business Ethics* 22(4): 311–326.

Sutherland, E.H., and D.R. Cressey. 1970. *Principles of criminology*, 8th ed. Philadelphia: Lippincott.

Tang, T.L.-P., and R.K. Chiu. 2003. Income, money ethic, pay satisfaction, commitment, and unethical behavior: Is the love of money the root of evil for Hong Kong employees? *Journal of Business Ethics* 46(1): 13–30.

Teal, E.J., and A.B. Carroll. 1999. Moral reasoning skills: Are entrepreneurs different? *Journal of Business Ethics* 19(3): 229–240.

Tenbrunsel, A.E. 1998. Misrepresentaiton and expectations of misrepresentation in an ethical dilemma: The role of incentives and temptation. *Academy of Management Journal* 41(3): 330–339.

Tenbrunsel, A.E., and D.M. Messick. 1999. Sanctioning systems, decision frames, and cooperation. *Administrative Science Quarterly* 44(4): 684–707.

Trevino, L.K. 1986. Ethical decision making in organizations: A person-situation interactionist model. *Academy of Management Review* 11(3): 601–617.

Treviño, L.K. 1990. A cultural perspective on changing and developing organizational ethics. *Research in Organizational Change and Development* 4: 195–230.

Treviño, L.K. 1992. Experimental approaches to studying ethical-unethical behavior in organizations. *Business Ethics Quarterly* 2(2): 121–136.

Treviño, L.K., and G.R. Weaver. 1994. Business ethics/business ethics: One field or two? *Business Ethics Quarterly* 4(2): 113–128.

Trevino, L.K., and G.R. Weaver. 2001. Organizational justice and ethics program "follow-through": Influences on employees' harmful and helpful behavior. *Business Ethics Quarterly* 11(4): 651–671.

Trevino, L.K., K.D. Butterfield, and D.L. McCabe. 1998. The ethical context in organizations: Influences on employee attitudes and behaviors. *Business Ethics Quarterly* 8(3): 447–476.

Tse, A.C.B., and A.K.M. Au. 1997. Are New Zealand business students more unethical than non-business students? *Journal of Business Ethics* 16(4): 445–450.

Tsui, J., and C. Windsor. 2001. Some cross-cultural evidence on ethical reasoning. *Journal of Business Ethics* 31(2): 143–150.
Udas, K., W.L. Fuerst, and D.B. Paradice. 1996. An investigation of ethical perceptions of public sector mis professionals. *Journal of Business Ethics* 15(7): 721–734.
Uddin, N., and P.R. Gillett. 2002. The effects of moral reasoning and self-monitoring on CFO intentions to report fraudulently on financial statements. *Journal of Business Ethics* 40(1): 15–32.
Upchurch, R.S. 1998. A conceptual foundation for ethical decision making: A stakeholder perspective in the lodging industry (U.S.A.). *Journal of Business Ethics* 17(12): 1349–1361.
Valentine, S., and G. Fleischman. 2003. Ethical reasoning in an equitable relief innocent spouse context. *Journal of Business Ethics* 45(4): 325–339.
VanSandt, C.V. 2003. The relationship between ethical work climate and moral awareness. *Business & Society* 42(1): 144–152.
Vardi, Y. 2001. The effects of organizational and ethical climates on misconduct at work. *Journal of Business Ethics* 29(4): 325–337.
Verbeke, W., C. Uwerkerk, and E. Peelen. 1996. Exploring the contextual and individual factors on ethical decision making of salespeople. *Journal of Business Ethics* 15(11): 1175–1187.
Victor, B., and J.B. Cullen. 1988. The organizational bases of ethical work climates. *Administrative Science Quarterly* 33: 101–125.
Volkema, R.J., and M.T.L. Fleury. 2002. Alternative negotiating conditions and the choice of negotiating tactics: A cross-cultural comparison. *Journal of Business Ethics* 36(4): 381–398.
Wagner, S.C., and G.L. Sanders. 2001. Considerations in ethical decision-making and software piracy. *Journal of Business Ethics* 29(1/2): 161–167.
Waller, D.S. 2002. Advertising agency-client attitudes towards ethical issues in political advertising. *Journal of Business Ethics* 36(4): 347–354.
Weaver, G., and L.K. Trevino. 1994. Normative and empirical business ethics: Separation, marriage of convenience, or marriage of necessity? *Business Ethics Quarterly* 4(2): 129–143.
Weaver, G.R., and L.K. Trevino. 1999. Compliance and values oriented ethics programs: Influences on employees' attitudes and behavior. *Business Ethics Quarterly* 9(2): 315–335.
Weber, J. 1992. Scenarios in business ethics research: Review, critical assessment, and recommendations. *Business Ethics Quarterly* 2(2): 137–159.
Weber, J. 1996. Influences upon managerial moral decision making: Nature of the harm and magnitude of consequences. *Human Relations* 49(1): 1–22.
Weber, J., and J. Gillespie. 1998. Differences in ethical beliefs, intentions, and behaviors: The role of beliefs and intentions in ethics research revisited. *Business and Society* 37(4): 447–467.
Weber, J., and J.E. Seger. 2002. Influences upon organizational ethical subclimates: A replication study of a single firm at two points in time. *Journal of Business Ethics* 41(1/2): 69–84.
Weber, J., L.B. Kurke, and D.W. Pentico. 2003. Why do employees steal? Assessing differences in ethical and unethical employee behavior using ethical work climates. *Business & Society* 42(3): 359–380.
Weeks, W.A., C.W. Moore, J.A. McKinney, and J.G. Longenecker. 1999. The effects of gender and career stage on ethical judgment. *Journal of Business Ethics* 20(4): 301–313.
Weick, K.A. 1979. *The social psychology of organizing*. Reading: Addison-Wesley.
Whitcomb, L.L., C.B. Erdener, and C. Li. 1998. Business ethical values in China and the U.S. *Journal of Business Ethics* 17(8): 839–852.
Wimalasiri, J.S., F. Pavri, and A.A.K. Jahl. 1996. An empirical study of moral reasoning among managers in Singapore. *Journal of Business Ethics* 15(12): 1331–1341.
Wu, C. 2003. A study of the adjustment of ethical recognition and ethical decision-making of managers-to-be across the Taiwan Strait before and after receiving a business ethics education. *Journal of Business Ethics* 45(4): 291–307.
Yetmar, S.A., and K.K. Eastman. 2000. Tax practitioners' ethical sensitivity: A model and empirical examination. *Journal of Business Ethics* 26(4): 271–288.

Chapter 12
Judging the Morality of Business Practices: The Influence of Personal Moral Philosophies

Donelson R. Forsyth

Ethical issues in business are intimately tied to more general moral values held by members of the community-at-large. Certain untoward practices – such as routine violations of employees' rights, deceiving consumers through misleading advertising, illegal price-fixing, insider trading, and the sale of merchandize that is known to be defective – may be unique to the business world, but individuals' reactions to such practices ultimately depend upon the same psychological and interpersonal processes that determine judgments of any morally evaluable action. Because appraisals of business practices are, at core, only a special case of general moral decision making, we approach the study of moral judgments of business practices by examining: (1) contrasting personal moral philosophies and their relationship to classical ethical philosophies; (2) the influence of personal moral philosophies on moral judgments; and (3) the implications of this psychological analysis of moral judgment for ethical debates over business practices.

Four Moral Philosophies

Most would morally condemn a company that deliberately violates government regulations designed to protect employees from harm, a business that knowingly sells faulty products that cause severe injury to uninformed consumers, or an unscrupulous executive who steals money from the pension fund, but this consensus is lost when the discussion turns to less clear-cut issues. This disagreement, however, is not unique to questions of business ethics. As early as 1898 Sharp complained that his studies of moral judgment were hindered by the lack of agreement

D.R. Forsyth (✉)
Jepson School of Leadership Studies, University of Richmond,
Richmond, VA 23173, USA
e-mail: dforsyth@richmond.edu

A.C. Michalos and D.C. Poff (eds.), *Citation Classics from the Journal of Business Ethics*, Advances in Business Ethics Research 2,
DOI 10.1007/978-94-007-4126-3_12, © Springer Science+Business Media B.V. 2013

among his subjects concerning what was moral and what was not. Although he speculated that people might be too incompetent or careless when they make moral judgments, he eventually concluded that disagreements concerning morality surface because people adopt different personal ethical systems.

The behavioral sciences offer a number of theoretical models that examine the nature of these divergences in moral judgment, including cognitive-developmentalism (Kohlberg 1983), social learning theory (Bandura 1990), and psychoanalytic theory (Freud 1927). The current approach, however, assumes that individuals' moral beliefs, attitudes, and values comprise an integrated conceptual system or personal moral philosophy. Moreover, although the number of personal moral philosophies is unlimited, most can be contrasted in terms of relativism and idealism. At one end of the relativism dimension, highly relativistic individuals espouse a personal moral philosophy based on skepticism. They generally feel that moral actions depend upon the nature of the situation and the individuals involved, and when judging others they weigh the circumstances more than the ethical principle that was violated. People who are low in relativism, in contrast, argue that morality requires acting in ways that are consistent with moral principles, norms, or laws. The second distinction, idealism, describes the individual's concern for the welfare of others. Highly idealistic individuals feel that harming others is always avoidable, and they would rather not choose between the lesser of two evils which will lead to negative consequences for other people. Those who are less idealistic, in contrast, do not emphasize such ideals, for they assume that harm will sometimes be necessary to produce good (Forsyth 1980; Schlenker and Forsyth 1977).

These two dimensions, relativism and idealism, parallel distinctions made by both moral philosophers and psychologists (Boyce and Jensen 1978; Waterman 1988). Philosophers have traditionally contrasted moral theories based on principles (deontological models) and models that stress the consequences of actions (teleological models) (Forsyth 1981a). Piaget (1932) believed that younger children tend to stress the consequences of an action – to the point of overlooking good intentions – whereas older children are able to take into consideration ethical rules when making judgments. Gilligan (1982, p. 65), in her analyses of sex differences in moral thought, notes that females' "hope that in morality lies a way of solving conflicts so that no one will be hurt" (concern for positive consequences), while males' moralities tend to stress the rational application of principles. Similarly Derry (1989) argues that first-level managers' moral dilemmas are often caused by their desire to meet the demands of their role as well as protect the human needs and welfare of others, and that often role-responsibilities overshadow one's concern for others' welfare (cf., Kelley 1989).

This model of personal moral philosophies, rather than assuming individuals are either rule-oriented or consequence-oriented, assumes individuals can range from high to low in their emphasis on principles and in their emphasis on consequences. The model thus identifies the four distinct personal moral philosophies shown in Table 12.1: situationism (relativistic and idealistic), subjectivism (relativistic but not idealistic), absolutism (not relativistic but idealistic), and exceptionism (neither relativistic nor idealistic).

Table 12.1 A taxonomy of personal moral philosophies

Ideology	Dimensions	Approach to moral judgment
Situationists	High relativism High idealism	Reject moral rules; ask if the action yielded the best possible outcome in the given situation
Subjectivists	High relativism Low relativism	Reject moral rules; base moral judgments on personal feelings about the action and the setting
Absolutists	Low relativism High idealism	Feel actions are moral provided they yield positive consequences through conformity to moral rules
Exceptionists	Low relativism Low idealism	Feel conformity to moral rules is desirable, but exceptions to these rules are often permissible

Situationism

Individuals who eschew universal moral principles (high relativism) but still insist that one should produce positive consequences that benefit all involved (high idealism) are termed situationists. Because these individuals favor the close inspection of potential benefits their outlook is most similar to philosophies approaches based on ethical skepticism. For example, Fletcher in his *situation ethics* (1966) argues that an action, to be moral, must be appropriate given the particular context; not necessarily good or right, but be "fitting". *Utilitarianism* similarly maintains that one must act in ways that will generate the greatest good for the greatest number of people, and James's (1891/1973) *value pluralism* suggests that the consequences of an action determine its moral value.

Subjectivism

Subjectivists, like situationists, reject moral rules (high relativism); they are not, however, particularly positive about the possibility of achieving positive outcomes for everyone concerned. Because such individuals described their moral decisions as subjective, individualistic judgments that cannot be made on the basis of moral absolutes or the extent to which the action benefits others their viewpoint parallels an *egoistic* moral philosophy. This position maintains that no moral judgments can be considered valid except in reference to one's own behavior. The only moral conclusion possible is that all people should act to promote their own self-interest, rather than focus on producing positive outcomes for others in general. This teleological outlook admits that consequences must be considered when formulating moral judgments, but unlike the more idealistic situational ethics it does not insist that one strive to produce positive outcomes. Indeed, because each person must determine the weights and values of the outcome obtained, individuals will differ dramatically in their moral conclusions.

Absolutism

Absolutists believe that one should strive to produce positive consequences (high idealism) but at the same time maintain strict adherence to general moral principles (low relativism). These individuals condemn certain actions, because (a) they harm people and (b) they violate fundamental moral absolutes. Such an outlook corresponds closely to a system of ethics known as *deontology.* To deontologists, acts are to be judged through their comparison with some exceptionless, universal moral rule. Immanuel Kant, generally regarded as the foremost proponent of the deontological position, prescribed that one must make certain that all actions adhere to categorical imperatives: exceptionless universal moral principles that can be derived through reason rather than empirical evaluation. Kant, for example, proposed that "to be truthful in all declarations is. . . a sacred unconditional command of reason and is not to be limited by any expediency" and that "all practical principles of justice must contain strict truths . . . since exceptions destroy the universality, on account of which alone they bear the name principles" (1873/1973, p. 258). In support of his position Kant maintained that a principle such as "Keep your promises only when it works to your advantage" negates the concept of a promise and therefore cannot qualify as a categorical imperative. The maxim "Always keep your promises," in contrast, does not generate any inconsistencies and therefore qualifies as a moral absolute.

Exceptionism

Exceptionists agree with the absolutist's appreciation of moral absolutes but they are not idealistic: they do not believe that harm can be avoided, that innocent people can always be protected, or that risking others' welfare is always wrong. They are, therefore, deontological, for they prefer to rely on moral principles as guidelines for action. At the same time, however, they are utilitarian in that they pragmatically admit that judgments should be made by balancing the positive consequences of an action against the negative consequences of an action. Their outlook thus corresponds most closely to a moral philosophy based on *rule-utilitarianism*: moral principles are useful because they provide a framework for making choices and acting in ways that will tend to produce the best consequences for all concerned. Following principles, however, will sometimes cause one to act in ways that will cause harm to innocent people, and in such instances exceptions are allowable.

Applications in Business Settings

The theoretically predicted differences among these four ethical types become clearer when their outlooks on various ethical issues that occur in business settings are contrasted. Consider, for example, a businesswoman reviewing an advertising campaign that describes the product somewhat inaccurately. The situationist is most concerned with the benefits to be obtained, both for the company and for the consumer.

If she feels that the product is a good one and that, in the long run, the buyer will be benefitted, then she will likely overlook any small inaccuracies in the ad copy. The subjectivist, in contrast, will most likely be fundamentally concerned with maximizing the company's profits, and will probably be perplexed if ethical issues are even raised. The absolutist will likely object to inaccuracies if she labels them as *lies*; if, however, they are described as mere puffery and the benefits of a successful campaign are made clear to her, then even the absolutist may be willing to overlook the inaccuracies. The exceptionist, too, is likely to overlook inaccuracies. Although she would agree that "truth in advertizing" is essential, she would likely point out that the need to make a profit and competitors' deceptive advertisements justify an exception in this case.

A businessman's decision to retain or let go a veteran employee who violates a company rule (e.g., personal long-distance phone calls, use of company credit card for personal purchases, pilfering, freelancing) provides a second example. The situationist would prefer to gather background information about the incident before making a decision, for he would wonder if circumstances justified or at least mitigated punishment for the employee's behavior. The subjectivist, in contrast, would be more likely to consider the practical consequences of the action for the company, but would also act on the basis of personal feelings. If, for example, the individual was a friend or relative, then the incident would probably be overlooked. The absolutist, in contrast, would likely react the most negatively provided the rule was stated publicly and clearly in company guidelines. He might regret the harm done to the individual, but he would feel that following company policy takes precedent over individual outcomes. Lastly, an exceptionist would be willing to overlook the untoward action if practical concerns weighed against termination. If the employee managed an important account, could make financial restitution to the company, or was very difficult to replace, then an exceptionist would not take action.

Personal Moral Philosophy and Moral Judgment

Do these individual differences in personal moral philosophy influence other aspects of morality, including moral cognition, action, and effect? Although Hartshorne and May (1928), in their early studies of morality, concluded that moral behavior was more the product of the situation than the person, more recent models of moral phenomena advocate an transactional view of personality and behavior. Haan (1978, 1986; Haan et al. 1985), for example, argues that individuals' moral behavior varies because interpersonal demands vary across situations. Haan feels that moral action is "informed and influenced by variations in contexts" and by individuals' "own strategies of problem solving" when they confront a moral dilemma (Haan 1986, p. 1282). Kurtines, by asking individuals to predict how they would behave in various social roles, found that individuals' use of principled moral reasoning varied across these role-settings (1984, 1986). Similarly, the approach described here assumes that the individual differences in personal moral philosophies influence behavior, but that the magnitude of this influence depends upon a number of situational factors.

Measuring Personal Moral Philosophy

The Ethics Position Questionnaire (EPQ) assesses personal moral philosophy by asking individuals to indicate their acceptance of items that vary in terms of relativism and idealism. The relativism scale includes items like "Different types of moralities cannot be compared as to 'rightness'" and "What is ethical varies from one situation to another." The idealism scale, in contrast, measures one's perspective on positive and negative consequences with such items as "A person should make certain that their actions never intentionally harm another even to a small degree" and "If an action could harm an innocent other then it should not be done" (Forsyth 1980). Overall, high scorers on the idealism subscale of the EPQ more strongly endorse items that reflect a fundamental concern for the welfare of others, whereas those who receive high scores on the relativism subscale of the EPQ tend to espouse a personal moral philosophy based on rejection of moral universals (Forsyth et al. 1988).

Moral Attitudes

Relative to the other three types, absolutists tend to be more conservative in their position on contemporary moral issues and practices. Leary et al. (1986), for example, found that scores on the Machiavellianism Scale correlated positively with relativism, but they correlated negatively with idealism. When Forsyth (1980) examined the relationship between one's moral philosophy and personal opinion on such issues as the artificial creation of human life, mercy killings, marijuana use, capital punishment, homosexuality, and abortion he found that absolutists, and male absolutists in particular, were relatively negative in their appraisals of test-tube babies, euthanasia, marijuana use, homosexuality, and abortion. This critical attitude was also noted in a follow-up study that focused specifically on sexual practices, including premarital sex, extramarital sex, and homosexuality (Singh and Forsyth 1989). Although not yet examined empirically, these findings suggest that absolutists would be the most negative toward illegal business practices, such as bait-and-switch advertising, employee exploitation, inadequate waste management strategies, the sale of off-standard products, job or wage discrimination, kickbacks, or misuse of authority for personal gain. They would also be more likely to object to legal, but ethically questionable, behavior. Absolutists might, for example, react harshly to co-workers who adopt alternative lifestyles, are sexually promiscuous in the work place, or adopt nontraditional sexual preferences. They may prefer to work for a company that sells trucks rather than IUDs.

Moral Judgment

The negativity of the absolutists in their moral attitude corresponds to an overall negativity when formulating moral judgments. When judging actions that led to positive and negative consequences, absolutists were significantly harsher in their appraisals, whereas situationists based their judgments on both negative and positive consequence data. Absolutists also attributed more responsibility to people who produced negative consequences, evaluated specific consequences less favorably, and condemned the morality of the person being appraised more often than other judges. Exceptionists were the most positive (Forsyth 1978). Similarly, when evaluating the morality of 16 ethically controversial psychological studies, absolutists were more negative than all other types (Forsyth and Pope 1984). They apparently focused on the potential harm for subjects created by researchers.

In many cases, however, situational and cognitive factors mediate the strength of the personal moral philosophy-judgment relationship. Forsyth (1981b), for example, found that absolutists were more negative than exceptionists, but only when the individual was clearly responsible for his action and the consequences of the action were extremely negative. In a related study, Forsyth (1985) asked individuals to appraise the morality of someone who, by either violating or conforming to a moral principle (such as "tell the truth," "do not steal," or "keep your promises"), produced positive or negative consequences for innocent others. As predicted, idealistic subjects (both absolutists and situationists) more strongly condemned individuals who caused extremely negative consequences, whereas the relativistic subjectivists and situationists were more lenient when judging individuals who violated a moral norm. In terms of information integration, an averaging model with differential weights accounted for idealists' (situationists and absolutists) judgments since conformity to moral principles was discounted when the consequences were extremely negative or positive. Subjectivists' judgments conformed to an averaging model of information integration since mildly positive consequences lowered moral judgments of conforming actions, and exceptionists combined information in a strictly linear, additive fashion; the more positive the consequences or the greater the conformity of the action to a moral norm, the more positive the moral judgment.

Moral Behavior

The analysis of individual differences immoral and immoral behavior has traditionally stymied researchers, but the taking of personal moral philosophies into account yields some insight into this empirical puzzle. Forsyth and Berger (1982), in a study of cheating, found that 36% of the college students they studied cheated on a test when left alone with the answer key, but cheating was not related to either idealism or relativism. These researchers also tested resistance to moral temptation in a second study by adding a confederate who urged subjects to take answers from the answer key. Cheating increased to 83% in this study, but once again propensity to cheat wasn't linked to personal moral philosophy.

These studies suggest that personal moral philosophy does not influence moral behavior in most settings. A more circumspect approach, however, proposes that features of the social setting may possibly enhance – or reduce – the causal impact of moral values on behavior. For example, because absolutists and exceptionists emphasize the importance of moral rules, individuals who subscribe to these two types of personal moral philosophies may be more reluctant to engage in immoral behavior when moral rules are made salient by situational factors. Similarly, since the idealistic ideologies – situationism and absolutism – stress the need to achieve positive, humanitarian consequences, then individuals who accept these ideals might be more likely to engage in immoral action if such actions are the means to help others.

This revised approach was supported in a study of lying (Forsyth and Nye 1990). Situationists, absolutists, subjectivists, and exceptionists were placed in a situation in which they were asked to tell a deliberate lie to another person. In making this request, the researcher emphasized that the information was simply a form of feedback (nonsalient moral norm) or that the information was a lie (salient moral norm). In addition, one half of the subjects were told that they would receive a bonus of three dollars by giving the information (either lie or feedback), while the remaining subjects were told that the information would probably have positive consequences for the person being mislead (i.e., it was for "his own good").

As anticipated, the two situational variables – the salience of moral norms and the consequences of action – had a strong impact on moral action. While only 50.0% of the subjects agreed to lie when they were offered $3 and were told that they would be lying rather giving feedback, this percentage increased to 76.2% across the other three conditions. In addition, idealism influenced moral behavior, but in a surprising fashion. Although high idealists espouse a philosophy that condemns harming others, they were more likely to lie than the low idealists. Fully 91.66% of the situationists and absolutists (high idealists) agreed to tell the lie, while only 70.83% of the subjectivists and exceptionists (low idealists) complied with the experimenter's request. In fact, situationists and absolutists usually lied no matter what the consequences or salience of moral norms. Exceptionists, in contrast, were less likely to lie if offered money to lie and subjectivists were less likely to lie if they stood to gain from the lie and the action was labeled a lie.

This study supports the commonsense notion that people who espouse lofty moral values may tend to behave the most immorally. Although both situationists and absolutists strongly endorse such beliefs as "One should never psychologically or physically harm another person" and "It is never necessary to sacrifice the welfare of others," both groups were willing to tell a total stranger a lie. While these findings are not too damaging for situationists since these individuals believe that lying is permissible in some settings, absolutists staunchly maintain that lying violates fundamental moral principles, and are quite harsh when judging others who have broken this moral absolute. Yet, when they themselves were tempted to lie, they were more likely to succumb. Although additional research is needed to further explore the moral thought of absolutists, the current research attests to a "hypocrisy effect" that may be obscuring the link between moral values and moral behaviors: People who say they are the most morally upright may be most likely to fall prey to temptation (Forsyth and Nye 1990).

Reactions to One's Own Moral Transgressions

Klass (1978), after reviewing a number of previous studies of individuals' feelings of guilt, shame, and self-esteem after breaking moral norms, concludes that "the same overt action seems to make some people feel better and others feel worse, and for still others, has no effects" (p. 766). The personal moral philosophy model accounts for these divergences by suggesting that individuals who emphasize obedience to moral norms (low relativists) but nonetheless find themselves acting contrary to a salient moral norm should display much more negative post-transgression reactions than other subjects. In contrast, idealistic individuals who achieve positive consequences for others should display more positive affective reactions following their transgression.

In the study of cheating mentioned earlier, these predictions were partially confirmed. The more absolutists cheated the more negatively they rated themselves, and exceptionists rated themselves more positively the more they cheated (Forsyth and Berger 1982, Study 1). In a second study, absolutists who were prodded into cheating on a test rated themselves as more negative, weak, unlikable, and dirty than individuals in all the other personal moral philosophy categories (Forsyth and Berger 1982, Study 2). Similarly, Forsyth and Nye (1990), in their study of lying, found that when subjects were lying to secure positive consequences for themselves, no differences due to personal moral values were obtained. When lying was motivated by a desire to help another person, situationists rated themselves very positively, especially in comparison to the absolutists.

Personal moral philosophies also tempered self-evaluations in a study of reactions to failure and success when working for personal profit or for a charity. Given high idealists' desire to achieve positive outcomes for others, they should feel more positive following charitable actions rather than for themselves. Relativists, in contrast, should not feel as positive about themselves after they help others than would non-relativists. In a preliminary test of this prediction subjects assigned to the self-interest condition were informed that any money they earned during the study should be considered their salary. Subjects in the charity condition were told that any money they earned would be donated to the State Charity Foundations, and they were given a booklet describing this organization. After completing their work subjects were told their performance was a success (they were paid) or a failure (they were not paid), at which time they completed measures of affect, morality, and self-esteem.

Overall subjects' self-ratings were more positive when they succeeded rather than failed. Differences due to personal moral philosophy, however, were obtained after failure. Once again absolutists demonstrated an hypocrisy effect, for they felt more moral when they failed in a charitable action than when they failed while trying to secure personal gain. Exceptionists, in contrast, rated themselves as particularly moral when they failed when working for personal gain. Lastly, low relativists' self-esteem scores were more positive when they failed rather than succeeded, irrespective of the nature (selfless vs. selfish) of the action (Forsyth and Matney 1990).

The Wider Implications

In sum, predictions derived from the personal moral philosophy model have shown that individuals who differ in relativism and idealism divaricate when making moral judgments, in attitudes toward many contemporary moral issues, when attributing responsibility after wrongdoing, when judging the ethics of behavioral science research, and in resistance to moral temptations. Researchers have also reported theoretically predicted correlations between idealism, relativism, and other individual difference variables, including machiavellianism, an ethic of responsibility, and an ethic of caring. These studies, however, also suggest that the impact of relativism and idealism on moral judgment and behavior depends on the nature of the social situation. Consistent with an interactional approach to personality-behavior relationships, idealism and relativism are maximally influential when factors in the situation heighten the salience of these personal moral values. They also raise a number of issues pertaining to ethics, science, and applications.

Studying Morality Scientifically

In many cases researchers have sought to combine both science and philosophy in the study of moral phenomena (Haan 1982). Kohlberg (1983), for example, deliberately accepted a deontological model as the most mature approach to making moral judgments, and ranked other views as inferior. He argued that because only older individuals learn to generate principles of morality based on autonomy and cooperation, then any morality based on other considerations is immoral or immature. He therefore committed the naturalistic fallacy by moving from "This is how individuals make judgments" to "This is how individuals should make judgments."

The current approach, however, strives to maintain a distinction between a philosophical analysis of moral issues and a scientific analysis of an individual's personal moral philosophy. Unlike philosophy, the scientific analysis of morality advocates the long-term goal of increasing and systematizing our knowledge about the subject matter via theory construction. These theories, once developed, must also be tested using objective, empirical methods rather than logical claims, subjective feelings, or authorities' opinions. Studies of morality, if they are to be scientific, must remain within these boundaries. Hypotheses offered must be empirically testable, using methods that other scientists accept as adequate. Although the personal moral philosophies draw on distinctions made within moral philosophy, these philosophical distinctions are not used as evidence attesting to the validity of the psychological theory of individual differences. The model also merely describes individual differences in moral thought, and does not argue that any one philosophy is more morally advanced than another (Forsyth 1992).

Science and Application

Studies of morality are not, however, completely independent of moral issues, for in many cases research can inform moral judgment processes. For example, a business practice may be adopted based on the moral principle that all people should be paid an equitable wage. When this principle is accepted as the basis for action, information regarding how equity can be calculated and how inequities can be reduced is required. Scientific procedures then become useful in identifying solutions to problems, the short-and long-term implications of implementing certain actions or programs designed to fulfill the standards expressed in the moral principle, and the psychological, political, sociological, and economic reactions that may accompany the implementation of the programs.

Scientific research may also influence moral judgments by providing an indication of the validity of factual statements made in the moral judgment process. Individuals may decide an action is moral because they feel that it will have certain results that are desirable. A scientific analysis becomes relevant if it can provide evidence that the action being considered will lead or not lead to the desired consequences. If, for example, installing air bags in cars is deemed just since it reduces the likelihood of severe injury in an automobile accident, then data that speak to the validity of this claim are relevant to the moral approbation of the practice. Similarly, an advertising campaign featuring a spokesperson who deliberately and blatantly lies about the product may be viewed as allowable if it can be shown that viewers recognize that they are being given false information. Even this information, however, may be irrelevant to certain individuals. Absolutists, for example, may find that the practice is immoral simply because it violates the rule that prohibits lying.

Resolving Moral Controversies

Given that individuals seem to adopt a variety of different personal moral philosophies, perfect consensus regarding any given business practice can never be expected. Indeed, given that disagreement is the rule not the exception, then why bother to search for solutions to ethical dilemmas? The current approach suggests that problems of ethics can be addressed most profitably through open, reasoned discussion of ethical questions from each of four perspectives: situationism, subjectivism, absolutism, and exceptionism. Although a common ground on any given question cannot always be located, the discussion itself sparks greater understanding of the problems and is, of itself, progress. Individuals in the business community must operate within the limits that society places upon them; so long as these limits are violated, ethical and value conflicts will continue to disrupt our economic system, and endanger both the reputation and the effectiveness of business. However, if the relative importance of the many factors that influence moral judgments can be enumerated, clarified, and weighed through research and informed discussion, business ethicists will be able to deal effectively with problems that confront them. While the concept of individual differences in personal moral philosophy suggests that we will probably never reach the ideal of complete agreement, at least we can aim for a fuller understanding of our own and others' reactions to various types of business practices.

References

Bandura, A. 1990. Selective activation and disengagement of moral control. *Journal of Social Issues* 46(1): 27–46.

Boyce, W.D., and L.C. Jensen. 1978. *Moral reasoning: A psychological–philosophical integration*. Lincoln: University of Nebraska Press.

Derry, R. 1989. An empirical study of moral reasoning among managers. *Journal of Business Ethics* 8: 855–862.

Fletcher, J. 1966. *Situation ethics*. Philadelphia: Westminster Press.

Forsyth, D.R. 1978. Moral attribution and the evaluation of action. Unpublished doctoral dissertation, University of Florida, Gainesville, Fl.

Forsyth, D.R. 1980. A taxonomy of ethical ideologies. *Journal of Personality and Social Psychology* 39: 175–184.

Forsyth, D.R. 1981a. A psychological perspective on ethical uncertainties in behavioral research. In *New directions for methodology of social and behavioral science: Ethics of human subject research*, vol. 10, ed. A.J. Kimmel. San Francisco: Jossey-Bass.

Forsyth, D.R. 1981b. Moral judgment: The influence of ethical ideology. *Personality and Social Psychology Bulletin* 7: 218–223.

Forsyth, D.R. 1985. Individual differences in information integration during moral judgment. *Journal of Personality and Social Psychology* 49: 264–272.

Forsyth, D.R. 1992. Values, conceptions of science, and the social psychological study of morality. In *The role of values in psychology and human development*, ed. M. Azmitia, W.M. Kurtines, and J. Gewirtz. New York: Wiley.

Forsyth, D.R., and R.E. Berger. 1982. The effects of ethical ideology on moral behavior. *Journal of Social Psychology* 117: 53–56.

Forsyth, D.R., and L. Matney. 1990. The emotional consequences of selfish and selfless actions. Paper presented at the second annual convention (June 1990) of the American Psychological Society, Dallas TX.

Forsyth, D.R., and J.L. Nye. 1990. Personal moral philosophies and moral choice. *Journal of Research in Personality* 24: 398–414.

Forsyth, D.R., and W.R. Pope. 1984. Ethical ideology and judgments of social psychological research. *Journal of Personality and Social Psychology* 46: 1365–1375.

Forsyth, D.R., J.L. Nye, and K. Kelly. 1988. Idealism relativism, and the ethic of caring. *Journal of Psychology* 122: 243–248.

Freud, S. 1927. *The psychopathology of everyday life*. London: Hogarth Press.

Gilligan, C. 1982. *In a different voice*. Cambridge, MA: Harvard University Press.

Haan, N. 1978. Two moralities in action context. *Journal of Personality and Social Psychology* 36: 286–305.

Haan, N. 1982. Can research on morality be "Scientific". *American Psychologist* 37: 1096–1104.

Haan, N. 1986. Systematic variability in the quality of moral action, as defined in two formulations. *Journal of Personality and Social Psychology* 50: 1271–1284.

Haan, N., E. Aerts, and B. Copper. 1985. *On moral grounds: The search for practical morality*. New York: New York University Press.

Hartshorne, H., and M.A. May. 1928. *Studies in the nature of character*. New York: Macmillan.

James, W. 1891/1973. The moral philosopher and the moral life. In *Introduction to moral philosophy*, ed. P.E. Davis. Columbus: Merrill.

Kant, I. 1873/1973. Critique of pure reason and other works on the theory of ethics. Trans. T.K. Abbott, In *Introduction to moral philosophy*, ed. P.E. Davis. Columbus: Merrill.

Kelley, M. 1989. Commentary on "An empirical study of moral reasoning among managers". *Journal of Business Ethics* 8: 863–864.

Klass, E.T. 1978. Psychological effects of immoral actions: The experimental evidence. *Psychological Bulletin* 85: 756–771.

Kohlberg, L. 1983. *Essays in moral development*, vol. 2. New York: Harper & Row.

Kurtines, W.M. 1984. Moral behavior as rule governed behavior: A psychosocial role-theoretical approach to moral behavior and development. In *Morality, moral behavior, and moral development: Basic issues in theory and research*, ed. W. Kurtines and J.L. Gewirtz. New York: Wiley.

Kurtines, W.M. 1986. Moral behavior as rule governed behavior: Person and situation effects on moral decision making. *Journal of Personality and Social Psychology* 50: 784–791.

Leary, M.R., P.D. Knight, and B.D. Barnes. 1986. Ethical ideologies of the Machiavellian. *Personality and Social Psychology Bulletin* 12: 75–80.

Piaget, J. 1932. The moral judgment of the child. New York: Macmillan.

Schlenker, B.R., and D.R. Forsyth. 1977. On the ethics of psychological research. *Journal of Experimental Social Psychology* 13: 369–396.

Sharp, F.C. 1898. An objective study of some moral judgments. *The American Journal of Psychology* 9: 198–234.

Singh, B., and D.R. Forsyth. 1989. Sexual attitudes and moral values: The importance of idealism and relativism. *Bulletin of the Psychonomic Society* 27: 160–162.

Waterman, A.S. 1988. On the uses of psychological theory and research in the process of ethical inquiry. *Psychological Bulletin* 103: 283–298.

Chapter 13
A Review of Empirical Studies Assessing Ethical Decision Making in Business

Terry W. Loe, Linda Ferrell, and Phylis Mansfield

Introduction

Current ethical decision making models present numerous variables that influence ethical choice, providing a theory base for how ethical decisions are made in organizations. There is general agreement among scholars concerning the individual variables and organizational learning processes that influence ethical decisions. The positive ethical decision making models (Ferrell and Gresham 1985; Hunt and Vitell 1986; Jones 1991; Trevino 1986) and their theoretical underpinnings identify key constructs that assist in understanding the factors that have the greatest effect on an individual's ethical decision making in organizations. Criticisms of normative models of business ethics, which often assume absolute truths about appropriate decision making, led to the development of positive perspectives and models. Positive models describe what actually occurs in the organization, versus normative models that address what *should* occur. Unlike normative models that specify decision rules for how to make an optimum or correct decision, positive models are more readily evaluated, using scientific modes of inquiry (Thorne and Ferrell 1993).

Insights into the strength of positive models of ethical decision making come from empirical study that has assessed these relationships. Positive models guide or increase our understanding of business phenomena (Hunt 1991). Hunt continues,

T.W. Loe (✉)
Department of Marketing, Hankamer School of Business, Baylor University,
P.O. Box 98007, Waco, TX 76798-8007, USA
e-mail: tloe@coles2.kennesaw.edu

L. Ferrell
University of Tampa, 401 W. Kennedy, Tampa, FL 33606, USA

P. Mansfield
Department of Management and Marketing, Andrews University,
Berrien Springs, MI 49104, USA

A.C. Michalos and D.C. Poff (eds.), *Citation Classics from the Journal of Business Ethics*, Advances in Business Ethics Research 2,
DOI 10.1007/978-94-007-4126-3_13, © Springer Science+Business Media B.V. 2013

"Scientific knowledge thus rests on the bedrock of empirical testability" (1991, p. 197). In 1994, Ford and Richardson published a comprehensive review of the empirical literature related to ethical beliefs and decision making. This project updates their work by evaluating empirical studies in organizational settings and relating these studies to the Jones (1991) Synthesis of Ethical Decision Making Decision Making Model. Summaries of the findings of these empirical studies are provided along with suggestions for future research.

Theoretical Models of Organizational Ethical Decision Making

The Jones model (1991) provides the most comprehensive synthesis model of ethical decision making. The model integrates previous ethical decision making models and represents overall agreement regarding the variables that influence ethical decision making and introduces the concept of "moral intensity." Jones believed previous studies failed to consider the nature of the ethical issue. Moral intensity is the "extent of issue-related moral imperative in a situation" (Jones 1991, p. 372). The foundation of Jones' model lies in Rest's (1986) four-stage process: recognizing moral issues, making moral judgments, establishing moral intent, and engaging in moral behavior. Jones (1991) uses Rest's (1986) four stages to link the positive ethical decision making models and assumes that ethical choices are not just individual decisions, but are determined by social learning in the organization.

"Recognizing an issue" is encompassed in the works of Ferrell and Gresham (1985), Hunt and Vitell (1986), and Trevino (1986). Trevino (1986) and Rest (1986), who discuss moral evaluation via moral philosophy (deontological and teleological), support "making a moral judgment." Ferrell and Gresham (1985) established that "moral intent" of the individual is moderated by significant others, individual moderators, and opportunity. Trevino (1986) identified both individual and situational moderators as affecting the relationship between making a moral judgment and engaging in moral behavior. The most comprehensively examined variables are discussed below and include gender, moral philosophy, education and work experience (individual factors), culture and climate, codes of ethics (organizational factors), awareness, rewards and sanctions, and significant others (organizational factors). Other studies with less empirical examination are discussed in a miscellaneous category section, and include individual factors: cognitive moral development, moral philosophy, gender, age, education and work experience, nationality, religion, locus of control, and intent; the organizational factor opportunity, and moral intensity.

Empirical Studies of Ethical Decision Making in Business

Studies addressing the ethical decision making process in business can be categorized into two distinct pursuits: (1) studies that directly examine the hypotheses set forth by ethical decision making models, and (2) studies identifying the moderators

Table 13.1 Number of empirical studies of ethical decision-making in business by category

Construct	# of empirical studies
Awareness	15
Individual factors	
Cognitive moral development	6
Moral philosophy	21
Gender	26
Age	15
Education and work experience	18
Nationality	10
Religion	3
Locus of control	4
Intent	4
Organizational factors	
Opportunity	3
Codes of ethics	17
Rewards and sanctions	15
Culture and climate	18
Significant others	11
Moral intensity	2

of ethical decision making within the organization. Table 13.1 provides a summary of empirical studies of ethical decision making in business by general category of inquiry. Table 13.2 provides a summary of the empirical studies that address the direct linkages in ethical decision making models (awareness, individual factors and intent). Table 13.3 details the studies of the moderating factors of ethical decision making in the organization (organizational factors such as organizational culture, opportunity, codes, significant others, etc.) and moral intensity. The overall findings of these studies are reviewed with the most comprehensively researched areas discussed first.

Gender in Ethical Decision Making

Table 13.1 reviews the studies related to each established dimension of ethical decision making and reveals that the bulk of empirical studies address individual factors that influence ethical decision making. These types of inquiries accompany most ethics studies as control mechanisms and therefore, generate a greater volume of findings than any other single area. Particularly, the role of gender in ethical decision making has received significant examination (26 studies in business). The bulk of studies either determined no significant gender differences or found females tend to be more ethically sensitive than males. Even though gender is one of the most researched or tangentially researched areas, the findings are mixed and inconclusive. More reflection on the methodology of these studies is necessary; how was ethical behavior measured, what was the composition of the study, and where was the study conducted? The bulk of gender related studies were reported in the *Journal*

Table 13.2 Empirical research of ethical decision-making in business

Year/Author: Journal	N: Sample composition	Findings
Awareness		
1961 Baumhart: *HBR*	1,700: HBR subscribers	Industry climate influences ethical behavior
1992 Tyson: *JBE*	495: Students	Individuals perceive their own behavior to be more ethical than others
1992 Dubinsky et al.: *JPSSM*	218: Salespeople	Salespeople differ in their view of what is or is not an ethical situation
1992 Henthorne et al.: *JBE*	311: Sales managers	Managers have more critical view of questionable behavior than salespeople
	329: Salespeople	
1993 Kawathatzopoulos: *JBE*	31: Students	Simple instruction is sufficient for a shift in subject's mode of ethical problem solving
1993 Morgan: *AMR*	385: Managers	Individuals perceive their own behavior to be more ethical than others
1993 O'Clock and Okleshen: *JBE*	195: Students	Individuals perceive their own behavior to be more ethical than others
1993 Robertson and Schlegelmilch: *JBE*	813: Managers	U.S. managers consider most ethical issues to be more important than U.K. managers; U.S. managers differ in their perception of the importance of ethical issues
1993 Shaub et al.: *BRA*	207: Audit CPAs	Ethical orientation influences ethical sensitivity.
1993 Stevens et al.: *JBE*	171: Students and faculty	Freshman and faculty differ in their awareness levels in some instances. Seniors were more ethically conservative than Freshman
1993 White and Dooley: *JBE*	184: Students	Awareness of codes of conduct has no significant impact on ethical decision or behavior
1994 Kohut and Corriher: *SAM AMJ*	86: MBA students	Awareness of codes of conduct has no significant impact on ethical decision or behavior; no significant difference in level of awareness by position or level
1994 Simpson et al.: *JBE*	209: Students	Awareness of codes of conduct has no significant impact on ethical decision or behavior
1996 Armstrong: *JBE*	197: Students (three different countries)	Cultural environment influences the perception of ethical situations.
1996 Wimalasiri et al.: *JBE*	157: Managers and students (Singapore)	Gender and ethnicity is not significantly related to ethical sensitivity; business managers and students demonstrate the same ethical sensitivity

(continued)

Table 13.2 (continued)

Year/Author: Journal	N: Sample composition	Findings
Individual factors: cognitive moral development		
1990 Trevino and Youngblood: *JAP*	94: MBA students	CMD influences ethical decision-making
1992 Goolsby and Hunt: *JM*	269: AMA members	CMD is positively related to socially responsible behavior
1993 Elm and Nichols: *JBE*	243: Managers	Age and education level are negatively related CMD
1990 Weber: *HR*	37: Managers	Level of moral reasoning in a business context is lower than in nonbusiness
1996 Wimalasiri et al.: *JBE*	109: Managers	Age, education and religious affiliation influences CMD
	48: Business students	
1993 Sridhar and Camburn: *JBE*	246: Students	Organizations develop along similar stages and levels as individuals
Individual factors: moral philosophy		
1978 Hegarty and Sims: *JAP*	120: Graduate students	Machiavellianism is a significant covariant of unethical behavior
1989 Swinyard et al.: *JBE*	568: Students (U.S. and Chinese)	U.S. students base ethical behavior more on teleological philosophy; students are equivalent in their moral acceptance of a decision
1990 Mayo and Marks: *JAMS*	104: Marketing researchers	Deontological and teleological philosophies have a significant influence on ethical judgments
1992 Fraedrich and Ferrell: *JAMS*	184: Marketing managers	Managers change moral philosophy based on the situation
1993 Allen and Davis: *JBE*	207: Consultants	Individual values are positively related to professional ethics
1993 Cohen et al.: *JBE*	113: Accounting academics	Accountants use different philosophies
1993 Fraedrich: *JBE*	189: Managers	Rule deontologists rank higher on ethical behavior scale than any other philosophy types
1993 Galbraith and Stephenson: *JBE*	107: Students	Type of situation leads to different decision criteria for males vs. females; neither males nor females use one decision making criteria
1993 Glenn and Van Loo: *JBE*	1,668: Students	Students are less ethical than managers and have lower ethical attitudes
1993 Hunt and Vasquez-Parraga: *JMR*	747: Managers	Deontological unethical behavior with negative consequences is disciplined more severely and is rewarded more with positive consequences
1993 Singhapakdi and Vitell: *JBE*	492: AMA members	Professional values and certain personal values are factors in ethical judgments

(continued)

Table 13.2 (continued)

Year/Author: Journal	N: Sample composition	Findings
1993 Vitell et al.: *JAMS*	508: AMA members	Ethical climate has no significant effect upon personal norms; relativism is a poor predictor of norms; established 5 dimensions of ethical marketing norms
1993 Zabid and Alsogoff: *JBE*	81: Malaysian managers	Malaysian managers have high ethical values
1994 Cyriac and Dharmaraj: *JBE*	68: Middle and senior level managers	Machiavellianism influences ethical decisions
1994 Grover and Hui: *JBE*	248: Students	Individuals change philosophies based upon the situation
1994 Tansey et al.: *JPSSM*	104: Sales people	Moral philosophy affects ethical decision
1996 Brady and Wheeler: *JBE*	141: Financial institution employees	Ethical philosophy is more behavioral-oriented (people tend to behave before they think)
1996 LaFleur et al.: *JAMS*	251: Advertising practitioners	Rule configuration (moral philosophy) influences ethical intentions and judgment
1996 McDonald and Pak: *JBE*	4,044: MBA students employed full time; business association members	Multiple cognitive frameworks (philosophies) are used to evaluate ethical content of marketing activities
1996 Verbeke et al.: *JBE*	185: Salespeople	Personality traits (Machiavellianism) affects ethical decision-making
1997 Akaah: *JBR*	452: AMA members	People form research ethics judgments based primarily on deontological considerations secondarily on teleological considerations
Individual factors: gender		
1978 Hegarty and Sims: *JAP*	120: Graduate students	No significant gender differences
1983 Browning and Zabriskie: *IMM*	145: Purchasing association	No significant gender differences
1984 Beltramini et al.: *JBE*	2,856: Students	Females act more concerned with ethical issues
1985 Chonko and Hunt: *JBR*	1,076: Managers	Males acknowledged fewer ethical problems than females
1985 Dubinsky and Levy: *JAMS*	122: Retail sales people	No significant gender differences
1985 McNichols and Zimmerer: *JBE*	1,178: Students	No significant gender differences
1987 Kidwell et al.: *JBE*	100: Managers	Males and females differ slightly; males are more likely to hide their mistakes
1988 Ferrell and Skinner: *JMR*	602: Marketing researchers	Gender is a significant predictor of ethical behavior

(continued)

Table 13.2 (continued)

Year/Author: Journal	N: Sample composition	Findings
1988 Jones and Gautschi: *JBE*	455: MBA students	Females are less likely than males to be loyal to the organization in an ethically questionable environment
1989 Akaah: *JBE*	420: AMA members	Females indicate higher ethical judgment than males
1989 Barnett and Karson: *JBE*	513: Insurance company employees	Females more ethical than males
1989 Bellizi and Hite: *JM*	452: Sales managers and executives	Gender influences ethical behavior
1989 Betz et al.: *JBE*	213: Students	Males more than twice as likely as females to engage in unethical behavior
1989 Derry: *JBE*	40: Fortune 100 industrial corporate employees	Gender not related to reported experience of moral conflict
1990 Kelley et al.: *JBE*	550: Marketing researchers (AMA)	Females more ethical than males
1990 Singhapakdi and Vitell: *JMM*	529: AMA members	No significant gender differences
1992 Borkowski and Ugras: *JBE*	90: Students	Males and MBAs are more utilitarian; females have more definite ethical positions
	40: MBA students	
1992 Callan: *JBE*	2,261: State employees	No significant gender differences
1992 Dawson: *JPSSM*	89: Students	Females operate with higher standard of ethical behavior than males
1992 Goolsby and Hunt: *JM*	269: AMA members	High CME profile more likely to be female and highly educated
1992 Ruegger and King: *JBE*	2,196: Students	Females more ethical than males
1992 Serwinek: *JBE*	423: Insurance employees	No significant differences in majority of indices
1992 Tyson: *JBE*	495: Students and accountants	Females have greater ethical sensitivity
1992 Whipple and Swords: *JBE*	319: Students	Females are more critical of ethical issues than males
1993 Galbraith and Stephenson: *JBE*	107: Students	Genders differ in use of decision approach when making ethical judgments
1996 Brady and Wheeler: *JBE*	14: Financial institution employees	Gender is not a significant indicator of ethical disposition

(continued)

Table 13.2 (continued)

Year/Author: Journal	N: Sample composition	Findings
Individual factors: age		
1983 Browning and Zabriskie: *IMM*	145: Purchasing association members	Younger managers have a more ethical viewpoint than older managers
1984 Stevens: *ABER*	349: Students 113: Executives	No significant age differences
1987 Kidwell et al.: *JBE*	100: Managers	No significant age differences
1988 Izraeli: *JBE*	97: Managers	No significant age differences
1988 Jones and Gautschi: *JBE*	455: MBA students	Minimal significance on 2 of 14 items
1989 Barnett and Karson: *JBE*	513: Insurance company employees	Later career stages generally more ethical
1990 Kelley et al.: *JBE*	550: Marketing researchers (AMA)	Older respondents and those with greater than 10 years experience are more ethical
1992 Muncy and Vitell: *JBR*	569: Consumers	Individuals with greater ethical concern are older, have lower income and less education
1992 Ruegger and King: *JBE*	2,196: Students	Older students are more ethical
1992 Serwinek: *JBE*	423: Insurance employees	Older workers have stricter interpretations of ethical standards
1992 Tyson: *JBE*	495: Students and accountants	Regardless of age, individuals rated themselves as more ethical than others
1993 Stevens et al.: *JBE*	171: Students and professors	Seniors are more ethically conservative than freshmen
1993 White and Dooley: *JBE*	184: Students	Students respond more practically than ethically
1994 Kohut and Corriher: *SAM AMJ*	86: MBA students	No significant age differences
1996 Brady and Wheeler: *JBE*	141: Financial institution employees	Age is a powerful determinant regarding ethical disposition
Individual factors: education and work experience		
1972 Hawkins and Cocanougher: *JM*	225: Students	Business majors tend to be more tolerant of questionable business practices
1974 Goodman and Crawford: *PJ*	1,500: Students	No significant differences found
1980 Arlow and Ulrich: *ABER*	120: Students 103: Executives	Executives are more ethical than students
1981 Dubinsky and Gwin: *JPMM*	226: Sales and purchasing managers	Purchasing managers see more questionable business practices than sales managers
1983 Browning and Zabriskie: *IMM*	145: Purchasing association	Managers with higher level of education viewed gifts as unethical

(continued)

Table 13.2 (continued)

Year/Author: Journal	N: Sample composition	Findings
1984 Beltramini et al.: *JBE*	2,856: Students	Business majors are more concerned with ethical issues than other majors
1984 Dubinsky and Ingram: *JBE*	116: Salespeople	No significant differences
1984 Stevens: *JBR*	349: Students 113: Executives	Executives more ethical than students
1985 Chonko and Hunt: *JBR*	1,076: Managers	Technical majors tend to be more ethical than nontechnical majors
1985 McNichols and Zimmerer: *JBE*	1,178: Students	No significant differences
1987 Kidwell et al.: *JBE*	100: Managers	The greater the work experience, the more ethical the responses
1987 Laczniak and Inderrieden: *JBE*	113: MBA students	Education (technical versus nontechnical) has no effect
1988 Lane et al.: *JBE*	335: Graduate and Undergraduate students	Minimal significant differences
1989 Stevens et al.: *AMAP*	382: Students, managers and Attorneys	No significant differences
1992 Callan: *JBE*	226: State employees	Length of employment not related to ethical values
1992 Henthorne et al.: *JBE*	311: Sales mangers 329: Salespeople	Substantial variance between the responses from retail managers vs. retail sales-people; managers viewed the scenarios more critically than salespeople
1992 Serwinek: *JBE*	423: Insurance employees	No significant differences
1994 Kohut and Corriher: *SAM AMJ*	86: MBA Students	No relationship between experience or position and ethical decision-making
Individual factors: nationality		
1978 Hegarty and Sims: *JAP*	120: Graduate students	Foreign students are more ethical than U.S. students
1987 Becker and Fritzsche: *JBE*	72: French; 70: German; 124: U.S. managers	French managers have strongest beliefs in codes of ethics
1992 Abratt et al.: *JBE*	52: South African and Australian managers	South African and Australian managers show no significant differences in responses
1992 Kaye: *JBE*	50: Australian and U.S. companies	U.S. firms have more formal ethical structures than Australian firms
1992 Small: *JBE*	179: Students	U.S. and Australian students have similar attitudes; U.S. students slightly stronger ethical sensitivity
1992 Whipple and Swords: *JBE*	319: U.S. and U.K. students	No significant differences

(continued)

Table 13.2 (continued)

Year/Author: Journal	N: Sample composition	Findings
1992 White and Rhodeback: *JBE*	118: Graduate students 267: Taiwanese managers	U.S. managers have a higher ethical rating than Taiwanese managers
1993 Alam: *JBE*	99: Top 200 New Zealand companies	New Zealand CEOs give low priority to ethical values
1993 Robertson and Schlegelmilch: *JBE*	813: U.S. managers 860: U.K. managers	U.S. managers consider ethical issues to be more important than U.K. managers
1993 Zabid and Alsagoff: *JBE*	81: Malaysian managers	Malaysian managers have relatively high ethical values
Individual factors: religion		
1978 Hegarty and Sims: *JAP*	120: Graduate students	No significant findings
1985 McNichols and Zimmerer: *JBE*	1,178: Students	Strong religious beliefs related to a negative attitude toward certain acceptable behaviors
1987 Kidwell et al.: *JBE*	100: Managers	No significant findings
Individual factors: locus of control		
1978 Hegarty and Sims: *JAP*	120: Graduate students	Locus of control is not related to ethical decision-making
1989 Zahra: *JBE*	302: Managers	Managers with an external locus of control perceived organizational politics as ethical
1990 Klebe-Trevino and Youngblood: *JAP*	94: MBA students	Locus of control influences ethical decision-making directly and indirectly through outcome expectancies
1990 Singhapakdi and Vitell: *JMM*	529: AMA members	No significant findings
Individual factors: intent		
1989 Dubinsky and Loken: *JBR*	305: Salespeople	Subjective norms and attitudes are good predictors of intentions
1990 Mayo and Marks: *JAMS*	104: Marketing researchers	Deontological and Teleological evaluations have a significant influence on ethical intent
1990, Reidenbach and Robin: *SMA*	103: Sales personnel	Ethical attitudes are strongly linked to ethical intentions
1996 Robin et al.: *JBR*	251: Advertisers	Perceived importance of ethical issue influences behavioral intention
Individual factors: moral intensity		
1996 Robin et al.: *JBR*	251: Advertisers	Perceived importance of ethical issue influences behavioral intention
1996 Singhapakdi et al.: *JBR*	453: AMA members	Moral intensity influences the ethical decision-making process

Table 13.3 Moderating factors of ethical decision-making in business

Yr./Author: Journal	N: Sample composition	Findings
Organizational factors: opportunity		
1979 Zey-Ferrell et al.: *HR*	133: AMA marketing managers	Opportunity and significant others are better indicators of ethical behavior than personal factors
1982 Zey-Ferrell and Ferrell: *HR*	225: Advertising managers	Opportunity is a predictor of ethical behavior
1993 Wahn: *JBE*	565: Human resource professionals	The greater the organizational dependence, the more likely the compliance with organizational pressure to behave unethically
Organizational factors: opportunity; codes of ethics		
1977 Brenner and Molander: *HBR*	1,227: HBR subscribers	Codes are second to superior behavior in influencing ethical behavior
1977 Weaver and Ferrell: *AMAP*	280: AMA members	Codes and enforcement improve ethical behavior
1978 Ferrell and Weaver: *JM*	236: Marketing managers	Existence/enforcement of a corporate policy does not support more ethical conduct
1990 Trevino and Youngblood: *JAP*	94: MBA students	Formal policies generate an increased level of awareness and subsequent reporting of unethical incidents
1992 Barnett: *JBE*	240: Business executives	Formal policies generate an increased level of awareness and subsequent reporting of unethical incidents.
1992 Dubinsky et al.: *JPSSM*	218: Salespeople	Employees desire more direction through formal policies and codes of ethics.
1992 Kaye: *JBE*	50: Australian companies	Formal policies generate an increased level of awareness and subsequent reporting of unethical incidents.
1993 Allen and Davis: *JBE*	207: Consultants	Codes must be enforced to be effective
1993 Barnett et al.: *JBE*	295: Business executives	Formal policies generate an increased level of awareness and subsequent reporting of unethical incidents
1993 Beneish and Chatov: *JAPP*	160: Managers	Contents of codes vary according to industry
1993 Glenn and Van Loo: *JBE*	1,668: Students	Codes are less effective than earlier research indicated
1993 Kawathatzopoulos: *JBE*	31: Students	Simple instruction is sufficient for a significant shift in the subject's mode of ethical problem solving
1993 Robertson and Schlegelmilch: *JBE*	813: Managers	U.K. companies' communicate policies through senior executives and U.S. communicate policies through the HR department
1994 Bruce: *PPMR*	522: Managers	Codes are necessary, but not as effective as example, support and education

(continued)

Table 13.3 (continued)

Yr./Author: Journal	N: Sample composition	Findings
1994 Kohut and Corriher: *SAM AMJ*	86: MBA students	Knowledge of code has no significant impact on ethical decisions
1996 McCabe et al.: *BEQ*	318: People employed in business	Codes of conduct are positively associated with ethical behavior
1996 Verbeke et al.: *JBE*	185: Salespeople	Internal communication and choice of control system affects ethical decision-making
Organizational factors: opportunity; rewards and sanctions		
1961 Baumhart: *HBR*	1,700: HBR subscribers	Rewards for ethical behavior increases ethical behavior
1978 Hegarty and Sims: *JAP*	120: Graduate students	Rewards for unethical behavior increases its frequency
1989 Bellizi and Hite: *JM*	452: Managers and executives	Poor performers are disciplined more harshly when caught in questionable activity than good performers; when negative consequences result from the behavior there is harsher punishment
1990 Hunt et al.: *JAMS*	330: Advertising executives	Neither penalties nor rewards are associated with socially responsible actions
1990 Trevino and Youngblood: *JAP*	94: MBA students	Rewards influence ethical decision-making indirectly through outcome expectations
1992 Barnett: *JBE*	240: Executives	Executives report increased frequency of employee-voiced concerns in larger or non-unionized organizations; unionized companies perceive higher levels of whistleblowing
1992 Callahan and Collins: *JBE*	276: NY state employees	Belief that there is an informal hierarchy for whistleblowing; fear of reprisal deters whistleblowing
1992 Dabholkar and Kellaris: *JBR*	198: Sales managers	Controversial sales practices with direct $ consequences and practices involving transgressions against customers are judged most severely
1992 DeConinck: *JBE*	246: Sales managers	Consequences of unethical behavior reflect the strength of the discipline received with poor performers receiving the harshest discipline.
1992 Trevino and Victor: *AMJ*	478: Students	Unethical behavior tends to be reported by those with responsibility and when others are perceived to be hurt.
1993 Barnett et al.: *JBE*	295: Executives	Policies encouraging disclosure are positively associated with increased reporting; ethics policies are positively associated with greater disclosure
1993 Hunt and Vasquez-Parraga: *JMR*	747: Managers	Unethical behavior is disciplined more severely when results are negative and rewarded for positive results

(continued)

Table 13.3 (continued)

Yr./Author: Journal	N: Sample composition	Findings
1993 Schultz et al.: *JAR*	145: Managers	Organizational prosperity is not related to reporting, but the situation relates positively to reporting
1993 Victor et al.: *JBE*	159: Fast food employees	Inclination to report peers is positively associated with role perception, interest of group members and procedural justice
1997 Akaah: *JBR*	452: AMA members	Assessment of the appropriateness of reward/discipline for ethical unethical research behavior is guided solely by ethical judgments in the case of reward, and partly by ethical judgments and partly by teleological considerations in case of discipline
Organizational factors: culture and climate		
1961 Baumhart: *HBR*	1,700: HBR subscribers	Industry climate influences ethical decision-making
1977 Weaver and Ferrell: *AMAP*	280: AMA members	Existence and enforcement of a corporate policy on ethics may improve some ethical beliefs
1988 Ferrell and Skinner: *JMR*	602: Marketing researchers	Organizational structure or bureaucracy is related to ethical behavior
1988 Victor and Cullen: *ASQ*	872: Managers	Identifies 5 dimensions in ethical work climate
1992 Dabholkar and Kellaris: *JBR*	198: Sales managers	Organizational controversial practices which are targeted to customers are judged most severely
1992 DeConinck: *JBE*	246: Sales managers	Poor performers receive the harshest discipline for unethical behavior
1992 Kaye: *JBE*	50: Australian companies	U.S. firms have more cultural support of ethics throughout the organization than Australian firms
1992 Small: *JBE*	179: Students	Similarities exist between U.S. and Australian attitudes toward business ethics
1992 Wang and Coffey: *JBE*	78: Fortune 500 Board of Directors	Social responsibility receives greater support when more outsiders are on the board
1993 Alam: *JBE*	99: New Zealand companies	New Zealand companies give low priority to ethical values within the organization
1993 Elm and Nichols: *JBE*	243: Managers	Ethical climate is unrelated to moral reasoning
1993 Posner and Schmidt: *JBE*	1,059: Managers	Supports values congruence model
1993 Vitell et al.: *JAMS*	508: AMA members	Support such as a code of ethics contributes to ethical climate
1994 Judge: *JBE*	162: Hospitals	Organizational size and economic scarcity are negatively related to the social performance of the organization

(continued)

Table 13.3 (continued)

Yr./Author: Journal	N: Sample composition	Findings
1994 Soutar et al.: *JBE*	105: Western Australian managers	Organizational factors have a significant impact on the ethicalness of the firm
1995 Jones and Hiltebeitel: *JBE*	250: Members of the institute of management accountants	Organizational support influences ethical decision processes
1997 Schwepker et al.: *JAMS*	152: Employees of Sales and marketing executive member firms	Ethical climate is negatively associated with perceived ethical conflict
1996 Verbeke et al.: *JBE*	185: Salespeople	Ethical climate affects ethical decision-making
Organizational factors: significant others		
1961 Baumhart: *HBR*	1,700: HBR subscribers	Significant others influence ethical decision-making
1977 Brenner and Molander (77): *HBR*	1,227: HBR subscribers	Significant others influence ethical behavior; codes second to supervisor behavior
1979 Zey-Ferrell et al.: *HR*	133: AMA marketing managers	Significant others and opportunity better indicators of ethical behavior
1982 Zey-Ferrell and Ferrell: *HR*	225: Managers and ad agency managers	Significant others predictor of ethical behavior; significant others best predictor of ethical behavior
1992 Tyson: *JBE*	495: Students	A relationship exists between significant others and ethical decision-making in the organization
1993 Morgan: *AMJ*	385: Managers	Perception of manager varied according to perspective of rater; ethical behavior enhances managers' stature in eyes of subordinates
1993 Wahn: *JBE*	565: Human Resource Professionals	A relationship exists between significant others and ethical decision-making in the organization
1993 Zabid and Alsagoff: *JBE*	81: Malaysian managers	Behavior of immediate supervisor most important variable in influence to act unethically
1994 Bruce: *PPMR*	522: Managers	Significant others more effective than code in influencing ethical conduct
1994 Grover and Hui: *JBE*	248: Students	A relationship exists between significant others and ethical decision-making in the organization
1994 Soutar et al.: *JBE*	105: Western Australian managers	A relationship exists between significant others and ethical decision making in the organization

of Business Ethics (17) and of the 26 studies conducted, 11 used a student sample. Perhaps the use of student samples to measure organizational ethics related issues should be examined. Student samples often are younger than organizational samples and have some imbedded characteristics associated with the sample's inexperience both in life and in the workplace.

Moral Philosophy

Moral philosophy ranks second in number of studies conducted (21). Evaluations of moral philosophy range from examining deontological perspectives versus teleological (Hunt and Vasquez-Parraga 1993; Mayo and Marks 1990) to Machiavellianism's influence on ethical decision making (Cyriac and Dharmaraj 1994; Hegarty and Sims 1978). Student or faculty samples were utilized in one third of the studies and 13 appeared in the *Journal of Business Ethics.* Generally, these studies reveal that moral philosophy is related to ethical decision making and individuals may decide upon using different philosophies based upon experience (early career versus later) or based upon industry. Moral philosophy has not been systematically related to the level of ethical behavior in ethical decision making, which represents opportunity for future research.

Education, Work Experience and Culture and Climate

Eighteen studies explored education and work experience and culture and climate. Education and work experience were found to have negligible or no influence on ethical decision making in half of the studies. The other nine studies produced mixed findings, while some of the studies indicated that higher educational levels are associated with greater ethical sensitivity. The mixed nature of the findings suggests we do not clearly understand the role of experience and education in ethical decision making in organizations. Similar studies of age related to ethical decision making found a positive correlation between age and ethical decision making. Additional research can assist in understanding the role of education, intra-company experience, and cross industry and multi-company experience on ethical decision making. Culture and climate have been found to be pervasive in influencing and adapting organizational ethics. Findings in this area strongly support the theoretical and managerial beliefs that managing the culture of the organization contributes to managing organizational ethics.

Codes of Ethics

The structural elements of an ethics and compliance program contribute to ethical decision making in organizations following the importance of the organizational culture and climate. Key in this understanding is the articulation of the organizational risk areas and the values of top management expressed through the code of ethics (or conduct). Seventeen studies address the role of codes of ethics in influencing organizational ethical decision making. A majority of the studies revealed that codes influence ethical decision making and assist in raising the general level of awareness of ethical issues. The passage of the Federal Sentencing Guidelines for Organizations in 1991, which outlined seven fundamental steps to developing effective compliance programs, spotlighted codes of ethics as key to effectuating higher levels of ethical climate. Perhaps our greatest opportunities for research relate to evaluating the effectiveness of codes, structuring of codes, and their communication and integration with other aspects of the organization's culture.

Awareness

Fifteen studies address awareness of ethical issues. A majority of these studies utilized student samples (nine). The findings were widely diverse based upon the goals of the studies. Several evaluate the role of codes of conduct in generating awareness of ethical issues (Kohut and Corriher 1994; Simpson et al. 1994; White and Dooley 1993). Others consider individuals' awareness of their own ethical behavior relative to others' (Morgan 1993; O'Clock and Okleshen 1993; Tyson 1992), while some evaluated singular issues with respect to awareness. Researchers fail to relate awareness to ethical behavior in organizations, representing a significant opportunity for study.

Rewards and Sanctions

Rewards and sanctions, which are the major components of opportunity, were investigated in 15 studies. A relationship between rewarding unethical behavior and the continuation of such behavior was revealed in a majority of these projects. Generally, rewarded and supported behaviors occur more frequently. Sanctions and their enforcement minimize opportunity. Additional research of rewards and sanctions should address communication issues at different levels in the organization, how other organizational members are informed of violations, and continuous improvement mechanisms for revising policies.

Significant Others

Eleven studies address significant others. Significant others (within the organization) greatly influence ethical decisions of their co-workers and peers as suggested by Ferrell and Gresham (1985). These studies show over-whelming support for the importance of managing relationships within the work group and the pervasive influence of peers in ethical decision making. Perhaps the greatest strides in understanding the influence of significant others can come from a better understanding of group decision making and the role of peer influence in ethical decision making. We know peers are influential, but is that influence greater in day-to-day decision making or with major ethics related decisions? When does the collectivity of the system break down and group members report behavior and decisions to other organizational members? Future research should address these questions.

Miscellaneous Categories

The remaining areas of study provide very mixed findings (i.e., the role of nationality) or only a few studies addressing a particular issue (i.e., cognitive moral development in business, religion, locus of control, intent, general opportunity, and moral intensity). Areas such as moral intensity represent relatively new topics for investigation. This variable originated with Jones' (1991) synthesis model and additional research in this area is anticipated. Topics such as cognitive moral development and religion represent difficult areas of study to report and relate the findings to managerially actionable conclusions. Opportunity has often been assessed through the structural mechanisms within the organization (codes and policies, rewards and sanctions). Intent has proven to be a very difficult area to assess in organizational ethical decision making. And finally, locus of control relates to an individual's susceptibility to influence (external locus of control-particularly concerned with significant others versus an internal locus of control which indicates less susceptibility to peer influence). Locus of control closely parallels, in ethical decision making, the concept of peer influence-which has been extensively researched.

Discussion and Conclusions

Organizational ethical decision making theory needs to be empirically tested to further our knowledge in the area of business ethics. Numerous researchers have contributed to our knowledge in this area through the testing of current ethical decision making models. A few researchers (i.e., Ford and Richardson 1994; Tsalikis and Fritsche 1989) have provided helpful reviews of ethics research. This article reviews the empirical studies related to organizational ethical decision making theory and evaluates the general findings while observing areas that would benefit from further inquiry. Such an analysis is necessary for ethics researchers to evaluate the progress of knowledge development.

The tables provided offer a synopsis of the studies, their findings, samples researched, and the scope of the research. The *Journal of Business Ethics* published an overwhelming number of the studies (61), reaffirming the journal's status as the major outlet for business ethics research. Other outlets included the *Journal of Business Research* (eight) the *Journal of Marketing Science* (seven), and the *Journal of Marketing* (four). The paucity of articles published in other journals indicates a need to more thoroughly integrate ethics issues in other areas of research. Robin and Reidenbach (1987) indicate a need for the gap between ethics and marketing strategy to narrow. Further study integrating the ethical constructs suggested by ethical decision making theory with other marketing related variables, such as marketing orientation, quality and performance would be appropriate in narrowing the gap.

The studies reviewed here indicate a need to consider methodological issues when conducting ethics research. Longitudinal studies are necessary to more fully gain understanding of how ethical climate is impacted by ethics training and, as indicated above, how ethics constructs influence performance over time. Additional studies using industry samples is important to gaining face validity and in providing research results that will be given serious consideration by practitioners.

Understanding why and how individuals and groups make ethical decisions in a business context should improve the ethical decisions made in the organizational context. There is a difference between studying ethics in the personal lives of individuals and the ethical decisions made in organizations. People in organizations are influenced by the corporate culture and role relationships. While there is great difficulty in describing precisely how or why individuals in the work group make the decisions they do, ethical decision models attempt to generalize about the average or typical behavior patterns within organizations. The empirical studies undertaken should help managers who attempt to influence the ethical environment of their organizations through ethics training and compliance programs.

Though all of the constructs set forth in ethical decision making have been empirically examined, more research needs to be conducted on intent and moral intensity. This study chronicles research in business that has tested the major organizational ethical decision making constructs. These studies were related specifically to the constructs and relationships set forth in positive theories, which is one of the first steps to assess our overall level of understanding of organizational ethical decision making. Aristotle (1943) suggested that when such observations fail to support theory, the theory must be abandoned for theory that can be supported by empirical testing. Our efforts should assist in guiding the efforts of organizational ethics researchers.

References

Abratt, R., D. Nel, and N.S. Higgs. 1992. An examination of the ethical beliefs of managers using selected scenarios in a cross-cultural environment. *Journal of Business Ethics* 11: 29–35.

Akaah, I. 1989. Differences in research ethics judgments between male and female marketing professionals. *Journal of Business Ethics* 8: 375–381.

Akaah, I. 1997. Influence of deontological and teleological factors on research ethics evaluations. *Journal of Business Research* 39: 71–80.

Alam, K.F. 1993. Ethics in New Zealand organisations. *Journal of Business Ethics* 12: 433–440.
Allen, J., and D. Davis. 1993. Assessing some determinant effects of ethical consulting behavior. The case of personal and professional values. *Journal of Business Ethics* 12: 449–458.
Aristotle. 1943. In *Aristotle: On man in the universe*, ed. Louise Ropes Loomis. New York: Gramercy Books.
Arlow, P., and T.A. Ulrich. 1980. Business ethics, social responsibility and business students: An empirical comparison of Clark's study. *Akron Business and Economic Review* 11(3): 17–23.
Armstrong, R.W. 1996. The relationship between culture and perception of ethical problems in international marketing. *Journal of Business Ethics* 15(11): 1199–1208.
Barnett, T. 1992. A preliminary investigation of the relationship between selected organizational characteristics and external whistleblowing by employees. *Journal of Business Ethics* 11: 949–959.
Barnett, J.H., and M.J. Karson. 1989. Managers, values, and executive decisions: An exploration of the role of gender, career stage, organizational level, function, and the importance of ethics, relationships and results in managerial decision making. *Journal of Business Ethics* 8: 747–771.
Barnett, T., D. Cochran, and G.S. Taylor. 1993. The internal disclosure policies of private-sector employers: An initial look at their relationship to employee whistleblowing. *Journal of Business Ethics* 12: 127–136.
Baumhart, R. 1961. How ethical are businessmen? *Harvard Business Review* 39(4): 6–19.
Becker, H., and D.J. Fritzche. 1987. Business ethics: A cross-cultural comparison of managers' attitudes. *Journal of Business Ethics* 6: 289–295.
Bellizi, J.A., and R.E. Hite. 1989. Supervising unethical salesforce behavior. *Journal of Marketing* 53: 36–47.
Beltramini, R.F., R.A. Peterson, and G. Kozmetsky. 1984. Concerns of college students regarding business ethics. *Journal of Business Ethics* 3: 195–200.
Beneish, M.B., and R. Chatov. 1993. Corporate codes of conduct: Economic determinants and legal implications for independent auditors. *Journal of Accounting and Public Policy* 12: 3–35.
Betz, M., L. O'Connell, and J.M. Shepherd. 1989. Gender differences in proclivity for unethical behavior. *Journal of Business Ethics* 8: 321–324.
Borkowski, S., and Y. Ugras. 1992. The ethical attitudes of students as a function of age, sex, and experience. *Journal of Business Ethics* 11(12): 961–979.
Brady, F.N., and G.E. Wheeler. 1996. An empirical study of ethical predispositions. *Journal of Business Ethics* 15: 927–940.
Brenner, S.N., and E.A. Molander. 1977. Is the ethics of business changing? *Harvard Business Review* 55(1): 57–71.
Browning, J., and N.B. Zabriskie. 1983. How ethical are industrial buyers? *Industrial Marketing Management* 12: 219–224.
Bruce, W. 1994. Ethical people are productive people. *Public Productivity & Management Review* 17(3): 241–252.
Callahan, E.S., and J.W. Collins. 1992. Employee attitudes toward whistleblowing: Management and public policy implications. *Journal of Business Ethics* 11: 939–948.
Callan, V.J. 1992. Predicting ethical values and training needs in ethics. *Journal of Business Ethics* 11: 761–769.
Chonko, L.B., and S.D. Hunt. 1985. Ethics and marketing management: An empirical examination. *Journal of Business Research* 13(August): 339–359.
Cohen, J., L. Pant, and D. Sharp. 1993. A validation and extension of a multidimensional ethics scale. *Journal of Business Ethics* 12: 13–26.
Cyriac, K., and R. Dharmaraj. 1994. Machiavellianism in Indian management. *Journal of Business Ethics* 13: 281–286.
Dabholkar, P.A., and J.J. Kellaris. 1992. Toward understanding marketing students' ethical judgment of controversial personal selling practices. *Journal of Business Research* 25: 103–109.
Dawson, L.M. 1992. Will feminization change the ethics of the sales profession? *Journal of Personal Selling and Sales Management* 12(1): 21–32.

DeConinck, J.B. 1992. How sales managers control unethical sales force behavior. *Journal of Business Ethics* 11: 789–798.

Derry, R. 1989. An empirical study of moral reasoning among managers. *Journal of Business Ethics* 8: 855–862.

Dubinsky, A.J., and J.M. Gwin. 1981. Business ethics: Buyers and sellers. *Journal of Supply Chain Management* 17(4): 97–103.

Dubinsky, A.J., and T.N. Ingram. 1984. Correlates of salespeople's ethical conflict: An exploratory investigation. *Journal of Business Ethics* 3: 343–353.

Dubinsky, A.J., and M. Levy. 1985. Ethics in retailing perceptions of retail salespeople. *Journal of the Academy of Marketing Science* 13(1): 1–16.

Dubinsky, A.J., and B. Loken. 1989. Analyzing ethical decision making in marketing. *Journal of Business Research* 19: 83–107.

Dubinsky, A.J., M.A. Jolson, A. Marvin, R.E. Michaels, M. Kotabe, and C.U. Lim. 1992. Ethical perceptions of field sales personnel: An empirical assessment. *Journal of Personal Selling and Sales Management* 12(4): 9–21.

Elm, D.R., and M.L. Nichols. 1993. An investigation of the moral reasoning of managers. *Journal of Business Ethics* 12: 817–833.

Ferrell, O.C., and L.G. Gresham. 1985. A contingency framework for understanding ethical decision making in marketing. *Journal of Marketing* 49(Summer): 87–96.

Ferrell, O.C., and S.J. Skinner. 1988. Ethical behavior and bureaucratic structure in marketing research organizations. *Journal of Marketing Research* 25: 103–109.

Ferrell, O.C., and M.K. Weaver. 1978. Ethical beliefs of marketing managers. *Journal of Marketing* 42(3): 69–73.

Ford, R.C., and W.D. Richardson. 1994. Ethical decision making: A review of the empirical literature. *Journal of Business Ethics* 13: 205–221.

Fraedrich, J.P. 1993. The ethical behavior of retail managers. *Journal of Business Ethics* 12: 207–218.

Fraedrich, J.P., and O.C. Ferrell. 1992a. Cognitive consistency of marketing managers in ethical situations. *Journal of the Academy of Marketing Science* 20(3): 245–252.

Fraedrich, J.P., and O.C. Ferrell. 1992b. The impact of perceived risk and moral philosophy type on ethical decision making in organizations. *Journal of Business Research* 24: 283–295.

Galbraith, S., and H.B. Stephenson. 1993. Decision rules used by male and female business students in making ethical value judgements: Another look. *Journal of Business Ethics* 12: 227–233.

Glenn Jr., J.R., and M.F. Van Loo. 1993. Business students' and practitioners' ethical decisions over time. *Journal of Business Ethics* 12: 835–847.

Goodman, C.S., and C.M. Crawford. 1974. Young executives: A source of new ethics? *The Personnel Journal* 53(3): 180–187.

Goolsby, J.R., and S.D. Hunt. 1992. Cognitive moral development and marketing. *Journal of Marketing* 56(1): 55–68.

Grover, S.L., and C. Hui. 1994. The influence of role conflict and self-interest on lying in organizations. *Journal of Business Ethics* 13: 293–303.

Hawkins, D.I., and A.B. Cocanougher. 1972. Student evaluations of the ethics of marketing practices: The role of marketing education. *Journal of Marketing* 36(April): 61–64.

Hegarty, W.H., and H.P. Sims Jr. 1978. Some determinants of unethical decision behavior: An experiment. *Journal of Applied Psychology* 63: 451–457.

Henthorne, T.L., D.P. Robin, and R.E. Reidenbach. 1992. Identifying the gaps in ethical perceptions between managers and salespersons: A multi-dimensional approach. *Journal of Business Ethics* 11: 849–856.

Hunt, S.D. 1991. *Modern marketing theory: Critical issues in the philosophy of marketing science*. Cincinnati: South-Western Publishing Company.

Hunt, S.D., and A.Z. Vasquez-Parraga. 1993. Organizational consequences, marketing ethics, and salesforce supervision. *Journal of Marketing Research* 30(February): 78–90.

Hunt, S.D., and S. Vitell. 1986. A general theory of marketing ethics. *Journal of Macromarketing* 6(Spring): 5–16.

Hunt, S.D., P.L. Kiecker, and L.B. Chonko. 1990. Social responsibility and personal success: A research note. *Journal of the Academy of Marketing Science* 18(3): 239–244.

Izraeli, D. 1988. Ethical beliefs and behavior among managers: A cross-cultural perspective. *Journal of Business Ethics* 7: 263–271.

Jones, T.M. 1991. Ethical decision making by individuals in organizations: An issue-contingent model. *Academy of Management Review* 16(2): 366–395.

Jones, T.M., and F.J. Gautschi III. 1988. Will the ethics of business change? A survey of future executives. *Journal of Business Ethics* 7: 231–248.

Jones, S.K., and K.M. Hiltebeitel. 1995. Organizational influence in a model of the moral decision process of accountants. *Journal of Business Ethics* 14: 417–431.

Judge Jr., W.Q. 1994. Correlates of organizational effectiveness: A multilevel analysis of a multidimensional outcome. *Journal of Business Ethics* 13: 1–10.

Kawathatzopoulos, I. 1993. Development of a cognitive skill in solving business ethics problems: The effect of instruction. *Journal of Business Ethics* 12: 379–386.

Kaye, B.N. 1992. Codes of ethics in Australian business corporations. *Journal of Business Ethics* 11: 857–862.

Kelley, S.W., O.C. Ferrell, and S.J. Skinner. 1990. Ethical behavior among marketing researchers: An assessment of selected demographic characteristics. *Journal of Business Ethics* 9: 681–688.

Kidwell, J.M., R.E. Stevens, and A.L. Bethke. 1987. Differences in the ethical perceptions between male and female managers: Myth or reality. *Journal of Business Ethics* 6: 489–493.

Klebe-Trevino, L., and S.A. Youngblood. 1990. Bad apples in bad barrels: A causal analysis of ethical decision making behavior. *Journal of Applied Psychology* 75(4): 378–385.

Kohut, G.F., and S.E. Corriher. 1994. The relationship of age, gender, experience and awareness of written ethics policies to business decision making. *S.A.M. Advanced Management Journal* 59(1): 32–39.

Laczniak, G., and E.J. Inderrieden. 1987. The influence of stated organizational concern upon ethical decision making. *Journal of Business Ethics* 6: 297–307.

LaFleur, E.K., R.E. Reidenbach, D.P. Robin, and P.J. Forrest. 1996. An exploration of rule configuration effects on the ethical decision processes of advertising professionals. *Journal of the Academy of Marketing Science* 24(1): 66–76.

Lane, M.S., D. Schaupp, and B. Parsons. 1988. Pygmalion effect: An issue for business education and ethics. *Journal of Business Ethics* 7: 223–229.

Mayo, M.A., and L.J. Marks. 1990. An empirical investigation of a general theory of marketing ethics. *Journal of the Academy of Marketing Science* 18: 163–171.

McCabe, D.L., L.K. Trevino, and K.D. Butterfield. 1996. The influence of collegiate and corporate codes of conduct on ethics-related behavior in the workplace. *Business Ethics Quarterly* 6(4): 461–476.

McDonald, G., and P.C. Pak. 1996. It's all fair in love, war, and business: Cognitive philosophies in ethical decision making. *Journal of Business Ethics* 15: 973–996.

McNichols, C.W., and T.W. Zimmerer. 1985. Situational ethics: An empirical study of differentiators of student attitudes. *Journal of Business Ethics* 4: 175–180.

Morgan, R.B. 1993. Self and co-worker perceptions of ethics and their relationships to leadership and salary. *Academy of Management Journal* 36(1): 200–214.

Muncy, J., and S. Vitell. 1992. Consumer ethics: An investigation of the ethical beliefs of the final consumer. *Journal of Business Research* 24: 297–311.

O'Clock, P., and M. Okleshen. 1993. A comparison of ethical perceptions of business. *Journal of Business Ethics* 12: 677–687.

Posner, B., and W. Schmidt. 1993. Value congruence and differences between the interplay of personal and organizational value systems. *Journal of Business Ethics* 12: 341–347.

Reidenbach, R.E., and D.P. Robin. 1990. A partial testing of the contingency framework for ethical decision making: A path analytical approach. Southern Marketing Association Proceedings: Southern Marketing Association. Tuscaloosa, AL: University of Alabama 121–128.

Rest, J.R. 1986. *Moral development: Advances in research and theory*. New York: Praeger.

Robertson, D.C., and B.B. Schlegelmilch. 1993. Corporate institutionalization of ethics in the United States and Great Britain. *Journal of Business Ethics* 12: 301–312.
Robin, D.P., and R.E. Reidenbach. 1987. Social responsibility, ethics, and marketing strategy: Closing the gap between concept and application. *Journal of Marketing* 51(January): 44–58.
Robin, D.P., R.E. Reidenbach, and P.J. Forrest. 1996. The perceived importance of an ethical issue as an influence on the ethical decision making of Ad managers. *Journal of Business Research* 35: 17–28.
Ruegger, D., and E.W. King. 1992. A study of the effect of age and gender upon student business ethics. *Journal of Business Ethics* 11: 179–186.
Schultz Jr., J.J., D.A. Johnson, D. Morris, and A. Dyrnes. 1993. An investigation of the reporting of questionable acts in an international setting. *Journal of Accounting Research* 31(Supplement): 75–103.
Schwepker Jr., C.K., O.C. Ferrell, and T.N. Ingram. 1997. The influence of ethical climate and ethical conflict on role stress in the sales force. *Journal of the Academy of Marketing Science* 25(2): 99–108.
Serwinek, P.J. 1992. Demographic and related differences in ethical views among small businesses. *Journal of Business Ethics* 11: 555–566.
Shaub, M.K., D.W. Finn, and P. Munter. 1993. The effects of auditors' ethical orientation on commitment and ethical sensitivity. *Behavioral Research in Accounting* 5: 145–169.
Simpson, P.M., D. Banerjee, and C.L. Simpson Jr. 1994. Softlifting: A model of motivating factors. *Journal of Business Ethics* 13: 431–438.
Singhapakdi, A., and S.J. Vitell. 1990. Marketing ethics: Factors influencing perceptions of ethical problems and alternatives. *Journal of Macromarketing* 10(1): 47–65.
Singhapakdi, A., and S.J. Vitell. 1993. Personal and professional values underlying the ethical judgements of marketers. *Journal of Business Ethics* 12: 525–533.
Singhapakdi, A., S.J. Vitell, and K.L. Kraft. 1996. Moral intensity and ethical decision making of marketing professionals. *Journal of Business Research* 36: 245–255.
Small, M.W. 1992. Attitudes towards business ethics held by Western Australian students: A comparative study. *Journal of Business Ethics* 11: 745–752.
Soutar, G., M.M. McNeil, and C. Molster. 1994. The impact of the work environment on ethical decision making: Some Australian evidence. *Journal of Business Ethics* 13: 327–339.
Sridhar, B.S., and A. Camburn. 1993. Stages of moral development of corporations. *Journal of Business Ethics* 12: 727–739.
Stevens, G.E. 1984. Business ethics and social responsibility: The response of present and future managers. *Akron Business and Economic Review* 15(3): 6–11.
Stevens, R., J. Harris, and S. Williamson. 1993. A comparison of ethical evaluations of business school faculty and students: A pilot study. *Journal of Business Ethics* 12(8): 611–619.
Swinyard, W.R., T.J. DeLong, and P.S. Cheng. 1989. The relationship between moral decisions and their consequences: A tradeoff analysis approach. *Journal of Business Ethics* 8: 289–297.
Tansey, R.G., H. Brown, M.R. Hyman, and L.E. Dawson Jr. 1994. Personal moral philosophies and the moral judgements of salespeople. *Journal of Personal Selling and Sales Management* 14(1): 59–75.
Thorne, D.M., and O.C. Ferrell. 1993. Assessing the application of cognitive moral development theory to business ethics. *Journal of Business Ethics* 10: 829–838.
Trevino, L.K. 1986. Ethical decision making in organizations: A person-situation interactionist model. *The Academy of Management Review* 11(3): 601–617.
Trevino, L.K., and B. Victor. 1992. Peer reporting of unethical behavior: A social context perspective. *Academy of Management Journal* 35(1): 38–64.
Trevino, L.K., and S.A. Youngblood. 1990. Bad apples in bad barrels: A causal analysis of ethical decision making behavior. *Journal of Applied Psychology* 75(4): 378–385.
Tsalikis, J., and D.J. Fritsche. 1989. Business ethics: A literature review with a focus on marketing ethics. *Journal of Business Ethics* 18: 695–753.

Tyson, T. 1992. Does believing that everyone else is less ethical have an impact on work behavior? *Journal of Business Ethics* 11: 707–717.
Verbeke, W., C. Ouwerkerk, and E. Peelen. 1996. Exploring the contextual and individual factors on ethical decision making of salespeople. *Journal of Business Ethics* 15: 1175–1187.
Victor, B., and J.B. Cullen. 1988. The organizational bases of ethical work climate. *Administrative Science Quarterly* 33(1): 101–125.
Victor, B., L.K. Trevino, and D.L. Shapiro. 1993. The influence of justice evaluations and social context factors. *Journal of Business Ethics* 12(4): 253–263.
Vitell, S., K.C. Rallapalli, and A. Singhapakdi. 1993. Marketing norms: The influence of personal moral philosophies and organizational ethical climate. *Journal of the Academy of Marketing Science* 21(4): 331–337.
Wahn, J. 1993. Organizational dependence and the likelihood of complying with organizational pressures to behave unethically. *Journal of Business Ethics* 12: 245–251.
Wang, J., and B.S. Coffey. 1992. Board composition and corporate philanthropy. *Journal of Business Ethics* 11: 771–778.
Weaver, K.M., and O.C. Ferrell. 1977. The impact of corporate policy in reported ethical beliefs and behavior of marketing practitioners. In AMA Proceedings 477–481.
Weber, J. 1990. Managers' moral reasoning: Assessing their responses to three moral dilemmas. *Human Relations* 43(7): 687–702.
Whipple, T.W., and D.F. Swords. 1992. Business ethics judgments: A cross-cultural comparison. *Journal of Business Ethics* 11: 671–678.
White, C.S., and R.S. Dooley. 1993. Ethical or practical: An empirical study of students' choices in simulated business scenarios. *Journal of Business Ethics* 12: 643–651.
White, L.P., and M.J. Rhodeback. 1992. Ethical dilemmas in organization development: A cross-cultural analysis. *Journal of Business Ethics* 11: 663–670.
Wimalasiri, J.S., F. Pavri, and A.A.K. Jalil. 1996. An empirical study of moral reasoning among managers in Singapore. *Journal of Business Ethics* 15: 1331–1341.
Zabid, A.R.M., and S.K. Alsagoff. 1993. Perceived ethical values of Malaysian managers. *Journal of Business Ethics* 12: 331–337.
Zahra, S.A. 1989. Executive values and the ethics of company politics: Some preliminary findings. *Journal of Business Ethics* 8: 15–29.
Zey-Ferrell, M., and O.C. Ferrell. 1982. Role-set configuration and opportunity as predictors of unethical behavior in organizations. *Human Relations* 35(7): 587–604.
Zey-Ferrell, M., K.M. Weaver, and O.C. Ferrell. 1979. Predicting unethical behavior among marketing practitioners. *Human Relations* 32(7): 557–569.

Chapter 14
A Study of the Effect of Age and Gender upon Student Business Ethics

Durwood Ruegger and Ernest W. King[†]

Many empirical surveys have been given to business students for the purpose of obtaining their views on acceptable ethical behavior. However, survey results are rarely conclusive and ethical beliefs change as the nation's view of morality changes. During the past decade, women have continued to gain prominence in corporate management. Also, the nation's population has continued to gray. It is estimated that the number of workers age 35 and older will increase by approximately 70 million by the year 2000 (Schachter and Dellaverson 1985). These expected gender and age changes in the nation's workforce will probably influence future empirical decision making. The present survey polled 2,196 students for the purpose of obtaining their ethical beliefs. The intent of the survey was to determine whether or not age or gender played a role in a person's perception of proper ethical conduct.

It is never easy to define the term "ethics" or the term "business ethics." The first draft of John Locke's *Essay Concerning Human Understanding* grew out of a meeting in 1690 between friends who had gathered to discuss philosophical questions (Locke 1947). John Locke asked the group the following question: "Why must a man keep his word?" In answering the question, he proposed three different answers. "If a Christian be asked, he will give as his reason: because God who has the power of eternal life and death, requires it of us. But if a Hobbyist is asked why? He will answer: because the public requires it, and the Leviathan will punish you if you do not, and if one of the old philosophers had been asked, he would have answered: because it is dishonest, below the dignity of a man, and opposed to virtue, the highest perfection of human nature to do otherwise" (Locke 1963).

D. Ruegger (unable to contact)

E.W. King[†] (Deceased)

A.C. Michalos and D.C. Poff (eds.), *Citation Classics from the Journal of Business Ethics*, Advances in Business Ethics Research 2,
DOI 10.1007/978-94-007-4126-3_14,

The "depends upon who you ask" theory of John Locke has not changed. Nations differ, cultures differ, and certainly individuals differ in their perception of acceptable moral or ethical behavior.

Business students have been exposed to ethical teachings through family, religion, vocation, education and other experiences. This early development of moral or ethical training will carry over to their business occupations. Self-interest, profits, and other motives, however, may eventually cloud their best ethical judgment. The crucial question in boardroom meetings where social responsibility is discussed is not, "Are we morally obligated to do it?" but, rather, "What will happen if we don't do it?" (Carr 1989).

Corporate senior executives are placed under extreme pressure to balance shareholder earnings against corporate social responsibility. A poll of corporate executives revealed that 76% of those surveyed believed that social responsibility is basically a question of ethics (Carrol 1975). Another study by Edmonds and Hand (1976) indicated that senior corporate executives were confident that they could maximize shareholder wealth and also achieve social responsibility. Price fixing, the savings and loan scandal, and numerous insider trading prosecutions have harmed the public's perception of business ethics. As the public's concern over business ethics continues, schools of business will be expected to do a better job of teaching ethics in their undergraduate and graduate courses. "Good ethics is good business because of readily understandable quid pro quo concepts; a business that behaves ethically induces others to behave ethically toward it" (Learned et al. 1989).

Prior Research

Some of the prior research in this area found females to be more ethical than males (Betz et al. 1989) and older students to be more ethical than younger students. The surveys used small samples of 200 students or less. On the other hand, McNichols and Zimmer (1985) surveyed a larger sample of 1,178 students and found that there was no significant difference in the ethical beliefs of males and females.

Research Design

This survey, consisting of ten questions, was prepared to measure reader response in six areas of ethical conduct: performing work or engaging in practices that may be unethical or harmful (Questions 1, 2 and 3); the employer's responsibility for the safety and welfare of its workers (Question 4); using company time for personal business (Question 5 and 6); informing on your employer (Question 7); informing on fellow employees (Questions 8 and 9); and the company's duty to restrain itself when there is a lack of competition (Question 10).

Students were asked to evaluate the ethical acceptability of each hypothetical question. They were encouraged to base their answers upon how they would react if faced with that particular problem. Each question was rated as being either

[A] acceptable, [SA] somewhat acceptable, [SU] somewhat unacceptable or [U] unacceptable. The survey questions are as follows:

1. Working for a company during the Vietnam War that manufactured Agent Orange. The sometimes lethal chemical was used to defoliate jungle foliage. Many people, including U.S. soldiers, were contaminated by the aerial applications.
2. A mechanic intentionally adds charges to a customer's bill because the customer continuously calls to check on the car.
3. A pharmacist gives pills to a regular customer even though the customer's prescription has expired.
4. A sports owner ordering a player to take prescription drugs and to play, even though playing while injured could end the player's career.
5. Looking for a better job while you are on company time.
6. Paying your bills and performing various personal services on company time.
7. An auto plant employee knows that a defective part is being installed in new cars. After failing to convince the company to correct the problem, the employee elects to remain silent in order to protect his/her job. Evaluate the conduct of the employee.
8. You have a personal knowledge that a fellow employee is padding his/her company expense account (a few dollars per week). You notify your supervisor and the employee is fired.
9. You have observed a fellow employee taking drugs in the restroom. Also, you have noticed a deterioration in the employee's work. You elect to remain silent.
10. Action by an industry (i.e., sugar, oil, etc.) to intentionally and falsely create conditions that indicate that there is a severe shortage of the commodity. The action is taken in order to inflate the product's selling price.

Survey Respondents

The survey was voluntarily and anonymously completed by 2,196 students taking business courses at the University of Southern Mississippi. The University has an enrollment of approximately 13,000 students. The survey was conducted during the fall and spring semesters for the years 1989 and 1990. Participants provided a blend of urban and rural backgrounds. The rural group was comprised of students primarily from the southern part of Mississippi, the eastern part of Louisiana, the western part of Alabama and northwestern Florida. Students from the metropolitan areas of Mississippi, New Orleans, Louisiana, and Mobile, Alabama made up the urban group. Table 14.1 depicts the statistical breakdown of the survey sample.

Research Problem

The null hypotheses that we chose to test are as follows:

Hypothesis statement #1
There will be no significant difference at the 0.05 level in the attitude of males and females when determining acceptable ethical behavior in the six areas of study.

Table 14.1 Survey sample statistics

Females	1,042	Business majors	1,862
Males	1,154	Nonbusiness majors	334
21 years or less	1,286	Freshmen	70
22–30 years	765	Sophomores	440
31–40 years	105	Juniors	778
40 plus years	40	Seniors	886
		MBA	22
International	111		
United States	2,085		

Table 14.2 Chi square calculations for hypothesis # 1 (males-females)

Question #	df	Chi sq.	Chi sq. (0.05)	Hypothesis status
1,2,3	3	93.6911	7.815	Rejected
4	3	58.4599	7.815	Rejected
5,6	3	7.6704	7.815	Accepted
7	3	153.4731	7.815	Rejected
8,9	3	7.3165	7.815	Accepted
10	3	46.6198	7.815	Rejected

Hypothesis statement #2
There will be no significant difference at the 0.05 level in the attitude of students of different ages when determining acceptable ethical behavior in the six areas of study.

Survey Results

Since the survey information is categorical, the Chi Square method was chosen as the best method to analyze the data. The data for the questions that showed a significant difference were then plotted and are shown in graph form to visually aid the reader's interpretation of the respondents' answers. The survey result is also shown for each individual question.

Males and Females

Table 14.2 details the results of Chi Square calculations for male and female students.

The Chi square level of significance (with 3 degrees of freedom) at the 0.05 level is computed to be 7.815 (Borg 1981). In questions 5, 6, 8 and 9, there was no significant difference in the ethical beliefs of males and females. Males and females did differ significantly in their answers to the remaining questions. The greatest significant differences obtained from the Chi square test cells are listed for the purpose of aiding the reader's interpretation of the graphs.

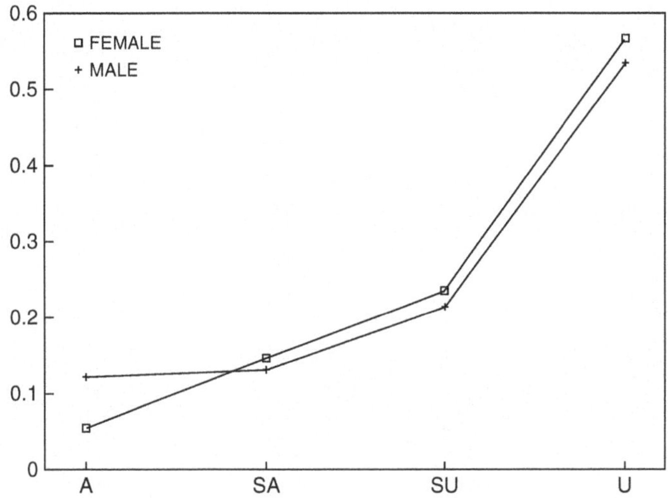

Fig. 14.1 Performing work or engaging in unethical or harmful practices

1. Performing work or engaging in practices that may be unethical or harmful, (Questions 1, 2, 3). *Greatest significant difference*: Acceptable [A] category. 12.1% of the males and 5.3% of the females thought the conduct of the parties was acceptable. (Result: Females are more ethical than males.) Figure 14.1 shows the pattern of response by gender for category 1.
2. Employers responsibility for the safety and welfare of its workers. (Question 4.) *Greatest significant difference*: Unacceptable [U] category. 72.4% of the males and 85% of the females thought the conduct of the parties was unacceptable. (Result: females are more ethical than males.) Figure 14.2 shows the pattern of response by gender for category 2.
3. Using company time for personal business. (Questions 5, 6.) No significant difference was found between males and females in this category.
4. Informing on your employer. (Question 7.)
   Greatest significant difference: Unacceptable [U] category. 23.2% of the males and 42.3% of the females thought the conduct of the parties was unacceptable. (Result: females are more ethical than males). Figure 14.3 shows the pattern of response by gender for category 3.
5. Informing on fellow employees. (Questions 8, 9.) No significant difference was found between males and females in this category.
6. The company's duty to restrain itself when there is a lack of competition. (Question 10.)
   Greatest significant difference: Unacceptable [U] category. 56.6% of the males and 64.7% of the females thought the conduct of the parties was unacceptable. (Result: females are more ethical than males.) Figure 14.4 shows the pattern of response by gender for category 4.

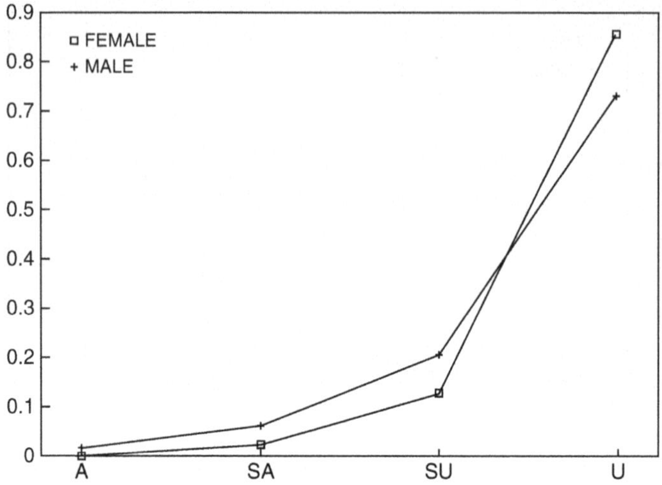

Fig. 14.2 The employer's responsibility for the safety and welfare of its workers

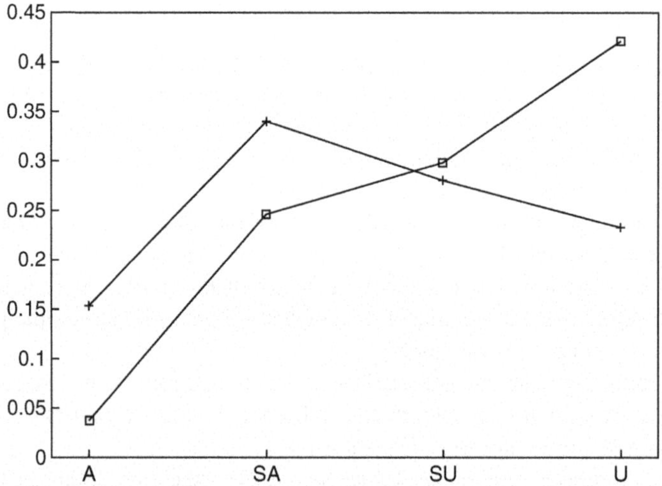

Fig. 14.3 Informing on your employer

Age

Table 14.3 details the results of Chi square calculations for students by age groups.

The Chi square level of significance (with 9 degrees of freedom) at the 0.05 level is computed to be 16.919 (Borg 1981). In questions 8 and 9, there is no significant difference. Age is a significant determining factor when expressing ethical beliefs in all of the remaining questions.

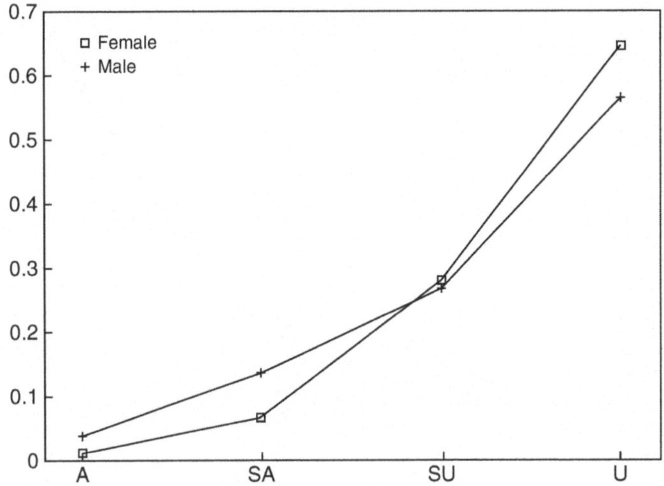

Fig. 14.4 Company's duty to restrain itself when competition is lacking

Table 14.3 Chi square calculations for hypothesis # 2 (age)

Question #	df	Chi sq.	Chi sq. (0.05)	Hypothesis status
1,2,3	9	30.3807	16.919	Rejected
4	9	21.9727	16.919	Rejected
5,6	9	51.2022	16.919	Rejected
7	9	32.8738	16.919	Rejected
8,9	9	14.2796	16.919	Accepted
10	9	40.8676	16.919	Rejected

1. Performing work or engaging in practices that may be unethical or harmful. (Questions 1, 2, 3.)
   Greatest significant difference: Somewhat acceptable [SA] category. 18.3% of the –21 age group and 9.2% of the age 40 and over group found the conduct of the parties to be somewhat acceptable. (Result: most ethical, in order, 40+ years; 31–40 years; 22–30 years; –21 years.) Figure 14.5 shows the pattern of response by age for category 1.
2. Employer's responsibility for the safety and welfare of its workers. (Question 4.)
   Greatest significant difference: Somewhat unacceptable [SU] category. 5.7% of the age 31–40 group and 18.7% of the –21 age group found the conduct of the parties to be somewhat unacceptable. (Result: most ethical, in order, 40+ years; 31–40 years; 22–30 years; –21 years.) Figure 14.6 shows the pattern of response by age for category 2.
3. Using company time for personal business. (Questions 5, 6.)
   Greatest significant difference: Unacceptable [U] category. 27.7% of the –21 age group and 62.5% of the age 40 and above group thought the conduct of the parties was unacceptable. (Result: most ethical, in order, 40+ years; 31–40 years; 22–30 years; –21 years.) Figure 14.7 shows the pattern of response by age for category 3.

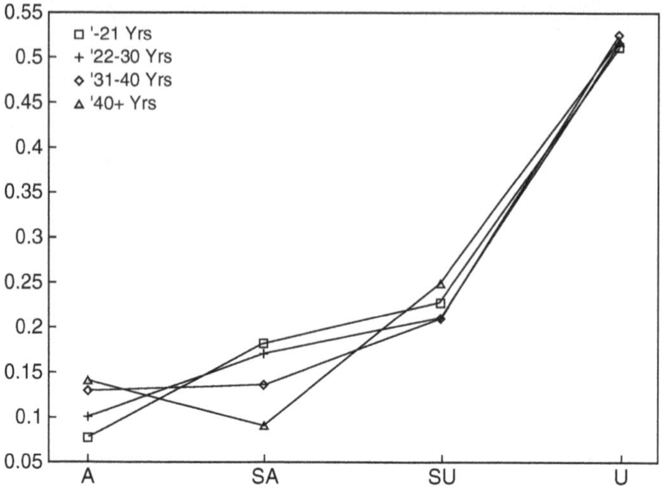

Fig. 14.5 Performing work or engaging in unethical or harmful practices

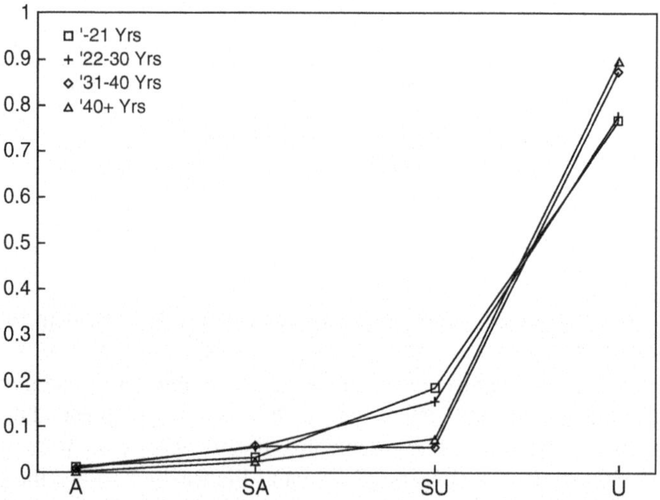

Fig. 14.6 The employer's responsibility for the safety and welfare of its workers

4. Informing on your employer. (Question 7.)
   Greatest significant difference: Unacceptable [U] category. 42.3% of the −21 age group and 23.2% of the age 40 and over age group approved of the action of the worker. (Result: most ethical, in order, 40+ years; 31–40 years; 22–30 years; –21 years.) Figure 14.8 shows the pattern of response by age for category 4.
5. Informing on fellow employees. (Questions 8, 9.) No significant difference was found between the age groups in this category.

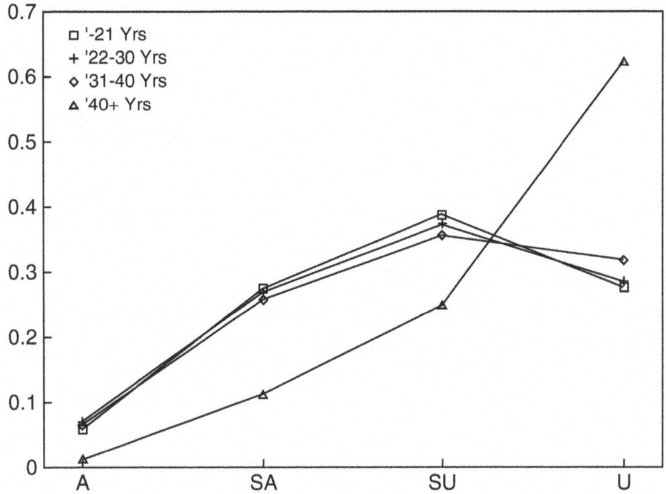

Fig. 14.7 Using company time for personal business

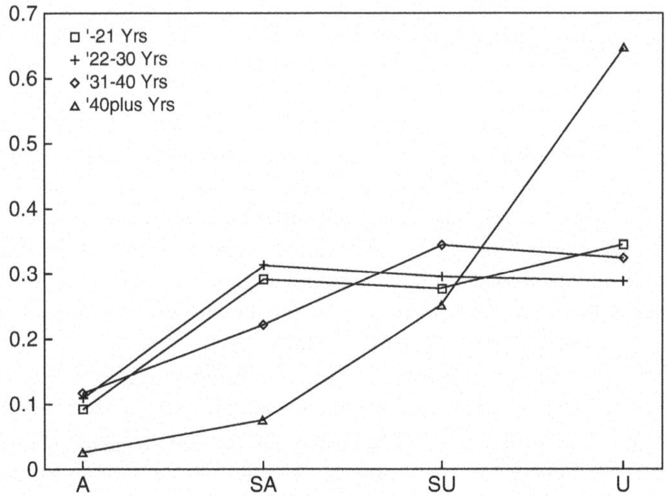

Fig. 14.8 Informing on your employer

6. The company's duty to restrain itself when there is a lack of competition. (Question 10.)
   Greatest significant difference: Unacceptable [U] category. 25% of the –21 age group and 50% of the age 40 and over group approved of the action of the industry. (Result: most ethical, in order, 40+ years; 31–40 years; 22–30 years; –21 years.) Figure 14.9 shows the pattern of response by age for category 6.

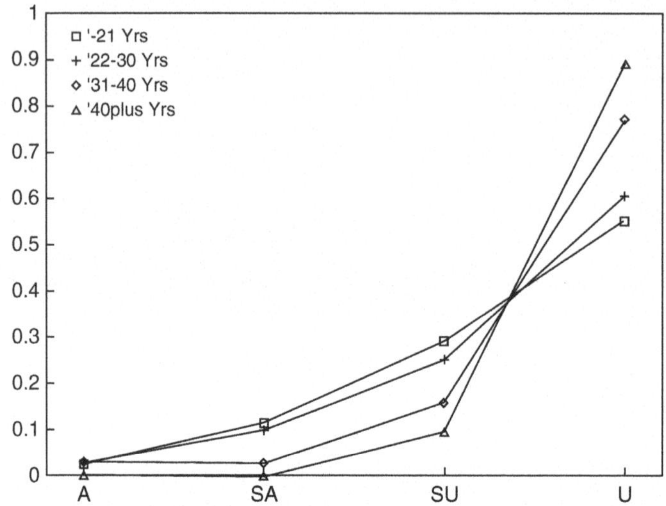

Fig. 14.9 Company's duty to restrain itself when competition is lacking

Summary and Conclusions

The present study surveyed 1,042 females (47.4%) and 1,154 males (52.6%). The survey suggests that gender is a significant factor in the determination of four of the six categories tested. However, no significant differences were found at the 0.05 level between females and males when considering the use of company time for personal business or when asked to evaluate the acceptability of informing on a fellow employee. Answers to the four remaining questions suggest that females are more ethical in their perception of business ethical situations. The responses for the ten questions are summarized by gender in Table 14.4.

In addition, this survey suggests that age is a determining factor in five or six categories tested. The one exception in which no significant difference was found at the 0.05 level between students of different ages occurred when students were asked to evaluate the acceptability of informing on a fellow employee. Students were divided into groups according to age as follows: –21 years, 22–30 years, 31–40 years, and 40 plus years. Although the survey covered a large sample, some limitations may occur due to the small size of the 40 plus age group. We tested only 40 students in that particular group. We do not know what effect, if any, the smaller sample will have on the validity of the survey.

The study suggests that those students falling in the 40 plus years age group were the most ethical, followed in order by the 31–40 group, the 22–30 group and those 21 years of age and under. Thus, age does appear to have a significant affect upon how students view business ethics. The responses for the ten questions are summarized by age in Table 14.5.

The finding of this survey lends support to the surveys of Betz et al. (1989) which asserted that females are more ethical than males. However, it appears to contradict

Table 14.4 Overall survey results in percentage form by gender

	Acceptable		Somewhat acceptable		Somewhat unacceptable		Unacceptable	
Questions	Male	Female	Male	Female	Male	Female	Male	Female
1, 2, 3[a]	12.1	5.3	13.0	14.5	21.4	23.5	53.5	56.7
4[b]	1.7	0.3	5.9	2.3	20.0	12.4	72.4	85.0
5, 6[c]	7.7	6.5	27.3	26.1	38.4	37.2	26.6	30.1
7[d]	15.1	3.6	33.9	24.4	27.8	29.7	23.2	42.3
8, 9[e]	23.0	22.0	23.0	24.3	27.0	26.2	25.0	27.5
10[f]	3.6	1.1	13.3	6.5	26.4	27.7	56.6	64.7

Males n = 1,154
Females n = 1,042
[a] Approval of unethical or harmful practices. (Agent Orange, mechanic, pharmacist)
[b] Approving owner's right to order player to take drugs so that he/she may play
[c] Using company time for personal business
[d] Remaining silent in order to protect your job
[e] Willing to inform on a fellow employee
[f] Approval of a company's practice of using false information in order to inflate the product's price

Table 14.5 Overall survey results in percentage form by age

	Acceptable				Somewhat acceptable			
Questions	–21	22–30	31–40	40+	–21	22–30	31–40	40+
1, 2, 3[a]	7.8	10.2	13.0	14.2	18.3	17.1	13.7	9.2
4[b]	1.1	0.8	1.0	0.0	3.3	5.5	5.7	2.5
5, 6[c]	5.9	7.1	6.7	2.5	27.5	26.8	25.7	24.0
7[d]	9.0	10.7	11.4	2.5	28.9	31.1	21.9	7.5
8, 9[e]	21.9	18.8	20.5	19.0	25.9	23.9	19.5	23.5
10[f]	2.5	2.9	2.9	0.0	11.5	9.9	2.9	2.5
	Somewhat unacceptable				Unacceptable			
Questions	–21	22–30	31–40	40+	–21	22–30	31–40	40+
1, 2, 3[a]	22.9	21.1	21.0	25.0	51.0	51.5	52.4	51.7
4[b]	18.7	15.8	5.7	7.5	76.9	77.9	87.6	90.0
5, 6[c]	38.9	37.5	35.7	39.0	27.7	28.6	31.9	43.5
7[d]	27.5	29.4	34.3	25.0	34.5	28.8	32.4	65.0
8, 9[e]	26.4	29.3	32.0	27.5	25.8	27.9	28.0	30.0
10[f]	29.7	25.5	16.2	7.5	56.3	61.7	78.1	90.0

n=2,196
[a] Approval of unethical or harmful practices. (Agent Orange, mechanic, pharmacist)
[b] Approving owner's right to order player to take drugs so that he/she may play
[c] Using company time for personal business
[d] Remaining silent in order to protect your job
[e] Willing to inform on a fellow employee
[f] Approval of a company's practice of using false information in order to inflate the product's price

the assertion of McNichols and Zimmer (1985) that males and females share similar ethical beliefs. Overall, the findings tend to suggest that there is a close correlation between gender and age when considering business ethical problems.

Follow-up voluntary class discussions indicate similar traits between age and gender. The female and older students (male and female) who volunteered to speak were more comfortable with recognizing a practice as either being right or wrong. Thus, females and older students seem to be less troubled by ethical dilemmas. However, the males and younger students who spoke appeared to be more flexible in their ability to justify a less than perfect ethical performance. One reason for the differences in ethical reasoning by males and females could possibly be traced to the family. The traditional family allowed the male to be aggressive and to behave in a manner that would not be acceptable for a female. On the other hand, females were taught to be loving and caring and to be supportive of the needs of other people. Because of federal legislation to eliminate job discrimination and the fact that two salaries are needed in most households, the roles of females have changed. However, it is possible that some of the traditional role traits for females have carried forward to this date.

Finally, the study reinforces the theory that gender and age affects the way students view business ethics. Class discussions indicate that those students who have worked for long periods of time appear to be more ethical than those students with limited work experience. The differences in male and female ethical perceptions are likely to change as females become more deeply entrenched in all areas of the workplace.

References

Betz, M., L. O'Connell, and J.M. Shepard. 1989. Gender differences in proclivity for unethical behavior. *Journal of Business Ethics 8*:321–324; See also: Beltramini, R.F., R. Peterson, and G. Kozmetsky. 1984. Concerns of college students regarding business ethics. *Journal of Business Ethics 3*:195–200.

Borg, W.R. 1981. *Applying educational research*, 301. New York: Longman Inc.

Carr, A.Z. 1989. Can an executive afford a conscience? In *Ethics in practice*, 32. Boston: Harvard Business School Press.

Carrol, A.B. 1975. Managerial ethics: A post-watergate view. *Business Horizons*, April, p. 18.

Edmonds, C.P., and J.M. Hand. 1976. What are the real long-run objectives of business. *Business Horizons* 19(December): 75–81.

Learned, Edmund P., A.R. Dooley, and R.L. Katz. 1989. Personal values and business decisions. In *Ethics in practice*, 52. Boston: Harvard Business School Press.

Locke, J. 1947. *On politics and education*, 6. New York: Walter J. Black, Inc.

Locke, J. 1963. Concerning human understanding. In *Great books of the western world*, vol. 35, Chap. 2, 105. Chicago: Encyclopaedia Britannica.

McNichols, C.W., and T.W. Zimmer. 1985. An empirical study of differetiators of student attitudes. *Journal of Business Ethics* 4: 301.

Schachter, V., and J. Dellaverson. 1985. Cleaning out the old deadwood. *Across the Board*, January.

Chapter 15
Some Initial Steps Toward Improving the Measurement of Ethical Evaluations of Marketing Activities

R. Eric Reidenbach and Donald P. Robin

The study of marketing ethics is assuming a level of importance approaching the more traditional managerial and strategic concerns of marketing inquiry. The study of marketing ethics has evolved along three related, but differentially developed paths, which DeGeorge (1986, pp. 16–18) identifies as normative ethics, metaethics, and descriptive ethics.

Normative ethics in marketing consists of attempting to develop and justify a moral system of the discipline. Such a system would rely, most likely, on developed moral philosophies but would also adapt them to the special needs and problems of marketers. Metaethics involves the analysis of moral reasoning. It is concerned with the formal language system of normative ethics and especially the meaning of terms. Relatively little published work in marketing addresses these two streams of marketing ethics.

Two approaches dominate descriptive ethics: model building (e.g., Ferrell and Gresham 1985; Hunt and Vitell 1986), and, the ethical evaluation of marketing practices and activities (e.g., Sturdivant and Cocanoughen 1973; Krugman and Ferrell 1981; Browning and Zabriskie 1983; Dubinsky and Rudelius 1980; Shuptrine 1979). Beauchamp and Bowie (1983, p. 5) refer to this second descriptive approach as the scientific study of ethics citing as an example studies reported in the *Harvard Business Review* that describe "what business executives think is morally acceptable and morally unacceptable." Recognition of the value of this type of marketing ethics research is provided also by Donaldson and Werhane (1983, p. 2) who state: "Because business ethics involves relating business activities to some concept of

R.E. Reidenbach
Department of Marketing, Center for Business Development and Research, University of Southern Mississippi, Southern Station, Box 5094, Hattiesburg, MS 39406, USA

D.P. Robin (✉)
Department of Marketing, College of Business, Louisiana Tech University, Ruston, LA, USA
e-mail: robind@wfu.edu

A.C. Michalos and D.C. Poff (eds.), *Citation Classics from the Journal of Business Ethics*, Advances in Business Ethics Research 2,
DOI 10.1007/978-94-007-4126-3_15, © Springer Science+Business Media B.V. 2013

human good, it is a study which has as one of its aspects the *evaluation* of business practices." It is primarily but not exclusively toward this second evaluative or scientific approach to descriptive marketing ethics that the concerns expressed in this research are directed.

The Weakness of "Scientific Studies" of Marketing Ethics

There are, we believe, two basic problems which reduce the utility of so-called scientific studies of marketing ethics and which must be addressed if we are to proceed to a higher level of study. These two problems have to do with the pluralistic nature of moral philosophy and the single global measures which marketers tend to use in obtaining evaluations of marketing activities.

The field of ethics contains a number of individual philosophies, many of which posit conflicting ideas, rules, and interpretations which in turn, can lead to conflicting evaluations of what is ethical/unethical, right/wrong, or moral/immoral. Both Beauchamp and Bowie (1983) and Donaldson and Werhane (1983) provide concise, yet thorough discussions of the different philosophies of ethics. These include relativism, egoism, theories of justice, deontology, and utilitarianism. Most marketing writers and researchers, if they even discuss the different moral philosophies, tend to limit their discussions to the philosophies of utilitarianism and/or deontology (e.g., Hunt and Vitell 1986; Ferrell and Gresham 1985; Robin and Reidenbach 1987). These reductionistic approaches assume that individuals engage in some sort of "cognitive calculus" invoking the tenets of either deontology or utilitarianism or possibly some hybrid of the two philosophies in making an ethical evaluation. In fact, the assumption often made regarding the use of moral philosophy in marketing is that individuals "knowingly or unknowingly use a set of philosophical assumptions as a basis for making ethical decisions" (Ferrell and Gresham 1985, p. 88). Little, if any consideration is given to the other competing strains of moral philosophy such as relativism, egoism, or justice. That individuals may use other moral philosophies is a distinct possibility that is addressed by James R. Rest (1979) who argues that individuals pass through a moral development process ranging from Obedience – "Do what you are told" to Nonarbitrary Social Cooperation wherein individuals rely on abstract principles much like those that dominate utilitarianism and deontological reasoning. Rest argues that the final state of moral development wherein individuals rely on the prescribed notions of moral philosophy (e.g., deontology and utilitarianism) is one which is sought but not yet attained. The issue then becomes: Should descriptive studies of marketing ethics rely solely on the normative philosophies of deontology and utilitarianism?

The second problem concerns the instrumentation used to assess the evaluations. Typically, marketers rely on a single global measure of the ethics of a marketing situation. This measure is generally made using a seven point ethics scale anchored by such adjective phrases as "not at all unethical/very unethical" or "ethical/unethical". Single item measures may be relatively less reliable than multi-item measures (Kerlinger 1986, p. 415; Nunnally 1967, p. 192) and consequently more heavily error laden. Thus, the results of research using single item measures of the ethical evaluation of given marketing activities may be less than optimal.

A second aspect of the global measure problem is that it does not or cannot detail the dynamics of the evaluation. By this we mean it is impossible to understand the ethical perspective(s) that is or are invoked in making the evaluation. Is the individual using a relativist, deontological, utilitarian perspective or some other set of criteria in making the evaluation? A single global measure is incapable of revealing this information. If we are to improve our understanding of the evaluation process and to make positive reactions to situations which warrant a reaction, it is important to address the problems inherent in the pluralistic nature of ethical theory and its measurement.

Hypotheses

The following hypotheses are offered which address the different concerns expressed in the previous section of this paper.

H_1: Individuals will invoke either a deontological, utilitarian, relativist, egoist, or justice perspective in evaluating the ethical content of a marketing activity.

This hypothesis addresses the emphasis that marketers place on what are often considered to be the two dominant streams of ethical philosophy (Hunt and Vitell 1986; Robin and Reidenbach 1987; Ferrell and Gresham 1985), and is concerned with the first problem cited earlier. The work of Rest (1979) suggests that most individuals have not yet reached this level of moral development. Thus, to utilize deontology or utilitarianism exclusively as the basis for a growing body of descriptive marketing ethics knowledge may be premature at best and can only be defended on a normative basis. Moreover, the hypothesis suggests that in making evaluations, individuals rely on a *specific* moral philosophy. That is, they rely on, in its entirety, one single philosophy and not a hybrid of two or more philosophies.

H_2: Individuals will use the same patterns of ethical evaluative criteria to assess different marketing activities which contain differing perceived levels of ethical consequence.

This hypothesis suggests that patterns of ethical evaluative criteria are developed and set within individuals. Further, this hypothesis suggests that these patterns are not situation specific. It is likely, as the work of Ferrell and Gresham (1985) suggests, that situational variables may impact the evaluation process. However, if these situational variables are held constant, the criteria employed by the individual should also be constant.

H_3: Individuals will use the same ethical evaluative criteria in assessing the ethical content of the marketing activity as they use in assessing their own probability of behavior under similar situations.

This hypothesis examines whether the pattern of criteria are task specific. In other words, do individuals organize the criteria differently in performing the evaluation task than they do when asked to assess the probability of their future behavior? Patterns of criteria have been shown to be task specific in other types of marketing evaluations (Reidenbach and Grimes 1985).

Methodology

As suggested in the title, this study is offered as an initial step toward improving the measurement of ethical evaluations of marketing activities. Accordingly, one of the first steps involves the development of scales to measure the different strains of moral philosophy which an individual might invoke in the evaluation process. To this end, a search of the business ethics literature focusing on the discussions of Beauchamp and Bowie (1983), DeGeorge (1986), and Donaldson and Werhane (1983) was undertaken to identify the relevant concepts associated with the different strains of moral philosophy. For example, the egoist school of ethical philosophy relies heavily on the ideas of prudence, self promotion, best self interests, selfishness, and personal satisfaction. These concepts were then translated into seven point semantic differential scales. This process was repeated for each of the following strains of ethical philosophy: deontology, utilitarianism, relativism, and justice. The resultant concepts for each ethical philosophy are shown in Fig. 15.1.

Two hundred and eighteen basic marketing students at the University of Mississippi were exposed to three different scenarios designed to test the three hypotheses discussed earlier. The student sample was chosen principally for its convenience. However, the use of student respondents under controlled conditions should not mitigate the value of the outcome of this study. Previous research (Dubinsky and Rudelius 1980) into student versus professional evaluations showed a high degree of congruence. About 50% of the evaluations were not significantly different. In those that did differ, students were generally more ethical than their professional counterparts. Differences between any respondent groups can be expected. However, since this is an initial effort at generating the proper measuring devices and at understanding the evaluative process, the student group was felt to be justified.

The three scenarios involved ethical issues situated within a retailing context and are shown in Fig. 15.2 (Dornoff and Tankersley 1975). These scenarios depict situations which are not unfamiliar to marketing students and scenarios which were judged that the respondents would be capable of evaluating from an ethical perspective. Scenarios were used to provide the contextual stimulus and to motivate the evaluation process (Alexander and Becker 1978). For each scenario, respondents were asked to rate the action of the individual on each of the 29 scales developed from the concepts shown in Fig. 15.1. Seven point bipolar scales utilizing the following format were used:

Fair	1	2	3	4	5	6	7	Unfair
Just	1	2	3	4	5	6	7	Unjust
Efficient	1	2	3	4	5	6	7	Inefficient

Fig. 15.1 *A priori* normative philosophy scales

Justice Scales:
- Just/Unjust
- Fair/Unfair
- Results/Does not result in an equal distribution of good and bad

Relativist Scales:
- Culturally acceptable/Unacceptable
- Individually acceptable/Unacceptable
- Acceptable/Unacceptable to people I most admire
- Traditionally acceptable/Unacceptable
- Acceptable/Unacceptable to my family

Egoism Scales:
- Self promoting/Not self promoting
- Selfish/Not selfish
- Self sacrificing/Not self sacrificing
- Prudent/Not prudent
- Under no moral obligation/Morally obligated to act otherwise
- Personally satisfying/Not personally satisfying
- In the best interests of the company/Not in the best interests of the company

Utilitarian Scales:
- Efficient/Inefficient
- OK/Not OK if actions can be justified by their consequences
- Compromises/Does not compromise an important rule by which I live
- On balance, tends to be good/Bad
- Produces the greatest/Least utility
- Maximizes/Minimizes benefits while minimizes/maximizes harm
- Leads to the greatest/Least good for the greatest number
- Results in a positive/Negative cost-benefit ratio
- Maximizes/Minimizes pleasure

Deontology Scales:
- Violates/Does not violate an unwritten contract
- Violates/Does not violate my ideas of fairness
- Morally right/Not morally right
- Obligated/Not obligated to act this way
- Violates/Does not violate an unspoken promise

In addition, each respondent was asked to indicate the probability that (s) he would behave in the same manner as did the individual in the scenario. This rating was done on a seven point scale anchored by highly probable/highly improbable.

Scenario A:

A person bought a new car from a franchised automobile dealership in the local area. Eight months after the car was purchased, he began having problems with the transmission. He took the car back to the dealer, and some minor adjustments were made. During the next few months he continually had a similar problem with the transmission slipping. Each time the dealer made only minor adjustments on the car. Again, during the thirteenth month after the car had been bought, the man returned to the dealer because the transmission still was not functioning properly. At this time, the transmission was completely overhauled.

Action: Since the warranty was for only one year (12 months from the date of purchase), the dealer charged the full price for parts and labor.

Scenario B:

A young man, recently hired as a salesman for a local retail store, has been working very hard to favorably impress his boss with his selling ability. At times, this young man, anxious for an order, has been a little over-eager. To get the order, he exaggerates the value of the item or withholds relevant information concerning the product he is trying to sell. No fraud or deceit is intended by his actions, he is simply over-eager.

Action: His boss, the owner of the retail store, is aware of the salesman's actions but he has done nothing to stop such practice.

Scenario C:

A retail grocery chain operates several stores throughout the local area including one in the city's ghetto area. Independent studies have shown that prices do tend to be higher and there is less of a selection of products in this particular store than in the other locations.

Action: On the day welfare checks are received in the area of the city, the retailer increases prices on all of his merchandise.

Fig. 15.2 Scenarios used in the study

The Reliability and Validity of the Scales

The reliability and validity of the measuring instrument are crucial to the objectives of this research. Consequently, the reliability of the instrument was examined using Cronbach's alpha to assess the internal consistency of the instrument. Because three different measures were taken (one for each of the scenarios), three different coefficient alphas were calculated. Coefficient alpha for each of the three scenarios ranged from 0.85 for Scenario A to 0.87 for Scenarios B and C. These are relatively high reliability measures indicating a high degree of internal consistency among the scale items further suggesting that they all belong to the same domain of content (Nunnally 1967, p. 226). In addition, the reliability measures compare favorably to those reliability measures obtained in other marketing research efforts (Peter 1979).

Several measures of validity were used. Scale items were broken down into the different philosophical strains which they purport to measure and which are shown in Fig. 15.1. To the extent that they converge, operationalized by high intraclass correlations, the items can be said to measure a common ethical philosophy. The relativism scales evidenced the highest degree of convergence (average $r = 0.54$), followed by the justice scales (average $r = 0.53$), the utilitarian scales (average $r = 0.42$), the deontology scales (average $r = 0.31$), and finally the egoist scales (average $r = 0.20$). No measure of divergence was made. However, many of the individual scale items correlated highly with items in other classes indicating some lack of divergence, perhaps attributable to the high degree of internal consistency and/or possible conceptual overlap of the different moral philosophies.

A second validity measure involved the average correlations between the grouped item evaluations of the situations and a seven point univariate measure (ethical/unethical) of the evaluation of the situation. The correlations were relatively high. The relativism scales had the highest average correlation with the single ethics measure. The correlation for Scenario A was 0.41, for Scenarios B and C 0.57 and 0.62 respectively. The next highest average correlations were for the justice scales: 0.34, 0.56, and 0.49, while the utilitarian scales correlated 0.22, 0.38, and 0.38 for the three scenarios. Finally, the egoist scales correlated 0.19, 0.32, and 0.30. The relatively high and consistent correlations between the item pooled scales and the univariate measure of ethics compares favorably to other correlations between attitude models and univariate measures of affect (see: Mazis et al. 1974) indicating a relatively strong degree of construct validity.

Results

The evaluations of the three different scenarios were subjected to a factor analysis using an orthogonal rotation. An orthogonal rotation was chosen to provide as maximally different structures as possible. Highly correlated factors, such as those obtained with an oblique rotation, are sometimes difficult to distinguish from one another (Tabachnick and Fidell 1983, p. 401). It was felt that identification of the character of the factors was a key consideration to the study and thus an orthogonal rotation was performed.

The factor analysis produced ten factors for Scenario A which explained 62% of the variance in the individual items. Five factors, each explaining 60% of the variance were generated from Scenarios B and C. In all cases, only those factors with an eigenvalue greater than one were retained for subsequent analysis.

Substantial parallelism existed between the factors for Scenarios B and C, but the results for Scenario A were different in both the number of factors and their content. This difference might be accounted for by the following possible explanations. First, Scenario A was the first scenario presented to the respondents and personal decision criteria were not yet in place to make the evaluations. Thus the difference in factor patterns may be due to a "practice effect". This would suggest that the respondents needed to become more familiar and comfortable with the evaluative criteria. Second, the differences in the scenarios may have radically changed the decision criteria and their organization. Thus, a situation effect might have occurred. Finally, the personalized nature of Scenario A (i.e., a single individual was injured as opposed to the somewhat more generalized character or injury where several individuals were injured) may have elicited a different organization of response criteria from the respondents. Because of the radically different structure of Scenario A, the remaining analysis will concentrate on the results obtained from Scenarios B and C.

The results of the study will be presented by examination of each of the hypotheses. Because of the interrelatedness of hypothesis one and hypothesis two, they will be discussed together.

Hypothesis One and Hypothesis Two

Comparing the factor patterns of the evaluations of Scenarios B and C with the expected patterns developed on an a priori basis argues for rejection of Hypothesis 1. The comparisons are shown in Table 15.1. The factor patterns that emerged bear little resemblance to the hypothesized patterns, leading to the conclusion that individuals do not use either a purely deontological or utilitarian or any other philosophically based set of criteria in evaluating the ethical content of marketing activities. For example, in the results from Scenario B, the first and most significant factor contained three justice, two utilitarian, three relativist, one deontological, and one egoist item. The second factor contained five utilitarian, three egoist, and one relativist item. While it is possible to describe this factor (on a *post hoc* basis) as teleological in character, it must also be noted that respondents appeared to have combined two radically different teleological philosophies (egoism and utilitarianism). The third factor contained three deontological items, two egoist, one justice and one relativist item. Factor four was primarily deontological, with two of the three items being

Table 15.1 Factor relationships for thirty scale items on two scenarios

Scale items	Factor structures				*A priori* judgement of normative philosophy
	B[a]	C	B	C	
Just/unjust	1[b]	1	0.79	0.84	Justice
Fair/unfair	1	1	0.78	0.81	Justice
On balance tends to be good/bad	1	1	0.66	0.76	Utilitarianism
Individually acceptable/unacceptable	1	1	0.65	0.68	Relativism
OK/Not OK if actions can be justified by their consequences	1	1	0.59	0.73	Utilitarianism
Culturally acceptable /unacceptable	1	1	0.57	0.66	Relativism
Acceptable/unacceptable to people I most desire	1	1	0.52	0.81	Relativism
Violates/does not violate my ideas of fairness	1	1	–0.63	–0.62	Justice/Deontology
Selfish/not selfish	1	5	–0.46	0.66	Egoism
Obligated/not obligated to act this way	3	1	0.71	0.73	Deontology
Duty bound/not duty bound to act this way	3	1	0.67	0.58	Deontology
Morally right/not morally right	3	1	0.58	0.83	Deontology
Acceptable/unacceptable to my family	3	1	0.58	0.71	Relativism
Self sacrificing/not self sacrificing	3	1	0.57	0.36	Egoism
Results/does not result in an equal distribution of good and bad	3	1	0.45	0.62	Justice
Leads to the greatest/least good for the greatest number	3	1	0.60	0.62	Utilitarianism
Under no moral obligation/morally obligated to act otherwise	3	2	0.41	0.44	Egoism
Results in a positive/negative cost-benefit ratio	2	2	0.76	0.68	Utilitarianism
Produces the greatest/least utility	2	2	0.71	0.72	Utilitarianism
Self promoting/not self promoting	2	2	0.69	0.47	Egoism
Maximizes/minimizes benefits while minimizes/maximizes harm	2	2	0.63	0.47	Utilitarianism
In the best interests/not in the best interests of the company	2	2	0.62	0.69	Egoism
Efficient/inefficient	2	2	0.59	0.66	Utilitarianism
Maximizes/minimizes pleasure	2	2	0.58	0.49	Utilitarianism
Personally/not personally satisfying	2	2	0.53	0.50	Egoism

(continued)

Table 15.1 (continued)

Scale items	Factor structures				*A priori* judgement of normative philosophy
	B[a]	C	B	C	
Traditionally/not traditionally acceptable	2	1	0.49	0.61	Relativism
Violates/does not violate an unwritten contract	4	3	0.73	0.81	Deontology
Violates/does not violate an unspoken promise	4	3	0.68	0.84	Deontology
Compromises/does not compromise an important rule by which I live	3	4	0.67	–0.62	Utilitarianism
Prudent/not prudent	5	4	0.70	0.76	Egoism

[a]Refers to scenario (see Fig. 15.2)
[b]Indicates on which factor an item loads most heavily

deontological and the third an ambiguous rule-based item that could be considered either deontological or rule utilitarian. The factors from the other scenarios produced similarly mixed results.

The results also argue in favor of rejecting hypothesis two. Individuals appear to organize and use the evaluative criteria differently from situation to situation. Table 15.1 indicates that respondents evaluated Scenario C (the least ethical situation) differently than they did Scenario B. The major difference appears to be the manner in which they combined factors one and three that emerged in evaluating Scenario B into one large factor in evaluating Scenario C. Thus, to the extent that the hypothesized items accurately measure the individual normative ethical philosophies, the evidence suggests that individuals do not use clearly defined normative ethical philosophies in evaluating the ethics of marketing activities.

Because of the similarity of the factor patterns that emerged from the evaluation of Scenarios B and C the attempt to name the underlying constructs focuses on the results from Scenario B. Factor one seems to identify learned, personalized values where ideas of justice and fairness are combined with ideas of individual and cultural acceptance. The construct seems to include those rules of society that the respondents have internalized but perhaps have not formalized in any specific manner. Alternatively, the construct identified by factor three seems to suggest a more formalized set of rules and duties, perhaps based on family and religious training since most of the respondents are indigenous to the so called "Bible Belt". A review of the text of Scenarios B and C is suggestive of why the two constructs might have been pulled together in the evaluation of Scenario C. Scenario B was judged to be the least ethically offensive ($x=5.15$) and therefore was less influenced by formalized rules but rather was dominated by broader cultural taboos. However, Scenario C was judged the most ethically offensive ($x=6.42$) and consequently respondents may have invoked not only the cultural guidelines but also the formal rules of their upbringing. This influence may also be related to the level of involvement with the two scenarios. This cannot be determined since no check on involvement was made.

The underlying construct identified by factor two (Scenario B) might be labeled the psychologically removed, cognitive calculus factor. The construct seems to represent the rational side of the respondent. However, the construct does not seem to separate personal welfare from the welfare of society. The combination of egoism and utilitarianism descriptors that are part of the factor seem to support the lack of separation that occurred.

Factor four (Scenario B) seems to represent a construct that could be described as an internalized, situational commitment. If the situation is ego- involving arising from an implied personal commitment (e.g., if the individual perceives the action as a violation of an unspoken promise), the reaction to the situation will be different from those situations which do not evoke a personal commitment. This factor exactly paralleled factor three for Scenario C.

Table 15.2 Correlations with dependent variables (significance)

	Scenario B (least unethical)		Scenario C (most unethical)	
Factors[a]	7 point ethical/ unethical	Probability of response	7 point ethical/ unethical	Probability of response
Factor # 1	0.71[b]/0.50 (0.0001)	−0.54/0.29 (0.0001)	0.78/0.61 (0.0001)	−0.67/0.45 (0.0001)
Factor #2	0.22/0.05 (0.0001)	−0.34/0.12 (0.0001)	0.15/0.02 (0.03)	−0.23/0.05 (0.0005)
Factor #3	0.27/0.07 (0.0001)	−0.23/0.05 (0.0005)	−0.08/0.006 NS	0.18/0.03 (0.008)
Factor #4	−0.21/0.04 (0.001)	−0.18/0.03 (0.009)	0.25/0.06 (0.0002)	−0.11/0.01 NS
Factor #5	0.05/0.003 NS	−0.12/0.01 NS	0.009/0.01 NS	−0.09/0.008 NS

[a]Factor scores were used for these correlations, and since the factors were generated using an orthogonal rotation, they are virtually uncorrelated

[b]r/r^2

Hypothesis Three

Hypothesis three suggests that individuals will organize the ethical evaluative criteria that they use in assessing the ethical content of marketing activities in the same manner that they do when they assess the probability of their own ethical behavior under similar circumstances. Table 15.2 shows the correlations and squared correlations between the factor scores for the two factor patterns (Scenarios B and C) with the seven point univariate measure of the ethical content of the scenarios and the seven point estimate of the respondent's probability of acting in a similar manner as the individuals in the scenarios.

The results suggest that individuals rely on similar patterns of criteria in evaluating the situation as they do in making an estimate of their own behavior. Factor one has the biggest impact on the evaluation as well as on their estimate of their own behavior under similar circumstances. Factor four (Scenario C) has a larger relative impact on the evaluation than it does on the assessment of the individual's behavior.

Overall, the results suggest that individuals tend to rely most heavily on one factor for making ethical evaluations of marketing activities ($r^2=0.50$ for Scenario B, and $r^2=0.61$ for Scenario C), and marginally so on the other factors. The same statement can be made for the probability estimate of the individual's behavior under similar circumstances.

Implications for Ethics Research

There are several implications that the results of this research have for the continued study of marketing ethics. First, this study has generated an initial set of scales which measure various dimensions of the different strains of moral philosophy.

These scales evidence a high degree of reliability and a modest degree of convergent validity. In addition, the scales correlate relatively highly with a univariate measure of the ethical content of situations. This would indicate that the scales embody a relatively high degree of construct validity. The value of these scales is to be realized in their application to other situations, respondent groups, under varying experimental conditions. Continued scale development is necessary.

Secondly, the results suggest that individuals do not use clearly delineated concepts of ethical philosophy in making ethical evaluations of marketing activities. This in turn suggests that models of the evaluation or decision making process should not rely solely on the philosophies of deontology or utilitarianism. The evidence presented in this study suggests that individuals typically evolve perspectives that can be measured using the concepts derived from the different ethical philosophies including relativism, egoism and justice theories. These derived perspectives may reflect, as Rest (1979) suggests, different stages in moral development, confusion in sorting out relatively descriptive elements of the cases, confusion in applying norms or maybe something else, for that matter a lack of awareness of the normative moral philosophies.

A third implication is that there appears to be no single standard of evaluation. That is, the nature and organization of the ethical evaluative criteria appear to be situation specific. It will be recalled that individuals used different patterns of criteria in evaluating the two different scenarios which were notably distinct with respect to the degree of ethical consequence contained within them. This may be a function of factors other than the degree of ethical consequence. Other factors might include harm to individuals as opposed to harm to a general aggregate, the level of personal involvement in the situation depicted, and the level of the individual's moral development, to name but a few.

Fourth, there is a question as to whether these patterns of ethical evaluative criteria are to be found in different groups of individuals. This study used students and the results may be limited in that regard. Similar studies of different groups of individuals may produce generalizations regarding the way in which individuals organize their ethical reactions to the ethical content of marketing activities. This same concern should also be extended to examine the cultural and subcultural implications of the different ethical theories.

References

Alexander, Cheryl S., and Henry Jay Becker. 1978. The use of vignettes in survey research. *Public Opinion Quarterly* 42: 93–104.

Beauchamp, Tom L., and Norman E. Bowie. 1983. *Ethical theory and business*, 2nd ed. Englewood Cliffs: Prentice-Hall, Inc.

Browning, John, and Noel B. Zabriskie. 1983. How ethical are industrial buyers? *Industrial Marketing Management* 12: 219–224.

DeGeorge, Richard R. 1986. *Business ethics*, 2nd ed. New York: Macmillan Publishing.

Donaldson, Thomas, and Patricia H. Werhane. 1983. *Ethical issues on business*, 2nd ed. Englewood Cliffs: Prentice-Hall, Inc.

Dornoff, Ronald J., and Clint B. Tankersley. 1975. Perceptual differences in market transactions: A source of consumer frustration. *Journal of Consumer Affairs* 9(Summer): 97–103.

Dubinsky, Alan J., and William Rudelius. 1980. Ethical beliefs: How students compare with industrial salespeople. In *Proceedings of the American Marketing Association Educators Conference*, 73–76. Chicago: American Marketing Association.

Ferrell, O.C., and Larry G. Gresham. 1985. A contingency framework for understanding ethical decision-making in marketing. *Journal of Marketing* 49(Summer): 87–96.

Hunt, Shelby, and Scott Vitell. 1986. A general theory of marketing ethics. *Journal of Macromarketing* 6(Spring): 5–16.

Kerlinger, Fred N. 1986. *Foundations of behavioral research*, 3rd ed. New York: Holt, Rinehart, and Winston.

Krugman, Dean M., and O.C. Ferrell. 1981. The organizational ethics of advertising: Corporate and agency views. *Journal of Advertising* 10: 21–30.

Mazis, Michael B., Olli T. Ahtola, and R.Eugene Klippel. 1974. A comparison of four multi-attribute models in the prediction of consumer attitudes. *Journal of Consumer Research* 2(June): 38–52.

Nunnally, Jum C. 1967. *Psychometric theory*. New York: McGraw-Hill Book Company.

Peter, J.Paul. 1979. Reliability: A review of psychometric basics and recent marketing practices. *Journal of Marketing Research* XVI(February): 6–17.

Reidenbach, R Eric, and Sharon Grimes. 1985. How concept knowledge affects concept evaluations. *Journal of Innovation Management* 14(Winter): 25–26.

Rest, James R. 1979. *Development in judging moral issues*. Minneapolis: University of Minnesota Press.

Robin, Donald P., and R.Eric Reidenbach. 1987. Social responsibility, ethics, and marketing strategy. Closing the gap between concept and application. *Journal of Marketing* 51(January): 44–58.

Shuptrine, F.Kelly. 1979. Evaluating the ethics of marketing practices: Student perceptions. In *Proceedings of the American Marketing Association Educators Conference*, 124–127. Chicago: American Marketing Association.

Sturdivant, Frederick D., and A.Benton Cocanoughen. 1973. What are ethical marketing practices? *Harvard Business Review* 51(November–December): 10–12.

Tabachnick, Barbara G., and Linda S. Fidell. 1983. *Using multivariate statistics*. New York: Harper & Row, Publishers.

Chapter 16
Differences in Ethical Perceptions Between Male and Female Managers: Myth or Reality?

Jeaneen M. Kidwell, Robert E. Stevens, and Art L. Bethke

Introduction

As recently as 15 years ago very few women pursued careers in management (*Time*, March 10 1964). Because of this the study of pertinent issues in the management field focused on the male manager. The 1980s, however, present quite a contrasting picture.

Today women are entering management careers in record numbers, and therefore psychologists and organizational behavior theorists are faced with a new challenge in the study of those same pertinent issues. One specific issue involves the area of ethical management decision making. As Mark Pastin, editor of *Business Horizons* magazine stated:

> As management problems become more complex, they become more ethical. As management problems become more ethical, they become more complex. (Pastin 1983).

An illustration of this can be found in the Bendix case. In 1979, Mary Cunningham, a 28-year-old Harvard Business School graduate, was hired by William Agee, 43, Chairman of Bendix Corporation, to serve as his executive assistant. Within a year Agee promoted Cunningham to the position of vice-president for corporate and

J.M. Kidwell
Avon Products, Inc., 701 Orange Drove Av., Number 106,
South Pasadena, CA 91030, USA

R.E. Stevens (✉)
Department of Marketing, Northeast Louisiana
University, Monroe, LA, USA
e-mail: rstevens@sosu.edu

A.L. Bethke
Department of Management, Northeast Louisiana
University, Monroe, LA, USA

A.C. Michalos and D.C. Poff (eds.), *Citation Classics from the Journal of Business Ethics*, Advances in Business Ethics Research 2,
DOI 10.1007/978-94-007-4126-3_16,

public affairs (Velasquez 1983). Rumors quickly spread about the relationship between Agee and Cunningham and sparks began to fly at Bendix. Although the then-married Agee denied all rumors, claiming that Ms. Cunningham was a “close friend and a friend of my family”, the pressure became too much and in October of 1980 Cunningham resigned from Bendix (Velasquez 1983). Since that time William Agee and Mary Cunningham have been married.

Did Mary Cunningham’s rapid rise at Bendix have anything to do with her personal relationship with William Agee? Were the decisions and behaviors of Agee and Cunningham ethical or unethical? If Ms. Cunningham had been a ‘he’ instead of a ‘she’ would the issue have arisen at all? Although we may never arrive at a consensus on what is right and what is wrong, in the Bendix Case, it is essential that the ethical dilemma presented not be ignored.

Prior research has dealt with the practice of ethical governance in business (Andrews 1984), and professional codes of ethics in management (Mc-Nulty 1975). Additional research has studied the ethics of businessmen (Brennan et al. 1961), and the ethics of managers as a whole (Ruch and Newstrom 1975). However, little published research is available which specifically compares and contrasts the ethical decisions of male and female managers. This study was undertaken for the purpose of filling that gap.

Research Objectives

The specific objectives of this study were:

1. To identify whether or not differences existed between the ethical decisions of male and female managers.
2. If differences do exist, to identify the areas in which they occur.
3. To determine how each gender perceived their counterparts would respond to the same ethical decision making situations.
4. To determine if there were business or demographic variables which could be used to predict the ethical decision responses of managers whether male or female.

Research Methodology

The population of interest in this study consisted of men and women, in comparable managerial positions. Given the pilot nature of the study, a nonprobability, quota sampling procedure was employed. Self-administered questionnaires were hand delivered to 60 male and 60 female managers in three midwestern states. Since a person other than the researcher delivered the questionnaires, they were briefed on the purpose of the study and asked to adhere to that purpose by not biasing their choices of managers who would be asked to participate in the study. To increase the response rate a cover letter was attached to each questionnaire.

The questionnaires were used to gain information in three areas: business background, ethical decisions, and demographic characteristics. To measure ethical decisions a closed response questionnaire was chosen. Two-way frequencies and a median version of the chi-square test were used to test for significant differences between all variables. Also, the *t*-test for independent means was utilized to test for significant differences in business background/ethical decision responses and demographic characteristics/ethical decision responses. A 0.05 level of significance was used.

Findings

Of the 120 questionnaires distributed, 107 were returned; a response rate of 89%. Because a predetermined sample size had been established, only questionnaires from the first 50 male and first 50 female respondents were used. Table 16.1 provides a breakdown of respondent characteristics.

Two of the objectives of this study were to identify whether differences existed between the ethical decisions of male and female managers and, if they did exist to identify areas in which the differences occurred. To obtain this information respondents were asked to rate 17 ethical decision situations by assigning each a score between 1 and 5; with 1 equaling 'Very Unethical' and 5 signifying "Not At All Unethical". Results showed a significant difference between the responses of men and women in only *one* ethical situation – *concealing one's errors.* When comparing responses to that decision situation it was found that females viewed such behavior as more unethical than did their male counterparts. Twenty-four percent of female respondents answered that concealing one's errors was very unethical, while only 15% of males responded in like manner. Although 2% of the males responded that the situation was not at all unethical, none of the females responded that way. See Table 16.2 for the results of the self ratings.

Another objective of the study was to determine how each gender perceived their counterparts would respond to the same set of ethical decision situations. Findings revealed several significant differences. Men viewed their female counterparts as significantly different than themselves in every situation *except* concealing one's errors. Women, on the other hand, felt that men would react in a different manner in every situation except 'Not reporting other's violations of company rules and policies.' Table 16.3 provides a breakdown of the decision situations and the mean scores associated with the perceptions of the genders.

The results showed only one area where significant differences existed between males and females on what they considered to be ethical. However, there were significant differences in 16 out of 17 situations when they rated the ethical behavior of their male/female counterparts, i.e., males rated females as being significantly less ethical than themselves and vice versa.

The last objective of the study was to determine if there were business background or demographic variables which could be used to predict the ethical decision responses

Table 16.1 Characteristics of respondents

Gender:		Age:	
Male	50%	Under 25	4%
Female	50%	25–34	31%
		35–44	33%
		45–54	20%
Number of years in work force:		Marital status:	
Less than 1	3%	Single	19%
1 but less than 6	19%	Married	74%
6 but less than 11	21%	Divorced	6%
11 or more	57%	Widowed	1%
Management level:		Education:	
Supervisory	57%	High school/GED	11%
Middle	39%	Attended college	15%
Upper	3%	College graduate	36%
		Graduate work	38%
Number of employees supervised:		Before tax annual income:	
0	10%	Under $20,000	9%
1–5	36%	$20,000–$34,999	30%
6–10	22%	$35,000–$49,999	26%
More than 10	32%	$50,000–$64,999	19%
		$65,000 and over	16%
Gender of supervisor:			
Male	85%	Religious preference:	
Female	15%	Protestant	82%
		Catholic	15%
		Jewish	0%
		Other	3%
Industry:			
Finance/banking	9%		
Oil and gas	71%		
Consumer goods	20%	Church attendance:	
		More than weekly	11%
Resident state:		Weekly	27%
Oklahoma	86%	Monthly	16%
Illinois	11%	Special occasions	27%
Missouri	3%	Rarely, if ever	18%

of managers. Responses to several of the survey questions were analyzed against the responses to the ethical decision making situations. Variables analyzed were:

1. Number of years in the work force
2. Age
3. Highest level of education attained, to date
4. Before tax annual income level
5. Religious preference
6. Frequency of church attendance

Table 16.2 Ethical decision situations[a]

Situation	Mean score Males	Mean score Females
Using company services for personal use	2.38	2.34
Padding an expense account up to 10%	1.50	1.52
Padding an expense account in excess of 10%	1.24	1.16
Giving gifts/favors in exchange for preferential treatment	1.56	1.64
Taking longer than necessary to do a job	2.34	1.84
Doing personal business on company time	2.64	2.74
Divulging confidential information	1.22	1.22
Concealing one's errors	2.06[b]	1.80[b]
Passing blame for errors to an innocent co-worker	1.24	1.10
Claiming credit for someone else's work	1.56	1.28
Falsifying time/quality reports	1.30	1.28
Calling in sick to take a day off	1.90	1.82
Authorizing a subordinate to violate company rules or policies	1.62	1.26
Using company materials and supplies for personal use	2.44	2.70
Accepting gifts/favors in exchange for preferential treatment	1.50	1.66
Taking extra personal time (long lunches, late arrivals,…)	2.54	2.52
Not reporting others' violations of company rules and policies	2.66	2.56

Self ratings (1 = very unethical, 5 = not at all unethical)

[a]Reprinted by permission of the publisher, from Ruch and Newstrom (1975), p. 18. © 1975 AMACOM, a division of American Management Associations, New York

[b]Denotes a significant difference at the 0.05 level of significance

Table 16.3 Ethical decision situations

Situation	Mean score How females view males	Mean score How males view females
Using company services for personal use	2.68*	2.29*
Padding an expense account up to 10%	2.46*	1.32*
Padding an expense account in excess of 10%	1.80*	1.18*
Giving gifts/favors in exchange for preferential treatment	2.40*	1.72*
Taking longer than necessary to do a job	2.14*	2.28*
Doing personal business on company time	3.14*	2.72*
Divulging confidential information	1.32*	1.63*
Concealing one's errors	2.30*	2.08
Passing blame for errors to an innocent co-worker	1.78*	1.32*
Claiming credit for someone else's work	2.22*	1.62*
Falsifying time/quality reports	1.72*	1.42*
Calling in sick to take a day off	2.26*	2.41*
Authorizing a subordinate to violate company rules or policies	1.78*	1.72*
Using company materials and supplies for personal use	3.06*	2.64*
Accepting gifts/favors in exchange for preferential treatment	2.16*	1.78*
Taking extra personal time (long lunches, late arrivals,…)	3.28*	2.72*
Not reporting others' violations of company rules and policies	2.54	2.52*

Perceptions of the opposite gender (1 = very unethical, 5 = not at all unethical)

*Denotes a significant difference at the 0.05 level of significance

Results showed that the only characteristic which had a consistent significance on the entire set of decision situations was number of years in the work force. According to the chi-square test and t-test for independent means, those respondents who had been employed in the work force for a longer period of time tended to exhibit more ethical responses to the decision making situations.

Conclusions and Implications

One major finding of this study was that male and female managers generally do not differ in their perception of what is ethical and what is unethical. With only one exception they tended to agree completely regarding what one should or shouldn't do in the ethical decision situations they were presented with. The only significant difference in responses was in the decision situation of whether or not to conceal one's errors. In this decision situation, male managers indicated more of a propensity to conceal errors than did the female managers. Perhaps the explanation for that could be found in the larger culture and the socialization process. Before these managers entered the work force they all received the role prescriptions that the larger society metes out. Male managers enter the world of work with a general idea of what they *must* do and *cannot* do. The same, of course, is true for females. One common stereotype that exists is that men shouldn't make mistakes or errors. Obviously, given the role prescription, men would be more inclined than females to conceal one's errors. Generally though, this study tends to confirm that when faced with decision situations that contain an ethical component both male and female managers tend to react the same. Further evidence that there are few differences between male and female managers.

More significant was the second major finding of the study. When male and female managers were asked to estimate the ethics of the opposite sex in each of the decision situations, almost universally each sex viewed the opposite sex as being more unethical than themselves. The significance of this is that one tends to act as one perceives. When male managers have to interact with female managers in the organization and this interaction includes an ethical component then, given each's perception of the other, major problems could develop, communications could breakdown and cooperative behaviors could cease. The solution to this potential problem scenario is perhaps suggested in the third major finding, that years in the work force tended to correlate positively with ethical decision making. Over time, male and female managers will learn that the other sex is no more unethical than themselves. Other evidence also suggests that as female managers became more commonplace in the work force, the incidence of stereotypical behaviors tended to decrease and individuals started treating others as individuals regardless of sex.

References

Andrews, Kenneth R. 1984. Difficulties in overseeing ethical policy. *California Management Review* 26(Summer): 133–137.

Brennan Jr., John, Valtz James, Shallenberger John, and Stanton Vincent. 1961. How ethical are businessmen? *Harvard Business Review* 39(July–August): 6–10.

McNulty, Nancy. 1975. And now, professional codes for the practice of management. . . but not in the U.S. *The Conference Board Record* 26(April): 21–25.

Pastin, Mark. 1983. Why? *Business Horizons* 13(January–February): 2.

Ruch, William, and John Newstrom. 1975. How unethical are we? *Supervisory Management* 8(November): 16–21.

*Time.*1964. Difference that sex makes. March 20.

Velasquez, Manuel. 1983. Organizational statesmanship and dirty politics: Ethical guidelines for the organizational politician. *Organizational Dynamics* 12(Autumn): 65–68.

Chapter 17
Business Ethics: A Literature Review with a Focus on Marketing Ethics

John Tsalikis and David J. Fritzsche

The ethical sensitivity of all professionals – lawyers, physicians, educators, and business executives – has come under close scrutiny in recent years. Post-Watergate morality has dictated that the past level of ethics exhibited by professionals is no longer adequate and perhaps never was. This renewed ethical concern represents the recurrence of an established issue: the lack of ethical behavior exhibited by many persons in positions of responsibility.

New articles appear almost daily in newspapers stating that another company has come under investigation by the justice Department for illegal activities such as illegal campaign contributions, bribes to foreign countries, insider trading, etc. In response to these pronouncements, policy statements on business ethics have poured forth from corporations, recognizing the apparent fact that some of this country's most distinguished executives do not care how results are obtained, even if it means breaking the law.

In addition, Frederick (1986) argues that the social environment is bound to become more turbulent and disorderly. Scott and Mitchell (1985) underscore that claim with their concern over widespread corruption. Scott and Mitchell refer to the plethora of articles reporting such managerial excesses as exhorbitant bonuses, golden parachutes, "greenmail", ego-motivated takeover wars, and even fraud.

The most scathing indictment on the state of corporate ethics was voiced by Amitai Etzioni who concluded that in the past decade, two-thirds of the 500 largest U.S. corporations have been involved in varying degrees in some form of illegal behavior (Gellerman 1986).

J. Tsalikis (✉)
Marketing Department, Florida International University,
University Park, Miami, FL 33199, USA
e-mail: tsalikis@fiu.edu

D.J. Fritzsche
School of Business Administration, Marketing Department,
University of Portland, Portland, OR, USA

A.C. Michalos and D.C. Poff (eds.), *Citation Classics from the Journal of Business Ethics*, Advances in Business Ethics Research 2,
DOI 10.1007/978-94-007-4126-3_17,

However, the majority of situations that business people face today do not involve strictly legal matters. Instead they must make judgments concerning what is "right" or ethical to do. It is one of the tasks of ethics to distinguish between ethical and unethical business practices. The task of determining what is ethical or not is not easy. Kenneth Andrews once said, "if it's black and white, and a man has normal courage and security, he'll say no. It's in the gray areas that the businessman may more likely flounder."

Johnson (1981) argues that "most business decisions involve choices between two or more goods or two undesirable options." A related challenge to ethical decision making is that sometimes good and evil seem to be joint products. In other words, a desirable result is accompanied by a negative one. An example of this is the pollution and exhaustion of resources which often accompanies high standards of living and technology.

Within the business firm, the functional area most closely related to ethical abuse is marketing. This is because marketing is the function of business charged with communicating and openly satisfying customers. Thus, marketing is closest to the public view and, consequently, is subject to considerable societal analysis and scrutiny (Murphy and Laczniak 1981).

This paper will review the literature on business ethics with a special focus in marketing ethics. In addition, the majority of the reviewed literature has an American perspective. For an excellent collection of articles dealing with business ethics in Canada see Poff and Waluchow (1987). However, before proceeding any further it is necessary to: (1) define ethics, and (2) present the various philosophical normative theories of ethics.

Definition of Ethics

"Unethical" acts were committed throughout history. Christianity has Adam eating the forbidden fruit, Cain murdering his brother. The majority of the ancient Greek philosophers devoted much of their time to developing theories of ethics. The early theories studied ethics from a normative perspective, meaning that they were concerned with "constructing and justifying the moral standards and codes that one ought to follow" (Vitell 1986). On the other side, a positive perspective of ethics attempts to describe and explain how individuals actually behave in ethical situations.

One of the major preoccupations of ethical theorists was to create a definition of ethics. As with the majority of concepts, ethics was defined differently by different theorists.

Beauchamp and Bowie (1983, p. 3) define ethics as the "inquiry into theories of what is good and evil and into what is right and wrong, and thus is inquiry into what we ought and ought not to do." Similarly, Runes (1964, pp. 98–100) states that "ethical behavior refers to 'just' or 'right' standards of behavior between parties in a situation." On the same line, Barry (1979a, b) defines ethics as "the study of what constitutes good and bad human conduct, including related actions and values."

Ethics, according to DeGeorge (1982, pp. 13–15), is the study of morality. DeGeorge argues that:

> Morality is a term used to cover those practices and activities that are considered importantly right and wrong, the rules which govern those activities, and the values that are imbedded, fostered, or pursued by those activities and practices. The morality of a society is related to its mores or the customs accepted by a society or group as being the right and wrong ways to act, as well as to the laws of a society which add legal prohibitions and sanctions to many activities considered to be immoral.

Similarly, Taylor (1975, p. 1) defines ethics as an "inquiry into the nature and grounds of morality," where morality means "moral judgments, standards, and rules of conduct." Vitell (1986) applied Taylor's definition to define marketing ethics as "an inquiry into the nature and grounds of moral judgments, standards, and rules of conduct relating to marketing decisions and marketing situations."

From the above definitions of ethics, we see that the term ethics is used interchangeably with morals. Although this usage is acceptable, it is more accurate to restrict the terms morals and morality to the conduct itself. The terms ethics and ethical refer to the study of moral conduct or to the code one follows.

For an extensive treatment of "business ethics" definitions see Lewis (1985).

Philosophical Normative Ethical Theories

Recognizing that the number of these theories is quite significant, only the ethical theories most commonly refered to in the business literature will be presented.

The ethical theories are usually divided into three groups: (1) consequential theories – those that deal exclusively with the consequences of an action; (2) single-rule nonconsequential – those that deal with a single rule; and (3) multiple-rule nonconsequential – those that deal with multiple rules. Some philosophers call the first group teleological, while group two they call deontological. Group three is a hybrid of both teleological and deontological theories.

Cavanagh et al. (1981) divided the theories of ethics into three categories: (1) utilitarian theories – evaluating behavior in terms of their consequences; (2) theories of rights – emphasizing the entitlements or rights of individuals, including the right to free consent, the right to privacy, the right to freedom of conscience, the right to free speech, and the right to due process; (3) theories of justice – focusing on the distributional effects of actions.

Consequential Theories

Traditionally, many theorists contend that the moral rightness of an action can be determined by looking at its consequences. If the consequences are good, the act is ethical; if bad, the act is unethical. In other words, an ethical act is one that produces at least as great a ratio of good to evil as any other course. An obvious question arises in regard to the consequences. In deciding what to do should we consider the consequences only to oneself? Or should one consider them with respect to everyone involved? That decision hinges on the two main consequential theories – egoism and utilitarianism.

Egoism

Egoism contends that an act is ethical when it promotes the individual's best longterm interests. If an action produces a greater ratio of good to evil for the individual in the long run than any other alternative, then that action is ethical. A major misconception is that all egoists are exponents of hedonism – the view that only pleasure is good in itself and worth seeking. True, some egoists are hedonistic, as was the ancient Greek philosopher Epicurus. But other egoists identify the good with knowledge, rational self-interest and self-actualization.

Among the weaknesses of ethical egoism are: (a) ethical egoism would take no stand against even the most blatant business practices, e.g. discrimination, pollution, unsafe products, etc., and (b) egoism cannot resolve conflicts of egoistic interests among two individuals.

Utilitarianism

Utilitarianism asserts that we should always act so as to produce the greatest ratio of good to evil for everyone. It emphasizes the best interest of everyone involved with the action. As originally formulated by notable reformers Jeremy Bentham and John Stuart Mill, utilitarianism has been associated with reform or social improvement.

Utilitarianism argues that if it were possible to accurately calculate pleasure and pain, we would subtract the total unhappiness from the total happiness our action would produce, and choose the action which produces the greatest net happiness. While all utilitarians agree on the principle of greatest net utility, they disagree on how this principle should be applied. Some utilitarians would apply it to the act itself; others, to the rule the act falls under. Thus we get act utilitarians and rule utilitarians.

Act utilitarianism maintains that the right act is the one that produces the greatest ratio of good to evil for all concerned. On the other side, rule utilitarians ask us to determine the worth of the rule under which an action falls. If keeping the rule produces more total good than breaking it, we should keep it.

Act utilitarianism has provided the basis for an ethical position termed situational ethics proposed by Joseph Fletcher. Fletcher (1966) advocates acting in a way that produces the most "Christian love", that is, the greatest amount of love fulfillment and benevolence. For Fletcher it is crucial when making moral decisions to be fully aware of all the facts surrounding the case, as well as the probable consequences of each alternative. But he also argues that after all calculations have been completed, one must choose the act that will best serve "love" as defined in the Christian tradition.

Fletcher views situational ethics as one of three primary avenues for making moral decisions. The other two are: (a) the legalistic, which contends that moral rules are absolute laws that must always be obeyed; and (b) the antinomian, which contends that no guidelines exist, that each situation is unique and requires a new decision.

Among the weaknesses of utilitarianism are: (a) it seems to ignore actions that are wrong in themselves – with utilitarianism the ends justify the means which sometimes can be unethical; and (b) the principle of utility may come into conflict with that of justice.

The views of utilitarianism seem to come out of the writings of Douglas Sherwin. Sherwin (1983) asks the question "what does it mean to be an ethical business person?" In order to answer that question he presented business as being a system of interdependent members that can thrive only when all its members are given equal emphasis. So, "to act ethically a manager has to ensure that the owners, employees, and customers all share fairly in the business's gain."

Sherwin also argues that the American society has purposefully left a place for business among its institutions to secure economic performance in the production and distribution of goods and services. It follows that business leaders have the responsibility to try to deliver the benefits society seeks through this strategy. The values that govern their behavior must therefore be grounded in this purpose, must implement it, and must be constrained by it. Sherwin seems to argue that a business person is behaving ethically if he/she behaves according to the society's best interest. His view seems to correspond with the view of utilitarianism.

Single-Rule Nonconsequential Theories

Whereas consequential theories argue that we should consider the consequences of an action in evaluating its morality, nonconsequential theories contend that we should consider other factors. Some such theories have even argued that we should not consider consequences at all. One such theory found considerable acceptance in business: the Golden Rule.

Golden Rule

In modern culture, the Golden Rule is most commonly interpreted as, "Do unto others as you'd have them do unto you." It commands us to treat others the way we would want to be treated. The other single-rule nonconsequential theory is credited to Kant (1959).

Kant's Categorical Imperative

Kant's ethical theory stands as the premier illustration of a purely deontological theory, one that attempts to exclude a consideration of consequences in ethical decision making. To understand Kant's theory one should grasp the concept of "good will" or, in a loose interpretation, good intentions. Contained in good will is the concept of duty. Only when we act from duty do our actions have moral worth. Still we are left wondering what duties we have and how we can know them. Kant believes that through reason alone we could arrive at a moral law, based not on religion like the Golden Rule, nor on empirical evidence relating to consequences as in utilitarianism. If we arrive at such a law, it would oblige everyone without exception to follow it. Kant believes that he formulated such a law in his "categorical imperative." Kant's categorical imperative says that we should act in such a way that we could wish the maxim or principle of our action to become a universal law.

Multiple-Rule Nonconsequential Theories

Unlike single-rule nonconsequential theories, some nonconsequential theories, while relying on factors other than consequences in determining the morality of an action, appeal not to one rule, but several. Three such theories deserve special attention.

Ross's Prima Facie Duties

Ross's theory is seen as an attempt to join aspects of utilitarianism with those of Kantianism. Ross (1939) believes that it is necessary to introduce consequences into ethical decision making while insisting that consequences alone donot make an act right. Ross contends that there are duties or obligations which bind us morally. In any ethical decision, we should weigh options with respect to the duties involved, and from the alternatives determine the duty that is most obligatory. So, an act may fall under a number of duties. For example, a business person may have the duty to maximize profits and, at the same time, be obliged to refrain from injuring people. The problem here lies in choosing the most obligatory duty.

To solve this problem Ross proposes "prima facie duties." The term prima facie means "at first sight" or "on the surface." By prima facie duties, Ross means the duties that at first sight dictate what we should do when other moral factors are not considered. In other words, a prima facie duty is one we recognize at first sight as being obligatory when all other things arc equal and when there are no conflicting duties.

Ross presents six main categories of prima facie duties:

1. Duties of fidelity – included are the duty not to lie, the duty to remain faithful to contracts, and the duty to keep promises.
2. Duties of gratitude.
3. Duties of justice.
4. Duties of beneficence – those that rely on the fact that there are other people in the world whose happiness we can improve.
5. Duties of self-improvement.
6. Duties of noninjury.

Rawl's Maximin Principle of Justice

Rawls (1971) proposes a theory of ethics that tries to use the strengths of consequential and nonconsequential ethics while avoiding their pitfalls. Rawls proposes two principles to ensure justice: the equal liberty principle and the difference principle. By equality Rawls means the impartial and equitable administration and application of rules which define a practice. In other words, each person participating in a practice or affected by it should have an equal right to the greatest amount of liberty that is compatible with a like liberty for all.

Crucial to any theory of social justice is the determination of when inequality is permissible. After all, a just society is not one in which all are equal, but one in which inequalities are justifiable. Rawls addresses this problem with his difference principle. The difference principle defines what kinds of inequalities are permissible. It specifies under what conditions the equal liberty principle may be violated.

Garrett's Principle of Proportionality

According to Garrett (1966), any moral decision involves three elements: what we intend, how we carry out the intention, and what happens (or intention, means, and end). We have seen that consequentialists are primarily concerned with the end of an action, whereas nonconsequentialists generally put more emphasis on the intention behind it (as in Kant's case) or on one or more characteristics of the means itself. In the proportionality principle, Garrett brings together intention, means, and end to form a synthesis. Garrett's principle of proportionality states:

> I am responsible for whatever I will as a means or an end. If both the means and the end I am willing are good in and of themselves, I may ethically permit or risk the foreseen but unwilled side effects if, and only if, I have a proportionate reason for doing so (Garrett 1966, p. 8).

Ethical Relativism

Protagoras, a Greek philosopher who lived in the fifth century B.C., seems to have believed two things: first, that moral principles cannot be shown to be valid for everybody; and second, that people ought to follow the conventions of their own group.

Protagoras's views can be classified as forms of ethical relativism. The term "ethical relativism," however, is used in different senses. Sometimes one is said to be a relativist if he thinks that an action that is wrong in one place might not be in another. If relativism is used in this sense, then practically everyone is a relativist, for practically everyone believes that certain circumstances make a difference to the morality of an act. Other times one is said to be a relativist if he believes: (a) that different social groups sometimes have different values and ethical opinions, and (b) an individual's values are near-replicas of the values of his group.

The previous ethical theories have been accused of "ethical absolutism" because they suggested that there is only one true ethical code. Robin (1980) argues that an extreme version of ethical relativism "takes the position that, since there are two sides to every moral dilemma, and since every individual is entitled to their own system of values, neither side is more correct than the other."

This extreme position would not be very helpful to marketers faced with important ethical decisions. A more moderate version of ethical relativism is presented excellently by Robin:

> According to the philosophy of ethical relativism, limited moral principles are open-ended in several respects. These philosophers believe that there are no moral principles which constitute a complete solution for every moral circumstance. They believe that there can be no resolution of a moral problem which is equally satisfactory for all people or for all time. They also believe that circumstances are constantly changing in important respects and that these changing circumstances produce the need for constant reevaluation of basic values and moral principles. Thus, moral decisions are always tentative and risky, but they are also constantly necessary. It is apparently true that societies throughout the world and over time have always held people responsible for their actions. In addition to being held responsible by others, the individual must constantly answer to his severest critic – his own conscience... Under the ethical relativist's philosophy, no theoretical work can provide complete and concise advice on specific decisions. At best, it can explain the means for making moral decisions and suggest the methods that are involved (p. 142).

The major implication of ethical relativism is that all moral norms are relative to particular cultures. The rules of conduct that are applicable in one society do not apply to the actions of people in another society. Each community has its own norms, and morality is entirely a matter of conforming to the standards and rules accepted in one's own culture. To put it simply: What is right is what my society approves of; what is wrong is what my society disapproves of.

Literature Review

Direct concern for business ethics appeared strongly during the 1920s. The business literature of that period contains many titles dealing with ethics per se, such as "Adventures on the Borderlands of Ethics," "The Ancient Greeks and the Evolution of Standards in Business," and "Book of Business Standards."

Since the 1920s the literature in marketing and business ethics has grown even more voluminous and diversified. The extensiveness of this literature is best demonstrated by the review article by Murphy and Laczniac (1981), which has over 100 references relating to marketing and business ethics, the *Bibliography of Business Ethics* by Jones and Troy (1982), and the creation of two journals dealing with the subject of business ethics (*the Journal of Business Ethics,* and *the Business and Professional Ethics Journal*). In addition, Dr. Kenneth Bond has published the 4th edition of his *Bibliography of Business Ethics and Business Moral Values.* Dr. Bond's bibliography contains approximately 2,500 journal and text citations; in addition to annotated audio-visual citations, lists of active journals, and other bibliographies.

In order to present this literature, Murphy and Laczniac divided it into specific areas such as marketing research ethics, advertising ethics, marketing education ethics, and others.

DeGeorge (1982, pp. 12–15) divides ethical study into three related phases: normative ethics, descriptive ethics, and metaethics. The three constitute what DeGeorge calls general ethics, as opposed to special ethics.

Normative ethics seeks to uncover, develop, and justify the basic principle or the basic values of amoral system. Descriptive ethics is concerned with studying and describing the morality of people, culture, or society. It also compares and contrasts different moral systems, codes, practices, beliefs, principles and values. Metaethics analyzes moral reasoning. It is concerned with the formal language system of normative ethics and especially the meaning of terms. Relatively little published work in marketing addresses this particular stream of marketing ethics.

Special ethics applies general ethics: first, to solve particular problems, and second, to investigate the morality of specialized areas of human endeavor. This yields business ethics, engineering ethics, professional ethics, social ethics, and so on. Business ethics also has a descriptive, normative and meta-ethical aspect. In most cases, it is difficult to decide whether an issue is one of general ethics raised by a business problem or an issue that is particular to business ethics itself. But since the division between the two is rough and not exact, the question of whether or not an issue is one of general or business ethics needs seldomly to be decided.

Another way to categorize the literature is presented by Vitell (1986). Vitell divides the literature into two broad categories: (1) normative literature, and (2) positive literature. The normative literature includes articles of a general nature that are primarily concerned with what managers "ought to do." This includes: (a) present decision models which managers can apply in situations that have ethical content, (b) a set of guidelines for managers to follow in such situations, and (c) articles that relate to a specific area of marketing such as marketing research, advertising, or marketing education.

The positive or empirical literature, on the other hand, includes articles that survey what certain groups of people consider as ethical or unethical conduct. Such groups include business and marketing executives, business students, consumers and others. These surveys either use direct questions on the ethicality of an act or specific scenarios having ethical content.

Normative Literature

The normative literature includes articles of a general nature which are primarily concerned with what managers "ought to do" when confronted with an ethical dilemma.

This literature is further divided into: (A) ethical codes or guidelines for managers to follow in situations that have ethical content, (B) normative decision models that managers can apply in such situations, (C) articles that relate to a specific area of marketing such as marketing research, advertising, or marketing education, and (D) articles about ethical abuses in marketing. (However, out of a necessity for clarity of presentation some empirical articles will be presented in the normative section and vice versa).

A. Ethical Codes

Several approaches have been suggested for attaining high ethical standards in business. One is a return to common sense, reason, and religion to discourage seeking personal gain at the expense of the common good (Byron 1977). Other suggestions include codes of ethics, government regulation, and corporate models of ethical behavior (Berkman 1977; Boling 1978; Kramer 1977; Allen 1977).

Codes of conduct is one of the most pervasive responses used by the business community as a way to improve ethical conduct. In the last decade, most major corporations have introduced some form of written code of ethics (Lewin 1983). White and Montgomery's (1980) survey of CEOs in major corporations revealed that almost all of the large firms, about 75% of the medium sized firms, and about 50% of the smaller companies have a code of ethical conduct. Written codes of ethics are also used by nine out of ten state governments (Hays and Gleissner 1981).

An early effort in developing operational guidelines for marketing managers when faced with ethical decisions is presented by Patterson (1966). Patterson attempts to answer the question "what workable guides are available to help a marketing executive to evaluate alternative courses of action in a specific concrete situation?" (p. 12). These ethical guidelines are necessary because of the market power that companies hold. If this power is not used in a wise and ethical way, the government might be forced to intervene and curtail this power. Patterson contends that these guidelines can not generally be taken from ethical theory, law, or political science, because generally these guidelines were too abstract to be applied to the specific dilemmas that decision makers face. He proposes the appointment of Customer Review Boards which could consider and react to most proposed marketing decisions.

Purcell (1977a, b) argues that "good ethics is good business in the long run," even though he admits that this is not always true in the short run. But however difficult the trade-off is, ethics must prevail if the free market system is to survive. He endorses the implementation of ethical codes by several professional associations, but stresses that ethical codes are not a panacea, even when they can be enforced on association members, something not too common. Purcell goes as far as to propose the institutionalization of ethics at the top management by appointing a corporate officer to be the corporation's ethical 'devil's advocate,' or better yet an 'angel' sadvocate.' This ethical advocacy idea, however, received mostly negative feedback by top management executives.

The term "institutionalizing ethics" simply means incorporating ethics formally and explicitly into daily business life, and making it a regular and normal part of business. It means including ethics into company policy making at the board and top management levels and, through a formal code, integrating ethics into all daily decision making and work practices for all employees. According to Weber (1981), a corporation may institutionalize ethics by three principal methods: (1) a company policy or code of ethics, (2) a formally designated ethics committee on the board of directors, and (3) a management development program that incorporates ethics into its curriculum. Weber found that 67% of the firms he surveyed had ethics codes, and about 6% had ethics board committees. Management development programs concerned, however, with ethics were rare. Weber understands that each corporation is unique and so should adjust each of the above methods to its environment and size.

In a survey of *Fortune* 1,000 industrial and service corporations, the Center for Business Ethics (1986) reveals that corporations are beginning to take steps to institutionalize ethics. However, they recognize that in most cases additional mechanisms and strategies are needed to make their ethics efforts more effective, including ethics committees, judiciary boards, ethics training, and even changes in corporate structure.

Hite et al. (1988) performed a content analysis of ethical policy statements regarding marketing activities. Their results show that the topics covered most often are: misuse of funds/improper accounting, conflicts of interest, political contributions, and confidential information.

Gossett (1975) suggests that corporate legal counsel is uniquely situated and prepared to act as an arbitrer to social conflict between the corporation and society and also to lend "a deep sense of personal morality to this task." Similarly, Erteszek (1975) states that:

> the chief executive could use a man with knowledge in this area as a sounding board and as a spiritual counselor. The advisor should be a compassionate man who understands the problems and trials and tribulations of a chief executive who is often very lonely.

Steiner (1976) is also in favor of using some kind of ethical advisor or, as he calls them, "moral iconoclasts in the corporate inner sanctum." Steiner argues that the very presence of ethical advisors would bolster public confidence in the business system. Conversely, Steiner saw that this injection of ethical values into market decisions might lead businessmen to confuse their economic mission with altruistic concerns so that they fail to fulfill the basic business function of producing goods and services efficiently.

Boling (1978) agrees with Petit (1967), who declared that there was a "moral crisis in management", defined as a conflict between classical business ideology – an operational ethic which calls for profit through economic action – and managerial ideology, an ethic which stresses social responsibility. Boling argues that ethical codes are necessary to serve as the leading edge of law, because laws cannot prescribe that ethical conduct should be for everyone in all situations. These codes of ethics should be developed through the cooperation of both supervisors and subordinates. As a result, this cooperation will hopefully develop "group ethics," as opposed to "personal ethics."

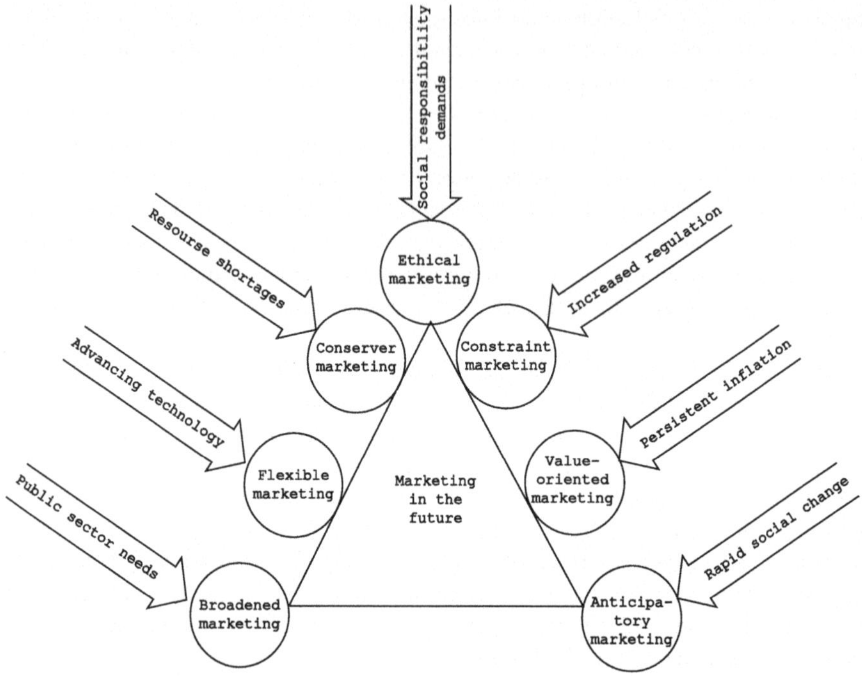

Fig. 17.1 Trends in marketing and the forces shaping them

Support for this principle of superiority of group ethics over personal ethics was established by Fulmer (1967). This argument conforms with Simon's (1976) theory that organization decision making can set the stage for and give direction to individual moral development.

Fritzsche and Becker (1982) argue that a set of response rules or codes which can be used by managers as a guide to action when faced with specific types of ethical problems should be developed. These rules should reflect the general values and expectations of society. The response rules should result in raising the ethical behavior of organizations over the long run via the expectations and practices of future managers as they enter the work force.

Laczniak and Udell (1979) view the future trends in marketing as presented in Fig. 17.1. They argue that the attempts of marketers to meet the challenge of being more ethically responsible will take the following forms: (1) enhanced professionalism, (2) ethical codes, (3) ethical consultants, and (4) ethics seminars.

Robin (1980) introduces the theory of ethical relativism in the field of marketing ethics. He argues that all of the parties involved in business and society interface and look upon their value systems as absolutes. Business people in particular are acting in a way that they might consider ethical according to their own values. Society, on the other hand, has different values and views the same act as not so ethical.

A solution to this problem is for business people to adapt the relativist's philosophy and recognize the right of others to have different value systems.

Based on the theory of ethical relativism, Robin proposes certain guidelines for formulating codes of behavior in marketing. First, he proposes certain guidelines for establishing boundaries for ethical codes because ethical codes "over which the concerned parties have little or no control are meaningless." Second, he discusses the primary methods for settling value differences when they occur.

Finally, on the subject of corporate ethical codes' effectiveness, Weller (1988) proposed several hypotheses that need to be addressed in future research.

Criticism of Ethical Codes

Murphy and Laczniak (1981) conclude that corporate codes of ethics are somewhat controversial as to their effectiveness in resolving ethical conflict. Brenner and Molander (1977) in their follow up to Baumhart's (1961) classic study on business ethics report that respondents believed that ethical codes are limited in their ability to change human conduct. Nevertheless, "the mere existence of a code, specific or general, can raise the ethical level of business behavior because it clarifies what is meant by ethical conduct."

Coe and Coe (1976) cite four criteria that distinguish professions from other occupations. One of these is "governance through a code of ethics and disciplinary procedures for the violation of the code of ethics" (p. 257). If these ethical codes are to be useful, they must be specific. The AMA code, as well as codes of other related professional associations, lack specificity. The AMA code is not alone in not addressing many of the important issues confronting managers. A survey conducted by the Ethics Resource Center (1979) indicated that about 75% of the responding firms had written codes of ethics, but that these too were lacking in specificity.

Codes of conduct are not likely to provide adequate guidance for future managers, at least as they are presently constituted. In a study of corporate codes of conduct, Chatov (1980) finds 14 types of behavior which were most frequently prohibited. Two-thirds of the codes appear to deal to some extent with the issues of coercion and control and conflict of interest. However, paternalism and personal integrity were totally ignored. No mention was made as to the proportion of the codes which were window dressing, relative to the codes which were incorporated into company policy.

Patterson (1966) searches for "workable guides to help a marketing executive to evaluate alternative courses of action in a specific concrete situation."The marketing executive should frame his problem in a way that he is able to solve it for himself. The approach to marketing ethics should be practical, concrete, and realistic. It should emphasize the "case" approach and not the "principles-to-solution" approach of the more traditional ethical theory.

Patterson also contends that a set of structural limitations on private power would be more effective than codes of conduct. Although competition could be an effective structural limitation on the private sector of the economy, marketing executives should attempt to forestall potential government intervention by establishing customer review boards or by surveying customers on future marketing plans.

Like Patterson, Ohmann (1962) acknowledges some value in codes of ethical behavior, but he feels that codes are subtly directed to keep "others" in line. That is, an executive might easily conclude: "I want to live up to my own high moral standards but I cannot, because of the sharp practices of others." What is needed, claims Ohmann, is an ethics of moral principles contained in the interdependent relationships of society.

Ethical codes of conduct are especially needed in the area of international business which has always been criticized for its plethora of routine unethical practices (Schollhammer 1978 – for further discussion see 'Ethical Issues in International Marketing' later in this paper). Prasad and Rao (1981) argue that codes of ethics for international firms "require more than the public relations announcements by companies rushing to 'reemphasize a long-standing policy.'" An example of the failure of international codes of ethics was reported in the *Wall Street Journal* (February 28, 1979). According to the report, the Grumman Corporation adopted a written policy prohibiting overseas payoffs. While the board was trying to crack down on violators, the company's top managers ignored the rules against payoffs. Consequently the board established an audit committee composed entirely of outside directors. The committee issued a report revealing that company managers had: (1) circumvented the rules by camouflaging questionable payments, (2) withheld information from the board, and (3) defied orders from the company's special counsel. These acts were not confined to low-rank employees but were also performed by top ranking officials of the firm. (For additional discussion of ethical codes see marketing research ethical codes.)

B. Normative Ethical Decision Models

The study of ethical issues in modern organizations, argues Payne (1980), has not reached the sophistication of other behavioral science pursuits. The social science literature examining ethics and values is immense in both volume and scope. Academic disciplines such as philosophy, anthropology, sociology, psychology, and social psychology can each provide countless textbooks and myriad approaches to questions concerning ethics. There has been reluctance, however, to apply this theoretical framework to common business ethics. Payne identifies the behavioral theories of social comparison, equity, social exchange, social distance, reference group, and reinforcement as promising theories to be applied in the study of business ethics.

Bartels (1967) argues that the previous literature on ethics has emphasized subjective factors, actions, and the performer's viewpoint, rather than objective factors, interactions, and the relationships between individuals. In other words, emphasis has been given to lists of actions regarded as ethical or unethical, rather than to the determinants which place an action on the list. Bartels argues also that previous literature emphasized the absolute rather than the relative character of ethics. Once determined, the universality of ethical standards has been assumed. Bartels constructed a model for ethics in marketing. In his model, Bartels uses matrices to illustrate the complex relationships that are the basis for ethical decision making. This model attempts to answer the questions: (1) how are ethical standards set? and (2) how are ethical decisions made?

Bartels' model includes two parts: (1) Creation of ethical standards – standards derived from the culture, from various institutional processes and structures, and from the expectations nurtured among the economic participants, (2) ethical decision making – with standards having been determined, one then must select a course of action.

According to Bartels's model, cultural characteristics color all social institutions (e.g., church, government, economy). Non-economic institutions (e.g., family, church) influence the economic roles of participants in a business organization. And the interaction of economic participants (e.g., managers, employees, competitors, consumers) affects ethical standards within the economic sphere. These three matrices merely identify roles and interrelationships among participants, yet the fourth matrix determines ethical behavior in specific situations.

In these situations, the ethical decision maker is guided by the level of his "ethical sensitivity", the strength of complementary and contrasting claims, and finally in some instances by economic capacity to act.

Cavanagh et al. (1981) developed a decision tree which can be used for incorporating ethics into decision making. Their normative model integrates three kinds of ethical theories: utilitarianism, theories of moral rights, and theories of justice. A modified version of Cavanagh et al. model is presented in Fig. 17.2. This model requires a decision to "pass" the test of all three ethical theories, unless there is an "overwhelming factor" that precludes the application of any of the three theories. An "overwhelming factor" is any situational factor that may, in a given case, justify overriding one of the three ethical criteria: utilitarian outcomes, individual rights, or distributive justice. Situations that can lead to an overwhelming factor are: conflicts between criteria, conflicts within criteria, and lack of capacity to employ the criteria.

Laczniak (1983a, b) argues that ethical decision rules presented in the literature have been limited to the citation of simple ethical maxims. Typically these maxims include:

The Golden Rule:	act in the way you would expect others to act toward you.
The Utilitarian Principle:	act in a way that results in the greatest good for the greatest number.
Kant's Categorical Imperative:	act in such a way that the action taken under the circumstances could be a universal law or rule of behavior.
The Professional Ethic:	take only actions which would be viewed as proper by a disinterested panel of professional colleagues.
The TV Test:	a manager should always ask: "would I feel comfortable explaining to a national TV audience why I took this action."

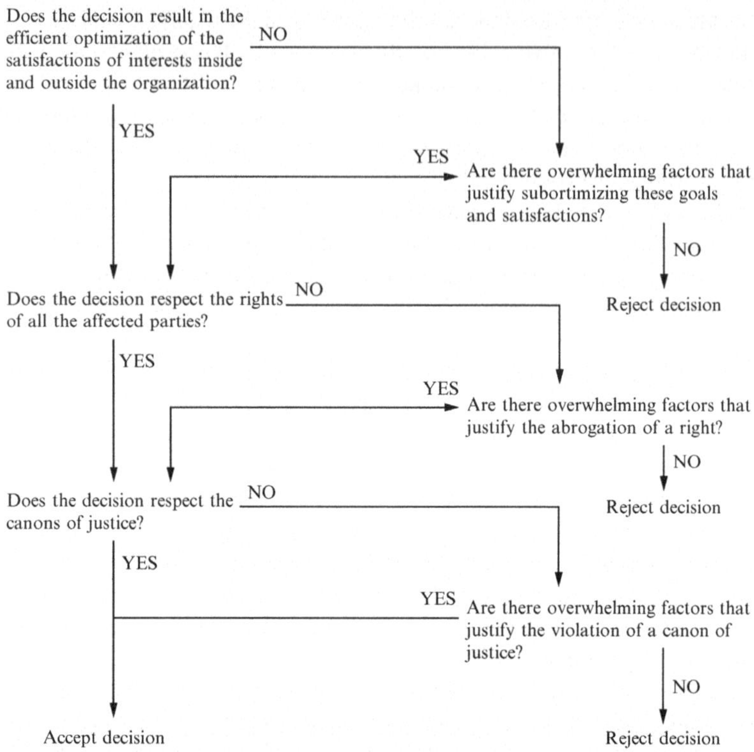

Fig. 17.2 A decision tree for incorporating ethics into a decision

Laczniac argues that these limited ethical frameworks are simplistic, lack theoretical rigor, and have hampered the ethical analysis of marketing managers. Laczniac presents a framework that includes the theories developed by Ross, Garrett, and Rawls (as presented in the introduction). Similar to Cavanagh et al.'s decision tree, Laczniac presents several questions which, if can be answered negatively, the action is probably ethical. These questions are:

Does action *A* violate the law?

Does action *A* violate any general moral obligations:

- duties of fidelity?
- duties of gratitude?
- duties of justice?
- duties of beneficence?
- duties of self-improvement?
- duties of nonmaleficence?

Does action *A* violate any special obligations stemming from the type of marketing organization in question?

Is the intent of action *A* evil?

Are any major evils likely to result from or because of action *A*?

Is a satisfactory alternative *B*, which produces equal or more good with less evil than *A*, being knowingly rejected?
Does action *A* infringe on the inalienable rights of the consumer?
Does action *A* leave another person or group less well off?
Is this person or group already relatively under-privileged?

Laczniac admits that the major purpose of his framework is to be used as a pedagogical tool to sensitize managers to the factors that are important in coming to grips with ethical issues. In addition this framework may suggest some of the components necessary for the construction of a model describing ethical behavior in marketing.

In addition Laczniak (1983b) gave 14 propositions that should enable managers to deal with the subject of business ethics. He grouped these propositions into three categories: (1) propositions that serve as useful foundations; (2) descriptive propositions; and (3) proscriptive propositions.

Dixon (1982) argues that "conventionally, marketing activity is seen to occur in a market directed economic system which is self-regulating; the market mechanism transforms private interests into public interest" (p. 38). This point of view is the center of Adam Smith's "invisible hand" hypothesis. In an analysis of Smith's and his contemporaries' work, Dixon found that their conceptual models did not rely solely upon the completely free reign of self interest, but required a coexistent ethical system. Dixon saw the existence of ethics and justice as crucial for the survival of the economic system. If an ethical system is present, then there is no need for intervention by a central authority. According to Vitell (1986), Dixon's article "is useful in giving a historical perspective to marketing and business ethics in our society, and in anchoring the need for an ethical component to marketing within this historical perspective" (p. 15).

Clasen (1967) suggests a more concrete marketing ethics theory. Employing the T-group technique to develop sensitivity to ethical issues in marketing decision making, Clasen concludes by means of group consensus, that no one traditional "well-spring" of ethics is sufficient in itself to determine the ethics of a complex marketing situation. That is, personal conscience, law, corporate policy, technical knowledge, and market expertise contribute in varying degrees to the final decision, but none of them touch the nerve of a marketing decision.

Through analysis of his own marketing decisions, Clasen observed two sources of ethical standards that were always present: professional expertise and consumer acceptance. The first "allows one to know what is good for someone else even when the other is unaware of the factors and the ethics involved" (p. 84). The second assumes that the company marketing executives' decisions "must in fact constitute what the consumer would do or choose: (a) if she had the best technical education, or (b) if she had the most modern tools for testing and evaluating" (p. 85).

Jurgen (1976) argues that ethical behavior must consider the value systems of society as a whole. He argues:

> if good and meaningful change is to take place, two vital ingredients become mandatory: an understanding of the concerns of others so that value emphasis will serve the greatest good, and an awareness of, and dedication to, the values underlying ethical behavior, by both individuals and institutions (p. 177).

Fig. 17.3 Three ethical frames of reference for the marketer

Pruden (1971) presents three ethical frames of reference for marketers (see Fig. 17.3). These ethical frames are: an individual ethic, an organizational ethic, and a professional ethic. An individual is influenced by each of these three ethical frames. The model in Fig. 17.3 rests upon the notion of power: the power of organizational rewards and punishments supporting authority, the power of an individual to withdraw his essential services, and finally the power of a profession to exercise sanctions through the collective action of a professional group. A marketer's behavior would probably be guided by an ideology which was the synthesis of these three ethics. This synthesis, however, would likely be a dynamic balance since there are likely to be fundamental points of conflict among the three ethics. Pruden argued that the professional ethic is the most appropriate for marketers in view of mounting social demands and radically changing technology, and that its development is the responsibility of the American Marketing Association.

Fisk (1982) develops five general principles of ethical marketing conduct, hoping to progress to-ward a general theory of marketing ethics. The five ethical principles, which are based on the premise that human behavior is selfish and that people are motivated to seek personal gain, are:

1. Principle of trade – "ethical behavior is trading behavior. The exchange of value for value" (p. 257).
2. Principle of noncoercion – "ethical behavior requires rejection of coercive behavior. Coercion is the suppression of someone's rights and freedoms."
3. Principle of fairness – "the ethical individual treats others as independent equals."

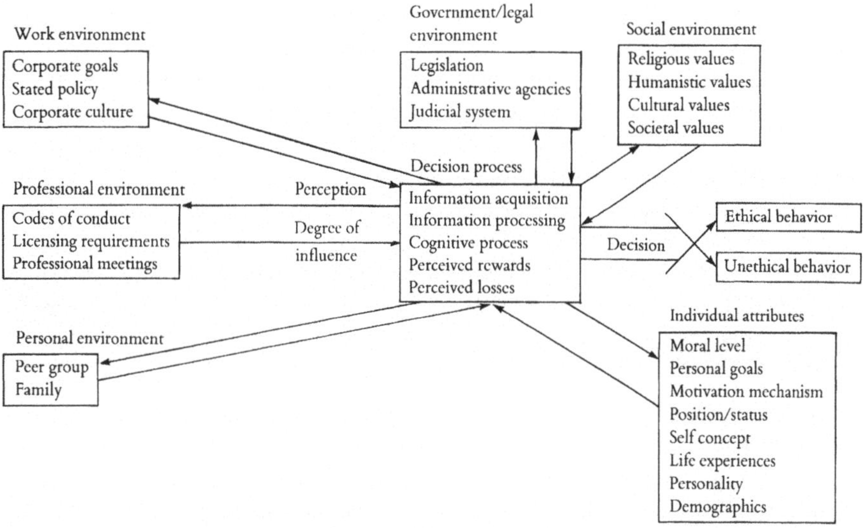

Fig. 17.4 A behavioral model of ethical/unethical decision making

4. Principle of independent judgement – "the ethical individual exercises independent judgement and expects the same of trading partners."
5. Principle of marketing – "satisfying consumer needs is *the key* to satisfying the needs of the marketer. Profits are maximized in the longrun by satisfying consumer needs" (p. 258).

These ethical principles are consistent with the ideas of exchange relationships and the marketing concept. The principles, argues Fisk, evolved from Libertarian thought (Rand 1964), and are based on ideas contained in Equity theory (Adams 1963) and Austrian Economics (Meager 1950).

The most recent normative ethical decision model is proposed by Bommer et al. (1987). The model, according to the authors, links the influencing factors of ethical/unethical behavior with the mediating structure of the individual's decision making process. The Bommer et al. model is presented in Fig. 17.4.

C. Articles Related to a Specific Area of Marketing

This part of the literature includes: (1) articles on marketing research ethics, and (2) ethical issues in marketing management.

Ethical Issues in Marketing Research

Bogart's (1962) ground beaking article on "The Researcher's Dilemma" introduces ethical issues in the area of marketing research. Bogart argues that marketing researchers face a dilemma on how to resolve his dual orientation as a professional and as a businessman. As a professional, he thinks of himself as a scientist concerned with the pursuit of truth for its own sake; as a businessman, on the other hand, he has to be concerned with means and ends and corporate goals. The ethical problems which confront the marketing researcher are intensified by the absence of accepted codes of ethics, and by the pressures of the company to be productive in ways which have nothing to do with research at all.

Since the publication of this article, ethical issues in marketing research have received the most attention in the field of ethical marketing literature. According to Murphy and Laczniac (1981), the four major foci of this literature are: (a) the issues and rights of researchers and clients; (b) the attitudes of professionals toward research ethics; (c) the role of codes of ethics; and (d) the discussion of ethics in marketing research textbooks.

a. Issues and rights of researchers and clients. This part of the marketing literature deals with the delineation of the rights of all parties involved in the research process.

Bogart (1962) identifies four major types of problems in marketing research: (1) the extent of the researcher's honesty in doing what he purports to do; (2) the question of manipulating research techniques in order to produce desired findings; (3) the propriety of business judgement exercised in undertaking research (e.g., when a client chooses to define a problem in terms the researcher cannot accept); and (4) the forthright relationship of the researcher to those interviewed regarding the study's true purpose and sponsorship (1962, p. 9).

Blankenship (1964) raises three potential ethical problems. The first deals with ownership and management of research firms. In the case of a research firm owned or controlled by a bigger firm (let's assume an advertising company), the question is "can the subsidiary do unbiased work for its parent?" What subsidiary will risk a study showing that its parent is doing a poor job, if this study is designed to be used by one of the parents accounts. A similar problem can result in the case of interlocking directorates.

Second, ethical problems could be caused by financial aspects in the buying and selling of research. In this case, Blankenship considers the practice of excessive entertaining and giving presents to the potential buyer of research unethical. Ethical questions can also be raised when the salesman of research has an incentive to sell more research than necessary (this occurs when he is paid commission only).

Finally, ethical problems will arise if shoddy or fictional data are gathered. This can be avoided by installing quality standards and controls, and by filtering the concern for high quality down to the actual interviewers.

Tybout and Zaltman (1974) discuss the subjects's (respondents's) rights in marketing research and how their violation may affect the quality of data. They introduce the respondents, "bill of rights," which contain the "right to choose," the "right to safety," and the "right to be informed." A respondent's "right to choose" might be violated if he is pressured to make a "forced compliance" decision in the course of a laboratory experiment. Similarly, if confidentiality is promised but not kept, the respondent's "right to safety" is breached. Finally, the "right to be informed" is breached when the respondent is not debriefed at the end of an experiment that involved manipulation.

The breach of any of these rights may affect the quality of data. For example, if anonymity is regarded as suspicious by subjects, they may refuse to respond to personal or controversial questions, or not participate in the research at all. Individuals that do respond might be less than candid. In both cases, the quality of the data suffers.

Tybout and Zaltman offer solutions for all these possible problems. For example, to insure anonymity when responding to sensitive or embarrassing questions they proposed the use of the "randomized response technique." This procedure allows the respondent to reply to a question selected at random from two or more questions without the interviewer knowing which question he is responding to.

Day (1975), in his reply to the Tybout and Zaltman article, say that while Tybout and Zaltman are to be congratulated for exploring a neglected topic in marketing ethics, they confine their analysis to subjects' rights and ignore the rights of practitioners and clients. Day contended that the arguments presented in the Tybout and Zaltman article are severely weakened by being based solely on experimental psychological research, rather than on survey research which constitutes by far the greater part of marketing research.

In their rejoinder to Day, Tybout and Zaltman (1975) argue that Day confused the terms "market" and "marketing" research. Tybout and Zaltman argue that while in market research – a study of the market for a product – survey research is prevalent, in marketing research – research on consumer behavior, information processing etc. – experimental research is mostly used.

Similar to Tybout et al., Schneider (1977) studies several types of respondent abuse in both survey and experimental research. Schneider's three ethical considerations in the treatment of subjects or respondents are: (1) deceptive/fraudulent practices – including unrealized promise of anonymity, faked sponsor identification, and others; (2) lack of consideration or concern for subjects/respondents –including poorly conducted interviews, failure to debrief, etc.; and (3) invasion of privacy – including projective techniques, one-way mirrors, etc. This issue of respondents' privacy was also examined by Frey and Kinnear (1979). Schneider recommended a research project by professional researchers to determine what research practices the public considers unethical.

Hawkins (1979) focused on the impact of sponsor identification and disclosure of the respondent's right to refuse to participate on the quality and quantity of data generated in a mail survey. He found that a department store being the sponsor reduced the response rate significantly from that obtained from a research firm or university sponsor. Presumably, the response rate was lower because respondents suspected an ulterior motive (profits). In addition, a definite statement of the respondent's right to refuse to participate had a significant negative impact on the response rate when the department store was identified as the sponsor. It appeared to have only limited impact with other sponsor types. Finally, Hawkins found that neither treatment had a major effect on the nature of the obtained responses.

b. Attitudes toward research ethics. This category includes mainly surveys of marketing professionals regarding their attitudes toward ethics in marketing research.

Crawford (1970) reports the reactions of research directors and top marketing executives to fourteen "situations" which occur in the process of marketing research.

Crawford found that respondents disapproved of the use of ultraviolet ink, hidden tape recorders, and one way mirrors. Yet the majority of the respondents in their experience had encountered such or similar situations. Hawkins (1979) argues that:

> except in areas involving at best questionable law, nothing but one's conscience operates to inhibit these practices. There is no broadly applicable code, no board of investigation, no licensing authority, and no federal statement of research practice guidelines … thus a situation seems to prevail where objectionable practices occur at least occasionally, if not frequently, without formal resistance.

An interesting finding was that top marketing managers have a similar set of ethical standards as that of researchers.

Coney and Murphy (1976) examine the opinions of practicing and academic marketing researchers on the present state of affairs with respect to ethical and professional practices in marketing research. The extremely high response rate (nearly 75%) indicates that the respondents were concerned about ethical issues in marketing research. The most important finding, however, was that marketers perceive a significant gap between the ideal of ethical marketing research behavior and what is now common practice. For all seven practices examined, marketers felt that such a gap exists. The fact that a large proportion of AMA members are either unaware or unfamiliar with the Marketing Research Code of Ethics indicated the effectiveness of such ethical codes.

Beltramini (1986) surveyed a nationally representative sample of 500 marketing researchers and found that those researchers involved in competitive information acquisition are willing to misrepresent themselves and even take liberties beyond the limitations of official ethical policy.

c. *Marketing research ethical codes*. Gilbert Sabater (1982) argues that:

> the diversity of activities and the range of problems in the practice of marketing research make it difficult to reach consensus on ethics and standards. Yet, underlying the practice of most professionals in the field, there is a strong shared sense of responsibility for the proprieties of what marketing researchers do and the integrity of what they produce.

Gilbert Sabater chaired an AMA committee established to address problems raised by unethical practices and to set guidelines and standards for the marketing research profession.

While abuses are the short term reasons for ethical codes, a long-range reason is protection of the marketing research field. Twedt (1963) points out that the consumer must be protected against unethical research approaches if his cooperation is to continue. Blankenship (1964) mentions three other reasons: the risk of government intervention, protection of the users of research, and protection of the researcher. The user has to be assured of receiving honest research of acceptable quality. The researcher must be protected against the behavior of others less scrupulous than he. But, Blankenship continues:

> codes alone cannot provide the answer. They merely provide a few guideposts. And even the guideposts don't make the marketing research field any more ethical; they merely provide a broad written framework within which to determine when the behavior of a researcher is within or out of bounds … There is another reason why these codes alone will never provide the full answer. They can cover only the principles of honesty; they cannot

> hope to cover integrity. For integrity is a far tougher thing to specify. Honesty is merely an avoidance of incorrect behavior. Integrity is a voluntary, spontaneous, positive form of honesty, where one takes initiative in being honest by being almost aggressive about it … the codes can never legislate integrity.

Frey and Kinnear (1979) warn the profession that the absence of strong professional/ethical codes might lead to restrictive government regulation. Specifically, they argue that practices such as the guise of research as a sales ploy (called "sugging") and the research utilized as a disguise in a direct mail scheme might force FTC to step in and regulate the industry.

A specific code of ethics governing the relationship between client and consultant was advocated by Bezilla et al. (1976). Some of the solutions for client-consultant problems and for ensuring fair treatment of both parties are: a strong professional association for policing illegitimate behavior; partial payment for a proposal; and consultation fee for proposal writing.

The development of ethical codes should coincide with the development of "professionalism" in the practice of marketing research. Bogart (1962) was the first to recognize the importance of that linkage. Bogart's article was followed by Gerhold (1974) who proposed four requirements for professionalism in marketing research. These requirements are: (1) an agreed upon definition of the marketing research field; (2) group or professional identification; (3)proof of competence; and (4) principles manifested in a code of ethics (p. 10). Coe and Coe (1976)conclude that (1) a code of ethics, and (2) a procedure for disciplining violators are essential to professionalism. On the other hand, Murphy and Conney (1976) believe that professionalism in marketing research may best be achieved through accreditation.

d. Discussion of research ethics in textbooks. It is encouraging that recent textbooks on marketing research include at least a chapter on the subject of marketing research ethics. Such textbooks are by Zaltman and Burger (1975), Kinnear and Taylor (1979), and Tull and Hawkins (1987). The most thorough analysis on the subject of marketing research ethics is a chapter in the Handbook of Marketing Research by Hollander (1974).

Ethical Issues in Marketing Management

A recent study by Chonko and Hunt (1985) surveys the ethical beliefs of marketing managers. Their results show that: (a) bribery is the most often mentioned problem faced by marketing managers followed by fairness, honesty, and pricing strategy; (b) ethical conflict is mainly felt when they tried to balance the demands of the corporation against customer needs; (c) marketing managers perceive plenty of opportunities in their companies to engage in unethical behavior, but, in general, such behavior does not lead to success; and (d) the existence of ethical codes is not related to the extent of unethical behavior by marketing managers.

In addition to the general article above, several articles about marketing managers have appeared in the literature dealing with ethical issues in purchasing, retailing, advertising, pricing, distribution, sales, international marketing and others.

a. Purchasing managers' ethics. Cummings (1979) contends that the only person who can have a more significant influence on the firm's bottom line than the salesman is the purchaser. A survey for the National Association of Purchasing Management reveals that accepting small items like tickets for sporting events or theater, advertising souvenirs, free lunches or dinners was not considered unethical; where as accepting larger gifts like loans, clothing, and appliances was deemed unethical. Cummings also found that most large companies have formal written policies on purchasing ethics. In a similar study, Rudelious and Buchholz (1979) argue that although written policies cannot cover every ethical situation, these policies can help the purchasing agent make a more consistent decision.

Dempsey et al. (1980) surveyed industrial buyers in order to determine the influence of gifts and other personal inducements on making industrial sales. Their results show that buyers generally agree that business lunches and advertising specialties are appropriate or "ethical" forms of inducements. On the other side, "an-evening-on-the-town" or a gift worth more than $10 were considered inappropriate or "unethical".

b. Product managers' ethics. Ethical issues regarding product decisions have also occupied marketing researchers. Practices such as the proliferation of nonfunctional packaging (Hartley 1976), planned obsolescence (Gwinner et al. 1977), and arbitrary product elimination (Hise and McGinnis 1975), were deemed as at least ethically suspect, if not outright unethical. Hise and McGinnis argue that most companies deciding to eliminate a product evaluate only the profit potential of the product and ignore any effects such an act might have on consumers. An example of that behavior is the lack of replacement parts of a discontinued product line or the termination of a necessary but unprofitable pharmaceutical product.

The way a product is priced can be ethically-suspect, if not outright unethical. For example, Sturdivant (1968) discovered that ghetto consumers pay more for the same product than the more affluent suburban consumers. An article in the *Wall Street Journal* ("Consumer Find … 1977") discussed the practice of altering the quality and/or size of a product in order to keep the price at the same level (e.g., chocolate bars). Sonnefeld and Lawrence (1978) found that ethical codes on pricing and specifically on price discrimination circulates only at the top levels and the word seemed to have trouble getting down the line. Even those documents that circulated among all the employees seemed to be "broadly written, toothless versions of the golden rule." Sonnefeld and Lawrence propose a specific code of ethics for dealing with price fixing and price discrimination problems.

c. Ethics in the channel of distribution. Ethical problems in the channel of distribution can range from unresponsiveness by retailers in dealing with customer complaints (Andreason and Best 1977), coercion of channel members by the channel leader and to franchisors charging high prices to products they sold to their captive customers (Weigand 1980).

d. Salespeople's ethics. Dubinsky et al. (1980) argue that salespeople are key links between an organization and its customers, who often face ethical dilemmas when forced to choose between short-run pressures from management to meet a sales quota and long-run goals of achieving customer confidence and satisfaction. The inability to handle such dilemmas – due partly to a lack of management guidelines – may lead to job stress, poor sales performance, and dissatisfied customers.

In order to address this potentially problematic situation, Dubinsky et al. identify what kind of situations are viewed by salespeople as problematic, whether stated company policy existed that apply to these situations, and whether sales personnel want such stated policies. Situations or practices considered as presenting an ethical problem were: (1) allowing personalities – liking for one purchaser and disliking for another – to affect price, delivery, and other decisions regarding terms of sale; (2) having less competitive prices or other terms for buyers who use a firm as the sole source of supply; and (3) making statements to an existing purchaser that exaggerate the seriousness of his problem in order to obtain a bigger order or other concessions. Finally, sales personnel seem to want more guidelines to help them resolve ethical questions.

Given that salespeople are likely to experience ethical conflict in their jobs, it is incumbent for sales managers to design work environments that mitigate ethical conflict. Walker et al. (1977) argue that ethically troubled salespeople will experience increased levels of job-related tension, frustration, and anxiety; these disfunctional consequences could further lead to lower job performance and increased turnover. A later article by Walker et al. (1979) reports that the inability of salespeople to resolve ethical problems can result in conflict between salespeople and their managers; again resulting in reduced job satisfaction and low productivity. In addition, they found that performing the sales job in an unethical fashion may lead to customer dissatisfaction, unfavorable word-of-mouth, as well as reduced sales and profits for the firm.

Sales management writers such as Dalrymple (1982), Futrell (1981), Russell et al. (1978), and Stanton and Buskirk (1978) agree that ethical issues confronting sales personnel can be categorized in two groups: (1) ethics in dealing with customers and (2) ethics in dealing with employers. Customer-related concerns include bribes, gifts, entertainment, reciprocity, and conflict of interest. Employer-related concerns include moonlighting, relationships with fellow salespeople, the use of company assets, expense accounts, and sales contests.

Snyder (1976) studied the practice of bribing in order to make a sale. He admits that berbery is not only a problem with dealings abroad but also inside the USA. Snyder found that 22% of his respondents have been asked to make an illegal payment abroad, while 49% were asked to make such a payment in the USA. Snyder argues, however, that post-Watergate morality has forced most companies to develop codes of international sales ethics.

Bellizzi and Murdock (1981) focus on industrial sales management in the 1980s, and recommend the development of an ethical code for industrial sales. This code should outline the proper sales techniques, as well as gift giving and entertainment issues.

Ebejer and Morden (1988) proposed a "realistic" professional ethic for sales people – "limited paternalism." According to the authors:

> Limited paternalism implies that a salesman should 'be his buyer's keeper' in the sense that he should serve the interests of his customers by identifying their needs, while disclosing all relevant information about products or services in order to facilitate mutual exchange to mutual advantage (p. 337).

e. Retailing ethics. Norris and Gifford (1988) collected both comparative and longitudinal data between 1976 and 1986 from retail store managers and retail students concerning their perceptions of ethical practices in retailing. Contrary to the popular belief that ethics have eroded over time, their results indicate a significant increase in the ethics of retail store managers. However, a significant decrease was evident in the ethics of retail students.

Other one time studies in the field of retailing ethics have been conducted in retail communications (Levy and Dubinsky 1983), retail theft(Fitzmaurice and Radolf 1961; Tatham 1974), retail sales personnel (Dubinsky and Levy 1985), and retail store managers (Dornoff and Tankersley 1975a, b).

f. Advertising ethics. To understand better the ethics in advertising issue, it is helpful to examine some of the history that underlies the morality of advertising issues. Murphy and Laczniak (1981) provide the following useful summary.

The ethics of advertising, like sales, has come under question almost continuously (Packard 1957; Galbraith 1958). Because advertising is such a visible element of marketing, this situation is not surprising. Furthermore, ethical issues come up with respect to the role of advertising agencies' dealing with their clients as well as the advertiser-consumer linkage.

A thorough discussion of advertising ethics is contained in Wright and Mertes's (1974) readings book. In this work, selections about advertising ethics were written by Alderson, who discussed the reconciliation of Christian ethics with the U.S. economy; Levitt (1970); and a variety of scholars from outside the field of marketing who used their fields of religion, philosophy, and history to comment on advertising ethics.

Despite the appearance of an advertising code of ethics in the 1920s, the various authors chronicle many continuing abuses, including puffery and exaggerated claims. Several prescriptions for raising the level of ethics in advertising were presented by these writers, including Levitt's (1970) classic defense of advertising ethics. In that article, Levitt admits that advertisers typically try to persuade and manipulate consumers but that these efforts are not fundamentally different or as controversial as the efforts of artists, politicians, and editorial writers to manipulate ideas in the minds of citizens. Levitt states that "embellishment and distortion are among advertising's legitimate and socially desirable purposes." To reject these techniques of advertising would be to deny man's honest needs and values.

At the 1971 AMA Educators' Conference, Boulding (1971) gave a speech on the ethics of persuasion. He listed four major ethical criticisms of the persuasion industry:

1. The contention that persuasion of an individual violates the person's inherent right.
2. The fact that the persuasion industry leads to certain human addictions.
3. Simple dishonesty – that is, persuaders are only trying to make money but not propagate the truth.
4. The idea that persuasion frequently degenerates into vulgarization.

Boulding's thoughtful analysis concludes with the call for a continuing search by marketers for answers to tough ethical questions in advertising.

Several new topics have surfaced in the area of advertising ethics. Consoli (1976) advocates that advertisers display a high standard of ethics in using comparative advertising. Also, the stereotyping of women in advertising is mentioned as another ethical issue in this article. Turk (1979) examines what he labeled as the "ethical morass" of advertising to children. He feels both government and industry are caught in this trap. He argues that marketers and broadcasters feign concern for children's health but also want to perpetuate highly profitable television programs aimed at children. At the same time, Turk likened the FTC staff to moral crusaders of another era and states that their proposals are too severe for acceptance.

Krugman and Ferrell (1981) investigated the ethical perceptions held by advertising practitioners, ad agency account managers, and corporate ad managers regarding their peers in the organization and others with whom they interact. It is not surprising that they found that respondents believe that they possess higher ethical standards than their peers. The authors conclude that favorable ethical performance will be rewarded and widely disseminated and that top management should use their perceived higher ethical standards to influence the members of the firm.

Recently, the popular press has taken notice of current advertising campaigns that make extensive use of sex appeal. Bronson (1980) examined several campaigns and discussed the role of the network censor in deciding which ads are not in good taste. The use of sex appeal is especially prevalent in promoting designer jeans (Frons 1980; Bronson and Birnhaum 1980). The use of models clad provocatively in jeans and the use of suggestive language in television commercials are commonplace in this type of advertising. One writer captured the flavor of these campaigns: "Almost all TV ads for designer jeans exploit fantasy in campaigns that seem to stretch the tenets of truth in advertising" (Frons 1980, p. 85).

One thing seems certain: The overt nature of advertising lays it open to questions of an ethical nature. This point was noted by Greyser and Reece (1971) when introducing their classic survey of business people's attitudes toward advertising:

> Perhaps because it touches the public in so many ways and throughout the day, advertising seems to be receiving a constant barrage of criticisms from both activists and the public.

After concentrating on the business perspective toward advertising, Greyser and Reece (1971) concluded that subscribers to a leading business publication were increasingly uneasy about the truthfulness and ultimate social impact of advertising.

Krugman and Ferrell (1981) reached the conclusion that advertisers clearly distinguished between the acceptability of certain practices. Ethics is seen to be a matter of degree rather than either absolutely wrong or absolutely right. Issues of a more overt nature that need more than tacit approval are judged to be more unethical than issues that are more covert and easily rationalized. For example, padding an expense account more than 10% or manipulating a situation to make a superior or subordinate look bad are seen as highly unethical, while not reporting the violations of others and taking extra personal time are seen as more acceptable behavior. In sum, the less overt and more easily rationalized behaviors are believed to be more acceptable and more widely practiced.

In the late 1970s, Maidenform started the advertising appeal, "The Maidenform woman. You never know where she'll turn up." The advertisements featured a scantily clad model standing around fully clothed men. Women Against Pornography have given Maindenform a ZAP award for sexist advertising. The company maintains that the only way their merchandise can be properly shown is to put it on models. Ferrell (1985) argues that the Maidenform ethical dilemma is a good example of ethical relativism. Ethical relativism recognizes that while there may be different value systems, analysis of moral consequences and the establishment of limited moral principles are extremely important (Robin 1980). In the Maidenform example, one party sees the use of live models in advertisements as the logical way to promote lingerie, while another group perceives such provocative photos as exploitative and unethical.

g. Ethics in international marketing. Business has been accused of unethical practices in international dealings since international trade began. Multinational corporations, with their major role in international trade, have attracted much of the criticism concerning unethical behavior (Rosenberg 1987; Donaldson 1985; Hagg 1984; Berleant 1982; Naor 1982; Simpson 1982).

Marketing activities have also been central to international trade and thus have attracted their share of criticisms concerning unethical behavior. Marketing has been criticized for offering harmful products to underdeveloped countries (e.g., DDT), and promoting its products through bribes and payoffs (Longenecker et al. 1988; Lane and Simpson 1984; Johnson 1985).

Efforts to legislate such practices, including the Foreign Corrupt Practices Act of 1977 (Shaw 1988), have been ineffective because it is difficult to legislate ethics. Kaikati and Label (1980) argue that in order to cope with the Foreign Corrupt Practices Act strong top management support for the corporate code of ethics is essential. In addition, strong disciplinary action should be taken against the violators of that code.

Post and Baer (1978) criticize severely the marketing of infant formula in foreign countries and propose an extensive "demarketing" strategy as a way to solve this ethical problem. For a complete presentation of the infant formula controversy, see Baker (1985).

Fritzsche and Becker (1984) argue that ethical practices of business tend to vary from country to country. In their study, marketers were asked to evaluate the ethical standards in various countries. Germany was perceived as the most ethical country followed by the United Kingdom and then the U.S. and France. Mexico was ranked lowest. The authors concluded that the level of ethical behavior tends to increase with the level of economic development of the country. Whether this increase is caused by developments in the legal system of the country or by society's expectations and the needs of the participants is unknown.

Fritzsche (1985) offers a model of ethical decision making that can be used by international marketers (see Fig. 17.5). This model is a modification of the one proposed by Cavanaugh et al. (1981). The macro part of the model deals with the utilitarian benefits to society and serves as a screening device for the micro portion of the model. The micro part deals with individuals. Stage 2 of the micro part is concerned with the effect of the decision on individuals' freedom. If stage 3 is reached, the issue of individual justice is considered.

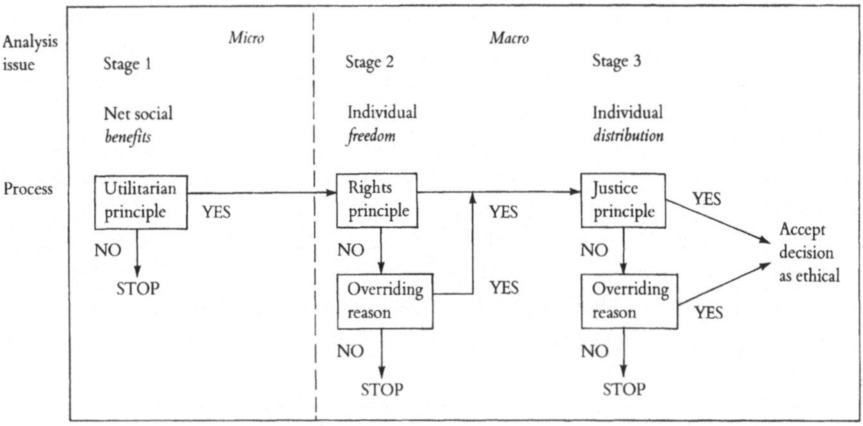

Fig. 17.5 A model for ethical decision making

Schollhammer (1979) argues that the continued rapid expansion of multinational corporations and the inordinate economic power they hold has brought their activities under close scrutiny and criticism. This criticism has been fueled by sensational revelations of unethical practices, such as undue political influence, bribery, and corruption committed by prominent multinational firms. However, some of this criticism might be unjustifiable because, as Schollhammer found, corrupt payments are far more often asked of than offered by the multinational corporations. So, these firms seem to be more the victims of a social practice pervasive among many of the developing countries of the world.

Schollhammer further argues that, although relatively few multinationals have been implicated, their unethical practices affect the ethical perception of all. The author found that the ethical standards of the multinationals are viewed with suspicion by the majority of the respondents he surveyed.

Barry (1979a, b) surveyed 65 major multinational corporations and found that only a small number even have explicit statements and directives that the business be lost, or other adverse economic consequences be accepted, in order to comply with the corporation's ethical policies. Only 25% of the firms have taken any steps to prevent unethical practices abroad.

Finally, Prasad and Rao (1982) argue that ethics and morals are subject to changing societal values as well as subjective interpretations. For these reasons, questions concerning business ethics in general are difficult to deal with, and those concerning the ethics of multinational companies are even more difficult because of the heterogeneity of societal values by which these firms are affected.

h. Ethics in marketing education. Arlow and Ulrich (1985) argue that there are two basic approaches to improve business ethics. One approach entails reforming organizational practices such as developing corporate ethical codes, and providing more top management ethical leadership. The second approach advocates the incorporation of business ethics into the curriculum of business schools.

It is possible and may be essential that ethics and business ethics become an integral part of each business student's academic preparation for the business world. Unfortunately, according to Kreitner (1981), Kreitner and Reif (1980), and Moore (1982), no concerted effort is being made along these lines. Most business administration curricula contain a single course relating business to its external environment. Typically, only a chapter or two is devoted to business ethics or social responsibility.

Gelb and Brien (1971) suggest that universities must share the burden of guilt for business executives failing fully to recognize the need for social responsibility in business decisions. They argue that universities are partially responsible for the personal and organizational value systems that influence managerial decision making.

Lane et al. (1988) designed a survey to assess the impact of business education on the ethical beliefs of business students. They concluded that "business programs, rather than reinforcing positive ethical perceptions and actions on the part of students may, in fact, have a negative impact on certain ethical actions and perceptions" (Lane et al. 1988, p. 229). Included in the negative impact were engagement in dirty tactics, selling one's soul for grades, and pandering to professors' wishes.

In discussing possible future directions for marketing education, Lazer (1970) states that attempts to teach business students how to cope with socially related issues have not been as successful as efforts directed at the development of marketing technicians.

From 1975 to 1980, several studies attempted to identify the position of higher education vis-à-vis instruction in business ethics. Buchholz's (1979) survey reports that over 82% of 307 responding AACSB schools are offering courses in corporate social responsibility, business and society, or public policy where business ethics is usually covered. About 71% of the sample reported that they covered the subject of ethics and values in these courses. Similar results were reported by Holloway and Hastings (1978). Other schools have introduced separate courses in business ethics (Lewin 1983).

However, Huber (1979) and McMahon (1975) report that at least 60% of the institutions surveyed did not have a course in business ethics. According to George (1987) "this discrepancy seems to suggest that the respondents did not perceive the public policy or business environment types of offerings as being primarily ethical in their orientation" (George 1987, p. 514).

In 1968, Marks and Scott reported that 35% of the AACSB responding schools offered a course dealing with ethics or social responsibility. This study has since been invalidated because it did not distinguish between ethics courses and business and society courses.

Murphy and Laczniac (1980) found that only 2% of the schools offered a course in marketing ethics specifically. The other 98% said that the topic of ethics was covered in some other marketing course. Even for the few schools that offered a specific marketing ethics course, they offered it as an elective and not as a required one. Some additional surveys on the subject were reported in the *Journal of Business Ethics* (Hoffman and Moore 1982; Hosmer 1985).

The logic behind the absence of courses on business ethics was presented by Miller and Miller (1976) in their article "It's Too Late for Ethics Courses in Business Schools." The authors argued that:

> It seems to us that it is impossible to deal effectively with the problems of integrity in business at any level other than the highly personal one of the integrity of the executive. If you accept that premise, then most of the courses at the university level become an exercise in futility (p. 40).

Hosmer (1987) proposes three reasons why some business schools do not offer a course in business ethics: (1) a lack of understanding about the complexities of ethical decisions in business, (2) a reliance on the concept of Pareto Optimality in economics, and (3) an objection to managerial ethics on the grounds that the field is unscientific and subjective.

In addition, the Harvard Business School did not offer any courses in business ethics because the faculty felt that by the time students enrolled in graduate school, their ethical values were ingrained.

Contrary to the Harvard Business School, Konrad (1978) argues that the fact that the ethical values of students are ingrained is not an excuse for not offering business ethics courses. Konrad admits that such courses will not transform the student's values in the course of a few months, but the course will make them more sensitive to ethical issues, and promote the use of the already ingrained values.

Empirical evidence, although scant, tends to support Konrad's view. Purcell (1977a, b) in a long term study measured ethical reactions of business students just before taking a business ethics course and 10 years later when they were in the business world making actual ethical decisions. He found that the respondents were more apt to recommend ethical behavior 10 years after graduation than when they were asked to make similar judgments just before taking the business ethics course. Barach and Nicol (1980) found that a business ethics course positively affected students not only on the subjects covered in the course but affected their business behavior in general.

A related string of literature measured the level of ethical awareness of students. Hawkins and Cocanougher (1972) studied students' reactions to ethical issues in business. They found that business majors were more tolerant of business practices than non business majors. Similar findings were reported by Gelb and Brien (1971), Shuptrine (1979), and Losser and Hasty (1979).

Murphy and Laczniak (1981) argue that marketing educators and authors of marketing textbooks should take steps to increase the emphasis on ethical issues in marketing courses. These steps include: (1) ethical issues should be woven throughout marketing courses and texts instead of being left to the end; and (2) create some marketing cases that deal with ethical issues.

Because of the fundamental antagonism of the various normative ethical theories and the conflicting codes of action they propose, teachers, such as Vivien Well, have become disillusioned with ethical theory and have eliminated it entirely from their courses (Brady 1985). The reason for this action is that the complexity far outweighs the relevance of theory (Milesko-Pytel 1979). Emphasizing in a recent essay the inapplicability of ethical theory, Archie Bahm (1982) argues that we are "teaching ethics without ethics to teach."

Mathison (1988) argues that business ethics courses, as they are presently being taught, have an excessively philosophical bent and may not be relevant to real business people facing real business problems.

In addition, Mathison contends that the majority of textbook examples and cases (over two-thirds of the cases in Velasquez 1982; Luthans et al. 1987; and Hosmer 1987) reflect a strong bent toward top executives' dilemmas, ignoring middle and supervisory level positions' ethical concerns. Mathison proposes that the core foundational concepts of egoism, utilitarianism, and moral idealism still need to be dealt with. However, three additional tools should also be presented: (1) Mathison's "synthesis model," which attempts to integrate the best aspects of the traditional models (Mathison 1988, 1987), (2) the Nash model (Nash 1981), and (3) the Pagano model (Pagano 1987) both of which constitute a series of simple but probing practical questions.

Pamental (1988) reviews several texts used in business ethics courses and he commends them for the use of case materials and for the manner by which they involve the students in decision making situations. Pamental argues that, unlike earlier texts, these texts do not warrant the criticism that "cases shed little light on how the ethical component is incorporated into the decision-making process" (Walton 1979). However, he criticized them for: (1) concentrating too heavily on cases of a general management nature, ignoring the various functional areas of the firm in which most graduates begin their careers, and (2) concentrating too heavily on manufacturing firms, at the expense of service firms.

In conclusion, two major viewpoints on teaching business ethics in business schools exist. One suggests that business ethics is a necessary part of an undergraduate business student's education and that the subject can be taught either by challenging student values or by making students aware of ethical behavior (Baily 1968; Bok 1976; Donaldson 1978; Konrad 1978; Purcell 1981; Saul 1981). Powers and Vogel (1980) cite a variety of reasons for the growing interest in the subject of business ethics and why it is important in the education of business students.

The other viewpoint is that efforts by business schools are already too late to build ethical values, as these values must be assimilated as part of a total educational philosophy instead of a single course (Miller and Miller 1976). Similarly, Andrews (1979) indicates that ethics instruction did not change the ethical predispositions of graduate business students, and that while other business skills can be taught, corporate ethics cannot be. Available studies in the area do not support either view. For example, on one side Barach and Nicol (1980), and Purcell (1977a, b) report that MBA graduates perceive that a business and society course has a positive effect on business ethics.

Stead and Miller (1988) argue that even though there was very little post-course reordering of priorities, students did display an increased perception of the importance of social issues.

On the other side, Arlow and Ulrich (1980, 1985) report that both the short term and long term effects of a business and society course on undergraduate business students' ethical values are negligible, but the results varied by academic major.

In addition, Arlow and Ulrich (1983) report an initial overall improvement in ethical scores 4 months after a course in ethics, but 4 years later respondents reverted back to the initial low scores measured before they took the course.

Martin (1981) found that there was no significant improvement in the ability of undergraduate business students to analyze ethical problems after a two-course exposure to ethics compared with the ability of engineering students who did not take the courses.

i. Information explosion. Another area of ethical concern whose prominence has been growing dramatically in this age of high technology is the information explosion due to the introduction of computers in all business functions. New innovations and applications in the fields of computers and telecommunications are introduced so rapidly that most businesses have not had the time to assess the ethical implications of that explosion. Hutzler (1982) argues that corporate decision makers need to be aware of the potential problems arising from these changes, not only from an operational perspective but also from legal and ethical viewpoints.

Burger and Schmidt (1983) present some of the issues that might create ethical problems in this area. These include privacy of consumer information, security of information, the question of possible consumer manipulation, and the storing of information for multinational corporations in foreign countries.

Weston (1979) found that even though the majority of the public feel that computers have improved the quality of life, even more people see dangers in the way computers are being used to process personal data.

j. Social responsibility of marketing managers. A group of researchers from Yale University has divided ethical meaning into two categories. Into the first category falls all that behavior based on the "moral minimum" of not harming others. The second category represents the "affirmative duty" to attack social problems of poverty, discrimination, or urban decay (Simon et al. 1972). The authors accepted the first view, that the moral minimum which confronts business people is only the reduction of injuries caused by the processes they manage. Contrary to Simon and Powers, proponents of social responsibility seem to take the second view.

The concepts of social responsibility and social auditing are conceptually close to ethics. Social responsibility is especially close to utilitarian theories of marketing ethics. But in spite of this relationship, the social responsibility and social auditing literature will not be reported in this literature review. For more information on these subjects see Bauer and Fenn (1973), Kizilbash et al. (1979), Moser (1986), Filios (1986), Spencer and Butler (1987), Zahra and LaTour (1987), and Orpen (1987).

D. Articles on Ethical Abuses in Marketing

Within the business firm, the functional area most closely related to ethical abuse is marketing. This is because marketing is the function of business charged with communicating and openly satisfying customers. Thus, marketing is closest to the public view and, consequently, is subject to considerable societal analysis and scrutiny (Murphy and Laczniak 1981).

Some years ago Farmer (1967) argued that the field of marketing is basically unethical; that businesses push consumption of unnecessary goods and services causing scarce resources to be squandered. Although Farmer took a more moderate position in a later article (1977), ethical questions about marketing practices remain a critical concern for practitioners as well as academicians.

Farmer provides two explanations of why marketing is viewed as unethical. The first is that for the past 6,000 years the field of "marketing" has been thought of as made up of "fast-buck artists, con-men, wheeler-dealers, and shoddy-goods distributors." The second explanation is that "what is visible about marketing is not the intriguing, truly exciting research work in a variety of behavioral and technical areas. Instead, it is the picture of some pitchman selling hair spray on television!"

Marketing's problem of perceived ethical abuse is made clearer by the following two studies: Baumhart (1961) identifies the major ethical problems that business people want to eliminate: (1) gifts, gratuities, bribes, and "call girls," (2) price discrimination and unfair pricing, (3) dishonest advertising, (4) miscellaneous unfair competitive practices, (5) cheating customers, unfair credit practices, and overselling, (6) price collusion by competitors, (7) dishonesty in making or keeping a contract, and (8) unfairness to employees and prejudice in hiring. Note that five of the eight most important ethical problems have to do with marketing activities. Brenner and Molander (1977) conducted a follow-up study and found the same set of undesirable practices.

This prejudice against marketing is further explored by Steiner (1976) in his excellent article "The Prejudice Against Marketing." One of the major points is that marketing is seen as unethical partly because it deals only with time and place utility and not form utility.

Finally, Hunt and Chonko (1986) designed a research project to explore the question of whether marketing is manipulative, unethical, or "Machiavellian" in nature. They conclude that marketing has its "share of Machiavellians – no more, no less." In addition, "marketers high in Machiavellianism are not disproportionately located in any particular marketing occupation (such as sales)." Finally, the authors show that one does not need to be a Machiavellian to succeed in marketing. Actually, the reverse seems to occur.

Positive Studies

Wokutch and Fahey (1981) identify a number of methods used in ethical research:

1. The utilization of laboratory experiments and business game simulations in which unethical behavior is measured. This method allows the researcher to measure the influence of various factors such as business experience, age and completion of a business ethics course. One example of the use of this methodology is the study by Hegarty and Sims (1978) in which they measured the effects of potential rewards and punishments on students paying kickbacks in simulated business situations.

2. Ex post facto research in which actual ethical decision situations are reconstructed. Such an approach permits the study of real life situations. Some researchers have avoided this line of research because of its problem of getting accurate and complete information.
3. Participant observation approach, which permits the researcher to observe behaviors as they take place and then infer cause and effect relationships. Unfortunately, this approach is seldom used because of problems involved in gaining access to organizations.
4. The survey research approach in which subjects report on their own ethical behavior and beliefs.

The majority of instruments used in collecting ethical data utilize some form of scenarios presenting some ethical/unethical situation to which the subjects have to react. The use of scenarios, according to Fritzsche and Becker (1982), allows one to inject a greater amount of background information and detail into an ethically questionable issue. Scenarios therefore are thought to elicit a higher quality of data in this type of research than is possible from simple questions (Alexander and Becker 1978).

Scenarios and "paper and pencil" questionnaires have been traditionally used in ethics research, because they can "create dilemmas that can induce respondents to realistically modify their choices of alternatives in a given situation" (Vitell 1986). Scenarios, in addition, can induce the respondent to experience "the task as a problem and must therefore do some fresh thinking" (Gibbs and Widaman 1982, p. 13).

Fritzsche and Becker (1983) used scenarios that presented various types of ethical dilemmas. The ethical dilemmas addressed dealt with the issues of: (1) coercion and control, (2) conflict of interest, (3) the physical environment, (4) paternalism, and (5) personal integrity. The authors concluded that marketing managers reacted differently to different types of dilemmas.

Positive studies in business ethics can be divided into six main categories: (1) causes of unethical behavior, (2) ethics of future executives, (3) the relationship between ethical behavior and profitability, (4) social marketing ethics, (5) cross cultural ethics, and (5) surveys of various publics.

1. Causes of Unethical Behavior

In 1961, Raymond Baumhart undertook one of the early examinations of corporate ethics. Baumhart (1961) surveyed more than 1,700 business people and found that almost 80% believed that unethical practices occur in business. The unethical practices that 82% of the respondents would most like to see eliminated were associated with the traditional marketing functions of pricing and promotion. Some respondents felt that marketing affords the greatest number of opportunities for unethical behavior; the marketing structure itself encourages questionable business practices.

The two key influences felt to be leading to unethical behavior were business superiors and the ethical climate of the industry. Nossiter (1964) argues that these responses do not reflect a world of amoral executives, accepting the business life as it is; instead, the respondents display a marked uneasiness about their role and that of their fellows.

Baumhart also found that students have a lower opinion of the ethics of a business person than that of the business person himself. In addition, business people tended to attribute significantly higher ethical standards to themselves than they did to their associates in business.

Arlow and Ulrich (1988) compare the results of Baumhart's study with their business graduate sample's ranking of factors that influence ethical conduct. These rankings are:

Baumhart stud	*Arlow & Ulrich study*
1. Personal codes of behavior	1. Family training
2. Behavior of superiors	2. Conduct of superiors
3. Formal company policy	3. Practices in industry
4. Industry ethical climate	4. Conduct of peers
5. Behavior of peers	5. Religious training
	6. School training

The strong consistency among the priority attached to factors influencing ethical conduct is obvious from the above listing.

Brenner and Molander (1977) replicated Baumhart's study and found that 67% of 1,227 business executives surveyed felt that unethical practices occur in business. Furthermore, this study indicated that pressure imposed by superiors and the absence of a corporate ethical policy were the two main causes of unethical behavior. Other factors influencing "unethical" decisions were: (1) the industry ethical climate, and (2) the behavior of one's coworkers in the firm. These factors were the same in both the Baumhart and Brenner and Molander studies, although their rank order was slightly different.

Another explanation for unethical business behavior is the use of two ethical standards – personal and business (Bowman 1976; Carroll 1975). Personal standards tend to be more strict than business ones. Bowman's and Carroll's research found that people feel under pressure to compromise their personal standards in order to achieve the goals of the organization. Carr (1968) suggested yet another reason for unethical business behavior. In a controversial article, he likened the strategies people employ in business to those used by individuals playing a game, such as poker, where the players' standards differ from those generally employed in their nonworking lives. Carr stated that "most businessmen are not in different to ethics in their private lives, everyone will agree. The point is that in their office lives they cease to be private citizens; they become game players who must be guided by a somewhat different set of ethical standards" (p. 145). Perhaps, then, as long as one does not transgress the law – the business player's "rules of the game" – it is necessary to adhere to higher laws (that is, ethical standards). It is to the advantage of business people to follow only the rules of the game in plotting a strategy to achieve victory.

It is possible that a kind of Gresham's Law of ethics operates in a business environment. That is, "the ethic of corporate advantage invariably silences and drives out the ethic of individual restraint" (Carr 1970). The results of a study by Newstrom and Ruch (1975) suggest that managers have a propensity to act unethically if it is to their advantage – and if the barriers to unethical practices are reduced or removed. If a Gresham's law of ethics is applicable in industry, then personal codes will probably be compromised, forcing adherence to a code of business ethics. To do otherwise could cause mavericks to suffer peer ostracism or even lose their jobs.

Newstrom and Ruch (1975) surveyed business executives and found that: (1) ethics is personal –each of the situations was seen as "highly unethical" by some respondents, whereas they were seen as "not at all unethical" by others; (2) ethical beliefs of employees are similar to perceptions of top management ethics – the explanation for this finding was that employees either project their beliefs onto top management or else pattern their thoughts after this critical reference group; (3) managers have the propensity to capitalize on opportunities to be unethical, if those situations arise; and (4) managers believe their colleagues to be far more unethical than they themselves claim to be.

Fritzsche and Becker (1982) examine the business ethics of college students using ten vignettes which pose five different types of ethical problems. Their data appear to indicate that the students respond to the vignettes on an individual basis. There are also indications that the responses are elicited by the type of problem. Finally, the authors conclude that students may possess no hard and fast rules for dealing with specific types of ethical problems. Each problem is likely to be dealt with individually, based upon the values the student holds at that point. According to the authors:

> this finding may tend to explain the great variation in the ethical behavior of today's managers. With no instilled rules to follow, the ethics of the individual are likely to reflect the ethics of the organizations with which they associate. In the long run, one might thus expect the ethical behavior of managers to sink to the lowest common denominator.

Carroll (1975) concluded that the impact of social interaction on ethical behavior is a major internal environmental consideration in understanding ethical behavior toward consuming publics. Carroll's survey found that young managers in business said they would go along with their superiors to show their loyalty in matters that related to judgments of morality. Almost 60% of the respondents agreed that young managers would have done just what junior members of Nixon's re-election committee had done.

A survey by Pitney-Bowes Inc. (1977), a manufacturer of business equipment, revealed that 95% of its managers feel pressure to compromise personal ethics to achieve corporate goals. A similar study of Uniroyal managers found 70% feel pressure to compromise ethics. Most managers at Pitney-Bowes and Uniroyal believe most of their peers would not refuse orders to market off standard and possibly dangerous products.

Tarnowieski (1973) concluded that only 27% of the business respondents were able to say that they have never been expected to compromise personal principles to conform to organizational standards. Furthermore, more than half the businessmen reported that they could see no decrease in the organizational pressures to conform to various unethical standards. The survey reveals a perceived ethical decay since a majority of the respondents argued that prevailing youth attitudes are symptomatic of a moral breakdown in American society.

Concerning the actions of top management, several writers have stated that top management sets the ethical tone for the organization. This has been implicitly referred to as "the organization ethic" by Alderson (1964), Westing (1984), and Pruden (1971).Weaver and Ferrell (1977), in their studies of marketing managers, called upon top management to "establish a policy as well as express a commitment to ethical conduct." In a later paper, Ferrell and Weaver (1978) concluded that top management must assume at least part of the responsibility for ethical conduct of marketers within their organization. The authors went on to state that top management must establish and enforce policies, thereby developing a frame of reference for ethical behavior.

Similarly, Kaikati and Label (1980), in their examination of American bribery legislation, concluded that no code of ethical behavior is likely to be observed unless the chief executive officer declares that violators will be punished. When a company fails to take strict disciplinary action, many employees assume that their unethical acts are accepted standards of corporate behavior.

Ferrell and Weaver (1978) compare the ethical beliefs of marketing managers with those of top management. The important finding of their study is that respondents believe that they make decisions in an organizational environment where peers and top management have lower ethical standards than their own. Also, respondents believe that the existence and enforcement of corporate policy do not encourage more ethical conduct than their existing personal beliefs. Actually, it is perceived that the existence and enforcement of corporate policy sanctions less ethical conduct than respondents believe is appropriate.

In studying the correlates of salespeople's ethical conflict, Dubinsky and Ingram (1984) found that role conflict, role ambiguity, length in present position, length in sales, level of education, major source of income, and intensity of market competition were unrelated to salespeople's ethical conflict. Because all the variables in their study were found to be unrelated to ethical conflict, Dubinsky and Ingram list several additional variables that may be related to ethical conflict and should be the focus of future research. Among these variables are:

Intrapersonal –	sex, personality
interpersonal –	kinds of customers contacted, power
organizational –	span of control, closeness of supervision, quality of sales training programs
environmental –	current economic conditions, primary demand for the product.

In replicating the Ferrell and Weaver studies using Israeli managers, Izraeli (1988) concluded that the best predictor of managers' ethical behavior is their perceptions concerning their peers' behavior.

Weaver and Ferrell (1977) surveyed marketing practitioners and found that the existence and enforcement of corporate policy may improve some ethical beliefs and behavior. That finding challenged the findings of Brenner and Molander (1977) that company policy is a somewhat secondary influence in ethical beliefs and behavior. According to Vitell (1986) this study is important in that it studied the importance of organizational sanctions on individual ethical behaviors.

Finally, Laczniak and Inderrieden (1987), using an experimental design, studied the influence of "stated organizational concern" for ethical conduct upon managerial behavior. According to the authors, "only in the case of suggested illegal behavior tempered by high organizational concern were managers influenced by organizational policy to modify the morality of their actions" (p. 297).

2. The Ethics of Future Executives

There are those who believe that business schools have the opportunity to influence the ethical behavior of tomorrow's business leaders. Others are convinced that today's business students are more ethical than present day managers.

A study by Goodman and Crawford (1974) failed to find any meaningful difference in the ethical behavior of marketing executives, MBA students, and undergraduate business students. These results did not support the belief that students are more ethical than managers. Goodman and Crawford tried to determine to what extent the emerging ethics of the younger generation may have influenced their attitudes toward various potential business practices of the established order. They surveyed both business students and marketing executives to see the differences in ethical perceptions between the two groups. The results showed that business students do not represent an upcoming influx of new ethical standards, since their ethical standards were not significantly different from the marketing executives. In the same study, a comparison of the business student with liberal arts students arts did show a significant difference, although liberal students were slightly more critical of certain business practices.

Purcell (1977a, b), using a slightly different approach than Goodman and Crawford, found that a group of students who took his management ethics course were less ethical when they took the course than they were a decade later. Purcell's conclusion was that greater ethical consciousness and sophistication developed through business experience. A more recent study by Arlow and Ulrich (1982) sampled 120 undergraduate business students. A comparison of the students with a group of business executives revealed that students had lower personal business ethics than did the executives. These results are consistent with those of Hollon and Ulrich (1979), who found the personal business ethics of managers actually exceeded those of business students. Similar results were reported by Stevens (1984), using a questionnaire developed by Clark (1966).

Beltramini et al. (1984) surveyed 2,856 students and found that college students are quite sensitive to ethical issues, major, years in school, or gender. In addition, female students are more concerned about ethical issues in business than their male counterparts. Similar results were reported by Jones and Gautschi (1988).

Krackhardt et al. (1985) studied MBA students in an effort to discover the determinants of the student's judgements regarding ethical issues in business. They found that MBA students are utilizing a utilitarian perspective in analysing ethical issues in business. Regarding codes of ethics the authors concluded that:

> ...Within a business context, witnessing unethical behavior does not seem to carry any heavy responsibility for reporting the behavior. This finding may explain why there is such controversy over 'whistle-blowing' inorganizations. Although organizations may encourage employees to report unethical behavior, it is clear that failure to report such behavior is not considered highly unethical ... (p. 14)

3. Relationship Between Ethical Behavior and Profitability

Several CEOs have come to the conclusion that ethical business is good business. Donald V. Seibert, CEO and Chairman of J. C. Penny, is quoted as saying, "in the long run, the best business decision is that which is founded on the most ethical judgements" (Solomon and Hanson 1985, p. xi). In addition, Rance Crain (1983), President of Crain Communications and Editor-in-chief of Advertising Age, argues that "business ethics makes good business sense ...ethical business conduct is a pragmatic, no-nonsense, bottom-line way of running your business for the long-term welfare of everybody involved."

Powers and Vogel (1980), and Callahan and Bok (1980) argue that the linking of managerial competence with moral competence should be the major goal of any course in business ethics.

Hill (1977) argues that public opinion and ultimately the long term survival of the firm depend partly on keeping high ethical standards in its business dealings, and partly on being honest in its statements of public concern.

Solomon and Hanson (1985) argue that ethical behavior promotes improved performance in the organization. They claim that "the most powerful argument for ethics in business is success. Ethical businesses are successful businesses" (Solomon and Hanson 1985, p. 22).

Ohmann (1955) argues that businesses should acknowledge that "idealism" is not only for holy days but should be part of the everyday business routine. Such an acknowledgement, argues Saul (1981), will entail corporate decision makers conceding that they can be ethical and still stay in business, and ridding themselves of the notion that the only truly ethical companies are those that are also going out of business. Business leaders must realize that ethical behavior is good business (Miller 1979). It results in greater drive and motivation, it attracts better quality people who appreciate working with a respected company; and it improves relations with customers, competitors, and the public.

In a recent literature review of the relationship between profitability and social responsibility, Abratt and Sacks (1988) concluded that "organizations who adopt the societal marketing concept will be the ones most likely to make long-run profits as well as be beneficial to society as a whole" (p. 497).

Friedman and Friedman (1988) propose a framework for organizational success in which the marketing concept must work together with good management approaches and ethical business practices in order for the organization to be successful in the long run.

Sturdivant and Ginter (1977) surveyed 130 senior executives of various corporations. Managers with the most profitable corporations tended to be more favorable toward minorities, the poor, and other aspects of human rights than were executives in the less profitable firms. Johnson (1981) interpreted these results as meaning that "profitable business is, by and large, ethical business."

Sturdivant and Ginter examined the profitability of companies that are high and low in social or ethical performance. The authors in their findings implied that "ethical" firms are profitable firms. This implied causation of being "ethical" leading to higher profits does not stand in firm grounds in that the same relationship can be explained by reversing the causal flow. In other words, firms that are profitable can "afford" to be more "ethical."

As seen before, Purcell (1977a, b) argued that "good ethics is good business in the long run" even though he admitted that this is not always true in the short run. But however difficult the trade-off is, ethics must prevail if the free market system is to survive.

Palmer (1986) cites a study that concludes that permeating an entire organization with negative ethical attitudes can result in "increased labor costs, loss of goodwill, major losses due to theft, purposefully counterproductive behavior, and direct market share losses."

In the international market arena, Barry (1979a, b) found that the multinational corporations that have not had serious improper payments problems are also among the leaders in their industries and enjoy a strong competitive advantage over the corporations that were involved in unethical payoffs.

A different opinion is expressed by Learned et al. (1959), who conclude that the view that good ethics is good business is not a fully adequate or satisfying guide for action.

Finally, the subject of how ethical dilemmas on the job would affect worker productivity will not be dealt within this paper. For the most current critique of the literature on the subject and recommendations for future research, see Moser (1988).

4. Social Marketing Ethics

Murphy et al. (1978) made a distinction between marketing ethics and social marketing ethics and offered guidelines for both social and business marketing. Similar arguments were presented in an article in the *Journal of Marketing* a year later about the ethical dimensions of social marketing (Laczniak et al. 1979).

In a related article, Laczniak et al. (1981) confirmed the hypothesis that certain marketing techniques were considered less acceptable for political candidates and drug education than for the selling of soap, dishwashers, or TV dinners.

In yet another article, Lusch et al. (1980) tested the hypothesis of whether the public is able to make a distinction between the "ethics of social ideas" versus the "ethics of marketing social ideas." Their results showed that individuals cannot totally separate the social idea from the marketing technique used to promote the idea. Consumer advocates would probably argue that professional marketers must assume partial responsibility for the impact of any social program or idea which has been professionally marketed. They would suggest the marketer is as responsible for subsequent actions as the gun shop owner who illegally sells a handgun to a minor. Finally, they also found that certain social issues are more likely to foster strong ethical concerns than others.

5. Cross-Cultural Studies

As was argued in the introduction, most ethically sensitive marketing decisions fall into the "gray" area, where the difference between an ethical and an unethical action is not so clear, creating an ethical dilemma about which action to choose. This ethical dilemma facing business people is further compounded by two other factors. The first is that historically the ethical yardstick for business has been profit – the bottom line. Milton Friedman expresses the view that there is one and only one social responsibility of business – to increase its profits for the benefit of the stockholders (Friedman 1962).

The second factor is that business is continually getting more complex and intertwined with other publics than in the past. With more and more companies expanding into foreign markets, the problem of cross cultural ethics is getting more prevalent. Business practices that are considered ethical in the U.S. are not viewed as such in different cultures. How different cultures view various business practices has only been given slight attention by the ethics literature.

England (1975) believes that people brought up in different cultures hold different values and ethical beliefs (the moral dimension of personal values). McClelland (1961) studied the achievement motive in different countries and concluded that different cultures have different effects on business practices. Although McClelland does not treat the topic of ethics as such, he states that the diverse value patterns and religious beliefs pointed toward the diversity of ethical beliefs among different cultures. Textbooks in international business are filled with examples warning international managers of potential cultural conflicts. For example, the way Hindus view business would be different from the way Christians view business. Terpstra (1978) points out that Hindus are taught that concern with earthly achievements is a snare and a delusion, while Christians praise the value of hard work and achievement.

Similarly, Prasad and Rao (1982) argue that, although certain ethical norms such as honesty, integrity, self-discipline, loyalty, and compassion are widely proclaimed and are part of any civilization, adherence to these standards varies greatly among people.

The majority of the cross-cultural studies in marketing ethics have been "coincidental;" meaning that culture was not the main variable of focus in the study. Two such studies are by Hegarty and Sims (1978, 1979).

Hegarty and Sims (1978) regard ethical decision making as a phenomenon of learning. As such, it may be possible that ethical behavior can be strengthened or weakened, according to environmental consequences of the behavior reinforcement theory of Skinner (1938, 1953, 1969). More specifically, the authors hypothesize that: (1) when unethical behavior is followed by a positive reinforcement (reward), subsequent decisions tend to be less ethical than the non reward conditions; (2) when unethical behavior is followed by the "threat of punishment," subsequent decisions become more ethical; (3) competitiveness tends to increase unethical decision making; and (4) some personality and demographic variables, used as covariates in the experiment, explain a significant variance in ethical decision making.

The most significant of these covariates is "foreign nationality" ($F=8.74$), followed by "Machiavellianism" ($F=7.63$), "economic values orientation" ($F=5.43$), "locus of control" ($F=4.84$), and "political value orientation" ($F=3.84$). Other variables such as sex, extraversion, neuroticism, and religious value orientation were not significant covariates.

Foreign nationals, comprising 20% of a sample of 120, were found to be significantly less ethical than U.S. nationals. But according to the authors, "the finding that foreign nationals were more unethical was ambiguous but interesting and deserves much further investigation." Similar results are found in two subsequent experiments (Hegarty and Sims 1979). In all three experiments, Hegarty and Sims make the mistake of grouping all foreign nationals in one group, as if they are homogeneous. But if we accept the premise that culture and its values have an effect on the individual's ethics, we would expect individuals with different cultures to have different ethical beliefs and different ethical behavior.

Tat (1981) replicate, the study of Hawkins and Cocanougher (1972) using black students. Tat argues that previous studies found business students more tolerant of questionable business practices than non-business students (Hawkins and Cocanougher 1972; Shuptrine 1979). However, Tat's study provides conflicting results. Black business majors are not more tolerant of questionable business practices than are non business majors. Tat attributes that difference between black and white students to the type of environment under which these two groups of students were raised. Tat argues that:

> the majority of minority students, regardless of majors, were raised under a disadvantaged environment and had been exploited. The unpleasant experiences may lead them to have such deep-rooted attitudes toward the business community that the exposure to a business education could not change their perceptions of business practices.

In addition, Tat concludes that the mean ratings of both business and nonbusiness majors in his study are lower than those in Hawkins and Cocanougher's study. Tat explains that difference as follows:

> being raised under a disadvantaged environment, the minority students may view the situations presented to them as mild, compared to their actual experiences in dealing with merchants in low income areas.

The important finding of this study is that the ethical perceptions of black subjects are different from the ethical perceptions of white subjects. In other words, members of different subcultures have different ethical beliefs.

The only cross-cultural study in business ethics that had culture as its focal variable is by Kam-Hon Lee. Lee (1981) studies the impact of culture and management level on ethics in marketing practices. In his study, he compares the ethical beliefs of Chinese managers with the ethical beliefs of British managers working in Hong Kong. He hypothesizes that the culture in which a manager is brought up plays a significant role in ascertaining the differences of ethical practices. However, neither a significant effect due to culture, nor a significant interaction effect of the two independent variables (culture, level of management) was found in any of the ten scenarios used. That led Lee to conclude that the evaluation frameworks of British and Chinese managers is extremely similar. Lee attributes that finding to a possible acculturation of the British managers. The author argues that the British managers practiced the principle of "when in Rome, do as the Romans do."

Kam-Hon Lee's findings seem to contradict the widely accepted view that people raised in different cultures hold different ethical beliefs (England 1975). Two recent studies seem to support Lee's (1981) findings. Tsalikis and Nwachukwu (1988) compare the ethical beliefs of black and white business students and found them to be, with a few exceptions, quite similar. In a similar study, Tsalikis and Nwachukwu (1989) found that, despite the cultural differences, Greek business students had similar ethical beliefs with their American counterparts.

6. Surveys of Various Publics

This branch of the ethical literature includes surveys of various groups in order to determine whether they consider certain business practices as "ethical" or "unethical." Groups surveyed include business executives from various types of business, business and non business students (both graduate and undergraduate), and comparisons among business executives and students.

Vitell (1986) argues that the majority of these studies measured only people's beliefs and opinions without having a theoretical or conceptual foundation. However, Vitell finds these studies useful to the extent they provided an insight to the ethical decision making process and to the development of a positive theory of ethical decision making.

The best known surveys were by Baumhart (1961), Brenner and Molander (1977), and Carroll (1975). The results of these studies were reported previously under the heading "causes of unethical behavior" and need not be repeated here.

Another important study is Sturdivant and Cocanougher's (1973) survey of corporate executives, business school students, blue collar workers, and housewives. These four groups were asked to evaluate the ethics of various business practices. The results revealed that there is a substantial "ethical gap" between the ethical perceptions of these four groups. This gap was more obvious between house-wives and corporate executives.

Hawkins and Cocanougher (1972) compared the ethical views of undergraduate business and non-business majors. The two groups were questioned about their ethical beliefs on 20 scenarios involving ethical issues. The results showed that business students rated many questionable practices more "ethical" than did nonbusiness majors. This permitted the authors to argue that the pursuit of a business education will lead to relatively more tolerant attitudes toward questionable business practices. An additional hypothesis that a student's father's career would have an effect on his/her ethical perceptions was not accepted.

In a series of articles in the *Wall Street Journal*, based on a WSJ/Gallup survey, Ricklefs (1983a, b, c, d) reported that business executives and general citizens often see ethical issues very differently. On many issues, the executives apply a far stricter ethical standard, at least in the abstract. In addition, citizens were considerably more inclined than executives to condone wrongdoing if there are mitigating circumstances. Despite that, a large share of surveyed citizens have adopted a cynical view of the ethics practiced by the country's business leaders. More alarmingly for employers, people who condemn taking advantage of an individual commonly seem to shrug their shoulders over doing the same thing to an employer.

In the same survey, young Americans consistently indicated that they are more likely to take an unethical path than their elders. Women were found to behave consistently more ethically than men. In addition, Americans who attend a church or feel a religious affiliation appear only slightly more ethical than their less-pious compatriots.

Posner and Schmidt (1984) surveyed 1,460 executives in an effort to learn something about their values. They concluded that, contrary to popular opinion, profit maximization and the stockholders are not the main focus of business executives, but the public-at-large and the government were paid substantial attention. In addition, the authors found that pressures to conform to organizational standards were perceived as very strong, without any hope of these pressures diminishing in the future.

Clinard (1983) studied middle-level managers using a series of interviews. Although no statistical analysis could be performed to that data, several inferences were drawn. Among these inferences were: (a) the CEO sets the ethical tone for the whole organization – a result which is shared by Dagher and Spader (1980); (b) pressures to show profits were substantial enough to lead to unethical behavior, and (3) corporate codes of ethics are not sufficient and government intervention is necessary. Another less well-structured series of interviews of top executives was performed by Silk and Vogel (1976).

Krugman and Ferrell (1981) surveyed the ethical perceptions of advertising practitioners, advertising agency account managers, and corporate advertising managers. In addition to presenting their own beliefs, respondents were asked to assess the ethical beliefs of peers and superiors. The results indicated that respondents believe they are more "ethical" than their peers. On the other side, respondents reported that their superiors have the same or higher ethical standards than themselves. Corporate advertising managers believe their advertising agency counterparts hold lower ethical standards than their own. The converse did not hold true.

In a survey by Neill (1965); both the general public and business executives rated advertising and public relations executives below professionals, small businessmen, average workers, and federal workers. Business executives rated themselves just below scientists, who are in the first place, and rated labor union officials the lowest. The general public assigned the best ethical reputation to banks, telephone companies, life insurance companies and electric utilities. The respondents felt that automobile dealers, advertising agencies, and cosmetic and drug firms were the most guilty of misleading advertising, claims and promotions, high prices, and poor quality products. A survey of business by Harris et al. (1966) indicated that more than half the general public approved of the way government is regulating business. In other words, the general public felt that corporate executives are too business oriented and care little for the individual.

Dornoff and Tankersley (1975a, b) surveyed both retailers' and consumers' perceptions of retailers' actions taken in market transactions. This particular study did not explicitly deal with the ethical dimensions of the retailers' actions but the study's design justifies its placement in the ethical literature.

Trawick and Darden (1980) surveyed marketing educators' and practitioners' perceptions of ethical standards in the marketing profession. The results revealed that marketing practitioners felt that they are as ethical as those in other professions. Marketing educators, on the other side, were more slightly skeptical about the ethical standards of the marketing profession. However, this difference in opinion was not significantly different. Vitell (1986) observed that in both the Krugman and Ferrell (1981), and Trawick and Darden study "both practitioners and educators have a basically teleological ethical perspective."

Browning and Zabriskie (1983) surveyed members of a state purchasing association to gain insights into their ethical beliefs and behavior. Their results showed that industrial buyers had a high level of ethical beliefs and an even higher level of ethical behavior when specific situations are referenced. On the other hand, there was some evidence that giving favors may still be part of doing business with some buyers.

Dubinsky et al. (1980) compared the ethical perceptions of industrial salespeople and business students. Their results showed a significant difference between salespeople's and business students' perceptions of ethical issues facing industrial salespeople. Students see more situations as raising ethical questions than salespeople do. They also feel a greater need to have a company policy addressing several of the selling situations examined. Interestingly, students perceive the giving of gifts to a purchaser as less ethically troubling than salespeople.

Wood et al. (1988) compared the ethical attitudes of students and business professionals. The results show that students are significantly more willing to engage in unethical behavior than their professional counterparts.

The majority of the above articles have surveyed business people or business students. Both of these groups represent the producer's side of the market. Davis (1979) argues that, in addition to their rights, consumers also have certain ethical responsibilities. These responsibilities are to offer intelligent suggestions and complaints when necessary to business, to use information that is available from labels, owner's manuals, etc., and to be honest and fair in all dealings and call attention to errors that are to their disadvantage as well as those that are to their advantage.

In a related article, Stampfl (1979) developed a consumer's ethical code based on ethical principles borrowed from disciplines such as economics, sociology, law, psychology, marketing, and political science. Stampfl's ethical code is quite similar to Davis's consumer responsibilities.

In a survey of management's attitudes on corruption in business, Pitt and Abratt (1986) found that while their sample of top and middle managers condemned corruption and corruptive practices, the perceived participation by their peer group was higher than expected.

Additional surveys were conducted on marketing executives (Crawford 1970 – reported under marketing research), sales personnel (Dubinsky et al. 1980– reported under sales management), and purchasing managers (Rudelius and Buchholz 1979; Cummings 1979; Dempsey et al. 1980 – reported under purchasing management).

Ethical differences between males and females. The phenomenon of women rising to top management positions is a relatively new one. According to *Time* (March 10, 1984), very few women pursued careers In management 16 years ago. Because of this the majority of ethical studies focused on male managers. As more and more women entered the ranks of top management, the question of their ethical reactions versus their male counterparts came into prominence.

Kidwell et al. (1987) studied the differences in ethical perceptions between 50 male and 50 female managers. They found that ethical perceptions between males and females are quite similar. However, when they rated the ethical behavior of the other sex, females rated males as being significantly less ethical than themselves and vice versa. Similar results were reported by McNichols and Zimmerer (1985).

On the other side, Beltramini et al. (1984), in a survey of students' concerns regarding business ethics, found that female students are more concerned about ethical issues than are their male counterparts.

Similarly, Jones and Gautschi (1988) argue that women MBA students are more sensitive to ethical issues than their male counterparts. Women also "display a greater tendency to take action when they perceive a questionable business practice … As women managers become commonplace, it may well follow that corporate behavioral norms will be affected positively" (Jones and Gautschi 1988, p. 245).

These studies/surveys were attacked from three sides:

1. An article by Morgan (1981) questions the methodology used in most of the empirical studies in marketing ethics. Morgan contends that differences found among the various groups might be the result of the experimental design used, rather than actual differences. In Morgan's words, " … if one desired to show that housewives disagreed extensively with the business community, one could package a series of hypothetical situations to support this contention" (1981, p. 238).

2. Reidenbach and Robin (1986) criticize the use of a seven or five point Likert scale ranging from "very unethical" to "very ethical" to measure respondents' ethical perceptions. The authors propose that ethical measurements should be treated as dichotomous and interval level variables. According to Reidenbach and Robin:

> if a marketing practice is somewhat, marginally, or mostly ethical it also stands to reason that, at the same time it would be somewhat, marginally, or mostly unethical. This leaves one in the perplexing position of reconciling the question of how an act or activity can be both ethical and unethical when judged by the same individual.

3. Vitell (1986) criticizes most of the previous studies as lacking a strong theoretical foundation. According to Vitell:

> none of the studies reviewed was concerned with establishing any kind of positive theoretical framework that could be used to explain how decision makers choose particular courses of action in situations having ethical content.

Because of that, Vitell (1986) set out to develop a positive model or theory of marketing ethics.

Studies Leading to a Positive Theory of Marketing Ethics

The most recent development in the business ethics literature should be credited to Hunt, Vitell, and some other researchers attempting to develop a "positive" theory of marketing ethics. Following Vitell's (1986) lead, the articles leading to the development of this positive theory will be divided into (1) conceptual, and (2) empirical.

Conceptual Studies

Kohlberg (1981) studied the meaning and measurement of moral development influenced by the work of Jane Loevinger on the meaning and measurement of ego development. Kohlberg hypothesized that people go through six stages of moral development. These are:

1. The stage of punishment and obedience – where right is the literal obedience to rules and authority.
2. The stage of individual instrument purpose and exchange – where right is serving one's own needs and making fair deals.
3. The stage of mutual interpersonal expectations, relationships and conformity – where right is being concerned about others, keeping loyalties and being motivated to follow rules.
4. The stage of social system and conscience maintenance – where right is doing one's duty to society.

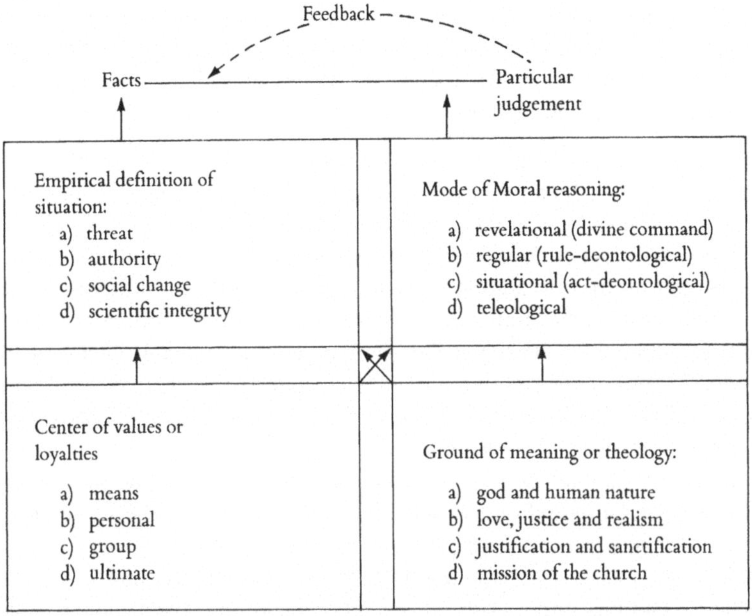

Fig. 17.6 Elements involved in justifying an ethical decision (Stassen's model)

5. The stage of prior rights and social contact or utility–where right is upholding the basic rights, values, and legal contracts of society.
6. The stage of universal ethical principles – where right is determined by universal ethical principles that all should follow.

One of the major caveats of Kohlberg's theory is that it was developed with psychology in mind and, as many other theories transplanted from psychology to marketing, might be unreliable.

The major contribution of Kohlberg is that individuals may behave differently in similar ethical situations over time. This might occur because these individuals have progressed to another ethical stage in their moral development.

Stassen (1977) presented a streamlined version of Ralph Potter's analytical scheme for portraying the main elements involved in justifying an ethical decision. Stassen's model is presented in Fig. 17.6. According to Fig. 17.6, a particular ethical judgment is affected by four dimensions. These dimensions are:

1. The empirical definition of the situation – it includes various situationspecific variables (such as perceived risk and legitimacy of various alternative courses of action) that might affect the individual's perception of the situation.
2. The moral reasoning dimension – it includes the three major normative theories of ethics, rule-deontological, act deontological, and teleological, and adds that of divine command, "where principles are justified because they are God-given" (Vitell 1986, p. 35).

3. The theological dimension – one explanation of this dimension is that ethical thought requires some answer to the existential question, "Why ought I be moral?"
4. The loyalties dimension – it focuses on the groups that might influence the individual's ethical perceptions.

This model was criticized as normative and empirically untestable. However, the main contribution of the above model, is that it can be used in grasping the most important elements in reasoning about moral decisions.

Dayton (1979) argues that, even in ethical situations, individuals will attempt to maximize their utilities. In addition, Dayton argues that these "utility maximizers" might "adopt cooperative strategies in order to solve mutual problems, and that the adoption of cooperative strategies can produce optimal mutual outcomes for the cooperators" (pp. 131–132). Dayton seems to recognize the importance of others to the individual faced with an ethical decision, even though he is mainly concerned with the maximization of his own utility.

Alderson (1965), in his theory of marketing systems argues that there exist three types of sanctions imposed on the individual decision maker. These sanctions are: (1) organizational sanctions – sanctions imposed by your supervisors for example, (2) market sanctions – sanctions imposed by the marketplace, and (3) ecological sanctions – sanctions imposed by the society as a whole. Even though Alderson presented his theory as a normative one, his conceptualizations can be used for the development of a positive theory of ethical decision making.

Empirical Studies

The previous studies, even though normative in nature, set the stage for the development of a positive theory of marketing ethics. Other studies, however, approached the question of ethical decision making from the positive side.

Mayer (1970) was concerned with the causes of unethical behavior among purchasing managers. Mayer argued that purchasing managers will be more prone to act "unethically" if certain conditions exist. These conditions are: (1) the individual's inclination toward "unethical" behavior, (2) the expected penalties versus the expected gains of the behavior, and (3) the opportunity to engage in unethical practices. Numbers one and two were later studied by Hegarty and Sims (1978, 1979). Hegarty and Sims conducted a laboratory experiment using graduate business students to study ethical decision making under different contingencies of reinforcement. They found that "when subjects were rewarded for unethical behavior, the unethical behavior was higher than when subjects were not rewarded" (1978, p. 451). Increased competition also tended to promote unethical behavior.

Finally, their results indicated that four personality variables (locus of control, economic and political value orientation, and Machiavellianism) acted as covariates

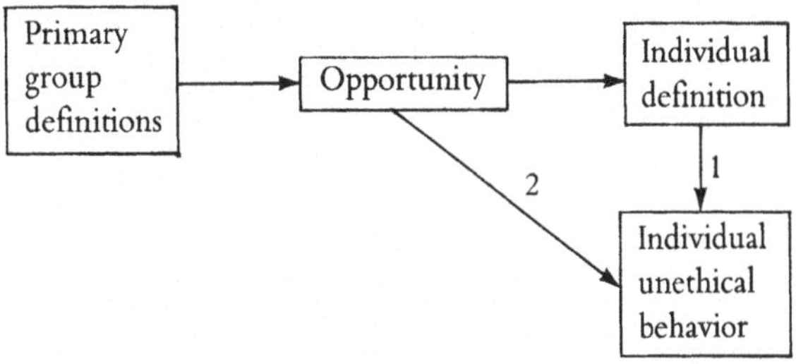

Fig. 17.7 A model of differential association plus opportunity

of unethical behavior. The second experiment by the same authors confirmed the notion that personality variables are related to unethical decision making. In addition, they found that an organizational ethics policy significantly reduced unethical behavior. In both studies, foreign nationality was found to be related to unethical decision behavior.

Zey-Ferrell et al. (1979) utilized Sutherland's "differential association" model (Sutherland 1970) to predict unethical behavior among marketing practitioners. The authors used Newstrom and Ruch's 17-item scale to develop six types of predictor variables. These variables are: (1) the marketer's beliefs; (2) what the marketer thought his peers believed; (3) what the marketer thought top management believed; (4) what the marketer thought his peers did; (5) the opportunity the marketer thought his peers had to become involved in unethical behavior; and (6) the opportunity the marketer himself had to become involved in unethical behavior. Their findings showed that the marketer's perceptions of what his/her peers did and his/her own opportunity to commit unethical behavior were the best predictors of actual unethical behavior. Their results seem to indicate that the individual's own attitudes are important in predicting unethical behavior. This finding contradicts Hegarty and Sims's assertions that various personality variables were significant covariates of unethical behavior.

These findings were represented by the authors in their "model of differential association plus opportunity" (Fig. 17.7). According to this model unethical behavior comes about in two ways. First, the individual may behave unethically after having altered his own definition or attitude toward the behavior due to peer pressure. Second, the individual may behave unethically without any change in the way he perceives the behavior. Similar findings were reported in later articles by the same authors (Zey-Ferrell and Ferrell 1982; Ferrell et al. 1983).

The Zey-Ferrell and Ferrell 1982 study expanded the model to include interorganizational influences. The results showed that interorganizational influences were not significant. In other words, reference groups that are "closer" to the individual had a greater effect on his behavior.

A more recent article by Ferrell and Gresham (1985) presented a positive model of ethical decision making in marketing (Fig. 17.8). This model was criticized by Vitell (1986), who presented his own more comprehensive "marketing ethics model" (Fig. 17.9).

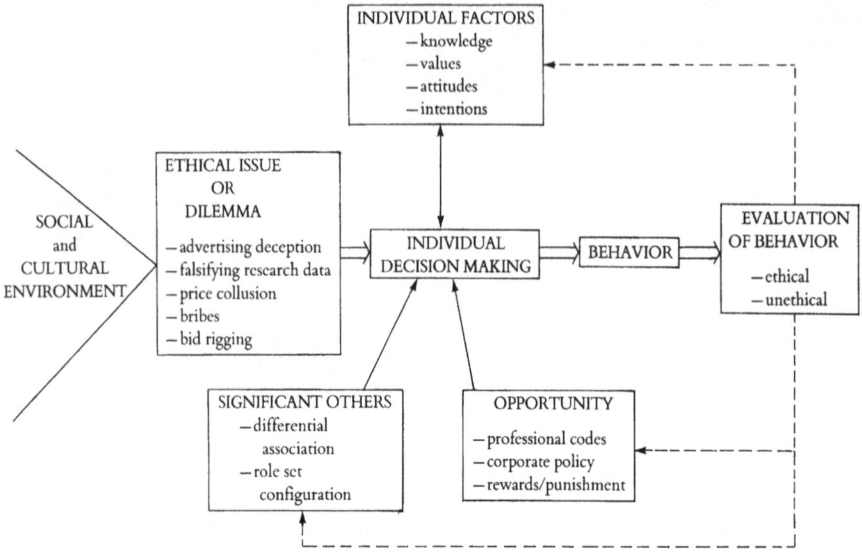

Fig. 17.8 A contingency model of ethical decision making in a marketing organization

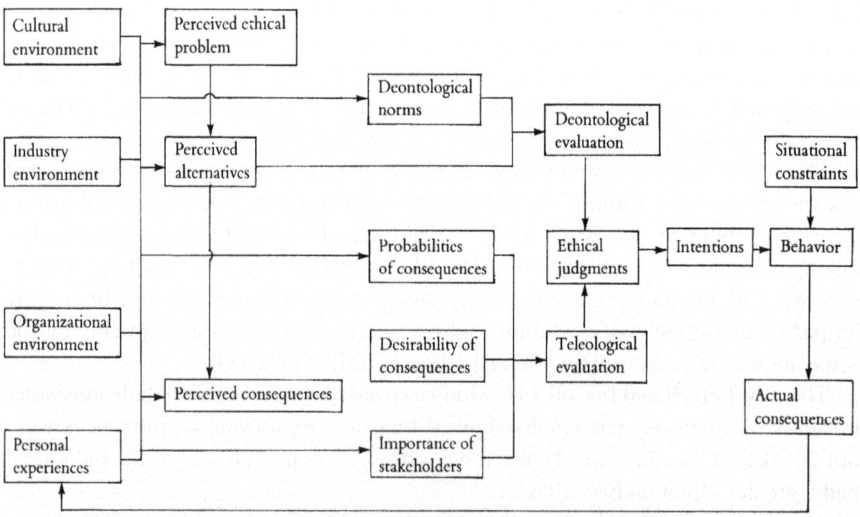

Fig. 17.9 Marketing ethics model (MEM)

Conclusion

The Weaknesses of "Scientific Studies" of Marketing Ethics

There are two basic problems which reduce the utility of so-called scientific studies of marketing ethics and which must be addressed if we are to proceed to a higher level of study. These two problems have to do with (1) the pluralistic nature of moral philosophy and (2) the single global measures which marketers tend to use in obtaining evaluations of marketing activities.

The field of ethics contains a number of normative theories, many of which pose conflicting ideas, rules, and interpretations which, in turn, can lead to conflicting evaluations of what is ethical or unethical. These normative theories were presented in the introduction of this paper. Excellent discussions of these theories can also be found in both Beauchamp and Bowie (1983) and Donaldson and Werhane (1983). However, most marketing writers and researchers, if they even discuss the different ethical philosophies, tend to limit their discussions to the philosophies of utilitarianism and/or deontology (e.g. Hunt and Vitell 1986; Ferrell and Gresham 1985).These reductionistic approaches assume that individuals engage in some sort of cognitive calculus, invoking the tenets of either deontology or utilitarianism or possibly some hybrid of the two philosophies in making an ethical evaluation. Little, if any, consideration is given to the other competing strains of moral philosophy such as relativism, egoism, or justice.

For example, Fritzsche and Becker (1984) attempted to link management behavior with normative theories of ethics. They classify the responses of managers to a series of vignettes according to the normative ethical theory represented by the response. More specifically, following the presentation of each of five vignettes, respondents were asked to decide whether they would behave in accordance with the requested unethical behavior. After this decision, respondents reported the reasons why they would behave like this. These responses were classified according to the type of normative ethical theory they represented. The results show that the majority of the respondents use utilitarian logic to justify their decision. The utilitarian responses were equally divided between act and rule utilitarianism.

The major caveat of this study is that "when a complete response contained elements from several response categories, it was classified according to the first response category discussed" (p. 169).

In addition, Brady (1985) argues that both deontological theories of ethics and utilitarian theories of ethics have traditionally claimed to be the exclusive process through which ethical decisions are made. Brady contends that it is disconcerting to be offered an analytic framework that consists of a fundamental antagonism between formalism (a term Brady is using as equivalent to "deontological") and utilitarianism and then to be invited to "take your pick." Brady develops a model that views the two ethical theories of utilitarianism and formalism not as antagonistic but as complementary. According to Brady, the relationship between formalism and utilitarianism is not a "zero-sum relation", but one that can be described more as

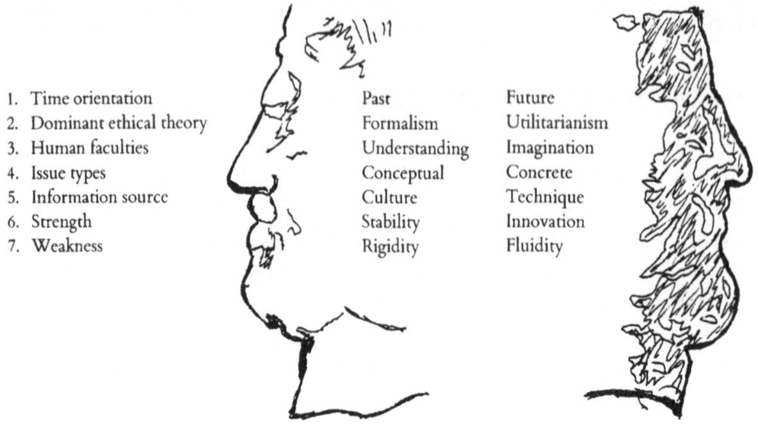

Fig. 17.10 A Janus-headed model of ethical process

"division of labor." Using the two-faced Roman god Janus, Brady portrays the process of resolving ethical issues as simultaneously looking to the past, as well as to the future, with utilitarianism looking to the future and formalism looking to the past (see Fig. 17.10).

In this model, ethical decision makers are presented as doing two things at once:

1. As formalists, they are looking to the cultural heritage established by law, language, and tradition and assessing the relevance and adequacy of the store of knowledge to the issue at hand.
2. As utilitarians, they are simply seeking to discover a solution that will give the best possible results according to some idea of what it means to be fully human. (Because the latter requirement is a notoriously difficult one, utilitarians usually 'liberalize' the requirement by surveying the personal preferences of all interested or affected persons, rather than explicating the concept of 'humanity').

Finally, Rest (1979) argues that individuals pass through a moral development process, ranging from Obedience ("Do what you are told") to "Nonarbitrary Social Cooperation" wherein individuals rely on abstract principles much like those which dominate utilitarian and deontological reasoning. Rest argues that the final stage of moral development wherein individuals rely on the prescribed notions of moral philosophy (e.g., deontology and utilitarianism) is one which is sought but not yet attained. The issue then becomes: should descriptive studies of marketing rely solely on the normative philosophies of deontology and utilitarianism?

The second problem concerns the instrumentation used to assess the evaluations. Typically, marketers rely on a single global measure of the ethics of a marketing situation. Measuring usually occurs on a seven point ethics scale anchored by such adjective phrases as "not at all unethical" to "very unethical" or form "ethical" to "unethical." A single measure is highly unreliable (Kerlinger 1986, p. 415; Nunnally

1967, p. 192) and unreliable measures are heavily error laden. Thus the results of research, using single global measures of the ethical evaluation of given marketing activities, are questionable.

A second aspect of the global measure problem is that it does not or can not detail the dynamics of the evaluation. This means that it is impossible to understand the ethical perspectives that are invoked in making the evaluation. Is the individual using a relativist, deontological, utilitarian perspective or some other set of criteria in making the evaluation? A single global measure is insufficient in revealing this information. If we are to improve our understanding of the evaluation process and if we are to make positive reactions to situations which warrant a reaction, it is important to address the problems inherent in the pluralistic nature of ethical theory and its measurement.

In order to solve these weaknesses of scientific studies of marketing ethics, Reidenbach and Robin developed an instrument that includes the theories of relativism, egoism, and justice in addition to utilitarianism and deontologicalism (see Appendix A).

Appendix A

Sample Questionnaire

Fair	____:____:____:____:____:____:____	unfair
Just	____:____:____:____:____:____:____	unjust
culturally acceptable	____:____:____:____:____:____:____	culturally unacceptable
self promoting	____:____:____:____:____:____:____	not self promoting
efficient	____:____:____:____:____:____:____	inefficient
violates an unwritten contract	____:____:____:____:____:____:____	does not violate an unwritten contract
OK if actions are justified by the result	____:____:____:____:____:____:____	not OK even if the actions are justified by the results
compromises an important rule by which I live	____:____:____:____:____:____:____	does not compromise an important rule by which I live
individually acceptable	____:____:____:____:____:____:____	individually unacceptable
selfish	____:____:____:____:____:____:____	unselfish
on balance, tend to be good	____:____:____:____:____:____:____	on balance, tend to be bad
violates my idea of fairness	____:____:____:____:____:____:____	does not violate my of idea fairness
results in an equal distribution of good and bad	____:____:____:____:____:____:____	does not result in an equal distribution of good and bad
acceptable to people I most admire admire	____:____:____:____:____:____:____	not acceptable to people I most
ethical	____:____:____:____:____:____:____	unethical
duty bound to act this way	____:____:____:____:____:____:____	not duty bound to act this way
produces the greatest utility	____:____:____:____:____:____:____	does not produce the greatest utility
traditionally acceptable	____:____:____:____:____:____:____	traditionally unacceptable
morally right	____:____:____:____:____:____:____	not morally right
maximizes benefits while minimizing harm	____:____:____:____:____:____:____	minimizes benefits while maximizing harm
obligated to act this way	____:____:____:____:____:____:____	not obligated to act this way
leads to the greatest good for the greatest number	____:____:____:____:____:____:____	does not lead to the greatest good for the greatest number
results in a positive cost-benefit ratio	____:____:____:____:____:____:____	results in a negative cost-benefit ratio
violates an unspoken promise	____:____:____:____:____:____:____	does not violate an unspoken promise
maximizes pleasure	____:____:____:____:____:____:____	minimizes pleasure
self sacrificing	____:____:____:____:____:____:____	not self sacrificing
acceptable to my family prudent	____:____:____:____:____:____:____	not acceptable to my family not prudent
under no moral obligation to act otherwise	____:____:____:____:____:____:____	under a moral obligation to act otherwise
personally satisfying	____:____:____:____:____:____:____	not personally satisfying
in the best interests of the company	____:____:____:____:____:____:____	not in the best interests of the company

Overall, how would you rate the actions of would you say they were:

_______ethical	_______unethical
_______proper	_______improper
_______right	_______wrong
_______responsible	_______not responsible
_______moral	_______immoral
_______just	_______unjust

If you were responsible for making the decision that was just described in the scenario, what is the probability you would make the same decision?

highly probable _____:_____:_____:_____:_____:_____:_____ highly improbable

References

Abratt, Russell, and Diane Sacks. 1988. The marketing challenge: Toward being profitable and socially responsible. *Journal of Business Ethics* 7: 497–507.

Adams, J.Stacy. 1963. Toward an understanding of inequity. *Journal of Abnormal and social Psychology* 67: 422–436.

Alderson, Wroe. 1964. *Ethics, ideologies and sanctions', in report of the committee on ethical standards and professional practice*. Chicago: AMA.

Alderson, Wroe. 1965. *Dynamic marketing behavior*. Homewood: Richard D. Irwin, Inc.

Alexander, C.S., and H.J. Becker. 1978. The use of vignettes in survey research. *Public Opinion Quarterly* 42: 93–104.

Allen, Fred T. 1977. Should corporate ethics be regulated? *Management Review* 66(March): 16–17.

Andreason, Alan, and Arthur Best. 1977. Consumers complain – Does business respond? *Harvard Business Review* 55(July–August): 93–101.

Arlow, P., and T.A. Ulrich. 1980. Business ethics, social responsibility and business students: An empirical comparison of Clark's study. *Akron Business and Economic Review* 11(Fall): 17–22.

Arlow, P., and T.A. Ulrich. 1982. Can ethics be taught to business students? *The Collegiate Forum* 14: 17.

Arlow, P., and T.A. Ulrich. 1985. Business ethics and business school graduates: A longitudinal study. *Akron Business and Economic Review* 16(Spring): 13–17.

Arlow, P., and T.A. Ulrich. 1988. A longitudinal survey of business school graduates' assessments of business ethics. *Journal of Business Ethics* 7: 295–302.

Bahm, A.J. 1982. Teaching ethics without ethics to teach. *Journal of Business Ethics* 1: 43–47.

Baily, N.A. 1968. The role of business and business schools in raising ethical standards in business. *MSU Business Topics* 16(Spring): 29–32.

Baker, James C. 1985. The international infant formula controversy: A dilemma in corporate social responsibility. *Journal of Business Ethics* 4: 181–190.

Barach, Jeffery A., and Elizabeth A. Nicol. 1980. Teaching ethics in business school. *Collegiate News and Views* 34(Fall): 5–8.

Barry, Richmon. 1979a. Can we prevent questionable foreign payments? *Business Horizons* 22(June): 14–19.

Barry, V. 1979b. *Moral issues in business*, 39–70. New York: Wadsworth Publishing Co.

Bartels, Robert. 1967. A model for ethics in marketing. *Journal of Marketing* 31(January): 20–26.

Bauer, Raymond, and Dan H. Fenn Jr. 1972. *The corporate social audit*. New York: Russell Sage.

Baumhart, Raymond S.J. 1961. How ethical are businessmen? *Harvard Business Review* 39(July–August): 6–31.

Beauchamp, Tom L., and Norman E. Bowie. 1983. *Ethical theory and business*, 2nd ed. EnglewoodCliffs: Prentice Hall, Inc.

Bellizzi, Joseph A., and Gene W. Murdock. 1981. Industrial sales management in the 1980s. *Industrial Marketing Management* 10(October): 299–304.

Beltramini, Richard F. 1986. Ethics and the use of competitive information acquisition strategies. *Journal of Business Ethics* 5: 307–311.

Beltramini, Richard F., Robert A. Peterson, and George Kozmetsky. 1984. Concerns of college students regarding business ethics. *Journal of Business Ethics* 3: 195–200.

Berkman, H.W. 1977. Corporate ethics: Who cares? *Journal of the Academy of Marketing Science* 5(Summer): 154–167.

Berleant, Arnold. 1982. Multinationals, local practice, and the problem of ethical consistency. *Journal of Business Ethics* 1: 185–193.

Bezilla, Robert, Joel B. Haynes, and Clifford Elliot. 1976. Ethics in marketing research. *Business Horizons* 19(April): 83–86.

Blankenship, A.B. 1964. Some aspects of ethics in marketing research. *Journal of Marketing Research* 1(May): 26–31.
Bogart, Leo. 1962. The researcher's dilemma. *Journal of Marketing* 26(January): 6–11.
Bok, D.C. 1976. Can ethics be taught? *Change* 8(October): 26–30.
Boling, T.Edwin. 1978. The management ethics crisis: An organizational perspective. *Academy of Management Review* 3(April): 360–365.
Bommer, Michael, Clarence Grato, Jerry Gravander, and Mark Tuttle. 1987. A behavioral model of ethical and unethical decision making. *Journal of Business Ethics* 6: 265–280.
Bond, Kenneth: *Bibliography of Business Ethics and Business Moral Values*. For printed copies contact the Center for Business Ethics at Bentley College, Waltham, MA 02254. Computer disks can be obtained from the author at the College of Business, Humboldt State University, Arcata, CA 95521.
Boulding, Kenneth. 1971. The ethics of persuasion. Paper presented at the AMA Educators' Conference, Minneapolis, MN, August 30.
Bowman, J.S. 1976. Managerial ethics in business and government. *Business Horizons* 19(October): 48–54.
Brady, Neil F. 1985. A Janus-headed model of ethical theory: Looking two ways at business/ society issues. *Academy of Management Review* 7: 568–576.
Brenner, Steven N., and Earl A. Molander. 1977. Is the ethics of business executives changing? *Harvard Business Review* 55(January–February): 57–71.
Bronson, Gail. 1980. Sexual pitches in ads become more explicit and more pervasive. *The Wall Street Journal*, 1+, November 18.
Bronson, Gail, and T. Birnbaum. 1980. Some people believe that blue jean ads are a little too blue. *The Wall Street Journal*, 1, October 7.
Browning, John, and Noel B. Zabriskie. 1983. How ethical are industrial buyers? *Industrial Marketing Management* 12: 219–224.
Buchholz, R.A. 1979. *Business environment/public policy: A study of teaching and research in schools of business and management*. Washington, DC: American Assembly of Collegiate Schools of Business.
Burger, Kenneth, and Sandra L. Schmidt. 1983. The information explosion: Students need to consider the ethical issues. In *Southern Marketing Association Proceedings*.
Byron, William J. 1977. The meaning of ethics in business. *Business Horizons* 20(December): 31–34.
Callahan, D., and S. Bok. 1980. *Ethics teaching in higher education*. New York: Plenum Press.
Carr, Albert Z. 1968. Is business bluffing ethical? *Harvard Business Review* 46(January–February): 143–167.
Carr, Albert Z. 1970. Can an executive afford a conscience? *Harvard Business Review* 61(July–August): 58–64.
Carroll, Archie B. 1975. Managerial ethics: A post-watergate view. *Business Horizons* 18(April): 75–80.
Cavanagh, Gerald F., Dennis J. Moberg, and Manuel Velasquez. 1981. The ethics of organizational politics. *Academy of Management Review* 6(3): 363–374.
Center for Business Ethics. 1986. Are corporations institutionalizing ethics. *Journal of Business Ethics* 5: 85–91.
Chatov, Robert. 1980. What corporate ethics statements say. *California Management Review* 22(Summer): 20–29.
Chonko, Lawrence B., and Shelby D. Hunt. 1985. Ethics and marketing management: An empirical exatnination. *Journal of Business Research* 13: 339–359.
Clark, John W.S. 1966. *Religion and moral standards of American businessmen*. Cincinnati: South-Western.
Clasen, Earl A. 1967. Marketing ethics and the consumer. *Harvard Business Review* 45(January–February): 79–86.
Clawson, Joseph C., and Donald E. Vinson. 1978. Human values: A historical and interdisciplinary analysis. In *Advances in consumer research*, vol. 5, ed. H.Keith Hunt, 396–402. Provo: Association for Consumer Research.

Clinard, Marshal B. 1983. *Corporate ethics and crime: The role of middle management*. Beverly Hills: Sage Publications.
Coe, Ted L., and Barbara J. Coe. 1976. Marketing research: The search for professionalism. In *Marketing: 1776–1976 and beyond*, ed. Kenneth L. Berthardt, 257–259. Chicago: AMA.
Coney, Kenneth A., and John H. Murphy. 1976. Attitudes of marketers toward ethical and professional marketing research practices. In *Proceedings: Southern Marketing Association*, ed. Henry W. Nash, Donald P. Robin, 172–174.
Consoli, John. 1976. Comparative print ads more credible: Kershaw. *Editor and Publisher*, 14 and 16, May 22.
Crain, Rance. 1983. Ethics: It makes good sense. *Advertising Age*, 54, M-50, August 15.
Crawford, C.Marie. 1970. Attitudes of marketing executives toward ethics in marketing research. *Journal of Marketing* 34(April): 46–52.
Cummings, Gary F. 1979. Are purchasing ethics being put to the test? *Iron Age*, 222, 21–24, September 24.
Dagher, S.P., and P.H. Spader. 1980. Poll of top managers stresses education and leadership by example as strong forces for higher standards. *Management Review* (March): 54–57.
Dalrymple, D.J. 1982. *Sales management: Concepts and cases*. New York: Wiley.
Davis, Rose M. 1979. Comparison of consumer acceptance of rights and responsibilities. In *Ethics and the Consumer Interest*, ed. Norleen M. Ackerman, American Council of Consumer Interests, 25 Annual Conference Proceedings, 68–70.
Day, Robert L. 1975. A comment on 'ethics in marketing research'. *Journal of Marketing Research* 12(May): 232–233.
Dayton, Eric. 1979. Utility maximizers and cooperative undertakings. *Ethics* 90(October): 130–141.
DeGeorge, Richard R. 1982. *Business ethics*, 2nd ed. New York: Macmillan Publishing.
Dempsey, William, F.Antony Bushman, and Richard E. Plank. 1980. Personal inducements of industrial buyers. *Industrial Marketing Management* 9: 281–289.
Dixon, D.F. 1982. The ethical component of marketing: An eighteenth-century view. *Journal of Macromarketing* 2(Spring): 38–46.
Donaldson, T. 1978. Ethics in business schools: A proposal. *National Forum* 63(3): 11–14.
Donaldson, T. 1985. Multinational decision-making: Reconciling international norms. *Journal of Business Ethics* 4: 357–366.
Donaldson, Thomes, and Patricia H. Werhane. 1983. *Ethical issues in business: A philosophical approach*, 2nd ed. Englewood Cliffs: Prentice Hall, Inc.
Dornoff, Donald J., and Clint B. Tankersley. 1975a. Perceptual differences in market transactions: A source of consumer frustration. *Journal of Consumer Affairs* 9: 97–103.
Dornoff, Donald J., and Clint B. Tankersley. 1975b. Do retailers practice corporate responsibility? *Journal of Retailing* 51(Winter): 33–42.
Dubinsky, Alan J., and Thomas N. Ingram. 1984. Correlates of salespeople's ethical conflict: An exploratory investigation. *Journal of Business Ethics* 3: 343–353.
Dubinsky, Alan J., and M. Levy. 1985. Ethics in retailing: Perceptions of retail salespeople. *Journal of the Academy of Marketing Science* 13(Winter): 1–16.
Dubinsky, Alan J., Eric N. Berkowitz, and William Rudelius. 1980. Ethical problems of field sales personnel. *MSU Business Topics* 28(Summer): 11–16.
Ebejer, James M., and Michael J. Morden. 1988. Paternalism in the marketplace: Should a salesman be his buyer's keeper? *Journal of Business Ethics* 7: 337–339.
England, G.W. 1975. *The manager and his values: An international perspective*. Cambridge: Ballinger Publishing Co.
Erteszek, Jan J. 1975. An interview with Jan Erteszek in Los Angeles. *Business and Economics I*(Fall).
Ethics Resource Center. 1979. *Codes of ethics in corporations and trade associations and the teaching of ethics in graduate business schools*. Princeton: Opinion Research Corporation.
Farmer, Richard N. 1967. Would you want your daughter to marry a marketing man? *Journal of Marketing* 31(January): 1–3.

Farmer, Richard N. 1977. Would you want your son to marry a marketing lady? *Journal of Marketing* 41(January): 15–18.
Ferrell, O.C. 1985. Implementing and monitoring ethics in advertising. In *Marketing ethics*, ed. G.R. Laczniak and Patric E. Murphy, 26–40. Lexington: Lexington Books.
Ferrell, O.C., and Larry G. Gresham. 1985. A contingency framework for understanding ethical decision making in marketing. *Journal of Marketing* 49(Summer): 87–96.
Ferrell, O.C., and Mark Weaver. 1978. Ethical beliefs of marketing managers. *Journal of Marketing* 42(July): 69–73.
Ferrell, O.C., Mary Zey-Ferrell, and Dean Krugman. 1983. A comparison of predictors of ethical and unethical behavior among corporate and agency advertising managers. *Journal of Macromarketing* 3(Spring): 19–27.
Filios, Vassilios P. 1986. Review and analysis of the empirical research in corporate social accounting. *Journal of Business Ethics* 5: 291–306.
Fisk, Raymond P. 1982. Toward a theoretical framework for marketing ethics. In *Southern Marketing Association Proceedings*, 255–259.
Fitzmaurice, T.J., and H. Radolf. 1961. Preventing theft in retail stores. *Journal of Retailing* 37(Summer): 1–8.
Fletcher, Joseph. 1966. *Situation ethics: The new morality*, 95. Philadelphia: Westminster Press.
Frederick, W.C. 1986. Commentary on Vogel', in 'A debate on the future of research in business and society. *California Management Review* 28: 152–153.
Frey, Cynthia J., and Thomas C. Kinnear. 1979. Legal constraints and marketing research: A review and call to action. *Journal of Marketing Research* 16(August): 295–302.
Friedman, Milton. 1962. *Capitalism and freedom*. Chicago: University of Chicago Press.
Friedman, Hershey H., and Linda W. Friedman. 1988. A framework for organizational success. *Journal of Business Ethics* 8: 219–221.
Fritzsche, David J. 1985. Ethical issues in multinational marketing. In *Marketing ethics: Guidelines for managers*, ed. G.R. Laczniak and P.E. Murphy, 85–96. Lexington: Lexington Books.
Fritzsche, David J., and Helmut Becker. 1982. Business ethics of future marketing managers. *Journal of Marketing Education* 4(Fall): 2–7.
Fritzsche, David J., and Helmut Becker. 1983. Ethical behavior of marketing managers'. *Journal of Business Ethics* 2: 291–299.
Fritzsche, David J., and Helmut Becker. 1984. Linking management behavior to ethical philosophy – an empirical investigation. *Academy of Management Journal* 27(1): 166–175.
Frons, Mark. 1980. The Jeaning of America. *Newsweek,* 83, 85.
Fulmer, Robert M. 1967. Ethical activities of associations. *Association Management* 19: 24–27.
Futrell, C. 1981. *Sales management: Behavior, practice and cases*. Hinsdale: Dryden Press.
Galbraith, John Kenneth. 1958. *The affluent society*. Boston: Houghton Mifflin.
Garrett, Thomas. 1966. *Business ethics*. Englewood Cliffs: Prentice Hall, Inc.
Gelb, B.D., and R.H. Brien. 1971. Survival and social responsibility: Themes for marketing education and management. *Journal of Marketing* 35(April): 3–9.
Gellerman, Saul. 1986. Why good managers make bad ethical choices. *Harvard Business Review* 64(July–August): 85–90.
George, Richard J. 1987. Teaching business ethics: Is there a gap between rhetoric and reality. *Journal of Business Ethics* 6: 513–518.
Gerhold, Paul E. 1974. Why we need a profession, and how to get one. *Journal of Advertising Research* 14(October): 9–13.
Gibbs, John C., and Keith F. Widaman. 1982. *Social intelligence: Measuring the development of sociomoral reflection*. Englewood Cliffs: Prentice-Hall, Inc.
Goodman, Charles S., and Merle C. Crawford. 1974. Young executives: A source of new ethics? *Personnel Journal* 53(March): 180–187.
Gossett, William. 1975. Legal counsel as a social adjuster. *Harvard Business Review* 53(May–June): 6–7.
Greyser, Steven A., and Bonnie Reece. 1971. Businessmen look hard at advertising. *Harvard Business Review 50*(May–June).

Gwinner, Robert F., et al. 1977. *Marketing: An environmental perspective*, 480–481. St. Paul: West Publishing Co.
Hagg, Claes. 1984. The OECD guidelines for multinational enterprises: A critical analysis. *Journal of Business Ethics* 3: 71–76.
Harris, Louis, and Associates. 1966. What Americans really think of business. *Newsweek* 67 # 18, 84–85, May 2.
Hartley, Robert F. 1976. *Marketing fundamentals*, 336. New York: Donnelly.
Hawkins, Del I. 1979. The impact of sponsor identification and direct disclosure on respondent rights on the quantity and quality of mail survey data. *Journal of Business* 52(4): 577–590.
Hawkins, Del I., and A.Benton Cocanougher. 1972. Student evaluations of the ethics of marketing practices: The role of marketing education. *Journal of Marketing* 36(April): 61–72.
Hays, S.W., and R.R. Gleissner. 1981. Codes of ethics in state government: A nationwide survey. *Public Personnel Management Journal* 10(1): 48–58.
Hegarty, Harvey W., and Henry P. Sims. 1978. Some determinants of unethical behavior: An experiment. *Journal of Applied Psychology* 63(4): 451–457.
Hegarty, Harvey W., and Henry P. Sims. 1979. Organizational philosophy, policies, and objectives related to unethical decision behavior: A laboratory experiment. *Journal of Applied Psychology* 64(3): 331–338.
Hill, John W. 1977. Corporations – the sitting ducks. *Public Relations Quarterly* 22(Summer): 8–10.
Hise, Richard T., and Michael A. McGinnis. 1975. Product elimination: Practice, policies, and ethics. *Business Horizons* 18(June): 25–32.
Hite, Robert E., Joseph A. Bellizzi, and Cynthia Fraser. 1988. A content analysis of ethical policy statements regarding marketing activities. *Journal of Business Ethics* 7: 771–776.
Hoffman, Michael W., and Jennifer M. Moore. 1982. Results of business ethics curriculum survey. *Journal of Business Ethics* 1(2): 81–83.
Hollander Jr., Sidney. 1974. Ethics in marketing. In *Handbook of marketing research*, ed. Robert Ferber, 1–127. New York: McGraw Hill.
Hollon, Charles J., and Thomas A. Ulrich. 1979. Personal business ethics: Managers vs. Managers-to-be. *Southern Business Review* 5: 17–22.
Holloway, Robert, and Delbert Hastings. 1978. The business and society course and its discontents. Working paper, College of Business Administration, University of Minnesota.
Hosmer, L.T. 1985. The other 338: Why a majority of our schools of business administration do not offer a course in business ethics. *Journal of Business Ethics* 4: 17–22.
Hosmer, L.T. 1987. *The ethics of management*. Homewood: Irwin.
Huber, C.E. 1979. *The promise and perils of business ethics*. Washington, DC: American Association of Colleges.
Hunt, Shelby, and Scott Vitell. 1986. A general theory of marketing ethics. *Journal of Macromarketing* 6: 5–16.
Hunt, Shelby D., and Lawrence B. Chonko. 1986. Marketing and Machiavellianism. Working paper at Texas Tech University.
Hutzler, Laurie H. 1982. The legal ramifications of information privacy. *Administrative Management* (September): 36–38.
Izraeli, Dove. 1988. Ethical beliefs and behavior among managers: A cross-cultural perspective. *Journal of Business Ethics* 7: 263–271.
Johnson, Harold L. 1981. Ethics and the executive. *Business Horizons* 24(May–June): 53–59.
Johnson, Harold L. 1985. Bribery in international markets: Diagnosis, clarification and remedy. *Journal of Business Ethics* 4: 447–455.
Jones, Thomas M., and Frederick H. Gautschi III. 1988. Willthe ethics of business change? a survey of future executives. *Journal of Business Ethics* 7: 231–248.
Jones, Donald G., and Helen Troy. 1982. *A bibliography of business ethics: 1976–1980*. Charlottesville: Colgate Darden Graduate School of Business Administration, University of Virginia.
Jurgen, Robert J. 1976. The business of business ethics. *Intellect*, 177–178, December.

Kaikati, Jack, and Wayne A. Label. 1980. American bribery legislation: An obstacle to international marketing. *Journal of Marketing* 44(Fall): 38–43.
Kant, Immanuel. 1959. *Foundations of the metaphysics of morals*. Trans. Lewis White. New York: Bobbs-Merrill.
Kerlinger, F.N. 1986. *Foundations of behavioral research*. New York: Holt.
Kidwell, Jeaneen M., Robert E. Stevens, and Art L. Bethke. 1987. Differences in ethical perceptions between male and female managers: Myth or reality? *Journal of Business Ethics* 6: 487–493.
Kinnear, Thomas C., and James R. Taylor. 1979. *Marketing research: An applied approach*, 66–77. New York: McGraw Hill, Inc.
Kizilbash, A.H., William O. Hancock, Carlton A. Maile, and Peter Gillet. 1979. Social auditing for marketing managers. *Industrial Marketing Management* 8: 1–6.
Kohlberg, Lawrence. 1981. *The meaning and measurement of moral development*. Worcester: Clark University Press.
Konrad, R. 1978. Are business ethics worth studying? *Business and Society Review* 27(Fall): 54–57.
Krakhardt, David, Sharon McCarthy, and Dick Wittink. 1985. What makes it unethical? Determinants of ethical evaluation in business. Paper presented at the Academy of Management Annual Meeting, San Diego.
Kramer, Otto P. 1977. Ethics programs can help companies set standards of content. *Administrative Management* 38(January): 46–49.
Kreitner, Robert, and William Reif. 1980. Ethical inclinations of tomorrow's managers: Cause for alarm? *Journal of Business Education* 56(October): 25–29.
Kreitner, Robert. 1981. Needed: Formal instruction in business ethics for tomorrow's managers. Presentation at the Academy of Management Annual Meeting, San Diego, August.
Krugman, Dean M., and D.C. Ferrell. 1981. The organizational ethic of advertising: Corporate and agency views. *Journal of Advertising* 10(1): 21–30.
Laczniak, Gene R. 1983a. Framework for analysing marketing ethics. *Journal of Macromarketing* 1(Spring): 7–18.
Laczniak, Gene R. 1983b. Business ethics: A manager's primer. *Business* 33: 23–29.
Laczniak, Gene R., and Edward J. Inderrieden. 1987. The influence of stated organizational concern upon ethical decision making. *Journal of Business Ethics* 6: 297–307.
Laczniak, Gene R., and J.G. Udell. 1979. Dimensions of future marketing. *MSU Business Topics* 27(Fall): 33–44.
Laczniak, Gene R., Robert F. Lusch, and John H. Murphy. 1979. Social marketing: Its ethical dimension. *Journal of Marketing* 43(Spring): 29–36.
Laczniak, Gene R., Robert F. Lusch, and William A. Strang. 1981. Ethical marketing: Perceptions of economic goods and social problems. *Journal of Macromarketing* 1(Spring): 48–57.
Lane, Henry W., and Donald G. Simpson. 1984. Bribery in international business: Whose problem is It? *Journal of' Business Ethics* 3: 35–42.
Lane, Michael S., Dietrich Schaupp, and Barbara Parsons. 1988. Pygmalion effect: An issue for business education and ethics. *Journal of Business Ethics* 7: 223–229.
Lazer, William. 1970. Marketing education: Commitments for the 1970s. *Journal of Marketing* 35(July): 11.
Learned, Edmund, Arch Dooley, and Robert Katz. 1959. Personal values and business decisions. *Harvard Business Review* 37(March–April): 115–116.
Lee, Kam-Hon. 1981. Ethical beliefs in marketing management: A cross cultural study. *European Journal of Marketing* 15(1): 58–67.
Levitt, Theodore. 1970. The morality of advertising. *Harvard Business Review* 48(July–August): 84–92.
Levy, M., and A.J. Dubinsky. 1983. Identifying and addressing retail salespeople's ethical problems: A method and application. *Journal of Retailing* 59: 46–66.
Lewin, T. 1983. Business ethics' new appeal. *New York Times,* F4, December 11.
Lewis, Phillip V. 1985. Defining 'business ethics': Like nailing jello to a wall. *Journal of Business Ethics* 4: 377–383.

Longenecker, Justin G., Joseph A. McKinney, and Carlos W. Moore. 1988. The ethical issue of international bribery: A study of attitudes among U.S. Business professionals. *Journal of Business Ethics* 7: 341–346.

Losser, S.V., and R.W. Hasty. 1979. Curriculum choice and student evaluation of business ethics. Paper presented at Southwestern Marketing Association, Texas, Houston, March.

Lusch, Robert F., Gene R. Laczniak, and Patrick E. Murphy. 1980. The ethics of social ideas versus the ethics of marketing social ideas. *Journal of Consumer Affairs* 14(Summer): 156–163.

Luthans, Fred, Rich M. Hodgetts, and Hen R. Thompson. 1987. *Social issues in business*. New York: Macmillan.

Marks, Norton E., and Richard A. Scott. 1968. Ethics for marketing executives: The educational environment. In *Changing marketing systems*, ed. Reed Moyer, 379–381. Chicago: AMA.

Martin, T. R. 1981. Do courses in ethics influence the ethical evaluations of students?, Marquette University, Working Paper.

Mathison, David L. 1987. Teaching an ethical decision model that skips the philosophers and works for real business students. In *Proceedings, National Academy of Management*, New Orleans, 1–9.

Mathison, David L. 1988. Business ethics cases and decision models: A call for relevancy in the classroom. *Journal of Business Ethics* 7: 777–782.

Mayer, R.R. 1970. Management's responsibility for purchasing ethics. *Journal of Purchasing* 4: 13–20.

McClelland, D.C. 1961. *The achieving society*. Princeton: VanNostrand.

McMahon, Thomas. 1975. *Report on the teaching of socio-ethical issues in collegiate schools of business*. Chicago: Loyola University.

McNichols, Charles W., and Thomas W. Zimmerer. 1985. Situational ethics: An empirical study of differentiators of student attitudes. *Journal of Business Ethics* 4: 175–180.

Meager, Carl. 1950. *Principles of economics*. Trans. and ed. James Dingwall and Bert F. Hoselitz. Glencoe: The Free Press.

Milesko-Pytel, D. 1979. With a dose of morality. *American Education* 15(1): 31–36.

Miller, A. 1979. A report card on the M.B.A. *New York Times*, Section 3, p. 4, March 18.

Miller, Mary S., and Edward A. Miller. 1976. It's too late for ethics courses in business schools. *Business and Society Review* 17(Spring): 39–42.

Moore, Thomas. 1982. Industrial espionage at the Harvard B-School. *Fortune*, 70–72, 76, September 6.

Morgan, Fred. 1981. Bias in research on marketing ethics. In *Southeastern Marketing Association 1981 Proceedings*, 235–238.

Moser, Martin R. 1986. A framework for analyzing corporate social responsibility. *Journal of Business Ethics* 5: 69–72.

Moser, Martin R. 1988. Ethical conflict at work: A critique of the literature and recommendations for future research. *Journal of Business Ethics* 7: 381–387.

Murphy, John H., and Kenneth A. Conney. 1976. Accreditation of marketing researchers. In *Marketing: 1776–1976 and beyond*, ed. Kenneth L. Bernhardt, 260–265. Chicago: AMA.

Murphy, P.E., and Gene R. Laczniak. 1980. *Marketing education: Current status and a view to the 1980*. Chicago: AMA.

Murphy, P.E., and Gene R. Laczniak. 1981. Marketing ethics: A review with implications for marketers, educators and researchers. *Review of Marketing* 251–266.

Murphy, P.E., Gene R. Laczniak, and Robert F. Lusch. 1978. Ethical guidelines for business and social marketing. *Journal of the Academy of Marketing Science* 6(Summer): 195–204.

Myrick, Fred L. 1975. Student evaluations of the ethics of marketing practices: The role of marketing education – A replication and extension. In *Proceedings: Southern Marketing Association Annual Meeting*, Henry W. Nash, and Donald P. Robin, eds., 102–104.

Naor, Jacob. 1982. A new approach to multinational social responsibility. *Journal of Business Ethics* 1: 219–225.

Nash, Laura L. 1981. Ethics without sermon. *Harvard Business Review* 59(6): 79–90, November–December.

Neill, Harry W. 1965. The ethics of American business. In *Business in a changing social order*, ed. Daniel N. DeLucca, 151–187. Philadelphia: St. Joseph's College.
Newstrom, John W., and William A. Ruch. 1975. The ethics of management and the management of ethics. *MSU Business Topics* 23(Winter): 29–37.
Norris, Donald G., and John B. Gifford. 1988. Retail store managers' and students' perceptions of ethical retail practices: A comparative and longitudinal analysis (1976–1986). *Journal of Business Ethics* 7: 515–524.
Nossiter, Bernard D. 1964. *The mythmakers*, 85. Boston: HoughtonMifflin Co.
Nunnally, J.C. 1967. *Psychometric theory*. New York: McGraw Hill.
Ohmann, O.A. 1962. Ethical concepts for marketing managers', talk given at the sixth Conference on Marketing Management, University of Michigan, March 30.
Orpen, Christopher. 1987. The attitudes of United States and South African managers to corporate social responsibility. *Journal of Business Ethics* 6: 89–96.
Packard, Vance. 1957. *The hidden persuaders*. New York: Pocket Books.
Pagano, Anthony M. 1987. Criteria for ethical decision making in managerial situations. In *Proceedings, National Academy of Management*, New Orleans, 1–12.
Palmer, R.E. 1986. Let's be bullish on ethics. *The New York Times*, 23, June 20.
Pamental, George L. 1988. A different look at texts. *Journal of Business Ethics* 7: 531–536.
Patterson, James M. 1966. What are the social and ethical responsibilities of marketing executives? *Journal of Marketing* 30(July): 12–15.
Payne, Steven L. 1980. Organizational ethics and antecedents to social control processes. *Academy of Management Review* 5: 409–414.
Petit, Thomas A. 1967. *The moral crisis in management*. New York: McGraw Hill.
Pitney-Bowes Inc. 1977. The pressure to compromise personal ethics. *Business Week,* 107, January 13.
Pitt, Leyland F., and Russell Abratt. 1986. Corruption in business – are management attitudes right? *Journal of Business Ethics* 5: 39–44.
Poff, Deborah, and Wilfrid Waluchow. 1987. *Business ethics in Canada*. Scarborough: Prentice-Hall Canada Inc.
Posner, Barry Z., and Warren H. Schmidt. 1984. Values and the American manager: An update. *California Management Review* 26(3): 202–216.
Post, James E., and Edward Baer. 1978. Demarketing infant formula: Consumer products in the developing world. *Journal of Contemporary Business* 7(Fall): 13–34.
Potter Jr., Ralph B. 1969. *War and moral discourse*. Richmond: JohnKnox Press.
Powers, C.W., and D. Vogel. 1980. *Ethics in the education of business managers*. New York: Institute of Society Ethics and the Life Sciences, The Hastings Center, Hastings on Hudson.
Prasad, Jyoti N., and C.P. Rao. 1982. Foreign payoffs and international business ethics: Revisited. In *Southern Marketing Association Proceedings*, 260–264.
Pruden, Henry O. 1971. Which ethics for marketers. In *Marketing and social issues*, ed. John R. Wish and Stephen H. Gamble, 98–104. New York: Wiley.
Purcell, Theodore V. 1977a. Institutionalizing ethics into top management decisions. *Public Relations Quarterly* 22(Summer): 15–20.
Purcell, Theodore V. 1977b. Do courses in business ethics pay off? *California Management Review* 19: 50–58.
Purcell, Theodore V. 1981. Practices, promises and pitfalls of business ethics instruction. Paper presented at the 41st annual meeting of the Academy of Management, San Diego, CA, August.
Rand, Ayn. 1964. Objective ethics. In *The virtue of selfishness: A new concept of egoism*, ed. Ayn Rand. New York: New American Library, Inc.
Rawls, John. 1971. *A theory of justice*. Cambridge, MA: Harvard University Press.
Reidenbach, Eric, and Don Robin. 1986. some initial steps toward improving the measurement of ethical evaluations of marketing activities. Working paper, University of Mississippi.
Rest, James R. 1979. *Development in judging moral issues*. Minneapolis: University of Minnesota Press.

Ricklefs, Roger. 1983a. On many ethical issues, executives apply stiffer standard than the public. *The Wall Street Journal*, November 1.
Ricklefs, Roger. 1983b. Honesty and ethical standards. *The Wall Street Journal*, October 2.
Ricklefs, Roger. 1983c. Executives apply stiffer standards than public to ethical dilemmas. *The Wall Street Journal,* 27, October 3.
Ricklefs, Roger. 1983d. Executives and general public say ethical behavior is declining in US. *The Wall Street Journal*, 25, October 31.
Robin, Donald P. 1980. Value issues in marketing. In *Theoretical developments in marketing*, ed. C.W. Lamb and P.M. Dunne, 142–145. Chicago: AMA.
Rokeach, M. 1968. *Beliefs, attitudes, and values*. San Francisco: Jossey-Bass.
Rosenberg, Harriet. 1987. The kitchen and the multinational corporation: An analysis of the links between the household and global corporations. *Journal of Business Ethics* 6: 179–194.
Ross, William D. 1930. *The right and the good*. Oxford: Clarendon.
Rudelius, William, and Rogene A. Buchholz. 1979. Ethical problems of purchasing managers. *Harvard Business Review* 57(March–April): 11–14.
Runes, Dagobert D. 1964. *Dictionary of philosophy*, 98–100. Patterson: Littlefields, Adams and Co.
Russell, F.A., F.H. Beach, and R.H. Buskirk. 1978. *Textbook of salesmanship*. New York: McGraw Hill Co.
Sabater, Gilbert. 1982. Professional standards committee comes to grips with issues of marketing ethics. *Marketing News*, 3, September 3.
Saul, George K. 1981. Business ethics: Where are we going? *Academy of Management Review* 6(2): 269–276.
Schneider, Kenneth C. 1977. Subject and respondent abuse in marketing research. *MSU Business Topics* 25(Spring): 13–20.
Schollhammer, Hans. 1978. Ethics in international business context. In *International business 1979: MSU international business and economic studies*, 299–308. East Lansing: Michigan State University.
Scott, W.C., and T.R. Mitchell. 1985. The moral failure of management education. *The Chronicle of Higher Education*, 35, December 11.
Shaw, Bill. 1988. Foreign corrupt practices act: A legal and moral analysis. *Journal of Business Ethics* 7: 789–795.
Sherwin, Douglas S. 1983. The ethical roots of the business system. *Harvard Business Review* 61(November–December): 183–192.
Shuptrine, F. Kelly. 1979. Evaluating the ethics of marketing practices: Student perceptions. In *1979 educators' conference proceedings*, Neil Beckwith et al., eds. Chicago: AMA, 124–127.
Silk, Leonard, and David Vogel. 1976. *Ethics and profits: The crisis of confidence in American business*. New York: Simon and Schuster.
Simon, Herbert A. 1976. *Administrative behavior*. New York: The Free Press.
Simon, John, Charles W. Powers, and Jon P. Gunneman. 1972. *The ethical investor: Universities and corporate responsibility*. New Haven: Yale University Press.
Simpson, James R. 1982. Ethics and multinational corporations vis-a-vis developing nations. *Journal of Business Ethics* 1: 227–237.
Skinner, B.F. 1938. *The behavior of organisms*. New York: Appleton Country-Crofts.
Skinner, B.F. 1953. *Science and human behavior*. New York: Free Press of Glencoe.
Skinner, B.F. 1969. *Contingencies of reinforcement*. New York: Appleton Country-Crofts.
Snyder, James D. 1976. Bribery in selling: The scandal comes home, *Sales and Marketing Management*, 35–38, May 10.
Solomon, Robert C., and Kristine Hanson. 1985. *It's good business*. New York: Harper & Row.
Sonnefeld, Jeffrey, and Paul R. Lawrence. 1978. Why do companies succumb to price fixing? *Harvard Business Review* 58(July–August): 145–157.
Spencer, Barbara A., and John K. Butler Jr. 1987. Measuring the relative importance of social responsibility components: A decision modeling approach. *Journal of Business Ethics* 6: 573–577.
Stampfl, Ronald W. 1979. Multi-disciplinary foundations for a consumer code of ethics. In *Ethics and the consumer interest*, ed. Norleen M. Ackerman, 12–19. American Council of Consumer Interests, 25th Annual Conference Proceedings.

Stanton, W.J., and R.H. Buskirk. 1978. *Management of the sales force*. Homewood: Richard D. Irwin, Inc.

Stassen, Glen. 1977. A social theory model for religious social ethics. *Journal of Religious Ethics* 5(1): 9–37.

Stead, Bette A., and Janice J. Miller. 1988. Can social awareness be increased through business school curricula. *Journal of Business Ethics* 7: 553–560.

Steiner, John F. 1976. The prospect of ethical advisors for business corporations. *Business and Society* 16(Spring): 5–10.

Stevens, George E. 1984. Business ethics and social responsibility: The responses of present and future managers. *Akron Business and Economic Review* (Fall): 6–11.

Sturdivant, Frederick D. 1968. Better deal for ghetto shoppers. *Harvard Business Review* 46(March–April): 130–132 and 135–139.

Sturdivant, Frederic D., and James L. Ginter. 1977. Corporate social responsiveness: Management attitudes and economic performance. *California Management Review* 19(Spring): 30–39.

Sturdivant, Frederic D., and A. Benton Cocanougher. 1973. What are ethical marketing practices? *Harvard Business Review* 51(November–December): 10–12 and 176.

Sutherland, E., and D.R. Cressey. 1970. *Principles of criminology*. Chicago: J. B. Lippincott.

Tarnowieski, Dale. 1973. *The changing business ethics*, 2. New York: AMACOM.

Tat, Peter K. 1981. Minority student perceptions of the ethics of marketing practices. In *Southern Marketing Association Proceedings*, 214–216.

Tatham, R.L. 1974. Employee views of theft in retailing. *Journal of Retailing* 50: 49–55.

Taylor, Paul W. 1975. *Principles of ethics: An introduction*. Encino: Dickerson Publishing Co., Inc.

Terpstra, V. 1978. *The cultural environment of international business*. Cincinnati: South-Western Publishing Co.

The Wall Street Journal. 1977. Consumers find firms are paring quantities to avoid price rise, 1+, February 15.

The Wall Street Journal. 1979. Evading an edict: Grumman board finds payoffs continued despite board's policy, 1, February 28.

Trawick, F., and W.R. Darden. 1980. Marketer's perceptions of ethical standards in the marketing profession: Educators and practitioners. *Review of Business and Economic Research* 16(Fall): 1–17.

Tsalikis, John, and Osita Nwachukwu. 1988. Cross-cultural business ethics: Ethical beliefs' difference between blacks and whites. *Journal of Business Ethics* 7: 745–754.

Tsalikis, John, and Osita Nwacliukwu. 1989. Cross cultural marketing ethics: An investigation on the ethical beliefs' differences between Greeks and Americans. *Journal of International Consumer Marketing* 1(Spring)# 3.

Tull, D.S., and D.I. Hawkins. 1987. *Marketing research*. New York: MacMillan Publishing Co.

Turk, Peter. 1979. Children's television advertising: An ethical morass for business and government. *Journal of Advertising* 8(Winter): 4–8.

Twedt, D.W. 1963. Why a marketing research code of ethics? *Journal of Marketing* 27: 48–50.

Tybout, Alice M., and Gerald Zaltman. 1974. Ethics in marketing research: Their practical relevance. *Journal of Marketing Research* 11(November): 357–368.

Tybout, Alice M., and Gerald Zaltman. 1975. A reply to comments on 'ethics in marketing research: Their practical relevance'. *Journal of Marketing Research* 12(May): 234–237.

Velasquez, Manuel G. 1982. *Business ethics*. Englewood Cliffs: Prentice Hall.

Vitell, Scott J. Jr. 1986. Marketing ethics: Conceptual and empirical foundations of a positive theory of decision making in marketing situations having ethical content. Unpublished dissertation, Texas Tech University.

Walker, O.C., G.A. Churchill, and N.M. Ford. 1977. Motivation and performance in industrial selling: Present knowledge and needed research. *Journal of Marketing Research* 14(May): 156–168.

Walker, O.C., G.A. Churchill, and N.M. Ford. 1979. Where do we go from here? Selected conceptual and empirical issues concerning the motivation and performance of the industrial salespeople. In *Critical issues in sales management: State-of-the-art and future research needs*, ed. G. Albaum and G.A. Churchill. Eugene: College of Business Administration, University of Oregon.

Walton, C.C. 1979. To break the pentameter – Ethics courses? Implications for business education. *Modern values in business and management*, Proceedings of the 1979 AACSB Annual Meeting.

Weaver, K.Mark, and O.C. Ferrell. 1977. The impact of corporate policy on reported ethical beliefs and behavior of marketing practitioners. *American Marketing Association Proceedings* 41: 477–481.

Weber, James. 1981. Institutionalizing ethics into the corporation. *MSU Business Topics* 29(Spring): 47–52.

Weigand, Robert E. 1980. 'Buying in' to market control. *Harvard Business Review* 58 (November–December): 141–149.

Weller, Steven. 1988. The effectiveness of corporate codes of ethics. *Journal of Business Ethics* 7: 389–395.

Westing, J.Howard. 1967. Some thoughts on the nature of ethics in marketing. In *Changing marketing systems*, ed. Reed Moyer, 161–163. Chicago: AMA.

Weston, Alan F. 1979. The impact of computers on privacy. *Datamation,* 190–194, December.

White, B.J., and B.R. Montgomery. 1980. Corporate codes of conduct. *California Management Review* 23(2): 80–87.

Wokutch, Richard E., and Louis Fahey. 1981. Methodological issues in business ethics research. Symposium at the Academy of Management Annual Meeting, San Diego, August.

Wood, John A., Justin G. Longenecker, Joseph A. McKinney, and Carlos W. Moore. 1988. Ethical attitudes of students and business professionals: A study of moral reasoning. *Journal of Business Ethics* 7: 249–257.

Wright, John S., and John E. Mertes. 1974. *Advertising's role in society*, 252–300. St. Paul: West, Part VI.

Zahra, Shaker A., and Michael S. LaTour. 1987. Corporate social responsibility and organizational effectiveness: A multivariate approach. *Journal of Business Ethics* 6: 459–467.

Zaltman, Gerald, and P.C. Burger. 1975. *Marketing research*, 614–637. Hinsdale: Dryden Press.

Zey-Ferrell, Mary, and O.C. Ferrell. 1982. Role-set configuration and opportunities as predictors of unethical behavior in organizations. *Human Relations* 35(7): 587–604.

Zey-Ferrell, Mary, K.Mark Weaver, and O.C. Ferrell. 1979. Predicting unethical behavior among marketing practitioners. *Human Relations* 32(7): 557–569.

Chapter 18
An Integrative Model for Understanding and Managing Ethical Behavior in Business Organizations

W. Edward Stead, Dan L. Worrell, and Jean Garner Stead

"The question of ethics in business conduct has become one of the most challenging issues confronting corporate America in this era," is the conclusion of a recent Business Roundtable report (Business Roundtable 1988: p. 4). Indeed, support for this point abounds. Whether it be Wall Street, the defense industry, the savings and loan industry, or some local mom-and-pop operation, examples of unethical behavior in business appear daily in the national and local media. In the last couple of years, virtually every major business and news periodical in the nation (i.e., *Fortune, Newsweek, Time* and *Wall Street Journal*) has depicted the business ethics of the 1980s as greedy, selfish distortions of the free enterprise system with excessive emphasis on personal wealth and fame. Ninety-four percent of the 1082 respondents to a 1988 Touche Ross survey of business executives, directors, and business school deans, said that the business community as a whole is troubled by ethical problems. Sixty-eight percent of the respondents said that they did not believe these ethical problems were overblown in the press (Touche Ross 1988). In their recent book, Freeman and Gilbert (1988) strongly contend that all strategies have some ethical foundation, and that managers must recognize that they do not operate in an ethical vacuum. They say that strategic decision makers must address the issues facing them in moral terms or risk moral decay.

Managing ethical behavior is thus no doubt a critical social problem for business organizations. It is also a very complex problem which requires an in-depth understanding of the many factors which contribute to employees' decisions to behave ethically or unethically. The purpose of this article is to develop an integrative model

W.E. Stead (✉) • J.G. Stead
Department of Management and Marketing, College of Business and Technology, East Tennessee State University, P.O. Box 70625, Johnson City, TN 37614, USA
e-mail: steade@etsu.edu; steadj@etsu.edu

D.L. Worrell
Walton College of Business, University of Arkansas, Fayetteville, AR 72701-1201, USA
e-mail: dworrell@walton.uark.edu

A.C. Michalos and D.C. Poff (eds.), *Citation Classics from the Journal of Business Ethics*, Advances in Business Ethics Research 2,
DOI 10.1007/978-94-007-4126-3_18,

of ethical behavior based on an extensive review of empirical and conceptual literature related to this issue. This model provides some important clues as to how ethical behavior can be effectively managed in business organizations.

Understanding Ethical Behavior in Organizations

Current behavioral research strongly supports a person-situation interaction explanation of human behavior in which both individual and situational factors influence the behavioral choices made by individuals (Jones 1985; Luthans and Kreitner 1985; Terborg 1981; Trevino 1986). In this section, we will focus on discussing the individual and situational factors identified in the current literature which seem to influence employees' decisions to behave ethically or unethically at work.

Individual Personality and Socialization Factors

There is little doubt that personality and background will influence a person's ethical system – his or her system of ethical philosophies and behavioral patterns. Researchers have suggested three personality measures that may influence ethical behavior – ego strength, machiavellianism and locus of control (Hegarty and Sims 1978; Preble and Miesing 1984; Trevino 1986). Ego strength is defined as an individual's ability to engage in self-directed activity and to manage tense situations (Crandall 1973). Machiavellianism is a measure of deceitfulness and duplicity (Robinson 1973). Locus of control is a measure of whether or not a person believes that his or her outcomes in life are determined by his/her own actions (internal) or by luck, fate or powerful others and institutions (externals) (Levenson 1974).

Socialization also seems to influence a person's ethical system. Researchers have identified sex role differences, religious beliefs, age, work experience and nationality as factors which may influence the ethical decisions made by individuals (Hegarty and Sims 1978; Preble and Miesing 1984).

A critical socialization factor for business managers is the influence of significant others. Research in social learning theory strongly supports the idea that we learn appropriate behavior by modeling the behavior of persons we perceive as important – parents, siblings, peers, teachers, public officials, etc. (Jones 1985; Luthans and Kreitner 1985). Managers no doubt represent significant others to employees, and thus the ethical behavior of managers will certainly influence the ethical behavior of employees.

Ethical Philosophies and Decision Ideologies

As we discussed above, a person's personality and socialization will likely influence his or her ethical system. Both the content of an individual's ethical system – the norms that guide his or her ethical behavior – and the individual's perceptions about when and how to apply these ethical norms will likely vary according to differences in personality and socialization factors. For example, it has been found that machiavellians are likely to believe that ethics are situational rather than absolute (Leary et al. 1986).

The content of one's ethical system, the network of ethical norms and principles one holds, constitutes a person's ethical philosophy. Social psychologists have contended for years that these normative structures influence the behavioral decisions made by individuals (Hogan 1973). Thus, an individual's ethical philosophy will likely influence his or her ethical decisions.

Cavanagh et al. (1981) identified three basic ethical philosophies, each of which represents a unique part of the total ethical situation faced by individuals in business organizations. The first is utilitarianism. The central concept of utilitarianism is a belief that ethics is best applied by considering the greatest good for the greatest number. The second philosophy is individual rights. This philosophy focuses on protecting individual rights such as the right to be informed, the right to free consent, the right to due process, etc. The third ethical philosophy is justice. Such an ethical system stresses social justice and the opportunity for all to pursue meaning and happiness in life. Researchers have concluded that these philosophies accurately represent the ethical normative structures of individuals (Boal and Peery 1985). Most individuals allow one of these philosophies to dominate their ethical decisions with the utilitarian philosophy being dominant among business managers (Fritzche and Becker 1984).

As mentioned above, when and how persons apply their ethical philosophies will also vary from individual to individual. Forsyth (1980) contends that individuals differ in terms of the moral judgments they make, and that the actions they take resulting from these moral judgments also differ. He refers to these differences as ethical decision ideologies and says that they are based on two dimensions. First is idealism – the degree to which an individual believes that ethical behavior always results in good outcomes. Second is relativism – the degree to which an individual believes that moral rules are situational. Persons high in both idealism and relativism are called situationists. They reject the use of universal or individual moral principles, preferring to analyze each situation and to determine appropriate moral behavior based on this analysis. Subjectivists are individuals low in idealism and high in relativism. They base their moral judgments on individual rather than universal principles. Absolutists are individuals low in relativism but high in idealism. They believe that they achieve the best outcomes in life by following strict, universal moral codes. Finally, exceptionists, those low in both dimensions, believe in universal moral rules as guides, but are open to practical exceptions. Researchers have found that persons with different ethical decision ideologies vary in terms of how they integrate ethical information, how they judge their own ethical dilemmas, and how they judge the moral decisions of others (Forsyth 1981, 1985; Forsyth and Pope 1984). They also differ in terms of their sense of moral obligation, responsibility and caring for other people (Forsyth et al. 1988).

Ethical Decision History

Social learning theorists contend that past decisions play a key role in current and future decisions. Once reinforced, a decision made by an individual will influence future decisions that he or she makes (Jones 1985; Luthans and Kreitner 1985). Thus as ethical decisions are made and reinforced over time, the individual develops an ethical decision history. Through this process ethical philosophies and decision ideologies are likely to become relatively enduring.

Decision history is unique in the sense that it is both situational, because of its reinforcement foundation, and individual, because of the influence of the person's own ethical system and unique behavioral history. The fact that it is both individual and situational may explain why researchers have found that decision history has a strong direct influence on ethical decisions made by individuals (Stead et al. 1987).

Organizational Factors

Another set of factors influencing the ethical behavior of employees exists in the organizational context. Researchers have concluded that a variety of organizational variables influence ethical behavior among employees. Further, because of their immediate situational impact on employee behavior, these variables, like with decision history, have been shown to have a strong direct influence on specific ethical decisions made by employees, usually overwhelming individual variables such as personality and socialization (Hegarty and Sims 1978; Stead et al. 1987; Trevino 1986).

The philosophies of top managers as well as immediate supervisors represent a critical organizational factor influencing the ethical behavior of employees. Copious research over a period of more than 25 years clearly supports the conclusion that the ethical philosophies of management have a major impact on the ethical behavior of employees (Arlow and Ulrich 1980; Baumhart 1961; Brenner and Molander 1977; Carroll 1978; Hegarty and Sims 1978, 1979; Posner and Schmidt 1984; Touche Ross 1988; Vitell and Festervand 1987; Worrell et al. 1985).

Another organizational factor is managerial behavior. According to Nielsen (1988), managers behaving unethically contrary to their ethical philosophies represents a serious limit to ethical reasoning in the firm. Much of the research cited in the above paragraph implicitly or explicitly states that ethical philosophies will have little impact on employees' ethical behavior unless they are supported by managerial behaviors which are consistent with these philosophies. If normative structures help explain behavior patterns as social psychologists contend (Hogan 1973), then, conversely, norms not supported by appropriate behaviors are not likely to be accepted as legitimate by employees. One of the keys to understanding the influence of managerial philosophy and behavior on the ethical behavior of employees lies in a point made earlier that managers represent significant others in the organizational lives of employees and as such often have their behavior modeled by employees.

One of the most basic of management principles states that if you desire a certain behavior, reinforce it. Another critical organizational variable that influences ethical behavior is the firm's reinforcement system. Research in ethical behavior strongly supports the conclusion that if ethical behavior is desired, the performance measurement, appraisal and reward systems must be modified to account for ethical behavior (Hegarty and Sims 1978, 1979; Trevino 1986; Worrell et al. 1985). According to Nielsen (1988, p. 730),

> In many cases, managers choose to do, go along with or ignore the unethical … because they want to avoid the possibility of punishments [or] to gain rewards …

Several dimensions of the job itself may also influence the ethical behavior of employees. Researchers believe that the more centrally located a job is in the communication network of the firm, the more ethical decisions will likely have to be made by the occupant of that job (Trevino 1986). Also jobs involving external contacts are believed to have more potential for ethical dilemmas than jobs with purely internal contacts (Vitell and Festervand 1987). Further, management often responds less severely to breaches of ethics by employees on whom they rely for technical expertise, because these employees represent a scarce resource for the firm (Rosen and Adams 1974).

External Forces

There are a variety of external factors which will likely influence the ethical philosophies and behaviors of managers, the reinforcement system established to control employee behavior, the discretion given employees to behave ethically or unethically, etc. Two-thirds of the respondents to the Touche Ross survey (1988) believed that the most threatening condition to American business ethics today is the decay in political, social and cultural institutions.

Two-thirds of the respondents to the Touche Ross survey (1988) also believed that competitive pressures represent a significant threat to American business ethics. Two key competitive factors which affect ethics were mentioned by these executives. One was the ever increasing competitive pressure to concentrate on short-term earnings. Another was related to the current multinational business environment with its varying ethical standards from country to country. James Sammons, Executive Vice President of the American Medical Association, says that economic pressures associated with health care delivery in todays' high-tech, high-cost environment represents the most serious ethical problem facing the health care industry (Sammons 1988).

Volatile economic conditions, resource scarcity and pressures from stakeholders may also serve to undermine ethical behavior in organizations. The ethical trap provided by external factors such as these is obvious. It places the firm in a position of having to choose between being an ethical role model for its industry and the environment in general or succumbing to the situational pressures and engaging in unethical practices. While it is certainly encouraging that 65% of the Touche Ross survey respondents believed that high ethical standards strengthened the firm's competitive position, it is somewhat discouraging that 35% of those respondents believed that high ethical standards either weakened or had no effect on the firm's competitiveness (Touche Ross 1988).

This discrepancy in the opinions of the respondents to the Touche Ross survey (1988) as to whether high ethical standards enhance or detract from a firm's competitive position probably reflects the fact that ethical decisions have several potential competitive outcomes. Being ethical may directly increase a firm's profitability (i.e., reducing costs by reducing employee theft) or it may directly decrease a firm's profitability (i.e. increasing costs by installing an expensive pollution control system or insuring a safe workplace). Further, ethical actions may have a less direct but nonetheless real effect on a firm's competitiveness. For example, decisions to recall a defective product (i.e., Tylenol) or to withdraw from a market for moral reasons (i.e., South Africa) may have immediate costs but may also enhance a firm's image and thus its long-term profitability. In their casebook, Matthews et al. (1985) present several cases which clearly demonstrate each of these potential competitive outcomes.

A Model of Ethical Behavior in Organizations

The model depicted in Fig. 18.1 conceptually demonstrates the relationships among the factors discussed above. Hopefully, the model will help to improve managers' understanding of both why employees behave ethically or unethically in business organizations and what managers can do to influence this behavior.

The initial linkage in the model reflects the relationship between the individual factors and the development of the person's ethical philosophy and decision ideology. Essentially this linkage demonstrates that the ethical beliefs that one holds and how and when those beliefs are applied, are strongly influenced by personality and background.

The interactions between one's ethical philosophy and decision ideology will likely influence the ethical decisions a person makes. These decisions are usually reinforced – rewarded, punished, etc. Over time, the individual's ethical choices and the nature of the reinforcement that accompanies these choices lead to his or her ethical decision history.

As the individual enters and gains experience in an organization, his or her ethical behaviors are influenced by managerial philosophy and behavior, the reinforcement system and the characteristics of the job itself. This work experience with its reinforcement and significant influence by management in turn become critical socialization forces influencing the individual.

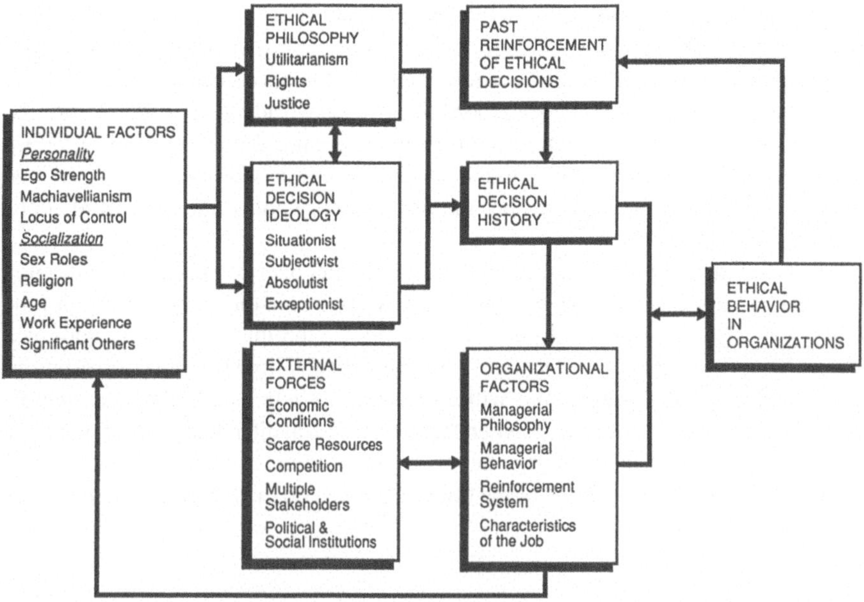

Fig. 18.1 Model of ethical behavior

Of course, these organizational factors do not exist in isolation, but are instead heavily influenced by outside forces such as competitive pressures, economic conditions, resource needs, stakeholder demands, etc. As mentioned above, maintaining high ethical standards may directly increase or decrease a firm's competitiveness, or it may have both of these outcomes over time. However, Goodpaster and Matthews (1982, p. 139) contend that if "moral demands are viewed as containments – not replacements – for self-interest" then firms can for the most part be competitive while maintaining moral responsibility. This will not always be the case of course, but cases in which being ethical requires self-sacrifice are rare (Goodpaster and Matthews 1982).

Note that the model depicts a direct relationship between decision history and organizational factors and the ethical choices made by the individual in the organization. These factors have consistently overshadowed personality and socialization factors in research. Also note that as the ethical choices the employee makes are reinforced over time by the organization, they become a part of the employee's decision history which in turn can influence the ethical culture of the organization.

Conclusions and Recommendations

Our position, of course, is that ethical behavior needs managing and can be managed in business organizations. However, influencing ethical behavior in business organizations is a multi-faceted problem with many traps and pitfalls. In developing a system for managing ethical behavior, a firm may have to modify its structure, selection and training procedures, reporting system, reward system, communication system and internal auditing procedures. These modifications cannot be made in an organization unless those who spearhead the effort have adequate leadership skills, a reasonable period of time, and support from the organization's authority structure and culture (Nielsen 1989). Thus, implementing the ethical management suggestions discussed in this section will require the firm to have total commitment and cooperation from top to bottom.

As the model and research review above indicate, decision history and organizational factors have the most significant impacts on the ethical behavior of employees. Thus, managers do not have to rely on the integrity of the employee alone. They have the power to structure the organizational context to promote ethical behavior. If managers are willing to take the actions necessary to support ethical behavior, then employees, when faced with ethical dilemmas such as improper gifts, kickbacks, improper pricing, nepotism, favoritism, etc., may be encouraged to make the right choices. Some of the things firms can do to manage ethical behavior are presented below.

Behave Ethically Yourself

This is first and foremost in influencing ethical organizational behavior. As Ranken (1987) points out, it is not the corporation itself that exerts moral responsibility, but rather the individual members of the corporation. Therefore, the institutionalization of high ethical standards in corporations "stems from the character of persons who occupy the relevant positions (Ranken 1987, p. 634)." Managers cannot expect ethical behavior from employees if they do not behave ethically themselves. Managers are the most significant role models in the organizational setting; thus they have a major socializing influence on lower level employees. The key to being an effective ethical role model for employees is to demonstrate consistency between one's ethical philosophy and ethical behavior.

None of the other suggestions made in this section are likely to have much influence on ethical behavior if managers do not behave ethically. This is especially true for top managers. Remember, as stated above, that ethical management systems in organizations require the support of the organizational culture and authority structure (Nielsen 1989). The dominant core values of the firm's culture are formulated at the top, and the authority structure of the firm begins at the top. Thus, ethical behavior must begin at the top.

Managers who wish to influence ethical behavior without support from the top will likely have to do so by initiating individual action against the unethical behavior in the organization. Behaving ethically may mean that a manager refuses to carry out unethical policies, threatens to blow the whistle, or actually blows the whistle. Individuals who take such actions often risk high anxiety and loss of potential livelihood. Thus, engaging in ethical behavior may require a great deal of courage for the individual (Nielsen 1989).

Screen Potential Employees

Since individuals are likely to face ethical issues most of their lives, there is little doubt that potential employees have significant ethical decision histories when they apply. Thus the first line of defense against unethical behavior in the organization is the employment process. There are several methods available to organizations for ethical screening. These techniques vary widely in terms of costs and benefits. Further, these techniques may vary widely in terms of their legality and may themselves have ethical implications.

Paper and pencil honesty tests are one technique which may be used for ethical screening in organizations. These tests seem to be reasonably valid with low costs and short time periods involved in administration (Sackett and Harris 1984).

Background investigations, which can range in scope from simply checking résumé information, calling references and requiring transcripts to hiring investigators, can be valuable tools in screening employees. Of course, full-blown investigations can be very expensive and time consuming and thus are cost effective only in cases of very sensitive positions. Further, before conducting such an investigation, the organization should inform the applicant and get his/her permission. On the other hand, since researchers have found that between 30% and 80% of all credentials may contain at least some misstatement of fact (Bayes and McKee under review), it seems that firms would be well advised to require official transcripts, call references and former employers, etc. These methods are not very costly, and can help the company in avoiding problems down the road. Interestingly, relatively few firms seem to bother to invoke these simple procedures.

Other means for screening the ethics of employees were revealed in the Business Roundtable report (1988). For example, Chemical Bank requires all potential employees to read and sign a statement obligating them to abide by the company's values and ethical standards as part of the application process; Johnson and Johnson includes its code of ethics in all of its recruiting material; and Norton specifies honesty and integrity as characteristics it wants search firms to screen for when finding applicants for positions with the firm.

As mentioned above, there are both legal and ethical issues involved in screening employees. For example, one screening mechanism, the much maligned polygraph (often referred to as twentieth century witchcraft), is no longer available for employee screening except for a few sensitive government positions. Its use in employment decisions has been seriously restricted by Federal legislation. Also, firms must be careful to consider the privacy rights of both potential and former employees when checking references, conducting background investigations, etc.

Develop a Meaningful Code of Ethics

Codes of ethics are probably the most visible sign of a company's ethical philosophy. In order for a code of ethics to be meaningful, it must clearly state its basic principles and expectations; it must realistically focus on the potential ethical dilemmas which may be faced by employees; it must be communicated to all employees; and it must be enforced. Further, a meaningful code of ethics cannot rely on blind obedience. It must be accepted and internalized by the employees who are required to implement it. This means that managers must attend not only to the content of the code but also to the process of determining that content. To be most effective, a code should be developed and disseminated in an open, participative environment involving as many employees as possible.

All ten firms in the Business Roundtable report (1988) had strict codes of ethics. These firms stressed several factors related to successful institutionalization of their codes including giving the codes to new employees as part of their selection and orientation, conducting seminars on the codes, and requiring communication of the codes at all levels. This last factor seemed to be of particular importance to these firms. They stressed that communication of their codes takes place in open discussion environments where employees are encouraged to ask questions and make suggestions concerning the codes. For example, many of these companies encouraged separate units to develop their own specific codes which dealt with the unique ethical dilemmas they faced. They believe that participative methods like this improve the potential that the codes will play a central role in the management of ethical behavior within their organizations.

On the other hand, it appears that not all firms stress their ethical codes to this degree, and that many of the codes themselves ignore certain crucial ethical issues. The conclusions of one study indicated that very few CPAs have a good working knowledge of the AICPA code of ethics (Davis 1984). William Frederick has found that many codes of ethics seem to be little more than lip service documents which focus primarily on profit oriented issues while often ignoring other critical issues such as personal character matters and environmental problems (Wartzman 1987).

Provide Ethics Training

Employees need to have an experiential awareness of the types of ethical dilemmas they may face, and they need to know what actions to take in these dilemmas. Providing ethics training for employees is one key to increasing this awareness.

Ethics training normally begins with orientation sessions and open discussions of the firm's code of ethics. Employees should be encouraged to participate at a high level in these sessions as well as in other training that follows. This is often followed by the use of fictitious ethical scenarios which simulate situations that employees may face on the job. Providing salespersons with scenarios involving improper gifts or kickback offers gives employees a chance to make ethical decisions in realistic situations and to discuss these decisions openly with peers, supervisors, etc. Organizations such as McDonnell Douglas and General Dynamics have used scenario training to transform their codes of ethics from simple documents to tools for training, education and communication about ethical standards (Otten 1986).

Nielsen (1988) believes that this traditional approach to ethics training may not be completely effective because it relies too heavily on ethical reasoning as an action (praxis) strategy for managing unethical behavior. He says that traditional training approaches may improve an employee's intellectual understanding of what ethics is. However, there are many limitations (i.e., bounded rationality and time constraints) which can impede the employee's ability to translate this intellectual understanding into practice. He suggests an alternative approach in which the actual ethical experiences, values and intuitions of the participants become the primary elements of ethics training. He believes that such an approach may achieve a better balance between experiential and abstract classroom learning than more traditional methods.

Reinforce Ethical Behavior

The reinforcement system of the company must support ethical behavior. Employees should be rewarded for behaving ethically, and they should be punished for behaving unethically. This is not as simple as it sounds, however. It involves developing a clear understanding of how ethical behavior is defined by the organization, developing a system to measure and report ethical behavior, and developing a performance appraisal and feedback system that includes ethical behavior. Chemical Bank, for example, has a comprehensive internal and external audit system in place, and its employees are encouraged and provided mechanisms to report any suspected improprieties. General Mills uses integrity and social responsibility as a key factor in its performance appraisal and reward distribution decisions (Business Roundtable 1988).

Effective reinforcement also involves being willing to make tough decisions in situations involving unethical behavior. Remember, employees in positions to make ethical decisions are often those who play some central role in the organization or on whom the organization relies for technical expertise, etc. Disciplining employees who are critical to the organization's success is not easy. And yet, successful management of ethical behavior requires the resolve on management's part to be willing to severely punish unethical performance. There was consensus among the firms in the Business Roundtable (1988) on this point. Most said that ethics violators would be fired summarily and prosecuted for their actions if possible. They also said that punishment for unethical behavior must be followed-up by immediately spreading the news of the offense and the punishment through the firm's grapevine.

Create Positions, Units and Other Structural Mechanisms to Deal with Ethics

As noted earlier, no cooperative effort for influencing ethical behavior from within an organization is going to be successful unless it is supported by the authority structure and culture of an organization (Nielsen 1989). One way to operationalize such support for ethical behavior is by creating structural mechanisms for managing ethics. A variety of structural mechanisms designed to advise management about ethics, monitor ethical behavior among employees, communicate ethical policies, serve as ombudsman for reporting ethical violations, etc., can be put into place in business organizations. Raelin (1987) calls for a professional ethical aide-de-camp for top managers. Xerox has established an internal audit committee to monitor ethics; Norton has established an ethics committee of the board of directors. Employee newsletters and magazines are frequently used to publish codes of ethics, ethical policies, etc. (Business Roundtable 1988).

In sum, ethical behavior in business organizations is a complex, multi-faceted problem with significant individual and situational dimensions. Effective management of ethical behavior requires that organizations espouse ethics, expect ethical behavior from managers, screen potential applicants effectively, provide meaningful ethical training for employees, create ethics units, measure ethics, report ethics, reward ethics and make the tough decisions when none of this works. Developing systems with these characteristics requires sound leadership and support from the organizational culture and authority. Managers must often be willing to take risks in effectively implementing such a system. Yes, managing ethical behavior in business organizations is possible, but it is no easy task.

References

Arlow, P., and T.A. Ulrich. 1980. Auditing your organization's ethics. *Internal Auditor* 39(4): 26–31.

Baumhart, R. 1961. How ethical are businessmen? *Harvard Business Review* 39(4): 26–31.

Bayes, P., and McKee, T. 'Do CPA firms have adequate internal control over hiring? Unpublished manuscript.

Boal, K.B., and N. Peery. 1985. The cognitive structure of corporate social responsibility. *Journal of Management* 11(3): 71–82.

Brenner, S., and E. Molander. 1977. Is the ethics of business changing? *Harvard Business Review* 55(1): 55–71.

Business Roundtable. 1988. *Corporate ethics: A prime business asset*. New York: Business Roundtable.

Carroll, A.B. 1978. Linking business ethics to behavior in organizations. *Advanced Management Journal* 43(3): 4–11.

Cavanagh, G., D. Moberg, and M. Valasquez. 1981. The ethics of organizational polities. *Academy of Management Review* 3: 363–374.

Crandall, R. 1973. The measurement of self-esteem and related constructs. In *Measures of social psychological attitudes*, ed. J.P. Robinson and P.R. Shaver, 45–167. Ann Arbor: Institute for Social Research.

Davis, R.R. 1984. Ethical behavior reexamined. *CPA Journal* 54(December): 33–36.

Forsyth, D.R. 1980. A taxonomy of ethical ideologies. *Journal of Personality and Social Psychology* 39(1): 175–184.

Forsyth, D.R. 1981. Moral judgment: The influence of ethical ideology. *Personality and Social Psychology Bulletin* 7(2): 218–223.

Forsyth, D.R. 1985. Individual differences information integration during moral judgment. *Journal of Personality and Social Psychology* 49(1): 264–272.

Forsyth, D.R., and W.R. Pope. 1984. Ethical ideology and judgments of social psychological research: Multidimensional analysis. *Journal of Personality and Social Psychology* 46(6): 1365–1375.

Forsyth, D., J. Nye, and K. Kelley. 1988. Idealism, relativism, and the ethic of caring. *Journal of Psychology* 122(3): 243–248.

Freeman, E., and D. Gilbert. 1988. *Corporate strategy and the search for ethics*. Englewood Cliffs: Prentice-Hall Inc.

Fritzche, D., and H. Becker. 1984. Linking management behavior to ethical philosophy: An empirical investigation. *Academy of Management Journal* 1: 166–175.

Goodpaster, K.E., and J.B. Matthews Jr. 1982. Can a corporation have a conscience? *Harvard Business Review* 60(1): 132–141.

Hegarty, W., and H. Sims Jr. 1978. Some determinants of unethical decision behavior: An experiment. *Journal of Applied Psychology* 63(4): 451–457.

Hegarty, W.H., and H.P. Sims Jr. 1979. Organizational philosophy, policies and objectives related to unethical decision behavior: A laboratory experiment. *Journal of a Applied Psychology* 64(3): 331–338.

Hogan, R. 1973. Moral conduct and moral character: A psychological perspective. *Psychological Bulletin* 79(4): 217–232.

Jones, E.E. 1985. Major developments in social psychology during the past five decades. In *The handbook of social psychology*, ed. G. Lindzey and E. Aronson, 47–107. New York: Random House.

Leary, M.R., P.D. Knight, and B.D. Barnes. 1986. Ethical ideologies of the Machiavellian. *Personality and Social Psychology Bulletin* 12(1): 75–80.

Levenson, H. 1974. Activism and powerful others: Distinctions within the concept of internal-external control. *Journal of Personality Assessment* 38: 377–383.

Luthans, F., and R. Kreitner. 1985. *Organizational behavior modification and beyond: An operant and social learning approach*. Glenview: Scott Forsman.

Matthews, J.B., K.E. Goodpaster, and L.L. Nash. 1985. *Policies and persons: A casebook in business ethics*. New York: McGraw-Hill.

Nielsen, R.P. 1988. Limitations of ethical reasoning as an action (praxis) strategy. *Journal of Business Ethics* 7: 725–733.

Nielsen, R.P. 1989. Changing unethical organizational behavior. *The Academy of Management Executive* 3(2): 123–130.

Otten, A.L. 1986. Ethics on the job: Companies alert employees to potential dilemmas. *Wall Street Journal*, July 14, p. 23.

Posner, B., and W. Schmidt. 1984. Values and the American manager: An update. *California Management Review* 24(3): 206–216.

Preble, J.F., and P. Miesing. 1984. Do adult MBA and undergraduate business students have different business philosophies? In *Proceedings of the National Meeting of the American Institute for the Decision Sciences*, November, 346–348.

Raelin, J.A. 1987. The professional as the executive's ethical aide-de-camp. *The Academy of Management Executive* 1(3): 171–182.

Ranken, N.L. 1987. Corporations as persons: Objections to Goodpaster's principle of moral projection. *Journal of Business Ethics* 6: 633–637.

Robinson, J. 1973. General attitudes toward people. In *Measures of social psychological attitudes*, ed. J.P. Robinson and P.R. Shaver, 587–627. Ann Arbor: Institute for Social Research.

Rosen, B., and J.S. Adams. 1974. Organizational coverups: Factors influencing the disciplining of information gatekeepers. *Journal of Applied Psychology* 4(4): 375–384.

Sackett, P.R., and M.M. Harris. 1984. Honesty testing for personnel selection: A review and critique. *Personnel Psychology* 37(2): 221–245.

Sammons, J.H. 1988. How economics threatens quality care: The challenge of medical ethics today. In *Ethics in American business: A special report*. New York: Touche Ross and Co.

Stead, W.E., D.L. Worrell, J.B. Spalding, and J.G. Stead. 1987. Unethical decisions: Socially learned behaviors. *Journal of Social Behavior and Personality* 2(1): 105–115.

Terborg, J.R. 1981. Interaction psychology and research on human behavior in organizations. *Academy of Management Review* 6(4): 569–576.

Touche Ross. 1988. *Ethics in American business: An opinion survey*. New York: Touche Ross and Co.

Trevino, L.K. 1986. Ethical decision making in organizations: A person-situation interactionist model. *Academy of Management Review* 11(3): 601–617.

Vitell, S., and T. Festervand. 1987. Business ethics: Conflicts, practices and beliefs of industrial executives. *Journal of Business Ethics* 6: 111–122.

Wartzman, R. 1987. Nature or nurture? Study blames ethical lapses on corporate goals. *Wall Street Journal*, October 9, p. 31.

Worrell, D.L., W.E. Stead, J.G. Stead, and J.B. Spalding. 1985. Unethical decisions: The impact of reinforcement contingencies and managerial philosophies. *Psychological Reports* 57: 355–365.

Chapter 19
Concerns of College Students Regarding Business Ethics*

Richard F. Beltramini, Robert A. Peterson, and George Kozmetsky

The increasingly complex and competitive business environment has resulted in new pressures being brought to bear on the traditional values and ethics of business decision makers and managers. As institutions continue to be challenged, the issue of business ethics has become the subject of considerable attention (e.g., Carr 1970; Carroll 1975; Ruch and Newstrom 1975; Coney and Murphy 1976; Brenner and Molander 1977; Purcell 1977). Researchers have reported a need for educators to reinforce childhood moral and ethical values, and clarify them for individuals participating in the current business environment. Simultaneously, business managers need to selectively evaluate competing value systems to develop an ethical framework guiding their decision making.

Since business ethics made the headlines in the scandals of the early 1960s, the traditional response to the challenge of developing ethical decision makers and managers has been to turn to educators. Trawick and Darden (1980) believe that, "Academicians are responsible for preparing future [managers] for their positions in business… formal education makes a person more sensitive and articulate about ethical issues, but that knowledge does not necessarily assure ethical action".

*This research was supported in part by the Institute for Constructive Capitalism, The University of Texas at Austin. The opinions expressed in this paper are those of the authors and do not necessarily reflect the views of the Institute.

R.F. Beltramini (✉)
Department of Marketing, Wayne State University, Tempe, AZ, USA
e-mail: R_Beltramini@wayne.edu

R.A. Peterson
Department of Marketing Administration, The University of Texas, Austin, TX, USA

G. Kozmetsky
Institute for Constructive Capitalism, The University of Texas, Austin, TX, USA

A.C. Michalos and D.C. Poff (eds.), *Citation Classics from the Journal of Business Ethics*, Advances in Business Ethics Research 2,
DOI 10.1007/978-94-007-4126-3_19, © Springer Science+Business Media B.V. 2013

While some research has focused on assessing the ethical attitudes of *current* business decision makers and managers (e.g., Ferrell and Weaver 1978; Dagher and Spader 1980), relatively little attention has been directed toward the attitudes of *future* business decision makers and managers, today's college students, toward business ethics (e.g., *Management Review* 1978).

Many of the attitudes of these future decision makers and managers regarding ethical practices in business are currently in the process of being shaped. Yet, there is relatively little empirical documentation of college students' concerns and attitudes concerning business ethics.

Although exploratory research has been conducted regarding the relationship between educational environment and business ethics (Hawkins and Cocanougher 1972; Shuptrine 1979), the results have been based on relatively restrictive samples (e.g., small sizes and business majors from only a single educational institution) and have utilized a situational approach (e.g., asking study participants to rate twenty situations on seven point 'ethical/unethical' semantic scales) rather than a more direct approach. However, to maximize the usefulness of any findings, a sample should be generalizable to the population of interest ('college students') and be of sufficient size to permit detailed and reliable analysis. Further, to adequately assess general attitudes toward business ethics, questions used in an investigation should not be function specific (i.e., relate only to marketing, finance, etc.).

The purpose of the present investigation, therefore, was to address the current attitudes of college students toward specific business ethics issues. The approach utilized involved a national sample of college students and a direct questioning of study participants with respect to a series of general business ethics issues. That is, rather than presupposing the ethical nature of student solutions to posed problem scenarios, this investigation incorporated student-defined concerns. The combination of expanded generalizability and direct questioning versus presupposition provides a unique contribution to advance research in this area.

Methodology

Data were collected from a sample of 2,856 college students attending 28 different universities located in 23 different states. Both public (e.g., University of Washington, University of Massachusetts) and private (e.g., University of Pennsylvania, Southern Methodist University) institutions were included in the sample. At each university selected, a faculty member was requested to assume responsibility for distribution of study questionnaires to three types of individuals – students majoring in business, students majoring in liberal arts or social sciences, and students majoring in engineering or natural sciences. Representation was sought from all undergraduate classifications (freshman through senior), and both sexes.[1]

The business ethics issues investigated were derived in the following manner. Initially, some 200 undergraduate students were requested to simply list, in unaided form, their concerns regarding business ethics. These concerns were then tabulated and content analyzed, and the ten concerns receiving the greatest number of mentions selected for further investigation. These ten concerns were posed in question form and study participants were requested to indicate, on a six-point ('extremely concerned' to 'extremely unconcerned') scale, how concerned they were with respect to the issue addressed by each question. Hence, in this instance 'attitude' was investigated in the context of 'concern'. This approach appeared to be realistic, given the insights obtained from the pilot study.

Analysis and Findings

Table 19.1 presents the ten business ethics issues investigated, together with selected descriptive statistics. These descriptive statistics reflect the study participants' levels of concern on each of the ten business ethics issues. While the ten items are ranked in the table in order of relative concern, from 'high' to 'low' concern, each of the issues obtained percentage responses that, on balance, placed it on the 'concerned' half of the response continuum. That is, in general, study participants reported they were concerned with all of the ethical issues investigated, although some more so than others.

Differences in the concern ratings across academic classification (freshman, sophomore, junior, and senior), academic major (students majoring in business, students majoring in liberal arts or social science, and students majoring in engineering or natural sciences), and sex (male and female) were analyzed by means of analysis of variance. Specifically, analysis of variance was respectively applied utilizing academic classification, academic major, and sex in turn as the independent variable and concern ratings on each of the ten business ethics scale items as the dependent variables. Tables 19.2, 19.3 and 19.4 contain the results of each analysis of variance conducted.

Differences in academic classification yielded statistically significant ($p<0.05$) differences in concern ratings on only one scale item – "Are the ethics of business people worse than the ethics of individuals in government?" Study participants who were seniors stated they were relatively less concerned about this issue than were the remaining study participants.

Differences in academic major resulted in statistically significant concern mean rating differences for five of the ten issues investigated. Study participants who were business students generally stated they were relatively more concerned with respect to the issues than were study participants indicating they were either liberal arts/social science majors or engineering/natural science majors.

Finally, sex differences yielded significant concern rating differences for eight of the ten ethics issues. Females were consistently more concerned than males with each issue.

Even though certain of the concern mean ratings differences were statistically significant, in a practical sense (i.e., proportion of variance explained) the differences were not substantial. Indeed, a detailed analysis of the concern responses

Table 19.1 Descriptive statistics for business ethics issues

Issue	Percentage response: Extremely concerned 1	2	3	4	5	Extremely unconcerned 6	Mean	Standard deviation
Is it possible to improve ethics in business?	17.9	30.3	30.5	12.7	5.7	2.9	2.7	(1.2)
Do current ethical standards meet the needs of society?	17.9	28.1	31.7	13.5	5.9	2.9	2.7	(1.2)
How will change in business ethics affect our living standard and way of life?	17.4	28.8	30.9	14.7	5.8	2.4	2.7	(1.2)
Will business ethics get better or worse in the future?	17.4	29.1	30.1	13.5	6.7	3.2	2.7	(1.3)
Have business ethics deteriorated over the years?	17.8	28.9	28.7	14.1	6.8	3.7	2.7	(1.3)
How much importance should ethical considerations be given in designing corporate policies?	17.1	27.6	30.6	14.9	6.9	2.9	2.8	(1.3)
Are business ethics being sacrificed due to government regulation and inflation?	16.3	27.3	30.9	15.3	6.6	3.6	2.8	(1.3)
Do current ethical standards meet the needs of business?	12.6	25.4	32.2	17.3	7.4	5.1	3.0	(1.3)
Should U.S. businesses be expected to operate on a higher ethical level than businesses in other countries?	14.2	23.5	31.3	17.9	8.4	4.7	3.0	(1.3)
Are the ethics of business people worse than the ethics of individuals in government?	13.2	22.2	28.2	20.0	9.8	6.6	3.1	(1.4)

reveals that there was nearly as much response variation within groups as across groups, and that the statistically significant differences observed were due in part to the large sample size employed

Table 19.2 Mean concern ratings for selected academic classifications

Items	Mean[a]			
	Freshman	Sophomore	Junior	Senior
Is it possible to improve ethics in business?	2.8	2.7	2.7	2.6
Do current ethical standards meet the needs of society?	2.8	2.6	2.6	2.8
How will change in business ethics affect our living standard and way of life?	2.7	2.6	2.7	2.7
Will business ethics get better or worse in the future?	2.7	2.6	2.7	2.8
Have business ethics deteriorated over the years?	2.7	2.7	2.8	2.8
How much importance should ethical considerations be given in designing corporate policies?	2.9	2.7	2.8	2.7
Are business ethics being sacrificed due to government regulation and inflation?	2.8	2.8	2.8	2.8
Do current ethical standards meet the needs of business?	3.0	3.1	2.9	3.0
Should U.S. businesses be expected to operate on a higher ethical level than businesses in other countries?	2.9	3.0	2.9	3.0
Are the ethics of business people worse than the ethics of individuals in government?*	3.0	3.0	3.0	3.2

*$p<0.05$
[a] 1 = extremely concerned, 6 = extremely unconcerned

Conclusions

This study investigated the attitudes of a national sample of college students toward selected business ethics issues. The methodological approach employed operationalized attitudes in terms of concern regarding the ethical issues. Results of the study indicate that college students are currently concerned about business ethics in general. Moreover, they appear somewhat more concerned about improving business ethics ("Is it possible to improve ethics in business?") than with 'finger pointing' ("Are the ethics of business people worse than the ethics of individuals in government?").

Somewhat surprisingly, the ethical concerns of the students surveyed were not substantially different across academic classification or academic major. Although certain differences were statistically significant, this was due as much to the relatively large sample size as to the magnitude of the differences.

Table 19.3 Mean concern ratings for selected academic majors

Items	Mean[a]		
	Business	Liberal arts/ Social science	Engineering/ Natural science
Is it possible to improve ethics in business?*	2.6	2.8	2.8
Do current ethical standards meet the needs of society?	2.7	2.7	2.8
How will change in business ethics affect our living standard and way of life?*	2.7	2.6	2.8
Will business ethics get better or worse in the future?	2.7	2.7	2.8
Have business ethics deteriorated over the years?	2.7	2.8	2.8
How much importance should ethical considerations be given indesigning corporate policies?*	2.7	2.8	2.9
Are business ethics being sacrificed due to government regulation and inflation?*	2.7	2.8	2.9
Do current ethical standards meet the needs of business?*	2.8	3.1	3.1
Should U.S. businesses be expected to operate on a higher ethical level than businesses in other countries?	3.0	2.9	3.0
Are the ethics of business people worse than the ethics of individuals in government?	3.1	3.0	3.2

*$p < 0.05$
[a]1 = extremely concerned, 6 = extremely unconcerned

However, there was a consistent tendency for the females in the sample to express more concern than the males in the sample, regardless of the issue. While it is difficult to speculate on the precise implications of this finding, one interpretation is that the increasing participation of females in the workforce will have a significant impact on what are considered ethical business practices. Not only are the attitudes of future decision makers and managers regarding ethical practices currently in the process of being shaped by educators, but to an extent it is the female students' concerns which may well be establishing a new moral force in tomorrow's business world.

Additional work in researching student concerns regarding business ethics is clearly needed. This empirical investigation has highlighted the influence of academic classification, academic major, and sex on these concerns. However, as ethical norms evolve, reflecting changing societal patterns, the need emerges to

Table 19.4 Mean concern ratings for males and females

Items	Mean[a]	
	Male	Female
Is it possible to improve ethics in business?*	2.7	2.6
Do current ethical standards meet the needs of society?*	2.8	2.6
How will change in business ethics affect our living standard and way of life?*	2.8	2.6
Will business ethics get better or worse in the future?*	2.8	2.6
Have business ethics deteriorated over the years?*	2.8	2.6
How much importance should ethical considerations be given in designing corporate policies?*	2.8	2.7
Are business ethics being sacrificed due to government regulation and inflation?	2.8	2.8
Do current ethical standards meet the needs of business?*	3.0	2.9
Should U.S. businesses be expected to operate on a higher ethical level than businesses in other countries?	3.0	2.9
Are the ethics of business people worse than the ethics of individuals in government?*	3.2	3.0

*$p<0.05$
[a]1 = extremely concerned, 6 = extremely unconcerned

continually investigate and monitor attitudes regarding business ethics. Additional information on the concerns of today's college students regarding business ethics can serve as input for intelligent decision making among policy makers, educators, and business people alike.

Note

1 The sample consisted of 7%, freshmen, 12% sophomores, 35% juniors, and 46% seniors (academic classification); 50% business, 23% liberal arts/social science, and 27% engineering/natural science (academic major); and 57% male and 43% female (sex). Even though strict probability sampling was not employed, the resulting variance in schools suggests the sample was a fairly representative one.

References

Brenner, S.N., and E.A. Molander. 1977. Is the ethics of business changing? *Harvard Business Review* 55(January/February): 57–71.

Carr, A.Z. 1970. Can an executive afford a conscience? *Harvard Business Review* 48(July/August): 58.

Carroll, A.B. 1975. Managerial ethics: A post-Watergate view. *Business Horizons* 18(April): 77–80.
Coney, K.A., and J.H. Murphy. 1976. Attitudes of marketers toward ethical and professional marketing research practices. In *Proceedings of the Southern Marketing Association*, 172–174.
Dagher, S.P., and P.H. Spader. 1980. Poll of top managers stresses education and leadership by example as strong forces for higher standards'. *Management Review* 69(March): 54–57.
Ferrell, O.C., and K.M. Weaver. 1978. Ethical belief of marketing managers. *Journal of Marketing* 42: 69–73.
Hawkins, D.I., and A.B. Cocanougher. 1972. Student evaluations of the ethics of marketing practices: The role of marketing education. *Journal of Marketing* 36: 61–64.
Management Review. 1978. Managers 0, Students 1 in an ethics contest. June, 58.
Purcell, T.V. 1977. Do courses in business ethics pay off? *California Management Review* 19: 50–58.
Ruch, W.A., and J.W. Newstrom. 1975. How unethical are we? *Supervisory Management* 20(November): 16–21.
Schutte, T.F. 1963. 'Marketing implications of executives' perceptions of business ethics'. In *Proceedings of the American Marketing Association*, 186–199.
Shuptrine, F.K. 1979. Evaluating the ethics of marketing practices: Student perceptions. In *Proceedings of the American Marketing Association*, 124–127. Chicago: American Marketing Association.
Trawick, I.F., and W.R. Darden. 1980. Marketers' perceptions of ethical standards in the marketing profession: Educators and practitioners. *Review of Business and Economic Research* 16: 1–17.

Chapter 20
Gender Differences in Proclivity for Unethical Behavior

Michael Betz, Lenahan O'Connell, and Jon M. Shepard

Introduction

The issue of ethics has been on the front pages of America's newspapers for several years. Over 100 individuals associated with the Reagan administration have been under an "ethical or legal cloud". The newswire has carried information exposing unethical business practices from insider trading on Wall Street (Ivan Boeksy, Michael Milken, Dennis Levine) to Norelco's sale of a water filter that apparently contaminates with methylene chloride the water it is supposed to purify. Anyone teaching ethics in the professions seems to have only to wait for the next evening's newscast to obtain fresh lecture and discussion material.

These scandals have shaken the public's confidence in the ethics of our institutional leaders. Business leaders are now looking for ways to restore public confidence (*Corporate Ethics: A Prime Corporate Asset*, NY: The Business Roundtable, 1988) and business schools are rushing to institute courses in business ethics (Harvard University has been given some $20 million by a Wall Street alumnus for the purpose of creating a professional ethics program).

One aspect often ignored in discussions of business ethics is the sex of the offender. In this paper, we explore the possible connection between gender and the

M. Betz
Department of Sociology, University of Tennesee,
Knoxville, TN 37919, USA

L. O'Connell
Department of Sociology, Carson-Newman College,
Jefferson, TN, USA

J.M. Shepard (✉)
Department of Management, Department of Sociology,
University of Kentucky, Lexington, KY, USA
e-mail: jshepard@vt.edu

A.C. Michalos and D.C. Poff (eds.), *Citation Classics from the Journal of Business Ethics*, Advances in Business Ethics Research 2,
DOI 10.1007/978-94-007-4126-3_20,

willingness to engage in unethical business behavior. After discussing some approaches to this issue, we present data from a sample of undergraduate and graduate business majors.

Approaches to Gender and Unethical Behavior

According to Carol Gilligan (1982) males and females have distinctly different moral orientations. Although women conceptualize moral questions as problems of care involving empathy and compassion, men conceptualize them as problems of rights. Some research on the relation of gender to work indicates that females are more concerned with helping people; males are more interested in income and advancement (David 1974; Lueptow 1981; Betz and O'Connell 1987). Other studies show that men and women working in, or planning for, business careers have generally different values and work-related interests (Keys 1985; Statham 1987; Shann 1983; Brenner and Tomkiewicz 1979).

Two broad explanations are used to explain gender differences in values and work interests. According to the "structural" approach, differences between men and women, due to early socialization and other role requirements (e.g., wife, mother), will be overridden by the rewards, and costs associated with occupational roles (Blauner 1964; Collins 1975; Kanter 1977; Markham et al. 1985; Feldberg and Glenn 1979). Since the nature of present (or anticipated) work shapes behavior through the structure of rewards, men and women will respond similarly in the same occupational environment. In other words, men and women in a given occupation (or in training for a particular occupation) will exhibit the same priorities on a wide range of occupational attributes: money, working with people, helping people, advancement, freedom from supervision, and so on (Lacy et al. 1983).

Although the structural approach predicts that women will become more like men under similar occupational conditions, the "gender socialization" approach asserts that the sexes bring different values and traits to their work roles, which, in turn, differentially shapes their work-related interests, decisions, and practices. Consequently, men and women will respond differently to the same set of occupational rewards and costs (Lueptow 1981; Veroff 1977). According to proponents of this approach, men will seek signs of competitive success – money and advancement – and deemphasize relationships and intrinsic satisfaction derived from work itself. This approach suggests that men are more likely to work long hours and break rules because men view achievement as competition, as a game to be won. Conversely, women are thought to place less emphasis on competitive success and more on doing tasks well and promoting harmonious relationships. Thus, women are expected to work fewer hours, show less concern for money and advancement, and adhere more often to rules and laws.

Presumably, a concern for money and advancement spurs a willingness to be less ethical and a concern with relationships and people promotes ethical behavior. The structural approach predicts that the sexes will be equally willing to be unethical

Table 20.1 Work-related values and interests

	Male	Female
Reasons for career goals at age 40		
(a) Money and power	14.6%	1.8%
(b) Growth, stimulation, and development	20.0	29.1
Expected income at age 40	$92,270	$65,532
Organization rank at age 40	4.6	3.7
Compete for leadership	4.3	4.0
Help people	3.8	4.2

when occupation is held constant. The gender socialization approach assumes differences in willingness to be unethical will exist among men and women in the same occupation.

Sample and Methods

To explore these issues, data were obtained from 213 business school students in 11 classes in finance and management at The University of Tennessee in the fall of 1986. A response rate of 91% was obtained. Of these students, 46.5% were female and the remaining 53.5% were male; 37.1% were undergraduates.

Female enrollment in all the masters degree programs in business at The University of Tennessee is 37%, but the percentage of graduate females in our sample is 41%; these response rates are partially explained by males being less likely to respond to questionnaires. The research instrument included measures that assess: (1) the willingness to engage in unethical conduct, (2) work orientations and interests, (3) career goals, and (4) demographic information.

Results

In answering an open-ended question on the reasons for their career goals, males more than females gave monetary and power reasons for goals at age 40 (14.6% versus 1.8%) as shown in Table 20.1. Females more than males indicated a concern with rewards that are intrinsic to the work – opportunities for growth, stimulation, and development (29.1% versus 20.0%). Table 20.1 also shows that men are more concerned than women with income, organizational rank, and leadership.

More female than male students want to help people. For example, the average score on a five point Likert scale (5 = agree strongly) is significantly higher for females than for males (4.2 versus 3.8), indicating that they agree more with the statement "It is important to me that the work I do helps people". In addition,

Table 20.2 Percentages on willingness to engage in unethical behavior by sex

	Males $n=114$	Females $n=99$
Willing to use shortcut estimating method[a]	39.3	19.6
Claim $50 extra on travel expenses[b]	14.9	6.1
Willing to buy stock with inside information[c]	50.0	31.3
Willing to transfer $20,000 by computer from their employer[d]	12.3	4.0
Willing to make $100,000 from a marijuana deal	17.5	2.0

[a]You are working for a large company. Your job is to determine the cost of supplying a complex service. From experience you know you can make a quick estimate of the service. The quick method overestimates or underestimates by 5% the figure obtained from the company's elaborate, time-consuming procedure. The company tells you to follow the time-consuming procedure. However, the company rarely checks on how thoroughly people follow procedures, so there is little chance of getting caught if you don't follow the procedure

[b]Your job requires travel. Your company pays for travel expenses. A co-worker tells you that some employees claim more expense than actually spent. If you claim $350 but spent only $300 you could earn an additional $50 at the company's expense. There is only a small chance you will be caught, but you could lose your job

[c]You are working as a stockbroker. You have a friend who works for a large corporation who gives you inside information that the value of the company's shares will double overnight. By buying shares in this company you can double your wealth. It is illegal for a stock-broker to take advantage of inside information. If discovered you face prosecution, but there is only a 1% chance you would get caught

[d]You working for a large company and you discover a way to transfer funds from that company to an account from which you can draw money. If you transfer these funds, you can obtain $20,000. Due to the technical complexities involved there is only a small chance you will be caught

females more than males disagree with the statement "It is more important to earn a lot of money than to help people".

We asked five questions about unethical behavior. One concerned taking shortcuts in paperwork. Four questions focused on financially self-aggrandizing conduct: padding expenses accounts, selling marijuana, profiting from insider information in the stock market, and computerized theft (the wording of these questions is in Table 20.2).

To determine how oriented to company's procedures students thought they would be, we asked whether they would seek to find a short cut in the procedure prescribed for estimating costs of their employer's service. Two times the proportion of males (39.3%) to females (19.6%) indicated they would skirt company rules (see Table 20.2).

With the exception of insider trading, few respondents were willing to break laws for personal gain. Regarding the willingness to pad expense accounts, 14.9% of the males and 6.1% of the females indicated they would be willing to claim unwarranted expenses on their expense account. The question on insider trading elicited nearly twice the willingness to buy stock illegally on the part of males (50.0%) than females (31.3%). (It is interesting to note that none of those arrested in the recent insider trading scandals have been women.) As shown in Table 20.2, 12.3% of the males and 4.0% of the females indicated they might or would be willing to transfer illegally money to themselves by computer. Finally, more males than females (17.5% versus 2.0%) expressed a willingness to sell marijuana for a $100,000 profit.

Summary and Conclusions

In this paper, we examined a range of possible gender differences in work-related values and interests as well as in the expressed willingness to engage in unethical work behavior. On questions pertaining to work-related values and interests, we found gender differences. Men were more concerned with money and advancement; women were more interested in relationships and helping people.

The gap between the sexes was widest on the questions pertaining to unethical behavior. Males were more than twice as likely to say they would engage in actions regarded as less ethical on five measures: using a shortcut estimating procedure that was opposed by the employer, padding travel expenses, selling marijuana, engaging in insider trading, and embezzling money via the computer.

We do not know what, if any, courses on ethics the respondents have had. But our results suggest that ethics courses need to focus on the rules that govern the stock-market. It appears that many otherwise ethical students are willing to engage in insider trading. Perhaps students fail to apprehend the negative consequences of insider trading including the harm done to other investors.

Overall, the results support the gender socialization approach but it should be emphasized that very-few would engage in any of these actions regarded as unethical except the issue of insider information. Although these men and women were preparing for similar careers, they possess distinct differences in work-related values and interests, and in professed proclivities for unethical behavior. A stronger test would involve a before-after design among people who have been in the labor force for a period of time, however, our results are strongly suggestive.

References

Betz, M., and L. O'Connell. 1987. Gender and work: A look at sex differences among pharmacy students. *American Journal of Pharmaceutical Education* 51: 39–43.

Blauner, R. 1964. *Alienation and freedom: The factory worker and his industry*. Chicago: The University of Chicago Press.

Brenner, O., and C. Tomkiewicz. 1979. Job orientation of males and females: Are sex differences declining? *Personnel Psychology* 32: 741–750.

Collins, R. 1975. *Conflict sociology: Toward an explanatory science*. New York: Academic.

David, D. 1974. Occupational values and sex: The case of scientists and engineers. Unpublished paper presented at American Sociological Association meetings in Montreal, Canada.

Feldberg, R., and E. Glenn. 1979. Male and female: Job versus gender roles. *Social Problems* 26: 524–539.

Gilligan, C. 1982. *In a different voice*. Cambridge, MA: Harvard University Press.

Kanter, R. 1977. *Men and women of the corporation*. New York: Basic Books.

Keys, D.E. 1985. Gender, sex role, and career decision making of certified management accountants. *Sex Roles* 13: 33–46.

Lacy, W.B., J.L. Bokemeier, and J.M. Shepard. 1983. Job attribute preferences and work commitment of men and women in the United States. *Personnel Psychology* 36: 315–329.

Lueptow, L.B. 1981. Sex-typing and change in the occupational choices of high school seniors: 1964–1975. *Sociological Education* 54: 16–24.

Markham, W.T., S.J. South, C.M. Bonjean, and J. Corder. 1985. Gender and opportunity in the federal bureaucracy. *The American Journal of Sociology* 91: 129–150.

Shann, M.H. 1983. Career plans of men and women in gender dominant professions. *Journal of Vocational Behavior* 22: 343–356.

Statham, A. 1987. The gender model revisited: Differences in the management styles of men and women. *Sex Roles* 16: 409–429.

Veroff, J. 1977. Process vs. impact in men's and women's achievement motivation. *Psychology of Women Quarterly* 1: 283–293.

Chapter 21
Predicting Unethical Behavior: A Comparison of the Theory of Reasoned Action and the Theory of Planned Behavior

Man Kit Chang

Introduction

For the past 10 years, a numbers of studies have proposed frameworks and models to represent the determinants of unethical behavior (Bommer et al. 1987; Ferrel and Gresham 1985; Hunt and Vitell 1986; Trevino 1986). Most of them pulled from past business ethical studies the factors found to influence ethical decision making and behavior. They have been criticized for not contributing to theoretical development, but were only summaries of prior research (Brady and Hatch 1992). Most of the models have not been validated.

Predicting behavior has been the major objective of psychological theories, and some of them have been doing a very good job. The theories may be very useful in investigating unethical behavior. Some of the models mentioned earlier do draw on social psychological theories in their formulation, for example, the theory of reasoned action (TRA) (Ajzen and Fishbein 1980; Fishbein and Ajzen 1975). Theory of reasoned action and its extension, theory of planned behavior (TPB) (Ajzen 1991), have been found to be very useful in predicting a wide range of behavior (Sheppard et al. 1988; Madden et al. 1992). Therefore, it is reasonable to believe that theory of reasoned action and theory of planned behavior will provide a very good foundation for us to investigate unethical behavior. Heretofore, the theories have rarely been applied to this behavioral domain. Randall (1989) reviewed empirical studies of business ethics from 1960 to 1988, and concluded that the theory of reasoned action has rarely been applied to the study of business ethical decision making and only a few of the linkages proposed by the theory have

M.K. Chang (✉)
Department of Finance and Decision Sciences, School of Business,
Hong Kong Baptist University, Kowloon Tong, Hong Kong
e-mail: mkchang@hkbu.edu.hk

A.C. Michalos and D.C. Poff (eds.), *Citation Classics from the Journal of Business Ethics*, Advances in Business Ethics Research 2,
DOI 10.1007/978-94-007-4126-3_21,

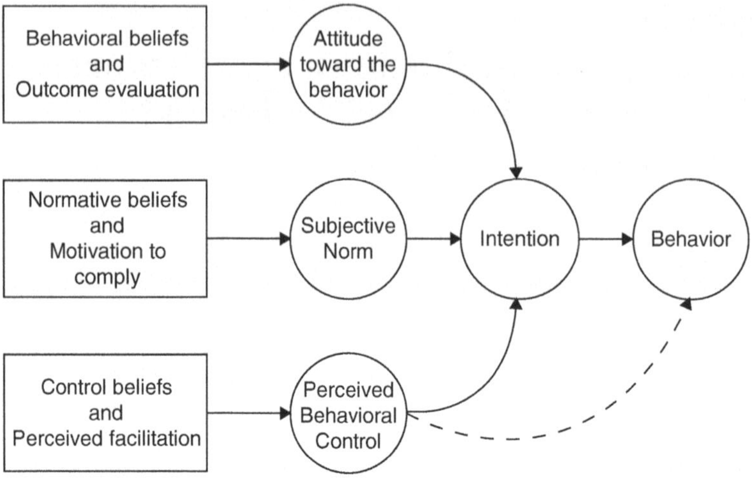

Fig. 21.1 Theory of planned behavior (Adopted from Mathieson 1991; Ajzen 1991)

been tested. Randall suggested that additional tests of the hypothesized linkages in the model should be performed.

The first objective of this study is to test the validity of the theory of reasoned action and theory of planned behavior as applied to an unethical behavior in information systems area – software piracy. Software piracy results in software companies losing billions of dollars in potential software sales (Smiddy and Smiddy 1985). Since it is an unethical and illegal behavior widely practiced worldwide, it is easy to solicit responses from people about their own behavior. The second purpose of the current study is to compare the utility of theory of reasoned action and theory of planned behavior in predicting unethical behavior. The third purpose of this study is to test whether the inclusion of a causal path which has not been hypothesized previously by the theory of planned behavior will improve the predictive power of the theory, as found by other studies (Shepherd and O'Keefe 1984; Shimp and Kavas 1984; Timko 1987; Vallerand et al. 1992).

Theory of Reasoned Action and Theory of Planned Behavior

Figure 21.1 depicts the theory of planned behavior which is an extension of theory of reasoned action. The difference between these two theories is that the theory of planned behavior has added perceived behavioral control as the determinant of behavioral intention, as well as control beliefs which affect the perceived behavioral control. Both theories assume that human beings are basically rational and make systematic use of information available to them when making decisions. Theory of reasoned action also assumes that the behavior being studied is under total volitional control of the performer (Madden et al. 1992).

Theory of reasoned action is based on the proposition that an individuals behavior is determined by the individuals *behavioral intention* (BI) to perform that behavior, which provides the most accurate prediction of behavior (Fishbein and Ajzen 1975). Behavioral intention is a function of two factors: one's *Attitude* toward the behavior (A) and *Subjective Norm* (SN).

Attitude toward the behavior is defined as "a persons general feeling of favorableness or unfavorableness for that behavior" (Ajzen and Fishbein 1980). Subjective Norm is defined as a person's "perception that most people who are important to him think he should or should not perform the behavior in question" (Ajzen and Fishbein 1980). Attitude toward behavior is a function of the product of ones salient belief (B) that performing the behavior will lead to certain outcomes, and an evaluation of the outcomes (E), i.e., rating of the desirability of the outcome. Attitude thus is defined as:

$$A = \sum B_i E_i$$

Subjective Norm is a function of the product of one's normative belief (NB) which is the "person's belief that the salient referent thinks he should (or should not) perform the behavior" (Ajzen and Fishbein 1980), and his/her motivation to comply (MC) to that referent. Thus Subjective Norm can be defined as:

$$SN = \sum NB_i MC_i$$

Variables that are external to the model are assumed to influence intentions only to the extent that they affect either attitudes or subjective norms (Fishbein and Ajzen 1975). The theory of reasoned action has been successfully applied to a large number of situations in predicting the performance of behavior and intentions, such as predicting turnover (Prestholdt et al. 1987); education (Fredricks and Dossett 1983); and breast caner examination (Timko 1987). In a meta-analysis of research on the theory of reasoned action, Sheppard et al. (1988) concluded that the predictive utility of the theory of reasoned action was strong across conditions.

However, the predictive validity of the theory of reasoned action becomes problematic if the behavior under study is not under full volitional control. Sheppard et al. (1988) pointed out two problems. First, the prediction of behavior from intention is problematic because a variety of factors in addition to one's intentions determine whether the behavior is performed. Second, there is no provision in the model for considering either the probability of failing to perform one's behavior or the consequences of such failure in determining one's intentions. To deal with these problems, Ajzen (1985) extended the theory of reasoned action by including another construct, perceived behavior control (PBC), to predict behavioral intentions and behavior. The extended model is the Theory of Planned Behavior. Perceived behavioral control refers to "people's perception of the ease or difficulty of performing the behavior of interest" (Ajzen 1991). If behavior is not under complete volitional control, the performers need to have the requisite resources and opportunities in order to perform the behavior. The perception of whether they have the resources will affect their intention to perform the behavior, as well as the successful performance of the behavior.

Perceived Behavioral Control is a function of control beliefs (CB) and perceived facilitation (PF). Control belief is the perception of the presence or absence of requisite resources and opportunities needed to carry out the behavior. Perceived facilitation is one's assessment of the importance of those resources to the achievement of outcomes (Ajzen and Madden 1986). PBC can be defined as

$$PBC = \sum CB_i PF_i$$

Theory of planned behavior has been successfully applied to various situations in predicting the performance of behavior and intentions, such as predicting user intentions to use a new software (Mathieson 1991), to perform breast self-examination (Young et al. 1991), and to avoid caffeine (Madden et al. 1992). Madden et al. (1992) found that the theory of planned behavior has a better predictive power of behavior than the theory of reasoned action.

Since our study is cross-sectional, we investigated only the relationship between attitude, subjective norm, perceived behavioral control, and behavioral intention. We did not include the prediction of actual behavior in our research design. This study did not attempt to test every component of the theory of reasoned action and theory of planned behavior; it instead attempted to establish the relationships between attitudes, subjective norm, perceived behavioral control, and behavioral intention using confirmatory modeling techniques. We chose to leave the belief components to a more comprehensive study once we have established the validity of the core part of the theories in our present study.

Application of the Theory of Reasoned Action and Theory of Planned Behavior to Moral Behavior

Only a few investigators have used theory of reasoned action or theory of planned behavior to explain unethical decision making. Two recent studies were conducted by Randall and Gibson (1991) and Vallerand et al. (1992). Randall and Gibson (1991) used the theory of planned behavior to investigate the ethical decision making of medical professionals. The results showed that attitude explained a large portion of the variance of intention while subjective norm explained a moderate amount of the variance. The addition of perceived behavioral control did not increase predictive power. Randall and Gibson (1991) explained that the insignificant impact of perceived behavioral control might be due to the behavior studied, reporting misconduct of colleagues, which was under one's total volitional control. Since most unethical behavior, such as corruption and computer hacking, require substantial resources and opportunities to perform successfully, it is reasonable to hypothesize that the theory of planned behavior will better explain unethical behavior than the theory of reasoned action. Vallerand et al. (1992) investigated the moral behavior in sports by asking the respondents to answer their behavioral choice in two hypothetical situations. The results provided support to the validity of using theory of reasoned action to explain unethical decision making.

The theory of reasoned action and theory of planned behavior are not without their critics. Randall and Gibson (1991) noted that when researchers used theory of reasoned action, they only tested linkage hypothesized by the theory without considering other linkages between constructs. However, a number of studies have shown that attitudinal and normative structure are not independent; subjective norm was found to influence attitude (Shepherd and O'Keefe 1984; Shimp and Kavas 1984; Vallerand et al. 1992). In our analysis, we compared the original formulation of the theory of planned behavior and a modified version of it with a causal path from subjective norm to attitude.

Method

Subjects

A total of 181 (99 male and 82 female) university students participated in this study. They were from several Hong Kong universities. Questionnaires were distributed inside the library and canteens of the universities; the investigators then collected the completed questionnaires.

Measures

Ten measured variables were used to reflect the components of the theory of reasoned action and the theory of planned behavior. The measures were modeled after Ajzen and Fishbein (1980) and Madden et al. (1992). In addition, some demographic variables such as sex, age and university major were collected. The following discussion describes the questions used to measure the constructs.

Behavioral Intentions

The respondent's intention to make unauthorized software copy was measured using three 7-point items. "I intend to make unauthorized software copy in the future" (INT1); "I will try to make unauthorized software copy in the future" (INT2); and "I will make an effort to make unauthorized software copy in the future" (INT3). The scales for these questions ranged from *extremely probable to extremely improbable*.

Attitude

Attitude was measured using a three-item semantic differential scale. On a 7-point fully anchored scale, respondents were asked whether they felt making unauthorized software copies were *good-bad (A1), harmful-beneficial (A2),* and *wise-foolish (A3).*

Subjective Norm

The subjective norm was measured by one question: "Most people who are important to me think that I should make unauthorized software copies" (SN). The SN was rated on a 7-point scale ranging from extremely probable (1) to extremely improbable (7).

Perceived Behavioral Control

It was measured using three items: "I have complete control of making unauthorized software copies" (PCB1); "For me to make unauthorized software copies is easy" (PCB2); "If I want to, I could easily make unauthorized software copies" (PCB3). They were rated on a 7-point scale ranging from strongly agree (1) to strongly disagree (7).

Data Analysis

The method of data analysis used in this study was structural equation modeling with latent variables. The statistical program EQS (Bentler 1993) was used to perform the structural modeling analysis. Structural Equation Modeling (SEM) is a confirmatory approach to data analysis (Byrne 1994), which is highly appropriate in the present context. Since the theory of reasoned action and the theory of planned behavior have been applied and validated in a large number of studies, we have strong theoretical support to specify our models and to test their validity. One additional advantage of using SEM is that it can test the measurement model and the path model simultaneously.

Model fit was evaluated using the Comparative Fit Index (CFI). CFI has an advantage over other fit indices in that it avoids the underestimation of fit in a small sample (Bentler 1990). A CFI value of over 0.90 is desirable and indicates an acceptable fit of the model to the data (Bentler 1992).

The data were analyzed using the two-step approach suggested by Anderson and Gerbing (1988). In the first step, a confirmatory factor analysis (CFA) was performed to determine whether the measured variables reliably reflect the hypothesized latent variables (attitude, perceived behavioral control and behavioral intention). Since Subjective Norm was measured with only one variable, the measured variable itself was used as the construct and allowed to covariate with the latent variables in the CFA.

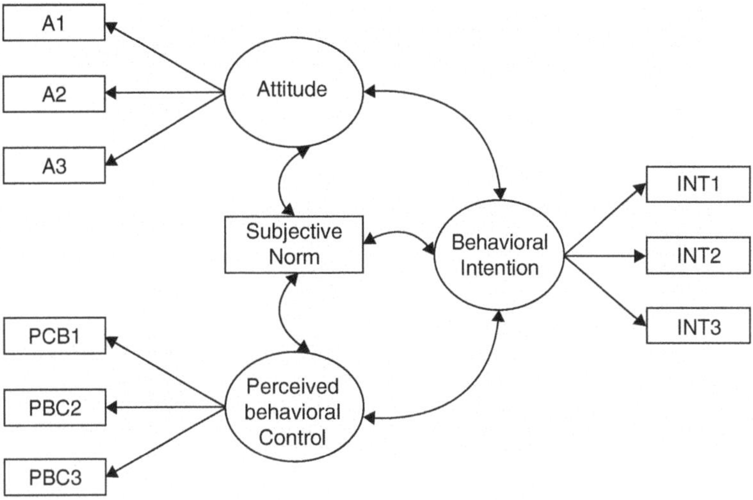

Fig. 21.2 The confirmatory factor analysis model

All latent variables were allowed to intercorrelate freely without attribution of a causal order.

In the second step, a series of structural equation path models were tested: (1) to determine the adequacy of the theory of reasoned action in explaining the software piracy behavioral intention (Model 1); (2) to test whether the theory of planned behavior better predicts the software piracy behavior than the theory of reasoned action (Model 2); (3) to test whether the direct causal path from subjective norm to attitude improved significantly the fit of the data (Model 3).

Nested-model comparison was used to find out which model best explains the sample covariance. Models are nested if "a more restricted model is obtained by imposing constraints on a more general model" (Bentler 1992). In our analysis, theory of reasoned action is nested within theory of planned behavior by setting to zero the path from PBC to BI. While theory of planned behavior is nested within Model 3 by setting to zero the path from SN to Attitude. Chi-square difference test or the likelihood ratio (Bollen 1989) was used to analyze whether the improvement in the model fits are significant.

Results

Confirmatory Factor Analysis

To assess the adequacy of the measurement model, we performed a confirmatory factor analysis in the first step of data analysis. Figure 21.2 shows the confirmatory factor analysis model. The factor variances were fixed at unity and all constructs

Table 21.1 Standardized confirmatory factor loadings

Factors	Cronbach's alpha	Factor loading[a]
Attitude	0.65	
A1		0.86
A2		0.48
A3		0.48
Perceived behavioral control	0.70	
PBC1		0.33
PBC2		0.88
PBC3		0.90
Behavioral intention	0.94	
INT1		0.94
INT2		0.97
INT3		0.82

[a] All factor loadings are significant at $p=0.05$

Table 21.2 Relationships among latent variables in the CFA

Latent variables	1[a]	2	3	4
1. Attitude	–			
2. Subjective norm	0.758	–		
3. Perceived behavioral control	0.319	0.333	–	
4. Behavioral intention	0.480	0.498	0.514	–

[a] All correlations are significant at $p=0.05$

were allowed to correlate freely. The confirmatory factor model adequately reflects a good fit to the data, $\chi^2(30, N=181)=54.664, p=0.004$, CFI=0.973. The high CFI indicates that the 3-factor structure is a valid one. Table 21.1 shows the factor loadings of the observed variables on the latent constructs as estimated from the confirmatory factor analysis. All factor loadings are significant at an alpha level of 0.05, and the factor loadings are fairly high. This supports that the measurement shows convergent validity (Anderson and Gerbing 1988).

Table 21.2 shows the correlations between the latent variables. These correlations are in the expected direction and all are significant at an alpha level of 0.05.

Structural Path Model

The second step in our data analysis was to compare various structural models. Figure 21.3 shows the specification of the models we tested; and Table 21.3 shows the results of the model comparisons. Fit statistics (Chi-square, degree of freedom,

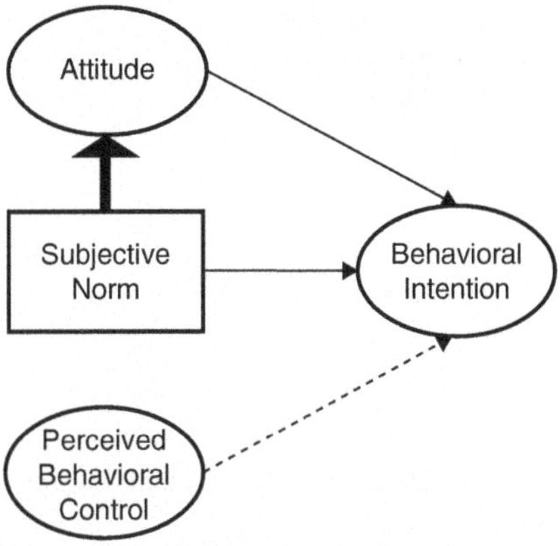

Fig. 21.3 Model specification for Model 1, the theory of reasoned action (*full thin arrows*). Model 2, the theory of planned behavior (*full thin arrows* and *broken arrow*), and Model 3 (*all arrows*)

Table 21.3 Chi-square, normed fit index (NFI) and comparative fit index (CFI) of the models

Models	χ^2	df	$\Delta\chi^2$	NFI	CFI
Null model	953.960	45			
Model 1 – TRA	134.620	34	819.340*	0.859	0.889
Model 2 – TPB	101.395	33	33.225*	0.894	0.925
Model 3 – TPB + SN → Attitude	69.269	32	32.126*	0.927	0.959

*$p<0.05$

normed fit index, and CFI) associated with the models and information about the Chi-square difference tests associated with specific model comparisons are provided.

Model 1 was evaluated to test the validity of theory of reasoned action in predicting behavioral intention. Using maximum likelihood estimation, the model did not provide a good fit to the data, χ^2 (34, $N=181$), $p\leq0.001$, and a poor CFI of 0.889.

Model 2 representing the theory of planned behavior was also evaluated using maximum likelihood estimation. This model provides a reasonable fit to the data with $\chi^2(33, N=181)=101.395$, $p\leq0.001$. A highly significant Chi-square difference test for the comparison of Model 1 and Model 2 suggests that Model 2 (TPB) provides an important improvement in fit over that of Model 1. However, the value of CFI (0.925) and NFI (0.894) are somewhat low but marginally acceptable.

Finally, based on the results of past studies, we tested Model 3 which is created by adding a causal path linking subjective norm to attitude to the theory of planned behavior. The final maximum likelihood model fit is X^2 (32, $N=181)=69.269$, $p\leq0.001$, CFI=0.959. The high CFI value implies that the model provides an adequate fit to the data. The chi-square difference test for the comparison of Model 2 and Model 3 is highly significant. Combining with the high incremental CFI, it can be concluded that Model 3 provides a better fit than Model 2.

Table 21.4 presents the standardized structural model coefficients for Model 3. The pattern of causal relationships is consistent with that predicted by the theories.

Table 21.4 Standardized path coefficients (without factor loadings) for Model 3

Path	Coefficient
A–BI	0.341*
SN–BI	0.086
PBC–BI	0.425*
SN–A	0.492*

Note: A Attitude, *BI* Behavioral intention, *SN* Subjective norm
*$p<0.05$

Table 21.5 Direct, indirect, and total effect (non-standardized) of Model 3

Relations	Direct	Indirect	Total
Attitude			
SN	0.382*		0.382
Intention			
Attitude	0.425*		0.425
Subjective norm	0.083	0.163*	0.246
Perceived behavioral control	1.373*		1.373

*$p<0.05$

In predicting behavioral intention, perceived behavioral control contributes more than attitude. The beta for the path linking subjective norm and behavioral intention was not significant. However, as shown in Table 21.5, the indirect effect of subjective norm on behavioral intention through attitude is significant at an alpha level of 0.05.

Discussion

The principal objective of this study was to assess the applicability of two social psychological theories, theory of reasoned action and theory of planned behavior, to the predicting of unethical behavior. We also compared the usefulness of these two theories. The result shows that theory of planned behavior is better than theory of reasoned action in predicting unethical behavior. This result is inconsistent with one found by Randall and Gibson (1991) in a study of ethical decision making in the medical profession. Perceived behavioral control was found to add little explanation power in predicting behavioral intention. Our results show that perceived behavioral control is the most important predictor of intention to use illegal software copies. Our findings support Ajzen's (1991) conclusion after reviewing 16 studies of predicting intention using theory of planned behavior that the addition of perceived behavioral control improved significantly the prediction of intentions.

The usefulness of perceived behavioral control in predicting (un)ethical behavior has been substantiated by our results and is consistent with most situations involving decisions of performing unethical behavior. As mentioned before, the performers of unethical behavior do not have total control in most situations. Opportunities and resources must exist before they can be performed. In the case of illegal software copying, the perpetrators must be able to obtain a copy of the software before they can make the duplication. Without this, their intention to perform the action will be lower, no matter how favorable their attitudes are towards software copying and how much their significant others agree on the behavior. To perform successfully the behavior requires much greater effort if the software is not readily available. Therefore, in order to prevent software piracy or other unethical behavior, it is important that responsible authorities should curtail any opportunity that the perpetrators has to perform the unethical behavior.

The results also show the validity of the theory of planned behavior as applied to the domain of unethical behavior. This provides a much more solid theoretical basis for the study of ethical and unethical behavior. The theories can be used to structure past studies as well as to guide future research design.

The determinants of attitude, subjective norm, and perceived behavioral control are their corresponding beliefs. This theory provides a relatively simple basis for identifying where and how to target behavioral change attempts by understanding various beliefs about unethical behavior (Sheppard et al. 1988).

Another objective of our study was to test causal links that have not been included in the theory of planned behavior. Specifically, we included the causal path linking subjective norm to attitude in our final model. Our results show that attitude and subjective norm are not as independent as the models predict. The addition of the causal path from subjective norm to attitude improves the model fit considerably and the beta for this path is highly significant. This result is consistent with past findings (Shepherd and O'Keefe 1984; Shimp and Kavas 1984; Vallerand et al. 1992). The significant causal path from subjective norm to attitude suggests that the attitude formation, that is the favorableness or unfavorableness towards the behavior, is affected by how significant others consider the performance of the behavior. The theory of planned behavior predicts that behavioral belief will affect one's attitude. The question is, where does the person get these beliefs? One possible source is, and quite reasonably so, from their parents, teachers, peers, etc. In short, they are the person's significant others. If this is true, the effect of the significant others on attitude formation cannot be ignored. In a company, colleagues may affect greatly the ethical behavior of a person, both through social pressure and formation of attitudes. Therefore, if we want employees to act ethically, creating an ethical atmosphere is of utmost importance.

Limitation and Future Research

Ajzen (1991) pointed out that the relative importance of attitude, subjective norm, and perceived behavioral control in the prediction of intention is expected to vary across behavior and situations. Although this study found that perceived behavioral control is the most important construct in predicting unauthorized software copying, different results may be obtained in other unethical behavior. More research needs to be carried out to test the validity of theory of planned behavior in predicting unethical behavior.

Our study tested only part of the theory of planned behavior. We deliberately did this in order to establish the validity of the theory before a full study is launched. We are now carrying out a study of the full model by incorporating the belief components in our design.

Since a number of studies including this one have found that there is causal path from the subjective norm component and attitude component, we should test for the presence of the causal path routinely as Vallerand et al. (1992) suggested.

Conclusion

The present study attempted to evaluate the applicability of the theory of reasoned action and theory of planned behavior to the moral behavior domain. Results from the present study show that theory of planned behavior can be used quite successfully to predict the intention to perform unethical behavior. As such, it provides a solid theoretical basis for the study of unethical behavior, and it is better than the theory of reasoned action, which does not take the resources and opportunity into account, in predicting unethical behavior. However, the attitude and subjective norm components are not as independent as the theory predicts, which has been supported by previous studies. Therefore, future research should take the path linking subjective norm to attitude into account.

References

Ajzen, I. 1985. From intentions to actions: A theory of planned behavior. In *Action-control: From cognitions to behavior*, ed. J. Kuhland and J. Beckman, 11–39. Heidelberg: Springer.

Ajzen, I. 1991. The theory of planned behavior. *Organizational Behavior & Human Decision Processes* 50: 179–211.

Ajzen, I., and M. Fishbein. 1980. *Understanding attitudes and predicting social behavior*. Englewood Cliffs: Prentice-Hall.

Ajzen, I., and T.J. Madden. 1986. Prediction of goal-directed behavior: Attitudes, intentions, and perceived behavioral control. *Journal of Experimental Social Psychology* 22: 453–474.

Anderson, J.C., and D.W. Gerbing. 1988. Structural equation modeling in practice: A review and recommended two-step approach. *Psychological Bulletin* 103: 411–423.

Bentler, P.M. 1990. Comparative fit indexes in structural models. *Psychological Bulletin* 107: 238–246.

Bentler, P.M. 1992. On the fit of models to covariance and methodology to the *Bulletin*. *Psychological Bulletin* 112: 400–404.

Bentler, P.M. 1993. *EQS structural equations program manual*. Los Angeles: BMDP Statistical Software.

Bollen, K.A. 1989. *Structural equations with latent variables*. New York: Wiley.

Bommer, M., C. Gratto, J. Gravander, and M. Tuttle. 1987. A behavioral model of ethical and unethical decision making. *Journal of Business Ethics* 6: 265–280.

Brady, F.N., and M.J. Hatch. 1992. General causal models in business ethics: An essay on colliding research traditions. *Journal of Business Ethics* 11: 307–315.

Byrne, B.M. 1994. *Structural equation modeling with EQS and EQS/windows: Basic concepts, applications, and programming*. Thousand Oaks: Sage.

Ferrel, O.C., and G. Gresham. 1985. A contingency framework for understanding ethical decision making in marketing. *Journal of Marketing* 49: 87–96.

Fishbein, M., and I. Ajzen. 1975. *Belief, attitude, intention, and behavior: An introduction to theory and research*. Reading: Addison Wesley.

Fredricks, A.J., and D.L. Dossett. 1983. Attitude-behavior relations: A comparison of the Fishbein-Ajzen and the Bentler-Speckart models. *Journal of Personality and Social Psychology* 45: 501–512.

Hunt, S.D., and S. Vitell. 1986. A general theory of marketing ethics. *Journal of Macromarketing* 6: 5–16.

Madden, T.J., P.S. Ellen, and I. Ajzen. 1992. A comparison of the theory of planned behavior and the theory of reasoned action. *Personality and Social Psychology Bulletin* 18: 3–9.

Mathieson, K. 1991. Predicting User intentions: Comparing the technology acceptance model with the theory of planned behavior. *Information Systems Research* 2: 173–191.

Prestholdt, P.H., I.M. Lane, and R.C. Mathews. 1987. Nurse turnover as reasoned action: Development of a process model. *Journal of Applied Psychology* 72: 221–227.

Randall, D.M. 1989. Taking stock: Can the theory of reasoned action explain unethical conduct? *Journal of Business Ethics* 8: 873–882.

Randall, D.M., and A.M. Gibson. 1991. Ethical decision making in the medical profession: An application of the theory of planned behavior. *Journal of Business Ethics* 10: 111–122.

Shepherd, G.J., and D.J. O'Keefe. 1984. Separability of attitudinal and normative influences on behavioral intentions in the Fishbein-Ajzen model. *The Journal of Social Psychology* 122: 287–288.

Sheppard, B.H., J. Hartwick, and P.R. Warshaw. 1988. The theory of reasoned action: A meta-analysis of past research with recommendations for modifications and future research. *Journal of Consumer Research* 15: 325–343.

Shimp, T.A., and A. Kavas. 1984. The theory of reasoned action applied to coupon usage. *Journal of Consumer Research* 11: 795–809.

Smiddy, J.D., and L.O. Smiddy. 1985. Caught in the act. *Datamation* 31: 102–104.

Timko, C. 1987. Seeking medical care for a breast cancer symptom: Determinants of intentions to engage in prompt or delay behavior. *Health Psychology* 6: 305–328.

Trevino, L.K. 1986. Ethical decision making in organizations: A person-situation interactionist model. *Academy of Management Review* 11: 601–617.

Vallerand, R.J., P. Deshaies, J. Cuerrier, L.G. Pelletier, and C. Mongeau. 1992. Ajzen and Fishbein's theory of reasoned action as applied to moral behavior: A confirmatory analysis. *Journal of Personality and Social Psychology* 62: 98–109.

Young, H.M., L. Lierman, G. Powell-Cope, D. Kasprzyk, and J.Q. Benoliel. 1991. Operationalizing the theory of planned behavior. *Research in Nursing & Health* 14: 137–144.

Chapter 22
Consumer Ethics: An Investigation of the Ethical Beliefs of Elderly Consumers

Scott J. Vitell, James R. Lumpkin, and Mohammed Y.A. Rawwas

Introduction

As Peter Drucker (1981) has observed, ethical concerns in business have become very important to many people:

> Business ethics is rapidly becoming the "in" subject ... 'it' is now being taught in departments of philosophy, business schools, and theological seminaries. There are countless seminars on it, speeches, articles, conferences and books, not to mention the many earnest attempts to write business ethics into the law.

Additionally, since marketing is the functional area, within business, that interfaces with the consumer, it tends to come under the greatest scrutiny, generates the most controversy and receives the most criticism with respect to potentially unethical business practices. Advertising, personal selling, pricing, marketing research and international marketing are all the subject of frequent ethical controversy (Murphy and Laczniak 1981).

In the last decade, much attention has been given to marketing ethics. Murphy and Laczniak (1981) cite well over 100 articles dealing with this topic and an update by Murphy and Priden (1987) shows several dozen more since 1981, including recent attempts to develop theoretical models in the marketing ethics area (Ferrell and Gresham 1985; Hunt and Vitell 1986; Ferrell et al. 1989). However, the marketing

S.J. Vitell (✉)
Department of Marketing, School of Business Administration, University of Mississippi, University, MS 38677, USA
e-mail: svitell@bus.olemiss.edu

J.R. Lumpkin
Dean, College of Business, Louisiana Tech University, Ruston, Louisiana 71272, USA

M.Y.A. Rawwas
Department of Marketing, College of Business Administration, University of Northern Iowa, Cedar Falls, IA 50614, USA

A.C. Michalos and D.C. Poff (eds.), *Citation Classics from the Journal of Business Ethics*, Advances in Business Ethics Research 2,
DOI 10.1007/978-94-007-4126-3_22, © Springer Science+Business Media B.V. 2013

discipline has been remiss in its examination of the inextricably related phenomenon of *consumer* ethics. While various studies have examined the major ethical problems confronting marketers (e.g., Chonko and Hunt 1985 – marketing management; Tybout and Zaltman 1974 – marketing researchers; Bellizzi and Murdock 1981 – industrial sales managers; Hunt et al. 1984 – marketing researchers; and Hunt and Chonko 1987 – advertising executives), few have systematically examined the ethical beliefs and attitudes of the final consumer. Murphy and Laczniak (1981) cite only a handful of articles examining the topic of consumer ethics while Murphy and Pridgen (1987) do not report any.

Consumers have often been surveyed in ethics-related studies (e.g., Sturdivant and Cocanougher 1973; Ricklefs 1983), but usually they have been surveyed regarding their ethical perceptions of business and marketing practices, *not* regarding their ethical perceptions of *consumer* practices. One notable exception to this is a study by Wilkes (1978) that examined consumer attitudes toward consumer-initiated fraud against business. Overall, however, there is a "gap" in the marketing ethics literature concerning the ethical beliefs and attitudes of the final consumer regarding potentially unethical consumer practices.

In addition, virtually no studies have examined the ethical beliefs of elderly consumers despite the fact that this represents an important and rapidly growing segment of the population. Petre (1986) noted that in the United States, households in the elderly population are wealthier, more numerous, and more willing to spend than ever before, making this segment important as consumers. The number of people 65 years or older in the United States is currently 28 million, or 11.9% of the population. This 65-and-over group has been growing at twice the rate of the population as a whole and is projected to reach 64.6 million by the year 2030, accounting for over 21% of the population (French and Fox 1985). Further, since elderly consumers may differ from younger ones in terms of their moral thinking (see Pratt et al. 1983), it is important to examine the ethical beliefs of this segment of the population.

The present study will attempt to correct this omission in the literature by examining the ethical beliefs of U.S. elderly consumers regarding various consumer practices and by examining the ethical ideologies of elderly consumers.

Literature Review

Within the consumer behavior literature, there is little mention of consumer activities that fall beyond the boundaries of what is considered as normative or ethical, and what little there is has typically been very narrow in its scope (e.g., Davis 1979; Moschis and Powell 1986). Most models of consumer behavior focus upon one's decision processes with respect to the acquisition, usage and disposition of products, but these models typically do not take into account the ethics component. By contrast, this research is specifically concerned with examining consumer behavior (acquisition, usage and disposition) involving an ethical component.

Previous research involving consumer ethics can be classified into six major categories. First, some authors have empirically examined a single component of "unethical" consumer behavior. The area most commonly examined has been shoplifting (e.g., Kallis et al. 1986; Moschis and Powell 1986), but even topics such as the ethics component of consumer energy conservation have been research (e.g., Haldeman et al. 1987).

A second stream of research has examined the apparent "double standard" that exists between what consumers perceive as acceptable consumer behavior and what consumers believe are acceptable business practices. Historically, consumers have tended to hold business to a higher standard than they, themselves, are willing to follow. Two studies supporting this concept of a double standard are a study by Davis (1979), which used an adult population, and one by DePaulo (1986), using a student population. A third research stream has attempted to provide normative guidelines for consumer rights and responsibilities. For example, Stampfl (1979) outlines a code of ethics for consumers.

Recommendations on how business can best cope with unethical consumer behavior and consumer abuse typify a fourth area of research. An example is a study by Schubert (1979) which developed strategies for combatting consumer abuses. A fifth stream of research has attempted to examine consumer attitudes relative to a variety of potentially unethical consumer practices. The study by Wilkes (1978) is one of the relatively few studies that can be included within this stream. In this study, the author examined 15 fraudulent retail situations in terms of consumer perceptions of how wrong each was and, also, how often one's friends might behave in the manner described in the situation. Additionally, Wilkes asked consumers what would be the appropriate management action for dealing with each situation.

Finally, a sixth stream of research involves the development of theoretical models. An example of this stream is an article by Grove et al. (1989) which presents a model based upon the techniques of neutralization, borrowed from sociology. Their paper discusses how consumers justify non-normative consumer behavior.

Regarding the issue of the age of consumers and their ethical beliefs, very little research has been conducted. However, what research there has been tends to indicate that age does make a difference in terms of ethical beliefs, with older individuals appearing to be "more ethical" than younger ones. While this relationship between age and "ethicalness" could be a spurious one, there is evidence that these two variables are closely related. For example, a cross-cultural study by Ma (1985) found that there was a positive relationship between age and a law-abiding orientation. A study by Pratt et al. (1983) found that older individuals tended to be better organized and more consistent in their moral thinking. They tended to be more philosophically reflective than the young. Finally, Vitell (1986) found that age influenced the way in which sales executives made ethical judgments. More specifically, older executives seemed to have fewer ethical conflicts between what was ethical and what was beneficial for the firm.

The present study would tend to come closest to the "fifth stream" of research that has examined consumer attitudes concerning various questionable practices. However, this study will go beyond the previous research of Wilkes (1978) in that it will examine the links between ethical ideologies, Machiavellianism and attitudes toward potentially unethical consumer practices. In addition, this study departs from previous research in that it examines an elderly population.

Several hundred studies have examined Machiavellianism, including several that have researched the degree of Machiavellianism among current and future business executives (Hegarty and Sims 1978; Chonko 1982; Hunt and Chonko 1984; Singhapakdi and Vitell 1990). However, no previous studies have attempted to examine the extent of Machiavellianism among consumers.

In describing Machiavellianism, Hunt and Chonko (1984, p. 30), noted that "the label Machiavellian [is] becoming a negative epithet, indicating at least an amoral (if not immoral) way of manipulating others to accomplish one's objectives." It would be inappropriate, however, to equate "Machiavellian" with such extreme labels like "dishonest" or "deceitful." Christie and Geis (1970), based on their studies, cautioned against this interpretation. More appropriately, Machiavellian persons possess a kind of *cool detachment* that makes them less emotionally involved with others or with saving face in potentially embarrassing situations. Therefore, the more Machiavellian the individual, the less ethical they are and vice-versa. Thus, this is an appropriate construct to examine in relation to consumers' ethical beliefs.

Forsyth (1980) has developed a classification system based upon one's preferred ethical ideology. In this, Forsyth divides people into four different ethical types. "Situationists" are those who reject moral rules while asking if their actions yield the best possible outcomes given the situation. These individuals would use deception if it yielded the best possible outcome in a situation. "Absolutists" believe that their actions are moral only if they yield positive consequences through conformity to moral absolutes. They believe that deception is always wrong since it violates fundamental moral principles. "Subjectivists" are those who reject moral rules and base their moral judgment on personal feelings about their actions. They believe that deception is a personal matter to be decided upon by the individual. Finally, "exeptionists" believe that conformity to moral rules is desirable, but that exceptions are permissible. They believe that if deception cannot be avoided, then it is allowable as long as safeguards are used (Forsyth and Pope 1984).

Clearly, this typology can be related to consumer ethical beliefs as "absolutists" would tend to have the most rigid ethical belief systems while "subjectionists" would have the most flexible ones. "Situationists" and "exceptionists" would be likely to be found between these two extremes in terms of their ethical beliefs.

Specifically, the objectives of this research are as follows:

1. To determine to what extent elderly consumers are Machiavellian.
2. To determine the preferred ethical ideologies of the elderly.
3. To examine the ethical beliefs of elderly consumers concerning various questionable consumer practices
4. To examine the relationships between Machiavellianism, preferred ethical ideology and ethical beliefs for elderly consumers.

Methodology

Sample

Self-administered questionnaires were mailed to 1,600 residents above the age of 60 in one large Southeastern United States metropolitan area. Of these, 431 responses were returned for a response rate of 27% with 394 being usable for the purpose of this study. The sample ranged in age from 60 to 79 with a mean of 68.

Seventy-two percent of the respondents were married with 70% being male. Thirty-three percent of the respondents were retired, while 20% held either part-time or full-time jobs. A comparison between this sample and population characteristics taken from the Statistical Abstracts of United States (1989) for this metropolitan area, shows this sample to be more educated and to have less retirees. The percentage of retirees among the elderly population were 86% and the levels of education for the elderly population showed that 10% had only a high school diploma. In other respects the sample is representative of the population from which it was drawn.

Measures

Machiavellianism was measured using the MACH IV scale developed by Christie and Geis (1970). This scale contains 20 items with 10 items worded in a Machiavellian direction and 10 items worded in the opposite direction. These items appear in the Appendix. Each respondent was asked to indicate the extent of his or her agreement or disagreement with each of the 20 items using a five-point Likert scale. A Cronbach's alpha coefficient of 0.623 was obtained for this scale. This compares to one of 0.76 obtained by Hunt and Chonko (1984) in a study of marketing practitioners and split-half reliability of 0.79 reported by Christie and Geis (1970) using a student sample.

A second construct measured was one's predominant ethical perspective. This was measured using the Ethics Position Questionnaire (EPQ) developed by Forsyth (1980). The EPQ consists of two scales, each containing 10 items (see the Appendix). One is designed to measure idealism and the second is designed to measure relativism, or the rejection of universal moral principles. Respondents were asked to indicate their agreement or disagreement with each item using a five-point Likert format. Cronbach's coefficient alpha for the idealism scale was 0.849 and for the relativism scale it was 0.830.

These two scales were then used to classify respondents into one of four ethical ideologies. The mean score of one's responses to the idealism scale and the mean score of one's responses to the relativism scale are combined to determine one's ethical ideology. Respondents who had high scores on both scales are considered "situationists." Those who are high on the idealism scale but low on relativism are

Table 22.1 Factor analysis for consumer ethics scale

Dimension name and items	Factor loading	Cronbach's alpha
I. Actively benefiting from illegal activity		0.760
Drinking a can of soda in a supermarket without paying for it	0.788	
Using a long distance access code that does not belong to you	0.740	
Giving misleading price information to a clerk for an unpriced item	0.682	
Reporting a lost item as "stolen" to an insurance company in order to collect the money	0.536	
Changing price-tags on merchandise in a retail store	0.532	
II. Passively benefitting		0.755
Not saying anything when the waitress miscalculates the bill in your favor	0.817	
Getting too much change and not saying anything	0.773	
Lying about a child's age in order to get a lower price	0.715	
Moving into a new residence and finding that the cable TV is still hooked up, and using it rather than signing up and paying for it	0.713	
III. Actively benefitting from questionable action		0.730
Stretching the truth on an income tax return	0.732	
Using a coupon for merchandise you did not buy	0.655	
Using an expired coupon for merchandise	0.600	
Not telling the truth when negotiating the price of a new automobile	0.548	
IV. No harm/no foul		0.747
Taping a movie off the television	0.747	
Returning merchandise after trying it and not liking it	0.722	
Recording an album instead of buying it	0.681	
Using computer software or games that you did not buy	0.618	
Spending over an hour trying on different dresses and not purchasing any	0.596	

classified as "absolutists." Respondents low on idealism but high on relativism are "subjectivists," and those low on both scales are considered "exceptionist."

The third construct used in the study measured one's beliefs regarding 20 consumer situations having potentially ethical implications. This "consumer ethics" scale was developed by Muncy and Vitell (1989). Respondents were asked to rate whether they perceived these actions as being wrong (unethical) or not wrong (ethical) on a five-point scale.

Principal components factor analysis with a varimax rotation was performed on the data yielding a four factor solution. The results appear in Table 22.1. Two of the questions did not load on any of the four factors; however, the factor structure for the remaining items was consistent with the Muncy and Vitell study. The first factor might be labeled as "actively benefitting from an illegal activity." The most distinguishing characteristics of these actions are that they are all initiated by the consumer (e.g., changing price tags on merchandise in a store) and they are all likely to be perceived as illegal by most consumers. Five questions loaded on this factor, with the coefficient alpha being 0.760.

The second factor can be labeled as "passively benefitting at the expense of others." Here the consumer benefits from the seller's mistake (e.g., getting too much change and not saying anything) rather than his own actions. The coefficient alpha for this factor was 0.755 with four items loading on it. The third factor might be labeled as "actively benefitting from a questionable, but not necessarily illegal, action." Here, as in the first factor, the consumer initiates the action, but these are not as likely to be perceived as illegal (e.g., not telling the truth when negotiating the price of a new automobile). The four items loading on this factor yielded a coefficient alpha of 0.730.

The fourth factor can be labeled as "no harm/no foul." These are actions that consumers perceive as not resulting in any harm and, therefore, at least some consumers perceive them as acceptable actions. The five questions loading on this factor have a coefficient alpha of 0.747.

Findings

Elderly Consumers and Machiavellianism

The MACH IV scale was used to determine the extent to which elderly consumers might be Machiavellian. To compare the results of this study to previous ones using the MACH IV scale, 40 points were added to all scores so that a score of 100 would represent the neutral point. After doing this, the mean score for the sample was 90.9 with overall scores ranging from a minimum of 70 to a maximum of 126.

Comparing this result to previous studies indicates that elderly consumers are somewhat *more* Machiavellian than those in other groups. For example, in examining the degree of Machiavellianism among marketing professionals, Hunt and Chonko (1984) obtained a mean score of 85.7, and in researching Machiavellianism among an adult population, Christie and Geis (1970) obtained a mean of 84.5.

This result is somewhat unexpected as younger people are generally considered to be less "ethical" and, therefore, more Machiavellian. However, based on only one study, it would be premature to claim that elderly consumers are more Machiavellian than their younger counterparts, especially since it may be inappropriate to compare this sample to previous ones. Nevertheless, the results, if supported in future research, could have significant implications for marketers who are concentrating their efforts towards elderly markets.

Elderly Consumers and Ethical Ideology

The Ethics Position Questionnaire (EPQ) was used to determine the dominant ethical ideologies of respondents. The mean score on the idealism scale was 40.4 and on the relativism scale it was 26.0. Since the neutral point for each scale is represented by a score of 30 (scores range from 10 to 50), it appears that elderly consumers generally believe that morally "right" behavior leads to good or positive consequences (idealism scale). It also appears that they do *not* reject the notion that absolute moral principles do exist (relativism scale). This relatively high position on the idealism scale and low one on the relativism scale tends to indicate that the elderly are relatively "ethical" as a group. This result is consistent with the previous research involving age and ethics (Ma 1985; Pratt et al. 1983; Vitell 1986).

However, these results are somewhat in conflict with the finding that elderly consumers are relatively Machiavellian since it would be expected "that highly Machiavellian persons would endorse ethical beliefs that were more relativistic and less idealistic than low Machs" (Leary et al. 1986, p. 76). However, respondents in the present study, even though they scored fairly high on the MACH IV scale, seem to be *more* idealistic and *less* relativistic.

When respondents are grouped into the four ethical ideologies, the picture becomes clearer, however. Of the 394 respondents, 78 (19.8%) are exceptionists, 81 (20.6%) are subjectivists, 122 (30.9%) are absolutists and 113 (28.7%) are situationists. If one examines just the subjectivists, since they are the most likely to be Machiavellian due to their rejection of moral rules, one observes a MACH IV score of 96.2. This is considerably higher than the overall mean for the other three groups (89.5), and higher than the mean for each individual group: 87.2 for absolutist; 90.4 for exceptionists; and 91.2 for situationists.

These results indicate that there is a significant group of elderly consumers who tend to be high Machiavellian subjectivists. At the same time, however, the majority of elderly consumers seem to accept the tenets of idealism while rejecting relativism. This majority is about average, or slightly higher, in terms of its Machiavellianism. Thus, while most elderly consumers appear to be relatively ethical, a significant segment exists that believes ethics are a matter of personal feelings.

Elderly Consumers and Consumer Ethics

One factor generated from the consumer ethics scale was comprised of those activities where one "actively benefits from an illegal activity." Respondents overwhelmingly believed that these activities were unethical as the mean for the five items was 1.19, with 1 corresponding to "definitely wrong" and 5 to "definitely not wrong." The mean for these same five items in the Muncy and Vitell (1989) study was 1.42, indicating that elderly consumers tend to be less accepting of this type of behavior than the general population.

A second factor generated from this scale was described as "passively benefitting at the expense of others." The mean for the four items of this factor was 1.51 indicating that, while these activities were still considered unethical, they were somewhat less unethical than those where one *actively* does something to benefit oneself. The mean for these same four items in the Muncy and Vitell (1989) study was 1.98. This, again, indicates that elderly consumers tend to also view these behaviors as being more unethical than do consumers in general.

"Actively benefitting from a questionable, but not necessarily illegal, action" described the third factor generated from the consumer ethics scale. The mean for the four questions related to this factor was 1.69. Thus, these activities too were clearly viewed as unethical by elderly consumers. However, in the Muncy and Vitell (1989) study, the average mean of these same items was 2.16, indicating that, at least some, younger consumers must have viewed these behaviors as being somewhat acceptable.

Finally, five questions formed the factor, "no harm/no foul." These were the least unethical practices as viewed by elderly consumers with the mean of these being 2.86. Thus, overall, elderly consumers were somewhat neutral as to whether these were ethical or unethical behaviors. As before, the mean for the same items in the Muncy and Vitell (1989) study was higher (3.38).

In summary, it appears that elderly consumers are more inclined to view all types of "questionable" consumer activities as more unethical than are younger consumers. This result is consistent with the previous research on age and ethics. However, as mentioned, the comparison of this sample with previous ones may be inappropriate. The relative relationships between the various factors was the same for elderly consumers and for younger consumers, however.

Determinants of Ethical Beliefs

Finally, multivariate analysis of covariance was performed with the four dimensions of the consumer ethics scale as dependent variables and the EPQ ideologies as an independent variable with Machiavellianism and age as covariates. In addition, gender was included as an independent variable in the analysis.

The purpose of this analysis was to determine whether or not one's ethical ideology and the extent of one's Machiavellianism would have any impact on one's ethical beliefs relative to various consumer practices, and whether or not this would vary depending upon the type of consumer practices involved. Gender and age were included to see if there might be any differences in ethical beliefs based on these demographic variables. Even though this was an elderly population, it was felt that there was a sufficient age distribution to warrant an examination of this variable.

The results appear in Tables 22.2 and 22.3 and indicate that one's ethical ideology is a significant overall determinant of a consumer's ethical beliefs. More specifically, univariate tests indicate a significant relationship between the EPQ and both "passively benefitting at the expense of others" and "no harm/no foul" activities. An examination of the means for the different EPQ ideologies indicates that for all four

Table 22.2 Results of Mancova analysis – independent variables

Source	*F*-test
I. Multivariate tests	
Ethical ideology	2.04*
Gender	4.65**
Interaction	ns
II. Univariate tests	
A. Dependent variable – actively benefitting from illegal activity	
Ethical ideology	ns
Gender	ns
Interaction	3.21*
B. Dependent variable – passively benefitting	
Ethical ideology	3.55*
Gender	ns
Interaction	ns
C. Dependent variable – actively benefitting from questionable action	
Ethical ideology	ns
Gender	14.43**
Interaction	ns
D. Dependent variable – no harm/no foul	
Ethical ideology	4.35*
Gender	ns
Interaction	ns

*$p=0.05$; **$p=0.01$
Note: ns = not statistically significant

Table 22.3 Results of Mancova analysis – covariates

Source	T-test
I. Univariate tests	
A. Dependent variable – actively benefitting from illegal activity	
Machiavellianism	2.53*
Age	ns
B. Dependent variable – passively benefitting	
Machiavellianism	3.68**
Age	ns
C. Dependent variable – actively benefitting from questionable action	
Machiavellianism	5.99**
Age	ns
D. Dependent variable – no harm/no foul	
Machiavellianism	2.58**
Age	−2.40*

*$p=0.05$; **$p=0.01$
Note: ns = not statistically significant

categories of consumer activities, "subjectivists" are the ones who most believe that these activities *are* ethical. In addition, "absolutists" are consistently those who most believe these activities to be ethical. These results are as expected since subjectivists and absolutists are relative "extremists" with subjectivists rejecting moral rules, on the one hand, and absolutists believing in moral absolutes, on the other.

The multivariate main effect for gender was significant. However, univariate tests show that gender was only significant in determining beliefs for those consumer practices described as "actively benefitting from a questionable, but not necessarily illegal, action." In this instance and for the other three categories of consumer practices as well, women tended to find these as more unethical than men. This may be explained, in part, by the fact that men tended to be somewhat more Machiavellian than women.

Machiavellianism was a significant covariate for each category of consumer beliefs, with those who were Machiavellian believing the practices to be more acceptable than their less Machiavellian counterparts.

Finally, age was only a significant covariate in relation to the "no harm/no foul" behaviors with older consumers believing that these practices were more unethical than younger consumers. The fact that an elderly population, with a limited diversity in age, was used might explain why this variable had no impact on the other categories of consumer practices.

Conclusions and Implications

Overall the elderly consumers sampled are somewhat more Machiavellian than the general population as reported in previous research. However, it appears that it is a small, but significant segment that are Machiavellian with the majority of those surveyed being about the same as the rest of the population in terms of this particular personality variable.

In terms of their ethical ideologies, the largest single group (30.9%) was "absolutists," or those who strictly conform to moral absolutes and norms. A second group, "exceptionist," represent 19.8% of the sample. These are individuals who believe in conformity to moral rules, but who further believe that under certain extraordinary circumstances exceptions are permissible. Thus, a majority of elderly consumers have strong ethical norms that guide their behavior.

Additionally, the second largest group of respondents (28.7%) was "situationists" who, while they do reject moral rules, judge the ethics of a situation by the consequences and outcomes of the situation. Most of these individuals are probably utilitarians who seek out those alternatives that generate the greatest good for the greatest number of individuals.

Only the "subjectivists" (20.6%) have questionable ethics since these are the consumers who not only reject moral rules, but base their ethical judgments on personal feelings. This was supported by the finding that the "subjectivists" were the ones who consistently felt that each of the four groups of questionable consumer activities were "less wrong" as compared to the beliefs of other elderly consumers.

Given the percentage of "subjectivists," we might conclude that the vast majority of elderly consumers are relatively ethical. This fact was supported by the finding that elderly consumers tended to view each of the four groups of consumer activities as "more wrong" than did the general population. One's beliefs concerning the ethicalness of the various consumer practices examined was a function of one's ethical ideology, the extent of one's Machiavellianism and one's gender. This latter finding showed that elderly women were somewhat more ethical than elder men in terms of their ethical beliefs.

Overall, the results of this study tend to show that elderly consumers, while generally being more ethical than younger consumers, are quite diverse in terms of their ethical beliefs. They are represented by a variety of ethical ideologies; their numbers include both Machiavellians and those who are not; and they possess very divergent beliefs about selected consumer practices. Just as it would be a mistake to consider elderly consumers as a homogeneous group in terms of their general attitudes and beliefs, it would be a mistake to consider them as homogeneous in terms of their ethical beliefs.

Appendix

List of scale items

Machiavellian scale

1. Never tell anyone the real reason you did something unless it is useful to do so.
2. The best way to handle people is to tell them what they want to hear.
3. One should take action only when sure it is morally right.
4. Most people are basically good and kind.
5. It is safest to assume that all people have a vicious streak and it will come out when given the chance.
6. Honesty is the best policy in all cases.
7. There is no excuse for lying to someone else.
8. Generally speaking, people won't work hard unless they're forced to do so.
9. All in all, it is better to be humble and honest than to be important and dishonest.
10. When you ask someone to do something for you, it is best to give the real reasons for wanting it rather than giving reasons which carry more weight.
11. People who get ahead in the world lead clean, moral lives.
12. Anyone who completely trusts others is asking for big trouble.
13. The biggest difference between criminals and others is that the criminals are stupid enough to get caught.
14. Most people are brave.
15. It is wise to flatter important people.
16. It is possible to be good in all respects.
17. Barnum was wrong when he said that there's a sucker born every minute.

18. It is hard to get ahead without cutting corners.
19. People suffering from incurable diseases should have the choice of being put painlessly to death.
20. Most people forget more easily the death of their father than the loss of their property.

Ethics position questionnaire (EPQ)

I. Idealism scale

1. A person should make certain that their actions never intentionally harm another even to a small degree.
2. Risks to another should never be tolerated, irrespective of how small the risks might be.
3. The existence of potential harm to others is always wrong, irrespective of the benefits to be gained.
4. One should never psychologically or physically harm another person.
5. One should not perform an action which might in any way threaten the dignity and welfare of another individual.
6. If an action could harm an innocent other, then it should not be done.
7. Deciding whether or not to perform an act by balancing the positive consequences of the act against the negative consequences of the act is immoral.
8. The dignity and welfare of people should be the most important concern in any society.
9. It is never necessary to sacrifice the welfare of others.
10. Moral actions are those which closely match ideals of the most "perfect" action.

II. Relativism scale

1. There are no ethical principles that are so important that they should be a part of any code of ethics.
2. What is ethical varies from one situation and society to another.
3. Moral standards should be seen as being individualistic; what one person considers to be moral may be judged to be immoral by another person.
4. Different types of moralities cannot be compared as to "rightness".
5. What is ethical for everyone can never be resolved since what is moral or immoral is up to the individual.
6. Moral standards are simply personal rules which indicate how a person should behave, and are not to be applied in making judgments of others.
7. Ethical considerations in interpersonal relations are so complex that individuals should be allowed to formulate their own individual codes.
8. Rigidly codifying an ethical position that prevents certain types of actions stand in the way of better human relations and adjustment.
9. No rule concerning lying can be formulated; whether a lie is permissible or not permissible totally depends upon the situation.
10. Whether a lie is judged to be moral or immoral depends upon the circumstances surrounding the action.

References

Bellizzi, J.A., and W. Murdock. 1981. Industrial sales management in the 1980's. *Industrial Marketing Management* 10(October): 299–304.

Chonko, L. 1982. Are purchasing agents machiavellian? *Journal of Purchasing and Materials Management* 18(Winter): 15–20.

Chonko, L., and D. Hunt. 1985. Ethics and marketing management: An empirical examination. *Journal of Business Research* 13: 339–359.

Christie, R., and F.L. Geis. 1970. *Studies in machiavellianism*. New York: Academic.

Davis, R.M. 1979. Comparison of consumer acceptance of rights and responsibilities. In *Proceedings, 25th annual conference of the American Council on Consumer Interests*, ed. N.M. Ackerman, 68–70. Columbia: American Council on Consumer Interests.

DePaulo, P.J. 1986. Ethical perceptions of deceptive bargaining tactics used by salespersons and customers: A double standard. In *Proceedings of the division of consumer psychology*, ed. J.G. Saegert. Washington, DC: American Psychological Association.

Drucker, P.F. 1981. What is business ethics? *Across the Board*, October, pp. 22–32.

Ferrell, O.C., and L. Gresham. 1985. A contingency framework for understanding ethical decision making in marketing. *Journal of Marketing* 49(Summer): 87–96.

Ferrell, O.C., L. Gresham, and J. Fraedrich. 1989. A synthesis of ethical decision models for marketing. *Journal of Macromarketing* 9(Fall): 55–64.

Forsyth, D.R. 1980. A taxonomy of ethical ideologies. *Journal of Personality and Social Psychology* 39(1): 175–184.

Forsyth, D.R., and W.R. Pope. 1984. Ethical ideology and judgments of social psychology research: Multidimensional analysis. *Journal of Personality and Social Psychology* 46(6): 1365–1375.

French, W.A., and R. Fox. 1985. Segmenting the senior citizen market. *Journal of Consumer Marketing* 2(Winter): 61–74.

Grove, S.J., S.J. Vitell, and D. Strutton. 1989. Non-normative consumer behavior and the techniques of neutralization. In *Proceedings of the 1989 AMA winter educators' conference*, ed. Richard Bagozzi and J.Paul Peter, 131–135. Chicago: American Marketing Association.

Haldeman, V.A., J.M. Peters, and P.A. Tripple. 1987. Measuring a consumer energy conservation ethic: An analysis of components. *Journal of Consumer Affairs* 21(1): 70–85.

Hegarty, W.H., and H.P. Sims Jr. 1978. Some determinants of unethical decision behavior: An experiment. *Journal of Applied Psychology* 63(August): 451–457.

Hunt, S.D., and L. Chonko. 1984. Marketing and machiavellianism. *Journal of Marketing* 48(Summer): 30–42.

Hunt, S.D., and L. Chonko. 1987. Ethical problems of advertising agency executives. *Journal of Advertising* 16(4): 16–25.

Hunt, S.D., and S. Vitell. 1986. A general theory of marketing ethics. *Journal of Macromarketing* 6(Spring): 5–16.

Hunt, S.D., L. Chonko, and J. Wilcox. 1984. Ethical problems of marketing researcher. *Journal of Marketing Research* XXI(August): 309–324.

Kallis, M.J., K.A. Krentier, and D.J. Vanier. 1986. The value of user image in quelling aberrant consumer behavior. *Journal of the Academy of Marketing Science* 14(Spring): 29–35.

Leary, M., P. Knight, and B. Barnes. 1986. Ethical ideologies of the machiavellian. *Personality and Social Psychology Bulletin* 12(March): 75–80.

Ma, Hing-Keung. 1985. Cross-cultural study of the development of law-abiding orientation. *Psychological Reports* 57: 967–975.

Moschis, G.P., and J. Powell. 1986. The juvenile shoplifte. *The Marketing Mix* 10(1, Winter-Spring): 1.

Muncy, J.A., and S.J. Vitell. 1989. Consumer ethics: An empirical investigation of the ethical beliefs of the final consumer. Working paper.

Murphy, P., and G. Laczniak. 1981. Marketing ethics: A review with implications for managers, educators and researchers. In *Review of marketing 1981*, ed. B. Enis and K. Roering, 251–266. Chicago: American Marketing Association.

Murphy, P., and M.D. Pridgen. 1987. Ethical and legal issues in marketing. Paper presented at A.M.A. Marketing Ethics Workshops, University of Southern Mississippi.

Petre, P. 1986. Marketers mine for gold in the old. *Fortune*, March 31, pp. 70–78.

Pratt, M., G. Golding, and W. Hunter. 1983. Aging as ripening: Character and consistency of moral judgment in young, mature, and older adults. *Human Development* 26: 277–288.

Ricklefs, R. 1983. Executive apply stiffer standards than public to ethical dilemmas. *The Wall Street Journal* 3(November): 27, 43.

Schubert, J.G. 1979. Consumer abuse: Some recommendations for change. In *Proceedings, 25th annual conference of the American Council on Consumer Interests*, ed. N.M. Ackerman, 12–20. Columbia: American Council on Consumer Interests.

Singhapakdi, A., and S.J. Vitell. 1990. Marketing ethics: Factors influencing perceptions of ethical problems and alternatives. *Journal of Macromarketing* 10(Spring): 4–18.

Stampfl, R.W. 1979. Multi-disciplinary foundations for a consumer code of ethics. In *Proceedings, 25th annual conference of the American Council on Consumer Interest*, ed. N.M. Ackerman, 12–20. Columbia: American Council on Consumer Interests.

Sturdivant, F.D., and A.B. Cocanougher. 1973. What are ethical marketing practices? *Harvard Business Review* (November–December): 10–12 & 176.

Tybout, A.M., and G. Zaltman. 1974. Ethics in marketing research: Their practical relevance. *Journal of Marketing Research* 11(November): 357–368.

Vitell, S.J. 1986. Marketing ethics: Conceptual and empirical foundations of a positive theory of decision making in situations having ethical content. Unpublished doctoral dissertation, Texas Tech University.

Wilkes, R.E. 1978. Fraudulent behavior by consumers. *Journal of Marketing* 42(October): 67–75.

Chapter 23
The Role of Moral Intensity in Moral Judgments: An Empirical Investigation

Sara A. Morris and Robert A. McDonald

A recent *Newsweek* editorial applauded the four on-lookers who rescued truck driver Reginald Denny from being beaten to death during the Los Angeles riots of 1992. Upon hearing the court testimony of one of the rescuers about why he chose to get involved, the editorial writer deduced: "He assumes that there is a moral imperative that would be obvious to everybody. . ." (Greenfield 1993, p. 80). The issue-related moral imperative in a decision situation has been conceptualized as the issue's moral intensity (Jones 1991, p. 372). The current study investigated the relationship between the moral intensity of an issue and an individual's moral judgment, in the context of business situations. A moral judgment is a considered opinion of what *should* be done (i.e., a decision about the morally right thing to do) when confronted with an ethical dilemma (Rest 1986).

The moral judgment is one component of the ethical decision making process (Jones 1991). By ethical decision making, we mean the decision under consideration involves an ethical or moral issue, as opposed to not involving ethical/moral issues. The ethical decision making process may work well or poorly. When it works well, a good, right, fair, and/or just decision is implemented. When it works poorly, the result is the implementation of a bad, wrong, unfair and/or unjust decision. Developing a better understanding of the ethical decision making process is important for business scholars and practitioners who want the process to work well. Developing a better understanding of the moral judgment component will contribute to our understanding of the overall ethical decision making process.

Jones (1991) assumed that the moral intensity construct represents an issue-specific contingency rather than an individual's perceptions about the issue, but we disagree.

S.A. Morris (✉)
Department of Management, Old Dominion University, Norfolk, VA 23529, USA
e-mail: smorris@odu.edu

R.A. McDonald† (Deceased)

A.C. Michalos and D.C. Poff (eds.), *Citation Classics from the Journal of Business Ethics*, Advances in Business Ethics Research 2,
DOI 10.1007/978-94-007-4126-3_23,

Cognitive models are widely accepted in the organizational behavior literature (Thomas and Velthouse 1990), and are deemed descriptive of some dimensions of strategic management (e.g., Schwenk 1988; Thomas et al. 1993) and organization theory (e.g., Duncan 1972; Weick 1979). This study compared the objective and perceived characteristics of three moral issues. Such a comparison is reminiscent of the longstanding debates over the effects of objective versus perceived environmental uncertainty (e.g., Boyd et al. 1993; Jauch and Kraft 1986).

We then investigated the relationship between perceived moral intensity and moral judgment. Because Jones (1991) described moral intensity as a six-dimensional construct, an additional purpose of the current study was to investigate the various dimensions of moral intensity. To date, only two empirical tests of the construct have been reported, namely, Jones and Huber (1992) and Weber (1993). Weber (1993) tested just one of the six dimensions. Jones and Huber (1992) tested five of six dimensions, but found only one to be significant.

Conceptual Foundations

Rest (1986) considered moral judgment to be one of the psychological processes involved in producing moral behavior, but others (Ferrell et al. 1989; Hunt and Vitell 1986; Jones 1991; Trevino 1986) have conceptualized moral judgment as a component of ethical decision making. Given that behavior and decision making are clearly related, we use the decision making framework in this paper. Within ethical decision making, the term moral judgment has been used with both process and content connotations. When used to connote the decision process, moral judgment refers to the moral reasoning process required to identify a morally superior alternative (e.g., Waterman 1988). Kohlberg (1969) and Rest (1986) articulated theories of cognitive moral development, which explain how an individual's moral reasoning process evolves over the person's lifetime.

When used to connote the decision content, moral judgment can refer to either the alternative chosen (e.g., Jones 1991) or an individual's evaluation of the alternatives chosen (e.g., Jones and Huber 1992). We use the term to mean the decision content, more specifically, to refer to the alternative chosen. Thus, we examined the relationship between perceived moral intensity and the alternative chosen.

Correlates of Moral Judgment

Except for Collins (1989) and Jones (1991), conceptual models and empirical studies of ethical decision making have assumed that individual differences, often in conjunction with organizational and/or environmental factors, would explain variations in moral judgments (choices made). Theoretical models have commonly included individual differences in cognitive moral development (e.g., Ferrell et al. 1989; Trevino 1986) and/or philosophical orientation or ideology (e.g., Ferrell et al. 1989;

Forsyth 1980; Hunt and Vitell 1986) to predict and explain moral judgment. Relevant empirical studies have examined individual differences in cognitive moral development (e.g., Logsdon et al. 1992; Malinowski and Smith 1985; Trevino and Youngblood 1990), philosophical orientation or ideology (e.g., Forsyth 1981; Fraedrich and Ferrell 1992; Fritzsche and Becker 1984), and such factors as locus of control (e.g., Hegarty and Sims 1978; Trevino and Youngblood 1990). In a departure from this line of inquiry, Dubinsky and Loken (1989) applied the theory of reasoned action (Ajzen and Fishbein 1980) to ethical decision making and examined individual differences in expectancies and subjective norms.

With regard to organizational influences on moral judgment, theoretical models have included such factors as significant others and opportunity (Ferrell and Gresham 1985) and organizational culture (Ferrell et al. 1989; Trevino 1986). Empirical studies have examined the relationship between moral judgment and the following organizational variables, among others: ethical work climate (e.g., Elm 1989; Gaertner 1991), group decision making (e.g., Nichols and Day 1982), role responsibility/codes of conduct (e.g., Trevino and Victor 1992), and rewards and/or punishment (e.g., Hegarty and Sims 1978; Trevino and Youngblood 1990).

With regard to environmental influences on moral judgment, some theoretical models (e.g., Ferrell et al. 1989; Ferrell and Gresham 1985; Hunt and Vitell 1986) have more explicitly considered the social, economic, and/or cultural environment than others, but few environmental variables have been specified or tested empirically. However, Hegarty and Sims (1978) and Miller et al. (1990) did find cross-cultural (i.e., national) differences in moral judgment.

Collins (1989) argued that moral judgment is contingent on the nature of the issue under consideration. Jones (1991) developed an expanded model of ethical decision making which incorporated issue-specific contingencies into the mix of individual differences, organizational variables, and environmental factors. Essential to this issue-contingent model was a new construct, moral intensity, to which we now turn.

Underpinnings of Moral Intensity

Moral intensity "captures the extent of issue-related moral imperative in a situation" (Jones 1991, p. 372). The moral intensity construct has its underpinnings in moral philosophy (Jones 1991) and in the legal system (Collins 1989), more specifically, tort law (Weber 1993) and retribution (Jones 1991). In moral philosophy, proportionality is the basis for distinguishing degrees of moral responsibility (Jones 1991). The level of moral responsibility depends on such factors as the nature of the benefits/harms involved, the urgency of the situation, and the decision maker's freedom of choice in the situation.

Collins (1989) pointed out that the legal system designates a hierarchy of harms; the most serious harms, deserving of the greatest condemnation, are physical, followed by economic harms and psychological harms, in that order. Legal precedents from tort actions demonstrate that, in general, greater compensation is exacted from wrongdoers for physical harm than for any other type, and greater penalties are imposed for economic wrongs than for psychological wrongs (Weber 1993). Jones (1991) believes that criminal law contains an element of proportionality, because the extent of retribution is intended to be proportional to the crime committed.

Dimensions of Moral Intensity

When identifying influences on moral judgment, both Collins (1989) and Jones (1991) specified six characteristics of moral issues, albeit not the same six. For Collins (1989), the intentionality, visibility, severity, repetition, permanency, and verifiability of a wrongful act affected the degree of moral condemnation of the act. For Jones (1991), the obligation to act in a situation, or the moral imperative, was related to the seriousness of the ethical consequences that would flow from the situation; a social consensus about what should be done; the probability of the effect; the temporal immediacy of consequences; the proximity of affected parties; and/or the number of people affected.

We adopted the Jones model for the current paper. Specifically, Jones (1991, pp. 374–378) identified the following six dimensions of moral intensity:

1. the magnitude of consequences, which he defined as the aggregate harm done to victims [or aggregate benefits accruing to beneficiaries],
2. social consensus, described as the level of agreement about the goodness or evil of a proposed act,
3. the probability of effect, defined as a joint function of the likelihood of occurrence of an act and the expected consequences of the act,
4. temporal immediacy, defined as the length of time between the act and its ethical consequences,
5. proximity, which taps the degree to which the actor can identify with potential victims or beneficiaries, and
6. concentration of effect, the degree to which costs or benefits of the act apply to only a few people.

Jones (1991) argued that the combined effects of these dimensions define the moral intensity of a particular issue.

Given its multidimensionality, Jones (1991) expected moral intensity to vary noticeably from issue to issue. We suspected that different dimensions of moral intensity could be subject to cognitive biases that would increase their variability. Therefore, we next discuss the perceptual aspects of moral judgments.

Role of Perception in Decision Making

Ethical decision making is a specialized form of decision making in general, a topic which has provoked considerable scientific research. In terms of generic decision making, judgment refers to evaluation of alternatives and making a choice among them (Bazerman 1986). Making a judgment involves information processing (Hogarth 1987) and sensemaking (Thomas et al. 1993).

Simon (e.g., March and Simon 1958) theorized and research in cognitive psychology subsequently established that human beings have limited information processing capacity (Hogarth 1987). This condition limits the individual's capacity for rational choice because it forces decision makers to construct simplified mental models to grapple with complex problems (Schwenk 1988).

Because of limited information processing capacity, individuals perceive information selectively, as opposed to comprehensively (Hogarth 1987), and use heuristics, or rules of thumb, to simplify information processing in the decision making task (Tversky and Kahneman 1974). Heuristics save time and usually produce satisfactory decision results, but nevertheless create biases (Bazerman 1986). Heuristics and biases affect the decision maker's assumptions and cognitive frames for problem solving (Schwenk 1988). Thus, the basic tools of decision making – heuristics, biases, assumptions, and cognitive frames – are cognitive in nature.

Hypotheses

According to Jones (1991), the six dimensions of moral intensity are characteristics of the issue under consideration, not characteristics of the individual decision maker or the organizational or environmental context. It is the combined effects of the dimensions which define the overall moral intensity of an issue. The hypotheses involve the perceptual nature of the dimensions (HI) and the relationship between either the combined dimensions (H2) or the separate dimensions (H3) and moral judgments.

Given that perception plays such an important role in decision making in general, it is reasonable to suppose that an individual's perceptions play an important role in ethical decision making, especially with regard to assessing the dimensions of moral intensity, as a prelude to moral judgment. The first hypothesis resulted from this logic.

Hypothesis 1: For a given issue, the perceived dimensions of moral intensity differ from the objective dimensions.

From the theoretical arguments, we expected an issue's perceived moral intensity to affect the individual's moral judgment, but research evidence which might support or refute a relationship between moral intensity and moral judgment was scarce. Only two explicit tests of the moral intensity construct have been reported. Jones and Huber (1992) found that the combined effects of five moral intensity dimensions predicted moral judgment, where moral judgment was operationalized in terms of decision content (specifically, the person's evaluation of the alternative chosen). However, only one of the five dimensions, namely, social consensus, had a separate effect.

Two studies examined the relationship between moral intensity and moral judgment, where moral judgment was operationalized in terms of the decision process, i.e., the type of moral reasoning used to reach a decision. The findings of Weber's Pittsburgh study (1990) supported the notion of a link between moral intensity and moral reasoning, but this study was not designed as a test of the moral intensity construct, as it pre-dates Jones' (1991) model. Weber's Milwaukee study (1993) was designed as an explicit test of one dimension of moral intensity, the magnitude of the consequences. Like the former study, the findings of the latter study indicate a link between moral intensity and moral reasoning. Neither of these studies examined the decision content, and neither tested other dimensions of moral intensity.

In the aggregate, the evidence indicates that moral intensity may be important and that two dimension of moral intensity, social consensus and the magnitude of the consequences, may be more significant than others. The positive correlations between moral intensity and certain aspects of the process and content of moral judgment lend credence to the possibility that moral intensity is related to the alternative chosen, i.e., to the moral judgment itself.

From these considerations, we derive our remaining hypotheses. In Hypotheses 2 and 3, moral intensity refers to the combined effects of the six dimensions defined by Jones (1991) and each dimension is a function of the decision makers perceptions. Moral judgment refers to the decision content and means the alternative chosen.

Hypothesis 2: The overall moral intensity of an issue, as perceived by a decision maker, affects the individual's moral judgment.

Hypothesis 3: Two dimensions of moral intensity, namely, the perceived magnitude of the consequences and the perceived social consensus, are more significant than others.

Research Methodology

Sample and Procedure

The sample consisted of 182 undergraduate students enrolled in an introductory management course. Subjects in the sample ranged from 17 to 51 years old with 50% of the sample 21 years old or younger. Forty-nine percent were female and 51% were male.

Questionnaires were distributed to subjects during class-time. The questionnaires consisted of three scenarios and accompanying questions. Subjects were asked to complete the questionnaires at home and return them to the researchers at the following class meeting. Participation was voluntary.

The response rate was approximately 75%. The response rate must be estimated because we did not require the instructor to call roll in order to ascertain the exact number of students present on the day the questionnaires were distributed.

Instruments

Scenarios

In order to represent a variety of ethical dilemmas and situations, three scenarios were utilized in the study. Previous researchers (e.g., Fritzsche and Becker 1984; Reidenbach et al. 1991) have demonstrated that the use of multiple scenarios is preferable in ethics research. Moreover, multiple scenarios were used since Jones (1991, p. 373) suggested that "moral intensity is likely to vary substantially from issue to issue."

The three scenarios used in this study were adapted versions of scenarios found in the literature. For each scenario, two moral intensity variables were manipulated such that there was a high and a low intensity situation for each manipulated variable. In total, four versions of each scenario were developed, i.e., every combination of the two manipulated variables – high/high, high/low, low/high, low/low.

The first scenario, adapted from Fritzsche and Becker (1984, p. 169), involved a bribe situation. In this scenario, a bicycle company has the choice of making a payment that will ensure future business profits. Social consensus and magnitude of consequences were manipulated in this scenario. For low social consensus, the scenario involved payment for entry into a foreign market. For high social consensus, the scenario involved payment in exchange for a contract with a domestic company. Magnitude of consequences was manipulated by varying the amount of payment and profits; $1 million after tax profits and $100,000 payment for low magnitude of consequences and $8 million after tax profits and $800,000 payment for high magnitude of consequences.

The second scenario, adapted from Hosmer (1991, p. 22), outlined an environmental pollution situation. In this scenario, managers of a manufacturing plant consider dumping solvents and cleaning solutions down a storm drain that runs off into a body of water. Proximity and temporal immediacy were manipulated in this scenario. Proximity was manipulated by varying the location of the scenario; local area for high proximity and a distant location for low proximity. For temporal immediacy, the length of time between action and harm was varied; immediate harm for high temporal immediacy and decades before harm for low temporal immediacy.

The third scenario, adapted from Reidenbach et al. (1991, p. 85), described an over-promising situation. In this scenario, a book store promises that a book will be delivered by a certain date; however, the book store knows that there is a possibility that the book will not be delivered on this date. Concentration of effect and probability of effect were manipulated in this scenario. Probability of effect was manipulated by varying the probability that the book would be delivered on the promised date; 30% for high probability of effect (i.e., only 30% chance of on-time delivery) and 75% for low probability of effect. For concentration of effect, the type of customer was varied; state agency for low concentration of effect and individual student for high concentration of effect.

Moral Judgment

Following each scenario, respondents were asked to indicate their degree of agreement with a series of questions. The questions used a five-point Likert scale, ranging from (1) strongly agree to (5) strongly disagree. The first question indicated moral judgment; respondents were asked to indicate their level of agreement with a moral judgment concerning the scenario (e.g., Rollfast should pay the $100,000).

Moral Intensity

The remaining seven questions covered the six dimensions of moral intensity outlined by Jones (1991) (e.g., Most people would agree that the current practice is wrong [social consensus]). There were seven questions about moral intensity rather than six because we decomposed magnitude of consequences into magnitude of benefits and magnitude of costs.

Jones (1991) did not specify how to measure the combined effects of the six dimensions of moral intensity, but Jones and Huber (1992) assumed that each of the six dimensions act independently of the others.

Social Desirability Bias

Self-report instruments are particularly susceptible to social desirability bias (Moorman and Podsakoff 1992). Social desirability is commonly defined as "some individuals' tendencies to overreport socially desirable personal characteristics and to underreport socially undesirable characteristics" (Arnold et al. 1985, p. 955). Social desirability bias can result in spurious results or suppress or moderate relationships (Ganster et al. 1983). Randall and Gibson (1990) reported that, unfortunately, only 1 out of 96 empirical articles appearing in the *Journal of Business Ethics* considered the effect of social desirability bias on results.

A version of the revised Balanced Inventory of Desirable Responding (BIDR-6) scale developed by Paulhus (1991; shortened after personal communication in 1992) was used to measure social desirability bias. The BIDR-6 instrument contained two sub-scales, self-deception (SD) and impression management (IM). Self-deception is defined as the propensity of individuals to "deny having psychologically threatening thoughts or feelings" (Paulhus 1991, p. 4). Impression management is defined as the propensity of respondents to "consciously over-report their performance of a wide variety of desirable behaviors and under-report undesirable behaviors" (Paulhus 1991, p. 4).

Respondents were asked to indicate the extent of their agreement with the 20 items. The measure used a 5-point response scale, ranging from 1 (not true) to 5 (very true). To score the scales, one point is added to the SD score for each '5' response and one point is added to the IM score for each '4' or '5' response (Paulhus 1991).

Results

Descriptive Statistics

Means, standard deviations, and correlations for the variables in the study are presented in Table 23.1. The moral intensity variables were recoded such that a high value indicated high moral intensity and the moral judgment variable was recoded such that a high value indicated an ethical (i.e., right, just, good, fair) judgment. Interestingly, moral judgment was the best or most just/fair for the pollution scenario (mean of 4.48) and worst or most unjust/unfair for the bribe scenario (mean of 2.80).

Comparison of Means

The first hypothesis stated that the perceived dimensions of moral intensity would differ from the objective dimensions. The objective dimensions were manipulated; for each dimension, half of the questionnaires contained high scores and half contained low scores. After respondents indicated their perceptions about each dimension, f-tests (Table 23.2) were used to compare the differences between mean scores for the people assigned to the low and high groups.

The hypothesis was partially supported. Four of the seven manipulations produced statistically different ($p<0.10$) means. Moreover, for the bribery scenario ($t=1.84$, $p=0.068$), the means for the low and high magnitude of costs groups were 3.19 and 2.90, respectively, in the opposite direction from what would be expected.

Regression Analysis

To test the second and third hypotheses, two-step hierarchial regression analysis was used. Three analyses were conducted, one for each scenario. For each regression model, the dependent variable was the moral judgment for the scenario. Independent variables included age, gender, impression management, self-deception, and the seven moral intensity variables for each scenario. The regression equations are presented in Table 23.3.

In the first step, control variables (i.e., age, gender, impression management, and self-deception) were entered into the regression model. Since Jones (1991, p. 372) suggested that traits and characteristics of the decision-makers are separate from moral intensity, these control variables were entered in the first step. Only the R^2 value for the bribery scenario ($R^2=0.13$, $p<0.001$) was significant, with age as a significant predictor (P=0.34, $p<0.001$).

Table 23.1 Descriptive statistics

Variables:
1. Age
2. Gender [a]
3. Impression management
4. Self deception
5. Judgment
6. Magnitude of consequences/benefits
7. Magnitude of consequences/costs
8. Social consensus
9. Probability of effect
10. Temporal immediacy
11. Proximity
12. Concentration of effect

Vars	Means	s.d.	1	2	3	4	5	6	7	8	9	10	11
1.	25.28	7.07											
2.			−0.10										
3.	2.82	2.31	0.20**	0.13									
4.	1.59	1.53	−0.07	−0.18*	0.04								
Bribery scenario													
5.	2.80	1.30	0.35**	0.03	0.13	−0.07							
6.	4.10	0.99	−0.01	−0.16**	−0.01	0.11	−0.24**						
7.	3.08	1.06	−0.07	0.10	0.04	−0.03	0.22**	−0.05					
8.	3.34	1.14	0.17*	−0.03	0.15*	0.06	0.28**	−0.03	0.15				
9.	3.62	0.98	−0.08	−0.03	0.06	−0.01	−0.26**	0.29*	−0.12	−0.04			
10.	3.24	0.78	0.04	−0.17*	−0.01	−0.16*	−0.11	0.02	−0.11	0.05	0.22**		
11.	3.33	0.90	0.11	0.05	0.02	0.09	−0.02	0.15*	0.03	0.10	−0.22**	−0.06	
12.	2.42	0.99	−0.03	0.07	0.08	0.01	−0.02	−0.19**	−0.04	−0.06	−0.08	−0.17*	0.06

Pollution scenario													
5.	4.48	0.96	−0.06	0.06	−0.03	−0.02							
6.	2.48	1.15	−0.03	−0.06	−0.04	−0.01	−0.24**						
7.	3.39	1.32	0.17*	0.06	0.09	0.07	0.12	−0.17					
8.	4.37	0.78	0.06	−0.00	0.06	0.11	0.42**	−0.18*	0.18*				
9.	4.52	0.75	0.10	0.14	0.18*	0.02	0.32**	−0.18*	0.18*	0.36**			
10.	3.68	1.16	0.10	0.01	0.06	−0.01	0.05	−0.05	0.10	0.14	0.01		
11.	3.76	1.01	0.04	0.17*	0.10	0.01	0.23**	−0.06	0.03	0.31**	0.17*	0.06	
12.	1.61	0.90	−0.15*	−0.07	−0.08	−0.03	−0.31**	0.20**	−0.19*	−0.39**	−0.60**	0.07	−0.14
Over-promising scenario													
5.	3.67	1.09	−0.12	0.08	−0.02	−0.04							
6.	3.30	1.11	−0.02	−0.05	0.03	−0.07	−0.32**						
7.	3.22	0.97	−0.04	0.08	0.05	−0.06	0.23**	−0.03					
8.	3.39	1.04	−0.01	0.10	0.03	−0.06	0.59**	−0.27**	0.25**				
9.	3.10	1.18	0.01	0.01	0.14	0.04	0.21**	0.22**	0.16*	0.29**			
10.	3.30	0.80	0.06	−0.16	0.06	0.04	0.02	0.05	−0.26**	−0.12	0.22**		
11.	3.46	0.86	−0.01	0.24**	−0.01	−0.13	0.17*	−0.12	0.05	0.22**	0.16*	−0.05	
12.	3.18	0.98	0.11	−0.04	0.06	0.01	0.07	−0.08	−0.23**	0.07	0.03	0.26**	0.17*

*$p<0.05$; **$p<0.01$

[a] Gender was coded 1 for men ($n=92$) and 2 for women ($n=90$)

Table 23.2 Comparison of means

Variables manipulated (scenario)	Assigned group	*n*	Means	s.d.	t^a	*df*
Magnitude of benefits	Low	113	4.02	1.05		
(Bribery)	High	69	4.23	0.86	–1.50[b]	165.27
Magnitude of costs	Low	113	3.19	1.09		
(Bribery)	High	69	2.90	0.99	1.84†	180
Social consensus	Low	91	3.30	1.23		
(Bribery)	High	92	3.38	1.06	–0.50	181
Probability of effect	Low	91	2.42	1.09		
(Over-promising)	High	90	3.79	0.81	–9.62***[b]	166.86
Temporal immediacy	Low	69	3.71	1.02		
(Pollution)	High	114	3.67	1.25	0.26[b]	165.55
Proximity	Low	88	3.47	1.02		
(Pollution)	High	92	4.04	0.93	–3.99***	178
Concentration of effect	Low	112	2.98	0.89		
(Over-promising)	High	69	3.51	1.04	–3.62***	179

†$p<0.10$; *$p<0.05$; **$p<0.01$; ***$p<0.001$
[a]Based on pooled variance estimate unless otherwise noted
[b]Based on separate variance estimate

Table 23.3 Results of hierarchical regression analyses (betas)[a] with moral judgments as DVs

	Bribery scenario	Pollution scenario	Over-promising scenario
Step 1 (controls)			
Age	0.34***	–0.04	–0.11
Gender	0.05	0.05	0.05
Impression management	0.06	–0.03	–0.00
Self deception	–0.04	–0.02	–0.04
ΔR^2	0.13***	0.01	0.02
Step 2 (intensity)			
Magnitude of benefits	–0.17*	–0.13†	–0.15*
Magnitude of costs	0.18**	0.04	0.11†
Social consensus	0.19**	0.30***	0.54**
Probability of effect	–0.16*	0.05	0.05
Temporal immediacy	–0.09	0.02	0.15*
Proximity	–0.10	0.16*	–0.00
Concentration of effect	–0.05	–0.15†	0.02
ΔR^2	0.18***	0.28***	0.41***
Overall R^2	0.31	0.29	0.43
F	6.86***	6.09***	11.43***
df	(11,167)	(11,166)	(11,166)

†$p<0.10$; *$p<0.05$; **$p<0.01$; ***$p<0.001$
[a]Regression coefficients for manipulated variables are underlined

In the second step, the moral intensity variables were added to the regression model. The increases in R^2 values for all three scenarios were highly significant ($p<0.001$). This provides strong support for Hypothesis 2; i.e., perceived moral intensity, in the aggregate, affected moral judgment.

For the bribery scenario, perceived magnitude of benefits, perceived magnitude of costs, perceived social consensus, and perceived probability of effect were significant terms ($p<0.10$) in the regression model. For the pollution scenario, perceived magnitude of benefits, perceived social consensus, perceived proximity, and perceived concentration of effect were significant terms ($p<0.10$) in the regression model. For the over-promising scenario, perceived magnitude of benefits, perceived magnitude of costs, perceived social consensus, and perceived temporal immediacy were significant terms ($p<0.10$) in the regression model.

Therefore, 3 is supported by the regression analysis; i.e., some dimensions of moral intensity were more important than others. Examination of the regression equations reveals that perceived magnitude of benefits and perceived social consensus were significant ($p<0.10$) predictors in all three scenarios. Perceived magnitude of costs was a significant predictor ($p<0.10$) for the bribery and over-promising scenarios. Noteworthy, perceived social consensus was the highest β for all three scenarios. Also, the β for perceived magnitude of benefits is always negative.

Discussion

The results of this study lend support to Jones' (1991) assertion that moral intensity affects ethical judgment. After controlling for several personal characteristics and traits, the moral intensity variables, in the aggregate, accounted for a significant proportion of the total variation in moral judgment.

Jones and Huber (1992) found only one significant dimension of the moral intensity construct (namely, social consensus). Weber (1990, 1993) examined only one dimension, magnitude of the consequences, and found it significant. Our findings indicate that multiple dimensions of moral intensity contributed to the variation in moral judgment: magnitude of consequences (magnitude of benefits, always; magnitude of costs, usually), social consensus, and one other dimension that varied depending on the issue. A possible explanation for our finding of multiple significant dimensions is our use of perceptual rather than objective measures of the dimensions.

Some of the moral intensity variables had a greater effect on moral judgment than others. Two moral intensity variables (i.e., the perceived magnitude of benefits and perceived social consensus) consistently were significant predictors of moral judgment. Interestingly, perceived social consensus is the strongest predictor for all three scenarios. More research is needed to substantiate the importance of social consensus and magnitude of benefits in the making of moral judgments.

Managerial Implications

We study the process of decision making with regard to ethical dilemmas in organizations in order to encourage decisions that are good, fair, just, and right. With this in mind, important managerial implications derive from the findings regarding Hypothesis 3.

The significant positive regression coefficients for perceived social consensus across all scenarios suggest that social consensus regarding what is good or evil, relative to a particular issue, is a major determinant of what should be done in the judgment of the decision maker. The significance of perceived social consensus in this study is consistent with Trevino's (1986) contention and prior research (e.g., Weber 1990) that American managers operate at Kohlbergs (1969) conventional level of cognitive moral development. Trevino (1986, p. 608) stated: "Therefore, most managers will look outside themselves for cues about what is right (appropriate) behavior and what is wrong (inappropriate) behavior."

The significant positive regression coefficient for age in the bribery scenario but not in the other scenarios reinforces the importance of social consensus. Older people are more likely both to remember the scandals regarding foreign bribery in the 1970s and to be aware of legal injunctions against bribery. Younger people are more likely to be unaware of these social norms. In the pollution and over-promising scenarios, how the law and/or other social norms apply is equally ambiguous to younger and older respondents. Therefore, age was not significant in these scenarios.

The significance of perceived social consensus implies that we can improve the goodness, justness, and/or fairness of decisions by informing or reminding organizational decision makers of the social consensus regarding various ethical issues. Relevant training is warranted.

The results regarding the decomposed magnitude of consequences variables, i.e., perceived magnitude of benefits and perceived magnitude of costs, suggest implications for managerial training as well. The significant negative regression coefficients for perceived magnitude of benefits across all scenarios indicate that greater perceived benefits induced less morally justifiable decisions about what should be done. The perceived magnitude of costs variable was significant and positive for two of three scenarios/issues, but only marginally significant (i.e., $0.05 < p < 0.1$) for one of these two. Positive coefficients for perceived magnitude of costs suggest that higher perceived costs induced judgments that were better, more fair, and/or more just.

Should future studies yield a consistently negative relationship between magnitude of benefits and moral judgment and a consistently positive relationship between magnitude of costs and moral judgment, training decision makers to be more aware of the negative consequences, social costs, and spillover effects of their decisions should improve the likelihood of good, just, and fair moral judgments.

Limitations

There are several limitations to this study. First, the convenience sample of undergraduate students made sense in terms of the preliminary, if not exploratory, nature of the current research. Generalizing from undergraduates becomes precarious to the extent that the dimensions of moral intensity are susceptible to maturity effects. Does one's perception of magnitude of benefits or costs, social consensus, probability, time, proximity, or concentration of effect change with age or experience? Intuitively, we would answer "yes." However, Table 23.1 shows few significant correlations between age and these moral intensity variables. Nevertheless, the study needs replication among more mature respondents with more business experience.

In this preliminary study, we attempted to establish the significance of perceived moral intensity to moral judgment. The positive results of this study suggest that future studies should apply a more rigorous test which includes more individual, organizational/situational, and/or environmental contingencies in the regression models.

We narrowly operationalized the dimensions of moral intensity. For example, we defined magnitude of consequences in terms of a dollar amount. Future researchers will want to operationalize the intensity dimensions in more sophisticated ways.

Despite these limitations, this exploratory study contributes to the literature by demonstrating that moral intensity is a concept that warrants further empirical study.

References

Ajzen, I., and M. Fishbein. 1980. *Understanding attitudes and predicting social behavior*. Englewood Cliffs: Prentice-Hall.

Arnold, H.J., D.C. Feldman, and M. Purbhoo. 1985. The role of social desirability response bias in turnover research. *Academy of Management Journal* 28: 955–966.

Bazerman, M.H. 1986. *Judgment in managerial decision making*. New York: Wiley.

Boyd, B.K., G.G. Dess, and A.M.A. Rasheed. 1993. Divergence between archival and perceptual measures of the environment: Causes and consequences. *Academy of Management Review* 18: 204–226.

Collins, D. 1989. Organizational harm, legal condemnation and stakeholder retaliation: A typology research agenda and application. *Journal of Business Ethics* 8: 1–13.

Dubinsky, A.J., and B. Loken. 1989. Analyzing ethical decision making in marketing. *Journal of Business Research* 19: 83–107.

Duncan, R.B. 1972. Characteristics of organizational environments and perceived environmental uncertainty. *Administrative Science Quarterly* 17: 313–327.

Elm, D.R. 1989. Managers reasoning about ethical issues: The impact of ethical climate and self-monitoring. Unpublished doctoral dissertation, University of Minnesota, Minneapolis.

Ferrell, O.C., and L.G. Gresham. 1985. A contingency framework for understanding ethical decision making in marketing. *Journal of Marketing* 49(3): 87–96.

Ferrell, O.C., L.G. Gresham, and J. Fraedrich. 1989. A synthesis of ethical decision models for marketing. *Journal of Macromarketing* 9(Fall): 55–64.

Forsyth, D.R. 1980. A taxonomy of ethical ideologies. *Journal of Personality and Social Psychology* 39: 175–184.

Forsyth, D.R. 1981. Moral judgment: The influence of ethical ideology. *Personality and Social Psychology Bulletin* 7(2): 218–223.

Fraedrich, J.P., and O.C. Ferrell. 1992. The impact of perceived risk and moral philosophy type on ethical decision making in business organizations. *Journal of Business Research* 24: 283–295.

Fritzsche, D.J., and H. Becker. 1984. Linking management behavior to ethical philosophy: An empirical investigation. *Academy of Management Journal* 27: 166–175.

Gaertner, K.N. 1991. The effect of ethical climate on managers' decisions. In *Morality; rationality and efficiency: New perspectives on socio-economics*, ed. R.M. Coughlin, 211–223. Armonk: M. E. Sharpe.

Ganster, D.C., H.W. Hennessey, and F. Luthans. 1983. Social desirability response effects: Three alternative models. *Academy of Management Journal* 26: 321–331.

Greenfield, M. 1993. Ignoring the "Why Nots". *Newsweek* CXXII (11) (September 13): 80.

Hegarty, W.H., and H.P. Sims. 1978. Some determinants of unethical decision behavior: An experiment. *Journal of Applied Psychology* 63: 451–457.

Hogarth, R.M. 1987. *Judgment and choice*. New York: Wiley.

Hosmer, L.T. 1991. *The ethics of management*, 2nd ed. Homewood: Irwin.

Hunt, S.D., and S. Vitell. 1986. A general theory of marketing ethics. *Journal of Macromarketing* 6(Spring): 5–16.

Jauch, L.R., and K.L. Kraft. 1986. Strategic management of uncertainty. *Academy of Management Review* 11: 777–790.

Jones, T.M. 1991. Ethical decision making by individuals in organizations: An issue-contingent model. *Academy of Management Review* 16: 366–395.

Jones, T.M., and V.L. Huber. 1992. Issue contingency in ethical decision making. *International Association for Business and Society Proceedings*: 156–166.

Kohlberg, L. 1969. Stage and sequence: The cognitive-developmental approach to socialization. In *Handbook of socialization theory and research*, ed. D.A. Goslin, 347–480. Chicago: Rand McNally.

Logsdon, J.M., J.K. Thompson, and R.A. Reid. 1992. Software piracy: Is it related to stage of moral development? *International Association for Business and Society Proceedings*: 31–37.

Malinowski, C.I., and C.P. Smith. 1985. Moral reasoning and moral conduct: An investigation prompted by Kohlberg's theory. *Journal of Personality and Social Psychology* 49: 1016–1027.

March, J.G., and H.A. Simon. 1958. *Organizations*. New York: Wiley.

Miller, J.G., D.M. Bersoff, and R.L. Harwood. 1990. Perceptions of social responsibilities in India and in the United States: Moral imperatives or personal decision? *Journal of Personality and Social Psychology* 58: 33–47.

Moorman, R.H., and P.M. Podsakoff. 1992. A meta-analytic review and empirical test of the potential confounding effects of social desirability response sets in organizational behavior research. *Journal of Occupational and Organizational Psychology* 65: 131–149.

Nichols, M.L., and V.E. Day. 1982. A comparison of moral reasoning of groups and individuals on the "defining issues test". *Academy of Management Journal* 25: 201–208.

Paulhus, D.L. 1991. BIDR reference manual for version 6. Unpublished report, University of British Columbia.

Randall, D.M., and A.M. Gibson. 1990. Methodology in business ethics research: A review and critical assessment. *Journal of Business Ethics* 9: 457–472.

Reidenbach, R.E., D.P. Robin, and L. Dawson. 1991. An application and extension of a multidimensional ethics scale to selected marketing practices and marketing groups. *Journal of the Academy of Marketing Science* 19: 83–92.

Rest, J. 1986. *Moral development: Advances in research and theory*. New York: Praeger.

Schwenk, C.R. 1988. *The essence of strategic decision making*. Lexington: Lexington Books.

Thomas, K.W., and B.A. Velthouse. 1990. Cognitive elements of empowerment: An "interpretive" model of intrinsic task motivation. *Academy of Management Review* 15: 666–681.

Thomas, J.B., S.M. Clark, and D.A. Gioia. 1993. Strategic sensemaking and organizational performance: Linkages among scanning, interpretation, action, and outcomes. *Academy of Management Journal* 36: 239–270.

Trevino, L.K. 1986. Ethical decision making in organizations: A person-situation interactionist model. *Academy of Management Review* 11: 601–617.
Trevino, L.K., and B. Victor. 1992. Peer reporting of unethical behavior: A social context perspective. *Academy of Management Journal* 35: 38–64.
Trevino, L.K., and S.A. Youngblood. 1990. Bad apples in bad barrels: A causal analysis of ethical decision-making behavior. *Journal of Applied Psychology* 75: 378–385.
Tversky, A., and D. Kahneman. 1974. Judgment under uncertainty: Heuristics and biases. *Science* 185: 1124–1131.
Waterman, A.S. 1988. On the uses of psychological theory and research in the process of ethical inquiry. *Psychological Bulletin* 103(3): 283–298.
Weber, J. 1990. Managers' moral reasoning: Assessing their responses to three moral dilemmas. *Human Relations* 43: 687–702.
Weber, J. 1993. Assessing the role of the moral issue and its intensity upon managerial decision making. *International Association for Business and Society Proceedings*: 390–394.
Weick, K. 1979. *The social psychology of organizing*, 2nd ed. Reading: Addison-Wesley.

Chapter 24
Will the Ethics of Business Change? A Survey of Future Executives

Thomas M. Jones and Frederick H. Gautschi III

Introduction

The late 1970s and early 1980s are described by Lipset and Schneider (1983) as a period in which American institutions experienced a "crisis of confidence." Their thesis is not surprising given what even the most casual observer might recall from that time period – for example revelations of: (1) illegal political contributions by corporations, (2) bribery of foreign officials, and (3) American governmental helplessness in the presence of foreign terrorists. Since shortly after the advent of the Reagan years, the public mood seems to have become more positive with regard to those same institutions. A July 1985 Gallup poll showed public confidence in the following institutions to have risen over the 1980–1985 period: churches, the military, the U.S. Supreme Court, public schools, Congress, television, and big business. With regard to the last category, those expressing a great deal of confidence had risen from a low of 20% in 1980 to 31% in 1985. Still, big business ranked behind each of the other institutions, with the exception of television.

The reasons for the low level of public confidence are open to debate, but, in part, the explanation lies in a public perception that big business is marked by unethical practices. Union Carbide's role in the Bhopal tragedy, Manville's culpability in the asbestos crisis, and E. F. Hutton's involvement in financial misdealings are only a few examples of well-publicized questionable behavior on the part of big business. The impact of such well known misdeeds manifests itself in the results of another

T.M. Jones (✉)
Department of Management and Organization, Foster School of Business,
P.O. Box 353226, 512 Paccar Hall, University of Washington, Seattle, WA 98195, USA
e-mail: rebozo@u.washington.edu

F.H. Gautschi III
Gautschi Law Firm, LLC, 2200 Sixth Avenue, Suite 1250, Seattle, WA 98121, USA

A.C. Michalos and D.C. Poff (eds.), *Citation Classics from the Journal of Business Ethics*, Advances in Business Ethics Research 2,
DOI 10.1007/978-94-007-4126-3_24,

Gallup poll taken in August 1985. Respondents were asked the following question: how would you rate the honesty and ethical standards of people in these different fields – very high, high, low, or very low? Business executives received very high or high marks from only 23% of the respondents. This result placed executives behind: clergymen (67%), druggists/pharmacists (65%), medical doctors (58%), dentists (56%), college teachers (54%), engineers (53%), policemen (47%), bankers (37%), TV reporters/commentators (33%), journalists (31%), newspaper reporters (29%), and lawyers (27%). In an identical Gallup poll 2 years earlier, business executives had achieved a very high/high rating from only 18% of the respondents. However, in the 1983 poll the rating for each of the other occupations was also lower than that for 1985.

The low esteem in which the public has held business executives has not been unnoticed by the business community or professional schools of business. Codes of ethics, rare 15 years ago, are commonplace among America's large corporations. Various texts and casebooks discuss the efficacy of such codes and their implementation. Molander (1980), for example, provides an interesting case history of Weyerhaeuser's tribulations involved in designing and implementing a code of ethics in the mid-1970s. Harvard Business School, in a response to a charge from the university's president, has instituted a special project on ethics in business. Business and Society textbooks typically contain a section on business ethics. (See, for example, Sturdivant 1985; Steiner and Steiner 1985; Davis et al. 1980.) In addition, the study of business ethics has become the subject of distinct courses and textbooks in recent years as the result of the shared interests of business scholars and philosophers. Recent texts include DeGeorge (1982), Velasquez (1982), and Matthews et al. (1985). Finally, the recent advent of two journals, the Journal of Business Ethics and the Business and Professional Ethics Journal, demonstrates further the heightened academic interest in ethics in business.

During the 1960s and 1970s the business press explained that business leaders were becoming increasingly concerned with business ethics and corporate social responsibility. Baumhart (1961) and Brenner and Molander (1977), in the two most frequently cited studies, reported results of extensive surveys of business executives that demonstrated this heightened concern. A particularly striking finding of the latter study was the ranking of customers ahead of stockholders as "the group to whom executives feel the greatest responsibility" (p. 69). The authors argued that the traditional caveat emptor relationship had given way to the firm's being the "customer's servant."

At present, however, much attention is being given to making the American economy better able to compete with foreign firms. Productivity, not responsibility, seems to be the major concern for the American business community. A question worth exploring is: How does this changing, muddied environment translate into attitudes toward business ethics and social responsibility held by future executives? It is the aim of this study to provide some answers to this question.

Previous Research

Previous research on attitudes comes under one of three headings: surveys of business executives, interviews with selected executives, and surveys of college/professional school students. In the first category the best known studies are those of Baumhart (1961) and Brenner and Molander (1977). Both studies involved surveys of Harvard Business Review readers. Baumhart focused his attention on the ethical norms of business executives, finding, among other things, that executives surveyed viewed their own behavior to be more ethical than that of their peers.

Brenner and Molander updated and expanded the Baumhart study by adding material on social responsibility. In comparing the results of their analysis of 1,227 responses to Baumhart's results, the authors conclude (p. 59) that:

1. Respondents evince considerable disagreement regarding whether ethical standards have changed.
2. Respondents view the ethical standards of their peers less optimistically than they view their own.
3. Respondents favor ethical codes, but feel that such codes will not be effective by themselves.
4. Respondents embrace the concept of social responsibility and rank responsibility to customers ahead of responsibility to stockholders.

These conclusions from responses to survey questions are based on aggregate measures, and, consequently, do not allow one to draw inferences regarding the views of persons at different levels of the organizational hierarchy, or to determine, for example, whether older executives differ from younger executives in attitudes. Further, the male to female ratio in the sample was approximately 19:1. As a result, the authors could not confidently compare the attitudes of men and women executives.

Carroll (1975) conducted a random survey of 400 managers selected from various corporate listings. Using a four point scale (agree, somewhat agree, somewhat disagree, disagree) he asked his respondents to react to a series of statements alleging unethical business behavior as printed in newspapers and magazines. From the 238 respondents Carroll learned that on some issues top managers expressed different views from those of middle and lower level managers. For example, a majority of top managers disagreed with the following statement while a majority of middle and lower level executives agreed with the statement.

> The illegal business campaign contributions of the last year or so are realistic examples of the ethics of today.

On the aggregate level 47% of the respondents expressed at least some level of agreement with the statement "Business ethics today are far superior to ethics of earlier periods," a result similar to that found by Brenner and Molander two years later. Similar to the analysis conducted by Brenner and Molander, Carroll's study relies primarily on aggregate measures. Further, as in the Brenner and Molander study, Carroll does not subject his data to any statistical analysis.

In contrast with the three studies just noted is the work of Posner and Schmidt (1984). The study sought to learn something about the values of American managers. To do so the authors polled 6,000 executives. The results of the analysis of the responses of 1,460 managers allowed the authors to conclude, among other things, that (pp. 214–215):

> Profit maximization and stockholders, contrary to popular opinion and stereotypes [sic] are not the central focus of managers . . . attention to the public-at-large, or government is also not very substantial.
>
> Managers perceive that pressures to conform to organizational standards are strong (and very few see these pressures diminishing).

Although Posner and Schmidt confine much of their analysis to the aggregate level, they do give some attention to ascertaining the nature of differences among managers by level in the organization. For example, an analysis of variance (p. 206) demonstrates that upper, middle, and lower level managers rank differently the importance of 16 categories of organizational stakeholders. Interestingly, it is only upper level managers who rank customers first. Whether the scaled value of importance for the customer category is statistically different across management levels is a question not addressed by the authors. Further, although they have the data that would allow them to do so, the authors do not try to assess the extent to which educational levels and gender differences are associated with varying sets of values of the respondents.

A contrasting approach to the survey is that of the series of interviews. A particularly good example of this approach is found in Clinard (1983). [An earlier, less well-structured use of the approach was used by Silk and Vogel (1976) in their frequently cited study of top level executives.] Clinard conducted lengthy, in-depth interviews with 64 retired middle-level managers from a variety of Fortune's 500 companies. Although the nature of his sample was such that he could not subject his data to statistical analysis, he was able, through a careful reading of the records of the interviews, to draw numerous inferences. For example, the evidence was quite convincing that the respondents believed that top management is an important determinant of ethical behavior within the corporation, in that "...the chief executive officer (CEO), sets the corporate ethical tone." (p. 132) In addition, those persons interviewed provided considerable support for the argument that pressures to show profits are, at least at times, substantial enough to lead middle managers to engage in unethical behavior. Finally, in a finding that bears on the perceived efficacy of corporate codes of ethics, the majority of respondents felt that:

> ... industry cannot police itself effectively without some government intervention. . . . [The] unethical behavior of certain top management personnel within an industry, plus the greed and unethical practices of some corporations, have made government regulation necessary. Moreover, they could visualize no way in which industry rules might be effectively enforced. (p. 153)

The last finding reported above contrasts with that reported by Trawick and Darden (1980). Although the sample is not described, this study of the attitudes of marketing academics and practitioners concludes:

1. Improving marketing ethics can be achieved best through formal education.
2. A formal code of ethics coupled with self-regulation is good means of improving marketing ethics.
3. Government regulation to upgrade marketing ethics is not well received by marketing practitioners.

Upon subjecting the responses of the practioners and academics to a chi-square test for differences, the authors found that there were no major differences between the two groups. Instead, any differences were in degree and not substance.

Do external groups share the views on business ethics demonstrated in the studies discussed above? Clearly, the Gallup Poll results cited earlier suggest that the public has a less than sanguine view of the ethical norms of business executives. For the purposes of the current study, it is useful to refer to studies of the attitudes of college and professional school students.

A recent study of the attitudes of college students regarding business ethics is that conducted by Beltramini et al. (1984). In their study the authors analyzed the questionnaire responses from 2,856 students in 28 universities, private as well as public, after having conducted a pre-test on 200 students. The pre-test led to the development of the ten item questionnaire used in the study. The major finding of the study is that women students are more concerned about ethical issues in business than are their male counterparts, regardless of the issue. Although statistically significant differences were found on some items across academic classification and major, these differences were not particularly large in a substantive sense. In fact the authors conclude that college students are quite sensitive to ethical issues in business, regardless of major, gender, or year in school. Still, the authors are led to assert that:

> Not only are the attitudes of future decision makers and managers regarding ethical practices currently in the process of being shaped by educators, but to an extent it is the female students' concerns which may well be establishing a new moral force in tomorrow's business world. (p. 200)

The assertion is worth pondering given the size of the sample and the results obtained. Responses to the ten questions were measured on a six point scale, ranging from Extremely Concerned to Extremely Unconcerned. The magnitude of difference between and among the various groups ranged from 0.1 to 0.3, hardly a large number on a six point scale. Given the size of the sample, and the fact that the male to female breakdown is 57–43%, one ought to expect statistically significant differences between the two groups. Consequently, it is not clear that the results of the study allow for a statement quite as bold as the one quoted above.

Krakhardt et al. (1985) conducted a sophisticated statistical study on MBA students at a particular institution so as to try to discover determinants of the students' judgements regarding ethical issues in business. At the time of its presentation, the study did not address itself to differences within the respondent pool according to demographic factors. Still, the study in its early form provides some useful findings. Specifically, the authors note that there is a strong tendency among MBA students to display a utilitarian perspective on business ethics. When addressing codes of ethics that contain a requirement that employees report code violations, the authors note that:

> … [W]ithin a business context, witnessing unethical behavior does not seem to carry any heavy responsibility for reporting the behavior. This finding may explain why there is such controversy over `whistle-blowing' in organizations. Although organizations may encourage employees to report unethical behavior, it is clear that failure to report such behavior is not considered highly unethical by this sample of MBA students. (p. 14)

What remains to be studied is an extension of the studies just discussed. While we know a good deal about the attitudes of business decision makers, our knowledge of the attitudes of future executives is not extensive. Nor are we particularly well informed as to the effect of demographic factors on attitudes. A systematic, carefully constructed study of current MBA students' attitudes should allow us to learn, for example, whether tomorrow's executives reflect the views of what is considered to be an increasingly conservative American public. It is to this and other similar questions that we turn our attention.

The Study

During the 1984–1985 academic year, we administered a questionnaire to students enrolled in a required MBA course, Context of the Business System, at the University of Washington. The questionnaire contained a series of open-ended questions that asked students, "What would you do if …" followed by the description of a situation that involved an ethical issue or issues. For example, one question asked what the student would do if s/he were told to fire a once productive 62 year old employee in order to make room for a younger employee. In addition to the open-ended questions, bounded questions appeared that asked the students to: (1) rank a series of ethical issue categories according to their perceived importance, (2) compare their own ethical standards to those of other groups, (3) rank stakeholder groups according to their claim upon the firm, and (4) comment on the current and expected future state of ethics in business. From the responses to the questionnaires we were able to refine the survey instrument. (See the Appendix for a reprint of the questionnaire.) Subsequently, we decided to administer the questionnaire to MBA students within a set of schools offering the MBA degree. The set of schools (Harvard, California-Berkeley, Michigan, Duke, Minnesota, Penn State, Pittsburgh, Oregon State, Portland State, Santa Clara, and Cal. State-L.A.) was chosen to provide a diversified sample according to: (1) geographical region, (2) public versus private, (3) academic stature (international, national, and regional), and (4) size. From approximately 1,000 questionnaires that were sent out in 1985 we received 455 usable responses.

For analysis of the responses we developed a series of aggregate measures and a series of comparative measures by age, education, and gender of the respondents.

(The reader who wishes to see a full statement of each of the questions should refer to the Appendix to this paper.)

The responses to questions 1, 2, 4 and 5 can be considered to represent interval level data. Consequently, the mean aggregate values are appropriate for summary statistic purposes. In addition, we were able to perform t-tests on these questions for differences in means for: (1) older versus younger students, (2) male versus female students, and (3) those students with graduate degrees versus those with undergraduate degrees only. Although we conducted t-tests for differences of means whenever appropriate, we shall report only those intergroup differences that are statistically significant. Question 3, which asks students to rank stakeholder groups, results in the generation of ordinal level data, which lends itself to less powerful statistical tests. Consequently, for the responses to that question we chose to avoid performing non-parametric tests on rank order across the several demographic categories in the set of respondents.

The open-ended questions required that we develop some sort of classification scheme for summary purposes. For question 7, which asked respondents to suggest ways of upgrading corporate ethical norms, the responses fell rather neatly into one or more of five categories: (1) improved legislation/stronger punishment, (2) improved legislation/external audits, (3) increased consumer awareness through media/consumer interest groups, (4) improved education of managers (future and present) to include ethics, and (5) improved corporate culture. The remaining open-ended questions were somewhat less easy to fit neatly into a classification scheme. After some deliberation, we decided that the response pattern could accommodate a classification scheme first articulated by Hirschman (1970). According to Hirschman, organization members, when faced with decision making situations in which their own values conflict with those of the organization and/or a superior, display behavior that fits into one or more of three types: exit (the individual leaves the organization), voice (the individual "speaks out" regarding the conflict), or loyalty (the individual acts in way consistent with the values of the organization and/or the superior). While not all of the responses to the hypothetical situations we posed fit into this taxonomy, the overwhelming majority did. As with the data for question three, we were left with a sizable set of ordinal level data for questions 8–15.

Results

As Table 24.1 shows, our respondents display considerable diversity within the six demographic categories for which we collected data. Notice, though that the "typical" respondent is male, under 30, with a B.A., 1–6 years of experience, previously earning between $20,000 and $30,000 annually, and specializing in finance.

Not surprisingly, our results at times are consistent with those found in studies described earlier, while at other times our results conflict with those of other researchers, as will become clear in the discussion that follows. We begin by describing the responses to the various questionnaire items.

Table 24.1 Profile of respondents

Age		Sex		Education	
Range	Frequency	Category	Frequency	Highest degree	Frequency
20–24	113 (25.3%)	Male	290 (64.4%)	B.A.	343 (76.4%)
25–29	213 (47.7%)	Female	160 (35.6%)	B.S.	46 (10.2%)
30–34	64 (14.3%)	No answer	5 (1.1%)	M.A.	51 (11.4%)
35–39	43 (9.6%)			M.S.	0
40–44	10 (2.2%)			J.D.	1 (0.2%)
45–49	2 (0.4%)			Ph.D.	3 (0.7%)
50 and over	2 (0.4%)			Other	5 (1.1%)
No answer	8 (1.8%)			No answer	6 (1.3%)
MBA concentration		Experience		Income	
Area	Frequency		Frequency		Frequency
Finance	151 (39.7%)	None	59 (13.3%)	Under $10k	50 (12.8%)
Info. Sys.	21 (5.5%)	1–3 years	146 (33.0%)	$10k–14,999	20 (5.1%)
Int. Bus.	12 (3.2%)	4–6 years	129 (29.2%)	$15k–19,999	43 (11.0%)
Mkting.	87 (22.9%)	7–9 years	41 (9.3%)	$20k–24,999	67 (17.1%)
Hum. Res. Mgmt.	9 (2.4%)	10 and over	64 (14.5%)	$25k–29,999	74 (18.9%)
Bus. Econ.	1 (0.3%)	Other	3 (0.7%)	$30k–34,999	61 (15.6%)
Gen. Mgmt.	43 (11.3%)	No answer	13 (2.9%)	$35k–39,999	38 (9.7%)
Logistics	2 (0.5%)			$40k and up	36 (9.2%)
Accounting	21 (5.5%)			Other	2 (0.5%)
Operations	9 (2.4%)			No answer	64 (14.1%)
Other	24 (6.3%)				
No answer	75 (16.5%)				

As Table 24.2 shows, respondents display considerable sensitivity toward the 14 ethical issue categories listed in the table. (Recall that the list was derived from the pre-test that we conducted in 1984. The question asks the respondent to indicate the extent to which the business community should give attention to the issue category listed).

At the aggregate level there are three findings that are worth noting. First, clearly, "product related" issues rank highest. Second, a closer examination of the responses shows that product safety has a dominant position in the view of our respondents, since 71.6% gave the category a 1 and 93.6% gave it a 1 or a 2. Finally, some of the "timeless" social policy issues – apartheid, comparable worth, and minority hiring – have relatively little salience with MBA students, while others – whistle-blowing and bribery – retain their importance. This result, as it pertains to apartheid, is a bit of a surprise, given the substantially increased divestment activity taking place among colleges/universities and public sector agencies in recent months. Recall, though, that the questionnaire was completed several months prior to the accelerated divestment activity.

Another point of note regarding the social policy issues is illustrated by a comparison of females and males in the sample. There are three statistically significant

Table 24.2 Importance of ethical issues

Issue	Mean response	Rank
Product safety	1.324	1
Product quality	1.522	2
Product information	1.753	3
Bribery	2.053	4
Whistle-blowing	2.145	5
Disclosure to shareholders	2.148	6
Community relations	2.231	7
Plant closures	2.355	8
Arbitrary discharges	2.448	9
Relations with foreign governments	2.476	10
Minority hiring	2.506	11
Executive compensation	2.695	12
Comparable worth	2.794	13
Apartheid	2.827	14

Measured on a 5 point scale, where *1* – a great deal of attention

Table 24.3 Intergroup differences on ethical issues

Issue	Score (women)	Rank	Score (men)	Rank
Product information	1.610	3	1.834	3
Minority hiring	2.340	9	2.583	11
Comparable worth	2.439	12	2.993	14

differences between male and female MBA students on question 1, as the table below shows.

Each of the differences is significant at the 0.05 level with the difference on comparable worth significant at better than the 0.01 level. Notice that, in general, women and men do not show sizable differences in their views. In the first two items from Table 24.3, it is clear that although there is a difference between the two groups, the magnitude of the difference is not large, being approximately 0.2 for each. It is only when one looks at comparable worth that there is a substantial difference. Specifically, the difference in magnitude is greater than 0.5, or large enough to suggest that women feel considerably more strongly about where this issue ought to be on corporate America's agenda than do men. Interestingly, although it is an issue that affects them directly, women rank the issue 12th on the list of 14.

The only other statistically significant intergroup differences on ethical issues occur for older students (30 and older) versus younger students. Similar to what was just discussed, the differences are of rather modest degree. Specifically, the two groups differ on only two issues, executive compensation and apartheid, with older students showing more concern regarding the first category and younger students showing more concern regarding the latter issue. But the ranks for the two groups are very close, 12 versus 12 and 13 versus 14, respectively. The two sets of scores are within 0.2 of each other, hardly a striking magnitude. One can speculate that the

Table 24.4 Comparison of respondents ethical norms

Reference group	Score
Current business school faculty	2.858
Fellow MBA students	2.479
Past peers	2.358
Past supervisors	2.280
Current business executives	2.136

differences are explained as follows. First, older students are more concerned about executive compensation because they are more aware of compensation levels. Second, those same students may show less concern about Apartheid because of their more sophisticated sense of the limits of corporate influence in this area.

Consistent with the results of earlier research, our respondents indicate that they regard their own ethical standards to be higher than those of other groups. In question 2, we asked the respondents to compare their own ethical standards to those of five other groups: (1) current MBA students, (2) current business executives, (3) past peers, (4) past supervisors, and (5) current business school faculty members. The responses on a 5 point scale range from "much higher than" (1) to "much lower than" (5). The mean values for the four groups are shown in Table 24.4.

In addition to the general result noted above, there are other points of significance suggested by the table. First is the result that our respondents hold the norms of current executives in rather low regard. What this suggests is that the students have views similar to those expressed by the general public as evidenced by recent Gallup Polls. This result is even more striking in that 329 of the 455 respondents saw their own standards as higher than those of current executives, while only 4 respondents considered their own standards to be lower than those of executives. Second, there is an encouraging note in that current business school faculty rank highest in terms of ethical norms. 100 respondents saw their own norms as higher than those of faculty members; 57 respondents viewed their own norms as being lower than those of faculty members. There is the possibility that the business school faculty member, and the business school itself, can serve as a model for MBA students. This is particularly true for students with undergraduate degrees only (versus students with graduate degrees). The mean score for the former group is 2.894 and for the latter, 2.679. The difference between the two scores is significant at the 0.05 level. Although the magnitude of the difference is not large, we have reason to conclude that the first group of MBA students is more confident of the ethical standards of current faculty members. Finally, consistent with what Brenner and Molander (1977) found, our respondents viewed their own norms to be higher than those of their peers.

Interestingly, when respondents were asked to comment on progress made in the improvement in the state of business ethics to date and likely to be made in the future (Questions 4 and 5), they were generally optimistic on both counts. Although there was considerable disagreement regarding the current state of ethics in comparison to that of 10 years ago (another finding consistent with that of Brenner and Molander), the mean score on this question, 2.796 (1 indicates strong agreement with the statement, "There is good reason to believe that business practices are more

Table 24.5 Stakeholders rankings

Stakeholder group	Score	Ranking
Stockholders	2.440	1
Customers	2.562	2
Employees	2.754	3
Society-at-large	4.816	4
Local community	4.830	5
"Neighbors"	5.533	6
Suppliers	6.049	7
Government agencies	6.810	8

ethical today than 10 years ago."), shows that, overall, respondents feel that ethical standards have improved over the last 10 years. By a slightly less positive score, 2.804, respondents feel, overall, that ethical norms are likely to improve over the next 10 years, a period in which they will be in a position to influence business practices.

A striking feature of the response patterns for question 5 is that very few respondents expressed strong feelings about the future state of business practices – only 7.5% strongly agreed or strongly disagreed with the statement. Although the respondents view themselves as having high ethical standards, they appear to feel that their own high standards will be of rather modest consequence in the typical corporate "culture." Or, it may be as Clinard (1983) learned, that pressure for profit can make even the most high minded individual willing to compromise his/her standards. Finally, we are able to understand more fully the meaning of the results for questions 2, 4 and 5 by examining the response pattern in question 3.

In question 3 we presented the respondents with a list of eight corporate stakeholder groups. We asked the respondents to rank "… the groups [in] the order in which constituency interests ought to be served by the firm." Table 24.5 shows the result of the ranking.

One of the major findings from the Brenner and Molander study was that the concept of social responsibility had taken hold within corporate America, as evidenced by the respondents' ranking responsibility to customers ahead of responsibility to stockholders. More recently, Posner and Schmidt (1984) reached a similar conclusion, as it applies to the views of upper level executives. Our results indicate that a more traditional ranking exists within tomorrow's executives. We suggest that this outcome helps to explain our respondents' reactions to question 5. That is, notice that our respondents rank stockholders, customers, and employees quite close to one another, with the scores for other stakeholder groups being quite distant from those of the first three groups. Recall that in discussing the responses to question 1 we noted that MBA students tend to be more sensitive to product issues than to, for example, "timeless" social issues. This suggests that their concerns about ethical issues in business focus primarily on product rather than process issues. The results for question 3 are consistent with this outcome in that process issues are typically associated with groups outside the traditional tri-partite conception of the corporation, i.e., stockholders, customers, and employees.

Table 24.6 Means of upgrading corporate ethical norms

Approach	Response frequency (%)
Improved legislation/stronger punishment	18.3
Improved legislation/external audits	4.4
Increased consumer awareness through media/ consumer interest groups	12.8
Improved education to include ethics	20.5
Improved corporate culture	30.0
Other	13.9

The second clustering in question 3 is of societal groups (society-at-large, local community, and "neighbors"). In contrast, Posner and Schmidt's respondents displayed little attention to the public-at-large.

Two other characteristics of the response pattern are noteworthy. First, the fact that the MBA students ranked governmental agencies last suggests a continuation of an adversarial (versus cooperative) relationship with government. Posner and Schmidt showed a similar result. Second, the ranking of suppliers (seven out of eight) suggests a substantial difference in attitude towards "arm's length transaction" constituents – the firm owes little to firms from which it buys, but much to those to whom it sells, its customers.

Whether despite or because of the views expressed in the responses to questions 1–5, the students surveyed were quite clear in their feelings toward upgrading corporate ethical norms. Only 17% of the respondents felt that the norms did not need to be upgraded, while 11% were uncertain. Fully 72% expressed a need for upgrading ethical norms. Consistent with some of the results that we presented earlier, women were seen to differ significantly from their male counterparts on this issue, in a direction that one might predict. Specifically, women were more positive than men on the need to upgrade ethical norms. (Statistical significance obtained at the 0.05 level). Similarly, students with prior graduate degrees were more convinced than their peers without graduate training of the need for upgrading ethical norms. (Again, statistical significance obtained at the 0.05 level.)

The 72% who indicated that ethical norms needed to be upgraded suggested a variety of means for bringing about the improvement as Table 24.6 shows.

In summarizing the figures in the table we note three results. First, 22.7% favor legal means of improving ethics either through stiffer penalties or increasing the chances of getting caught. Second, 35.5% favor external monitoring of corporate ethics, either through legal means (above) or improved monitoring by outside groups. Finally, 50.5% favor improvement in the ethical content of professional curricula or in the ethical component of corporate culture. Recall that Clinard's respondents were quite clear that some sort of external intervention is necessary to upgrade ethical behavior. Trawick and Darden's marketing professionals, on the other hand, were not particularly sympathetic toward increased external intervention. Interestingly, the Trawick and Darden respondents support Beltramini et al.'s (1984) assertion that student perceptions are shaped by educators. The Trawick and Darden respondents indicated that improved formal education held the greatest potential for improving marketing ethics.

The fact that a sizable portion of our respondents indicated that improved formal education could help is somewhat encouraging, particularly in comparison to the call for improved corporate culture. Recall that our respondents indicated that they viewed their own ethical norms to be (1) about on a par with current business school faculty members and (2) clearly superior to those of current business executives. Given these views, one could argue that there is good reason for devoting resources of business schools to upgrading the ethical content of the various curricula. Surely, doing so is not an easy task, but compared to the suggestion to improve corporate culture, the potential for success is bright. (Of course, it can be argued that the two suggestions are neither mutually exclusive nor necessarily independent. Further, our interpretation is not likely to resolve the debate in academic circles regarding whether courses in ethics are worth including in the professional school curricula – see, for example, Cavanaugh (1984), Chap. 5, for a discussion of the issue – but it should lend some comfort to the proponents of the idea.)

Further, recall that various studies have shown that professionals and students alike have expressed some confidence in the ability of formal codes of ethics to improve behavior. In addition, studies of specific companies have suggested the same confidence. For example, Tuleja (1985) argues (p. 203) that codes can be of great value, because "… [t]here are corporations that actually try to live by the principles set forth in their codes …." For whatever reasons, our respondents are overwhelmingly unsympathetic toward the possibility of a code of ethics being of much value. In fact, the frequency of the ethical code suggestion was negligible. One can infer that even those MBA students who suggested improving the corporate culture did not have the institution of ethical codes in mind.

Finally, the majority view expressed by our respondents is consistent with that of Trevino (1986) who argues that

> Codes of ethics will affect ethical/unethical behavior significantly only if they are consistent with the organizational culture and are enforced.

The eight open-ended questions that concluded the questionnaire required the respondents to forecast what they would do when faced with a decision in an ethically difficult situation. The difficulty could be caused by uncertainty as to what constitutes the "right" thing to do in the situation or by the individual's proximity to the behavior at issue and/or by the individual's position within the organizational hierarchy. The set of hypothetical situations chosen for this portion of the questionnaire allowed us to vary each of the three dimensions just mentioned. Although it was not always possible to do so, we attempted to fit the response patterns into Hirschman's exit, voice, and loyalty taxonomy. The results of our attempt are discussed below.

Question 8 asked the respondent to consider a situation in which s/he has been told by a supervisor to fire a 62 year old employee in order to: (1) make room for a younger employee, (2) make room for a member of a minority race, or (3) save the firm the cost of full benefits. As Table 24.7 shows, as the reason for pressuring the

Table 24.7 Response summary for question 8

	Frequency (%)		
Response	(1)	(2)	(3)
Pure loyalty	22.5	19.1	14.9
Voice and loyalty	3.0	2.8	3.4
Modified loyalty	18.6	17.5	17.0
Highly modified loyalty	26.4	25.0	20.5
Total loyalty	70.1	64.4	55.8
Voice	15.4	19.8	25.5
Voice (?)(a)	2.5	3.0	4.1
Voice (?)(b)	5.1	5.7	5.1
Total voice	26.0	31.3	38.1

Where the various categories above are made up of the following sets of raw responses:

Do it, unqualified (loyalty)
Object, but do it (voice and loyalty)
Transfer, demote, etc., but do not fire (modified loyalty)
Suggest early retirement, but do not pressure (highly modified loyalty)
Don't do it, not right (voice)
Don't do it, not my job (voice (?)(a))
Point out possible legal problems (voice (?)(b))

older employee into retirement changes, respondents change their preferences for voice versus loyalty responses. Specifically, making room for a younger employee found relatively few willing to voice objections in either a pure or modified form but many willing to adopt loyalty positions. Making room for a minority employee made respondents less "loyal" and more willing to voice disagreement. Finally, saving the cost of full benefits elicited even fewer loyalty responses and even more voice responses. Apparently, making room for a younger employee is more acceptable to these respondents than is making room for a minority employee, which, in turn, is preferable to simply trying to save the company the full cost of benefits. Interestingly, in each variation of the question men were significantly (at the 0.01 level) more likely to "do as ordered" than were women. Finally, the number of exit responses was negligible.

Questions 9 and 10 pertain to the respondent's being a company president who had the opportunity to hire away a competitor's employee. Question 10 adds the fact that the employee asks for a guaranteed annual salary of $100,000 for his 5 years of experience. As Table 24.8 shows, in the first case the vast majority (76.5%) would hire the competitor's employee. In the second case a majority (50.8%) would still opt to hire the employee, assuming that it was profitable to do so. Clearly, the high level of the salary demand prompted some misgivings in our respondents. Two intergroup differences are of significance here. First, on question 9 older students were more inclined to consider legal implications before acting than were

Table 24.8 Response summary for question 9

Response	Frequency (%)
Hire him	55.0
Hire, if legal	17.5
Hire, if profitable	4.0
Don't hire, increase research and development	7.5
Don't hire, unqualified	8.9
Wait, monitor competition	2.0
Depends on industry practice	0.4

Table 24.9 Response summary for question 10

Response	Frequency (%)
Hire him	7.9
Hire, if profitable	42.9
Hire, if at competitive salary (i.e. don't hire)	11.3
Don't hire, questionable loyalty	3.6
Don't hire	26.6

their younger counterparts (significant at the 0.01 level). This perhaps reflects an increased awareness of legal ramifications (that indeed may exist) on the part of older students. Second, on question 10, women and men differed significantly in their willingness to hire the employee under the modified circumstances (at approximately the 0.05 level), with women being less inclined to hire.

Comparison of the response patterns for questions 9 and 10 along with the questions themselves leads to the following conclusions. In question 10 a high salary is specified, suggesting a purchase of information as well as an employee (Table 24.9). This caused: (1) respondents to choose don't hire options in strikingly greater numbers (41.5% versus 16.4%), and (2) among those who would still hire the employee, many more apparently delve into the economics of the situation before hiring; this suggests no higher ethical standard, but simply an increased awareness that costs may exceed benefits when the price goes up.

Question 11 asked the respondent what s/he would do as a middle manager when s/he discovered that the company's executives had given false testimony before a governmental agency. As Table 24.10 shows, 28.3% gave responses that fit into the loyalty category, 44.0% gave responses that fit into the voice category, and 6.6% gave responses that fit into the exit category. The only intergroup difference of significance is for students with graduate degrees versus all others. In this case nearly 30% of those with undergraduate degrees only chose the loyalty response compared to less than 19% for those with graduate degrees. (This difference reaches statistical significance at the 0.1 level, but not quite at the 0.05 level.)

Table 24.10 Response summary for question 11

Response	Frequency (%)
Pure loyalty	28.3
Internal voice	22.9
External voice	21.1
Total voice	44.0
Exit	6.6
Here the four general categories are composites from the following raw responses:	
Do nothing (loyalty)	
Do nothing, bad politics (loyalty)	
Do nothing unless it affects me directly (loyalty)	
Confidentially discuss with superior (voice, internal)	
Pressure executive, expose him if necessary (voice, internal)	
Leak information to outside party (voice, external)	
Disclose the information (voice, external)	
Resign (exit)	
Depends on the issue (no category)	
Other	

Note: 21.2% of the responses fell into the last two categories just above

Question 12 places the respondent in three separate positions within the organizational hierarchy: president, middle level manager, and entry level manager. The respondent is asked to indicate what s/he would do after learning of an unsuspected potentially harmful flaw in one of the company's products. The tendency for respondents to choose "action or voice" options did not change much with changes in organizational authority, but the strength of their preferred response did; strong responses (action or voice) were almost universal at the "president" level (as Table 24.11 shows) – chosen with an 88.8% frequency – but considerably less common at the middle and entry levels. At these lower levels, respondents chose less strong voice options, commensurate with their reduced power in the organization. Finally, exit responses were uncommon as were loyalty or "economically expedient" responses. (There were no statistically significant intergroup differences for this question.)

Question 13 asked the respondent to indicate what s/he would do as a middle level manager upon learning that one of the company's recalled products was to be sold to the government of an African country. As Table 24.12 shows, the response pattern is a bit different from that seen for some of the earlier questions. Specifically, although nearly one quarter of the responses fall into the loyalty category, exit responses are up compared to earlier response patterns (11.5% compared to 6.6% for question 11). Further, there are more intergroup differences than we have seen heretofore.

The gender differences are the most striking for this question. First, more than 15% of the women in the sample indicated that they would leave the organization, while less than 10% of the men selected the same option. This difference is statistically significant at the 0.1 level but not quite significant at the 0.05 level. Second, nearly

Table 24.11 Response summary for question 12

Response	Frequency (%) (1)	(2)	(3)
Stop production	88.1	32.6	29.9
Stop production indirectly	0.7	3.8	4.1
Voice	5.9	57.3	58.3
Exit	0.5	2.7	3.4
Loyalty or economic expediency	3.1	2.5	3.0

The five composite categories above were developed from the following raw responses:
(Try to) Stop production (stop production)
(Try to) Stop production, publicize (stop production)
Inform superiors (voice)
Lobby for production halt (voice)
Do nothing (economic expediency)
Halt production only if not profitable (economic expediency)
Do as ordered (N.A., loyalty)
Resign (N.A., exit)

Table 24.12 Response summary for question 13

Response	Frequency (%)
Loyalty	23.2
Voice, external	19.6
Voice, internal	22.5
Voice, ambiguous	14.5
Total voice	56.5
Exit	11.5

The five categories above were developed from the following response categories:
Do nothing (loyalty)
If the foreign government is aware, do nothing (loyalty)
If the foreign government is unaware, inform it (voice, external)
Leak to an outsider (voice, external)
Question publicly (voice, external)
Voice opposition through channels (voice, internal)
Discuss with top management (voice, internal)
Try to stop sale (voice, ambiguous)
Resign in protest (exit)

26% of the men surveyed chose the loyalty response compared to less than 18% of the women surveyed. This difference is statistically significant at the 0.05 level.

The other intergroup difference pertains to age. Those respondents under age 30 were considerably more likely to chose the loyalty response compared to their older counterparts (approximately 25% versus approximately 16%). This difference is statistically significant at the 0.05 level.

Question 14 asked the respondent what s/he would do after learning of confidential information that, were it disclosed, obviously would be judged as unethical by the

Table 24.13 Response summary for question 14

Response	Frequency (%)
Loyalty	22.0
Voice, external	22.0
Voice, internal	25.7
Total voice	47.7
Exit	28.1
Judge the situation myself	15.7

The five categories above were developed from the following raw responses:
Do nothing (loyalty)
Read and burn (loyalty)
Do nothing if common behavior (loyalty)
Leak to outsider (voice, external)
Disclose publicly, resign (voice, external, exit)
Talk to superior (voice, internal)
Keep in house, correct problem (voice, internal)
Resign (exit)
Personally judge ethical value

public. As Table 24.13 shows, the response pattern is affected by the respondent's position in the organizational hierarchy, in that while the frequency of the loyalty response is roughly equivalent to that seen for other questions (22%), the frequency of the exit response jumps substantially (28.1%). Note, too, that the responses required that we add another category, "judge the ethical situation personally." Finally, the only significant intergroup difference that obtains is between students with graduate degrees and those with undergraduate degrees only. In this case more than 22% of the students with undergraduate degrees only chose the loyalty option compared to just over 12% of those with graduate degrees. This result is significant at the 0.05 level. (Note: although the differences were not statistically significant, men and women as well as older and younger students differed in a direction consistent with what we found for other questions. Nearly 24% of the men chose the loyalty response compared to less than 19% of the women. Only 17% of the students over age 30 chose the loyalty response compared to nearly 24% of their younger counterparts.)

Question 15 placed the respondent on the board of directors and asked her/him what s/he would do upon learning of an illegal political campaign contribution made with company money by the CEO and chairman of the board. As Table 24.14 shows, the response pattern is consistent with those found for many of the earlier questions. When the responses are collapsed we see that roughly one quarter of the responses fit into the loyalty option. Further, just over half of the responses fit into the voice category (55.2%). Finally, a small percentage of the responses fall into the exit category (6.7%). (No statistically significant intergroup differences obtained for this question.)

Table 24.14 Response summary for question 15

Response	Frequency (%)
Loyalty	26.2
Voice, external	16.6
Voice, internal	38.6
Total voice	55.2
Exit	6.7

The four response categories above were drawn from the following raw responses:
Do nothing (loyalty)
Go public (voice, external)
Leak information (voice, external)
Expose/resign (voice, external, exit)
Confront, blow whistle internally (voice, internal)
Consider his dismissal (voice, internal)
Force resignation (voice, internal)
Argue against in closed meeting (voice, internal)
Resign (exit)

Table 24.15 Summary of responses for questions tapping Hirschman's taxonomy

	Question number									
Response category	8a	8b	8c	11	12a	12b	12c	13	14	15
Voice – pure, strong, external – or action	15.4	19.8	25.5	21.1	88.8	36.4	34.0	19.6	22.0	16.6
Voice – modified, weak, internal	10.6	11.5	12.6	22.9	5.9	57.3	58.3	22.5	25.7	38.6
Total voice	26.0	31.3	38.1	44.0	94.7	93.7	92.3	56.6	47.7	55.2
Pure loyalty or economic expediency	22.5	19.1	14.9	28.3	3.1	2.5	3.0	23.2	22.0	26.2
Modified loyalty	47.6	45.3	40.9	–	–	–	–	–	–	–
Total loyalty	70.1	64.4	55.8	28.3	3.1	2.5	3.0	23.2	22.0	26.2
Exit	–	–	–	6.6	0.5	2.7	3.4	11.5	28.1	6.7

Note: Numbers in the table are percentages

Summary

The salient features of the response patterns to our hypothetical situations, as reflected in Table 24.15 below, can be summarized as follows.

1. Responses that reflect pure loyalty (or economic expedience) are infrequent overall – in only two cases do they constitute more than 25% of all responses. This suggests that, overall, most respondents faced these ethically questionable situations with some measure of protest, whether in the form of voice, exit, or modified loyalty. This result must be viewed as encouraging.

2. Exit responses are an infrequent form of protest; in only two cases were the exit responses greater than 10%.
3. The "product safety" related question (12) elicited the highest number of voice responses (pure and total) and the lowest number of loyalty responses (pure and total). This corresponds well with the responses to question 1 in which respondents ranked product safety as the most important issue.
4. The response pattern for question 8 yields some striking results. Specifically, these questions:

   (a) ranked lowest in overall voice responses
   (b) ranked lowest in overall exit responses
   (c) ranked highest in overall loyalty responses (albeit with a substantial component of "modified loyalty" which gives some vent for disagreement or some substitute for "voice").

   These personal "equity" issues may elicit more loyalty and less protest (either through "exit" or "voice") because of the moral ambiguity associated with equity issues – respondents may be uncertain as to what is right or wrong.
5. Overall, our respondents displayed a strong tendency to take action in those situations in which they were witnesses to unethical behavior, regardless of their level of authority. Whether they would expect others to do the same we did not attempt to ascertain. Consequently, we are unable to state whether our findings support or conflict with that of Krakhardt et al. (1985) that their respondents did not consider failure to report unethical behavior unethical itself.
6. On balance, women differed from men in their tendency to protest by being less likely to: "do as ordered," "do nothing," "be loyal," or hire in an ethically questionable environment. In addition, they displayed a greater willingness to "exit" than did men.
7. On balance, we observed very little difference in the response patterns according to age.
8. On balance, students with graduate degrees were less likely to choose loyalty options than were their counterparts with undergraduate degrees only.

Conclusions

We asked in the tide of our study, "Will the ethics of business change?" Although it is hazardous to forecast behavior from expressed attitudes, we think that a tentative forecast is warranted here. On the basis of the results of our survey we feel that there is reason to be optimistic. The attitudes of future executives suggest that they are persons who may fit well into what Neilson (1984) refers to as the "manager as institution citizen." The three identifying characteristics of this ideal type manager are as follows:

1. Independent thinking and judgment
2. Resistance to evil ideal types
3. Acting with a civic orientation.

The future executives in our study display a sensitivity toward ethical issues that is tempered primarily by their perceived organizational authority and the requisites of the prevailing organizational culture. This sensitivity is particularly strong among women MBA students, as they display a greater tendency to take action when they perceive a questionable business practice than do their male counterparts. As women managers become commonplace it may well follow that corporate behavioral norms will be affected positively.

Appendix

1. The following is a list of ethical issue categories that have been discussed in the popular and/or business press. By checking the appropriate box please indicate how much attention you feel that the business community should give to each of the issue categories.

	Great deal Attention	Considerable Attention	Some Attention	Little Attention	No Attention
a. (1) Product information disclosure to consumers	[ ]	[ ]	[ ]	[ ]	[ ]
(2) Information disclosure regarding operations to stockholders	[ ]	[ ]	[ ]	[ ]	[ ]
b. Employment practices:					
(1) Minority hiring/ promotions	[ ]	[ ]	[ ]	[ ]	[ ]
(2) Comparable worth	[ ]	[ ]	[ ]	[ ]	[ ]
(3) Arbitrary discharges	[ ]	[ ]	[ ]	[ ]	[ ]
c. Product quality	[ ]	[ ]	[ ]	[ ]	[ ]
d. Product safety	[ ]	[ ]	[ ]	[ ]	[ ]
e. Firms' relations with foreign governments	[ ]	[ ]	[ ]	[ ]	[ ]
f. Community relations	[ ]	[ ]	[ ]	[ ]	[ ]
g. Rights of employees to disclose company wrong doing	[ ]	[ ]	[ ]	[ ]	[ ]
h. Bribery of Government officials	[ ]	[ ]	[ ]	[ ]	[ ]
i. Executive compensation	[ ]	[ ]	[ ]	[ ]	[ ]
j. Dealing with apartheid in South Africa	[ ]	[ ]	[ ]	[ ]	[ ]
k. Plant closures	[ ]	[ ]	[ ]	[ ]	[ ]
l. Other (please specify)	[ ]	[ ]	[ ]	[ ]	[ ]

2. How would you compare your own ethical standards to those of:

	Much Higher Than	Higher Than	About the Same as	Lower Than	Much Lower Than
Your fellow MBA students	[ ]	[ ]	[ ]	[ ]	[ ]
Current business executives	[ ]	[ ]	[ ]	[ ]	[ ]

Past peers	[ ]	[ ]	[ ]	[ ]	[ ]
Past supervisors	[ ]	[ ]	[ ]	[ ]	[ ]
Current business school faculty members	[ ]	[ ]	[ ]	[ ]	[ ]

3. Publicly held firms are required by law to give primacy to the financial interests of their stockholders. Below is a list of various corporate constituencies/stakeholder groups. Putting aside the apparent legal mandate, please indicate by ranking the groups the order in which constituency interests ought to be served by the firm. (A rank of 1 indicates first place for the affected group.)

[ ] Stockholders
[ ] Society-at-large
[ ] The local community in which the firm operates
[ ] Neighbors in close proximity to the firm's operations
[ ] Customers
[ ] Employees
[ ] Governmental agencies
[ ] Suppliers

4. There is good reason to believe that business practices are more ethical today than 10 years ago.

Strongly agree	Agree	Uncertain	Disagree	Strongly disagree
[ ]	[ ]	[ ]	[ ]	[ ]

5. There is good reason to believe that business practices are likely to be more ethical 10 years from now compared to today.

Strongly agree	Agree	Uncertain	Disagree	Strongly disagree
[ ]	[ ]	[ ]	[ ]	[ ]

6. Do you believe that corporate ethical norms ought to be upgraded?

[ ] Yes
[ ] No
[ ] Uncertain

If you answered yes, please answer question 7, otherwise move to question 8.

7. How would you propose that the upgrading of corporate ethical norms be accomplished?

Now we are going to ask you to respond to a series of 8 hypothetical situations. Try to place yourself in each of the situations.

8. What would you do if…

… you were told by your superior to pressure a 62 year old employee into early retirement in order to:

1. make room for a younger employee
2. make room for a member of a minority race; or
3. save the firm the cost of full benefits.

The employee, once productive but now worth considerably less than his salary, has been with the firm for 30 years.

9. … as the president of a company in a highly competitive industry, you learn that a competitor has made an important scientific discovery that will substantially reduce, but not eliminate, your profit for about a year? There is a possibility of hiring one of the competitor's employees who knows the details of the discovery.
10. … In the previous situation, the employee, an engineer with 5 years of experience, was asking a guaranteed annual salary of $100 000 for the 5 years.
11. Suppose that you, a middle level executive, discovered that one of your company's executives had given false testimony before a governmental agency and that there appeared to be no action forthcoming by top management to deal with the situation. What action, if any, would you take?
12. Suppose that you, (a) as president of the company, (b) as a middle manager, (c) as an entry level manager, discovered an unsuspected flaw in one of your company's products and that if the product were to be marketed a higher than expected incidence of serious injuries to consumers would result. What action would you take?
13. Suppose that a governmental agency ordered your company to withdraw a highly profitable product from the U.S. market because of safety concerns. You, as a middle level manager, learn that top management has decided to sell the product to the government of an African nation. What action would you take?
14. Suppose that you as an entry level manager were given access to confidential information that if disclosed would show your company to be engaging in what would obviously be judged by the public as unethical behavior. What action would you take?
15. Suppose that as a member of a board of directors you learned that the chairman of the board and CEO had made an illegal contribution of company money to a recent presidential candidate. The contribution appears to have been given in exchange for future government contracts. What would you do?

The following questions are for statistical classification purposes only.

16. Age ______
17. Sex: M______ F______
18. Highest education level attained prior to entering M.B.A. program

    BA., B.S. _______
    Masters _______
    J.D. _______
    Ph.D. _______
    Other _______

19. Area of concentration in the M.B.A program (please specify)
20. Years of full-time work experience _______
21. Approximate annual income immediately prior to entering the M.B.A program __________

Thank you for your cooperation in completing the survey.

References

Baumhart, Raymond C. 1961. How ethical are businessmen? *Harvard Business Review* 6–19: 156–176.

Beltramini, Richard F., Robert A. Peterson, and George Kozmetsky. 1984. Concerns of college students regarding business ethics. *Journal of Business Ethics* 3: 195–200.

Brenner, Steven N., and Earl A. Molander. 1977. Is the ethics of business changing? *Harvard Business Review* 35: 57–71.

Carroll, Archie B. 1975. Managerial ethics: A post-Watergate view. *Business Horizons* 18: 75–80.

Cavanaugh, Gerald F. 1984. *American business values*, 2nd ed. Englewood Cliffs: Prentice-Hall.

Clinard, Marshal B. 1983. *Corporate ethics and crime: The role of middle management*. Beverly Hills: Sage Publications.

Davis, Keith, William C. Frederick, and Robert L. Blomstrom. 1980. *Business and society: Concepts and policy issues*, 4th ed. New York: McGraw-Hill.

DeGeorge, Richard T. 1982. *Business ethics*. New York: Macmillan Publishing Company.

Hirschman, Albert O. 1970. *Exit, voice, and loyalty*. Cambridge: Harvard University Press.

Krakhardt, David, Sharon McCarthy, and Dick Wittink. 1985. What makes it unethical? Determinants of ethical evaluation in business. Paper presented at the Academy of Management Annual Meeting, San Diego.

Lipset, Seymour M. and William Schneider. 1980. The confidence gap: Business, labor, and government in the public mind. New York: Free Press.

Matthews, John B., Kenneth E. Goodpaster, and Laura L. Nash. 1985. *Policies and persons: A casebook in business ethics*. New York: McGraw-Hill.

Molander, Earl A. 1980. Responsive capitalism: Case studies in corporate social conduct. New York: McGraw-Hill.

Neilson, Richard P. 1984. Toward an active philosophy for management based on Arendt and Tillich. *Journal of Business Ethics* 3: 153–161.

Posner, Barry Z., and Warren H. Schmidt. 1984. Values and the American manager: An update. *California Management Review* 26(3): 202–216.

Silk, Leonard, and David Vogel. 1976. *Ethics and profits: The crisis of confidence in American business*. New York: Simon and Schuster.

Steiner, George A., and John F. Steiner. 1985. *Business, government and society: A managerial perspective*, 4th ed. New York: Random House.

Sturdivant, Frederick D. 1985. *Business and society: A managerial approach*, 3rd ed. Homewood: Richard D. Irwin.

Trawick, Fred, and William R. Darden. 1980. Marketers' perceptions of ethical standards in the marketing profession: Educators and practitioners. *The Review of Business and Economic Research* 16(1): 1–17.

Trevino, Linda Klebe. 1986. Ethical decision making in organizations: A person situation interactionist model. *Academy of Management Review* 11: 601–617.

Tuleja, Tad. 1985. *Beyond the bottom line: How business leaders are turning principles into profits*. New York: Facts on File Publications.

Velasquez, Manuel G. 1982. *Business ethics: Concepts and cases*. Englewood Cliffs: Prentice-Hall.

Chapter 25
Situational Ethics: An Empirical Study of Differentiators of Student Attitudes

Charles W. McNichols and Thomas W. Zimmerer

Introduction

The philosopher Aristotle, in his discussion of the 'road of the mean', emphasized that for every virtue there were two vices. These vices represented the two extremes that bounded the road of the mean. The road, we imagine, could be very broad indeed. There was no defined absolute standard, but a standard that emphasized the need to avoid the excesses or extremes of behavior. The actual path may be twisted at times or even distorted by society, its leaders and the leaders of our major institutions of society.

Few Americans would subscribe to the philosophical doctrines of Nietzsche who emphasized the right of the strong to dominate the weak. Yet, with very little insight into the workings of our society we must conclude that for the past our society, like others, has reflected a domination of the powerful over the weak. Power is an essential element for effective administration of any system, be it a business or society in general. The rich and powerful do possess more economic power than the poor; they also possess more political influence and, definitely, the capability to structure sociological relationships. Rules are just and equitable, to most, because we are a 'nation of laws.' However, those laws were written, legislated, approved and enforced by an extremely small segment of our society. Economic policies are chosen, enacted and carried out by a select handful of citizens. Though an unpopular idea at first glance, the strong (powerful) do dominate the weak.

From whom, then, do ethics flow? Have ethics become, or have they always been, a product of the values and behaviors of the powerful of a society? The powerful, be they kings, presidents, priests or corporate executives do actively work to 'set the

C.W. McNichols • T.W. Zimmerer (unable to contact)

A.C. Michalos and D.C. Poff (eds.), *Citation Classics from the Journal of Business Ethics*, Advances in Business Ethics Research 2,
DOI 10.1007/978-94-007-4126-3_25, © Springer Science+Business Media B.V. 2013

rules of the game.' Laws, religious values, moral doctrine are never traced to the masses, but to a small or even singular force.

The shape and direction of Aristotle's road of the mean seems to be shaped by a continuously interacting societal dynamic which is not guided by a singular force, but evolves gradually as men and events crash together through what we call history. Ethics evolve. For the most part, this evolutionary process has probably made more humane the recommended behaviors of society as well as increased, over all, the standard practiced by men and women.

The authors have no delusions; the high standards of ethical behavior we now enjoy are, to a very large measure, a product of our superior economic conditions, if thrown without notice into an economic catstrophy which ripped away our fundamental security, would we find our society continuing to adhere to the same high ethical standards, or would it evolve downward toward its so recent past? Little more than a century ago we found slavery an acceptable and necessary element of our life. The American people found it quite acceptable to slaughter or cage the original inhabitants of our land 'in the name of progress.' The ethical standards of our Protestant forefathers did not seem to find the loss of life of 'savages' as important as new land, opportunity and potential wealth.

The powerful in government, commerce and religion spoke out loudly through their actions or lack of action. Ethical standards are living values. They represent a vital and critical guiding force in the functioning of our society.

For years, colleges and universities have struggled with how to 'teach' the subject of ethics. Few would argue that an understanding of philosophy and its impact on the shaping of our values and behavior is an essential element of education, but how does one know what the real meaning of the 'road of the mean' is? Is ethics, like beauty, in the eye of the beholder? The world which surrounds each of us is viewed in so many different ways. Ethics is not something which we can take out to examine or separate neatly from our daily activities.

Stace suggested that "any ethical position which is equally applicable to all men at all times may fairly be called a species of ethical relativity" (Stace 1979). Ethical absolutists would hold that every real work situation can be judged in terms of a standard which is both universal and unchanging. The authors are not philosophers, but professors of management who are both concerned for the quality of decisions which managers make and are interested in measuring the responses of future managers when presented with a variety of questionable ethical situations. In each of these situations, the ethical absolutist would deem the actions as unethical. Brenner and Molander (1977) published in the *Harvard Business Review* an article entitled, 'Is the Ethics of Business Changing?' The conclusions of this article are:

> Respondents are somewhat more cynical about the ethical conduct of their peers than they were.
>
> Most respondents favored ethical codes, although they strongly prefer general precept codes to specific practice codes.
>
> There is substantial disagreement among respondents as to whether ethical standards in business today have changed from what they were.

In our study we were interested in measuring any differences that might exist between how potential managers (students) responded to a series of ethically questionable situations, and how they feel society and business managers would judge the behavior. By examining these students attitudes, we may gain insights into the likely behavior of our future leaders, as well as expand on the work of Brenner and Molander.

Specific Research Issues

The following specific research questions were investigated in the study:

1. Do male and female students differ in their attitudes toward the ethical acceptability of behaviors in specific situations?
2. Are attitudes toward the ethical acceptability influenced by the sex of the individual exhibiting the behavior?
3. Do male and female students' attitudes toward the ethical acceptability of behavior depend on whether the individual is of the same versus the opposite sex?
4. Do business majors differ in their attitudes toward what constitutes ethical behavior from other academic majors?
5. Does the strength of spiritual/religious beliefs affect attitudes toward the acceptability of behavior?
6. Do individual attitudes toward what constitutes ethical behavior differ from perceptions of what society or the business managers will accept?

Research Design

The study was based on an instrument consisting of narrative descriptions of ten situations involving an ethical question, along with demographics and a question eliciting a self-report of the strength of spiritual/religious beliefs. A typical situation is presented in Fig. 25.1.

The remaining descriptions presented the following situations:

1. A theft of money left in an unlocked car committed by an unemployed individual with a sick child.
2. Providing a female companion for a recently divorced business client who is about to award a big advertising contract.
3. Hinting that a competitor for a promotion has had a drinking problem.
4. Creating a phony church to avoid income taxes.
5. Failing to call overcharges paid by a customer to the customer's attention.
6. Using company time, materials, and equipment to prepare a church bulletin.
7. See Fig. 25.1.
8. Using the company WATS line to make personal telephone calls.

Fig. 25.1 Example situation description

Situation 7: David works at a factory that uses a time clock. Each and every person is required to punch in and out. Employees are not allowed to punch in more than 10 minutes before 8:00 AM, the starting time. On Friday, he arrives a half-hour early, but doesn't punch in until 8:00 AM. Quitting time is 5:00PM but he wants to leave early to begin his weekend. David knows that it is a company violation to have someone 'punch you out,' but he feels that by 4:30 PM, he has already put in an 8 hour day. David convinces Ralph to punch him out at 5:00 PM, knowing that both of them could lose their jobs if Ralph is caught punching him out.

9. Admitting under-age teenagers into an X-rated drive-in movie theater.
10. An athlete endorsing a real estate development that is know to be a 'rip-off'.

Each respondent was asked to provide three opinions about the acceptability of the behavior described in the situation:

What is your opinion about this person's behavior in this situation?
What is your opinion about how our society would judge this person's behavior?
What is your opinion about how business would judge this situation?

Each of the resulting 30 responses involved a four point scale with values of (A) Acceptable: (SA) Somewhat Acceptable; (SU) Somewhat Unacceptable; and (U) Unacceptable.

Four versions of the instrument were used in the study. For the first, the names of individuals in all ten of the situations were clearly male. The second version used all female names. The third and fourth versions alternated the gender of the names, beginning with the male name in the third version and a female name in the fourth.

The sample consisted of 1,178 randomly selected undergraduate students. 1,130 usable responses were obtained. The question concerning strength of religious belief received 912 responses, and this sample was used in correlation analysis. Basic sample statistics follow:

Males: (47%)		Females: (53%)	
Business Majors: (38%)		Other Majors: (62%)	
Version 1: (17%)	2: (29%)	3: (30%)	4: (24%)

Response patterns were examined using contingency tables. Then, t-Tests and correlation coefficients were evaluated after converting the responses to a numeric scale, with (1) representing acceptable; (2) somewhat acceptable; (3) somewhat unacceptable behavior, and (4) unacceptable.

Results

General Results

Mean responses for the 30 questions (10 situations × 3 opinions) ranged from 2.2 to 3.5,with standard deviations between 0.78 and 1.1.The mean scores are summarized in Table 25.1.Means of three or greater represent a population view of the behavior as unacceptable.

The mean response to the strength of spiritual/religious belief question was 6.12 with a standard deviation of 1.9. These results suggest that the sample includes a substantial diversity of opinion concerning the ethics of the reported behaviors, as well as a substantial range of strength of religious beliefs.

Correlations among the 30 questions ranged from 0.0000 to 0.53, with the highest correlations among the personal, societal, and business opinions for the same situation. The highest correlation among opinions on different situations was 0.42. However, most such correlations were below 0.10 and statistically insignificant. As a consequence, this paper discusses univariate results.

Male/Female Differences

Three sets of t-Tests were used to examine male/female response differences.

(a) Overall acceptability of behavior scores – male/female examples: To perform this test, mean scores were formed for responses to each of the 30 items for the questionnaires describing behavior of a male and for the questionnaires describing the behavior of a female. Two sample T-Tests comparing the opinions of

Table 25.1 Sample means ($N = 1{,}130$)

	Opinions		
Situation	Personal	Society's	Business
1	3.33	3.18	3.48
2	2.59	2.63	2.23
3	3.20	2.99	2.79
4	3.21	3.10	2.91
5	2.83	2.77	2.36
6	2.86	2.54	3.22
7	2.85	2.65	3.35
8	3.04	2.83	3.21
9	2.96	3.10	2.48
10	2.76	2.76	2.34

male/female behavior yielded 11 results significant at the 5% level or better. Two of these were in the personal opinion questions, four were in the opinion of how society would view the behavior, and five were in the views of how business would view the behavior. There is some evidence in these results that respondents think society and the business world have different views of the acceptability of behavior for males and females. However, the absolute magnitudes of the differences in means were small (0.2 or less), and were not consistent in direction: the male behavior was seen as more unacceptable than the female in roughly 50% of the significant comparisons.

(b) Composite scores – male/female behavior: For this test, the two questionnaire formats describing the behavior of a mixture of individuals with names of alternating gender were used. Composite scores, formed by summing the respondent's personal view of the acceptability of behavior for the five male and five female examples, were compared with a paired t-Tests. It was thus possible to look for respondents' tendencies to find either male or female behavior more unacceptable. Summing five questions results in 20 point scales, and the following t-Test results:

Mean acceptability score (male behavior described): 14.7478
Mean acceptability score (female behavior described): 14.6547
Mean paired difference: 0.1031, significance level: 0.303

In this case, no significant sex bias is indicated.

(c) Sex match/mismatch between respondent and individual described in the example: Reported acceptability of described behavior was compared between situations where the sex of the respondent matched the sex of the individual in the example and situations where the sex did not match. The same two questionnaire formats described in (b) were used. All 30 responses were separately examined with two – sample t-Tests. The objective here was to compare respondents' judgement of the behavior of their own sex with their judgment of behavior of the opposite sex. The largest of these 30 mean-differences was significant at $p=0.048$, and this was the only difference significant at greater then the 10% level. Again, no sex bias is suggested by the data.

Differences Among Business/Non-business Majors

Mean scores for each of the 30 items were computed for respondents from the College of Commerce and Industry and for all other academic units. There were five differences significant at the 5% level or below, although the mean scores on the four point scale in these cases differed only by a tenth of a point. The five significant differences involved three in which business majors were more negative

Table 25.2 Sample correlations: religious belief and opinions of ethical acceptability ($N=912$)

Situation	Opinions Personal	Society's	Business
1	0.12[a]	−0.02	0.06
2	0.13[a]	−0.08	−0.07
3	0.11[a]	−0.01	−0.05
4	0.21[a]	0.04	0.01
5	0.08	0.05	−0.09[b]
6	0.05	−0.01	0.06
7	0.13[a]	−0.01	0.12[a]
8	0.17[a]	0.01	0.07
9	0.21[a]	0.04	−0.04
10	0.15[a]	0.09[b]	−0.04

[a] Significant at $p<0.0005$
[b] Significant at $p<0.01$

about the ethics of a behavior than the non-business majors, so no clear trend is indicated by these differences.

Impact of Spiritual/Religious Beliefs

Table 25.2 summarizes sample correlation coefficients comparing religious belief with expressed opinions of ethical acceptability for the ten situations.

The most significant correlations are between individual strength of religious belief and attitude toward the ethical acceptability of behavior reported in a situation. A significant positive correlation means that more strongly expressed religious belief implies a more negative attitude toward the reported behavior. It is interesting to note that the strength of a respondent's religious beliefs seems to impact personal attitudes about the behavior, but does not seem to color his or her perceptions of what society or the business community will think about the behavior.

Comparison of Personal/Societal/Business Attitudes

To look for significant differences among the three responses provided for each situation, paired t-Tests were used comparing the personal/societal, personal/business, and societal/business responses for each individual. Twenty-seven of the resulting differences were significant at $p<0.0005$, one was significant at the 3% level and two were insignificant. Respondents generally judged each behavior more harshly from an ethical standpoint than they thought society as a whole or the business world would judge the behavior. Respondents also thought society would have a more negative attitude toward behavior in most of the examples than the business community.

Discussion

While the survey results show substantial variation in individual attitudes toward ethics, and in opinions of society's and the business world's attitudes toward this subject, little explanation of the source of these differences was obtained from the study.

Major study objectives included investigating differences in the acceptability of behavior based on sex of the respondent and of the individual exhibiting the behavior, strength of religious beliefs, and academic major. There is a pattern suggesting that strength of religious belief affects individual opinions of what is acceptable, but not the view of what society as a whole or the business world will view as acceptable. The study did not find evidence of ethics differences based on sex or academic major.

The researchers had hypothesized that the sex of the person involved in the ethically questionable action would produce statistically significant differences. The age and educational level of the participants may have influenced the results. It may be that for these persons there no longer exists a dual code of ethics. The researchers intend to investigate the same issues with participants who are older.

Further, the image of business as less ethical than society as a whole generally held by nonbusiness students in the 1960s and 1970s seems to have evaporated. The researchers can only surmise that the animosity and distrust which was held by students toward business no longer exists.

Individuals tended to report a more negative personal view of behavior in the ten example situations than they thought either society or the business world would have. It is interesting to speculate on whether this is the result of social desirability, or accurately reflects personal ethics which are stronger than those believed to exist in society and the business community.

Future analysis of these data will look in more detail at specific situations, since some of these have stronger business or societal implications than others and, as a consequence, variables explaining attitudes toward behavior may differ among the situations.

References

Brenner, Steven N., and Earl A. Molander. 1977. Is the ethics of business changing. *Harvard Business Review* 55: 57–71.

Stace, Walter T. 1979. In *Ethical relativity and ethical absolution in ethical issues in business*, ed. T. Donaldson and P.H. Werhand, 82. Englewood Cliffs: Prentice-Hall.

Chapter 26
The Relationship Between Corporate Social Performance, and Organizational Size, Financial Performance, and Environmental Performance: An Empirical Examination

Peter A. Stanwick and Sarah D. Stanwick

Introduction

An area that has received an increased focus of attention is the corporate social performance (CSP) of organizations (i.e. Carroll 1979; Wartick and Cochran 1985; Wood 1991a, b). Previous work has focused primarily on the relationship between CSP and financial performance (i.e. Anderson and Frankle 1980; Ingram and Frazier 1980; McGuire et al. 1988). This study builds on this existing research base by examining the relationship between corporate social performance and three organizational variables: organizational size, financial performance and environmental performance.

Theoretical Background

Corporate Social Performance

Wood (1991a) describes Corporate Social Performance (CSP) as being comprised of three major components. The first component is the level of corporate social responsibility which is based on legitimacy within society, public responsibility within the organization, and managerial discretion by each individual within the organization.

P.A. Stanwick(✉)
Department of Management, Auburn University,
415 W. Magnolia, Auburn, AL 36849-5241, USA
e-mail: pstanwick@cob-1.business.auburn.edu

S.D. Stanwick
School of Accountancy, Auburn University,
415 W. Magnolia, Auburn, AL 36849-5241, USA

A.C. Michalos and D.C. Poff (eds.), *Citation Classics from the Journal of Business Ethics*, Advances in Business Ethics Research 2,
DOI 10.1007/978-94-007-4126-3_26, © Springer Science+Business Media B.V. 2013

The second component is the processes of corporate social responsiveness which includes environmental assessment, stakeholder management and issues management. The third component refers to the outcomes of corporate behavior and includes social impacts, social programs, and social policies. As a result, CSP is a critical factor to consider for all organizations since CSP components such as: "(s)ocial issues, environmental pressures, stakeholder concerns are sure to affect corporate decision making and behavior far into the future" (Wood 1991b, p. 400).

Corporate Social Performance and Financial Performance

Previous research on the relationship between CSP and financial performance has provided conflicting results. A positive relationship has been identified in a number of studies (i.e. Bowman 1978; Fry and Hock 1976; Preston 1978; Anderson and Frankle 1980; Belkaoui 1976). This research supports the view that the cost of having a high level of corporate social responsibility is more than offset by the increased benefits in employee morale and productivity (Soloman and Hansen 1985). However, additional studies have found a negative relationship (i.e. Ingram and Frazier 1980; Freedman and Jaggi 1982). This research supports the view that the costs of being socially responsible forces the firm into an unfavorable financial position versus firms that are not socially responsive (Aupperle et al. 1985).

One explanation why these studies may have yielded inconsistent results could be the method in which the social performance variable has been measured (Ullmann 1985). However, a number of recent studies (i.e. McGuire et al. 1988; Fombrun and Shanley 1990; Thomas and Simerly 1994) have been consistent in the use of the same variable to measure corporate social performance. This measurement variable is the *Fortune* Corporate Reputation Index.

The Use of the Corporate Reputation Index as a Measurement of CSP

In a number of recent studies, the firm's corporate reputation has been used as a measurement of CSP (i.e. McGuire et al. 1988; Fombrun and Shanley 1990; Thomas and Simerly 1994). The firms corporate reputation is based on *Fortune*'s Corporate Reputation Index. Using the Corporate Reputation Index, both McGuire et al. (1988) and Fombrun and Shanley (1990) found a positive relationship between CSP and financial performance.

However, Fryxell and Wang (1994) warn that there will be a strong relationship between the Corporate Reputation Index and the firm's financial performance since, they argue, the Corporate Reputation Index is heavily weighted based on the financial position of the firm. Therefore, a fundamental question that needs to be addressed is whether the Corporate Reputation Index is a valid measurement of a firm's corporate social performance. By examining the relationship between CSP and three organizational variables, including the firm's environmental performance, the results of this study will provide empirical support as to whether the Corporate Reputation Index does indeed represent the firm's environmental commitment.

Corporate Size and Corporate Social Performance

Based on past research, it is expected that the size of the firm will play a role in the firm's CSP (i.e. Dierkes and Coppock 1978; Trotman and Bradley 1981). Larger firms receive a high level of attention from the general public, which may, in turn, "encourage" the firms to have a higher level of CSP. In their study, Fombrun and Shanley (1990) found that larger firms had a higher value of their Corporate Reputation Index. As a result, it is expected that larger firms would have a higher level of CSP.

Corporate Social Performance and Environmental Performance

Based on the principles of corporate social responsibility (Wood 1991a), it is expected that one of the critical components in the measurement of CSP will be based on the environmental performance of the organization. This is supported by research conducted by Poduska et al. (1992) and Reilly (1992). In examining the social responsibility at Eastman Kodak, Poduska et al. (1992) found that Kodak made a conscious effort to reduce the level of pollution emissions through technological innovations. Reilly (1992) also supports this relationship by examining the pollution reduction activities at Minnesota Mining and Manufacturing.

In this study, environmental performance of the organization is represented by the level of pollution emissions released by the organization. Based on the CSP model and subsequent research, it is expected that organizations will have an obligation to implement actions that will benefit society (Wood 1991a). As a result, it is predicted that there will be an inverse relationship between CSP and the level of pollution emissions.

Therefore, the hypothesis to be empirically tested in this study is:

Hypothesis 1: Corporate Social Performance of a firm will have a positive relationship with the size of the firm and the profitability of the firm and an inverse relationship with the level of pollution emissions released by the firm.

Methodology

Sample

This study is based on a sample of firms that meet the following criteria for each year from 1987 to 1992:

1. The firm was listed in the *Fortune* Corporate Reputation Index;
2. The firm was listed in the top 500 companies of pollution emissions in the United States Environmental Protection Agency's Toxic Release Inventory Report; and
3. Information was available about the firm's level of profitability and sales from the *Fortune* 500 listing.

This criteria resulted in the selection of 111 firms in 1987; 102 firms in 1988; 120 firms in 1989; 125 firms in 1990; 118 firms in 1991; and 121 firms in 1992.

Measures

Corporate Social Performance

Corporate Social Performance is based on the *Fortune* Corporate Reputation Index. Over 8,000 executives and outside industry experts are asked to evaluate organizations within their own industry on eight different variables on a scale from zero (poor) to ten (excellent). The eight attributes are: (1) quality of management, (2) quality of products or services, (3) innovativeness, (4) long-term investment value, (5) financial soundness, (6) ability to attract, develop, and keep talented people, (7) wise use of corporate assets, and (8) responsibility to the community and the environment. Based on the ranking of these eight variables, an overall reputation number is derived.

Since responsibility to the community and the environment is one of the eight attributes of the Corporate Reputation Index, the Corporate Reputation Index is used as a proxy measurement of CSP. The measurement of CSP based on the Corporate Reputation Index which has been used in previous research studies (i.e. McGuire et al. 1988; Fombrun and Shanley 1990; Wokutch and Spencer 1987; Thomas and Simerly 1994) supports the validity of the instrument.

In addition, the benefits of using the Corporate Reputation Index include the high number of respondents and high quality level of respondents to the survey. The respondents are familiar with the performance of the firms and the overall characteristics of the industry and, therefore, can make a well informed evaluation of the organization.

Size

Based on previous work by Fombrun and Shanley (1990) and Cowen et al. (1987), the size of the organization is based on the annual sales of the firm.

Financial Performance

The financial performance of the organization is based on the level of profitability (Cowen et al. 1987). To control for the variation in the size of the organization, the profitability of the firm is based on the yearly profits of the firm divided by the annual sales level of the firm.

Environmental Performance

The environmental performance of the organization is based on the level of pollution emissions released by the firm. The level of pollution emissions is obtained from the EPA's Toxic Release Inventory Report which generates a listing of the top 500 firms based on pollution emissions. The EPA sent the authors this summary for the years 1987 through 1992. This summary report was unavailable beginning in 1993. This report provides information on air releases, water releases, underground injections, land releases, and transfers from publicly owned treatment works and other transfer facilities. To control for the variation in the size of the organization, the emissions level of the firm is based on the annual pollution emissions of the firm, as reported on the Toxic Release Inventory Report, divided by the annual sales level of the firm.

Results

The yearly descriptive statistics are shown in Table 26.1. As can be seen from the results presented in Table 26.1, there is significant variation of all the variables in the study. In the 6 years examined in this study (1987–1992), the sales of the firms in the sample varied from $123.4 million to $132.7 billion. The Corporate Reputation Index of the companies varied from 3.24 to 9.02. The level of emissions also varied significantly from 5186.3 to 14,396,995. There was also a high level of variation in profitability (−59.49 to 57.96).

The correlation between CSP and the other three variables is shown in Table 26.2. As highlighted in Table 26.2, there is a significant positive correlation between CSP and profitability for all 6 years of the study. In addition, there is a significant inverse relationship between CSP and pollution emissions in 1987 and a significant positive relationship between CSP and sales in 1988, 1989, and 1990. Furthermore, there is a significant positive relationship between level of pollution emissions and profitability from 1987 to 1991. There is also an inverse relationship between sales and profitability and pollution emissions in 1987.

The results of the regression analysis are shown in Table 26.3. The data in Table 26.3 support Hypothesis 1. The data in the 1987 and the 1990 sample support the relationship of all the variables presented in the hypothesis. In the years 1988, 1991 and 1992, the regression analysis demonstrated the positive relationship between CSP and sales and profitability, and the 1989 sample highlighted the positive relationship between profitability and CSP.

Discussion

The results of this study show that for 2 of the 6 years of the study (1987, 1990), a firm's size, financial performance, and environmental performance do impact the firm's level of CSP. Firms that are larger in size, have higher levels of profitability and lower levels of pollution emissions have higher levels of CSP. In addition, 3 of

Table 26.1 Descriptive statistics

Panel 1: 1987 results ($n=111$)	Mean	Std Dev	Minimum	Maximum
S87	10,662	15,591	123.4	101,782
P87	6.30	4.61	−12.82	20.10
EMS87	1,389,876	2,511,325	27,964	14,396,995
REP87	6.50	0.96	3.24	9.0
Panel 2: 1988 results ($n=102$)				
S88	11,789	18,454	529.8	121,085
P88	5.66	9.19	−59.49	20.32
EMS88	625,178	1,381,953	16,941	9,373,648
REP88	6.50	0.87	3.88	8.87
Panel 3: 1989 results ($n=120$)				
S89	11,304	17,061	597.5	126,974
P89	5.57	4.62	−10.92	22.5
EMS89	358,697	927,845	6163.92	8,695,437
REP89	6.57	0.86	3.86	8.90
Panel 4: 1990 results ($n=125$)				
S90	12,598	19,509	594.8	126,017
P90	4.48	5.49	−10.55	22.77
EMS90	299,687	816,258	5186.33	6,193,903
REP90	6.34	0.97	3.57	8.86
Panel 5: 1991 results ($n=118$)				
S91	12,998	19,244	983.6	123,780
P91	3.85	8.76	−26.66	57.96
EMS91	495,276	1,409,281	18,064	10,045,919
REP91	6.33	0.96	3.70	9.02
Panel 6: 1992 results ($n=121$)				
S92	12,791	20,123	624.4	132,775
P92	0.93	7.79	−23.89	20.25
EMS92	442,706	1,126,479	14,430	9,382,278
REP92	6.38	0.92	3.58	8.74

Index:
SXX = yearly sales in millions of dollars
PXX = yearly profits/yearly sales
EMSXX = yearly pollution emissions/yearly sales
REPXX = yearly Fortune Corporate Reputation Index number

the 4 remaining years (1988, 1991, 1992) showed the positive relationship between CSP and sales and profitability. As a result, this study extends previous research on CSP. The results show that CSP is a multi-faceted construct which is impacted by various organizational variables. The results show that corporate social performance is indeed a complex construct. For firms to be acknowledged as leaders in corporate social responsibility, they need to focus not only on their financial performance, but also on their environmental performance. Although a significant relationship was

Table 26.2 Correlation analysis results

Panel 1: 1987 ($n = 111$)			
	REP87	S87	P87
S87	0.15293		
	0.1114		
P87	0.39218	−0.15846	
	0.0001	0.0967	
EMS87	−0.22306	−0.18927	0.20588
	0.0186	0.0466	0.0302
Panel 2: 1988 ($n = 102$)			
	REP88	S88	P88
S88	0.17154		
	0.0847		
P88	0.47964	0.00799	
	0.0001	0.9365	
EMS88	0.00678	−153,333	0.19007
	0.9461	0.1239	0.0557
Panel 3: 1989 ($n = 120$)			
	REP89	S89	P89
S89	0.18696		
	0.0409		
P89	0.40401	−0.05995	
	0.0001	0.5154	
EMS89	−0.06639	−0.12224	0.19482
	0.4713	0.1835	0.0330
Panel 4: 1990 ($n = 125$)			
	REP90	S90	P90
S90	0.19198		
	0.0320		
P90	0.54999	−0.05291	
	0.0001	0.5579	
EMS90	−0.03764	−0.13975	0.25748
	0.6769	0.1201	0.0037
Panel 5: 1991 ($n = 118$)			
	REP91	S91	P91
S91	0.11948		
	0.1975		
P91	0.43468	−0.10937	
	0.0001	0.2384	
EMS91	0.04555	−0.14140	0.37548
	0.6243	0.1267	0.0001
Panel 6: 1992 ($n = 121$)			
	REP92	S92	P92
S92	0.10412		
	0.2558		
P92	0.38932	−0.14246	
	0.0001	0.1191	

(continued)

Table 26.2 (continued)

EMS92	−0.00050	−0.13616	0.10119
	0.9956	0.1365	0.2694

Index:
SXX = yearly sales in millions of dollars
PXX = yearly profits/yearly sales
EMSXX = yearly pollution emissions/yearly sales
REPXX = yearly Fortune Corporate Reputation Index Number

Table 26.3 Regression analysis results

Panel 1: 1987					
Source	DF	Sum of squares	Mean square	F value	Prob > F
Model	3	28.10759	9.36920	13.778	0.0001
Error	107	72.76155	0.068001		
Total	110	100.86914			
R square = 0.2787			Adjusted R square = 0.2584		
Variable	DF	Parameter estimate	Standard error	T for Ho: Parameter = 0	Prob > T
Intercept	1	5.911502	0.15486903	38.171	0.0001
S87	1	0.000017	0.000006	2.055	0.0423
P87	1	0.099607	0.0017580	5.666	0.0001
EMS87	1	−0.00000011	0.000000	−3.398	0.0010
Panel 2: 1988					
Source	DF	Sum of squares	Mean square	F value	Prob > F
Model	3	20.16139	6.72046	11.586	0.0001
Error	98	56.84653	0.58007		
Total	101	77.00793			
R square = 0.2618			Adjusted R square = 0.2392		
Variable	DF	Parameter estimate	Standard error	T for Ho: Parameter = 0	Prob > T
Intercept	1	6.177282	0.106402	58.056	0.0001
S88	1	0.000007	0.000004	1.799	0.0752
P88	1	0.046597	0.008410	5.541	0.0001
EMS88	1	−3.927157E-8	0.000000	−0.694	0.4892
Panel 3: 1989					
Source	DF	Sum of squares	Mean square	F value	Prob > F
Model	3	19.80151	6.60050	11.134	0.0001
Error	116	68.77015	0.59285		
Total	119	88.57166			
R square = 0.2236			Adjusted R square = 0.2035		
Variable	DF	Parameter estimate	Standard error	T for Ho: Parameter = 0	Prob > T

(continued)

Table 26.3 (continued)

Intercept	1	6.0451	0.123156	49.085	0.0001
S89	1	0.0000100	0.000004	2.397	1.0181
P89	1	0.082336	0.015590	5.281	0.0001
EMS89	1	−0.0000001	0.000000	−1.526	0.1297
Panel 4: 1990					
Source	DF	Sum of squares	Mean square	F value	Prob > F
Model	3	43.56269	14.52090	24.349	0.0001
Error	121	72.15953	0.59636		
Total	124	115.72222			
R square = 0.3764			Adjusted R square = 0.3610		
Variable	DF	Parameter estimate	Standard error	T for Ho: Parameter = 0	Prob > T
Intercept	1	5.800674	0.1028680	56.389	0.0001
S90	1	0.000010	0.0000036	2.770	0.0065
P90	1	0.106152	0.0130791	8.116	0.0001
EMS90	1	−0.0000002	0.0000001	−2.200	0.0297
Panel 5: 1991					
Source	DF	Sum of Squares	Mean Square	F Value	Prob > F
Model	3	24.60510	8.20170	11.294	0.0001
Error	114	82.78313	0.72617		
Total	117	107.38823			
R square = 0.2291			Adjusted R square = 0.2392		
Variable	DF	Parameter estimate	Standard error	T for Ho: Parameter = 0	Prob > T
Intercept	1	6.063533	0.1055127	57.467	0.0001
S91	1	0.000008	0.0000041	1.886	0.0618
P91	1	0.054285	0.0097211	5.584	0.0001
EMS91	1	−8.061886E-8	−1.329	0.1864	
Panel 6: 1992					
Source	DF	Sum of squares	Mean square	F value	Prob > F
Model	3	18.34049	6.11350	8.444	0.0001
Error	117	84.71031	0.72402		
Total	120	103.05080			
R square = 0.1780		Adjusted R square = 0.1569			
Variable	DF	Parameter estimate	Standard error	T for Ho: Parameter = 0	Prob > T
Intercept	1	6.249765	0.100076	62.450	0.0001
S92	1	0.000007383	0.000004	1.879	0.0628
P92	1	0.049257	0.010105	4.875	0.0001
EMS92	1	−1.6939E-8	0.000000	−0.243	0.8088

Index:
SXX = yearly sales in millions of dollars
PXX = yearly profits/yearly sales
EMSXX = yearly pollution emissions/yearly sales

only present in 2 of the 6 years of the study for all three variables examined, it does confirm that pollution emissions are important when considering the relationship between CSP and organizational variables.

The results of the study also support the belief that a strong relationship exists between profitability and corporate social performance. This study supports the view that profitability of the firm allows and/or encourages managers to implement programs that increase the level of corporate social responsibility.

In addition, the results show that larger firms recognize the need to be leaders in their commitment to corporate social performance. The leadership role may be due not only to the firm's access to additional resources used to implement corporate social performance programs, but also to the increased influence of additional stakeholders (i.e. environmental groups, government regulations) rather than a primary focus on stockholders.

In addition, this study extends the research using *Fortune's* Corporate Reputation Index. The results show that the Corporate Reputation Index is a valid indicator of the firm's overall corporate social performance. The significant relationship between CSP and the three organizational variables, which include pollution emissions, demonstrates that the Corporate Reputation Index does represent the environmental pro-activeness of organizations.

Limitations and Suggestions for Future Research

There are a number of limitations in this study that can be addressed in future research. A primary limitation is the use of pollution emissions to measure environmental performance in all sizes of firms. The use of pollution emissions ignores the measurement of environmental performance of firms in relatively low polluting industries. Therefore, this study is biased toward heavy manufacturing firms and limits the generalizability of the results.

In addition, the use of pollution emissions will not capture extraordinary environmental impacts, such as major oil spills and toxic gas releases. However, the focus of this study is to examine the consistency of the relationship presented over a 6 year time period. The focus of this study was not to examine the short term measurement of this relationship based on one time unique extraordinary circumstances. Despite these limitations, the authors believe that pollution emissions are a valid proxy to measure the level of environmental performance of an organization. However, the authors suggest that future research should examine other variables which could be used as a proxy for environmental performance.

Another limitation of this study is the bias toward large organizations due to the selection criteria of the firms. Future studies could examine the relationship presented in this study to see if it is also applicable to smaller firms which may be included in the Toxic Release Inventory Report, but not included in the *Fortune* company listing.

Summary

The purpose of this study was to examine the relationship between the corporate social performance (CSP) of an organization and three variables: the size of the organization, the financial performance of the organization, and the environmental performance of the organization. By empirically testing data from 1987 to 1992, the results of the study show that firm size, financial performance and environmental performance do impact the level of corporate social performance.

References

Anderson, J., and A. Frankle. 1980. Voluntary social report: An iso-beta portfolio analysis. *The Accounting Review* 55: 468–479.

Aupperle, K., A. Carroll, and J. Hatfield. 1985. An empirical examination of the relationship between corporate social responsibility and profitability. *Academy of Management Journal* 28: 446–463.

Belkaoui, A. 1976. The impact of the disclosure of the environmental effects of organizational behavior on the market. *Financial Management* 5: 26–31.

Bowman, E. 1978. Strategy, annual reports, and alchemy. *California Management Review* 20: 64–71.

Carroll, A. 1979. A three-dimensional conceptual model of corporate social performance. *Academy of Management Review* 4: 497–505.

Cowen, S., L. Ferreri, and L. Parker. 1987. The impact of corporate characteristics on social responsibility disclosure: A typology and frequency-based analysis. *Accounting, Organizations and Society* 12: 111–122.

Dierkes, M., and R. Coppock. 1978. Europe tries the corporate social report. *Business and Society Review* 16(Spring): 21–24.

Fombrun, C., and M. Shanley. 1990. What's in a name? Reputation building and corporate strategy. *Academy of Management Journal* 33: 233–258.

Freedman, M., and B. Jaggi. 1982. Pollution disclosures, pollution performance and economic performance. *Omega* 10: 167–176.

Fry, F., and R. Hock. 1976. Who claims corporate responsibility? The biggest and the worst. *Business and Society Review/Innovation* 18: 62–65.

Fryxell, G., and J. Wang. 1994. The Fortune Corporate "Reputation" Index: Reputation for what? *Journal of Management* 20: 1–14.

Ingram, R., and K. Frazier. 1980. Environmental performance and corporate disclosure. *Journal of Accounting Research* 18: 614–622.

McGuire, J., A. Sundgren, and T. Schneeweiss. 1988. Corporate social responsibility and firm financial performance. *Academy of Management Journal* 31: 854–872.

Poduska, R., R. Forbes, and M. Bober. 1992. The challenge of sustainable development: Kodak's response. *Columbia Journal of World Business* 27: 286–291.

Preston, L. 1978. Analyzing corporate social performance: Methods and results. *Journal of Contemporary Business* 7: 135–150.

Reilly, W. 1992. Environment, Inc. *Business Horizons* 35: 9–11.

Soloman, R., and K. Hansen. 1985. *It's good business*. New York: Atheneum.

Thomas, A., and R. Simerly. 1994. The chief executive officer and corporate social performance: An interdisciplinary examination. *Journal of Business Ethics* 13: 959–968.

Trotman, K., and G. Bradley. 1981. Associations between social responsibility disclosure and characteristics of companies. *Accounting, Organizations and Society* 6: 355–362.

Ullmann, A. 1985. Data in search of a theory: A critical examination of the relationships among social performance, social disclosure, and economic performance. *Academy of Management Review* 10: 540–577.

Wartick, S., and P. Cochran. 1985. The evolution of the corporate social performance model. *Academy of Management Review* 10: 758–769.

Wokutch, R., and B. Spencer. 1987. Corporate saints and sinners: The effects of philanthropic and illegal activity on organizational performance. *California Management Review* 29: 62–77.

Wood, D. 1991a. Corporate social performance revisited. *Academy of Management Review* 16: 691–718.

Wood, D. 1991b. Social issues in management: Theory and research in corporate social performance. *Journal of Management* 17: 383–406.

Chapter 27
Business Codes of Multinational Firms: What Do They Say?

Muel Kaptein

Introduction

The interest in corporate social responsibility, sustainable business practice, corporate governance, business ethics, and integrity and compliance management has grown markedly in the past decade (Waddock et al. 2002). It is not only stakeholders who expect companies to pay greater attention to norms, values and principles; companies themselves are acknowledging the importance of responsible business practice (Waddock et al. 2002). But what are a company's responsibilities? And how can the board and management ensure that the company meets its responsibilities? A much recommended management instrument to achieve this is a business code (also referred to as a corporate code of ethics (e.g. Cressey and Moore 1983), a code of conduct (e.g. White and Montgomery 1980) or an integrity code (e.g. Petrick and Quinn 1997). Scholars (see for example McIntosh et al. 2002), international governing bodies (e.g. the United Nations, the European Union and the Organization for Economic Cooperation and Development), business associations (e.g. the international Chamber of Commerce) as well as special interest groups (e.g. the International Labor Organization and Transparency international) have been calling on companies to develop their own business codes. But what is a business code and what is its function?

A business code is a policy document that defines the responsibilities of the corporation towards its stakeholders and/or the conduct the corporation expects of employees (Kaptein and Wempe 2002). A code clarifies the objectives the company pursues, the norms and values it upholds and what it can be held accountable for.

M. Kaptein (✉)
Department Business-Society Management, Erasmus University Rotterdam,
P.O. Box 1738, 3000 DR Rotterdam, The Netherlands
e-mail: mkaptein@rsm.nl

A.C. Michalos and D.C. Poff (eds.), *Citation Classics from the Journal of Business Ethics*, Advances in Business Ethics Research 2,
DOI 10.1007/978-94-007-4126-3_27,

A code aims to reduce the occurrence of incidents, to improve the extent to which stake-holder expectations are realized, to boost stake-holder confidence in the company and to encourage the authorities to relax regulations and controls (see, for example, Ethics Resource Center 1980; Raiborn and Payne 1990).

How common are codes among companies? And what is their content? Many studies have been conducted into the prevalence of codes in specific countries (see Table 27.1). Various publications have also appeared on the content of codes in specific countries. Research has also been conducted into the content of business codes of multinational firms with reference to one or more issues such as bribery, child labor and human rights (see Table 27.2).

To date, no research has been conducted to examine the prevalence and full content of business codes of the largest corporations in the world.

This paper presents the results of an analysis of the codes of the 200 largest multinational firms. What do they tell us? What are the most cited issues? Which issues are barely mentioned? What wording do companies choose to express their responsibilities? How uniform and diverse are the codes? Is there a core set of universal norms that multinational firms uphold and, if so, how can they be described?

A content analysis of business codes delineates the responsibilities multinationals proclaim. To be sure, the existence of codes does not imply that companies strictly adhere to them (Sims and Brinkmann 2003), but an analysis of the content of business codes nevertheless reveals what kind of ethics companies claim to uphold. The results could, among other things, serve as benchmark in evaluating and developing individual and international business codes (e.g. the OECD Guidelines for Multinational Enterprises, the UN's Global Compact and the Caux Principles).

Clearly, it is not to implied here that the moral obligation of companies to include an issue in their codes is directly proportional to the frequency with which an issue presents itself. The moral legitimacy of an ethical standpoint is not determined by numbers (Donaldson and Dunfee 1999). The frequency with which issues are included in codes does, however, allow us to deduce that the more an issue is mentioned, the greater the number of companies there are who endorse it. It can thus be asserted that the greater the frequency with which an issue is addressed the greater reason a company should have for not incorporating this issue in its business code.[1]

An examination of the prevalence of codes and the issues they deal with subsequently generates the question of how the similarities and differences among the codes could be explained. In this paper, the collected data will be used to carry out an in-depth analysis of the different code types that can be found in practice. Is there uniformity among business codes with the same objective and target group and what bearing do differences in this regard have on the issues that are addressed? Thereupon, the influence of cultural and continental divisions on code type and content will be examined.

This paper aims to give the reader a better grasp of the content of business codes. The empirical effectiveness of business codes, however, falls beyond the scope of this paper (see for example Schwartz 2001). The content of individual codes is not evaluated either.

Table 27.1 Research conducted on the prevalence of business codes

Country	Most recent study	Researcher	Research method	Percentage of codes (%)
United States	1999b	Weaver et al.	Survey of Fortune 1000 with a response rate of 26%	78
Canada	2002	KPMG Canada	Survey of largest 800 companies and 200 public sector organizations with a response rate of 13%	77
Japan	1997	Nakano	Survey of largest 2199 companies with a response rate of 7.2%	37
India	2002	KPMG India	Survey of largest 800 companies with a response rate of 20%	78
South Africa	2002	KPMG South Africa	Survey of 1026 public and private organizations with a response rate of 16%	71
Australia	1996a	Farrell and Cobbin	Survey of largest 537 companies with a response rate of 42%	42
England	2000	London Business School and Arthur Andersen	Survey of largest 350 companies with a response rate of 12%	78
Germany	1999	KPMG Germany and the University of Erlangen-Nürnberg	Survey of largest 1000 companies with a response rate of 25%	54
Belgium	2002	KPMG Belgium	Telephonic survey of all of the largest 100 companies	53
Netherlands	2003	Employer association VNO-NCW, KPMG and Ethicon	Telephonic survey of all of the largest 100 companies	54

Table 27.2 Research conducted on the content of codes

Researchers	Year	Object of research	Themes researched
White and Montgomery	1980	30 codes of U.S. companies	Several issues
Cressey and Moore	1983	119 codes of largest companies in U.S.	Several issues
Mathews	1987	202 codes of 485 companies in U.S.	Several issues
Schlegelmich and Houston	1989	31 codes of the largest 200 companies in England	Several issues
Langlois and Schlegelmich	1990	189 English, French and West German company codes	Several issues
Employer association VNO-NCW, KPMG and Ethicon	1991, 1999 and 2003	Respectively, 21, 38 and 54 codes of the largest 100 companies	Several issues
Lefebvre and Singh	1992	75 of the largest 500 companies in Canada	Several issues
Farrell and Cobbin	1996a	95 codes of the largest 537 companies in Australia	Several issues
Council of Economic Priorities	1998	71 codes of 360 companies	Sourcing Guidelines for Labor Rights
OECD	1998	98 codes of randomly chosen companies	Fair business practice, labor rights, environmental stewardship and corporate citizenship
ILO	1999	215 codes of multinationals	Labor rights
Van Tulder and Kolk	2000	13 international companies in the sporting goods industry	Several issues
Ashridge Centre for Business and Society	2000	52 business codes of Fortune 500 companies	Human rights
Gordon and Miyake	2001	246 codes of international companies	Bribery
Kolk and Van Tulder	2002a	55 business codes of Fortune 500 companies	Child labor
KPMG Belgium	2002	53 codes of the largest 100 companies	Several issues

This paper starts with a discussion of the methodology of the research conducted. Following this, the issues in the analyzed codes are arranged according to theme and prevalence. On the basis of this analysis, we distinguish three types of codes. The paper concludes with an overview of the most significant findings and a number of suggestions for companies to improve their business codes.

Methodology

This study focuses on the 200 largest corporations in the world, using the SCOPE Core Company list (Van Tulder et al. 2001). In 2001, the respective company headquarters were contacted by phone with the inquiry of whether the company had a business code. A business code was defined as an independent, company-specific policy document which delineates company responsibilities towards stakeholders and/or employee responsibilities. Documents that formulate responsibilities towards a single stake-holder (e.g. a code for suppliers), a mission statement that merely formulates economic objectives, or rules of conduct for employees with regard to a single issue (e.g. a code for the use of e-mail and the Internet) were excluded from this definition.

In the telephonic contact, a connection with the department of Public Affairs or Corporate Communications was requested. The company representative was addressed in the official local language. Since a range of terms are used to refer to business codes in practice, the company representative was assisted as much as possible with synonyms and different descriptions of a code. If the person in question had doubts, we asked to be put in contact with a colleague (from another department). In some cases, we were put through to Human Resources, Legal Affairs or Corporate Security. The companies that claimed to have a code were requested to send us an original copy. Two companies that claimed to have a code but did not want to make it public due to its confidential nature were not included in the list of companies with a code given that it could not be verified.

At the beginning of 2002, the managing directors of the companies that maintained that they did not have a code were contacted by mail to establish whether this was indeed the case. The letters were written in the official language of the country where headquarters was based. Two additional codes were eventually received. Finally, a search was conducted on the web sites of companies that repeatedly stated that they did not have a code and other public resources on company codes were also consulted. This did not yield any additional codes. The search was ended on 1 August 2002.

The aim of this approach was to collect as many codes as possible so that the proportion of companies with a code could be represented as reliably as possible. This contrasts with a few of the studies listed in Table 27.1 that have been conducted. Simply approaching companies with a questionnaire could have an adverse effect on the reliability of one's findings. Companies with a code are more likely to respond with the result that on the basis of the total response rate, the percentage of companies with a code could appear higher than what is actually the case (see for example the study conducted in England by the London Business School with a response rate of 12%).

The Japanese codes that were received were translated into English by a native speaker and checked by a second native speaker. This was followed by a content analysis. In this analysis, an inventory was made of the different items contained in the codes. The corporate integrity model developed by Kaptein and Wempe (2002) served as basis for classification. The model distinguishes between (1) company responsibilities towards stakeholders, (2) principles governing stakeholder relationships, (3) corporate values and (4) employee responsibilities towards the company. In addition, the codes were analyzed for the degree to which they contained references to implementation, compliance and monitoring along with their length and tone. The analysis left aside the distinction that can potentially be drawn between ethical and economical norms and responsibilities (Robin et al. 1989). It is, after all, not possible to deduce from the text of a company's business code whether the commitment, for example, to deliver high quality products is motivated by ethical and/or economic considerations. This is also why this study employs the concept of business codes rather than codes of business ethics.

The Prevalence, Title and Size of Codes

How many multinational firms, then, have a code? Of the 100 largest companies in the world, 58% have a code. Of the successive group of 100 companies, 47% have a code. This means that of the 200 largest multinationals, 52.5% have a business code.

Business codes are most prevalent among U.S. companies, a finding that is consistent with an earlier study of Langlois and Schlegelmilch (1990). The U.S. has a long tradition of business codes (see for example White and Montgomery 1980). The large number of Japanese companies in the top 200 and the relatively small proportion of Japanese companies with a code lower the total percentage of company codes. The prevalence of company codes by country is outlined in Table 27.3.

The vast majority of the analyzed codes (79%) belong to companies based in the U.S., France, Germany and Japan. In the analysis below, we will examine the differences among codes from the Americas (largely represented by the U.S.), Europe (largely represented by Germany and France) and Asia (largely represented by Japan).

The titles of the codes diverge strongly, for instance, "Standards of Business Conduct" (Exxon Mobil), "What We Stand For" (BP Amoco), and "Legal and Ethical Policy" (BTR). Of all the titles employed, 36% contain the word "conduct", 17% "principles/guidelines", 9% "ethics", 6% "values" and 4% "integrity".

The size of the different codes varies, as presented in Table 27.4, from 1 page (e.g. Nichemen) to 79 pages (3 M), and from 50 words to almost 18,000 words.

Table 27.3 Prevalence by country

Country	Top 100	Top 101–200	Total
More than 10 companies in top 200			
1. United States	71%(17/24)	66% (23/35)	68%(40/59)
2. France	60%(6/10)	33% (4/12)	45%(10/22)
3. Germany	50%(7/14)	38% (3/8)	45%(10/22)
4. Japan	50%(15/30)	27% (8/30)	38%(23/60)
Fewer than 10 companies in top 200			
5. Netherlands	100%(1/1)	100% (2/2)	100%(3/3)
6. England/Netherlands	100%(2/2)	–	100%(2/2)
7. England/United States	100%(1/1)	–	100%(1/1)
8. Canada	–	100% (1/1)	100%(1/1)
9. Sweden	100%(1/1)	–	100%(1/1)
10. Switzerland	100%(3/3)	67% (2/3)	83%(5/6)
11. England	50%(1/2)	100% (3/3)	80%(4/5)
12. Italy	50%(2/4)	100% (1/1)	60%(3/5)
13. South Korea	33%(2/6)	–	33%(2/6)
14. Venezuela	0%(0/1)	–	0%(0/1)
15. Mexico	0%(0/1)	–	0%(0/1)
16. Brazil	–	0% (0/2)	0%(0/2)
17. Spain	–	0% (0/3)	0%(0/3)
Total	58%	47%	52.5%

Table 27.4 Number of pages of business codes

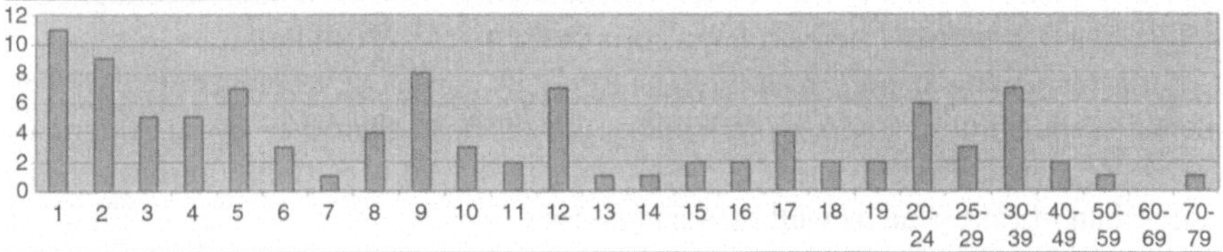

The Content of Business Codes

In the following section, the content of the codes of the 200 largest companies are analyzed and discussed with reference to (i) stakeholder responsibilities, (ii) stakeholder principles, (iii) corporate values, (iv) internal employee conduct and (v) implementation and compliance. Thereupon, we shall identify the types of codes that can be distinguished on the basis of the content analysis that has been carried out.

Stakeholder Responsibilities

In its "Global Business Standards", Sara Lee declares that "we have a responsibility to ourselves, to each other, to our consumers, to our stockholders, to our business partners and to our communities". But what are these responsibilities? What kind of responsibilities do companies embrace? In Table 27.5, the issues that are addressed in the examined codes are depicted by stake-holder.

Most corporate codes, whether extensively or concisely, pay attention to consumers, investors, employees, society and the natural environment. Specifying responsibilities towards competitors and suppliers is significantly less widespread. Although some issues are frequently referred to (such as delivering quality and achieving returns) the terms in which this is stated may differ. The quality levels companies pledge to deliver to customers are subject to a number of qualifications such as "high quality" (Nestle), 'highest quality' (Merck/HP), "excellent quality" (Coca-Cola) and "customer's first choice for quality" (British Telecom). Greater divergence can be found in the level of returns to shareholders: "acceptable" (Shell), "sufficient" (Hewlett Packard), "satisfactory" (Philips), "superior" (Ito Yokado Group), "best possible" (Merck), "excellent long term" (British Telecom) and "maximize long term" (BP). With respect to the natural environment and competitors, there is greater textual uniformity. The terms in which companies express their position towards society are more diverse. A few examples include "a harmonious relationship with society" (Ito Yokado Group), "contributing to the well-being of society" (AT&T), "benefit humankind" (Bayer), "major contribution to development of society" (Deutsche Telekom), "betterment of society" (Coca-Cola), "meeting legal obligations" (Fiat) and "being a good corporate citizen" (Toshiba).

Striking is that when the results are analyzed by continent, references to environmental responsibilities appear 45% more in European than they do in American codes. Responsibilities towards competitors are referred to 52% more in American codes than in European as well as Asian codes.

Stakeholder Principles

In addition to articulating stakeholder interests, a code can also communicate and elaborate on the principles the company upholds. Stakeholder principles are general requirements for company and employee conduct: they govern the relationship between company and stakeholders (Kaptein and Wempe 2002). Table 27.6 depicts the most cited stakeholder principles.

Stakeholder principles generally do not receive as much attention as stakeholder interests. Transparency (55%), honesty (50%) and fairness (45%) are the most cited principles. Fairness, for example, is referred to in connection with the selection of suppliers, the distribution of benefits and burdens and the assessment of employee performance. As Merck declares "… we treat our suppliers with honesty, fairness and respect". Shell applies fairness also to its competitors: "… to compete fairly …will

Table 27.5 Responsibilities towards stakeholders

		Degree to which it is mentioned (n = 105) (%)
I.	*Customers (or: consumers, clients, buyers)*	
	Supplying sufficient/good/high/highest/superior/excellent/reliable/top quality/original products and services and offering good value	67
	Sustaining or enhancing the health and safety of consumers	35
	Providing reasonable/competitive/fair prices (and payment conditions) commensurate with quality	34
	Continually improving quality of products and services	28
	Providing products and services at the right place and time and in the right amount (accurately, timely, continuity)	10
	Preventing misuse/abuse of products	3
	Helping consumers to use products responsibly	2
	Providing customized products for minorities	1
II.	*Capital providers (or: stockholders, owners, investors)*	
	Achieving a maximum/superior/satisfactory/sound/competitive/acceptable/above-the- market-average return on the capital in the long term, in fair proportion to the market-related risk	41
	Conserving, protecting and (above-the-market-average/maximize) increasing the owners'/investors' assets/capital	9
III.	*Employees (or personnel, staff, human capital, including applicants and temporary employees)*	
	Encouraging/optimizing personal development/growth/use of talents	40
	Treating employees with dignity/respect	39
	Valuing diversity/equal opportunity	31
	Offering productive/responsible/challenging/pleasant/enriching work and working environment	23
	Offering good/competitive/excellent terms of employment/compensation	12
	Providing stable and secure job opportunities	9
	Making the best possible use of each person's skills, abilities and knowledge	9
	Conforming to sound labor standards	8
	Refraining from child labor	4
	Creating/enabling/guaranteeing a balance between work and private life	2
IV.	*Suppliers, joint ventures, contractors and distributors*	
	Ensuring equal opportunity	14
	Seeking mutually beneficial/long-term relationships	12
	Paying competitive market prices in timely manner	6
	Making reasonable demands	3

(continued)

Table 27.5 (continued)

	Degree to which it is mentioned (n = 105) (%)
V. *Society (or local community)*	
Observing, both directly and indirectly, all relevant local laws and regulations	57
Being a good corporate citizen through charitable donations, educational and cultural contributions, and employee participation in community and civic affairs	36
Enhancing the quality of life/contributing to sustainable development/improvement	18
Respecting human rights/dignity (of those affected by the activities) and promoting them wherever practicable	11
Supporting public policies and practices that promote human development and democracy	8
Supporting/participating in local initiatives that promote peace, security, diversity and social integration. E.g. collaborating with community organizations (for example government agencies and industry groups) dedicated to raising standards of health, education, product safety, workplace safety and prosperity	7
Recognizing government's legitimate obligation to society (legitimizing government authority)	6
Doing business with stakeholders who do not systematically violate national and international social standards	4
Abandoning commercial activities in countries where it is made impossible to promote/respect human rights	2
Setting an example in countries where human rights are seriously and systematically violated	2
Adopting practices that permit the transfer and rapid diffusion of technologies and know-how	2
Timely payment of taxes	1
VI. *Competitors*	
Refraining from seeking access to competitors' assets through improper means	21
Refraining from casting competitors in a bad light or criticizing them publicly	2
VII. *Natural environment (health, safety and environment)*	
Preventing/preserving/restoring the natural environment or treating the environment with due care	56
Offering safe, clean, orderly and healthy working conditions; eliminating/preventing injuries/incidents	49
Preventing/limiting/reducing/controlling negative environmental impacts such as the direct and indirect pollution of soil, water and air, noise, creation of waste products and use of hazardous materials	31
Collecting and having waste processed separately and re-using or recycling it where possible	21
Using energy and other natural resources effectively and prudently/efficiently	20

(continued)

Table 27.5 (continued)

	Degree to which it is mentioned (n = 105) (%)
Preventing incidents	16
Promoting development of environmentally friendly products	10
Supporting research and development of environmental technologies	7
Preventing harm to animals and helping to optimize animal welfare	2

Table 27.6 Stakeholder principles

	Extent to which it is cited (n = 105) (%)
1. Transparency	55
2. Honesty/truth	50
3. Fairness/ impartiality	45
4. Trust	23
5. Empathy/respect/diversity	20
6. Stimulating stakeholders to raise concerns	19
7. Accountability	18
8. Dialogue/open communication	14
9. Equality	12
10. Responsiveness	11
11. Keeping promises	10
12. Coherence/uniformity	4
13. Freedom/autonomy of stakeholders	3

not prevent others from competing freely …" Good stake-holder communication (e.g. transparency, honesty, dialogue, and responsiveness) is mentioned most. For example, Nestlé "… invites government officials, health professionals and consumers to draw its attention to any Nestle infant formula marketing practices in developing countries which they consider are not in conformity with the above commitment" and BT states that it will "…. use [its] values and principles in dialogue with other organizations …".

Comparing the most frequently mentioned principles in the business codes by continent shows that American codes specifically emphasize the principle of honesty (64% in comparison with 45% in European and 38% in Asian codes); European companies place relative more emphasis on the principles of transparency (68%, compared to Asian 54% and American companies 52%) and the principle of empathy (30%, compared to Asian 21% and American companies 11%); and Japanese companies place somewhat more emphasis on the principle of trust (29%, in contrast with American 22% and European companies 17%). The principle of fairness is mentioned less often in American codes (35%) than in European (50%) and Asian (46%) codes.

Table 27.7 Core values of/within the organization

	Extent to which it is mentioned (n = 105) (%)
1. Teamwork/mutual support/interdependence/co-operation/ team-spirit	43
2. Responsibility/conscientiousness	33
3. Open communication	29
Innovation, creativity, pioneering	29
5. Customer oriented	19
6. Flexibility	17
7. Efficiency	16
8. Professionalism	14
Entrepreneurship	14
Pride/dignity	14
11. Loyalty	13
12. Motivation/enthusiasm/energy/spirit/encouragement	12
13. Participation	11
14. Shared purpose/unity	10
15. Exchanging ideas/learning	9
Independence	9
17. Consistent and unequivocal public image	8
18. Effectiveness	6
Productivity	6
20. Cost-awareness	5
21. Discipline	4
Diligence/perseverance/dedication	4
23. Courage/daring	3
24. Harmony	2
25. Humility	1

Corporate Values

Apart from stakeholder principles which pertain specifically to stakeholder relationships, organizations also express their core values in a code. Core values refer to those qualities a company deems desirable and which should ground all business conduct and outcomes (Kaptein and Wempe (2002)). Table 27.7 presents a summary of the organizational values that can be found in the examined codes.

The core values cited in the codes diverge strongly. Merck, for example, asserts that "… we strive to create an environment of mutual respect, encouragement and teamwork…" while AT&T states that "We treat each other with respect and dignity…" The most often cited values are teamwork (43%), responsibility (33%), open communication (29%) and innovation (29%). Noteworthy is that the value of effectiveness is seldom mentioned explicitly. Shell is one of the exceptions in asserting that "The most important contribution… to the social and material progress of countries… is in per forming basic activities as effectively as possible." American codes make comparatively less mention of values than do European codes.

Open communication can be found in 35% of the European codes, while it amounts to 25% in American codes. European codes mention teamwork 1.5 times more often than do Japanese and American codes. Humility, harmony, dedication, innovation, creativity and team spirit are largely found in business codes of Asian origin. Innovation and creativity, for example, are respectively mentioned 73% and 46% more in Asian codes than in American and European codes. By contrast, the value responsibility/ conscientiousness can be found just as often in American (30%) as in Asian (35%) and European codes (33%).

Internal Conduct

Business codes can also clarify what is expected of employees in their engagement with one another and their treatment of organizational assets. Contrary to the categories discussed above, the latter refers to employee conduct versus the company as opposed to employee conduct on behalf of the company (Mathews 1987). Table 27.8 provides an overview of the items referred to in this area.

Many codes include a diverse range of rules of conduct employees must obey among themselves (particularly discrimination (44%) and intimidation (43%)) and with respect to the company. Most forms of conduct listed in Table 27.8 such as engaging in fraudulent practices, leaking confidential information and sexual invitations is mostly subject to certain conditions, for example, that the value is below $50 (GTE) or "purely symbolic" (Fiat), that their acceptance is "always agreed with the supervisor" (Deutsche Telecom), "a social courtesy" (NTT), that the "company officer or his/her delegate [has] approve[d] its acceptance" (Kodak), that it is "generally accepted business practices of one's country and industry" (Sara Lee) or that its purpose is "to create goodwill" (Xerox).

Implementation and Compliance

A quarter of the codes make reference to implementation of the code. GTE for instance, points out the central role of managers: "GTE supervisors have an additional responsibility for maintaining a climate in which legal and ethical business conduct is the norm; communicating to employees the seriousness of GTE's commitment to such conduct; encouraging open discussion of employees' business concerns; accepting and processing reports filed by employees of possible misconduct; and, never compromising GTE's standards to achieve a goal or objective, no matter how important that goal or objective seems at the moment." GTE also refers to a Business Conduct Line for employees with questions about interpretation and compliance with the code.

Table 27.8 Employee conduct towards the company and among themselves

		Extent to which it is mentioned (*n*= 105) (%)
I.	Corporate funds	
	Adherence to sound financial accounting principles	46
	No fraud	45
	No diversion of funds (embezzlement)	19
	No misuse of funds for personal gain	18
	No misuse of funds for business purposes	16
	Correct handling of expense returns	8
	No unjustified billing of hours	7
II.	*Corporate equipment*	
	Proper use of equipment and goods	29
	Protection and conservation of equipment and goods	18
	No theft of business equipment or goods	18
	Prohibition of or restriction on taking business equipment home for private use	17
	Prohibition or restriction on private use of means of communication	14
	No neglect of maintenance	3
III.	*Corporate information*	
	No leakage of confidential information (like trade secrets)	50
	No use of insider information when trading shares of other securities	44
	No unauthorized use of access codes	10
IV.	*Authorities*	
	No conflicting side-line activities/ conflict of interests	52
	No corruption or bribery	46
	Prohibition or restriction on acceptance of gifts	47
	No favoring of family and friends	34
V.	*Corporate time*	
	No alcohol and drug use	17
	No private surfing on the internet during working hours	3
	Sufficient effort	2
	Keeping to stipulated times	1
	No unjustified calling in sick	1
	No arms/weapons in the workplace	1
VI.	*Staff*	
	No discrimination	44
	No intimidation/harassment/threatening	43
	Treating one another with respect	35
	No sexual harassment	26
	Treating one another fairly	20
	No unwelcome or unsolicited physical and verbal sexual advances	16
	Respect for privacy	14
	No racism or racist insinuations	12
	No verbal abuse	11

(continued)

Table 27.8 (continued)

	Extent to which it is mentioned (n= 105) (%)
No physical violence	11
No tasteless/obscene jokes/gestures or material	10
No bullying	10
No gossiping/ridiculing/insulting	6
No favoritism	3

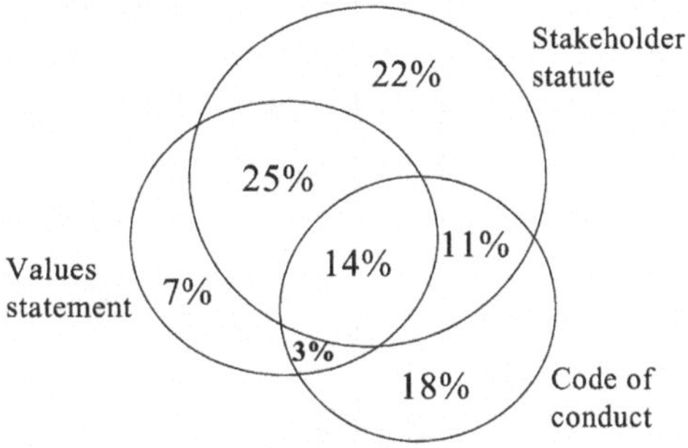

Fig. 27.1 Frequency of type of codes

Some 52% of the codes indicate that compliance with the code is monitored. British Telecom, for instance, sheds light on its monitoring practices as follows: "We are committed to communicating, measuring and appropriate reporting of our performance against these principles."

Profiles of Business Codes

The analysis thus far (in keeping with most scientific analyses of codes) has treated business codes as a uniform concept. The question, however, is whether the diversity in the codes' content is not (partly) the result of the type of code individual companies have in mind. On the basis of the collected and analyzed codes, we can distinguish three clusters of codes: (1) the stake-holder statute/business principles, (2) the values statement and (3) the code of conduct. 72% of the codes formulate responsibilities towards stake-holders (the so-called stakeholder statute or business principles), 49% express the corporate core values in a coherent manner (the so-called values statement) and 46% set down norms and rules for employee conduct (the so-called code of conduct).[2] A number of codes integrate two or even three approaches. Each type is elaborated on in Figure 27.1. The types of corporate codes differ, among other things, in focus (for internal and/or external use), level of abstraction, size, use of pronoun and attention to compliance.

Based on a content analysis of codes of business in the U.S., Mathews (1987) concludes that U.S. companies are more concerned with conduct against the company

Table 27.9 Types of code

	Focus	Objects	Level-of abstraction	Size	Use of personal pronoun	Tone	Compliance paragraph	Countries
Stakeholder statute/ business principles	Internal and external use	Responsibilities and principles towards stakeholders	Mostly high	A single to a few pages	Often first person plural	Predominantly descriptive	Mostly, in terms of e.g. external reporting and mechanisms for complaints of stakeholders	Especially European (46%) and Asian (40%) companies
Values statement	Primarily for internal use and to a lesser degree for external use	Organizational values	Mostly high	A single to a few pages	Often first person plural	Predominantly descriptive	Hardly	Especially Asian (47%) and European (32%) companies
Code of conduct	Primarily for internal use	Desirable employee conduct	Mostly detailed	A few to many pages	Often second or third person singular	Predominantly prescriptive	Largely, in terms of e.g. sanction mechanisms and whistle-blowers procedures	Especially U.S. companies (53%)

than on behalf of the company. From this study, it would indeed appear that codes of conduct are a particularly American phenomenon. Asian and European companies, however, choose for a stakeholder statute/business principles or a values statement more often than do American companies. Mathews's conclusion with respect to American codes is also only a partial reflection of the present state of affairs. Many American codes (74%) address stakeholder responsibilities, stake-holder principles and/or, to a lesser extent, core values. As this is often (64%) accompanied by a detailed explication of the norms and rules for employee conduct in regard to the company, the latter often overshadows the rest (at least as far as number of words and visual impact are concerned) (Table 27.9).

Calculating anew the frequency with which issues are referred to by code type shows that more uniformity can be found especially among codes of conduct. For example, the percentage of codes of conduct that address fraud, bribery, use of confidential information and upholding proper social norms between employees increase by a factor of 1.8 compared to the total percentage of business codes that refer to these items.[3] Of all the codes of conduct, 91% address these issues. Regarding business codes which can be defined as values statements, much variation can still be found in the corporate values that are mentioned.

Conclusion

This paper consisted of three steps. First, we made an inventory of the codes of the 200 largest companies in the world. Second, we analyzed the content of the collected codes. Finally, we examined to what extent the content of the codes can be related to the type and origin of codes.

It was found that 58% of the 100 largest companies (and 52.5% of the 200 largest companies) in the world have a code of conduct. On the one hand, this figure can be viewed as positive: more than half of the largest multinational firms acknowledge and define their responsibilities, principles, values and/or norms in a written policy document. On the other hand, almost half of the largest multinational firms – at the time of this study – do not have a code.

Although a business code is not a statutory requirement, it would appear advisable for companies who do not have a code to (re)consider whether it might be desirable to develop and introduce a business code (Schwartz 2002). As more companies adopt a code, those who refrain from doing so will increasingly be confronted with stakeholders who will want to know why a code is not viewed a desirable instrument to manage ethics, integrity and social responsibility. This study did not examine the reasons companies may have for not adopting a code. A follow-up study could focus on this question and examine to what extent companies have ethically justifiable reasons for not having a code.

This paper has shown that both similarities and differences can be found in the content of codes, both with respect to responsibilities towards stakeholders, stakeholder principles, corporate values, as well as conduct against the company. Codes generally describe the responsibilities a company assumes with respect to employees, customers, capital providers and society as a whole. In general, companies do not employ opposing norms. They specifically differ in what they include and exclude from their codes and the wording that is used (for instance in terms of levels of commitment).

Finally, this paper has shown that an important determining factor in the content of a code is the target group the company has in mind: external and/or internal stakeholders. In the case of the former, the code will focus mostly on responsibilities towards stakeholders and the principles that apply. In the case of the latter, the code will mostly formulate rules for conduct. If the analyzed codes are grouped according to type, uniformity in content increases markedly.

The diversity in the content of corporate codes (also within countries) is not necessarily a negative sign. It could very well be an indication of the authenticity of the codes in the sense that companies draw up codes to suit their particular circumstances as opposed to merely copying those of other companies, model codes or codes of international institutions. At the same time, a number of topical social issues such as human rights receive slight attention in the codes.

This study offers a benchmark for companies to assess their codes against other corporate codes and the items they address. As companies become more international, comparisons with the corporate codes of companies in the countries where they do business become more desirable. Stakeholders judge the quality of individual business codes partly with reference to the quality of other corporate codes in that country. For example, in an Asian country, a typically American code of conduct could be regarded as too comprehensive and forceful while the business principles of a European company could be viewed as too ambitious and abstract.

The benchmark that is presented in this paper is neither a proposal for a model code nor does it suggest that uniformity among business codes is necessarily desirable. The benchmark gives companies and stakeholders cause for examining the reasons why a company does not take a stand on a given issue. If a company decides to address an issue in its code, it is important that it uses its own words and tailors it to its own circumstances. This overview is especially useful for companies who do not have a code but who would like to develop such a policy document. One of the first steps in developing a code is to decide on the type of code the company deems fitting (a stakeholder statute/business principles, a values statement and/or a code of conduct), the issues it elects to address and the terms in which the code will be shaped.

The benchmark offers stakeholders support in questioning companies on the content of the code: Why does your company include issue X but not issue Y? Why do you, as company, formulate it like this and not like other companies do? Why do you not mention, for example, fair play, knowing that 45% of companies do? For international institutions that have issued a standard for corporations (e.g. the UN and the OECD) this overview offers an aid in evaluating their own standards on comprehensiveness and the extent to which companies have adopted their standard.

The more companies embrace a given issue, the more reason exists for other companies to ask themselves why they have omitted it.

By performing a periodical analysis of the content of business codes, we can track the extent to which there is evidence of further homogenization or diversification in codes (for example in terms of structure, issues and wording).

Recommendations

An assessment of content is just one aspect of the overall evaluation of a business code. Another factor concerns the extent to which a code demonstrates a company's awareness of relevant and topical issues, organizational dilemmas and stakeholder expectations (Kaptein and Wempe 1998). Judging individual codes merely based on desk-research and just in terms of comprehensiveness is therefore not justified. Moreover, some norms may be so self-evident – for instance the prohibition on killing someone in the workplace – that it need not be included in the code despite the fact that it remains valid.

Another significant aspect is the process through which the code is established and institutionalized. A code is nothing, coding is everything (Kaptein and Wempe 1998). The quality of individual business codes can therefore only be determined by conducting research on these aspects as they manifest in practice.

We can, nevertheless, in random order, put forward a number of general suggestions for improving codes.

- Accountability: The impact and credibility of a code can be enhanced by making a commitment to stakeholders to periodically account for implementation and compliance with the code, for example in an annual report (Van Tulder and Kolk 2000). Only 4% of the analyzed codes address external reporting.
- Feedback: A company can use a code as a means to invite internal and external stake-holders to share their ideas on improving the code or even its implementation. Although many companies have institutionalized and refer to an internal ethics hotline (Kaptein 2002), it is often unclear to external stakeholders who they can turn to. Only 5% of the examined codes indicate that the company would appreciate external stakeholders to report incidents and who they can contact.
- A stimulating work environment: A key factor in the proper implementation of a code is that managers create a work environment which enables and encourages employees to observe the code (Benson 1989; Tucker et al. 1999). Few codes give a clear and convincing account of its implementation (25%) and the role fulfilled by management (16%). Companies could therefore consider placing more emphasis on the responsibility the organization (and management in particular) has in stimulating and creating the conditions for employees to comply with the code.

- Periodic update: If a code is to be a relevant and meaningful document, it is not only its implementation that should be attended to in great detail; it should also be updated at regular intervals (Ethics Resource Center 1990). Some business codes have not been modified in more than ten years, which increases the likelihood that new issues will not be attended to. It is therefore advisable that companies consider stipulating (maximum) intervals between updates in their codes. If a company refrains from doing so updates might repeatedly be postponed. Moreover, in the event that updates do occur unexpectedly, it could create suspicion among stakeholders that something must be (fundamentally) amiss to have prompted adjustment of the code. Apart from that, most companies (86%) make no mention of the process through which the code came into being.
- Clear status of the code: Most codes are unclear about the status of the code, that is, to what extent the codes express declarations of intent or actual business practice. It is often also unclear how the code relates to other regulations within and beyond the boundaries of the company. In 67% of the codes it is not clarified whether the norms and values subscribed to in the code are also worked out in greater detail in separate policy documents and regulations.
- Availability of the code: Through this research project, first hand experience was gained of how cumbersome it can be to obtain company codes (in a few cases it took more than 4 months and in another few it took between 12 and 15 telephone calls before the document was sent by mail). It also appeared that some companies regard their code as confidential or classified information. Apart from that, codes are often unavailable via the intranet or in English (despite the fact that these companies maintain business relations in English-speaking countries).
- Convincing message: Some codes are abstractly formulated. In theory, an abstract code could be as effective (or even more effective) as a detailed code (Kaptein and Wempe 1998). In that case, it is important that (even more of) an effort is made with implementation (due to the demand it places on employees to translate it to their specific functions). Companies with abstract codes should therefore examine how it can be made clear to users and readers that abstraction is not an admission of weakness but rather a considered admission of strength.
- Clear structure: As we have seen, there is strong divergence among the codes in terms of structure. The structure depends, among other things, on the type of code the company has in mind (for instance organizing it according to stakeholder group or values). At the same time, some codes display considerable lack of coherence and issues appear to have been assembled at random. Organizational values especially are at times scattered in the text or mentioned only in the introduction. The impact of core values in particular, lies in their selection (Collins and Porras 1994).
- Appropriate presentation: Despite the fact that the content of and process through which codes are established are of chief importance, the appearance of codes also says something about a company's regard for its code (White and Montgomery 1980). A glossy publication, for example, can generate suspicion that the company is more concerned about its appearance than its content. On the other hand,

taking care with a code's presentation and style reflects a company's regard for the code and, by implication, the length of time it expects the code to serve (from being of one-off use to being a reference). The examined codes vary from being presented in the form of a few standard photocopies to full color text and photos printed on quality paper.

- Unique identity: The strength of and commitment to the code is largely reflected in the extent to which the code is tailored to the company's unique circumstances (Pemberton and Pendergraft 1990). The texts of the codes display strong similarities particularly with regard to the natural environment and rules of conduct with respect to fraud and corruption. The current growth of international codes increases the likelihood that companies will adopt these texts (almost) literally in their codes. If external stakeholders and employees are to regard the code seriously, companies should avoid appearing to have been led by one or more codes of other companies or international organizations without having thoroughly thought through their position is on the issue at hand.

Finally, another important question is whether some types of codes are more effective than others (Schwartz 2001). A general code that appeals to employees' sense of responsibility could be more effective than a very detailed code which can easily be interpreted as a vote of no confidence (Treviño et al. 1999). We may likewise ask what a code actually says about the factual situation. The current growth in sustainability reporting (KPMG 2002) could perhaps serve as point of departure in formulating an answer to this question. As yet, this study shows that on paper, many companies have an eye for the responsible treatment of stakeholders along with the principles, values and norms that ground sound conduct.

Acknowledgement Thanks to the two referents for their very useful comments on an earlier version of this paper.

Notes

1. An analysis of business codes unravels the norms and values companies endorse and provides insight into the extent to which companies actually share the principles that have been developed in the academic field of business ethics. An inventory of so-called micro-norms is also in keeping with the call of Donaldson and Dunfee (1999) to supplement their Integrated Social Contracts Theory with empirical research on the ethics of business.
2. In calculating the prevalence of code types, each code was examined to establish whether it elaborates on at least two specific responsibilities towards stake-holders, values or rules of conduct. Codes were treated for instance as values statements only if the company named the values as such and clustered them as such in the code. If only a few scattered values appeared in the text, the codes were not treated as values statements.
3. This factor was calculated by dividing the number of times an item occurs by the total number of codes of conduct instead of by the total number of business codes as was done earlier. This percentage was then divided by the percentage of this item of the total number of codes as presented in Table 27.8.

References

Ashridge Centre for Business and Society. 2000. Business responses to human rights. Hertfordshire.

Benson, G. 1989. Codes of ethics. *Journal of Business Ethics* 8: 305–319.

Collins, J.C., and J.I. Porras. 1994. *Built to last: Successful habits of visionary companies*. London: Century Business.

Council on Economic Priorities. 1998. SCREEN. CEP's International Social Responsibility Research Service (New York: Council on Economic Priorities).

Cressey, D.R., and C.A. Moore. 1983. Managerial values and corporate code of ethics. *California Management Review* 25(4): 53–77.

Donaldson, T., and T. Dunfee. 1999. *Ties that bind: A social contracts approach to business ethics*. Boston: Harvard Business School Press.

Ethics Resource Center. 1980. *Implementation and enforcement: Codes of ethics in corporations and associations*. Princeton: Opinion Research Corporation.

Ethics Resource Center. 1990. *Creating a workable company code of ethics*. Washington, DC: ERC.

Farrell, B.J., and D.M. Cobbin. 1996a. A content analysis of codes of ethics in Australian enterprises. *Journal of Managerial Psychology* 11(1): 37.

Farrell, B., and D. Cobbin. 1996b. Mainstreaming ethics in Australian enterprises. *The Journal of Management Development* 15(1): 37–50.

Gordon, K., and M. Miyake. 2001. Business approaches to combating bribery: A study of codes of conduct. *Journal of Business Ethics* 34: 161–174.

International Labor Organization. 1999. *A social conscience in the global market place: Labor dimensions of codes of conduct, social labeling and investor initiatives*. Geneva: ILO.

Kaptein, M. 2002. Guidelines for the development of an ethics safety net. *Journal of Business Ethics* 41: 217–234.

Kaptein, M., and J. Wempe. 1998. Twelve Gordian Knots when developing an organizational code of ethics. *Journal of Business Ethics* 17: 853–869.

Kaptein, M., and J. Wempe. 2002. *The balanced company: A theory of corporate integrity*. Oxford: Oxford University Press.

Kolk, A., and R. Van Tulder. 2002a. Child labor and multinational conduct: A comparison of international business and stakeholder codes. *Journal of Business Ethics* 36: 291–301.

Kolk, A., and R. Van Tulder. 2002b. The effectiveness of self-regulation: Corporate codes of conduct and child labor. *European Management Journal* 20: 260–270.

KPMG Belgium. 2002. *Business codes in Belgium 2002*. Brussels: KPMG.

KPMG Canada. 2002. *Ethics and corporate social responsibility survey 2002: Ethical leadership*. Toronto: KPMG Forensic.

KPMG Germany and Universitat Erlangen-Nürnberg, and U. Erlangen-Nürnberg. 1999. *Unternehmensleitbilder in Deutschen Unternehmen*. Frankfurt: KPMG.

KPMG India. 2002. *India fraud survey report 2002*. New Dehli: KPMG Forensic.

KPMG International and University of Amsterdam. 2002. *KPMG international survey of corporate sustainability reporting 2002*. De Meern: KPMG.

KPMG South Africa. 2002. *Southern Africa fraud survey 2002*. Johannesburg: KPMG Forensic.

Langlois, C.C., and B.B. Schlegelmilch. 1990. Do corporate codes of ethics reflect national character? Evidence from Europe and the United States. *Journal of International Business Studies* 4: 519–539.

Lefebvre, M., and J.B. Singh. 1992. The content of focus of Canadian corporate code of ethics. *Journal of Business Ethics* 11: 799–808.

London Business School, and Arthur Andersen. 2000. *Ethical concerns and reputation risk management: A study of leading U.K. companies*. London: Arthur Andersen.

Mathews, M.C. 1987. Codes of ethics: Organizational behavior and misbehavior. *Research in Corporate Social Performance and Policy: Empirical Studies of Business Ethics and Values* 9: 107–130.

McIntosh, M., R. Thomas, D. Leipziger, and G. Coleman. 2002. *Living corporate citizenship: Strategic routes to socially responsible business*. London: Prentice Hall/Financial Times.

Nakano, C. 1997. A survey study on Japanese managers' views of business ethics. *Journal of Business Ethics* 16: 1737–1751.

OECD (Organization of Economic Cooperation and Development). 1998. *Corporate governance: Improving competitiveness and access to capital in global markets*. Paris: OECD.

Pemberton, J.M., and L.O. Pendergraft. 1990. Toward a code of ethics: Social relevance and the professionalization of records management. *ARMA Quarterly* 24: 2–15.

Petrick, J.A., and J.F. Quinn. 1997. *Management ethics: Integrity at work*. Thousands Oaks: Sage.

Raiborn, C.A., and D. Payne. 1990. Corporate codes of conduct: A collective conscience and continuum. *Journal of Business Ethics* 9: 879–889.

Robin, D., M. Giallourakis, F. David, and T. Moritz. 1989. A different look at codes of ethics. *Business Horizons* 32: 66–73.

Schlegelmilch, B.B., and Houston, J.E. 1989. Corporate Codes of ethics in large UK companies: an empirical investigation of use, content and attitudes. *European Journal of Marketing* 23: 7–24.

Schwartz, M.S. 2001. The nature of the relationship between corporate codes of ethics and behavior. *Journal of Business Ethics* 32: 247–262.

Schwartz, M.S. 2002. A code of ethics for corporate code of ethics. *Journal of Business Ethics* 41: 27–43.

Sims, R.R., and J. Brinkmann. 2003. Enron ethics (Or: Culture matters more than codes). *Journal of Business Ethics* 45: 243–256.

Treviño, L.K., G.R. Weaver, D.G. Gibson, and B.L. Toffler. 1999. Managing ethics and legal compliance: What works and what hurts? *California Management Review* 41(2): 131–151.

Tucker, L.R., V. Stathakopolous, and C.H. Patti. 1999. A multidimensional assessment of ethics codes: The professional business association perspective. *Journal of Business Ethics* 19: 287–300.

Van Tulder, R., and A. Kolk. 2000. How multinationality affects ethics: Codes of conduct in the sporting goods industry. *Journal of International Business Studies* 32(2): 267–283.

Van Tulder, R., D. Berghe, and A. Muller. 2001. *Erasmus (S)Coreboard of core companies: The world's largest firms and internationalization*. Rotterdam: Rotterdam School of Management.

VNO-NCW, KPMG and Ethicon. 1991, 1999, 2003. The business code. The Hague.

Waddock, S.A., C. Bodwell, and S.B. Graves. 2002. Responsibility: The new business imperative. *The Academy of Management Executive* 16(2): 132–147.

Weaver, G.R., L.K. Trevino, and P.L. Cochran. 1999a. Integrated and decoupled corporate social performance: Manager commitments, external pressures, and corporate ethics practices. *Academy of Management Journal* 42(5): 539–552.

Weaver, G.R., L.K. Treviño, and P.L. Cochran. 1999b. Corporate ethics practices in the mid-1990s: An empirical study of fortune 1000. *Journal of Business Ethics* 18: 283–294.

White, B.J., and B.R. Montgomery. 1980. Corporate codes of conduct. *California Management Review* 23(2): 80–87.

Chapter 28
Consumer Ethics: An Empirical Investigation of Factors Influencing Ethical Judgments of the Final Consumer

Scott J. Vitell and James A. Muncy

Concerns for ethical issues in business have dramatically increased over the last decade. Both academics and practitioners are showing an intense interest in ethical issues faced in the business world. For example, both the *Journal of Business Ethics* and the *Business & Professional Ethics Journal* came into existence in the early 1980s. There have also been numerous ethics conferences such as the Arthur Anderson sponsored conferences on teaching business ethics, Penn State's G. Albert Shoemaker Program in Business Ethics, and the Conference Board's recent "Integrating Business Ethics" conference. Much of the research that has been done on business ethics has focused on marketing and marketing related activities (Ferrell and Gresham 1985; Hunt and Vitell 1986; Ferrell et al. 1989). This is probably due to the fact that marketing in general, and the buyer/seller dyad in particular, is a place where a lot of ethical problems in business arise (Baumhart 1961; Brenner and Molander 1977; Vitell and Festervand 1987).

Thus, a large body of literature is developing concerning ethics in the marketplace; however, almost all of this research has focused on the seller side of the buyer/seller dyad. In two major reviews of marketing ethics, Murphy and Laczniak (1981) cite only a handful of articles examining consumer ethics and Murphy and Pridgen (1987) do not cover the topic at all. After an extensive search of the literature, fewer than 20 studies could be found which studied ethical issues in the marketplace from the consumer's perspective and most of these studies focused on very specific and limited situations having ethical content (such as shoplifting). Given that, in the words of Bernstein (1985), consumers are "out-doing big business and the government at

S.J. Vitell (✉)
Department of Marketing, School of Business Administration,
University of Mississippi, University, MS 38677, USA
e-mail: svitell@bus.olemiss.edu

J.A. Muncy
Department of Marketing and Economics, Langdale College of Business,
Valdosta State University, Valdosta, GA 31698, USA

A.C. Michalos and D.C. Poff (eds.), *Citation Classics from the Journal of Business Ethics*, Advances in Business Ethics Research 2,
DOI 10.1007/978-94-007-4126-3_28, © Springer Science+Business Media B.V. 2013

unethical behavior" (p. 24), there seems to be a definite need to study the ethical decision making of consumers. Consumers are a major participant in the business process and not considering them in ethics research will likely result in an incomplete understanding of business ethics.

The current paper describes a study that investigated consumers' judgments about a variety of situations with ethical content and that studied the relationship between these factors and selected attitudinal variables. This is the first study that has investigated consumers' ethical beliefs across a wide cross-section of the population in order to investigate consumer ethical judgments and the factors that may relate to these judgments.

Previous Research on Consumer Ethics

As stated earlier, research on consumer ethics has been quite limited. The little that has been written about consumer ethics can be placed into three categories. First, some authors have empirically examined very specific behaviors that have ethical implications. The two most commonly investigated areas are shoplifting (Kallis et al. 1986; Moschis and Powell 1986) and ecologically related consumption (Antil 1984; Haldeman et al. 1987).

A second set of papers have focused on providing normative guidelines for business and consumers on ethically related issues. For example, Stampfl (1979) outlined a code of ethics for consumers and Schubert (1979) developed a set of strategies for combatting consumer abuse.

The third set of papers has focused on developing a conceptual and empirical basis for understanding ethical decision making by consumers. Conceptually, Grove et al. (1989) presented a model, based upon the techniques of neutralization developed in sociology by Sykes and Matza (1957), that helps explain how some people may justify non-normative consumer behavior. Specifically, they stated that consumers may justify their non-normative consumer behavior through the denial of responsibility, denial of injury, denial of victim, condemning the condemners, and appeal to higher loyalties. Given the paucity of research in this area, the techniques of neutralization seems capable of giving some direction for studying consumers' ethical judgments.

Empirically, only three studies could be found that investigated the ethical judgments of the final consumer. Based on John F. Kennedy's "Consumer Bill of Rights," Davis (1979) investigated the extent to which people are willing to take on the responsibilities corresponding to their rights as consumers. She found that more subjects were likely to insist on their rights as consumers than were willing to accept their corresponding responsibilities. Specifically, on average, 95% of the respondents accepted their rights while only 74% accepted their responsibilities.

In a similar study, DePaulo (1987) investigated students' perceptions about how wrong they believed certain behaviors to be. Some situations presented to various subjects focused on the behavior of sellers and some focused on the behavior of buyers. There were pairs of behaviors that were conceptually similar but different in terms of whether it was the buyer or seller engaging in the unethical behavior (e.g., the buyer misleading the seller when negotiating versus the seller misleading the buyer when negotiating). Consistent with Davis (1979), consumers were more critical of sellers when they engaged in potentially unethical behavior than they were of buyers when they engaged in the same potentially unethical behavior.

A study by Wilkes (1978) investigated consumers' judgments concerning how "wrong" certain activities are. Though statistics are readily available on the extent of illegal or fraudulent consumer behavior, this is the only study that investigated peoples' perceptions of such behavior. Though some fraudulent activities were disapproved of more than others, most of these activities were seen as being wrong. There were a few activities that consumers seemed to perceive as tolerable. These "points of tolerance" seem to relate to those activities where business rather than the consumer was at fault.

Though the research by DePaulo et al. does give some insight into ethical judgments, more research is still needed. There are at least three ways in which the research on consumer ethics should be extended.

First, all three of the above-mentioned studies used a limited sample. DePaulo used student subjects, Wilkes studied the beliefs of housewives in a small university community, and the specifics of Davis' sample were not given, although it seems clear that her sample was not representative of an adult population since 49% of her sample was under the age of 25. To gain a better understanding of the consumer's ethical beliefs, research is needed that studies a broader cross-section of the adult population. This is needed to insure that the results identified are not idiosyncratic to any given segment of society.

Second, research is needed that investigates a broader set of beliefs within a single study. Though the breadth of issues investigated by these three studies, taken together, is considerable, insight into ethical judgments can be gained by studying the breadth of these issues within one single study. This will help in understanding how consumers make a wide range of judgments, and in determining if certain types of potentially unethical behaviors are viewed as more acceptable than others.

Third, there is very little information on the attitudinal factors that may contribute to the ethical judgments made by consumers. Though the ethical judgments, themselves, in these three studies potentially indicate a relationship between ethical beliefs and underlying attitudes towards business and government, among others, these studies did not explicitly study these issues. Thus, research that studies the relationship between selected attitudinal variables and the consumer's ethical beliefs would be useful in helping to understand the factors that may affect the consumer's ethical judgments.

In sum, what we know about the consumer's ethical decision making is very limited. There is a need to investigate ethical judgments of consumers across a broad cross-section of the adult population to see if these are related to underlying attitudes toward business and government as well as other groups. The current research was designed specifically to address these research needs. The specific research questions are presented in the following section.

Research Questions

The purpose of the current research was to further explore the nature of ethical judgments. Given the small amount of research that has been done, there was little that could be stated in terms of specific research hypotheses. Thus, the current research was done within the context of discovery (Hunt 1991); therefore, the specific issues being researched were stated in terms of research questions and not research hypotheses.

Specifically, the current research extends the work of Wilkes (1978), Davis (1979), and DePaulo (1987) in several ways. First, the sample used in the current study was much broader than was used in any of these other studies. Second, the current study combined the situations investigated by these previous studies, as well as adding a few more, in order to assess consumer judgments across a wider cross-section of situations having ethical content. Third, consumer attitudes toward business, salespeople, government, mankind in general and illegal acts were assessed, and these were related to ethical judgments. Specifically, the current research was designed to address the following two broad research questions:

Research Question 1: What are consumers' judgments concerning a wide range of situations that have ethical content and that they may face as consumers?
Research Question 2: Are there certain attitudinal differences that relate to the ethical judgments made by consumers?

Additionally, there were specific research subquestions that related to each of these broader questions.

General Ethical Judgments

Though most, but not all, of the situations having ethical content investigated in the current study were investigated by *either* Wilkes (1978), Davis (1979), or DePaulo (1987), the current research investigates more situations than any of these studies did individually. This should give greater insight into how consumers make judgments across a wide set of situations having ethical content. It was expected that certain behaviors would be perceived as being more "tolerable" than others. Consistent with Wilkes (1978) it was expected that these "points of tolerance" would relate to situations where the seller rather than the buyer was at fault. However, it seems likely that there are other reasons why consumers may show greater tolerance for certain potentially unethical acts than others. The data was analyzed *purely within the context of discovery* to see if other factors could be identified that explain why people differ in their ethical judgments. Thus, related to the first research question, the following three research subquestions were addressed:

Research Question 1a: Are consumers more tolerant of certain kinds of potentially unethical behavior than others?
Research Question 1b: If differences do exist across situations, are these differences due primarily to who is at fault for the potentially unethical behavior (i.e., the buyer or the seller)?
Research Question 1c: If differences do exist across situations, are there factors other than who is at fault which could potentially explain why these differences exist?

Attitudinal Characteristics

Both Davis (1979) and Depaulo (1987) indicated that there is a "double-standard" in terms of what is wrong for consumers versus what is wrong for buyers. However, all consumers did not exhibit this double standard. Consistent with the techniques of neutralization discussed earlier, it seems that those who have a more positive attitude towards business would be less likely to have this double standard and thus, would make different ethical judgments than those who have a negative attitude towards business. This question also was investigated separately within the context of salespeople since they are the point of contact at the buyer/seller interface. This may also apply to the government which has the responsibility of enforcing certain societal norms. In addition, it seems plausible that a consumer's general attitude towards others may impact how he or she makes ethical judgments. Finally, one's attitude about the inherent ethicalness of an illegal act may relate to ethical judgments. Thus, relating to the second research question, the current research investigated the following five research subquestions:

Research Question 2a: Do consumers who have a more positive attitude towards business in general make different ethical judgments than those who have a negative attitude?
Research Question 2b: Do consumers who have a more positive attitude towards salespeople make different ethical judgments than those who have a negative attitude?
Research Question 2c: Do consumers who have a more positive attitude towards government make different ethical judgments than those who have a negative attitude?
Research Question 2d: Do consumers who have a more positive attitude towards others make different ethical judgments than those who have a negative attitude?
Research Question 2e: Do consumers who believe that illegal acts are inherently unethical make different ethical judgments than those who do not believe this?

Methodology

Questionnaire

Since response rates in this type of research are typically low, one of the primary concerns for developing the current study was to minimize the number of nonrespondents. Thus, a short, one page (front and back) survey was administered. There were three parts to this survey.

Part 1 of the survey presented consumers with a set of 27 situations potentially faced by consumers that may have ethical content. These statements were developed through a review of the literature and through discussions with people who have worked in this area. Though it would be very difficult to derive a set of statements which exhaustively cover all ethical situations facing consumers, it is believed that these 27 statements cover the breadth of such potential situations. To check this assumption, 160 undergraduate students enrolled in a marketing research class were asked to indicate situations in which consumers may face ethical decisions. Of the 381 situations given by these students, 256 (67%) were conceptually equivalent to the behavior presented in these 27 statements. Thus, it is believed that these statements adequately (though not exhaustively) represent the domain of ethical judgments faced by consumers. The respondents were instructed to rate the 27 ethical belief statements as to whether they perceived these actions as being "wrong" (unethical) on a five point scale with the anchor points being "strongly believe that it is wrong" and "strongly believe that it is *not* wrong" and the middle point being "do not have an opinion."

Part 2 of the survey presented ten attitudinal statements. These statements were used to gain insight into consumers' attitudes towards business in general (three statements), salespeople in particular (two statements), government (two statements), mankind (two statements) and illegal acts or behaviors (one statement). Consumers were asked to rate their agreement with these ten statements on a five point scale from strongly agree to strongly disagree with the middle point being neither agree nor disagree.

Part 3 consisted of six demographic questions. There were four closed-ended questions used to assess family income, gender, age, and education. There were also two open-ended questions used to assess occupation and, for those who attended college, college major.

Sample

The sample consisted of 1,900 heads of households within the United States. These names were obtained from a large mailing list with a database comprising most U.S. households. This mailing list company guarantees an accuracy rate of 93%.

A two-stage random sample was conducted. First, 50 three-digit zip codes were randomly selected from among all three-digit zip codes in the United States. Second, a random selection was made from all households in these 50 zip codes.

Two waves were sent. A system was devised, implemented, and explained to respondents that assured anonymity while monitoring which surveys were returned. The response rate was 360 (19%) for the first wave and 209 (11%) for the second wave for a total response of 569 (30%). This response rate is consistent with comparable studies on marketplace ethics (see Chonko and Hunt 1985). To check for nonresponse bias as suggested by Armstrong and Overton (1977), the responses from the first wave were compared to the responses from the second wave. Of the 41 questions that could be compared (27 ethical judgment statements, 10 attitudinal statements, and 4 demographic questions) 5 showed significant differences at the 0.05 level (3 ethical judgment statements, 1 attitudinal statement, and 1 demographic question) and 2 were significant at the 0.01 level (both ethical judgment statements). Thus, though some nonresponse bias does appear to be present, such bias does not seem to be pervasive.

One of the most important considerations of the current research was to get a sample that included the diversity present in the U.S. population. A demographic summary of the respondents is as follows: on gender, the sample was split with there being 62.8% males and 37.2% females; on age, the sample was split with 26.9% being under the age of 35, 35.4% being between the ages of 36 and 55, and 38.7% being over the age of 55; on annual family income, 26.6% had an income of $20,000 and less, 40.8 had an income of $20,001–$40,000, 19.6% had an income of $40,001–$60,000, and 13.0% had an income of over $60,000; and on education, 30.4% did not go beyond high school, 29.4% had some college, 18.7% finished their education with a college degree, and 21.6% had at least some graduate work. Thus, the goal of sample diversity seems to have been achieved in that a large portion of the major demographic segments of the U.S. society were represented.

Analysis and Results

General Ethical Judgments

The first research question is "What are consumers' judgments concerning a wide range of situations that have ethical content and that they may face as consumers?" To answer this general research question as well as its three subquestions, consumers were asked to respond to the 27 consumer ethics statements described above.

Most of these actions were generally perceived as being wrong. However, 5 of the 27 statements had a mean response over the neutral point of the scale (3.0) indicating that these 5 were perceived as acceptable. As Table 28.1 indicates, "taping a movie off the television" was the least wrong action while "changing price-tags on merchandise in a retail store" was perceived as the most wrong.

Table 28.1 Means and percent responses to consumer ethics statements

Consumer ethics statement	Mean	Strongly believe that it is wrong 1 (%)	2 (%)	3 (%)	4 (%)	Strongly believe that it is not wrong 5 (%)
1. Actively benefiting						
Changing price-tags on merchandise in a retail store (563)[a]	1.25	81	16	1	0	2
Drinking a can of soda in a supermarket without paying for it (563)	1.33	71	28	1	0	1
Using a long distance access code that does not belong to you (562)	1.42	65	30	3	1	1
Reporting a lost item as "stolen" to an insurance company in order to collect the money (561)	1.55	58	34	5	2	1
Giving misleading price information to a clerk for an unpriced item (563)	1.55	53	42	3	1	1
Returning damaged merchandise when the damage is your own fault (561)	1.59	54	39	4	2	1
2. Passively benefiting						
Getting too much *change* and not saying anything (563)	1.77	42	45	6	5	1
Observing someone shoplifting and ignoring it (562)	1.88	38	43	15	4	1
Lying about a child's age in order to get a lower price (559)	1.89	36	46	11	6	1
Not saying anything when the waitress miscalculates the bill in your favor (563)	1.94	32	54	7	7	1
3. Deceptive, "legal" practices						
Removing the pollution control device from an automobile in order to get better mileage (563)	1.97	39	41	9	9	3
Breaking a bottle of salad dressing in a supermarket and doing nothing about it (563)	2.04	26	52	15	6	1
Stretching the truth on an income tax return (560)	2.06	34	41	12	10	3

Returning merchandise to a store by claiming that it was a gift when it was not (560)	2.07	35	39	12	12	2
Taking an ashtray or other "souvenir" from a hotel or restaurant (563)	2.08	30	47	11	11	2
Using a coupon for merchandise you did not buy (549)	2.1	26	48	18	7	1
Using an expired coupon for merchandise (560)	2.19	24	49	13	12	2
Joining a record club just to get some free records without any intention of buying records (564)	2.23	29	41	13	13	4
Not telling the truth when negotiating the price of a new automobile (554)	2.27	31	35	16	11	6
Moving into a new residence, finding that the cable TV is still hooked up, and using it rather than signing up and paying for it (560)	2.34	22	44	17	14	4
Tasting grapes in a supermarket and not buying any (563)	2.39	21	45	11	20	3
4. No harm/indirect harm						
Using computer software or games that you did not buy (543)	2.81	12	25	39	18	6
Recording an album instead of buying it (554)	3.12	12	22	20	33	13
Returning an item after finding out that the same item is now on sale (555)	3.16	12	24	16	31	16
Returning merchandise after trying it and not liking it (554)	3.48	8	14	15	46	16
Spending over an hour trying on different dresses and not purchasing any (557)	3.69	6	10	20	38	26
Taping a movie off the television (561)	3.8	4	9	20	37	30

[a] Figures in parentheses are N's for consumer ethics statements

Clearly, research subquestion 1a, "Are consumers more tolerant of certain kinds of potentially unethical behavior than others?" was answered in the affirmative. While the overwhelming majority disapproved of most of the actions tested, some of the actions were acceptable to many of the respondents. Thus, while most actions were viewed as unacceptable, there was more tolerance for some actions, and even a degree of acceptance of other actions.

Research subquestion lb asks, "If differences do exist across situations, are these differences due primarily to who is at fault for the potentially unethical behavior (i.e., the buyer or the seller)?" This too can be answered in the affirmative. Those actions that were considered to be the most unacceptable appear to be those where the consumer is actively benefiting at the expense of the seller (i.e., the first six items in Table 28.1). A typical example would be "changing price-tags on items in a retail store." A distinguishing characteristic of these actions is that all of them are initiated by the consumer; the consumer is actively involved in the behavior.

The next "set" of actions (i.e., the next four items in Table 28.1) appear to be those where the consumer is passively benefiting at the expense of others. An example would be "getting too much change and not saying anything." Most of these are initiated by the seller; that is, consumers benefit because of the seller's mistake. While, "Lying about a child's age …" may seem to be more active than passive, it may be that consumers interpreted this as simply "saying nothing and letting the seller make the mistake" that the child was younger than he or she really was. Thus, it appears that consumers *do* make some ethical distinctions in terms of who is at fault. It seems that consumers are more likely to accept passive unethical behavior than active unethical behavior, although both were considered to be wrong.

The next group of actions does not seem to fit this pattern, however. These 11 actions (see Table 28.1) also seem to be ones where the consumer is actively involved. However, these may differ from the first set in that, while the consumer is actively involved in some deception, these actions are not as likely to be seen as illegal as those in the first group. For instance, "not telling the truth when negotiating the price of a new automobile," may be an active deception, but it is probably not seen as illegal.

The issue of "perceived legality" is, perhaps, what makes these actions more acceptable. This also answers, in part, research subquestion 1c, "If differences do exist across situations, are there factors other than who is at fault which could potentially explain why these differences exist?" The answer to this is that the perceived illegality of an act might also influence its perceived ethicalness.

Additionally, the final six actions, which appear to be acceptable to many, may be so rated because there is no direct harm to anyone (although there may be indirect harm). Interestingly, three of these six deal with copying or taping something rather than buying it, a good example of indirect rather than direct or immediate injury to the seller. Thus, in deciding upon the severity of an action, consumers apparently consider whether or not direct harm is involved. This also leads one to answer research subquestion 1c in the affirmative.

Table 28.2 Descriptive statistics – general attitude statements

Attitude statement	Mean	Agree (%)	Disagree (%)
1. Attitude toward business			
Most businesses in America do not truly care about individual consumers	3.40	29	55
Most businesses generally try to deal with me in a fair way and, thus, I try to deal in a fair way with them	2.10	81	6
Free enterprise is the best form of an economic system	1.78	82	3
2. Attitude toward salespeople			
I never purchase anything from a door-to-door salesperson	3.37	27	47
Most salespeople cannot be trusted; they will say whatever they need to in order to make a sale	3.08	39	41
3. Attitude toward government			
The government has too many laws regulating business	2.57	50	23
The government has too many laws governing my life	2.65	46	26
4. Attitude toward mankind			
Man is basically good	2.29	72	15
If you deal honestly with a person, he or she will deal honesty with you	2.71	51	29
5. Attitude toward illegal acts			
If something is illegal, then it is ethically wrong to do it	2.41	61	24

Attitudinal Characteristics

Our second research question is, "Are there certain attitudinal differences that relate to the ethical judgments made by consumers?" An examination of its five separate research subquestions will help us to answer this broader research issue. To answer these subquestions, consumers were asked ten questions concerning general opinions and attitudes. These questions, their means and the percentage agreeing/disagreeing appear in Table 28.2.

As can be seen by examining the questions in Table 28.2, the average respondent felt somewhat alienated from government, believing that there are too many laws affecting both themselves and business. However, consumers seemed to be generally satisfied with businesses, believing that they care about consumers and deal fairly with them. The greatest consensus among respondents was that the best economic system is the free enterprise system. Only about 3% of respondents disagreed with this assertion.

Nevertheless, consumers were somewhat divided concerning their trust of salespeople with 39% agreeing that you cannot trust salespeople and 41% believing that you can trust them. In addition, about 27% of respondents said that they would not purchase from a door-to-door salesperson. Still, most respondents felt that man was basically good and that generally people deal honestly with each other.

Finally, the average respondent believed that if something is illegal, it is also ethically wrong, with only about 24% disagreeing with this statement.

Research subquestions 2a–2e were tested using correlation analysis with the results appearing in Table 28.3. Where more than one statement was used to measure an attitude, these were summated.

Relating to one's attitude toward business, as per research subquestion 2a, it was expected that consumers who felt a greater alienation from business would make ethical judgments that were more tolerant of unethical consumer behavior. This is based, to a large extent, on the work of Sykes and Matza (1957) regarding "techniques of neutralization." As previously mentioned, Sykes and Matza, in studying juvenile delinquency, identified five ways that juveniles justify aberrant behavior. One of the primary methods identified for justifying such behavior was labeled "condemning the condemners." Here, the person justified behavior that is socially disapproved of by making accusations towards those who do the disapproving. Thus, those that find it easier to condemn the buying side of the buyer/seller dyad would see greater justification in engaging in behavior that might be considered by others to be unethical. Similarly, as expressed in research subquestion 2b, it was expected that those with a more negative attitude toward salespeople, would also make ethical judgments that were more tolerant of unethical consumer behavior.

Question 2a, "Do consumers who have a more positive attitude towards business in general make different ethical judgments than those who have a negative attitude?" received moderate support in that 16 of the 27 correlation coefficients were significant. Given the way the constructs were scored, these positive correlations indicate that consumers who do have a more negative attitude toward business also tend to be more accepting of potentially unethical consumer behavior. However, the same was not true of one's attitude toward salespeople as only 7 of the 27 correlation coefficients were significant. Apparently, one's general attitude toward business does influence one's ethical judgments, but one's specific attitude toward salespeople has a much lesser influence on a consumer's ethical judgments.

Research subquestion 2c asks, "Do consumers who have a more positive attitude towards government make different ethical judgments than those who have a negative attitude?" Thus, it was also expected that there would also be a positive relationship between a consumer's ethical standards and their attitude toward government. Since many of the activities in the study may be perceived as coming under some form of government regulation, then greater consumer justification for these "questionable" actions may come through condemning the government rather than business.

However, this was not the case as only 2 of the 27 correlation coefficients relating attitude toward government to consumer ethical practices were significant. Thus, research subquestion 2c was not supported. The only strong relationship was between attitude toward government and removing pollution control devices. This may be explained by the fact that "alienated" consumers probably considered prohibitions against the removal of pollution control devices as *a specific* example

Table 28.3 Correlation of general attitude and consumer ethics statements

Consumer ethics statement	BUSAT	GOVAT	MANAT	SALEAT	ILLAT
Changing price-tags on merchandise in a retail store (1.25)[a]	0.09*	–0.02	0.08	0.02	0.11**
Drinking a can of soda in a supermarket without paying for it (1.33)	0.13**	–0.05	0.03	0.04	0.11**
Using a long distance access code that does not belong to you (1.42)	0.15**	–0.04	0.01	0.07	0.16**
Reporting a lost item as "stolen" to an insurance company in order to collect the money (1.55)	0.15**	–0.02	0.05	0.01	0.16**
Giving misleading price information to a clerk for an unpriced item (1.55)	0.16**	0.04	0.07	0.06	0.10*
Returning damaged merchandise when the damage is your own fault (1.59)	0.15**	–0.04	0.05	0.06	0.11**
Getting too much change and not saying anything (1.77)	0.23**	–0.03	0.09*	0.13**	0.16**
Observing someone shoplifting and ignoring it (1.88)	0.15**	0.05	0.06	0.05	0.16**
Lying about a child's age in order to get a lower price (1.89)	0.20**	–0.06	0.01	0.08*	0.22**
Not saying anything when the waitress miscalculates the bill in your favor (1.94)	0.18**	–0.06	0.10*	0.09*	0.23**
Removing the pollution control device from an automobile in order to get better mileage (1.97)	0.13**	–0.20**	0.00	0.09*	0.11**
Breaking a bottle of salad dressing in a supermarket and doing nothing about it (2.04)	0.08	–0.08	0.00	0.11*	0.15**
Stretching the truth on an income tax return (2.06)	0.11*	–0.08	0.04	0.04	0.22**
Returning merchandise to a store by claiming that it was a gift when it was not (2.07)	0.08	–0.02	–0.03	0.02	0.23**
Taking an ashtray or other "souvenir" from a hotel or restaurant (2.08)	0.11**	–0.05	0.08*	0.03	0.22**
Using a coupon for merchandise you did not buy (2.10)	0.09	–0.06	0.00	0.05	0.13**
Using an expired coupon for merchandise (2.19)	0.11**	–0.04	0.03	0.02	0.27**
Joining a record club just to get some free records without any intention of buying records (2.23)	0.07	–0.04	0.01	0.01	0.21**
Not telling the truth when negotiating the price of a new automobile (2.27)	0.19**	–0.02	0.08	0.10*	0.27**

(continued)

Table 28.3 (continued)

Consumer ethics statement	BUSAT	GOVAT	MANAT	SALEAT	ILLAT
Moving into a new residence, finding that the cable TV is still hooked up, and using it rather than signing up and paying for it (2.34)	0.08	−0.10*	0.02	0.12**	0.22**
Tasting grapes in a supermarket and not buying any (2.39)	0.06	0.00	−0.01	0.01	0.14**
Using computer software or games that you did not buy (2.81)	0.03	−0.05	0.03	0.02	0.20**
Recording an album instead of buying it (3.12)	0.02	−0.03	0.05	0.01	0.16**
Returning an item after finding out that the same item is now on sale (3.16)	0.14**	−0.02	−0.00	0.07	0.14**
Returning merchandise after trying it and not liking it (3.48)	0.01	−0.04	0.05	−0.01	0.10*
Spending over an hour trying on different dresses and not purchasing any (3.69)	−0.06	−0.03	0.05	−0.02	0.11**
Taping a movie off the television (3.80)	0.03	0.02	0.02	−0.05	0.25**

BUSAT attitude toward business, *GOVAT* attitude toward government, *MANAT* attitude toward mankind, *SALEAT* attitude toward salespeople, *ILLAT* attitude toward illegal acts
*Significant at 0.05 level; **Significant at 0.01 level
[a] Figures in parentheses are means for consumer ethics statements

of government "interference" in their lives. However, there is no *general,* overall relationship between attitude toward government and the acceptance and/or rejection of questionable consumer actions.

It was also expected that those who have a more positive attitude toward others, in general, would have stricter ethical standards. This is research sub-question 2d, "Do consumers who have a more positive attitude towards others make different ethical judgments than those who have a negative attitude?" Again the rationale is based, in part, on Sykes and Matza's techniques of neutralization. It seems as though it would be easier for someone to justify questionable behavior if they had a less trusting attitude towards others, in general. This question was not supported either, however, as only two correlations were significant. Thus, a person's overall view of mankind does not seem to influence his or her ethical beliefs as a consumer.

Research subquestion 2e stated, "Do consumers who believe that illegal acts are inherently unethical make different ethical judgments than those who do not believe this?" It was expected that consumers who believe that illegal acts are inherently unethical would be less tolerant of questionable consumer actions than those who did not believe this. This question was very strongly supported as all 27 correlations were significant. Thus, consumers who equated "illegal with unethical" were significantly less tolerant of the consumer actions examined than those who did not equate these two concepts.

Conclusions and Implications

There are certain limitations to this study. For example, the sample was drawn exclusively from the United States. There is no certainty that similar results would have been obtained if other nationalities had been sampled. In fact, the extent to which ethical beliefs differ across cultures and nationalities might provide beneficial insight into the determinants of these ethical beliefs.

It should be emphasized that this research was done purely within the context of discovery. Given the results, however, it appears that the goal of discovery was accomplished in that many interesting findings deserving of further investigation were revealed. This research presents a viable starting point for developing a body of knowledge on consumer ethics.

The present study did show that several important factors are likely to contribute to how consumers make ethical judgments: whether or not the buyer or the seller is at fault, whether or not the activity is perceived as illegal, whether or not there is direct harm to the seller, whether or not the consumer has a negative attitude toward business, and whether or not the consumer equates unethical with illegal.

One explanation of the results dealing with "fault" is that consumers view passive, unethical behavior as more acceptable than active, unethical behavior because they believe that if it is the seller's mistake or the seller's fault that leads to the seller being harmed, then he or she is just getting what they deserve. This explanation fits within the techniques of neutralization model of "condemning the condemners" and/or "denial of victim."

Similarly, the fact that indirect, less immediate harm to the seller is more acceptable than direct, immediate harm can be explained by the "denial of injury" technique. One implication of this is that a consumer education campaign could be useful in clarifying the magnitude of losses due to practices such as copying software, tapes, and movies. Some consumers may not be aware of the problem caused by these practices since they have been made possible by relatively new technology.

Since consumers who believe themselves alienated from business seem to be more likely to accept questionable consumer acts, business can help itself by "cleaning up" its own image. This can only be done through a "real" improvement in business ethics across the board, in conjunction with a campaign to inform the consumer of this effort. Unfortunately, there will always be some "dishonest" firms who will find it to their advantage to ignore any such efforts, but stronger attempts at self-regulation such as the example of self-regulation within the U.S. advertising industry could be beneficial.

Future research in this area should look at issues such as the extent to which ethical beliefs differ across cultures and nationalities and at the determinants of these ethical beliefs. In addition, comparisons of a consumer's ethical beliefs with various personality variables such as Machiavellianism or ethical ideology would add to our limited knowledge in this area. Ultimately, the development of a general theory of consumer ethics which could be used to guide research in this area and to help develop a body of knowledge on consumer ethics is imperative.

References

Antil, J.H. 1984. Socially responsible consumers: Profile and implications for public policy. *Journal of Macro-marketing* 4(Fall): 18–39.

Armstrong, J.S., and T.S. Overton. 1977. Estimating non-response bias in mail surveys. *Journal of Marketing Research* 14(August): 396–402.

Baumhart, R. 1961. How ethical and businessmen? *Harvard Business Review* 38(July–August): 6–31.

Bernstein, P. 1985. Cheating – The new national pastime? *Business* 35(October–December): 24–33.

Brenner, S.N., and E.A. Molander. 1977. Is the ethics of business executives changing? *Harvard Business Review* 55(January–February): 57–71.

Chonko, L.B., and S.D. Hunt. 1985. Ethics and marketing management: An empirical examination. *Journal of Business Research* 13(July): 339–359.

Davis, R.M. 1979. Comparison of consumer acceptance of rights and responsibilities. In *Proceedings, 25th annual conference of the American Council on Consumer Interests*, ed. N.M. Ackerman, 68–70. Columbia: American Council on Consumer Interests.

DePaulo, P.J. 1987. Ethical perceptions of deceptive bargaining tactics used by salespersons and consumers: A double standard. In *Proceedings of the division of consumer psychology*, ed. J.G. Saegert, 201–203. Washington, DC: American Psychological Association.

Ferrell, O.C., and L. Gresham. 1985. A contingency framework for understanding ethical decision making in marketing. *Journal of Marketing* 49(Summer): 87–96.

Ferrell, O.C., L. Gresham, and J. Fraedrich. 1989. A synthesis of ethical decision models for marketing. *Journal of Macromarketing* 9(Fall): 55–64.

Grove, S.J., S.J. Vitell, and D. Strutton. 1989. Non-normative consumer behavior and the techniques of neutralization. In *Proceedings of the 1989 AMA winter educators' conference*, ed. R. Bagozzi and J.P. Peter. Chicago: American Marketing Association.

Haldeman, V.A., J.M. Peters, and P.A. Tripple. 1987. Measuring a consumer energy conservation ethic: An analysis of components. *Journal of Consumer Affairs* 21(1): 70–85.

Hunt, S.D. 1991. *Marketing theory*. Cincinnati: Southwestern.

Hunt, S.D., and S.J. Vitell. 1986. A general theory of marketing ethics. *Journal of Macromarketing* 6: 5–16.

Kallis, M.J., K.A. Krentier, and D.J. Vanier. 1986. The value of user image in quelling aberrant consumer behavior. *Journal of the Academy of Marketing Science* 14(Spring): 29–35.

Moschis, G.P., and J. Powell. 1986. The juvenile shoplifter. *The Marketing Mix* 10(Winter–Spring): 1–14.

Murphy, P., and G. Laczniak. 1981. Marketing ethics: A review with implications for managers, educators and researchers. In *Review of marketing 1981*, ed. B. Enis and K. Roering, 251–266. Chicago: American Marketing Association.

Murphy, P., and M.D. Pridgen. 1987. Ethical and legal issues in marketing. Paper presented at A.M.A. *Marketing ethics workshop*, University of Southern Mississippi.

Schubert, J.T. 1979. Consumer abuse: Some recommendations for change. In *Proceedings, 25th annual conference of the American Council on Consumer Interests*, ed. N.M. Ackerman, 146–149. Columbia: American Council on Consumer Interests.

Stampfl, R.W. 1979. Multi-disciplinary foundations for a consumer code of ethics. In *Proceedings, 25th annual conference of the American Council on Consumer Interests*, ed. N.M. Ackerman, 12–20. Columbia: American Council on Consumer Interests.

Sykes, G.M., and D. Matza. 1957. Techniques of neutralization: A theory of delinquency. *American Sociological Review* 22(December): 664–670.

Vitell, S., and T. Festervand. 1987. Business ethics: Conflicts, practices and beliefs of industrial executives. *Journal of Business Ethics* 6: 111–122.

Wilkes, R.E. 1978. Fraudulent consumer behavior. *Journal of Marketing* 42(October): 67–75.

Chapter 29
The Morality of Software Piracy: A Cross-Cultural Analysis

William R. Swinyard, Heikki Rinne, and Ah Keng Kau

Introduction

As long as the personal computer has existed, software piracy has been an important issue. Software producers have tried just about everything to protect themselves from losses due to unauthorized copying. They have made the copying difficult, using unformatted or oddly formatted disk sectors, laser holes and burns, and special error codes. They have created software which works only with key disks or plug-in port keys. They use license-agreements or lease-contracts with probably unenforceable break-seal acceptance provisions. And through it all, ADAPSO (an anti-piracy trade association representing 750 computer and software companies) promotes an understanding of copyright law and the moral notion, "Thou Shalt Not Dupe" (ADAPSO 1984).

Despite these efforts, as the personal computer industry has grown, so has software piracy. The International Trade Commission, for example, estimates that theft of "intellectual property" costs the U.S. more than US$40 billion annually in lost sales and royalties. For software, it is estimated that one illegal copy is made for every software program sold (Bailey 1984).

Though software piracy is a troublesome issue in every corner of the globe, the popular press has singled out Asia for particular condemnation. Articles in the U.S. computer press often comment with disdain about Hong Kong's "Golden Arcade", Singapore's "Funan Center" and "People's Park," or Taipei's "Computer Alley" – retail outlets where the computer shopper can buy pirated copies of virtually any

W.R. Swinyard • H. Rinne
Institute of Business Management, Brigham Young University, 660 TNRB, Provo, UT 84602, USA

A.K. Kau
Department of Marketing, National University of Singapore, Kent Ridge, Singapore

A.C. Michalos and D.C. Poff (eds.), *Citation Classics from the Journal of Business Ethics*, Advances in Business Ethics Research 2,
DOI 10.1007/978-94-007-4126-3_29,

copyrighted software for little more than the costs of a blank disk (see Hebditch 1986, for example). The illegal sales from these outlets are impossible to measure. Lotus Development Corporation believes that software piracy from Taiwan alone cost them lost sales of US$200 million annually (Eduardo Lachica 1989). In a single 1986 raid on one Hong Kong shopping arcade US$130,000 worth of pirated software was confiscated (Warner 1986). The shops stop making and selling pirated copies for only a few hours after such raids.

A casual reader of these articles could logically conclude that the people of these Asian nations are behaving immorally about software copyright law. Possibly even that they are immoral people. If we hold a belief – say, that Asians pirate software – we may form a belief structure that leads to broader conclusions about them (Bern 1970).[1] Are these conclusions warranted? By copying software are Asians behaving immorally? What *drives* their morality on this? How do they justify it? Is their moral development here different than that of Westerners? Or do they have similar moral development but different moral behaviors?

This paper investigates such issues. In particular, it contrasts the historical cultural development of proprietary intellectual property in Asia with that of the U.S. The piracy issue is specifically addressed using data collected in the United States and Singapore.

Cultural Foundations

Protection legislation originated in the Western World. This legislation, which deals with patents, copyrights, trademarks, trade secrets, etc., reflects the traditional value of the West on the preservation and protection of individual creative efforts. Software can be protected through a variety of legal means. Program code has received both patent and copyright protection, but its most popular protection is under international copyright law (Harris 1985). Copyright law originated centuries ago with British common law. In the U.S. its origins are found in the first draft of the Constitution. Article I, Section 8 of that document contain these clauses:

> The Congress shall have power to promote the progress of science and useful arts, by securing for limited times to authors and inventors the exclusive right to their respective writings and discoveries …
>
> and
>
> To make all laws which shall be necessary and proper for carrying into execution the foregoing powers, and all the powers vested by this constitution in the government of the United States, or in any department or officer thereof.

However, more thorough protection provided by statutory copyright law became available in 1909. These laws were strengthened with the 1976 Copyright Act (Davis 1985) and the 1980 Software Amendments to that act (Benheshtian 1986), which specifically included the visual representation of program code as appropriate to copyright.

Copyright Laws and the West

Copyright and patent protection reflect a characteristic value of the Western World in general and the U.S. in particular. In the United States, individual freedom and benefits are emphasized over societal benefits. That and many other western nations generally hold that individual creative developments have individual ownership. This view is reflected widely: artists' signatures on their creative work, journalists' bylines in newspaper articles, authors' names on their work, individual claims to design or copyright ownership, individual patent ownership.

Not only have artists and authors have historically taken full credit for and signed their work, but also glass-blowers, ceramicists, silversmiths, photographers, clock-makers, leatherworkers, woodworkers and furniture-makers, welders, inventors of all kinds, and even sometime masons, cement-layers, clothing inspectors, and automobile workers.

The West's preoccupation with protecting original creative work led it to originate copyright, patent, and trade-secret legislation.

Copyright Laws and the East

Asia presents quite a contrast. Asian cultures (and particularly the Chinese culture, which has dramatically influenced the culture of most Asian nations), has traditionally emphasized that individual developers or creators are obliged to share their developments with society. A Chinese proverb heralds this view: "He that shares is to be rewarded; he that does not, condemned." Indeed, third-world and Asian nations "traditionally believe that copyright is a Western concept created to maintain a monopoly over the distribution and production of knowledge and knowledge-based products" (Altbach 1988).

Barnes (1989) suggests that, "the inclination to create identical clones of a single product can be explained by [Asian] calligraphy." Becoming a master calligrapher in Japan takes countless hours of copying the works of a master until the student's work is indistinguishable from the original (Sanson 1943). Barnes (1989) points out that moveable type – not accidentally a Chinese invention – allowed exact copies of the master's original calligraphy. A likely motivation for the Chinese to invent moveable type was that it permitted them to precisely reproduce classically elegant calligraphy time after time, thus reflecting their cultural value of sharing creative work.

It is also noteworthy that in Asia books often feature both the name of the translator and the author with equal standing on the title page. Asian paintings often are signed with the name of the school that produced the work, rather than the name of the artist. Indeed, these schools typically have numerous artists, all precisely duplicating the same creative work.

We can see the legislative reflections of such values. Software was slow to achieve copyright protection in Japan and the Philippines, and it still does not exist in Indonesia, Malaysia, and Thailand (Greguras and Langenberg 1985). And while mainland China is an attractive market for U.S. software firms, their major concern for that country is its lack of legal protection for software (Blois 1988; Greguras and Foster-Simons 1985).

And so we see that the cultural history of Asia does not generally support the notion of protecting proprietary creative work. In many Asian nations the highest compliment one can be paid is to be copied. Emulation is not only admired, it is encouraged. It is no surprise then that protection concepts would be adopted slowly.

Moral Decision-Making

Asians also have a different perspective on moral decision-making than people of many western nations. Americans, in particular, tend to be more rule-oriented in their decisions than Asians, who tend to be circumstance-oriented. Swinyard et al. (1989) reported that Americans tend to make moral decisions based on fundamental value rules of right and wrong. That study found that Americans see little relativity in their moral choices; what is moral in one situation is also moral in another. The research concluded that they are relatively rule-oriented or deontological in their moral decisions.

By contrast, the study found that Asians (at least, Singaporeans) seem to make moral decisions less on rules and more on the basis of the consequences of their moral behavior. Thus, it concluded that Asians seem to follow a more utilitarian ethic. This tendency, too, suggests that Americans would be more likely be obedient to copyright laws than Asians, who would more carefully examine the situation, outcomes, or benefits which would result from a copyright violation.

Hypotheses

As a result of the above discussion we are led to expect that,

1. Americans will have both attitudes and intentions which are more congruent with copyright laws than Asians, and
2. Asians will tend to base their moral decisions on the outcomes of the behavior, while Americans will tend to base their moral decisions on the nature of the decision itself.

Methodology

Sample

Our study uses a pilot sample of 371 student subjects: 221 attending a major western U.S. university and 150 attending the National University of Singapore.

Extensively pretested versions of a questionnaire were administered in classroom settings to students all across both campuses. The questionnaires were completed in private and subjects were assured of complete anonymity in their responses. The courses chosen typically contained students of all major fields of study in the respective schools of management for the two universities. While the sample does not represent "Americans" and "Singaporeans," it does reasonably represent the business management students of two Universities within those countries.

Measures of Cognition, Attitudes, and Intentions

The questionnaire measured cognition of or *knowledge* toward pirating copyrighted software using three summed statements. Using five-point scales (anchored with 1 = "strongly disagree" and 5 = "strongly agree"), subjects were asked to indicate their view toward these statements:

- Making a copy of copyrighted software and giving it to a friend is illegal,
- When you buy a copyrighted software program, you usually are only buying the right to *use* the software. The program itself remains the property of the publisher, and
- It is illegal to copy "public domain" software (reverse scored).

Three measures were also summed to obtain subjects' *attitudes* toward software copyright laws:

- I would feel guilty about even *having* unauthorized copies of copyrighted software,
- I would not feel badly about making unauthorized copies of software (reverse scored), and
- I would feel badly about giving even my close friends copies of copyrighted software.

And, similarly, three measures were summed to obtain their *behavioral intentions* toward these laws:

- I wouldn't hesitate to make a copy of a copyrighted software program for my own personal use (reverse scored),
- I wouldn't hesitate to accept a copy of copyrighted software if someone offered (reverse scored), and
- I would never offer a friend a copy of a copyrighted software program.

For these three measures, then, higher scale values correspond with greater *knowledge* of copyright law, and *attitudes* and *behavior* more consistent with software copyright law.

Measures of Personal Utility

Tradeoff analysis was used to measure personal utility. The first moral reasoning study to use tradeoff analysis was that by Swinyard et al. (1989). Tradeoff analysis

Table 29.1 Decision alternatives

Do not copy the software and do not use it,
Copy the program and destroy the copy after using it for the assignment,
Copy the program and keep a copy for use on other projects, or,
Copy the program and sell copies to other people that ask for it.

is a powerful method of analysis most often used to measure the relative importance of one product attribute (say, the quality or durability of a product) compared with another (for example, price). Tradeoff analysis requires that people ask themselves, "Are some attributes so important to me that I should sacrifice others to get them?" It takes into consideration context and situational contingencies.

It also fits comfortably with the requirements of a circumstantial study of moral decision-making. For example, suppose a manager of research is faced with both a depleted budget and a need for a second copy of a new but costly business software package to complete a project. She has some choices. Among them: she can make the sacrifice and buy the package, perhaps by using budget allocated to another necessary area, but escape any threat of prosecution, or spasm of conscience. Or she can make an illegal duplicate copy of the software package and risk an entanglement with the law or even her own boss, but preserve her meager budget. If the project had important outcomes for her, she would undoubtedly be more inclined to *somehow* obtain the software. What should she do? Tradeoff analysis permits the computation of her *utility* or preference level for her alternative actions, given the results or outcomes that face her.

Similar to this example, our questionnaire asked the subjects to role-play each of three different scenarios. Each scenario placed the subjects in charge of an important business project which could be successfully completed with some new software, but there was no money available for its purchase. The scenarios explained, however, that a friend who owns this software has offered to let it be illegally copied. Subjects were given several alternatives in dealing with this software dilemma, shown in Table 29.1.

But each alternative carried with it some consequences or outcomes or benefits for the completion of a project in which the copied software will be used. The three scenarios differed, in fact, only in these outcomes (shown in Table 29.2), which were those having personal benefits, family benefits, or community benefits. For each of these sets of benefits, some outcomes may be viewed as a more attractive incentive to pirate the software, while others are not. One scenario shown to subjects is found in Appendix 1.

Moral Acceptability and Tradeoff Measures

In each scenario subjects completed a measure of "moral acceptability" for each of the four alternative decisions shown in Table 29.1 (scaled on a seven-point "acceptable" to "unacceptable" scale (with "7" as "acceptable")). This is illustrated

Table 29.2 Possible outcomes from successful completion of the project

Personal Benefits

1. Provide you with a significant promotion and raise – a much better position and a 50% salary increase, or it could
2. Provide you with a modest promotion and raise – a somewhat better position and a 10% salary increase or it could
3. Not affect your job, position, or salary with the company

Family Benefits

1. A large financial reward – one which will totally pay all family bills, and completely relieve your family from its critical financial condition, or
2. A modest financial reward – one which will pay some of the family bills, and provide temporary relief from your family's critical condition, or
3. No financial reward – thus providing no relief for your family's critical financial condition.

Community Benefits

1. Significantly benefit thousands of people in your community, or
2. Significantly benefit hundreds of people in your community, or
3. Provide no benefits to people in your community.

in Appendix 1. After reading the scenario, subjects were then asked to complete a 16-cell "tradeoff" table having the moral choices in the columns, and the outcomes (Table 29.2) in the rows. One tradeoff table, using "personal benefits" as the outcomes, is shown in Appendix 2.

Results

Cognition, Attitude, and Intentions Measures

As shown in Fig. 29.1, compared with the U.S. group, the Singaporean subjects were more *knowledgeable* about software copyright law ($t=4.70$, $p<0.001$). Despite this however, their attitudes were *less* supportive of those laws ($t=7.78$, $p<0.001$). And their behavioral intentions were consistent with their attitudes – the Singaporeans were significantly more inclined to make pirated copies of software than the Americans ($t=10.59$, $p<0.001$). These data support our first hypothesis – that Americans will have attitudes and intentions more congruent with copyright laws than Asians.

Moral Acceptability

Figure 29.2 provides further support for the first hypothesis. This Figure shows that the U.S. subjects differed from the Singaporeans on measures of moral acceptability. Of the four decision measures shown in Table 29.1, the two groups were similar in

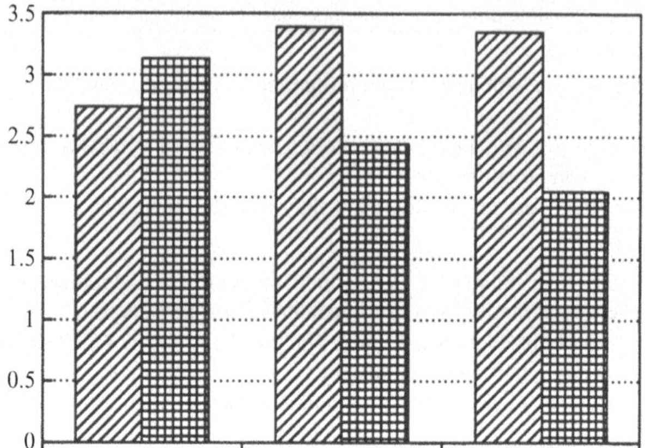

	Cognition	Attitudes	Behavioral Intent
US Subjects	2.74	3.39	3.35
S'n Subjects	3.13	2.44	2.05

N - 221 (US), 150(singapore)

Fig. 29.1 Response toward software copying, cognition, attitudes, behavioral intent

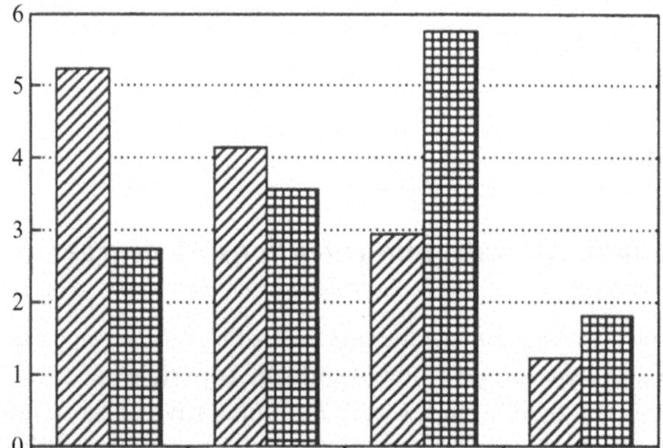

	Do Not Copy	Destroy Copy	Keep Copy	Sell Copies
US Subjects	5.24	4.14	2.94	1.22
S'n Subjects	2.73	3.56	5.76	1.81

N-221 (US), 150 (Singapore)

Fig. 29.2 Moral acceptability

their evaluations of the "destroy copy" and "sell copies" decisions ("copy the program and destroy the copy after [use]": $t=0.85$, n.s. and "copy the program and sell copies": $t=0.056$, n.s.). But "do not copy" and "keep copy" were rated very differently.

Table 29.3 Tradeoff table results

Software alternatives	Do not copy or use	Copy, but destroy after use	Copy and keep a copy	Copy and sell copies	
Outcome for you:	1	2	5	10	–U.S.
Benefit thousands of people in your community	5	2	1	6	–Asian
Benefit hundreds	3	4	7	11	–U.S.
of people in your community	7	4	3	8	–Asian
Provide no benefit	6	8	10	12	–U.S.
to people in your community	11	10	9	12	–Asian

The Singaporeans found "copy the program and keep a copy . . ." significantly *more* acceptable ($t=3.53$, $p<0.001$), and "do not copy the software" significantly *less* acceptable than the Americans ($t=3.58$, $p<0.001$).

Tradeoff Utilities

The tradeoff results reflect the above tendencies. For example, a typical tradeoff table is shown in Table 29.3 for the U.S. and the Asian groups.

As Table 29.3 shows, in completing the tradeoff table the U.S. group tended to favor the columns. In particular, their low numbers in the first column show that they preferred the "do not copy" alternative over all others, followed next by the "copy and destroy" column. Indeed, five of their first six preferences are in these first two columns. Thus, the U.S. students showed preference for their "decisions" over the "outcomes." That is, in making a moral decision, the U.S. group was more influenced by the legality of the copying than its impact on people.

The Singaporean subjects, on the other hand, specifically favored the "copy and keep a copy" over the other alternatives. They also tended to favor the rows – their lower numbers in Table 29.3 show concern toward the row variables of having a desirable outcome, rather than showing compliance with copyright laws. Thus, the Singaporean students showed preference for the "outcomes" over the "decisions."

The calculated tradeoff utilities from these data (and the two other tradeoff tables which were completed similarly) confirm this. The utilities are shown in Fig. 29.3.[2] These utilities are simply calculated representations of what we have already observed in Table 29.3. For example, because the U.S. subjects tended to favor the "do not copy" column more than the Singaporeans, it is no surprise to us that Fig. 29.3 shows that the calculated utilities for "do not copy" are substantially greater for the U.S. subjects than for the Singaporeans. And for "copy and keep a copy", the utility is somewhat greater for the Singaporeans than for the Americans.

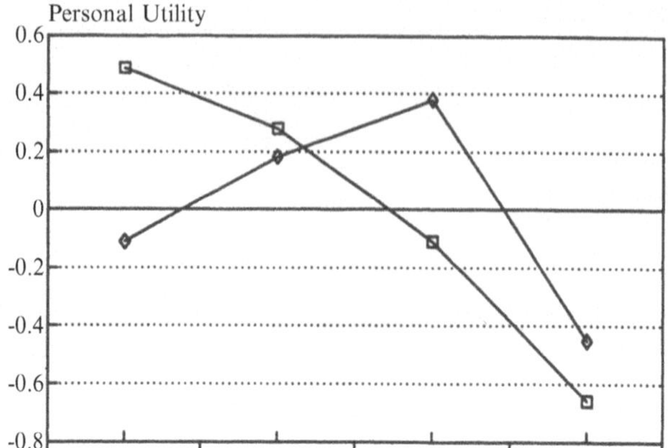

	Do Not	Destroy	Keep	Sell
US Subjects	0.488	0.28	-0.109	-0.659
S'n Subjects	-0.11	.0183	0.379	-0.452

--- Decision About Copying the Software ---

N - 221 (USA), 150 (Singapore)

Fig. 29.3 Utility of copying decision

The calculated tradeoff utilities representing the importance of the copying decision versus the outcome are shown in Fig. 29.4. Figure 29.4 plots four points along the horizontal axis. The first three of these – "self," "family," and "community" – represent utilities or importance for the *outcomes* to come from copying the software:

- personal benefits, or benefits to *self*
- *family* benefits, and
- *community benefits*.

The fourth point on the horizontal axis of Fig. 29.4 – "copy" – represents the utility or importance of the copying *decision*. Thus, Fig. 29.4's utility shown for "copy" represents the value or importance subjects are placing on the legality of the copying decision over the outcomes. On the other hand, the utilities shown for "self", "family", and "community" represent the value or importance subjects are placing on the actual outcomes of the project.

And so we see that, for the Singaporean subjects, the higher utilities in Fig. 29.4 show their greater interest in the outcomes or benefits of the copying decision than in the legality of the copying. That is, in making a moral decision, the Singaporean group was more influenced by the benefits of their actions on self, family, or community than by the legality of copying the software. By contrast, the U.S. group was more influenced by the legality of the decision than by the benefits of the decision.

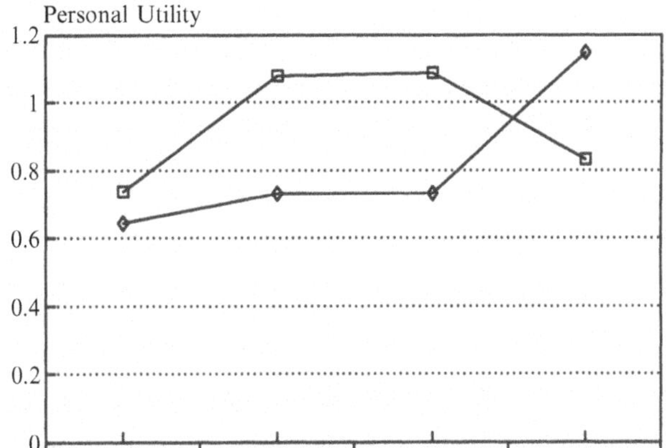

	Self	Family	Community	Copy
US Subjects	0.643	0.731	0.731	1.147
S'n Subjects	0.737	1.077	1.086	0.831

-221 (US), 150(singapore)

Fig. 29.4 Importance of decision vs outcome

We view these results in support of our second hypothesis – that Asians will base their moral decisions more on the outcomes of the behavior, while Americans will base their moral decisions more on the nature of the decision itself.

Discussion and Conclusions

While Asians seem to have a more casual attitude than Americans toward software piracy, those in the West must understand that it is not simple law-breaking we are dealing with. Copyright and other protection legislation goes firmly against the grain of Asian culture, which supports the concept of sharing, not protecting, individual creative work. One should not expect Asians to quickly support copyright legislation, nor to immediately embrace it in their attitudes or behavior.

Meanwhile, police-action enforcements of copyright laws are being used in Asia. Despite the fact that many Asians are behaving illegally, to conclude that they are behaving immorally is inappropriate. More accurately, it appears that their moral values respecting this matter are simply very different from Westerners. Software copyright runs afoul of deeply rooted and somewhat fundamental Asian-cultural beliefs. Not only does their culture provide *less* support for copyright legislation, it provides *more* support for the human benefits which might come from the piracy.

We should expect relatively little voluntary compliance, until the Asian cultural norms change. Culture changes slowly, and people in the U.S. and other Western nations must have patience with Asia as it changes. Achieving Asian congruence of thought on it will likely take years; perhaps even generations.

Appendix 1

The Scenario

Suppose you are working for a private company on a government consulting project. The timing and the completion of the project is critical, and you are committed to the project.

You have just found out that there is *a computer software program which is essential to finish the project correctly and on time*. The software is copyrighted and costs $800. However, the company has not budgeted for the software and is not willing to purchase it.

You have a friend who has purchased this software program. Your friend has offered to let you copy the programs and use the copy however you wish.

Alternatives

You have the four alternatives listed below available for you. Please check the space which best reflects your personal view how acceptable or unacceptable each alternative is for you.

Acceptable	Unacceptable	
–	–	A. Do not copy the software and do not use it.
–	–	B. Copy the program and destroy the copy after using it for the assignment.
–	–	C. Copy the program and keep a copy for use on other projects.
–	–	D. Copy the program and sell copies to other people that ask for it.

Outcomes for Your Decision

Suppose that if you get the project finished correctly and on time, the following three alternatives exist for you. The successful completion of the project could:

1. Provide you with a significant promotion and raise – a much better position and a 50% salary increase, or it could
2. Provide you with a modest promotion and raise – a somewhat better position and a 10% salary increase, or it could
3. Not affect your job, position, or salary with the company.

Appendix 2

Tradeoff Table for the Scenario

Now please consider both the four alternatives (A, B, C, and D) available to you with regards to the software, and the three personal outcomes (1, 2, and 3) and indicate the order of your preference for each combination, by numbering each box from 1 to 12:

Alternatives				
	Do not copy or use	Copy, but destroy after use	Copy and keep a copy	Copy and sell copies
Outcome for you: Provide you with a significant promotion and raise				
Provide you with a modest promotion and raise				
Not affect your position with the company				

Notes

1 In this case, the belief structure would be "vertical" and resemble a syllogism:

1. The Asians pirate software.
2. Software piracy is both illegal and immoral, and so …
3. The Asians must be immoral law-breakers.

2 While tradeoff analysis provides no difference tests of significance, it does provide a "badness of fit measure." Measures above 0.2 are to be considered unreliable. Our measures were all at 0.03 or lower, and no more than 6.5 inconsistencies out of a possible 198 comparisons, which suggests a very good fit with the original data.

References

ADAPSO. 1984. *Thou shalt not dupe*. Arlington: ADAPSO.

Altbach, Philip G. 1988. Economic progress brings copyright to Asia. *Far Eastern Economic Review* 139(9): 62–63.

Bailey, Douglas M. 1984. A war of attrition: Software companies vs crafty pirates. *New England Business* 6(6): 22–23.

Barnes, Howared W. 1989.Cost leadership and differentiation: Contrasting strategies of Japan and the Federal Republic of Germany. Working Paper, Brigham Young University, Provo.

Benheshtian, Mehdi. 1986. Computer copyright law. *Journal of Systems Management* 37(9): 6–11.

Bern, Daryl. 1970. *Beliefs, attitudes, and human affairs*. Belmont: Brooks/Cole.

Blois, Keith. 1988. Supermarkets in China. *Retail & Distribution Management* 16(1): 40–42.

Davis, G.Gervaise. 1985. *Software protection*. New York: Van Nostrand Reinhold.

Eduardo, Lachica. 1989. Trade thievery: U.S. companies curb pirating of some items but by no means all. *Wall Street Journal* (March 16).

Greguras, Fred, and Frances Foster-Simons. 1985. Software protection in the People's Republic of China. *Information Age* 7(4): 220–228.

Greguras, Fred, and Peter M. Langenberg. 1985. Trends in proprietary protection in Asia and the Pacific Region. *Information Age* 7(1): 3–9.

Harris, Thorne D. 1985. *The legal guide to computer software protection*. Englewood Cliffs: Prentice-Hall.

Hebditch, David. 1986. Pirate's paradise. *Datamation* 32(17): 71–72.

Sanson, G.B. 1943. *Japan: A short cultural history*. New York: Appleton.

Swinyard, William R., Thomas L. DeLong, and Peng Sim Cheng. 1989. The relationship between moral decisions and their consequences: A tradeoff analysis approach. *Journal of Business Ethics* 8: 289–297.

Warner, Edward. 1986. U.S. attempts to take wind from Asian software pirates' sails. *Computerworld* 20(18): 123.

Chapter 30
The Association Between Corporate Social Responsibility and Financial Performance: The Paradox of Social Cost

Moses L. Pava and Joshua Krausz

It is generally assumed that common stock investors are exclusively interested in earning the highest level of future case-flow for a given amount of risk. This view suggests that investors select a well-diversified portfolio of ecurities to achieve this goal. Accordingly, it is often assumed that investors are unwilling to pay a premium for corporate behavior which can be described as "socially-responsible".

Recently, this view has been under increasing attack. According to the Social Investment Forum, at least 538 institutional investors now allocate funds using social screens or criteria. In addition, Alice Tepper Marlin, president of the New York-based Council on Economic Priorities has recently estimated that about $600 billion of invested funds are socially-screened (1992).

While the notion of socially-responsible investing is often a vague and ill-defined concept and therefore extremely difficult to quantify, there are nevertheless, a cluster of core issues which describe the practice. Among the most common issues are the following: environmental concerns, community relations, military contracts, nuclear energy, product quality, consumer relations, employee relations, philanthropy, and South African investments. There are many other issues which individual investors might use in classifying corporations as socially-responsible. One important example is the issue of the economic boycott of Israel. Because of the absence of this issue and many others, it is important to recognize that while socially-responsible investing represents an economic philosophy, in practice, it also tends to correlate with a political world-view, as well. Screening on the basis of social-responsibility refers merely to those rules which current practitioners employ in selecting corporate investments, in addition to the traditional economic screens. In this sense, it is a descriptive term only.

Although the practice of using both traditional economic criteria and social-responsibility screens to allocate funds is becoming more common, and while the legal

M.L. Pava (✉) • J. Krausz
Sy Syms School of Business, Yeshiva University, New York, NY 10033, USA
e-mail: mpava@yu.edu

A.C. Michalos and D.C. Poff (eds.), *Citation Classics from the Journal of Business Ethics*, Advances in Business Ethics Research 2,
DOI 10.1007/978-94-007-4126-3_30, © Springer Science+Business Media B.V. 2013

constraints associated with the practice are apparently being removed, the implications are still not well understood. What are its financial benefits and costs? Is there a measurable financial impact? Therefore, the objectives of this study are four-fold. First, in the next section, we will review over twenty empirical studies which have attempted to measure both the direction and the degree of association between CSR and financial performance. Second, because of limitations inherent in the previous work, we further explore the association between corporate social-responsibility and traditional financial performance. In this study we examine the long-term financial performance of a group of 53 firms which have been identified by the Council on Economic Priorities (CEP) as being socially-responsible, and compare the financial performance of this group to a control sample matched by size and industry (Council on Economic Priorities et al. 1991). The rationale for basing our study on the CEP firms will be discussed in Sect. 2, where we describe the methodology and results of the study. Third, we hope that by further studying the statistical association between CSR and financial performance to shed additional light on both the benefits and the costs associated with socially-responsible actions, and in this way to formulate a better understanding of the nature and limitations of CSR. Finally, we conclude our study with implications for academics, investors, and corporate executives.

Section 1

In an attempt to understand the relationship between CSR and financial performance, there have been numerous studies which have measured the statistical association between perceived corporate social-responsibility and traditional financial performance. We have identified and reviewed 21 empirical studies which explicitly addressed this question as the major research objective. Our investigation reveals an important, and (we believe) unappreciated, empirical regularity. It can be succinctly stated as follows:

> Nearly all empirical studies to date have concluded that firms which are perceived as having met social-responsibility criteria have either outperformed or performed as well as other firms which are not (necessarily) socially-responsible.

This surprising empirical regularity, which we label the "paradox of social cost", demands an explanation. To the extent that social activities are costly to the firm (even while creating positive externalities), one would expect a negative relationship between social performance and financial performance at the individual firm level.

The Traditionalists' View of the Corporation

Milton Friedman is most closely associated with the traditional view of the corporation (See Friedman 1962, 1970; Friedman and Friedman 1980). His position can be summarized as follows: Business managers have a responsibility to shareholders – the owners of the corporation – to maximize firm value. Managers, acting as agents of the shareholders, have no mandate to embark on socially-responsible projects that do not enhance the income generating ability of the firm. In addition, managers should not refrain from profitable investments which satisfy all legal constraints but do not conform to managers' own personal social agenda. Rather, as Friedman put it, "The social responsibility of business is to increase profits." He further emphasized, "Few trends would so thoroughly undermine the very foundations of our free society as the acceptance by corporate officials of a social responsibility other than to make as much money for their stockholders as they possibly can. This is a fundamentally subversive doctrine." (1962: p. 133)

Friedman's primary assumption which leads to his conclusion that CSR is a "subversive doctrine" is his belief that the term social-responsibility as applied to the corporate context, if it means anything at all, implies that the business manager "must act in some way that is not in the interest of his employers." (1970: p. 33) Thus managers who act out of a sense of social-responsibility are engaging in a form of taxation without representation.

Further, Friedman believes that business managers have no comparative advantage when it comes to implementing social programs. Managers are experts in producing products, selling them, or financing them. Management has no necessary expertise in fighting social-ills.

We believe that Friedman's argument is both rigorous and somewhat convincing. His voice, although the loudest, clearest, and least apologetic, is by no means solitary.[1] Numerous economists, accountants, corporate executives, and social critics either explicitly or implicitly accept a similar view of the corporation.

Empirical studies often assume the traditionalists' view as a starting point. For example, Baldwin et al. (1986), in investigating the relationship between CSR and financial performance, wrote that the purpose of their study was to produce quantitative estimates of the penalty, as non-market risk, that investors would have to bear as a result of not being able to invest in various equity securities. The implicit assumption is that there must be a cost. The only relevant question remaining according to these authors is: Is the cost material?

---

[1] Having spelled out what we believe in an unbiased view of Friedman's writings, it should be pointed out that even his "unequivocal" argument is ambiguous enough to provide some sanction for corporate management to engage in what they might view as socially-responsible actions. For example, in describing the proper role for corporate executives, Friedman has written that their responsibility is to conduct the business in accordance with the desires of stockholders, "which generally will be to make as much money as possible *while conforming to the basic rules of the society, both those embodied in law and those embodied in ethical custom.*" (1970: p. 33, emphasis added) Although he certainly does not accept the term "social-responsibility", even Friedman recognizes the existence of corporate obligations beyond mere legal requirements. Even corporate managers of the Friedman-type need to make moral decisions about "ethical custom", and can not escape formulating an answer to Friedman's rhetorical question: "If businessmen do have social responsibility other than maximizing profits for stockholders, how are they to know what it is?" (1962: p. 133) Is this question different in kind to the following: If businessmen need to conform to the basic rules of society, which include those embodied in ethical custom, how are they to know what they are? In his book (co-authored with Rose Friedman 1980) the author further elaborated:

> Narrow preoccupation with the economic market has led to a narrow interpretation of self-interest as myopic selfishness, as exclusive concern with immediate rewards. Economics has been berated for allegedly drawing far-reaching conclusions from a wholly unrealistic "economic man" who is little more than a calculating machine, responding only to monetary stimuli. That is a great mistake. Self-interest is not myopic selfishness. It is whatever it is that interests the participants, whatever they value, whatever goals they pursue. (p. 18)

Not unexpectedly corporate executives often explain and defend their economic decisions along similar lines. One example should suffice. An important national newspaper has been criticized for publishing advertisements from the Kingdom of Saudi Arabia. The paid advertisements have described a large and varied number of available professional and technical positions. Critics point out that Saudi Arabia has never concealed the fact that its laws forbid women to work with men, and indeed women are barred from most occupations (a practice which is prohibited in the United States). In response to a suggestion that the newspaper require all advertisers to declare themselves as equal opportunity employers, an executive at the newspaper replied that it would not be acceptable to refuse advertisements just because "we might disagree with the policies pursued by the countries in which advertisements are located." He went on to state (echoing an extreme interpretation of Friedman's position) that the policy of the newspaper was that it is "improper to use an economic sanction: the declination of advertising in furtherance of our editorial view." (as quoted in Boycott Report 1992)

Although, Friedman's critics often attempt to paint him as a lone-wolf, his views are arguably "mainstream". In the introduction to his book, New Challenges to the Roles of Profit, Benjamin Friedman suggested that the traditional view is still dominant. Accordingly, he wrote that "The standard textbook view is that firms seek to make as much profit as possible within the constraints imposed by production technology (supply factors) and market conditions (demand factors). The great preponderance of scholarly research in economics … either implicitly or explicitly accepts this proposition, in order to provide a guide for determining firms' behavior." (1978: p. 3)

We conclude this section with what, for the purposes of our study, is the most important implication of the traditionalists' view. It can be stated in the form of a testable hypothesis as follows:

The Traditionalists' Hypothesis

Firms which are screened on the basis of social-responsibility will be characterized as inferior investments using traditional financial statement analysis criteria.

This hypothesis follows directly from Friedman's observation that social responsibility, if it means anything at all, implies that the business manager "must act in some way that is not in the interest of his employers." As stated above, however, a review of the literature is inconsistent with this hypothesis. And, therefore, although Friedman's view may be both rigorous and somewhat convincing, it is apparently not descriptive in the sense that it is not supported by the available empirical evidence. We now turn to a discussion of these studies.

The Paradox of Social Cost: Empirical Evidence

Each of the studies discussed in this section explicitly examined the statistical relationship between perceived corporate social-responsibility and traditional financial performance. Appendix A to this report briefly describes the important characteristics of these 21 studies. In the appendix we disclose the social responsibility and financial performance criteria used in each study. In addition, we briefly summarize the main results and some additional comments.

The studies which we reviewed were published over a 20 year time span. The first study was published in 1972, and the last in 1992. The studies used a wide variety of methodologies and variables to test for an association. For example, Belkaoui (1976) compared risk- adjusted market returns of companies that disclosed pollution control information in their annual reports versus a control sample of non-disclosing firms during a 4 month period following annual report disclosure. By extreme contrast, Sturdivant and Ginter (1977) examined the difference in 10 year earnings per share growth between firms which scored high on a CSR reputational index versus low scoring firms. Both of these studies were interested in answering the same basic research question: To what degree is CSR related to traditional financial performance? However, both studies chose different ways to measure CSR (annual report disclosure versus reputational index), different ways to measure financial performance (market returns versus a financial accounting measure), and different time horizons (4 months versus 10 years).

In addition to using alternative methodologies and variables, there also exists a wide diversity in terms of industries examined. Among the industries were: chemical, electric power, food processing, iron and steel, pulp and paper, and others. Further, some of the reported studies went beyond individual industry analysis and examined inter-industry effects (see for example Cotrill 1990).

Finally, underscoring the inter-disciplinary nature of the research question, studies have been published in numerous academic journals. Five were published in the Academy of Management Journal, three in Accounting Review, two in Accounting, Organizations, and Society. The 11 remaining studies were each published in different journals ranging from Journal of Economic Studies to Journal of Business Ethics. The alternative approaches and assumptions adopted in each of the studies reflects the unique contributions of each of the academic disciplines that have participated in this research including: accounting, business ethics, economics, finance, and management. This diversity should mitigate problems associated with experimental deficiencies which might result from any one approach. The most important observations which suggest themselves from our literature review are listed below:

1. Our single most important observation is that of the 21 studies, 12 reported a positive association between CSR and financial performance, 1 reported a negative association, and 8 reported no measurable association. As opposed to Ullmann (1985), we conclude that there is a consistent pattern in terms of this association. While we agree with Ullmann, when he wrote that "conflicting results were reported even in cases based on the same sample of firms" (p. 543), we strongly disagree with his interpretation that "no clear tendency can be found." Table 30.1 compares the results of our literature review to Ullmann's. Notice that even according to Ullmann's accounting, of the 13 studies which he identified as examining the relationship between CSR and financial performance, 8 found positive correlations, 1 found negative correlations, and the remaining 4 studies reported no correlations. While it is evidently true that not all studies

Table 30.1 CSR and traditional financial performance: summary of 21 empirical studies – principal findings

	Column A	Column B
Direction of association	1993– results	Ullmann (1985)
Positive association	12	8
Negative association	1	1
No association	8	4
Totals	21	13

Column A of this table summarizes the principal findings of the 21 studies reviewed in Appendix A to this report. Column B summarizes the principal findings of the 13 studies reviewed by Ullmann (1985)

Table 30.2 CSR and traditional financial performance: summary of 21 empirical studies – CSR criteria used

Social-responsibility criteria	Studies using criteria	Studies using criteria and reporting positive association	Studies using criteria and reporting negative association
Environmental performance	9	4	0
Reputational index	6	4	1
CSR disclosure	2	3	0
South African investment	2	0	0
CEO attitudes	1	0	0
Multiple criteria	1	1	0
Totals	21	12	1

report that CSR firms perform better than non-CSR firms, the overwhelming preponderance of the evidence indicates that CSR firms perform at least as well as other firms. We believe that this finding directly contradicts the traditionalists' view of the corporation. This surprising empirical regularity constitutes prima facie evidence for the existence of the "paradox of social cost". To the extent that social activities are costly to the firm (even while creating positive externalities), one would predict a negative relationship between social performance and financial performance at the individual firm level. In the next section, we will discuss five plausible explanations to these findings.

2. In examining CSR performance, numerous surrogates have been employed. As per Table 30.2, of the 21 studies, 9 used a measure of environmental performance, 6 used reputational indexes, 2 each used disclosure and South African related criteria. Of the 12 studies that reported some positive association there is no predominance of any one variable. Four of the 9 studies that employed environmental performance as the CSR surrogate, and 4 of the 6 studies that used a reputational index, reported a positive association.
3. In addition to using alternative measures for CSR, the studies have also employed a wide variety of measures for financial performance. Table 30.3 provides additional details. Note that 6 of the 21 studies focused solely on financial accounting returns, 7 based their results on market based returns, and still others used multiple

Table 30.3 CSR and traditional financial performance: summary of 21 empirical studies – financial performance criteria used

Financial performance criteria	Studies using criteria	Studies using criteria and reporting positive association	Studies using criteria and reporting negative association
Stock price returns	7	4	0
Financial accounting returns	6	3	1
Market-based measure of risk	2	1	0
Multiple criteria	6	4	0
Totals	21	12	1

Table 30.4 CSR and traditional financial performance: summary of 21 empirical studies – sample size

Sample size	Studies using criteria	Studies using criteria and reporting positive association	Studies using criteria and reporting negative association
Less than 20	7	4	0
21–40	6	3	1
41–60	2	1	0
More than 61	6	4	0
Totals	21	12	1

criteria. The 12 studies which reported positive associations are not driven by any one variable. For example, 3 of the studies which reported positive associations were based on accounting data alone, and 4 each were based on either market data alone or multiple criteria.

4. The observation that researchers employed many different methodologies is corroborated by Table 30.4. Six of the studies examined CSR and financial performance of more than 61 firms, 7 of the studies included less than 20 in their sample. There are advantages and disadvantages to both large and small sample studies. For example, small sample sizes may result in better estimates of CSR. Large sample sizes will minimize sample bias. We simply observe, as above, that methodological diversity should mitigate problems associated with experimental deficiencies which might result from any one approach.

To conclude this part of our discussion, we note two possible limitations in interpreting and generalizing the results. First, most of the studies were relatively short term in nature. Only 5 of the 21 studies examined more than 5 years of data. The implications of this deficiency will be discussed in the next section. Second, only 6 studies examined data after 1975 (even though 13 studies were published after 1979). There exists, therefore, a need to update some of these earlier studies. Nevertheless, the body of work reviewed here represents a strong case against the traditionalists' conception of CSR. Friedman observed that CSR, if it means anything at all, implies that the business manager "must act in some way that is not in the interest of his employers." We suggested that this view implies the following formal hypothesis:

The Traditionalists' Hypothesis

Firms which are screened on the basis of social-responsibility will be characterized as inferior investments using traditional financial statement analysis criteria.

Most studies to date have presented evidence which is inconsistent with this hypothesis. We next turn to an extensive discussion of five plausible explanations to this seeming paradox.

The Paradox of Social Cost: Five Explanations

We discuss five possible explanations to the empirical results presented in the previous section. The explanations should not be viewed as mutually exclusive. In fact, each explanation provides additional insight into the nature of CSR, and thus provides a more realistic understanding of a complex phenomenon.

Explanation 1 – Socially-responsible firms are identical to non-socially-responsible firms.

As we emphasize throughout this study, the notion of socially-responsible investing is often a vague and ill-defined term. It is almost impossible to provide a precise definition. Further, social-responsibility is always a function of perception. Even if there is a growing consensus on a number of issues like environmental concern or employee relations, there is still enough disagreement that all general observations about the degree of CSR will be met with some opposition. It is therefore tempting to suggest that because of the uncertainty surrounding definitions of CSR there is no such thing as CSR, and therefore firms which may have been identified as socially-responsible are, in fact, no different from other, non-socially-responsible firms. If this proposition holds, then the paradox described in the previous section disappears.

There is ample anecdotal evidence which is consistent with this explanation. For example, the New York Times recently reported (February 11, 1993) that the Sun Oil Company of Philadelphia, the 12th-largest oil company in the United States became the first Fortune 500 company to endorse the Valdez Principles (or at least a watered-down version in which some of the original principles were negotiated). These principles are a code of corporate environmental conduct which were devised following the 1989 Alaskan oil disaster. According to Robert H. Campbell, Sun's chairman and chief executive, there is a tremendous "philosophical congruence" (as quoted by the N. Y. Times) between what Sun already does and the environmental principles. In fact, Campbell emphasized, at the signing ceremony, that he did not foresee any major changes in company operations. To the extent that Sun Oil's observations are generalizable to other oil companies and other industrial corporations, one should not anticipate any negative financial repercussions following the signing of the Valdez Principles.

That there may be minimal direct costs associated with CSR (relative to the size of the corporation) is suggested in a recent comment in Prudential's annual report. Robert Winters, the CEO, wrote that the firm considers social-responsibility "critical to our success." He further disclosed that, "The Prudential Foundation gave more than $16 million to various worthy causes." The discussion about CSR in the CEO's letter consumes about 10% of the total disclosures (in terms of paragraphs), whereas the $16 million charitable contribution consumes less than one tenth of 1% of reported net income.

Support for the idea that there is no difference between socially-responsible firms and other firms is the possibility that all major U. S. corporations who abide by the law are by definition socially-responsible. Regulatory requirements, and the constant threat of increased regulatory actions, coupled with an increasingly hostile tort system, may provide ample incentive for U. S. corporations to engage in socially-responsible behavior. Any attempt therefore to distinguish between socially-responsible firms and other firms is essentially arbitrary. At least in the area of pollution control there is some evidence to support this conjecture. Shane and Spicer (1983), in studying pollution ratings produced by the Council on Economic Priorities, stated that the Council's criteria "to rate the overall efficacy of companies' pollution-control systems correspond fairly closely to legislative requirements promulgated under the Clean Air Act Amendments ... and the Federal Water Pollution Control Act." (p. 524)

There is no doubt that in some instances CSR is nothing more than self-advertising. On the other hand, there is also no doubt that this explanation is not complete. There are often substantial costs associated with CSR behavior. For example, Freedman and Jaggi (1982) reported that in highly polluting industries as much as 20% of the total amount of capital expenditures have been devoted to pollution abatement. Belkaoui (1976) suggested that in the steel industry the percentage may reach as high as 25%.

While it is true that some of the surrogates that have been used to measure CSR are not precise, it is extremely unlikely that there are no differences between firms that are perceived as having met CSR criteria and others. It is unlikely that all, or even most, of the attempts to distinguish between socially-responsible firms and non-socially-responsible firms have been meaningless. The ability to obtain information about socially-responsible actions has become less difficult. Rockness and Williams (1988) surveyed managers of socially-responsible mutual funds about sources of "social information." Among the most important sources of information were the companies themselves and government agencies. In addition, private social responsibility organizations like Franklin Research, and Investor Responsibility Research Center were also mentioned. In total, the authors listed 39 different sources of social information which were cited by at least one fund manager.

At the same time CSR information has become easier to obtain, mutual funds which advertise themselves as socially-responsible have begun to define the practice with more and more exactness. Table 30.5 summarizes both the positive and negative screens used by nine of the most important and influential socially-responsible mutual funds. Issues like environmental concern, South Africa, weapons production, and employee relations were cited by almost all of the mutual funds examined.

Table 30.5 Social responsibility screens used by nine mutual funds

Negative screens	Number of funds using screen
South Africa	8
Weapons	7
Nuclear power	6
Tobacco, alcohol, gambling	3
EPA violations, polluters	1
Positive screens	
Environmental issues	8
Employee relations	6
Corporate citizenship	4
Product quality and safety	4
Alternative energy	3

Source: Social Investment Forum – updated August 1991
This table reports the number of mutual funds that explicitly cited the above social-responsibility screens in the fund prospectuses. It is based on the following nine mutual funds: *1*-Calvert-Ariel Appreciation Fund, *2*-Calvert Social Investment Fund, *3*-Domini Social Index Trust, *4*-Dreyfus Third Century, *5*-New Alternatives, *6*-Parnassus Fund, *7*-Pax World Fund, *8*-Rightime Social Awareness Fund, and *9*-Schield Progressive Environmental Fund

Therefore, if there exists real differences between socially-responsible firms and other firms, the original question remains. We now turn to a second plausible explanation.

Explanation 2 – *The experiments to test the association between CSR and traditional financial performance have not been carefully designed or controlled.*

According to this explanation, socially-responsible firms may not be identical to non-socially-responsible firms. However, the experiments to test the association between CSR and financial performance have not documented an inferior performance for CSR firms because the tests have not been well-designed.

For example, Vance (1975) argued that earlier association studies had not been "validated." His main concern was the that earlier studies adopted an extremely short window to measure financial performance. Cochran and Wood (1984) further noted that earlier studies (including Vance) lacked methodological rigor in the sense that they failed to measure "risk-adjusted" returns. Ullmann (1985) concluded that "studies of the relationship between social performance and economic performance are highly questionable when social disclosure is used as a proxy for social performance." (p. 545)

Cochran and Wood suggested that reputational indexes used to measure CSR are "highly subjective and thus may vary significantly from one observer to another." (p. 43) Further, and perhaps a more severe criticism, is whether or not the reputational indexes are even purporting to measure CSR. For example, at least two studies have used Fortune magazine's annual survey of "corporate reputations" as the surrogate for CSR (McGuire et al. 1988; Cotrill 1990). The appropriateness of this measure can be questioned given that of the eight key attributes respondents were queried about to determine corporate reputations, arguably, only two were directly related to issues of CSR.[2]

In addition, it has been suggested that reported results may be a function of "spurious correlations." Chen and Metcalf (1980) criticized an earlier study which documented a positive association between pollution control records and financial performance by stating that the earlier "evidence rests on spurious relationships created through one or more intervening variables. The reported significant associations might not have been observed had the effect of intervening variables been controlled (or adjusted)." (p. 168) Chen and Metcalf showed that when they controlled for size, the positive association between CSR performance and financial performance is eliminated. In their words, "The results indicate that the conclusion of a moderate to strong association between pollution control record and financial indicators is not justified." (p. 174)

Roberts (1992) further suggested that, in general, many of the studies in this area are merely "ad hoc" attempts to relate corporate social responsibility actions to selected corporate characteristics. Roberts suggested that the earlier work lacked a "theoretical foundation." (p. 610) Ullmann (1985) made a similar point when he explained that, "The generally ambiguous nature of the results of the studies surveyed in the previous sections suggests that the models may be incompletely specified." (p. 551)

In spite of these important criticisms, the possibility of methodological limitations is by no means a complete explanation. As stated in the previous section, the overwhelming preponderance of the evidence indicates that CSR firms perform at least as well as other firms. Examining the observations delineated above, there is no reason to believe that a systematic bias has been introduced. We therefore turn to a third possible explanation.

Explanation 3 – A conscious pursuit of corporate social-responsibility goals causes better financial performance.

This third possibility represents an alternative view to the traditional conception of the business enterprise. The prediction that social-responsibility might lead to better firm performance cuts across the ideological spectrum. Variants of this positions have been boldly articulated by conservative thinkers (including George Gilder, Michael Novak, and Irving Kistol), centrists (including Arthur Okun and Clarence Walton), and by radical writers (including the sociologist Severyn Bruyn, and economists like Samuel Bowles and Herbert Gintis). This idea has also been periodically suggested by empirical researchers and corporate executives, as well.

---

[2] The eight key attributes (of corporate reputation) listed *by Fortune* magazine (February 8, 1993) were the following: quality of management, financial soundness, quality of products or services, use of corporate assets, value as long-term investment, innovativeness, ability to attract, develop, and keep talented people, and community and environmental responsibility.

In stark contrast to Adam Smith's view, George Gilder celebrated the role of the entrepreneur (1984).

> Even if we do not ask economists to perform as moral philosophers, we should demand that they accurately observe the world. Observing the world, one can see scarce factual foundation for the prevailing view of entrepreneurial activity. The capitalist is not merely a dependent of capital, labor, and land; he defines and creates capital, lends value to land, and offers his own labor while giving effect to the otherwise amorphous labor of others. He is not chiefly a tool of markets but a maker of markets; not a scout of opportunities but an inventor of them; not a respondent to existing demands but an innovator who evokes demand; not chiefly a user of technology but a producer of it. He does not operate within a limited sphere of market disequilibria, marginal options, and incremental advances. For small changes, entrepreneurs are unnecessary; even a lawyer or bureaucrat would do. (p. 17)

He concluded this discussion by emphasizing, "It is the entrepreneurs who know the rules of the world and the laws of God. Thus they sustain the world. In their careers, there is little of optimizing calculation, nothing of delicate balance of markets … They are the heroes of economic life." (p. 19)

Michael Novak (1984) has also criticized the traditional views. In reviewing the theories about democratic capitalism inherited from Adam Smith, Jeremy Benthan, Ludwig von Mises, Frederik von Hayek, and Milton Friedman, he wrote,

> The typical mistake of classic thinkers on this subject is to have laid too small a foundation to support the lived world of democratic capitalist society as we have experienced it. They have too chastely considered the economic system in abstraction from the real world, in which the political system and the moral-cultural system also shape the texture of daily life. (p.36)

Accordingly, he described a central element of democratic capitalism, "virtuous self-interest", as follows:

> The laws of free economic markets are such that the real interest of individuals are best served in the long run by a systematic refusal to take short-term advantage. Apart from internal restraints, the system itself places restraints upon greed and narrowly constructed self-interest. Greed and selfishness, when they occur, are made to have their costs. A firm aware of its long-term fiduciary responsibilities must protect its investments for future generations. It must change with the time. It must maintain a reputation for reliability, integrity, and fairness … Thus a firm committed to greed unleashes social forces that will sooner or later destroy it. Spasms of greed will disturb its own inner disciplines, corrupt its executives, anger its patrons, injure the morale of its workers, antagonize its suppliers and purchasers, embolden its competitors, and attract public retribution. In a free society, such spasms must be expected; they must also be opposed. (p. 93)

Among the so-called neo-conservatives, Irving Kristol has also voiced concern over the traditional view of the corporation, especially as advocated by Friedman. (See Two Cheers For Capitalism 1978, pp. 63–64.) In discussing the rationale for corporate philanthropy, Kristol recognized that the only justification for corporate charity (as distinct from individual charity which "refines and elevates the soul of the giver" p. 134) is that it must "serve the longer-term interests of the corporations." He continued, "Corporate philanthropy should not be, and cannot be, disinterested." (p. 134) Kristol's view is consistent with the possibility that a conscious pursuit of corporate social-responsibility goals (Kristol himself used the term "social responsibility" to describe controllable philanthropic expenditures) may cause better financial performance, especially in the long run.

Arthur Okun concluded his book, Equality and Efficiency, by stating, "the market needs a place, and the market needs to be kept in its place." (1975: p. 119) Even while recognizing the limitations of a market-based system, Okun justified the profit motive along the lines we are discussing here. In defending his belief that a reliance on self-interest is not offensive as an organizing principle for the economy, he wrote that "self-interest is consistent with an enlightened selfishness that creates loyalties to family, community, and country, as institutions that benefit the individual and extend his range of interests." (p. 49)

Clarence Walton, one of the earliest proponents of CSR similarly noted that "Corporations will be around a long time and durable organizations exist by doing things right – right in the fullest sense of the word." (1992: p. 60)

At the other end of the ideological spectrum, more radical theorists have, from time to time, also entertained the possibility that social-responsibility may lead to better financial performance. Bowles and Gintis (1987) suggested that democratically controlled firms may be more efficient than the traditional corporate form of organization. This prediction is suggested by the possibility that "the change in the locus of command" that would be necessarily a part of a democratically controlled firm "may be expected to reduce the wage and surveillance costs of generating a given level of labor performed." (p. 78)

Severyn Bruyn has also predicted a positive link between social performance and economic performance. Unlike the traditional perspective, he dismissed the notion that there must be a tradeoff between them, rather the relationship between CSR and financial performance is a synergistic one. Bruyn (1987) wrote:

> In reality, social considerations in the investment process can actually enhance the possibilities of economic return. The fact is that the two values are not necessarily exclusive. Social and economic values can be maximized together, this creative synergism is the practical direction taken by social investors today. (p. 12)

The possibility that the association between CSR and financial performance may be the result of a causal relationship, as discussed here, has also been periodically suggested by empirical researchers, as well. In presenting evidence that CSR firms in the food-processing industry outperformed non-CSR firms, Bowman and Haire (1975) explained that while there is not a one to one relationship between CSR and financial performance, nevertheless CSR is "a signal of the presence of a style of management that extends broadly across the entire business function and leads to more profitable operation." (p. 54) The authors continued that "it is exactly this ability to sense, adapt, negotiate with, and cope with these forces that is … the sign of managerial excellence and hence profitability." (p. 54)

Sturdivant and Ginter (1977) provided evidence that socially-responsible firms (as measured by a reputational index) outperformed a control sample in terms of 10 year earnings per share growth. They elaborated:

> It would appear that a case can be made for an association between responsiveness to social issues and the ability to respond effectively to traditional business challenges . . . A company management group which reflects rather narrow and rigid views of social change and rising

expectations might also be expected to respond less creatively and effectively in the traditional but also dynamic arenas in which business functions. Hence there is the stronger economic performance . . . (p. 38)

Kahneman et al. (1986) have provided survey evidence which supports the causal link between CSR and financial performance. They argued that a realistic description of our economic system must include the fact that consumers, suppliers, and employees care about being treated fairly and treating others fairly. In addition, they are willing to resist unfair firms even at a positive cost to themselves. Satisfying the "fairness constraint" may lead to better long-run financial performance.

Executives have attempted to describe the connection between CSR and financial performance through the vehicle of the annual report. For example, the president of Ben and Jerry's Homemade Inc. recently defended his commitment to a social agenda in his president's letter to shareholders as follows:

> We have a two-part bottom line. This Annual Report presents both our financial progress and our progress in contributing to the quality of life in our communities ... We believe that if we focus on the quality of everything we do, the traditional business measures will fall into place. We are master ice cream and frozen dessert makers. We want to be a force for progressive social change. And our staff is perpetually enthusiastic about our future. If we can continue to grow these values as fast as we grow the company we'll be fine.

In summary, the view discussed here is a powerful countervailing paradigm to the traditional view of the corporation. Further, it is apparently more consistent with the available empirical evidence than the alternative view. Nevertheless there are major limitations. First, it is highly doubtful whether the variables which have been used as surrogates for CSR in the empirical studies are always closely related to the notions of "social-responsibility" which have been emphasized by Gilder, Novak, Okun, and, even Bowles and Ginter. We observe here that while there is a clear overlap between CSR as it has developed in practice over the last 20 years and the notions of responsibility as discussed in this section, the overlap is not exact. Therefore the explanation offered here may not be entirely appropriate for the empirical findings previously reported.

Second, intuitively, the explanation is not completely compelling. Simply put, if doing good is always costless, why isn't everyone good? By the logic offered here, even a scoundrel would eventually notice that it is in his or her best interest to choose CSR. We therefore need a view which can explain the persistence of scoundrels, as well as saints.

Finally, the explanation as stated here is too general. In Explanation 5, below, its scope is limited. First, however, we discuss the following alternative explanation.

Explanation 4 – Only firms which perform better in terms of financial criteria can afford a conscious pursuit of corporate social-responsibility goals.

Social-responsibility does not cause enhanced financial performance, but rather, financial performance allows for the performance of discretionary social actions. Anecdotal evidence supports this view For example, in response to poor financial performance, firms with "no layoff" policies have been forced to shrink their employee base. What was once viewed as a permanent part of corporate strategy to meet corporate social-responsibility goals is no longer economically viable.

According to this view, especially as it has been articulated by Ullmann (1985), the motivation for engaging in socially-responsible actions is external to the corporation. Ullmann suggested that social performance should be viewed as a result of a "strategy for dealing with stakeholder demands." (p. 552) He continued, "When stake-holders control resources critical to the organization, the company is likely to respond in a way that satisfies the demands of the stakeholders."

A central component to Ullmann's "stake-holder model" is the link between financial performance and social-responsibility. In Ullmann's view, economic performance is posited as an independent variable. Therefore, economic performance explains CSR, and not vice versa. "Economic performance determines the relative weight of a social demand and the attention it receives from top decision makers. In periods of low profitability and in situations of high debt, economic demands will have priority over social demands . . . Economic performance influences the financial capability to undertake costly programs related to social demands." (p. 553)

McGuire et al. (1988), following Ullmann, concluded their empirical study by noting that "Firms with high performance and low risk may be better able to afford to act in a socially responsible manner." (p. 869) Echoing Ullmann, they continued, "In essence, it may be more fruitful to consider financial performance as a variable influencing social responsibility than the reverse."

Chen and Metcalf (1984) examining the relationship between pollution control and financial performance similarly suggested that "economically, a firm with high earnings is more likely to incur pollution abatement costs than one with low earnings." (p. 173)

More recently, Roberts (1992) in presenting empirical evidence which is consistent with Ullmann's stakeholder model, concurred that it is economic performance which leads to higher levels of CSR and not the other way around.

> The importance placed on meeting social responsibility goals may be secondary to meeting the economic demands that impact directly on a company's continued viability. Economic performance directly affects the financial capability to institute social responsibility programs. Therefore, given certain levels of stakeholder power and strategic posture, the better the economic performance of a company the greater its social responsibility activity and disclosures. (p. 599)

Ullmann's stakeholder model is consistent with the traditional view of the corporation in the sense that both view social responsibility as a net cost to the corporation. In addition, a benefit of the stakeholder model is that it is compatible with much of the empirical evidence which was reviewed above.

We believe that this approach represents an important development in understanding the nature of CSR. Effective managers need to satisfy all important stakeholders, not simply the demands of shareholders. Further, it is plausible to assume that meeting the needs of consumer groups, environmental activists, labor unions, the government, and other stakeholders is becoming more important to corporate managers. Nevertheless, it may not be accurate to suggest that the demands for social-responsibility are always external to the corporation, as the stakeholder model (as developed by Ullmann) implies.

Further, an important and unappreciated implication to the stakeholder model is that if there is a net cost to CSR, in the long run it should be detected. In other words, firms which start out with a financial advantage and can therefore afford to engage in socially-responsible actions, should over time (assuming they continue to engage in CSR) forfeit their financial advantage. That CSR activities represent a material cost is directly suggested in Ullmann's observation quoted above that economic performance influences the financial capability to undertake costly programs related to social demands. This testable implication of the stake-holder model has never been formally examined. Therefore, one of the main goals of the current research is to examine the long run financial performance of a group of socially-responsible firms.

Explanation 5 – Sometimes, *a conscious pursuit of corporate social-responsibility goals causes better financial performance.*

Explanation 3, as suggested above, it too extreme. Explanation 5 limits its applicability. According to this last explanation, there are two types of socially-responsible actions. Some social actions have no net costs, and in fact may benefit the firm in the long run, while other socially-responsible actions (even while creating positive externalities) are costly to the firm. This explanation suggests that the traditional view (and Explanation 4 above) is wrong in assuming that social actions do not benefit the firm. The position adopted here proposes that Friedman's statement that the very term "social responsibility" must imply behavior that is not in the interest of the corporation is needlessly provocative. (See Friedman 1970: p. 33.) Our disagreement with Friedman is a definitional one. Friedman's view is that any action which benefits the firm is, by definition, not "socially-responsible." Alternatively, we suggest that whether or not an action benefits the firm (in terms of increased financial performance) is irrelevant to its classification as "socially-responsible."

If Explanation 5 is to help unravel the paradox of social cost, we must add the plausible assumption that the major corporations which have been studied in the empirical literature, and which are perceived as being socially-responsible, are pursuing corporate goals which are consistent with financial performance goals. Corporate management, on average, rejects those activities which are not congruent with shareholder demands. Under this assumption, we do not anticipate a negative association between CSR and financial performance.

The possible existence of two types of social actions, although intuitively appealing, has received little attention. The important advantages of this explanation are that:

1. it is consistent with the empirical studies examined above,
2. it does not assume that the motivation for CSR is always external to the firm (as in Explanation 4), and
3. it is consistent with the views of corporate executives and board members.

The explanation offered here is based, in part, on Peter Drucker's definition of corporate social-responsibility (1989). In his book The New Realities, Drucker wrote:

> We know in rough outline the social responsibility of the pluralist institutions of society. We know that their first social responsibility is to do their job. We know secondly that they have responsibility for their impacts – on people, on the community, on society in general. And finally we know that they act irresponsibly if they go beyond the impacts necessary for them to do their own job, whether it is taking care of the sick, producing goods, or advancing learning. (p. 86)

In describing the responsibility for organizational impacts Drucker amplified:

> It has to exercise considerable control over the people who work for it; otherwise, it cannot do its job. It has considerable impact on people who are customers whether they buy a company's goods or are patients in a hospital. And it has impacts on bystanders. The factory that closes at four-thirty in the afternoon creates a traffic jam for everyone in the community. Responsibility for one's impacts is the oldest principle of the law. It does not matter whether the institution is at fault or is negligent. The Roman lawyers who first formulated this principle called it the "doctrine of the wild animal." If the lion gets out of its cage, its keeper is responsible. Whether the lion's keeper was careless and left open the door of the cage, or whether an earthquake released the lock, is irrelevant. (pp. 87–88)

Drucker's "doctrine of the wild animal" thus insures that the "institution has a duty – but also a self-interest – to limit its impact to what is actually needed for the discharge of its social function." (p. 88)

Consistent with Explanation 5 above, Drucker also underscored the existence of two types of socially-responsible actions. He pointed out that social-responsibility is effective only under stringent conditions. It must fit the organization's value system. "It must be an extension of what it is doing rather than a diversion." (p. 92) In a recent article, Drucker (1992) continued on the theme of social responsibility. He wrote that "we had better be watchful because good intentions are not always socially responsible. It is irresponsible for an organization to accept – let alone pursue – responsibilities that would impede its capacity to perform its main task and mission or to act where it has no competence." (p. 99)

In addition to Drucker, a number of attempts have been made to distinguish between socially-responsible actions which lead to better financial performance and those that do not. It is often assumed that there may be a link between pollution control and financial performance. For example, in discussing the compatibility between high levels of pollution control and high profit levels, Bragdon and Marlin (1972) suggested that the poor performance of the domestic steel industry must be viewed as a consequence of poor management. They believed that "good managements are likely both to earn higher profits and to be more careful in protecting the environment." (p. 10) According to their view, while Japanese and European firms were investing in new equipment with lower pollution levels, American steel companies refused to change over to the new technology. That foreign companies have outperformed domestic steel producers is in part a "reflection of lower costs associated with better pollution control." (p. 9)

Coffey and Fryxell (1991) in suggesting that corporate social-responsibility involves taking actions pursuant to obligations beyond the economic and legal sphere, isolated four components of CSR that may lead to better firm performance. "Evidence of corporate social responsiveness may be related to a broad range of issues including: pollution abatement, product safety, advertising messages, the role of women and minorities in the firm. That the capability to change with social climate is important for long-term economic performance is a basic tenet of strategic management." (p. 439)

A major limitation to Explanation 4 above is its insistence that the motivation for CSR is always external to the organization. This observation is plainly seen in Ullmann's prediction that firms with poor economic performance, low stakeholder power, and a passive strategic posture are not likely to engage in CSR. (p. 553) Explanation 5, however, predicts that even in a period of poor economic performance, a corporation may find it in its own interest to pursue CSR objectives. The motivation for CSR can thus be an internal decision to increase long term financial performance, while simultaneously meeting responsibilities for corporate impacts.

Cornell and Shapiro (1987) further explored this possibility. What are the advantages – to the shareholder – of honoring product warranties beyond legal requirements? Cornell and Shapiro suggested that what motivates corporate executives to honor implicit contracts (with no legal ramifications) is that executives' believe that the long term value of the firm is a direct function of its ability to sell (not only explicit claims) but also implicit claims. In the authors words, the market value of a corporation includes "organizational capital which equals market value of all future implicit claims the firm expects to sell." (p. 10)

To clarify the distinction between implicit and explicit claims the authors used the following example:

> The price at which IBM's PC_{jr}, included both the price of the hardware and the prices of the implicit claims for future support, software, product enhancements, and the like. As it became clear that PC_{jr}'s success in the market was limited, IBM faced a difficult decision. If the company chose to discontinue the product line it would clearly lessen the organization liabilities connected with PC_{jr}. On the other hand, discontinuing the product reduces the payout on implicit claims previously issued by the company, which in turn reduced the firm's organizational capital by causing the prices of future implicit claims to fall. (p. 9)

The problem that IBM and other corporations face is that if they fail to honor implicit claims for one product, stakeholders will rationally assume that they are less likely to honor implicit claims for other products, including items yet to be marketed. "For firms such as IBM that choose to identify all their products with the company name, the spillover effect is likely to be particularly strong." (p. 9)

In this example, IBM chose what we might label the socially-responsible solution. The company chose to discontinue the production of PC_{jr} but it also undertook a major advertising campaign to let PC_{jr} owners and other stake-holders know that "If you own a PC_{jr} you can be sure it is still a well-cared for member of the IBM PC family." (p. 10) They chose this solution, not out of a sense of altruism, but because of concern with their long term financial performance.

By contrast, when Exxon phased out its office systems division, Exxon "provided minimal support for customers and other stakeholders of that division." (p. 9) Presumably, Exxon executives perceived little spillover effect as a result of this decision, as the office systems division was incidental to their main line of business.

Cornell and Shapiro extended their analysis beyond customer warranties. They wrote:

> When a firm hires a new employee, he or she frequently receives promises about the work environment, the evaluation process and the opportunity for advancement, as well as an explicit employment contract … In a similar fashion, implicit claims are sold to stakeholders, such as suppliers and independent firms that provide repair services and manufacture supporting products. (pp. 6–7)

To conclude this section, we note what for our purposes is the most important implication of Explanation 5. Explanation 5 states: SOMETIMES, a conscious pursuit of corporate social-responsibility goals causes better financial performance. If this explanation holds, and if we add the plausible assumption that the major corporations choose, on average, to pursue those CSR goals consistent with financial goals, in the long run, socially-responsible firms may actually outperform non-socially responsible firms in terms of traditional financial performance. Firms identified as socially-responsible, should maintain, or even increase, their relative financial advantage over non-socially-responsible firms.[3] This implication, is in direct opposition to the implication of Explanation 4 above. According to *Explanation 4: Only firms which perform better in terms of financial criteria can afford a conscious pursuit of corporate social-responsibility goals*. As we pointed out above, this implies that firms which start out with a financial advantage and can therefore afford to engage in socially-responsible actions, should over time (assuming they continue to engage in CSR) forfeit their financial advantage.

Section 2

A major goal of this study is to explore the association between CSR and traditional financial performance. In this way, we can begin to distinguish between Explanations 4 and 5 discussed in the previous section.

Creating the Sample

In particular, we examine the long-term financial performance of a group of 53 firms which have been identified by the Council on Economic Priorities (CEP) as being socially–responsible (GROUP 1), and compare their performance to a control

[3] Our point here is that CSR may cause better long run financial performance. We also recognize, however that firms experiencing extreme financial distress may cut back first on CSR programs. In this special case, a deteriorating financial performance may directly lead to fewer CSR activities. This is true because there are fewer legal requirements associated with CSR commitments (implicit claims) than other more traditional corporate activities (explicit claims). It may be less costly to break CSR commitments than other more formal contractual agreements.

Table 30.6 Characteristics of Groups 1 and 2 firms

Characteristics	Group 1 53 Firms		Group 2 53 Firms	
Domini 400 social index	44	83%	12	23%
100 best companies to work for	24	45%	2	4%
75 best companies for working mothers	12	23%	0	0%
50 best places for blacks to work	12	23%	0	0%
Best companies for women (50)	8	15%	1	2%
More than 20% employee ownership	4	8%	0	0%
Top 100 defense department contractors	3	6%	1	2%
Direct investment in South Africa	2	4%	6	11%
Top 50 manufacturers releasing toxic chemicals	1	2%	1	2%
Top 100 nuclear weapons contractors	0	0%	1	2%
Tobacco companies	0	0%	1	2%

sample matched by both industry and size (GROUP 2). In addition, to test for changes over time, we compare the relative performance of the GROUP 1 and 2 firms in two time periods (1985–1987 and 1989–1991). A listing of the 106 firms selected for our study is included in Appendix B.

The CEP described the companies in GROUP 1 as "ethical" portfolio companies. The advantages of choosing the CEP firms for our study are as follows[4]:

1. The CEP is highly regarded as a credible source of information on CSR. Numerous published studies have used previous CEP studies as the basis for forming measures of CSR. For example, of the 21 studies we reviewed in the previous section, 5 used CEP studies. We concur with Shane and Spicer (1983) who concluded that "The most detailed, consistent, and comparable data bearing on corporate social performance has been published by the CEP. It appears to be the most active external producer of information in this area." (p. 522)
2. The CEP ratings are not unique. The firms included in GROUP 1 tend to be rated high in terms of CSR by numerous external groups. Table 30.6 summarizes some characteristics of the GROUP 1 and GROUP 2 firms, and provides additional support to the CEP ratings. There is significant overlap between the GROUP 1 firms, as identified by the CEP, and firms included in the Domini 400 Social Index. Only 12 of the GROUP 2 firms were included in the Domini Index. About half the GROUP 1 firms (24 firms) were rated among the "100 Best Companies to Work For", while only 2 of the GROUP 2 firms were included on this list. Further, 12 of the GROUP 1 firms were among the "75 Best Companies for Working Mothers", and none of the GROUP 2 firms were identified among the "75 Best Companies for Working Mothers".

[4] In selecting these firms the CEP "drew both on the holdings listed in the prospectuses of the socially responsible mutual funds and on lists provided by the SIF." (p. 19) Additional information was drawn from reports prepared by Franklin Research and Development and Clean Yield.

Table 30.7 Industry classifications for socially-responsible firms

SIC codes	Industry classification	Number of firms
2000–2099	Food and kindred products	9
2300–2399	Apparel and other finished products	2
2500–2599	Furniture and fixtures	1
2600–2699	Paper and allied products	1
2700–2799	Printing, publishing and allied	3
2800–2899	Chemicals and allied products	9
3000–3099	Rubber and misc plastic products	1
3100–3199	Leather and leather products	1
3500–2599	Indl, Comml Machy, Computer Eq	4
3600–3699	Electr, Other Elect Eq, Ex Comp	3
3700–3799	Transportation equipment	1
3800–3899	Meas Instr; Photo Gds; Watches	3
4500–4599	Transportation by air	3
4800–4899	Communication	1
4900–4999	Electric, gas sanitary services	3
5300–5399	General merchanise stores	3
5600–5699	Apparel and accessory stores	1
6500–6599	Real estate	1
7300–7399	Business services	1
7500–7599	Auto repair, services, parking	1
7900–7999	Amusement and Recreation Services	1

Table 30.6 also indicates that few of the GROUP 1firms are listed among the "Top 100 Defense Department Contractors", or among the "Top 50 Manufacturers Releasing Toxic Chemicals". Finally, and not surprisingly, none of the GROUP 1 firms were included among the "Top 100 Nuclear Weapons Contractors," or were identified as "Tobacco Companies".

3. To achieve the goals of this study we needed an aggregate measure of CSR, as opposed to a measure of one or more of the components of CSR. The CEP ratings, based on an assessment of 12 specific CSR components, provided a convenient and well respected third party assessment. Further, we believe that the CEP ratings provide a more precise measure of CSR, per se, than those obtained from the next best competitor, Fortune magazine's annual survey of "corporate reputations". As discussed in the previous section, the appropriateness of the survey results can be questioned given that of the eight key attributes respondents were queried about to determine corporate reputations, arguably, only two were directly related to issues of CSR.
4. The GROUP 1 firms were selected from diverse industries, thus enhancing the generalizability of the results. Table 30.7 reveals that 21 industries are represented among the 53 GROUP 1 firms. Nine firms were selected from both Food and Kindred Products (SIC codes 2000–2099) and Chemicals and Allied Products (SIC codes 2800–2899). Eleven industries had just one member among the GROUP 1 firms. The relatively large proportion of firms in Food and Kindred

Products and Chemical categories might be considered prima facie evidence of an industry effect. The possibility that there exists an association between perceived social-responsibility and industry has been documented by Cotrill (1990), Bowman and Haire (1975).

To conclude this discussion, many of the 53 firms in GROUP 1 have been described as socially-responsible by a wide variety of outside evaluators. The CEP is one of the most highly regarded external producers of social-responsibility information. The 53 firms represent a diverse sample of companies. The sample thus provides an important, and inherently interesting, point of departure.

Financial Performance Criteria

We compared firm characteristics between GROUPS 1 and 2 over a broad range of traditional financial variables. The variables fall into one of four major categories. Specifically, we examined:

A. Market-based Measures of Performance including market return, price to earning ratio, and market value to book value,
B. Accounting-based Measures of Performance including return on assets, return on equity, and earnings per share,
C. Measures of Risk including current ratio, quick ratio, debt to equity ratio, interest coverage, Altman's Z-score,[5] and market beta,
D. Other Firm-specific Characteristics including capital investment intensity, size, number of lines of business, and dividend-payout ratio.

In all we examined and report results for 16 traditional financial statement variables. Each of the variables is constructed from data available on COMPUSTAT. (COMPUSTAT is a machine-readable data base with historical financial information for over 1,500 publicly traded corporations.) Individual year mean and median results are displayed in Tables 30.8, 30.9, 30.10, and 30.11.

In general, our results indicate that there is little evidence that the GROUP 1 firms, that is firms screened on the basis of CSR criteria, can be characterized as inferior investments relative to the GROUP 2 firms. This finding, once again, contradicts what we called in the previous section, the traditionalists' hypothesis. In addition, some evidence exists which supports the stronger proposition that the GROUP 1 firms can be characterized as superior investments relative to GROUP 2 firms.

[5] The Altman's Z-Score has been found useful in predicting bankruptcy. It is actually a combination of five additional financial ratios. For a full discussion see Stickney (1990) or Altman (1968).

Table 30.8 Market-based measures of performance Group 1 (G1) versus Group 2 (G2) 1985–1991

	1985	1986	1987	1988	1989	1990	1991	Mean
Market returns								
G1 – Mean	24.96	16.01*	–3.87	4.18*	21.69	–0.30	32.33	13.57
G1 – Med.	33.25	12.80	–4.10	2.50	25.20	–7.40	26.50	12.68
Market returns								
G2 – Mean	26.69	5.15	3.19	15.97	16.48	–11.10	24.39	11.54
G2 – Med.	32.70	13.00	–0.50	15.10	18.10	–17.60	22.00	11.83
P/E ratio								
G1 – Mean	19.52	21.06	18.78	15.08	20.59	19.91*	24.43	19.91
G1 – Med.	15.79	17.48	14.94	13.57	17.59	15.69	20.99	16.58
P/E ratio								
G2 – Mean	23.07	22.72	20.63	16.29	22.30	15.68	22.87	20.51
G2 – Med.	17.16	17.73	15.35	13.45	14.96	13.47	18.85	15.85
Market to book value								
G1 – Mean	2.94	2.99	3.20	3.00	3.39**	2.90	3.67**	3.16
G1 – Med.	2.29	2.28	2.65	2.61	3.06	2.39	2.79	2.58
Market to book value								
G2 – Mean	3.30	3.37	2.84	2.56	2.96	2.70	3.02	2.96
G2 – Med.	1.97	2.79	2.09	2.23	2.18	1.76	1.94	2.14

*10% level of significance; **5% level of significance

Table 30.9 Accounting-based measures of performance Group 1 (G1) versus Group 2 (G2) 1985–1991

	1985	1986	1987	1988	1989	1990	1991	Mean
Return on assets								
G1 – Mean	7.54	6.01	8.55**	8.23	7.98*	6.91	6.69	7.42
G1 – Med.	6.55	6.30	8.00	6.70	7.10	6.20	6.45	6.76
Return on assets								
G2 – Mean	5.99	7.70	6.67	7.10	6.07	6.23	4.81	6.37
G2 – Med.	6.15	6.60	6.90	7.00	6.70	6.60	5.15	6.44
Return on common equity								
Gl – Mean	16.53	14.28	19.45**	19.86	19.93	16.81	15.89	17.54
G1 – Med.	15.35	15.30	18.80	19.60	18.30	16.50	15.70	17.08
Return on common equity								
G2 – Mean	14.04	17.68	15.50	17.39	17.70	40.63	15.93	19.84
G2 – Med.	15.80	18.10	15.70	16.90	16.60	15.20	11.80	15.73
EPS G1 – Mean	3.14	2.29	2.55	2.45	2.61	1.96	1.60	2.37
G1 – Med.	2.69	2.22	2.20	2.46	1.90	2.14	2.12	2.25
EPS G2 – Mean	3.08	2.35	2.36	2.49	2.43	2.00	1.45	2.31
G2 – Med.	3.09	1.96	2.13	2.20	2.30	2.05	1.43	2.17

*10% level of significance; **5% level of significance

Table 30.10 Measures of risk Group 1 (G1) versus Group 2 (G2) 1985–1991

	1985	1986	1987	1988	1989	1990	1991	Mean
Current ratio								
G1 – Mean	2.09	2.02	1.96	1.85	1.85	1.87*	1.79	1.92
G1 – Med.	1.86	1.91	1.86	1.77	1.85	1.77	1.67	1.81
Current ratio								
G2 – Mean	2.14	1.87	1.97	1.99	1.99	1.62	1.77	1.91
G2 – Med.	1.91	1.55	1.73	1.67	1.59	1.43	1.40	1.61
Quick ratio								
G1 – Mean	1.30	1.14	1.22	1.07	1.08	1.08	1.04	1.13
G1 – Med.	1.15	1.04	0.99	0.96	0.99	0.93	0.89	0.99
Quick Ratio								
G2 – Mean	1.21	1.17	1.13	1.15	1.11	0.90	1.01	1.10
G2 – Med.	1.10	0.90	1.00	1.00	0.95	0.75	0.78	0.93
Debt/equity ratio								
G1 – Mean	61.29	75.30	78.79	106.57	139.40	229.43	315.75	143.79
G1 – Med.	33.71	29.89	36.77	39.77	60.92	61.27	54.61	45.28
Debt/equity ratio								
G2 – Mean	76.69	74.93	68.39	93.89	95.05	121.78	147.12	96.84
G2 – Med.	40.28	39.98	48.43	41.75	52.20	45.02	40.76	44.06
Interest coverage								
G1 – Mean	7.81	7.38	9.19**	8.43	7.54	6.41	7.63	7.77
G1 – Med.	4.14	4.78	5.72	4.52	3.60	3.43	3.74	4.28
Interest coverage								
G2 – Mean	9.30	8.80	6.40	6.02	5.50	5.52	5.82	6.77
G2 – Med.	4.12	4.77	4.18	4.03	3.34	3.21	3.19	3.83
Altman's Z–score								
G1 – Mean	10.46	10.08	12.27	13.56	20.61	17.31	19.37	14.81
G1 – Med.	8.12	7.26	7.19	5.89	5.49	5.22	6.24	6.49
Altman's Z–score								
G2 – Mean	10.91	9.87	12.97	13.68	10.22	14.37	15.20	12.46
G2 – Med.	5.99	4.68	5.53	5.40	5.08	5.60	6.02	5.47
Market beta								
G1 – Mean	1.17*	1.15	1.17*	1.14	1.15	1.14	1.17*	1.16
G1 – Med.	1.20	1.30	1.20	1.10	1.10	1.20	1.20	1.19
Market beta								
G2 – Mean	1.04	1.06	1.04	1.06	1.07	1.09	1.04	1.06
G2 – Med.	1.10	1.10	1.10	1.20	1.20	1.10	1.10	1.13

*10% level of significance; **5% level of significance

A – Market-Based Measures of Performance

According to Table 30.8, the market returns for GROUP 1 were slightly better than the market returns for GROUP 2. The overall means for the 7 year period were 13.57% and 11.54%, respectively. Further, in 4 of the 7 years the GROUP 1 firms

Table 30.11 Other firms-specific characteristics Group 1 (G1) versus Group 2 (G2) 1985-1991

	1985	1986	1987	1988	1989	1990	1991	Means
Capital investments assets								
G1 – Mean	0.11**	0.09	0.10**	0.10**	0.09	0.09	0.08	0.09
G1 – Med.	0.09	0.06	0.08	0.08	0.08	0.08	0.07	0.08
Capital investments assets								
G2 – Mean	0.09	0.10	0.07	0.08	0.08	0.08	0.07	0.08
G2 – Med.	0.08	0.09	0.05	0.07	0.07	0.06	0.06	0.07
Total assets								
G1 – Mean	3040.60*	2870.02	3647.38*	4809.14*	5240.85**	5413.71*	6267.24*	4469.85
G1 – Med.	1715.56	2140.20	2019.36	2460.40	2743.90	2975.71	3254.84	2472.85
Total assets								
G2 – Mean	2358.00	3366.32	2949.88	3112.53	3449.99	4243.84	4228.39	3386.99
G2 – Med.	1555.26	1879.12	1896.30	1793.80	1971.60	2149.62	2027.39	1896.16
Lines of business								
G1 – Mean	NA	2.35	2.02	2.21	2.17	2.08	2.14	2.16
G2 – Med.	NA	2.00	1.00	2.00	1.00	1.00	1.00	1.33
Lines of business								
G2 – Mean	NA	2.02	2.20	2.08	2.02	2.02	2.02	2.06
G2 – Med.	NA	1.50	2.00	2.00	2.00	2.00	2.00	1.92
Dividend payout								
Ratio G1 – Mean	48.70	41.15	40.35	35.66	45.69	44.94	56.52	44.72
G1 – Med.	37.96	32.50	34.73	33.61	36.86	40.65	41.74	36.86
Dividend payout								
Ratio G2 – Mean	54.20	50.42	40.79	32.07	35.09	35.36	48.07	42.29
G2 – Med.	39.26	38.91	27.19	26.34	29.73	33.68	33.28	32.63

*10% level of significance; **5% level of significance

had higher returns than GROUP 2 firms. In 1986 GROUP 1 outperformed GROUP 2 firms at the 10% level of significance, and in 1988 this relationship was reversed.

There was almost no difference between the price to earning ratios for the two groups. The overall mean for GROUP 1 firms was 19.91 for the 7 year period, and 20.51 for the GROUP 2 firms. The only year in which there was a statistically significant difference at the 10% level was 1990 when the price to earning ratios were 19.91 and 15.68, favoring the GROUP 1 firms.

Among the market-based measures, the most consistent results were related to the market value to book value ratios. This ratio relates the market capitalization of the firm to the accounting valuations. The overall means for the 7 year period was 3.16 versus 2.96 for GROUPS 1 and 2, respectively. From 1987 through 1991, GROUP 1firms had a higher ratio in each year. In 1989 and 1991, the differences were significant at the 5% level.

B – Accounting-Based Measures of Performance

Table 30.9 presents the accounting-based measures of performance. These results are similar to the market-based results in indicating either no difference, or a slight advantage to the socially-responsible firms.

The first variable presented in Table 30.9 is return on assets. It has been suggested that return on assets "takes the particular set of environ-mental factors and strategic choices made by a firm as given and focuses on the profitability of operations relative to the investments (assets) in place." (Stickney 1990: p. 161) An important characteristic of this accounting measure is that it separates financing activities from both operating and investing activities. The overall means for the 7 year period were 7.42% and 6.37%, for GROUPS 1 and 2, respectively. In 2 of the 7 years, 1987 and 1989, the GROUP 1 firms had significantly higher return on assets. In 1987, the mean for the GROUP 1 firms was 8.55% versus 6.67% for the GROUP 2 firms. Similarly, in 1989, the mean for the GROUP 1 firms was 7.98% versus 6.07% for the GROUP 2 firms. Further, in only one year, 1986, did the GROUP 2 firms outperform the GROUP 1 firms, and this difference was not statistically significant. We conclude from these results that the GROUP 1 firms were certainly no less efficient in generating income from assets in place than the GROUP 2 firms, and, in fact, were slightly more efficient.

Although return on common equity is usually correlated with return on assets, it is useful to report this variable as an additional measure of financial performance. It has been argued that return on common equity, which relates income available to common shareholders to average amount of common equity in use during a period, should be emphasized as the appropriate tool for assessing the profitability "from the view-point of an investor in a firm's common stock." (Stickney 1990: p. 219) Not surprisingly, the results here also indicate a slight advantage to the GROUP 1 firms. Although the overall means for the 7 year period were slightly higher for the GROUP 2 firms, this result was primarily driven by the 1990 results, which must be interpreted with care. Notice that in 1990, although the return on common equity for GROUP 2 was apparently much higher than the GROUP 1 results, the difference is not significantly different, and, in fact, GROUP 1 had a higher median. The difference in the reported means between GROUPS 1 and 2 is thus the result of statistical outliers in GROUP 2. The only significant difference was 1987 in which the GROUP 1 firms had a mean of 19.45% versus GROUP 2's mean of 15.50%.

The last variable included in Table 30.9 is earnings per share. The overall means for the 7 year period were $2.37/share versus $2.31/share for GROUPs 1 and 2, respectively. Although the GROUP 1 firms outperformed the GROUP 2 firms in 4 of the 7 years, in none of the years were the results significant at even the 10% level.

C – Measures of Risk

Table 30.10 presents results related to traditional measures of risk. The first two variables presented in the table, the current ratio and the quick ratio, provide an assessment of the corporations' ability to meet its short term obligations as they come due. These measures are often labelled short-term liquidity ratios. For both the current ratio and the quick ratio, the overall means for the 7 year period were nearly identical. For the current ratio the GROUP 1 mean was 1.92 and the GROUP 2 mean was 1.91. Similarly, for the quick ratio the GROUP 1 mean was 1.13 and the GROUP 2 mean was 1.10. The only significant difference (at the 10% level) was for the current ratio in 1990. The GROUP 1 mean was 1.87, which was higher, and thus slightly less risky, than GROUP 2's mean of 1.62.

In addition to examining short-term liquidity ratios, Table 30.10 summarizes results for three long-term solvency measures: interest coverage, debt to equity ratio, and Altman's Z-score. Each of these measures indicate the firms' ability to meet interest payments and principal payments as they come due.

First, for the interest coverage variable, the overall means for the 7 year period were slightly higher (less risky) for the socially-responsible firms. For the GROUP 1 firms the mean was 7.77 and for the GROUP 2 firms the mean was 6.77. (These numbers show that for ever $1 of interest expense there was, on average, $7.77 and $6.77, respectively, of income before interest expense and income taxes.) In 1987, the difference between the two groups was significant at the 5% level; GROUP 1 was 9.19 and GROUP 2 was 6.40. Further, in every year, from 1987 through 1991 GROUP 1 had higher interest coverage than GROUP 2 in terms of both means and medians.

Second, with respect to the debt to equity ratio, which measures the amount of long-term debt financing in a firms' capital structure, although there is some indication that the socially-responsible firms may be more risky, these results should not be overstated. Although the overall mean for the 7 year period is higher for the GROUP 1 firms than for the GROUP 2 firms, this result is, in part, a function statistical outliers among the GROUP 1 firms. In fact, the mean of the median results for the entire 7 year period, which are unaffected by the outliers, and arguably more relevant for our purposes, are nearly identical between GROUPS 1 and 2. The mean of the median results for 7 year period were 45.28% and 44.06%, respectively for GROUPS 1 and 2. Further, in none of the individual years were the differences between the two groups statistically significant.

Altman's Z-Score, a weighted average of five financial statement ratios, has been found useful in predicting bankruptcy. It thus captures a different dimension of corporate risk. In interpreting the Z-Score, the lower the outcome, the greater the probability of bankruptcy. The results summarized in Table 30.10 indicate that in 5 of the 7 years the GROUP 1 scored higher than GROUP 2. The overall mean results for the 7 year period was 14.81 and 12.46, respectively.

The last variable examined in Table 30.10 is market beta. This variable compares the variability of stock returns for a given company with the variability of the stock market as a whole. Higher levels of beta more stock market variability in relation to the market. It is the only one of the 16 variables examined which consistently favored the GROUP 2 firms. Once again, however, the differences should not be over-stated. The overall mean results indicate that the GROUP 1 betas (overall mean 1.16) are about 9% higher than the betas for GROUP 2 (overall mean 1.06). Focusing on the individual year results, in each year the GROUP 1 firms had higher betas than the GROUP 2 firms. In 3 years, 1985, 1987, and 1991, these differences were significant at the 10% level.

D – Other Firm-Specific Characteristics

In addition to examining the performance and risk measures discussed above, Table 30.11 reports comparative statistics for four additional variables: capital investment intensity, total assets, number of lines of business, and dividend-payout ratio.

The capital investment intensity variable was created by deflating new capital investments each year by total assets. The results show that the GROUP 1 firms had higher investment ratios in all but 1 of the 7 years. In fact, in 1985, 1987, and 1988, the capital investment intensity variable is significantly higher (at the 5% level) for the GROUP 1 firms than it is for the GROUP 2 firms. The ratio for the GROUP 1 was 11%, 10%, and 10% respectively for 1985, 1987, and 1988, compared to 9%, 7%, and 8% for GROUP 2. The overall means for the 7 year periods are consistent with these findings.

In addition to greater investment activity, the GROUP 1 firms are also larger than the GROUP 2 firms, in terms of total assets. These results are interesting and

Table 30.12 Distribution of industry rankings of socially-screened firms

	1	2	3	4	5	6	7	⇒ 8	Total
Number of firms	21	10	4	2	5	3	3	5	53
%	40	19	8	4	9	6	6	9	100

This table displays the number and percentage of socially-screened firms that were the largest firm in the industry, the second largest firm, etc.

important. By 1991, as per Table 30.11, the mean asset size of GROUP 1 firms is over $6 billion, compared to a mean asset size of over $4 billion for GROUP 2 firms. Although the disparity is mitigated somewhat in focusing on median results rather than mean results, nevertheless the difference is statistically significant at the 10% level.

The differences in terms of size between the two groups is somewhat surprising. This is especially true since our strategy in creating the control sample (GROUP 2) was to select firms "as close as possible" in terms of asset size. In some cases, however, this strategy did not result in extremely close matches. Table 30.12 illustrates the difficulty. According to the table, about 40% of the firms in Group 1 were the biggest firms in their respective industries (ranked on the basis of total assets). For example, Group 1 includes K- Mart and Johnson and Johnson. These are the number one firms in the Variety Stores industry and the Pharmaceutical Preparation industry, respectively. Because the socially-responsible firms were so big, many of the control firms, by construction, had to be smaller than their socially-responsible counterparts.

This size effect documented here confirms results of previous research. For example, Trotman and Bradley (1981) concluded that companies which provide social responsibility information are, on average, larger in size than companies which do not disclose this information. Arlow and Gannon (1982), in reviewing the literature, suggested that social responsiveness might be linked to such factors as industry and organizational size. Finally, McGuire et al. (1988) using Fortune Magazine's annual survey of corporate reputations concluded that total assets were positively linked to social-responsibility reputations.

Returning to Table 30.11, it is interesting to note that even given the substantial size differences between GROUPS 1 and 2, there are no statistically significant differences between the groups in terms of number of lines of business. This is true, even though for 5 of the 6 years (data were not available for 1985), GROUP 1 had a higher mean than GROUP 2.

Similarly, there were no significant differences for the last variable examined, the dividend payout ratio. Again, this is true, even though GROUP 1 had higher means from 1988 through 1991. The overall 7 year means were 44.72% and 42.29%, for GROUPS 1 and 2, respectively.

An Examination of Time Trends

In addition to comparing the performance of the GROUP 1 and 2 firms over the entire 7 year period as above, we also test for changes over time. Specifically, we compare the relative performance of the GROUP 1 and 2 firms in two time periods (1985–1987 and 1989–1991).

To assess the relative performance, we first divided the sample into two time periods, an early and late period. Next, for the early period, we compared the 3 year means for each of the 16 variables between GROUPS 1 and 2. We repeated the identical procedure for the later period. Table 30.13 lists those variables in which there were statistically significant differences in one time period, but not the other.

Our analysis shows that in terms of the market-based measures of performance, risk measures, and other firm-specific characteristics there is no evidence that the GROUP 2 firms performed better relative to the GROUP 1 firms in the later period than in the earlier period. The single piece of evidence supporting the enhanced performance of the GROUP 2 firms in the later period is one of the three accounting-based measure of performance, return on common equity. There was no relative improvement for either return on assets or earnings per share. Thus, most of our data is inconsistent with Explanation 4, of the previous section, which posits a net cost associated with social-responsibility actions.

Table 30.13 Trend analysis early period (1985–1987) versus late period (1989–1991)

	Early period means (1985–1987)	Late period means (1989–1991)
Market returns – G1	10.29	17.85*
Market returns – G2	16.04	9.85
P/E ratio – G1	20.48*	23.50
P/E ratio – G1	23.15	23.07
Market to book value – G1	3.18	3.32*
Market to book value – G2	3.03	2.90
Return on common equity – G1	17.99**	18.33
Return on common equity – G2	14.83	24.83
Interest coverage – G1	8.50	7.65**
Interest coverage – G2	8.16	5.47
Capital investments/assets – G1	0.10**	0.09
Capital investments/assets – G2	0.08	0.08
Total assets – G1	3366.36	5608.93**
Total assets – G2	2684.18	3949.48

This table lists each of the 16 variables in which there was a statistically significant (at either the 5% or 10% level) difference between GROUPS 1 and 2 in one time period, but not the other
*10% level of significance; **5% level of significance

By contrast, the preponderance of evidence is that GROUP 1 firms performed relatively better than GROUP 2 firms in the later period. This is especially true for the market-based measures of performance. As indicated in Table 30.13, the market returns for the GROUP 1 firms were nearly twice as high in the later period than the market returns for the GROUP 2 firms. Similarly, the mean of the market value to book value in the later period is significantly higher for the GROUP 1 firms. Notice also, that the in early period, the price to earnings ratio favored GROUP 2, but the effect reverses in the later period. All three of these findings indicate a relatively enhanced performance of the socially-responsible firms in the later period.

In addition to improvements in market-based measures of performance, our results also indicate a relative improvement in one of the risk measures. The interest coverage ratio, which is not significantly different between the two groups in the early period, is significantly higher (less risky) for GROUP 1in the later period. None of the other risk measures indicate any changes over time.

Finally, examining other firm-specific characteristics, Table 30.13 shows that, although there is no significant difference in terms of size in the early period between the two groups, in the later period, the socially-responsible firms are significantly larger than the control sample. The only other variable which showed changes over time was the capital investment intensity variable. In the early period, GROUP 1 had significantly higher investment ratios than GROUP 2.

To summarize the results of this section, most of the variables, although not every variable, showed either no change between the two time periods, or indicated an improved performance over time for the socially-responsible firms relative to the control sample. It is certainly pre-socially-responsible firms perform better over time.

The issues involved in assessing socially-responsible actions, and measuring financial performance are too complex and nuanced to expect definitive answers. However, based on our results to date, and to the extent they are corroborated by additional studies using alternative samples, and even longer testing periods, Explanation 5 above, becomes more plausible. Recall, Explanation 5 suggested that, at least, some CSR activities might cause better financial performance. A relative improvement in the performance of socially-responsible firms over time is consistent with this hypothesis.

The tone of our discussion and the formulation of the conclusions to our empirical work are purposely tentative. This underscores the exploratory nature of the research project. Nevertheless, the consistency of the results reported here, and the persistent finding, across numerous studies, that socially-responsible firms certainly perform no worse, and perhaps, perform better than non-socially responsible firms, is an important and intriguing finding which demands additional attention. Although our understanding of the relationship between corporate social-responsibility and traditional financial performance is not complete, in the next section we conclude our study with a general discussion of six propositions about corporate social-responsibility.

Section 3

The specific purpose of our study has been to explore the association between corporate social-responsibility and traditional financial performance. In this study we examined the long-term financial performance of a group of 53 firms which have been identified by the Council on Economic Priorities (CEP) as being socially-responsible, and compared the financial performance of this group to a control sample matched by both size and industry (Council on Economic Priorities et al. 1991). Many of the 53 firms in GROUP 1 have been described as socially-responsible by a wide variety of outside evaluators. The CEP is one of the most highly regarded external producers of social-responsibility information. The 53 firms represent a diverse sample of companies. Thus the sample provides an important, and inherently interesting, point of departure.

Our analysis of the data suggested that there is almost no evidence that firms which are screened on the basis of social-responsibility criteria performed worse than other firms. By contrast, there is some evidence to suggest a positive association between social-responsibility and traditional financial performance. Further, there was little to suggest that the control sample performed relatively better in the later period compared to the social-responsibility group. In fact, once again, most of the evidence suggested that the socially-responsible firms performed relatively stronger in the later period. This was particularly true for the market-based measures of performance, but also held for one risk measure. In terms of other firm characteristics, the evidence showed that the socially-responsible firms were significantly larger than the control group in the later period.

This concluding section extends our discussion of CSR. We examine six formal propositions. Although there will continue to be constructive debates about many of the specific issues concerning the relationship between social activities and financial performance, the following general propositions are warranted.

1 – Managers, board members, and investors are increasingly confronted by business decisions with social and therefore ethical implications.

As our economy begins to spill over domestic borders, as corporations continue to expand in size, as technological impacts multiply, society's well-being becomes more tightly linked with corporate decision-making. Simply put, as corporate power increases, the ramifications of its actions multiply. Many of the most important ethical decisions individual face are with-in the corporate context. The executive decisions which ultimately lead to the Exxon Valdez disaster were surely not only economic decisions (even if that is how they were framed by the principal actors) but also involved an ethical component, as well. The question of whether or not a beer distillery should specifically target urban areas for a high-alcohol malt liquor must be answered both with economic and ethical criteria. The decision to continue marketing or to withdraw a record album advocating the killing of police officers, regardless of its solution, demands recourse not only to profit considerations, but also requires a formulation, and at least, an implicit understanding of corporate obligations to society.

We emphasize this point, although it would seem obvious, because it is apparently not universally accepted. Milton Friedman, for example, has explicitly stated that "The really important ethical problems are those that face an individual in a free society." We, of course, do not disagree that individuals face importance ethical problems, but we believe that more and more ethical problems are faced by individuals within the corporate context.

2. – A difference of opinion regarding social and ethical obligations does not prove that CSR is unnecessary or perhaps (as some might suggest) meaningless.

Arguments against managers adopting CSR criteria often take the following form: Since it is obviously true that well-intentioned individuals disagree about CSR issue X, managers must, therefore, disregard issue X in formulating business policy Y. Once again, Friedman provides the clearest and most unequivocal formulation of this position. Friedman has written, "If businessmen do have social responsibility other than maximizing profits for stockholders, how are they to know what it is?" (1962: p. 133) Friedman's succinct formulation captures one of the most difficult aspects related to CSR.

Advocates of this argument point out that managers are hired exclusively to maximize profits. Further, they have no special expertise in evaluating ethical considerations. Managers must therefore avoid arbitrarily usurping corporate funds in pursuit of subjective personal goals. An executive who pursues issue X is there-fore in violation of his or her contract with employers.

On proposition 2, we offer three observations: First, as has often been observed by philosophers, an awareness and recognition of diversity of opinion and practice with regard to ethical issues does not imply ethical relativism. For example, the philosopher Robert Nozick (1981) has shown that, although it is not the intention of philosophy to produce uniformity of belief, nevertheless good reasons can be put forth to show how there can be objective values and ethical truths.

If the traditionalists' point is merely that it is difficult to precisely specify the contours of social-responsibility, it is obviously true. If traditionalists' are only pointing out that we have not reached a consensus on many of the issues surrounding the ethical obligations of the business corporation, again, we would have no quarrel. If, however, the traditionalists' view suggests that these reasons necessarily imply that social-responsibility is an untenable option (as Friedman's position would seem to imply), it is unwarranted. The notion of CSR is difficult to implement in practice. This does not imply that it is impossible.

Second, even accepting the strong assumption that executives and investors explicitly agree that the sole legitimate corporate goal is profit maximization, it certainly does not follow that the ethical world thus evaporates. It is, at best unclear, why if both parties to a transaction agree to disregard an ethical obligation, their joint obligation thus disappears. It may very well be the case that each of the parties may have an a priori, and higher level obligation, to pursue issue X. Any contract therefore which supersedes X may not be binding from an ethical perspective.[6]

Finally, and perhaps most importantly, there is little evidence to suggest that investors and managers, in fact, agree to remove ethical and social-responsibility constraints from executive decision-making. The assumption that corporate management can not use ethical criteria in making good business decisions is at the core of the traditionalists' view. It appears, on the face of it, that this is a strange suggestion.

Friedman has written that if social-responsibility means anything at all it must mean that managers act in some way that is not in the interest of employers. It maybe, however, that investors' have a preference for social-responsibility. At minimum, the core assumption of the traditionalists' argument should be subject to empirical investigation. Mulligan (1986) has summarized the counter-argument as follows:

> There is no good reason why this remarkable claim must be true. The exercise of social responsibility in business suffers no diminishment in meaning or merit if the executive and his employers both understand their mutual interest to include a proactive social role and cooperate in undertaking that role. (p. 266)

We articulate this alternative view as a separate proposition.

3. – Some shareholders will willingly forfeit profits for enhanced CSR performance.

Epstein and Pava (1992) have presented survey evidence consistent with this possibility. Though the stereotype is that investors are worried only about profits, when individual investors were explicitly asked to rank their preferences as to how corporate funds should be allocated, pollution control and product safety were rated significantly higher than increased dividends.

4. – Little empirical evidence exists which documents that firms rated high in terms of CSR perform poorly in terms of financial performance.

In the course of this study we identified 22empirical studies (including this one) which attempted to gauge the degree of association between CSR and financial performance. Of these 22 studies which we have examined, only one reported a negative correspondence between social responsibility and financial performance.

5. – Some forms of CSR may enhance, and not detract, from financial performance.

This proposition is the most controversial of our observations. However, we believe that it is the most consistent reading of the available empirical data. The

[6] Nevertheless, the contract may be extremely relevant from a legal perspective. See Martin Luther King's, "A Letter From a Birmingham jail" (in Newton 1989).

conclusion is also intuitively appealing. This is especially true that if by social responsibility we focus on the following limited set of socially responsible activities: environmental pollution, employee and consumer relations, and product quality. Each of these areas are inextricably linked with financial performance.

What this last proposition does not imply is that one should expect corporations to go beyond their areas of expertise, and to solve social problems of which they are not even indirectly responsible for. Peter Drucker (1989) perhaps put it best when he recently wrote that "We know that corporations first social responsibility is to do their job. We know secondly that they have responsibility for their impacts – on people, on the community, on society, in general. And finally we know that they act irresponsibly if they go beyond the impacts necessary for them to do their own job, whether it is taking care of the sick, producing goods, or advancing learning." (p. 86)

6. – Stakeholder theory, especially as developed by Ullmann, is a useful but not a complete paradigm to model CSR.

To the extent that proposition 5 holds, it suggests a limitation of the stakeholder theory. As Ullmann (1985) has written, "Economic performance determines the relative weight of social demand and the attention it receives from top decision makers. In periods of low profitability and in situations of high debt, economic demands will have priority over social demands … Economic performance influences the financial capability to undertake costly programs related to social demands." A model, however, which, a priori, disallows the possibility that CSR causes better financial performance is incompletely specified.

Conclusion

What makes this area of inquiry so interesting is that with each answer, new and exciting questions emerge. The relationship between CSR and financial performance is complex and nuanced. This study has emphasized the recurrent and paradoxical finding that firms which have been perceived as having met social-responsibility criteria have generally been shown to have financial performance at least on a par, if not better, than other firms.

Two areas of further interest are the role of the CEO in establishing CSR goals, and how corporations, through the annual report, defend and justify CSR expenditures. Although our understanding of CSR is by no means complete, it is an area of research that has proven to yield interesting and important results.

Acknowledgment This research project was funded by a generous grant from The Lupin Foundation. The Sy Syms School of Business is grateful for the opportunity. In addition, the authors would like to thank former Dean Michael Schiff for his guidance and wisdom in helping develop the research agenda, and Dean Harold Nierenberg for providing an environment conducive to completing this project.

Appendix A: Summary of 21 Empirical Studies

Authors/Date	Social responsibility criteria	Financial performance criteria	Results	Comments
Bragdon and Marlin (1972)	Council on economic priorities air and water pollution measures	Various measures of financial accounting returns	Lower levels of pollution were correlated with better financial performance (+)	Authors correlated the pollution control indexes with profitability indexes (1965–1971) for 17 companies in the pulp and paper industry
Vance (1975)	Milton Moskowitz's social responsibility ratings	Percentage change in stock price	All but one of the 14 firms in the sample had performance records considerably worse than the NYSE composite index (–)	Author examined updated financial performance (1972–1975) of original Moskowitz sample
Bowman and Haire (1975)	Proportion of annual report prose devoted to social responsibility issues	Return on equity	Mean return on equity for firms with "some discussion" was 14.3%, while the mean return on equity for firms with "no discussion" was 9.1% (+)	Authors examined 82 firms in the food-processing industry between 1969 and 1973. Authors claim social disclosure is a surrogate for social responsibility. Some evidence provided which suggests relationship between social responsibility and financial performance may be U-shape
Fogler and Nutt (1975)	Three pollution indexes	Financial accounting earnings and stock price data	No significant relationship was found between financial performance and pollution ratings (0)	Authors examined performance of 9 firms between March 1971 and March 1972 after substantial publicity was released about their pollution tendencies
Belkaoui (1976)	Disclosure of pollution control information in 1970 annual reports	Market-based returns adjusted for risk	The 50 experimental firms, in which pollution information was disclosed, out-performed the control sample in terms of stock returns (+)	In the 4 month period following disclosure, the market made a temporary conversion of the positive effect of pollution control expenditures in higher share valuation

Sturdivant and Ginter (1977)	Milton Moskowitz's social responsibility ratings	Ten year earnings per share growth	There was a significant difference in EPS growth between the best and worst social performers. Socially responsible firms outperformed their non responsible counterparts (+)	Authors examined 28 firms between 1964 and 1974 who passed data requirements. They conclude that there is evidence that, in general, the responsively managed firms will enjoy better economic performance
Alexander and Buchholz (1978)	Milton Moskowitz's social responsibility ratings	Market-based returns adjusted for risk	No significant relationship between social responsibility ratings and market-based returns (0)	Authors examined stock market performance of 46 firms between 1970 and 1974. They concluded that their results are consistent with efficient markets. Further, the effects of the degree of social responsibility on stock prices were either non-existent or had occurred prior to 1970
Chugh et al. (1978)	Firms belonging to high pollution industries	Market-based estimates of beta	Between 1970 and 1972 estimated betas of "polluter" firms shifted up (+)	Authors compared 59 experimental firms, in high pollution industries, to 60 control firms. The authors attributed the shift in estimated betas to the increased water and air pollution control legislation during the 1970 to 1972 time period
Anderson and Frankle (1980)	Annual report disclosures (1972) related to social responsibility issues	Market-based returns adjusted for risk	In 6 month period following annual report disclosure there is no difference between disclosing and non-disclosing firms. Examination of March returns, however, gives credence to the possibility of a positive impact (+)	Authors compared stock market returns between 210 disclosing firms and 113 non-disclosing firms. The authors concluded that the results strongly support the contention that the market values social disclosure positively. The ethical inventors may exist and, in fact dominate the market

(continued)

Appendix A (continued)

Authors/Date	Social responsibility criteria	Financial performance criteria	Results	Comments
Freedman and Jaggi (1982)	Council on economic priorities air and water pollution measures	Various measures of financial accounting returns	In general there is no association between pollution measures and financial performance. However, evidence is reported which suggests that for very large firms with poor economic performance, pollution disclosure are more detailed (0)	The authors examined the relationship among pollution disclosures, pollution performance, and economic performance for 109 firms in highly polluting industries during 1973 and 1974
Shane and Spicer (1983)	Council on economic priorities air and water pollution measures	Market-based returns adjusted for risk surrounding publication of CEP studies	The results indicated that the CEP firms experienced, on average, relatively large negative abnormal returns. Moreover, returns for those companies that revealed to have low pollution-control performance rankings were found, on average, to have significantly more negative returns than companies with high rankings (+)	The authors examined stock market performance of 58 firms (pulp and paper, electric power, iron and steel, and petroleum industries only) between 1970 and 1975. The purpose of this paper was to investigate the question of potential information content of socially-oriented disclosures produced outside the firm
Cochran and Wood (1984)	Milton Moskowitz's social responsibility ratings	Various measures of financial accounting based returns and excess market valuations	Firms with older assets have lower social responsibility ratings. There is also a marginally significant positive association between social responsibility and financial performance (+)	Financial performance was examined for nearly 40 firms between 1970 and 1979

Chen and Metcalf (1984)	Two pollution indexes	Various measures of financial accounting based returns, estimated betas, and price earnings ratios	Controlling for firm size, there is no statistical association between pollution indices and financial indicators (0)	In re-examining an earlier study by Spicer, the authors concluded that there is no relationship between a pollution index and financial indicators. The authors concluded that given the visibility of large firms and the severe effects of pollution from large operations on the environment, a large firm tends to do more, either voluntarily or involuntarily on pollution control
Aupperle et al. (1985)	CEOs' concern for society as reflected in mail questionnaire	Return on assets adjusted for risk	No significant relationships were found between a strong orientation toward social responsibility and financial performance (0)	The authors examined the association between attitudes of CEOs (for 241 firms who were listed in Forbes 1981 Annual Directory and answered a mail questionnaire) and financial performance
Freedman and Jaggi (1986)	A pollution index	Market-based returns adjusted for risk surrounding annual report date	The test results did not indicate any difference between investor reaction to extensive disclosures and investor reaction to minimal disclosures (0)	This study examines investors' differential reaction to extensive pollution disclosures in annual statements compared with those firms that make minimal disclosures. All 88 firms belonging to chemical, paper and pulp, oil refining, and steel industries that disclosed some information were examined for 1973 and 1974
Baldwin et al. (1986)	Investment in South Africa	Market-based estimates of beta	Excluding firms which do business with South Africa from investment portfolio produces a "minute" increase in risk (0)	Authors attempted to estimate the penalty (as non-market risk) that would have to be incurred as a result of not being able to invest in firms that do business with South Africa. The procedure was to delete excluded companies from S&P 500, and to then come up with the combination of stocks that eliminated the most non-market risk

(continued)

Appendix A (continued)

Authors/Date	Social responsibility criteria	Financial performance criteria	Results	Comments
Rockness et al. (1986)	Amount of chemical waste disposal as reported by EPA and US House Subcommittee on Oversight and Investigations	Various measures of financial accounting based returns	Higher ROE was associated with smaller amounts of on-site chemical waste disposal (+)	This study examined 21 firms in the chemical industry between 1980 and 1983. It also examines the disclosure of environmental performance in the annual report with respect to hazardous waste disposal
McGuire et al. (1988)	Fortune magazine's annual survey of corporate reputations	Various measures of financial accounting based returns, market-based returns adjusted for risk, and market-based estimates of beta	ROA and total assets showed positive relationships and operating income growth had a negative correlation. Accounting and stock-market based risk measures tended to be negatively associated with social responsibility (+)	The authors examined the association between financial performance and social responsibility for 98 firms during the 1977–1984 time period. The authors concluded that it may be more fruitful to consider financial performance as a variable influencing social responsibility than the reverse
Cotrill (1990)	Fotune magazine's annual survey of corporate reputations	Market concentration, market share, industry	There was a positive association between market share and CSR. In addition there was an industry effect as well (+)	The author examined 118 firms in over 18 industries during 1982 and 1983. The author wrote that the biggest surprise was that the industry effect was not more fully accounted for by competition levels
Patten (1990)	Sullivan principles (A code of behavior mandating equal economic opportunities for non-white workers in South Africa)	Market-based returns adjusted for risk and trading volume around the signing of the principles	No price reaction. Authors did report a volume reaction (0)	The author compared price and volume reaction between 37 firms who signed Sullivan principles in 1977 and 37 control firms. The results indicated that, at least in terms of volume, the information did impact upon stock market behavior

Roberts (1992)	Council of economic priorities evaluations of social disclosure, dollars contributed by PACs, public affairs staff members, sponsorship of philanthropic foundation	Various measures of financial accounting based returns, market-based estimates of beta, size, etc.	There was a positive association between CSR and economic performance	The purpose of this study was to test “a stakeholder theory”. The author examined 80 firms between 1984 and 1986 which met data requirements. The author concluded that the empirical results support stakeholder theory

Appendix B: Socially-Screened (Group 1) Versus Control Firms (Group 2)

	Group 1 – Socially-screened	Group 2 – Control
1	Campbell Soup Co	Unilever PLC – Amer Shrs
2	Quaker Oats Co	Borden Inc
3	Sara Lee Corp	Smithfield Companies Inc
4	Ben & Jerry's Homemde – CL A	Dreyer's Grand Ice Cream Inc
5	Heinz (H. J.) Co	CPC International Inc
6	General Mills Inc	Ralston Purina Co
7	Kellogg Co	American Maize-Prods – CL A
8	Hershey Foods Corp	Savannah Foods & Inds
9	Tootsie Rool Inds	Mel Diversified Inc
10	Hartmarx Corp	Crystal Brands
11	Liz Claiborne Inc	Benetton Group SPA – ADR New
12	Miller (Herman) Inc	Kimball International – CL A
13	Weyerhaeuser Co	Georgia-Pacific Corp
14	Gannett Co	Times Mirror Co-Del – SER A
15	Knight-Ridder Inc	New York Times Co – CL A
16	Houghton Mifflin Co	Western Publishing Group Inc
17	Wellman Inc	Courtaulds Plc – ADR
18	Baxter International Inc	Smithkline Beecham PLC – ADS
19	Merck & Co	American Home Products Corp
20	Johnson & Johnson	Bristol Myers Squibb
21	Marion Merrell Dow Inc	Imcera Group Inc
22	Procter & Gamble Co	Colgate-Palmolive Co
23	Clorox Co-Del	NCH Corp
24	Avon Products	Intl Favors & Fragrances
25	Fuller (H. B.) Co	Loctite Corp
26	Rubbermaid Inc	Illinois Tool Works
27	Stride Rite Corp	Wolverine World Wide
28	Cummins Engine	Brunswick Corp
29	Digital Equipment	Hewlett-Packard Co
30	Apple Computer Inc	Tandy Corp
31	Pitney Bowes Inc	General Binding Corp
32	Tennant Co	Tokheim Corp
33	Maytag Corp	Whirlpool Corp
34	Lifeline Systems Inc	Pico Products Inc
35	Huffy Corp	Harley-Davidson Inc
36	Easstman Kodak Co	Canon Inc – ADR
37	Xerox Corp	Fuji Photo Filmm – ADR
38	Polaroid Corp	Ricoh Co Ltd – ADR
39	Delta Air Lines Inc	AMR Corp-Del
40	Federal Express Corp	Airborne Freight Corp
41	Nynex Corp	Bellsouth Corp
42	Hawaiian Electric Inds	Puget Sound Power & Light

(continued)

Appendix B (continued)

	Group 1 – Socially-screened	Group 2 – Control
43	Brooklyn Union Gas Co	Peoples Energy Corp
44	Chambers Development – CL A	Attwoods Plc – ADR
45	Penney (J. C.) Co	Ito Yokado Co Ltd – ADR
46	K Mart Corp	Coles Myer Ltd – ADR
47	Wal-Mart Stores	Woolworth Corp
48	Dayton Hudson Corp	Price Co
49	Nordstrom Inc	TJX Cos Inc – New
50	Rouse Co	Vornado Inc
51	Safety-Kleen Corp	Sotheby's Holdings – CL A
52	Ryder System Inc	Rollins Truck Leasing
53	Disney (Walt) Company	Bally Mfg Corp

References

Alexander, G.J., and R.A. Buchholz. 1978. Corporate social responsibility and stock market performance. *Academy of Management Journal* 21: 479–486.

Altman, E. 1968. Financial ratios, discriminant analysis, and the prediction of corporate bankruptcy. *Journal of Finance* 23(September): 589–609.

Anderson, J.C., and A.W. Frankle. 1980. Voluntary social reporting: An iso-beta portfolio analysis. *The Accounting Review* 55(3): 467–479.

Arlow, P., and M. Gannon. 1982. Social responsiveness, corporate structure, and economic performance. *Academy of Management Review* 7: 235–241.

Aupperle, K.E., A.B. Carroll, and J.D. Hatfield. 1985. An empirical examination of the relationship between corporate social responsibility and profitability. *Academy of Management Journal* 28(2): 446–463.

Baldwin, S.A., J.W. Tower, L. Litvak, J.F. Karpen, H.F. Jackson, and B. McTigue. 1986. *Pension funds and ethical investment*. New York: Council on Economic Priorities.

Belkaoui, A. 1976. The impact of the disclosure of the environmental effects of organizational behavior on the market. *Financial Management* 5(4): 26–31.

Bowles, S., and H. Gintis. 1987. *Democracy & capitalism: Property, community and the contradictions of modern social thought*. New York: Basic Books.

Bowman, E.H., and M.A. Haire. 1975. A strategic posture toward corporate social responsibility. *California Management Review* 18(2): 49–58.

Boycott Report. 1992. Developments and trends affecting the Arab Boycott and Arab Influence in the USA. Vol. 16, No. 8. New York: American Jewish Congress.

Bragdon, J.H., and J.A.T. Marlin. 1972. Is pollution profitable? *Risk Management* 19(4): 9–18.

Bruyn, S.T. 1987. *The field of social investment*. Cambridge: Cambridge University Press.

Chen, K.H., and R.W. Metcalf. 1980. The relationship between pollution control record and financial indicators revisited. *Accounting Review* 55(1): 168–177.

Chen, K.H., and R.W. Metcalf. 1984. The relationship between pollution control record and financial indicators revisited. *The Accounting Review* 55(1): 168–177.

Chugh, L., M. Haneman, and S. Mahapatra. 1978. Impact of pollution control regulations on the market risk of securities in the U.S. *Journal of Economic Studies* 5(1): 64–70.

Cochran, P.L., and R.A. Wood. 1984. Corporate social responsibility and financial performance. *Academy of Management Journal* 27(1): 42–56.

Coffey, B.S., and G. Fryxell. 1991. Institutional ownership of stock and dimensions of corporate social performance: An empirical examination. *Journal of Business Ethics* 10: 437–444.

Cornell, B., and A.C. Shapiro. 1987. Corporate stakeholders and corporate finance. *Financial Management* 16: 5–14.

Cotrill, M.T. 1990. Corporate social responsibility and the marketplace. *Journal of Business Ethics* 9: 723–729.

Council on Economic Priorities, M. Alperson, A. Tepper Marlin, J. Schorsch, and R. Will. 1991. *The better world investment guide*. New York: Prentice Hall.

Drucker, P.F. 1989. *The new realities: In government and politics/in economics and business/in society and world view*. New York: Harper and Row.

Drucker, P.F. 1992. The new society of organizations. *Harvard Business Review*, Sept.–Oct.: 95–104.

Epstein, M.J., and M.L. Pava. 1992. Corporations and the environment: Shareholders demand accountability. *USA Today Magazine* 121(2570): 32–33.

Fogler, H.R., and R. Nutt. 1975. A note on social responsibility and stock valuation. *Academy of Management Journal* 18(1): 155–160.

Freedman, M., and B. Jaggi. 1982. Pollution disclosures, pollution performance and economic performance. *The International Journal of Management Science* 10(2): 167–176.

Freedman, M., and B. Jaggi. 1986. An analysis of the impact of corporate pollution disclosures included in annual financial statements on investors' decisions. *Advances in Public Interest Accounting* 1: 193–212.

Friedman, M. 1962. *Capitalism and freedom*. Chicago: The University of Chicago Press.

Friedman, M. 1970. A Friedman doctrine – The social responsibility of business is to increase its profits. *The New York Times Magazine* Sept. 13: 32–33, 123–125.

Friedman, B.M. (ed.). 1978. *New challenges to the role of profit*. Lexington: Lexinton Books.

Friedman, M., and R. Friedman. 1980. *Free to choose*. New York: Avon Books.

Gilder, G. 1984. *The spirit of enterprise*. New York: Simon and Schuster.

Kahneman, D., J.L. Knetsch, and R.H. Thaler. 1986. Fairness and assumptions of economics. *Journal of Business* 59(4): 285–300.

Kristol, I. 1978. *Two cheers for capitalism*. New York: Basic Books.

McGuire, J., A. Sundgren, and T. Schneeweis. 1988. Corporate social responsibility and firm financial performance. *Academy of Management Journal* 31(4): 854–872.

Mulligan, T. 1986. A critique of Milton Friedman's. Essay 'the social responsibility of business is to increase its profits'. *Journal of Business Ethics* 5: 265–269.

New York Times (February 11, 1993).

Newton, L. 1989. *Ethics in America: A source reader*. Prentice Hall: Englewood Cliffs.

Novak, M. 1984. *The spirit of democratic capitalism*. New York: American Enterprise Institute/ Simon and Schuster.

Nozick, R. 1981. *Philosophical explanations*. Cambridge, MA: The Belknap Press of Harvard University Press.

Okun, A. 1975. *Equality and efficiency: The big tradeoff*. Washington, DC: The Brookings Institution.

Patten, D.M. 1990. The market reaction to social responsibility disclosures: The case of the Sullivan principles signings. *Accounting, Organizations and Society* 15(6): 575–587.

Roberts, R.W. 1992. Determinants of corporate social responsibility disclosure: An application of stakeholder theory. *Accounting, Organizations and Society* 17(6): 595–612.

Rockness, J., and P.F. Williams. 1988. A descriptive study of social responsibility mutual funds. *Accounting, Organizations and Society* 13(4): 397–411.

Rockness, J., P. Schlachter, and H. Rockness. 1986. Hazardous waste disposal, corporate disclosure, and financial performance in the chemical industry. *Advances in Public Interest Accounting* 1: 167–191.

Shane, P., and B. Spicer. 1983. Market response to environmental information produced outside the firm. *The Accounting Review* 58(3): 521–538.

Social Investment Forum 1991. *Socially responsible mutual funds* (August, Minneapolis, MN).

Stickney, C.P. 1990. *Financial statement analysis: A strategic perspective*. Orlando: Harcourt Brace Jovanovich.

Sturdivant, F.D., and J.L. Ginter. 1977. Corporate social responsiveness. *California Management Review* 19(3): 30–39.

Trotman, K., and G. Bradley. 1981. Association between social responsibility disclosure and characteristics of companies. *Accounting, Organizations and Society* 6: 355–362.

Ullmann, A.A. 1985. Data in search of a theory: A critical examination of the relationships among social performance, social disclosure, and economic performance of U. S. firms. *Academy of Management Review* 10(3): 540–557.

Vance, S.C. 1975. Are socially responsible corporations good investment risks? *Management Review* 64(8): 18–24.

Walton, C. 1992. *Corporate encounters: Ethics, law & business environment*. Fort Worth: The Dryden Press.

Chapter 31
Corporate Ethics Practices in the Mid-1990s: An Empirical Study of the Fortune 1000

Gary R. Weaver, Linda Klebe Treviño, and Philip L. Cochran

Various forms of corporate ethics structures and activities have become common in U.S. business organizations over the last 20 years, to the point that previous studies suggested that formal ethics programs were becoming institutionalized in corporate America (Berenbeim 1987, 1992; Center for Business Ethics 1986, 1992; White and Montgomery 1980; Sweeney and Siers 1990). This empirical study of *Fortune* 1000 service and industrial firms returns to that topic for an updated view of corporate ethics practice in the mid-1990s. Specifically, it reports on firms' usage of formal ethics policies or ethics codes, formal ethics structures or offices, formalized activities such as ethics training programs, and on the involvement of key corporate personnel in ethics program activities. Our study is distinguished in part by the degree of specificity with which different aspects of corporate ethics activity are delineated and measured; it provides, in effect, a snapshot of the "state of the art" in formalized corporate ethics function.

Our results show a high degree of corporate adoption of ethics policies, but wide variability in the extent to which these policies are implemented by various supporting structures and managerial activities. In effect, the vast majority of firms have committed to the lower cost, possibly more symbolic side of ethics activity: the

G.R. Weaver
Department of Business Administration, Alfred Lerner College of Business & Economics University of Delaware, Newark, DE 19716, USA
e-mail: gweaver@udel.edu

L.K. Treviño (✉)
Department of Management and Organization, Pennsylvania State University, University Park, PA 16802, USA
e-mail: LTreviño@psu.edu

P.L. Cochran
Kelley School of Business Indianapolis, Indiana University, 801 West Michigan Street, Indianapolis, Indiana 46202, USA
e-mail: plcochra@iupui.edu

A.C. Michalos and D.C. Poff (eds.), *Citation Classics from the Journal of Business Ethics*, Advances in Business Ethics Research 2,
DOI 10.1007/978-94-007-4126-3_31,

promulgation of ethics policies and codes. But firms differ substantially in their efforts to see that those policies or codes actually are put into practice by organization members. Despite a flurry of attention to formal ethics codes and policies, many firms at most are relying on pre-existing corporate structures or processes to put these policies into action. Moreover, significant importance still attaches to the informal, harder-to-assess side of ethics in corporate America, including factors such as the norms of corporate cultures and subcultures or executive role modeling (cf. Treviño 1990). But if preexisting corporate structures and informal cultural processes prove insufficient to implement now popular ethics policies, then those policies will have a largely symbolic organizational role.

Our intention in this report is to describe the current state of formal ethics practice; in this context, we offer no additional empirically-based explanations of why contemporary corporate ethics programs take the forms they do. In particular, we do not presume to explain the reasons for ethics programs by appeal to corporate pronouncements. Such reports are subject to various biases, especially, but not exclusively, insofar as some motives for ethics management (a) may be more ethically acceptable than others, (b) may be subject to multiple interpretations by different persons in the same organization, and (c) may reflect externally imposed imperatives for executives to use particular symbols and structures to maintain certain appearances (Pfeffer 1981). Executive reports of corporate goals are important data points for various purposes, but – at least for understanding the origins of corporate ethics activity – should be considered in conjunction with other influences on organizational activity using more complex analytical techniques (cf. Beneish and Chatov 1993; Weaver et al. 1995). Similarly, we do not report here any assessments of ethics program effectiveness.

Method and Measures

Data Collection Method

The population studied consists of the Fortune 500 industrials and 500 service corporations, as listed in 1994. (Except for the year, this is the same database used in the Center for Business Ethics studies published in 1986 and 1992.) These firms are likely to be sufficiently large to enable them to develop corporate ethics offices, and are representative of the diversity of larger U.S. business firms. In particular, they are subject to varying internal and external pressures (e.g., from government, industry associations, boards of directors, labor, etc.) which might encourage various forms of ethics activity.

In order to see that our confidential questionnaire on current ethics practices went to an informed respondent, we initially contacted the public affairs or corporate communications office of each firm by telephone in mid-1994, asking for the name and address of the "officer most responsible for dealing with ethics and conduct issues in the firm." Public affairs/corporate communications offices were identified in the 1994 *National Directory of Corporate Public Affairs* (Close et al. 1994); for firms not listed in the directory, a call was made to the human resources department. This preliminary research produced a 990-firm mailing list. Missing firms either refused to identify an ethics-knowledgeable officer, or were holding companies owning essentially independent subsidiaries.

The survey instrument queried a range of formal corporate ethics policies, structures, activities, and personnel. The content of the survey was determined in light of preliminary on-site interviews with ethics-responsible persons at several service and industrial firms. Initial and follow-up questionnaires were distributed by mail to all 990 firms during late 1994. Two hundred and fifty-four returns were received during late 1994 and early 1995, for a 26% response rate. We believe this is a good response rate given the length of the survey and the fact that most contacts were high level officers (vice presidents or higher). The response rate compares well with other surveys of corporate executives (e.g., Hambrick et al. 1993).

Potential Response Biases

Statistical analyses (t-tests) revealed no significant difference in reporting rates between the service and industrial firms. It is possible, however, that firms in particular circumstances would not respond to a questionnaire of this nature; for example, firms under financial duress might be less able or willing to devote an officer's time to providing answers. Non-response bias was tested by comparing the responding firms to a randomly selected and roughly equal number of non-responding firms on four measures: size measured in number of employees; size measured as gross revenues; size measured as total assets; and net profit. Responding and non-responding firms were compared as a whole, and as divided into responding/non-responding services and responding/non-responding industrials. No significant differences were discovered, except in the case of number of employees for combined lists of service and industrial firms. In that case, responding firms were larger (mean number of employees for responding firms = 25,865; for non-respondents, 17,637; $t = -2.33$, $p < 0.05$). This is not surprising. Larger firms may be more likely to confront the organizational and environmental complexities which provide an impetus for formal ethics practices, and also will have the economies of scale which can make formalized practices affordable (as opposed to informal efforts to deal with ethical issues within the firm). Such firms, then, should have less motive to casually discard the questionnaire on the grounds that "this doesn't pertain to us," and also may be more likely to have officers who feel competent and interested enough to respond on behalf of the firm.

Business ethics research routinely confronts questions of social desirability biases in data collection (Fernandes and Randall 1992; Randall and Fernandes 1991). Standard methods of assessing and compensating for such biases exist regarding measures of individual behavior, but not for the kind of organization-level structural reporting used in this study. However, many of the questions in the study were focused simply on the existence of various types of corporate structures, programs, and policies, and thus do not lend themselves to as much interpretive license as do questions concerning personal behavior. The relatively objective character of most survey questions, plus the fact that companies were asked only to report on formal policies and programs, and not on ethical problems, should reduce social desirability bias.

Formal Corporate Ethics Practices, 1995

Our study examined the following aspects of formalized corporate ethics activity: ethics-oriented policy statements; formalized management responsibilities for ethics; free-standing ethics offices; ethics and compliance telephone reporting/advice systems; CEO involvement in ethics activities; training, communication, and education programs; investigatory functions; and evaluation of the ethics program activities. (Totals for specific results may not equal 100% due to rounding of fractional percentages.)

Ethics Policy Statements

Our study examined a number of factors related to ethics codes and policy statements, including their usage, age, rate of revision, degree of dissemination, and employee acknowledgement of the policy.

Codes and Other Policy Statements

A number of academic and practitioner writings on corporate ethics practice have focused on the usage and content of codes of ethics or conduct (Mathews 1988; Chatov 1980; Cressey and Moore 1983; White and Montgomery 1980; Weaver 1993). However, it is possible that many firms address ethical issues in the context of regular employee policy manuals, etc., instead of, or in addition to, separate codes of conduct (Center for Business Ethics 1992). Just because a firm does not have a distinct code of ethics should be no reason to assume that it has given no attention to ethical concerns in its formal policies. Consequently, we asked each firm whether or not it "addresses business ethics and business conduct issues in formal documents" of any kind. For those firms that claimed to address ethics or conduct issues formally, we then asked whether this was done in the context of "regular company policy and procedure manuals," a "separate code of ethics/code of conduct," or "in other ways." Ninety-eight percent of firms claimed to address ethics and conduct issues in some kind of formal document. Of those 98%, 67% did so through regular policy manuals, and 78% did so through separate codes of ethics, indicating that the majority of organizations take a multi-pronged approach to setting forth their standards of appropriate conduct. Twenty-two percent noted the

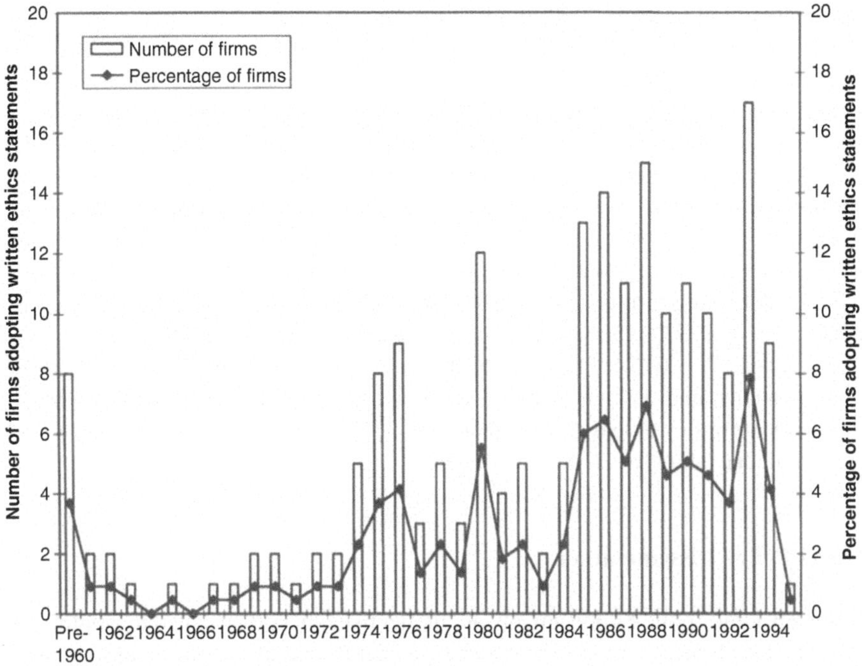

Fig. 31.1 Ethics standards adoptions by year ($n = 217$; 1995 January/February only)

use of other means of specifying company ethics policies, including (for example) occasional letters, bulletins and memoranda, video documents, posters, mission statements, and top executive speeches.

Age of Ethics Codes/Standards

Figure 31.1 indicates the number and percentage of firms adopting a formally specified ethics code or standard in a given year. Dividing the data set into quintiles helps reveal variations in the intensity of code adoption activity. The first quintile of code adoptions occurs up to and including 1975; followed by the periods 1976–1983, 1984–1987, 1988–1990, and 1991–1995. Overall, this indicates the relative recency of formally identified ethics codes or policies; most have been introduced in roughly the last 20 years. That certain years (1980, 1993) stand out from their neighbors suggests triggering events in the business environment immediately prior to those years (allowing time for the dissemination of the influence of such events, or for the workings of organizational decision processes). For example, implementation of the United States Sentencing Commission guidelines in 1991 may account for the higher level of ethics code introduction noted for 1993 and 1994.

Policy Revision as an Indication of Ethics Importance

Company ethics policies may be actively attended to or else ignored or marginalized in everyday company affairs. One possible indication of active attention to an ethics code or policy statement is the degree to which it is routinely revised. Consequently, we asked each firm to indicate the number of code revisions which occurred during the previous 10 years. We do not report results for firms that introduced their code in the period 1993–1995. It would be unrealistic for firms which so recently adopted a code to engage in substantial revisions of it, and inclusion of data from such firms would risk biasing results downward. Of the 185 firms which had ethics policies or codes prior to 1993, 19% reported no revisions during the 1985–1994 period; 18% one revision; 20% two revisions; 19% three revisions; 7% four; 7% five; 5% six to nine revisions, and 5% ten or more revisions. More simply: 17% of firms revise their code or policy at least every other year, 37% have revised it at most once, and the remainder fall between those extremes.

Ethics Policy Dissemination

Company ethics policies presumably are ineffective unless distributed to employees. We asked each firm to report the percentage of different classes of employees who received a copy of the company ethics code or policy. The vast majority of firms distribute ethics policies to 80% or more of their (i) high level executives (100% of firms), (ii) middle managers and professionals (98% of firms), and (iii) lower level management/supervisory staff (87% of firms). Code or policy distribution is less widespread but still common among nonsupervisory employees (clerks, hourly workers, etc.); 75% of firms report distributing their code or policy to at least 80% of employees in this category. Some respondents indicated that this lower rate of distribution reflected the constraints of contractual job specifications with labor unions.

Acknowledgment of Receipt and Obedience

Merely distributing a code or policy, however, does not guarantee that anyone reads it or abides by it. Therefore, we also asked whether a firm requires employees to (a) acknowledge receipt of the company policy or code, and (b) acknowledge compliance with it. Roughly 90% of firms provided easily coded answers to these questions. (Other firms provided complex answers which specified different requirements for different ranks or particular categories of ethics and compliance issues (e.g., insider trading).) These results show that nearly all firms (90%) require acknowledgment of receipt of the ethics policy or code at least once in an employee's career. Only 45%, however, require such acknowledgment on an at-least-annual basis (Fig. 31.2). Results are similar for acknowledging compliance with the policy or code; 85% require this at least once in an employee's career, while 51% require it on an at-least-annual basis. In summary, although roughly half of firms require

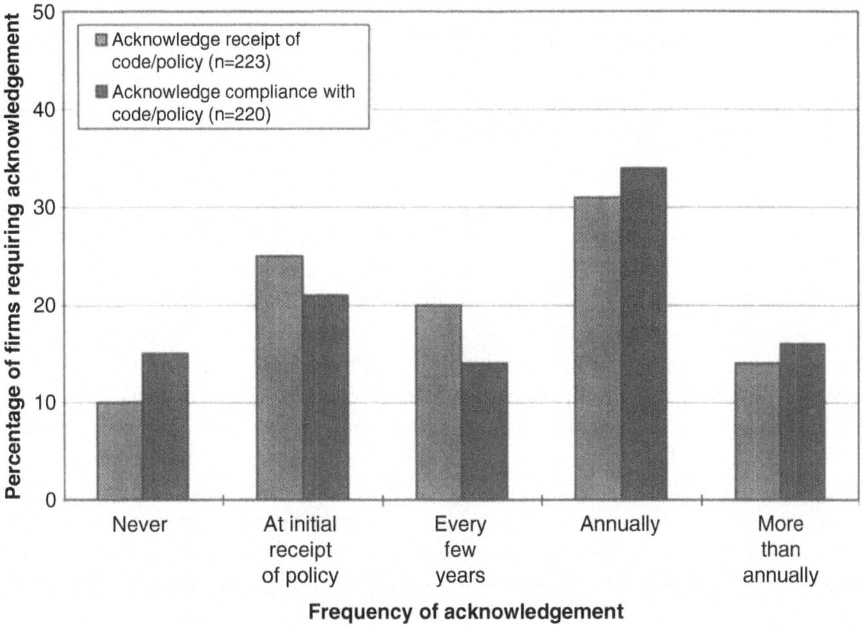

Fig. 31.2 Employee acknowledgement of ethics code or policy

employees repeatedly to acknowledge or recommit to the firm's ethics policies, nearly similar proportions of firms make no such effort, risking a situation in which codes are noted once and then forgotten.

Ethics Personnel and Offices

Ethics Personnel

Delineation of corporate ethics policies can be achieved through regular policy manuals or separate codes of ethics, and managerial responsibilities for implementing or supporting ethics policies similarly can be diffused among a collection of officers or focused on one single officer. Assignment of responsibility for ethics program activities to a single individual may look like it offers a higher degree of firm commitment to ethics, but that need not be the case, as such individuals actually may devote only a small portion of their time to ethics-related tasks, even when their titles include the terms "ethics" or "compliance."

Fifty-four percent of firms reported having a single officer specifically assigned to deal with ethics and conduct issues, in keeping with the United States Sentencing Commission's recommendations for an effective ethics program. But firms with a single officer assigned responsibility for ethics indicated a wide disparity in the proportion of time that person devotes to ethics activities, ranging from as little as 1% (10% of respondents) to as much as 100% (13% of respondents). Of the firms reporting a single officer responsible for ethics, 54% indicated that this officer spends not more than 10% of his or her time in ethics-related activities. At the other extreme, 14% reported 91–100% of the officer's time spent in ethics-related functions. Formally assigning ethics to someone does not in itself guarantee that ethics-related issues garner much executive attention.

Ninety-eight percent of firms reported the titles of their ethics-responsible officers, thereby giving a clue as to where ethics responsibilities are lodged functionally within firms. Most prominent are legal departments (33% of firms) and ethics/compliance offices (32%), followed by audit (10%), human resources (9%), and high-level general administration (10%, spread among corporate secretary, chief financial officer, chief operating officer, or chief executive officer).

Firms also may divide some responsibilities for ethics and conduct issues among multiple officers. This practice may be in lieu of assigning responsibility to a single officer, or may reflect a secondary assignment of supporting roles to persons other than the primary ethics officer. Sixty-nine percent of firms report that they spread ethics- related responsibilities among different officers ($n=247$), with the large majority sharing responsibilities among four or fewer different positions (90%).

Ethics Offices/Departments

Thirty percent of firms report that they have specific departments or offices created specifically to deal with ethics and conduct issues (e.g., corporate ethics office, corporate compliance office, etc.). Creation of these offices is a recent phenomenon, however, with 63% having been created in the 1990s (Fig. 31.3). Interestingly, comparisons of the year of office creation with the year of code adoption shows that 25% of ethics offices have been created in the same year that an ethics code is adopted, and 15% actually were created *prior* to the adoption of a formal code of ethics.

Ethics Office Staff

Most (55%) ethics offices have at most one full-time non-clerical employee (and in some cases, no non-clerical employees who devote all of their time to the office). The suggests that the majority of ethics offices serve in largely coordinating or supporting roles. Thirty-one percent of ethics offices have two to five non-clerical staff, 6% six through ten staff, and 8% more than ten staff. In most cases, the person in charge of the ethics office reports to a very high level of administration, however, with 72% of ethics office heads reporting to persons at the level of executive vice president or higher (including 18% who report directly to the CEO).

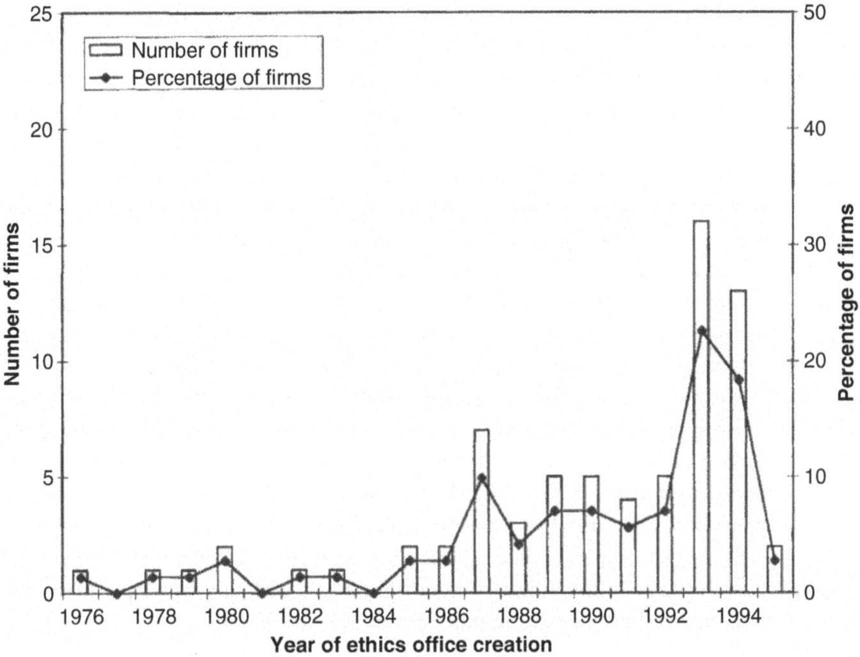

Fig. 31.3 Ethics office creation by year (1995 data for January/February only)

Corporate-Level Ethics Evaluations

Firms may use various means to evaluate the achievements or failures of their ethics-oriented activities, structures and personnel. Willingness to resort to external evaluation may indicate that the ethics program is not a purely symbolic, decoupled feature of the organization. We asked firms to respond to three questions regarding corporate-level external ethics evaluations. Each question was answered on a 1–5 Likert-type scale, with 1 anchored as "never" and 5 as "very frequently." Twenty-three percent of firms selected 4 or 5 on the scale when asked how often the firm "compares its ethical performance with that of other companies," 22% answered "never" (1) to this question (mean: 2.6; standard deviation: 1.2). Ten percent answered 4 or 5 when asked whether they "survey external stake-holders (e.g., customers, suppliers) regarding the firm's ethics and values," 46% answered "never" (1) (mean: 1.9; standard deviation: 1.1). Ten percent answered 4 or 5 when asked whether external parties are used "to help evaluate [the] ethics program"; 51% answered "never" (1) (mean: 1.9; standard deviation: 1.1). In summary, although some firms are quite active in externally assessing their corporate ethical performance and programs, roughly equal to much greater numbers of firms do not resort to external evaluations.

Standardized Procedures for Dealing with Ethics-Related Problems

The introduction of an ethics program not only can impose behavioral expectations on employees, but can also raise the expectations employees have of their employing organization. Companies that preach ethics, in short, may expect to be held to higher ethical standards. In part, this can involve seeing that standards of procedural propriety or justice are upheld in the administration of company ethics policies. In most U.S. settings, this will call for clearly identified routines and procedures for dealing with any complaints or allegations brought against employees under the ethics policies of the firm. Although employees may dispute the fairness of particular procedures, having some kind of procedure established for confronting ethical problems is a minimal requirement of procedural justice. Consequently, we asked companies to respond to the statement: "The firm has standardized procedures for following up on allegations of ethics violations." Respondents answered on a 1–5 Likert-type scale, anchored "strongly disagree" (1) and "strongly agree" (5). The mean answer was 3.9 (standard deviation: 1.2). Seventy percent of respondents answered by selecting 4 or 5 on the scale, indicating agreement that the firm had standardized procedures in place for dealing with ethics allegations. Six percent selected 1 on the scale, indicating strong disagreement with any suggestion that the firm had standardized procedures in place for ethics problems.

Telephone Reporting and Advice Systems

Fifty-one percent of firms have adopted some kind of telephone-based system whereby ethics and compliance complaints and queries can be raised by employees. Thirty-four percent of these telephone lines are answered in an ethics or compliance office, with legal departments and audit departments also playing a major role as the focal point of calls (19% and 18%, respectively). Other departments and external parties less commonly answered the telephone line (human resources, 8% of firms; security, 4%; external consultants, 9%; and miscellaneous other functions or combined functions, 8%).

Twenty-five percent of firms reported that their ethics telephone line receives no more than one call per month per 10,000 employees. Forty-six percent reported 2–9, 12% 10–19, and 18% 20 or more calls per month per 10,000 employees. One potential factor driving such variations in call rates is the perceived role of the ethics program and related activities and structures. Some ethics programs may be oriented toward controlling or regulating employee behavior in order to comply, for example, with legal requirements. Other programs may contain emphases on encouraging employees to embody particular values is their own decision making, or toward offering help and assistance to employees grappling with one or another ethical complexity in business (Weaver et al. 1996; Paine 1994). Some firms may pursue both tasks to varying degrees. To the extent that the ethics program and associated telephone line are perceived as fulfilling a regulating or policing role, employees may be dissuaded from using it either to aid themselves or to correct or guide coworkers.

With the foregoing distinction in mind, we examined the names of companies' ethics-related telephone lines. Ninety-seven of the 129 firms having a telephone line for ethics issues provided the line's name. We analyzed these names in terms of several categories. Fifty-seven percent of these telephone lines are labeled at least in part by use of the term "hotline," conveying some sense of reactive response to a problem. Of that group, 18% strongly suggested regulation or control of behavior (e.g., "compliance hotline"), 29% were simply labeled "ethics hotline," 47% were simply described as "hotlines," and 5% had other, idiosyncratic names using the term "hotline." Of the 43% of telephone lines not labeled "hotline," the largest group (45%) were labeled in terms of values, aspirations or counseling (most typically as "helpline"). Twelve percent of the non-"hotline" group, however, invoked strong senses of control and regulation. The remainder of the non-"hotline" group were not easily categorized (e.g., "the XYZ Corporation line"). If we consider all telephone names using the term "hotline," plus all those suggesting compliance, to convey a sense of reaction and control, and the other easily categorized names as conveying a sense of value-commitment and ethical aspirations, the set of 97 telephone line names break down as follows: 62% reaction and control oriented; 20% aspirations and values oriented; 19% neutral or otherwise not easily categorized.

Top Management Involvement in Corporate Ethics

Much writing on corporate ethics practice has suggested the importance of top management involvement in and commitment to ethics program effectiveness. Consequently, we were interested in seeing just how active chief executives are in corporate ethics activities. Most of our respondents were in reasonably close proximity to their CEOs. Eight percent had offices adjacent to the CEO's; 38% were not adjacent, but on the same floor; 39% were on a different floor of the same building; and the remainder were located in a different building at the same site (7%) or at a different site (8%). Insofar as the respondents were identified as the "officer most knowledgeable about ethics and conduct issues in the firm," this suggests a strong potential for a CEO to be actively informed of and involved in corporate ethics activities.

However, when we asked what CEOs actually were doing in regard to ethics issues, responses did not suggest a high level of activity or visible forms of concern. Specifically, we asked (1) how frequently a CEO communicated directly with the respondent about ethical issues, policies or programs; (2) the number of meetings attended by the CEO annually which have ethical issues, policies or programs as their primary focus; (3) the frequency with which the CEO sends out company-wide communications about business ethics and conduct; and (4) the number of live or taped ethics-oriented messages the CEO delivered in the last year to employee groups.

The largest number of CEOs communicated with respondents about ethics-related issues one to two times per year (46%). Twenty percent of CEO's engaged in no ethics-related communication with respondents. Twenty-one percent discussed ethics three to six times per year, and 13% seven or more times per year.

The largest number of CEOs attended no meetings which had ethics as their primary focus (32%). Thirty percent attended one meeting per year with ethics as a primary focus. Twenty-three percent attended two or three such meetings annually, and 15% four or more meetings annually.

When asked how often their CEO sends out company-wide written communications on ethics, 11% of respondents replied that their CEO never does such. Thirty-eight percent indicated such communications were delivered on an "every few years basis"; 46% said annually; and 5% indicated more than annually. Live or taped messages to employees were used less frequently. Sixty-two percent of firms reported that their CEO never provides live or taped messages on ethics to employees. The remainder indicated that the CEO provided live or taped ethics messages to employee groups at least annually.

Summarizing this CEO activity, we observe that the greatest proportion of CEOs discussed ethics-related issues with our ethics-responsible respondents once or twice a year (46%), attended no meetings with ethics as a primary focus (32%), sent out company-wide communications about business ethics and conduct annually (46%), and provided no live or taped messages about ethics to employees (62%). Although an annual formal message from the CEO may seem, at first glance, to constitute a respectable level of CEO commitment, we tend to disagree. Given the number of different messages organization members receive, and given that pro forma communiqués may be taken considerably less seriously than other forms of communication, our results suggest that from the standpoint of most employees, many CEOs convey minimal official commitment to corporate ethics programs. Of course, our data indicate many exceptions to these modal descriptions as well. But the data do suggest that for many firms, CEO attitudes toward ethics program activities likely are unclear in the eyes of employees. If so, employees of necessity will form their opinions of a CEO's ethics commitment largely from information provided by their immediate supervisors and/or company rumor "grapevines." Whether or not these sources accurately portray the CEO's stance on ethics, and provide support for any formal ethics program, is an open question.

Communication, Training, and Investigation

Not only do CEOs typically send out no more than one formal message annually to employees about ethics, employees generally do not receive more than one such message annually, regardless of its source (not counting the ethics code or policy itself). We asked how frequently different classes of employees received communications – other than the code or policy – which reminded them about ethics and conduct issues. Results are summarized in Fig. 31.4, but note that regardless of

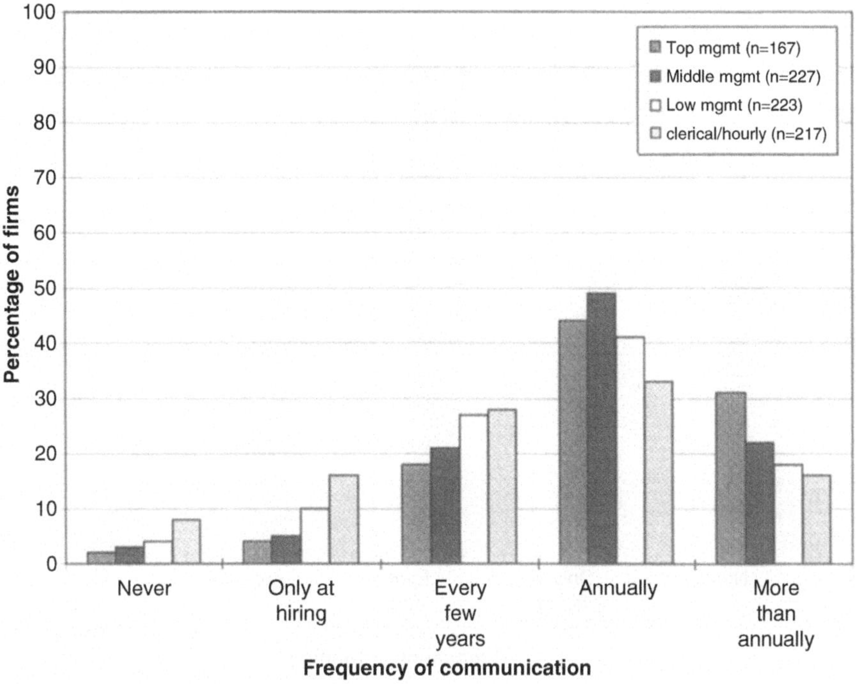

Fig. 31.4 Frequency of ethics communications received by employees

organizational rank, never more than a third of employees received any message about ethics more than once a year (percent receiving more than annual messages: high-level management – 31%; middle management – 22%; low-level management/supervisors – 18%; non-supervisory employees – 16%). If the target of communication is a reliable guide, the data presented in Fig. 31.4 also suggest that firms see higher-level managers as more responsible for implementing company ethical standards (or perhaps as more in need of reminders, because of their greater decision-making authority in most firms).

Depending upon employee rank, fully one-fifth to one-third of employees receive no ethics training or education of any sort (Fig. 31.5). In many firms, ethics and conduct issues appear relegated to the domain of formal documents and occasional written reminders, plus whatever messages (good or bad) are conveyed informally through the "grapevine" or as part of the company's culture(s). Similarly, only one-fifth to one-fourth of employees receive any ethics education or training on an at-least-annual basis. For the largest group of employees, ethics training and education is occasional, occurring "every few years."

On average, ethics training itself is most prominently the responsibility of ethics officers, human resources staff, and legal counsel. Respondents were asked to rate the involvement level of various corporate functions in ethics-training activities on a 1–5 scale (from "not at all involved" to "very involved"); only those three functions averaged above the midpoint of the scale (ethics office: mean 3.1, s.d. 1.8; human

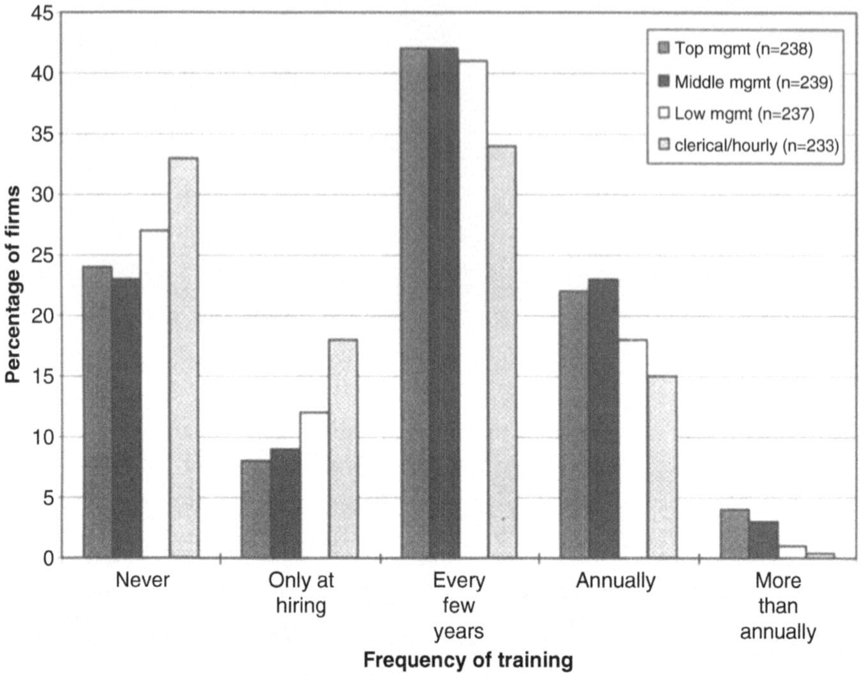

Fig. 31.5 Ethics training for employees by rank

resources: mean 3.4, s.d. 1.4; legal department: mean 3.4, s.d. 1.5). When the issue was changed to "who investigates alleged ethical violations," the audit and control function joined those rating above the midpoint of the scale (ethics office: mean 3.6, s.d. 1.8; human resources: mean 3.9, s.d. 1.1; legal: mean 4.3, s.d. 1.0; audit/control: mean 4.0, s.d. 1.2).

Conclusion

The findings discussed above suggest that major American corporations generally have adopted one or another form of ethics-oriented company policies, but vary substantially in the extent to which those policies are supported by ethics-specific structures, personnel, and activities. The attention devoted by business news media and practitioner associations to extensively developed ethics programs may convey a sense that such programs are common. Our results suggest instead that such programs are considerably less common; it may be a more limited set of high-profile ethics programs which is given repeated attention by observers of corporate ethics initiatives.

Some organizations have developed various ways to support their ethics policies, whether through training, communication, or other means. Without wishing to denigrate the work that is done in the context of formal ethics programs, however, one must admit that on their present scale in many firms, ethics programs and policies risk being swamped by other, often more persistent influences on organization members. These other influences may be part of the formal organization (such as compensation policies), or reflect the informal side of the organization (such as supervisor role-modeling or elements of organizational cultures and subcultures). At least in their current form, we should assume that corporate ethics programs are not self-sufficient; they depend heavily for their success on support from other organizational systems and informal norms and practices. In the long run, the implementation of ethics policies by persons not directly involved in ethics program activities will be crucial for encouraging good corporate behavior. For example, what department heads say during performance appraisals can be as important as any ethics officer's comments during a training session. This indicates the value of additional inquiry into the relationship of ethics programs and policies to other aspects of organizational life, and into the reasons why some firms develop extensive ethics programs while others do not.

For managers and policy makers, these results indicate that giving attention to formalized ethics programs alone may be ineffective at fostering corporate ethics. If the organizations that participated in this study are representative, we may surmise that there is a limited amount of organizational attention and resources that can be focused on formal ethics program activities and structures. As a result, there is only so much one can expect from an ethics program alone in a large organization, and to place all expectations and responsibilities for ethics on such a program may be asking for more than it can deliver. Thus, in addition to asking how an ethics program can be used to encourage good corporate behavior, managers and policy makers should consider how the rest of the organization's activities and structures contribute to or detract from that program specifically, and good behavior generally.

Much talk in the current business and legal environment, such as the work of the United States Sentencing Commission, encourages the growth of formal ethics programs (Kaplan et al. 1993; Dalton et al. 1994). Formalized ethics programs may now be the societally taken-for-granted method for fostering corporate ethics, but just because they are taken for granted is no guarantee that they alone are adequate to the task. Nor does it mean they are the only or necessary means for completing the task; one should not assume that firms reporting little in the way of formal ethics program activity thereby are unethical firms. But the common focus on formal ethics programs can distract attention from other organizational processes that are central to fostering good business ethics. There is, in the end, only a certain amount that can be accomplished by formal activity, and there are countless other messages organization members receive. Therefore, any effort to assess what corporations are doing to encourage good ethics ultimately must look at the rest of the organization, in both its formal and informal aspects.

Acknowledgement This research was supported by the Ethics in Business Research Fund of the American Institute of Certified Public Accountants. The authors are grateful for this support.

References

Beneish, M.D., and R. Chatov. 1993. Corporate codes of conduct: Economic determinants and legal implications for independent auditors. *Journal of Accounting and Public Policy* 12: 3–35.

Berenbeim, R. 1987. *Corporate ethics*. New York: The Conference Board.

Berenbeim, R. 1992. *Corporate ethics practices*. New York: The Conference Board.

Center for Business Ethics. 1986. Are corporations institutionalizing ethics? *Journal of Business Ethics* 5: 85–91.

Center for Business Ethics. 1992. Instilling ethical values in large corporations. *Journal of Business Ethics* 11: 863–867.

Chatov, R. 1980. What corporate ethics statements say. *California Management Review* 22(4): 20–29.

Close, A.C., J. Valerie Steele, and M.E. Buckner. 1994. *National directory of corporate public affairs: 1994*. Washington, DC: Columbia Books.

Cressey, D.R., and C.A. Moore. 1983. Managerial values and corporate codes of ethics. *California Management Review* 25(4): 53–77.

Dalton, D.R., M.B. Metzger, and J.W. Hill. 1994. The "New" U.S. sentencing commission guidelines: A wake-up call for corporate America. *The Academy of Management Executive* 8(1): 7–13.

Fernandes, M.F., and D.M. Randall. 1992. The nature of social desirability response effects in ethics research. *Business Ethics Quarterly* 2: 183–206.

Hambrick, D.C., M.A. Geletkanycz, and J.W. Fredrickson. 1993. Top executive commitment to the *status quo:* Some tests of its determinants. *Strategic Management Journal* 14: 401–418.

Kaplan, J.M., J.E. Murphy, and W.M. Swenson. 1993. *Compliance programs and the corporate sentencing guideline*. Deerfield: Clark Boardman Callaghan.

Mathews, M.C. 1988. *Strategic intervention in organizations: Resolving ethical dilemmas*. Newbury Park: Sage.

Paine, L.S. 1994. Managing for organizational integrity. *Harvard Business Review* 72: 106–117.

Pfeffer, J. 1981. Management as symbolic action. *Research in Organizational Behavior* 3: 1–52.

Randall, D.M., and M.F. Fernandes. 1991. The social desirability response bias in ethics research. *Journal of Business Ethics* 10: 805–817.

Sweeney, R.B., and H.L. Siers. 1990. Ethics in corporate America. *Management Accounting* June, 34–40.

Treviño, L.K. 1990. A cultural perspective on changing and developing organizational ethics. *Research in Organizational Change and Development* 4: 195–230.

Weaver, G.R. 1993. Corporate codes of ethics: Purpose, process, and content issues. *Business and Society* 32(1): 44–58.

Weaver, G.R., L.K. Treviño, and P.L. Cochran. 1995. Environmental and managerial influences on the intensity and integration of corporate ethics programs: An empirical study. Presented at Academy of Management Annual Meeting, Aug 1995.

Weaver, G.R., L.K. Treviño, and P.L. Cochran. 1996. Defining and explaining the character of corporate ethics programs, *Proceedings of the International Association for Business and Society.*

White, B.J., and R. Montgomery. 1980. Corporate codes of conduct. *California Management Review* 23(2): 80–87.

Chapter 32
Concepts and Definitions of CSR and Corporate Sustainability: Between Agency and Communion

Marcel van Marrewijk

Abbreviations

CS	Corporate sustainability
CSR	Corporate Social Responsibility
ECSF	European Corporate Sustainability Framework
SRI	Socially Responsible Investing
VNO-NCW	Dutch Employers Association
WBCSD	World Business Council for Sustainable Development

Introduction

In academic debates and business environments hundreds of concepts and definitions have been proposed referring to a more humane, more ethical, more transparent way of doing business. This point in time is an important if not critical moment in the development process of new generation business frameworks facilitating sustainable growth. A continuation of the creativity period – "let 100 flowers blossom" – will lead to unclear situations: by the time real progress is at hand a clear and unbiased definition and concept will be needed to lay a strong foundation for the following steps in the development process of corporate sustainability and especially in its implementation.

In the section "Aspects of Corporate Sustainability and Corporate (Social) Responsibility", I will start with the contemporary critique on CSR. From there

M. van Marrewijk (✉)
Van Linden van den Heuvellsingel 7, 3135 KH, Vlaardingen, The Netherlands
e-mail: marcel@vanmarrewijk.nl

A.C. Michalos and D.C. Poff (eds.), *Citation Classics from the Journal of Business Ethics*, Advances in Business Ethics Research 2,
DOI 10.1007/978-94-007-4126-3_32,

I will investigate historical and philosophical arguments (section "A Philosophical Contribution to CS") supporting or falsifying the proposal to differentiate the notion of corporate sustainability according to the development stages of the organisations. In the section "A Practical Contribution to Corporate Sustainability", I will deal with the major trends supporting corporate sustainability and elaborate on the changing relationships between corporations, governments and civil society. In the section "Proposals for Defining CSR and Corporate Sustainability", I will list some recent proposals on the concept and definitions of CSR and CS and will finally propose a set of differentiated definitions of corporate sustainability, each related to a specific ambition level c.q. development level of organizations.

Aspects of Corporate Sustainability and Corporate (Social) Responsibility

Various Notions

An intensive debate has been taking place among academics, consultants and corporate executives resulting in many definitions of a more humane, more ethical and a more transparent way of doing business. They have created, supported or criticized related concepts such as sustainable development,[1] corporate citizenship,[2] sustainable entrepreneurship, Triple Bottom Line,[3] business ethics,[4] and corporate social responsibility.[5]

The latter term particularly has been thoroughly discussed (Göbbels 2002) resulting in a wide array of concepts, definitions and also lots of critique. It has put business executives in an awkward situation, especially those who are beginning to take up their responsibility towards, society and its stakeholders, leaving them with more questions than answers.

Problems with Current Definitions

According to Göbbels (2002), Votaw and Sethi (1973) considered social responsibility a brilliant term: "it means something, but not always the same thing to everybody". Too often, CSR is regarded as the panacea which will solve the global poverty gap, social exclusion and environmental degradation. Employers' associations emphasize the voluntary commitment of CSR. Local governments and some Non-Governmental Organizations (NGOs) believe public–private partnerships can, for instance rejuvenate neighbourhoods. Also various management disciplines have recognised that CSR fit their purposes, such as quality management, marketing, communication, finance, HRM, and reporting. Each of them present views on CSR that align with their specific situation and challenges. The current concepts and definitions are therefore often biased towards specific interests.

Banerjee (2001, p. 42) states that corporate social responsibility is "too broad in its scope to be relevant to organizations" and Henderson (2001, pp. 21–22) "there is no solid and well-developed consensus which provides a basis for action". The lack of an "all-embracing definition of CSR" (WBCSD 2000, p. 3) and subsequent diversity and overlap in terminology, definitions and conceptual models hampers academic debate and ongoing research (Göbbels 2002, p. 5).

On the other hand, an "all-embracing" notion of CSR has to be broadly defined and is therefore too vague to be useful in academic debate or in corporate implementation. A set of differentiated approaches, matching the various ideal type contexts in which companies operate, could be the alternative.

Jacques Schraven, the chairman of VNO-NCW, the Dutch Employers Association, once stated[6] that "there is no standard recipe: corporate sustainability is a custom-made process". Each company should choose – from the many opportunities – which concept and definition is the best option, matching the company's aims and intentions and aligned with the company's strategy, as a response to the circumstances in which it operates.

A Historical Perspective

Past eras have shown acts of charity, fairness and stewardship, such as the medieval chivalry and Scholastic view on pricing, the aristocracy's noblesse oblige, the early twentieth century paternalistic industrialists and the contemporary ways of corporate (and private) sponsoring of arts, sports, neighbourhood developments, etcetera.

In academic literature, various authors[7] have referred to a sequence of three approaches, each including and transcending one other, showing past responses to the question to whom an organization has a responsibility.

According to the *shareholder approach*, regarded by Quazi and O'Brien (2000) as the classical view on CSR, "the social responsibility of business is to increase its profits" (Friedman 1962). The shareholder, in pursuit of profit maximization, is the focal point of the company and socially responsible activities don't belong to the domain of organizations but are a major task of governments. This approach can also be interpreted as business enterprises being concerned with CSR "only to the extent that it contributes to the aim of business, which is the creation of long-term value for the owners of the business" (Foley 2000).

The *stakeholder approach* indicates that organizations are not only accountable to its shareholders but should also balance a multiplicity of stakeholders interests that can affect or are affected by the achievement of an organization's objectives (Freeman 1984).

According to the *societal approach*,[8] regarded as the broader view on CSR (and not necessarily the contemporary view), companies are responsible to society as a whole, of which they are an integral part. They operate by public consent (licence to operate) in order to "serve constructively the needs of society – to the satisfaction of society".[9]

The philanthropic approaches might be the roots of CS, but the different approaches to corporate responsibility clearly show that CSR is a new and distinct phenomenon. Its societal approach especially appears to be a (strategic) response to changing circumstances and new corporate challenges that had not previously occurred. It requires organizations to fundamentally rethink their position and act in terms of the complex societal context of which they are a part. This is a new perspective.

A Philosophical Contribution to CS

Value Systems

Abraham Maslow (1968/1982) declared the five basic needs of human individuals, implying that individuals would strive for the next need as soon as the former had been fulfilled. His contemporary Clare Graves concluded that there are many ways of achieving these needs. Individual persons, as well as companies and societies, undergo a natural sequence of orientations [Survival, Security, Energy & Power, Order, Success, Community, Synergy and Holistic Life System]. These orientations brighten or dim as life conditions (consisting of historical *Times*, geographical *Place,* existential *Problems* and societal *Circumstances)* change. The orientations impact their worldview, their value system, belief structure, organizing principles and mode of adjustment (Beck and Cowan 1996).

If, for instance, societal circumstances change, inviting corporations to respond and consequently reconsider their role within society, it implies that corporations have to re-align all their business institutions (such as mission, vision, policy deployment, decision-making, reporting, corporate affairs, etcetera) to this new orientation.

Graves, and his successors Beck and Cowan, have made clear that entities will eventually try to meet the challenges their situation – featuring specific life conditions – provide or risk the danger of oblivion or even extinction. The quest to create an adequate response to specific life conditions results in a wide variety of survival strategies, each founded on a specific set of values and related institutions. These value systems reflect their specific vision on reality (worldview), their awareness, understanding, and their definition of truth.[10] This is why in Seattle, Genoa, Prague representatives of the Global Civil Society clashed with politicians and industrialists; their value systems do not align, there are conflicting truths and worldviews and opposite strategies as to how to deal with (their interpretation of) the situation.

The Principles Behind Evolutionary Development

Ken Wilber (1995), having studied evolutionary developments in great depth, supports Graves when stating: "Evolution proceeds irreversibly in the direction of increasing differentiation/integration, increasing organization and increasing complexity".[11] This "growth occurs in *stages*, and stages are *ranked* in both a logical and chronological order. The more *holistic* patterns appear *later* in development because they have to wait the emergence of the parts that they will then integrate or unify".[12] This ranking refers to normal hierarchies (or holarchies) converting "heaps into wholes, disjointed fragments into networks of mutual interconnection".[13]

As the natural orientations emerged, they clearly show an increase of integratedness and complexity, each stage including and transcending the previous ones.

Wilber drafted 20 "patterns of existence" or "tendencies of evolution" which I shall briefly summarize: reality is not composed of things or processes; it is not composed of wholes nor does it have any parts. Rather it is composed of whole/parts, or holons.[14] This is true of the physical sphere (atoms), as well as of the biological (cells) and psychological (concepts and ideas) sphere, or simply said, apply to matter, body, mind and spirit. Atoms or processes are first and foremost holons, long before any "particular characteristics" are singled out by us.

Holons display four fundamental capacities: self-preservation, self-adaptation, self-transcendence and self-dissolution. Its *agency* – its self-asserting, self-preserving tendencies – expresses its *wholeness*, its relative autonomy; whereas its *communion* – its participatory, bonding, joining tendencies – expresses its *partness,* its relationship to something larger. Both capacities are crucial: any slight imbalance will either destroy the holon or make it turn into a pathological agency (alienation and repression) or a pathological communion (fusion and dissociation). Self-transcendence (or self-transformation) is the system's capacity to reach beyond the given, pushing evolution further, creating new forms of agency and communion. Holons can also break down and do so along the same vertical sequence in which they were built up.

These four capacities or "forces" are in constant tension: the more intensely a holon preserves its own individuality, preserves it wholeness, the less it serves its communions or its partners in larger and wider wholes and vice versa. This tension can be manifested, for instance in the conflict between rights (agency) and responsibilities (communions), individuality and membership and autonomy and heteronomy.

If holons stop functioning, all the higher holons in the sequence are also destroyed, because those higher wholes depend upon the lower as constituent parts.

In the same way organizations and employees are mutually dependent, as a strike clearly shows. Naturally, organizations support their employees (vertical relationship), creating value as an (horizontal) agency, in constant exchange with its stakeholders (horizontal communion).

Holons emerge holarchically, in a natural hierarchy, as a series of increasing whole/parts. Holons transcend and include their predecessor(s), forming a hierarchical system. What happens if the system itself goes corrupt, turns into a pathological hierarchy? Given the characteristics of holons and hierarchies, a disruption or pathology in one field can reverberate throughout an entire system.

The negative consequences of globalization are good examples of outcomes of a pathological system. With multinationals over-emphasizing their self-preservation (agency), and thus ignoring their participatory role within the community at large, the "threefold global crisis of deepening poverty,[15] social disintegration, and environmental degradation" (Korten 2001, p. 13) gave rise to major critique on the business environment.[16] It inspired a few individual entrepreneurs to immediately transform their businesses. The majority, however, try to ignore it and continue to disregard their responsibility for its impact on the physical and social environment.

As can be expected from theoretical exercises, countervailing power is emerging in the growth, both in number and impact, of the (global) civil society Non-Governmental Organisations (NGOs) especially, are building up impact, influencing business and politics towards acting more responsibly and operating in a more sustainable way In the next chapter I will return to the relationship between Business, Civil Society and Government.

Lessons to Be Learned

In addition to the previously mentioned principles of charity and stewardship, often regarded as the roots of CSR, I would like to define two other principles, based on the "natural tendencies of evolution" (Wilber 1995). These are the Principle of Self-determination (or agency, self-preservation) and the Principle of Communion. In combination, the two principles allow each entity, individual or group to act according to its awareness,[17] capabilities and best understanding of its situation, provided it does not conflict with current regulations or interfere with the freedom of others to act in obtaining a similar objective. "Freedom stops when it interferes with the freedom of others" (Levinas 1940–1945).

The right to be, the right to define its role within a given situation – the manifestation of agency or autonomy – is balanced by the moral obligation to be accountable for its impact on the environment. It is communion that stops freedom when it interferes with the freedom of others. Being an entity within something larger, obliges to adapt to the environment, adjust itself to changing circumstances and be accountable for one's impact on others. These principles apply to water molecules as well as human beings and their organizations.

When the chosen role and corresponding awareness appear not to be adequate responses to current circumstances, the system, other related entities in this situation, will influence the subject and try to correct and, as an ultimate response, bring the existence of the subject into jeopardy An increasing number of experiences can demonstrate this principle.

So far we have seen that evolution provides a sense of direction, inspiring both in individuals and corporations goals for transformation.[18] Challenged by changing circumstances and provoked by new opportunities, individuals, organizations and societies develop adequate solutions that might be new sublimations, creating synergy and adding value at a higher level of complexity. Since instability increases at higher complexity levels, entities can shift to lower levels should circumstances turn unfavourable or should competences fail to meet the required specifications.

A Practical Contribution to Corporate Sustainability

Why will companies adopt CS practices? Simply stated: they either feel obliged to do it; are made to do it or they want to do it. In this chapter we briefly investigate trends within companies and within society that support the development of CS.

Corporate Challenges

Many companies have mastered their business operations and at the same time created “separate kingdoms”.[19] This manifests for instance in employees being more loyal to the business unit than the company, business metrics supporting unit management even at the expense of the performance of the mother company, transfer pricing and information asymmetry between HQ and its divisions. Another contemporary corporate challenge is managing issues in the supply chain. This is even more complex.

In quality management terms these phenomena relate to making shifts or progress in the sequence of quality orientations. Quality management can be oriented at a product level, at process level, at the organization as a systemic entity, at the supply chain and at the society as a whole. Each level includes and transcends the previous ones and each orientation represents a higher level of complexity.

The former ones – product and process quality – can be managed with rather technical and statistical instruments. Creating an organization that functions as a whole instead of separate de*part*ments or with managing issues in the supply chain, management needs a shift of approach: the employees and their suppliers have become more important. For instance, to be successful, management has to develop a climate of trust, respect and dedication and allow others to have their fair share of mutual activities (together win). We can conclude that organizations which continue to improve their quality, ultimately have to adopt a more social management style, in other words, move towards (higher levels of) corporate sustainability.

Changing Concepts of Business, Governments and Civil Society

System theorists recommend, as “a cure to any diseased system, rooting out any holon that have usurped their position in the overall system by abusing their power . . .”[20] and ignoring their duties and responsibilities, I would add. To root out cancer cells, medics developed surgical techniques and chemical cocktails. By fully abandoning business we would remove ourselves from the creation of wealth and necessary supplies, making the cure much worse than the disease. Mankind needs more subtle approaches to, for instance, increase the individual and collective level of awareness and understanding, support favourable behaviour and restore the imbalance of global institutions.[21]

Business forms an important triangular relationship with the State and the Civil Society. Each has a specific mechanism that coordinates their behaviour and fulfils a role within society Generally, the State is responsible for creating and maintaining legislation (control), Business creates wealth through competition and cooperation (market), and Civil Society structures and shapes society via collective action and participation.

Both market and control mechanisms have shown major fallacies with respect to organizing societal behaviour. Since civil society has gained importance, both business and government have to respond to the collective actions of civilians, churches and especially NGOs. Corrective actions such as jeopardizing companies' reputations, challenge companies to apply more sustainable approaches in their business (Zwart 2002).

Once, there were circumstances which resulted in clear-cut roles and responsibilities for both companies and governments, both relatively independent, and an impact on civil society that could be neglected. As complexity grew business and government became mutually dependent entities. Since their coordinating mechanisms were incapable of adequately arranging various contemporary societal topics, the importance of civil society increased. Various representatives stressed "new" values and approaches which politics and business no longer could ignore.

Business has to learn how to operate within interfering coordination mechanisms, with blurred boundaries and surrounding layers of varying degrees of responsibility, overlapping one other. Nowadays, governments increasingly leave societal issues within the authority of corporations. For instance, Schiphol Airport is supposed to limit noise and pollution, and at the same time accommodate the increasing demand for flights. NGOs and other stakeholders expect participation and involvement and request new levels of transparency.

According to various sources in academic literature (e.g. Wartick and Wood 1999) common values and norms play a major role in shaping society. Once it was the government elite that stated the societal values, later business leaders added theirs. Along with the process of democratization, representatives of the civil society have increasingly been introducing "common" values and norms and acting upon them to make government and business respond to these values. We see moving panels, changing circumstances and new existential problems arousing various members in society to act and transform into value systems and corresponding institutional arrangements (Fig. 32.1).

Accepting their new position in society, companies develop new values, new strategies and policies and new institutional arrangements that support their functioning in areas that were once left to others, redefining their roles and relationships with others.

Proposals for Defining CSR and Corporate Sustainability

I will introduce three proposals to define CSR and Corporate Sustainability. I will also deal with the relationship between the two notions.

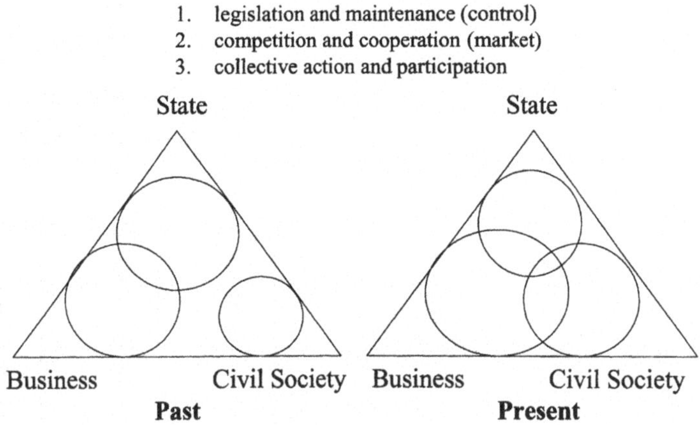

Fig. 32.1 State, business and civil society

Corporate Societal Accountability (CSA)

The first one is suggested by Math. Göbbels (2002). He concludes that the inconsistency and sometimes ambiguity of CSR is also due to language problems. Andriof and McIntosh's (2001, p. 15) introduced the term "corporate *societal* responsibility" in order "to avoid the limited interpretation of the term 'social responsibility', when translated into Continental European cultures and languages, as applying to social welfare issues only. The term 'societal responsibility' covers all dimensions of a company's impact on, relationships with and responsibilities to society as a whole".

He continued investigating the linguistic approach and concluded in line with Brooks (1995) and Klatt et al. (1999, pp. 17–33) that the word "responsibility" should be replaced by "accountability", for it causes similar problems as "social". This would imply a preference to use *corporate societal accountability* (CSA) as the contemporary term for CSR.

Although I fully agree with its reasoning and suggestion, I expect it will be difficult for policy makers and executives to get used to another new generic notion.

A Hierarchical Relationship Between CSR, CS and Corporate Responsibility

The second proposal was suggested to me by Lassi Linnanen and Virgilio Panapanaan (2002) from Helsinki University of Technology. They consider Corporate Sustainability (CS) as the ultimate goal; meeting the needs of the present without compromising the ability of future generations to meet their own needs (WCED 1987). In spite of the traditional bias of CS towards environmental policies, the various

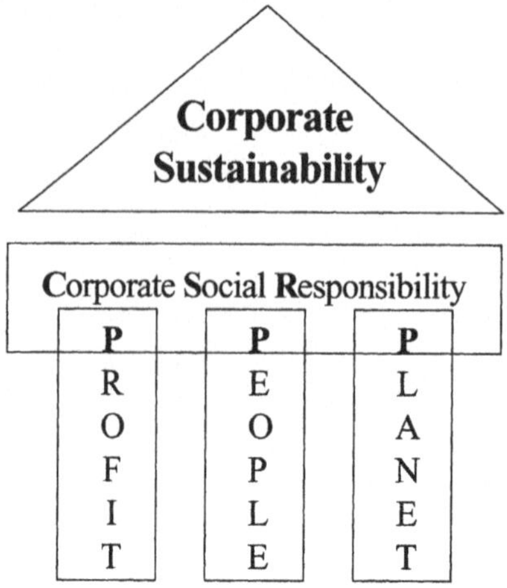

Fig. 32.2 Relationship 3P, CS and CSR (*Source:* Erasmus University, Wempe & Kaptein)

contributions at the Corporate Sustainability Conference 2002 at the Erasmus University Rotterdam in June clearly showed sufficient interest in integrating social and societal aspects into CS. The Erasmus University's Business Society Management has also placed CS as the ultimate goal, with CSR as an intermediate stage where companies try to balance the Triple Bottom Line (Wempe and Kaptein 2002) (see Fig. 32.2). Moreover, the theme of the EU Communication was *CSR: a business contribution to Sustainable Development.*

The Finnish proposal implies a distinct disaggregation of dimensions – distinguishing sustainability from responsibility (CR) – to draw a more consistent picture. The three aspects of sustainability (economic, environmental, and social) can be translated into a CR approach that companies have to be concerned with. The simple illustration below (Fig. 32.3) depicts the relationship of CS, CR and CSR, plus, the economic and environmental dimensions. This is also to show how CSR as a new tool fits into the current CR or CS framework to complete the picture of corporate sustainability.

Although I fully agree with this new domain of CSR and consequently smaller interpretation of the social dimension of the organization, I doubt if the clock can be reversed.

CSR and CS as Two Sides of a Coin

Keijzers (2002) have indicated that the notions of CSR and CS have shown separate paths, which recently have grown into convergence. In the past sustainability related to the environment only and CSR referred to social aspects, such as human rights. Nowadays many consider CS and CSR as synonyms. I would recommend to keep a

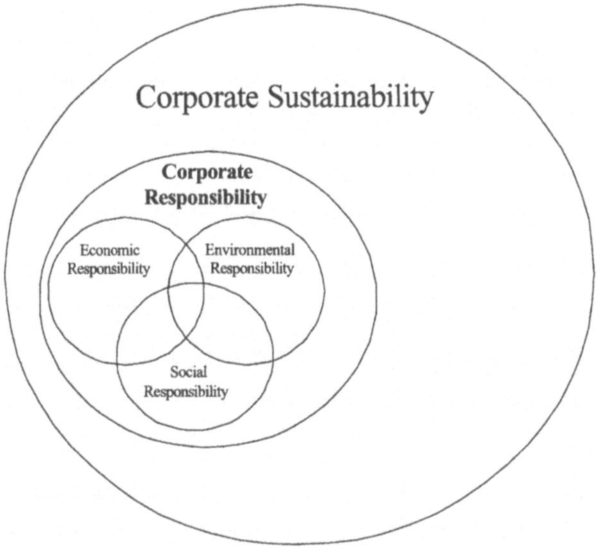

Fig. 32.3 General model of CS/CR and its dimensions (*Source:* Lassi Linnanen and Virgilio Panapanaan, Helsinki University of Technology)

small but essential distinction: Associate CSR with the communion aspect of people and organisations and CS with the agency principle. Therefore CSR relates to phenomena such as transparency, stakeholder dialogue and sustainability reporting, while CS focuses on value creation, environmental management, environmental friendly production systems, human capital management and so forth.

In general, corporate sustainability and, CSR refer to company activities – voluntary by definition – demonstrating the inclusion of social and environmental concerns in business operations and in interactions with stakeholders. This is the broad – some would say "vague" – definition of corporate sustainability and CSR.

I will now differentiate this definition into five interpretations, c.q. ambition levels of corporate sustainability. Each definition relates to a specific context, as defined in *Spiral Dynamics.* Also the motives for choosing a particular ambition is provided for [read CS as CS/CSR]:

1. *Compliance-driven CS* (Blue): CS at this level consists of providing welfare to society, within the limits of regulations from the rightful authorities. In addition, organizations might respond to charity and stewardship considerations. The motivation for CS is that CS is perceived as a duty and obligation, or correct behaviour.
2. *Profit-driven CS* (Orange): CS at this level consists of the integration of social, ethical and ecological aspects into business operations and decision-making,

provided it contributes to the financial bottom line. The motivation for CS is a business case: CS is promoted if profitable, for example because of an improved reputation in various markets (customers/employees/shareholders).

3. *Caring CS* (Green): CS consists of balancing economic, social and ecological concerns, which are all three important in themselves. CS initiatives go beyond legal compliance and beyond profit considerations. The motivation for CS is that human potential, social responsibility and care for the planet are as such important.
4. *Synergistic CS* (Yellow): CS consists of a search for well-balanced, functional solutions creating value in the economic, social and ecological realms of corporate performance, in a synergistic, win-together approach with all relevant stakeholders. The motivation for CS is that sustainability is important in itself, especially because it is recognised as being the inevitable direction progress takes.
5. *Holistic CS* (Turquoise): CS is fully integrated and embedded in every aspect of the organization, aimed at contributing to the quality and continuation of life of every being and entity, now and in the future. The motivation for CS is that sustainability is the only alternative since all beings and phenomena are mutually interdependent. Each person or organization therefore has a universal responsibility towards all other beings.

The above defined principle of self-determination allows each and everyone to respond to outside challenges in accordance to its own awareness and abilities. Any organization has the right to choose a position from 1 to 5. However not all these positions are equally adequate responses to perceived challenges offered in the environment. The principle of self-determination is balanced by the principle of communion: entities are part of a larger whole and thus ought to adapt itself to changes in its environment and respond to corrective actions from its stakeholders.

The right to be and the capacity to create added value equals the duty to be responsible for its impact and to adjust itself to changes in its environment. Without conforming to this principle, organizations ultimately risk extinction.

A differentiated set of CS/CSR definitions implies that there is no such thing as *the* features of corporate sustainability or CSR. Each level practically manifests specific CS and CSR activities, manifesting the corresponding intrinsic motivations. In other words, the various CSR and CS activities can be structured into coherent institutional frameworks supporting a specific ambition of CS/CSR. Some levels include a wide range of advanced developments within CS and CSR, while others, the more traditionally oriented, have almost none.

The coherent institutional frameworks supporting specific levels of CS/CSR, can be difficult thresholds preventing companies from adopting higher levels of corporate sustainability. This might explain why, according to worldwide research by Ernst & Young[22] among 114 companies from the Global 1,000, 73% confirmed that corporate sustainability is on the board's agenda; 94% responded that a CS strategy might result in a better financial performance, but only 11% is actually implementing it.

In *Multiple Levels of Corporate Sustainability,* Marcel van Marrewijk and Marco Werre (2003) show that specific interventions can only be adequately addressed within a specific context and situation. A higher ambition level and specific CS interventions require a supporting institutional framework and value system. The authors developed a matrix distinguishing six types of organizations at different developmental stages, their corresponding institutional frameworks, demonstrating different performance levels of corporate sustainability.

Acknowledgements While writing the basic draft of this article in the beautiful valley of the Ardech, France, I made particular use of an overview article on CSR by Math. Göbbels [see Chaps. 2, 5] and the work of Ken Wilber [see Chap. 3].

Furthermore, I wish to acknowledge the constructive and useful comments of earlier versions of this article by Teun Hardjono, Marco Werre and my wife, Erna Kraak.

Notes

1 World Commission on Environment and Development's (Our Common Future, Brundland-1987): Sustainable development is the development that meets the needs of the present without compromising the ability of future generations to meet their own needs.

2 Marsden and Andriof (1998) define good corporate citizenship as "understanding and managing a company's wider influences on society for the benefit of the company and society as a whole".

3 Elkington (1997): "Triple Bottom Line" or "People, Planet, Profit", refers to a situation where companies harmonize their efforts in order to be economically viable, environmentally sound and socially responsible.

4 Kilcullen and Ohles Kooistra (1999): business ethics is "the degree of moral obligation that may be ascribed to corporations beyond simple obedience to the laws of the state" (p. 158).

5 EU-Communication July 2002: "CSR is a concept whereby companies integrate social and environmental concerns in their business operations and in their interactions with their stakeholders on a voluntary basis."

6 Quote in the Volkskrant: "Er zijn geen standaardrecepten: MVO is maatwerk".

7 See e.g. Göbbels (2002), Van Marrewijk (2001), Quazi and O'Brien (2000), Freeman (1984).

8 With early contributions of McGuire (1963) and Committee for Economic Development – CED (1971), but also van Marrewijk (2001) and Gobbels (2002).

9 Committee for Economic Development – CED (1971, p. 16).

10 See also M. Foucault, The order of things (1970): "truth" is simply an arbitrary play of power and convention.

11 Wilber, K., *Sex, Ecology and Spirituality*, 2nd ed. (Boston: Shambhala, 1995, 2000), pp. 19, 74.

12 Wilber, K. SES (p. 28) italics by Wilber.

13 Wilber, K. SES (p. 26).

14 Koestler: "a holon is a whole in one context and simultaneously a part in another".

15 About 2.3 billion people live on less than $2 per day. The income of the top 20 in developing countries is 37 times the income of the bottom 20 and it has doubled in the last decade: See also Korten (2001), WRI, UNEP, WBCSD.

16 See f.i. Drucker (1984), Hawken (1993), Elkington (1997), Zadek (2001).

17 According to Wilber, consciousness (or awareness) is directly related to depth, i.e. the level in the hierarchy (p. 65).

18 See also: Pirsig, R. Lila, an inquiry into morals (1991).

19 Eli Goldratt during a lecture at RSM, October 1998.

20 Wilber, K. SES (2000, p. 30).

21 Henry Minzberg, at the inaugurating conference of the European Academy of Business in Society, Fontainebleau, 6 July 2002. "The economically oriented institutions such as the WTO, IMF and the Worldbank are not balanced by as powerful institutions, defending social and environmental interests."

22 Press release at 6 Sept 2002: www.account-ingweb.nl.

References

Andriof, J., and M. McIntosh, (eds.) 2001. *Perspectives on corporate citizenship*. Sheffield: Greenleaf Publishing.

Banerjee, S.B. 2001. Corporate citizenship and indigenous stakeholders. *Journal of Corporate Citizenship, Issue* 1: 39–55.

Beck, D., and C. Cowan. 1996. *Spiral dynamics*. Oxford: Blackwell Publishers.

Brooks, T. 1995. *Accountability: It all depends on what you mean*. Clifton: Akkad Press.

Committee for Economic Development. 1971. *Social responsibilities of business corporations*. 16 New York: CED.

Drucker, P. 1984. The new meaning of corporate social responsibility. *California Management Review* 16(2): 53–63.

Elkington, J. 1997. *Cannibals with forks. The triple bottom line of 21st century business*. Oxford: Capstone Publishing Ltd.

Foley, J.A., S. Levis, M.H. Costa, et al. 2000. Incorporating dynamic vegetation cover within global climate models. *Ecological Applications* 10: 1620–1632.

Foucault, M. 1970. *The order of things*. New York: Random House.

Freeman, R.E. 1984. *Strategic management: A stakeholder approach*. Marshfield: Pitman Publishing Inc.

Friedman, M. 1962. *Capitalism and freedom*. Chicago: University of Chicago Press.

Göbbels, M. 2002. *Reframing corporate social responsibility: The contemporary conception of a fuzzy notion*.

Hawken, P. 1993. *The ecology of commerce: A declaration of sustainability*. New York: Harper Business.

Henderson, D. 2001. *Misguided virtue. False notions of corporate social responsibility*. Wellington: New Zealand Business RoundTable.

Keijzers, G., R. van Daal, and F. Boons. 2002. *Duurzaam Ondernemen, strategie van bedrijven*. Deventer: Kluwer.

Kilcullen, M., and J. Ohles Kooistra. 1999. At least do no harm: Sources on the changing role of business ethics and corporate social responsibility. *Reference Services Review* 27(2): 158–178.

Klatt, B., S. Murphy, and D. Irvine. 1999. *Accountability: Practical tools for focusing on clarity, commitment and results*. London: Kogan Page.

Korten, D. 2001. *When corporations rule the world*, 2nd ed. San Fransisco: Berrett-Koehler Publishers.

Levinas, E. 1961. *Totality and infinity*. New York: Taylor and Francis.

Linnanen, L., and V. Panapanaan. 2002. *Roadmapping CSR in Finnish companies*. Helsinki: Helsinki University of Technology.

Marsden, C., and J. Androf. 1998. Towards an understanding of corporate citizenship and how to influence it. *Citizenship Studies* 2(2): 329–352.

Maslow, A. 1968/1982. *Toward a psychology of being*. New York: Van Nostrand Reinhold.

Marrewijk, M., and T.W. Hardjono. 2001. The social dimensions of business excellence. *Corporate Environmental Strategy* 8(3): 223.

Marrewijk, M., and M. Werre. May 2003. Multiple levels of corporate sustainability. *Journal of Business Ethics* 44(2 and 3): 107–119.

McGuire, J.W. 1963. *Business and society*. New York: McGraw-Hill.

Pirsig, R. 1991. *Lila, an inquiry into morals*. New York: Bantam Books.

Quazi, A.M., and D. O'Brien. 2000. An empirical test of a cross-national model of corporate social responsibility. *Journal of Business Ethics* 25(1): 33–51.

Steiner, G.A., and F.S. Steiner. 2000. *Business, government and society. A managerial perspective*. New York: McGraw-Hill.

van Marrewijk, M. 2003. European corporate sustainability framework. *International Journal of Business Performance Measurement* 5(2/3): 121–132.

van Marrewijk, M., and T.W. Hardjono. May 2003. European corporate sustainability framework for managing complexity and corporate change. *Journal of Business Ethics* 44(2–3): 121–132.

Votaw, D., and S.P. Sethi. 1973. *The corporate dilemma: Traditional values versus contemporary problems*. New York: Prentice Hall.

Wartick, S.L., and D.J. Wood. 1998. *International business and society*. Malden: Blackwell Publishers.

WCED – World Commission on Environment and Development or the Brundtland Commission 1987.

Wempe, J., and M. Kaptein. 2002. *The balanced company. A theory of corporate integrity*. Oxford: Oxford University Press.

Wilber, K. 1995. *Sex, ecology, spirituality: The spirit of evolution*. Boston: Shambhala.

Wilber, K. 2000. *A theory of everything: An integral vision for business, politics, science and spirituality*. Boston: Shambhala.

World Business Council for Sustainable Development WBCSD. 2000. *Corporate social responsibility: Making good business sense*. Geneva: WBCSD.

Zadek, S. 2001. *The civil corporation*. London: Earthscan Publications.

Zwart, A. van der. 2002. *Reputatiemechanisme in beweging: doelstreffend bij issues aan MVO?* Master thesis, Erasmus University Rotterdam, Rotterdam.

Chapter 33
An Experimental Examination of the Effects of Individual and Situational Factors on Unethical Behavioral Intentions in the Workplace

Gwen E. Jones and Michael J. Kavanagh

Unethical behavior in the workplace has become a serious and costly problem in society and in organizations. On almost a daily basis the popular press is replete with accounts of unethical behavior on the part of corporate managers and employees. In recent years there have been numerous accounts of insider trading, defense contract fraud, marketing of dangerous products, health risk coverups, discrimination against minorities, and embezzlement of funds in our savings and loan industry. Security analysts contend that economic crimes such as employee theft are on the rise, and that the cost of these crimes will increase from $114 billion in 1990 to $200 billion by the end of the decade (Knight-Ridder 1993). Not surprisingly, business educators, organizational researchers, legislators, and members of the general public have become increasingly concerned with reducing the incidence of unethical behavior in the workplace. In spite of the increased interest in business ethics, surprisingly little research in the related fields of organizational psychology have focused on understanding the factors that influence individuals to engage in unethical behavior. By understanding what leads to incidences of un-ethical behavior on the part of employees in the work environment, we can better foresee and perhaps inhibit its pervasiveness in organizations.

Several causal models of unethical behavior (i.e., Ferrell and Gresham 1985; Hung and Vitell 1986; Hegarty and Sims 1978, 1979; Trevino 1986; Trevino and Youngblood 1990), depict the dependent variable of unethical behavior as influenced by a person-situation interaction. Specifically, individuals are influenced to engage in unethical behaviors by characteristics of the situation as well as by characteristics of the individual.

G.E. Jones (✉)
Department of Management, Fairleigh Dickinson University,
285 Madison Ave, Madison, NJ 07940
e-mail: gjones@fdu.edu

M.J. Kavanagh
Department of Management, State University of New York, Albany, NY, USA

A.C. Michalos and D.C. Poff (eds.), *Citation Classics from the Journal of Business Ethics*, Advances in Business Ethics Research 2,
DOI 10.1007/978-94-007-4126-3_33,

The purpose of this study was to examine the relative effects of a set of situational characteristics variables and a set of individual characteristics variables on an individual's decision to engage in an unethical behavior in the work place. Based on an extensive review of various bodies of literature, including psychology, sociology, and criminal justice, three situational variables were chosen: quality of work experience, peer influences and behavior, and managerial influences and behavior; and three individual variables were chosen: locus of control, Machiavellianism, and gender.

Situational Variables

Quality of Work Experience

After a review of the literature, Merriam (1977) concluded that employee dissatisfaction with their work experience was a major, yet little understood determinant of employee theft. In an interview study reported by Altheide et al. (1978), they explained that ". . . many employees steal for revenge or dignity. They see their wages-in-kind as not only something they are entitled to, but also as a way of 'getting back' at a boss or supervisor who made an unkind remark or, probably more common, insisted that a worker show up for overtime." (p. 102) Kemper termed this "reciprocal deviance," which he asserts occurs in reaction to when the organization, or someone who represents the organization, such as a supervisor, defaults on its obligations to employees. In other words, individuals may seek redress in the form of unethical acts, such as property or time theft, in order to restore felt negative inequities in the psychological contract between the employer and themselves. Hollinger and Clark (1982, 1983) provided empirical support by exhibiting a significant relationship between job dissatisfaction and counterproductive or deviant work behaviors. Also, Greenberg (1990) found that when manufacturing plant workers' pay was temporarily reduced by 15% (without adequate explanation from management), employee theft rose to a significantly higher rate. Greenberg explained the phenomenon in terms of equity theory (Adams 1965), specifically that pilfering from their employer was an attempt to restore feelings of inequity by increasing their outputs. He also suggests that the theft could have been motivated by feelings of resentment and frustration (as reported by the workers) toward the organization, that resulted from the pay reduction (Greenberg 1989).

H_1: Individuals will report higher unethical behavioral intentions when the quality of work experience is perceived to be poor than when the quality of work experience is perceived to be good.

Peer Influence

An individual's peers have been found to influence unethical behavior. These referent peers may be others within the organization, or lateral others in the field but employed by other organizations. A survey of managers by Zey-Ferrell et al. (1979) and Zey-Ferrell and Ferrell (1982) found that the manager's perceptions of what their peers do was a better predictor of unethical behavior than their own values and beliefs, or those of top management.

There are two ways in which peers may influence unethical behavior: through norms and through differential association. In a weak organizational culture, peers provide the normative structure, or guides to decision making (Schein 1984). Peers set the standards and serve as referents for behavior. Also, Sutherland's (e.g., 1949, 1983) differential association theory of criminal behavior assumes that unethical behavior is learned through the association with a peer group. This learning includes the techniques of committing the unethical act, as well as the motives and rationalizations which serve to legitimize the unethical behavior.

Hollinger and Clark (1983) asserted, and empirically supported, the notion that the attitudes and sanctions of one's primary work group about employee deviant behaviors against the organization, including property and time theft, were significant predictors of the frequency of these acts. They argue that these norms guide the individual in determining the certainty of getting caught. Through interviews with manufacturing plant workers, Horning (1970) found that employee deviant behavior is often group sup-ported, but the actual act is done alone or in secret. Through the same methodology, Altheide et al. (1978) found that coworkers set the standards for which types of deviant acts are acceptable as well as the limitations on these acts, so as to not call attention to management.

> H_2: Individuals will report higher unethical behavioral intentions when their peer group is perceived to regularly engage in the unethical behavior than when the peer group is perceived to not regularly engage in unethical behavior.

Managerial Influences

Several surveys of executives (Baumhart 1961; Brenner and Molander 1977; Bowman 1976; Lincoln et al. 1982; Carroll 1978; Newstrom and Ruch 1975) have shown that these individuals felt pressure from management to engage in behavior that compromises their own ethical principles. They felt it was necessary to comply with these requests to succeed in their organizations. Thus, pressures from superiors within an organization seem to exert a major impact on unethical behavior.

Also, unethical behavior on the part of managers can influence the unethical behavior of subordinates, through what Kemper (1966) called "parallel deviance." Deviance at upper levels legitimates the imitation of these deviant acts at lower levels. For example, in the case of "… the violation of work rules in open conspiracy with foremen so that production goals can be met. (or) When a boss gives his secretary an obviously padded expense account, the secretary may conclude that a bit of theft on her own part is therefore legitimate." (p. 296). Unethical behavior on the part of individuals who represent the organization to the employee sends a message to that employee that "the worker's deviance is legitimated and the standards of compliance to organizational principle are shown to be simply myth and of no account." (p. 296)

H_3: Individuals will report higher unethical behavioral intentions when their supervisors are perceived as engaging in unethical behavior than when supervisors are perceived as not engaging in unethical behavior.

Individual Variables

Locus of Control

An individual antecedent that has received empirical support in the ethical decision making literature is the locus of control (LOC) construct. According to Rotter (1966), an individual with an internal LOC perceives outcomes to be a direct result of his or her efforts whereas an individual with an external LOC perceives outcomes to be from external forces beyond his or her control, such as others or fate. Externals feel less responsible for outcomes than do internals. Individuals with a high internal LOC are more likely to recognize a direct relationship between their behavior and outcomes. As a result, internals are more likely to attribute responsibility for outcomes to themselves and hence tend to choose to engage in ethical behaviors and not to engage in unethical behaviors. Conversely, externals are more likely to attribute responsibility to others or situational factors and thus engage in unethical behavior (Lefcourt and Wine 1969; Seeman 1963; Trevino and Young-blood 1990). This relationship has been empirically supported in the investigations of such ethical and unethical behaviors as prosocial acts (Spector 1982; Lefcourt 1982), whistleblowing (Dozier and Miceli 1985), cheating and resistance to pressure (Lefcourt 1982), and taking kickbacks (Hegarty and Sims 1979). The literature supports the following hypothesis regarding the relationship between LOC and unethical behavior.

H_4: Individuals with an external locus of control will report higher unethical behavioral intentions than those with an internal locus of control.

Machiavellianism

Machiavellianism is a personality construct based on the writings of Niccolo Machiavelli (1966/1513), who advocated principles for behavior that are opportunistic and influential of others in interpersonal relations. Individuals high on Machiavellianism (high Machs) are characterized by the "cool syndrome" (Christie and Geis 1970), meaning an affective detachment (e.g., they tend not to be easily swayed by loyalty or friendships). They typically lack concern for conventional morality, and are effective manipulators of others. Results of three studies by Hegarty and Sims (1978; 1979) found Machiavellianism to be correlated with unethical behavior (engaging in kickbacks). Flynn et al. (1987) found that high Machs were not more likely to cheat than individuals who were low Machs, however high Machs cheated significantly more often to avoid punishment than to attain rewards. Consistent with previous research, the following hypothesis was posited.

H_5: Individuals high on the Mach scale will report higher unethical behavioral intentions than individuals low on the Mach scale.

Gender

Several studies have empirically investigated the influence of gender on ethical decision making. Interest in this individual variable stems from the fact that women are increasingly entering management and executive positions (Akaah 1989). Thus, as a greater portion of these positions are occupied by women, will the result be more or less ethical behavior exhibited in management? The empirical results, however, on the relation between gender and ethical behavior have been inconsistent. In two experimental studies examining kickback behavior, Hegarty and Sims (1978, 1979) found no gender differences, however Stratton et al. (1981) found females to be slightly more adverse to padding expenses than were males. Chonko and Hung (1985) found that women perceived more ethical problems in marketing management than did males, thus indicating women are more sensitive to ethical problems. In a study of decisions based on ethical vignettes, Fritzsche (1988) found no differences across gender.

Research where individuals have been asked to rate whether certain behaviors are unethical have also yielded mixed results. Kidwell et al. (1987) found no differences except in one ethical situation – concealing one's errors – where females reported this to be more unethical than did men. Akaah (1989) found a large significant difference between males and females, with females overall evincing higher ethical standards than their male counterparts.

In a large, nationally representative survey done by Patterson and Kim (1991), it was found that less than half as many women as men reported believing that the only way to get ahead was to cheat. Moreover, it was found that women are less willing to compromise their values in order to get ahead, and women are less likely to engage in deviant behaviors at work, such as employee theft and time theft. Patterson and Kim present the astounding assertion that "If valuable company property is stolen, the thief will be a man six times out of seven" (p. 158).

Thus, the research results have not been consistent, however, the empirical literature tends to support the following hypothesis.

H_6: Males will report higher unethical behavioral intentions than will females.

Dependent Variable

Actual behavior is what is ultimately of interest. However to adequately assess the effects of the above variables it would be very difficult or unethical to measure actual behaviors of this nature. That is, we may be violating individuals' rights to privacy by asking about unethical behavior or by setting up a situation where we can observe them engaging in unethical behavior. Behavioral intentions are arguably an adequate surrogate measure. In his discussion of white collar crime, Coleman (1991) notes that this type of crime is not driven by passion or compulsion. The behavior is *of rational* choice. Therefore, if unethical behavior in organizations is of rational choice, we could assume that intentions are indicative of actual behavior. Also, Fishbein and Ajzen (1975; Ajzen 1988) have argued that individuals generally behave in a consistent manner with their espoused beliefs, attitudes, and values. In responses to a situation (such as an ethical dilemma), there is consistency between the way people think and feel and the way they act. Thus one's reported behavioral intentions in response to a situation should be consistent, or at least indicative of their actual behaviors.

Experiment 1 – Method

Overview

Using a 2×2×2 experimental design, two studies were conducted which examined the effects of the three situational variables: (1) quality of the work experience (good versus poor); (2) peer influences (unethical versus ethical); and (3) managerial influences (unethical versus ethical) on individuals' behavioral intentions in an ethically ambiguous dilemma in an work setting. The hypothesized effects of the three individual variables, (1) locus of control (internal versus external), (2) Machiavellianism (high versus low), and (3) gender (male versus female), were also examined.

Procedure

Data were collected in one session. Subjects were randomly assigned to experimental conditions, with proportional numbers of males and females assigned to each condition. Participants were asked to (1) read and sign a consent form, (2) complete a questionnaire measuring locus of control, Machiavellianism, social desirability, (3) read a scenario depicting an ethically ambiguous situation, (4) complete a questionnaire indicating their reactions to the dilemma, (5) complete a short questionnaire checking the experimental manipulations, and (6) complete a demographics questionnaire. Subjects were debriefed on the purpose and procedures of the study and thanked for their participation.

Subjects

Participants were 138 upper level undergraduate students (70 females and 64 males, 4 subjects with missing data) enrolled in a management course at a large northeastern university. The average age of the sample was 21, and approximately 70% indicated that they had work experience, primarily in the retail or service industries. Thirty-six percent indicated that they were currently employed. Students were remunerated with extra credit points for their participation. Participants were guaranteed anonymity. Individuals who did not want to participate in the research were given the opportunity to earn extra credit by reading a short article put on reserve at the library on unethical behavior in organizations.

Manipulations

Subjects were asked to read a short scenario which asks the subject to assume they are in a situation in which there is an ethical dilemma. The scenario was based on a case presented in Johnson (1974) depicting an employee tempted to pad his or her trip expense report.

All scenarios of the eight conditions began with the following: Irving Brockbank International is a fast-paced, reputable advertising firm in the Northeast. You have been with the firm as an accounts executive for about 6 months. Among other responsibilities, you consult with smaller advertising agencies promoting local area businesses. This requires that you periodically visit your clients, and you typically travel about once a month.

Quality of Work Experience

Quality of work experience was depicted in the scenario as being either good or poor. The following operationalizations were used.

> *Good.* Since working for the firm, you have been given a nice office, a competitive salary and good benefits. The company values you as an employee, and your immediate supervisor has been very appreciative of your efforts. In general, you have been very satisfied with the quality of your employment in the firm.
>
> or
>
> *Bad.* Since working for the firm, you've discovered that your salary is below industry average, the benefits are not very good, and your "office" is a tiny cubicle you share with two other people. The company doesn't seem to value you as an employee, and your immediate supervisor has not been very appreciative of your efforts. In general, you have not been very satisfied with the quality of your employment in the firm.

Peer Influences

Peers were depicted as either ethical or unethical. Wording of this manipulation was as follows:

> After coming back from a trip, you show your expense report to one of your friends in the office who basically does the same job you do. After looking at your expense report, he:
> *Ethical:* raises his eyebrows, and says, "You need to be very careful in reporting you expenses. For instance, I see you spent $30.00 for the cab fare from the airport. That could look very

suspicious to payroll. I know that some people in the company do inflate their trip report expenses, but most people are pretty accurate. If we aren't, payroll will start requiring even more verification of expenses. Plus, company travel funds will get depleted, and it'll be harder to justify a trip."

or

Unethical: laughs and says, "You actually put down what you really spent!" He then says to you, "Let me tell you, most of us add a few bucks here and there – its sort of a private perk." He then proceeds to show you which expenses you could increase (for example taxi fares, meals, and tips) and why (for example, a receipt is not required). He also tells you by how much you could increase expenses, without it being noticed by payroll as excessive.

Managerial Influences

Wording of this manipulation was as follows:

Ethical: Later, you happen to see the expense report of your boss from when he did the same trip about a month ago. You notice that his expenses are reported as much less than you reported. For example, you went ahead and put down estimates of meals of about $40.00 per day. Your boss reported that he spent about $15.00 per day. Obviously, the boss is very meticulous and accurate in reporting trip expenses.

or

Unethical: Later, you happen to see the expense report of your boss from when he did the same trip about a month ago. You notice that his expenses are reported as much greater than you know it really cost, from having just taken the same trip. For example, you stayed in the same hotel as he did and it cost you $7.00 cab fare between the hotel and airport. He reported that it cost $20.00 each way. You notice other expenses as well that are most likely inflated.

Measures

Locus of Control

Rotter's (1966) forced-choice measure of locus of control was adapted to a 5-point Likert-type response format. The scale was reduced to ten items based on a principle components analysis, varimax rotation, of pilot study data; combined with inspection of the item content. Items were coded and added such that a low score indicated an internal locus of control and a high score indicated an external locus of control. Coefficient alpha = 0.76.

Machiavellianism

The scale developed by Christie and Geis (1970) was reduced to ten items in the same manner as the locus of control scale above, i.e., through principle components analysis of pilot study data. Items were endorsed with a 5-point Likert-type scale in lieu of the original true-false format. Coefficient alpha = 0.72.

Biographical Information

The biographical information collected from each subject included: sex, age, race, whether currently employed, months of full time work experience, industry in which the subject had the majority of his or her work experience, and academic major.

Behavioral Intentions

Individuals' reactions to the scenarios were measured with a questionnaire developed for this study based on refinements of the results from two pilot studies. Four items were rated on a Likert-type 5-point scale ranging from strongly disagree to strongly agree. An example item is: "If I were actually in this situation, I would most likely increase the expense report total." Items were coded such that high scores indicated a more unethical response. Coefficient alpha = 0.87.

Social Desirability

A social desirability measure was included to determine if subjects were simply trying to "look good," instead of answering frankly about their intentions. Ten items form the Marlowe-Crowne Social Desirability Scale (Crowne and Marlowe 1964) were selected for this study, and subjects endorsed items with a 5-point Likert-type scale. Coefficient alpha = 0.56.

Results

Manipulation Checks

ANOVA results indicated that the manipulations for this study were successful: quality of work experience [$F(7, 129) = 32.38$, $p < 0.001$], peer influence [$F(7, 129) = 17.68$, $p < 0.001$], and manager influence [$F(7, 129) = 56.21$, $p < 0.001$].

Tests of the Hypotheses

Table 33.1 presents descriptive statistics and correlations among the study variables. Hierarchical regression analyses were used to test the effects of the situational and individual variables on the likelihood of engaging in the unethical behavior. The analysis involved regressing the dependent variable on three dummy coded variables representing the situational variables as well as the four individual variables all on step 1, and variables representing interactions among the situational variables

Table 33.1 Experiment 1 means, standard deviations, minimum and maximum range values, and inter-correlations for all variables

Variable	M	SD	Min	Max	Inter-correlations						
					1	2	3	4	5	6	7
1. Quality of work experience	0.51	0.05	0	1	–						
2. Manager influence	0.51	0.50	0	1	0.000	–					
3. Peer influence	0.52	0.50	0	1	0.000	0.000	–				
4. Locus of control	26.26	6.12	11	44	0.107	–0.111	0.026	–			
5. Machiavellianism	29.32	5.23	16	45	–0.101	–0.109	0.015	0.272***	–		
6. Gender	0.49	0.50	0	1	–0.058	0.015	0.002	–0.036	0.106	–	
7. Social desirability	27.10	4.29	17	40	0.013	0.070	–0.051	–0.184	–0.295***	–0.121	–
8. Unethical behavioral intentions	7.64	3.23	3	15	0.235**	0.066	0.247**	0.211**	0.216**	0.033	0.124

*$p<0.05$; ** $p<0.01$; *** $p<0.001$

Table 33.2 Results of regression analysis for Experiment 1

	Behavioral intentions	
Independent variable	*B*	*t*
Quality of work experience	0.236	3.051***
Manager influence	−1.371	0.172
Peer Influence	−0.007	−0.068
Locus of control	0.152	1.882*
Machiavellianism	0.181	2.226*
Gender	0.049	0.640
Manager/Peer interaction	0.431	3.176***

$R=0.506$; $F(7, 128)=6.307$, $p<0.0001$
* $p<0.05$; ** $p<0.01$; *** $p<0.001$

on step 2. Only one interaction term was significant, manager × peer, thus the model was trimmed, and for the final analysis only this interaction was entered on step 2. The results of the regression analysis are shown in Table 33.2. These results showed that, of the individual variables, there were significant main effects in the hypothesized direction for locus of control ($p<0.05$) and Machiavellianism ($p<0.05$), but not for gender. The hypotheses for the situational variables were supported by the results, specifically there was a strong main effect for Quality of Work Experience ($p<0.001$), and an interaction effect of manager influence and peer influence ($p<0.001$).

Social Desirability

The correlational results indicated that individuals who had a low Machiavellian or internal locus of control score tended to have a high social desirability score, and conversely, individuals who exhibited high Machiavellian or external locus of control scores tended to have a low social desirability score. Thus from these results it could be inferred that there was a response bias on the Machiavellian and locus of control, by the desire to "look good."

Discussion

Results revealed that individuals that are externally locused are more likely to behave unethically than individuals with an internal locus of control. This finding supported hypothesis one, and is consistent with prior research (e.g., Trevino and Youngblood 1990). The findings also supported hypothesis two, specifically that individuals with a high Machiavellian personality are more likely to behave unethically than individuals low on this construct. Gender was not found to affect whether an individual indicated they would or would not act unethically. Thus, hypothesis three was not supported. Quality of work experience was found to exhibit a strong main effect in support of hypothesis four. Hence, the results indicated that when individuals who are in a work environment that treats them poorly, they are more likely to act unethically than when the work environment treats them well. On step 1 of the regression analysis, managerial influence did not exhibit a significant main effect, whereas peer influence did exhibit a significant strong main effect. When the interaction term between these two variables was entered on step 2 of the regression analysis, the main effect for peer influence was no longer significant, and is represented in the interaction effect between manager influence and peer influence.

To determine whether the results were robust, Experiment 1 was replicated with a different sample. Subjects in Experiment 2 were Masters of Business Administration evening students, and most were employed in profession positions. This sample was considered to be more representative of professional employees.

Experiment 2 – Method

As noted above, Experiment 2 was designed to replicate Experiment 1 with a more generalizable sample, and to test the robustness of the results across different samples. Experiment 2 used the same experimental design, experimental procedure, and analyses reported in the method section of Experiment 1 above.

Subjects

Participants were 154 students (63 females and 86 males, 5 subjects with missing data) enrolled in MBA evening classes at the same university as subjects in Experiment 1. The average age was 27 years with an average of 5 years work experience. Sixty-three percent indicated that they were currently employed. The majority of their work experience was represented in four industries: services (30% of subjects), government (16%), finance-related (14%), and manufacturing (12%). All subjects volunteered during regular class sessions to participate, and were assured anonymity.

Procedures

The role play scenarios and manipulations were identical to those used in Experiment 1. The only change was the wording of the manipulation checks (not the manipulations themselves) in an effort to obtain stronger results for the manipulations. This was successful: quality of work experience [$F(7, 135)=89.16, p<0.001$], peer influence [$F(7, 135)=p<0.001$], and manager influence [$F(7, 135)=51.07, p<0.001$].

Results

Table 33.3 presents the descriptive statistics and correlations among the independent and dependent variables for Experiment 2. Table 33.4 shows the results of the regression analysis. No inter-action terms were significant, thus all variables were entered on one step. The results showed that there was not a significant effect of locus of control on behavioral intentions, and thus hypothesis one was not supported. However, there was a strong main effect for Machiavellianism in the hypothesized direction. Again, gender did not exhibit a significant effect on behavioral intentions. Hypotheses four, five, and six were all supported by the results, specifically, there were significant main effects in the hypothesized directions for quality of work experience, peer influence, and managerial influence.

Discussion

Two experimental studies were designed to empirically test hypotheses of individual and situational variables proposed to affect an individual's unethical behavioral intentions. The results indicated that the majority of the hypothesized relationships were supported, and that the effects of the individual and situational variables were relatively robust across the samples.

The quality of work experience was supported as having a significant main effect by the results of both experiments. A content analysis of an open-ended question (i.e., Why would you be more or less likely to engage in padding the expense report?) indicated that individuals may have felt justified in acting unethically toward the organization since they were being underpaid and overworked with no appreciation from the organization. This is consistent with prior research on employee theft (e.g., Hollinger and Clark 1983; Greenberg 1989).

Peer influence showed a significant causative effect in both experiments. This effect was masked by the significant interaction between peer and managerial influence in Experiment 1. While both peer influence and managerial influence showed effects in the hypothesized directions in Experiment 1 and Experiment 2, only peer influence was significantly correlated with behavioral intentions in Experiment 1 and only managerial influence was significantly correlated with behavioral intentions in Experiment 2. Perhaps the younger group with less job-related experience tended to give more weight to group norms (what everyone else was doing) and felt there was "safety in numbers," whereas the older, more work-experienced group felt that one should look to what the boss does to determine whether the behavior was an "accepted business practice."

Of the individual variables, the hypothesized influence of Machiavellianism exhibited the strongest and most robust relationship with the dependent variable across the samples. A caveat should be noted, specifically that the Machiavellian personality construct measure was significantly correlated with social desirability, indicating a possible response bias, which may have inhibited illustration of the true

Table 33.3 Experiment 2 means, standard deviations, minimum and maximum range values, and inter-correlations for all variables

					Inter-correlations						
Variable	M	SD	Min	Max	1	2	3	4	5	6	7
1. Quality of work experience	0.52	0.50	0	1	–						
2. Manager influence	0.52	0.50	0	1	–0.013	–					
3. Peer influence	0.51	0.50	0	1	–0.024	0.045	–				
4. Locus of control	26.53	6.03	12	42	0.009	0.014	–0.055	–			
5. Machiavellianism	27.71	4.70	14	40	0.017	–0.025	–0.151*	0.369***	–		
6. Gender	0.60	0.49	0	1	–0.014	–0.014	0.039	0.033	0.099	–	
7. Social desirability	28.31	4.23	19	39	0.066	–0.013	0.079	–0.215	–0.454***	–0.052	–
8. Unethical behavioral intentions	6.83	2.93	3	15	0.149*	0.242***	0.120	0.070	0.239***	0.122	0.008

*$p<0.05$; ** $p<0.01$; *** $p<0.001$

Table 33.4 Results of regression analysis for Experiment 2

	Behavioral intentions	
Independent variable	B	t
Quality of work experience	0.153	2.131*
Manager influence	0.246	3.432***
Peer influence	0.147	2.029*
Locus of control	−0.028	−0.359
Machiavellianism	0.265	3.387***
Gender	0.097	1.346

$R = 0.416$; $F(6, 161) = 5.631$, $p < 0.0001$
* $p < 0.05$; ** $p < 0.01$; *** $p < 0.001$

effect of Machiavellianism on behavioral intentions. A possible surrogate scale that may be a less obvious measure of Machiavellianism is the California Personality Inventory Socialization scale (Gough 1990). This scale measures a construct suspiciously similar to the Machiavellian construct. High scorers on this scales are described as conscientious, responsible, conforming, and honest. Low scorers are described as guileful and deceitful, opportunistic and manipulative. Recently, Collins and Schmidt (1993) reported a study which sought to discover personality constructs that distinguished white-collar incarcerated offenders from other white-collar employees. Their data showed that the socialization scale exhibited a mean standard deviation difference between the two samples of 1.00 or greater. Exploration of this construct is certainly worth pursuing.

Locus of control exhibited mixed results across the two experiments. For Experiment 1, the correlation between locus of control and behavioral intentions was in the hypothesized direction, specifically, the degree to which the individual was externally locused was positively related to higher unethical behavioral intentions. This result was not supported by data of Experiment 2.

The assertion that men tend to be more likely to endorse unethical behavior than do women was not supported in either experiment. Future research might examine constructs, such as sex-role orientation (e.g., Bern 1974), which would provide more explanatory mechanisms if differences were found.

Limitations and Implications for Future Research

Several limitations of the present research should be mentioned. First is the issue of generalizing from a laboratory experiment to the actual work setting. Although the subjects were asked to put themselves in the situation, there were no real pressures, benefits, or consequences. For several reasons cited elsewhere (e.g., Cavanagh and Fritzsche 1985), the scenario technique used was deemed as most appropriate for addressing the research question. Internal validity was enhanced at the expense of external validity. We felt it was important to first establish that there exists a causal relationship. Future research can then determine whether the relationships are found in actual work settings. Effectively conducting field quasi-experimental research in the ethics area will require extreme creatively on the part of researchers, which few to date have achieved without the research itself being equivocally ethical.

Generalizability is somewhat limited by the focus on intentions rather than actual behavior. However, as Trevino and Victor argue (1992), attitudes and intentions are important and worthy of scientific inquiry in and of themselves. As mentioned earlier, attitudes and intentions have been researched in other areas of organizational behavior such as motivation and turnover (Fishbein and Ajzen 1975; Steel and Ovalle 1984; Tubbs and Ekeberg 1991) and have supported the predictive relationship between intentions and subsequent behavior.

Finally, only one type of unethical behavior, expense report padding, was examined. The findings from this study may not be generalizable to other types of unethical behavior, such as engaging in kickback behavior, insider trading, or discrimination against minorities.

Implications for Management

The potential practical implications of these results are rather encouraging. If indeed situational characteristics exert significant influence on a person's likelihood of engaging in unethical behavior, as the present study would indicate, organizations can focus on structuring the organizational environment rather than on recruiting and selecting individuals who are more likely to behave ethically. Selecting for integrity has been found to be problematic (e.g., Sackett et al. 1989; Sackett and Harris 1984), and several states have passed legislation prohibiting the use of integrity tests.

The behavior on the part of managers and that of the peer group can be managed to curb unethical behavior on the part of employees, as is indicated by the positive influence of ethical managers and peers. Through training and other techniques for influencing the norms of the organization, organizations should focus on developing a climate which clearly engenders ethical norms for behavior. Also, since the behavior on the part of managers appears to be quite influential on an individual's decision to engage in unethical behavior, organizations might impose more severe organizational sanctions against managers for engaging in these acts.

The results suggest that an individual's quality of work experience affects his or her likelihood of engaging in unethical behavior. Therefore, maintaining a good quality of work experience for employees may be an important technique for controlling unethical behavior in the workplace. Organizations may want to regularly diagnose employee attitudes through employee attitude surveys and subsequently act upon suggestions generated for improving work conditions.

References

Adams, J.S. 1965. Inequity in social exchange. In *Advances in experimental social psychology*, vol. 2, ed. L. Berkowitz, 267–299. San Diego: Academic.

Ajzen, I.P. 1988. *Attitudes, personality and behavior*. Milton Keynes: Open University Press.

Akaah, I.P. 1989. Differences in research ethics judgments between male and female marketing professionals. *Journal of Business Ethics* 8: 375–381.

Altheide, D.L., P.A. Adler, P. Alder, and D.A. Altheide. 1978. The social meanings of employee theft. In *Crime at the top*, ed. J.M. Johnson and J.D. Douglas. Philadelphia, PA: Lippincott.

Baumhart, R.C. 1961. How ethical are businessmen? *Harvard Business Review* 39(4): 6–8.

Bern, S.L. 1974. The measurement of psychological androgeny. *Journal of Consulting and Clinical Psychology* 42: 155–162.

Bowman, J.S. 1976. Managerial ethics in business and government. *Business Horizons* 19: 48–54.

Brenner, S.N., and E.A. Molander. 1977. Is the ethics of business changing? *Harvard Business Review* 55(1): 57–71.

Carroll, A.B. 1978. Linking business ethics to behavior in organizations. *SAM Advance Management Journal* 43: 4–11.

Cavanagh, G.F., and D.J. Fritzsche. 1985. Using vignettes in business ethics research. *Research in Corporate Social Performance and Policy*, ed. L.E. Preston 7: 279–393. JAI Press.

Chonko, L.B., and S.D. Hung. 1985. Ethics and marketing management: An empirical examination. *Journal of Business Research* 13: 339–359.

Christie, R., and F.L. Geis. 1970. *Studies in Machiavellianism*. New York: Academic.

Coleman, J.W. 1991. Respectable crime. In *Criminology*, ed. J.F. Sheley. Belmont: Wadsworth.

Collins, J.M., and F.L. Schmidt. 1993. Personality, integrity, and white collar crime: A construct validity study. *Personnel Psychology* 46: 295–311.

Crowne, D.P., and D. Marlowe. 1964. *The approval motive*. New York: Wiley.

Dozier, J.B., and M.P. Miceli. 1985. Potential predictors of whistle-blowing: A prosocial behavior perspective. *Academy of Management Review* 10: 823–836.

Ferrell, O.C., and L.G. Gresham. 1985. A contingency framework for understanding ethical decision making in marketing. *Journal of Marketing* 49: 87–96.

Fishbein, M., and I.P. Ajzen. 1975. *Belief, attitude, intention and behavior: An introduction to theory and research*. Boston: Addison-Wesley.

Flynn, S., M. Reichard, and S. Slane. 1987. Cheating as a function of task outcome and Machiavellianism. *The Journal of Psychology* 121: 423–427.

Fritzsche, D.J. 1988. An examination of marketing ethics: Role of the decision maker, consequences of the decision, management position, and sex of the respondent. *Journal of Macromarketing* 8: 29–39.

Gough, H.G. 1990. The California psychological inventory. In *Testing in counseling practice*, ed. C.E. Watkins Jr. and V.L. Campbell, 37–62. Hillsdale: Lawrence Erlbaum Associates.

Greenberg, J. 1989. Cognitive re-evaluation of outcomes in response to underpayment inequity. *Academy of Management Journal* 32: 174–184.

Greenberg, J. 1990. Employee theft as a reaction to underpayment inequity: The hidden cost of pay cut. *Journal of Applied Psychology* 75: 561–568.

Hegarty, W.H., and H.P. Sims. 1978. Organizational philosophy, policies, and objectives related to unethical decision behavior: A laboratory experiment. *Journal of Applied Psychology* 64: 331–338.

Hegarty, W.H., and H.P. Sims. 1979. Some determinants of unethical decision behavior: An experiment. *Journal of Applied Psychology* 63: 451–457.

Hollinger, R.C., and J.P. Clark. 1982. Employee deviance: A response to the perceived quality of the work experience. *Work and Occupations* 9: 97–114.

Hollinger, R.C., and J.P. Clark. 1983. *Theft by employees*. Lexington: Lexington Books.

Horning, D.N.M. 1970. Blue collar theft: Conceptions of property, attitudes toward pilfering, and work group norms in a modern industrial plant. In *Crimes against bureaucracy*, ed. E.O. Smigel and H.L. Ross. New York: Van Nostrand Reinhold.

Hung, S.D., and S. Vitell. 1986. A general theory of marketing ethics. *Journal of Macromarketing* 5: 5–16.

Johnson, R.J. 1974. Conflict avoidance through acceptable decisions. *Human Relations* 27: 71–82.

Kemper, T.D. 1966. Representative roles and the legitimation of deviance. *Social Problems* 13: 288–298.

Kidwell, J.M., R.E. Stevens, and A.L. Bethke. 1987. Differences in ethical perceptions between male and female managers: Myth or reality? *Journal of Business Ethics* 6: 489–493.

Knight-Ridder. 1993. Stealing from work – bad for business. *Times Union Extra* 1–2.

Lefcourt, H.M. 1982. *Locus of control: Current trends in theory and research*, 2nd ed. Hillsdale: Erlbaum.

Lefcourt, H.M., and J. Wine. 1969. Internal versus external control of reinforcement and the deployment of attention in experimental situations. *Canadian Journal of Behavioral Science* 1: 167–181.

Lincoln, D.J., M.M. Pressley, and T. Little. 1982. Ethical beliefs and personal values of top level executive. *Journal of Business Research* 10: 475–487.

Machiavelli, N. 1966. *The prince*. New York: Bantam (Originally published in 1513).

Merriam, D. 1977. Employee theft. *Criminal Justice Abstracts* 9: 380–386.

Newstrom, J.W., and W.A. Ruch. 1975. The ethics of management and the management of ethics. *MSU Business Topics* 23: 29–37.

Patterson, J., and P. Kim. 1991. *The day America told the truth*. New York: Prentice Hall.

Rotter, J.B. 1966. Generalized expectancies for internal versus external control of reinforcement. *Psychological Monographs: General and Applied* 80: 1–28.

Sackett, P.R., and M.N. Harris. 1984. Honesty testing for personnel selection: A review and critique. *Personnel Psychology* 37: 221–245.

Sackett, P.R., L.R. Burris, and C. Callahan. 1989. Integrity testing for personnel selection: An update. *Personnel Psychology* 42: 491–529.

Schein, E.H. 1984. Coming to a new awareness of organizational culture. *Sloan Management Review* 25: 3–16.

Seeman, M. 1963. Alienation and social learning in a reformatory. *American Journal of Sociology* 69: 270–284.

Spector, P.E. 1982. Behavior in organizations as a function of employees' locus of control. *Psychological Bulletin* 91: 482–497.

Steel, R.P., and N.K. Ovalle. 1984. A review and meta-analysis of research on the relationship between behavioral intentions and employee turnover. *Journal of Applied Psychology* 69: 673–686.

Stratton, W.E., W.R. Flynn, and G.A. Johnson. 1981. Moral development and decision making: A study of student ethics. *Journal of Enterprise Management* 3: 35–41.

Sutherland, E.H. 1949. *White collar crime*. Rhinehart/New York: Holt/Winston.

Sutherland, E.H. 1983. *White collar crime: The uncut version*. New Haven: Yale University Press.

Trevino, L.K. 1986. Ethical decision making in organizations: A person-situation interactionist model. *Academy of Management Review* 11: 601–617.

Trevino, L.K., and B. Victor. 1992. Peer reporting of unethical behavior: A social context perspective. *Academy of Management Journal* 35: 38–64.

Trevino, L.K., and S.A. Youngblood. 1990. Bad apples in bad barrels: A causal analysis of ethical decision-making behavior. *Journal of Applied Psychology* 75: 378–385.

Tubbs, M.E., and S.E. Ekeberg. 1991. The role of intentions in work motivation: Implications for goal-setting theory and research. *Academy of Management Review* 18: 180–199.

Zey-Ferrell, M., and O.C. Ferrell. 1982. Role set configuration and opportunity as predictors of unethical behavior in organizations. *Human Relations* 35: 587–604.

Zey-Ferrell, M., K.M. Weaver, and O.C. Ferrell. 1979. Predicting unethical behavior among marketing practitioners. *Human Relations* 32: 557–569.

Chapter 34
Pinto Fires and Personal Ethics: A Script Analysis of Missed Opportunities

Dennis A. Gioia

In the summer of 1972 I made one of those important transitions in life, the significance of which becomes obvious only in retrospect. I left academe with a BS in Engineering Science and an MBA to enter the world of big business. I joined Ford Motor Company at World Headquarters in Dearborn Michigan, fulfilling a long-standing dream to work in the heart of the auto industry. I felt confident that I was in the right place at the right time to make a difference. My initial job title was "Problem Analyst" – a catchall label that superficially described what I would be thinking about and doing in the coming years. On some deeper level, however, the title paradoxically came to connote the many critical things that I would *not* be thinking about and acting upon.

By that summer of 1972 I was very full of myself. I had met my life's goals to that point with some notable success. I had virtually everything I wanted, including a strongly-held value system that had led me to question many of the perspectives and practices I observed in the world around me. Not the least of these was a profound distaste for the Vietnam war, a distaste that had found me participating in various demonstrations against its conduct and speaking as a part of a collective voice on the moral and ethical failure of a democratic government that would attempt to justify it. I also found myself in MBA classes railing against the conduct of businesses of the era, whose actions struck me as ranging from inconsiderate to indifferent to simply unethical. To me the typical stance of business seemed to be one of disdain for, rather than responsibility toward, the society of which they were prominent members. I wanted something to change. Accordingly, I cultivated my social awareness; I held my principles high; I espoused my intention to help a troubled world; and I wore my hair long. By any measure I was a prototypical "Child of the 1960s."

D.A. Gioia (✉)
Department of Management and Organization, Smeal College of Business Administration, Pennsylvania State University, University Park, PA 16802, USA
e-mail: dag4@psu.edu

A.C. Michalos and D.C. Poff (eds.), *Citation Classics from the Journal of Business Ethics*, Advances in Business Ethics Research 2,
DOI 10.1007/978-94-007-4126-3_34, © Springer Science+Business Media B.V. 2013

Therefore, it struck quite a few of my friends in the MBA program as rather strange that I was in the program at all ("If you are so disappointed in business, why study business?"). Subsequently, they were practically dumbstruck when I accepted the job offer from Ford, apparently one of the great purveyors of the very actions I reviled. I countered that it was an ideal strategy, arguing that I would have a greater chance of influencing social change in business if I worked behind the scenes on the inside, rather than as a strident voice on the outside. It was clear to me that somebody needed to prod these staid companies into socially responsible action. I certainly aimed to do my part. Besides, I liked car.

Into the Fray: Setting the Personal Stage

Predictably enough, I found myself on the fast track at Ford, participating in a "tournament" type of socialization (Van Maanen 1978), engaged in a competition for recognition with other MBA's who had recently joined the company. And I quickly became caught up in the game. The company itself was dynamic; the environment of business, especially the auto industry, was intriguing; the job was challenging and the pay was great. The psychic rewards of working and succeeding in a major corporation proved unexpectedly seductive. I really became involved in the job.

Market forces (international competition) and government regulation (vehicle safety and emissions) were affecting the auto industry in disruptive ways that only later would be common to the wider business and social arena. They also produced an industry and a company that felt buffeted, beleaguered, and threatened by the changes. The threats were mostly external, of course, and led to a strong feeling of we-vs-them, where we (Ford members) needed to defend ourselves against them (all the outside parties and voices demanding that we change our ways). Even at this time, an intriguing question for me was whether I was a "we" or a "them." It was becoming apparent to me that my perspective was changing. I had long since cut my hair.

By the summer of 1973 I was pitched into the thick of the battle. I became Ford's Field Recall Coordinator – not a position that was particularly high in the hierarchy, but one that wielded influence for beyond its level. I was in charge of the operational coordination of all of the recall campaigns currently underway and also in charge of tracking incoming information to identify developing problems. Therefore, I was in a position to make initial recommendations about possible future recalls. The most critical type of recalls were labeled "safety campaigns" – those that dealt with the possibility of customer injury or death. These ranged from straight-forward occurrences such as brake failure and wheels falling off vehicles, to more exotic and faintly humorous failure modes such as detaching axles that announced their presence by spinning forward and slamming into the startled driver's door and speed control units that locked on, and refused to disengage, as the car accelerated wildly while the spooked driver futilely tried to shut it off. Safety recall campaigns, however, also encompassed the more sobering possibility of on-board gasoline fires and explosions....

The Pinto Case: Setting the Corporate Stage

In 1970 Ford introduced the Pinto, a small car that was intended to compete with the then current challenge from European cars and the ominous presence on the horizon of Japanese manufacturers. The Pinto was brought from inception to production in the record time of approximately 25 months (compared to the industry average of 43 months), a time frame that suggested the necessity for doing things expediently. In addition to the time pressure, the engineering and development teams were required to adhere to the production "limits of 2,000" for the diminutive car: it was not to exceed either $2,000 in cost or 2,000 lb in weight. Any decisions that threatened these targets or the timing of the car's introduction were discouraged. Under normal conditions design, styling, product planning, engineering, etc., were completed prior to production tooling. Because of the foreshortened time frame, however, some of these usually sequential processes were executed in parallel.

As a consequence, tooling was already well under way (thus "freezing" the basic design) when routine crash testing revealed that the Pinto's fuel tank often ruptured when struck from the rear at a relatively low speed (31 mph in crash tests). Reports (revealed much later) showed that the fuel tank failures were the result of some rather marginal design features. The tank was positioned between the rear bumper and the rear axle (a standard industry practice for the time). During impact, however, several studs protruding from the rear of the axle housing would puncture holes in the tank; the fuel filler neck also was likely to rip away. Spilled gasoline then could be ignited by sparks. Ford had in fact crash-tested 11 vehicles; 8 of these cars suffered potentially catastrophic gas tank ruptures. The only three cars that survived intact had each been modified in some way to protect the tank.

These crash tests, however, were conducted under the guidelines of Federal Motor Vehicle Safety Standard 301 which had been proposed in 1968 and strenuously opposed by the auto industry. FMVSS 301 was not actually adopted until 1976; thus, at the time of the tests, Ford was not in violation of the law. There were several possibilities for fixing the problem, including the option of redesigning the tank and its location, which would have produced tank integrity in a high-speed crash. That solution, however, was not only time consuming and expensive, but also usurped trunk space, which was seen as a critical competitive sales factor. One of the production modifications to the tank, however, would have cost only $11 to install, but given the tight margins and restrictions of the "limits of 2,000," there was reluctance to make even this relatively minor change. There were other reasons for not approving the change, as well, including a widespread industry belief that all small cars were inherently unsafe solely because of their size and weight. Another more prominent reason was a corporate belief that "safety doesn't sell." This observation was attributed to Lee Iacocca and stemmed from Ford's earlier attempt to make safety a sales theme, an attempt that failed rather dismally in the marketplace.

Perhaps the most controversial reason for rejecting the production change to the gas tank, however, was Ford's use of cost-benefit analysis to justify the decision. The National Highway Traffic Safety Association (NHTSA, a federal agency) had approved the use of cost-benefit analysis as an appropriate means for establishing automotive safety design standards. The controversial aspect in making such calculations was that they required the assignment of some specific value for a human life. In 1970, that value was deemed to be approximately $200,000 as a "cost to society" for each fatality. Ford used NHTSA's figures in estimating the costs and benefits of altering the tank production design. An internal memo, later revealed in court, indicates the following tabulations concerning potential fires (Dowie 1977):

Costs: $137,000,000

(Estimated as the costs of a production fix to all similarly designed cars and trucks with the gas tank aft of the axle (12,500,000 vehicles × $11/vehicle))

Benefits: $49,530,000

(Estimated as the savings from preventing (180 projected deaths × $200,000/death) + (180 projected burn injuries × $67,000/injury) + (2,100 burned cars × $700/car))

The cost-benefit decision was then construed as straightforward: No production fix would be undertaken. The philosophical and ethical implications of assigning a financial value for human life or disfigurement do not seem to have been a major consideration in reaching this decision.

Pintos and Personal Experience

When I took over the Recall Coordinator's job in 1973 I inherited the oversight of about 100 active recall campaigns, more than half of which were safety-related. These ranged from minimal in size (replacing front wheels that were likely to break on 12 heavy trucks) to maximal (repairing the power steering pump on millions of cars). In addition, there were quite a number of safety problems that were under consideration as candidates for addition to the recall list. (Actually, "problem" was a word whose public use was forbidden by the legal office at the time, even in service bulletins, because it suggested corporate admission of culpability. "Condition" was the sanctioned catchword.) In addition to these potential recall candidates, there were many files containing field reports of alleged component failure (another forbidden word) that had led to accidents and, in some cases, passenger injury. Beyond these existing files, I began to construct my own files of incoming safety problems.

One of these new files concerned reports of Pintos "lighting up" (in the words of a field representative) in rear-end accidents. There were actually very few reports, perhaps because component failure was not initially assumed. These cars simply were consumed by fire after apparently very low speed accidents. Was there a problem? Not as far as I was concerned. My cue for labeling a case as a problem either required high frequencies of occurrence or directly-traceable causes. I had little time for speculative contemplation on potential problems that did not fit a pattern that suggested known courses of action leading to possible recall. I do, however, remember being disquieted by a field report accompanied by graphic, detailed photos of the remains of a burned-out Pinto in which several people had died. Although that report became part of my file, I did not flag it as any special case.

It is difficult to convey the overwhelming complexity and pace of the job of keeping track of so many active or potential recall campaigns. It remains the busiest, most information-filled job I have ever held or would want to hold. Each case required a myriad of information-gathering and execution stages. I distinctly remember that the information-processing demands led me to confuse the facts of one problem case with another on several occasions because the tell-tale signs of recall candidate cases were so similar. I thought of myself as a fireman – a fireman who perfectly fit the description by one of my colleagues: "In this office everything is a crisis. You only have time to put out the big fires and spit on the little ones." By those standards the Pinto problem was distinctly a little one.

It is also important to convey the muting of emotion involved in the Recall Coordinator's job. I remember contemplating the fact that my job literally involved life-and-death matters. I was sometimes responsible for finding and fixing cars NOW, because somebody's life might depend on it. I took it *very* seriously. Early in the job, I sometimes woke up at night wondering whether I had covered all the bases. Had I left some unknown person at risk because I had not thought of something? That soon faded, however, and of necessity the consideration of people's lives became a fairly removed, dispassionate process. To do the job "well" there was little room for emotion. Allowing it to surface was potentially paralyzing and prevented rational decisions about which cases to recommend for recall. On moral grounds I knew I could recommend most of the vehicles on my safety tracking list for recall (and risk earning the label of a "bleeding heart"). On practical grounds, I recognized that people implicitly accept risks in cars. We could not recall all cars with *potential* problems and stay in business. I learned to be responsive to those cases that suggested an imminent, dangerous problem.

I should also note, that the country was in the midst of its first, and worst, oil crisis at this time. The effects of the crisis had cast a pall over Ford and the rest of the automobile industry. Ford's product line, with the perhaps notable exception of the Pinto and Maverick small cars, was not well-suited to dealing with the crisis. Layoffs were imminent for many people. Recalling the Pinto in this context would have damaged one of the few trump cards the company had (although, quite frankly, I do not remember being overtly influenced by that issue).

Pinto reports continued to trickle in, but at such a slow rate that they really did not capture particular attention relative to other, more pressing safety problems. However, I later saw a crumpled, burned car at a Ford depot where alleged problem components and vehicles were delivered for inspection and analysis (a place known as the "Chamber of Horrors" by some of the people who worked there). The revulsion on seeing this incinerated hulk was immediate and profound. Soon afterwards, and despite the fact that the file was very sparse, I recommended the Pinto case for preliminary department-level review concerning possible recall. After the usual round of discussion about criteria and justification for recall, everyone voted against recommending recall – including me. It did not fit the pattern of recallable standards; the evidence was not overwhelming that the car was defective in some way, so the case was actually fairly straightforward. It was a good business decision, even if people might be dying. (We did not then know about the pre-production crash test data that suggested a high rate of tank failures in "normal" accidents (cf., Perrow 1984) or an abnormal failure mode.)

Later, the existence of the crash test data did become known within Ford, which suggested that the Pinto might actually have a recallable problem. This information led to a reconsideration of the case within our office. The data, however, prompted a comparison of the Pinto's survivability in a rear end accident with that of other competitors' small cars. These comparisons revealed that although many cars in this subcompact class suffered appalling deformation in relatively low speed collisions, the Pinto was merely the worst of a bad lot. Furthermore, the gap between the Pinto and the competition was not dramatic in terms of the speed at which fuel tank rupture was likely to occur. On that basis it would be difficult to justify the recall of cars that were comparable with others on the market. In the face of even more compelling evidence that people were probably going to die in this car, I again included myself in a group of decision makers who voted not to recommend recall to the higher levels of the organization.

Coda to the Corporate Case

Subsequent to my departure from Ford in 1975, reports of Pinto fires escalated, attracting increasing media attention, almost all of it critical of Ford. Anderson and Whitten (1976) revealed the internal memos concerning the gas tank problem and questioned how the few dollars saved per car could be justified when human lives were at stake. Shortly thereafter, a scathing article by Dowie (1977) attacked not only the Pinto's design, but also accused Ford of gross negligence, stonewalling, and unethical corporate conduct by alleging that Ford knowingly sold "firetraps" after willfully calculating the cost of lives against profits (see also Gatewood and Carroll 1981). Dowie's provocative quote speculating on "how long the Ford Motor Company would continue to market lethal cars were Henry Ford II and Lee Iacocca serving 20 year terms in Leavenworth for consumer homicide" (1977, p. 32) was particularly effective in focusing attention on the case. Public sentiment edged toward labeling Ford as socially deviant because management was seen as knowing that the car was defective, choosing profit over lives, resisting demands to fix the car, and apparently showing no public remorse (Swigert and Farrell 1980–1981).

Shortly after Dowie's (1977) expose, NHTSA initiated its own investigation. Then, early in 1978 a jury awarded a Pinto burn victim $125 million in punitive damages (later reduced to $6.6 million, a judgment upheld on an appeal that prompted the judge to assert that "Ford's institutional mentality was shown to be one of callous indifference to public safety" (quoted in Cullen et al. 1987, p. 164)). A siege atmosphere emerged at Ford. Insiders characterized the mounting media campaign as "hysterical" and "a crusade against us" (personal communications).

The crisis deepened. In the summer of 1978 NHTSA issued a formal determination that the Pinto was defective. Ford then launched a reluctant recall of all 1971–1976 cars (those built for the 1977 model year were equipped with a production fix prompted by the adoption of the FMVSS 301 gas tank standard). Ford hoped that the issue would then recede, but worse was yet to come.

The culmination of the case and the demise of the Pinto itself began in Indiana on August 10, 1978, when three teenage girls died in a fire triggered after their 1973 Pinto was hit from behind by a van. A grand jury took the unheard of step of indicting Ford on charges of reckless homicide (Cullen et al. 1987). Because of the precedent-setting possibilities for all manufacturing industries, Ford assembled a formidable legal team headed by Watergate prosecutor James Neal to defend itself at the trial. The trial was a media event; it was the first time that a corporation was tried for alleged *criminal* behavior. After a protracted, acrimonious courtroom battle that included vivid clashes among the opposing attorneys, surprise witnesses, etc., the jury ultimately found in favor of Ford. Ford had dodged a bullet in the form of a consequential legal precedent, but because of the negative publicity of the case and the charges of corporate crime and ethical deviance, the conduct of manufacturing businesses was altered, probably forever. As a relatively minor footnote to the case, Ford ceased production of the Pinto.

Coda to the Personal Case

In the intervening years since my early involvement with the Pinto fire case, I have given repeated consideration to my role in it. Although most of the ethically questionable actions that have been cited in the press are associated with Ford's intentional stonewalling after it was clear that the Pinto was defective (see Cullen et al. 1987; Dowie 1977; Gatewood and Carroll 1981) – and thus postdate my involvement with the case and the company – I still nonetheless wonder about my own culpability. Why didn't I see the gravity of the problem and its ethical overtones? What happened to the value system I carried with me into Ford? Should I have acted differently, given what I knew then? The experience with myself has sometimes not been pleasant. Somehow, it seems I should have done *something* different that might have made a difference.

As a consequence of this line of thinking and feeling, some years ago I decided to construct a "living case" out of my experience with the Pinto fire problem for use in my MBA classes. The written case description contains many of the facts detailed above; the analytical task of the class is to ask appropriate questions of me as a figure in the case to reveal the central issues involved. It is somewhat of a trying experience to get through these classes. After getting to know me for most of the semester, and then finding out that I did *not* vote to recommend recall, students are often incredulous, even angry at me for apparently not having lived what I have been teaching. To be fair and even-handed here, many students understand my actions in the context of the times and the attitudes prevalent then. Others, however, are very disappointed that I appear to have failed during my time of trial. Consequently,

I am accused of being a charlatan and otherwise vilified by those who maintain that ethical and moral principles should have prevailed in this case no matter what the mitigating circumstances. Those are the ones that hurt.

Those are also the ones, however, that keep the case and its lessons alive in my mind and cause me to have an on-going dialogue with myself about it. It is fascinating to me that for several years after I first conducted the living case with myself as the focus, I remained convinced that I had made the "right" decision in not recommending recall of the cars. In light of the times and the evidence available, I thought I had pursued a reasonable course of action. More recently, however, I have come to think that I really should have done everything I could to get those cars off the road.

In retrospect I know that in the context of the times my actions were *legal* (they were all well within the framework of the law); they probably also were *ethical* according to most prevailing definitions (they were in accord with accepted professional standards and codes of conduct); the major concern for me is whether they were *moral* (in the sense of adhering to some higher standards of inner conscience and conviction about the "right" actions to take). This simple typology implies that I had passed at least two hurdles on a personal continuum that ranged from more rigorous, but arguably less significant criteria, to less rigorous, but more personally, organizationally, and perhaps societally significant standards:

X	X	?
Legal	Ethical	Moral

It is that last criterion that remains troublesome.

Perhaps these reflections are all just personal revisionist history. After all, I am still stuck in my cognitive structures, as everyone is. I do not think these concerns are all retrospective reconstruction, however. Another telling piece of information is this: The entire time I was dealing with the Pinto fire problem, I owned a Pinto (!). I even sold it to my sister. What does that say?

What Happened Here?

I, of course, have some thoughts about my experience with this damningly visible case. At the risk of breaking some of the accepted rules of scholarly analysis, rather than engaging in the usual comprehensive, dense, arms-length critique, I would instead like to offer a rather selective and subjective focus on certain characteristics of human information processing relevant to this kind of situation, of which I was my own unwitting victim. I make no claim that my analysis necessarily "explains more variance" than other possible explanations. I do think that this selective view is enlightening in that it offers an alternative explanation for some ethically questionable actions in business.

The subjective stance adopted in the analysis is intentional also. This case obviously stems from a series of personal experiences, accounts, and introspections. The analytical style is intended to be consistent with the self-based case example; therefore, it appears to be less "formal" than the typical objectivist mode of explanation.

I suspect that my chosen focus will be fairly non-obvious to the reader familiar with the ethical literature (as it typically is to the ethical actor). Although this analysis might be judged as somewhat self-serving, I nonetheless believe that it provides an informative explanation for some of the ethical foibles we see enacted around us.

To me, there are two major issues to address. First, how could my value system apparently have flip-flopped in the relatively short space of 1–2 years? Secondly, how could I have failed to take action on a retrospectively obvious safety problem when I was in the perfect position to do so? To begin, I would like to consider several possible explanations for my thoughts and actions (or lack thereof) during the early stages of the Pinto fire case.

One explanation is that I was simply revealed as a phony when the chips were down; that my previous values were not strongly inculcated; that I was all bluster, not particularly ethical, and as a result acted expediently when confronted with a reality test of those values. In other words, I turned traitor to my own expressed values. Another explanation is that I was simply intimidated; in the face of strong pressure to heel to company preferences, I folded – put ethical concerns aside, or at least traded them for a monumental guilt trip and did what anybody would do to keep a good job. A third explanation is that I was following a strictly utilitarian set of decision criteria (Velasquez et al. 1983) and, predictably enough, opted for a personal form of Ford's own cost-benefit analysis, with similar disappointing results. Another explanation might suggest that the interaction of my stage of moral development (Kohlberg 1969) and the culture and decision environment at Ford led me to think about and act upon an ethical dilemma in a fashion that reflected a lower level of actual moral development than I espoused for myself (Trevino 1986, 1992). Yet another explanation is that I was co-opted; rather than working from the inside to change a lumbering system as I had intended, the tables were turned and the system beat me at my own game. More charitably, perhaps, it is possible that I simply was a good person making bad ethical choices because of the corporate milieu (Gellerman 1986).

I doubt that this list is exhaustive. I am quite sure that cynics could match my own MBA students' labels, which in the worst case include phrases like "moral failure" and "doubly reprehensible because you were in a position to make a difference." I believe, however, on the basis of a number of years of work on social cognition in organizations that a viable explanation is one that is not quite so melodramatic. It is an explanation that rests on a recognition that even the best-intentioned organization members organize information into cognitive structures or schemas that serve as (fallible) mental templates for handling incoming information and as guides for acting upon it. Of the many schemas that have been hypothesized to exist, the one that is most relevant to my experience at Ford is the notion of a script (Abelson 1976, 1981).

My central thesis is this: *My own schematized (scripted) knowledge influenced me to perceive recall issues in terms of the prevailing decision environment and to unconsciously overlook key features of the Pinto case, mainly because they did not fit an existing script. Although the outcomes of the case carry retrospectively obvious ethical overtones, the schemas driving my perceptions and actions precluded consideration of the issues in ethical terms because the scripts did not include ethical dimensions.*

Script Schemas

A *schema* is a cognitive framework that people use to impose structure upon information, situations, and expectations to facilitate understanding (Gioia and Poole 1984; Taylor and Crocker 1981). Schemas derive from consideration of prior experience or vicarious learning that results in the formation of "organized" knowledge – knowledge that, once formed, precludes the necessity for further active cognition. As a consequence, such structured knowledge allows virtually effortless interpretation of information and events (cf., Canter and Mischel 1979). A *script* is a specialized type of schema that retains knowledge of actions appropriate for specific situations and contexts (Abelson 1976, 1981). One of the most important characteristics of scripts is that they simultaneously provide a cognitive framework for *understanding* information and events as well as a guide to appropriate *behavior* to deal with the situation faced. They thus serve as linkages between cognition and action (Gioia and Manz 1985).

The structuring of knowledge in scripted form is a fundamental human information processing tendency that in many ways results in a relatively closed cognitive system that influences both perception and action. Scripts, like all schemas, operate on the basis of prototypes, which are abstract representations that contain the main features or characteristics of a given knowledge category (e.g., "safety problems"). Protoscripts (Gioia and Poole 1984) serve as templates against which incoming information can be assessed. A pattern in current information that generally matches the template associated with a given script signals that active thought and analysis is not required. Under these conditions the entire existing script can be called forth and enacted automatically and unconsciously, usually without adjustment for subtle differences in information patterns that might be important.

Given the complexity of the organizational world, it is obvious that the schematizing or scripting of knowledge implies a great information processing advantage – a decision maker need not actively think about each new presentation of information, situations, or problems; the mode of handling such problems has already been worked out in advance and remanded to a working stock of knowledge held in individual (or organizational) memory. Scripted knowledge saves a significant amount of mental work, a savings that in fact prevents the cognitive paralysis that would inevitably come from trying to treat each specific instance of a class of problems as a unique case that requires contemplation. Scripted decision making is thus efficient decision making but not necessarily good decision making (Gioia and Poole 1984).

Of course, every advantage comes with its own set of built-in disadvantages. There is a price to pay for scripted knowledge. On the one hand, existing scripts lead people to selectively perceive information that is consistent with a script and thus to ignore anomalous information. Conversely, if there is missing information, the gaps in knowledge are filled with expected features supplied by the script (Bower et al. 1979; Graesser et al. 1980). In some cases, a pattern that matches an existing script, except for some key differences, can be "tagged" as a distinctive case (Graesser et al. 1979) and thus be made more memorable. In the worst case scenario, however, a situation that does not fit the characteristics of the scripted perspective for handling problem cases often is simply not noticed. Scripts thus offer a viable explanation for why experienced decision makers (perhaps *especially* experienced decision makers) tend to overlook what others would construe as obvious factors in making a decision.

Given the relatively rare occurrence of truly novel information, the nature of script processing implies that it is a default mode of organizational cognition. That is, instead of spending the predominance of their mental energy thinking in some active fashion, decision makers might better be characterized as typically *not* thinking, i.e., dealing with information in a mode that is akin to "cruising on automatic pilot" (cf., Gioia 1986). The scripted view casts decision makers as needing some sort of prod in the form of novel or unexpected information to kick them into a thinking mode – a prod that often does not come because of the wealth of similar data that they must process. Therefore, instead of focusing what people pay attention to, it might be more enlightening to focus on what they do *not* pay attention to.

Pinto Problem Perception and Scripts

It is illustrative to consider my situation in handling the early stages of the Pinto fires case in light of script theory. When I was dealing with the first trickling-in of field reports that might have suggested a significant problem with the Pinto, the reports were essentially similar to many others that I was dealing with (and dismissing) all the time. The sort of information they contained, which did not convey enough prototypical features to capture my attention, never got past my screening script. I had seen this type of information pattern before (hundreds of times!); I was making this kind of decision automatically every day. I had trained myself to respond to prototypical cues, and these didn't fit the relevant prototype for crisis cases. (Yes, the Pinto reports fit a prototype – but it was a prototype for "normal accidents" that did not deviate significantly from expected problems). The frequency of the reports relative to other, more serious problems (i.e., those that displayed more characteristic features of safety problems) also did not pass my scripted criteria for singling out the Pinto case. Consequently, I looked right past them.

Overlooking uncharacteristic cues also was exacerbated by the nature of the job. The overwhelming information overload that characterized the role as well as its hectic pace actually forced a greater reliance on scripted responses. It was impossible to handle the job requirements *without* relying on some sort of automatic way of assessing whether a case deserved active attention. There was so much to do and so much information to attend to that the only way to deal with it was by means of schematic processing. In fact, the one anomaly in the case that might have cued me to gravity of the problem (the field report accompanied by graphic photographs) still did not distinguish the problem as one that was distinctive enough to snap me out of my standard response mode and tag it as a failure that deserved closer monitoring.

Even the presence of an emotional component that might have short-circuited standard script processing instead became part of the script itself. Months of squelching the disturbing emotions associated with serious safety problems soon made muffled emotions a standard (and not very salient) component of the script for handling *any* safety problem. This observation, that emotion was muted by experience, and therefore de-emphasized in the script, differs from Fiske's (1982) widely accepted position that emotion is tied to the top of a schema (i.e., is the most salient and initially-tapped aspect of schematic processing). On the basis of my experience, I would argue that for organization members trained to control emotions to perform the job role (cf., Pitre 1990), emotion is either not a part of the internalized script, or at best becomes a difficult-to-access part of any script for job performance.

The one instance of emotion penetrating the operating script was the revulsion that swept over me at the sight of the burned vehicle at the return depot. That event was so strong that it prompted me to put the case up for preliminary consideration (in theoretical terms, it prompted me cognitively to "tag" the Pinto case as a potentially distinctive one). I soon "came to my senses," however, when rational consideration of the problem characteristics suggested that they did not meet the scripted criteria that were consensually shared among members of the Field Recall Office. At the preliminary review other members of the decision team, enacting their own scripts in the absence of my emotional experience, wondered why I had even brought the case up. To me this meeting demonstrated that even when controlled analytic information processing occurred, it was nonetheless based on prior schematization of information. In other words, even when information processing was not automatically executed, it still depended upon schemas (cf., Gioia 1986). As a result of the social construction of the situation, I ended up agreeing with my colleagues and voting not to recall.

The remaining major issue to be dealt with, of course, concerns the apparent shift in my values. In a period of less than 2 years I appeared to change my stripes and adopt the cultural values of the organization. How did that apparent shift occur? Again, scripts are relevant. I would argue that my pre-Ford values for changing corporate America were bona fide. I had internalized values for doing what was right as I then understood "rightness" in grand terms. They key is, however, that I had not internalized a *script* for enacting those values in any specific context outside my limited experience. The insider's view at Ford, of course, provided me with a specific and immediate context for developing such a script. Scripts are formed from salient experience and there was no more salient experience in my relatively young life than joining a major corporation and moving quickly into a position of clear and present responsibility. The strongest possible parameters for script formation were all there, not only because of the job role specifications, but also from the corporate culture. Organizational culture, in one very powerful sense, amounts to a collection of scripts writ large. Did I sell out? No. Were my cognitive structures altered by salient experience? Without question. Scripts for understanding and action were formed and reformed in a relatively short time in a way that not only altered perceptions of issues but also the likely actions associated with those altered perceptions.

I might characterize the differing cognitive structures as "outsider" versus "insider" scripts. I view them also as "idealist" versus "realist" scripts. I might further note that the outsider/idealist script was one that was more individually-based than the insider/realist script, which was more collective and subject to the influence of the corporate milieu and culture. Personal identity as captured in the revised script became much more corporate than individual. Given that scripts are socially constructed and reconstructed cognitive structures, it is understandable that their content and process would be much more responsive to the corporate culture, because of its saliency and immediacy.

The recall coordinator's job was serious business. The scripts associated with it influenced me much more than I influenced it. Before I went to Ford I would have argued strongly that Ford had an ethical obligation to recall. After I left Ford I now argue and teach that Ford had an ethical obligation to recall. But, *while I was there*, I perceived no strong obligation to recall and I remember no strong *ethical* overtones to the case whatsoever. It was a very straightforward decision, driven by dominant scripts for the time, place, and context.

Whither Ethics and Scripts?

Most models of ethical decision making in organizations implicitly assume that people recognize and think about a moral or ethical dilemma when they are confronted with one (cf., Kohlberg 1969; Trevino 1992). I call this seemingly fundamental assumption into question. The unexplored ethical issue for me is the arguably prevalent case where organizational representatives are not aware that they are dealing with a problem that might have ethical overtones. If the case involves a familiar class of problems or issues, it is likely to be handled via existing cognitive structures or scripts – *scripts that typically include no ethical component in their cognitive content.*

Although we might hope that people in charge of important decisions like vehicle safety recalls might engage in active, logical analysis and consider the subtleties in the many different situations they face, the context of the decisions and their necessary reliance on schematic processing tends to preclude such consideration (cf., Gioia 1989). Accounting for the subtleties of ethical consideration in work situations that are typically handled by schema-based processing is very difficult indeed. Scripts are built out of situations that are normal, not those that are abnormal, ill-structured, or unusual (which often can characterize ethical domains). The ambiguities associated with most ethical dilemmas imply that such situations demand a "custom" decision, which means that the inclusion of an ethical dimension as a component of an evolving script is not easy to accomplish.

How might ethical considerations be internalized as part of the script for understanding and action? It is easier to say what will *not* be likely to work than what will. Clearly, mere mention of ethics in policy or training manuals will not do the job. Even exhortations to be concerned with ethics in decision making are seldom likely to migrate into the script. Just as clearly, codes of ethics typically will not work. They are too often cast at a level of generality that can not be associated with any specific script. Furthermore, for all practical purposes, codes of ethics often are stated in a way that makes them "context-free," which makes them virtually impossible to associate with active scripts, which always are context-bound.

Tactics for script *development* that have more potential involve learning or training that concentrates on exposure to information or models that explicitly display a focus on ethical considerations. This implies that ethics be included in job descriptions, management development training, mentoring, etc. Tactics for script *revision* involve learning or training that concentrate on "script-breaking" examples. Organization members must be exposed either to vicarious or personal experiences that interrupt tacit knowledge of "appropriate" action so that script revision can be initiated. Training scenarios, and especially role playing, that portray expected sequences that are then interrupted to call explicit attention to ethical issues can be tagged by the perceiver as requiring attention. This tactic amounts to installing a decision node in the revised scripts that tells the actor "Now think" (Abelson 1981). Only by means of similar script-breaking strategies can existing cognitive structures be modified to accommodate the necessary cycles of automatic and controlled processing (cf., Louis and Sutton 1991).

The upshot of the scripted view of organizational understanding and behavior is both an encouragement and an indictment of people facing situations laced with ethical overtones. It is encouraging because it suggests that organizational decision makers are not necessarily lacking in ethical standards; they are simply fallible information processors who fail to notice the ethical implications of a usual way of handling issues. It is an indictment because ethical dimensions are not usually a central feature of the cognitive structures that drive decision making. Obviously, they should be, but it will take substantial concentration on the ethical dimension of the corporate culture, as well as overt attempts to emphasize ethics in education, training, and decision making before typical organizational scripts are likely to be modified to include the crucial ethical component.

References

Abelson, R.P. 1976. Script processing in attitude formation and decision-making. In *Cognition and social behavior*, ed. J.S. Carroll and J.W. Payne, 33–45. Hillsdale: Erlbaum.

Abelson, R.P. 1981. Psychological status of the script concept. *American Psychologist* 36: 715–729.

Anderson, J., and L. Whitten. 1976. Auto maker shuns safer gas tank. *Washington Post* (December 30), B–7.

Bower, G.H., J.B. Black, and T.J. Turner. 1979. Scripts in memory for text. *Cognitive Psychology* 11: 177–220.

Cantor, N., and W. Mischel. 1979. Prototypes in person perception. In *Advances in experimental social psychology*, vol. 12, ed. L. Berkowitz, 3–51. New York: Academic Press.

Cullen, F.T., W.J. Maakestad, and G. Cavender. 1987. *Corporate crime under attack*. Chicago: Anderson Publishing Co.

Dowie, M. 1977. How Ford put two million firetraps on wheels. *Business and Society Review* 23: 46–55.

Fiske, S.T. 1982. Schema-triggered affect: Applications to social perception. In *Affect and cognition*, ed. M.S. Clark and S.T. Fiske, 55–78. Hillsdale: Erlbaum.

Gatewood, E., and A.B. Carroll. 1981. The anatomy of corporate social response: The Rely, Firestone 500, and Pinto cases. *Business Horizons* 24(5): 9–16.

Gellerman, S. 1986. Why "Good" managers make bad ethical choices. *Harvard Business Review* (July–August), 85–90.

Gioia, D.A. 1986. Symbols, scripts, and sensemaking: Creating meaning in the organizational experience. In *The thinking organization: Dynamics of organizational social cognition*, ed. H.P. Sims Jr. and D.A. Gioia, 49–74. San Francisco: Jossey-Bass.

Gioia, D.A. 1989. Self-serving bias as a self-sensemaking strategy. In *Impression management in the organization*, ed. P. Rosenfeld and R. Giacalone, 219–234. Hillsdale: LEA.

Gioia, D.A., and C.C. Manz. 1985. Linking cognition and behavior: A script processing interpretation of vicarious learning. *Academy of Management Review* 10: 527–539.

Gioia, D.A., and P.P. Poole. 1984. Scripts in organizational behavior. *Academy of Management Review* 9: 449–459.

Graesser, A.C., S.G. Gordon, and J.D. Sawyer. 1979. Recognition memory for typical and atypical actions in scripted activities: Test of script pointer and tag hypothesis. *Journal of Verbal Learning and Verbal Behavior* 18: 319–332.

Graesser, A.C., S.B. Woll, D.J. Kowalski, and D.A. Smith. 1980. Memory for typical and atypical actions in scripted activities. *Journal of Experimental Psychology* 6: 503–515.

Kohlberg, L. 1969. Stage and sequence: The cognitive-development approach to socialization. In *Handbook of socialization theory and research*, ed. D.A. Goslin, 347–480. Chicago: Rand-McNally.

Louis, M.R., and R.I. Sutton. 1991. Switching cognitive gears: From habits of mind to active thinking. *Human Relations* 44: 55–76.

Perrow, C. 1984. *Normal accidents*. New York: Basic Books.

Pitre, E. 1990. Emotional control. Working paper, the Pennsylvania State University.

Swigert, V.L., and R.A. Farrell. 1980–1981. Corporate homicide: Definitional processes in the creation of deviance. *Law and Society Review* 15: 170–183.

Taylor, S.E., and J. Crocker. 1981. Schematic bases of social information processing. In *Social cognition 1*, ed. E.T. Higgins, C.P. Herman, and M.P. Zanna, 89–134. Hillsdale: Erlbaum.

Trevino, L. 1986. Ethical decision making in organizations: A person-situation interactionist model. *Academy of Management Review* 11: 601–617.

Trevino, L.K., 1992. Moral reasoning and business ethics: Implications for education, research and management. *Journal of Business Ethics* 11: 445–459.

Velasquez, M., D.J. Moberg, and G.F. Cavanaugh. 1983. Organizational statesmanship and dirty politics: Ethical guidelines for the organizational politician. *Organizational Dynamics (Autumn)* 12(3): 65–80.

Van Maanen, J. 1978. People processing: Strategies of organizational socialization. *Organizational Dynamics (Summer)* 7(1): 18–36.

Chapter 35
Reflections on Careers, *JBE* and Business Ethics

Alex C. Michalos and Deborah C. Poff (eds.)

To join us in celebrating the first 30 years of publication, we invited scholars who authored citation classics or distinguished papers, as well as those who had served on our Editorial Board and/or are recognized as leaders in the field to write short essays (600 words or less) for this volume. Those who authored citation classics or distinguished papers were invited to answer two questions.

1. What has been the impact, if any, of your citation classic (or distinguished paper) on your career?
2. What has been the impact, if any, of the *Journal of Business Ethics* on the field of business ethics?

Current or former Editorial Board members and leading scholars were only asked the second question.

The essays that follow include all those sent to us, as sent to us, except for some standardizing stylistic changes. Some authors provided titles for their reflections and these have been retained. Those that did not have titles have simply been entitled 'Relections'.

We are grateful to all these authors for sharing their reflections with us. Some are particularly biographical and some are more academic assessments of the *Journal* and the field from a variety of very interesting and important perspectives.

A.C. Michalos (✉)
Professor Emeritus, Political Science, University of Northern British Columbia, (home) 463 13th Street, Brandon, R7A 4P9, MB, Canada
e-mail: michalos@brandonu.ca

D.C. Poff (eds.)
President and Vice Chancellor, Brandon University, 18th Street, R7A 6A9, Brandon, MB, Canada

A.C. Michalos and D.C. Poff (eds.), *Citation Classics from the Journal of Business Ethics*, Advances in Business Ethics Research 2,
DOI 10.1007/978-94-007-4126-3_35, © Springer Science+Business Media B.V. 2013

Antonio Argandona

Some Challenges for the Journal of Business

The decision to launch the *Journal of Business Ethics* was undoubtedly an act of academic entrepreneurship, resulting, as it did, in a publication that has done great service to business ethics and management. Its founders therefore deserve our recognition and congratulations. At the same time, a quick comparison of the contents of the *Journal* today with the contents 30 years ago shows how our discipline has evolved. Here I shall venture to point out some of the future challenges of business ethics that I hope we will see reflected in the pages of the *Journal of Business Ethics* in the years ahead.

The first of those challenges has to do with what I consider to be one of the *Journal*'s great strengths, namely, its multidisciplinarity. The challenge now is to move beyond collections of articles, each representing a different approach, towards articles in which all, or several, of those approaches are combined. This is no easy task because in order to write in the overlap between paradigms you have to be an expert in all of them, and that is not readily compatible with the way in which our social scientists work. If any field can do it, though, it is the field of management, which is not the monopoly of any one discipline. And this is a fitting challenge for the *Journal of Business Ethics*.

Which leads us to the second challenge. Business ethics is not an applied ethics that brings abstract principles to bear on a particular area. If economics is the science of human action, business must be the field in which decisions are made that are relevant to the manager, to other stakeholders, and to the whole of society. Beyond our arguments about the goals of companies, business ethics must start by asking how the woman or man to whom we attribute responsibility for managing a company acts. We cannot construct business ethics from outside the theory of human action, that is to say, from outside the manager's decision-making process. And this is a task precisely for business ethics because it adds the holistic dimension that marketing, finance or strategy otherwise lack.

And that brings me to yet another challenge for business ethics and the *Journal*. Although this is an academic journal, it must make an effort to offer guidelines, suggestions and recommendations to managers about how they can manage companies in a moral way. I am not proposing that it become a management journal; I am proposing that it make an effort to confront academicians with the question of how their theoretical and empirical studies can be converted into ideas that are useful to managers.

Finally, I shall point to two further challenges. One: that of restoring the ethical dimension that Corporate Social Responsibility (CSR) has frequently lost, having become little more than a repertoire of techniques. No doubt there are many exceptions, but there is a danger that the practical dimension of CSR will defeat its purpose.

And two: the challenge of reigniting the debate about foundations, about the kind of ethics we are applying in companies. I realize that this is countercultural and perhaps even anti-academic, at least the way scientific research is currently understood in our field. The new generations, however, will be grateful for some serious reflection on these topics. And the *Journal of Business Ethics* is undoubtedly the right place for it.

Richard F. Beltramini and Robert A. Peterson

Reflections

First author: Having our article identified as a "citation classic" by the *Journal of Business Ethics* is a large honor, and I credit its original publication with making a significant impact on my professional career. As the first empirical article published in *JBE*, the national survey employed allowed us to project our findings broadly, and to call attention to an important research area. In fact, feedback on its publication helped me identify my primary research focus, and encouraged me to conduct several additional studies published in *JBE* over the years, including our replication with extension in 1991.

The *Journal of Business Ethics* represents the leading publication of its kind on this topic, and consistently ranks quite highly among the rankings based on the *Social Sciences Citation Index*. This is due in large part to the editorial leadership of the *Journal*, and its rigorous manuscript review process. But additionally, it is worth noting the multi-disciplinary backgrounds of its Editorial Review Board members and of *JBE*'s contributors. Readers find a healthy mix of methodological techniques in each issue, coupled with solid coverage of both theoretical and practical direction supplied by the articles published. Seeing the importance of business ethics on the careers of future business leaders, I've incorporated coverage in all of my classes, and encouraged my colleagues to do the same.

While the field of business ethics has grown, recent industry abuses have underscored the ongoing need to focus more attention to the topic, both in classrooms and in boardrooms. As such, I guest edited a special issue of *JBE* on advertising ethics in 2003, and am currently guest editing a special issue of the *Journal of Advertising Research* as a "call to action" on the topic. I applaud *JBE* for 30 years of impact, and remain proud to have participated modestly over the years.

Second author: The impact of our 1984 *Journal of Business Ethics* article, "Concerns of College Students Regarding Business Ethics," has been extremely gratifying. As one of the first articles to report empirical research results in the *Journal*, the article demonstrated the contribution that survey research could make when investigating ethics. Moreover, with its emphasis on college student study participants, the article was the genesis of two research streams that I have pursued the past quarter-of-a-century and that have led to numerous publications. One stream has been methodological in nature in that it has focused on when it is appropriate in general to use college students as study participants. The other research stream has continued the focus on ethical attitudes of college students and has resulted in several publications, including a 2005 book (*Business Ethics*: *New Challenges for Business Schools and Corporate Leaders*) and a 2010 article in *JBE* ("Effects of Nationality, Gender, and Religiosity on Business-Related Ethicality," *Journal of Business Ethics*, Vol. 96, 573–587). The topic of college students' business-related ethics remains one that needs to be objectively and robustly investigated, and I am pleased that our 1984 article has both catalyzed and stimulated research for more than 25 years.

John R. Boatright

What Has Been the Impact of the Journal of Business Ethics on the Field of Business Ethics?

As a member of that dwindling band of intrepid souls who were present at the beginning of the field of business ethics in the 1970s, I can recall my receipt of the first issue of the *Journal of Business Ethics* in February 1982. It still sits on my bookcase, high up at the beginning of five shelves of volumes, now numbering 104. The stapled spines of the first two volumes and their relative thinness are daily visual reminders of the distance the journal has come in 30 years of publication.

The founding of *JBE* was both a risky gamble on the future of a not yet established field and a critical step in assuring its establishment. At the time, business ethics was developing rapidly as a curricular area, with courses and textbooks abounding, but it had yet to make the all-important leap into academic respectability as a distinct subject for research. The Society for Business Ethics, which had been formed 2 years earlier, in 1980, was still largely a special interest group of philosophers, who found that the potential for publication in the few receptive philosophy journals was limited to a narrow range of philosophically interesting topics, which, even collectively, did not form the basis for a viable separate field of study. The earliest publications in business ethics, aside from textbooks, were edited volumes from conferences held in the late 1970s. Despite their significant contribution to the development of business ethics, these books could not substitute for a journal as a vehicle for scholarly output, which is the *sine qua non* for academic recognition. By 1980, everyone in the field recognized that business ethics had a future only if there was at least one journal devoted solely to the subject, and yet there was no recognized field to support such a journal.

We can be thankful to Alex Michalos for taking the initiative to found *JBE*. Without it, the field of business ethics would probably exist today, but not with the rapid development and solid respectability that it has experienced. In re-reading Alex's editorial statement "Purpose and Policy" in the first issue, I am struck by his declaration that the journal would provide a "public forum" for debate among all people with an interest in business from "a variety of methodological and disciplinary perspectives." He seemed to recognize at the time that this nascent field could not be merely a sub-specialty of philosophy but had to encompass diverse methodologies and disciplines. Moreover, by omitting any mention of academic developments and emphasizing the public interest nature of the *Journal*, the statement of purpose and policy side-stepped any question of the "parentage" of business ethics and created space for a new, independent field of study. More than any other journal in business ethics – fortunately, there are now several good ones – *JBE* can lay claim to an instrumental role in the field's development.

Over the years, I have been a close observer of the growth of the *Journal,* not only in my use of the research in its pages but also as an editorial board member of *JBE* and two of its rivals. Like a parent with more than one child, I find it difficult to compare journals with which one is closely associated. I am constantly impressed, however, with the broad range of contributors, many of whom are not primarily in business ethics; *JBE* has succeeded, more than other business ethics journals, in drawing researchers around the world to the field. Moreover, given that the preponderance of articles published today are empirical, which contrasts with the original theoretical bent of the field, *JBE* has succeeded in its founding vision of being a journal that makes business ethics a truly interdisciplinary field. So thanks should be given not only for the founding of this great journal and its role in launching a field, but also for what it has contributed in 30 years to the body of business ethics research. May it continue its fine work for many years to come.

Clive Boddy

The Impact of the Journal of Business Ethics on the Field of Business Ethics

I write this essay about the impact of the *Journal of Business Ethics* on the field of business ethics from the point of view of myself as a formerly successful business practitioner who has now gone into academia as a second career and only recently become a full time academic and only just been appointed to the editorial board of *JBE*. This viewpoint may therefore be different from that of a longer term academic. One of the differences is that I very strongly believe that business research should be relevant to business practitioners just as medical research is relevant to doctors and nurses, and this is, I think, one of the key strengths of the *Journal of Business Ethics*. It is relevant, it is accessible and it is current and up to date in the areas it covers.

For example, two nights ago in the UK there was a documentary on BBC2, as part of the "Horizon" series, about psychopaths in society and psychopaths as corporate leaders. The newspaper follow-up commentary and the on-line discussion stimulated by this debate about toxic managerial leaders was large and vocal, just as it always is when toxic leadership is discussed. Toxic leadership is directly relevant to all people in business because toxic leaders bully others, destroy careers, create emotional and psychological destruction, parasitically use the resources, savings, investments and earnings of others for their own ends and destroy the long term feasibility of the businesses that they manage.

The *Journal of Business Ethics* is outstanding in reflecting this debate in society, in its pages, and it has certainly long been concerned with toxic leaders as unethical managers and in particular with the dark triad of narcissists, Machiavellians and psychopaths. Papers about Machiavellians have been appearing in *JBE* since at least 1996 and a search within the journal for Machiavellianism results in 160 papers being identified. Narcissists have been written about in *JBE* since 1997 in about 15 papers and psychopaths have been written about since 2008 with 17 papers about them. These types of selfish and unethical managers, although small in numbers, are destructive and damaging to everyone who works with them for any extended length of time and this is why their presence is so relevant to business and to business ethics. The *JBE* is one of the few academic journals that has kept itself up to date with these issues and with the public debate around toxic leadership.

Other elements of the mission and objectives of the *JBE* also add to its impact on business ethics and society. One of these is its objective to avoid jargon in favor of dialogue. *JBE* is not one of those management journals where the academic language used is so dense and academically colloquial as to obscure meaning and camouflage relevance. There is no language barrier and practitioners can pick up the journal, read it and understand it. It also aims to be all-inclusive and multi-disciplinary and this fosters a wide reach that extends across all areas of business and includes marketing, ethics, accountancy, economics, law and organizational behavior, among others. These factors of importance, relevance and accessibility make *JBE*, I believe, one of only a tiny handful of business journals that would be as highly ranked by business practitioners as it is by business academics.

The overall aim of the *Journal of Business Ethics*, to improve the human condition, marks the journal as one of the most noble in intent, ambitious in scope and important in substance of all business journals. It is this that marks the journal out as being important to society and to ethics. Articles are not chosen for publication merely because they are mathematically elegant or sophisticated in their statistical analysis, but rather because their content and substance is important to society and to the world in which we live. That is what makes the impact of *JBE* so outstanding.

Susan C. Borkowski and Yusuf J. Ugras

Reflections

The article, "Business Students and Ethics: A Meta-Analysis" was the second one that we collaborated on that specifically addressed the issues and concerns associated with business ethics. This was also the first meta-analysis we ever undertook. In order to actually collect the data for the meta-analysis, we had to first read and research as many of the existing studies on business ethics from the student perspective that we could locate. I do remember my surprise when I realized how much of the existing research we were analyzing had been published in prior issues of *JBE*.

Our study grew out of our mutual developing interest in ethics in the early 1990s. Borkowski's work in this area started with Mary Anne Gaffney at Temple University analyzing accounting codes of ethics, and led to studying ethics in the accounting publishing process from both the author and the editor viewpoints with Mary Jeanne Welsh at La Salle University. These early studies on ethics led to my [Borkowski] current interest in corporate sustainability reports, working with Welsh and Kristin Wentzel, also at La Salle University.

Ugras' early interest in ethics stemmed from his observations of the students' responses to ethical dilemmas, especially between traditional undergraduate and part-time adult learners. These observations led into a research inquiry with Borkowski, "The Ethical Attitudes of Students as a Function of Age, Sex and Education", which was also published in *JBE* back in December 1992. The literature review that we undertook for this first study was the impetus for the meta-analysis. When we realized the breadth and depth of existing research on business students and ethical behavior, a meta-analysis seemed the best approach to trying to make sense of all the varied and sometimes contradictory findings of prior researchers in this area.

Without understanding business ethics from the bottom up and undertaking the meta-analysis that led to our article, we would not have had the theoretical underpinnings to continue in this area. Did it help our careers? Well, one of us is a full professor (Borkowski) and the other a Dean (Ugras), so we would unreservedly say "Yes!"

For us, our interest in business ethics aligns with, and is reinforced and strengthened by our University's mission – "the free search for truth by teaching its students the basic skills, knowledge, and values that they will need for a life of human dignity…preparing students for informed service and progressive leadership in their communities and to fulfilling the immediate and final goals of their lives." Working together, our faculty and students embrace these values and strive to achieve these goals both on a personal and on a professional level. Articles published in the *Journal of Business Ethics* definitely shape how both faculty and students discuss and think about business ethics. Many articles have been used in our accounting, business law, and senior capstone strategy course to augment to traditional textbook material, bringing to the classroom an awareness of, and an appreciation for, the continued relevance of business ethics to our everyday business decisions. We would like to extend our gratitude for *JBE* and its specific focus on business ethics, which is needed now more than ever!

Norman E. Bowie

Relections

Although business ethics has a long history, this current wave of business ethics teaching and research began in the late 1970s with the publication of a number of textbooks in business ethics. However, at that time there was no organized business ethics society and no scholarly journal devoted specifically to business ethics. Under the leadership of Alex Michalos and Deborah Poff, the *Journal of Business Ethics*

(*JBE*) was created and began publication in 1982. For nearly a decade *JBE* was **the** journal for those of us writing in business ethics and a number of classic articles appeared there. Between 1982 and 1988 I published three articles in *JBE* including what I believe to be one of my better pieces "Fair Markets." My most recent piece in *JBE*, "How Empirical Research in Human Cognition Does and Does Not Affect Philosophical Ethics" appeared in the tribute volume for my late dear friend Tom Dunfee in 2010. I dare say that all the founders of The Society for Business Ethics have published several papers in *JBE*.

But that was just the beginning. Several generations of business ethics scholars have gotten their start by publishing articles in *JBE*. As the number of papers submitted to scholarly journals has increased and the number of pages in scholarly journals has remained roughly the same, scholars in all disciplines have had an increasing difficulty finding an outlet for their scholarly work. *JBE* has been an exception and has steadily increased the number of pages over the years. As a result a number of scholars at non research institutions and young scholars have had a better chance at getting their research published.

In addition, *JBE* embodies a number of characteristics that we as business ethicists endorse. *JBE* is open to researchers who conduct business ethics research from a number of different methodological perspectives. Of course it has provided a major outlet for philosophical thinking. But at the empirical level it has been more open to survey research than many traditional management journals. Scholars interested in religion and management have had a voice.

From the beginning *JBE* has published work on international business ethics and has been open to business ethics scholars around the world. It has been the major outlet for scholars in developing countries. Thus *JBE* has contributed significantly to the development of a community of international business ethics scholars.

So happy 30th birthday *JBE* and congratulations to Alex Michalos and Deborah Poff for their contribution to this journal and to the field of business ethics in general.

Leonard J. Brooks

Thirty-Year Impact of the Journal of Business Ethics

For several reasons, the *Journal of Business Ethics* has played the dominant role in defining business ethics thought, education, and practice during the last 30 years.

From the beginning, *JBE* published articles that featured new ideas or practices from both academics and practitioners. Many of these articles were very creative and thoughtful, but not highly rigorous in a scientific or research sense – an approach that afforded an opportunity for new ideas to be expressed, broadly discussed by individuals and in classes, and nurtured. Over time, *JBE* has transitioned to include more rigorously researched articles, but continues to provide the most comprehensive source of business ethics ideas and topical discussion.

Without *JBE*'s editorial stance and accessibility, the pace of development and impact of business ethics would have been delayed significantly. When the number of submissions became too large, the editors and publisher expanded to almost a monthly publication schedule. Other journals have simply not been publishing enough articles to perform this nurturing role, nor have they been as widely read. It took foresight and fortitude on the part of the editors to formulate their vision and to stick to it – and I applaud them for it.

A list of 51 of the most highly cited of the 4,747 articles *JBE* published during the last 30 years appears elsewhere in this issue, and it demonstrates the breadth and significance of *JBE*'s impact. While there are other excellent journals for specific business ethics topics, none, either alone or in combination, have done as much to create the frameworks that now exist for our understanding of business ethics and its many dimensions. Indeed, the other journals – that publish scientifically rigorous studies that deepen our knowledge on many issues – have been enabled in their mandates by the exploratory and formative roles played by *JBE*.

In the years to come, as the business ethics field becomes more mature, *JBE* will modify its vision, but hopefully will continue to embrace the formative nurturing of ideas for the benefit of both academics and practitioners, and indeed for society as a whole.

It has been a welcome honour and privilege to serve as an early member of the *JBE* Editorial Board, and more recently as a reviewer. Most hearty congratulations to Alex and Deb on the first 30 years, and best wishes for the next.

Edmund F. Byrne

What, If Any, Has Been the Impact of the Journal of Business Ethics on the Field of Business Ethics?

The precise impact that a purveyor of words has on a widely practiced field of study is not easy to determine. But there are clear indications that this journal has had a profound effect on both internal and external aspects of business ethics.

Internally, the journal has greatly facilitated the sharing of ideas in the field. This can be seen by noting the greatly expanded number of issues (regular and special) that are published even as the rejection rate remains high. Also noteworthy is the numerical and geographical expansion over time of its contributors, its readers via hard copy and increasingly via online availability, and its library subscribers. In these respects this journal is unsurpassed in the field, as may someday be its spinoff, the *Asian Journal of Business Ethics*. Equally significant, however, is the ever widening range of sub-specialties that have been assigned a section in the journal (now more than four times as many as the original four).

Important as are these developments to an appreciation of the field of business ethics, even more important is the identifiable role they represent in distributing the content of *JBE* not only to but beyond the attention of academics. It would be hyperbolic to say that *JBE* has discernibly changed the business world as a whole. But failing this it has contributed to the falsification of two criticisms of business ethics: (1) that the discipline has no effect on business in the real world and (2) that it tends to focus only on large corporations.

As for the first criticism, *JBE*, in consort with scholars, activists, and concerned government officials, has helped stimulate the ever growing movement to impose responsibility standards on business institutions. Key among these are efforts to implement corporate social responsibility in the world via codes of ethics and social responsibility charters as well as adoption of business-oriented human rights in international law via governmental and UN documents. To say that these developments are controversial misses the key point that they are now a significant ingredient of ongoing debate, within and beyond this discipline, regarding acceptable business practices and regulatory concerns. Moreover, they are consonant with the undeniable fact that transnational corporations have become a major component of business in today's world and accordingly call for increased scrutiny.

This said, it is not the case that less global aspects of business are ignored in the pages of *JBE*. Even a casual perusal of its contents negates the assertion that business ethics overlooks issues more prevalent among middle-management, workforce, and small business owners and operators. For, in these pages will be found countless careful studies using diverse theories and methods to improve the ethical quality of work on all levels and in just about every part of the globe. Moreover, the journal provides an invaluable mechanism for understanding in depth and proposing solutions to problems encountered in the workplace. Theories proposed and tested in one setting become models for further research elsewhere, and over time the panoply of studies that result from this academic colloquy provides well intentioned business professionals with relevant and carefully reasoned suggestions for enhancing the ethical aspects of their business.

Allowing, then, that there is always room for improvement, I am persuaded that the *Journal of Business Ethics*, under the wise tutelage of its founding Editor and Editor in Chief, has done an awe-inspiring job of advancing the quality and the efficacy of business ethics.

Cam Caldwell

Meeting Today's Demands and Tomorrow's Hopes

As one of the top 45 journals used by the *Financial Times* (2010) to determine a business school's research rank, the prestige of the *Journal of Business Ethics* (*JBE*) is well acknowledged internationally – but the reason that the *JBE* has received this ranking is that it is bridging the gap between scholar and practitioner to confront values-based issues and challenge traditional thinking that have plagued academic thinking for decades (cf. Pfeffer and Fong 2004). In today's business schools where much of the value of learning is "taken on faith," (Pfeffer 2009) the need to provide a forum for examining new ideas about values, leadership, and ethical expectations has come to the forefront in a world described by David Callahan (2004) as "the cheating culture."

JBE opens the door for considering new ideas that challenge the status quo while requiring that scholars demonstrate high standards of academic rigor. In a world characterized by change, chaos, creativity, and conflict (Buchholz and Rosenthal 2005), *JBE* has become a vehicle for identifying options for old and ineffective models (Pfeffer 1998) of thinking that are the underlying causes of many organization problems associated with leadership and governance (Covey 2004). The evidence has proven that businesses are in serious trouble when they are satisfied with simply trying to be "good," since "Good is the enemy of great" (Collins 2001:1). Good, ironically, was probably never good enough – the clear lesson for the American economy over the past 50 years (Reich 2011).

JBE offers an opportunity to challenge the moral courage of those who wear the mantle of leadership, but whose performance has been stunningly inadequate at a time when we are desperate for great leaders and rational long-term decision-making (Friedman 2009). Whether at the organizational or the individual level, whether regarding business schools or the leaders of Wall Street, scholars who have written in *JBE* have questioned the status quo, challenged sloppy thinking (and worse conduct), and advocated for accountability.

Today's business leaders and scholars need to heed the counsel offered by the University of Michigan's Robert Quinn (1996:158), who wrote that whenever leaders "sacrifice their principles for pressure, both they and the system take another step toward slow death." But, like Quinn, *JBE* provides an opportunity to challenge tomorrow's leaders to "accept the necessary risk (of living by correct principles) because it is the right thing to do.... (and to) care enough to risk dying for the organization which would kill them for caring" (Quinn 1996:158). In the world of tomorrow, we are fortunate to have the *JBE* to enable us to be an ethical conscience and a forum for moral conduct in both business and education.

References

Buchholz, R.A., and S.B. Rosenthal. 2005. Toward a contemporary conceptual framework for stakeholder theory. *Journal of Business Ethics* 58:137–148.

Callahan, D. 2004. *The cheating culture: Why more Americans are doing wrong to get ahead.* Orlando: Harcourt Books.

Collins, J. 2001. *Good to great: Why some companies make the leap... and others don't.* New York: HarperCollins.

Covey, S.R., and S.R. Covey. 2004. *The 8th habit: From effectiveness to greatness.* New York: Free Press.

Financial Times. 2010. 45 journals used in FT research rank. http:www.ft.com/intl/cms/s/2/bd9e8b74-fd17-11dd-1103-000077b07658.html#axzz1f3DPqI4D. Accessed 24 June 2010.

Friedman, T.L. 2009. *Hot, flat, and crowded: Why we need a green revolution… and how it can renew America*. New York: Picador.

Pfeffer, J. 2009. Leadership development in business schools: An agenda for change. *Stanford Graduate School of Business Faculty Working Papers*.

Pfeffer, J., and C.T. Fong. 2004. The business school 'Business': Some lessons from the US experience. *Journal of Management Studies* 41(8): 1501–1520.

Quinn, R. E. 1996. *Deep change: Discovering the leader within*. San Francisco: Jossey-Bass.

Reich, R.B. 2011. *Aftershock: The next economy and America's future*. New York: Vintage.

Joanne B. Ciulla

Reflections

Looking back through 30 years of the *JBE*, I was struck by the ways in which it is distinctive. At 30, the *JBE* is arguably the oldest journal that focuses on business ethics. It was born and nurtured over the years by the dedication and hard work of its editors, Alex Michalos and Deborah Poff. Editing a journal takes an enormous amount of time. Most editors perform the job for about 5 years – so to do it over a span of 30 years is extraordinary. All of us in the field owe our thanks to Alex and Deborah for their service to the journal and to business ethics.

Not only is the *JBE* old, it is also plentiful in terms of the number of articles it has published. The journal started with one volume, four issues a year in 1982 and grew to its current seven volumes (28 issues per year). At the end of 2011, the *JBE* had printed 4,747 articles. By opening up so much space for ideas, the *JBE* has provided the field with a bounty of food for thought that was vital to the development of business ethics.

In the 1990s, I served on the editorial board and as book editor. In the early days, the quality of the articles was not always great, but what was lacking in quality was offset by the variety of interesting topics. Today, academia is obsessed with journal statistics about rejection rates, impact scores, etc. One result of this is that many of the articles in the so-called "A" journals are not very interesting. As a matter of fact, I suspect that many academics only read the "top" journals when they are doing research, have an article in them, or are checking to see if their work is being discussed or cited in an article – but I digress. My point is that the diversity of approaches and topics in the *JBE* make it a journal that is appealing to read and welcoming to new voices.

The range of ideas in the *JBE* is partly due to the fact that its articles are by scholars from all over the world. Thirty years ago, most of the publications in business ethics were by North Americans. The internationalization of the *JBE* evolved with remarkable speed, which is testament to the quality and commitment of its editors and reviewers. When necessary, they were willing to go the extra mile and help authors, who were writing in a second language, to effectively communicate their ideas. Without this help, many fine articles by non-native English speakers might not have seen their way into print. And without input from all corners of the world, the field of business ethics would be greatly impoverished.

Many of the articles that were written 20 or 30 years ago are still relevant today. In the first issue of the *JBE*, Alex Michalos wrote that the purpose of the journal is to examine all aspects of business from "the point of view of human action aimed at securing the good life." As Europe and the US work their way through their financial crises, we still ponder some of the same questions about business and capitalism as vehicles for securing the good life. In this respect, one could say that the *JBE* and business ethics scholars have been fighting the good fight even if they have not won the war. Perhaps for this happen, we will have to wait and see what the next 30 years bring. Until then, happy birthday *JBE* and thank you!

Thomas Clarke

The Impact of the Journal of Business Ethics

The *Journal of Business Ethics* is a consistent and rigorous reminder that, "Business decision-making is a moral exercise." Since the origin of commerce, the ethical basis of business has been in question. In the ancient Greek civilization Aristotle could readily distinguish between the basic trade required for an economy to function, and trade for profit which could descend into unproductive usury (Solomon 1992, 321). Most major world religions cast a skeptical eye on business including Christianity, Islam and Confucianism. Shakespeare immortalized the potential venality of business in *The Merchant of Venice*, "All that glitters is not gold." Frentrop (2003) graphically records how greed, speculation, deceit and frequent bankruptcy punctuated the fortunes of the earliest of the great trading companies beginning with the Dutch East India Company.

Adam Smith in 1776 in *The Wealth of Nations* made a withering comment on company management that would echo through the ages: "Being managers of other people's money than their own, it cannot well be expected that they should watch over it with the same anxious vigilance with which the partners in a private co-partner frequently watch over their own ... Negligence and profusion, therefore, must always prevail more or less in the management of the affairs of a joint stock company" (Smith 1976, 264–265).

As technological change advanced with the industrial revolution, there occurred a wider diffusion of ownership of many large companies as no individual, family or group of managers could provide sufficient capital to sustain growth. Berle and Means chronicled the profound implications of this *separation of ownership and control:* 'the dissolution of the old atom of ownership into its component parts, control and beneficial ownership' (1933:8). Berle and Means expressed hope that with this different concept of a corporation there might develop a much wider accountability to the community recognizing the significance of the diffusion of ownership and the concentration of control in the modern corporation: "The economic power in the hands of the few persons who control a giant corporation is a tremendous force which can harm or benefit a multitude of individuals, affect whole districts, shift the currents of trade, bring ruin to one community and prosperity to another" (Berle and Means 1933, 46).

However any hope of a wider sense of fiduciary duty in corporations was eroded away in the later decades of the twentieth century in the Anglo-American world, as capital markets became more aggressive and unstable, and executive compensation was propelled upwards by stock options. A succession of cycles of booming economies followed by market collapse and recession, culminated in 2007/2008 in the first global financial crisis, which was also a crisis in governance and regulation. The most severe financial disaster since the Great Depression of the 1930s exposed the dangers of unregulated markets, nominal corporate governance, and neglected risk management. What also appeared in stark relief was an economic system, corporations and managers singularly lacking in any moral compass.

It has been argued that the dominant logic in this era in both finance and law of *agency theory*, has reduced managers to mere agents of shareholder principals. Agency theory asserts *shareholder value* as the ultimate corporate objective which managers are incentivized and impelled to pursue: "The crisis has shown that managers are often incapable of resisting pressure from shareholders. In their management decisions, the short-term market value counts more than the long-term health of the firm" (Segrestin and Hatchuel 2011, 484; Jordi 2010). Agency theory has become "a cornerstone of … corporate governance" (Lan and Heracleous 2010, 294). As governments, regulators, and financial institutions examined what had gone wrong during the crisis, a new sense of the importance of robust regulation, alert corporate governance, and stronger ethical guidelines became widespread. In effect what is now emerging is an integration of corporate governance, corporate social responsibility and corporate sustainability which potentially offers a new framework for ethical business.

The *Journal of Business Ethics* has helped us navigate through the moral dilemmas and ethical compromises of the last three decades. It has stared into the soul of business and not flinched from offering a courageous and principled account of what it sees.

References

Berle, A., and G. Means. 1933. *The modern corporation and private property.* New Brunswick: Transaction Publishers.

Frentop, F. 2003. *A history of corporate governance.* Brussels: Deminor.

Jordi, C.L. 2010. Rethinking the firm's mission and purpose. *European Management Review* 7: 195–204.

Lan, L.L., and L. Heracleous. 2010. Rethinking agency theory: The view from law. *Academy of Management Review* 35: 294–314.

Segrestin, B., and A. Hatchuel. 2011. Beyond agency theory, a post-crisis view of corporate law. *British Journal of Management* 22: 484–499.

Smith, A. 1976. *The wealth of nations.* Chicago: Chicago University Press

Solomon, R.C. 1992. Corporate roles, personal virtues: An Aristotelean approach to business ethics. *Business Ethics Quarterly* 2(3): 317–339.

Denis Collins

JBE: The Path to More Ethical Organizations and Societies

Journal of Business Ethics (*JBE*) fans, we have much to celebrate. More than 30 years of continuous publication! Because of *JBE*, thousands of excellent articles have been published that may never have seen the light of day in traditional management journals; thousands of professors are writing articles on relevant topics; thousands of professors have been tenured due to the presence of a high quality publication outlet; and hundreds of mainstream journals are now forced to publish ethics-related research. That is quality management-by-objectives!

Social change theory has long established that change is not dependent on 100% participation – the tipping point rests at around 20%. *JBE* provided those of us in that 20% with a vehicle through which we could share ideas with like-minded scholars – and with those who took a little longer to catch on.

JBE is within the core of capitalism. Successful capitalism requires ethical behaviors in the economic and political systems. Adam Smith conceptualized capitalism as an economic system to eradicate poverty. Under mercantilism, constant food shortages meant that my Irish ancestors ate tree bark in the 1700s to survive, which really didn't help matters. Try economic liberty, Smith insisted, bounded within an ethical legal system.

Led by *JBE*, our broad mission remains that of reform – of organizations and by extension society. As an academic field, we are committed to transforming organizations and stakeholders from their current moral status to one that generates even more ethical relationships while serving the interests of owners, employees, customers, suppliers, the community, and the natural environment. What more noble life can one aspire, as the earth spins on its axis and around the sun every day. Well, there is one other major task, personal improvement along Lawrence Kohlberg's levels of moral reasoning.

Remember that first acceptance letter from *JBE*? Mine came in 1987, for an article trying to rescue Aristotle from business ethics ignominy by contextualizing his writing, forgiving him for slavery, and noting that at the core of his writing is a full-fledged communitarian business model, with a central place for liberty. In 1989, *JBE* published my typology on legal condemnation and stakeholder retaliations, which Tom Jones later reconceptualized as an issue's "moral intensity." In between, I published a well-grounded radical reinterpretation of Adam Smith; overlooked now because it was published in a now-defunct journal.

JBE truly blossomed under the guidance of those who gave it birth, Alex Michalos and Deborah Poff. Volumes appeared full of theoretical, empirical, and just overall interesting thoughts. If you wanted to create a special issue around a relevant topic you could do it. All you needed to do was ask, round up the scholars, and do the yeoperson's work of editing them to tell a story. Through this process I made new friends with like minded colleagues concerned about service learning (1996) and how to design and support an ethical economy in Mexico and Central America (2009).

I now look forward to the electronic *JBE* Table of Contents arriving regularly. The last one I received was yesterday – volume 103, issue 1 – which includes discussions and research on an innovative voluntary code of conduct to protect stakeholders; transnational corporate corruption and regulation fluidity; ethics and spirituality in the Latino-Hispanic American reality; and women being more likely to provide socially desirable survey responses; to mention a few.

What an amazing array of leading research! Where would these have been published if *JBE* didn't exist? How further maligned would management education be without these contributions?

We have indeed entered a new age of responsibility and accountability. *JBE* is one entry point on that path, constructed so that we can guide our colleagues from Business Schools and other academic disciplines through the entry ramp. Let's keep at it until ethics is sincerely integrated in all courses and in the design and implementation of all organizations.

Christopher J. Cowton and Russell Sparkes

What, If Any, Has Been the Impact of Your Distinguished Article on Your Career?

As co-authors, our careers have been very different. One (Sparkes) is an ethical investment/socially responsible investment (SRI) practitioner who also writes on the subject, while the other (Cowton) is an academic who has published on a wide variety of subjects but with a focus on financial ethics – though from that background he has also made some contributions to SRI practice.

The article – which was subsequently translated into Italian (Cowton and Sparkes 2005) – was published as part of a special issue on ethical investment and corporate social responsibility (CSR), edited by Grant Michelson, Nick Wailes, Sandra van der Laan and Geoff Frost. The call for papers for the special issue was a helpful prompt to consider the impact of SRI. We had both been involved in SRI from its early days in the UK and we both had, in separate but connected writings, tried to lay the foundations for analysis of, and reflection upon, SRI. Thus the special issue provided an excellent opportunity for the two of us, with our differing career trajectories but closely allied interests, to collaborate and reflect on how SRI might fit into the "bigger picture" of corporate social responsibility (CSR).

What, If Any, Has Been the Impact of the Journal of Business Ethics on the Field of Business Ethics?

The growth in the annual publication quantity of the *Journal of Business Ethics* mirrors, and has helped to make possible, the growth of business ethics as a distinctive and flourishing area of academic research and scholarship. Together with the appearance of other leading journals such as *Business Ethics Quarterly* and *Business Ethics: A European Review*, this growth, and the imposition of appropriate review procedures, has meant that business ethics as an academic field of study has achieved a level of output and sophistication barely imaginable a quarter of a century ago. Gratifyingly, the early commitment to the publication of papers from a wide range of perspectives, especially philosophy and the social sciences, has continued through to the present day, contributing to the vibrancy of business ethics scholarship.

With the continual advances in academic disciplines and evolution of business practices, many questions and opportunities lie before us and much work remains to be done. In the case of the practice of SRI, it has grown to a size where it has a significant impact on global capital markets; for example, 850 investment institutions, whose investment assets amount to $25 trn, are currently signed up to the UN Principles for Responsible Investment. However, beyond assessment of the possible impact of SRI upon investment returns, there is relatively little rigorous academic scrutiny of this activity, and the high level of citation of our article demonstrates the value of the *JBE*'s work in this field.

In SRI and other areas of business ethics, thanks to the contributions of those who have made the *Journal of Business Ethics* what it is today – editors, reviewers and authors – the scholarly community is in a strong position to face the challenges and opportunities of the future. We are pleased that our own paper has been a small part of that process and are proud to have it cited alongside many other fine pieces in this celebratory issue.

Reference

Sparkes, R., and C.J. Cowton. 2005. 'La Maturazione dell Investimento Socialmente Responsabile: Una Revisione del suo Legame con la Responsabilita Sociale d'Impressa'. In *Etica e Finanze*, eds. Signori, S., G. Rusconi, and M. Dorigatti, 222–244. Milano: FrancoAngeli.

Wesley Cragg

The Journal of Business Ethics: Contributions and Impacts

While there are many ways to assess the scholarly contribution the *Journal of Business Ethics* has made to academic research in general and business ethics in particular, one way is to look at the journal's impact on the development of business ethics research over its 30 year life span. Seen from this perspective, the journal's impact can be divided into three phases.

Phase one, the launch of the journal and it first years of operation were ground breaking. The 1970s saw the first wave of post war scandals. Watergate investigations and related inquiries laid bare business practices involving the bribery of foreign public officials, e.g. the Lockheed and the Japanese government, attempted covert collaboration of business with government in pursuit of questionable foreign policy objectives, e.g. ITT and the CIA in Chile, and the exercise of covert and illegal political party funding via off-shore agents again in the United States. Passage of the American Foreign Corrupt Practices Act in response to raising concerns about the ethical standards of some of the world's largest and most prestigious multinational corporations was one response. Another was a growing realization of the need to explore, understand and critically evaluate the ethical dimensions of business conduct. What was lacking at the time, however, was a vehicle for publishing business ethics research. The *Journal of Business Ethics* was a response to that need. It therefore played a foundational role in creating business ethics as an academically and intellectually credible field of scholarly research.

With the launch of the journal came the need to define the scope of the field. Was the field to be understood as narrowly defined by normative methodologies or opened to a wide range of empirical and normative disciplinary and interdisciplinary approaches? Were contributions to the field to be judged against narrow and conventional disciplinary criteria or against a broader range of both disciplinary and interdisciplinary criteria designed to encourage and publish a wide range of approaches? The editorial response was to open the door to a broad range of approaches and strategies judged against a broad range of disciplinary and interdisciplinary editorial guidelines and standards. This editorial stance was then (phase three) to have a decisive impact on the eventual infiltration of business ethics into management education.

Equally important was whether contributions and contributors to the journal would be restricted to narrow geographical, e.g. North American or western, boundaries? Or would it welcome contributions from diverse geographical and cultural backgrounds? Again the editorial decision to choose the latter path played a leadership role in internationalizing the field and discipline of business ethics. These were its central contributions and impacts in phase two.

In its third and current phase, the journal has played a central role in broadening the field of management education to include a focus on values, value based management assumptions and ethics. Over the past two decades, the need to sensitize corporations and their managers, boards of directors, and investors to think more explicitly and articulately about the role of ethics in good management has become increasingly evident. Over the same period it has also become increasingly clear that business schools had an important role to play in this regard. The integration of ethics into management education, however, required an expansion of professional knowledge and skills to include ethics on the part of a broad cross section of management faculty. It also required access to publishing opportunities in recognized scholarly journals willing to publish management oriented business ethics research. Over the past decade, the *Journal of Business Ethics* has provided that vehicle. Its status as a leading research journal in the field has provided the credibility required to ensure the inclusion of business ethics research in the international ranking of business schools, in hiring decisions and in tenure and promotion decisions. Had that not happened, persuading business school faculty to take the field seriously would have been and would continue to be much more difficult.

In summary, the *Journal of Business Ethics* has played a decisive role in launching business ethics as a field of research, defining its boundaries and finally opening the door to the integration of business ethics into the field of business and management education. For all of this, the editors and the Journal are to be congratulated for a remarkable contribution to the world of teaching and scholarship.

Richard T. DeGeorge

Reflections

Some articles that are frequently cited make the reputations of their authors. Some become the publication by which the author is known. This article [The Status of Business Ethics – Past and Future (1987)] was neither in my case. But it did mirror my career and was something of a blueprint for it. The article was published in a Japanese translation, in an Italian translation, in a German anthology on business ethics, and in an American anthology. So it had some international appeal. It was written 25 years ago when business ethics as an identifiable area was only about 10 years old. It presents the history of those 10 years; it claims business ethics is a distinctive field of academic research and attempts to define what the field is and what its limits are; and it outlines what remains to be done. It claims that by 1987 business ethics had reached a plateau. During the previous 10 years a relatively small group formed what was to become the field. The time was obviously ripe because a number of us independently hit on the same ideas and came out with the first textbooks. They all sold well which shows there was a market, and with texts available courses proliferated across the country both in business schools and in philosophy departments. The core group amounted to no more than 20, and those active in the field other than teaching numbered perhaps 50. We soon came to know one another. Despite the cool reception we received from the establishment, those of us working in the area found it exciting. Everything was new, the territory was virgin land, and without consciously doing it we were setting the bounds of the emerging field. The legitimacy of the field was still somewhat in question in 1987 when I wrote the article, and by describing and defining the field of business ethics I was defending what I knew was a controversial claim. My book *Business Ethics* was an attempt to cover the whole field as I described it. I think it is correct to say that by 1987 the field had been defined, the basic work had been done, and that since then development has been incremental, with no big discernible leaps in the academic realm. For businesses the leap probably came in 1991 with the U. S. Federal Sentencing Guidelines for Corporations, which led to wholesale adoption of codes, training programs, corporate ethics officers, and so on. The article describes what I then saw as tasks to be done in the future, and those formed a blueprint for what I did in the ensuing years.

I was on the Editorial Board of the *Journal for Business Ethics* from 1982 to 1992 and appreciate the contributions it has made to business ethics from the start. The *Journal* immediately became the major outlet for those writing in the area and essential reading for all interested in it. The *Journal* grew from one volume (four issues) a year to seven volumes (28 issues) per year. It helped define business ethics, and from the start it has been open to all orientations and disciplines in our multidisciplinary field. It has also filled a gap by publishing the best papers from conferences and meetings as university presses came to shy away from them. Alex Michalos was one of the early pioneers in the field. That he is still editor-in-chief 30 years later proves that he is a marathon runner rather than sprinter. He deserves our thanks and awe.

Robbin Derry

Essay for the Journal of Business Ethics, *Citation Classics Celebration*

This award of distinction falls on my first published article, "An Empirical Study of Moral Reasoning Among Managers". The article, reporting my dissertation research, challenged both Kohlberg's and Gilligan's theories on gender and moral reasoning. Launching into the research, I was eager to hear the voices of women and men describing their experiences of moral conflict and considered moral reasoning at work. The results surprised me, as a third of my interviewees described work lives with no moral conflicts, while those who faced conflicts reported moral reasoning that defied gendered explanations. As I struggled to understand this pattern of unexpected responses, I was forced to disagree with theories I loved and counted on. In doing so, I grew up intellectually, taking responsibility for my findings and interpretations, and making meaning out of confusion. In writing an article from this experience, I staked my claim as an academic. The publication of this article convinced me that I was an accepted member of a community of scholars who shared my interests. This conviction and the sense of belonging, gave me essential confidence as I moved into job interviews, conference presentations, and future research projects. I had an article published in THE journal in my field! For these reasons, this article was certainly the most important of my career, letting me know that I could succeed in meeting the initial standards of the academic world.

The *Journal of Business Ethics* was launched just as I began working on my PhD. I had been trying to figure out how and where I could study business ethics for several years. Even the question of who to talk to about ethics in business was a challenge. The *JBE* was for me a lifeline. Its presence announced the existence, however tenuous and strung out, of a network of people who were sufficiently interested to call themselves business ethicists. For many of us, alone within our academic institutions in studying ethical issues, the arrival of the *JBE* was akin to the delivery of an occasional newspaper to a household on the prairies in the early 1800s. Its reminder of not-aloneness was received with joy and relief. Over the decades since its debut, *JBE* has accepted and published research from authors in dozens of countries, providing each of them perhaps with a similar lifeline connection to the growing community. The role of the journal in establishing the field of business ethics can be described as pioneering, leading, innovating, diversifying, outreaching, and teaching. As it has grown in stature, recognition, breadth and quality, it has continued to make a name for outstanding scholarship in business ethics. I am proud to have been sustained by *JBE* for so long.

Tom Donaldson

What Sex and Business Ethics Have in Common?

It seems odd to compare the field of business ethics to that of human sexual behavior. In the popular imagination one field is topped by a halo of supererogatory, perhaps even "impossible," idealism; while the other is weighed down by popular conceptions of "lower" instincts. But at least in their genesis, key similarities between the two fields are striking. Both fields at their inception were subordinated to the status of non-academic interest. Both were dismissed as popular topics fit for media attention and casual conversation, not for high-level empirical and theoretical research. Both were subject to entrenched prejudices that covertly blocked inquiry. And both in the ensuing decades have proven conclusively how silly that prejudice was.

The catapulting of both fields into serious consideration demanded singular initiatives, ones that galvanized the attention of serious researchers and pointed the way to their possible future. In the instance of sexual behavior, it was the *Kinsey Reports*, two books on human sexual behavior that appeared in 1948 and 1953 (Institute for Sex Research and Kinsey 1953; Kinsey et al. 1948). In the instance of business ethics, it was the launching of the *Journal of Business Ethics* in February of 1982.

The significance of the appearance of a journal devoted to business ethics that immediately attracted hundreds of submissions from academic scholars is difficult to exaggerate. To be sure, other attempts at publication and research in the area of business ethics had been mounted; and to be sure, some scholars had already published business ethics research in other scholarly outlets. But the climate in 1982 inside philosophy departments and sociology departments was inhospitable to novelty, especially novelty addressing commercial motives. Most philosophers and sociologists were disdainful of business ethics largely because of their unexamined assumption that business must march to the drum of profit and nothing else. Interestingly, it was this naïve assumption about business ethics that researchers rigorously put to test in hundreds of later pieces of research published in *JBE.* Inside business schools, the climate was similarly stifling, but for different reasons. Business schools saw "business ethics" as tantamount to business bashing; anyone who believed that business ethics needed special study must be someone who sought to shame business.

Just as now, in 1982 there were four main academic stakeholders in business schools: deans/administrators; students; alumni; and faculty. The first three categories were, and still are, welcoming. The last category, however, i.e., the business school faculty, rallied against business ethics; and as any thoughtful person knows, without faculty support, a field is dead. I recall painfully a day in 1981 when, having been invited by the MBA students of the business school of the University of Chicago, I debated the school's Dean on the question of "Should Business Ethics be taught in Schools of Business?" The dean steadfastly denied that business ethics should be admitted to the business school curriculum; he insisted that its mere teaching reflected a bias against the practice of business. Oddly enough, he also offered the view that teaching business ethics was unnecessary because graduate business schools attracted on average more ethical people than other areas. Throughout, the dean's arguments reflected the prevailing attitudes of business school faculty members that business ethics could never rise to academic maturity.

The only way to persuade some people that a thing *can* be done is to *do* it. The *Journal of Business Ethics* did it, and showed business school faculty that business ethics could come of age by publishing hundreds of pieces of insightful research over the next three decades, both empirical and theoretical. Indeed, the *Journal of Business Ethics* not only succeeded in lowering faculty resistance to teaching and research in business ethics, but opened the door to the appearance of other scholarly journals in the area.

Much has changed since the day in 1981 when I debated the dean at the University of Chicago. Faculty resistance to the study of business ethics in business schools remains but has long since passed the tipping point of barring tenure. And while much remains to be done; we this year celebrate one of the seminal achievements of academe in the last half century: the launching of the *Journal of Business Ethics*.

References

Institute for Sex Research., and A.C. Kinsey. 1953. *Sexual behavior in the human female*. Philadelphia: Saunders.

Kinsey, A.C., W.B. Pomeroy, and C.E. Martin. 1948. *Sexual behavior in the human male*. Philadelphia: W. B. Saunders Co.

Paul Dunn

Corporate Governance Research and the Journal of Business Ethics

The *Journal of Business Ethics* allows researchers to explore non-traditional aspects of business behaviour. It is a forum to "bring something new or unique to the discourse" by approaching the topic "from the moral viewpoint." In the area of corporate governance, for example, this has allowed researchers to focus on the ethical aspects of governance. Furthermore, by having a specialized journal it has allowed the quantity and quality of ethical research into corporate governance to keep pace with the general increasing interest in the field as a whole.

The Web of Science lists 5,394 articles on the topic of corporate governance that have been published in scholarly journals since 1980, 2 years before the *Journal of Business Ethics* began. At that time, the focus was on the legal, financial and economic aspects of corporate governance. In the 1990s, there was an expanded interest in the topic. From 1992 onwards there was a dramatic increase in the number of articles and the number of citations. In 1992, for example, there were 185 citations; in 2010 there were 11,149. The articles that were cited the most were from the *Journal of Political Economy*, the *Journal of Finance*, and the *Journal of Financial Economics*.

Prior to 1992 there were only a handful of cited articles that addressed the social and ethical aspects of governance. But then, as the general interest in governance increased so too did the interest in examining this topic from social and ethical perspectives. The number of articles and citations that focussed on the social aspects rose substantially from only two in 1992 to 1,207 in 2010. A similar pattern occurred with respect to published research that examined ethics and corporate governance. In 1992 there was only one citation; in 2010 there were 329. However, the influential articles that addressed these aspects of corporate governance were not published in the traditional mainstream law, economic and finance journals. Instead the cited articles that adopted a social perspective tended to appear in such journals as *Administrative Science Quarterly*, *The Academy of Management Review* and *The Academy of Management Journal*. The articles that address the ethical aspects of corporate governance were published in the more specialized journals such as *Journal of Business Ethics* and *Business Ethics Quarterly*, as well as *The Academy of Management Review*.

Topics such as corporate governance are many faceted. It is essential that we have a firm understanding of the legal, economic and financial aspects of governance. This is the bedrock for most of our studies. This is why these articles are so well cited. In turn, by standing on their shoulders, we have enlarged the field of study. We have, since 1992, greatly expanded our understanding of the social and ethical aspects of corporate governance. This has been facilitated by having specialized journals that publish new and non-traditional research. The number of quality papers published in *Journal of Business Ethics* on corporate governance has kept pace with the general increase in the number of high quality papers that are published on the topic of corporate governance in general. Hence, there is a critical need for both the traditional journals and the specialized ones. Specialized ones, such as the *Journal of Business Ethics*, enrich our understanding of a variety of business topics. By adopting an ethical perspective we develop a more holistic understanding of business.

Dawn R. Elm

What Has Been the Impact of the Journal of Business Ethics on the Field of Business Ethics?

In the 30 years since its inception, the *Journal of Business Ethics* has had a substantial impact on the field of business ethics. The journal started when the field was beginning to move past mainstream publications in the field of management. There was an increasing need for a journal that reflected the focused research on ethics in business organizations from a philosophical and social science perspective.

Although there continued to be articles on business ethics published in *Academy of Management Review*, *Academy of Management Journal*, *Organizational Dynamics* and *Human Relations*; the value of having a journal that was specifically dedicated to business ethics research was a milestone for the field. It started with articles on topics that were still related to mainstream management research such as organizational influences on individual ethical behavior in public accounting; the ethics of purchasing professionals in government; and the relationship between ethics and job satisfaction. These "bridging" types of articles began a pathway for more targeted research in business ethics which helped to articulate the field as a distinct and valuable realm of study.

The *Journal of Business Ethics* became a primary publication outlet for the research in business ethics and corporate social responsibility with a specific focus on the ethical dimensions of the business world. The scope of the articles moved from bridging management and business ethics to research at the forefront of the field. We began to see articles on the theory of moral personhood, the role of ethics in global corporate culture, and the moral reasoning of managers. The accessibility of these types of articles helped to expand and further define the field.

The journal was instrumental in delineating crucial distinctions within the field of business ethics. By publishing empirical studies, social scientifically oriented studies, philosophical articles and combinations of social science and philosophical articles, the field evolved to consider a wide range of potential research streams that could contribute to continued learning in business ethics.

Today the *Journal of Business Ethics* is one of the top journals in a field which now has several publication outlets. Articles today reflect the evolution of the field to include recent research on meaningful work, corporate citizenship and social responsibility, ethics and aesthetics, moral disengagement, values assessment, and ethical decision making across industry and global dimensions. The evolution and impact of the field is related to the continuing quality of research and the increasing scope of the journal as we move forward from the past 30 years.

Georges Enderle

Four Achievements and One Hopefully in the Making

When Alex Michalos and Deborah Poff started the *Journal of Business Ethics* in February 1982, there was little public discussion about business ethics. If it was not ignored, it was dismissed as an "oxymoron" or a contradiction in itself. As I remember, those working in the field of business ethics had to defend and justify their endeavor, and for those in Europe, the reference to North America that business ethics as an emerging academic field actually existed, did not help much. Over the past 30 years, however, this situation has changed considerably. Ethical issues related to business have become a widespread public concern all over the world.

Obviously, it would be presumptuous to assume that the *Journal of Business Ethics* has brought about this change. Many factors have contributed to this change, not the least corporate scandals, the downsides of globalization and the financial crises in the plural. Nevertheless, it is astounding that the scope of the *Journal* defined by the editors has remained the same and the purpose and the policy set up at the beginning are still relevant today.

What impact has the *Journal* had on the field of business ethics? As such an assessment is quite difficult to make, I would like to highlight four achievements. First, the *Journal,* certainly, has contributed significantly to the promotion and strengthening of public discussion and debate on ethical issues related to business. This is true for academia where the *Journal* with its A-ranking is a crucial publication site for tenure track professors of business ethics in business schools and other academic institutions. But it also holds, to some extent, for the media and business and other organizations searching for clarification and guidance on ethical matters in business. Online access to over 100 volumes provides an immensely rich source of information.

Second, from the beginning, the concept of business ethics has been defined by the *Journal* in a broad sense including "all systems involved in the exchange of goods and services", which are studied from a moral point of view that encompasses "all human action aimed at securing a good life." This means that business ethics has not been reduced to individual ethics as it tends to be in many Anglo-American business ethics discussions. Nor has the *Journal* focused exclusively on ethical issues of the economic system as Continental European traditions used to define business ethics during most of the twentieth century. Rather, this broad understanding proposed by the *Journal* has provided sufficient conceptual room for individual, organizational and systemic ethics in the context of globalization.

Third, the *Journal* has struck a fair balance overall between conceptual, theoretical and empirical articles and advanced a wide variety of methodological and disciplinary perspectives. This ambitious goal is not easy to achieve and, admittedly, has not always been successful. But the *Journal* has not stifled the emerging field of business ethics; it has helped it to grow and has been a trail-blazer over many years.

Fourth, as for the geographic spread represented by the members of the editorial team, the leadership of the *Journal,* first, was located predominantly in the USA and Canada. By 2009, the North American part remained strong, with a substantial increase of Canadian and European members. However, compared to 51 North Americans and Europeans, only five members represented the rest of the world. So Alex and some Asian friends thought the time had come to help fill this gap (along with the *Business Ethics – A European Review* and the *African Journal of Business Ethics*) and launched in 2011 the *Asian Journal of Business Ethics.* All those engaged in the global business ethics movement can only wish that this child will grow as strong and productive as its parent.

Loren Falkenberg

The Evolution of the Journal of Business Ethics

In 1982 the first issue of the *Journal of Business Ethics* was published, and I had my first and only MBA class in business ethics. In the first issue Hoffman and Moore (1982) reviewed a survey sent to over 1,200 colleges and universities, and they found less than 14% of the responding institutions offered business ethics courses. Prior to the launch of the *Journal of Business Ethics* there were only two other journals with a stated mandate of publishing articles on ethical issues: *Business and Society* and *Business and Professional Ethics* Journal.

The minimal level of journal activity in 1982 reflects the level of instruction and discussion that occurred in my single business ethics class. The assigned case was "Nestle Infant Formula", and the class was an unstructured discussion of sales practices by Nestle. The professor ended the discussion by commenting that each of us would have to monitor for potential ethical issues and respond on the basis of our gut feelings. At the time there was not an electronic retrieval system for the professor to access relevant articles from the two available journals. So I am giving the professor the benefit of the doubt, and conclude a lack of access to academic articles and cases limited the introduction of business ethics into my MBA program.

Since my MBA class in 1982 the evolution of the *Journal of Business Ethics* has paralleled the increased value placed on academic research and teaching in business ethics. The number of journals focusing on business and professional ethics has expanded from three in 1982 to greater than 20 journals in 2011. Two journals in 1982 were published in the United States, while *JBE* was published in the Netherlands. The first volumes of the *Journal of Business Ethics* were dominated by American authors, and it wasn't until after 2000 that there was a significant contribution from European researchers. The globalization of the field and the journal are reflected in the balance of authors from Europe, Asia and North America in the 2010 volume.

I examined the growth trajectory of the *Journal of Business Ethics* by reviewing the table of contents of the first issue of each volume. A number of trends in this analysis illustrate the key role the journal has played in the expanding interest and demand for academic articles in business ethics. First, the rapid growth in published issues reflects both the need and interest for articles that further our understanding of the complexities of decision making in business, and the growth in society's expectations for business leaders. The number of articles published per year rapidly expanded, with the journal having only four issues per year in the first 2 years, followed by six issues per year, and increasing to 12 issues (3 volumes) per year in 1988. By 2011 the *Journal of Business Ethics* was publishing seven volumes per year (28 issues) and had published a total of 103 volumes.

The leadership role of the *Journal of Business Ethics* in this evolution is reflected in a recent review of the classification of professional and business ethics journals. Serenko and Bontis (2009) found *Journal of Business Ethics* was one of only two journals classified as "A" level journals; and the *Journal of Business Ethics* is the only business ethics journal on the *Financial Times* top 45 journals list. The parallel in the growth of the *Journal of Business Ethics* and the expansion of business ethics courses is noted in a recent survey of the top 50 global business schools. Over 84% of the top 50 business schools require students to take courses in business ethics, corporate social responsibility and/or sustainable business.

There are many benchmarks one could use to analyze the role a journal plays in the evolution of a field. It only requires a small snapshot of the publication history of the *Journal of Business Ethics* to conclude that the journal has led the field from a nascent academic area in 1982 to a critical field in the study of business decisions.

References

Hoffman, W.M., and J.M. Moore. 1982. Results of a business ethics curriculum survey conducted by the Center for Business Ethics *Journal of Business Ethics* 1: 81–83.

Serenko, A., and N. Bontis. 2009. A citation-based ranking of the business ethics scholarly journals. *International Journal of Business Governance and Ethics* 4: 390–399.

Marilynn Fleckenstein

Reflections on the Journal of Business Ethics

For many years, early in my career, the thought of working in the field of ethics was absolutely frightening. Ethics was messy; metaphysics was much more structured and therefore more appealing to my mind. However, ethics which deals with human behavior has held a prominent, if not central place in the thought of such great intellectuals as Plato, Aristotle and Thomas Aquinas.

In the early 1970s, in the light of the war in Vietnam, the woman's movement and civil rights movement, questions began to be asked about the role and responsibility of business in these social movements. In particular, the questions focused on the production of materials of war, especially chemicals such as Agent Orange. It was in this era that the discipline of business ethics moved to the forefront and began to evolve. However, very few philosophers paid much attention and for the most part, any discussion of ethical concerns was hidden in the business courses themselves.

It was not until the American Assembly of Collegiate Schools of Business insisted that ethics become an integral part of the curriculum that a diverse and sophisticated body of literature began to be formed. The *Journal of Business Ethics* played a significant role in this development as it came to be recognized as providing a high quality venue for the research of scholars.

It was then, that I along with my students were interested in pursuing these questions. But it seemed that the disciplines of management and ethics were worlds apart. How could these be brought together in a coherent and meaningful way? What could ethics contribute to the study of management and what could management say to ethics?

Ethics could provide language and a conceptual framework which one could utilize to discuss the ethical issues that arise in the practice of business management and in the world of business. Ethics teaches through careful reasoning on how one ought to make distinctions and avoid fallacies. Ethics also offers an opportunity to think through complex ethical issues. The study of management introduces one to specialized areas such as employment, intellectual property and international business. It can, then be said that the function of the discipline of business ethics is to delineate the duties and obligations that business persons have precisely as business persons.

Recognizing the growing interest in and importance of the field of business ethics, the three Vincentian universities in the United States, DePaul University, Niagara University and St. John's University, embarked on a collaboration focused on bringing together scholars from business and the humanities with business practitioners for open discussion of the ethical issues involved in the practice of business. An annual conference was begun in the fall of 1994. This conference was conceived as a natural extension of the basic mission and values of these institutions which share a commitment to the vision of St. Vincent DePaul and his dedication to education and service. The annual conference seeks to promote business ethics through excellence in academic research and the practical application of that research to business situations.

The dissemination of the work of this conference has been primarily through *The Journal of Business Ethics,* which generously publishes a special issue each year composed of articles developed from the work of the conference participants. Without this vehicle much of the work produced from the conference might never have found an audience. As we prepare for our 18th conference we are grateful to have this relationship with *The Journal of Business Ethics* and look forward to this collaboration for many years to come.

Gary M. Fleischman

JBE: 30 Years of Enhancing the Public Good of Business Ethical Behavior

Few could have imagined in 1982, *Journal of Business Ethics* (hereafter "*JBE*"), would so transform the literature. It is clear that the goals, purposes, and policy that Alex Michalos championed in his 1982 editorial have been achieved, namely that *JBE* has provided a highly effective public forum for sustained public scrutiny of all ethical issues related to the pure public good of business ethical behavior. In 1982 business ethics was considered a specialized, fringe topic that was mostly ignored. However *JBE* has been instrumental in transforming, developing, and incorporating business ethics into the academic mainstream. Specifically, *JBE* has fostered empirical assessment of the gap between normative ethical rhetoric versus reality in organizations.

The purpose of this essay is to elucidate noteworthy arenas of business ethics inquiry where *JBE* has been especially proficient. Specifically, I focus on *JBE*'s noteworthy contributions relating to (1) ethical dilemmas relating to employee-specific as well as employee-manager interactional dyads; (2) implications for the organizational ethical context; and (3) the impact of business ethics on stakeholders and society as illustrated by contrasting an ethical versus unethical organizational environment.

JBE has transformed our understanding of ethical dilemmas that employees experience in the workplace.

Specifically, much literature has utilized Rest's (1986) moral reasoning framework that involves investigation of ethical sensitivity to recognize ethical dilemmas, ethical judgments about these dilemmas, and intentions to act out ethical judgments. This research underscores the tension between knowing what is moral versus acting morally due to moral agent internal conflicts that may vary based on relativistic versus idealistic ethical ideologies. Conflict may also emanate from the ethical context. Studies have augmented this inquiry with ethical dilemmas that highlight the employee-manager dyadic relationship. In short, literature promulgates that management has a nontrivial impact on subordinates, and the "tone at the top" is key to institutionalizing the organizational ethical context.

JBE has made a superlative impact on the field by using empirical finding implications to pragmatically offer solutions to management. *JBE* therefore bridges the academic versus professional chasm by offering pragmatic training suggestions to enhance the ethical context, including ideas relating to the content and enforcement of codes of conduct. These implications may involve building organizational focus on corporate social responsibility, sustainability, and corporate governance initiatives.

JBE has elucidated the interactive relationships among employees, management, and the organizational environment, which ultimately impacts stakeholders and society. For example, research involving employee deviance provides excellent contrast in terms of these interactions compared with those of ethical organizations. Contexts tolerant of bullying, narcissism, or Machiavellianism are often characterized by turnover, low productivity, and poor job satisfaction and employee emotional and physical health, ultimately impairing stakeholders and society. Contrast employees who shape quality ethical contexts and harmonization of individual and organizational morals by exemplifying extra role and altruistic behaviors. Research concludes these employees are healthier, happier, have high job satisfaction, and are productive, leading to business profitability, greater philanthropy and corporate social responsibility, and reductions in poverty, all benefiting stakeholders and society.

During the past 30 years *JBE* has fostered a forum of sustained public scrutiny that has encouraged research to bridge the gap between normative ideals versus reality. Implications of this research provide management tools to enhance the ethical environment and behavior. Future research should focus on managerial decision-making ethical dilemmas, because managers are key drivers of moral behavior in the workplace, and are responsible for the ethical tone. Strengthening the ethical context makes employee's lives better and more productive. This enhances the pure public good of business ethical behavior, which benefits society, the ultimate goal of *JBE* for the past 30 years.

Robert C. Ford and Woodrow D. Richardson

Reflections

In the late 1980s, Woody and I were teaching and researching social responsibility, business ethics, and decision making at the University of Alabama at Birmingham. Since I was interested in the intersection of ethical and decision theories, I had sought out and organized the literature on ethical decision making. In early 1990, my review of this literature led me to develop a model of ethical decision making that I submitted to the *Academy of Management Review.* Unfortunately, the same month I submitted my paper, *AMR* published an article by Thomas Jones that had many overlapping points with my work. The reviewers rightly stated that my paper did not add enough new to the literature to justify publication. Nonetheless, I felt that the review of the literature done to support its arguments was so extensive that others interested in this topic might benefit from the work. Woody had been working along a similar line of research, and with his assistance we updated and organized this literature into the article that appeared. This article marked the end of our intense interest in the topic as we moved to new universities (me as chair of hospitality management at University of Central Florida and Woody as faculty at Ball State) and different research agendas (me as author of multiple works on service management and Woody as a case writer).

We are pleased to learn of the value of the article to other scholars who have benefited from the effort we put into accumulating and categorizing this still growing literature. The 550 plus cites reported by Google Scholar as of this writing is a rewarding testimonial to its value. In the concluding section of the article we noted that the review of literature revealed many interesting research opportunities and issued a call to scholars to investigate them. It is clear that many took advantage of that call. We are delighted that so many colleagues have benefited from our work.

R. Edward Freeman

The Importance of the Journal of Business Ethics

The Journal of Business Ethics has had a profound impact on the teaching and scholarship in business ethics, and in business schools. From its inception the *Journal* has taken a rather broad approach to what counts as business ethics. It has always published more than simply the latest analytic philosopher's analysis of a particular problem in business. The *Journal* has encouraged empirical research as well as theoretical work for many years. Today we see other business ethics journals also taking up this approach that was pioneered by *JBE*.

As the ratings mania has swept business schools, especially in the US and Canada, *JBE* has maintained its place as a premier publication outlet in the *Financial Times* and *Business Week* rankings. It also counts for a number of schools who have very strict rules about publications "counting" for academic issues such as grants and leaves.

A third way that *JBE* has been important to the development of our discipline is through the publication of special issues that are often the result of conferences all over the world. I have benefited greatly from reading the work of scholars from all over Asia. I'm afraid I would not have such access to their work if not for *JBE*. Conference publications can be a tricky business, but erring on the side of providing a voice to many, is a great contribution, that few journals are willing to undertake.

Finally, *JBE* has been an important outlet for me personally. Here I mean not only the papers that I have been fortunate enough to publish there, but also that some of the most sharply critical papers on stakeholder theory have appeared in the pages of *JBE*. These papers have often moved my colleagues and I to write responses, and even where we have not, the papers have made the development of stakeholder theory much more interesting and exciting. In a recent book, *Stakeholder Theory: The State of the Art* (Cambridge 2010), my colleagues (Jeffrey Harrison, Andrew

Wicks, Bidhan Parmar, and Simone DeColle) and I referred to more than 20 papers from the pages of *JBE*, and there were many more references that were connected to research programs that have appeared in the *journal*. In an even more recent book, *Stakeholders Matter: A New Paradigm for Strategy and Society* (Cambridge 2011), Sybille Sachs and Edwin Ruhli refer to more than 30 articles from *JBE*. That the *Journal of Business Ethics* has had a remarkable impact on the development of stakeholder theory is unquestionable.

Donelson R. Forsyth

Judging the Morality of Business Practices: The Influence of Personal Moral Philosophies: 20 Years Later

The theory of personal moral philosophies stole quietly into the world of ethics in the early 1980s. At that time most psychologists who studied morality were cognitive developmentalists interested in age-related changes in morality. The theory of ethics positions, in contrast, focused on adults' moral thoughts, actions, and judgments, but most of the initial empirical work was conducted with young adults in laboratory settings. These early studies tested basic predictions about the relationship between individual differences in idealism and relativism and morality and were published in good journals in the field of social psychology and personality, but the theory gained few adherents and generated little empirical attention.

That changed in 1992 with the special issue of *Journal of Business Ethics* (*JBE*) edited by Robert Giacalone dealing with the behavioral aspects of business ethics. Dr. Giacalone was intrigued by the laboratory-based studies of ethics positions and believed that the theory could be usefully applied in organizational and business situations. Buoyed by his optimism, I wrote "Judging the Morality of Business Practices: The Influence of Personal Moral Philosophies" to describe the basic theory, summarize the evidence up to that point, and point out possible applications.

That publication gave the theory new life. The paper offered investigators a way to deal with a fundamental problem in ethics: moral diversity. Even people who agreed on such matters as politics, fine dining, and the weather often disagree when the conversation turns to issues of ethics. Investigators searching to explain some of this variance among individuals in terms of moral outlook turned to the pages of *JBE* and found the Ethics Position Questionnaire (EPQ). The EPQ provided one way, of many, to conceptualize this variation and researchers used it to explain differences in moral thought and action in various business contexts, workers' responses to a peer's wrongdoing, variations in codes of ethics in different cultures and corporations, sex differences in moral outlook, the use of relatively unscrupulous accounting practices, consumers' reactions to various marketing ploys, leaders' moral values, and so on. By 2008, when my colleagues and I collected up the findings from various studies for a meta-analytic review (Forsyth et al. 2008), we identified over 200 publications that cited the original 1992 paper and used the EPQ to study over 30,000 people in 29 different countries. The publication of the theory in *JBE* was a career highlight, for it proved to be the catalyst that transformed a relatively unknown theory into a familiar and well-studied one.

The secret to the paper's impact lies in the scope, defined focus, and quality of the *Journal of Business Ethics*. Previous publications in psychological journals interested only a few researchers, whereas *JBE*'s boundary spanning reach across disciplines pushed the theory into prominence in the field of ethics. *JBE* is theoretical yet applied, both conceptually and empirically rigorous, and open to new ideas and orientations. Its focus is narrower than any disciplinary journal – on ethics, specifically – but it is this focus that heightens its impact. When *JBE* first began publishing papers, those who studied ethics published their results in various professional journals, for there was no one primary outlet for the field. Now, the empirical study of ethics has emerged as a field in its own right, in part in response to growing interest in the business world in issues of integrity, justice, and ethics, but also because of the existence of an excellent journal that "brings something new or unique" to the study of ethics.

Reference

Forsyth, D.R., E.H. O'Boyle, and M.A. McDaniel. 2008. East meets West: A meta-analytic investigation of cultural variations in idealism and relativism. *Journal of Business Ethics* 83: 813–833.

Elisabet Garriga and Domenec N. Mele

Reflections

First of all, Prof. Elisabet Garriga and Prof. Domènec Melé would like to congratulate the *Journal of Business Ethics* for its 30 years and they hope that it will have another 30+ years, and so, they will have more opportunities to contribute to the dialogue about business ethics by publishing there.

Both authors think that the *Journal of Business Ethics* has a high impact on the business ethics field for its rigorous, relevant and diverse ethical research, with both theoretical and empirical approaches, tackling the central and main ethical debates. In their view this journal contributes to building a serious discourse and dialogue in business ethics. Regarding the field of Corporate Social Responsibility, this journal has tried to emphasize its ethical perspective, and hopefully it will continue in this way.

Due to the journal's great impact, the article "Corporate Social Responsibility Theories: Mapping the Territory" (Garriga and Melé 2004) has had a big influence on the professional career of the authors. The main impact on the first author's career, Professor Elisabet Garriga, has been at the level of acknowledgement, reputation and expertise in the CSR field. In her own words:

"Since its publication, the paper has given me a great amount of recognition. When I am attending a conference, it is always a pleasure to find a doctoral student who says to me "Thank you for your paper, it helped to make sense of the field of CSR" or simply a Professor telling me "I liked your paper a lot". It truly makes me happy. Nevertheless, my main source of satisfaction is when I notice that my research has helped others to develop their own research agenda, which consequently has helped to move the CSR field forward".

This paper also gave Professor Garriga a reputation in the field of CSR and the privilege to work with some important authors of CSR theories and to continue this integrative approach based on a relational view of the CSR concept (accepted paper for publication forthcoming). Furthermore, the first author has been frequently invited to review articles on CSR and to become a reviewer of several journals; the first journal in doing so and the most appreciated was the *Journal of Business Ethics*. In addition, this paper helped her to advance her research agenda by identifying new innovative areas of research in the field of Corporate Social Responsibility, and new opportunities for publishing have arisen. For example, her article "Cooperation in Stakeholder Networks: Firm's 'Tertius Iungens Role" (2009) presented a new approach to stakeholder cooperation based on network theory where the research up to then was scant.

The article has provided the second author, Professor Domènec Melé, a reputation as an expert on Corporate Social Responsibility Theories. He was invited to write a chapter on this topic in *The Oxford Handbook of Corporate Social Responsibility* (2008a) and has often been invited to review papers on the theoretical foundations of CSR. The idea of an integrative approach, suggested in this article, has inspired his further work, including a special issue of the *Journal of Business Ethics* (see Melé 2008b, for the introductory editorial) and two books (Melé 2009, 2012), in which ethics is at the core of corporate responsibility.

References

Garriga, E., and D. Melé. 2004. Corporate social responsibility theories: Mapping the territory. *Journal of Business Ethics* 53(1–2, August): 51–71.

Garriga, E. 2009. Cooperation in stakeholder networks: Firms' 'Tertius Iungens' role. *Journal of Business Ethics* 90:623–637.

Melé, D. 2008a. Corporate social responsibility theories. In *The oxford handbook of corporate social responsibility*, eds. Crane, A., A. Williams, D. Matten, J. Moon, and D.S. Siegel, 47–82. Oxford/New York: Oxford University Press.

Melé, D. 2008b. Integrating ethics into management. *Journal of Business Ethics* 78(3): 291–297.

Melé, D. 2009. *Business ethics in action. Seeking human excellence in organizations.* New York: Palgrave-MacMillan.

Melé, D. 2012. *Management ethics: Placing ethics at the core of good management.* New York: Palgrave-MacMillan.

Robert A. Giacalone

On the Impact of the Journal of Business Ethics

The impact of the *Journal of Business Ethics* has been significant, for it has engaged in a systematic expansion of the field, primarily by focusing on three areas: behavioral business ethics, interdisciplinary research, and internationalization of the journal.

First, at a time when business ethics was primarily philosophically driven and focused on ethical theory, it took the courageous and ground-breaking approach of accepting papers on behavioral business ethics. This approach has had considerable implications on the development of the field in that it shifted the focus from a strictly philosophical to a behavioral approach. In turn, this shift is now witnessed in other journals and in how we view business ethics inquiry. More critically, with this behavioral approach, we see a closer alignment with what organizations want. With no intent to undermine philosophical approaches, the reality is that philosophical approaches without the ability to alter and measure behavioral change would leave us far removed from the realities of organizational life. Because measurement has become a reality in the field, we have legitimized our discipline with practitioners by speaking the assessment language that organizations understand. But with this shift has come an underlying concern, however, that a great deal of what we now see as business ethics is often heavily focused on organizational behavior and psychological concepts that ultimately may turn the study of business ethics into a kind of "ethics light," where organizational behavior and psychology are really the focus.

Second, what has characterized the *Journal* over the years is the breadth of its offerings. In it, business ethics grew to be more broadly defined, to include areas of research and practice that were beyond the traditional strictures. Indeed, what we have seen is an interdisciplinary compendium of business ethics work in which both the criterion and the predictor variables have been expanded. It is a field now where, for example, one can easily recognize that the unethical components of deviance, the predictive values of positive organizational scholarship variables and spirituality are connected to business ethics concerns. Here, too, a bit of unease emerges because the major focus so often may not be business ethics criterion and predictor variables, but variables largely in other research disciplines. For example, articles focused primarily on organizational approaches to justice, using mostly citations from non-ethics journals, are more about organizational behavior and less about ethical issues. Striving for a true interdisciplinary integration will be essential.

Finally, at a time when research on organizations had a more North American slant, the *Journal* remained steadfast in publishing the work of researchers across the world. This has had the important impact both of internationalizing the field and of expanding the worldview of what business ethics and social responsibility are all about. With the different religious, cultural, economic, language, values, and historical approaches emergent in the *Journal*, a confluence of what the field could be has emerged in the often disparate approaches of these international authors.

Where does the *Journal of Business Ethics* go from here? The answer to that question will be the challenge for the *Journal* over the next 30 years and 100 volumes. Other journals in the area have increasingly emulated the pattern that the *Journal* proffered for the field. So the issue will be what distinctive additions the *Journal* will bring forth to lead the field. How it evolves to be different, and in so doing, challenges researchers and educators in business ethics and social responsibility to grow, should be the central question that guides it.

Kevin Gibson

Reflections

The *Journal of Business Ethics* by itself may not have made the corporate world more moral: However, it has provided us with language and frameworks that have changed the narrative about business actions and leaves me optimistic about the future. At the time the *Journal* was first published, the term Ethics had a whiff of remedial Sunday school. The emergent texts in the area concentrated on the philosophical foundations and some of the special problems for people in business, such as insider trading, bribery, coercive sales techniques and whistleblowing, with a strong implication that judicious application of an appropriate moral theory would solve the issue. While those sorts of problems are still with us, we now have a much richer and sophisticated moral discourse about business activity that draws on empirical research, systems approaches, post-modern and feminist literature, and a broader philosophical base that recognizes the importance of metaphysics and epistemology in these discussions. Moreover, the dialogue now actively involves non-Western voices. For example, 20 years ago, the corporate mission statement, if there was one, probably had no references to stakeholder welfare, sustainability, or social responsibility, whereas they have now become an integral part of business thinking. The change in the story we tell ourselves about business has expanded in no small part due to the wide mission and scope of *JBE*. The *Journal* has been a valuable asset in providing an integrative forum that brings together the quantitative and qualitative research which grounds speculative ideas. Indeed, the legitimacy of the *Journal* now underwrites a discourse in business, professional training and scholarship that has emerged during its history.

The *Journal* also has a direct impact on my professional life. I am employed at a University that maintains its faculty should be teacher/scholars. This description is not exclusive: it means that the institution expects that research should be incorporated into the classroom – that is, research from across the field, not just my personal interests. Not unusually, administration demands effectiveness in teaching in a subject that is notoriously hard to evaluate. The fact that the *Journal* includes pedagogical articles along with research means that it is my resource of first resort.

Dennis A. Gioia

Pinto Fires and Personal Ethics: 20 Years Before and After Publication

If you have read my tale of the Pinto Fires saga, published 20 years ago in *JBE* in 1992, you might remember that the story actually began 20 years before that, when I joined Ford in 1972. The fact is that it took me until 1982 to come clean and acknowledge to my Penn State colleagues that I was a central figure in the case. Then it took until 1986 to write up the teaching case about it, and yet another 5 years to write the *JBE* article about the experience. You might say I was a little slow in coming out. So, what has happened since the publication of the public confession?

In the wake of the article, what happened initially was akin to a small public hanging. The piece received quite a bit of attention from fellow academics – people attuned to a juicy story, especially if it has a whiff of corporate misdeed. Some were appalled at my decisions, disappointed in my actions, and took the occasion to make a few (somewhat sanctimonious) pronouncements. One even threw me in the same rogues' gallery as fraud artists like Joe Jett and Michael Milken. Some others thought my analysis in terms of cognitive scripts that were missing an ethical component, thus leading to a lack of ethical awareness, was disingenuous, self-serving and evasive. Others thought the description of how decision making in organizations actually happens was revealing, if troubling. To be fair, though, many thought the account compelling and the explanations enlightening, particularly because they revealed the complex interplay of cognition, information overload, organizational culture/knowledge/learning, and corporate ethics and social responsibility. The academic conversation was pretty spirited for a while. Then, after about 2 years, Pinto Fires dropped out of sight, its half-life apparently exhausted, my 15 min of fame (infamy, actually, in some peoples' eyes) apparently over.

Around the year 2000, the damn thing came roaring back. I started getting calls from all kinds of journalists wanting my commentary on recalls – and not just car recalls, all recalls (hair dryers!). I became a go-to guy – an instant expert reincarnated to feed the media beast. Why? Why all this sudden new interest? Initially it was a mystery… until I realized that all the renewed attention was because of the rise of the Internet and Google's little invention. All you had to do was google "Pinto fires" and my name popped up. Now everybody knew my name. Lord, what had I done with a well-intended, unwitting publication in *JBE?*

Then in 2005 *Fortune* magazine was celebrating its 75th anniversary. As part of their historical coverage, they formed an editorial team whose charge was to nominate the 20 most significant decisions – good or bad – in *Fortune*'s 75 years. Their list was filled with stunningly successful decisions (e.g., Sears' big box stores; Pan Am's initiation of international flights, IBM's 360 computer, CitiBank's ATMs, etc.). Only a very few decisions were nominated as debacles, one of which was … Ford's decision "to let the Pinto explode." Oh, good grief. Predictably enough, the editors googled Pinto and got two insider names: Lee Iacocca (President of Ford at the time of the Pinto case) and me. Iacocca had some savvy and declined to comment when contacted. Not me. I sang like a canary. At one point, I let slip that when I was at Ford, we referred to the depot where failed parts were returned as the "Chamber of Horrors." My, how they dearly loved that quote. In the end, though, *Fortune* treated me fairly (and even cited *JBE* in the article), but it was quite the experience.

Around this same time Linda Trevino arranged to videotape me teaching the Pinto Fires case to a class. So now if you google "Pinto Fires, the Living Case," you can get the whole story on DVD too. And to think, I owe it all to *JBE.* Was it worth it? Maybe. Perhaps. Probably. Even if I still get calls from people who, 40 years after the fact and 20 years after the article (but who only recently read it)), still want to take me to task for my role in this damnably visible case.

Kenneth Goodpaster

Reflections

RE: What, if any, has been the impact of the *Journal of Business Ethics* on the field of business ethics?

JBE has been a venue for practical reflection and reflective practice

For the past 4 years, I have been shepherding an ambitious book project, a history of corporate responsibility in the United States, to be published by Cambridge University Press during 2012. One of the most profound "takeaways" from this philosopher's journey through more than two centuries of business history is the *tenacity* of the American mindset when it comes to the moralization of the modern corporation. Despite numerous occasions for disappointment and discouragement over the behavior of business toward its stakeholders, and despite clearly articulated alternative social arrangements from Marxism in the nineteenth century to democratic forms of socialism in the twentieth, the pursuit of *business ethics* by thought-leaders and practitioners in America is remarkable. For the very idea of business ethics as a field of thought and practice *presupposes* a shared conviction that the institutions inhabiting a market economy are *capable* of ethical responsibility, not simply legal compliance. In the United States, business scandals and tragedies involving workers or consumers or local communities have always given rise to protests, regulations, legislation, and judicial discipline; but it is significant that they have *not* led to revolution or to the dismantling of the private sector. Instead, the American public has demanded higher levels of business ethics. This persistence appears to be culturally embedded in ways that are less evident in other countries.

By the end of the 1970s, the field of business ethics had taken on new energy with the academic alliance of empirical work on corporate responsibility by management scholars and normative work by philosophers, theologians, and others in the humanities. This new energy needed a multi-disciplinary outlet for peer-reviewed research, for "engaging the profession." The founders of the *Journal of Business Ethics* responded to this need with courage, generosity and a spirit of servant leadership. Over the past 30 years, *JBE* has displayed noteworthy breadth in its editorial criteria, providing a venue for professional contributions from an array of disciplines including all of the social sciences, the liberal arts, and professional studies. Without gatekeepers for the exchange of practical reflection and reflective practice, a hybrid field like business ethics could not have matured and cannot continue to grow. The contribution and impact of *JBE* lies in this "exchange" space. I have seen in its regular and special issues innovative work that would not have found entry into the business ethics conversation but for the existence of this journal's editorial philosophy and publication criteria.

Speaking as a subscriber since Volume 1 Number 1, as an editorial board member and manuscript reviewer for well over 20 years, and as a contributing author of several articles in the *Journal of Business Ethics*, I can say with confidence that *JBE's* impact has been salutary. Formidable competitors have emerged, to be sure, with distinctive strengths and standards, but these rivals are not threats to *JBE*; indeed, they represent its legacies. Congratulations!

Irene M. Gordon

The Impact of the Journal of Business Ethics

Several of us, long associated with the *Journal of Business Ethics* (*JBE*), have been asked to address the question: "What impact has the *JBE* had on the field of business ethics?" I suspect our collective answers will reflect common themes. From my perspective, there are three important effects.

Perhaps the most visible effect is *JBE* being listed on the *Financial Times* 45 (previously the FT 40). The *JBE* provides a respected outlet for business ethics research that is cross-, multi- and inter-disciplinary. *JBE* is a journal that allows people from inside and outside of business academe to publish ethics related articles. As evidence to support my statement, I looked at my own university for the period

November 2008 through October 2011. From a library database search, I found eight articles published during this period (Robinson et al. 2011; Gordon 2011; Abramson 2011; Barnea and Rubin 2010; Herremans et al. 2009; Boutilier 2009; Poitras and Meredith 2009; Peloza et al. 2009). These eight Simon Fraser University contributions came from the disciplines of accounting (Gordon), finance (Poitras and Rubin), marketing (Meredith and Peloza), strategy (Abramson), technology and operations management (Bertels) and from one non-business discipline (Boutilier). The breadth of disciplines represented reflects the interest in ethics and the existence of the *JBE* clearly meets an important function and need within the community of business researchers working on business and ethics.

More specifically related to my field of accounting, the *JBE* has provided many of us interested in both accounting and business ethics an important outlet for our research. I find that some accounting research questions of interest to me are unlikely to be published in some of the accounting discipline's journals. *JBE* allows for broader types of accounting-related research to be published.

JBE supplies articles that serve as valuable sources of educational material that may be included in our teaching. I have personally used *JBE* articles in preparing for seminars and for assigned course readings. In particular, I have used articles directly related to ethics as well as articles specifically focused on Corporate Social Responsibility (CSR). Students have benefited from the quality of the research and the types of questions *JBE* researchers ask. The chosen articles offer areas for debate and questions that make students think beyond disciplinary boundaries. These challenges allow our business students opportunities to grow and expand their knowledge and understanding of business ethics.

Without the *JBE* business ethics research would have been poorer over the past 30 years. We have benefited from the *JBE* as a respected research outlet and an important source of educational material for business students.

References

Abramson, N.R. 2011. Kierkegaardian confessions: The relationship between moral reasoning and failure to be promoted. *Journal of Business Ethics* 98(2): 199–216.

Barnea, A., and A. Rubin. 2010. Corporate social responsibility as a conflict between shareholders. *Journal of Business Ethics* 97(1): 71–86.

Boutilier, R. 2009. Globalization and the careers of Mexican knowledge workers: An exploratory study of employer and worker adaptations. *Journal of Business Ethics* 88(Supplement 2): 319–333.

Gordon, I.M. 2011. Lessons to be learned: An examination of Canadian and U.S. Financial accounting and auditing textbooks for ethics/governance coverage. *Journal of Business Ethics* 101(1): 29–47.

Herremans, I.M., M.S. Herschovis, and S. Bertels. 2009. Leaders and laggards: The influence of competing logics on corporate environmental action. *Journal of Business Ethics* 89(3): 449–472.

Peloza, J., S. Hudson, and D.N. Hassay. 2009. The marketing of employee volunteerism. *Journal of Business Ethics* 85(Supplement 2): 371–386.

Poitras, G., and L. Meredith. 2009. Ethical transparency and economic medicalization. *Journal of Business Ethics* 86(3): 313–325.

Robinson, M., A. Kleffner, and S. Bertels. 2011. Signaling sustainability leadership: Empirical evidence of the value of DJSI Membership. *Journal of Business Ethics* 101(3): 493–505.

Michelle Greenwood

What, If Any, Has Been the Impact of the Journal of Business Ethics on the Field of Business Ethics?

In the academic area of business, dominated by empirical and positivistic journals, the *Journal of Business Ethics* (affectionately known as *JBE*) offers a crucial alternative: the exploration of philosophical and normative interpretations of business dilemmas. Unique amongst journals, it deals with a broad range of ethical issues as they pertain to business, offering opportunities to emerging scholars and those new to the business ethics, whilst at the same time attracting senior and expert specialists from the field.

JBE is frequently characterized in terms of both its breadth and its proliferation. The journal embraces expansive and liberal interpretations of ethical theories; diverse methodological approaches and heuristics; and wide-ranging praxis in varied organizational settings. The journal publishes many regular and special issues each year, has raised the profile of business ethics in the broader academy, and is widely cited both within the field business ethics and more broadly. However, as noted by Phillips et al. (2003) with regard to one of the major subjects of *JBE* – stakeholder theory – such exposure can be at once a project's making and its weakness.

It is frequently commented that the best articles in *JBE* surpass those published elsewhere, but that they are diluted by the publication in the journal of many less significant papers. Yet, it is the accessibility of *JBE* that allows for varied, non-traditional and dissenting voices. Based, in part, on well-positioned rankings (especially its FT45 listing) and impact factors, *JBE* has become a magnet for scholars subjected to the vicissitudes of journal ranking for research assessment exercises. Research not conceived or framed in relation to business ethics is now commonly submitted and in many cases published. The manner in which this further opening of the gates strengthens or dilutes the journal – and the field more generally – remains to be seen.

Whilst the sheer quantity of *JBE* issues published per year is a conversation stopper, what rarely gets mentioned is the large number of special issues the journal supports. Special issues allow for deep exploration of hitherto neglected topics and involvement in the editorial process of scholars with fresh or atypical perspectives. The forthcoming special issue on Ethics and HRM (human resource management) provides a case in point. As an ethical laden project within business and society, and a positive discipline within academia, HRM requires comprehensive and rigorous ethical analyses. *JBE* is laying the groundwork for this endeavor, bringing critical and ethical exploration to both scholarship and education in HRM.

JBE has shown leadership in specific areas of business ethics scholarship. Although every commentator is likely to have his or her own favorites, the areas of religious ethics, codes of conduct, and geographically specific studies have been identified as particular strengths of the journal. On a personal note, I regard highly *JBE's* support of two important developments in the field of business ethics: the refinement of stakeholder theory, in particular considerations of the moral treatment of stakeholders (Freeman 2010; Freeman et al. 1988); and the development of CSR theory, in particular the political conception of corporate social responsibility (Palazzo and Scherer 2006).

Being involved with *JBE* is synonymous with being part of the study of business ethics. It is hard to imagine that there is one researcher, one student, one syllabus, one (academically-read) practitioner with interest in the field that has not in some way been impacted by the journal.

References

Freeman, R.E. 2010. Managing for stakeholders: Trade-offs or value creation. *Journal of Business Ethics* 96(0): 7–9.

Freeman, R.E., D.R. Gilbert, and E. Hartman. 1988. Values and the foundations of strategic management. *Journal of Business Ethics* 7(11): 821–834.

Palazzo, G., and A. Scherer. 2006. Corporate legitimacy as deliberation: A communicative framework. *Journal of Business Ethics* 66(1): 71–88.

Phillips, R., R.E. Freeman, and A.C. Wicks. 2003. What stakeholder theory is not. *Business Ethics Quarterly* 13(4): 479–502.

Sally Gunz

The Impact of the Journal of Business Ethics on Business Ethics

These observations consider the impact of the *Journal* on the academic community. While the *Journal* undoubtedly influences business practice, I am simply ill equipped to measure that effect.

When asked to contribute to this collection I sought counsel from those whom I admire in the accounting ethics discipline. It is remarkable the consistency in response and how these coincide with my own thoughts. To understand the observations, we must begin by acknowledging a key underlying tension. Most (perhaps all) business and professional programs report the examination of ethical issues to be an important element of their curricula. However, consider more closely the two critical exemplars of 'commitment' in an academic environment: mandatory courses and tenure track positions. Now examine the woeful evidence of either in a large proportion of business and professional programs at least across North America. Business ethics is really important, but not *so* important as to replace a course or tenured position in marketing, or accounting, or operations research, etc. Instead we 'integrate' ethics across many courses – not a bad idea if done right, but is it? The alternative to 'right' is a class that is abandoned when time is tight or subject matter that is signaled to be secondary to primary course content.

The above tension is reflected in leading academic business journals. Until recently, few would accept an ethics article to be relevant to their mandates. Advice to junior faculty interested in ethics was consistently: 'wait till after tenure' and even then understand your work may be marginalized by your colleagues. In this context, consider the insight of Deborah Poff and Alex Michalos in establishing the *JBE* and thereby giving business ethicists a legitimate arena for their work. Looking back at my own CV, I see a *JBE* article as one of my first. And I remember with real gratitude the encouragement from Alex to submit a paper, ironically entitled "Are Academics Committed to Accounting Ethics Education?" 1998.

This is, however, part only of the contribution made by the *JBE*. It is genuinely international where many of the leading business academic journals are unashamedly North American-centric. It continues to defend a broad subject mandate. And perhaps most importantly, it is effectively overseeing a mandate for increased quality without discouraging innovation or creativity. The inclusion of the *JBE* in the Financial Times 40 (now 45) was a landmark in the *Journal's* history. This ranking signals value to even the most reluctant academic administrator.

Two fields of scholarly interest further illustrate the *JBE* contribution. In the past decade academic interest in corporate social responsibility has increased dramatically. A more hidebound journal would require submissions in an emerging field to fit within the constraints of an existing one. The *JBE* created first one and then two sections to address the demands of the academic community. Recent financial crises have led to a renewed interest in ethical behaviour at both reporting and market levels and the increased volume of submissions resulted in a separate finance section. This, however, is not a journal jumping on academic 'bandwagons' with no respect for quality. The demands on authors for improved theory and methodology are constant and the days of applying one successful tool to a variety of contexts with little thought to relevance are long since gone.

In sum: the impact of the *JBE* is immeasurable to those working in the business ethics discipline. This journal is our academic 'home' and one that tests us and demands much of us. It has earned its FT ranking and for this we have all benefited. It is an important step to establishing business ethics as an accepted component of all business and professionals programs, not just in thought but also in actuality.

Christine A. Hemingway and Patrick W. Maclagan

What Has Been the Impact, If Any, of Your Citation Classic on Your Career? And What Has Been the Impact, If Any, of the Journal of Business Ethics on the Field of Business Ethics?

An apparent dualism between structure and agency, reification or voluntarism, is at the essence of what has exercised the minds of philosophers since the ancients (Rabinow 2000). And whilst the philosophy of critical realism regards this as a non-duality, with structural and agential forces, in turn, informing and transforming the other, our own presupposition regarding personal values as a driver of CSR was congruent with this epistemological perspective. We have always regarded the impact of personal values as an operating mechanism which, despite structural pressures, is causally efficacious through judgemental rationality and reflexivity (Archer 2000). Social change *is* possible, albeit tremendously difficult. Thus, in the context of CSR, this focus on individuals' actions could range from senior managers' influence over policy formulation to the opportunities which may be open to all staff for the exercise of discretion, despite their position in the organisational hierarchy.

Indeed, we both felt that personal values as a driver of CSR had largely been overlooked in the CSR literature, which has tended to emphasise the more obvious economic drivers of both governments and corporate reputation management. It cannot be a coincidence that both of us – at an earlier stage in our respective careers – were employed for a decade or more in industrial management. Perhaps this has inclined us to empathise with individuals and the situations which they face in corporate life, and encouraged us to address matters accordingly. This was certainly the case for the first author and as such, this paper represented an initial step in the articulation of an intellectual position regarding CSR which she has since developed further. As a consequence, she was awarded a Visiting Fellowship from the Nottingham University Business School, U.K. She has also recently accepted a nomination for a Fellowship of the Royal Society of Arts (FRSA). The second author, now at a late stage in his career, was already widely published, including the authorship of a book on *Management and Morality* (Maclagan 1998) in which, although the primary focus is on individual action, questions of structure and agency are recognised (as noted by Pataki 2000). He regards the success of this paper [Managers' personal values as drivers of corporate social responsibility] as vindication of his view, held for several decades, that the role of the individual should be emphasised more than is often the case in the literature on CSR.

And so we turn to the impact of The *Journal of Business Ethics*. With its broad coverage of the field, it is well positioned to address matters such as the complex relationship between individuals' values, judgements and corporate behaviour. As interest in the subject (not least in the pedagogical context) has grown, so the *Journal* has made a significant contribution, especially since 1998 when the annual number of articles published was increased. Indeed, this has provided a platform for more academics to present their work. Nevertheless, the impact of the *JBE* remains high with a factor of 1.125 according to the Thomson Reuters *Journal Citation Reports* (Web of Knowledge). This is a highly regarded measure of quality and we would support the *Journal* in its efforts to retain its reputation as a leading international journal in the field of business ethics.

References

Archer, M.S. 2000. *Being human: The problem of agency*. Cambridge: Cambridge University Press.

Maclagan, P.W. 1998. *Management and morality: A developmental perspective.* London: Sage.

Pataki, G. 2000. Patrick Maclagan: Management and morality: A developmental perspective. Book review. *Organisation Studies* 21(4): 836–841.

Rabinow, P. 2000. *Michael Foucault, ethics: Subjectivity and truth*. London: Penguin.

W. Michael Hoffman

Business Ethics: The Beginnings

A Brief Essay for the *Journal of Business Ethics* in Celebration of 30 Years of Publication

Most scholars mark the beginning of the formal discipline of business ethics as the 1970s. It was then that courses and conferences began to emerge, textbooks and articles began to be published, and centers for business ethics were founded in universities such as Bentley, Delaware, and Virginia and outside the academy in institutions such as the Ethics Resource Center in Washington, DC.

What gave rise to this sudden flurry of activity is multifaceted. One might mention the ongoing maturation of the field of applied ethics generally along with particular events such as the Watergate scandal, high profile corruption cases in which bribes were paid in order to secure foreign contracts, and the passage of the Foreign Corrupt Practices Act in 1977, among others.

When I founded the Center for Business Ethics (CBE) at Bentley University in 1976, social circumstances were ripe for growth in the field. Despite the skepticism and occasional derision, there was an expanding awareness that given the ever increasing influence of business on society, progress was needed in articulating its ethical context. One thing, however, was missing… a professional journal. It is essentially impossible for a field to be accorded credibility without at least one respected academic journal that serves as the reservoir of the best in professional research and reflection. Back in 1982, the *Journal of Business Ethics* (*JBE*) was created to serve that function. And ever since, it has had an indispensible role in the flourishing of the field. I can speak from experience because back in May 1982, along with my colleague Jennifer Moore, I served as the guest editor for *JBE*'s second issue. There we published a collection of articles drawn from the first three Bentley national conferences on business ethics, organized by CBE. It was an important event, and *JBE* was just the publication needed to provide a forum for these views.

It will come as no surprise to note that the period since the founding of *JBE* has been one in which the world of business has undergone unprecedented change. In 1979, the United States established diplomatic relations with the then poor underdeveloped country of China. The personal computer was introduced in 1981 to be followed by the creation of the internet. The term "globalization" was coined in the 1980s around the time when the interests of shareholders was challenged by a broader notion of "stakeholder" interests. *JBE* was founded before both Enron and WorldCom came into being and disappeared under the weight of their own corruption. These and many other developments changed the context of business and even helped to change our understanding of what a business is.

Changes such as these brought with them new ethical dilemmas and new challenges to our understanding. Throughout this amazing period, the *Journal of Business Ethics* has been both the guidebook to the ever-changing ethical landscape of business, as well as the town square where the global community of scholars could come together to share ideas and discoveries, and engage in debates and disagreements. Ultimately, *JBE* has been where scholars have sought to shine a light on the vital importance of infusing the practice of business with something more important than the drive for profits – a social conscience.

And while the world of business has its hub in the United States, it took two brilliant and tenacious Canadians, Alex Michalos and Deborah Poff, to hold the reigns and guide this journal through this remarkable, tumultuous period. The business ethics community is indebted to *JBE* for providing the forum that has been indispensible for the flourishing of our field.

Bryan W. Husted

The Impact of National Culture on Software Piracy

This article is part of a stream of research dealing with the antecedents of ethical behavior at a macro-level. This particular paper focuses on software piracy and adds to a series that also includes corruption and environmental performance. This particular article was especially well received by scholars in information technology and has been cited in relevant journals in the field. In part I think this response has been due to the fact that this article was one of the first, if not the first, to examine how culture relates to an ethical behavior of interest into information technology using a quantitative methodology based on data available through the Business Software Alliance. This paper continues to attract attention because of the increasing prevalence of software piracy around the world. It offers the message that solutions must be consonant with the cultural context in which piracy occurs.

Clearly the *Journal of Business Ethics* has played and continues to play a major role in business ethics research. For many years it was the only scholarly outlet dedicated to research in the field. Although competition among journals has increased, the *Journal of Business* Ethics remains an important outlet for scholars from around the world. I know of no other outlet that regularly publishes research from such a diverse group of business ethicists. It has displayed an openness to theoretical and empirical approaches that is difficult to find elsewhere. In addition, it publishes much research from new scholars just beginning their careers in the academic world and provides a vital space for communicating heterodox ideas and using new methodological approaches. For many schools, publication in *JBE* is prized because of its privileged position in the journal list of the *Financial Times*. Hence its past is very rich and its future looks quite bright.

Po-Keung Ip

JBE – Celebrating 30 Years of Accomplishments

The Journal over the last two decades has witnessed a steady increase of publications on business ethics in Greater China, a region that covers China, Taiwan, Hong Kong and Macau. The bulk of these papers are authored by scholars and researchers in this region, reflecting a solid growth of interests and competence in this area. The issues tackled by these publications comprise a diverse lot, ranging from corruption, work values, environmental issues, corporate governance, consumer ethics, corporate culture, financial ethics, CSR, ethical perceptions, and accounting ethics to general business ethics. Many of these publications are of empirical nature reporting and interpreting data collected in the field, while a few are theoretical work focusing on the conceptual and normative dimensions of business ethics in this region.

Among this bulk of publications, two subject matters that have received extensive discussions conspicuously stand out. They concern issues about *guanxi* (Chinese version of social relationships) and Chinese values in business. Researching on these uniquely Chinese elements surely helps unravel the subtle yet entrenched social and cultural foundations of Chinese business ethics. As Chinese business is gaining global influence and attention in the wake of China's spectacular rise, to understand the nature of its culture and practices not only is imperative in academia but the world at large. The four Chinese societies in the region share some core Chinese-ness, however they also demonstrate discernable differences in institutions, cultures and collective preferences.

Taiwan is a newly developed democracy with a state-driven market economy and a globally influential high-tech sector. Hong Kong is China's Special Administrative Region that has a strong tradition of rule of law and free market, and is practicing a diminished form of democracy. Similar arrangements can be found in the tiny city of Macau, another China's SAR. And China is a one-party state with an evolving market socialism introduced some three decades ago, and is now the second largest economy in the world.

How business ethics is practiced in these four diverse Chinese societies with their different social, economic and political systems itself is a worthy topic of investigation. The *Journal* has been effective in providing a platform for discussing these issues and thus helps both strengthen the richness and diversity of the discourse and extend the research horizon of business ethics. In today's globalized world, business ethics is no longer confined to the Anglo-Saxon or European countries, but includes the increasingly important Asian region. By embracing the Chinese (and Asian) aspect of business ethics in its fold, the *Journal* has succeeded in making the scope of business ethics discourse authentically global and relevant, as it should be. This positive impact on knowledge and understanding that enriches the world is beyond measure.

The value of a good academic journal depends on its ability to facilitate the creation and dissemination of timely and useful knowledge and ideas that help make the world a better place. Over the last 30 years the *Journal* has been realizing this value to the full. Last but not least, a *Journal* of this significance is not possible without good leadership. It is through the leadership of its Founding Editor, Professor Alex Michalos, with his foresight, inclusiveness and steady execution that the *Journal* has achieved this crowning success. It is time to celebrate these remarkable accomplishments.

Jay J. Janney

Reflections

I tend to be a pretty lucky scholar. I stumbled onto my dissertation topic by accident, during the first 6 weeks of my first semester in the Doctoral program (at the University of Kentucky). Similarly, I'd have to classify this paper [An empirical investigation of the relationship between change in corporate social performance and financial performance: A stakeholder theory perspective] as another exemplar of my scholarly luck. Here's the quick story. I had just completed an independent study with Greg Dess (now at University of Texas-Dallas), creating an extensive literature review on the Resource – Based View of the firm. I was looking for gaps in the literature. The next day, Krish Muralidhar (one of the paper's co-authors) stopped by to chat with Greg. He and the other three co-authors wanted to frame the theory for their work using RBV, but hadn't studied RBV in depth: could Greg help?

Greg had a tight book deadline approaching, and had to decline. But with my RBV literature review in his hand, Greg recommended that they bring me on-board as a co-author, which they did. What a lucky break!

Overwhelmed at first, I read the paper, and liked it as is. I felt my co-authors had developed an excellent method for CSR that made a real contribution. It occurred to me, however, that the draft pointed to a gap in the literature that we could fill. There had been work on reputation and ethics, signaling theory, and reputation and RBV, but not (in my opinion) a tight integration of business ethics and RBV. While retaining the focus on the methods, I wanted to emphasize how perceptions of ethics matter (using RBV). We submitted it to the *Journal of Business Ethics*, where it was warmly received.

Professionally, the paper opened doors for me; this being my most heavily cited paper. I went onto the job market shortly after the paper was accepted (always a good thing), and the University of Dayton wanted to hire strategy/entrepreneurship faculty who were grounded in the ethics literature. The faculty liked the integration of the multiple domains. Hence this work differentiated me in their eyes and I joined the faculty in 2001, where I happily remain. Since then, I have published additional work on ethics, including a second paper (2009) in the *Journal of Business Ethics*. I also re-framed my dissertation to emphasize signaling, from which I published four journal articles.

In my humble opinion, most academic domains start as a phenomenon, where people describe what exists. At the next level, domains begin to appear as special cases in other domains. That is, people apply an existing theory to (in this case) a business ethics example. It is still descriptive work, but richer. Finally, at a maturity stage, insights from the domain begin to influence theory in other domains, and work is much more integrative. I think our work is an example of that with the *Journal of Business Ethics*, as are many of the "citation classics and distinguished papers". I believe the *Journal* itself leads the domain in integrating multiple theories. As a result, the *Journal's* scope offers a breadth and depth that in my opinion makes it the premiere business ethics outlet.

Muel Kaptein

Business Codes of Multinational Firms: What Do They Say?

I am honoured that an article I wrote has been selected to be included in this volume of citation classics. Being classified as a citation classic suggests that at least a few of my colleagues regard – or, at least, regarded – the article as meaningful, noteworthy and relevant to their own research. That the article was published less than a decade ago in 2004 shows that it has been taken up in a relatively short space of time.

The article contains the results of a study of the business codes of the 200 largest corporations in the world. What is unique about this study is that it was the first time that such research was conducted. It shows not only in which countries and continents the largest companies have a code, but also the content and the differences between them.

With regard to the editors' question about the impact of the article on my own career, my answer is as follows. Firstly, the article strengthened my view that considerable research into codes was still needed. Why is the content so diverse, and is this a positive or negative feature? And what, subsequently, determines the effectiveness of codes? Since then, I have conducted research on the effectiveness of business codes. Accordingly, I carried out a meta-analysis of studies of the effectiveness of business codes, and conducted empirical research into the factors that influence the effectiveness of business codes. I have also used the inventory of items from the business codes of the Global 200 to develop a generic, multidimensional scale to measure unethical behaviour within and by organizations, which was published in the *Journal of Management*.

Secondly, the article assisted me in my capacity as business consultant. Companies struggle with questions such as, 'What is a good business code?', 'Which issues should we include?', and 'How do we describe each issue?' The study provided me with broad insight into the content of codes which assisted me in advising clients. In addition to my own consultancy work, I know of other companies in different continents that have used the article as a benchmark in the development and actualization of their own codes.

In my view, this also illustrates the influence of the *Journal of Business Ethics* in the field – the second question the editors of this volume asked me to respond to in this short essay. The *Journal of Business Ethics* does not only have an impact in academia but also in practice. That is not only a welcome bonus but it is also a moral obligation. I have full confidence that the *Journal of Business Ethics* will continue to do so successfully. On the next 30 years!

Adam Lindgreen, Jon Reast and Joelle Vanhamme

Business Ethics: Fact or Fiction?

When international business schools that offer MBAs and executive MBAs voted to include the *Journal of Business Ethics* (*JBE*) in the *Financial Times'* list of the 45 top academic journals in business, it sent a strong sign that our journal exerts a strong impact. The *Financial Times* also compiles rankings of the best MBAs in the world, using as one of its criteria a business school's research rank, or the number of faculty publications in top academic journals. Since joining the list of top journals, we have enjoyed a growing number of manuscript submissions.

These developments imply that faculty in business schools are interested in publishing their best work on ethics in *JBE*. In turn, future managers may adjust their MBA school choices based indirectly on the university's publications in *JBE*. That is, schools with faculty publishing in top journals earn better rankings, and those rankings are utterly critical for attracting MBA students.

The ranking of *JBE* by renowned sources such as *Financial Times* also helps raise the profile and importance of business ethics for current and future managers. University curricula reflect the growing prominence of journals such as *JBE* and the associated interest in business ethics. For example, in many schools, specialized ethics-based modules constitute a key feature of degree programs. The most forward-looking institutions ensure that business ethics represents a constant, clearly visible theme in all business-related modules and programs, as well as a clear element of any interactions with business community members.

Alongside the increasing success of *JBE* and the development of the business ethics field (and related corporate responsibility research), universities in Europe, North America, and Australasia have been establishing research centers and institutes to encourage and support research and corporate engagement with business ethics. Such centers play their part in developing the field, according to aims such as:

- To build a stronger link between business ethics theory and practice.
- To promote knowledge sharing and partnerships within the business ethics field and across private, governmental, voluntary, and academic sectors.
- To strengthen business ethics education for present and future managers.
- To identify and disseminate exemplary business ethics policies and practices.

Some business schools go even further and explicitly work to move businesses along on their journey toward more ethical business. For example, Edhec Business School recently created an International Ethics Board "that seek[s] to encourage businesses to increasingly incorporate the value of Responsibility into all their actions." This board includes members of the academic community, but the majority of its members are prominent business leaders, including the chairpeople of Michelin and Auchan.

Such progress is encouraging, but it remains important to influence the thinking of current and future managers. Why? Even after the widely reported Enron (U.S.) and Bank of Credit & Commerce International (U.K.) scandals of the 1990s, recent events, such as the Parmalat (Italy), Sanlu baby milk (China), and Lehman Brothers (U.S.) scandals, indicate that business ethics–related problems are not abating. The search for profit maximization must be balanced by questions of ethics and, at a minimum, adherence to laws and regulations. Instead, a cynical balance of law breaking for enhanced profit versus fines, if caught, has become too prevalent. We cannot ignore the organizations that have, in a relatively short space of time, embedded business ethics into their culture and behavior, but too many just keep paying lip service to the principles, without altering their actual business ethics. Thus there is still work for journals such as *JBE* to do, not only in developing the field but also in disseminating business ethics throughout practitioner circles to change the values and behaviors of corporate entities worldwide.

The overriding message of this short essay needs no sugar coating: Business ethics is not fiction but a fact that managers absolutely must take seriously. The smart money is on organizations that make business ethics the very heart of their existence. If Shakespeare was right, and all the world is a stage, these are the organizations that will be neither the spectators nor the players, but rather the scribes who take charge of the script.

Jeanne M. Logsdon, Judith Kenner Thompson and Richard A. Reid

Reflections

Software piracy was emerging as a critical ethical and economic issue in the early 1990s, and college students were thought to engage in this questionable practice quite frequently. Thus, it provided an excellent topic for the three authors to collaborate on an empirical research study that appeared to have some important theoretical and practical implications. The research question was whether an individual's moral reasoning capability was related to attitudes and behaviors about using pirated software. This empirically-based study provided a great opportunity for us to learn much more about a number of research issues, including debates about various measurements of moral reasoning as well as the social desirability response bias.

The findings of the study were important because level of moral development, as measured by Rest's Defining Issues Test, was only weakly correlated to software piracy attitudes and behavior. This result was contrary to our working hypothesis, but not wholly unexpected. Our article concluded with a number of possible explanations for the findings, including the low level of "moral intensity" of the piracy issue, and this is what launched quite a large number of subsequent empirical studies, many of which have been published in the *Journal of Business Ethics*.

In terms of impacts on our careers, in the short term we were recognized favorably in our home institution for designing a scientifically rigorous study. Over the longer term we remained active in research productivity on separate projects for a number of years following publication of the software piracy paper. While we did not conduct any follow-on studies to this one, we did find inspiration in what we learned during this investigation. For example, later research often made reference to level of moral development, social desirability response bias, and the nature of issue moral intensity. We also have had the satisfaction of seeing the value of our work as inspiration for later scholars because we identified an important research question and established a sound empirical foundation upon which future investigative efforts could be based.

The *Journal of Business Ethics* has had a very significant impact on the field of business ethics by providing a widely-distributed and high-quality journal for dissemination of all types of research results related to business ethics. No other ethics-related journal has the breadth of coverage of *JBE*. Virtually every type of applied business ethics topic has appeared here. Both qualitative and quantitative research methodologies have been welcomed. There is broad geographical coverage – studies from just about every part of the globe have been published. Practitioners as well as scholars can find valuable contributions in the *Journal*. We can personally attest that selection of our article for publication by the *Journal of Business Ethics* has had a profound impact on nurturing this future research stream because of its focal position across a wide spectrum of business ethics scholars.

S. W. Kelly, O.C. Ferrell and S. Skinner

Reflections

What, If Any, Has Been the Impact of Your Citation Classics on Your Career?

Throughout our careers, we have been involved with a number of research projects associated with marketing research ethics. This article was a building block for several studies in the marketing ethics area for the coauthors. All of our careers have been enhanced by selecting this topic for research and publication.

The *Journal of Business Ethics* provided the best outlet for this article because of the diversity of audience in the business ethics arena. The coauthor team has gained visibility and the opportunity to network with those scholars interested in marketing research ethics. Being in the distinguished category in citation classics will continue to enhance our reputation in marketing ethics and increase the number of scholars that use this article in their research. We are also hopeful that this recognition will be a benefit to practitioners as they try to understand frameworks that can improve marketing research.

What, If Any, Has Been the Impact of the *Journal of Business Ethics* on the Field of Business Ethics?

Over the past 30 years, the *Journal of Business Ethics* has been the premier journal advancing knowledge in this field. In many ways, the *Journal of Business Ethics* has helped pioneer and advance business ethics from an academic and a practitioner perspective. Its articles have reflected the many changes in academic research, regulation of business ethics, and the development of corporate business ethics programs. In the early years of the *Journal of Business Ethics*, there appeared to be much more concern for individual ethics and philosophical orientations that could affect ethical decision making. Today there is a greater focus on organizational ethics, ethical culture, and the social influences of ethical decision making in an organizational context.

Without the *Journal of Business Ethics*, academic researchers would not have a common outlet to share their research and knowledge in advancing the discipline. The journal has covered a wide range of topics such as the impact of moral philosophy on ethical decision making, the role of organizations in developing ethics programs that are effective in preventing misconduct, the social and psychological characteristics of decisions makers, and many macro ethical issues related to social responsibility and sustainability.

We feel that the future of the *Journal of Business Ethics* is very bright. The journal has established its leadership position and is listed as a top journal in most rankings.

Its ranking in the *Financial Times* list of Top 40 Publications worldwide has given authors a significant ability to emphasize the value of their publications to their peers. The journal is leading the charge in institutionalizing business ethics in schools of business.

Ans Kolk

Reflections on Impact

To say something about the impact that a journal has had on a field, as this volume aims to do as part of the celebration of 30 years of publication of the *Journal of Business Ethics* (*JBE*), looking at citations is a logical and first step. This is indeed what the introductory chapter does, with interesting results. However, it also lists over 30 limitations of using citations, and the results clearly show the long time lag, with the 'newest' article in the top 20 articles dating back to 2006. This in itself illustrates the limited value of impact factors as other studies have underlined as well. Considering these caveats, what can we say about the impact of *JBE* beyond citations? And what may be perspectives for the future, if we do not look backward but forward?

As to the first question, in my view a further broadening of *JBE's* scope and coverage has taken place in the period since those articles in the most cited list were published. Business ethics as framed by *JBE*, and as reflected in the articles in recent years in particular, seem to have become rather eclectic, covering corporate governance, sustainability, development, partnerships, peace and conflict, to name just a few of the topics that received attention in the journal. While the citation classics give an impression of the state of the field and the impact of *JBE*, it is about the development and the history to a large extent.

What also remains underexposed when looking at citations is the peculiar function that *JBE*, as a relatively specialised outlet, appears to have in the landscape of journals that cover 'mainstream' business disciplines. This relates to critical observations made in and about various mainstream journals regarding the lack of relevance and of insufficient attention to new ideas that are still messy. Several authors have attributed this absence to mainstream journals' almost exclusive focus on methodological and technological sophistication, as well as to the difficulties of examining topics that cross boundaries and are at the margins of disciplines (McAlister 2005; MacInnis 2005; Miller 1998; Stealin 2005). It has also been noted that social science journals tend to be most concerned with the 'accuracy of the present' – in contrast to science journals that are more attentive to publishing potential path-breaking studies even if these are not yet fully perfect (Hopwood 2007, p. 1371). It is here where there has been a role for journals like **JBE** to add insights 'at the margins' (cf. Miller 1998) and across disciplines with emergent issues.

One might hope that at some point this function will be taken over by the mainstream journals in business, including most notably accounting, finance and marketing

(Hahn et al. 2010). In management studies, attention to business ethics, broadly defined, can be seen, although so far mostly written by those authors that are specialised in these topics and also publish in *JBE*; it is unclear to what extent this will spread to others. Such a development towards further mainstreaming may require a reconsideration of rigour and relevance, of the very notion of impact, and of the role of research and scholarly outlets in academia, business and society. Until then, a journal such as *JBE* will continue to be important, regardless of citation counts, to help set the agenda with novel ideas and approaches. While this may come with variability in terms of the quality of the research and the output at times, it can lead to "approximate answers to important problems or issues" that "are just as useful (if not more useful) than precise answers to wrong, well-defined, narrow problems" (Raju 2005, p. 18).

References

Hahn, T., A. Kolk, and M. Winn. 2010. A new future for business? Rethinking management theory and business strategy. *Business and Society* 49(3): 385–401.

Hopwood, A.G. 2007. Whither accounting research? *The Accounting Review* 82(5): 1365–1374.

MacInnis, D.J. 2005. Them versus us: Woes on the bifurcation of the academic marketing discipline. *Journal of Marketing* 69(October): 14–16.

McAlister, L. 2005. Unleashing potential. *Journal of Marketing* 69(October): 16–17.

Miller, P. 1998. The margins of accounting. *The European Accounting Review* 7(4): 605–621.

Raju, J.S. 2005. Revitalizing the role of marketing in business organizations: What can poor academics do to help? *Journal of Marketing* 69(October): 17–19.

Stealin R. 2005. Influencing the practice through big new ideas. *Journal of Marketing* 69(October): 21–22.

Terry W. Loe, Linda K. Ferrell and Phylis Mansfield

Relections

What Has Been the Impact, If Any, of Your Citation Classic on Your Career?

The review of empirical studies assisted us in gaining an understanding of the multitude of empirical studies on organizational ethics and how they supported well known frameworks of ethical decision making. This article, early in our careers, provided strong visibility and awareness of our interest in the ethics area. The fact the article was so heavily cited, confirms our experience that the study became a nice reference piece for work to understand organizational ethical decision making. The article, according to Google scholar, has been cited over 285 times. The work allowed us to review hundreds of articles and extrapolate commonalities in the findings to assist us in our future research, as well as to support others working in the area. We have also taken the insights gained from our study and applied them to businesses and also in the classroom to enhance future business leaders' appreciation and application of ethical principles in their careers. On a more personal note, we had a great time working on this article-sometimes we laughed so hard we cried. In reconnecting to discuss its impact and the *Journal of Business Ethics,* we renewed our connections and are planning to work together again on some future research projects.

What Has Been the Impact, If Any, of the *Journal of Business Ethics* on the Field of Business Ethics?

The *Journal of Business Ethics* has provided guidance to academics and industry. The goal to enhance the overall understanding of workplace ethical climate and culture as well as improving corporate and organizational interaction with society. There is no other journal systematically dealing with organizational ethics issues in a committed and pervasive fashion. There are competitor journals in the discipline which broaden their perspective to include more philosophical topics, or represent specific sub-discipline areas such as management, marketing, accounting and finance. But, the *Journal of Business Ethics* has remained squarely at the center of advancing our understanding of organizational ethical decision making. By providing the premier journal in the business ethics arena, the *Journal of Business Ethics* continues to have a significant impact on our careers as both a research resource and a publication outlet.

Steven Lysonski

Reflections

What, If Any, Has Been the Impact of Your Citation Classic on Your Career?

The catalyst that fueled my inquiry into the ethics of business students was the experience I was having in class when discussing marketing decisions with ethical implications. I witnessed a shift from the late 1970s to the late 1980s in sentiments by students regarding business. It appeared as if students were becoming less ethically minded or at least more accepting of some questionable business practices. I decided to examine cross cultural differences among business students in New Zealand, Denmark and the USA – countries in which I had taught marketing.

To my surprise students were not so different regarding ethical decision making when confronted with business problems. This realization stimulated my interest in understanding how students deal with ethical problems in a business context. The study, therefore, set the stage for the interest I would have in the topic for the next 20 or more years. Publishing that study gave me an entry point into other studies that I would conduct on ethical areas including the stereotyping of women in advertising, the influence of alcohol advertisements on college students, the downloading by students of MP3 music files illegally, among other topics.

The procedure of asking students to respond to actual scenarios with ethical dilemmas would be an approach that I would use in other studies during my career. Hence, this initial study affected my career in various indirect ways that only would become apparent to me as my career unfolded. The study also gave me various insights that would influence how I would teach some topics that relate to ethics. If you wish to conduct a small experiment of your own, ask students if there is an ethical implication regarding the conversion of corn into ethanol given that the diversion of corn from food products has resulted in higher prices of grains and even tortillas in third world countries. You will be surprised in what you hear. Hence, the study I conducted in 1990 continues as a work in progress as my career continues to explore the reactions of young people to ethical issues or dilemmas.

What, If Any, Has Been the Impact of the *Journal of Business Ethics* on the Field of Business Ethics?

We live in a world that surrounds us with increasing complexity, diversity and dynamism. As capitalism has diffused throughout the world in the form of globalization, ethical issues have become even more poignant and worthy of discussion. When I began my career in 1980, teaching business ethics was more of a side show in business school and clearly not mainstream. In marketing, we addressed the issue of business ethics in the area of macro-marketing, but the field was only in its infancy. There was no forum or journal that was devoted to unraveling, explicating or illuminating ethical issues in business.

JBE represents a beacon that has illuminated many areas of ethical understanding in business. There is no other journal that is committed to this singular goal. Its interdisciplinary nature gives readers a wide exposure to the gamut of ethical inquiry. Business ethics has emerged as a field with multiple and varied constituencies or stakeholders; it is no longer a backwater area. *JBE* serves as a mouth piece in this regard.

JBE has developed an international following with authors from around the world offering their research either conceptually or empirically. Hence, *JBE* has clearly had an impact on scholars in the academic community. Its articles are used in classroom settings, meaning that students are exposed to enlightening issues. It is likely that seeds are being planted in our students' young minds that may someday sprout in desired ways. Raising the consciousness of students and faculty to ethical issues is a good thing for obvious reasons. The commitment of *JBE* to guide our thoughts with ethical inquiries relevant to business is meritorious. The journal has evolved over the years with more attention being given to the theoretical underpinnings of empirical research. It has laid a foundation upon which others can add their building blocks in our development and understanding of business ethics.

Dirk Matten, Andrew Crane and Wendy Chapple

Reflections

To Question 1: By hindsight, we occasionally had to smile about the slight pretence in the title of this paper. In fact, it was the first publication of a new stream of research which we developed, together with Jeremy Moon, over the years into a broad stream of publications. The paper [Behind the mask: revealing the true face of corporate citizenship] then contains a first layout of a nascent research area which subsequently led to a number of papers in top ranked academic outlets, which in turn had a significant impact on the author's careers.

To Question 2: As the first academic journal specifically focusing on business ethics *JBE*, over the years, has published quite a number of classics. In particular in the first two decades many of the seminal, high quality, contributions to the field of business ethics and corporate social responsibility were published in *JBE*. As such *JBE* has been a seminal journal in adumbrating the academic field of business ethics. This is reflected in the inclusion of *JBE* into the criteria of assessing performance and quality of academic work in business schools by major ranking and evaluation bodies (e.g. the so-called *Financial Times* 45 List).

This success in defining a new sub-discipline in management in some ways has led to the emergence of more journals in the field and a growing openness of mainstream management journals for business ethics-related topics. Consequently, *JBE* now shares its role as an outlet for business ethics research with a number of other journals. It appears that *JBE*'s unique role now has shifted towards providing a wide base for scholars from various backgrounds to engage in the debate on business ethics. With now a nearly weekly publication schedule (e.g. 39 issues in 2010) it seems that *JBE* is certainly the leader in terms of quantity of published material in the business ethics field.

Joseph A. McKinney

Reflections

Our article, *Ethical Attitudes of Students and Business Professionals: A Study of Moral Reasoning*, was among the earlier articles on business ethics published by the co-authors. The reception given the article provided important incentive for the co-authors to do further research in the area of business ethics. We subsequently wrote and published about 10 additional business ethics articles on a variety of subjects.

The *Journal of Business Ethics* has provided an extremely valuable outlet for researchers from a wide variety of disciplines who are engaged in investigation of business ethics issues. It is the source that I most frequently consult when doing research in business ethics, and also is a most valuable resource for information on ethical issues that relate to my teaching. The field of business ethics would be much poorer and less developed without it.

Marcia P. Miceli

Reflections

Our essay concerns: Greenberger, D., M.P. Miceli, and D.J. Cohen. 1987. Oppositionists and group norms: The reciprocal influence of Whistle-Blowers and Co-Workers. *Journal of Business Ethics* 7: 527–542.

What Has Been the Impact, If Any, of Your Citation Classic on Your Career?

The publication of our article by the *Journal of Business Ethics* provided opportunities for us to connect with researchers and others in a variety of fields outside of business ethics, including management, social psychology, law, public policy and public management, and many others. For example, it provided a basis for discussing how co-workers' pressures for conformity may inhibit whistle-blowing and how observers of perceived wrongdoing could break those pressures, and under some circumstances, could influence others. Faculty and students at all levels (doctoral, masters', undergraduate), from around the world, have contacted us over the years. In addition, individuals with a practical stake in whistle-blowing, such as whistle-blowers and their attorneys, journalists, and support network representations, have expressed their interest and have shared information with us.

What Has Been the Impact, If Any, of the *Journal of Business Ethics* on the Field of Business Ethics?

As noted in another essay (for (Near and Miceli 1985)), the *Journal of Business Ethics* has had substantial impact on the research on whistle-blowing, as evidenced by research published in the journal and in other journals (e.g., where articles cite whistle-blowing research appearing in the *Journal of Business Ethics*, such as (Gundlach et al. 2003), published in the top-rated *Academy of Management Review*). This impact extends well beyond North America. One indicator of the international impact of the *Journal of Business Ethics* is its inclusion among the 45 representative leading journals that *The Financial Times* uses in assessing the research productivity of faculty. In summary, the *Journal of Business Ethics* has had a clear influence in stimulating, supporting, and shaping international interest in – and greater understanding of – whistle-blowing.

References

Gundlach, M.J., S.C. Douglas, and M.J. Martinko. 2003. The decision to blow the whistle: A social information processing framework. *Academy of Management Review* 28: 107–123.

Near, J.P., and M.P. Miceli. 1985. Organizational dissidence: The case of whistle-blowing. *Journal of Business Ethics* 4: 1–16.

Morgan P. Miles and Jeffrey G. Covin

A Note on the Impact of the Journal of Business Ethics on Practice and Theory

Impact on Practice

One measure of the significance of an academic journal is that it provides relevant guidance for decision making. By this measure the *Journal of Business Ethics' (JBE)* impact is significant as highlighted by its inclusion in the *Financial Times* annual list of the 45 most important academic journals for business leaders. *JBE* addresses the complex issues that surround businesses' relationship to ethics, sustainability, and cultural values. *JBE's* authors and audience include not only academics but business thought leaders and policy makers whose contributions greatly enhance its relevance. Papers published in *JBE* **do** impact practice and that is one of the most satisfying aspects for many scholars – that their work might influence the perspectives and practices of business and policy decision makers. Articles from *JBE* have helped stimulate discussions on issues as diverse as the value of "environmental marketing," the cost of social accountability certification, and the relevance of explicit ethical guidelines for firms, among many others relevant to ethical business practice.

Impact on Theory

Another measure of the relevance of an academic journal is its recognition as a forum for rigorous theory development and testing. *JBE's* contribution to business ethics theory is recognized by the tremendous number of its articles that are fundamental in other studies and journal articles, monographs, PhD courses, and dissertations.

JBE is included in the ISI citation index, the most prestigious index of the significance of social science scholarship, used by both universities and granting agencies to assess academic merit. Likewise, *JBE* is widely recognized as an "A grade" journal by many recruitment, merit, and promotion/tenure committees due to the reputation of its academically rigorous papers. *JBE* is a journal that has provided a very high quality open forum for scholars working on issues pertaining to a wide scope of topics at the business ethics and corporate social responsibility/sustainability interface.

What distinguishes *JBE* from many other scholarly journals in the business ethics space is that *JBE* has encouraged critical and *timely* academic discussions of the complex issues through its long-standing initiatives of special issues. Among scholars *JBE* has the well deserved reputation of allowing authors holding different perspectives on a topic the opportunity to contribute to a meaningful conversation on business's role in our society.

Impact on Academic Careers

Publishing in *JBE* has been one of the most important achievements in many academic careers, and it certainly was for me [Miles]. *JBE* has provided a needed high quality and relevant venue for exploring the role of values and ethics on business and society. The article that I feel may have been my most significant scholarly contribution to date was published in *JBE*. Over my two decade long career at universities I've been fortunate enough to publish in *JBE* several times and in every case it was always a great experience from submission, to revision, to the joy of ultimately seeing the paper in print. The editors should be proud that publication in *JBE* has enhanced the career opportunities for their authors. There is no other journal that I enjoy more as a reader, reviewer, or author, and none that is more important to business ethics scholars that seek to contribute to both practice and theory.

Sara Morris and Rob McDonald

Reflections

It is gratifying to discover that our article on the role of moral intensity in moral judgments is considered a classic by the *Journal of Business Ethics*. This is especially satisfying in light of *JBE*'s prominent position in the field both now (see Serenko and Bontis's (2009) study of citation rates in *International Journal of Business Governance and Ethics*) and over the years. Publication outlets play a crucial role in the development of academic disciplines and, cutting across content areas and national contexts, *JBE* has certainly provided the most inclusive journal home for scholarly research in business ethics/business and society over time.

Our publication on moral intensity is a tribute to synergy between co-authors. When I was an assistant professor and Rob McDonald was a doctoral student, his innate curiosity about research methods prompted him to search for opportunities to apply various techniques. I introduced him to some of the questions I had been studying in business ethics/business and society and we wrote conference papers that tweaked Brady's (1990) utilitarian/formalist aptitude scale and Aupperle, Carroll, and Hatfield's (1985) corporate social responsibility orientation instrument. I was impatient to do more than test possible marginal refinements in established measures, however, and wanted to examine theoretical constructs more than methods. Jones's (1991) new perspective on ethical decision making presented an attractive prospect as a compromise for our interests. Nevertheless, we had no funding to conduct an investigation among business practitioners and I had reservations about whether journal reviewers would accept a student sample. It was Rob's enthusiasm, not to mention persistent pestering, that prompted me to give it a try. Luckily, my fears were unfounded and now we have a classic.

As I reflect about how *JBE*'s publication of "The Role of Moral Intensity in Moral Judgments" affected us as individuals, several things come to mind. This piece was Rob's first published article and I am pleased to report that his interest in business ethics research methods continued for the rest of his life, which ended too soon. As it turned out, this article was a vital part of my tenure packet and I have subsequently benefited from the reputational halo of *JBE*'s inclusion in the *Financial Times* 45. I can't believe that my experience is atypical or that I am singular in my appreciation of the editorial workload carried out at the *Journal of Business Ethics* during the past three decades.

References

Aupperle, K.E., A.B. Carroll, and J.D. Hatfield. 1985. An empirical examination of the relationship between corporate social responsibility and profitability. *Academy of Management Journal* 28(2): 446–463.

Brady, F.N. 1990. *Ethical managing: Rules and results.* New York: Macmillan.

Jones, T.M. 1991. Ethical decision making by individuals in organizations: An issue-contingent model. *Academy of Management Review* 16(2): 366–395.

Patrick E. Murphy

Implementing Business Ethics in the Twenty-First Century

In examining my article from nearly 25 years ago, some aspects of it are timeless such as the following quote: "Recent events concerning unethical business practices not only on Wall Street, but also in many other places, appear to highlight the lack of attention to implementation of ethical policies." Several of the corporate examples did not stand the test of time such as Mc Donnell Douglas (acquired by Boeing in 1996). Furthermore, positive references about the following companies would now be questioned: Dow Corning (breast implant problems), Hewlett-Packard (board and top management failings) and Johnson & Johnson (product safety and recalls – Voreacos et al. 2011).

This article has had a significant impact on my career in several ways. First, the overall model for organizing and executing ethical policies proposed in the article was adapted for use in two textbooks that I coauthored on marketing ethics. In fact, the last chapter of both of these books is titled "Implementing Marketing Ethics". Second, the importance of ethics statements has been a focal point of my work since that article was published. I conducted a series of three separate empirical studies on the existence of and impact of ethics statements (values, credo, code and privacy policy) on ethical decision making in large corporations. The results of two of these three studies were published in the *Journal of Business Ethics* (Murphy 1995, 2005). Third, using both the original article and the empirical work as background, I assembled a number of ethics statements in a book – *Eighty Exemplary Ethics Statements* – and provided a commentary on each of them (Murphy 1998). Fourth, some of the topics in this article are still used in lectures that I give on ethical business practices. In particular, the four implementation responsibilities that were discussed in the article are paired with moral values – leadership with integrity, delegation with trust, communication with transparency/openness and motivation with reward/punishment. Finally, the essential aspect of corporate culture and its influence on the ethical posture of any company is a frequent topic of discussion in my business and marketing ethics courses.

The *Journal of Business Ethics* has been influential in the advancement of theoretical, empirical and practical components of the field. The journal has published the most extensive body of work on business ethics and the many sub-fields that it has spawned during its 30 years. *JBE* has been open to philosophical treatises, empirical studies, and more practically-oriented articles like mine. The specific area that I would like to focus on here is marketing ethics. *JBE* is to be complimented for having a section editor, Scott Vitell, for marketing ethics for many years. I know the *Journal* has devoted several special issues to marketing ethics over the years. The impact of *JBE* on the marketing ethics literature was chronicled in a recent review article (Schlegelmilch and Oberseder 2010) which found that over 160 articles out of nearly 550 have been published in *JBE* on marketing ethics, four times as many as the second ranked journal. Thus, the growth of the field of marketing ethics owes much to the receptivity of *JBE* to examinations of many aspects of the marketing field.

In conclusion, both my subsequent research and hopefully that of others has benefitted from the publication of this well cited article.

References

Murphy, P.E. 1995. Corporate ethics statements: Current status and future prospects. *Journal of Business Ethics* 14: 727–740.

Murphy P.E. 1998. *Eighty exemplary ethics statements*. Notre Dame: Notre Dame Press.

Murphy, P.E. 2005. Developing, communicating and promoting corporate ethics statements. *Journal of Business Ethics* 62: 183–189.

Schlegelmilch, B.B., and M. Oberseder. 2010. Half a century of marketing ethics: Shifting perspectives and emerging trends. *Journal of Business Ethics* 93: 1–19.

Voreaacos, D., A. Nussbaum, and G. Farrell. 2011. Johnson & Johnson fights to clear its once- Trusted Name. *Bloomberg Businessweek* (April 4–10): 64–71.

Samuel M. Natale

A Roadmap for Our Times

> "Cheshire Puss, asked Alice. Would you tell me, please, which way I ought to go from here? That depends a good deal on where you want to go, said the Cat. I don't much care where, said Alice. Then it doesn't matter which way you go, said the Cat."
>
> Charles "Lewis Carroll" Dodgson 1832–1898, English writer and mathematician, *Alice's Adventures in Wonderland,* 1865

> "To see what is right and not to do it is want of courage."
>
> Confucius 551 – 479 B.C., Chinese philosopher, *The Analects*, Book II, Chapter XXIV

One only has to read the papers to sense the conflicting forces that appear to be driving our lives. From the personal to the economic, arguments rage on ethical issues as disparate as gay marriage to what constitutes an ethically appropriate investment. Given the diversity that is now our everyday culture, agreement seems unlikely in the near future.

What are the duties and obligations of corporations? What are the factors of accountability? What are the norms or rules that might assist us in developing an honorable sense of direction? How do norms vary (or do they?) in variant geographies? In our current context, can anything be declared universal?

The dispute has continued for millennia as the briefest of literature searches will attest. In my experience, it was only with the emergence of the *Journal of Business Ethics* that the varied and sundry arguments could be more or less located in one place. For those of us who have been life-long academics and consultants, this publication has been a significant gift. Beyond locating the major points of view in one place, the *Journal's* rigorous, blind review process assures the reader that the work has been scrutinized carefully and vetted as internally integral and a contribution to often bewildering discussions.

The reader's response may vary from annoyance to delight but one thing has always been certain: the *Journal of Business Ethics* is a fountain of information to add to one's store of knowledge as well as data. Over the years, the journal has created a vast tapestry of various points of view to the benefit of many. There are, of course, increasing articles in the area of business ethics in many excellent journals but the foundational and encyclopedia foundation remains the *Journal of Business Ethics*.

An often unsung virtue of the *Journal of Business Ethics* is that it can be used in virtually any situation and materials can be found within its pages that examine an incredibly diverse geographic and cultural venue…no easy task in the contemporary scene. From classic authors to post modernists thinkers, the *Journal* continues to herald the diversity, quality and strength of our growing knowledge of one of humanity's greatest challenges.

A further intrapersonal gift that the journal offers is that it provides us with the data, information and wisdom that stokes the fires of courage…to empower individuals and organizations to make careful, ethical and directed decisions with clarity and conviction.

Janet P. Near and Marcia P. Miceli

Reflections

Our essay concerns: Near, J.P., and M.P. Miceli. 1985. Organizational dissidence: The case of whistle-blowing. *Journal of Business Ethics* 4: 1–16.

What Has Been the Impact, If Any, of Your Citation Classic on Your Career?

The publication of our article by the *Journal of Business Ethics* enabled us to connect with researchers around the world. It also helped facilitate the exchange of information with parties with a practical interest in whistle-blowing, such as journalists, whistle-blowers, their representatives, and individuals in organizations interested in promoting more ethical management, better public policy, or better practice in supporting valid whistle-blowing. For example, defining "whistle-blowing" has proven quite contentious: in 1985 we suggested a preliminary operational definition and this has led to a continuing debate, which in turn pushed us to empirically assess potential differences among types of whistle-blowers. Thus, our subsequent research was informed and guided by the work of many researchers who cited our *Journal of Business Ethics* article, and by inputs from non-academic researchers as well.

The cross-disciplinary nature of *Journal of Business Ethics* is invaluable. As with many papers it has published through the years, the topic of whistle-blowing is interdisciplinary, and relevant literature exists in multiple fields outside of business ethics, e.g., accounting, finance, information systems, law, business management, psychology, public policy and public management, and sociology. Popular and practical interest in the topic is evidenced by many newspaper and online articles that raise empirical questions. Without journals that embrace interdisciplinary work, knowledge of many topics such as whistle-blowing cannot advance as extensively or as richly.

What Has Been the Impact, If Any, of the *Journal of Business Ethics* on the Field of Business Ethics?

We see international influence of the *Journal of Business Ethics* specifically in research on whistle-blowing, as evidenced by research published in the *Journal*. Early research was conducted primarily in North America (e.g., Mesmer-Magnus and Viswesvaran 2005). Research not only continues there (e.g., MacNab and Worthley 2008), but also has been undertaken in many other countries, including several in Europe (e.g., Hassink et al. 2007; Tavakoli et al. 2003), Korea (Park et al. 2005), and China (e.g., Zhang et al. 2009).

A more general indication of its international impact is that the *Journal of Business Ethics* is among the 45 representative leading journals that the *Financial Times* uses in assessing the research productivity of faculty, as it updates its rankings of business curricula. Clearly, the *Journal of Business Ethics* has had a positive, respected influence in stimulating scholarly and popular interest in, and knowledge about, whistle-blowing.

References

Hassink, H., M. de Vries, and L. Bollen. 2007. A content analysis of whistleblowing policies of leading European companies. *Journal of Business Ethics* 75: 25–44.

MacNab, B., and R. Worthley. 2008. Self-efficacy as an intrapersonal predictor for internal whistleblowing: A US and Canada examination. *Journal of Business Ethics* 79: 407–421.

Mesmer-Magnus, J.R., and C. Viswesvaran. 2005. Whistleblowing in organizations: An examination of correlates of whistleblowing intentions, actions, and retaliation. *Journal of Business Ethics* 62: 277–297.

Park, H., M.T. Rehg, and D. Lee. 2005. The influence of Confucian ethics and collectivism on whistleblowing intentions: A study of Korean public employees. *Journal of Business Ethics* 58: 387–403.

Tavakoli, A.A., J.P. Keenan, and B. Crnjak-Karanovic. 2003. Culture and whistleblowing: An empirical study of Croatian and United States managers utilizing Hofstede's cultural dimensions. *Journal of Business Ethics* 43: 49–64.

Zhang, J., R. Chiu, and L. Wei. 2009. Decision-making process of internal whistleblowing behavior in China: Empirical evidence and implications. *Journal of Business Ethics* 88: 25–41.

Richard P. Nielsen

Praxeology and the Journal of Business Ethics

From a classical perspective, philosophical reflection can include ontology, epistemology, theoria, and praxeology (James 1911; Winch 1958; Toulmin 1992; Nielsen 1993; Tsoukas and Chia 2011). While most professional ethics journals as well as the *Journal of Business Ethics* regularly include articles about ontology, epistemology, and theoria, the *Journal of Business Ethics* has been unusual in its foundational concern for and continuing inclusion of action oriented praxeological work in organizational and business ethics. As illustrated and explained below, an action/praxis dimension is different from ontology, epistemology, and theoria; and, has been central to the mission and praxis of the *JBE*. As the founding Editor Alex C. Michalos (1982) explained in the very first issue of the *JBE,* "Ethics is … interpreted broadly to include all human *action* aimed at securing a good life.… In short, our basic concern is the study of business *activity* from a moral point of view [italics added]." This is a very important contribution both from the perspectives of service to practitioners and praxeological theory building. Praxeological work is not the same as work in ontology, epistemology, and theoria.

Ontological work in business and organizational ethics refers to how we categorize and identify the phenomena we study. An early *JBE* example of this type of article is the DeGeorge (1989) article, "There is ethics in business ethics; but there's more as well" that considered the different types of phenomena that can and should be studied in business ethics. Another example of this type of article is the Ashkanasy, Windsor, and Trevino (2006), "Bad apples in bad barrels revisited." In this article, the authors explain how it is important to identify and consider both individual (bad apples) and organizational (bad barrels) types of phenomena. A further example of a study that includes ontological dimensions is the Campbell (2007) article, "Why would corporations behave in socially responsible ways: An institutional theory of corporate social responsibility." This article explains how it is important to also consider more macro institutional phenomena as well and organizational and individual level phenomena in business ethics.

Epistemological work in organizational ethics refers to the types of questions we ask and how we know what we claim to know in the subject matter of organizational ethics. An early *JBE* example of this type of work is the Wilson (1982) article, "Mill's proof that happiness is the criterion of morality." In this article Wilson considers the question of how we might know whether it is true that happiness is the criterion of morality. Another example of this type of work is the Sandberg (2008) article, "Understanding the separation thesis" that considers whether we should ask ethical questions in our social science considerations of business phenomena or whether ethical questions need to be separated from business and social science questions. An example of an article that considers the epistemological limitations of ethical reasoning is Nielsen's (1988) "Limitations of ethical reasoning as an action (praxis) strategy."

Business and organizational ethics *theoria* focuses on understanding and explaining what behaviors and decisions are more and less ethical in organizational contexts and situations (Nielsen 1993). Tsoukas and Chia (2010) further explain: "The etymology of *theory* is revealing. As Toulmin (1982: 239) notes, the word *theoros* in classical Greece was mainly used to indicate the official delegate who was dispatched from the city-state to attend intercity athletic Games, especially the Olympic Games. He was not meant to take part in those games, only to observe them. Gradually *theoros* was used to refer to any spectator at the Games … in contrast with a participant. Eventually the abstract noun *theoria* acquired the meaning of spectating, in contrast to participating. With Aristotle, theoria came to refer to the philosopher's detached intellectual inquiry… Theoretical conjectures are in effect 'organized' collections of propositional statements making claims regarding the phenomenon under investigation that renders them plausible and logically coherent to a community of inquirers [scholars]."

An early *JBE* example of this type of conceptual work is the Goodpaster (1983) article, "The concept of corporate responsibility" in which Goodpaster, from the perspective of a scholar and the ethics literature, speculates and theorizes about what the idea of "corporate responsibility" could and should mean. A similar concept development article is Donaldson's (1985) *JBE* article, "Multinational decision making: Reconciling international norms," where Donaldson, again from the perspective of a scholar and the ethics literature, develops a conceptual scheme for integrating international and cross-cultural difference in norms and values. A related example of this type of work is Bowie's (1998) *JBE* article, "A Kantian theory of meaningful work" in which Bowie considers how Kantian ethical concepts might apply to the idea of "meaningful work" in business organizations. The focus of these types of theoria articles are concepts and ideas from the point of view of the more or less outsider, observer-scholar, and the ethics literature.

The difference between *theoria* and *praxeology* is not the difference between theory and practice (Bernstein 1971; Nielsen 1988, 1993, 2010; Toulmin 1992; Tsoukas and Chia 2010; Sandberg and Tsoukas 2011). According to Bernstein (1971, ix), "The Greek term 'praxis' has an ordinary meaning that roughly corresponds to the ways in which we now commonly speak of 'action' or 'doing' and it is frequently translated into English as 'practice.'" Bernstein further explains that praxis in a philosophical sense has a deeper meaning, "Praxis … signifies the disciplines and activities predominant in man's ethical and political life" within the polis, within the community, within the organization. The end of the praxis dimension of life is living well, appropriately, within the polis, within the community, within the organization. In contrast, the end of the theoria dimension of life is knowing or wisdom for its own sake. Within the whole person, both dimensions and perspectives are important, can, and should inform one another."

Praxeological theory building is developed inductively from the situations and perspectives of practitioners rather than deductively from the literature and perspectives of scholars who are trying to apply literature based theories to practice. Similarly, Sandberg and Tsoukas (2011: 339) explain that: "If practical rationality better captures the logic of practice … it is not because practical rationality deals with practice while scientific rationality allegedly does not .... Instead, it is because practical rationality ... makes theory a derivative of practice.... In contrast, scientific rationality ... makes practice derivative of theory...."

For example, in the first issue of *JBE*, Ellison (1982) in his article "Civil disobedience and whistleblowing: A comparative appraisal of forms of dissent," considers and theorizes from the perspective of practitioners the choices some make to maintain personal ethical integrity by acting as whistle-blowers that have important similarities to and implications for organizational citizenship and civil disobedience. An example from the 1990s is the Tsalikis and Latour (1995) article, "Bribery and extortion in international business: Ethical perspectives of Greeks and Americans." The authors examine, from the different perspectives of Greeks and Americans living and working in their different realities, how they perceive and respond to bribery and extortion problems differently. An example from the 2000s is the Taskin and Devos (2005) article, "Paradoxes from the individualization of human resources management: The case of telework." The authors consider from the ethical perspectives of individual employees working from home as well as the ethical perspective of human resources managers who try to serve these physically isolated employees, how the work life, activities, and satisfactions of these people are different and need to be managed and served differently. In a more recent article from 2010, Giacalone and Promisio (2010), "Unethical and unwell: Decrements in well-being and unethical activity of work." The authors examine the perspectives and experiences of practitioners who suffer severe, physiologically negative effects from the stress and trauma they experience in dealing with unethical behaviors at work.

As referred to above, an action, praxeological dimension has been central to the mission of the *JBE* as the founding Editor Alex C. Michalos (1982) explained and hoped for in the first issue of the *JBE,* "Ethics is ... interpreted broadly to include all human *action* aimed at securing a good life.... In short, our basic concern is the study of business *activity* from a moral point of view [italics added]." As illustrated and explained above, there are many and continuing examples of articles with praxeological dimensions in the *JBE* that are different from the ethics work in ontology, epistemology, and theoria. Further, almost every issue of *JBE* includes articles with praxeological dimensions. This espoused mission of *JBE* to include the praxelogical dimension has and is being fulfilled. Many thanks and great appreciation for the good work of the editors, authors, reviewers, and publisher of the *Journal of Business Ethics*.

References

Ashkanasy, N.M., C.A. Windsor, and L.K. Trevino. 2006. Bad apples in bad barrels revisited. *Business Ethics Quarterly* 16(4): 449–473.

Bernstein, R.J. 1971. *Praxis and action*. Philadelphia: University of Pennsylvania Press.

Bowie, N. 1998. A Kantian theory of meaningful work. *Journal of Business Ethics* 17(9): 1083–1092.

Campbell, J.L. 2007. Why would corporations behave in socially responsible ways: An institutional theory of corporate social responsibility. *Academy of Management Review* 32(2): 946–967.

DeGeorge, R. 1989. There is ethics in business ethics; but there's more as well. *Journal of Business Ethics* 8(5): 337–339.

Donaldson, T. 1985. Multinational decision making: Reconciling international norms. *Journal of Business Ethics* 4(4): 357–366.

Ellison, F.A. 1982. Civil disobedience and whistle-blowing: A comparative appraisal of forms of dissent. *Journal of Business Ethics* 1(1): 23–28.

Giacalone, R.A. 2010. Unethical and unwell: Decrements in well-being and unethical activity at work. *Journal of Business Ethics* 91(2): 275–297.

Goodpaster, K.E. 1983. The concept of corporate social responsibility. *Journal of Business Ethics* 2(1): 1–22.

James, W. 1911. *Some problems of philosophy*. Lincoln: University of Nebraska Press.

Michalos, A.C. 1982. Editorial: Purpose and policy. *Journal of Business Ethics* 1(1): 1.

Nielsen, R.P. 1988. Limitations of ethical reasoning as an action (praxis) strategy. *Journal of Business Ethics* 7(10): 725–735.

Nielsen, R.P. 1993. Organizational ethics from a perspective of praxis. *Business Ethics Quarterly* 3(2): 131–151.

Nielsen, R.P. 2010. Practitioner-based theory building in organizational ethics. *Journal of Business Ethics* 93(3): 401–406.

Sandberg, J. 2008. Understanding the separation thesis. *Business Ethics Quarterly* 18(2): 213–232.

Sandberg, J. 2011. Grasping the logic of practice: Theorizing through practical rationality. *Academy of Management Review* 36(2): 338–360.

Taskin, L., and V. Devos. 2005. Paradoxes for the individualization of human resources management. *Journal of Business Ethics* 62(1): 13–24.

Toulmin, S. 1982. *The return to cosmology*. Berkeley: University of California Press.

Tsalikis, J., and M.S. Latour. 1995. Bribery and extortion in international business: Ethical perspectives of Greeks compared to Americans. *Journal of Business Ethics* 14(4): 249–264.

Tsoukas, H., and R. Chia. 2010. Introduction: Why philosophy matters to organization theory. In *Philosophy and organization theory*, eds. Tsoukas, H., and R. Chia, 1–21. United Kingdom: Emerald.

Wilson, F. 1982. Mill's proof that happiness is the criterion of morality. *Journal of Business Ethics* 1(1): 59–72.

Winch, P. 1958. *The idea of a social science and its relation to philosophy*. London: Routledge, Kegan Paul.

Michael O'Fallon and Kenneth Butterfield

Reflections

What Has Been the Impact, If Any, of Your Citation Classic on Your Career?

This article began as a paper that the first author, Michael O'Fallon, was using to fulfill a seminar requirement while he was in the Ph.D. program at Washington State University. Michael and his advisor, Ken Butterfield, believed that since a number of years had passed since the last major review of the ethical decision-making literature was published, a review was timely and could make a contribution to the field. Ken also thought that a review would be an ideal way for Michael, then a second-year doctoral student, to get his arms around the ethical decision-making literature. We cannot help but reflect with some amusement that the seminar instructor, upon learning of Michael's fairly ambitious plan to review the empirical research in ethical decision making, warned him against writing such a paper, commenting that "it would never get published." Obviously we disagreed, and so Michael moved forward on the rather large task of gathering, summarizing, and categorizing the 174 articles that met the inclusion criteria. Approximately 1 year later, the manuscript was completed and submitted to *JBE*. Michael was pleased and somewhat surprised when the article was accepted, making it the first publication of his academic career.

Without question, this article holds significant meaning to us, and particularly to Michael. Beyond it being his first publication, he believes that it gave him an advantage when he began searching for an academic position. Although we did not know what impact, if any, the review would have on the field, we began to receive some acknowledgement of the article shortly after it was published. Michael remembers attending the Academy of Management annual meeting while on the job market and being approached by a fellow graduate student from another university. She asked if he was the Michael O'Fallon who had co-authored the ethics review article. When he responded that he was, she mentioned that her advisor had given her the article and told her that reading it would provide her with a good understanding of where the research in ethical decision-making stood at the time. Michael recalls it as one of the most humbling experiences of his life. To this day, Michael considers himself fortunate to have launched his publishing career with this article.

Although it was gratifying to see that Michael's efforts had paid off, we certainly would never have guessed that the paper would become one of *JBE*'s "Citation Classics." We have appreciated the generally positive response that this article has received.

JBE has made a significant mark in the field of business ethics. Due to its large number of published articles, in 2010 *Journal Citation Reports* ranked *JBE* #1 in total citations among all 38 ethics journals by a wide margin, and

11th out of 101 among all business journals in total citations. Recognition of *JBE*'s importance is also seen in its inclusion among the 40 journals in the prestigious *Financial Times* Business School journal list. In our opinion, some of the best and most influential business ethics articles ever written have appeared in *JBE*.

Mark Pastin

Reflections

The topic is the impact of the *Journal of Business Ethics* on the field of business ethics. I have had several relationships to the *Journal* – author, member of editorial board, and subscriber. I was one of the "early adopters" of business ethics and it seems like the *Journal* has been there every step of the way. I started out as a professor in a liberal arts college; became a professor in a business school; and left academia altogether to run the Council of Ethical Organizations and its related entities.

When I was in academia I was struck by the lack of connection between what academics think about and anything that happens in a business. To this rule, the *Journal of Business Ethics* was the exception, publishing practical articles and articles by practitioners as well as "pure" academic articles. If not for the *Journal*, I might have thrown in the academic towel earlier.

When I left academia, I was confronted by necessity of making whatever it is that I was knowledgeable about into something for which organizations would pay. For a time, that kept me occupied and I did little reading outside of what was on my desk or on the nightstand – mysteries. But I began to miss thinking about broader issues and that brought me back to the *Journal*. I feared not finding it as I remembered it. But it was better. Well written. Well edited. Relevant.

I have gone back to many of the other publications I read as an academic and found them to be useless for me. I am sure they are useful within their own frames of reference – or at least as notches on the tenure belt. But given that I have less time to read, I demand that what I read makes me enjoy what I am doing more – or enables me to do it better. And that is why I like the *Journal* every bit as much as I did 30 years ago. Its commitment to being cross disciplinary keeps me abreast of issues across fields. Some of its articles give me new ways to think about the perplexing problems presented by the organizations with which I interact. And it is still the publication I show to people when they ask what the heck business ethics is and whether it is really about anything.

I offer my profound gratitude to the *Journal* and to Alex and Deborah for keeping it going at the highest standard.

Moses L. Pava

First Encounter

As a newly minted PhD from the Stern School of Business at New York University in accounting (1990), I remember vividly grazing through the stacks at our library one morning at Yeshiva University. I was a young assistant professor at the Syms School of Business, and I was searching for something, but I was not quite sure what it was that I was searching for.

One thing I did know was that I was extremely uncomfortable with the efficient market hypothesis and the research paradigm based upon this ubiquitous hypothesis. There was no question my NYU education had provided me with an intellectually satisfying experience. I was truly dazzled by the beauty and possibilities of the newly emerging worldview that seemed to be corroborated by every new study published in the *Journal of Accounting Research* and the *Accounting Review*. With every new statistical refinement, the pervasive faith at NYU and other top business schools was strengthened to the point of what seemed to my teachers and colleagues as certainty. To this day, I see some of the potential benefits of judiciously applying such an elegant hypothesis to both theory and to practice. But, even then I knew something was not quite right with EMH. The efficient market hypothesis was one perspective among many others. It seemed to leave out too many important questions about finance, accounting, and business in general. The theory, my instincts told me, was too good to be true.

As I casually walked through the library, I picked up a copy of a strange looking journal. It seemed to be taller and wider than almost all of the other journals on the shelf. It included articles from a wide array of disciplines. As I began to read the articles, I thought to myself, this is interesting stuff! Perhaps the articles were written with somewhat less rigor than what I had been used to, but the subject of business ethics was just too compelling for me to forget easily.

That morning was a *defining moment* in my career. Although I had not yet read Joseph Badaracco's brilliant book by that name, nor did I immediately realize the importance of my chance encounter with the *Journal of Business Ethics*. I began to think more and more about business ethics, corporate social responsibility, integrity, and so many other related issues.

My first foray into business ethics research was an empirical study co-authored with Joshua Krausz on the association between perceived social responsibility and traditional financial performance. Josh and I chose the *Journal of Business Ethics* as our first choice, and we were gratified when the Editor, Alex Michalos, informed us that the paper had been accepted.

Over the years, the *Journal of Business Ethics* has expanded its scope, raised the level of scholarship, and has jumpstarted a high-level dialogue on the central importance of business ethics to our economy, society, and world.

Since my first publication, I have published numerous articles from empirical, theoretical, philosophical, and religious perspectives. I have read the published work of my teachers, peers, and students in its pages. My early hunch about the thinness of my formal education was truer than I could have ever known. Thanks to Alex and the entire field he has helped to deliver, the world of business research is richer, more colorful, and more significant than it was in 1990 when I first graduated with an impoverished view of the role business in society and a limited understanding of the real significance of business research. While this is my personal story, I am confident that I am not unique.

Dinah Payne and Brenda E. Joyner

Reflections

Career Impact of Citation Class Articles

The impact of having a distinguished article on our professional careers has been great and very positive. In part, it has allowed the authors to gain professional respect among academics and professionals, including recognition by the authors' own academic institutions for our scholarly efforts. It has aided in the maintenance or attainment of superior employment positions in eminent programs at excellent universities, as well. On a more personal career level, the use of the *Journal of Business Ethics* as a publication outlet has been most gratifying: to be allowed to publish in such a quality-oriented journal has given tremendous confidence to the authors and has incited us to continue to find and think about ethical dilemmas that confront and dismay business professionals. If our thought processes as presented in *Journal of Business Ethics* articles have helped a single business professional in the resolution of a moral dilemma, we are well satisfied and we take professional pride in our achievements.

Journal of Business Ethics' Impact on the Field of Business Ethics

The field of business ethics is full of serious and important issues for the business professional and for all of his stakeholders. In light of the importance of business in our society and the ethical conduct of such business, a resource like the *Journal of Business Ethics* is invaluable for business professionals and those who study business ethics as professors or students. We have used articles in the *Journal of Business Ethics* many, many times in a wide variety of research: *JBE* articles have been tremendously helpful in shaping the ethical dilemma targeted for study and in shaping the discussion and resolution of such ethical dilemmas. *JBE*'s impact on the field of business ethics is profound and profoundly good: it is an outlet for creative discussion on sensitive issues critically important to sound business practice. It is a venue to explore new thoughts on timely issues; it is a well-respected organ of suggested, measured change. It allows for the healthy exercise of intellectual curiosity with a final end to be a society positively impacted by critical thought, creativity and sensitivity.

Donna H. Randall and Ann Gibson

Journal of Business Ethics: A Celebration of Three Decades

If one were to anthropomorphize a publication, the *Journal of Business Ethics* would be a young adult. In 2012 the journal celebrates a 30-year publication history. In comparison to many other academic journals dating back to an earlier century, the journal indeed may still be regarded as the "new kid on the block." However, a 30-year publication history for any journal indicates that the journal is making significant contributions to the scholarly community and has staying power.

As researchers, we became acquainted with the journal during its formative early years. At the time, the late 1980s and early 1990s, it was not clear what direction the journal would take. There were other venues for publication of works on business ethics. However, there was something about the journal that made us want to stick around, to watch it grow, and to become part of its growth. The published articles were creative, inspiring and thought provoking.

In those early years, we felt an excitement about being associated with the journal. We were young management scholars sharing an interest in business ethics. We wanted to make a worthwhile contribution to a field that we viewed as having great importance to society. At the time, business ethics was an emerging sub discipline within the field of management and the journal to publish in was clearly the *Journal of Business Ethics*. In a 1990 article we described the *Journal of Business Ethics* as the "flagship" journal for business ethics; it remains so today.

By publishing in the journal, we joined an interdisciplinary community of scholars united by a singular interest. The authors and articles reflected a wide breath of disciplines and perspectives. Of particular note, we became part of an international community as the journal had a clearly stated interest in publishing research beyond domestic borders.

The articles that we published in the *Journal of Business Ethics* reflect, in a limited way, the diversity of issues and approaches that are characteristic of the field of business ethics. We explored issues such as why students take business ethics courses, ethical decision-making in the medical profession, and the application of the theory of reasoned action to explain unethical conduct.

However, as we approached the study of business ethics, we believed that we could make more significant and timely contributions to the field by encouraging methodological rigor in empirical business ethics research, specifically for those scholars seeking to study self-reported ethical conduct. Time shows that our hope has become a reality. According to the *Science Citation Index*, our article on methodology in business ethics research has been cited 108 times by social science scholars from around the world who have published in a wide variety of ethics and management journals. As we might expect, the largest percentage of these publications have been in the *Journal of Business Ethics*. It is gratifying to see that our work, in some fashion, may have guided and inspired others to introduce more methodological rigor, even into present publications (2010). We are thankful, as the work we have done is clearly built upon the generation of scholars who preceded us, especially those who published in the *Journal of Business Ethics*.

For 30 years Alex Michalos and Deborah Poff have carefully and thoughtfully guided *the Journal of Business Ethics*. They should be proud of the independent young adult journal that is celebrating a thirtieth birthday and is well positioned for many more decades of significant achievement.

Mohammed Y. A. Rawwas

Reflections

What Has Been the Impact of Your Citation Classic on Your Career?

The Citation classic [Consumer ethics – an investigation of the ethical beliefs of elderly consumers] helped me be promoted to Full Professor. It was one of the most important factors to determine my promotion. I had to include in my promotion file all articles that had cited my citation classic. Another benefit, the citation classic gave credibility and respect to my work.

What Has Been the Impact of the *Journal of Business Ethics* on the Field of Business Ethics?

The *Journal of Business Ethics* has introduced many theories, models and applications of business ethics that professors used in their classes and manuscripts. The journal has improved our business ethics knowledge and has given us a source to resort to it to understand the complexity of the topic.

Diana C. Robertson

Reflections

Publication of this article [Empiricism in business ethics – suggested research directions] the *Journal of Business Ethics* came at a time when empirical studies were in short supply. In the article I espoused the directions in which I believed the field should be moving and argued for the value of a greater empirical focus. In a sense the article outlined my own future research agenda. The paper called for further emphasis on the study of ethical behavior, in addition to the study of attitudes, and empirical work that would build theory as well as test it. The paper also delineated additional methodologies used in the social sciences that could be applied to the study of unethical behavior.

I wrote the article with the firm belief that normative and empirical research in business ethics are not in competition, but that each has much to contribute to the other. Perhaps more importantly, this mindset permeates my approach to both normative and empirical work. In advising doctoral students, I continuously reinforce the point that normative and empirical scholars can learn a great deal from each other. For example, in working with a student conducting experimental work on unethical behavior in negotiations, I underscored the importance of establishing the normative basis of such behavior.

The *Journal of Business Ethics* has been foundational to creating the field as we know it today. It was one of the first journals to focus explicitly on business ethics and, as such, helped legitimize the scholarly nature of business ethics research. In fact, it is difficult to imagine the field without the *Journal*. The *Journal* has allowed scholars to connect to one another around the topics about which we are most passionate. It has welcomed normative and empirical research, multiple and innovative methodologies, and has provided an outlet for international perspectives and research. In its nearly 30 years of publication, the journal has maintained its viability and importance to the field. We can only hope that it will continue to shape and define the field for at least the next 30 years.

Gedeon J. (Deon) Rossouw

The Impact of the Journal of Business Ethics on the Multi-disciplinary and Global Nature of the Field of Business Ethics

The *Journal of Business Ethics* made an important contribution in establishing the field of business ethics as a multi-disciplinary and a global field of study.

Business ethics has since its inception as an academic field been characterised as a multi-disciplinary field of study. This multi-disciplinary nature of the field of business ethics is at the same time one of the biggest attractors and one of the biggest detractors of the field of business ethics. As an attractor the multi-disciplinary nature of the field offers scholars from various academic disciplines the opportunity to move beyond the narrow confines of one specific field, and the possibility of multi- and inter-disciplinary collaboration. The multi-disciplinary nature of the field, however, is also a cause of frustration and alienation amongst scholars from various disciplines, each with their own disciplinary methodologies and epistemologies. This tension between various disciplines is visible in various collisions that have emerged in the field of business ethics, such as those between normative and descriptive approaches, between qualitative and quantitative approaches, and between reflective and managerial approaches. An achievement, but also a contribution that the *Journal of Business Ethics* has made to the field of business ethics over the past 30 years, is to provide a common dwelling for these diverse and often dissenting voices. The list of section editors of the *Journal of Business Ethics* underlines the extent to which this journal has been successful in not only accommodating a rich diversity of disciplinary perspectives, but also to enhance and entrench the multi-disciplinary nature of the field of business ethics.

The *Journal of Business Ethics* also played an important role in internationalising and globalising the field of business ethics. It succeeded in becoming a journal for the entire world, rather than a journal for, or of, a specific geographical region. On a global scale the *Journal of Business Ethics* has become the preferred journal of publication for business ethicists from all regions of the world (cf. Chan et al. 2010: 41). This was also demonstrated in the recent study by Albrecht et al. (2010). Although the *Journal of Business Ethics* is the preferred publication outlet of business ethicists around the world, the fact remains that the *Journal* has nevertheless been dominated by contributions from Western Europe and Northern America (and more specifically the USA and Canada). However, despite this domination, there was a gradual growth in contributions from other parts of the world, but especially from the Asia-Pacific region. The fact that the publishers of the *Journal of Business Ethics* recently launched the *Asian Journal of Business Ethics* is a clear recognition of the growth in contributions from that part of the globe. I have no doubt that the *Journal of Business Ethics* should once more be given at least some of the credit for internationalising and globalising the field of business ethics.

Despite the fact that the *Journal* became the world's preferred outlet for business ethics research, its readership still remains very much concentrated in the Global North and in the northern hemisphere. The cost of subscription to the journal remains prohibitively high for many countries in the Global South. Consequently despite the advances that have been made by the journal in attracting authors from around the world, the same can unfortunately not be said of readers around the world. It is my hope that ways will be found to also globalise the readership of the *Journal of Business Ethics.*

References

Albrecht, C., J.A. Thompson, J.L. Hoopes, and P. Rodrigo. 2010 Business ethics journal rankings as perceived by business ethics scholars. *Journal of Business Ethics* 95: 227–237.

Kam C., K.C. Cha, H-G. Fung, and J. Yau. 2010 Business ethics research: A global perspective. *Journal of Business Ethics* 95: 39–53.

Mark S. Schwartz

Reflections

What Has Been the Impact, If Any, of Your Citation Classic on Your Career?

My article "The Nature of the Relationship Between Corporate Codes of Ethics and Behaviour" (2001), which has somehow ended up as a *JBE* "Citation Classic", was based on my PhD dissertation. The study, which involved in-depth interviews of 57 employees, managers, and ethics officers at four large Canadian companies, examines several questions related to codes of ethics, including whether they in fact make any difference in affecting employee's behaviour. The primary finding of the study was that while under certain circumstances codes might affect one's behaviour, the nature of the impact was typically indirect rather than direct in nature. To help explain how codes impact behaviour, a series of eight metaphors were developed that include: (1) Rule-book (clarify); (2) Sign-post (consult); (3) Mirror (confirm); (4) Magnifying Glass (caution); (5) Shield (challenge); (6) Club (compliance); (7) Smoke Detector (convince); and (8) Fire Alarm (contact).

This initial study led me to publishing several other articles in *JBE* including: "A Code of Ethics for Corporate Codes of Ethics" (Schwartz 2002); "Effectiveness of Codes of Ethics: Perceptions of Code Users" (Schwartz 2004); "Universal Moral Values for Corporate Codes of Ethics" (Schwartz 2005), as well as "Tone at the Top: An Ethics Code for Directors?" (Schwartz et al. 2005).

Over time however, my research focus has shifted away from codes of ethics to other potentially more important factors that might influence employee ethical decision-making. I now believe that the key elements of developing and sustaining an ethical corporate culture include: (i) ethics programs (with codes of ethics as the key component); (ii) core ethical values that are infused throughout an organization's policies (i.e., not just within the code) as well as its processes and practices; along with (iii) ethical leadership.

What Has Been the Impact, If Any, of the *Journal of Business Ethics* on the Field of Business Ethics?

When I first began my PhD at York University in Toronto, Canada in 1993, there was no formal PhD program that specialized in the business ethics field that I was aware of. I was fortunate however to have Professor Wesley Cragg as my PhD supervisor. One of my first undertakings was to try to read all of the articles published in *JBE* (or at least the abstracts) since its inception (and there were already quite a few by the mid-1990s). Along with a review of the key textbooks published in the business ethics field, this initial review of *JBE* formed the backbone of all of my future research, and I suspect for many others in the field as well.

There is no question in my mind that without *JBE*, the field of business ethics would not have become accepted and appreciated as a legitimate academic field, now suffused with quality research. When *JBE* was added to the list of top journals by the *Financial Times* as part of its criteria for its business school rankings, this led to an even greater acceptance of the legitimacy and importance of the field's academic contribution.

In terms of my academic career, I am greatly appreciative that *JBE* exists, and that it welcomes all types of academic study from around the world, whether theoretical or empirical (including both quantitative and qualitative). *JBE* provides a critical publication outlet not just for those in the business ethics field, but for those entering or intersecting with the field from other disciplines. While there is much more business ethics research to be conducted and disseminated, I am certain that *JBE* will continue to play a dominant role in this endeavour.

References

Schwartz, M. 2001. The nature of the relationship between corporate codes of ethics and behaviour. *Journal of Business Ethics* 32(3): 247–262.

Schwartz, M.S. 2002. A code of ethics for corporate codes of ethics. *Journal of Business Ethics* 41(1): 27–43.

Schwartz, M. S. 2004. Effective corporate codes of ethics: Perceptions of code users. *Journal of Business Ethics* 55(4): 321–341.

Schwartz, M.S. 2005. Universal moral values for corporate codes of ethics. *Journal of Business Ethics* 59(1): 27–44.

Schwartz, M.S., T. Dunfee, and M. Kline. 2005. Tone at the top: An ethics code for directors? *Journal of Business Ethics* 58(1): 79–100.

S. Prakash Sethi

A New Milestone for the Journal of Business Ethics

It would be a monumental understatement to state that *Journal of Business Ethics (JBE)* has played a critical role in the development of academic inquiry into the general area of business ethics and corporate social responsibility. This definition of business ethics – or more accurately, the ethical context of business – continues to expand and now includes notions of sustainable business practices which emanate from a corporation's core business operations as opposed to voluntary non-business related responses to community needs. To wit, society's expectations regarding corporate performance have moved from corporate social responsibility to corporate social accountability.

This journey has not been easy or planned. We cannot be sure how it will evolve in the foreseeable future because of the difficulties in defining the "common good" and the legitimacy – ethical, social or political – of those individuals and groups who advocate an enlarged and multi-dimensional notion of responsibility and accountability on the part of business institutions.

From its inception, *JBE* has been an incubator nurturing the seeds of this new arena of academic inquiry. The primary credit and burden for this endeavor must rest with its two founding editors, Prof. Alex C. Michalos and Prof. Deborah C. Poff. They shepherded the journal from its infancy through a challenging youth to its mature state of vigorous and highly influential creation and dissemination of information on all issues pertaining to business conduct, including its moral underpinnings, and its real-time impact on both direct and indirect stakeholders.

I have been privileged to be a part of this process from its beginning, as a member of the editorial board and a frequent contributor and as an avid reader. From its very beginning, the two editors recognized that: (a) business ethics must be analyzed in the context of business practices in their various manifestations and competitive market condition, and (b) diverse social norms and cultural values influence the interpretation of the nature of ethics under different socio-cultural value frameworks. Therefore, the adequacy of business responses needs to be evaluated within their socio-political context, which may differ from the traditional notions of Judeo-Christian values that are taken for granted in the industrialized societies of the West.

The editors of *JBE* were cognizant of these questions and successfully bridged the gap between the East and the West by (a) continuously changing and enlarging the composition of the editorial board to incorporate diverse perspectives and practical experiences, and (b) by broadening the scope of *JBE*'s coverage in terms of issues addressed, new analytical frameworks, empirical data and findings, and widely divergent arguments as to ethically desirable outcomes.

This open-mindedness, in my opinion, was one of the most important reasons that allowed *JBE* to anticipate enormous changes in the world of business that would fundamentally alter and evolve with the advent of globalization and would de-link business (as owners of capital) from its two other important factors, i.e., labor and physical resources. This process has led to a dramatic shift in the locus of bargaining power and control of physical and human resources between political (mostly national) and economic (mostly global) economic institutions. As a consequence, there has been a relative diminution of the power of national governments to safeguard the wellbeing of their people as custodians of common good. Conversely, it has led to a tremendous increase in the power of large MNCs and their top executives to shape the economic structures of societies and in the distribution (in their favor) of added value, i.e., income, created through economic activity and efficient utilization of factors of production, i.e., capital, labor, and physical resources around the world.

JBE's success in envisioning these changes and capturing their impact is evident in the broad scope of the topics covered in its 100+ volumes and almost of 5,000 articles published in the 30 years of its existence. By any measure, *JBE* is the highest ranked journal in its field. Its roster of authors includes many of the most prominent and highly regarded authors from diverse academic fields who address common issues and challenge traditional orthodoxies in search of practical answers that cannot be viewed from the single lens of traditional academic disciplines.

In one sense, *JBE* and other journals dealing with ethical issues in business have become mainstream and their legitimacy and relevance are not in question, although this was not the case 30 years ago when the founders of *JBE* ventured to develop the new journal. In its early stages, the prevailing dogma of corporate social responsibility was best defined by the Noble laureate Milton Friedman, who declared that the "social responsibility of business is to increase profits." Business organizations were naturally quick to embrace this mission to the exclusion of everything else because it provided them with an iron-clad justification for their conduct. A review of corporate pronouncements around that period provides ample evidence that companies would vociferously argue against any notion of corporate social responsibility that could be construed as undermining their primary role of maximizing profits and enhancing shareholder value. They were also quite astute in not emphasizing the fundamental assumption made by Friedman that the competitive nature of markets, which were seldom as competitive as corporate leaders would want others to believe, and also the fact that business leaders continuously and invariably successfully strove to make markets less competitive so as to give them additional "pricing power" and profitability. Moreover, they were presenting Friedman's analysis as if it were akin to the definitive and incontrovertible statements of an expert in natural sciences. Also ignored was the fact that other Noble laureates in economics, such as Kenneth Arrow and Amartya Sen, had expressed starkly different views while still arguing within the boundaries of traditional economic theory.

In the subsequent three decades, there has been a remarkable and profound change in corporate expressions – if not actual conduct – on corporate social responsibility. The current state of corporate pronouncements could not be more different and yet equally self-serving. There is scarcely a corporation that does not profess its commitment to being socially responsible and adhering to the principles of ethical conduct and sustainable business practices; talking about social franchise; and, honoring a commitment to various types of codes of conduct as demonstration of voluntary self-regulation. Companies now publish voluminous annual social responsibility-sustainability reports publicizing their commitments to society's well-being and describing their activities as evidence of those commitments.

The Future Role of JBE

In my view, the future role of *JBE* is even more daunting than the challenges it faced at the time of its start-up 30 years ago. Globalization has brought about fundamental changes in how economic activities are conducted around the world, how the rules of the game are determined, and how major players influence the final economic and social outcomes, and their impact on various stakeholders.

JBE and other similarly oriented journals have had a profound influence on changing the nature of discourse between corporations and society-at-large. Corporate rhetoric now echoes the narrative advocated by stakeholders who profess to speak for the groups and issues that have suffered from negative externalities, i.e., adverse side-effects, of corporate actions.

Unfortunately, there is little evidence to show that corporate decision-making has changed in any significant manner to reflect integration of ethical norms – including the notions of common good – in corporate decision-making. One has only to look at the recent economic melt-down and resultant human suffering around the world and recognize the footprint of large corporations through questionable business practices of the leading financial institutions, insider trading, financial manipulation, widespread instances of bribery and corruption, price fixing, collusion and other instances of non-competitive behavior, fraud in marketing practices, environmental degradation and abuse of indigenous people on the part of extractive industries, and unfair and exploitative labor practices in poorer countries.

Instances of such unethical and illegal practices are not isolated. They are also not confined to certain industries, companies or countries. Instead, they seem to manifest corporate conduct that is hard-wired into the DNA of corporate persona and where voluntary adherence to higher legal and ethical norms would appear to be aberrant behavior.

I believe the future role for *JBE* is even more challenging and demanding *JBE* must find a way to induce changes in corporate behavior in a manner that combines economic efficiency with social justice, restraint in the use of economic power that voluntarily yields to the supremacy of political consensus for what is common good. In the final analysis, economic institutions can flourish only in the midst of social wellbeing. To think otherwise, would lead to the demise of free societies – including capitalism – as we know it and cherish it.

Roger A. Shiner

Reflections

I would like to congratulate the *Journal of Business Ethics* on 30 years of publication and over 100 volumes. Anyone working in the field has reason to thank deeply Alex Michalos and Deborah Poff for their foresight in the establishment of the *Journal* and their energy and dedication towards its continued existence. Even though an achievement like 100 volumes cannot occur without countless hours of time put in by other editors, reviewers and referees, and of course contributors, still the *Journal* will forever be linked to Alex and Deborah, and rightly so. When the *Journal* began publication, business ethics as a field for serious academic research, especially in my field of philosophy, barely existed. The foundation of a specialized, high-quality outlet for serious research served as an encouragement, an empowerment, and a reward for those of us working in the field as teachers to turn also to serious scholarship.

"Begin as you mean to continue" is a familiar saying. A brief look at the essays in the early volumes of the *Journal* reveals many that have become classics of the field, not matched since as to their insights and interest. Many of today's hot topics in the field of business ethics were seen as key issues even then by the editors and contributors to the *Journal* – corporate social responsibility, the ethics of advertising and business bluffing, anonymity and whistle-blowing, the ethical challenges of multinational corporations, computer ethics (now partitioned off as a separate field of endeavour). One could adopt glass-half-empty mode and see this as an indication of how little the *Journal* has affected anything. Or one could adopt glass-half-full mode and see this as an indication of the *Journal*'s willingness to take on the perennial issues with which the world of business struggles, and with which society struggles in trying to bring some measure of ethical accountability to the world of business.

The *Journal* was positioned from the beginning as a place for multidisciplinary approaches and studies. Nonetheless, from my own particular perspective as an academic philosopher, the content of the *Journal* has evolved over the last 30 years. It began with a considerable emphasis on more abstract and conceptual studies, but in recent times the emphasis has shifted to more empirical studies – field-work studies of attitudes and responses to ethical issues and challenges, rather than analysis of what would be good ethical reasons for action in some context or other. It is easily arguable that the empirical turn is justified: how can we begin to have a practical effect on the conduct of business unless we know what is out there in terms of existing attitudes and patterns of response? However, it is also fair to ask: how can we begin to have a practical effect on the conduct of business unless we know what goals and principles are ethically valid for business. Perhaps over the next stage of the *Journal*'s life, the pendulum will begin to swing back.

Well, there it is – my assumption that in the *Journal*'s future lie another 30 years of publication and another 100 volumes. May it be so. May the *Journal* continue as it has begun – a place to publish the leading-edge research in one of the most important fields of study in the humanities and social sciences that we academics presently occupy.

Shannon Shipp

Thinking About the Future of the Journal of Business Ethics

As an author in and a reviewer for *Journal of Business Ethics* for 11 years and an avid reader and follower for many more, I have had the privilege to observe how *JBE* has developed and shaped and been shaped by the rapidly developing field of business ethics. Another journal editor once told me that to have a successful journal, the editor must select a balance of timely and timeless articles. Elsewhere in this issue, the citation analysis of the articles published in *JBE*, the sheer number of articles published compared to other journals in the field of business ethics, and the inclusion in the *Financial Times* list of journals used to assess the quality of the publications of a given school or college of business shows that *JBE* has been able to reach that standard.

It has been interesting to observe how many of the articles published in ***JBE*** have addressed a few basic questions in business ethics:

1. What does it mean for businesses or individuals in business to be ethical in a business context?
2. Why do individuals or businesses act ethically (or unethically)?
3. How can we train individuals to act more ethically?
4. If training, selection, and development of ethical corporate culture fail, how do we effectively deter or punish unethical action?

Of these questions, the last has probably received the least attention. After all, this is the *Journal of Business Ethics*, not the *Journal of Corporate Punishment* or the *Journal of Deterrence*. However, according to the regulatory cycle proposed by Marianne Jennings, regulation is the end result of the companies' failure to meet the new ethical challenges they face when they develop new products, enter new markets, or develop new technologies. As a result, deterrence or punishment is a natural result of failing to meet new ethical challenges and deserving of more attention from business ethics scholars.

Punishment scholars such as Posner would argue that increasing the penalties for unscrupulous behavior would make individuals and companies less likely to engage in those activities. Yet increasing the level of regulatory oversight and associated penalties have not been the panacea one might expect. Sarbanes-Oxley in the U.S. was intended to be the law that would put an end to accounting shenanigans and manipulation of stock prices. To further strengthen the law, changes in the federal sentencing guidelines promoted even stiffer penalties for firms and individuals that violated securities laws. In the U.K., the Public Interest Disclosure Act and other regulations were enacted with the same end in mind. Unfortunately, the results were disappointing in controlling illegal or unethical behavior.

Since the passage of Sarbanes and other measures, accounting scandals such as abusive tax shelters promoted by some of the largest accounting firms in the world, ubiquitous use of backdating stock options, and the global financial crisis driven by widespread abuses in the mortgage industry and credit default swaps showed that simply writing new laws or increasing the amount of regulation will not result in the desired changes in behavior. In the wake of the mortgage meltdown, in 2010 the Dodd Frank bill was enacted to curb primarily banking institutions and I fear that the results will be the same.

But the types of ethical restraints often discussed in the pages of *JBE* and the new types of ethical oversight offered by new technologies might be part of the solution. I spoke at an all-day event where I discussed ethical awareness and ethical decision-making in the first half of the event and a partner at a Big 4 accounting firm spoke on curbing fraud and stiffening control and compliance measures in the second half.

When he stood up to speak, his first comment was, "If you listened to my colleague this morning and follow his advice to train your employees on ethics and to enact an ethical culture at your firm, you will probably not be calling my firm for assistance. If you did not, keep my number handy."

Employees and customers can help enact, monitor, and reinforce an ethical culture through new technological methods. Consumers can use such services as Angie's List, the Better Business Bureau business certification program, and web sites that target specific corporations such as Wal-Mart, Nike, and others to voice their concerns and be heard directly by high level managers in the affected firms. Employees can use confidential hotlines or other mechanisms to communicate with the audit committee of the firm. It may be that the future of dealing with unethical behavior is not to enact new laws and tighten the penalties but to focus on the informal means of affecting ethical behavior.

I look forward to many more years of timely and timeless articles from *JBE*

Randi L. Sims

Reflections

The research entitled "The influence of ethical fit on employee satisfaction, commitment, and turnover" was the starting point of my interest in employee ethical decision making. This particular study of hospital employees was among the first to demonstrate that ethical fit is significantly related to employee attitudes and behavioral intentions. The preliminary study laid the groundwork for my dissertation and became the foundation for much of my later work on employee ethical decision making. Before the establishment of the *Journal of Business Ethics*, research in business ethics appeared as a small sub-field within journals whose focus was primarily on other areas of business. With the launch of *JBE*, business ethics was more clearly established as an independent field of study, demonstrating the increasing importance of the study of business ethics.

Ronald R. Sims

The Institutionalization of Ethics, 1991

What, If Any, Has Been the Impact of Your Citation Classic on Your Career?

This citation classic has helped provide a platform during my career to not only dialogue with other academics who have an interest in business ethics, but also network and do increased interdisciplinary teaching, research and consulting work with practitioners, students and others, and overlap with others in the fields of organizational change and development who have a mutual interest in changing organizational culture. Further, the citation has been instrumental in being viewed as a resource by colleagues, students, and others on who want to publish relevant, current, innovative and accessible practical or applied writing on topics such as business ethics.

What, If Any, Has Been the Impact of the *Journal of Business Ethics* on the Field of Business Ethics?

Anyone who is familiar with the *Journal of Business Ethics* knows that it publishes original articles from a wide variety of methodological and disciplinary perspectives concerning ethical issues related to business that bring something new or unique to the discourse in their field. Articles published by contributors like myself examine moral or business ethics aspects of systems of production, consumption, marketing, advertising, social and economic accounting, labor relations, public relations and organizational behavior. Probably the most important impact that the *JBE* has had on the field of business ethics is the creation of a vehicle which has indeed promoted a dialogue between individual academics or researchers and a variety of interested professional and non-professional groups, be they from the business community, universities, government agencies, consumer groups or the society at large. More specifically, over the years the *JBE* has fulfilled its mission of improving the human condition by providing a forum for business ethics to be at the forefront in our understanding and analysis of the behavior of business organizations.

The *JBE* has been instrumental in shaping the identity of business ethics as an academic field through its published articles on a variety of research directions, inquiry methods and diversity of scholars who represent many leading academic (and non-academic institutions) from around the world. In addition, as a publication outlet the *JBE* continues to have a dramatic impact on the evolution, identity and future directions of the discourse or dialogue on business ethics. In my view, the *JBE* is a discipline-specific journal that has led the way in informing the overall academic community about the existence of business ethics as a scholarly domain. For example, when articles like the "Institutionalization of business ethics" was published in the *JBE* in 1991 the field of business ethics or research on the topic did not offer many options to publish my work on business ethics. However, over time several other specific journals emerged and as the business ethics discipline has progressed over the past few decades, more journals have opened up as outlets for a dialogue on the topic. For me, this is a sign of how business ethics has become a recognized academic domain since following the lead of the *JBE* many other business-oriented or general management journals now offer a space where scholars read new works, exchange ideas, share theories and accumulate references on the topic of business ethics. By staying true to its mission of publishing articles that examine moral or business ethics topics the *JBE* impact on the field of business ethics is quite obvious when one considers the number of non-business ethics or discipline researchers, practitioners, university administrators and members of business, not-for-profit and government organizations are able to form their understanding of business ethics as an academic field.

Ronald R. Sims

The Challenge to Unethical Behavior in Organizations, 1992

What, If Any, Has Been the Impact of Your Citation Classic on Your Career?

This citation classic has impacted my career as it has been utilized by fellow academics and practitioners who have an interest in the implications of ethical or unethical or ethical behavior on organizations. Whether as part of tenure and promotion decisions over the past 20 years, when colleagues, doctoral or undergraduate students are engaged in their own research or articles are published in journals which cite the article, or when I have submitted proposals to editors at book publishers, the article has served as a link between myself and others.

What, If Any, Has Been the Impact of the *Journal of Business Ethics* on the Field of Business Ethics?

Since the birth of the *Journal of Business Ethics* in 1982, the *JBE* has helped move the field of business ethics from what was once considered a relatively new niche discipline to a field or discipline viewed by scholars and others as the source for dialogue and research on the topic of business ethics. In 1992 when the *JBE* published my article "The challenge to unethical behavior in organizations", academics like myself, who were interested in business ethics topics were lucky if we could publish our research or work in more general outlets. Academic conferences, like the Academy of Management, also served as an outlet for those of us who were doing research on business ethics. The *JBE* helped the business ethics discipline mature over the past three decades. The *JBE* has allowed business ethics scholars like myself to have a research outlet that is indeed different from that of our colleagues in other academic domains and the *JBE* serves as a discipline-specific journal where business ethics researchers are able to directly communicate with like-minded audiences. Partially as a result of the *JBE*, a number of outlets include more traditional business-oriented journals now devoting substantial or more exclusive (i.e., special issues) on the topic of business ethics.

As corporate misconduct increased (e.g., Enron, WorldCom, Tyco), I believe the *JBE* has helped make the study of business ethics become more mainstream. The increased respectability of the *JBE* (i.e., the *JBE* is one of the 45 journals used by the *Financial Times* in compiling the prestigious Business School research rank) has helped those who do research on business ethics, which is still considered a niche discipline or field by some, to overcome or better address challenges like the recognition of their scholarly contribution by their peers, administrators and various committees. Fortunately, in my experience, more and more senior scholars and administrators serving on university tenure and promotion, merit pay and hiring committees are familiar with the research domain of academics or faculty, who work in what some view as the very narrow area of business ethics. As a result, as I can attest to when considering my experiences over my academic career during their deliberations, we no longer had to rely on personal subjective judgment, opinion of others or formal journal ranking lists. One need only pay attention to how many researchers who are not viewed as "those who focus on the niche field or discipline of business ethics" are now fighting to get their articles published in the *JBE*.

Ronald R. Sims, Hsing Cheng and Hildy Teegen 1996

Toward a Profile of Software Piraters, 1996

What Has Been the Impact, If Any, of Your Citation Classic on Your Career?

Perhaps the best way to answer the first question is by sharing the comments of one of my colleagues and co-authors at the time, Dr. Hsing Kenny Cheng, who when asked to respond to the question stated the following "Software piracy was a very serious problem (and still is) when I started my academic career at the College of William and Mary in 1992. I was intrigued by the software piracy problem; however, there was little research on software piracy at the time. My then-colleagues, Professors Ronald Sims and Hildy Teegen, and I decided to answer two key questions of software piracy – who pirates software and why? Our research into the first question resulted in the 1996 *Journal of Business Ethics* article entitled "Toward a Profile of Student Software Piraters". Building on the publication of this article in the *JBE* a follow-up study on why people pirate software appeared in *Journal of Management Information Systems* entitled "To Purchase or to Pirate Software: An Empirical Study" in 1997. Even though all of us have moved on to other research problems, we continue to experience the enormous impact of our software piracy studies on our career. None more evident than the comment of an outside reviewer quoted in the chair's letter in support of my promotion to full professor last year: "I know first-hand that Dr. Cheng's work laid the foundations that detailed the key triggers of software theft. His work has had a profound impact on research in software piracy which later evolved into addressing intellectual property issues surrounding other cultural products such as music, movies, and books." I must echo the comments of both Dr. Cheng and the outside reviewer as the article was but one thread of my more than 20 years of research, teaching and service in the business ethics arena. Research, teaching and service that has increasingly played an important role in my scholarly, teaching and service efforts here at the College of William and Mary Mason School of Business.

What Has Been the Impact, If Any, of the *Journal of Business Ethics* on the Field of Business Ethics?

The *JBE* has helped inform a large number of academics, practitioners, and others of the important issues that make up the field of business ethics and are of importance to teachers who teach business ethics, and in turn has influenced a large number of students who have gone on to be practitioners . Moreover, many of those in business have also turned to the writings in the *JBE* by those who one would consider in the fields of business ethics, or have looked to the *JBE* for guidance on issues or for help in writing corporate codes or designing training programs, all of which one finds as part of the discourse that make up the field of business ethics. In our experience, the media as well frequently turns to those who publish in research on business ethics in the *JBE* for guidance, help, or sound bites. Many of the academics one finds in the field of business ethics have been able to make an effort to open a dialogue with those in business, and have frequently been successful in doing so because of the *JBE*. The *JBE* has expanded the audience, not only for colleagues and students, but also corporate managers and the general public. We have also noticed that non-academic consultants have turned to the *JBE* for research and information which helps them better mediate between the academic arena and the corporate executive, many of whom use the business ethics scholarly material from the *JBE* to become informed about the state of the art and the arguments for or against various positions. Some of these act not only as intermediaries but, in a sense, as translators, translating information from the business ethics field found in the *JBE* into business-speak.

Ronald R. Sims and Johannes Brinkman 2003

Enron Ethics: (Or Culture Matters More Than Codes), 2003

What, If Any, Has Been the Impact of Your Citation Classic on Your Career?

This citation class has had an impact on our careers as it has provided important opportunities for us to network with other colleagues, present applied research papers at national and international conferences, and be sought out by organizations and those in the media who have an interest in how to develop and/or change cultures in organizations.

What, If Any, Has Been the Impact of the *Journal of Business Ethics* on the Field of Business Ethics?

First, business ethics which in our own view and (many other researchers) was once a niche-discipline or field has been elevated to a much higher status because of the *Journal of Business Ethics*. Since first publishing our article "Enron ethics: (or culture matters more than codes)" in the *Journal of Business Ethics* in 2003, we have found that we are no longer dramatically disadvantaged as compared to our colleagues because our research is published in a "niche" or lower quality journal as the *Journal of Business Ethics* as it is now included in the general journal ranking lists. Such a ranking has elevated the field of business ethics as very few of our colleagues (to include those who do research on business ethics and those who do not) now refer to the *Journal of Business Ethics* as a non-premier discipline outlet or label it as 'C' in a ranking of journals in management and related areas. This also applies to the field of business ethics. Clearly, times have changed over the years. And the change and impact on the business ethics field can partly be attributed to the *Journal of Business Ethics*.

Second, tying into the first two points above the *Journal of Business Ethics* has an impact on energizing the business ethics movement, or more specifically the field of business ethics itself, which has become firmly entrenched in the academic, business and broader communities. The concern for ethics in business is partially a result of the *Journal of Business Ethics*. The *Journal of Business Ethics* has helped business ethics as an academic field to contribute to discussion forums, research and teaching that inform both ethics in business and the business ethics movement. That is, the *Journal of Business Ethics* has helped the business ethics field be more responsive to the other two and in turn better interface or interact with them.

Finally, from an academic perspective, looking back over the past 30 years the *Journal of Business Ethics* has helped create a history of how the field of business ethics has evolved and just how far the field has come. The *Journal of Business Ethics* has helped us understand the past of the business ethics field. But it also continues to encourage us to look at the future of the field of business ethics. And especially the reality that there is still a lot for the business ethics field to do. For example, both globalization and the continued evolution of business organizations will change the way business is done and the ethical issues businesses face. As scholars from the United States and Norway we continue to see that the *Journal of Business Ethics* will remain relevant and have an impact on the field of business ethics, as business organizations change in the years to come. In closing, if there is anything that really stands out about the impact of the *Journal of Business Ethics* on the business ethics field, it is that the *Journal of Business Ethics* demonstrates that business ethics is neither a fad as some still claim, nor an oxymoron, as still others joke. The *Journal of Business Ethics* will continue to keep business ethics as a vibrant, complex field. We expect the *Journal of Business Ethics* will discuss ethical issues related to business ethics, from a wide variety of methodological and disciplinary perspectives, examine moral aspects of business organizations (i.e., their systems), serve as a vehicle for discourse and dialogue, and continue to portray the field of business ethics in dynamic and fascinating ways.

Anusorn Singhapakdi

An Essay on the Paper "The Perceived Role of Ethics and Social Responsibility: A Scale Development"

My primary research area has always been in the area of business ethics. Therefore, it is an honor to have a research paper recognized by the *Journal of Business Ethics (JBE),* the leading academic journal in business ethics. It is also an honor to be asked to write an essay about the impact of my *citation distinguished* paper (Singhapakdi et al. 1996) on my career and the impact of *JBE* on the field of business ethics. I believe *JBE* impacts the field of business ethics. Although my research program has always been in business ethics, as a marketing professor I also have my scholarly papers in business ethics published in traditional journals in the marketing discipline. Based on a recent citation analysis of my publication, it is interesting to find out that I generally have more citations for my *JBE* papers than for many of my business ethics papers published in marketing journals. It is also interesting that I seem to have more inquiries for my *JBE* papers, especially from scholars from developing and/or non-Western countries, than inquiries for my other business ethics papers published in traditional marketing journals. I would conclude *JBE* is more well-known among international scholars and, obviously, because *JBE* has a higher profile among *business ethics scholars*!

I believe my *citation distinguished* paper has been quite important for my career. The thrust of the paper is the development of a scale to measure a manager's perceived role of ethics and social responsibility (PRESOR). Since the scale has been widely adopted and successfully used by many scholars, the paper certainly has helped in establishing my reputation as a business ethics scholar. In fact, the paper has not only served as a good foundation for other scholars' work but has also served as a good foundation for my own subsequent work (e.g., Singhapakdi 1999; Singhapakdi et al. 2001, 2008).

For instance, the *citation distinguished* paper served as a strong foundation for the key assertion of my 1999 research (Singhapakdi 1999) that managers must first perceive ethics and social responsibility to be important to organizational effectiveness before their behaviors will become more ethical and socially responsible (the PRESOR scale was also used). The results, based on a mail survey of marketing managers in the U.S., generally supported this assertion and thus further validated the PRESOR scale. The results reveal a clear positive relationship between PRESOR and ethical decisions. In a sense, according to the results, managers believe that "Good ethics is good business" – a utilitarian motive can also result in ethical

BEHAVIOR (perhaps as easily as altruistic motives) and it's the behavior that ultimately matters.

As further examples of how this *distinguished* paper impacted my career, the PRESOR scale which was developed in the U.S. has also been adopted and translated for my research in different parts of the world. In Singhapakdi et al. (2001), my colleagues and I, among other things, investigated the variation in perceptions regarding the importance of ethics and social responsibility among marketing professionals from Australia, Malaysia, South Africa, and the U.S. The variation in those perceptions was explained by country differences (e.g., cultural differences and differences in the economic environment), organizational ethical climate, and selected demographic characteristics. In Singhapakdi et al. (2008), my colleagues and I further validated and extended the *distinguished* paper by investigating the relationship between selected antecedents and consequences of perceived importance of ethics within an economically growing non-Western culture (Thailand). I believe that my *citation distinguished* paper has been quite important for my career. I also believe that the *Journal of Business Ethics* significantly impacts the field of business ethics.

References

Singhapakdi, A. 1999. Perceived importance of ethics and ethical decisions in marketing. *Journal of Business Research* 45(1): 89–99.

Singhapakdi, A., M. Gopinath, J.K.M. Marta, and L.L. Carter. 2008. Antecedents and consequences of perceived importance of ethics in marketing situations: A study of Thai business people. *Journal of Business Ethics* 81: 887–904.

Singhapakdi, A., K. Karande, C.P. Rao, and S.J. Vitell. 2001. How important are ethics and social responsibility? A multinational study of marketing professionals. *European Journal of Marketing* 35(1/2): 133–152.

Singhapakdi, A., S.J. Vitell, K.C. Rallapalli, and K.L. Kraft. 1996. The perceived role of ethics and social responsibility: A scale development. *Journal of Business Ethics* 15(11): 1131–1140.

M. Joseph Sirgy

JBE's Impact on the Dissemination of Knowledge of Marketing Ethics in Books

What is the impact of *JBE* on the dissemination of knowledge of marketing ethics? One way to gauge *JBE*'s impact is to browse through marketing ethics books and look for *JBE* citations. During the last three decades, several major books were published on marketing ethics as well as marketing and society books and business ethics that incorporate a major component of marketing ethics. These are:

- Bloom, P.N., and G.T. Gundlach eds. 2001. *Handbook of marketing and society.* Thousand Oaks: Sage.
- Chonko, L.B. 1995. *Ethical decision making in marketing*. Thousand Oaks: Sage.
- Gundlach, G.T., Block, L.G., and W.L. Wilkie eds. 2007. *Explorations of marketing in society*. Mason: Thomson Higher Education.
- Laczniak, G.R., and P. Murphy. 1993. *Ethical marketing decisions: The higher road.* Boston: Allyn and Bacon.
- Michalos, A.C. 1995. *A pragmatic approach to business ethics*. Thousand Oaks: Sage.
- Murphy, P.E., G.R. Laczniak, N.E. Bowie, and T.A. Klein .2005. *Ethical marketing: Basic ethics in action*. Upper Saddle River: Pearson/Prentice-Hall.
- Peterson, R.A., and O.C. Ferrell eds. 2005. *Business ethics: New challenges for business schools and corporate leaders*. Armonk: M. E. Sharpe.
- Smith, N.C., and J.A. Quelch. eds. 1993. *Ethics in marketing*. Boston: Irwin.

Let's examine the evidence. *JBE* is cited in the book by Bloom and Gundlach (2001) in chapters dealing with changes on corporate practices in response to public interest advocacy and actions, corporate societal marketing, and macromarketing perspectives. The book by Chonko (1995) deals with ethical decision making in marketing. *JBE*'s imprint is felt throughout in discussions related to ethics and conflict, ethical decision making, ethics in the marketing work environment, marketing code of ethics, ethical issues in marketing information systems, ethics and product decisions, ethics and pricing decisions, ethics and advertising decisions, ethics and selling decisions, and ethics and distribution decisions. The book by Gundlach et al. (2007) has a major section dealing with marketing ethics. In that section, O. C. Ferrell addresses the nature and scope of marketing ethics. In this seminal article he cites research from *JBE*. *JBE* is also highly cited in the book by Laczniak and Murphy (1993) dealing with a variety of topics in marketing ethics, such as ethics in marketing research, product management ethics, ethical issues in distribution, ethical issues in advertising, personal selling ethics, and international marketing ethics. Alex Michalos, in his 1995 book, addresses several important marketing ethics topics based on research published in *JBE*. These include the impact of trust on business, international security, quality of life, and ethical considerations regarding public opinion polling during election campaigns. Murphy et al.'s (2005) book also covered topics such as ethical reasoning and marketing decisions, ethics in researching and segmenting markets, product management ethics, ethical issues in distribution channels and pricing, ethics in advertising and the internet, personal selling ethics, and implementing and auditing ethical marketing. Again, the book is replete with *JBE* citations. The edited book by Peterson and Ferrell (2005) [both editors are marketing professors] has countless *JBE* references. The book covers a large spectrum of topics related to marketing ethics such as ethics theory, personal moral codes, ethical leadership, and the conflict inherent between ethics and making a profit. Finally, with respect to the Smith and Quelch (1993) book, *JBE*'s imprint is evident through discussions of ethical issues in researching and targeting consumers, corporate policy and the ethics of competitor intelligence gathering, ethical issues in personal selling and sales force management, and ethical issues in advertising and sales promotion.

In sum, in its 30-years history *JBE* has made a significant impact on the dissemination of knowledge in marketing ethics through pedagogical books used in the classroom to teach marketing students, MBA students, and marketing professionals. I personally have used these books in teaching the subject matter, and I do strongly feel that *JBE* played an integral and indispensable role in the creation, dissemination, and utilization of knowledge directly related to marketing ethics. Thank you *JBE*, thank you Scott Vitell (editor of the Marketing Ethics section in *JBE*), and thank you Alex Michalos and Deborah Poff for leading this journal and making a fine and worthy contribution to the growing field of marketing ethics.

Alejo J. G. Sison

What, If Any, Has Been the Impact of the Journal of Business Ethics on the Field of Business Ethics?

I shall take a small detour in answering this question because sometimes, the shortest route isn't necessarily the best. First, I will try to respond to a query regarding the impact of the *Journal of Business Ethics* to those of us who work in the field by citing a personal experience. After earning my PhD I returned to the country of my birth, the Philippines, with a desire to lend a hand in a fledgling liberal arts college that had grown out of an institution that conducted graduate programs in business. This being the early 1990s, internet connection was at best spotty, if at all available. There was no alternative, therefore, to traditional libraries for sources of scholarly information. But resources at my college were unimaginably scarce, so I practically had to make do with the materials I had brought along with me from my graduate studies. Considering the 20 kilo airline baggage allowance and the limited funds I had for shipping, all told these books and journals occupied very little shelf-space.

However, there was one piece of advice from my mentor that stuck in my mind and to which I had tried to stay true even then: "Never resign yourself to simply repeating what other people have thought of and said." This, of course, implied that I should never give up furthering my own research interests, which was precisely the point in getting a PhD in the first place. But how?

Here is where the *Journal of Business Ethics* comes in. Early on I discovered that I could write the *Journal* managers and volunteer to come up with reviews of the new books they had received. That way, not only would I be able to keep abreast somewhat of recent developments, but I would also have a chance to publish short works. Best of all, my institution would be able to keep the books originally sent for review, for the use not only of myself and colleagues in the faculty, but of our students as well. To this day, I shall never forget this debt of gratitude that I owe to the *Journal.*

Since then I have moved on several times in my academic career, but the *Journal* has always accompanied me. I imagine it as an ever-dependable platform, both in print and electronically, from which to obtain, test and exchange knowledge. Given that knowledge doesn't come with its own voice or pair of legs, contact with it actually means contact with people of flesh and blood who are its purveyors and enablers. As a result, many of the people whom I have met through the *Journal*, in my multiple roles as reader, contributor, referee and editor, have in time turned out to be close acquaintances and friends. These include not only my fellow academics, but also managers, entrepreneurs, consultants, legislators, public administrators and publishing professionals, all of whom are usually covered by the catch-all term, "practitioners".

To some extent, my experience with the *Journal* mimics the one I have with the European Business Ethics Network (EBEN), the premier business ethics organization on the Continent and a major reference globally, in whose Executive Committee I serve. It is but logical and fitting that the *Journal* and EBEN regularly partner in the publication of special issues dedicated to the outstanding scholarship produced in EBEN conferences. In fact, we at EBEN do not consider the *Journal of Business Ethics* as just another journal, but as our journal, albeit extra-officially. Both perform the indispensable dual function of platform and gatekeeper or guardian of the best in business ethics scholarship and practice.

Laura J. Spence

Beyond the Usual Suspects: Leading the Field in Small Business Ethics

I still remember, back in 1997, receiving the proofs of my first article in the *Journal of Business Ethics* and feeling a real sense of pride to see my work in the familiar format. Then and now, the journal is highly visible as *the Journal of Business Ethics*, readily recognizable both within our field and by scholars outside it. Indeed, it is the journal's presence on the FT45 list which raises the profile and credibility of business ethics most obviously outside of our discipline, certainly within Europe. This is not at all to denigrate the other excellent publications in our field, which each make important contributions. Indeed, it is a regret of mine that the field does not have a wider range of high quality journals, which must be acknowledged to be in part a result of the extremely high number of issues of the *Journal of Business Ethics* absorbing much of the good work.

From my perspective the major contribution of the *Journal of Business Ethics* is the leadership the journal has shown in championing new and innovative approaches and aspects of business ethics. My personal favourite is unsurprisingly my own field, ethics in small firms. Like most others in mainstream management studies, not to mention the media and our own business school curricula, we business ethicists suffer from a blinkered obsession with large multinational corporations. Paradoxically these constitute a tiny minority of private sector businesses, literally, fewer than 5% in most countries, developed and developing alike. While there is no denying the individual impact that the 'usual suspects' can have (i.e. Nike, Philip Morris, Shell, Unilever, dare I say it, Enron), overlooking the majority business form of small and medium sized enterprises has in the past left our field bereft. This despite the enormous emphasis put on entrepreneurship and small business success by policy makers as the engines of the economy (around a third of turnover) and primary creators of employment (usually around 50% of private sector employment) and community cohesion. Indeed, with the global economic crisis engulfing us at the time of writing, still more emphasis is put on small firms as our saviours. Just in case there are any sceptics left out there, small firms cannot be treated as little big firms, they are different in nature as well as size from their larger counterparts, as all the published research testifies.

In 2004 a new section was established in the *Journal of Business Ethics* on Small Business, later developing to include Entrepreneurship and Social Enterprise, of which I am delighted to be the editor. This, I believe, was a major breakthrough in our field. Since that time, contributions have been published from all around the world on small business, embracing the critical developing country context (something else which we are not great at as business ethicists), and exploring the business ethics perspectives on entrepreneurship and social enterprise. I don't mean to imply that the *Journal of Business Ethics* was the first or is the only journal to publish in this area, but it has made a sustained commitment which has enhanced this research stream substantially. It is institutionalization as a stated section of the *Journal of Business Ethics* which I find so valuable, and which encourages me that our field is broadening in its focus and improving its contribution to knowledge by looking outside of – relatively speaking – a handful of well-known businesses. I look forward to still more innovative developments in the years to come.

Sebastian A. Sora

Journal of Business Ethics and Its Real Effect on Business Activities

In a world where it has become increasingly difficult to gather to exchange ideas, journals have become our *agora*. The *Journal of Business Ethics* is a particularly strong place where thoughtful businessmen and women grapple with dense, ambiguous, oft neglected ethical problems that abound in their professional and personal lives. The *Journal* provides businessmen and women with a source that helps them to enhance their own professional skills by skillfully publishing current, original thought that helps him or her to make more ethical, wiser decisions.

I have been a reviewer of the journal and two simple truths come to mind when reflecting on The *Journal's* importance: (1) it is a compendium of the finest thoughts in one place in the field of business ethics and (2) it has had an effect on the actions of many businesses. The *Journal* provides a platform in which original thinkers can share the ethical business problems that they face daily. This was evident in Jason Brennon's article on the evilness of profit: "For- Profit Business As a Civic Virtue" which argues that Google can be an example of a Civic Virtue. Brennon crafted the language so that we can better understand what it means to have virtue in a business world.

The *Journal of Business Ethics* also gives space to offer new perspectives to help people understand more subtle aspects of communication that often go overlooked. Thomas Li-Ping Tang "Detecting Honest People's Lies in Handwriting. The Power of the Ten Commandments and Internalized Ethical Values" encourages employers to better understand how people truthfully communicate. The *Journal* can also be a place where business executives can find the most current thought on issues that they face in strategic and tactical planning and give them a tool to navigate and reflect on the rocky terrain.

The *Journal's* uniqueness in publishing only original articles that are vetted by scholars in appropriate fields creates a brain trust of thinkers in the area that can give businessmen and women guidance when confronted by ethical issues. An executive's key skill and power rests in his/her ability to decide on a daily basis and often make those decisions in isolation. The *Journal* gives the executive a community in which some of those decisions may be made more easily and ethically, For example in a recent article by Martin and Parmar, "The Assumptions in Decision making Scholarship: Implications for Business Ethics Research," explore the rational model in the context of how core assumptions create decision paths. This awareness can make executive management more aware of how they are making decisions that effect the tactical and strategic future.

The writers of the *Journal* also engage in lively thought around increasingly sensitive and timely issues that face our multicultural world. Articles such as "Do Muslims Believe more in the Protestant Work Ethic than Christians? Comparison of People with Different Religious Backgrounds Living in the US" by Yavuz Fahir Zulfikar, allow business executives to change or modify or refresh their perceptions of what it means to lead a business in a multicultural environment. The journal also provides a space to examine the gender differences in the workplace. For example, "Examining Female Entrepreneurs' Management Style: An Application of a Relational Frame" by Holly Butner provides rich research to better understand how women entrepreneurs develop and manage their businesses.

It has become increasingly important to provide a place where meaningful ideas about ethics and business can be exchanged. For a business, timing and profit take precedence over the more intangible world of ethics and reflection. However, it is the examination of the vague, fuzzy world of ethics that will allow a business to prosper in the long run. As Ayn Rand writes, "Every aspect of Western culture needs a new code of ethics – a rational ethics – as a precondition of rebirth". The *Journal of Business Ethics* is helping to write that new code through insightful and timely research that helps business executives to understand the connection among their actions, the relationship with people they work with and for, and the growth of the businesses they work within.

Mark J. Somers

Reflections

Question 1. This study has helped me rethink organizational socialization and it shaped my thinking about outcome variables in organizational behavior especially job performance. As a result, I have studied aspects of job performance that are harmful to organizations in relation to work attitudes such as job satisfaction and organizational commitment. I don't think that I would have been as aware of the broader role that ethics plays in most aspects of organizational behavior had I not done this study. It also led me to pursue research on whistle-blowing in organizations with more vigor.

Question 2. The *Journal of Business Ethics* operates as a nexus for conceptual and empirical research in the broad area of ethics in business. As a result, it gave the field an identity and a voice that allowed it to grow and to expand its scope. Many papers focused on business ethics either shared space with unrelated articles in more general management journals or became confused with the related field of corporate social responsibility. *JBE* helped focus this field, define its domain, and establish its legitimacy.

Peter A. Stanwick

Reflections

Our article "The Relationship Between Corporate Social Performance, and Organizational Size, Financial Performance, and Environmental Performance: An Empirical Examination" has had a profound impact on my academic career. When this article was published in 1998, my research interests were broadly focused on strategy and other traditional management research streams. After this article was published in The *Journal of Business Ethics*, I realized that I could have a long and successful academic career examining issues related to business ethics, social responsibility and the natural environment. It allowed me the opportunity to broaden my perspective on how business ethics impact an organization. In addition, this article validated the belief that articles pertaining to business ethics can be published in journals classified in the 'top tier' of all academic business journals. We are very proud and pleased that so many people have used our article as a reference point for their research. The *Journal of Business Ethics* has had a phenomenal impact on academic research in business ethics. It has allowed many researchers to develop and extend existing research streams that are related to business ethics. In addition, The *Journal of Business Ethics* has converted business ethics research from a narrow niche focus to a broad and mainstream focus of academic research. The *Journal of Business Ethics* has pioneered the opportunity of business ethics researchers to develop and have published conceptual and empirical papers that cover a spectrum of topic areas and interests.

Sarah D. Stanwick

Reflections

In 1993, I completed my PhD at the Florida State University with an emphasis in accounting. My dissertation focused on environmental accounting, an area which was relatively unexplored by accounting researchers at the time. This research sparked my life-long interest in ethics, social issues and environmental accounting. As I began my teaching and research career at Auburn University, environmental and ethical issues continued to dominate my research agenda. In addition, I found myself integrating these issues into the accounting courses I taught. The publication of my article written with Peter Stanwick has had a tremendous impact on my career. The *Journal of Business Ethics* is considered one of the premier journals for publishing ethical, social and environmental research in our profession. Having our article accepted in 1998 was not only an honor, but a career milestone. Our colleagues recognize the rigor of journal and the value of our research has now been rewarded with the *JBE* Award. Over my 20 year career at Auburn University, I have watched the accounting profession go through unprecedented changes. These events have changed the face of the accounting profession. The *Journal of Business Ethics* has continued to explore these important ethical issues and present research findings that challenge researchers with new research questions. In the environmental accounting area, we now see a re-emergence of the importance of triple-bottom line reporting, an issue that I remember exploring when I was writing my dissertation. The future of business ethics research will continue to be conveyed through the *Journal of Business Ethics* for academics, business leaders and students.

Jean Garner Stead, W. Edward Stead and Dan L. Worrell

Reflections

Research is a deliberate process in which emerging themes and streams are built on the shoulders of work that has come before. From this perspective, the ultimate value of an academic article is determined by how much it contributes to this deliberate scientific process. Thus it is that the citations an article receives provide a valid record of the article's contributions to a given field. Thus, for all three authors the recognition of our 1990 *Journal of Business Ethics* article [An integrative model for understanding and managing ethical behavior in business organizations] as a Citation Classic is validation that our research has had a positive influence on the scientific development of the field of business ethics.

Since the publication of this article, the careers of the three authors have diverged a bit. Ed and Jean Stead have followed a traditional professorial path, and both are currently professors of management. Throughout their careers, Ed and Jean have underpinned their research on the belief that quality is ultimately the key to research value. The large readership and positive responses they have gotten to the *JBE* article have validated that belief. Besides its direct impact on the field of business ethics, the article also set the stage for their later work on the search for sustainability in the business arena. Dan Worrell has followed an administrative route since the publication of this article. He held his first administrative position when the article was published, and he has since gone on to hold many subsequent administrative positions in business higher education, including three deanships. For Dan the exploration of the ethical decision metrics and the development of the associated model in the article were very helpful in an application sense throughout his administrative career. Also, the article has had visibility in the field that has been helpful for his career growth and recognition.

The *Journal of Business Ethics* has long been recognized as a primary vehicle for the dissemination of important research in the field. It has played a key role over many years in creating important research space where dialogue can take place through both theoretical and empirical examination of significant ethical issues in business. Because of its reputation for publishing the best of the best business ethics research, articles that appear in the *JBE* are legitimized for both quality and relevance.

Betsy Stevens

Reflections

The impact of my research and publication of the article "An analysis of corporate ethical code studies: Where do we go from here?" has been significant for my career. It launched my interest and exploration into the field of corporate ethical codes and the role they play in articulating the ethics of an organization. Scholars were just beginning to explore this subject when the article was published in 1994. My article had only 17 footnotes as not many code studies had been published. Since then I have continued to study the impact of ethical codes in organizations with a focus on how ethics are communicated. I, and others, have published a number of articles since then exploring the role of corporate codes and the ways they can be successfully used to influence behavior in organizations. The literature is also much richer today and we know much more about how codes function in organizations today than we did in 1994.

Question 1.This article was an extension of my doctoral dissertation research where I analyzed 40 corporate ethical codes. I completed the research in 1993 at a time when little research about codes had been published. Corporate America began embracing ethical codes in the 1980s; some operating from a desire to embrace higher ethical values and others simply wanting to manage their images and appear more ethical to stakeholders. Because so many firms adopted codes in the 1980s, some companies were concerned that the absence of a code might reflect badly on them; a few adopted them simply as window dressing.

My article analyzed the codes studies that existed at the time and asked the question: Where do we go from here? Looking back, Mission statements and ethical codes were being discussed in the literature in ways that were confusing. The terms were sometimes interchanged and it became clear that good definition of corporate ethical codes was needed. My article devoted considerable space to defining a code and articulating the difference between a code and a mission statement. I pointed out the need for additional research in this emerging area of study and suggested new avenues of study, especially along the lines of how they were communicated to employees. I also noted the need to explore the degree to which codes may or may not impact employee behavior. Since 1994, a significant stream of important research in these areas has been developed by other scholars and published in the *Journal of Business Ethics* and other highly respected academic journals.

Thomas Li-Ping Tang

Making Contributions to the Literature

It is my great honor and privilege that I have been invited to write a short essay to celebrate the achievement of the *Journal of Business Ethics* for the past three decades. As an author and member of the Editorial Board, I am proud to present the following Chinese heritage. Confucius (551–479 BC) said, "Since the age of 15, I have devoted myself to learning; since 30, I have been well established; since 40, I have understood many things and have no longer been confused; since 50, I have known my heaven-sent duty; since 60, I have been able to distinguish right and wrong in other people's words; and since 70, I have been able to do what I intend freely without breaking the rules" (子曰:"吾十有五而志于學,三十而立,四十而不惑,五十而知天命,六十而耳顺,七十而从心所欲,不逾矩."). This reflects Confucius' personal biography of life-long learning and the development of personal ethics.

Age 30 is not only an important milestone for an individual, but also for our *Journal of Business Ethics* because it takes the time to accumulate the knowledge, establish a well-respected field of study, and become the selected corner stone of the business field. This important journal has been *chosen* to represent the field of business ethics in the top 45 business journals used by *Financial Times* and also in the top 20 journals used by *Business Week* to evaluate business professors' intellectual capital due to its important role of creating knowledge in ethics literature.

Let us turn to the word "knowledge" in Chinese: 學問. From the lowest to the highest, the word學 shows a young child (子) sitting at a desk (几) holding the literature (文) with both hands (手), depicting the act of "studying". The word – literature, 文, is a string connecting two pieces of bamboo, forming two crosses, X – one on top of the other, going through four holes on each piece, symbolizing a link between two pages of a book, or the knowledge that can be passed on from one generation to the next. The word, 問, has two components: a door, 門, and a mouth, 口. In order to gain entrance to a room or a field of knowledge, one must knock on the door, 門, open one's mouth, 口, and *ask* questions. It reflects the Western wisdom: "Ask and it will be given to you; seek and you will find; knock and the door will be opened to you" (Bible, Matthew 7: 7). Both studying (學) and asking questions (問) must exist in order to create new knowledge. Confucius also said: "Learning without thought is labor lost; thought without learning is perilous" (學而不思,则罔;思而不學,则殆.).

Our *Journal of Business Ethics* provides an open space and publishes only original articles from a wide variety of methodological and disciplinary perspectives concerning ethical issues related to business that bring something new or unique to the discourse in their field. Since 1982, it has published 103 volumes and almost 5,000 articles under the unique visionary leadership of Editor-in-Chief Alex C. Michalos and Editor Deborah C. Poff. Therefore, following Confucius' personal biography, scholars and practitioners may answer God's calling; accept an invitation for a banquet of studying (學) business ethics; fill our hearts with hope, joy, love, purpose, and meaning in our lives; take up a grand challenge with courage, faith, and passion; think deeply; cast the widest net; and ask (問) the most original, innovative, and counterintuitive questions in order to advance knowledge and serve the humanity because many are invited, but few are chosen.

Happy Birthday to the *Journal of Business Ethics*! It is your 30th Birthday! Congratulations!

Ann E. Tenbrunsel

Reflections

What, If Any, Has Been the Impact of the *Journal of Business Ethics* on the Field of Business Ethics?

The *Journal of Business Ethics* has been extremely instrumental in expanding the field of business ethics. The impact is driven in part by the encompassing view that the journal holds of business ethics, a view which has increased not only the journal's visibility but the visibility of business ethics itself. The journal has consistently opened its pages to a variety of approaches to the study of business ethics. In addition to normative approaches to ethics, the journal has embraced behavioral and empirical approaches and, in doing so, has expanded insight into the how and why of unethical behavior. We see this openness not only in the regular issues but also in special issues, which has allowed for in-depth coverage of a particular topic or conference devoted to business ethics. This embracing approach displayed by the editors and reviewers made "business ethics" accessible to a large group of researchers from a variety of disciplines, thus preventing the field from becoming an "ethics silo" in which only a small group of researchers talked among themselves.

The encompassing view of ethics exhibited by the journal has increased the attention paid to the journal and the research questions it addresses. This has helped make business ethics a topic deserving of attention by academics, their institutions and society at large. The *Financial Times* inclusion of the journal in their ranking of business school research is evidence of the recognition of the field and of the role that the *Journal* played in that recognition.

The *Journal of Business Ethics* has increased the accessibility of business ethics across domains, and in so doing, has enriched our understanding of business ethics by providing new perspectives that both challenged and enhanced more traditional views. For their substantial impact, the editors and reviewers of the *Journal* over the years are much appreciated by those of us who study business ethics and those that we hope benefit from the resulting research.

John Tsalikis

A Response to My Award for the "Classic" and "Distinguished" Articles

The *Journal of Business Ethics* is internationally recognized as the preeminent academic publication in the area of business ethics. At Florida International University it is classified as a "premier" journal (the highest ranking) in the College of Business Administration list. The main reason for the "premier" ranking is that the *Journal of Business Ethics* is used by both *Business Week* and *Financial Times* to rank U.S. schools.

The importance of *JBE* can be best described in the following statement: "Ethics remains crucial to business; without trust, the whole economic system could collapse."

All of my publications in *JBE* have helped my career immensely. However, having two articles in the top 50 makes me one of the leading experts in the world on the field of ethics. Hopefully this will help me be promoted to the rank of full professor, in addition to increasing the prestige and rankings of the department of Marketing, the college and FIU.

Sean Valentine

The Journal of Business Ethics: The Torchbearer for Positive Organizational Practices for 30 Years

For the past 30 years, the *Journal of Business Ethics* (*JBE*) has been recognized as one of the premiere academic outlets for high-quality research related to organizational ethics, corporate social responsibility, ethical reasoning, and other similar topics. *JBE* is often recognized as having a strong impact in the organizational sciences (i.e., the *Financial Times* list of top academic business journals), and the journal scores high on citation indexes that track how often published articles are referenced in other works. Such rankings and citation counts are particularly important because, when assessed together, they provide a more complete picture of the normative impact that a journal has on an academic discipline. Clearly, *JBE* has been instrumental not only in building interest in business ethics throughout universities and board rooms, but also in creating a critical mass of information that has shaped the direction of business ethics as a discipline. Additionally, many institutions of higher education recognize *JBE* as a high-quality publication on internal journal lists and rankings, with some schools even specifying it as an "A-level" outlet for the purposes of tenure and promotion, raise allocation and rewards distribution, and faculty awards and recognition.

JBE possesses a number of strengths that have positioned the *Journal* as a publication leader in business ethics. For instance, the *Journal* has historically published many different types of research, including issue-based articles, theoretical pieces, practitioner-based essays, and empirical studies. This strategy has enabled *JBE* to effectively differentiate itself from other outlets, which often focus on the dissemination of work representing a particular type or approach. The empirical nature of many of the studies published in *JBE* is what makes the journal exceptionally attractive. While philosophical and/or conceptual explorations of ethics are critical for theory development and expand the boundaries of the field, it is equally important to recognize that business ethics is a fundamentally applied discipline, requiring more objective (and often more quantitative) investigations of the real-world issues that affect managers and their employees. Consequently, researchers must ultimately interact with businesses and collect primary data for the purposes of identifying and describing important ethical issues that impact the workplace. Such efforts facilitate the development of prescriptive guidance that assists practitioners and ultimately disseminates research that shapes both theory and practice. It is this particular niche that *JBE* has been able to successfully fill, thereby garnering widespread recognition and respect.

The field of business ethics has evolved greatly over the years, and *JBE* has been instrumental in focusing attention on many of the most salient ethical challenges that scholars and business professionals face. From the early origins of the field that focused on model development to the latter empirical investigations of important focal variables, the *Journal* has provided a useful forum for the exchange of cutting-edge research with important academic and practical/managerial implications.

Its scope has grown to include the publication of unique international investigations of business ethics, new comprehensive assessments of multi-level relationships that exist within the organizational context, and more discipline-specific research related to such professions as human resource management, sales/marketing, and accounting. Given these qualities, *JBE* will continue to be the torchbearer for positive organizational practices well into the future.

Scott Vitell

Commentary on a Collection of Classic Articles: Journal of Business Ethics

The *Journal of Business Ethics* has played a major role in the field of business ethics and also in my own career. I was fortunate enough to serendipitously begin a research career in the field of marketing and consumer ethics at about the same time that the *Journal of Business Ethics* (*JBE*) was a nascent journal. Specifically, I completed my Ph.D. in 1986 while the *Journal* published its first issue four years earlier, in 1982. Given the *Journal's* interest in empirical research as well as conceptual pieces, it has provided a logical outlet for much of my ethics research over the years. My career has most clearly benefitted from the *Journal* in that it is both international and cross-disciplinary. Most of my other published articles in the business ethics field have primarily appeared in marketing journals, and many of these journals, until recently anyway, have tended to appeal mainly to a national readership, composed mostly of U.S. marketing scholars. Contrarily, my articles in the *Journal of Business Ethics* have been read by scholars from multiple disciplines and from all parts of the world leading to requests for reprints and/or assistance from researchers from other disciplines and other countries. This has even sometimes led to my finding new co-authors who would not have contacted me had my articles not appeared in *JBE*.

Since its inception, the *Journal of Business Ethics* quickly evolved into the premier journal in the business ethics field as exemplified by its high ranking in the *Financial Times'* list of 45 top business journals. It also ranks first among 20 scholarly business ethics journals according to a recent citation-based study by Serenko and Bontis (2009). The *Journal of Business Ethics* has served the field well by publishing articles from numerous subfields of business ethics research including teaching, religion, corporate governance, cross-cultural business ethics and consumer ethics, to name but a few. I mention the latter two areas specifically because my three co-authored papers that are being republished in this volume, as well as one of my "distinguished" articles that is also being recognized, all fall into one or the other of these two categories.

The 1993 "Effects of culture on ethical decision making: an application of Hofstede's typology" article, co-authored with Nwachukwu and Barnes, continues to be one of the most cited *JBE* articles (and the most cited cross-cultural *JBE* article) although I certainly never would have expected that at the time it was being written. Based upon Hofstede's typology, my co-authors and I were simply trying to conceptualize the potential impact of cross-cultural differences on various constructs/ relationships from the Hunt-Vitell General Theory of Marketing Ethics (Hunt and Vitell 1986). Apparently numerous readers have found those conceptualizations useful, and I am grateful for that and thank my co-authors for their insightful comments in framing the original paper.

My other articles mentioned above are consumer-related ethics articles. The *Journal of Business Ethics* has been at the forefront in terms of publishing research in the consumer ethics field, and this field would not have advanced nearly as much as it has were it not for *JBE.* The two consumer ethics articles re-published here are among the first in this field. Besides presenting the four original dimensions and individual items of the Muncy-Vitell scale, the 1992, "Consumer ethics: an empirical investigation of factors influencing ethical judgments of the final consumer" article co-authored with Jim Muncy examined the recently created (at the time) scale by analyzing the correlations between individual items of the scale and various consumer attitudes such as attitudes toward business, government and mankind in general, among others. Perhaps not surprisingly, one's attitude toward business seemed to generate the strongest correlations with the Muncy-Vitell items, with individuals having the strongest negative opinions of business being the one's most likely to condone unethical consumer behavior. While the results were not quite "cutting edge," since the scale had originally appeared in another journal (Muncy and Vitell 1992), the significance of the article was the exposure of the scale to the diverse readership of *JBE.* The 1991 "Consumer ethics: an investigation of the ethical beliefs of elderly consumers" article co-authored with Lumpkin and Rawwas essentially achieved the same results while specifically examining the ethical beliefs of an elderly population of consumers. I believe that these two articles, along with the initial presentation of the Muncy-Vitell scale, helped to generate much of the initial interest in this field. I give my thanks to *JBE* for publishing these articles at the time and, of course, my thanks and gratitude also to my co-authors for their immeasurable assistance, most especially Jim Muncy who first had the idea to develop a consumer ethics scale.

The more recent consumer ethics article, "Consumer ethics research: review, synthesis and suggestions for the future" (2003) was essentially a review piece. At the time that I wrote this article, I had "gotten away" from consumer ethics research for a few years, and was surprised to find that so much had been published in the interim. The writing of this paper helped to renew my interest in consumer ethics research once again and resulted in my co-authoring several subsequent consumer ethics pieces involving religiosity, many of which appeared in *JBE.* I am grateful to *JBE* for publishing consumer ethics articles over the years, not just mine but those of many other authors as well, and, of course, for publishing my aforementioned review of many of those articles.

Two articles that have been honored remain to be mentioned. One, a "citation classic," was actually my very first manuscript submitted to and accepted by *JBE.*

This was the 1987 article co-authored with Troy Festervand, "Business ethics: conflicts, practices and beliefs of industrial executives," that examined the views of executives regarding business ethics. It was patterned after Baumhart's original, ground breaking *Harvard Business Review* (1961) article and Brenner and Molander's (1977) follow-up article a decade later. I thank these early business ethics researchers and also my co-author for the parts they all played indirectly and directly in forming my career during those beginning years. Given that this was my first article published in *JBE,* one could perhaps state that it helped to launch my *JBE* publishing career.

My remaining honored *JBE* article was "The perceived role of ethics and social responsibility: a scale development" (1996) with Anusorn Singhapakdi as the lead author, and Rallapalli and Kraft as co-authors. In this manuscript we established a scale for measuring the extent to which an individual perceives that ethics and social responsibility play important roles in the success of an organization. Anusorn was my first doctoral student, graduating in 1988, and has been a valued colleague ever since. He was definitely the lead researcher on this article that continues to be cited as much, or more, today than when it was first published. My thanks to Anusorn for his contributions to this and to many more papers that we have worked on together over the years.

In conclusion, let me relate an incident that occurred while I was defending my doctoral dissertation in 1986. My dissertation defense involved presenting the theoretical model of the Hunt-Vitell theory of ethics as well as an initial empirical investigation of it. The "outside" member of the dissertation committee was a philosopher, and I remember his insisting that mine was not really an "ethics" dissertation. This essentially resulted in a debate between my dissertation chair, Shelby D. Hunt, who was joined by other marketers on the committee, and this particular philosopher. After a rather lengthy discussion on this issue, in which I was essentially a spectator, the philosopher admitted that positive/descriptive models and empirical research were indeed worthy of academic effort, but that they should never be called "ethics" because ethics is, by its very nature, inherently normative, never descriptive. Thankfully, the *Journal of Business Ethics* has never taken this restrictive position, so I conclude my comments with kudos to the *Journal of Business Ethics,* and its longstanding editor-in-chief, Alex Michalos, for recognizing the worthiness of positive theory and empirical research in the "ethics" field, and also for not being afraid to use the term, "ethics," to describe these worthy endeavors.

References

Baumhart, Raymond C. 1961. How ethical are businessmen? *Harvard Business Review* 39: 6–9.

Brenner, Steven N., and Earl A. Molander. 1977. Is the ethics of business changing? *Harvard Business Review* 55, 57–71.

Hunt, Shelby D., and Scott J. Vitell. 1986. A general theory of marketing ethics. *Journal of Macromarketing* 8 (Spring): 5–16.

Muncy, J.A., and S.J. Vitell. 1992. Consumer ethics: An investigation of the ethical beliefs of the final consumer. *Journal of Business Research* 24 (June): 297–311.

Serenko, Alexander., and Nick Bontis. 2009. A citation-based ranking of the business ethics scholarly journals. *International Journal of Business Governance and Ethics* 4(4): 390–399.

Gary R. Weaver

Authors' reflections on Weaver, G.R, Treviño, L. K. & Cochran, P.L., "Corporate ethics practices in the mid 1990s: An empirical study of the Fortune 1000", Journal of Business Ethics 1999

Our 1999 *JBE* article queried corporations about their ethics and legal compliance activity. It provided useful descriptive data about formal ethics programs at a key time in the development of these programs in corporate America – the mid-1990s. Although codes of ethics had existed in a few firms for some time, and the Defense Industry Initiative had seen the development of formal ethics programs in defense industry companies, the 1990s saw a spike in formal organizational activity related to ethics and legal compliance across a wide range of corporations. Decade after decade of corporate malfeasance had trained attention toward ways to reform corporate America, and the U.S. federal sentencing guidelines for organizations were passed in late 1991. The guidelines incorporated a "carrot and stick" approach. The idea was to encourage companies to proactively manage employees in a way that would support legal compliance by offering to treat companies more generously – to assess lower penalties for those in legal difficulty – if they could demonstrate that they had actively managed employee behavior in a way likely to discourage illegal action. This turned out to be a crucial time in the development of formal ethics and compliance activity in firms, and therefore a good time to take a "snapshot" of what was happening. Since that time, we have seen the development of an entire ethics and compliance profession represented by organizations such as the Ethics and Compliance Officers Association and the Society for Corporate Compliance and Ethics. We have also seen the development of consulting businesses that support organizational efforts in training, hotlines, investigations, and other signs of activity and attention to corporate ethics. The National Business Ethics Survey, conducted regularly by the Ethics Resource Center, asks some of the same questions we asked almost 20 years ago.

From the perspective of our research, this study provided a strictly descriptive backdrop for other, more in-depth explanatory studies (published elsewhere) that attempted to understand multiple influences on corporate ethics practices and employee ethical behavior. Perhaps one of the most important insights noted in our *JBE* article was our highlighting of the symbolic side of ethics and compliance management; many firms appeared to be implementing formal programs in a "check the box" fashion. Our other more in-depth analysis found that many firms were decoupling these programs from other important day-to-day activities of the firm, especially if their senior leaders were not highly committed to ethics as an end in itself (Weaver et al. 1999). Over the years, we (individually or together) also have examined multiple contextual influences on employee conduct (including the influence of corporate ethics programs). This research has generally supported our early sense that the formal side of ethics management is not the most important. For example, codes of ethics have only a small impact on employee behavior, especially if employees perceive that the codes are not enforced (Kish-Gephart et al. 2010). What matters much more are the climate and culture that are created in an organization. For example, employees' perceptions that leaders care about ethics and reinforce it by holding everyone accountable, and that ethics programs are not just "window dressing" but are part of the daily organizational conversation, are key contextual influences (Treviño and Weaver 2001).

The *Journal of Business Ethics* appears to have been at the right place at the right time to provide an outlet for the burgeoning of interest in the academic study of business ethics. Beyond academe, the rest of the world seems to have gotten the message too that business ethics is neither an oxymoron nor a fad but rather a legitimate focus of study.

References

Kish-Gephart, J.J., D.A. Harrison, and L.K. Treviño. 2010. Bad apples, bad cases, and bad barrels: Meta-analytic evidence about the sources of unethical decisions at work. *Journal of Applied Psychology* 95(1): 1–31.

Treviño, L.K., and G.R. Weaver. 2001. Organizational justice and ethics program 'follow-through': Influences on employees' harmful and helpful behavior. *Business Ethics Quarterly* 11(4): 651–671.

Weaver, G.R., L.K. Treviño, and P.L. Cochran. 1999. Integrated and decoupled corporate social performance: Management values, external pressures, and corporate ethics practices. *Academy of Management Journal* 42(5): 539–552.

Heidi von Weltzien-Høivik

Reflections

The *Journal of Business Ethics* has been instrumental in helping to internationalize research done in European countries. The *Journal* became the primary outlet for members of *the European Business Ethics Network (EBEN),* established in 1986, who wanted to publish in English.

No other journal set the standards so clearly from the start, yet allowed authors to remain true to the historical academic traditions of their own respective countries. Research approaches differ, in particular in the humanities and social sciences. The articles in the *Journal of Business Ethics* give evidence of the great variety of innovative approaches used in the constant search for knowledge in the different parts of the world.

As president of the *European Business Ethics Network* until 2005, I have had the pleasure of promoting the journal to all our members in most of the European countries. Ever since 1997, after each annual EBEN conference, the best papers are submitted for publication based on a double blind review process. This has been a huge encouragement and valuable help for all academics whose mother-tongue is not English.

Knowledge sharing is key to advancing learning and understanding in academia worldwide. The editors of the *Journal of Business Ethics* , Alex C. Michalos and Deborah C.Poff deserve to be recognized for their outstanding achievement in making this journal what it is.

William A. Wines

Response to JBE, September 18, 2011

1. When my citation classic came out in 1992 [Toward an understanding of cross-cultural ethics – a tentative model], I was a tenured full Professor at Boise State University in the College of Business & Economics. Prior to publication of the classic, I had published 21 other articles, not counting newspaper columns, published book reviews, and edited anthologies. I was a visitor at the University of Iowa before moving to Boise State in 1984. That move was forced by the farm crisis. I stayed at Boise State 18 years before leaving for greener pastures. My selection to be the John J. Aram Professor at Gonzaga University in 1999 probably was helped by the 1992 citation classic. I received some informal communication to that effect from a member of the selection committee. Other than that, I am not aware of any effect the article had on my career.
2. The impact of the *Journal of Business Ethics* on the field of business ethics is difficult to gauge. By providing an outlet for scholarly work, the *Journal of Business Ethics* provided a very positive service. In the United States, (the rest of my comment is limited to the U.S.A.) the significance of that service has been, I think, overshadowed by the "one true religion of the market" and by the college, university, and regulatory (accreditation) politics devolving from it. The business school deans I knew, with few exceptions, worshipped at the altar of the free market. The major donors did too. The result was that business ethics did not prosper in the U.S.A.; and some recent research tends to show ethics courses disappearing from business curriculae. A non-scientific and very small sample of six of the business schools with which I am familiar shows that: (a) four of the

six had business ethics courses 25 years ago; (b) only one of the six currently has a free-standing business ethics course now; and (c) three faculty positions (tenure track) that existed 25 years ago to teach the business ethics courses have dwindled to less than one position on tenure track (It was moved to the philosophy department which is not in the business school).

John A. Wood

Reflections

Since business ethics was only one area of the discipline of ethics that demanded my effort and attention, the article had little impact on my career. "Publish or perish" was not a part of the Baylor scene at that time (it is now). Publishing was encouraged but not required. The greater emphasis was on classroom performance. Except for reading an occasional paper on the subject at a regional professional meeting, I rarely addressed the subject outside of my classes. This article was the only one I authored in the field that was published in an academic journal. I did speak on the subject at various non-academic venues, but this article did not generate the invitation.
Regarding the *Journal,* it was clear from the very beginning that *JBE* would be a first-class publication. Each semester I used several articles either as a basis for class discussion or as required background reading. I began teaching business ethics in 1981 and quickly discovered that the *Journal* would be a major source in my teaching of the subject. The quality and scope of its articles pushed the *Journal* to the forefront of the burgeoning field of business ethics. It was the most reliable source to explore the major issues emerging in the discipline. Although my course was a religion course and I used biblical and theological concepts extensively, the more philosophical and utilitarian approach of the *Journal* was a natural companion to what I sought to accomplish in the course.

Congratulations to the *Journal* for 30 years of excellence.

Qin Qin Zheng

The Impact of the Journal of Business Ethics

Being a pioneer in business ethics, the *Journal of Business Ethics* (*JBE*) has witnessed the change and development of research in this field. For 30 years, *JBE* has been devoted to improving human welfare by publishing high-quality articles that bring new or unique perspectives in business ethics. Currently, *JBE* is one of the top 45 journals used by the *Financial Times* in business school research rank. The great impact of *JBE* has made it a world-wide leading journal in business ethics.

JBE is recognized as the premier journal with a high reputation because of its great and consistent contribution to the advancement of business ethics. Standing on the frontier of business ethics, *JBE* is dedicated to disseminating advanced knowledge about business ethics and publishing research that keeps pace with the latest development in social sciences. The broad scope of *JBE* provides a platform for diversified insight and advanced vision. The rigorous style of *JBE* sets the benchmark for peer journals. Therefore, *JBE* articles are cited with high frequency in relevant research. Meanwhile, *JBE* encourages scholars to use simple language to explain complex theories. *JBE*'s efforts benefit a wider range of readers without losing its depth and specialty. As a result, *JBE* gains high acknowledgment of business ethics scholars. Distinguished professors in business ethics constantly have articles published in *JBE*. *JBE* also cultivates many emerging stars. Some best papers at Academy Management (AOM) Meetings are published here. Increasing manuscript submissions and journal subscriptions indicate the popularity of *JBE*. Actually *JBE* has become an integral part of business ethics research.

In China, *JBE* establishes the unique and critical position for its profound influence. It is well known that the Chinese remarkable economy development is accompanied with great moral degradation. Such demoralization is exemplified in widespread fake products, massive unsafe goods sold, immodest power abuse, inundated crimes, and rampant corruption. Business ethics are therefore desperately needed and have become a subject of intense discussion. Enjoying high reputation worldwide, *JBE* undoubtedly becomes a flagship journal for business ethics research in China. *JBE* is a bridge that connects western and eastern ethical perspectives through high-level academic discussion. As a top business school in China [Fudan University], we regard *JBE* as an A level journal. Publishing in *JBE* represents the great achievement in the field of business ethics. We also use *JBE* articles in reading references for MBA teaching. The perspectives from *JBE* articles not only are highly cited by Chinese scholars in theoretical development but also enlighten Chinese business elites in actual practice.

The impact of *JBE* is universal, rather than country-specific. The leading position of *JBE* is derived from its long-established international reputation and is further strengthened by the strong support of scholars all over the world. *JBE*'s achievement in the past 30 years is impressive and remarkable. Cherishing the mission of human welfare improvement, *JBE* is paving the way to a sustainable and prosperous future.

Index

A.C. Michalos and D.C. Poff (eds.), *Citation Classics from the Journal of Business Ethics*, Advances in Business Ethics Research 2,
DOI 10.1007/978-94-007-4126-3, © Springer Science+Business Media B.V. 2013

C

F

G

T

The manufacturer's authorised representative in the EU is Springer Nature Customer Service Centre GmbH, Europaplatz 3, 69115 Heidelberg, Germany. If you have any concerns regarding our products, please contact ProductSafety@springernature.com

Printed and bound by CPI Group (UK) Ltd, Croydon, CR0 4YY
25/09/2026
02222831-0013